DICTIONARY OF
AMERICAN HISTORY

JAMES TRUSLOW ADAMS
Editor in Chief

R. V. COLEMAN
Managing Editor

VOLUME III

40-512

NEW YORK
CHARLES SCRIBNER'S SONS
1940

DICTIONARY OF
AMERICAN HISTORY

VOLUME III

Advisory Council

DICTIONARY OF
AMERICAN HISTORY

Habeas Corpus — Mixed Commissions

Habeas Corpus, The Writ of, like jury trial, has a history which runs well back into the Middle Ages. It is a device for freeing persons from illegal detention by governmental agencies. It is in the nature of an order of a court to the custodian of a person held, directing that the person be brought to a court hearing to determine whether he is lawfully detained. If the detention is deemed to be unlawful the prisoner is ordered released. The privilege of the writ was guaranteed in England by the Habeas Corpus Act of 1679, but it was suspended thereafter on occasion by special acts, so that its enjoyment was never fully assured. The American colonists valued it highly as a device for the preservation of civil liberties. In order to prevent suspensions of the privilege of the writ such as had taken place in England a provision was included in Section 9 of Article I of the Constitution^w of the United States to the effect that "The privilege of the writ of habeas corpus shall not be suspended, unless when in cases of rebellion or invasion the public safety may require it." Similar provisions are to be found in the constitutions of the several states.

The Judiciary Act of 1789^w empowered the Supreme Court and the district courts of the United States to issue writs of habeas corpus in circumstances involving the exercise of jurisdiction by Federal authorities. In 1833, when the nullification^w controversy brought the threat of state interference with Federal officers in the performance of their duties, Congress authorized the Federal courts to issue writs of habeas corpus to state officials by whom Federal officers might be detained. In 1842, when the McLeod^w case in New York had indicated the power of a state to embarrass the United States by interference with the representatives of a foreign government, Congress authorized the Federal courts to issue writs to state officials when the persons detained

were subjects of foreign governments and claimed to be acting under their sanction. The states, on the other hand, were held not to have a corresponding right to inquire by means of the writ of habeas corpus into the detention of persons held by the Federal Government (*see* Ableman v. Booth). Federal jurisdiction was expanded in 1867 to cover the broad field of cases in which detention was alleged to be in violation of the Constitution or of a law or treaty of the United States.

The Constitution does not say who may suspend the privilege of the writ of habeas corpus, within the exception clause which permits suspension. President Lincoln authorized its suspension at the beginning of the Civil War. In ex parte Merryman^w, a United States Circuit Court case decided early in 1861, Chief Justice Taney held that the power of suspension was in Congress and not in the President. President Lincoln ignored this opinion in preference for one of Attorney General Bates in which the power of the President to act in the absence of legislation was upheld. To meet the needs of this particular situation Congress later enacted a statute to cover suspension in circumstances arising out of the war. While the basic controversy has never been officially settled, the weight of opinion is now on the side of the interpretation given by Chief Justice Taney.

[John Mabry Mathews, *The American Constitutional System.*]

CARL BRENT SWISHER

Hague Court of Arbitration, officially called the Permanent Court of Arbitration, was established by the first Hague Conference of 1899, and was revised and improved by the second Hague Conference of 1907. It comprises three distinct bodies: First, there is the International Bureau, consisting of a Secretary-General and a small staff, which serves as a registry, a channel of communication, an administrative body, and a secretariat for matters relating to the Court and its work. This Bureau is subject to the general direction of an Administrative Council, composed of the diplomatic representatives at The Hague of the states parties to the Court, under the chairmanship of the Netherlands Minister for Foreign Affairs.

Secondly, there are the members or judges of the Court, consisting of four persons qualified in international law chosen by each of the states for a term of six years. With forty-seven states parties to the Hague Court (Ethiopia having adhered in 1935), the total number of judges might be 188, but has generally, due to unfilled vacancies, been about 150. These do not, however, at any time sit together as a court, but constitute merely a panel or list from which courts or tribunals may be made up.

Thirdly, there are the actual arbitral tribunals, which are constituted for particular disputes as they arise. These tribunals generally consist of five persons selected from the list of judges, the usual practice being for each of the disputing states to select one of its nationals and one non-national and for these four to agree upon the fifth, who becomes therefore the umpire.

Recourse to this Court is not in any sense compulsory, the machinery being available for states that care to use it, but these states having the complete right, even if they decide to arbitrate, to set up special tribunals quite outside this Hague Court. During a period of forty years (1899–1939), only twenty-one cases have been settled through this machinery, six of these having been submitted by the United States. Since the Permanent Court of International Justice, or World Court[w], was established in 1921, it has handed down sixty-odd decisions; and that Court, as a more genuine judicial court, seems to have replaced the Permanent Court of Arbitration.

[James Brown Scott, ed., *The Hague Court Reports*, Publications of the Carnegie Endowment for International Peace, 1st Series, 1916; 2nd Series, 1932; Manley O. Hudson, The Permanent Court of Arbitration, *American Journal of International Law*, Vol. XXVII, pp. 440-460, July, 1933.]   CLARENCE A. BERDAHL

Hague Peace Conferences, THE, were general international conferences which met at The Hague in 1899 and 1907, respectively, for the purpose of limiting armaments and of devising means to ensure world peace. Both were called by the Czar of Russia, although the second was actually initiated by President Theodore Roosevelt. Twenty-six states were represented in 1899

and forty-four in 1907, including in each case all the Great Powers.

Nothing at all was accomplished with respect to disarmament, but at the two Conferences thirteen Conventions were agreed upon, dealing with (1) the pacific settlement of international disputes through the machinery of good offices and mediation, inquiry and arbitration; (2) the use of force for the collection of debts; (3) the opening of hostilities; (4) the laws and customs of land warfare; (5) the rights and duties of neutrals in land warfare; (6) the status of enemy merchant ships at the outbreak of hostilities; (7) the conversion of merchant ships into warships; (8) the laying of mines; (9) naval bombardments; (10) the treatment of the sick and wounded in maritime warfare; (11) the right of capture at sea; (12) the creation of an International Prize Court; and (13) the rights and duties of neutrals in maritime warfare. In addition, four Declarations were adopted: for the prohibition of projectiles from the air, of asphyxiating gas, and of explosive or dum-dum bullets, and for compulsory arbitration; and several Wishes (*Voeux*) or Recommendations, the most important of which related to the limitation of armaments and the creation of a Court of Arbitral Justice. All of these conventions were widely ratified, except the one creating an International Prize Court.

[James Brown Scott, ed., *The Hague Conventions and Declarations of 1899 and 1907*, Publications of the Carnegie Endowment for International Peace, 3rd edition, 1918; Thomas K. Ford, The Genesis of the First Hague Peace Conference, *Political Science Quarterly*, Vol. LI.]

CLARENCE A. BERDAHL

Hague v. C. I. O. The feud between Mayor Frank Hague and the Committee on Industrial Organization[w] was one phase in the drab story of boss rule in Hudson County, N. J., which attracted national attention and on June 5, 1939, produced an important U. S. Supreme Court decision involving a review of the history and meaning of civil liberty (Frank Hague v. C. I. O.). The activities of the C. I. O. had produced disorder and industrial demoralization in so many communities that Mayor Hague's declaration that his bailiwick would have none of it commanded considerable support in various quarters. It was apparent, however, that suppression of C. I. O. activities involved principles and methods that could be used to the detriment of any minority group or unpopular organization. Ordinances empowering the Director of Public Safety to deny permits for public meetings where he considered public order might be endangered, forbidding distribution of printed matter, etc., became the legal bulwark of arbitrary governmental acts.

The groups adversely affected started proceedings in the Federal Court, which reached the Supreme Court in February, 1939. The difficulty of drawing a line between the proper exercise of police power and governmental oppression is apparent in the varied reasoning by which the justices in a five-to-two decision eventually declared the city ordinance a violation of the Fourteenth Amendment.

[*Index to Periodical Literature; New York Times Index*, 1935-39.]   W. A. ROBINSON

"Hail Columbia," our first national hymn, was the direct outgrowth of President Washington's neutrality policy in the war between France and England. Both countries had partisans in America, the Federalists*ᵂ* generally favoring England, the Republicans (Jeffersonian) *ᵂ*, France. Those sympathetic to the French Revolution made the "Marseillaise" their song while those who wished to avoid war adopted "The President's March" which had been written in the early 1790's by Philip Roth, an American citizen and former bandmaster in the British army. In 1798 feeling ran high as a result of the publication of the "XYZ" letters*ᵂ*, and George Fox, a popular Philadelphia actor, asked Joseph Hopkinson, a prominent young lawyer who had a reputation as a poet and patron of the arts, to compose a song to the music of the "March." Hopkinson, a strong Federalist and ardent admirer of Washington, avoided reference to either France or England, and gave voice to our national feeling of independence and our determination to protect our honor and rights. He succeeded so well that the song became popular with all classes and remained our national hymn until "America"*ᵂ* was written.

[B. A. Konkle, *Joseph Hopkinson, 1770-1842.*]
E. H. O'NEILL

Haines' Bluff, overlooking the Yazoo River about fourteen miles northwest of Vicksburg*ᵂ*, was fortified by the Confederates to protect Vicksburg's right flank and the Chickasaw Bayou region (*see* Chickasaw Bluffs, The Battle of). Sherman (U.) made a demonstration against the Bluff, April 30, 1863, to divert Confederate attention while Grant ran his transports past the Vicksburg batteries. Sherman then withdrew, but the success of Grant's movement on Vicksburg from the rear necessitated the evacuation of Haines' Bluff on May 18.

[Matthew F. Steele, *American Campaigns.*]
OSCAR S. DOOLEY

"Hair Buyer" was the epithet fixed upon Lt. Gov. Henry Hamilton of Detroit by his Kentucky opponent, George Rogers Clark*ᵂ*. As governor, Hamilton promoted Indian raids upon the settlements of the Ohio frontier. All civilized governments have utilized the Indians as military allies; the gravamen of Clark's charge was that the governor encouraged the savages to commit inhuman acts, which Hamilton denied. The epithet was a partisan atrocity accusation provoked by wartime hatred and suffering, and unsupported by trustworthy evidence.

[M. M. Quaife, George Rogers Clark and Detroit, *Indiana Historical Bulletin,* V, Extra No. 2, April, 1928.]
M. M. QUAIFE

"Hairdressers" were the scalping parties of Indians and bushrangers, who, incited by the bounties offered for enemy scalps, ravaged the frontiers during the colonial wars. Both the French and English were active in promoting such raids. In 1747 William Johnson paid £60 for six scalps; and Duchat, young captain in the French army, wrote from Ticonderoga in 1756 that "not a week passes but the French send them [the English] a band of hairdressers."

[F. W. Hodge, *Handbook of American Indians,* Part 2; George Friederica, Scalping in America, *Report,* Smithsonian Institution, 1906.]
A. C. FLICK

Haiti, Intervention in. Increasingly frequent revolutions, disputes between the Haitian government and American interests controlling the National Bank and the National Railroad, and a fear of European intervention were the principal reasons for the American military occupation of Haiti in July, 1915. The immediate occasion was the disappearance of organized government when a mob at Port au Prince, angered by the killing of 167 political prisoners, murdered President Guillaume Sam, after invading the French legation, in which he had taken refuge.

A new president, elected by the Congress under the protection of the American marines, signed the treaty of Sept. 16, 1915. Under this, Americans nominated by the President of the United States, but serving as officials of the Haitian government, assumed control of the country's finances, of its police force, of public works and of sanitation. The constitution of 1918, permitting foreign landownership, was adopted by a plebiscite, after the president and the American military authorities had arbitrarily dissolved the Haitian Congress.

The "caco" revolt of 1918, during which some 1500 Haitians were killed, led to an investigation by a committee of the United States Senate in 1921. The committee's report, criticizing the failure to co-ordinate the work of the American treaty officials and the general lack of a constructive policy, was followed by the appointment of Gen. John H. Russell as American High Commissioner, in 1922. Thereafter much constructive work was accomplished in road building, irrigation and sanitation. Order was maintained by a well-trained police force and the finances were placed on a sound basis. A $16,000,000 loan obtained in New York in 1922 provided funds for much of this development. In 1924 a fifth treaty service of "Agriculture and Professional Education" was established.

Under the transitory provisions of the constitution of 1918, an appointed council of state exercised the legislative power and elected the president. The indefinite continuance of this situation under President Borno (1922–30), as well as dislike of foreign control, caused much discontent. In 1930 President Hoover appointed a commission to study the problem of terminating the intervention. A popularly elected government under Stenio Vincent took office in 1930, and in 1931 American officials were withdrawn from the departments of public works, sanitation and agriculture. In 1934 the police was turned over to Haitian control and all American military forces were withdrawn. The United States continues to exercise a measure of control over Haiti's finances in accord with agreements under which the bonds of 1922 were issued.

[A. C. Millspaugh, *Haiti under American Control;* E. G. Balch, ed., *Occupied Haiti.*]   DANA G. MUNRO

Hakluyt's Voyages is the short title of a collection of original records of English voyages overseas before 1600. The full title is *The Principal Navigations, Voiages, Traffiques and Discoveries of the English Nation* (published, folio, 1589; expanded to three volumes, 1598–1600). The editor was Richard Hakluyt—pronounced Háklet —(1552–1616), clergyman and geographer, promoter and historiographer of the English expansion. The materials which he collected after 1600 were in part included in the more ambitious, but much less careful or complete, work of Samuel Purchas, *Purchas his Pilgrimes* (1625, four volumes, folio).

Hakluyt's American section, which occupies Vol. III of the *Voyages* and Part II of Purchas, is an admirable body of source materials for the early history of the English in the New World, the first such collection published for any European nation. For virtually every voyage of importance, Hakluyt procured a full narrative

by a participant, and added many official documents and private letters. He has thus preserved the original and often unique records of the voyages of Cartier, Hawkins, Drake, Frobisher, Davis, Cavendish, Raleigh (to Guiana) and (in Purchas) Hudson and Baffin; and of the colonial projects of French Florida, Gilbert's Newfoundland, Raleigh's Virginia and (in Purchas) Guiana, Virginia, New England and Newfoundland.

[Modern editions of Hakluyt, Glasgow 1903-05, 12 vols.; of Purchas, Glasgow 1905-07, 20 vols.]
GEORGE B. PARKS

Haldimand Negotiations. When the Republic of Vermont[w], established during the Revolutionary War at New York's territorial expense, failed to gain admission to the United States which it had been loyally assisting, Lord George Germain authorized the British commanders in America to offer Vermont self-government under the crown. In 1779 Sir Henry Clinton made overtures to Gen. Ethan Allen from New York, but these were not reciprocated. In 1780, however, the Vermont leaders sounded Gen. Frederick Haldimand, who commanded at Quebec, by proposing an exchange of prisoners. Haldimand sent Capt. Justus Sherwood to confer with Ethan Allen. In consequence, a cartel for exchange of prisoners was arranged and under this disguise Haldimand negotiated for the remainder of the war for the reunion of Vermont with Great Britain. These parleys were by conferences in isolated spots around Lake Champlain and by correspondence. On Germain's authority, Haldimand offered Vermont a liberal constitution, preferment for the leaders, confirmation of land titles and territorial expansion. The Vermonters, enjoying periodical truces because of the cartel, temporized and only promised to bring Vermont to neutrality. The defeat of Cornwallis in 1781 saved them from having to make a critical decision when Haldimand, impatient with delay, was threatening their frontiers. In 1782, considering that they had again been shabbily treated by Congress and that Vermont might even be suppressed after the war, they sent emissaries to Quebec with proposals for a reunion as soon as Great Britain could protect and subsidize them. But Haldimand, having received secret instructions to cease offensive warfare, temporized and avoided any commitment.

The Vermont negotiators were a small, influential group dominated by Ira and Ethan Allen, Gov. Chittenden and the Fays, whose guiding principles were to perpetuate Vermont and safeguard their landed interests irrespective of who won the war. Rumors were rife. Some Vermonters branded the negotiations as treason to America; others had confidence in the shrewd opportunism of their leaders; the loyalist minority, their numbers rapidly increasing by immigration, worked covertly for reunion. But the ruling clique was never forced by events to disclose precisely where it stood. Had the war ended in compromise—the Allens thought this likely—Vermont could have claimed favored treatment from Great Britain. The traditional view that the Vermonters negotiated only as a ruse and never seriously considered the British proposals is unwarrantable.

[C. W. Rife, Ethan Allen, an Interpretation, *The New England Quarterly*, October, 1929.]
                      CLARENCE W. RIFE

Hale, Nathan, Execution of. In September, 1776, when Washington desired information as to the British strength and positions, Hale volunteered to act as a spy. Posing as a country teacher, he entered the British lines on Long Island and Manhattan, procured the information and was returning when he was arrested on Sept. 21 and executed the following morning. His last words are said to have been, "I only regret that I have but one life to lose for my country," a paraphrase of a line from Addison's *Cato*.

[Henry P. Johnston, *Nathan Hale, 1776, Biography and Memorials*.]
                    ALVIN F. HARLOW

Half-Breed Tract, THE, was the triangular area of land, now part of the State of Iowa, lying between the Mississippi and Des Moines rivers south of the parallel forming the northern boundary line of Missouri. By a treaty signed on Aug. 4, 1824, the Sauk and Fox Indians^{qqᵛ} set this tract aside for the children of mixed white and Indian parentage. Before it was surveyed and divided, white settlers crowded in, some of the half-breeds sold their claims, and land companies were formed to handle sales in the tract. Congress and the territorial legislatures of Wisconsin and Iowa made laws regarding the various claims. The result was a succession of lawsuits, the last of which was decided by the Supreme Court of the United States in 1850.

[Jacob Van der Zee, The Half-Breed Tract, *Iowa Journal of History and Politics*, Vol. XIII; B. L. Wick, The Struggle for the Half-Breed Tract, *Annals of Iowa*, Third Series, Vol. VII.]
               RUTH A. GALLAHER

Half-Breeds. The children of white men and Indian women were called half-breeds; but the term was soon extended to include all degrees of such mixture of blood. White children were often captured and brought up as Indians, thus adding their quota. In Canada where the fur trade^{ᵛ} was for a time the chief interest, many white men lived among the Indians, fathering a class of "half-breeds" who tended to live in groups of their own, the best known being the half-breed settlements south of Lake Winnipeg. In the United States such separate groups were not found, Indians of mixed blood living among their own people and back-crossing. The consistent government policy of considering every person of part Indian descent as entitled to annuity rites and tribal status has discouraged mixed-bloods seeking regular white citizenship. In 1930 Indians possessing at least some fraction of white blood were estimated to exceed 48% of the registered Indian population.

[Indian Population in the United States and Alaska, *Bureau of the Census*, 1930.]
        CLARK WISSLER

"Half-Breeds," THE, represented the liberal wing of the Republican party^{ᵛ} during the Hayes and Garfield administrations. Favoring Hayes' liberal Southern policy and civil-service reform, the faction was nicknamed by the "Stalwarts"^{ᵛ} for its so-called "half-breed" Republicanism. Bitter factional rivalry continued for several years.

[E. E. Sparks, *National Development*.]
        GLENN H. BENTON

Half Moon, THE, was the ship which the Dutch East India Company provided for the voyage of exploration made by Henry Hudson in 1609, in the course of which the Hudson River^{ᵛ} was discovered. A vessel of eighty tons, it was a flat-bottomed two-master, of a type designed to navigate the difficult approaches to the Zuyder Zee. Called by the Dutch a *vlieboot*, a term derived from the Island of Vlieland, it has been translated into English, without reference to its derivations as "flyboat." Later employed in the East India trade, the *Half Moon* was wrecked in 1615 on the shore of the Island of Mauritius, then owned by the Dutch.

[Mrs. Schuyler Van Rensselaer, *History of the City of New York*.]
        A. C. FLICK

Halfway Covenant, THE. If, as they reached adulthood, children of the founders of Massachusetts and Connecticut gave no acceptable proof of that spiritual experience called "regeneration," should they be granted full church membership? In June, 1657, an intercolonial ministerial conference at Boston attempted to answer through the "Halfway Covenant," whereby membership was granted but, pending regeneration, participation in the Lord's Supper and voting in the church were withheld. Liberals objected, and though a Massachusetts Synod proclaimed it for all Massachusetts churches (1662), controversy continued for more than a century.

[Williston Walker, *The Creeds and Platforms of Congregationalism;* Perry Miller in *The New England Quarterly,* VI, 1933.]

RAYMOND P. STEARNS

Halifax, Fort, built in 1754 on a point of land at the confluence of the Sebasticook and the Kennebec rivers*ᵂ* in what is now Winslow, Maine, was one of the last of the line of forts erected by the British to enforce their claim to the Kennebec region.

[W. D. Williamson, *History of Maine.*]

ELIZABETH RING

Halifax Fisheries Award. The Marcy-Elgin Reciprocity Treaty of 1854*ᵂ* provided for extension of the inshore fishing "liberties" of the Convention of 1818*ᵂ* to all (instead of stipulated) Atlantic coastal waters of British North America, with reciprocal privileges for British subjects in American coastal waters as far south as 36° N. Lat. The treaty expired in 1866. The Treaty of Washington of 1871*ᵂ* provided for readmission of American citizens for ten years (extended to expire in 1885), without the reciprocal provision: instead a special mixed commission was to sit at Halifax to determine the amount of money that might be justly awarded to Great Britain as compensation for the abandonment of the reciprocal privilege in American territorial waters. The commission awarded $5,500,000 in gold to Great Britain as compensation.

[Samuel Flagg Bemis, *A Diplomatic History of the United States.*]

SAMUEL FLAGG BEMIS

Hall, Fort (Idaho), a fur-trading post located on the left bank of the Snake River near the junction of the Snake and Portneuf rivers, was built in the summer of 1834 by Nathaniel J. Wyeth. It was named in honor of Henry Hall of Boston, one of Wyeth's financial backers. In 1837 the fort was sold to the Hudson's Bay Company*ᵂ*, which operated the establishment until its abandonment in 1855. Fort Hall was a center for trade with Indians, and a stopping and trading point for Oregon Trail*ᵂ* immigrants, 1841–55. Here Idaho's first Protestant religious service was held, July 27, 1834, by the Rev. Jason Lee, a Methodist missionary. Under the Oregon Treaty*ᵂ* the United States Government reimbursed the Hudson's Bay Company for the value of the post.

[C. J. Brosnan, *History of the State of Idaho;* H. M. Chittenden, *The American Fur Trade.*]

CORNELIUS JAMES BROSNAN

Hamburg Riot, S. C., THE, of July 8, 1876, was the most important act of violence in the struggle between the Radical Republicans*ᵂ* and the Democrats for the control of South Carolina. Several hundred armed white men gathered in Hamburg to force the disarming of a Negro militia company guilty of obstructing the streets. In the melee which followed one white and seven Negroes were killed. Chamberlain, the Radical governor, called the affair a massacre engineered for political purposes. This alienated the white supporters of the governor and made certain the triumph of the faction of no compromise with the Radicals in the state Democratic convention of the following August.

[F. B. Simkins and R. H. Woody, *South Carolina during Reconstruction.*]

FRANCIS B. SIMKINS

Hamilton, Fort, was built by Gen. Arthur St. Clair*ᵂ* in September, 1791, during his ill-fated campaign against the northwestern Indians. Located on the Great Miami River at the present Hamilton, Ohio, it was the first and one of the most important, of a line of posts which constituted a chain between Fort Washington*ᵂ* (Cincinnati) and the Maumee Valley. A stockade fifty yards square with four substantial bastions, it was chiefly for storage purposes. In 1792, upon order of Gen. James Wilkinson, it was almost doubled in size by means of the enclosure with pickets of an area to the north.

[Henry Howe, *Historical Collections of Ohio,* I.]

FRANCIS PHELPS WEISENBURGER

Hamilton's Report on Manufactures (1791), made by him as Secretary of the Treasury in response to a House resolution, defended protective tariffs*ᵂ*, rejected Physiocracy's exaltation of agriculture, and argued that manufacturing is essential to the increase of society's income and the provision of a dependable home market for agriculture.

[F. W. Taussig, *Selected Readings in International Trade and Tariff Problems.*]

FRANK A. SOUTHARD, JR.

Hamlet Case, THE (1850), first recorded case under the Fugitive Slave Law of 1850*ᵂ*, exemplified the charge of abolitionists*ᵂ* that the law would facilitate the kidnapping of free Negroes. James Hamlet, free Negro of New York City, was arrested and taken to a Baltimore jail, in strict accordance with the law. He was shortly redeemed through the contributions of New York abolitionists.

[M. C. McDougall, *Fugitive Slaves.*]

GILBERT HOBBS BARNES

Hammer v. Dagenhart was decided by the Supreme Court of the United States in 1918, by a vote of five to four, in which the Court invalidated an act passed by Congress in 1916, designed to check the evil of child labor^{qv} by excluding from shipment in interstate commerce the products of mines and manufacturing establishments in which children under certain ages had been employed. The Court held the act unconstitutional on the ground that it was not a regulation of commerce, but an attempt to regulate the conditions of manufacturing and production—a matter that has been reserved to the states.

[Hammer v. Dagenhart, 247 U. S. 251, 1918; H. Hull and T. I. Parkinson, The Federal Child Labor Law, *Political Science Quarterly*, December, 1916; T. R. Powell, The Child Labor Law, the Tenth Amendment, and the Commerce Clause, *Southern Law Review*, August, 1918.]
P. ORMAN RAY

Hampden, Maine, Expedition (1814) was part of the general plan of the British to take possession of northeastern Maine in order to gain a direct route from Halifax to Quebec. The British occupied Castine^{qv} at the mouth of the Penobscot, Sept. 1, and proceeded up the river. The militia at Hampden offered but slight resistance, and Capt. Charles Morris of the United States corvette *Adams,* anchored there for repairs, was forced to fire his vessel and flee. Bangor (Sept. 3) and Frankfort (Sept. 6) surrendered without resistance. From then until the evacuation of Castine by the British, April 25, Maine east of the Penobscot was for the most part under the control of the British.

[W. D. Williamson, *The History of the State of Maine.*]
ROBERT E. MOODY

Hampton Roads Conference, THE. In response to an unofficial attempt of Francis P. Blair, Sr., to bring about peace when the collapse of the Confederacy was evident, Jefferson Davis wrote that he was willing to enter into a conference "with a view to secure peace to the two countries." On seeing this letter Abraham Lincoln wrote Blair of his readiness to bring peace "to the people of our one common country." In spite of the opposing points of view a conference was held, Feb. 3, 1865, on the *River Queen* in Hampton Roads between Lincoln and Seward on the one hand and Alexander H. Stephens, R. M. T. Hunter and J. A. Campbell representing the Confederacy. A veiled suggestion made by Blair for an armistice during which Confederate troops could be sent secretly to Mexico to assist the nationalist movement was rejected by Lincoln, who offered peace on the basis of (1) reunion, (2) emancipation, (3) disbanding of Confederate troops, with a personal promise of sympathetic treatment. The Confederate representatives were not empowered to accept any terms except independence, and the conference adjourned without further agreement.

[J. F. Rhodes, *History of the United States.*]
JAMES ELLIOTT WALMSLEY

Handcart Companies. *See* Mormon Handcart Companies.

Handicrafts. *See* Household Arts.

Hanging, as a method of execution, was carried over from England by the early settlers of this country. Other severe practices of inflicting death, while not extensive, were occasionally resorted to during the colonial period.

With the adoption of the Constitution, which prohibited "cruel and unusual punishment," these other methods were abandoned and hanging remained as the sole legal means of effecting capital punishment, until the innovation of electrocution and lethal gas^{qv}.

Notwithstanding the constitutional provision, a hanging, as it was conducted, was none the less cruel. Not only was it the occasion of festivities, during which a body was often left suspended for an entire day, but the method of execution lacked the slightest essentials of science. The condemned man was frequently flung from a ladder, or placed on a cart which was wheeled from under him; and instead of sustaining a quick, painless death, the victim, rather, suffered the agonies of slow strangulation.

The last century, however, brought about the adoption of more humane and scientific principles. The scaffold was established, the hangman's knot developed; and the combined effect of both created a snapping of the spinal column which results, presumably, in a swift and painless end.

Today, all hangings are private (with the exception of those that take place in a few Southern jurisdictions), and are conducted only in fourteen of the states and by the Federal Government.
LEWIS E. LAWES

Hanging Rock, S. C., Action at (Aug. 6, 1780). Gen. Sumter, with a force practically stripped of ammunition, attacked a mixed body of British regulars, Provincials and Tories, and defeated it with heavy loss. The Tories fled the field and, had not Sumter's men stopped to plunder the British camp of liquor, the American victory could have been made decisive.

[Francis V. Greene, *The Revolutionary War.*]
ROBERT S. THOMAS

Hannastown. When the Pennsylvania colonial government organized its westernmost lands into Westmoreland County in 1773, the county seat was established at Robert Hanna's tavern on the old Forbes Road[w], thirty-five miles east of Pittsburgh. Virginia claimed this area and sent Capt. John Connolly of Pittsburgh to arrest the Pennsylvania magistrates at Hannastown (see Pennsylvania-Virginia Boundary Dispute). The settlement continued to be the center of Pennsylvania county government during the Revolution, and was an important rendezvous for expeditions against the Indians who, on July 13, 1782, led by the Seneca, Guyasuta, attacked and burned it. In 1787 the county seat was moved three miles south to Greensburg on the newly created state turnpike.

[Edgar W. Hassler, *Old Westmoreland.*]

RANDOLPH C. DOWNES

Hannastown Resolution. Upon receipt of the news of the Revolutionary clash at Lexington[w], Mass., the frontier inhabitants of Westmoreland County, Pa., met at Hannastown[w] on May 16, 1775, and declared it the duty of Americans to resist English oppression. Stimulated by the danger of a frontier Tory-Indian co-operation with the English, the Association of Westmoreland County was organized to be ready to resist force with force.

[Edgar W. Hassler, *Old Westmoreland.*]

RANDOLPH C. DOWNES

Hannibal & St. Joseph Railroad, THE, was incorporated in 1847, work began on it in 1851, and it was completed in 1859. It was enormously important during the next two or three years when St. Joseph was the starting-point for the Pony Express[w], and the nearest railroad terminus during the Pikes Peak gold rush[w], for which this railroad carried the mails.

[R. I. Holcombe, ed., *History of Marion County, Missouri.*]   ALVIN F. HARLOW

Hanover (Pa.), Cavalry Engagement at (June 30, 1863), was an incident of the Gettysburg Campaign[w]. On June 25 Gen. J. E. B. Stuart (C.) left Lee's advancing army and raided around the Army of the Potomac[w]. Desiring to rejoin Lee he was forced to detour and moved northward toward Carlisle. In and about Hanover he was opposed by Gen. Judson Kilpatrick with whom he was engaged for the greater part of the day. Unable to break through, he turned eastward and arrived, July 1, in Carlisle via Jefferson and Dover, Pa.

[D. S. Freeman, *R. E. Lee.*]

ROBERT FORTENBAUGH

Harbors, in America, as elsewhere, have played a large part in the location of populations. The first explorers sought them, and there some of the earliest settlements began. That New York has the finest natural harbor on the Atlantic coast has something to do with the fact that the largest urban population in the Western Hemisphere is gathered in and around it. Boston was originally the leading port, but New York had deeper water and better waterways inland, and so took the supremacy in the 19th century. In 1902 work was begun on a 35-foot channel which reopened Boston harbor to the world's larger shipping. Portland (Maine), Philadelphia, Baltimore, Norfolk, Savannah, Mobile, Charleston, Galveston, San Francisco, Seattle and other cities are the natural developments of their sheltered anchorages. But on the Great Lakes, queerly enough, the large cities, Buffalo, Cleveland, Chicago, Milwaukee, Duluth, were built first, and artificial harbors were then created for them. Little was done in our earlier history toward the improvement of harbors. But under the colonial administrations of the 18th century, wharves, piers and docks at the Atlantic ports were brought to what was a high state of efficiency for those days. The United States Constitution vested all harbor rights and responsibilities in the Federal Government, and from that time all designing, construction and maintenance of harbors have been the care of army engineers, though in some cases cities have aided financially. The first congressional appropriation for harbor work was made in 1802, when $30,000 was spent in the erection of public piers at Philadelphia. In 1822 an appropriation was made for the building of a breakwater in Delaware Bay, and in 1826 funds were set aside for work in some twenty different places. With the completion of the Panama Canal[w] great improvements in harbors on the East and West coasts and in the Gulf of Mexico were carried out.

[Francis A. Collins, *Our Harbors and Waterways.*]

ALVIN F. HARLOW

Hard-Cider Campaign. *See* Campaign of 1840.

Hard Labor, Treaty of. At points along the frontiers the thrust of settlement in Virginia carried the whites across the Indian lines. One of these points was in southwest Virginia. To prevent war, Lord Shelburne sent from London instructions to the two superintendents of Indian affairs[w] in this country that the Indian tribes who claimed the western lands be called into separate conferences in which dividing lines might be agreed upon. At the south, Supt. John

Stuart convened the Cherokees[w] at Hard Labor in South Carolina, where on Oct. 14, 1768, a treaty was signed which fixed the line: to run from Tryon Mountain of the Blue Ridge by a straight line to Chiswell's Mine[w] on the New River; thence by a straight line to the confluence of the Kanawha with the Ohio River. Thus was recognized the claim of the Cherokees to lands west of that line. Virginians were not satisfied; the line as fixed left white settlers in the Indian country. Agitation led to a shift of the line farther west by the later treaty of Lochaber[w].

[S. C. Williams, *Dawn of Tennessee Valley and Tennessee History.*]   SAMUEL C. WILLIAMS

Hard Money is specie[w]. But those who favor hard money have, at different times, fought different opponents. In the 1830's the fight was against banks, which were opposed because they drove out specie, mixed in politics, and defrauded the people. The Specie Circular[w] of July 11, 1836, represents this point of view. In the 1870's and 1880's the fight was against the advocates of inconvertible government paper money as represented first by the Greenback party and later by the Populist party[qw]. This later group of hard money advocates had no objection to bank notes if they were redeemable in specie.

[D. R. Dewey, *Financial History of the United States.*]   JAMES D. MAGEE

Hard Roads. City pavements were the origin of hard roads. From cobblestones and roughly squared blocks on village streets transition was first to mud and later to gravel or crushed-stone surfaces, still known as "road metal." Gravel (stone broken by nature to pebbles) combined with sand and silt (or clay) and moisture forms a compact layer or carpet six to twelve inches thick on the soil or subgrade. Provided with adequate drainage, which was seldom, this served with fair satisfaction until the advent of automobiles. The only competitor of gravel was "macadam" or "macadamized surfaces"—the name from a Scotchman, John Loudon McAdam, first builder of crushed-stone roads bound with clay or stone dust and water, in England about 1815. Stone was broken by hand with hammers until 1858, when Eli Whitney Blake invented the "jaw" crusher, the first power-driven rock breaker. Macadam type surfaces were not used extensively outside of cities until the beginning of the state road movement (about 1891). From then until 1907, when motor cars began to replace horse-drawn vehicles, the macadam road maintained by continuous new applications was considered the "highest type." Pneumatic tires of motor cars changed the maintenance problem; they sucked out dust, or binder, and the surfaces speedily rutted and "corrugated." This led to application of asphaltic and tar oils for binder effect, supposed to have originated in California where asphaltic oils were plentiful and the process of extracting gasoline and other light oils had yet to be perfected. Next came application of mixtures of asphalt or tar with gravel or broken stone and sand, called "bituminous concrete," laid on the road and rolled with steam rollers, as ordinary or "water-bound" macadam had long been built. This type of bituminous surfacing, and the "mixed-in-place" type, where asphalt or tar is mixed with stone or gravel on the surface of the road with a kind of harrow, remain popular. The latest "high type" hard surface is a pavement of continuous slabs of portland cement concrete six to nine inches thick laid on a prepared subgrade, a kind of pavement old in cities (first in Bellefontaine, Ohio, 1884), but it was in Wayne County, Mich., and Milwaukee County, Wis., in 1909, that its practicability was first demonstrated for country roads. Brick on macadam foundation or on cement concrete foundation are used to some extent. Since hard-surfaced roads were introduced on state and county highways the progress has been toward constant straightening and widening of the paved surface. The first concrete pavements were fifteen feet wide for two-way traffic; this has changed to twenty-two feet; some main highways have two or four such lanes.

[Charles E. Foot, *Practical Road Building.*]   NATHAN C. ROCKWOOD

Hardware Trade. The earliest colonists brought articles of hardware from their European homes. As these needed replacing others were made by the colonists themselves, imported from Europe, or obtained from the village blacksmith. By 1800 a few importers specialized in the importation of hardware, and previous to the Civil War the majority of the articles entering the hardware trade were obtained from foreign sources, particularly Germany and England.

One of the earliest dealers to give most of his attention to American hardware was Amasa Goodyear, a manufacturer of Salem, who in 1826 opened a store in Boston. At this time domestic hardware only with difficulty could be sold without foreign labels. By the decade of the 1840's this situation was improved and by 1860 the majority of hardware items consumed in the United States were manufactured here. In 1929 there were 1789 wholesale and 25,330 retail establishments engaged in the hardware trade. The business of the wholesale establishments amounted to $866,158,332, that of the retail establishments to $706,052,831.

[V. S. Clark, *History of Manufactures in the United States, 1607-1929;* J. L. Bishop, *A History of American Manufactures;* Saunders Norvell, *Forty Years of Hardware.*]

FRED M. JONES

Hargis-Callahan-Cockrill Feud (1899–1903). This dispute arose over the outcome of the local election in Breathitt County, Ky., in 1899. Between December, 1901, and May, 1903, thirty-eight persons from the factions were killed.

[L. F. Johnson, *Famous Kentucky Tragedies and Feuds.*]

T. D. CLARK

Harlem, Battle of (Sept. 16, 1776). After the Battle of Long Island*ᵂ*, Washington, finding himself unable to hold New York City, withdrew to Manhattan Island and established a line from the mouth of the Harlem River across the island to Harlem (now Morningside) Heights. His army's morale was low, and groups of soldiers, sometimes whole companies, were leaving camp almost daily and going home. On the morning of Sept. 16 about 1000 British appeared on the Harlem Plains, and skirmishing began. Washington ordered Col. Knowlton's Connecticut Rangers and three Virginia companies under Maj. Leitch to strike at the enemy's rear. The movement was made too hastily, and both Knowlton and Leitch were killed; but with reinforcements sent down from the heights, the British were repulsed and driven back. This small victory greatly heartened the American troops, and Washington held his position for another month.

[Henry B. Carrington, *Battles of the American Revolution.*]

ALVIN F. HARLOW

Harlem in New York City. The first settler on the site of present-day Harlem came from Holland in 1636. Others soon followed, but between 1639 and 1647 the little colony was repeatedly ravaged and the settlers driven away by Indians. In 1658 a village christened New Haarlem was created by Gov. Stuyvesant and given military protection. It was declared annexed to New York in 1731, though several miles of open country separated the two places. A small nucleus of colored citizens in 1900 became within thirty years the largest Negro community on the continent.

[Carl Horton Pierce, *New Harlem, Past and Present.*]

ALVIN F. HARLOW

Harmar, Fort, was built at the junction of the Muskingum and Ohio rivers, on the west bank

of the Muskingum, in the fall of 1785 and spring of 1786, by Maj. John Doughty, and named for Colonel, later General, Josiah Harmar*ᵂ*, who occupied it for a time. The troops furnished protection to the surveyors of the seven ranges*ᵂ*, and later to the early settlers at Marietta*ᵂ*. After Wayne's victory at Fallen Timbers and the resulting treaty of Greenville*ᵠᵂ*, the troops were withdrawn.

[A. A. Graham, Military Posts in the State of Ohio, in Ohio Archaeological and Historical Society, *Publications,* III.]

T. N. HOOVER

Harmar, Fort, Treaties of. There were two Fort Harmar*ᵂ* treaties, both negotiated the same day, Jan. 9, 1789, by Arthur St. Clair, governor of the Northwest Territory*ᵂ*. The treaties were made separately so that the jealousy subsisting between the Six Nations*ᵂ* and the more westerly tribes should not be lessened. The treaty with the Six Nations (excepting the Mohawks, not represented) renewed and confirmed the Treaty of Fort Stanwix*ᵂ*, negotiated in 1784. This treaty fixed the western limits of the possessions of the Six Nations. A separate article provided severe punishment for Indians or whites guilty of stealing horses. Goods to the value of $3000 were given the Indians for these considerations.

The other treaty, with the Wyandot, Delaware, Ottawa, Chippewa, Potawatomi and Sauk nations*ᵠᵂ*, renewed and confirmed the treaty of Fort McIntosh*ᵂ*, of 1785. These nations were to serve as buffer nations against unfriendly Indians. For the consideration of $6000, the Indians relinquished all claim to lands beyond the limits set forth in the treaty.

[*American State Papers, Indian Affairs,* I, pp. 5-11.]

T. N. HOOVER

Harmar's Expedition (October–November, 1790). Before American settlers could occupy the Old Northwest*ᵂ*, the Indian confederacy opposed to them must be conquered. The war began in 1790, and in October, Gen. Josiah Harmar marched from Fort Washington*ᵂ* (Cincinnati) against the Indian towns at present-day Fort Wayne*ᵂ*. Two hotly contested battles were fought (Oct. 18, 22) in or near Fort Wayne, in both of which important detachments of Harmar's troops were defeated, whereupon Harmar retreated to Fort Washington. The hostile confederacy had not been conquered, and the campaign is well characterized as a "mortifying failure."

[B. J. Griswold, *The Pictorial History of Fort Wayne, Indiana.*]

M. M. QUAIFE

Harmony Society, THE, was established in Butler County, Pa., in 1804, by German Separatists under the leadership of George Rapp and his adopted son Frederick Reichert. The Harmonists emigrated from Württemberg to escape the persecutions to which their dissidence from the German Lutheran Church had subjected them. Economic necessity and the equalitarianism inherent in their pietistic beliefs led them to organize communistically Feb. 15, 1805. Their communism was based on contracts between the members and the trustees under which all property and authority was surrendered to the society in exchange for maintenance. In 1815 the society removed to Posey County, Ind., but returned in 1825 to a permanent home at Economy, Pa., twenty miles below Pittsburgh on the Ohio River. Here the Harmonists engaged in agriculture and industry with remarkable success, but toward the end of the century their wealth was dissipated by unwise investments and poor management. They had adopted celibacy in 1807 and despite the occasional accession of new members, their numbers gradually diminished. Most of the property was sold by 1903 and the society came to a practical end although it was continued as a legal entity for the support of the four surviving members.

[Aaron Williams, *The Harmony Society;* J. A. Bole, *The Harmony Society;* Charles Nordhoff, *Communistic Societies of the United States.*]
                                        EDGAR B. NIXON

Harness. For several generations the ox yoke took the place of harness in the American colonies. By 1750 saddles were made for sale in large towns but until after 1800 saddle trees and hardware were imported. About the latter date heavy draft harness appeared with the advent of post roads, cast-iron plows, and other light agricultural machinery, which helped to shift animal cultivation from oxen to horses and mules. Meanwhile the manufacture of harness and saddle hardware began with allied trades in Connecticut.

During the stage-coach[w] period, which lasted from early in the century until the Civil War, harness factories were established at Hartford, Newark, Wheeling, Louisville, Cincinnati and other market centers. With the popularization of the buggy about 1850 a demand arose for light harness which was graceful and decorative as well as durable. About the same time harness-making machinery culminating in the sewing machine[w] was perfected, and accelerated the concentration of manufacturing in quantity production factories.

Since motors have displaced animal traction, harness-making has declined. Between 1890 and 1935 the number of establishments engaged in this manufacture decreased from 8000 to 157 and the value of its output fell from $53,000,000 to $13,000,000.

[Leander Bishop, *History of American Manufactures;* Chauncey M. Depew, *One Hundred Years of American Commerce; U. S. Census of Manufactures,* 1935.]
                                        VICTOR S. CLARK

Harney Expedition (1855–56). Aroused by depredations of Sioux Indians[w] on the frontiers (*see* Grattan Incident) and along the California Trail[w], the Government, in March, 1855, ordered Gen. Harney to punish the offending tribes and occupy their country. He left Fort Leavenworth[w], Aug. 5, with 1200 troops, and on Sept. 3 almost annihilated Little Thunder's band of Brulé Sioux at Ash Hollow[w]. Marching thence by Fort Laramie[w] and the White and Cheyenne rivers, he reached the Missouri, Oct. 19, at Fort Pierre[w], where the troops wintered. The following spring Harney built Fort Randall, 150 miles farther down the Missouri.

[*South Dakota Historical Collections,* Vol. I, 1902, Vol. II, 1904.]
                                        JOSEPH MILLS HANSON

Haro Channel Dispute, THE, concerned the definition of the marine boundary between Washington and British Columbia under the Oregon Treaty of 1846[w]: which was the channel, the Haro Strait or the Rosario Strait? Between them lay the San Juan[w] archipelago, capable of being fortified. An arbitral decision, 1872, designating the Haro Strait, awarded the archipelago to the United States.

[Samuel Flagg Bemis, *A Diplomatic History of the United States.*]
                                        RICHARD W. VAN ALSTYNE

Harpers Ferry, Capture of. On Sept. 9, 1862, at Frederick, Md., Lee (C.) issued his famous "Lost Order"[w] outlining his plan of operations. To clear the enemy from his rear, Lee directed Jackson to make a wide march to the southwest, capture the garrison at Harpers Ferry as quickly as possible and then hurry northward to rejoin the main army, which was to advance westward through South Mountain[w], delaying McClellan (U.) as much as possible, and meet Jackson as he came northward from Harpers Ferry. The combined forces would then move through Hagerstown into Pennsylvania (*see* Maryland, Invasion of).

By Sept. 14, Jackson was beginning his investment of Harpers Ferry. The "Lost Order" had come into McClellan's possession and he knew Lee's plans. His movements became more energetic. On the 15th Harpers Ferry surrendered. Lee had advanced to Sharpsburg[qv], expecting Jackson. Delayed by the unlooked-for opposition at Harpers Ferry, Jackson was twenty-four hours behind Lee's schedule, a delay that was nearly disastrous.

[G. F. R. Henderson, *Stonewall Jackson and the American Civil War.*]   THOMAS ROBSON HAY

Harpers Ferry Raid, THE (Oct. 16–18, 1859), was the most positive blow struck by the antislavery forces in the half-century of agitation for the abolition of slavery in the United States. Yet it was not representative of the organized abolition societies; rather it was a one-man war upon the institution of slavery. The raid itself was abortive and ended disastrously, but it created such public discussion and political turmoil that, for the first time, national thought was thoroughly aroused on the issue with a resultant sharp cleavage between the proslavery and antislavery forces. In its influence on the stream of history, and as one of the chief contributing causes of the Civil War, the quixotical foray of Capt. John Brown and his small army of liberation looms up as a milestone.

John Brown, while yet following the peaceful pursuits of farmer and wool factor, nursed a plan to invade the South and forcibly liberate the slaves. As early as 1847 he talked of his scheme with Frederick Douglass, following in general outline the plan finally adopted for a series of raids along the line of the Allegheny mountains, liberating the slaves and organizing the country under a plan of government of his own devising. A convention was held at Chatham, Canada, on May 8, 1858, when a provisional constitution was adopted, a paper government set up, and a provisional army established of which Brown himself was selected as commander in chief. Brown's supporters in the Northern states were few in number and apparently none was in his full confidence; to them he imparted only the barest outlines of his scheme of liberation, not even disclosing the locale. Trusting him, and yet distrusting militant motives, these friends raised the necessary funds for the expedition.

Harpers Ferry, Va. (now West Virginia), was selected as the place of raising the standard of the new revolution because it offered an easy gateway to the South and the slave-holding sections and for the more practical reason that it was the site of the United States armory and arsenal where stores of arms and munitions were kept. Fresh from "bleeding Kansas"[qv] and slave raids into Missouri, John Brown made his appearance at Harpers Ferry on July 3, 1859, and

established headquarters at the near-by Kennedy farm in Maryland. Men and material assembled, he moved to the assault on Sunday night, Oct. 16, heading his army of liberation of seventeen white and five colored men. Ironically enough, the first man to lose his life was a free Negro, who was shot down by one of the raiders when he attempted to escape. The venture failed for lack of support; not one slave willingly joined the army of liberation. Besieged by Virginia and Maryland state troops, the survivors of the raiding party were driven into a fire engine house on the government reservation. Early Tuesday morning, the 18th, a force of United States Marines, commanded by Col. Robert E. Lee and Lt. J. E. B. Stuart, battered down the doors and captured the insurgents. Seventeen in all, ten of whom were raiders, were killed in the fighting. Brown and six of his men were later hanged at Charles Town, the county seat; the leader on Dec. 2, 1859.

[O. G. Villard, *John Brown, A Biography;* Boyd B. Stutler, *Captain John Brown and Harpers Ferry.*]

         BOYD B. STUTLER

Harper's Weekly, a pictorial magazine founded by Fletcher Harper of the publishing firm of Harper and Brothers in 1857. It exerted great political influence during the Civil War, and was famous for the cartoons of Thomas Nast[qv] who became its staff artist in 1862. These cartoons were responsible for the overthrow of the infamous Tweed Ring[qv] in 1872 when the *Weekly* was at the height of its power. In 1916 it was consolidated with the *Independent.*

[J. Henry Harper, *The House of Harper.*]

         HALLIE FARMER

Harpes, THE. Big and Little Harpe, brothers, were arch-criminals among criminals. They operated in pioneer times, chiefly in Kentucky and Tennessee. After Big Harpe was captured and beheaded by regulators in 1799, Little Harpe, under another name, joined Samuel Mason's band[qv] of highwaymen. He was legally hanged near Natchez in 1804.

[Otto A. Rothert, *The Outlaws of Cave-in-Rock.*]

         OTTO A. ROTHERT

Harris' Ferry (Harrisburg). John Harris, a native of England, settled on the Susquehanna River shortly before 1719, and later operated a public ferry there, which was much used by east- and west-bound travelers. His son, John Harris, Jr., became an important citizen during the French and Indian War[qv]. Councils with the Indians were held at his home in 1756 and 1757. In

1778 survivors of the Wyoming Massacre[w] came down the river in flatboats[w] and found shelter and protection with Harris. In 1785 Harris had a city laid out around his home, predicting that it would become the capital of the state, which it did in 1812.

[George W. Morgan, *Annals of Harrisburg.*]

ALVIN F. HARLOW

Harrisburg Convention. After the Tariff of 1824 proved unsatisfactory to the woolen interests and the "Woolens Bill" of 1827 had been defeated, the friends of protection[w] called a convention at Harrisburg, Pa., to agree upon a new bill. Meetings were held throughout the Northern states and 100 delegates from thirteen states met at Harrisburg, July 30–Aug. 3, 1827. A memorial to Congress was agreed upon in which the special needs of woolens and the general value of protection were set forth. However, because the Tariff of 1828 (*see* Tariff of Abominations) was drafted and passed for political ends, the demands of the memorial were ignored.

[Edward Stanwood, *American Tariff Controversies in the 19th Century.*]   ROBERT FORTENBAUGH

Harrison, Fort (Ind.), named for Gen. William Henry Harrison, was built in 1811 on the east bank of the Wabash River, where Terre Haute now stands, as a protection against depredations of Tecumseh[w] and the Prophet.

[Benson J. Lossing, *Pictorial Field Book of the War of 1812.*]   ROBERT S. THOMAS

Harrison Land Act, THE (May 10, 1800), named after William Henry Harrison, first delegate from the Northwest Territory[w] and chairman of the Committee on Public Lands responsible for its framing, is of the greatest significance in the history of the Federal Government's policy toward its public domain[w]. It amended and democratized the terms of the act of 1796, reflecting the demands of the frontier (*see* Land Act of 1796).

The chief complaint against the system established by the act of 1796 was that it encouraged the purchase of land by speculators and inhibited the acquisition of farm tracts by settlers. Nor had its operation resulted in large returns to the Government, for less than 50,000 acres of land had been sold between 1796 and 1800. The act of 1800, therefore, while retaining the rectangular system of survey established in 1796, was designed to facilitate individual purchase of land on easier terms (*see also* Division Act of 1800). Framed largely in accordance with the proposals of Harrison's report of Feb. 18.

1800, the act provided for the sale of land west of the Muskingum River in units as small as 320 acres. East of that river tracts of 640 acres were still to be offered. The credit system was made more flexible to meet the needs of the settlers, a four-year term being offered during which time payments might be completed, and the penalties for forfeiture abated. The minimum price of two dollars an acre and the auction system were retained but the administrative machinery was revised in the interests of the small purchaser. Four land districts were established, each with its respective land office—Cincinnati, Chillicothe, Marietta and Steubenville. Annual auction sales at stipulated dates were to be held in each office but private sales might take place in the intervening periods. The office of register was instituted to administer the land sales and records in each district. The act thus laid the foundations for the Government's democratic policy, and remains a monument to Harrison and to the influence of the frontier.

[B. H. Hibbard, *A History of the Public Land Policies;* D. B. Goebel, *William Henry Harrison.*]

DOROTHY BURNE GOEBEL

"Harrison's Landing Letter," McClellan's (July 7, 1862). Gen. McClellan had prepared a letter in which he desired to lay before President Lincoln, for private consideration, his personal views concerning the existing state of the rebellion, although they did not come strictly within the scope of his official duties. He handed it in person to the President at Harrison's Landing, on the James River, where Lincoln had come following the Seven Days Battles[w]. McClellan did not intend the letter to be published, but Lincoln showed it to his friends and the contents soon became publicly known. The views of McClellan were in opposition to those of the radical element of the Republican party (*see* Radical Republicans) and their personal hostility to him was vastly increased. This renewed opposition ultimately led to McClellan's downfall a few months later.

[George B. McClellan, *McClellan's Own Story;* W. S. Myers, *General George Brinton McClellan.*]

WILLIAM STARR MYERS

Harrodsburg. The earliest white settlement in Kentucky was begun at Harrod's Town (or -burg) in June, 1774, by James Harrod. Before the settlement was completed, however, Dunmore's War[w] occurred, and Harrod and his men left to participate in this struggle, returning in 1775. Harrodsburg became the principal base of operation for the Virginia pioneers, and it was here that George Rogers Clark[qv] planned (1777) his campaign against the British in the Northwest.

[Lewis Collins, *History of Kentucky.*]

T. D. CLARK

Hartford, Conn. *See* River Towns.

Hartford, THE, was a wooden-screw steam sloop-of-war, of 2790 tons, 226 feet by 43 feet, named for Hartford, Conn., and launched at the Charlestown Navy Yard, Boston, Nov. 22, 1858. She was armed with twenty-two 9-inch smooth-bore guns in broadside and two 20-pounder Parrott rifles. During the Civil War the ship became famous as the flagship of Admiral David Glasgow Farragut in the passage of Forts Jackson and St. Philip, in the bombardment and passage of the batteries at Vicksburg and later at Port Hudson, and in the Battle of Mobile Bay[qv]. In 1939 she was brought to Washington where, after being restored, she will become the nucleus of the Naval Museum.

[Frederic S. Hill, *Twenty-Six Historic Ships;* A. T. Mahan, *Admiral Farragut.*]   CHARLES LEE LEWIS

Hartford, Treaty of (1650), was between Peter Stuyvesant, governor of New Netherland, and the Commissioners of the United Colonies of New England[qv]. The Dutch and the New Englanders had quarreled over the ownership of the Connecticut Valley, the detention of fugitives, trade by the Dutch with the Connecticut Indians, the expulsion of English traders along the Delaware and the seizure of a Dutch ship in New Haven harbor. Stuyvesant visited Hartford, and it was agreed to submit these contested points to the arbitration of four disinterested persons. The four "delegates" presented an award which left the Delaware question open; accepted Stuyvesant's explanation of the seizure of a Dutch ship in New Haven harbor and established a boundary line between the English and Dutch that was drawn, on Long Island, across the island from Oyster Bay, and, on the mainland, from Greenwich twenty miles northward into the county. The Estates-General ratified this agreement in 1656; England never ratified it.

[F. G. Davenport, ed., *European Treaties Bearing on the History of the United States and Its Dependencies,* II.]

MAX SAVELLE

Hartford, Treaty of (1786). *See* Phelps-Gorham Purchase.

Hartford Convention, THE, called at the invitation of the Massachusetts legislature, was a meeting of twenty-six New England Federalists. Its inspiration was the opposition of New England mercantile interests, the Essex Junto and Federalists generally, to Jeffersonian Republican policies and to the War of 1812[qv]. Delegates, elected by the legislatures, were sent from Massachusetts, Connecticut and Rhode Island. Vermont and New Hampshire failed to co-operate, although two counties in the former and one in the latter sent delegates. The convention was held in secret sessions at Hartford, Conn. (Dec. 15, 1814–Jan. 5, 1815), for the declared purpose of considering the advisability of calling a general convention to revise the Constitution. It was a distinguished group, and, with one or two exceptions, was not drawn from the radical Federalist element, its most prominent figure being Harrison Gray Otis, who looked upon it as a safety valve for pent-up Federalist feeling.

Resentment in New England against commercial restrictions and westward expansion had been augmented by the unpopular war with England, which raised vexatious problems as to the control of state militia and the protection of the New England coast. The resolutions adopted for the consideration of New England legislatures recommended interstate co-operation in repelling British attacks, the use of Federal revenues in state defense, and the protection of citizens against unconstitutional military acts. The New England states were also urged to support constitutional amendments which would limit Southern political power, commercial embargoes and trade restrictions, declarations of war, admission of new states into the Union and officeholding by naturalized citizens.

Having made tentative plans for calling another meeting in six months, the convention adjourned. Both because of its secrecy and the immediate end of the war it was laid open to ridicule and charges of treasonable intent, and the doctrines of state and sectional rights which it advocated were temporarily discredited throughout the nation.

[Theodore Dwight, *History of the Hartford Convention;* Samuel Eliot Morison, *The Life and Letters of Harrison Gray Otis, 1765-1848.*]   ROBERT A. EAST

Hartford Wits, THE. In the last two decades of the 18th century a small group of youthful writers, chiefly Yale graduates, banded together as an informal literary club at Hartford, Conn., and achieved wide recognition through their timely satiric verse. The company was dubbed, first locally, later by a wider circle, "The Hartford (or Connecticut) Wits." The principal members were John Trumbull, Joel Barlow, David Humphreys, Timothy Dwight, Theodore Dwight, Richard Alsop and Lemuel Hopkins. Individually prolific writers, their chief productions in collaboration were *The Anarchiad, The Political Greenhouse* and *The Echo.* Contemporarily popular, but possessing scant literary merit, these effusions satirized educational curricula and the policies of Jeffersonian democracy[w].

[The Pleiades of Connecticut, *Atlantic Monthly,* February, 1865; H. A. Beers, *The Connecticut Wits and Other Essays;* Francis Parsons, *The Friendly Club and Other Portraits;* V. L. Parrington, ed., *The Connecticut Wits.*]

GEORGE B. UTLEY

Harvard College, the first collegiate foundation in the limits of the present United States, was established by the Massachusetts General Court's grant of £400, Oct. 28, 1636. Sept. 14, 1638, John Harvard of Charlestown, Mass., a Cambridge University graduate, died and left it his library and half of his property. In March the General Court named it Harvard. Its founding originated in the Puritans' conviction that learning was essential for godliness. Many Massachusetts settlers were graduates of English universities or had relatives who were, and their interest in higher education had popular support, testified to by individual gifts and grants from public funds to Harvard. The charter of 1650 defined the college's aim as "the aduancement of all good literature artes and Sciences" and the "education of the English and Indian Youth . . . in knowledge and godlines." It was to supply an educated clergy but it was never a mere ministerial training school. Budding preachers, like other students, took a liberal arts course essentially like that of Oxford and Cambridge, both of which for years recognized Harvard degrees as equivalent to their own. The first lay president was John Leverett, in office from 1708 to 1724, who upheld "a house of learning under the spirit of religion, not . . . the divinity school of a . . . sect" and "founded the liberal tradition of Harvard University" in spite of clerical conservatism. Harvard's 18th-century liberalism was, by modern standards, limited, but it kept "so far independent of sectarian control, as the times and circumstances made wise or possible." Before the Revolution mathematical and scientific instruction, originally weak, had been built up, and the first laboratory of experimental physics in this country had been started. The old system of having one tutor instruct a whole college class in all subjects was replaced by assigning tutors to instruction in special fields. Students came chiefly from New England but there were a few from the West Indies, the Carolinas and Bermuda. The largest graduating class before 1810 had sixty-three members (1771). In the Massachusetts constitution of 1780, Harvard was designated a university, and the founding of the Medical School (1782), the Law School (1817), the Divinity School (1819) and the Scientific School (1847) helped it to live up to the title. Its first two centuries were marked by devotion to a liberal arts tradition, progressive secularization of government and curriculum and increase in numbers of students. In the last hundred years its growth has been vast, and the elective system and the tutorial plan are but two of its contributions to American higher education. In 1938 its endowment was about $140,000,000, and in June, 1937, it conferred 2060 degrees.

[S. E. Morison, *Three Centuries of Harvard;* also his *Founding of Harvard College; Harvard in the Seventeenth Century; Development of Harvard University, 1869-1929.*]

KENNETH B. MURDOCK

Haskell Institute (Lawrence, Kans.), named for Dudley C. Haskell, congressman from Kansas, was established under an act of Congress of 1882 authorizing three nonreservation Indian schools for vocational training on the model of Carlisle[w] in Pennsylvania. It was opened September, 1884, with fourteen Indian students, offering, during its early years, training in four industries, carpentry, shoemaking, farming, and sewing and housework. The curriculum was expanded in variety of trades represented and came to include a four-year high school and a two-year commercial course. In 1927 the lower grades were limited. The high point of enrollment was reached in 1931 at 1173. Restrictions followed, diverting to regular institutions many who could finance their own education. After 1933 drastic changes were made; the attendance limit was set at 600; concentration focused on vocational work other than agriculture, which was transferred to Chilocco, Okla.; and the operation of the farm of about 1000 acres, built up from the 230 acres donated by Lawrence to secure the location of the institution, was abandoned.

JAMES C. MALIN

Hastings' Cutoff, named for Lansford W. Hastings who first advocated its use in 1846, followed a route to California which crossed the Salt Desert and the Sierra mountains instead of proceeding to Fort Hall[w], Idaho, and then branching southward. It shortened the route, but produced terrible suffering among emigrants driving slow-moving ox teams.

[L. W. Hastings, *Emigrants' Guide to California*, ed. by C. H. Carey.] CARL L. CANNON

Hatch Act (Aug. 2, 1939). This act marked the culmination of a long-drawn-out campaign to secure adequate Federal regulation of national elections, primaries and party conventions. Its author was Sen. Carl Hatch of New Mexico, who began agitating for "clean politics" in 1932. President Roosevelt, in his annual message to Congress on Jan. 5, 1939, suggested the need of legislation to eliminate "improper political practices" from relief[qv] activity. The Hatch Act, however, went far beyond his wishes and he signed it with obvious reluctance. The bill was supported by Republicans and those Democrats who reacted against the general use of relief workers for political purposes by the New Dealers.

Described as an act "To Prevent Pernicious Political Activities," the law lists nine "unlawful" actions. No one may "intimidate, threaten, or coerce" any person so as to influence his vote for or against any candidate for a Federal office. No promise of employment "or other benefit" may be made "directly or indirectly" for political support. Relief workers may vote as they please without intimidation. Political contributions may not be solicited from relief workers. Federal executive or administrative employees, except certain policy determining officials, may not "take any active part in political management or in political campaigns."

[*The United States News*, Aug. 7, 1939; 53 *Statutes at Large.*]
ERIK McKINLEY ERIKSSON

Hatcher's Run, Battle of. *See* Boydton Plank Road, Engagements at.

Hatchet, Burying the. This term appears in American literature as symbolizing a pledge of peace between Indian tribes or between Indians and whites. Often it is applied to an individual, Indian or white, who decides to withdraw from a controversy.

In the documents drawn up by historic Iroquois Indians (*Bulletin 184*, New York State Museum), explaining the principles of the League of the Five Nations[qv], a symbolic tree is mentioned, which is dug up, and all weapons of war cast into the hole and the tree replanted. This concept is certainly prehistoric. One of the first acts of white traders was to introduce the metal tomahawk[qv], in English, a hatchet, which soon became the symbol of Indian raids. Knox (1767), writing of Indians in New York and New England, tells that a hatchet painted red was thrown down in a friendly village as an invitation to join in a war. Acceptance was signified by picking it up or by "taking up the hatchet." In some instances war was declared by striking a hatchet into the ceremonial post in the center of the village. Priority in the literary use of "burying

the hatchet" is usually credited to Washington Irving. Thus while the actual origin of the term is obscure, the concept is found in Iroquois tradition where the burying of all weapons symbolized the making of peace. It was probably the existence of this symbolism and the subsequent place of the tomahawk in colonial speech, that led to the phrase "burying the hatchet."

[Lewis H. Morgan, *The League of the Iroquois.*]
CLARK WISSLER

Hatchet, Carrie Nation's. Carrie Nation (1846–1911) was a famous crusader in the temperance movement[qv]. She led public demonstrations against saloons, praying and preaching at the doors of the illegal "joints" in Barber County, Kans., where she lived. She finally decided that more drastic measures were necessary, and in 1900 wrecked several saloons with stones and iron bars, but failed to get herself arrested as, in arresting her, the town officials would have acknowledged the existence of the illegal saloons. However, the smashing of a luxurious saloon in Wichita ultimately brought arrest, but the charge of malicious destruction of property was dropped and she was freed following startling demonstrations from the Woman's Christian Temperance Union[qv] and almost nationwide attention. It was in Wichita, on Jan. 21, 1901, that she first used a hatchet. Saloon smashing was copied by women throughout the United States, urged on by Carrie Nation, who spent the rest of her life lecturing and attracting attention to the temperance movement by hatchet wielding even in New York City and Washington, D. C.

[Herbert Asbury, *Carrie Nation.*]
CHARLES MARION THOMAS

Hatfield–McCoy Feud, THE, was one of the most savage of mountain vendettas. Anderson (Anse) Hatfield, clan leader, and many of his kinsmen lived in Williamson County, W. Va., the McCoys just across the border in Kentucky. Their animosity dated back to the Civil War, but the feud proper began in 1880, after a Hatfield had been accused of stealing a semi-wild hog belonging to Randolph McCoy. In 1882 three sons of Randolph were seized by a squad of Hatfields led by a constable and a justice of the peace, on pretense of arrest for the killing of Ellison Hatfield, but instead, were brutally murdered. The feud continued, with frightful atrocities, suffered mostly by the McCoys, until 1888, when Kentucky officers made several raids into West Virginia, killing at least two Hatfield clansmen and capturing nine more, two of whom were executed, the others sent to state prison. By

1890, except for occasional killings, the war was ended.

[Charles G. Mutzenberg, *Kentucky's Famous Feuds and Tragedies.*]   ALVIN F. HARLOW

Hats, Restrictions on Colonial Manufacture of. Stimulated by the abundance of furs, colonial manufacturers, especially in New England and New York, were making and exporting hats to neighboring colonies, the West Indies and southern Europe. But in 1732 the influential Company of Felt-Makers in London persuaded Parliament to forbid colonial exportation of hats, to require a seven years' apprenticeship, to exclude Negroes and to limit each manufacturer to two apprentices. New York exported hats labelled "British" from 1733 to 1735 and John Adams stated the law was disregarded in Massachusetts, but the industry's rapid growth after 1783 suggests that the law had previously had an inhibiting effect.

[V. S. Clark, *History of Manufactures.*]
                                      LAWRENCE A. HARPER

Hatteras Inlet, Capture of (Aug. 28–29, 1861). At Hatteras Inlet, the key to Pamlico Sound, the Confederates had erected two weak forts with thirty-five guns. These were attacked by six Federal steam warships and one sailing sloop under Flag Officer S. H. Stringham, assisted by Maj. Gen. B. F. Butler and 860 soldiers. By using chiefly his large-shell guns and steaming at varying ranges, Stringham made it impossible for the defenders to reply effectively with their old short-range smooth-bores, and soon demolished the forts, forcing the garrison to surrender.

[Daniel Ammen, *The Navy in the Civil War.*]
                                      WALTER B. NORRIS

Haun's Mill Massacre, The, occurred Oct. 30, 1838, in Caldwell County, Mo. An armed mob of citizens, seeking to drive a colony of Mormons[w] from the state, suddenly appeared at the settlement, killed seventeen colonists, robbed their homes and ordered the survivors to leave the country on pain of death.

[Jenson, *Church Chronology;* H. H. Bancroft, *History of Utah.*]   J. F. SMITH

Havana Conference, The (Jan. 16–Feb. 20, 1928), was the Sixth International Conference of American States. President Coolidge attended the opening session. It improved the organization of the Pan American Union[w] and produced definite progress toward international conciliation and intellectual co-operation, but the principle of nonintervention was not agreed to.

[J. B. Scott, *The Sixth International Conference of American States.*]   HERMINIO PORTELL-VILÁ

Haverhill, Mass., Massacre at (March 15, 1697), was an incident of King William's War[w]. A band of Abnaki Indians burned the settlement at Haverhill, butchering twenty-seven women and children. Hannah Dustin and Mary Neff were carried off as captives. With the help of a boy previously captured by the Indians, these women, in the night, killed their entire Indian guard of twelve and brought their scalps back to Haverhill.

[Francis Parkman, *Count Frontenac and New France.*]
                                      ROBERT S. THOMAS

Haw River, N. C., Battle of the (Feb. 25, 1781). While in pursuit of Tarleton, Col. Henry Lee crossed the Haw, posed his forces as re-enforcements hurrying to Tarleton, and, completely deceiving Col. Pyle, nearly annihilated Pyle's Loyalist force. This American success deterred many local Tories from espousing the Loyalist cause.

[Henry B. Dawson, *Battles of the United States.*]
                                      ROBERT S. THOMAS

Hawaii, the Sandwich Islands, were visited by Gray and the *Columbia* in 1789–90, eleven years after their discovery by Cook[w]. Yankees trading in furs in the Pacific Northwest soon began visiting Honolulu (*see* China Trade). A thriving three-cornered trade developed; Hawaiian sandalwood was used in China in payment of goods for the American market. By 1820 American whalers[w] began to make Honolulu a repair port, some 400 visiting Hawaii annually from 1840–60. In 1820 Boston missionaries began the successful promotion of American influence. By 1840 Honolulu with its Yankee whalemen, missionaries and merchandise appeared as an American outpost.

To supervise growing American interests in Hawaii, President Monroe appointed a resident agent in 1820. American, as well as English and French, warships began visiting Hawaii. In 1826 the United States and Hawaii signed a treaty of peace and friendship. Though it was not ratified by the United States, Hawaii continued to respect it. Fearing French and English designs, Secretary of State Webster announced in 1842 that the independence of Hawaii be respected; that no power seek undue control or exclusive privileges. In 1843 Washington was represented in Hawaii by a diplomat, the first of his kind sent by any foreign power.

The acquisition of Oregon and California in the 1840's enhanced American interest in the Pacific and Asia. Honolulu, queen of the north Pacific, 2100 miles from San Francisco, became valuable as a naval station, a half-way point between Asia and California. Americans, including

President Pierce and Secretary Marcy, talked of the manifest destiny^{qv} of their country to include Hawaii. Influential Americans in Hawaii favored annexation. Fearing revolution from within, attacks by California filibusters or by some foreign power, King Hamehameha III consented to annexation on his terms. His death put a stop to the project.

Urged by the American sugar interests, the insular government appealed in 1848, 1852 and 1855 to Washington for a reciprocity treaty. In 1855 Secretary Marcy agreed, but the Senate, responding to the sugar interests of Louisiana, rejected the treaty. Attempts to revive the idea were made in 1863. In 1867 President Johnson signed it, but the Senate defeated it June 1, 1870. At the persistent urgings of the American sugar interests in Hawaii, King Kalakaua visited Washington in 1875 to exert some influence. Fearing that the islands might turn to England, President Grant signed the reciprocity treaty Jan. 30, 1875, and the Senate approved it a month and a half later. The treaty provided for free access of sugar and other products into American ports. When the treaty was renewed the United States was given the "exclusive right to enter the harbor of Pearl River."

This treaty stimulated Hawaiian industries, and American capital poured into the islands. When the McKinley tariff^{qv} of 1890 placed all sugar on the free list and Hawaii's basic industry lost its favored position, American growers demanded annexation as a means of restoring prosperity. When in 1893 Queen Liliuokalani attempted to eliminate American influence and restore autocratic rule, the influential Americans in Hawaii, with the connivance of United States Minister Stevens and the "moral" support of American marines, engineered a revolution, deposed the Queen, organized a provisional government, and opened negotiations with the United States for annexation. President Harrison signed the treaty, but before the Senate acted, Cleveland took office, withdrawing the document. When his special agent, Blount, reported the revolution a conspiracy between American planters and Minister Stevens, Cleveland ordered the restoration of the Queen. Refusing to obey, the provisional government converted itself into the Republic of Hawaii, soon recognized by foreign governments, including the United States.

The fear of Japanese designs upon the islands, and the value of the Hawaiian harbors, offered for the use of the United States during the Spanish-American War^{qv}, strengthened sentiment for annexation in Washington. On July 7, 1898, Hawaii was annexed by a joint resolution and on Aug. 12, the islands formally transferred sovereignty to the United States. In reply to Japan's protests, Washington assured Tokio that annexation would not affect the rights of Japanese in Hawaii.

By the Organic Act of April 30, 1900, Hawaii was made a full-fledged territory with American citizenship conferred on all citizens of the islands. The advantages of union have been mutual: practically the entire expanding Hawaiian trade is with the United States, while the islands furnish valuable naval bases for a strong American military and naval outpost. Hawaii favors even closer relations with the United States, statehood. Hawaii's "Bill of Rights," an act passed by Congress and signed by Coolidge April 10, 1924, meant greater benefits for the territory.

Hawaii's greatest social problem is the complexity of her population. Out of a total of 368,336 in 1930, pure and mixed natives were 49,167; whites, some 70,000; Chinese, 25,968; Filipino, 65,185; with the remainder Japanese.

[Ralph S. Kuykendall, *A History of Hawaii;* William D. Alexander, *A Brief History of the Hawaiian People;* Edmund J. Carpenter, *America in Hawaii.*]

J. W. ELLISON

Hawes-Cutting Act. *See* Tydings-McDuffie Act.

Hawkins, Fort, named after Benjamin Hawkins, Indian agent, was built in 1806 near the Ocmulgee River, on the site of the present city of Macon, Ga. After the defeat of the Creeks^{qv} by Andrew Jackson in 1813, Fort Hawkins lost its military importance.

[F. L. Paxson, *History of American Frontier.*]

CARL L. CANNON

Hawk's Peak Episode (March 6–9, 1846). When John C. Frémont was ordered by the Mexicans to leave California, he occupied Gavilan (Hawk's) Peak, some twenty-five miles from Monterey, built a log fort and raised the American flag. After three days he set out for Oregon. The affair helped to increase ill feelings between the Californians and the Americans and may be regarded as a direct cause of the Bear Flag Revolt^{qv}.

[J. C. Frémont, *Memoirs of My Life.*]

OSGOOD HARDY

Hawley-Smoot Tariff, THE, of 1930 was partly the outcome of unsatisfactory conditions in agriculture, and much of the discussion was concerned with farm products; but strenuous efforts were made to add further protection to certain manufactured products—a movement which the agricultural bloc was rather successful in stopping. On its way through Congress the bill was subjected to trading and logrolling, and both in method of construction and in final form was the antithesis of scientific tariff making. In spite of opposition, the act continued in modified form the "flexible clause" of the previous tariff. One section of the law prohibited the importation after Jan. 1, 1932, of goods produced by convict, forced or indentured labor. Forced labor was defined as "all work or service which is exacted from any person under the menace of penalty for its nonperformance and for which the worker does not offer himself voluntarily." Under some interpretations this statement might have described certain types of labor under communistic, or dictatorial, forms of government. The tariff stirred an unusual amount of hostility abroad. European critics associated the act with the payment of foreign war debts[qv] to the United States, and urged that not only did the high duties impose additional burdens on debtors, but that these nations were further embarrassed because of the decline of prices which made larger payments necessary, measured in goods, than was contemplated at the time the debt agreements were signed.

[F. W. Taussig, *Tariff History of the United States;* Isaac Lippincott, *Economic Development of the United States.*]   ISAAC LIPPINCOTT

Hay–Bunau-Varilla Treaty, THE, was signed on Nov. 18, 1903, by Secretary Hay and Philippe Bunau-Varilla, who, after the department of Panama revolted from Colombia, was made the envoy at Washington of the Panama Republic[qv]. This treaty provided that the United States should guarantee the independence of the republic of Panama, while that republic granted to the United States in perpetuity "the use, occupation, and control of a strip of land ten miles wide for the construction of a canal." Panama gave to the United States sovereign rights over this zone and the adjacent waters. In return, the United States agreed to pay the Panama Republic $10,000,000 when ratifications were exchanged and, beginning nine years thereafter, an annuity of $250,000. By this agreement the United States secured permission to construct the Panama Canal[qv] despite the fact that Colombia had refused to ratify the Hay-Herrán Treaty[qv].

[W. S. Robertson, *Hispanic-American Relations with the United States.*]   WILLIAM SPENCE ROBERTSON

Hay Burning. When settlement moved beyond the timber belt the homesteaders used up the scanty wood supply along the prairie streams, and having exhausted the buffalo chips[qv] turned to hay for fuel. It was twisted into convenient hanks

called "cats" and burned like sticks of wood. Mechanical devices were invented to twist these "cats." Special types of hay-burning stoves were invented and marketed on the plains. One known as a magazine type had several pipes like stove pipes which could be filled and inserted in the stove. A spring pushed the hay into the fire box.

[Everett Dick, *The Sod-House Frontier.*]
         EVERETT DICK

Hay-Herrán Treaty, THE, was signed by Secretary of State Hay and Minister Herrán of Colombia on Jan. 22, 1903. It provided that the New Panama Canal Company, which held an option on the canal route, might sell its properties to the United States. The treaty further provided that Colombia would lease to the United States a strip of land across the Isthmus of Panama for the construction of a canal. In return, the United States agreed to pay Colombia $10,000,000 cash and, after nine years, an annuity of $250,000. Although objections were made to this treaty because it did not give the United States complete governmental control over the proposed canal zone, yet it was ratified by the United States Senate. Evidently largely because of the expectation of securing greater financial returns, the Colombian Congress declined to ratify this convention.

[S. F. Bemis, *A Diplomatic History of the United States.*]
         WILLIAM SPENCE ROBERTSON

Hay-Pauncefote Treaties. The first Hay-Pauncefote Treaty, signed Feb. 5, 1900, modified the Clayton-Bulwer Treaty of 1850[qv], which provided for a joint protectorate by England and the United States of any transisthmian canal, to permit the construction and maintenance of a canal under the sole auspices of the United States. It was amended by the Senate to provide that it should supersede the Clayton-Bulwer Treaty, and to give the United States the right to fortify the canal. Great Britain declined to accept the Senate amendments, and the second Hay-Pauncefote Treaty was negotiated, and signed Nov. 18, 1901. Article I declared that it should supersede the Clayton-Bulwer Treaty. Article II provided that a canal might be constructed under the auspices of the United States and that she was to have all the rights incident to such construction as well as the right to regulate and manage the canal. However, Article III stipulated that the canal should be free and open to the vessels of all nations "on terms of entire equality" and that the charges of traffic should be "just and equitable" (*see* Panama Tolls Question). The United States was virtually accorded the sole power to assure the neutrality of transisthmian transit. Fortification of the canal was not mentioned, but during the negotiation the British foreign secretary admitted that the United States would have the right to fortify. This treaty made feasible the construction of a canal through Central America by the United States and enabled her to consider the Nicaragua route as an alternative to the Panama route.

[S. F. Bemis, *A Diplomatic History of the United States.*]

WILLIAM SPENCE ROBERTSON

Hayburn's Case (1792) was the first involving the constitutionality of an act of Congress to reach the Federal courts. It arose out of a pension^w law authorizing circuit judges to pass on claims subject to review by the Secretary of War and Congress. The decision of the Pennsylvania circuit on April 11, 1792, declining to hear the petition of William Hayburn on the grounds that it could not proceed because the law was inconsistent with the Constitution, led the Attorney General to appeal to the Supreme Court for a mandamus. The justices refused to act on the motion, but took under advisement one in behalf of Hayburn. Before a decision was announced other relief for pensioners was provided and, therefore, the Supreme Court never passed on the act. The decision in the Pennsylvania circuit is sometimes styled the "First Hayburn Case" to distinguish it from the motion before the Supreme Court.

[Charles Warren, *The Supreme Court in United States History.*]

L. J. MEYER

Hayes Award, a decision ending an Argentine–Paraguayan dispute over territory between the Verde and Pilcomayo rivers. In 1876 the two governments agreed to submit the question of title to the President of the United States, and on Nov. 12, 1878, Rutherford B. Hayes rendered an award upholding Paraguay's claims.

[*Foreign Relations of the United States*, 1878.]

MARY WILHELMINE WILLIAMS

Hayes–Tilden Controversy. *See* Campaign of 1876.

Hayfield Fight, THE, between a large number of Miniconjou Sioux^w and teamsters and soldiers of Fort C. F. Smith^w garrison, was one of the most stubbornly contested battles of the Sioux campaign in Montana. It occurred Aug. 1, 1867, in a hayfield about two and a half miles from the fort. The Americans, sheltered by a corral, were attacked repeatedly throughout the day, but held out until relieved in the evening. The American loss was three killed and four wounded.

[G. R. Hebard and E. A. Brininstool, *Bozeman Trail.*]

CARL L. CANNON

Haymarket Riot, THE (May 4, 1886), arose as an incident of the militant eight-hour movement of that year in Chicago which was frequently accompanied by conflicts between strikers and police. In protest against the shooting of several workmen, August Spies, editor of the semianarchist *Arbeiter-Zeitung*, issued circulars demanding revenge and announcing a mass-meeting at the Haymarket. Amidst general anticipation of violence, large police reserves were concentrated near by and Mayor Harrison attended the meeting; soon the mayor left, judging the speeches to be innocuous. Despite Harrison's advice, Capt. Bonfield and 180 police advanced on the meeting and ordered the crowd to disperse. At this point, a bomb, thrown by an unknown hand, fell among the police, resulting in seven deaths and numerous injured. Popular fears of a general anarchist plot made impartial investigation impossible; eight alleged anarchists^w were convicted on a conspiracy charge and four were hanged. The eight-hour movement collapsed beneath the stigma of radicalism^w. Gov. Altgeld pardoned the three surviving prisoners in 1893, declaring that the trial had been a farce—an opinion severely condemned by the conservative press, but highly praised by organized labor.

[H. David, *The History of the Haymarket Affair.*]

HARVEY WISH

Hays, Fort (Kans.), built in 1867 by Gen. John Pope, was one of a system of military posts established to combat hostile Plains Indians. Gen. Phil Sheridan for a time made his headquarters at Fort Hays, as did Gen. George A. Custer in the campaigns of 1867–69 (*see* Washita, Sheridan's Operations on).

Building of the Kansas Pacific Railroad^w to this point caused the rise of Hays City, which became the most turbulent town on the Plains while it was the rail head. Here James Butler Hickok, known as "Wild Bill," began his notable career as a frontier marshal in 1869. He maintained order with his revolvers until 1870, when, having killed three soldiers in an altercation, he fled to escape execution by Gen. Sheridan.

Moving of the rail head to Fort Sheridan, Colo., brought more peaceful conditions, although as late as 1874, citizens fought a street battle with Negro soldiers from the fort, in which six of the latter were killed.

[William J. Cutler, *The History of Kansas.*]

PAUL I. WELLMAN

Haywood-Moyer-Pettibone Case was one of the great criminal cases involving organized labor in the United States. It involved the principal officers of the old Western Federation of Miners*, generally viewed as a radical union, and developed from the killing of former Gov. Steunenberg of Idaho in 1905, by a bomb planted at his home by one Harry Orchard. The assassin turned state's evidence and accused the three union leaders Charles H. Moyer, president; William D. Haywood, secretary-treasurer; and George A. Pettibone, formerly prominent in the union but at that time retired. Through questionable extradition proceedings, these men were taken from Colorado to Idaho. A jury of farmers and ranchmen acquitted Haywood, the first to be tried. Later, Pettibone was tried and acquitted, and Moyer was released without trial.

[Luke Grant, Idaho Murder Trial, *Outlook*, Vol. LXXXV, and The Haywood Trial: A Review, *Outlook*, Vol. LXXXVI.]   GORDON S. WATKINS

Hazelwood Republic, THE, was organized July 29, 1856, by Rev. Stephen R. Riggs at his Hazelwood Mission near Yellow Medicine, Upper Sioux Agency, in western Minnesota. The constitution, signed first by seventeen Indians and eight half-breeds, professed belief in God and His Word, education, agriculture, adoption of the dress and habits of white men, and obedience to United States laws. A president, secretary and three judges were elected biennially. Recognized by the Indian agent as a separate band, the republic numbered eighty-two fullbloods by 1858. Weakened by hostilities of "blanket" Indians, it disbanded about 1860. Its leaders rescued many whites during the Sioux Outbreak, 1862*.

[S. R. Riggs, *Mary and I, Forty Years with the Sioux*, The Dakota Mission, *Minnesota Historical Collection*, Vol. III, and Protestant Missions in the Northwest, *ibid.*, Vol. VI.]   RUTH THOMPSON

"He Kept Us Out of War," epitomizing President Wilson's success, up to that time, in avoiding the European war, was first expressed in the Democratic platform of 1916, and echoed by William Jennings Bryan at the St. Louis convention. It became a campaign slogan and aided in Wilson's re-election.

[*The Democratic Textbook*, 1916; J. C. Long, *Bryan, The Great Commoner*.]   RICHARD E. YATES

Head Right was the system used in most of the English colonies, especially in the 17th century, of granting a certain number of acres, usually fifty, for each settler, the grant being made either for himself or to the person who paid for his transportation. This principle was also found in the early land laws of Texas (*see* Empresario System) .   HUGH T. LEFLER

"Headquarters in the Saddle." When Gen. John Pope was brought from the western front in 1862 to take command of the Federal Army of Virginia*, he issued a bombastic proclamation to the soldiers, and was credited with saying that his headquarters would be in the saddle. This latter expression was used by Gen. W. J. Worth as early as the Seminole War* in 1841. Pope said later that it was a standing joke at West Point before he graduated there in 1842, and he hotly denied that he would have used anything so stale.

[*Battles and Leaders of the Civil War*, Vol. II.]
                    ALVIN F. HARLOW

Health, Public. During the 17th and 18th centuries there were probably no permanent organizations in the United States intended for or devoted specifically to the promotion of the public health, although there may have been a few local officials who gave some small portion of their time to such matters. Whenever outbreaks of disease occurred, temporary committees or officers were appointed to apply the meager and mostly ineffective control measures then available, or persons voluntarily grouped themselves together to meet the emergency. During practically all of the period covered by the 17th and 18th centuries, except, possibly, the latter part, public health activities were devoted chiefly to attempts to control smallpox*, with spasmodic efforts to apply quarantine measures against yellow fever*, when that disease appeared in the cities of the Atlantic and Gulf coasts. Little or no attempts were made to control the other communicable diseases, which have been so remarkably reduced during the present century.

As elsewhere throughout the world, quarantine and isolation were the first important preventive measures adopted in the United States for the prevention and control of disease. To these public health measures were added others, such as immunization and disinfection. Measures regarding isolation were early adopted in New England, by law or regulation, and local provisions concerning smallpox were adopted by Boston and Salem as early as 1678. In 1721 Cotton Mather called attention to the protection against smallpox in Europe by artificial production of the disease; and it is reported that, in 1792, 8000 persons were inoculated in Boston. With the introduction of the milder preventive measure of vaccination*, inoculation ceased. Until fairly recently, disinfection was held to be of the greatest importance in prevention of disease, and the measure was adopted by Boston as early as 1678. While it is still used today, in certain cases, it is not accorded the importance that has been attached to it heretofore.

The measures just outlined constituted the first armamentarium of public health in the United States as well as elsewhere throughout the world. The second phase of public health in the United States, beginning with the discovery and adoption of vaccination against smallpox, was characterized by the extension of similar prophylactic measures, following the discoveries of Koch, Pasteur and others in the field of bacteriology. The next important advance in public health in the United States, which occurred early in the present century, is identified by the emphasis placed on public health education, and the following reduction in tuberculosis[qv] and infant mortality, in which knowledge of personal hygiene has played a large part. The most recent development is the broadening concept of the field of public health, the shift in emphasis to the chronic diseases of adult life, and the policy of making available the benefits of medical care to all.

Although the cities took the initiative in public health development in the United States, as in Europe, various conditions later emphasized the necessity for a national health service; and because of its early experience with quarantine, epidemics and sanitation[qv], the Marine Hospital Service (now the Public Health Service), created by an act of Congress in 1798, became the Federal health service.

The difference between the national public health service in the United States and that of most European countries is a difference inherent in the forms of government. Governments with highly centralized authority have centralized health organizations with plenary powers in health matters. The Federal Government of the United States is a government of enumerated powers under the Constitution, and local health matters remain in the police power of the states. The states, however, delegate certain authority in health matters to local civil divisions, whose ordinances and regulations must not, of course, be inconsistent with state or Federal laws. The Federal Government administers health laws and regulations of national import, such as the quarantine laws and regulations, enters into treaties with foreign nations regarding international health matters, and acts to protect the health of the people in interstate traffic and to suppress epidemics that threaten to spread from state to state.

The official governmental health services in the United States consist of the United States Public Health Service, the state departments of health, and the health organizations in cities, towns, incorporated villages, counties and rural districts. The state departments of health have jurisdiction over sanitation within their borders, control of communicable diseases, collection of vital statistics, maintenance of diagnostic laboratories, furnishing serums and other biologics free or at cost, and similar health matters.

The United States Public Health Service, while still conducting the marine hospitals and relief stations for the care of American merchant seamen and other beneficiaries, is engaged also in purely public health activities, such as the investigation of diseases and studies of improved methods of control, quarantine, epidemiological studies, surveys of disease prevalence, studies of health administration and co-operation with states in all health matters. The important recent developments include the expansion in the program for the control of the venereal diseases, the extension of research activities and aid to states in developing adequate health services and providing qualified personnel under the provisions of the Social Security Act[qv], the extension of aid to states in the control of venereal diseases under the Venereal Disease Control Act of 1938, and the intensive study of cancer and establishment of the National Cancer Institute under the National Cancer Institute Act of 1937. The United States Public Health Service was under the administrative jurisdiction of the Treasury Department from 1798 to June 30, 1939, when it was grouped with other welfare organizations under the new Federal Security Agency. It is administered by the Surgeon General and eight Assistant Surgeons General in charge of administrative divisions.

The first state department of public health was established in Massachusetts in 1869. Prior to 1900, thirty-eight other states had created similar departments, and at the present time all states have boards or departments of health. The most important advances in 1938 and 1939 in state health services were the additions of industrial hygiene, venereal disease and county health units to their departments and the increase in and improved qualifications of the personnel.

The development of full-time rural health organizations marks an important advance in public health service since 1908. Prior to that year, cities and towns had developed health services, but little advance had been made in rural areas. By 1911 the county health movement had started in three widely separated states. During the next ten-year period it had spread to 186 counties or rural districts in 23 states, and by 1939 full-time health services were available in 1371 counties in 42 states. The Territory of Hawaii also has such services.

In addition to the official health services, there are many unofficial and private health organizations, professional associations and various Funds or Foundations which have made valuable contributions to public health. Also, in the United States, other Federal agencies, such as the Children's Bureau, the Bureau of Mines, the Office of Education, the Bureau of Chemistry and Soils, and the Food and Drug Administration, and others, deal with some aspect of public health.

With a changing conception of the responsibility of government to society, with the public health objective that the benefits of preventive medicine, medical service and medical guidance and medical care should be available to all, and in view of the fact that insanitary conditions, epidemics and ill health are no longer looked upon as matters of purely local concern, the future will probably witness further expansion and broader interpretation of Federal powers in relation to the public health.

[Harry S. Mustard, *An Introduction to Public Health;* Harry H. Moore, *Public Health in the United States; A Half Century of Public Health,* American Public Health Association, New York, 1921; *Annual Reports* of the Surgeon General, United States Public Health Service; Annual Reports of State and City Health Departments.]   THOMAS PARRAN

Heath Patent (Oct. 30, 1629), a proprietary grant by Charles I to Sir Robert Heath, his attorney-general, of the region south of Virginia, between 31° and 36° N. Lat., to be known as Carolina. Heath was "about to lead thither a Colonye of men large & plentifull," but he failed to do so, as did Lord Maltravers, to whom he later assigned his patent. The grant of Carolina℗ to the eight proprietors in 1663 covered the same region as the Heath Patent, but the Privy Council℗ declared the latter forfeited because of failure to plant a settlement within the region.

[H. T. Lefler, *North Carolina History Told by Contemporaries.*]   HUGH T. LEFLER

Heating. The early colonists knew of no means of heating buildings and of cooking other than by open fireplaces. For more than a century, wood was the only fuel used in America. The late arrival at an inn, during winter, found his bedroom miserably cold, though a fire was hastily lighted on the hearth and a warming pan used on the bed. This was a flattish metal box filled with live coals which was passed back and forth by its long

handle between the sheets of a bed until the chill was taken off. Foot stoves, metal boxes filled with glowing charcoal, were used by well-to-do folk in church, in their traveling carriages and sometimes in stagecoaches, though often a hot brick or slab of soapstone wrapped in cloth had to serve. The first hint of new heating methods came between 1730 and 1740 when Christopher Sower of Germantown, Pa., invented a primitive stove which partly enclosed the fireplace. Benjamin Franklin in 1742 evolved what he called the Pennsylvanian Fireplace, really a sort of stove, though with the front open, like a fireplace; the smoke passed over the top of a separate air-chamber and down behind it before going up the chimney; and through small apertures, this air-chamber emitted heat into the room (*see* Franklin Stove). With the beginning of coal mining in Virginia in 1750, grates were introduced. The first enclosed stove, a box-shaped affair much like those used in the following centuries, was produced in 1752. Dozens of modifications were devised by succeeding generations. Mica windows and firebrick linings appeared in the early 19th century, and about 1830 the first base-burner, primarily for the use of anthracite℗, was introduced. The first hot-air furnace—then called a "basement stove"—is said to have been made and installed by William A. Wheeler of Worcester, Mass., about 1835. An early type of anthracite furnace was just a cast-iron stove surrounded by a brick air-chamber; the smoke, hot gases and hot air passed through large sheet metal drums on each succeeding floor above before escaping by the chimney. The hot-air furnace was the favorite type of central heating device for public buildings and large residences for half a century and more thereafter.

Hot water heating, which was used in the baths of ancient Rome, was revived in France in 1777, and was used in England and Canada for years before being brought to the United States from London in 1842 by Joseph Nason—who was also the first to warm a building in this country by steam, this in 1845–46. His first large steam-heating contract was that of the Eastern Hotel in Boston, his second, a woolen mill in Burlington, Vt. A few colleges and other institutions with groups of buildings were by 1880 warming them from a central steam-heating plant. Steam heat was one of several factors which contributed to the growing size and height of commercial buildings. After 1885 corporations in some of the larger cities distributed steam from central plants (frequently exhaust steam from electric lighting and power plants) through pipes under the street to customers. After 1895 many of these heating systems were made appendages of lighting and power organizations. In the latter 19th century gas^{qv}, mostly natural, though some artificial, was much used for fuel, usually with fireclay "gas logs" in grates and stoves. In the 20th century, as air conditioning^{qv} was developed, heating, of course, became an element in the scheme. Gas and oil also began slowly but steadily to supplant coal as fuel in heating furnaces. But all types of heating survive, and even in 1935, it was said that nearly half of the homes in the United States were still warmed by stoves, grates and fireplaces.

The first railroad passenger cars, being merely stagecoach bodies on tram-wheels, had no heating whatsoever; nor did they for a time after they assumed a box shape. Finally, a small stove was placed in one end of the car, making that portion uncomfortably hot, while the other end was cold. When a disaster occurred in winter, the stove, upset or smashed, frequently set the wreckage afire and consumed the trapped and injured passengers. The heating of cars with steam, piped from the locomotive, was introduced in Bavaria in 1869, but came more slowly in this country, and even on some important lines, the "deadly car stove" might still be found as late as 1900, though then rapidly disappearing. As in buildings, car heating was, after 1920, a part of the air conditioning problem. Horse cars and even electric street cars in Northern cities in the latter 19th century had small stoves in the front end in winter; but after 1895, electric heaters under the seats began to come into use, also being installed in subways and elevated lines. Next, the electric heating of automobiles, motor buses and airplanes became a requisite as those vehicles were developed to a high state of efficiency and comfort.

[Walter Bernan, *On the History and Art of Warming and Ventilating Rooms and Buildings;* Chauncey M. Depew, ed., *One Hundred Years of American Commerce;* Earl Vernon Hill, *Aerology for Amateurs and Others.*]

ALVIN F. HARLOW

Helderberg War. *See* Anti-Rent Agitation.

Helena, Battle at (July 4, 1863). A Confederate force of 7600 under Gen. T. H. Holmes attempted to take Helena, Ark., which was strongly fortified and held by Federal troops under Gen. B. M. Prentiss. The Confederate right wing stormed the Federal works, but the left was defeated, and the right was finally driven back, the whole attack failing. Confederate loss 1636, Federal 239.

[*Battles and Leaders of the Civil War*, Vol. III.]

ALVIN F. HARLOW

Helena Mining Camp, THE, started in 1864 with the discovery of gold in Last Chance Gulch in Prickly Pear Valley, just east of the Continental Divide. John Cowan, Robert Stanley and others, after spending the summer in unsuccessful prospecting, in September tried their "last chance," thus opening the most productive mining camp in Montana. Gold seekers from Bannack and Alder Gulch^{qv} and elsewhere hurried to the new "diggings," which soon adopted the name Helena, and the district took the name Rattlesnake. Red Mountain, Ten Mile and Unionville also produced large quantities of gold. On Silver Creek Thomas Cruse developed the Drum Lummon mine, which he sold in 1882 for $1,500,000. His North Star and Monarch mines showed almost equal wealth. As the placer mines were exhausted, quartz mining developed and silver and lead became important. In 1880, gold production was 8215 ounces, and silver 51,-379 ounces; in 1904 it had increased to 29,437 ounces for gold and 331,091 ounces for silver. In 1937 gold production amounted to 35,805 ounces and silver to 138,512 ounces.

[Michael A. Leesen, *History of Montana, 1739-1883;* Cornelius Hedges, Historical Sketch of Lewis and Clark County, in Montana Historical Society *Contributions*, Vol. II.]

PAUL C. PHILLIPS

Helium, the lightest gas known excepting hydrogen, is colorless, odorless, will not support combustion nor explode when mixed with air. It has 92.6% of hydrogen's lifting power, making it superior to the inflammable hydrogen for inflating balloons and dirigibles^{qv}. When the United States entered the World War the Government conducted an intensive search for an adequate supply. Helium was found with natural gas^{qv} in certain areas, and commercial production has since been so successful that millions of cubic feet have been produced at less than a cent per cubic foot. The United States (1939) has a virtual world monopoly of helium, owning reserves at Amarillo, Tex., Woodside and Harley Dome in Utah, Dexter, Kans., and Thatcher, Colo. The navy's nonrigid dirigible C-7 was the first airship to be inflated with helium, on Dec. 1, 1921. Under the Helium Act of Sept. 1, 1937, export of helium is forbidden except under license issued by the Secretary of State, approved by the Secretary of the Interior and all members of the National Munitions Control Board. Under this act the National Munitions Control Board refused (1938) export of helium to Germany for their new dirigible LZ-130.

[Paul H. Wilkinson, Helium, Hope of the Airship, in

Scientific American, August, 1938; C. de F. Chandler and W. S. Diehl, *Balloon and Airship Cases.*]

LOUIS H. BOLANDER

"Hell on Wheels" was a term applied, because of their turbulent character, to the temporary rails-end towns, or construction camps, of the Union Pacific Railroad^w (1865–69).

[Samuel Bowles, *Our Great West.*]

DAN E. CLARK

Helper's *Impending Crisis of the South*, published at New York in 1857, was an economic appeal to nonslaveholders of the South written by a North Carolinian of the small-farmer class. Using the census reports of 1790 and 1850 as sources, he contrasted Northern and Southern states to show that the South, with slave labor, was unable to keep pace with the "free" North in population, agriculture, industry and commerce. Applying opprobrious epithets to slaveowners, Helper claimed that they owed nonslaveholders of his section over seven billion dollars because slavery was responsible for the impoverished status of free labor. By selecting, twisting and misinterpreting his figures, he produced a volume which convinced many Northerners, who had been uninfluenced by the moral appeal, that slavery was an economic fallacy. By the end of 1857, 13,000 copies had been sold; by 1860, 142,000. A *Compendium,* published in 1859, was widely circulated as Republican campaign literature^w, and its endorsement by John Sherman was a factor in his defeat for the speakership. In the South newspapers and speakers refuted the work, copies were publicly burned, individuals were jailed for buying or possessing it, "Helperites" were dispossessed of positions and privileges, and a Virginian, Samuel M. Wolfe, wrote *Helper's Impending Crisis Dissected* (1860).

[H. T. Lefler, Hinton Rowan Helper, Advocate of a White America, in *Southern Sketches*, Number 1.]

WENDELL H. STEPHENSON

Hemp. Though England early sought hemp from the colonies to rig her sailing ships, and the British government and colonial legislatures tried to encourage its production by bounties, it never became an important export crop. But the virgin clearings and moderate climate of America invited its cultivation in a small way. Hemp patches were attached to many colonial homesteads, hemp and tow cloth were familiar household manufactures and local cordage supplied colonial shipyards.

After the Revolution, when settlers began to develop the rich Ohio Valley bottomlands, hemp became a staple crop in Kentucky. Mills for manufacturing it were erected at Lexington and elsewhere, and hemp cordage and bale cloth were used to pack the pioneer cotton crops of the Southwest. Output reached a maximum about 1860, when some 74,000 tons were raised in the United States, of which Kentucky produced 40,000 tons and Missouri 20,000 tons. Thereafter the advent of the steamship, the substitution of steel for hemp cordage, and the introduction of competing fibers lessened demand so that by 1930 output fell to less than 1000 tons. Nevertheless new hemp areas have appeared from time to time, notably in Wisconsin and California, and production for special purposes has not entirely ceased.

[Brent Moore, *The Hemp Industry in Kentucky; United States Census of Agriculture.*]   VICTOR S. CLARK

Hempstead, one of the oldest towns on Long Island, was settled in 1644 by Englishmen from Wethersfield and Stamford, Conn. The land was granted by Gov. William Kieft and sachems of the Massapeague, Merrick and Rockaway tribes of Indians. A fort, a meetinghouse and the first dwellings were built within a palisade. Hempstead is popularly thought to have been named for Hemel-Hempstead in England, but other authorities claim it was named by the Dutch for a town in Holland. Certainly until about 1700 the name was spelled in the Dutch way, Heemstede.

[Benjamin F. Thompson, *History of Long Island;* Bernice Schultz, *Colonial Hempstead.*]

JACQUELINE OVERTON

Henderson Land Company. After the voiding of the Transylvania^w title to lands in the Kentucky country by the Virginia legislature, Richard Henderson went to French Lick, the center of the Cumberland Settlements^w, and opened a land office for the promotion and sale of lands in the Tennessee country. Nashborough, later Nashville^w, was the center of the company's operations until 1783 when the North Carolina legislature followed Virginia's example in declaring the title of the company void.

[S. C. Williams, *Dawn of the Tennessee Valley and Tennessee History.*]   SAMUEL C. WILLIAMS

Hening's Statutes, a collection in thirteen volumes of all the public laws of Virginia from the first session of the legislature, in the year 1619, to the session ending Dec. 28, 1792, was compiled and edited by William Waller Hening, pursuant to an act of the Virginia Assembly, passed Feb. 5, 1808. The first four volumes, in a limited edition, were published in 1809. By an act of March 10, 1819, an enlarged edition, extending the series to thirteen volumes, was made possible, and by a later act of Jan. 24, 1823, the set was completed. In 1835 the first two of three supplemental volumes, covering the period, 1792–1803, were published as a continuation of Hening by Samuel Shepherd, Esq., of Richmond, Va., and the third and final volume, bringing the collection, comprising sixteen volumes in all, down to February, 1808, was published in 1836. An Index of the Personal Names occurring in the entire series of sixteen volumes was compiled and published by Joseph J. Casey in 1896.

SAMUEL M. WILSON

Hennepin Narratives, THE. Louis Hennepin was a Recollect friar, who accompanied LaSalle[*w*] on his first voyage to Illinois and was sent thence in 1680 with two companions to explore the upper Mississippi. He and his companions were taken captive April 11 by the Sioux Indians[*w*], and on their travels Hennepin saw and named, July 1, the Falls of St. Anthony[*w*], where the modern city of Minneapolis stands. The captives were rescued by Daniel Greysolon, Sieur Duluth[*w*], who carried them to Mackinac[*w*]. Subsequently Hennepin returned to France, where he wrote *Description de la Louisiane,* published in Paris in 1683. This is, in the main, a truthful narrative, while showing the author's traits of vanity and desire for self acclaim. Some years later he published *La Nouvelle Découverte* (Utrecht, 1697) which was translated and published in England as the *New Discovery* (London, 1698). In this work he claimed for himself the prior discovery of the lower Mississippi, declaring that Jolliet[*w*] had never made the trip, and that he had preceded LaSalle to the mouth of the Mississippi by two years. His descriptions of the lower river he plagiarized from those of his fellow Recollect, Zénobe Membré, who accompanied LaSalle on his voyage of 1682.

Hennepin wrote a third book of travels, *Le Nouveau Voyage* (Utrecht, 1698), which is a patchwork of citations from his other books and those of his contemporaries. At the time he applied to William III of England, under whose patronage the *New Discovery* appeared, he was likewise bidding for aid from Louis XIV, and asking to be returned to America. Louis, however, ordered the friar arrested if he appeared at any French port.

The writings of Hennepin were "best-sellers" in their day. As Thwaites remarks, "For a barefooted mendicant friar, Hennepin appears to have been uncommonly acute in making his narrative attractive to the uncritical public." His books first described Niagara Falls[*w*], which in *La Louisiane* he asserted were 500 feet in height; in *La Nouvelle Découverte* they were 600, and in *Le Nouveau Voyage,* 700. His descriptions of the manners and customs of the Indians were largely from the Siouan tribe. He gave European readers an account of the flora, fauna (animal and human) of North America, which was standard for a generation or more.

[R. G. Thwaites, ed., *The New Discovery,* Introduction; Abbé H. A. Scott, Un Coup d'Epée dans l'Eau, in Canada Royal Society *Proceedings,* 1927; *Minnesota History,* December, 1930; Father Louis Hennepin's *Description of Louisiana,* trans., Marion Cross.]

LOUISE PHELPS KELLOGG

Henry, Fort, formerly Fort Fincastle for one of Lord Dunmore's titles, was on the site of Wheeling, W. Va. The fort was built in June, 1774, by Col. William Crawford from plans drawn by George Rogers Clark. In 1776 the name was changed to Fort Henry in honor of Patrick Henry, governor of Virginia. In September of the following year Fort Henry was unsuccessfully attacked by Indians. Sept. 10, 1782, Fort Henry was attacked by Indians and British in what historians claim was "the last battle of the American Revolution."

[Wills De Hass, *History of the Early Settlement and Indian Wars of Western Virginia.*]

C. H. AMBLER

Henry, Fort, Capture of (Feb. 6, 1862). Seventeen thousand Union troops under Gen. U. S. Grant, supported by gunboats under Commodore Foote, moved by water against Fort Henry on the Tennessee River, initiating the successful Mississippi campaign. Outgunned by the river boats, outnumbered by the troops put ashore downstream, Gen. Tilghman (C.) safely evacuated most of his small garrison and fought well with a few artillerymen before surrendering. Grant disregarded previous plans to delay and moved straightway on Fort Donelson[*w*].

[A. L. Conger, *The Rise of U. S. Grant;* O. L. Spaulding, *The United States Army in War and Peace.*]

ELBRIDGE COLBY

Henry Letters. In 1808 John Henry, a British agent, investigated the extent of secession sentiment in New England (*see* Secession, The Right of). His very general reports omitted names and details (*see* Rose Intrigue). He later attempted unsuccessfully to dispose of these reports in London, finally surrendering them to a bogus "Count de Crillon" in exchange for "ancestral" properties in France. DeCrillon then sold the letters to the United States Government for

$50,000, bringing ridicule upon Madison's administration when they proved to be of no importance.

[Henry Adams, *History of the United States.*]

LOUIS MARTIN SEARS

Henry's Fork of Snake River in Montana was named for Andrew Henry, a partner of the St. Louis Missouri Fur Company[w], who built a fort there in 1809. The post was in the heart of the Blackfoot[w] fur country. The stream is frequently mentioned by early travelers.

[T. Stout, *Montana.*]

CARL L. CANNON

Hepburn Act of 1906, THE, was regulatory legislation designed to clarify certain powers previously granted to the Interstate Commerce Commission[w] and to further increase its authority over railroads and certain other types of carriers. It authorized the Commission to determine and prescribe just and reasonable maximum rates upon complaint and investigation; establish through routes and prescribe maximum joint rates and proper rate divisions between participating carriers; and determine, prescribe and enforce uniform systems of accounts. The Commission's orders upon carriers subject to its jurisdiction were made binding without court action, thus requiring the latter to assume the burden of initiating litigation that tested the validity of its orders. The law strengthened the Elkins Act[w] of 1903 as regards personal discrimination; forbade railroads from transporting any commodity, other than timber and its manufactured products, in which they were financially interested, except that which was necessary for their own use; restricted the granting of free passes to certain groups of individuals; and increased the number of commissioners from five to seven.

[F. H. Dixon, The Interstate Commerce Act as Amended, *Quarterly Journal of Economics*, Vol. XXI; H. S. Smalley, Rate Control under the Amended Interstate Commerce Act, *Annals of the American Academy of Political and Social Science*, Vol. XXIX.]

HOBART S. PERRY

Herd Law v. Free Grass was a manifestation of the age-old question of inclosures (*see* Fencing and Fencing Laws). It was common in the newly settled Western states and territories during the last quarter of the 19th century. The point at issue was as to whether livestock or the growing or ungathered crops must be fenced. The livestock grower who planted little or no crops favored free grass, or the fencing of fields and allowing animals to run at large. This was especially true when a considerable part of the land was still a part of the public domain[w]. The homesteader[w] who owned merely a pair of horses and a milk cow or two believed in herd law, or that pasture lands should be inclosed and cultivated fields left unfenced. State laws usually provided that each township or county unit should decide the question for itself by local election. Since the proponents of herd law were usually poor homesteaders, and those favoring free grass were well-to-do cattle raisers, the controversy sometimes took the form of a class struggle resulting at times in violence, the destruction of property and even loss of life. As communities became more thickly settled and prosperous, adequate fences were constructed and the controversy died out. (*See also* Barbed Wire.)

[E. E. Dale, The Passing of the Range Cattle Industry in Oklahoma, *The Cattleman*, Vol. XI, No. 6, November, 1924.]

EDWARD EVERETT DALE

Heresy Trials have not been as common in America as might be supposed. In the well-known Roger Williams (1635), Anne Hutchinson (1637) and John Wheelwright (1637) cases, though their theological teachings were involved, yet their conviction was not so much due to their heretical opinions as to the fact that they were considered enemies of the state (*see* Antinomian Controversy). The same was largely true of the Quakers and Baptists[qw] brought to trial in both Massachusetts Bay and the Virginia colonies.

The Presbyterians[w] have suffered more from heresy trials than any of the other American religious bodies because they possess both a rigid system of doctrine, Westminster Confession[w], and an efficient system of government. The influence of the frontier combined with revivalism[w] tended to undermine the Calvinistic[w] doctrines, with the result that a number of heresy trials took place on the Kentucky frontier. The best-known cases were those of Thomas B. Craighead and John Todd, tried by the Transylvania Presbytery in 1810. Another fruitful cause of heresy trials was the working of the Plan of Union of 1801, whereby Congregationalists[w] and Presbyterians united on the frontier. Thus a liberalizing influence from New England coming in contact with the more rigid Scotch-Irish Calvinism of the Presbyterians resulted in numerous heresy accusations and trials. The most famous were those of Albert Barnes (1831–36) and Lyman Beecher (1835), though during this whole period there was a veritable epidemic of heresy accusations.

Another period of heresy hunting came as a

result of the infiltration of new views of the Bible, known as the Higher Criticism[qv], and the growing acceptance of the evolutionary philosophy on the part of the more advanced religious leaders. Prof. C. A. Briggs of Union Theological Seminary was convicted of heresy by his Presbytery in 1893, and in 1905 Prof. H. G. Mitchell of the Boston University School of Theology, a Methodist, was dismissed because of heresy. There were numerous other cases during this period of the same general nature.

[C. F. Adams, *Three Episodes of Massachusetts History;* W. W. Sweet, *Religion on the American Frontier: The Presbyterians;* S. G. Cole, *The History of Fundamentalism;* W. E. Garrison, *The March of Faith.*]

WILLIAM W. SWEET

Hermitage Plantation, THE, near Nashville, Tenn., was bought by Andrew Jackson in 1795. He removed to it in 1804, and sold all but 6000 acres of the original 28,000-acre tract. The log cabin which served as Jackson's home was replaced by a brick house in 1819 and when this burned in 1834, the present Hermitage building was erected on the old site. After Jackson's death the Hermitage was occupied by Andrew Jackson, Jr., until 1888, although it had been bought by Tennessee in 1856 and preserved as a shrine.

[J. T. Faris, *Historic Shrines of America;* C. C. Sherlock, *Homes of Famous Americans.*]

R. S. COTTERILL

Hermosa, THE. On Oct. 19, 1840, the American schooner *Hermosa,* bound for New Orleans from Richmond, was wrecked on the key of Abaco. Wreckers took off the crew and cargo, including thirty-eight slaves, and put in at Nassau where the slaves were liberated on the ground that there was no recognition of slavery within the British Empire. The United States took the position that there could be no alteration of the status of master and slave in cases where the vessel was unwillingly taken within British waters. The case dragged on for many years, and was ultimately settled by an award of $16,000. (*See also Encomium,* The.)

[J. B. Moore, *Digest of International Law,* and *International Arbitrations.*]

JOHN G. VAN DEUSEN

Herrin Massacre, THE (June 22, 1922), was an outgrowth of an attempt to operate a strip mine in Williamson County, Ill., with nonunion labor during the coal strike of 1922. On June 22 forty-seven men working at the strip mine surrendered, under a promise of safe conduct, to an armed force of several hundred striking union miners. The captives were marched to a spot near Herrin and then ordered to run for their lives under fire. Twenty-one were killed, many more wounded. A special grand jury returned 214 indictments for murder and related crimes, but at the ensuing trial, which began on Nov. 13 and lasted nearly five months, local sentiment was such that convictions were impossible. On April 7, 1923, after several verdicts of acquittal had been returned, all the untried indictments were *nolle prossed.*

[*New York Times* for the period.]

PAUL M. ANGLE

Hessians, a designation often indiscriminately used for all the German mercenaries[qv] fighting on the side of the British in the Revolution, were, strictly speaking, the 17,000 men hired out by the landgrave of Hesse-Cassel, whose first wife was a daughter of George II. The 12,000 sent in 1776 included some of his best regiments, all drilled on the Prussian system and officered by experienced men. They took part in every campaign except Burgoyne's, distinguishing themselves especially at Long Island, Fort Washington, Brandywine, Newport and Charleston[qqv]. Their defeat at Trenton[qv], Christmas, 1776, raised the morale of Washington's men, who learned that even the Hessians were not invincible. The Jäger Corps, light troops, who rivaled the American riflemen, were the best soldiers on the British side. As prisoners the Hessians generally fared better than the British. Many deserted, partly induced by Congress' proclamations; others were bought out of prison by farmers and artisans; and many remained in the country after the war had ended.

[MS. collections, Clements Library and New York Public Library.]

B. A. UHLENDORF

Hester **Case** (N. J.). In December, 1698, the *Hester,* about to sail from Perth Amboy[qv] with a cargo of barrel staves for Madeira, was seized by New York authorities for nonpayment of duties to New York. The proprietors appealed to England, claiming port privileges under statutes of 1673 and 1696 and the action of the customs commissioners in erecting their port. In 1700, damages were awarded the vessel's owners and the right of New Jersey to ports of its own confirmed.

[H. L. Osgood, *The American Colonies in the Eighteenth Century.*]

C. A. TITUS

Hexing. The murder of a farmer named Rehmeyer in York County, Pa., Nov. 27, 1928, by a "witch doctor" and two youths brought to light the fact that witchcraft introduced into that region by early German settlers was still believed in and practised by many. Rehmeyer was accused of putting a "hex" or evil spell upon a certain family. A book on witchcraft published in Harrisburg in 1856 was found to be in many homes. It was believed that many previous deaths had been caused by this infatuation.

[Articles in *Nation*, Jan. 23, 1929, *Collier's*, May 25, 1929, *North American Review*, November, 1929.]

ALVIN F. HARLOW

Hiawatha was a Mohawk Indian chief known to the Iroquois Confederacy as Haionhwat'ha, who with Dekanawida and Jikonsasa founded the League of the Iroquois[w], a confederacy of the Mohawk, Oneida, Onondaga, Cayuga and Seneca tribes. The purpose of Hiawatha was to establish universal peace by uniting all known groups of the American continent. He began his mission among the Onondagas with whom he lived, probably attempting to build upon an older idea long prevalent among the Huron-Iroquois people. Since the Iroquois, later called the Six Nations, played an important part in colonial history, one must credit Hiawatha and his compeers with being the builders of one of the most formidable native empires on the continent, resulting in a military power entirely opposed to the peaceful plans of the founders. J. V. H. Clark is credited with relating the epic of Hiawatha to Henry R. Schoolcraft, whose writings attracted Henry W. Longfellow, who intermixed Algonkian and Iroquoian legends in the poem, "Hiawatha," but gave no facts relating to the hero's real character as a reformer and statesman.

[Horatio Hale, *Iroquois Book of Rites;* J. N. B. Hewitt, A Lawgiver of the Stone Age, *American Anthropologist,* April, 1892; Arthur C. Parker, *Constitution of the Five Nations.*]

ARTHUR C. PARKER

Hickory Ground was a Creek Indian town (Otciapofa) on the east bank of the Coosa, one mile below the falls. Just below the Hickory Ground, on the site of the old French Fort Toulouse[w], a detachment of Jackson's army after the battle of Horseshoe Bend[w] (March 27, 1814) erected Fort Jackson. Here, Aug. 9, 1814, Jackson made with the remnant of the Creeks[w] a treaty by which they ceded to the United States their land in southern Georgia and central Alabama.

[J. R. Swanton, *Early History of the Creek Indians,* Bulletin 73, United States Bureau of American Ethnology; J. S. Bassett, *Life of Andrew Jackson;* C. J. Kappler, *Indian Affairs: Laws and Treaties.*]

R. S. COTTERILL

Hicksites. A split in the Society of Friends in 1827, following the preaching of Elias Hicks, a Long Island Quaker[w], brought this sect into being. Several yearly meetings divided, e.g., Philadelphia, New York, Baltimore, with the Hicksites in the majority. They established Swarthmore College, and several schools. Recently they have come closer to the Orthodox, with whom they co-operate. They have about 20,000 members.

[*American Church History Series*, Vol. XII.]

AUGUSTUS H. SHEARER

Hide and Tallow Trade. In California under the Spanish regime missions and ranchmen depended chiefly upon the sale of hides and tallow for a livelihood. The plains and valleys were flooded with herds of cattle for which no market was available. Foreigners finally were attracted, and in 1822 William A. Gale, ex-fur trader, interested Bryant, Sturgis & Co. of Boston, and "Boston ships" soon took over the trade with a direct commerce between California and the eastern seaboard of the United States. The discovery of gold threatened to destroy the trade, but the coming of the railroad induced a gradual revival.

In the region east of California and west of the Mississippi, the cattle trade[w] began to boom after the Civil War, but in the Plains region few cattle were killed for hides alone. The buffalo hide had long been an important article of commerce. With the coming of the railroad, buffaloes[w] were slaughtered in huge numbers. In 1872 and 1873 the Atchison, Topeka and Santa Fé Railroad carried 424,000 buffalo robes and hides, and the Kansas Pacific and Union Pacific roads each carried as many. Both whites and Indians became hide hunters and from Texas to Canada the Plains were strewn with carcasses. By the mid-1880's the vast herds had been extinguished.

[H. H. Bancroft, *History of California;* E. D. Branch, *The Hunting of the Buffalo.*]   FRANK EDWARD ROSS

High Commission, Court of, was a term applied to a series of English commissions created by royal letters patent between 1535 and 1641. Originally instruments of the Privy Council[w] to protect the crown against heresy and treason, the commissioners were gradually increased in number (from 19 in 1559 to 108 in 1633), and they matured into a full-fledged court of law by 1580, "the Star Chamber for ecclesiastical cases." By new letters patent (1625) any three commissioners were authorized to conduct trials, whereby proceedings could be held simultaneously in several places. Thus constituted, the court became Laud's most effective means to root out Puritan nonconformity. Proceedings, or threat of proceedings, in High Commission caused Cotton, Davenport, Hooker and many other Puritan ministers to flee to Holland and the New World. Moreover, the trials were often rude, filled with personal insults, so that Puritans despised the court for its methods as well as its aims. In 1641 the Long Parliament abolished it and puritanically branded its work illegal, unjust and oppressive.

[Roland G. Usher, *The Rise and Fall of the High Commission.*]   RAYMOND P. STEARNS

High License. A method of regulating the liquor traffic through the exaction of high fees for licenses to sell liquors. The system originated in Nebraska in 1881 with radical temperance men who believed they were making a serious attack upon the traffic. Until then a license fee of $200 a year had been considered high; under the Nebraska law, fees ranged from a minimum of $500 to a maximum of $1000. High rates were intended to reduce the number and improve the character of the places licensed. The system was soon adopted in many states, some of which exacted even higher fees. By 1890, however, the system had become as thoroughly discredited in the eyes of all prohibitionists[w] as the saloon itself.

[W. D. P. Bliss, ed., *The Encyclopædia of Social Reform.*]   P. ORMAN RAY

High-Minded Men, THE, were forty (later fifty-one) anti-Clintonian Federalists[w] who urged the election of Vice-President Tompkins, the Republican candidate for governor of New York in 1820. In *An Address to the Independent Federal Electors, of the State of New-York, on the Subject of the Election of Governor and Lt. Governor of the State,* published at Albany and dated April 14, 1820, they deplored Gov. DeWitt Clinton's "personal party," declared the Federalist party dissolved and allied themselves with the Tammany faction. As they had often referred to themselves as "high-minded men" in the anti-Clintonian New York *American* (begun March 3, 1819), they were henceforth ridiculed by the opposition as "High-minded Federalists."

[D. R. Fox, *The Decline of Aristocracy in the Politics of New York.*]   STANLEY R. PILLSBURY

High School, THE, in the United States developed from the Latin Grammar School[w] (Boston, 1635), which was a direct imitation of secondary schools of England, and the academy[w] (Philadelphia, 1750). The first public high school was established in Boston in 1821 in order that any parent might secure for his child without expense an education that would fit him for life. In the early decades the East held that the public

high school could not compete with the academies in preparing youth for college; later it made such preparation its chief emphasis. The West always looked on the high school as a means of forwarding the education of all youth.

The number of public high schools increased slowly until about 1890; since then the growth has been phenomenal, the percentage of secondary-school pupils practically doubling every decade. In 1938 there were about 25,000 public high schools enrolling some 7,000,000 youth, about 65% of the age population. In several states this per cent rose to more than ninety. Nearly half of the enrollment was in schools with fewer than 100 pupils; 6% was in schools with more than 1000 enrolled. Private secondary schools, excluding those run by the Catholic Church, have slightly decreased.

In the early days high schools were based on elementary schools of seven, eight, or nine years; but all attempted almost the identical curriculum so far as they went. Finally the length of the high school was standardized, chiefly through the action of voluntary regional associations of colleges and secondary schools, at four years. But beginning about 1910 secondary education has claimed, from the elementary schools, the seventh and eighth grades, organizing grades 7–9 into a junior high school; and more recently, especially since 1927, it has extended the senior high school to include grades 13–14, the upper years being organized into a junior college. This unit now enrolls more than 100,000 students.

The typical public high school is now co-educational and comprehensive—that is, it aims at giving not only preparation for college but also the best possible preparation for life, including some degree of vocational guidance and education. Long proceeding without a well-thought-out plan, the public high school has been greatly influenced since 1894 by the reports of a series of committees appointed by the national professional organizations. The latest of these is the Committee on the Orientation of Secondary Education, which has published and popularized two important reports on the Issues and on the Functions of Secondary Education. The public high school in the United States has an importance in the education of all youth never paralleled in any other country.

[E. P. Cubberly, *Public Education in the United States;* E. W. Knight, *Education in the United States.*]

THOMAS H. BRIGGS

Higher Criticism, the term used to indicate the historical and textual study of the Bible[w], was introduced into America in the latter decades of the 19th century from Germany and England. Up to that time Christian people in the United States had generally believed in an infallible Bible, and the suggestions of the "Higher Critics" that it might not be the final and inerrant guide it was thought to be, came as a tremendous shock to many earnest people. President William R. Harper of the University of Chicago, Professors Charles A. Briggs of Union Theological Seminary and C. E. Bacon of Yale Divinity School, were among the most influential leaders in this new approach to the Bible, and for many years they and their colaborers were bitterly denounced by those who continued to hold the old views. By the end of the century, however, the findings of the Biblical scholars were beginning to receive wide acceptance among ministers and leading laymen, who came to hold that while the Bible may not be infallible on every question, it was nevertheless full of religious instruction and inspired men to look for experiences of God in their own times and in their own souls.

[C. A. Briggs, *General Introduction to the Study of Holy Scripture: Its Principles, Methods, History and Results;* A. C. Zenos, *The Elements of Higher Criticism.*]

WILLIAM W. SWEET

Higher Education. *See* Colleges and Universities.

Higher-Law Doctrine. In the debate on the Compromise of 1850[W] Sen. Seward declared that the proposed Fugitive Slave Act[W] might be constitutional, but there was a "higher law" than the Constitution. The higher-law doctrine was an appeal to conscience as being superior in authority to the laws of Congress.

JOHN G. VAN DEUSEN

Highlands, THE (1777-81). The strategic importance of the Hudson River in the Revolutionary War was recognized by both the British and the Colonials long before the outbreak of hostilities. A "sunken river," of sufficient depth to allow passage of deep-draft war vessels as high as Albany, it afforded the British a perfect opportunity to cut the colonies in two. On May 25, 1775, the Continental Congress[W] passed resolutions aimed at forestalling the British by fortifying the river line at various points. A survey, directed by the Provincial Congress of New York, settled on the Hudson Highlands, a rugged hill mass extending from approximately eight miles above West Point[W] to eight miles below, as the logical defense area.

In the fall of 1775 and the following winter, fortifications were constructed on Martelaer's Rock (now Constitution Island). Lying directly across from West Point, where the river makes a double right-angle bend in the course of a scant half-mile, the batteries of Fort Constitution[W] presented a solid obstacle to any British effort by water. However, early in 1776 the project was dropped. The defense effort was shifted to Forts Clinton and Montgomery, constructed on the rocky knobs flanking both sides of the mouth of Popolopen Creek (Pooploop's Kill), some four miles below West Point.

Early in October, 1777, Sir Henry Clinton moved from Manhattan with a force of 3500 men to open the Hudson to British navigation. (*See also* Burgoyne's Invasion.) Eluding Gen. Israel Putman's force, he stormed Forts Clinton and Montgomery on Oct. 6, taking them after heavy losses. A heavy steel chain, stretched across the river at Fort Montgomery and a protective log boom farther downstream were cut. With the capture of Fort Constitution on Oct. 7, and the breach of two other river obstructions, the Hudson Highland defenses were in British hands. The first of these obstructions was a log boom closing the river at Constitution Island; the second is described by writers of the period as a "chevaux-de-frize," consisting of log cribs loaded with stone, which blocked the channel between Storm King Mountain and Pollopel's Island (now Bannerman Island).

The withdrawal of the British ten days later was followed by the setting up of a defense system never again endangered, except by Arnold's treason[W]. Burgoyne's surrender at Saratoga[W] at the very hour when Clinton was moving north at high speed to attack Gates in the rear had saved the Revolution at a critical period. To render impossible a second British effort, Washington demanded that the Continental Congress provide an impregnable defense for the "key to America," as Washington termed it. Kosciusko was placed in charge of the construction of the works at West Point. A massive chain was stretched across the river, between West Point and Constitution Island; protected downstream by a log boom. Water batteries and redoubts on both sides of the river ensured a three-mile fire-swept zone along the line of the river—principally downstream. Redoubts and forts on the hills farther inland assured proper protection against a land attack.

To remove the last British threat Washington directed Gen. Anthony Wayne in July, 1779, to storm Stony Point[W], lying just below the southern gateway of the Highlands. Wayne's spectacular success was nullified later by Clinton's recapture of the position. However, with the shift of military operations to the Southern states in

1780 the last danger to American possession of the Highlands was removed.

[*George Clinton Papers*, Vol. III; *Washington's Writings;* J. R. Simms, *Frontiersmen of New York; The Centennial of the United States Military Academy; History of West Point,* Department of Economics, Government and History, U. S. M. A.]   HERMAN BEUKEMA

Highwaymen. *See* Bandits.

Highways. *See* Roads.

Hillabee Towns, THE, were Creek*ᵂ* Indian towns, five in number, located on a western tributary of the Tallapoosa in eastern Alabama. The Hillabee were one of the twelve major divisions of the Creeks; they numbered about 800 people. The Hillabee took part in the Creek uprising of 1813 and their towns were captured in November of that year by a combined force of Chero-kee*ᵂ* and Tennessee militia.

[J. R. Swanton, *Early History of the Creek Indians,* in Bulletin 73, United States Bureau of American Ethnology.]   R. S. COTTERILL

Hindman, Fort. *See* Arkansas Post, Battle of.

Hise Treaty, THE (June 21, 1849), was made with Nicaragua by Elijah Hise, an American agent acting on his own responsibility. In return for an exclusive right of transit, the United States guaranteed the territorial integrity of Nicaragua, including her claim to Mosquito*ᵂ*, which was a British protectorate. Though not adopted, the treaty was important as the first of a series of incidents which excited the American public against England (*see* Squier Treaty). The crisis thus threatened was averted by the Clayton-Bulwer Treaty*ᵂ*.

[Samuel Flagg Bemis, *A Diplomatic History of the United States.*]   RICHARD W. VAN ALSTYNE

Hispanic American Wars of Independence (1808–25). From the beginning of the Hispanic American independence movement the government and people of the United States took a keen interest in it. Their interest was centered more upon Spanish America than upon Brazil, where the movement began late, was of short duration, and ended in the establishment of a monarchy, and where British influence was at all times paramount. Though their interest in the wars of independence rose and fell with developments in Hispanic America, Europe and the United States itself, from 1815 to 1825 no other problem in our foreign relations received more sustained attention than did this one. Practically every one was theoretically in favor of Hispanic

American independence; but there was a great divergence of opinion as to whether the United States should do anything to promote it. As early as 1808 Jefferson's Cabinet asserted that the United States had a common interest with the revolutionists in excluding European influence, commercial as well as political, from the western hemisphere. European complications and the War of 1812 prevented the development of the larger policy implicit in this view; but after 1815 Henry Clay made himself the champion of it in Congress and urged the United States to give open encouragement to the revolutionists. The supporting arguments were both political and economic: sympathy (on the analogy of our own revolution) for peoples struggling to be free; our interest in spreading the "American system" of liberty and republican government, and our doctrine of neutral rights over the whole western hemisphere to counterbalance the Holy Alliance and England; and also in destroying the commercial monopoly of the European colonial systems. Important economic benefits were promised the United States: markets for its agricultural produce and manufactures; cargoes for its ships; a larger supply of specie; facilities for its China trade*ᵂ*, etc. Less was said about the considerable profit derived during the war from the munitions trade with the revolutionists and from privateering under their flags. Many Americans (notably J. Q. Adams, Secretary of State, 1817–25) were skeptical about most of these political and economic benefits; gave less weight to them than to the danger of European retaliation against any unilateral action by the United States in favor of the revolutionists; and were opposed on principle to the United States engaging in a crusade for democracy in any foreign country whatever. Other obstacles were the territorial interests of the United States in Florida, Texas and Cuba, and the antislavery measures of some of the new states. The divergence of views in the United States often cut across party, sectional and occupational lines, though generally speaking Clay's views seem to have found most support among agrarians of the interior and Adams' among Southern planters and Eastern merchants engaged in trade with England and the Continent. Monroe and probably most other Americans took a position somewhere between those of Adams and Clay. After 1825 the end of the wars of independence, the subsidence of the military menace from Europe, widespread disillusionment about Hispanic America (sharpened by the successes of our British rivals) and absorption in domestic affairs brought about a long-continued decline of interest on the part of the United States in the southern republics.

[J. F. Rippy, *Rivalry of the United States and Great Britain over Latin America;* C. C. Griffin, *The United States and the Disruption of the Spanish Empire;* A. P. Whitaker, *The Interest of the United States in Latin America.*]

A. P. WHITAKER

Historical Societies. Organizations for the study of history existed in Europe long before they began in America: the Society of Antiquaries of London was established as early as 1572. The first society of this sort in America was that of Massachusetts, founded in 1791 by Jeremy Belknap and a small group of Bostonians. John Pintard had attempted to attach a historical museum to the Society of St. Tammany in 1790 but this effort failed. The Massachusetts Historical Society grew out of the prevailing spirit of inquiry of the 18th century and also out of the Puritan atmosphere of New England which fostered a theistic interpretation of history—the latter a factor which helps to explain why such societies proliferated in New England, and in areas settled by New Englanders, more rapidly than in other sections of the country. Other historical societies followed that of Massachusetts in rapid succession: New York (1804), American Antiquarian Society, Worcester (1812), Rhode Island (1822), Maine (1823), New Hampshire (1823), Pennsylvania (1824), Connecticut (1825), Indiana (1830), Ohio (1831), Virginia (1831), Louisiana (1836), Vermont (1838), Georgia (1839), Maryland (1844), Tennessee (1849), Wisconsin (1849) and Minnesota (1849). During the early part of the 19th century numerous societies, local, state and national, were formed but soon disappeared. The founders of these societies had a broad and inclusive definition of history: the prospectus of the New York Society called for the preservation of books, pamphlets and manuscripts embracing orations, sermons, laws, journals of assemblies, Indian treaties, narratives of missionaries, transactions of political, literary and scientific societies, accounts of universities, colleges and other educational institutions, topographical descriptions of towns, cities, states at different periods, vital statistics, reports on commerce and transportation—in short, all sorts of data on the social, economic and political life of the people. Some societies specialized: the American Antiquarian Society developed the greatest collection of newspapers; later, religious, racial, scientific, business, genealogical and patriotic societies devoted to history came into existence. By the third quarter of the 19th century, such institutions were increasing rapidly; between 1850 and 1860 about a score were

founded, the same number in the next decade. With the centenary observances of 1876 and with the arrival of the chair of history in academic institutions, such societies increased more rapidly: some 200 were in existence in 1884 when the historians in the United States founded the American Historical Association[av], largest in membership of all such societies. From fifty to sixty state and local societies were formed in each of the last two decades of the 19th century. Today the number may be estimated at something over a thousand, if societies operating historical house museums are included. The New York Historical Society, with a great storehouse of manuscripts, rare books and newspapers and with an endowment of several million dollars, is the wealthiest of all such societies.

Publication of articles, essays, documents and memoirs constitutes one of the outstanding functions of these societies: their combined output would total several thousand volumes. One society alone has issued 720 publications totaling 75,000 pages. Many societies issue annual volumes of Transactions or Proceedings; others issue quarterly reviews. These institutions, by their very existence and by their co-operation, have made it possible for the Federal Government in recent years to project and carry far toward completion the most ambitious and inclusive inventory of historical and archival records that has been attempted in any country. Young as it is, the United States has, through its historical societies, exploited its history in a way that can be duplicated by no other country, in numbers of societies created, in their wealth or in their productivity.

[*American Historical Review,* XL, 1934, 10–37.]

JULIAN P. BOYD

History, American, Sources of. *Manuscript Archives.* The most important of these are to be found in the National Archives in Washington, in the Library of Congress, and in the libraries of the various governmental departments and bureaus in Washington. Archives of less general and more local value are to be found in governmental offices, both Federal and state, in various cities of the Union. Local archives abound in post offices, courthouses and churches. There are also great bodies of archival material in foreign countries which are indispensable to a study of American history.

The National Archives have been so recently established that few indexes or guides to its sources have been published. A historical records survey of archival material throughout the United States is in progress at the time this is written (*see* Archives).

The Library of Congress[v] has published many guides and indexes to its sources which since they are government documents will be found in the indexes to Federal printed documents mentioned later. Van Tyne and Leland's *Guide to the Archives of the Government in Washington,* 1907, and Leland and Mereness' *American Official Sources . . . of the World War,* 1926, are useful. A number of special studies exist, such as *Calendar of Archival Letters Received from the Organizations of the Government to 1820.* The National Association of State Libraries surveyed the field in 1914 and published a report in the American Library Association *Bulletin,* Vol. VIII, p. 271.

In the field of foreign archives relating to American affairs the most important group of guides has been published in the Papers of the Division of History of the Carnegie Institution of Washington. Almost all the important European archival collections have been examined and reported upon. A list of guides to *U. S. Archives, Manuscripts, Collections and Foreign Archives* will be found in Henry P. Beers' *Bibliographies in American History,* pages 70–76.

Printed Documents of the various governments, Federal, state, municipal and county, are important because they embody the official statement of fact. It is also probably the largest body of usable material, for most important documents find their way into print. The United States Government has printed a long series of indexes to its documents, some to the current series and afterward in cumulated indexes covering a period of years. There is so much literature on the subject that a study of the various indexes is necessary before progress can be made. A good introduction is to be found in I. G. Mudge's *Guide to Reference Books.* Special attention is directed to A. R. Hasse's *Index to U. S. Documents relating to Foreign Affairs,* and her *Index of Economic Material in Documents of the States of the United States.* Henry P. Beers in his *Bibliographies in American History,* previously referred to, devotes pages 56 to 81 to guides, indexes and lists of documents, mostly Federal.

Newspapers are valuable sources of history because they present a continuous chronological record, and include minor events not found in official documents, but of interest to the social historian.

The Library of Congress has perhaps the largest holdings of newspaper files in the country—certainly in those of the 19th century. In the period before 1820 the American Antiquarian Society at Worcester is possibly pre-eminent. The

New York Historical Society in New York City has excellent files before 1800 and good ones in the 19th century. Harvard University library through its Ebeling Collection is strong in the period 1795–1808. New York Public Library has an excellent collection and Yale has a good general collection of which a catalogue has been printed. Duke University has good files of Southern newspapers and the Wisconsin State Historical Society is good on the Mississippi Valley and its own state.

The best guide to library possessions is the *Union List of American Newspaper Files from 1821–1936, available in the United States and Canada, 1937.* The period before that date is in progress and eventually will be covered by Clarence S. Brigham in his Bibliography of American Newspapers, 1690–1820, published in the American Antiquarian Society *Proceedings.*

Good files of newspapers of the various states will usually be found either in the state library or the historical society library of that state.

Libraries. For the period of exploration and discovery the John Carter Brown Library of Providence (of which a printed catalogue is in process) and the James Lenox collection, now part of the New York Public Library, are probably the best, although the Bancroft Library at the University of California and the Ayer collection at Newberry are very good on Spanish beginnings. For the American Indian, the Ayer collection is excellent; the Bancroft collection is good for Central America, Mexico and the Pacific states; the New York Public Library and the Library of Congress have good general collections. For the colonial period and the Revolution the best collections will be found in the East. The Harvard, Yale, New York Public, New York Historical, American Antiquarian libraries and the Library of Congress are all strong. The William L. Clements Library at the University of Michigan has many important sources of colonial and Revolutionary interest. For the South in the same period the Virginia State and the Virginia Historical Society libraries, the Duke University library and, farther south, the University of Georgia with the DeRenne collection of Georgiana are unusually complete.

For sources of the beginnings of Mississippi Valley history the State Historical Society of Wisconsin is strong; the Burton Historical collection in the Detroit Public Library is good for French beginnings in the upper Mississippi and the Great Lakes; the Missouri Historical Society and the Louisiana Historical Society have much material on the history of the lower reaches of that great river. Good collections on the Southwest, including Spanish origins, are to be found at the University of Texas, the Ayer collection at Newberry, the Bancroft Library at Berkeley and the Southwest Museum at Los Angeles. The Far West is best represented in the Bancroft Library at Berkeley and at the Huntington Library at San Marino.

Bibliographies. The two fundamental bibliographies, other than official sources, are Sabin's *Dictionary of Books relating to America* in twenty-four volumes, and Evans' *American Bibliography, a Chronological Dictionary of all Books, Pamphlets and Periodical Publications printed in the U. S. from . . . 1639 to 1820.* The compiler died before the completion of his task. Twelve volumes have appeared including imprints of the year 1799.

An older work, but one still necessary, is Justin Winsor's *Narrative and Critical History of America,* in eight volumes. It contains many reproductions of old maps and an enormous number of bibliographical notes.

In the introductory chapter to Larned's *Literature of American History: a Bibliographical Guide,* Paul L. Ford gives an excellent summary of American historical sources to 1902, the date of publication. The remainder of the book is divided by periods and the important works on each period evaluated by historians in brief notes.

Writings on American History, an annual bibliography of books and articles on United States and Canadian history, covers a long period from 1906 to date. It is compiled by G. G. Griffin and there have been numerous publishers. It includes both books and periodical articles relating to American history, no matter where published. A more recently published work, *Bibliographies in American History: Guide to Materials for Research,* 1938, by Henry P. Beers, attempts to cover the whole field by periods, subjects and regions. Numerous special bibliographies exist. Examples are: Bemis and Griffin, *Guide to the Diplomatic History of the U. S.;* Wagner, *The Plains and the Rockies;* Bartlett, *Literature of the Rebellion.*   CARL L. CANNON

Hit or Miss was the first boat to be carried over the Allegheny crest on the Allegheny Portage Railway^{qv} (October, 1834). Bearing a westbound emigrant, Jesse Chrisman, with his family and possessions, at Hollidaysburg the flatboat was placed upon a railroad car, nestled overnight on the mountain summit, and at Johnstown was returned from the rails to canal waters. The experiment encouraged the building of "portable" boat-bodies whereby freight was sent over the

Pennsylvania Canal System^{qv} between Philadelphia and Pittsburgh without transshipment.

[A. F. Harlow, *Old Towpaths.*]
E. DOUGLAS BRANCH

Hitch-Hiking. Solicitation of rides from motorists on highways became prevalent about 1920. College boys "thumbed" their way to save expenses or to "see America." From 1930–38 unemployed men and even families hitch-hiked in search of work, often from coast to coast. Less dangerous and more respectable than hoboing by rail, the practice increased in spite of state legislation against it.

[Hugh Hardyman, The Art of Hitch-Hiking, *New Republic,* July 29, 1931.]   HARVEY L. CARTER

Hitchcock Reservations. At the time of the first vote by the Senate on the Peace Treaty of Versailles, and the embodied League of Nations^{qqv}, Sen. G. M. Hitchcock of Nebraska, Democratic leader, endeavored to reconcile the opposition to the treaty by the following reservations: the right of Congress to authorize or forbid the use of American forces for League sanctions; interpretation of the Monroe Doctrine^{qv} by the United States; equality of voting power in the League with the British Empire, inclusive of the Dominions; the right of withdrawal; exemption of domestic questions from the League's jurisdiction. On Nov. 19, 1919, the Senate rejected the treaty with these reservations: 41 for, 51 against.

[D. F. Fleming, *The United States and the League of Nations.*]   SAMUEL FLAGG BEMIS

Hitchman Case, THE (Hitchman Coal Co. v. Mitchell, 245 U. S. 229, 1917), arose from efforts of the United Mine Workers^{qv} to organize the West Virginia coal fields, and thereby protect their bargaining power in neighboring, unionized fields (*see* Coal Mining and Organized Labor). After a strike in 1906, the Hitchman Company required all returning employees to sign agreements to forego union affiliation (*see* Yellow-Dog Contract). Thereupon the union sent in organizers, and the company secured an injunction^{qv}. This was upheld by the Supreme Court on the ground that the economic interest of the union in fortifying its bargaining position did not constitute "just cause or excuse" for interfering with existing, amicable employment relations.

[Edw. Berman, *Labor and the Sherman Act;* W. W. Cook, Privileges of Labor Unions in the Struggle for Life, *Yale Law Journal,* Vol. XXVII, 1918.]
MYRON W. WATKINS

Hobkirk's Hill, Battle of (April 25, 1781). After the Battle of Guilford Court House[W], Gen. Greene invaded South Carolina, detached a force to reduce Fort Watson, and himself, with 1200 men, marched toward the British post at Camden[W], where Lord Rawdon was in command. At Hobkirk's Hill, north of Camden, he was attacked by Rawdon with 900 men. Greene's plan of battle was good, but two regiments fell into confusion through the loss of a commander and a misunderstanding of orders, and the battle was lost, though the Americans retired in good order, losing 264 men. The British loss was 258. But the fall of Fort Watson in his rear had made Rawdon's position untenable, and on May 10 he retreated southward, abandoning Camden to Greene.

[George Washington Greene, *Life of Major-General Nathanael Greene.*]   ALVIN F. HARLOW

Hobson's Choice, an old English racing term meaning one choice is as good as another, was the name given by Gen. Anthony Wayne, May 4, 1793, to the encampment site selected for his army. It was about 400 yards below the frontier village of Cincinnati on the north bank of the Ohio River. Here the troops remained for about six months undergoing training (*see* Wayne Campaign).

[Journal of Capt. T. T. Underwood in Filson Club.]   THOMAS ROBSON HAY

"Hoe Man, Damn Fool" (1875–90). As settlement crept onto the high plains beyond the rain belt, the Indians looked upon the agriculturist with disgust for his attempt to farm semiarid land and snorted, "Hoe man, damn fool!" Cowboys took up the refrain and unsuccessfully attemped to scare the "nester" out.

[Charles A. Siringo, *A Lone Star Cowboy.*]   EVERETT DICK

Hog Island Shipyard, THE, on the Delaware River, was built during the World War by the Government's Emergency Fleet Corporation[W], for the multiple fabrication of merchant ships and transports faster than German submarines could sink them. (Cost, $66,000,000.) Its maximum capacity was for fifty ships simultaneously on the ways while twenty-eight others fitted out at piers, completing one 7500-ton, steel, oil-burning vessel every seventy-two hours. Ships actually built totalled 110, the last finished in January, 1921. More than 41,000 men were employed at one time. It was probably the world's largest single-location industrial enterprise. (Sold in 1930.)

[E. N. Hurley, *The New Merchant Marine.*]   DUDLEY W. KNOX

Hog Reeve. A town officer in colonial New England, charged with the duty of impounding swine that strayed from the common lands, and with appraising damage done by them. The officer, now usually called field driver, is believed to be still in nominal existence in a few places.

P. ORMAN RAY

Hogs were introduced by the first colonists to furnish their customary meat, and multiplied rapidly in all sections. Abundance of forest nourishment supported wild droves and corn proved unexcelled for finishing. A pork surplus for export, mainly to the West Indies, early developed. The Connecticut Valley was the area of the first systematic hog raising and pork packing. The superior Dutch hogs mingled with the coarser English type in New York, and the Germans of Pennsylvania gave their usual care to this branch of husbandry. In the mild climate and luxuriant natural herbage of the South swine like other domestic animals flourished with little care; they ran wild in the western valleys and were often hunted like game. They established the region's main meat supply and a profitable export. Virginia hams and bacon early came to rival the famed Westphalian product.

On the frontier the ubiquitous porker was quite at home. The razor-back type was able to root its living and to do battle with or escape from most foes. The Southwest with its availability to markets led in the 1840's, but by the next decade the center of production had shifted to the Northwest where the natural conditions were most favorable for the strategic combination of corn[W] and hogs.

Early marketing was restricted to driving (by owners or large-scale drovers) to the Eastern cities, but with the extension of transportation processing was localized near the source of supply. Cincinnati started her first packing plant in 1818 and had forty-two by 1855. Southern Illinois towns were developing the business in the same period but by the 1850's the industry had definitely centered in Chicago (*see* Packing, Meat; Stock Yards). Along with packing a variety of by-product industries sprang up and before the rise of petroleum the refining of lard oil to compete with whale oil grew to major importance.

Hogs were the first domestic animals to undergo selective breeding. As early as the 1830's improvements were made by crossing mongrel sows with imported boars. The main American breeds in order of development have been the Chester White in southwestern Pennsylvania, the Poland-China in the Miami region of Ohio, and the Duroc-Jersey of New York and New Jersey.

Hog diseases—especially cholera, tuberculosis and influenza—have been combated by preventive inoculation and sanitary rearing.

[R. A. Clemen, *The American Livestock and Meat Industry;* P. W. Bidwell and J. I. Falconer, *History of Agriculture in the Northern United States, 1620-1860.*]

EARLE D. ROSS

Holden Peace Movement, THE (1863–64). Although the leader of this movement never completely revealed his plans, it is probable that William W. Holden, editor of the (Raleigh) *North Carolina Standard,* intended to detach North Carolina from the Confederacy and make a separate peace with the United States. Through editorials in his newspaper, public meetings which he inspired and petitions demanding peace negotiations he weakened the Southern cause and alarmed its leaders. For months Gov. Zebulon B. Vance disapprovingly watched the movement grow, but he hesitated to break political relations with Holden. When in January, 1864, he became convinced, however, that Holden planned to force the calling of a state convention for the negotiation of peace directly with the North, Vance severed political relations with him. Holden immediately announced his candidacy for the governorship, but Vance, after a brilliant stump-speaking campaign, crushingly defeated him in August, 1864, carrying every county in the state except three. This killed the peace movement in North Carolina. (*See also* Confederacy, Peace Movements in.)

[S. A. Ashe, *History of North Carolina;* R. D. W. Connor, *North Carolina: Rebuilding an Ancient Commonwealth.*]

RICHARD E. YATES

Holding Company, THE, broadly defined, is a type of business organization in which one corporation owns the securities, commonly the shares, of other companies and holds them for the purpose of influencing the management of the subsidiary companies, rather than for investment or other purposes. The two principal types of holding companies are first, those whose sole activity is the ownership of securities of other firms, and second, those which combine with such ownership business operations of their own.

The development of the holding company has coincided in the United States with the rise of "Big Business"^{qv} that began at the end of the 19th century. Previous to 1888 few companies were legally competent to hold shares of other firms. Most states followed the common law rule that business corporations could own the stock of others only when given specific permission by special legislation, and few such charters were granted. The exceptions were mainly in the railroad and communications industries. In 1888 the New Jersey general corporation law was amended so as to permit companies chartered under it to acquire the right to own shares in other firms. This change was quickly copied in other states, and the foundation was laid for the rise of the holding company as an important form of business organization.

The holding company offers special opportunities to the organizers and managers of business enterprises. It facilitates the combination of business units and permits of "tentative" consolidation in a way that the merger of two legal persons into one does not. It affords a convenient method of centralizing control of the policies of different businesses, while leaving control of their operations decentralized. The use of a number of holding companies placed "on top" of each other provides an easy way whereby business organizers can acquire control of a large volume of assets with relatively little investment on their own part. Separate incorporation by a large combine of properties located in different states often simplifies its accounting, taxation and legal problems and, commonly, frees the combine of legal restrictions to which it might otherwise be subject.

Such advantages led to the rapid growth of the holding company form. It spread from one type of business to another, even into the field of finance, and came to dominate the railroad and public utility^{qv} industries. (*See also* Electric Light and Power.) It united properties widely separated geographically and enterprises that, superficially, had little in common. It was bitterly attacked and as vigorously defended. It became the typical form of organization for large-scale enterprise in the United States in the first third of the 20th century.

[J. C. Bonbright and G. C. Means, *The Holding Company.*]

CHARLES C. ABBOTT

Holes of the Mountains was a term applied by fur trappers to mountain valleys where they were accustomed to camp, trap beaver and meet at annual rendezvous^{qv} for trading and social hilarity. Among the most famous of these were Gardner's Hole now in the Yellowstone National Park, Jackson's Hole along the east base of the Teton Range in Wyoming, Pierre's Hole^{qv} on the western slope of the same range, Ogden's Hole at the site of the present city of Ogden, Utah, and Brown's Hole (now Brown's Park), Wyo.

[H. M. Chittenden, *History of American Fur Trade in Early Far West.*]

CARL L. CANNON

Holladay Overland Stage Company. From 1850 to 1870, before railways were generally available for express, mail and passenger service between the Mississippi Valley and the Pacific coast, overland stage companies were organized and extensive lines were maintained. Among these was a service provided by Ben Holladay on March 21, 1862, when he bought at public auction the interests of Russell, Majors and Waddell[w]. By 1866 he operated over 2760 miles of western road, used 6000 horses and mules, 260 coaches, many wagons and employed hundreds of men. The Federal Government paid him annually $650,000 to carry the mail over these lines. In 1866 he sold his properties to Wells, Fargo and Company[w].

[LeRoy Hafen, *The Overland Mail;* A. L. Stimson, *History of the Express Business.*]   C. C. RISTER

Holland Land Company (1796–1846). Four Dutch banking houses, Stadnitski & Son, Van Staphorst, Van Eeghen and Ten Cate & Vollenhoven, decided to speculate in American funds, and in 1789, sent Theophile Cazenove to this country as agent.

In 1792 the other promoters, without Van Staphorst, authorized their agent to invest monies in lands in the United States. Regaining confidence, Van Staphorst soon joined, and the houses of Willink and Schimmelpenninck were added. Lands were purchased in the Genesees in November of that year. In December, Willink and others authorized Cazenove to purchase 500,000 acres in Pennsylvania.

Having decided to form a stock company, on May 20, 1795, the bankers made their declaration before a notary and on Feb. 13 of the following year the organization known as Hollandsche Land Compagnie was organized. The stock was divided into shares representing ownership of 1,300,000 acres in the Genesee, 900,000 east of the Allegheny and 499,660 west of that river. A director with six commissioners composed the management in Holland. In 1800 Cazenove was succeeded by Paul Busti as a general agent in America, and Joseph Ellicott became agent in the Genesees. The affairs of the Company in America were liquidated in 1846, or shortly thereafter.

[Paul D. Evans, *The Holland Land Company.*]
ROBERT W. BINGHAM

Holland Patent (1769). In accordance with a mandamus of King George III and Council, signed July 20, 1764, 20,000 acres of land were surveyed in Albany County, N. Y., north of the Mohawk River above German Flats for Lord Holland, and a patent was granted March 17, 1769. He sold the tract to Seth Johnson, Andrew

Craigie and Horace Johnson. Moses Wright was employed by the new owners to survey it into lots of 100 acres. A few settlers were on the property in 1797.

[*Calendar* of New York Colonial Manuscript Endorsed Land Papers.]   ROBERT W. BINGHAM

Holland Submarine Torpedo-Boat, THE, designed by John P. Holland, of Paterson, N. J., the most practical submarine built in the United States up to her time, was purchased, after exhaustive trials, by the Navy Department on April 11, 1900. Two months later Congress authorized the construction of five submarines of the Holland type. The Holland was a cigar-shaped craft, fifty-three feet long, propelled by a gasoline motor on the surface, and by an electric motor under water. The craft could dive, rise and be held at a desired level by the action of horizontal rudders placed at her stern. Air was furnished by compressors and reserve tanks. Her armament consisted of one bow torpedo tube, one bow pneumatic dynamite gun and three short Whitehead torpedoes. Holland had experimented with submarines for a quarter-century, and launched his first craft in 1877. He was the first to use an internal combustion engine in conjunction with an electric motor in a submarine.

[H. C. Fyfe, *Submarine Warfare, Past, Present, and Future;* William Hovgaard, *Modern History of Warships.*]
LOUIS H. BOLANDER

Holly Springs. Grant's 1862 overland campaign south from Tennessee depended upon accumulated supplies at Holly Springs, Miss. Gen. N. B. Forrest's raid incapacitated the railway, and Gen. Earl Van Dorn's surprise attack at Holly Springs, Dec. 20, destroyed Grant's depot. Grant withdrew northwards, living off the country, and thereafter approached Vicksburg[w] from the river.

[F. V. Greene, *The Mississippi.*]
ELBRIDGE COLBY

Hollywood, until 1911, was a quiet residential town, essentially a suburb of Los Angeles. Motion picture[w] producers had turned their eyes toward California as early as 1908, when William Selig placed a studio in Los Angeles. Two others followed, and in 1911 David and William Horsley took over an old tavern and its barn in Hollywood and turned them into a cinema studio. In 1912 the Universal Company located there, and when, in 1914, the new Paramount Corporation leased a big barn and began producing pictures, Hollywood's destiny was fixed. In rapid succession, other new giant movie companies built studios there; then, their owners' mansions began rising on its outskirts, followed by the palaces of high-salaried stars and directors, with their swimming pools, polo fields and other devices for luxurious living. The name of Hollywood as the world's movie capital became known to the uttermost parts of the earth; its glamor drew from all parts of America such hordes of would-be actors and actresses that they became a community problem. To intellectuals, its name connoted a pseudo-art-form, devoid of realism, naïvely illiterate. Its morals were long under fire, and after the mysterious murder of a director, stern measures were taken by the industry to improve its reputation.

[Benjamin B. Hampton, *A History of the Movies.*]

ALVIN F. HARLOW

Holmes County (Ohio) Rebellion (June, 1863) was a Civil War draft[w] resistance incident. After seizing four men from an enrolling officer, an armed group ignored Gov. Tod's order to disperse. A skirmish with troops in which two objectors were wounded ended the resistance. Thirteen men were surrendered for trial and the troops withdrew.

[E. O. Randall and D. J. Ryan, *History of Ohio.*]

CHARLES H. COLEMAN

Holmes Harbor, Indian Fight at. In March, 1854, William Young was murdered by Snohomish Indians. Found possessing Young's property, two were pursued to Holmes Harbor, Whidbey Island, Puget Sound, by Sheriff Russell and posse. In the ensuing fight five white men were wounded, one fatally. Nine Indians were killed.

[H. H. Bancroft, *History of Washington, Idaho and Montana;* Arthur A. Denny, *Pioneer Days on Puget Sound.*]

JOHN FRANCIS, JR.

Holmes v. Walton, a case decided by the Supreme Court of New Jersey in 1780, is cited as one of the so-called precedents for the doctrine of judicial review[w]. The Court declared unconstitutional a statute which provided that in certain classes of cases a jury might consist of six men. The legislature subsequently repealed the voided portion of the act. Thus the right of the courts to pass upon the constitutionality of legislation was not denied, but the legislature claimed the final power to define the functions of each department of Government. (*See also* Hayburn's Case.)

[W. S. Carpenter, *Judicial Tenure in the United States.*]

WILLIAM S. CARPENTER

Holston Treaty. On June 26, 1791, Gov. William Blount of the Southwest Territory (now Tennessee) met the representatives of the Cherokee[w] at White's Fort (Knoxville), some four miles below the junction of the French Broad and Holston rivers. On July 2 a treaty was signed making the Cherokee-American boundary the watershed between the Little and the Little Tennessee rivers and guaranteeing to the Cherokee the possession of the lands still retained by them. This ended a period of warfare on the upper Tennessee frontier in which the Indians had endeavored to get the United States to enforce the more favorable Treaty of Hopewell[w] of 1785 making the French Broad River the Cherokee-American boundary.

[Randolph C. Downes, *Cherokee-American Relations in the Upper Tennessee Valley, 1776-1791,* East Tennessee Historical Society's Publications, No. 8, 1936.]

RANDOLPH C. DOWNES

Holston Valley Settlements. James Patton of Augusta County, Va., claimed the honor of discovering in 1743 an unnamed river south of the New River. Stephen Holston about 1746 built his cabin at the headspring of the river. In 1748 Holston explored its lower reaches and in a canoe passed down the Tennessee, Ohio and Mississippi rivers as far as Natchez[w]. This adventure led to Holston's name being given to the river and valley. Progress of settlement down the Holston Valley was slow because of opposition of the Cherokees[w] to encroachments south of New River. Not until 1768 were there settlers as far down as the North Carolina line; but the treaty of that year at Fort Stanwix[w] caused an inrush and permanent settlements on the Holston and its tributaries below Virginia's southern boundary line. Donelson's line[w], run in 1771 under the Treaty of Lochaber[w], fixed the boundary between the Cherokees and Virginia at Holston River, severing this Holston Settlement from the one on the Watauga[w]. The first named, even the large part in North Carolina until 1777, was governed by Virginia. West of Donelson's line was formed on the Holston a distinct settlement known as Pendleton District. Virginians largely predominated in both Holston settlements, and took active parts in Lord Dunmore's War[w] and the Revolution.

[S. C. Williams, *Dawn of Tennessee Valley and Tennessee History.*]

SAMUEL C. WILLIAMS

Holt's Paper, during the American Revolution, was one of the staunch supporters of the revolting colonists. Forced from New York by the British, Holt soon established his *Journal* at Kingston, but before the British burned Kingston[w], Holt had removed to Poughkeepsie, where he remained with several interruptions until 1783 when he returned to New York City.

[V. H. Paltsits, *John Holt, Printer and Postmaster*.]

THOMAS ROBSON HAY

Holy Cross, Fathers of, are priests of the religious congregation of the same name, formed by Father Basile Antoine Moreau at Le Mans, France, in 1837 to teach and to do missionary work. They were introduced into the United States in 1841 by Father Edward Sorin, C.S.C., who settled first near Vincennes, Ind., and in November, 1842, moved his community to Notre Dame, Ind., where he founded the University of Notre Dame. These fathers also conduct Portland University, Portland, Oreg., and St. Edward's University, Austin, Tex., and publish *The Ave Maria*, a weekly magazine founded in 1865.

[Circular Letters of Father Edward Sorin, C.S.C., 2 volumes, 1885-94, Notre Dame, Indiana.]

THOMAS T. McAVOY, C.S.C.

Holy Experiment, THE, was Penn's term for the ideal government he established in Pennsylvania (1681) which laid "the foundation of a free colony for all mankind" and guaranteed civil liberty, religious freedom and economic opportunity. The people shared fully in government with a constitution and code of laws chosen by them. No restrictions were placed on immigration; religious or political oppression was unknown; oaths were abolished and peace established, hence no provision for war by forts, munition or militia was necessary. This government succeeded for seventy years.

[W. F. Dunaway, *History of Pennsylvania*.]

JULIAN P. BOYD

Holy Ground, Battle at. *See* Econochaca, Battle of.

"Holy Lord" Hinges. Commonest of house-door hinges used in colonial America were those shaped like the letters H and HL. Imported from England after 1700 they became universally popular. They were made of plain wrought iron and, when attached, were left unpainted. Legend has connected symbolic meaning—"Holy" and "Holy Lord"—to these shapes, explaining their widespread use as a protection against witchcraft.

[A. H. Sonn, *Early American Wrought Iron*.]

C. A. TITUS

Holy Name Society, THE, is a national organization of Catholic men, pledged to reverence the Name of God and of Jesus Christ by personal piety and group action of worship and by avoidance of blasphemy, perjury, cursing and all man-

ner of profane and indecent speech. Chiefly instrumental in its founding was Very Rev. Charles H. McKenna, O.P. In 1871 he wrote *The Manual of the Holy Name Society*, and that same year the first diploma or charter was obtained for the parish unit organized three years before by Rev. Stephen Byrne, O.P., at the Church of Saint Vincent Ferrer in New York City. The society is sponsored and directed by the Order of Preachers (O.P.), whose members are known as the Dominicans^q. At present (1939) the society numbers at least 2,000,000 members.

[M. J. Ripple, *The Holy Name Society and Its Great National Convention*.]   FRANCIS BORGIA STECK, O.F.M.

"Home, Sweet Home," was written by John Howard Payne while living in Paris, and was set to music by Henry Bishop from a Sicilian air which Payne had heard and with which Bishop was familiar. It was first sung by Maria Tree in Payne's operetta, *Clari*, produced at Covent Garden Theatre, London, May 8, 1823, and at the Park Theatre, New York, on Nov. 12. The version sung in *Clari* includes only the first two stanzas. The song became vastly popular and *Clari* was repeated on the American stage for over forty years.

[A. H. Quinn, *History of the American Drama*; G. C. D. Odell, *Annals of the New York Stage*.]

ARTHUR H. QUINN

Home Owners Loan Corporation, THE, was created by the Federal Home Loan Bank Board as directed by act of Congress, June 13, 1933. It was a "New Deal"^q Federal Government corporation, wholly owned and controlled by the United States and designed to refinance home owners who were threatened with foreclosure and loss of their homes. The H.O.L.C. was empowered to loan up to 80% of the appraised value of the property of homes not over $20,000 in value. The loans were made by exchanging bonds of the Corporation for mortgages. By the summer of 1937 the Corporation held over 1,000,-000 mortgages and as of June 30, 1936, it had issued over $3,000,000,000 in bonds guaranteed by the United States. The Corporation ceased lending operations on June 12, 1936, and has since been engaged in management of its mortgages, maintenance and sale of properties acquired through foreclosure and liquidation.

[*Annual Reports* of the Federal Home Loan Bank Board; *United States Government Manual*, 1937.]

HARVEY PINNEY

Home Rule is the term applied to the policy of allowing cities to make their own charters and thus determine their own form of government. The same right is sometimes given to counties.

Constitutional provisions for municipal home rule now exist in about one third of the states. But the right extends only to "strictly municipal matters," all other things being reserved for determination by the general laws. Since the line of demarcation between these two fields of local and general interest is not always clear, there has been much litigation in the state courts concerning the scope of home rule. The decisions have whittled down this scope considerably.

[Joseph McGoldrick, *The Law and Practice of Municipal Home Rule, 1916-1930.*]   WILLIAM B. MUNRO

Home Rule, Restoration of, in the South. After the establishment of carpetbag-Negro-scalawag[qv] governments in the South, it was clear that the native whites would submit only under compulsion. But with the Negro enfranchised, many ex-Confederates disfranchised, a black majority in some states, and a military-minded President, it was impossible for relief to come through ordinary political methods except in states where there was a white majority. This accounts for the resort to secret societies (Ku Klux Klan, Knights of the White Camelia[qv], etc.) designed to intimidate Negroes and their allies. Virginia, by a quick appeal to Congress, escaped the rigors of Reconstruction[qv]. In Tennessee a conservative constitution was ratified (March, 1870), and a Democratic administration elected (November) to take office in October, 1871. Georgia, although admitted to the Union, was reorganized under military direction when Negro members of the legislature were denied seats, and was forced to ratify the Fifteenth Amendment[qv] before being readmitted (July 15, 1870). The following election the Democrats gained control of the legislature (Nov. 1, 1871) and impeached Gov. Bullock. In North Carolina a "Reform Legislature" impeached Gov. Holden (1871) but it was not until Vance's election (1876) that the Democrats got full control. Texas was under carpetbag rule until Jan. 17, 1874, when the Radical governor, failing the support of Grant, surrendered his office to a Democrat. In Arkansas a Democratic-Conservative governor took office in 1874.

The excesses of Radical rule in the South alienated many in the North and made its defense more difficult for the Washington government. The Amnesty[qv] Act of 1872, the splits within the Radical party in most Southern states, together with the general dissatisfaction of the Negroes, made more hopeful the outlook for the opposition. In the remaining states to be "redeemed" the strife was more prolonged, the contest more violent, and the national significance greater. In 1875 the Mississippi Democrats, while ostensibly drawing no color line, organized on the "Mississippi Plan"[qv] of armed "companies." Despite several armed pre-election clashes, President Grant declined to aid the Republican governor, and on Election Day (Nov. 2) the Democrats, through threats and multiple voting, won a victory in the legislature. The lieutenant-governor was impeached, the governor resigned, and Radical rule came to an end on March 29, 1876. The South Carolina Democrats, taking their cue from Mississippi, nominated a "straight-out" ticket and organized the semimilitary "Red Shirts."[qv] The election (Nov. 7, 1876) was characterized by many irregularities and each side claimed the victory. The dangerous situation resulting from the establishment of a dual government continued until President Hayes withdrew the Federal soldiers and the Republicans gave way (April 11, 1877). A like situation in Florida came to an end when the Florida Supreme Court ruled against going behind the election returns and Gov. Drew was inaugurated, Jan. 2, 1877. A similar election and contest in Louisiana was not settled until Hayes sent a commission to negotiate an agreement. On April 24, 1877, the Packard "government" collapsed and home rule was established under Gov. Nicholls. The situation in the last three states was further complicated by the dispute over the national election of 1876.

[R. S. Henry, *The Story of Reconstruction.*]
      R. H. WOODY

Homestake Mine, THE, at Lead, S. Dak., was discovered on April 9, 1876. Since incorporation with others, Nov. 5, 1877, as the Homestake Mining Company, it has become the "greatest gold mine in the world." Since 1932 a gigantic three-compartment shaft, 13 x 19 feet, has been sunk four fifths of a mile deep. The company's 557 lode claims have seventy-five miles of narrow-gauge track underground, and 20,000 electric lights in continuous service. The milling plants require 7,000,000 gallons of water every twenty-four hours. From 1876 to 1936 the mine paid dividends of $97,062,202 and added $321,508,038 to the world's supply of gold and silver.

[R. Blackstone, The Homestake Mine, South Dakota, *Pahasapa Quarterly,* June, 1916; J. H. Curle, *Gold Mines of the World.*]
      PERCY S. FRITZ

Homestead Movement, THE. It would be difficult, if not impossible, to fix a date for the beginning of the movement which culminated in 1862 in the passage of the Homestead Law. Free land was engrained in the thoughts and desires of westward-moving settlers from early colonial days, but until the West became politically powerful the demand passed unheeded. The revenue motive was basic in determining the public land policy*ᵂ* of the new nation, and more than three quarters of a century were to elapse after the great land ordinance of 1785*ᵂ* before the advocates of free land to settlers were victorious.

Nevertheless, Congress began very early to receive petitions asking that land in certain regions be given without price to settlers. From the Ohio River came such a petition in 1797, and two years later one from Mississippi Territory. In 1812 Representative Morrow of Ohio presented a request from "The True American Society," whose members considered "every man entitled by nature to a portion of the soil of the country." Other instances could be cited to show that there was an insistence on the part of the pioneers that their services in making farms in the wilderness entitled them to land free of price. In 1825 Thomas Hart Benton moved that an inquiry be made into the expediency of donating lands to settlers. The House committee on public lands reported in favor of such a policy in 1828. In his message of Dec. 4, 1832, President Jackson expressed the opinion that "the public lands should cease as soon as practicable to be a source of revenue." Thus the basic doctrines of homestead legislation were steadily attracting adherents.

During the 1830's the Westerners gained an ally in organized labor. The National Trades Union Convention in 1834 and in 1836 adopted resolutions favoring the giving of land to settlers. Perhaps the most active leader in the movement was George Henry Evans, who became the editor of *The Working Men's Advocate,* established in 1844. About the same time there was organized the National Reform Association, which gave much of its attention to agitation for free land by means of public meetings, petitions and circulars. Horace Greeley also espoused the cause and brought it the powerful aid of his *New York Tribune.* In 1852 he presented a lengthy statement of the views of the "land reformers," the central idea being that the public land system should "be so modified that every person needing Land may take possession of any quarter-section not previously located, and that none other than a person needing land shall be allowed to acquire it at all."

The increasing public agitation was reflected in Congress by resolutions and petitions and finally, in 1846, by the introduction of homestead bills by Felix G. McConnell of Alabama and Andrew Johnson of Tennessee. The latter continued to be an ardent promoter of the homestead movement until success was achieved in 1862. It was not until 1852, however, that a general bill for free land actually came to a vote in Congress and then it was defeated in the Senate. Special laws donating land to settlers in Florida and Oregon, under certain conditions, were passed in 1842 and 1850, respectively.

The homestead movement first became a definite political issue in 1848, when the Free Soil party*ᵂ* declared in favor of free land to actual settlers "in consideration of the expenses they incur in making settlements in the wilderness . . . and of the public benefits resulting therefrom." Four years later the same party gave its support even more vigorously, but on different grounds. Now they asserted that "all men have a natural right to a portion of the soil; and that, as the use of the soil is indispensable to life, the right of all men to the soil is as sacred as their right to life itself." Therefore, they contended, "the public lands of the United States belong to the people, and should not be sold to individuals nor granted to corporations, but should be held as a sacred trust for the benefit of the people, and should be granted in limited quantities, free of cost, to landless settlers." These two platforms contained the main arguments used from first to last by the advocates of free land, namely, reward for public service in developing the country, and natural right.

No major political party came to the support of a homestead policy until 1860, but the adherents of the idea were far more numerous than the small votes polled by the Free Soil candidates indicated. In Congress the defeat of the bill of 1852 did not discourage the introduction of similar measures in both houses in the succeeding sessions. Until 1860, however, the formidable opposition to free land made it impossible to get a law through both houses.

Most Southerners were opposed to homestead legislation, mainly because they believed it would result in the peopling of the territories by anti-slavery settlers. Many Easterners disapproved of the movement because of their fear of the effect of its success on the economic situation in Eastern states. It would, they contended, accelerate the westward movement*ᵂ*, it would lower the value of land in the East, and it would deprive the Federal Government of an important source of revenue. Besides these sectional antagonisms to a measure so eagerly desired by Westerners, there was the opposition of the Know-Nothing party*ᵂ* and other antialien groups to any proposal to give free land to foreign immigrants.

The forces of opposition were sufficiently strong until 1860 to prevent the passage of a homestead law. In that year, however, a bill, introduced by Galusha A. Grow of Pennsylvania, and amended in the process of debate and conference, passed both houses. Although this law as finally passed retained a price of twenty-five cents an acre, it was vetoed by President Buchanan, who used most of the arguments which had hitherto been advanced against free land, including unconstitutionality. The effort to override the veto failed by a small margin, and the defeat was a bitter disappointment to the homestead cohorts.

As a matter of fact, however, victory was approaching. The very sectional conflict which had raised the most formidable obstacle to homestead legislation soon led to a situation which left the road to success entirely open. The new Republican party[q] in 1860 declared that "we demand the passage by Congress of the complete and satisfactory Homestead measure." The victory of the Republicans and the secession[q] of the South left the triumphant party free to carry out its program. On May 20, 1862, Abraham Lincoln attached his signature to the Homestead Law, and free land—the goal sought by generations of Westerners since the inception of the public-land polity—was attained.

The Homestead Law gave to "any person who is the head of a family, or who has arrived at the age of twenty-one years, and is a citizen of the United States, or who shall have filed his declaration of intention to become such," the privilege of obtaining a quarter-section of land free of charge, except a small filing fee, by living on the land for five years and meeting certain conditions with respect to cultivation. With numerous modifications, the basic features of the law are in force today.

[George M. Stephenson, *The Political History of the Public Lands from 1840 to 1862;* Thomas Donaldson, *The Public Domain;* Benjamin H. Hibbard, *A History of the Public Land Policies.*]

DAN E. CLARK

Homestead Strike of 1892, THE, is regarded as a landmark not only in the development of labor organization in the steel industry[q], but in the general history of organized labor in America as well. The Amalgamated Association of Iron, Steel and Tin Workers at this time was a powerful labor organization, which had established working relations with the Carnegie Company at Homestead. In 1892 negotiations with the company for a new agreement failed. A strike ensued in which the recognition of the union was the chief issue. Violence and disorder involving pitched battles between workers and a force of detectives were checked by the militia. The strike was lost. Thus, organized labor's first struggle with large-scale capital ended in failure

and, possibly, this is significant of the failure of unionism to penetrate the rising large-scale industries in later years.

[N. J. Ware, *Labor in Modern Industrial Society;* Commons and associates, *History of Labor in the United States,* Vol. II.]

HERBERT MAYNARD DIAMOND

Honduras, Proposed Loan Treaty. Signed Jan. 10, 1911, this would have made possible a loan by American bankers to refund British bonds long in default and to provide money for public works. It contemplated American control of Honduras' customs through a Collector General nominated by the fiscal agents of the loan with the approval of the President of the United States. The treaty was rejected by the Honduran congress and never approved by the United States Senate.

[*Foreign Relations of the United States,* 1912.]

DANA G. MUNRO

Honey Island, in the Pearl River, became a refuge for conscripts and deserters from the Confederate Army. In April, 1864, so many were in this region that Gen. Polk (C.) ordered Col. Lowry to "push his operations down the Pearl River" and "to move upon Honey Island and clear it out."

[Ella Lonn, *Desertion during the Civil War.*]

GEORGIA LEE TATUM

Honey War is the popular title applied to hostile activities in northeast Missouri between Missourians and Iowans in the fall of 1839 when the Iowa-Missouri boundary dispute was at its height. Aroused over resistance in collecting taxes and disagreement as to ownership of bee trees in the disputed area, the two governors ordered their militia to enforce the respective state laws. Compromise prevented armed conflict, and the Supreme Court of the United States made final approval of the boundary in 1851.

[Claude S. Larzelere, The Iowa-Missouri Disputed Boundary, in *Mississippi Valley Historical Review,* Vol. III; Walter B. Stevens, *Centennial History of Missouri.*]

FLOYD C. SHOEMAKER

"Honkey-Donk" Girls, or "Hurdy-Gurdies," were entertainers engaged by saloon keepers and proprietors of social resorts in frontier mining towns to dance with all comers. The music was usually furnished by a hurdy-gurdy or a fiddle; hence the designation of these dancers. They were usually engaged in sets of four with a chaperone who accompanied them at all times. They were mostly sturdy country girls, many of them Germans. Most of them saved their earnings and, when their contracts expired, many married men whose acquaintance they had made while following their vocation. As housewives and mothers they often became a substantial asset to the community.

[William J. McConnell, *Early History of Idaho.*]

WILLIAM S. LEWIS

"Honored Men" were the highest class of Choctaw[*w*] warriors who had performed deeds of valor, not to be confused with "Honored People," the hereditary caste of the Natchez[*w*] Indians, which included both men and women. Difficulty results from the French translation of both terms as *"considérés."*

[Dunbar Rowland and A. G. Sanders, *Mississippi Provincial Archives, French Dominion*, Vol. I.]

MACK SWEARINGEN

Hood's Tennessee Campaign (October–December, 1864). After the evacuation of Atlanta[*w*], Hood's (C.) army retired southward to rest and restore its organization and morale. President Davis visited the army and proposed a move northward to cut Sherman's (U.) communications to Chattanooga, with the possibility of moving on through Tennessee and Kentucky "to the banks of the Ohio."

Early in October, Hood was in the vicinity of Dalton in northern Georgia. Sherman followed from Atlanta. Hood marched off westward to Tuscumbia on the Tennessee River. Here he delayed three weeks awaiting Sherman's pursuit. Instead, Sherman, "forewarned" by Davis' speech, detached re-enforcements under Schofield to Thomas, commanding at Nashville, and himself returned to Atlanta. On Nov. 15 he began his raid to the sea (*see* Sherman's March to the Sea).

Hood decided to ignore Sherman and push into Tennessee to scatter the Union forces gathering at Nashville. He began his march on Nov. 19. On the 29th he nearly cut off Schofield's retreating army at Spring Hill[*w*]. The next day, chagrined and piqued at his failure and urged on by his own necessities, he assaulted Schofield's army at Franklin[*w*] and was repulsed with heavy losses. Schofield hurriedly retreated into Nashville. Hood followed, but did not attack. He delayed two weeks awaiting Thomas' move. The latter delayed to complete his preparations and to receive re-enforcements. On Dec. 15, Thomas attacked with fury and precision, crushed the left of Hood's line and caused the Confederate Army to withdraw to shorter lines. Thomas renewed his attack the next day and was completely successful (*see* Nashville, Battle of).

For the first time a veteran Confederate Army

was driven in disorder from the field of battle. Thomas' cavalry pursued vigorously, but was unable to disperse Hood's army, which crossed the Tennessee River and turned westward to Corinth, Miss. Hood soon relinquished his command to Gen. Richard Taylor. The war in the West was over.

[T. R. Hay, *Hood's Tennessee Campaign.*]

THOMAS ROBSON HAY

Hookworm Disease. Although the evidence is not conclusive, hookworms were probably brought to America by Negro slaves. They became widespread under the favorable climatic conditions of the Southeastern states, and undoubtedly played an important part in lowering the health and vitality of the rural people of that area. The insidious effects of hookworm infection caused many who were once proud, industrious, property-owning people to become indifferent, shiftless, languid and sickly, reduced to various degrees of poverty and ignorance.

The prevalence and importance of hookworm in the Southeastern states was first recognized by Dr. C. W. Stiles in 1901. In 1909 the Rockefeller Sanitary Commission was organized to study and control the disease in this country; it was out of this that the International Health Division of the Rockefeller Foundation[*w*] eventually grew. The effect of this attack on hookworm disease was to awaken an intelligent public interest in rural hygiene and to establish permanent agencies for the promotion of health in rural areas, which in this country took the form of county health organizations (*see* Health, Public).

[Asa C. Chandler, *Hookworm Disease, Its Distribution, Biology, Epidemiology, Pathology, Diagnosis, Treatment and Control.*]

ASA C. CHANDLER

Hoosac Mills Case (U. S. v. Butler, 297 U. S. 1, 1936). The Agricultural Adjustment Act[*w*] of 1933 empowered the Secretary of Agriculture to enter into contracts with farmers for the purpose of restricting production, to pay them cash benefits for their co-operation, and to lay processing taxes the proceeds of which were to be devoted to the benefit payments. In this case the processing taxes were declared invalid because the proceeds were devoted to an unconstitutional purpose. The payment of cash benefits to farmers to get them to co-operate was coercive, said the Court, and was an attempt on the part of Congress to do indirectly what it had no power to do directly, namely, regulate agricultural production—a matter solely within the jurisdiction of the states (*see* Reserved Powers of States).

HARVEY PINNEY

Hoosac Tunnel, THE, opened in 1876, extends 4.73 miles through the Hoosac Mountains of Massachusetts, a southern extension of the Green Mountains. It was started in 1855 by the Troy and Greenfield Railroad as part of a plan to divert western trade to Boston. The state aided, and was forced to take it over when the road failed in 1863. In 1887 it was turned over to the Fitchburg Railroad, now a part of the Boston and Maine. The first use of compressed air drills in the United States was in 1866 in the construction of this tunnel.

[F. A. Cleveland and F. W. Powell, *Railroad Promotion and Capitalization.*]   JAMES D. MAGEE

"Hoosier" is a term applied to the inhabitants of Indiana since pioneer days. It had a meaning well understood in the state as early as 1830. "Hoosier" occurs in a poem of that year printed in the Indianapolis *Journal* and was often used in letters and addresses during the first half of the 19th century. Its origin is obscure—incapable of satisfactory explanation. The oldest theory is that it is a corruption of "Who's here" (*hyer* or *yere*), as pronounced by the early inhabitants in answer to a late knock on a cabin door. Another explanation—highly improbable—is that it may have been derived from the word *Hussar*—often used by an early lecturer on the Napoleonic wars. Still another is that it originated from the word "husher," meaning a bully who at a cornhusking or a house-raising could quickly hush or quiet an antagonist.

[Meredith Nicholson, *The Hoosiers.*]
THOMAS L. HARRIS

Hoover Dam. *See* Boulder (Hoover) Dam.

Hopedale Community, THE (1842–56), was created in Milford, Mass., under the guidance of the Rev. Adin Ballou to be "an experiment in the science of a divine order of society, or an attempt to actualize in organic form the kingdom of God on the earth." It was a joint-stock company that shifted between the extremes of communism and individualism, but ended its existence after fourteen years by surrendering its property to its two wealthiest members and heaviest stockholders. Ballou believed it was not a financial failure, but too Christian in principle for its time.

[Adin Ballou, *The Hopedale Community.*]
ALLAN MACDONALD

Hopewell. A group of mounds and earthworks near Chillicothe, Ohio, described by Atwater in 1820, excavated in part by Squire and Davis in 1846, Moorehead in 1891, and finally thoroughly excavated by Shetrone, 1922–25.

As a type site it gives the name Hopewell to a complex of prehistoric mound-building cultures once flourishing in the Ohio drainage. Another type of mound-builder cultures in Ohio is called Fort Ancient[qqv]. Hopewell culture is characterized by cremation, finely carved stone pipes, copper ornaments, ceremonial use of sheets of mica and large use of fresh-water pearls. The pottery decorations are distinctive and influenced the ceramic art of many contemporary prehistoric cultures in the Mississippi drainage.

[H. C. Shetrone, *The Mound Builders.*]
CLARK WISSLER

Hopewell, Treaty of, was made at Hopewell, S. C., on Nov. 28, 1785, between the Cherokee Indians and commissioners of the United States; in the following January the same commissioners at the same place made almost identical treaties with the Choctaw and Chickasaw[qqv]. These treaties fixed boundaries between the different tribes and between Indians and whites, gave the United States sovereignty over the three tribes, and control of their trade. The treaty of Hopewell is significant as the first general Indian treaty made by the United States; its most important provision was the establishment of a definite boundary of Indian lands.

[*American State Papers, Indian Affairs,* I, 38–52; C. J. Kappler, *Indian Affairs: Laws and Treaties,* II, 8–16.]
R. S. COTTERILL

Hopewell Iron Works, THE, were located in southeastern Pennsylvania. There were two apparently independent enterprises by this name in the state: the Hopewell Forge belonging to the Cornwall mines opened by Peter Grubb in 1742 in Lancaster (now Lebanon) County; and the Hopewell Furnace and Forge begun by William Bird in 1744 in Berks County. The Bird venture failed in 1784 but the Lancaster forge continued for many years under the ownership of Robert Coleman.

[A. C. Bining, *Pennsylvania Iron Manufacture in the Eighteenth Century.*]
ELIZABETH W. MEADE

Hopi Indians, often called "Moqui," are a people of Uto-Aztecan stock, speaking a Shoshonean dialect but Pueblo[qv] in culture, occupying a large reservation in northeastern Arizona which centers around a cluster of pueblos atop, or close to, three mesas. They were evangelized during the 17th century, but from 1680 were persistently "apostates" and an asylum for numerous Pueblo fugitives from the Rio Grande towns.

Among the Hopi alone has survived the Snake

ceremony[w]; they are famous also for their foot-racers, and for their arts and crafts: pottery, textiles and basketry, sand painting and water-color work.

[F. W. Hodge, ed., *Handbook of American Indians*.]

LANSING B. BLOOM

Horizontal Tariff Bill, effective May 1, 1872, cut the protective duties 10%. Another act admitted tea and coffee free. This was a compromise by which the protectionists[w] prevented more drastic cuts in protective duties. The reduction was repealed in 1875 to meet an alleged need for more revenue.

[F. W. Taussig, *Tariff History of the United States*.]

JAMES D. MAGEE

Hornbook, THE, long used in England, was transplanted to America by the English colonists. It was the primer or first reading book used in the colonial schools. The Hornbook was really not a book at all but just a sheet of paper mounted on a board and covered with transparent horn. The board was projected to form a handle which the children held while reading. The handle was perforated so that it might be attached to the child's girdle. The Hornbook contained the alphabet in capital and small letters; the vowels followed by a combination with consonants to form syllables as ab, eb, ib, ob, ub, etc.; the Lord's Prayer and the Roman numerals.

[A. W. Tuer, *History of the Horn-book*.]

CHARLES GARRETT VANNEST

Hornet-Peacock Engagement, THE (1813). On Feb. 24, off British Guiana, the United States sloop *Hornet,* Master-Commandant James Lawrence, captured the British brig *Peacock,* Capt. William Peake, after a spirited action of fifteen minutes. Soon afterward the *Peacock* sank. The British had five killed, including Capt. Peake, and thirty-three wounded; the Americans, one killed and four wounded.

[A. T. Mahan, *Sea Power in Its Relations to the War of 1812;* Theodore Roosevelt, *The Naval War of 1812;* Albert Gleaves, *James Lawrence.*]

CHARLES LEE LEWIS

Hornet-Penguin Engagement, THE. On March 23, 1815, the American sloop of war *Hornet,* Master-Commandant James Biddle, commanding, encountered the British brig *Penguin,* Capt. J. Dickinson, commanding, off the island of Tristan d'Acunha in the south Atlantic. The American vessel carried twenty guns and the British nineteen. Each vessel was manned with 132 men. In the engagement which followed, the *Penguin* had her bowsprit and foremast shot

away, and Capt. Dickinson was killed. The *Penguin* was afterward sunk. The *Hornet* did not receive a single shot through her hull.

[Theodore Roosevelt, *Naval War of 1812;* J. F. Cooper, *History of the Navy of the United States.*]

LOUIS H. BOLANDER

Horse: Cow Horse. The original cow horse was essentially of the mustang[w] breed. Until the 20th century mares were seldom used for range work, and they are not much used yet, although a belled mare commonly led the remuda[w]. The cow pony had to have bottom, surefootedness and "cow sense"—a quality lacking in many finely bred horses. The average did not weigh a thousand pounds and was around fourteen hands high—"enough horse" to hold 1500 pounds of beef at the end of a rope. The cow pony often maintained the pitching proclivities of a bronco[w]. The elite of his kind were the cutting horses, agile, intelligent, superbly reined, trained to cut, or part, animals from a herd. The night horse was picked to stand guard, and to be relied upon when in pitchy darkness the herd stampeded across prairie-dog holes and gullies. In running after cattle, the cowboy's chief work often lay in staying with his horse, which would no more quit the running than a hound will quit a hot trail. "Cowboys are plentiful, good cow horses cost money," was a range saying.

[Old Granpa, in Frank R. Hastings, *Recollections of a Ranchman;* W. R. Leigh, *The Western Pony;* Ross Santee, *Men and Horses,* and *Cowboy.*]

J. FRANK DOBIE

Horse, THE, developing in the Americas only to the prehistoric stage, was early introduced into all the colonies from England and the continent. Before settled agricultural systems developed, oxen[w] were preferred for draft purposes, but horses and ponies were essential for inland travel. For the colonies as a whole, horses were valued mainly for riding, hunting and racing. The latter was a leading form of recreation throughout the colonies; there were sectional and intersectional meets, and races were a usual attraction of the market fairs. The jockey club founded at Charleston in 1734 is claimed to have been the first in the world and a similar organization was formed at Annapolis in 1745. Long Island was another famous racing center. Relatively high stakes and the sporting spirit gave the incentive for improvements through importations and a degree of selective breeding. New England carried on the first extensive breeding on the basis of early English and Flemish importations. From 1650 the region was exporting increasingly to the other continental colonies and especially to the West

Indies, where the sugar industry created a steady demand. Rhode Island developed one of the most distinctive and noted types of the period in the Narragansett pacer—a fast easy-gaited saddle horse but one not suited for driving or draft purposes. In direct contrast was the famous Conestoga of the Pennsylvania German farmers. The product of selection and careful handling, these animals were distinguished for size, strength and endurance. The development of such a suitable draft type was in harmony with the more settled and advanced cultivation and husbandry that prevailed in this region.

In all phases of the penetration, occupation and development of the continent the horse has played a major role. The stagecoach[*q*] was the first interregional utility. The post-rider opened communication with outlying settlements. The peddler[*q*] ministered to material needs, the doctor to physical and the circuit-rider[*q*] to the spiritual. Horses and mules[*q*] drew canal boat and rail car. The Western pony served the hunter, trapper and miner, and later provided the mounts for the long drive and herding activities of the cowboy. Pack horse, stager, freighter and express pony[*qq*] served the transportation needs of the Far West before the coming of the railroad. Extractive industries, manufactures and city distributive systems were all dependent on horse power. Cavalry[*q*] mounts and supply teams were adjuncts of military organization and of campaigning on every front. Sport and recreation, organized and unorganized, made increasing demands upon equine standardization and specialization.

Speed desires motivated the first systematic efforts at high breeding. The English thoroughbred, "Messenger," imported in 1788, was to become the progenitor of a group of racing families of whom the most noted have been the Hambletonian and the Mambrino. "Justin Morgan," foaled in Massachusetts in 1793, founded a line notable not only for speed but for light draft and provided the nearest attainment to a distinct American breed. The modern runners have been highly developed from thoroughbred strains and such races are still associated with high society and equally high stakes. From the first quarter of the past century, increasing attention has been given to harness racing, and selective breeding, careful training and improvement of track and equipment have brought a steady increase in speed. Racers' pedigrees and records are officially recorded in the registers established by John H. Wallace in 1871. The saddle-horse has continued to be bred for ever-lessening demand in the Kentucky bluegrass re-

gion. The heavy harness type—cob, hackney, coach—were imported and bred for a special pleasure-driving demand in the pre-automobile days and still appear in horse shows. The polo game has utilized small thoroughbreds and Western ponies.

Less spectacular but far more significant have been the uses of the horse in carrying on the nation's production and transportation. By 1860 the age-old controversy of the ox versus the horse for farm traction had been decisively settled. The ox's availability at the self-sufficing stage was overcome by the needs of increased and bettered production and the requirements of the new machinery. The general use of the standard draft breeds, pure or grade, was a condition of the "new agriculture" before the tractor stage. The Percheron was widely imported in the 1850's to become the most popular type. The other leading heavy breeds—Belgian, Clydesdale and Shire —were bred for the market from the 1870's. The Corn Belt from Ohio to Iowa has been the center of the draft-horse supply.

The revolution worked by the internal-combustion engine in auto and tractor[*q*] has resulted in a displacement of horses for power and transportation until the number on farms in 1936 was approximately that of a half century earlier. The decrease from 1918 had been nearly 48%. Whether the movement for small rural holdings and extended recreation programs will have an appreciable effect on the horse market the future alone can tell.

[John H. Wallace, *The Horse of America in His Derivation, History, and Development;* C. S. Plumb, *Types and Breeds of Farm Animals.*]

EARLE D. ROSS

Horse, The Spanish, in North America. There were no horses in America before the arrival of the Spaniards, whose steeds, derived from the Moors, were the finest of Europe. Their short backs revealed their Arabian blood; their legs, firmly jointed and not too long, made them sure on their feet. In America they lost weight and beauty, but were compensated by increased stamina. Unbelievable feats of their endurance are recorded.

Brought to the West Indies at the close of the 15th century, the Spanish horse was rapidly acclimated, and within thirty years formed the chief supply for the mainland expeditions. By the middle of the 16th century there were outstanding horse breeders in Cuba, Jamaica, Nicaragua, Chiapas and Oaxaca, who sold their products in two continents.

From the islands and Mexico the horse advanced with the Spaniard into the northern mainland in four salient columns. While Jamestown was being settled by the English on the Atlantic coast, Oñate[w] was establishing Spanish ranches in New Mexico. The tradition that the mustangs[w] of the Southwest sprang from the early expeditions of Coronado and DeSoto[qw] is apparently incorrect. By 1630 horses were plentiful around Santa Fé[w], but the Plains Indians seemingly had none, and no records are found of mounted Indians for three more decades. By 1660 the Indians had learned the value of horses, and had begun to steal them. During the next forty years the horse spread into the plains and mountains with great rapidity. In 1719 Dutisne found the Pawnees near Kansas with 300 horses, some bearing Spanish brands. The Snakes had horses by 1730 and two decades later the Blackfeet in present-day Canada were mounted. By the end of the 17th century the French of St. Lawrence Valley were obtaining a regular supply of Spanish horses from the Indians west of the Mississippi. (*See also* Indian and the Horse.)

Farther west Kino and his companions were pushing a second Spanish wedge into Arizona, where they established many stock ranches by 1700. Here also the horses multiplied and were acquired by the natives. Portolá from Lower California, and Anza from Arizona, took horses into Alta California, where they increased prodigiously. Exportation thence to Hawaii began in 1803 and reached extensive proportions by 1830. So numerous did horses become in California that thousands were slaughtered, or driven off cliffs or into the sea to drown. Simultaneously with the movement into Arizona, Spaniards from Coahuila introduced horses into Texas and Louisiana, where Patrick Henry, Daniel Boone, Philip Nolan and others from east of the Mississippi were buying stock before the end of the 18th century.

Just as the Western horse came from Mexico, so the foundation stock of the Atlantic coast came from the Spanish islands to Florida. By 1650 this district had many missions, several large towns, and two royal haciendas whence horses spread to the Indians—not from the remnants of DeSoto's mounts as has been commonly supposed. Indian revolts and English depredations at the close of the 1600's tended to spread the horse north into the English colonies. On the outskirts of Virginia they multiplied in a semiferal state—like the mustangs of the Southwest—until they were a menace to the crops and were hunted for sport. These horses were generally small, with bad points, but new blood was obtained from the Spanish stock west of the Mississippi.

Thus the first horses of North America were bred in the Spanish islands, and spread thence via Mexico, Florida and the Southwest into the whole continent. Indeed most of the horses imported even into the English colonies before the end of the 18th century were Spanish stock obtained from the Spanish islands of the Caribbean. Until the 19th century the Spanish horse presented the nearest, and, in many respects, the best, available horseflesh.

[Robert M. Denhardt, Spanish Horses and the New World, in *The Historian*, I, and The Southwestern Cowhorse, in *The Cattleman*, XXV; Francis Haines, Northward Spread of the Horse among the Plains Indians, in *American Anthropologist*, XXXX; Clark Wissler, Influence of the Horse in the Development of Plains Culture, in *American Anthropologist*, XVI.]

ROBERT DENHARDT

Horse Marines is a term ordinarily covering situations in which cavalrymen do the work of marines, or vice versa. In a broader sense it may designate, with humorous derision, almost any military or naval incongruity.

The expression became associated with an episode in Texas, 1836. San Jacinto[w] had been fought. Maj. Isaac Burton's Texas Rangers[w] were making a reconnaissance along the coast to establish the extent and speed of the Mexican withdrawal, which was being dictated more by food shortage than by military pressure from Houston. Near Copano, Burton sighted and by ruse captured three Mexican supply ships. Of course Burton's detachment became known as the "Horse Marines."

[Jim Dan Hill, *The Texas Navy.*]

JIM DAN HILL

Horse Racing. American turf history began in the year 1665, when Col. Nicolls, the first colonial governor of New York after it became a British possession, offered a silver cup to be raced for over a two-mile course that he had laid out on Long Island, where Garden City now stands. The great development of the sport, however, took place during the next century in Maryland, Virginia and the Carolinas, which became and long remained its strongholds. Then, as the West and South were colonized, Kentucky, Tennessee, Alabama and Mississippi became important racing and breeding regions, with Kentucky gradually gaining the ascendancy which it has ever since retained. When civilization crossed the Mississippi and the Great Plains it took the race horse with it, for not only was pioneering impossible without horses, but it rapidly developed that the high-bred horse was stronger, braver and more enduring than the common one, as well as swifter, and that his blood was indispensable for both progress and safety. In California the Spanish colonists had introduced a high grade of animals bred up from their own stock of Oriental ancestry (*see* Horse, The Spanish) and when the thoroughbred and the light-harness strains from the East were taken there they were quickly domesticated. In this manner the entire Union became a racing and breeding terrain, performers of high class being produced in all parts of the country.

While New York remained of the first importance as a center of the sport and the Union and Fashion Courses on Long Island were the scenes of contests that excited the attention of all America, it was nevertheless true that the real "race horse region" lay south of the Potomac and the Ohio rivers, Richmond, Charleston, Louisville and New Orleans giving the most important race meetings of the year. The devastation of the South in the Civil War wrecked its turf pre-eminence, its great breeding farms being not only laid waste but its impoverishment making it impossible to carry on racing as before. The sport, which had been virtually discontinued during the war, experienced its renaissance in New York, and ever since that city—its Courses and its influence—have been dominant. The metropolis today supports four "major" racing plants, three of them on Long Island—Belmont Park, Aqueduct and Jamaica—and one, Empire City Park, on the mainland; while a fifth, at Saratoga Springs, is also owned and controlled by its sportsmen. There is a group of important courses in New England; another in Maryland; Kentucky, while pre-eminent as a breeding state, has another group, including Churchill Downs, at Louisville, where the Kentucky Derby has been run annually since 1875; Ohio is dotted with tracks, but not of the first importance; Detroit has an elaborate plant; Chicago supports four, of which Arlington Park is one of the most extensive and imposing in existence; others will be found at Hot Springs, Ark., and Omaha, Nebr. In California the sport is maintained at five parks, headed by Santa Anita, at Los Angeles. There racing continues both summer and winter; while at New Orleans and in Florida, at Miami, which has two courses, there are also long winter seasons.

Race track betting has long been a subject of strife, both from the economic and the moral sides, but in recent years this has been superseded and the sport placed under state control in the various commonwealths where it flourishes, commissions appointed by the various governors supervising its conduct, while a substantial tax, levied upon both the betting and the admission fees, is exacted in return therefor. This rules almost without exception. The popularity of the sport under these conditions has become pronounced. The attendance upon great events runs as high as 70,000 (Kentucky Derby) , while it has also been possible to give such stakes as the Santa Anita Handicap, a race for all ages with $100,-000 added to the entrance fees. Everything is done to make the sport an attractive entertainment and the public response has been such that it is now a large revenue producer for nearly twenty different state treasuries. Political control has not, however, proved an unmixed blessing; though, all things considered, its introduction has perhaps been a step forward.

Harness racing flourishes in the United States as nowhere else in the world and the American standard-bred trotter has been accepted as the country's most important contribution to the ranks of domestic livestock. While there is no export demand for American thoroughbreds, standard-breds are exported every year in numbers to many different countries for both racing and breeding purposes. Harness racing is wholly unlike the thoroughbred sport. Race meetings are as a rule confined to a few days, the betting is a minor feature, a large proportion of the meetings given (over 800 in 1937) are features of state and county fairs[qq], and many of the contending horses are owned and trained by their drivers, who indulge in the sport as a matter of inclination or diversion rather than financial profit. The most important tracks are associated in what is known as the Grand Circuit, and at one of these meetings, that held at Goshen, N. Y., is annually decided the Hambletonian Stake, which is the richest event for trotters ever given, its value upon one occasion having ranged as high as about $75,000.

As is the case with the thoroughbred[p], trotting horse breeding is largely centralized in Kentucky. In both its breeding and its racing affairs, the light-harness industry presents more of an unprofessional aspect and touches much more nearly the every-day life of the people than does thoroughbred racing.

[*American Turf Register*, 16 vols., 1829-44; *Spirit of the Times*, 31 vols., 1831-61, and later vols. down to 1902; *Turf, Field & Farm*, 75 vols., 1865-1902; *American Stud Book*, 16 vols., 1873-1936; *Thoroughbred Record*, 127 vols., 1875-1939; *Goodwin's Turf Guide*, 43 vols., 1882-1908; *Daily Racing Form*, 45 vols., 1894-1939; *American Racing Manual*, 42 vols., 1897-1939; *Early American Turf Stock*, 2 vols., 1934-35; *American Trotting Register*, 28 vols., 1871-1932; *Horse Review*, 83 vols., 1888-1932.]

JOHN HERVEY

Horse Stealing has been practised all over America but it naturally became more dominant and more severely punishable where and when horses were most depended upon: in the West and Southwest. The culture of the Plains Indians was Horse Culture, and they raided horses from Mexico, from each other and from the settlers. The value range people put on horses is summed up in a saying, "A man on foot is no man at all." To be "left afoot" meant something like being scuttled on a desert island. Killings were not murders, and decent gun men went unmolested by law or society; cattle stealing was often justified by circumstances analogous to those that made "cattle lifting" on the Scotch border honorable (*see* Scott's *Rob Roy*) ; but "as lowdown as a horsethief" expressed the nadir of the social scale. A majority of "cottonwood blossoms"—men hanging, usually without benefit of jury, from limbs of cottonwood trees—were horse thieves.

During the lawless decades following the Civil War, gangs of horse thieves operated out of Texas into the Old South and over the West. They had hideouts for stolen horses, which would be sold or traded off only after having been driven hundreds of miles from home. It was not polite to inquire about the brand on any stranger's horse.

[J. Frank Dobie, *A Vaquero of the Brush Country;* J. Evetts Haley, *Charles Goodnight;* N. P. Lankford, *Vigilante Days and Ways.*]   J. FRANK DOBIE

Horsehead Crossing, a name frequently encountered in books of the Southwest, is confusing because there were two river crossings so designated, one in Texas, the other in Arizona. In Texas the Goodnight-Loving cattle trail[qv] passed the Pecos River at Horsehead Crossing near the present town of Ficklin. In Arizona, travel bound for Concho and Fort Apache passed the Puerco at Horsehead Crossing just below its junction with the Little Colorado.

[C. C. Rister, *Southwestern Frontier;* W. C. Barnes, *Arizona Place Names.*]   CARL L. CANNON

Horses, Wild. *See* Mustangs.

Horseshoe Bend, Battle of (March 27, 1814). After a six-months' campaign, involving four pitched battles, Maj. Gen. Andrew Jackson attacked 800 Creek Indians[qv] strongly entrenched at the Horseshoe Bend of the Tallapoosa River, within the present limits of Alabama. He had 2000 militia and regulars. The battle lasted about seven hours. Their breastworks overrun, the warriors refused to surrender and all but about fifty were killed. Jackson lost 49 dead, 157 wounded. The battle broke forever the military power of the southern Indians. Red Eagle, or Bill Weath-

erford, their able seven-eighths white leader, who was not present at the Horseshoe, perceiving the uselessness of further resistance, surrendered to Jackson.

[A. J. Pickett, *History of Alabama.*]
                                   MARQUIS JAMES

Hortalez et Cie owed its origin to Beaumarchais. The famous author of *Le Mariage de Figaro* in a pamphlet *La Paix ou la Guerre* influenced Louis XVI to secret assistance for the Americans. A corporation, nominally private, would safeguard the official neutrality of France while permitting substantial aid to the revolutionists. On May 2, 1776, the king authorized purchase of supplies to the value of 1,000,000 livres. In July the Spanish king extended similar assistance. In August the company was officially organized, and within a year it had sent to the Americans eight shiploads of military stores worth over 6,000,000 livres.

Notwithstanding the formal alliance of 1778 (*see* Franco-American Alliance), the company continued in business until 1783. Its total disbursements exceeded 21,000,000 livres and were of immeasurable importance to the *materiel* of the American Revolution. Confusion in reimbursements was responsible for the "Lost Million" of Beaumarchais.

[Blanche E. Hazard, *Beaumarchais and the American Revolution.*]   LOUIS MARTIN SEARS

Hospitals. The mediæval Church was the mother of hospitals, and its influence established hospitals in Catholic America before they were known in Protestant America. Still existent are the 16th-century Jesus Hospital of Mexico (1524) and the 17th-century Hôtels-Dieu of Quebec (1639) and Montreal (1644), but there was no general hospital on the soil of the United States until the 18th century. The orator's dramatic claim for the Philadelphia General Hospital, "This, Gentlemen, is the oldest hospital on this continent," is therefore incorrect. The Philadelphia General Hospital, known as Old Blockley, which opened as an almshouse (1732) ; Bellevue Hospital of New York, which opened as a workhouse (1736) ; and Pennsylvania Hospital, which opened as a hospital (1751), continue to contend for the title of "America's oldest hospital." William Shippen's private institution (1762) in Philadelphia, "a convenient lodging, under the care of a sober, honest matron, well acquainted with lying-in women," was our first maternity hospital. The Mad House (1768) at Williamsburg, Va., now the Eastern State Hospital, was the first insane asylum in the United States.

After the battle of Bunker Hill, in which the physician Joseph Warren died a hero's death, his youthful pupil and brother, John Warren, took charge of the wounded at Cambridge, "in several private but cummodious houses," which may be regarded as our first military hospital (1775). James Tilton, who introduced the hut system in the "hard winter of 1779–80, when the army was hutted near Morristown," advocated the plan of the Indian hut as the best hospital in cold weather. The army hospital located on a pasture in Boston afforded John Warren the material for lecturing on the cadaver. His sessions were conducted behind locked doors, as hostility to dissection of the human body was intense (lack of caution in New York caused prejudice to flare up in the Doctors' Mob, quelled only with the aid of militia). Despite the attempt at secrecy, this early anatomical course could not be hidden, and when it was repeated for two years it originated Harvard's medical school (1782–83), in which John Warren served as first professor of anatomy and surgery. His son, John Collins Warren, who succeeded to the dual chair, founded the Massachusetts General Hospital (1811), where in his old age he consummated his labors by giving anæsthesia[w] its first public demonstration (1846) —"and a new era for surgery began."

In the log-cabin period, Daniel Drake (1785–1852) was the medical builder of Ohio. Drake, battle-scarred from the "Thirty Years' War" with colleagues, gave the impulse to the hospital movement in the Mississippi Valley with the words: "All the tendencies of the age are to the study of medicine and surgery in hospitals. The laboratory is not more necessary for the study of chemistry, or a garden of plants for the study of botany, than a hospital for the study of practical medicine and surgery." The classic appeals for hospital instruction in America were made by Oliver Wendell Holmes (Scholastic and Bedside Teaching, 1867), who was a truant of Æsculapius; and by Abraham Flexner (Medical Education in the United States, 1910); who was not a physician. The hospital, designed for the reception and treatment of the sick, has emerged as the training field and teaching center of medicine and nursing.

Not until the 20th century did American hospitals, in number and equipment and personnel, begin to keep pace with the needs of the nation. There are now (1939) 1,124,548 hospital beds in the United States and 98.5% of our people live within thirty miles of a hospital. The present generation is the first that has grown up without a horror of hospitals, which was fully justified by the unspeakable conditions and mortality-rates of the past. (See also Army Hospitalization.)

[American and Canadian Hospitals, 1933-37; Journal of American Medical Association, July 16, 1938, p. 257.]

VICTOR ROBINSON

"Hot Oil" Case, THE, arose under the National Industrial Recovery Act of 1933[w], which, among other delegations of power, authorized the President to "prohibit the transportation in interstate and foreign commerce" of oil produced or withdrawn from storage in excess of the amount permitted to be produced by the state from which the oil was shipped. The Supreme Court invalidated this provision of the Recovery Act by holding that Congress had delegated essential legislative power to the President. Shortly afterward, Congress passed an act which avoided such broad delegation of power, but which contemplated substantially the same regulation of oil shipments.

[Panama Refining Co. v. Ryan, 293 U. S. 388, 1935; Code of the Laws of the U. S., p. 584; Public-No. 14, 74th Congress, 1935.]

P. ORMAN RAY

Hot Water, The Battle of, was a skirmish, June 26, 1781, about six miles from Williamsburg, Va., between Americans of the Pennsylvania Line, commanded by Col. Richard Butler, and a force of British troops led by Col. John Simcoe. It is also called the Battle of Jamestown and the Battle of Green Spring. Hot Water is the old name of the plantation adjoining Green Spring plantation.

[Joseph A. Waddell, Annals of Augusta County, Virginia.]

JOHN W. WAYLAND

Hot Water Rebellion. See Fries Rebellion.

Hours of Labor. See Wages and Hours of Labor.

Housatonic, THE, was a large sloop of war, one of the Federal fleet blockading Charleston[w] in 1863–64. H. L. Hunley of Mobile designed for the Confederates a hand-operated submarine only thirty-five feet long which, on Feb. 17, 1864, torpedoed the Housatonic and sank with her. Most of the Housatonic's crew were saved.

[Cyril Field, The Story of the Submarine.]

ALVIN F. HARLOW

"House Divided." Accepting the Republican[w] nomination to the United States Senate, at Springfield, Ill., June, 1858, Abraham Lincoln gave to Biblical truth a new fame in American politics when he declared:

" 'A house divided against itself cannot stand.' I believe this government cannot endure permanently, half slave and half free. I do not expect the Union to be dissolved—I do not expect the house to fall—but I do expect it will cease to be divided."

[Albert J. Beveridge, *Abraham Lincoln, 1809-1858.*]
THEODORE M. WHITFIELD

House-Grey Memorandum was an agreement in February, 1916, between Col. Edward House and Sir Edward Grey, British foreign secretary. President Wilson was to summon a conference for ending the World War^w. Should Germany refuse, "the United States would probably enter the war against Germany." If the conference met and failed, "the United States would [probably: *word inserted by Wilson*] leave the conference as a belligerent on the side of the Allies, if Germany was unreasonable." Grey took the memorandum *ad referendum*. The effect of Wilson's insertion is vigorously disputed. Nothing came of the plan.

[C. Seymour, *Intimate Papers of Colonel House;* Viscount Grey of Fallodon, *Twenty-Five Years;* R. S. Baker, *Woodrow Wilson: Life and Letters.*]
BERNADOTTE E. SCHMITT

House of David, a religious colony on communal basis, was founded at Benton Harbor, Mich., in 1903 by Benjamin Purnell, self-styled "seventh messenger" of the 144,000 elect. The cult practised celibacy, disdained shaves and haircuts. Purnell died in 1927 and the colony divided. In 1937 there were 350 members, 24 clergy and one church.

[E. S. Wooster, *Communities of the Past and Present.*]
WILLIAM J. PETERSEN

House of Hope, or Fort Good Hope, erected at Dutch Point in the South Meadow on the south bank of the Little or Park River at its junction with the Connecticut within the present city of Hartford, was the first European settlement in Connecticut and in the Connecticut Valley. The purpose of the post was to tap the trade of the Connecticut Valley, especially in furs. On June 8, 1633, Jacob van Curler, acting under orders from Wouter van Twiller, governor of New Netherland^w, purchased a small plot of land from the Indians and built the fort, which mounted two cannon. In the following September these Dutch threatened to stop Lt. William Holmes, of Plymouth, who sailed up the river and established a post at the present Windsor. In 1635-36 English from Massachusetts Bay Colony^w settled immediately north and west of the fort. Mutual recriminations followed and the English so narrowly circumscribed the fort that it had little value strategically or commercially.

When war broke out between England and the Dutch in 1653, Capt. John Underhill, with doubtful warrant, seized the fort, and in the following year the Hartford authorities occupied the premises definitely.

[Florence S. M. Crofut, *Guide to the History and Historic Sites of Connecticut.*]
GEORGE MATTHEW DUTCHER

House of Representatives. *See* Congress, The United States.

Houseboats. The habit of living in floating homes perhaps began when pioneers journeyed down the mid-western rivers in arks^w roughly equipped for housekeeping. Store boats^w and floating groggeries appeared in those times, then floating water mills (*see* Water Mills), and a little later the showboat^w. Gradually there came to be a class who made their home on the water, some by preference, some because they could not afford to own land. Some were nomadic, moving frequently, but most of them clung to one spot for many years. Some in flood time allowed their boats to settle on near-by waste land and remained there, often through several floods. For decades on end "shantytowns" of these boats have existed on mud banks at such cities as Cincinnati, Louisville and St. Louis. Shantyboatmen fish, catch floating logs and timber, search for the drowned and along the lower Mississippi cultivate gardens on the river banks by sufferance of the neighboring landowners.

[Harris Dickson, Shantyboats, *Saturday Evening Post,* Sept. 12, 1931.]
ALVIN F. HARLOW

Household Arts. The line of demarcation between household arts and the various crafts which developed in the course of American household economy is difficult to draw. Pioneer conditions forced the early settlers to make provisions for all of their needs from the simple essentials of food and shelter to the commodities involving more difficult crafts such as the making of furniture, utensils and clothing. The primitive ways of life required an extent of self-sufficiency and self-support which consumed a major portion of the time of the members of the family. Men, women and even children participated according to their capacities and physical strength.

The packing of butter in firkins, the pickling of pork in barrels, the smoking of hams and bacon, the chopping of headcheese and sausage meat, the trying of lard and similar means of preserving foods for the winter formed an important part of the task of household arts, and the tastiness and variety of such foods became a measure of the efficiency and thrift of the family.

In the matter of clothing, the problem of providing enough variety and sufficient quantity of clothes to meet all needs developed a whole series of crafts in the production of textiles. These persisted from the early part of the 17th century to the last quarter of the 18th century. Flax and wool were the two most important staples used in the weaving of cloth. Flax was made into linen, a very difficult process, and wool was made into heavy textiles for heavier clothing. The combination of wool and flax resulted in a material called linsey-woolsey^{qv}, a textile peculiar to colonial times. The raising of flax and its use for making cloth did not come into full fruition till 1670 when the English settlers migrated to New York. From that time on the making of beautiful linen became quite common and even fashionable and the spinning wheel took a prominent place in the equipment of the household. During the whole of the 18th century the making of woolen cloth played an important part in the home industries. In this both men and women participated. Large wool spinning wheels were developed which required that the spinner walk about twenty miles to produce six skeins of yarn. This was considered a day's work. The dyeing of the wool was developed as part of the production with blues and indigo the favorite colors. The indigo^{qv} produced in South Carolina eventually became an article of export. Iris, goldenrod, berries, the bark of red oak and hickory were also used as materials for the production of domestic dyes. After the American Revolution the production of wool cloth continued, but the fulling mill came into use for the treatment of wool so that it might be smoother, of closer texture and more practical for the making of clothing.

The making of household furniture^{qv}, outside of the very simplest conveniences, was left to the specialized craftsman, who made up special designs consistent with the needs of the times. In the matter of rugs, wall ornaments, embroidery and various forms of needlework the tradition of the Dutch and English settlers was followed. However, in the Southern states such as North Carolina and western Virginia there seems to have been a more persistent and a more varied development of the household arts which included the weaving of baskets out of native grasses, ferns and limbs of certain trees; the making of gloves, chair caning, quilting and similar arts. These have persisted to the present day. A survey carried on by the Agricultural Extension Service of the Rural Arts revealed many manifestations of household arts which have persisted from the earliest times of American settlement and have permeated most of the characteristically agricultural areas of the United States. It is quite evident that the desire for self-expression, the use of personal skills and the handiness of materials have encouraged a development of household arts which lean toward the creative rather than the utilitarian. Thus garden development, special skills in flower raising, the making of dolls and marionettes and the more personal application of skills to the making of quilts, dolls, etc., have taken the place of the older arts so important in the maintaining of a household.

[W. C. Langdon, *Everyday Things in American Life.*]

CAROL ARONOVICI

Housing. The history of the housing movement in this country begins in the middle of the 19th century with the rapid growth of our cities and the resulting congestion of population. Between 1849, when the first building code for New York City was enacted, and 1900, sporadic and more or less futile attempts were made to alleviate or remedy the ever-increasing menace of the slums, most of these efforts being concentrated in New York City. In 1867 the first Tenement House Law was passed in New York, setting up standards for light, air and ventilation. Most of its provisions, however, were repealed in 1872 and those that were left remained unenforced.

In 1901 another and far more drastic law was passed by the New York State legislature which became the model for legislation in many other states. This law contained high standards in regard to future construction, but did little toward remedying the conditions of buildings constructed before its enactment.

Between 1901 and 1933 the attack on bad housing conditions was restricted entirely to urban centers, the medium of attack being through the regulation of private enterprise and the setting of minimum standards by law. The result was better housing at higher costs which in turn demanded high rents. This meant that private enterprise could not build dwellings for the lower-income groups, and it can be safely stated that, during the above-mentioned period, 1901–33, a negligible number of new homes was provided for those groups.

These laws, however, dealt only with the question of the protection of life and health, and made no effort to control or regulate the use of land. In 1916 the city of New York passed its first zoning^{qv} ordinance, which attempted to set aside certain sections of the city for definite uses such as business, industrial, retail and residential. This represented the first effort of any city in the country to control its growth, with the exception of Washington, D. C., which was laid out by L'Enfant in the beginning of the 19th century. Other cities followed New York's lead shortly afterward, and some created planning commissions (*see* City Planning) for the definite purpose of replanning their areas. These ordinances helped considerably in the undeveloped areas, but had little effect on those already developed, as the laws were not retroactive.

In 1933 the first effort was made to house the poor with government financing and government subsidy. The National Industrial Recovery Act^{qv} of that year contained an appropriation of $150,-000,000 to be spent for slum clearance and low-rent housing on the basis of writing off 45% of the capital cost. The real purpose of this expenditure, however, was to put people to work and it was not until 1937 that the Federal Government took up the housing question seriously. In that year Congress created the United States Housing Authority, empowering it to make loans up to $500,000,000 over a period of three years to local housing agencies. Instead of writing off a part of the capital cost, this agency is permitted to make annual grants to these local agencies for the purpose of covering the difference between an economic rent and the rent which the low-income groups can pay.

In 1938 the New York State legislature passed a law permitting the city of New York to impose a special tax for the purpose of granting annual subsidies to meet the deficits of the New York City Housing Authority which is charged by law to build houses for the low-income groups. At this same session the legislature also passed resolutions amending the state constitution and empowering the state and its cities to lend money for slum clearance and low-rent housing.

[DeForest and Veiller, *The Tenement House Problem;* Edith Elmer Wood, *Recent Trends in American Housing;* James Ford, *Slums and Housing;* Catherine Bauer, *Modern Housing;* Langdon Post, *The Challenge of Housing.*]

LANGDON W. POST

Houston Ship Channel, THE, first opened in 1919 but deepened to a minimum of thirty feet and greatly improved since that time, furnishes the city of Houston a fifty-seven mile outlet to the Gulf for seagoing vessels. It has made Houston a close rival of New York City in volume of exports. Great industrial plants border the channel.

[*Texas Almanac,* 1925.]

L. W. NEWTON

Howard, Fort, built in 1816 on the site of the former French Fort La Baye, and the British Fort Edward Augustus, was the first American post at Green Bay^{qv}, Wis. Its garrison was called

out in the Red Bird uprising, 1827, and in the Black Hawk War^{qv}, 1832. The army post was of value in Americanizing the French settlement and upholding American laws and customs. The garrison was withdrawn in 1841; troops were again brought thither at the close of the Mexican War, when Lt. Col. B. L. E. Bonneville was the last commandant, and retired in 1852.

[Louise Phelps Kellogg, Old Fort Howard, in *Wisconsin Magazine of History*, Vol. XVIII.]

LOUISE PHELPS KELLOGG

Howland's Island (1600 miles SW. of Honolulu) was discovered in 1842 by Capt. George E. Netcher. In 1857 Capt. A. C. Benson of the U. S. S. *St. Mary's* formally took possession. Since 1935 the United States has maintained sovereignty over this island, and in 1936 an executive order placed it under the Division of Territories and Island Possessions.

[Alden P. Armagnac, Uncle Sam's New Ocean Empire, *Popular Science Monthly*, June, 1938.]

J. W. ELLISON

Hubbardton, Battle of (July 7, 1777). Gen. Fraser with troops from Burgoyne's army^{qv} defeated an American force under Seth Warner at Hubbardton, Vt., as it retreated from Ticonderoga^{qv}. One American detachment was completely surprised and the men "ran off." The leader of another was killed and his men dispersed. Warner fought courageously, but his command was dispersed by a bayonet charge. American militia, six miles away, under St. Clair refused to go to Warner's aid.

[Hoffman Nickerson, *The Turning Point of the Revolution.*]

THOMAS ROBSON HAY

Hudson-Fulton Celebration, THE, commemorated the 300th anniversary of Henry Hudson's discovery of the Hudson River^{qv} in 1609 and the 100th anniversary of the first successful application of steam to marine navigation upon that river by Robert Fulton^{qv} in 1807. Replicas of the *Half Moon* and the *Fulton*^{qqv} traveled up the Hudson Valley for local ceremonies, but the principal part of the celebration occurred in New York City from Sept. 25 to Oct. 11, 1909. It was non-commercial, dignified and successful in providing popular historical education and augmenting civic pride.

FRANK MONAGHAN

Hudson River. Verrazzano, an Italian explorer in French employ, was, so far as known, the first white man to have seen the Hudson River. In 1524, after entering New York Harbor, he wrote of "a very large river, deep at its mouth," which he had ascended for about half a league. The Spaniard Estevan Gomez noticed the Hudson in

1525. French traders traversed it, mostly from Canada, during that century, trading with the Mohawk Indians[*w*], and founded a small fort near the site of Albany in 1540, but this was later abandoned. Henry Hudson, exploring for the Dutch West India Company[*w*], ascended the river in 1609 as far as the neighborhood of Albany and sent some of his men to explore it some twenty-five miles farther, past the mouth of the Mohawk. It thereupon became an artery for Dutch colonization, Albany[*w*] being founded as a fur-trading station in 1614. Other settlement along the river soon followed. To vary the picture, a party of Walloons[*w*] who were suffering persecution in the Flemish Netherlands emigrated to what is now Ulster County in 1660, founding Kingston and other villages, while Germans from the Palatinate settled in the valley in 1710. After the British took over the Dutch possessions in 1664 the English population increased rapidly.

For more than two centuries after settlement began, this river was the chief and for more than one century almost the only avenue of travel and transportation between what is now New York State and New York City or the coast. During these two centuries, freight and passengers were carried up and down almost entirely in sloops. After the Erie Canal[*w*] was completed in 1825, all its great through traffic to and from New York State, the Great Lakes region and the Middle West traversed the Hudson between Albany and New York, the Champlain Canal adding more business to and from northern New York, Vermont and Canada. Fulton's *Clermont* was tested on the Hudson in 1807 (*see* Fulton's Folly), and thereafter steamboats began to displace the sloops. Tugs or towboats drew great fleets of Erie Canal boats, loaded, from Albany down to New York, bringing them back, sometimes loaded, sometimes empty. Large and elegant passenger steamboats plied the river in the mid-19th century, and were the pawns in traffic wars between Cornelius Vanderbilt, Daniel Drew and others. The completion in 1851 of the Hudson River Railroad along its eastern bank brought about a steady diminution of the river's freight traffic. The fine steamboats, because of their greater comfort and luxury, held a considerable share of the through passenger traffic for decades afterward.

The Hudson was perhaps the greatest single factor in making New York City the American metropolis; yet it handicapped the city, too. It is so vast that all railroads from the west (save the New York Central[*w*], coming via Albany and the east bank) must stop on the New Jersey shore

and transfer passengers and freight across by ferry. Only one railroad has succeeded in entering from the west—the Pennsylvania[*w*], which completed a tunnel connection under the river in 1910. The river is so wide and deep, its banks for the most part so rugged, that below Albany, nearly 150 miles from its mouth, it was not bridged until 1889, when a cantilever railroad structure was completed at Poughkeepsie. Thirty-six years elapsed before the next bridging, that at Bear Mountain in 1925; and not until the completion of the great George Washington suspension bridge in 1932, was it crossed at New York City. Because of its size and the fact that for the most part it is an estuary rather than a river, it has never been subject to serious floods.

[Nelson Greene, *History of the Valley of the Hudson.*]
ALVIN F. HARLOW

Hudson River Chain, THE. On May 1, 1778, between West Point and Constitution Island, the famous Hudson River Chain was stretched as a barrier to British shipping. It was constructed in approximately six weeks under the supervision of Capt. Thomas Machin, at the Stirling Iron Works, founded by "Lord" Stirling in 1751, of which Peter Townsend, chief iron-master of the Revolution, was then proprietor. Mined in Orange County, the individual links were slightly over two feet in length; were two and one half inches in thickness; and weighed 140 pounds. The chain, of 180 tons weight, was attached to huge blocks on either shore, supported by protecting batteries. It was buoyed at frequent intervals in midstream by logs sixteen feet in length and pointed at the ends. To weaken the chain was part of Arnold's plan of treason. Fragments of the chain are still preserved.

[Benson J. Lossing, *The Pictorial Field-Book of the Revolution.*]   LOUIS MARTIN SEARS

Hudson River Land Patents. The Dutch practice of making large grants was followed by the English with the result that by 1738 there was little unpatented land left on the Hudson below Albany. The great estates of the landed aristocracy, who played such a large part in the early history of the state, stretched from Albany to New York City. At Albany the great manor of Rensselaerswyck lay on both sides of the river. To the south, in Columbia County, was the manor of Livingston, Beekman's[*w*] great tract in Dutchess County, Philipse's[*w*] Highland patent in Putnam and the manors of Scarsdale, Pelham, Morrisania, Fordham and Philipsborough in Westchester. Although some of the "extravagant grants" made by Gov. Fletcher were annulled by his successor, large tracts such as the Great Nine Partners patent[w] in Dutchess County, the Kakiate[w] and Chesecocks patents in Orange County were secured and held for financial speculation.

[A. C. Flick, ed., *History of the State of New York*, Vol. III.]

A. C. FLICK

Hudson Tubes, THE, are two pairs of tunnels under the Hudson River connecting New York City with New Jersey. Started first in 1874 there were many delays. The company, headed by William G. McAdoo, which finally finished the work, started in 1902. The first operation was in February, 1908. Many of the modern methods of tunneling with a shield and compressed air were perfected during the building. Electrically operated passenger trains are run in the tunnels.

[W. G. McAdoo, *Crowded Years.*]

JAMES D. MAGEE

Hudson's Bay Company, THE, came into being as a result of the western explorations of Radisson[w] and DesGroseilliers in the middle of the 17th century. On trips into the Wisconsin and Minnesota country they learned from the Indians of a great fur country northwest of Lake Superior, which might be reached via Hudson Bay. This idea, linked with one of a probable Northwest Passage[w] through Hudson Bay, led the Frenchmen to England in the middle 1660's. There a sort of syndicate of wealthy and influential men was formed to try out their ideas. Out of this grew the Hudson's Bay Company, which received its charter on May 2, 1670, as The Governor and Company of Adventurers of England Trading into Hudson's Bay. Under that charter and supplemental charters the company still operates, though it has now lost its monopoly of trade, its territory and its administrative rights in the West, which were granted by the first document. It is thus one of the oldest commercial corporations in existence. During the heyday of the fur trade, the company had posts in most parts of what is now Canada. It also had a few forts on United States soil, but fewer than is currently believed. These were mostly along the boundary line west from Grand Portage[w], in the area where the chief impact of the company on United States history was felt. Some of that impact came with the bitter struggle carried on between the Hudson's Bay Company and the North West Company[w], which resulted largely from the establishment of Lord Selkirk's colony on the Red River of the North in 1811. Selkirk, it needs to be said, was one of the largest owners of stock in the English company. Just before the differences were composed by a union of the two

companies in 1821, Selkirk died, and for some years his colony was administered by the company. The colony's founding and struggles had a bearing on the founding of Fort St. Anthony (now Fort Snelling[w]) in 1819; the misfortunes of the colonists led to the emigration of many of them to Fort Snelling to be Minnesota's earliest settlers; the need of a market for the colony led to the development of the Red River Cart Traffic[w] with Minnesota settlements; and proximity to United States soil, and discontent of the colonists under company rule, led to annexation hopes and schemes both on the part of the colonists and the United States between 1849 and the surrender of the company's territories in 1869. Other effects of the company on Minnesota and North Dakota history are those resulting from the sending of missionaries to the Indians and half-breeds under the ægis of the company. Missionaries also played an important part in the company's relations to the history of the Oregon country[w], where company men appeared after the union of 1821 to carry on the fur trade begun years earlier by the North West Company, and where a joint occupation[w] agreement between the United States and Great Britain was in force between 1818 and 1846. By welcoming American traders, explorers, missionaries and settlers, Dr. John McLoughlin, the company's chief factor, helped Oregon to become American, though the decline of the fur trade is probably the basic reason for Great Britain's consent in 1846 to abandon its claims south of the forty-ninth parallel and thus avert a war which threatened (*see* Oregon Treaty of 1846).

[Douglas MacKay, *The Honourable Company;* The Hudson's Bay Company, *Hudson's Bay Company, A Brief History,* and *Books Relating to Hudson's Bay Company;* Arthur S. Morton, *History of the Canadian West.*]

GRACE LEE NUTE

Hue and Cry was a species of summary justice of mediæval English origin. In old English law when a felony was committed, the hue and cry was raised, and a man overtaken in this manner while he still had about him the signs of his crime would have short shrift. In the American colonies generally, individuals suspected of felonies, escaped prisoners and runaway servants and slaves could by law be pursued by hue and cry "from Town to Town, and from one County to another, as well by Horsemen as Footmen." Even where no person could be named in the warrant, the hue and cry would justify arrests made in consequence of it, including idlers, vagrants or other suspicious characters. In following persons on a hue and cry, officers were authorized to impress men, horses and boats, the expenses to be charged as part of the costs, and, in the case of recaptured servants, might entail additions to the term of service.

[Pollock and Maitland, *History of English Law;* A. P. Scott, *Criminal Law in Colonial Virginia.*]

RICHARD B. MORRIS

Huguenots in America, THE. The term Huguenot, of unknown origin, probably a diminutive of Hugo, had been applied to the followers of Calvin during the religious struggles of the 16th and 17th centuries. Henry IV had granted religious toleration to his Protestant subjects by the Edict of Nantes (1598), but this was revoked by Louis XIV in 1685. Approximately 300,000 persecuted French Huguenots fled to Prussia, Switzerland, Holland, England and America. Attempted settlements in Florida and South Carolina (1562 and 1564) failed (*see* Florida, French in; Port Royal). In 1623 Huguenots, largely French-speaking Walloons[w], settled New Amsterdam[w]. Peter Minuit was a Walloon, and Jean Vigne, first white child born on Manhattan Island, was French and probably Huguenot. Fort Orange (Albany), Kingston and New Paltz in New York were Huguenot settlements. Some 200 or 300 Huguenot families came to Boston after the Dragonades.

After 1685 increasing numbers came to America, settling in Rhode Island, in Hartford and Milford in Connecticut, and in New Rochelle, N. Y., mingling with other settlers in Delaware, Maryland and Pennsylvania, where they were called Dutchmen and confused with German settlers. In Virginia the first of the "French Protestant Refugees," as the name appears officially in the Virginia records, was Nicholas Martiau, coming before 1620 and being the earliest known Virginia ancestor of George Washington. The shipload coming to Manakintowne July 23, 1700, and two more shiploads in the same year, made up the largest single settlements of Huguenots in America. This group with its local church and pastor was absorbed into the Church of England. King William Parish was set aside for them, but their blood soon mingled with the English people of the colony.

In South Carolina Huguenots began coming in 1670, played a large part in the settlement of Charleston in 1680 and by 1687 had established four settlements largely or wholly French: Jamestown on the Santee, "The Orange Quarter" on the Cooper, Saint John's Berkeley and Charleston. In 1732, 360 French-Swiss Protestants settled Purysburg on the Savannah, and in 1764 the last French colony was founded, New Bordeaux in Abbeville County. In South Carolina, Huguenots preserved their identity more completely than in other colonies. The only Huguenot church in America is in Charleston, preserving its service, doctrine and organization unchanged. The Huguenot religion was Calvinistic in theology, ritual in form, Presbyterian in government and tolerant in principle. Until well within the 20th century one service each year was conducted in French in the Charleston Huguenot church. The same continuity of tradition is true of the people; there died in South Carolina in the last few years the last pure-blooded Huguenot in America, Hon. Isaac Porcher.

Huguenot contribution to American culture has been largely in the intellectual and artistic fields, giving a certain lightness and sureness of touch. Huguenot descendants have filled all places from Presidents, such as Washington, Adams, Garfield and Roosevelt; statesmen, such as Jay, Hamilton and Laurens; heroes, including Marion, Sevier and Schley; to artists like Paul Revere; scientists like Maury; educators like Vassar; and poets like Longfellow.

[Baird, *History of the Huguenot Emigration to America;* Walmsley, Huguenot Element in the Making of the United States, *The Huguenot,* No. 6.]

JAMES ELLIOTT WALMSLEY

Hull, Court-Martial of. Gen. William Hull's surrender of Detroit[w] was followed by his court-martial at Albany. Martin Van Buren and Philip S. Parker conducted the case for the Government; Hull acted in his own defense. He was charged with treason, cowardice and unofficerlike conduct. The Government's procedure gives the impression of attempting to "railroad" its victim. Hull was denied access to official records, denied, in effect, the right of representation by counsel, and tried before a "packed" court under Gen. Dearborn's presidency.

Hull should not have invaded Canada before perfecting his defenses at Detroit. He should have exercised greater care in preventing the severing of his communications. But the Government was to blame in placing a sixty-year-old general in command of an exposed post. The Secretary of War neglected to inform him that war had begun. Gen. Dearborn, judge of the court-martial, had contributed to Hull's disaster by signing an armistice in which Hull was not included and of which he was not informed, thus allowing the British to throw their entire force against Detroit. Instead of distributing the blame impartially, the Government made Hull the scapegoat of inefficiency everywhere.

Hull was acquitted of treason. He was found guilty of the other charges and sentenced to death, although the court recommended mercy.

President Madison pardoned the general on account of his Revolutionary record and his gray hairs.

[J. G. Van Deusen, Court-Martial of Gen. William Hull, *Michigan History Magazine*, October, 1928.]

JOHN G. VAN DEUSEN

Hull Treaty, THE (Nov. 17, 1807), followed a council with the Ottawas, Chippewas, Wyandots and Potawatomies*qqv* at Detroit. By this treaty much of the land in southeastern Michigan Territory was ceded by the Indians, the new Indian boundary becoming a line about seventy-five miles west of Detroit River, and extending north to the line of White Rock in Lake Huron.

[Cooley, *Michigan;* Campbell, *Outlines of the Political History of Michigan.*]

JOHN G. VAN DEUSEN

Hull's Escape from Broke's Squadron (1812). At 2 P.M. on July 17, the *Constitution*qv, commanded by Capt. Isaac Hull, off Barnegat, fell in with a British squadron of six vessels commanded by Commodore Broke. A chase lasting over sixty hours ensued, during which Hull, surpassing the British in the art of seamanship, escaped from what more than once appeared to be certain capture. Broke had even selected a prize crew from the *Shannon* to take the *Constitution* into Halifax.

[Theodore Roosevelt, *Naval War of 1812;* Ira Nelson Hollis, *The Frigate Constitution.*]

CHARLES LEE LEWIS

Hull's Trail was cut by Gen. William Hull through forest and swamp on his march to Detroit, 1812. Starting at Urbana, Ohio, the trail passed through Forts McArthur and Findlay, north through Portage and Bowling Green, and crossed the Maumee near Turkeyfoot Rock. Thence it went down the river through the site of Maumee and along Detroit Avenue in the city of Toledo; thence to Monroe (Frenchtown), Mich., on the River Raisin and on to Brownstown on the Huron. From here it followed the old river road northward through Monguagon, Wyandotte, Ecorse and Springwells to Detroit.

[George B. Catlin, Michigan's Early Military Roads, *Michigan History Magazine*, 1929.]

JOHN G. VAN DEUSEN

Hülsemann Incident, THE. During the Hungarian Revolution of 1848–49, President Taylor sent an agent to report its prospects of success, with a view toward recognition. This unneutral action, together with America's enthusiastic welcome in 1851 to Kossuth*qv*, the defeated hero, and her support in 1853 for the patriot Koszta*qv* against his former government, all inflamed the Austrian *chargé d'affaires,* Hülsemann, to a series of intemperate protests which were answered, first by Webster, later by Marcy, in the best spread-eagle manner.

[L. M. Sears, *A History of American Foreign Relations.*]

LOUIS MARTIN SEARS

Human Rights may be studied in their political, or in their economic, aspects, or, in a more comprehensive way, as social rights. From the political point of view, the earliest claims were upon the sovereign authority, however vested, to protect individuals in certain benefits, as with the Magna Carta and various bills of rights, including those in our Federal and state constitutions. In the course of time some of these rights came to be regarded as inalienable. Among these the American Declaration of Independence*qv* referred specifically to life, liberty and pursuit of happiness. In short, according to this concept certain rights are superior to constitutions and statute laws, and are inherent in man as a human creature. Modern bills of rights usually include freedom of speech, of religion, of assembly, of press and of petition for redress of grievances. Under the dictum of the Declaration of Independence the concept is susceptible of almost indefinite enlargement, and consequently, when applied as a practical policy, runs the danger of conflicts and inconsistencies. An impressive example is the recent doctrine which sets human rights in opposition to property rights. It is impossible to place these concepts in separate categories because one includes the other.

[William Graham Sumner, *What Social Classes Owe to Each Other;* Ernst Freund, *Standards of American Legislation.*]

ISAAC LIPPINCOTT

Humane Societies. The first, in America, such as those of Massachusetts and Philadelphia, organized in the 18th century, were devoted to the cause of Life Saving*qv* from sea or other waters. The Humane Society of New York, organized 1814, added to this the giving of aid to destitute debtors and other poor in prisons. With the creation of the Societies for the Prevention of Cruelty to Animals (1866) and to Children*qqv* (1875), humane work in America assumed a new phase. In 1877 the American Humane Association was formed at a meeting at Cleveland, Ohio, its immediate aim being a co-ordinating of state and local humane movements to curb cruelty to live cattle in interstate shipments from the West. Its agents watched for cases of brutal treatment of cattle by rail, and lobbyists were sent to Washington to procure legislation on the subject. The Association offered a prize of $5000 for the best design of a cattle car, and succeeded in bringing about many improvements in cars. In 1884 it won suits against two railroads in Massachusetts which set important precedents. It fought live-pigeon trap-shooting. Its chief function eventually became the co-ordinating of all state and local humane activities, under whatever name they operate—S. P. C. A., S. P. C. C., Humane Societies, the Anti-Cruelty Society of Chicago, etc.

[Roswell C. McCrea, *The Humane Movement;* Annual Reports of the early Humane Societies of Massachusetts, Philadelphia and New York.]

ALVIN F. HARLOW

Humanitarianism is a general concept the contents of which change with the evolution of human ideals and institutions—usually in the direction of enlargement. Once considered merely as a movement for the amelioration of human brutalities, it has since been extended to the treatment of animals, as with humane societies[w]. The earlier ideas included the abolition of slavery[w] and serfdom, diminishing the number of capital offenses, and ultimately the dispensing altogether with capital punishment[w]. The abolition of war, or at least, considerate treatment of wounded and prisoners, was a part of the program. Later extension of the concept included aid for the underprivileged, more and better schools, hospitals, asylums, benevolent institutions, care through community chests, provisions for the crippled and the blind. In most recent years have been added the ideals of social security—defense against the hazards of old age, out of work, accident. These objectives are more or less concrete. But, in addition, the professed humanitarian frequently adds vague concepts such as "expansion of democratic ideals," "development of liberalism," equal opportunities for all citizens and for peoples of every clime, and the further concept of humanity as one great family in which a benevolent spirit permeates the whole mass and becomes the guiding principle. In these respects the concept is broad enough to cover anything that moves the heartstrings. How contradictory the ideas may become is revealed by the fact that a few persons who call themselves humanitarians advocate "mercy death" for the incurables and the hopelessly insane.

[L. T. Hobhouse, *Liberalism;* James Ford, *Social Problems and Social Policy.*]

ISAAC LIPPINCOTT

Humiliation and Prayer, Days of. *See* Fast Days or Days of Humiliation, and Days of Thanksgiving.

Humphrey's Executor v. U. S. (1935) restricted the President's power to remove members of the so-called "independent" agencies. In the Federal Trade Commission Act, Congress provided that any commissioner might be removed by the President for inefficiency, neglect of duty, or malfeasance in office. In October, 1933, President Roosevelt removed Commissioner William E. Humphrey, not on any of the stipulated grounds, but because of differences of opinion as to policy. Humphrey denied the validity of this action, and after his death, his executor sued for recovery of the deceased's salary.

The Supreme Court held unanimously that Congress intended to create the Federal Trade Commission[w] as an independent body of experts, and therefore meant to limit the President's removal power to the causes enumerated in the act. It denied the Government's contention, based on Myers v. U. S.[w], that such limitation was unconstitutional. Whereas the Myers case involved a purely executive officer, the Federal Trade Commission's duties are predominantly quasi-legislative and quasi-judicial[w]. Congress has authority, the Court declared, to require such a body to act independently of executive control, and may forbid removal except for cause.

[E. P. Herring, *Public Administration and the Public Interest;* W. Anderson, *American Government.*]

RANSOM E. NOBLE, JR.

Hundred. The hundred in England was of varying size but generally supposed to have been originally an area occupied by 100 families. There were administrative officials and a court for the hundred. In the local government of English colonies in America there were evidences of the influence of the hundred, especially in Virginia, Maryland and Delaware.

Very early in Virginia the hundred was adopted as a territorial division and included, in theory at least, 100 families, but was far more extensive than in England and soon became strictly territorial, without regard to the number of persons. In Virginia, as in England, it was the unit for judicial, military and political purposes. By 1619 the borough, which included hundreds, was established and two burgesses from each borough were elected to the legislature. By 1634 Virginia was divided into eight large shires or counties. The hundreds thus gradually lost their influence but their names persisted because of their former importance.

In Maryland, as in Virginia, the hundreds were territorial units for elections, public levies and the preservation of the peace. The chief officer of the hundred, the constable or conservator of the peace, had the power of a justice of the peace in England. In the early period, the hundred was the unit of representation for the legislature (two burgesses from every hundred), also the unit for judicial, fiscal and military purposes. Even after counties were established, the importance of hundreds continued for a considerable period.

In Delaware under English control the hundred was adopted and was in operation by 1690. After counties were established the hundreds continued as the important subdivisions of them, persisting to the present. There are, for example, thirteen in Sussex County and the city of Wilmington has been made a separate hundred.

[P. A. Bruce, *Institutional History of Virginia in the Seventeenth Century;* H. C. Conrad, *History of Delaware;* J. L. Bozman, *History of Maryland;* H. L. Osgood, *The American Colonies in the Seventeenth Century.*]

PERCY SCOTT FLIPPIN

Hungarians, individually, have contributed to all periods of American history, but an important immigration dates only from the Revolution of 1848, and the visit of Louis Kossuth[qv] in 1851. Eight hundred Hungarians, more than eighty of them officers, fought in the Union armies during our Civil War. Political conditions caused the earlier migration; economic, that of the 1880's and later. The census of 1930 enumerated 247,450 persons of Hungarian birth. The mines of West Virginia and Pennsylvania, the vineyards of Ohio and California, have attracted many, though few settlements are now exclusively Hungarian.

[Joseph S. Roucek, Hungarians in America, in *The Hungarian Quarterly,* Vol. III, No. 2.]

LOUIS MARTIN SEARS

Hunkers, the conservative faction of New York's Democracy (1840's), favored spending state surpluses on canals in advance of canal earnings, internal improvements and liberal chartering of state banks[qv]. They deprecated antislavery agitation. Distribution of state patronage promoted party discord with Barnburner[qv] rivals. Hunkers favored Polk. They were charged with defeating Gov. Wright for re-election (1846). Barnburner revolt came in 1848. A coalition failed to elect Seymour governor in 1850. At this time Sen. Daniel S. Dickinson was a prominent Hunker. Pierce displeased the Hunkers. By 1853–55 the terms "Hards" and "Softs" appeared. Not all Hunkers became "Hards" (e.g., Seymour).

[D. S. Alexander, *Political History of the State of New York;* H. D. A. Donovan, *The Barnburners;* D. T. Lynch, *An Epoch and a Man: The Times of Martin Van Buren.*]

PHILIP G. AUCHAMPAUGH

Hunters. The American border settler was skilled in the use of his rifle and hunting knife and usually kept his family clothed in buckskins and his larder supplied with meat. The average frontiersman hunted for pleasure or to provide for his own household, but there were some who were hunters by profession. Commanders of border forts sometimes hired hunters to keep the troops supplied with deer and buffalo meat. From 1875 to 1885 hide buyers employed hundreds of expert marksmen to slaughter the great herds of buffalo[qv] on the Plains. This area was known as the "hunter's paradise," supporting millions of buffalo, deer, elk and antelope; and the scanty timber along its streams were havens for wild turkeys.

Since the first colony was planted on the Atlantic seaboard every border area has had its celebrated hunter. From 1765 to 1785 the Kentucky and Ohio regions talked much of James Harrod, Daniel Boone, Simon Kenton and Lewis Wetzel. Boone was more familiar with the Kentucky forests than he was with the streets of a Virginia town; a chronicler says that the years 1771–74 were the happiest of Kenton's life because "they were spent among men of the woods, hunters and trappers." David Crockett of Tennessee, who lost his life in the Texas revolution (1836), was a well-known bear and deer hunter, dubbed by H. H. Bancroft as a "mighty hunter and fearless soldier." The Great Plains and Rocky Mountains gave employment to many intrepid hunters during the 19th century, such as "Buffalo Bill" (W. F. Cody), "Kit" Carson, "Big Foot" Wallace, J. Wright Mooar, Thomas Forsythe and John Cook. Spending many years in the trackless wilds, all of these became expert guides and pathfinders for exploring parties.

[Albert L. Slager, General Simon Kenton, in *The Ohio State Archæological and Historical Quarterly,* Vol. XLV, No. 1, 46-67; Richard Irving Dodge, *Hunting Grounds of the Great West.*]

C. C. RISTER

"Hunters" Lodges. Formed in Vermont in May, 1838 to secure the independence of the Canadas after the failure of the Rebellions of 1837 (*see* Patriot War of 1837), the "Hunters" absorbed four similar secret societies formed between March, 1838, and March, 1839. At their height in 1839 they probably had 40,000 members. In September, 1838, they established headquarters at Cleveland and proclaimed the Republican Government of Upper Canada, to establish which they launched unsuccessful attacks against Prescott in November and Windsor in December. Three years of sporadic attacks on Canada followed. The lodges disintegrated after President

Tyler's proclamation of Sept. 25, 1841, and Alexander McLeod's[w] acquittal the following month.

[Orrin E. Tiffany, The Relations of the United States to the Canadian Rebellion of 1837-38, Buffalo Historical Society *Publications*, VIII.]

ALBERT B. COREY

Hunting Grounds. This term, as it appears in the literature relating to the Indians and the fur trade[w], is often used very loosely and may have different meanings, depending upon circumstances. It may, for instance, be applied to a vast area like the Great Plains, which was the range of the buffalo[w], and which was shared by many different tribes; or it may be used in referring to a limited and fairly well-defined region, recognized as the exclusive preserve of a certain tribe. Owing to the Indians' peculiar but characteristic conception of land ownership and utilization (*see* Land, Indian Conception of Ownership of), it is very difficult to describe or locate precisely any particular "hunting ground" at a given time. The geographical location and extent of the Indians' hunting grounds depended upon a number of factors, such as the character of animal life and its seasonal migration; the accessibility of such areas and the trails leading thereto; and tribal custom, together with the hostile or friendly relations between neighboring nations. Naturally, under these conditions, hunting grounds would be far from permanent or stable, and any accurate description would have to be laboriously pieced together from the innumerable accounts which have come down to us.

Many of the tribes which lived to the east of the Great Plains had more or less fixed abodes during certain seasons of the year, where they carried on a primitive agriculture. In the fall, they were accustomed to depart for their "wintering grounds," where they hunted the animals which supplied their food and the furs which they used for trade. They might return to their villages in March or April, where they disposed of their furs and did the spring planting. After the planting, some of the Indians might go off again on a summer hunt, lasting until July or August. The villages were naturally located in as close proximity to the hunting grounds as was practicable.

There were instances where different tribes shared the same hunting grounds. On the other hand, a tribal council might allocate certain limited areas to small hunting parties belonging to the tribe in question. It is apparent that encroachments by the whites upon the hunting grounds would threaten the livelihood and even the survival of the Indians in a given area. Jeal-ousy for these preserves led the Indians into innumerable intertribal conflicts as well as into the constantly recurring strife against the white man.

[F. W. Hodge, *Handbook of American Indians;* H. M. Chittenden, *The American Fur Trade of the Far West;* Emma H. Blair, *Indian Tribes of the Upper Mississippi Valley and Region of the Great Lakes.*]

WAYNE E. STEVENS

Huntsville, Ala., originally called Twickenham, was named for John Hunt, pioneer Tennessean, who erected a hut about 1805 on the bank of the "Big Spring" in the Tennessee Valley. When Madison County was organized out of the Mississippi Territory[w] in 1808, Huntsville became the county seat. As the first town in northern Alabama and inhabited by land-hungry immigrants from Tennessee, Georgia and Virginia, many of whom achieved prominence in social and political affairs, Huntsville soon became a thriving center of civilization, rivaling St. Stephens[w] in southern Alabama.

[E. C. Betts, *An Early History of Huntsville.*]

JOHN B. CLARK

Huron, Lake. That part of it known as Georgian Bay was discovered by Father Joseph Le Caron in 1615. Samuel de Champlain, who reached the lake the same year, by the same Ottawa River and Lake Nipissing route, named it the *Mer Douce.* Its present name was given it after the Huron Indians[w]. Etienne Brûlé in 1622 is thought to have skirted the shores of the lake from its southern end to the St. Mary River. It became the route for explorers, missionaries and fur traders to the Mississippi and the Western Plains.

[E. P. Morton, *Lake Huron and the Country of the Algonquins.*]

LAWRENCE J. BURPEE

Hurons, THE, were a confederation of more advanced Iroquoian tribes, visited by the French under Champlain in 1615, and estimated at from 20,000 to 30,000 people. Occupying what is often referred to as Huronia, around Lake Simcoe and south and east of Georgian Bay, their towns were often palisaded, more or less permanent and the site of many early French missions. From prehistoric times the Hurons had been at war with the Iroquois[w] tribes to the south. These latter, being the first to come into possession of firearms, fell upon the Hurons in 1648-50 with implacable fury. They ravaged their towns and country and killed or enslaved the greater part of the population. The history of the survivors is a tragic story. Some sought refuge with the French; others moved west to Michigan, Wisconsin and Illinois. Incurring the enmity of the Sioux[w], they were driven back to Wisconsin, moved to Michigan and finally to Ohio where, known as Wyandots, some were removed to Kansas in 1842 and, in the way of the white tide flowing westward, to what is now Oklahoma in 1867. Only a handful of this once great Indian people now remains.

[F. W. Hodge, *Handbook of the American Indians.*]
JOHN FRANCIS, JR.

Hurricanes. The word hurricane has come, in the United States, to mean a marine storm or one of those destructive tropical gales which arise in the West Indies and sometimes cross to our continent. Of a list of 355 such storms, all that are on record between 1493 and 1855, it was found that 245, including all of the worst ones, occurred in August, September and October. They follow some curious courses. The great hurricane of 1848 crossed Florida and moved with somewhat diminished force northwest to Nebraska, then turned sharply eastward, past the southern Great Lakes. The great hurricanes of 1873, 1879, 1881, 1885, 1886, 1893 and 1911 all occurred in August. That of 1879 destroyed 300 vessels along the Atlantic coast. That of 1881 killed 335 persons in and near Savannah. Two days later, its center was near Memphis, the next morning in Iowa, then in Minnesota. That of 1893 ravaged the Georgia and Carolina coasts, killing 1000 and doing $10,000,000 damage, and finally passed across Lake Ontario into Canada. Very frequently these storms—those of 1875, 1878 and 1896 being notable examples—sweep from Florida up the Atlantic coast to New York or New England. That of 1878 did enormous damage in Philadelphia. The most destructive hurricane in our history was that which struck Galveston[w], Tex., on Sept. 8, 1900. It fairly lifted the waters of the Gulf and hurled them through the city, drowning 6000 persons, more than one seventh of the population, and doing $20,000,000 damage, leaving not a house in the city uninjured. The barometer there fell to 28.48, the lowest figure on record in America up to that time. The year 1915 saw two major disasters, in August and September. The August storm entered through Texas, passed up the Mississippi Valley, then swerved northeastward across the Great Lakes; the September gale ravaged the Louisiana and Alabama coasts. In each of these some 275 persons were killed, and the property damage ran into many millions. In 1920 it was calculated that in the twenty years from 1900 to 1919 inclusive, Gulf coast hurricanes caused $105,642,000 damage and took

7225 lives. The September, 1926, hurricane almost wrecked Miami, Fla., killed 400, and did $25,000,000 damage. Two years later, September, 1928, a more terrible storm passed diagonally across southern Florida, driving Lake Okeechobee out of its bed, doing less property damage, but killing, as nearly as could be ascertained, about 2300 people. On Sept. 21, 1938, a West Indian hurricane, which had missed the whole east coast until it touched the New Jersey shore, devastated large areas of Long Island and New England; Providence, New London and other cities suffered enormous damage. More than 600 lives were lost.

[E. B. Garriott, *West Indian Hurricanes;* Isaac Monroe Cline, *Tropical Cyclones.*]
ALVIN F. HARLOW

Hurtado v. California. The issue in this case was whether a conviction for murder without grand jury indictment was a violation of the due process clause[w] of the Fourteenth Amendment. The State of California had provided a criminal procedure based merely on information or formal accusation by the prosecution. In 1884 the Supreme Court held such conviction was not outlawed. Due process of law meant old but it could also mean new procedure. In line with this principle, it was held in later cases, that states could even dispense with juries or permit self-incrimination.

[A. C. McLaughlin, *A Constitutional History of the United States;* R. E. Cushman, *Leading Constitutional Decisions.*]
LEONARD C. HELDERMAN

Husking Bee. *See* Bees, Husking, Quilting, etc.

Hutchinson Letters, THE, from Thomas Hutchinson, governor of Massachusetts, and other American Tories[w], soliciting troops and urging abridgment of American liberties, were transmitted from London to the colonies by Benjamin Franklin. Their receipt at Boston, early in 1773, caused a stir which encouraged the Massachusetts legislature to petition Hutchinson's removal. For his part in the affair Franklin was denounced before the Privy Council[w] and punished by the loss of his post as deputy postmaster-general of the colonies.

[W. V. Wells, *The Life and Public Services of Samuel Adams.*]
LLOYD C. M. HARE

Hutchinsonian Controversy, THE. *See* Antinomian Controversy, The.

Hyder Ali, THE, was a converted merchantman of sixteen guns belonging to Pennsylvania and commanded by Joshua Barney. On April 8, 1782, inside of Cape May, it captured the British brig *General Monk,* 18–20 guns. Barney secured a raking position with the *General Monk's* bowsprit entangled in his fore-rigging. In the thirty-minute fight, the British lost fifty-three in killed and wounded, the Americans fifteen.

[J. F. Cooper, *The History of the Navy of the United States.*]   WALTER B. NORRIS

Hydrographic Survey. Before the establishment of the Depot of Charts and Instruments in Washington in 1830, naval and merchant vessels purchased charts from foreign governments or private dealers. In 1837 were published four engraved charts, the first issued by the Navy Department. They were based on surveys made by naval officers, early encouraged to co-operate while cruising. During the following five years, eighty-seven similar charts were published, founded mainly on surveys of the Wilkes' Exploring Expedition*, 1838–42, in the South Seas and the Pacific.

In 1842, Matthew Fontaine Maury*, taking charge of the Depot (called after 1866 the Hydrographic Office), laid the foundation of systematic hydrographic work. Between 1847 and 1861 he issued his "Wind and Current Charts," accompanied by "Sailing Directions," covering all seas. They were based upon information collected from old logbooks of American men-of-war and information from mariners of all nations. Maury also issued forty-four general sailing charts and several coasting charts, based on the North Pacific Surveying Expedition, 1853–56, commanded successively by Commodore Cadwalader Ringgold and Commander John Rodgers, and on Commodore Matthew C. Perry's Expedition to Japan, 1852–54*.

In 1872 surveys of islands on the route between San Francisco and Australia were abandoned when Congress failed to renew the $50,000 appropriation. But Congress authorized surveys of the Amazon and Madeira rivers with their approaches in 1880, and of the west coast of Mexico in 1882. In December, 1883, a Pilot Chart of the North Atlantic was issued and in 1894 a similar chart of the North Pacific, both founded on Maury's work and showing magnetic variations, currents, tides, sail and steamship tracks, meteorological conditions, floating dangers, storm warnings, and other factors affecting the speed and safety of navigation. Similar charts, covering all oceans, are published monthly with frequent revisions based on new information from surveys authorized annually by Congress since 1889. Important new nautical data has also been supplied, since 1924, by naval vessels using sonic depth finders, the U. S. S. *Hull* and *Corey* by this invention having made a bathymetric chart of the Pacific coast and continental shelf of the United States. Lake surveys are made by the Engineer Corps* of the United States Army; surveys on the coasts of the United States and island possessions and in rivers to the head of tidal water and ship navigation, by the Coast and Geodetic Survey* of the Department of Commerce; and surveys on the high seas and in foreign waters, by the Hydrographic Office of the Navy Department.

[Gustavus A. Weber, *The Hydrographic Office: Its History, Activities, and Organization;* Charles Lee Lewis, *Matthew Fontaine Maury, Pathfinder of the Seas; Annual Report* of the Hydrographic Office for 1924, pp. 43-59.]
CHARLES LEE LEWIS

Hygiene. A generation ago hygiene was a personal matter, concerned with exercise, proper food, plenty of sleep and the correction of faulty habits in adolescence. Today, the term hygiene, extended from antenatal care to old-age pensions, has evolved into preventive medicine and public health*. Our early periodicals bore such names as the *Hygeian Record and Family Adviser,* the *Hygiest,* the *Herald of Health,* the *Doctor of Hygiene, Hygienic Family Almanac, Hygienic Monitor,* the *Hygienic Teacher and Water-Cure Journal.* Edited as a rule by faddists, they succumbed to editorial malnutrition or to financial marasmus. All the current periodicals in the field were established well within the 20th century.

The first important document in American hygiene was the *Report of the Massachusetts Sanitary Commision* (1850), a complete blueprint for public health organization, drafted by Lemuel Shattuck, which however "fell stillborn from the hands of the printer." Although its suggestions were adopted posthumously, the governor who signed it did not remember he had done so. In the year of this epochal report a farm boy named Stephen Smith went to the city of New York to complete his medical course. New York was then a perpetual fever-nest, and Smith heard the mayor refuse to summon the board of health, declaring it "more dangerous to the city than the cholera." Stephen Smith, the first sanitarian of New York, literally created the Metropolitan Board of Health (1866), just as later he founded the American Public Health Association (1871).

With the advent of the doctrine that each infectious disease is caused by a specific microorganism, hygiene moved into the new house of science. The American pioneers in the demonstration of the relationship of bacteria to public health were George Miller Sternberg with his work on disinfection (1886) and manual of bacteriology (1892); Theophil Mitchell Prudden, who investigated the dangers of dust (1890), drinking water and ice supplies (1891); William Henry Welch, who pointed out the colon bacillus (1891), and found the coccus of stitch-abscess and the bacillus of gas gangrene (1892). Prior to the European investigators, Theobald Smith and the veterinarian Daniel Elmer Salmon discovered the method of producing immunity from contagious diseases (1886). William Thompson Sedgwick traced typhoid epidemics to contaminated brooks and the fly. At the Lawrence Experiment Station Sedgwick undertook the fundamental investigation of water supply and sewage disposal^{qw} (1887), a landmark in American sanitation. Hermann Michael Biggs, whose watchfulness kept an epidemic of cholera^{w} out of America (1892), established in New York (1893) the first municipal bacteriological laboratories in the world, and organized the first municipal campaign against venereal diseases (1912).

Herbert William Conn was the first American to study the bacteriology of milk (1889). Countless infants, alleged to have perished from constitutional weakness or climatic conditions, had actually sucked death from the milk of the cow. Aside from tuberculosis and cholera infantum, contaminated milk has carried many epidemics of typhoid, scarlet fever, diphtheria, and septic sore throat. For years, New York drank its milk from diseased cows that never saw the sunlight, but were imprisoned in Long Island stables, feeding on brewer's swill. The merchant Nathan Straus began to save thousands of lives annually by establishing sterilized milk depots (1893). Henry Leber Coit, of New Jersey, originated the term and conception of certified milk (1892). Hervey D. Thatcher, of Potsdam, N. Y., devised the world's first milk bottle (1884). Now 30,000,000 bottles of milk are delivered to American doorsteps every morning—and there has been no milk-borne outbreak since the period of scientific inspection and pasteurization.

Industrial hygiene in America had an uneasy childhood, and was opposed not only by factory managers, but by the American Medical Association. Case reports on the menace of using white phosphorus in lucifer matches were published as early as 1851, but workers continued to exhibit the terrible affliction of phossy jaw until John Bertram Andrews sounded the alarm (1910) which caused this condition to disappear. Alice Hamilton investigated poisonous trades for the Illinois Commission, the hygiene of the lead industry and high explosives for the United States Department of Labor, and wrote *Industrial Poisons in the United States* (1925) and *Industrial Toxicology* (1934). The bibliographies by Ella M. Salmonsen on vitamins (1932) and silicosis (1934–37) are valuable as starting-points for future research.

The pioneer of naval hygiene was Albert Leary Gihon, author of the standard book on the subject (1871). Edward Lyman Munson wrote the main treatises on military hygiene (1902), sanitary tactics (1911), and the military shoe (1912). Clifford Whittingham Beers, who emerged from strait-jacket and asylum to write *A Mind that Found Itself* (1908), created the mental hygiene movement. Milton Joseph Rosenau, director of the United States Public Health Service and professor of preventive medicine at Harvard, published *Preventive Medicine and Hygiene* (1913). William Freeman Snow and Maurice Alpheus Bigelow long promoted social hygiene, which received a new impetus when Thomas Parran, surgeon-general of the United States Public Health Service, drove syphilis and gonorrhea into the light of open discussion (1936).

It can no longer be said that the United States is inhabited by an ailing population of frail physique. During the past quarter century we participated in the World War, passed through the most fatal pandemic of influenza^{w} in history, and suffered from a prolonged economic depression, yet the national environment was so modified in the light of the new hygiene, that there was a marked decline in infant mortality and a corresponding increase in the average duration of human life. The American attitude toward health is expressed in Emerson's exultant cry: "Give me health and a day, and I will make the pomp of emperors ridiculous."

[L. I. Dublin and A. J. Lotka, *Twenty-Five Years of Health Progress.*]   VICTOR ROBINSON

Hylton v. U. S. *See* Carriage Tax, Constitutionality of.

Hymns, American, are derived in part from New England's earlier psalmody. The *Bay Psalm-Book^{w}* (1640) superseded older (English) metrical versions of the Psalms. While its third edition (1650) appended a few hymns, none were of American origin, and the colonial churches looked to England for their sacred song. Probably the only book of hymns before the Revolution was one issued at Newport in 1766 by the Baptists^{w}. A Methodist^{w} selection of English origin, largely written by the Wesleys, appeared in 1790, was revised in 1802, and an American supplement added in 1808. During the last decade of the 18th century and the first third of the 19th century the Protestant Episcopal, Universalist, Lutheran, Unitarian, Congregational and Presbyterian churches^{qv} issued collections. Almost no hymns by Americans appeared in these books.

Samuel Davies (1723–61) was the first American to write hymns which have survived. Joel Barlow in 1785, Timothy Dwight in 1801, and James M. Winchell in 1818 attempted to adapt Isaac Watts' "imitations" of the Psalms to changing tastes. American missionary hymnody had its beginnings in Asahel Nettleton's *Village Hymns*, 1824. The writing of popular hymn tunes by William Billings (1746–1800), Daniel Read (1757–1836), Timothy Swan (1758–1842) and Oliver Holden (1765–1844) stimulated hymn writing. The tendency to write texts to familiar tunes is still characteristic of American hymn writers.

Pioneer conditions and the early Sunday Schools^{qv}, prayer-meetings and camp meetings^{qv} aided in the development of the "gospel song." Possibilities of its commercial exploitation were soon recognized, resulting in an enormous number being written. Very few have been included in carefully edited hymnals.

Bryant, Whittier, Holmes, Lowell and others wrote verse which has been the source of many of our best hymns, although originally not written for such use. Middle 19th century denominational hymnody suffered from sectarian controversies, and also deteriorated because of the inroads of gospel songs. Those who seemed least influenced by such distractions were the poets referred to and certain Unitarian and Universalist writers. Early in the 20th century there was a notable revival of hymn writing in the United States. Until 1880 hymns by native writers included in the chief denominational hymn books numbered less than 14%. In sixty years the number has risen to about 35%. Frank Mason North, Frederick Lucian Hosmer, Harry Emerson Fosdick, Ozora Stearns Davis, Earl Marlatt, John Haynes Holmes and others have made distinct contributions.

[Edward S. Ninde, *The Story of the American Hymn;* Frank J. Metcalf, *American Writers and Compilers of Sacred Music.*]

ROBERT G. McCUTCHAN

Hyphenate Groups. The term "hyphenated citizens" came into popular use with the outbreak of the World War in 1914. It was used by propagandists to discredit individuals of foreign birth and immigrant groups who were alleged to have a divided allegiance between the coun-

try of their birth and the country of their adoption. Although President Wilson never publicly used this term, it was clearly in his mind when in an address to naturalized citizens on May 15, 1915, at the time of the *Lusitania*^{qv} crisis, he stated that "A man who thinks of himself as belonging to a particular national group in America has not yet become an American." And in his annual message of 1915 he referred to naturalized citizens "who have poured the poison of disloyalty into the very arteries of our national life." Theodore Roosevelt, who was unsparing in his condemnation of "hyphen," spoke of "pillar of salt" citizens who, like Lot's wife, looked back. Specifically, hyphenate groups from 1914 to 1920 thought of American foreign policy and of the Treaty of Versailles^{qv} in terms of the interests of Ireland, Germany, Italy, Poland, and several racial groups in Europe. The most vociferous were the Irish-Americans and the German-Americans, because of their numbers and because of the vital issues at stake in those years.

[G. M. Stephenson, *A History of American Immigration;* H. P. Fairchild, *The Melting-Pot Mistake.*]

G. M. STEPHENSON

"I had rather be right than be President." This expression was used by Henry Clay, early in 1839, in a conversation with William C. Preston of South Carolina. Clay, alarmed by the growth of Abolitionism^{qv} in the North, had decided to attack the movement publicly. He consulted Preston, and the latter suggested that such a speech might be injurious to Clay's political fortunes. This advice, according to Preston, elicited the famous reply.

[*National Intelligencer,* March 15, 30, 1839; *Niles' Weekly Register,* March 23, 1839.]

GLYNDON G. VAN DEUSEN

Iberville River (Rio d'Iberville; now called "Bayou Manchac"), named for Iberville who traversed it on his return from the Mississippi to the Gulf Coast in 1699, leaves the Mississippi fifteen miles below Baton Rouge and empties into the Amite River about twenty-five miles to the eastward. It forms part of the northern boundary of the so-called "Isle of Orleans,"^{qv} and thus became a link in the international boundary between British and Spanish possessions after 1763. The British made it navigable by dredging, thus permitting their ships to enter the Mississippi via lakes Borgne, Pontchartrain and Maurepas, and the Amite and Iberville rivers, and rendering their commerce independent of the Spanish authorities at New Orleans. Fort Bute^{qv} (Manchac Post), established in 1763 at its junction with the Mississippi, remained an important British military and trading post, until captured by Spanish forces in 1779 during the American Revolutionary War. Spain regarded the Iberville as part of the international boundary between the Louisiana Purchase[w] and Spanish West Florida after 1803, though the United States claimed West Florida to the Perdido[w] as part of Louisiana. It formed part of the southern boundary of the short-lived West Florida Republic, established in 1810 after a successful revolt against Spain. Andrew Jackson closed the Iberville at the Mississippi end in 1814, as part of his defense system for New Orleans[w], to prevent a British attack in his rear. It remains leveed off from communication with the Mississippi, though many projects have been advanced for reopening this communication.

[Alcée Fortier, ed., *Louisiana*, Cyclopedic, I; Henry E. Chambers, West Florida in Its Relation to the Historical Cartography of the United States, in *Johns Hopkins University Studies*, XVI.]   WALTER PRICHARD

Icaria was the perfect commonwealth described by the French communist, Etienne Cabet (1788–1856), in the *Voyage en Icarie*. In Icaria all property was to be held in common, and all the products of labor were to be divided according to need. The book became enormously popular and led to a succession of attempts to put the theory into practice in the United States.

The initial effort was made in Fannin County, Tex., in 1848, by an "advance guard" from France. The colony was a failure. In 1849, under Cabet's personal leadership, a new start was made at Nauvoo, Ill. Here, after a period of prosperity, dissension developed, and in 1856 Cabet himself was expelled. Shortly afterward he died at St. Louis, Mo. His personal followers soon set up a community at nearby Cheltenham, which lasted until 1864.

After Cabet's death, Iowa was the scene of the principal Icarian experiments. Near Corning, emigrants from Nauvoo established a settlement and incorporated in 1860. Factional differences led to its dissolution in 1878. The next year, one of the factions organized a new community on the old site, which disintegrated in a few years. The other faction formed the "New Icarian Community" nearby. Its members lived in harmony, but their number dwindled steadily, and in 1895 the property was turned over to a receiver for distribution.

In 1881 former members of the Cheltenham group founded a community at Cloverdale, Calif. (Icaria-Speranza). It was dissolved in 1887.

[W. A. Hinds, *American Communities and Co-operative Colonies;* History and Constitution of the Icarian Community, in *Iowa Journal of History and Politics*, April, 1917.]   PAUL M. ANGLE

Ice, Artificial. *See* Refrigeration.

Idaho was part of the Oregon Country and later (1859–63) was included in Washington Territory until the region achieved political organization as a territory in 1863. The first recorded events in the area were those associated with the journeys of Lewis and Clark[w] (1805, 1806), and representatives of British and American fur companies. Between 1809 and 1834 the following posts were established: Kullyspell House, by the North West Company[w] on Lake Pend Oreille (1809); Fort Henry, an American post near St. Anthony (1810); Fort Boise[w]; and Fort Hall[w].

During the pre-territorial era three missions were founded: Lapwai Mission[w]; the Cœur d'Alene Mission of the Sacred Heart[w]; and the Latter-day Saints or Mormon Lemhi Mission, in the modern Lemhi County (1855). Thousands of Oregon Trail[w] emigrants crossed southern Idaho (1843–63) during the height of the emigration period, but made no settlements.

The discovery of placer[w] gold by E. D. Pierce on Oro Fino Creek (August, 1860) was a forerunner of settlement. Other camps were soon located to the southward. The miners needed a seat of government in the Salmon River country, as the region of the gold fields was called. This resulted in the creation of Idaho Territory, March 3, 1863.

The Nez Percé Indian War[w] (1877) is the best-known territorial event. During the decade 1880–90 the territory attained a population requisite to claim statehood. A state constitution was framed in August, 1889, and President Harrison signed an admission bill, July 3, 1890.

With the exception of the assassination of Gov. Frank Steunenberg, whose death resulted from his association with the Cœur d'Alene riots[w], the state's political history is of regional rather than of national importance. However, economic developments have had a continuous identification with Federal Government activities.

Idaho's chief industries are mining, forestry and agriculture. A major economic asset is the state's present rich, and future unpredictably extensive, water power resources.

The major money-producing metals, in order of rank, are: lead, silver, zinc, gold, copper and fire clay. The Bunker Hill and Sullivan Mine, in the Cœur d'Alene district, is North America's leading lead-silver mine. The phosphate fields near Montpelier contain 40% of the world's deposits. Since 1860, Idaho mines have yielded products estimated to be worth $1,000,000,000.

Idaho's lumber products—including (in their

"dollar" rank order) white (monticola) pine, yellow (ponderosa) pine, Douglas fir, larch, cedar and spruce—now supply national and international markets. The state's 25,000,000 acres of forest trees are owned by the Federal Government (80%), the state (16%) and privately (4%). There are sixteen national forests, which serve as vast playgrounds and perpetual conservators of Idaho's outdoors and of its game and fish.

Agriculture is today the state's chief industry. Leading crops are hay, wheat, potatoes, beans, sugar beets and peas. The ranking animal and poultry money producers are cattle, horses, sheep, swine and turkeys. The Idaho pea is supplying world markets. A notable pea production district is the rich "Palouse Country" in northern Idaho.

The state's vast wealth in water resources is indicated by the fact that Snake River[w], in its 1000-mile course through southern Idaho, drops one mile. In the valley of the Snake many homes are heated and lighted by electricity, and benefit from other almost countless services produced from the electrical energy stored in the eighty reservoirs built along that river and its tributaries.

The State University at Moscow, opened in 1892, enrolls more than 3000 students of collegiate rank. Only 7% of the population in 1930 was foreign born. The inhabitants are mainly descended from north European stocks: English, Scotch, Irish, Welsh, Scandinavian and German. Latter-day Saints, or Mormons, numbering 100,000, form by far the largest religious body. Next in order of rank are Catholics, followed by Methodists.

The state contains 83,880 square miles, with a small population (445,032), over 70% of which is rural. It is a land of villages and spacious countrysides. In 1931 the Primitive Area, 1,087,744 acres in central Idaho, was segregated as a perpetual playground. Sun Valley, founded in 1936, is a vacation spot in the Idaho Sawtooths, framed in an Alpine setting of "breathless" beauty. Objects of scenic interest are: the Craters of the Moon, geologic monuments of North America's most recent lava flow; the Canyon of the Salmon River; the Grand Canyon of the Snake River, the continent's deepest earth-gash; Idaho's hundred glacial lakes; and the City of Rocks, million-year-old green and white granite monuments, near Oakley, Cassia County.

The Shoshoni origin of the name Idaho, in poetic symbolism, provides a key word for understanding the spirit and genius of the aspiring citizenry of this young commonwealth: "E-dah-how!"—"Good morning, it is sun up!"

[C. J. Brosnan, *History of the State of Idaho;* United States Department of Agriculture, *Year Books of Agriculture.*]

CORNELIUS JAMES BROSNAN

Illinois. The Illinois Indians[w] and their country were known to the French by report for years before Jolliet[w] and Marquette in 1673 passed by the western edge of the present state in their exploration of the Mississippi River. Returning by the Illinois River and the Chicago portage[w], Jolliet sensed the possibilities of the fertile prairies and of a canal connection between the Mississippi and Great Lakes system. Between 1679 and 1687 Illinois was the center of the ambitious imperialistic schemes of LaSalle[w]. In January, 1680, he established Fort Crèvecœur[w] at the present Peoria. Two years later, he built a fort on Starved Rock[w], near the present town of LaSalle, on the Illinois River. This remained the base of operations for himself and, after him, of his lieutenants, Tonti and LaForest, until 1692, when their center of activity moved back to Lake Peoria. Near the beginning of the 18th century, the missions to the Kaskaskia and Cahokia tribes of the Illinois Indians, together with the chief French posts, were moved to the rich bottom lands on the east side of the Mississippi River from the mouth of the Missouri southward to the mouth of the Kaskaskia River. Here, stimulated by projects for mining and trade, grew up a permanent French settlement, with considerable numbers of Negro slaves, which, in the end, supplied foodstuffs both to New Orleans and to the French posts of the Great Lakes; here arose Fort de Chartres[w] on the bank of the Mississippi.

The Treaty of Paris[w] (1763) transferred the area of Illinois to the British. It was two years before they were able to send a garrison to Fort de Chartres. From it the territory was ruled during the British period by military authority. Although, intermittently, private persons and ministers considered establishing colonies within the area of the state with a measure of self-government, the Quebec Act[w] of 1774 finally annexed the territory to the province of Quebec. July 4, 1778, George Rogers Clark took possession of Kaskaskia[w] in the name of Virginia, and established Virginia's authority in the Mississippi River settlements and at Vincennes (*see* Clark's Northwest Campaign). Until 1782 the territory was included in the Virginia county of Illinois. Although Clark failed to occupy the whole territory of the present state, he kept the British out of it and maintained garrisons in the Illinois and Wabash villages. In 1783 the territory became part of the United States by the Definitive Treaty of Peace[w]. It was part of the Northwest

Territory^{w}, organized in 1788 under the Northwest Ordinance^{w}. It remained a part of Indiana Territory from 1800 to 1809, when Illinois Territory was established, including the present State of Wisconsin. At the outbreak of the War of 1812, the garrison of Fort Dearborn^{w} at Chicago was massacred by the Indians. Indian trouble continued in the state throughout the war, and one pitched battle was fought by the British and American forces near Rock Island.

At the end of the War of 1812 population flooded into the state. A series of Indian treaties between 1795 and 1833 cleared the state of Indian claims. On Dec. 3, 1818, it was admitted to the Union, with a population of about 40,000. In disregard of the Northwest Ordinance, the northeastern boundary of the state was set so as to include the site of Chicago^{w} within it.

The state's first major political battle was fought 1822–24 over the proposal of rewriting the state's constitution to include slavery. After slavery was defeated, from a period of factional politics, Illinois emerged in 1828 with an overwhelming majority for the Jacksonian and the later Democratic party$^{qq w}$. The increase of the state's population from 157,445 in 1830 to 476,183 in 1840, together with a congressional grant of land for the Illinois and Michigan Canal^{w}, to be constructed across the Chicago portage, induced the state in 1837 to pledge its credit for an elaborate system of internal improvements. The inevitable crash brought the state to the verge of bankruptcy, from which she was saved during the administration of Gov. Thomas Ford (1842–46) through an agreement by which the creditors postponed their claims and advanced enough additional money to complete the Illinois and Michigan Canal. With this stimulus, the state's population and prosperity once more began to expand. In 1860 it had reached a population of 1,071,951; by 1890 this had more than doubled. By July, 1936, its estimated population was 7,845,000.

The construction of railroads, mainly through private enterprise, in the 1850's, and the development of manufacturing combined to develop the state in industry and agriculture to the first rank in the Union. After 1856, with the election of its citizen, Abraham Lincoln, to the Presidency in 1860, Illinois became prevailingly Republican^{w}. Between 1856 and 1932, the state had only two Democratic governors, John P. Altgeld (1892–96) and Edward F. Dunne (1912–16). In 1932 and 1936 a Democrat, Henry Horner, was elected. The state bore its full share of the burden of the Civil War, despite the presence in the southern counties of a population

of immigrants from the Southern states who were inclined to sympathize with the cause of slavery. All told, Illinois furnished some 250,000 enlistments in the Federal Army, an excess of her quota. In 1917–18 the state gave 351,153 men to the armed forces recruited for the World War.

The Illinois constitution of 1818, like others of its type, placed authority in the hands of the state legislature, leaving the judiciary under its control and the governor a figurehead. The constitution of 1848 imposed various limitations upon the power of the state legislature. The constitution of 1870 is chiefly remarkable for restoring the customary balance of the three departments of government, and for introducing the principle of minority representation in the general assembly. The constitution was rapidly amended through popular referendum amendments, down to the year 1891, when a change of law as to the number of affirmative votes required to pass an amendment made further amendment almost impossible. The constitutional convention held in 1920–22 produced a new constitution which was rejected by the voters. Illinois' first capital, Kaskaskia, was succeeded by Vandalia in 1820; in 1837 the general assembly transferred the capital to Springfield, where it has since remained.

[*Centennial History of Illinois*, Illinois Historical Collections.]

THEODORE C. PEASE

Illinois, British Attempts to Reach (1763–66). By the Treaty of Paris (1763) ^{w}, title to the Illinois Country passed from France to Great Britain. At once boats were ordered made ready at Fort Pitt^{w} for an expedition destined for the Illinois posts. Before preparations were complete, however, Pontiac^{w} attacked the British frontier garrisons, and the approach from the east was necessarily abandoned.

The route from the south remained. Accordingly, a detachment from Mobile^{w} began fitting out at New Orleans in January, 1764. On Feb. 27 the ascent of the Mississippi was begun under the command of Maj. Arthur Loftus. Three weeks later an Indian attack, which resulted in several casualties, halted the expedition. His force weakened by desertion and disease, Loftus gave up the attempt.

By the summer of 1764 Pontiac's conspiracy had collapsed in the east, and diplomacy seemed to be worth trying in the west. From Mobile Lt. John Ross and Hugh Campbell were sent to treat with the Indians of the Illinois. Following the Tennessee and Ohio rivers, they reached their destination in February, 1765, but found the Indians defiant, and accomplished nothing.

The next attempt was made from the east by George Croghan[w], deputy Indian Superintendent, and Lt. Alexander Fraser. Preceding Croghan, Fraser reached Fort de Chartres[w] in late April, 1765, but found the Indians so hostile that it was only through Pontiac's own intervention that his life was spared. But the temper of the Indians was changing rapidly. By the time (July) Croghan reached Fort Ouiatenon[w], he was able to hold a great council at which Pontiac promised to abandon resistance to the advance of the British troops.

Croghan at once sent word of his success to Fort Pitt, where an expedition had been held in readiness. On Aug. 24, 100 men of the Black Watch under Capt. Thomas Stirling began the descent of the Ohio. On Oct. 9 they reached their destination, Fort de Chartres. The French garrison was formally relieved on the following day.

[C. W. Alvord and C. E. Carter, *The Critical Period, 1763-1765.*]   PAUL M. ANGLE

Illinois, Great Village of the (–1680), was located on the north side of the Illinois River about midway between the present cities of LaSalle and Ottawa. On this site, in 1673, Marquette found a Kaskaskia village comprising seventy-four cabins; four years later Allouez found eight Illinois tribes located there in 351 cabins. In 1680 the Great Village extended along the river for more than three miles, and contained perhaps 7000 inhabitants. In September of that year it was destroyed and its inhabitants dispersed by a devastating attack from the Iroquois[w]. At later dates the Illinois established other villages in the vicinity, but none approached the Great Village in size.

[Marion A. Habig, The Site of the Great Illinois Village, in *Mid-America*, July, 1933.]   PAUL M. ANGLE

Illinois and Michigan Canal, THE (1836–1930), connecting Lake Michigan and the Mississippi by a channel from Chicago to LaSalle on the Illinois River, was begun by the State of Illinois on July 4, 1836. In less than a year came the Panic of 1837[w], followed by a long period of stagnation. Financing became increasingly difficult with the result that in 1842, Illinois being virtually bankrupt, work was abandoned. However, under the leadership of Gov. Thomas Ford (1842–46), who saw in the revenues to be derived from the completed canal the only way to save the credit of the state, new methods of financing were devised and construction was resumed. On April 23, 1848, the first boat passed through the canal.

The Illinois and Michigan Canal became immediately profitable, and although the railroads which were constructed extensively in the next decade reduced its receipts, tolls exceeded expenses of operation until 1879. In the 20th century traffic dwindled almost to nothing, but sections of the canal were continued in use until 1930. So great was its influence on the development of its tributary region, that among North American artificial waterways only the Erie Canal[w] outranked it in importance.

[J. W. Putnam, *The Illinois and Michigan Canal.*]   PAUL M. ANGLE

Illinois and Wabash Company, THE, was formed by uniting the interests of the Illinois Land Company and the Wabash Land Company on March 26, 1779. The two original companies had been organized by the same man, William Murray of Philadelphia, and while the Illinois Company was comprised of Philadelphians, the Wabash Company included men from Virginia, Maryland, Philadelphia and London. Both companies held claims to land in the Illinois country[w] and both companies sought to establish towns and develop trade in the region. George Ross of Philadelphia was elected president of the combined companies; Bernard Gratz was chosen secretary; William Murray and John Campbell were designated as agents to carry out the actual operations of the company. This consolidation and reorganization, with the addition of new members, including Robert Morris, Conrad Gerard, the French minister, Silas Dean and others, increased tremendously the political and financial strength of the new company. The company's activity apparently terminated in 1784 after Virginia ceded her western lands[w] to the Federal Government.

[Thomas P. Abernethy, *Western Lands in the American Revolution.*]   R. J. FERGUSON

Illinois Band, THE, was organized in 1829 by seven students (Theron Baldwin, John F. Brooks, Mason Grosvenor, Elisha Jenney, William Kirby, Julian M. Sturtevant, Asa Turner) in the Yale Divinity School, who intended to engage in home missions in the West. They planned to go in a group to some frontier state in order that they might support one another in their religious activities, and to found there a college as a center of Puritan influence. John M. Ellis, a home missionary in Illinois, interested them in that state and in his plans for a college in Jacksonville. Bearing commissions from the American Home Missionary Society, the members of the Band went to Illinois about 1830, engaged in home missionary activities, and helped found Illinois College.

[J. M. Sturtevant, *Autobiography*.]

COLIN B. GOODYKOONTZ

Illinois Campaign of George Rogers Clark. *See* Clark's Northwest Campaign.

Illinois Central Railroad, THE, was originally projected in 1836 to connect Galena, Ill., with Cairo[w] at the confluence of the Ohio and Mississippi rivers, where a group of speculators planned to develop a great metropolis. The railroad became part of a state-wide program of internal improvements[w] undertaken by Illinois, the cost of which was far beyond the capacity of the state to finance. State aid ended after the Panic of 1837[w] and the Central Railroad remained in the blueprint stage until 1850 when Congress was induced to grant 2,595,000 acres of public lands[w] to aid in its construction. Congress stipulated the addition to the proposed route of a "branch line" to Chicago[w], then a lusty young city sprawling on the lake front. With the aid of Eastern and foreign capital the road was completed in 1856. Its 700 miles of track, built largely through undeveloped country, far exceeded anything under one management in the United States or abroad and was the marvel of the railroad world.

To sell its lands and thus provide for the cost of construction, and also to build up traffic, the Illinois Central advertised its land grant far and wide by distributing hundreds of thousands of pamphlets picturing highly idealized prairie farming, and by sending emigration agents through the Eastern states, Canada, England, Germany, Norway and Sweden. The result was a great flow of population into Illinois. The prairies of the central and eastern counties were soon settled, but land in the less fertile section of southern Illinois sold more slowly. Not until after 1900 was the land business closed out.

The Illinois Central was the first railroad to encourage crop diversification, sugar beet[w] cultivation, stock improvement, drainage, and the use of farm machinery[w], and has long pioneered in these and other efforts to aid farming. It established the general technique for advertising and colonizing large land tracts which was generally followed by other railroads, notably the Northern Pacific and the Atchison, Topeka & Santa Fé[qw], on a much larger scale.

Through the acquisition of other companies, the Illinois Central has become one of the more important railroad systems in the United States. Instead of promoting the growth at Cairo, it carried commerce north to Chicago and helped to make that city one of the most rapidly growing in the country. Its main line, once the "branch line," connects Chicago with New Orleans and taps the rich cotton section of Mississippi and Louisiana. The road has been conservative in its management, has never been in bankruptcy, and has prospered through most of its history.

The land grant to the Illinois Central was the first made by Congress to a railroad, and it opened the flood gates to a veritable deluge of grants which, until stopped in 1871, threatened to absorb most of the remaining public lands. (*See* Land Grants to Railways.)

[H. G. Brownson, *History of the Illinois Central Railroad to 1870;* P. W. Gates, *The Illinois Central Railroad and Its Colonization Work.*]

PAUL WALLACE GATES

Illinois Country, THE, or simply "The Illinois," was the term commonly applied in the 17th and 18th centuries to the region which eventually became the state of the same name. As originally used by the French explorers, the term designated the country occupied by the Illinois Indians[w]. When white settlements took root along the Illinois and Mississippi rivers, the reference was to the area of which these were nuclei. Not until the 19th century was the area definitely delimited.

PAUL M. ANGLE

Illinois County (Virginia) was created by Virginia in 1778 for the government of the Northwest Territory[w] after the conquest of that region by George Rogers Clark during the Revolution. By subsequent acts it was continued until 1782, when it expired.

[Clarence W. Alvord, *Cahokia Records, 1778-90,* Illinois Historical Collections, II.]

LEONARD C. HELDERMAN

Illinois Fur Brigade (1816?–27) was one of the several trading expeditions sent out annually by the American Fur Company[w] from its headquarters at Mackinac[w]. The brigade, usually numbering ten or twelve bateaux[w] loaded with trade goods, made its way down Lake Michigan and through the Chicago portage[w] and Des Plaines River to the Illinois River. There it divided into small parties which spent the winter bartering with the Indians for furs. In the spring it reassembled and returned by water to Mackinac.

After the re-establishment of Fort Dearborn[w] (1816), the Illinois brigade made annual expeditions until 1827, when the American Fur

Company sold its Illinois interests to **Gurdon S. Hubbard**, the brigade's commander.

[M. M. Quaife, *Chicago and the Old Northwest, 1673-1835; Autobiography of Gurdon Saltonstall Hubbard.*]

PAUL M. ANGLE

Illinois Indians. In the Journal of Father Jacques Marquette, describing his first visit to the Illinois country (1673), is found the expression: "When one speaks the word 'Illinois,' it is as if one said in their language, 'the men'—as if the other savages were looked upon by them merely as animals." He gives an account of the confederated tribes, the Illinois, which he encountered on the Mississippi and the Illinois rivers; the Cahokia, Tamaroa, Michigamea, Kaskaskia and Peoria.

In historic times the Illinois declined rapidly in number and lost much of their virility through wars, chiefly with the Iroquois*q*, or through disease and famine, and because of their contact with white traders and settlers. The Illinois lived by hunting and fishing and the products from the crude cultivation of the soil carried on by the squaws. Corn, beans, melons and squash were raised. In general, their cabins were large and were roofed and floored with mats made of rushes. Their utensils were made of wood, stone and crude pottery. Their weapon for all purposes was the bow and arrow supplemented for the chase with clubs, and knives and daggers of chipped flint.

The women are said to have outnumbered the men four to one and polygamy was a common practice. Missionaries refer to the ease with which the Illinois were converted to Christianity due to their belief in a "greater manitou," the "Great Spirit."*q* The calumet or pipe dance was the most important of their religious ceremonies used to unite them for war and in celebration of peace. (*See also* Illinois, Great Village of the.)

[C. W. Alvord, *The Illinois Country, 1673-1818.*]

JAMES A. JAMES

Illiteracy. The United States Census defines as illiterate "any person ten years of age or over who is not able to read and write, either in English or in some other language." This definition is unsatisfactory as a measure of inability to communicate by means of recorded symbols, since a person may be able to write his name and a few disconnected words, but wholly incapable of expressing his thoughts in writing. Consequently, recent studies have attempted to make a more realistic differentiation beween the formal literacy of the Census and effective literacy or "ability to read newspapers, and to write letters home." When this test for literacy was adopted in the United States Army psychological testing in 1918, 24.9% were returned as illiterate, although only 6% were so reported in the Census two years later.

Although the Census data probably understate the extent of illiteracy, since no tests are given, and it is likely that some persons will hesitate to report their inability on direct inquiry, the amount of error will remain constant if comparisons are confined to large population groups and geographical areas. This question was first included in the Census of 1840, but the data are comparable only since 1870, when the present definition of "formal literacy" was introduced. Since that time the reduction of illiteracy has been as follows:

Population Groups	Percent Illiterates	
	1870	1930
Total population	20.0	4.3
White	11.5	2.7
Native born	8.7*	1.5
Native born of native parentage	7.5†	1.8
Native born of foreign or mixed parentage	2.2†	0.6
Foreign born	12.0*	9.9
Negro	81.4	16.3
Other races	....	25.0

* Data for 1880.   † Data for 1890.

The reduction of illiteracy reflects the changing national attitudes toward education, toward compulsory school laws and their enforcement, and the effectiveness of the school system. The rate for those born before 1865 and educated under earlier conditions shows an illiteracy rate of 9.7%, while for those born since 1916 the rate is 1.2%. This indicates that if no further educational advances are made, the rate will sink to approximately 1% as the older generation dies off.

[Sanford Winston, *Illiteracy in the United States.*]

HOWARD E. JENSEN

Illuminati of New England. Certain meetings between 1790 and 1800 of New England clergymen, who discussed politics and had been influenced by the French Revolution, gave rise about 1798 to rumors that the Illuminati, the European cult inimical to government and religion founded by Adam Weisshaupt, had penetrated American society. Rev. Jedediah Morse and others declared in sermons and pamphlets that it was secretly engaged in propaganda looking to the overthrow of our civil and religious institutions. Statesmen viewed the matter with grave concern. The Freemasons were suspected of being involved, probably because of the fact that a cult in southern France, also calling itself the Illuminati, combined religion with certain methods of Freemasonry. Washington, a prominent Mason, said he knew of no "ill designs on our institutions." The Theistical Society of New York, organized in 1802, whose constitution allegedly expressed "opposition to all schemes of religious and political imposture," was also suspect, and was nicknamed the Columbian Illuminati. The alarm died out in a few years.

[Vernon Stauffer, *New England and the Bavarian Illuminati;* John Wood, *A Full Exposition of the Clintonian Faction, or the Society of the Columbian Illuminati.*]

ALVIN F. HARLOW

I'm Alone Case. On March 22, 1929, the *I'm Alone,* a vessel of Canadian registry engaged in the business of smuggling liquor into the United States, was sunk by gunfire from an American Coast Guard cutter while more than 200 miles offshore. A treaty of 1924 had given the United States rights of search^q and seizure over British vessels suspected of "rum-running," but had specified that these rights did not extend farther than a distance of one hour's steaming from the coast. The *I'm Alone's* destruction caused considerable outcry in Canada, the more so as a member of the crew had lost his life. At the suggestion of the United States Government, the question was arbitrated by a commission composed of the Chief Justice of Canada and a justice of the United States Supreme Court. The commission's final report (Jan. 5, 1935) recommended an apology by the United States to Canada, the payment of indemnities to the master and crew and to the dead man's widow, and the additional payment to Canada of $25,000 as a "material amend." These recommendations were fully carried out. As the actual ownership of the *I'm Alone* was found to have been American, compensation to the owners was denied.

[P. E. Corbett, *The Settlement of Canadian-American Disputes.*]   C. P. STACEY

Imboden-Jones Raid, THE (April 20–May 14, 1863). Entering West Virginia through mountain gaps near Harrisonburg, Gen. William E. Jones (C.) marched via Moorefield to the Baltimore and Ohio Railroad^q at Cheat River. Simultaneously, Imboden with 3365 men moved on Beverly and Weston.

Employing 2200 cavalry, Jones traversed 700 miles of territory, destroying railroad bridges, immense quantities of barreled petroleum, and other property, and collecting supplies and thousands of cattle and horses which he moved to

Virginia. Imboden accomplished similar results in a smaller territory. Both columns fought numerous engagements with Federal garrisons and other detachments.

[*Official Records, Union and Confederate Armies*, Vol. XXV; *Photographic History of the Civil War*, Vol. IV.]

JOSEPH MILLS HANSON

Immediatism (the immediate abolition of slavery), the slogan which the British antislavery movement employed in its drive to abolish West Indian slavery, was adopted for its prestige value by American abolitionists^q in 1831, but was officially altered by them to signify merely an immediate beginning of measures looking to the ultimate extinction of slavery.

[G. H. Barnes, *The Antislavery Impulse, 1830-1844.*]

GILBERT HOBBS BARNES

Immigrant Labor. Regarding the effects of the successive waves of different nationalities in lowering the price of American labor and affecting the labor situation in other ways, economists, sociologists and historians are of different minds. After the enactment of the drastic restrictive immigration laws, beginning in 1921 (*see* Immigration Act of 1924), there was a disposition to credit them in some measure for the prosperity of the years following; on the other hand, competent students concluded that the statistics of migration do not indicate that the laws caused much real change. The assertion that the immigrants, with a lower standard of living, replaced the American laborers and thus robbed them of their jobs has been refuted by the argument that the tides of immigration were self-regulatory: that the volume fluctuated according to business cycles. Notwithstanding, in every generation propaganda was spread in favor of laws restricting immigration as a means of protecting the American wage earner. It was so in the years of Know-Nothingism, in the 1850's; in the years of A. P. A.-ism and Populism, in the 1880's and 1890's; and in the years of the Ku Klux Klan, in the following century^{qq}. Moreover, speaking generally, leaders of organized labor favored restrictive legislation, though some of them, like George Henry Evans in the 1840's and Terence V. Powderly in the 1870's and 1880's, rather pinned their faith on reserving the public lands for actual settlers or on co-operative enterprises.

Undoubtedly, the successive waves of immigration retarded the progress of organized labor. It was not only the fact that during their first years in America the immigrants were engaged in ceaseless and hard work, and absorbed in orienting themselves in a new environment that made foreign-born communities stony soil for sowing the gospel of unionism, but also the fact that employers capitalized divisions among wage earners along nationalistic, racial and religious lines. Moreover, labor-baiting propagandists found a veritable arsenal of munitions in the inherent fear of and hatred for "alien agitators." In the Haymarket battle of 1886, the Pullman strike of 1894, the Lawrence strike of 1912, and the steel and coal strikes of 1919 and 1937, Anarchism, Bolshevism, Communism and Syndicalism—said to have been imported in the minds of men who harbored "un-American" ideas—were alleged to be at the bottom of these savage conflicts^{qv}.

During the years following the close of the Civil War and down to the World War, Europe was invaded by an army of immigration agents, many of whom bore commissions to enlist recruits for the American industrial army. In 1864, during the Civil War, Congress legalized contracts (*see* Contracts, Foreign Labor) by which immigrants pledged the wages of their labor for a term not to exceed twelve months, to repay the expenses of their journey to the United States. Under the protection of this law, and even after its repeal in 1868, corporations like the American Emigrant Company organized expressly for that purpose imported laborers upon orders from employers, who paid commissions for this service. And after Congress, in 1885, had made it unlawful to import contract labor, except under certain conditions, the law was honored more in the breach than in the observance. Some immigrants were imported merely under verbal contracts. In spite of subsequent legislation designed to close loopholes, Italians, Greeks, Mexicans, Jews and Slavs continued to be victims of such types of exploitation as the padrone system.

[I. A. Hourwich, *Immigration and Labor;* J. R. Commons and others, *The History of Labour in the United States;* L. I. Dublin, ed., *Population Problems in the United States and Canada.*]

G. M. STEPHENSON

Immigrants in Politics. Immediately upon arrival in the United States the immigrants fell under the watchful eyes of politicians who regarded them in the light of potential voters. Some immigrant stocks were even called "voting cattle," to be herded to the polls by bosses and ward heelers. In cities like Chicago and New York the days preceding elections witnessed the fraudulent naturalization^{qv} of hundreds, if not thousands. Moreover, many states conferred the right of suffrage^{qv} on immigrants who had taken out their first papers.

It is, of course, hazardous to label immigrant groups according to political affiliations. Politicians appealed to the racial pride and clannishness of naturalized voters—sometimes successfully—but in the long run they followed the channels cut by the native-born. The great bulk of the immigrants were conservative along political, social and religious lines.

Nevertheless, the student of American history must reckon with the "foreign vote" in certain presidential elections—notably in 1860, 1884, 1916 and 1920—and in state and local elections where the naturalized voters held the balance of power. For example, in the two decades preceding the election of Lincoln special efforts were made to capture the Irish and German vote, which had become self-conscious partly because of the anti-foreign Know-Nothing^{qv} party. The nativistic^{qv} and puritanical tinge of the Republican party, a heritage from the years of Know-Nothingism, determined to some degree the political affiliations of the old immigrants. The Irish, because of their religion and urban residence, remained Democratic, whereas the Germans, Scandinavians and Dutch showed favor to the Republican party^{qv}.

The immigrant vote perhaps did not seriously affect the outcome of elections, except during public excitement over questions that directly concerned the interests of the immigrants or injured their pride. The fact that politicians flattered them does not necessarily indicate that the immigrants were more gullible than the natives.

[G. M. Stephenson, *A History of American Immigration;* S. P. Orth, *Our Foreigners.*]

G. M. STEPHENSON

Immigration. The impact of rural America in the 19th century and of industrial America in the 20th jarred millions of Europeans loose from their old moorings to set them free from the political, social, religious and economic trammels of an Old World civilization. The migration of nearly thirty-eight million Europeans to the United States from 1820 to 1930 is the greatest movement of population in history.

For convenience the history of American immigration may be divided into three periods: (1) The Colonial Period, 1607 to 1776; (2) The Old Immigration, 1776 to 1885; and (3) The New Immigration, 1885 to the present. These more or less arbitrary divisions should be held loosely. Down to the close of the second period immigrants from northern and western Europe predominated; but the conditions that obtained in the United States and in Europe before 1820 were so vastly different from those that produced the great exodus from Europe after that date that it is justifiable to dismiss the colonial period lightly and to regard the movement after 1820 as constituting the history of American immigration. Moreover, this attempt at classification takes no account of Oriental immigration (mainly Chinese and Japanese) and immigration from the countries of the Western Hemisphere (mainly from Canada and Mexico). It is significant that general immigration legislation enacted by Congress has usually either exempted immigration from Asia and from North and South America or else has placed it in a special category.

Although the thirteen original colonies were settled largely by people from England, even before the Declaration of Independence there were immigrants from many countries of Europe, including Irish, Scotch-Irish, Scotch, Dutch, Swedes, Germans, French, Portuguese, Swiss and Jews. In Pennsylvania, for example, the Germans were so numerous that it was feared that the colony was in danger of losing its "American" characteristics. Proprietors, speculators and others encouraged immigration to the colonies. The stream of population that flowed from Europe to America before 1776 carried with it both colonists and immigrants, the former migrating from the mother country to one of its colonies and the latter severing allegiance from one government in favor of another. In terms of individual experiences this distinction was slight; but it is a distinction that ought to be drawn for purposes of clarity. After the Declaration of Independence, immigrants were aliens until such time as their residence entitled them to apply for citizenship[w], with its privileges and responsibilities. In other words, immigration implies expatriation. In a loose sense, Negro slaves and indentured servants who were brought to the colonies were immigrants; but in the strict sense, immigrants were persons who voluntarily uprooted themselves from the old environment in order to seek sustenance and fortune in the United States.

It is estimated that from 1776 to 1820 approximately 250,000 immigrants came to the United States; but it was not until after the close of the Napoleonic wars in Europe and the War of 1812 in America that the constant stream of immigration took its inception. And it was not until the decade of the 1840's that wave after wave of immigration deposited on American shores newcomers from practically every country of Europe —English, Irish, Scotch, Scotch-Irish, Welsh, Germans, Swiss, Dutch, French, Swedes, Norwegians, Danes, Icelanders, Finns, Slavs, Jews, Italians, Magyars, Portuguese, Spaniards, Greeks and peoples from the Balkan Peninsula.

Prior to 1883 about 85% of the immigrants came from the countries of northern and western Europe, the so-called old immigration composed mainly of people of Teutonic stock and in more recent years designated as the Nordic race. In 1907 about 80% came from the countries of eastern and southern Europe, usually designated as the new immigration. Some idea of the magnitude of this *Völkerwanderung* is conveyed by the fact that included in the total population of 76,000,000 in continental United States in 1900 were 10,500,000 born in a European environment and 26,000,000 of foreign parentage. According to the census of 1930, there were 13,366,407 foreign-born whites in a total population of 122,775,046.

In the decade preceding the election of Lincoln in 1860, 2,598,214 immigrants came to the United States, mainly from Great Britain, Ireland and Germany, with relatively few from Norway, Sweden and the Netherlands. After the Panic of 1857 and the outbreak of the Civil War, immigration declined; but after the collapse of the Confederacy, the stream assumed the huge volume that in the seventh decade deposited on American shores more than five million immigrants. This number was exceeded only in the two decades from 1900 to 1920, when the respective arrivals were 8,795,386 and 5,735,811. After 1900 immigration increased enormously. In 1905, for the first time, the number of immigrants arriving within a twelvemonth reached the million mark; and in 1907 the number was 1,285,349, the peak for all years before and after that date. From 1880 to 1890 the ranking countries were Germany, Ireland, England, Canada and Sweden; in the next decade the countries were Italy, Germany, Austria-Hungary, Russia and Ireland; and from 1900 to 1914 the order was Austria-Hungary, Italy, Russia, England and Ireland.

During the years of the World War and after (1914–38), the extraordinary situation in Europe and in the United States, coupled with drastic restrictive legislation, reduced the stream of immigration to a trickle, in contrast with the years preceding. When Congress enacted the immigration law of 1924[w], it closed a momentous chapter in American and European history. The generous, free-handed, laissez-faire policy was succeeded by legislation designed to close the doors to all but a few who could satisfy the drastic requirements enforced by immigration inspectors.

The complex forces that set in motion and accelerated immigration operated over a long period of time and varied with the conditions that obtained in each country. The individual immigrant was the product of the confluence of various forms of dissatisfaction with conditions in

Europe and favorable conditions in the United States. He fell victim to a class movement—popularly known as "America fever"—which spread from parish to parish. The fever sought its victims among those who were not inoculated with the virus of social distinction and economic prosperity. The epidemic was transmitted most effectively by hundreds of thousands of letters that were written by immigrants to relatives and friends back home. These "America letters" were read and pondered in cottages, at markets and fairs, in crowds assembled at parish churches, and in factories, and they were also broadcast by newspapers. In naive and simple language, disfigured by misspellings and faulty punctuation, the writers discoursed—often inaccurately—on the vista of opportunities that opened for them in the "Land of Canaan": the absence of onerous class distinctions, democracy and equality in government, religion and social intercourse, opportunities for education, low taxes and high wages, food and clothing denied men and women of their economic status in Europe, freedom from compulsory military service, the feverish development of the country—industrial expansion, railway construction, the opening of new territories, cheap, free and fertile land and large farms whose owners counted their chickens by the hundreds and their livestock by the scores. In this land of great distances, with billowing prairies of endless grain fields, its rivers and lakes swarming with fish, its abundance of coal and metals, the Government was rich enough to give to every man a 160-acre farm—referring to the Homestead Act^w of 1862.

Despite the good things awaiting them in the "Dollar Land," it is obvious that their longings for them could not have been satisfied without adequate means of transportation—cheap and rapid. The steamship and the railroad, together with inventions that revolutionized agriculture and manufacturing, not only brought tremendous adjustments in the lives of individuals in Europe and America but also shortened the span of the Atlantic Ocean from eight weeks in the days of sailing vessels to eight days in the era of the steam engine and the screw propeller. Rate wars between steamship companies and between railroad companies made it possible for hundreds of thousands of immigrants to travel from Liverpool, Hamburg, Stockholm, Oslo and Rotterdam to New York and Chicago for as little as $35.

During the last quarter of the 19th century and the opening years of the 20th, Europe was invaded by an army of emigration agents endowed with persuasive tongues and armed with broadsides and pamphlets published by steamship and railroad companies, land companies, industrial establishments and immigration commissions established by many states. Spurred on by attractive commissions, these agents distributed literature, made house-to-house canvasses, organized emigration societies, and delivered addresses that portrayed Europe in dark colors and America as a land without shadows.

The humble folk who hearkened to these evangelists brought with them little of the culture of their native lands; and their first years in America were ceaseless struggles with poverty and strange conditions. For the most part, they were free to work out their own religious, economic and social salvation. They established their own communities, societies, churches, educational institutions and newspapers; and soon the United States took on that polyglot appearance unknown in any other country.

[Edith Abbott, *Historical Aspects of the Immigration Problem;* M. R. Davie, *World Immigration with Special Reference to the United States;* J. W. Jenks and W. J. Lauck, *The Immigration Problem;* R. Mayo Smith, *Emigration and Immigration;* G. M. Stephenson, *A History of American Immigration;* Harry Jerome, *Migrations and Business Cycles.*]

                               G. M. STEPHENSON

Immigration Act of 1924, THE (commonly known as the Johnson Bill), passed by both houses of Congress by overwhelming majorities and signed by the President, May 26, 1924, provided a more drastic limitation of immigrants than the Act of 1921 by reducing the quota from 3% on the basis of the number of foreign-born of various peoples as recorded in the 1910 census to 2% on the basis of the 1890 census, thereby favoring prospective immigrants of the older racial stocks. This gave an annual quota of 164,-667, until July 1, 1927, when the statute provided that the annual quota be 150,000 and that the admission of persons of any race eligible for naturalization should be the percentage of this basic figure which that national group bore to the total population of the country in 1920 with no nationality having less than 100. This act carefully defined immigrants and non-quota arrivals, described the machinery of selection at American consulates in the country of departure, and provided certain humane preferences as well as drastic provisions of enforcement against fraudulent admissions. Criticism has come on the score of the difficulties in determining scientifically national origins in this country, from employers who prior to the depression of 1929 feared a shortage of manual labor, from religious and racial representatives who feared a numerical limitation of their groups, and from internationally minded persons who feel the free migrations of peoples should not be prevented.

[R. L. Garis, *Immigration Restriction.*]

RICHARD J. PURCELL

Immigration Restriction League, THE, was organized in 1894 in order to propagandize the country in favor of legislation designed to restrict the admission of emigrants from the countries of eastern and southern Europe. It sent questionnaires to governors inquiring whether or not immigrants were desired in their respective states and what stocks were preferred. The League was probably influential in obtaining the passage by Congress of a literacy test bill, in 1897, which was vetoed by President Cleveland.

[G. M. Stephenson, *A History of American Immigration.*]

G. M. STEPHENSON

Immunity Bath. This phrase seems to have been first used in March, 1906, when Judge J. O. Humphreys, of the United States District Court for Northern Illinois, was considering the question of ordering the discharge of sixteen defendants of the beef trust, then under indictment for violation of the Sherman antitrust law[w]. In his argument opposing such action, Atty. Gen. Moody declared ironically that the defendants' discharge would amount to giving them an "immunity bath." They were discharged, however, on the ground that, by furnishing evidence upon which the indictments were based, they had secured immunity from prosecution under the terms of the law creating the Federal Bureau of Corporations—a decision that seriously handicapped the Department of Justice in the prosecution of leading trust officials. The phrase has since been applied to the practice, under certain Federal and numerous state laws, of granting immunity from prosecution to implicated persons who disclose evidence of crime which otherwise would go unpunished.

[F. E. McGovern, Legal Repression of Political Corruption, American Political Science Association *Proceedings*, IV, 266-276.]

P. ORMAN RAY

Immunity of Private Property. Unlike the rule prevailing in land warfare, the law of maritime warfare recognizes the right of a belligerent[w] to capture and confiscate property belonging to nationals of the enemy state when found on the high seas. This liability of private property to capture encouraged the practice of privateering[w], by which a belligerent issued commissions to shipowners authorizing them to arm and to make prize[w] of the merchant vessels of the enemy. The irregularities resulting from the

practice of privateering led to its abolition by the states signing the Declaration of Paris of 1856[w]. The United States refused to become a party to the Declaration except on the condition that accompanying the abolition of privateering should be the immunity of private property from capture on the high seas. Again at the Hague Peace Conferences of 1899 and 1907[w] the United States proposed a rule abolishing the capture of private property in maritime warfare. This time not only Great Britain but a number of other maritime powers voted in the negative. The claim for immunity figures among the elements entering into the so-called "freedom of the seas."[w]

[H. S. Quigley, *The Immunity of Private Property from Capture at Sea.*]

C. G. FENWICK

Impeachment and conviction as a method of removal from public office was introduced from England into the revolutionary state constitutions[w]. It had been claimed in behalf of the colonial assemblies[w], but was denied except in the proprietary government of Pennsylvania. The Constitution[w] of the United States provides that "The President, Vice President and all civil Officers of the United States, shall be removed from Office on Impeachment for, and Conviction of, Treason, Bribery, or other high Crimes and Misdemeanors." Most of the states have drafted their constitutional provisions on this subject in similar language. Some difficulty has arisen in defining offenses so that they fall within the last two categories. But impeachable offenses were not defined in England, and it was not the intention that the Constitution should attempt an enumeration of crimes or offenses for which an impeachment would lie.

Impeachments have been voted by the House of Representatives and tried by the Senate of the United States upon ten occasions; upon two other occasions the proceedings were abandoned. The two-thirds vote of the Senate necessary to conviction has been obtained in only three cases (*see* Impeachment Trial of Andrew Johnson). The majority of impeachments have been directed against judges, who hold office during good behavior and whose removal can be effected in no other way. The first important use of impeachment was in the case of Samuel Chase[w], Associate Justice of the United States Supreme Court, in 1805. In obtaining an acquittal, counsel for Justice Chase insisted that indictable offenses alone were comprehended within the impeachment power. This restricted meaning of impeachable offenses was not transcended until the trial in 1913 of Robert W. Archbald, Associate Judge of the United States Commerce Court.

The charges against Judge Archbald, set forth in thirteen articles of impeachment, presented no indictable offenses. In all cases they alleged instances of misconduct in office which, if true, constituted breaches of the good-behavior tenure granted judicial officers. The conviction of the judge was a triumph for the broad view of the impeachment power.

Within the states the impeachment power has not been used extensively, because the short terms attached to public offices make enforced removals unnecessary. Where impeachments have been undertaken they have usually been instruments of party warfare. The impeachment of judges from partisan motives was carried out in several instances in Pennsylvania and Ohio at the beginning of the 19th century. More than 100 years later, Gov. Sulzer of New York was impeached and removed, the charges resting upon broad grounds of unfitness and involving offenses committed by Mr. Sulzer prior to his election. Subsequently governors were removed upon impeachment and conviction in Texas and Oklahoma. Although partisanship was the motivating force in these impeachments, they have served to give broader scope to the power of impeachment.

[W. S. Carpenter, *Judicial Tenure in the United States.*]
WILLIAM S. CARPENTER

Impeachment Trial of Andrew Johnson (1868). The greatest state trial in the United States was that of the impeachment of President Andrew Johnson in 1868. He was the first, and so far has been the only American President to suffer this ordeal.

After an eventful career in both houses of Congress, he had been elected Vice-President in 1864 as Lincoln's running mate. On Lincoln's death he became President and promptly took his stand for Lincoln's plan of reconstruction[w]. The Radical Republicans[w] began at once maneuvering to thwart him. Above all else they wanted Stanton continued as the Secretary of War. This was the object of the Tenure-of-Office Bill[w] passed on March 2, 1867, over Johnson's veto. It provided generally that all civil officers in whose appointment the Senate had participated could be removed only with the advice and consent of that body. A removal contrary to the act was made a "high misdemeanor." In August, 1867, Johnson found it impossible longer to tolerate Stanton, and when Stanton refused to resign, Johnson suspended him and appointed Gen. Grant as Secretary of War *ad interim.*

On Feb. 21, 1868, Johnson removed Stanton from office and on the following day the House of Representatives, by a vote of 126 to 47, decided to impeach[w] the President for removing Stanton in defiance of the Tenure-of-Office Act.

The Constitution[w] provides that the House of Representatives has the sole power to prefer charges against a President, i.e., articles of impeachment, and that the Senate sits as a court for the trial of the charges and is presided over by the Chief Justice. A two-thirds vote of the senators present is necessary for a conviction.

On March 13, 1868, the trial began. Benjamin F. Butler, a virulent partisan, opened for the prosecution with a vitriolic tirade, going far outside the charges. The evidence for the prosecution consisted largely in establishing that Johnson had in fact removed Stanton. The defense was that under the Constitution the President had this right and that the Tenure-of-Office Act in seeking to deprive him of this right was unconstitutional. Johnson himself did not attend the trial.

The scene in the high court on May 16, 1868, when the vote was taken, was a dramatic one. For days the Radicals had been working feverishly in and out of Congress to bring pressure to bear upon the senators to vote for a conviction. Finally the roll was called on the eleventh article (the first of the thirteen to be voted on). Sen. Grimes, suffering from a stroke of paralysis, was borne into the Senate chamber at the last moment to vote for an acquittal. In dead silence the galleries waited for the tally. At last it was announced that thirty-five senators had voted guilty and nineteen not guilty. Two-thirds not having pronounced guilty, the Chief Justice thereupon declared that the President was "acquitted on this article." He had been saved by one vote. But there were twelve articles which had not yet been voted on. The court thereupon adjourned to permit the representatives and senators to attend the National Republican Convention. It was hoped that on their return to Washington some of the wavering senators might change their minds in favor of conviction. On May 28 the high court reconvened to vote upon the second and third articles. Again the roll was called, but again thirty-five senators voted for conviction and nineteen for acquittal, and once more Johnson was saved by one vote. The remaining articles were never voted on. The court was then adjourned never to convene again, either for the trial of Andrew Johnson or thus far of any other President.

[Lloyd Paul Stryker, *Andrew Johnson, A Study in Courage.*]
LLOYD PAUL STRYKER

Impending Crisis. See Helper's *Impending Crisis of the South.*

Imperial Idea, Pre-Revolutionary. In general, before the Revolution, imperial theory was that of the Mercantilists[qv]. Colonies were to produce raw materials, and the home country be the entrepot for these to a large extent, and alone the center of manufacture as well as that of administration, and the ultimate arbiter of all legislation.

The approach of the Revolution, however, was marked, particularly in the 1770's, by discussion of this theory. The most important English views were those of Thomas Pownall, who advanced much the same ideas as those of the Imperial Federationists of a century or so later. He believed in centralization but with the colonists represented in a truly Imperial Parliament. On the other hand, some thinkers in New England suggested the method of decentralization which has actually been followed in "Dominion Status": local Parliaments, and the loose system of a Commonwealth of Nations, bound together only by the link of the crown. As one wrote: "the Government thus united in one Sovereign, though divided into distant Parliaments, will be actuated by one Soul. It will have all the advantages of a powerful Republic, and a grand extensive Monarchy . . . [with the King] as the common head of all his Parliaments, and exercising his authority with their several consents." These views found some echo in England but were too advanced for the time. The modern form of the British Empire was first glimpsed, however, by American and not British thinkers.

[Thomas Pownall, *The Administration of the Colonies; Boston Gazette*, Jan. 27 and Feb. 17, 1772; John Cartwright, *A Letter to Edmund Burke*; J. T. Adams, *Revolutionary New England*, pp. 380 ff.]

JAMES TRUSLOW ADAMS

Imperial Valley Canal. *See* All American Canal.

Imperialism is the term applied (usually by opponents of the policy) to the extension of governmental control by the United States over areas whose location or the character of whose population prevents their incorporation as integral parts of the United States with full rights of self-government. Such control may result from outright annexation[qv] or from arrangements which restrict the freedom of action of a nominally independent state.

The use of the term "agricultural imperialism" to describe such early annexations of territory as the Louisiana and Florida purchases[qv] is misleading, since these areas were destined to be populated by an overflow from the then existing area of the United States and to take their places as integral portions of the Federal Union. The same remark applies to Texas, the Mexican cessions of 1848 and 1853 (Gadsden Purchase) , and even to Alaska[qv]. A policy of imperialism was foreshadowed in the attempts of Seward and Grant, after the Civil War, to annex the Danish West Indies and the Dominican Republic, and in the early interest displayed in the Hawaiian and Samoan islands[qv], but the country was not squarely confronted with the issue until the 1890's, when government and people were forced to choose whether or not to accept the proffer of sovereignty over the republic of Hawaii and to exact from Spain the cession of her colonial empire as a consequence of the Spanish-American War[qv].

In the years just preceding these events, several influences had been at work which help to explain the course chosen by the United States. Renewed colonial activity on the part of the major European powers was rapidly bringing Africa, the islands of the Pacific, and portions of Asia under their control. The widely read treatises on sea power by Capt. A. T. Mahan were arousing American intellectuals to the importance of naval and colonial expansion if the United States were to play a leading role in world affairs. American manufacturers and exporters were becoming worried over markets and were especially concerned to find means for preserving a fair share of the Chinese market for American products (*see* Open Door Policy). Writers such as John Fiske and John W. Burgess were preaching the civilizing mission of the Germanic nations in general and the United States in particular; and their doctrines were powerfully re-enforced by the Protestant churches, which saw in Spain's crumbling empire enticing opportunities for Christian missionary activity. As a result of these diverse influences, the War with Spain, which had been entered upon avowedly as a humanitarian crusade, was utilized not only to destroy Spain's sovereignty in Cuba but to compel Spain to cede to the United States, Puerto Rico, the Philippine Islands and Guam[qv]. Hawaii, which had been renounced by the Cleveland administration in 1893, was annexed in 1898, as ancillary to the new interests in the Philippines; and in the following year, by agreement with Germany and Great Britain, the United States received the eastern islands of the Samoan group, thus reaching into the southwestern Pacific.

Meanwhile, the treaty with Spain had been ratified after a long debate over the wisdom of annexing the Philippines. In 1900 the Democratic party, with Bryan as its presidential candidate, opposed permanent retention of the Philippines and expostulated against an imperialist policy in general. The Republicans, with a platform justifying their course in the war and the accompanying annexations, won the election.

The United States made no further acquisitions of territory, with the exception of the purchase of the Virgin Islands[w] from Denmark in 1916. In 1903, however, it leased the Panama Canal Zone[w] from the Republic of Panama, and came to exercise wide authority in the Caribbean area through the establishment of protectorates, notably over Cuba (1901), Panama (1903), the Dominican Republic (1905, 1916), Nicaragua (1912) and Haiti (1915)[qw]. These relationships were defended, for the most part, as measures to prevent European intervention in the Caribbean, thereby upholding the Monroe Doctrine and safeguarding the Panama Canal[qw].

Since 1922, and more noticeably since 1929, the United States has shown a disposition to modify or abandon its imperialistic policy. It no longer acts in the role of protector to the states enumerated above; and in 1934 Congress provided for the complete independence of the Philippines—our most prized acquisition of 1898 —at a date not later than 1946 (*see* Tydings-McDuffie Act). Thus in a phase of its development in which, having a surplus of capital for investment, the United States might be expected to be increasingly imperialistic, it has in fact grown steadily less so. The explanation would appear to lie in the fact that imperialism has not paid the expected dividends—in material profit, national power and prestige or humanitarian uplift.

While American administrators in the possessions and protectorates have usually displayed a high sense of responsibility for the welfare of the native populations, the results of their endeavors have been partly vitiated by the American tariff policy, the absorption of land by American corporations and attempts at overrapid Americanization in economic, cultural and political matters.

[J. W. Pratt, *Expansionists of 1898.*]

JULIUS W. PRATT

Implied Powers. The Constitution[w] of the United States creates a national government of express or enumerated powers and state governments of reserved or residual powers. Thus the authority of Congress to enact laws is defined by the Constitution. This authority is found principally in seventeen express clauses in Article I, Section 8. These express powers are supplemented by a general grant of authority in the final clause of the section "to make all laws which shall be necessary and proper for carrying into execution the foregoing powers and all other powers vested by this Constitution in the government of the United States or in any department or officer thereof." It is in this general clause that the doctrine of implied powers finds its basis.

No sooner had the Constitution gone into operation than a bitter controversy arose between those persons who favored a strong central government and those who favored a central government of limited powers with strong governments in the states. The first group was known as Federalist[w] and the second as Anti-Federalist. The Anti-Federalists would have had the Constitution construed strictly, according to its letter; the Federalists favored a broad interpretation which would render the Constitution adequate to the expanding needs of the country. Thus the issue of strict v. broad construction of the Constitution, that is, whether or not Congress was to enjoy implied powers, became an important major issue between political parties.

Both Washington and Adams were Federalists as were Jay and Ellsworth, the first two chief justices of the United States Supreme Court. Jefferson, however, was the leader of the Anti-Federalists. After the success of the Anti-Federalists in the election of 1800, Adams appointed John Marshall, an eminent Federalist, as Chief Justice. He held the office until his death in 1835. It is difficult to overestimate the influence of Marshall in shaping the direction in which the new nation was to move. The fundamental constitutional decisions made by the Court under his leadership have stood unchallenged as precedents for subsequent courts to follow.

Chief Justice Marshall first enunciated the doctrine of implied powers in the case of United States v. Fisher (2 Cranch 358, 1805), but it was not until fourteen years later that the principle won national attention. In his decision in McCulloch v. Maryland[w] (4 Wheaton 316, 1819), Marshall took occasion to reassert the doctrine of implied powers. He upheld the validity of the act which created the Second Bank of the United States[w], notwithstanding the silence of the Constitution on the power of Congress to create corporations, or to establish banks. In this decision he said: "Let the end be legitimate, let it be within the scope of the Constitution, and all means which are appropriate, which are plainly adapted to that end, which are not prohibited, but consist with the letter and spirit of the Constitution, are constitutional."

He justified this doctrine on the necessities of constitutional interpretation. He said: "A constitution, to contain an accurate detail of all the subdivisions of which its great powers will admit and of all the means by which they may be carried into execution, would partake of the prolixity of a legal code, and could scarcely be embraced by the human mind. It would probably never be understood by the public. Its nature, therefore, requires that only its great outlines should be marked, its important objects designated, and the minor ingredients which compose those objects deduced from the nature of the objects themselves. . . . We must never forget that it is a constitution we are expounding."

Under this and subsequent decisions upholding the doctrine of implied powers the Constitution has been elaborated and expanded to meet the needs of a civilization which could never have been envisioned by its framers. Pure food and drug laws, lottery acts, a white slave law, a law against the transportation of stolen motor vehicles across state lines, a kidnapping law, a statute requiring the use of safety devices on interstate trains, and many others have been passed under the general authority given to Congress to regulate interstate and foreign commerce. The powers to tax and to establish post offices and post roads have similarly served as bases for Federal regulation. But when Congress sought to regulate child labor[w] under the taxing and commerce clauses the Supreme Court denied that such a power could be implied. Thus the powers reserved to the states (*see* Reserved Powers of States) under the Tenth Amendment may not be usurped under the excuse that they may be reasonably implied from some express power conferred upon Congress. The decisions upholding the constitutionality of the Wagner Act[w], however, indicate a tendency to permit a very broad construction of the commerce power which may result in a considerable diminution in the powers reserved to the states.

[A. J. Beveridge, *The Life of John Marshall;* W. W. Willoughby, *Principles of the Constitutional Law of the United States.*]

HARVEY WALKER

Imports. *See* Trade, Foreign.

Imports Essential for National Defense. Revolutionary America, John Hancock exclaimed, faced an "almost total Want of every thing necessary to carry . . . on" the war. Despite much building of saltpeter and powder mills and arsenals, Washington's army was largely dependent on munitions smuggled through the British blockade. Briefly during the War of 1812 the American army again felt the pinch of blockade,

but not until the Civil War did a serious problem of "strategic" imports emerge. In both food and materials of war the North was very largely self-sufficient, and in any event had access to foreign supplies. But the Confederacy was blockaded and lacked foodstuffs (until some agricultural diversification was achieved), was inadequately supplied with munitions, and even bought war vessels in England. In the 20th century the increasing complexity of warfare has multiplied the number of strategic raw materials[w], and while the United States is more nearly self-sufficient than any other major power the War Department lists twenty-six commodities which present wartime supply difficulties. Emeny (*see* below) concludes, however, that only in manganese, chromite, tin, antimony, tungsten and rubber is our dependence on imports of "really vital concern," incapable of solution by increased domestic production or use of substitutes.

[Claude H. Van Tyne, *The War of Independence;* Brooks Emeny, *The Strategy of Raw Materials.*]

FRANK A. SOUTHARD, JR.

Imposts. Article I of the Constitution[w] empowers Congress to levy "taxes, duties, imposts, and excises" (Sec. 8) ; and forbids the states to "lay any imposts or duties on imports or exports" (Sec. 10) . Inasmuch as Congress lacks the power to impose taxes on exports[w] (Sec. 9) , it is apparent that the little-used word "imposts" is synonymous with import duties. (*See* Tariff.)

FRANK A. SOUTHARD, JR.

Impressment, Confederate. From the early part of the Civil War, the Confederate War Department, first without, and after March, 1863, with, congressional approval, seized from producers supplies for the army and slaves for work on fortifications. Agents were ordered to impress only surplus supplies and slaves and to offer fair prices to the owners. Nevertheless, criticism of the administration of the law and the law itself increased with the growing suffering. By the winter of 1864–65 the whole system was abandoned.

[Frank L. Owsley, *State Rights in the Confederacy.*]

HENRY T. SHANKS

Impressment of Seamen was one of the harshest memories in the relations of Great Britain and the United States, which time and correct description have helped to soften. Recruits for the Royal Navy were forcibly mustered in the 18th century by the press gang[w]. While neutral vessels appear to have been so victimized prior to 1790, the problem became acute between that date and 1815. Under cover of the belligerent right of search[w] British boarding parties removed from the decks of foreign neutrals any seamen deemed British. The practice was steadfastly regarded in England as indispensable to sea power in the war with France. Improvement of the naval service and the application of psychological devices to induce enlistment, common to later days, were not then conceived of.

Although American seamen, in common with a few of other nationalities, were the occasional victims of the press gang in England, and although persons allegedly British subjects were removed from American ships in British ports, the real issue concerned the impressment of seamen *on the high seas*. The American merchant marine*ᵂ*, prospering and expanding under wartime conditions, offered unexcelled opportunities to British seamen. It is estimated that between 1790 and 1815 twenty thousand of them—including deserters from the Royal Navy—signed up on American ships. The conflict between the traditional doctrine of inalienable allegiance, held to by England, and the new, revolutionary American doctrine of the right of the individual to change his allegiance made an insuperable difficulty. As Canning put it, "when [British] mariners . . . are employed in the private service of foreigners, they enter into engagements inconsistent with the duty of subjects. In such cases, the species of redress which the practice of all times has . . . sanctioned is that of taking those subjects at sea out of the service of such foreign individuals. . . ." In no circumstances was naturalization*ᵂ* as an American citizen a protection to the seaman. (*See also* Expatriation.)

The British left the matter of determining nationality to the discretion of the press gangs and boarding officers. It is not recorded that these were careful in making distinctions. Use of the English tongue appears to have been the main test applied in the cases of likely-looking seamen. Of the 10,000 persons estimated to have been impressed from American ships, only one-tenth proved to be British subjects.

The British returned native-born American seamen to the United States, without indemnity, *if* their citizenship could be established. But the British authorities themselves took little responsibility to determine citizenship, and each separate case had to be handled by the American Government. In the meantime the impressed person had to remain in the service and go wherever he was commanded. As early as 1796 the United States issued certificates of citizenship to its mariners in an effort to protect them. These "protections" were soon abused, however. They were easily lost or sold by sailorfolk to British subjects. An American sailor could buy a "protection" from a notary public for one dollar and sell it to a Britisher for ten. The British consequently refused to honor the certificates.

American protest against impressment dates from 1787. Jefferson in 1792 tried to proceed on the simple rule "that the vessel being American shall be evidence that the seamen on board of her are such." But legally this doctrine was defensible only for the high seas. It had no pertinency to American vessels in British ports. On the other hand, Great Britain refused any concessions whatever to the principle. Thrice the United States tried to negotiate a treaty in which each party would deny itself the right to impress persons from the other's ships, and offered various concessions thereto. Impressment was linked with other issues of neutral trade, but it came to assume first place in American diplomacy. The climax occurred in 1807 when four men were removed from the frigate *Chesapeake*ᵂ. In 1812 Congress alleged impressment to be the principal cause of war, but in view of the ambitions of the Western War Hawks*ᵂ* this is subject to discount.

Impressment of seamen has been, since 1815, nothing but an historical curiosity. But there have been several modern derivatives: (1) On the basis of inalienable allegiance naturalized American citizens have been impressed into the armed services of the country of their birth upon their return to that country. (2) In the *Trent* Affair*ᵂ* the United States impressed citizens in rebellion from a British vessel. (3) In the World War the Allies removed enemy aliens, particularly military reservists, from American vessels.

[Edward Channing, *History of the United States*, Vol. IV.]   RICHARD W. VAN ALSTYNE

"In God We Trust" is the motto that has appeared on most issues of United States coins since 1864–66. Its presence there is due to increased religious sentiment resulting from the Civil War. Many devout persons throughout the country urged that the Deity be recognized on our coins. Accordingly, Secretary Chase asked the Director of the Mint at Philadelphia to have prepared a suitable device expressing this national recognition. Several forms of the desired motto were suggested—among them, "God our Trust" and "God and our Country," but the one we know so well was finally chosen. There is no law that requires it to be used.

[Government Document, *Catalogue of Coins of the United States*.]   THOMAS L. HARRIS

Inauguration of the President. This is the term denoting the great civic festival with which the President[w] is inducted into office. Aside from the oath administered the ceremonies are merely extraconstitutional customs. By an act of Sept. 15, 1788, the Congress of the Confederation supplied an omission of the Constitution by setting the first Wednesday of the following March (which then fell on the fourth) for starting the Government under the Constitution. The Twelfth Amendment (1804) made March 4 a permanent landmark until the Twentieth Amendment[qw] (1933) set Jan. 20 as the end of a presidential term. Since the inaugural ceremonies are extraconstitutional Congress could prescribe a more suitable season for them and has been importuned to do so whenever inclement weather has interfered with the program.

The body of customs constituting the inaugural ceremonies began accumulating with the first inauguration of Washington, whose colleagues generally believed that governments should be made impressive to the masses by imposing pageantry. The new Government not being ready on March 4, Washington was not inaugurated until April 30, 1789, when Chancellor Robert R. Livingston administered the oath on the balcony of Federal Hall in New York City, the first capital of the United States, in the presence of a great assembly in the streets. Washington had ridden to the hall in a coach of state with other carriages bearing prominent officials and foreign ministers, all escorted by military and followed by a long train of citizens—the first inaugural parade. His inaugural address was then delivered to both houses of Congress in the Senate Chamber, which became the regular place for it until 1817. After the first inauguration it became customary for a member of the Supreme Court, usually the Chief Justice, to administer the oath.

Thomas Jefferson, having criticized the first inauguration as "not at all in character with the simplicity of republican government, and looking as if wishfully, to those of European courts," walked from his lodgings in Washington over to the unfinished Capitol with only the salvos of artillery at twelve to mark his inauguration (1801). He delivered his inaugural address so modestly that only a few in the Senate Chamber heard him. Since Madison's second inaugural fell in the midst of the War of 1812, the military escorted the President to the Capitol, where 10,000 citizens were trying to crowd into the building. Consequently the next President, Monroe, set the precedent of speaking from the east portico of the Capitol (1817). In 1829 Jackson was escorted to his inauguration by aged Revolutionary veterans, while Gen. W. H. Harrison in 1841

rode a white horse in his inaugural parade. In 1853, 80,000 visitors came to see Pierce inaugurated. Lincoln's first inaugural (1861) took place in a setting of extraordinary military precautions against interference. Since his predecessor's term ended on Sunday, President-elect Hayes took the oath privately on Saturday, March 3, 1877, and publicly on Monday.

In recent years the inauguration has been attracting hundreds of thousands of visitors to Washington while the nation at large hears the radio broadcast of the President's address, the music of the marching bands and drum corps, and vivid word pictures of the passing parade from the lips of expert commentators.

[J. W. Garner and H. C. Lodge, *History of the United States.*]

W. E. BINKLEY

Income. Estimates of the total income of the American people prior to 1870 cannot be made, but the general trend during the last seventy years can be traced with a modicum of accuracy. In 1870, according to an early study of Dr. W. I. King, the estimated total national income was $6,720,000,000. By 1900 the total had increased to $17,965,000,000, and by 1920, according to a recent study of the Brookings Institution, to $75,397,000,000. In 1929, when the all-time peak was reached, the total was estimated to be $91,988,000,000. On the per-capita basis, according to the Brookings estimates, income was $251 in 1900, $707 in 1920 and $755 in 1929. Allowance for changes in the purchasing power of the dollar indicates that total realized income from all sources increased by 137.5% between 1900 and 1929, and by 48.6% on the per-capita basis. In consequence of the tremendous decline in physical production and of the price decline during the depression years of the 1930's, total national income, as estimated by the United States Department of Commerce and the Brookings Institution, probably fell to $44,900,000,000 by 1933. Thereafter it rose, and probably aggregated $62,100,000,000 in 1936.

Relative shares of the major claimants upon the national income have, of course, changed as the years have passed. In 1909, wages are estimated to have absorbed 38% of the national income, salaries 15.6%, the return of individual enterprisers 26.2%, the reward of investors and property owners 14.7% and business savings 4.7%. By 1920 the respective figures were: 43.9, 17.4, 22.8, 12.3 and 2.1. A characteristic of the 1920's was that wages did not increase as a percentage share of the national income, but that salaries—and therefore total employee income—rose appreciably as a share. By 1929, according to the Brookings Institution studies, wages absorbed 42.1% of the national income, salaries 21.7%, the return to individual enterprisers 17.3%, the return to investors and property holders 14.9% and business savings 2.7%.

In 1929, according to estimates from the same source, 59.5% of the families received incomes of less than $2000, these three fifths of the American families receiving 23.7% of the total national income. Approximately nine tenths (91.8%) of the families that year received incomes of less than $5000, and were the recipients of 57.9% of the total national income. When the upper limit of the income class is taken as $10,000, the figures reveal that 97.7% of the families received less than this amount, their share of all income being 72.0%. That same year, approximately 4000 American families received incomes of $500,000 per annum and over, their percentage of total income being 6.6%, although they constituted only 0.015% of all American families. A comparison of these data with studies for earlier years indicates some, but not a great deal, of lessening of the inequality in income distribution, even though absolute incomes of the lower-income groups were substantially greater in the immediate predepression years than they had been two decades before.

[W. I. King, *The National Income and Its Purchasing Power;* Maurice Leven, *Income Structure in the United States; Income in the United States*, National Bureau of Economic Research.]   ROYAL E. MONTGOMERY

Income Tax Cases. Prior to the Sixteenth Amendment[w] the Federal Government twice experimented with an income tax. The first endeavor (1862), designed as an emergency measure to assist in financing the Civil War, levied a tax on personal net incomes from whatever source derived. The constitutionality of the measure was questioned on the basis that an income tax was a direct tax and hence by constitutional provision had to be apportioned among the states according to population. In 1796 the Supreme Court had held that the only direct taxes in the constitutional sense were capitation and real-estate taxes (Hylton v. U. S.[w], 3 Dallas 171). This precedent was closely followed by the Court in the income-tax case (Springer v. U. S.[w], 102 U. S. 586) and its decision (1880) stated that the income tax was upon the use and not the ownership of property, hence it was in the nature of an excise or duty not requiring apportionment to population. Although ruled constitutional the tax had been abandoned in 1872.

Following popular demand from the South and West for a Federal income tax, the Gorman-Wilson Tariff Bill[w] (1894) introduced a 2% tax on all incomes over $4000. In view of the Springer decision Congress and the general public supposed the tax constitutional; nevertheless, the income-tax provisions of the tariff bill were presented almost immediately to the Supreme Court in Pollock v. Farmers Loan and Trust Co.[w] (157 U. S. 429). Questions to be decided were: (1) whether a tax on the income from real estate or from personal property was a direct tax and hence unconstitutional unless apportioned; (2) whether a tax on the income from state and municipal bonds was constitutional; and (3) whether the income tax as imposed violated the principle of uniformity. The Court's decision (April 8, 1895) declared taxes on income from real estate or bonds to be direct taxes. On the remaining questions the Court was equally divided and expressed no opinion. A rehearing of the case was granted and the second decision (158 U. S. 601) on May 20 held the income tax unconstitutional on all points.

In the period 1862–94 considerable sentiment for the taxation of wealth as such developed as well as the complementary feeling that thus property rights were being assailed. As a consequence, arguments for and against the 1894 law were much more ingenious and fundamental, questions of fiscal expediency being abandoned in favor of those on the basic principles of government and individual freedom. Proponents of the income tax triumphed eventually with the passage of the Sixteenth Amendment (1913) which gave Congress authority to levy taxes on income from any source and without apportionment. It was held subsequently (1920), however, that this did not extend congressional powers in taxing incomes but merely removed them from the restrictions of apportionment still applicable to other direct taxes (Evans v. Gore, 253 U. S. 245).

[E. R. A. Seligman, *The Income Tax;* E. D. Fagan and C. W. Macy, *Public Finance;* D. R. Dewey, *Financial History of the United States.*]   W. B. LOCKLING

Income Taxes. Personal income taxation in the United States began with the levy of a faculty tax by Massachusetts in 1643. Due to inadequate laws and administration, however, income proved an unsatisfactory basis for state taxation, so states gradually abandoned this form of revenue until a particularly successful Wisconsin law (1911) revived their interest. Today a majority of the states has an income tax of some sort.

The Federal Government adopted an income tax (1862–72) to help finance the Civil War, and attempted another in 1894. The latter was declared unconstitutional (*see* Income Tax Cases)

and it was not until the Sixteenth Amendment[w] was ratified (1913) that Federal taxation of personal income was validated.

Corporate income received attention when Virginia included it among taxable bases in 1844. A special corporation excise measured by net profits was levied by Congress in 1909 and the Revenue Act of 1913 included a corporation income tax. In 1917 the Federal tax structure was expanded to include excess and war profits. These were abandoned in 1921, the excess-profits tax[w] being reintroduced in 1933 and supplemented (1936) by an undistributed-profits tax[w]. Many states include corporate income among taxable sources also.

The administrative problems of an income tax are many. In the United States generally net income alone is subject to taxation and its computation raises many delicate points. Net taxable income is defined ordinarily as gross income minus expenses incurred in obtaining that income. Deductions and personal exemptions from the net taxable income are allowed in order to derive the net income subject to tax. Personal incomes, through a combination of normal and surtaxes, are ordinarily charged with progressive rates while corporate income is commonly, though not consistently, taxed at a uniform rate, the Federal law, for example, imposing progressive rates in the period 1913–21 and beginning again in 1936. Individual declaration of personal income and official review is the usual practice, the latter being aided by information supplied at the source. Publicity of returns, presumably as a check against evasion, was attempted by the Federal Government in 1924, 1925 and 1935, but was abandoned as undesirable. Unco-ordinated laws, particularly among the states, have made double taxation a serious problem. Some fiscal agencies tax incomes of residents regardless of where earned; others tax all income arising within their boundaries no matter where the receiver resides; some tax both types of income. Uniformity of laws and reciprocity offer solutions to this difficulty.

Although regarded as non-shiftable, the income tax has far-reaching social effects. The substantial exemptions and deductions granted in the United States release all but a small proportion of the population—approximately 2% for the Federal tax—yet the income tax has become the main support of the Federal Government in ordinary times (see Internal Revenue) and contributes substantially to state revenues.

[J. J. Klein, *Federal Income Taxation;* Alzada Comstock, *State Taxation of Personal Incomes;* National Industrial Conference Board, *State Income Taxes;* H. L. Lutz, *Public Finance;* Tax Research Foundation, *Tax Systems of the World.*]   W. B. LOCKLING

Indemnities, or payments for losses or injuries suffered by a state or its citizens at the hand of another state or its citizens, have been demanded on numerous occasions by the United States. In 1864, the United States participated with Great Britain, France and the Netherlands in the naval attack upon the batteries of the daiymo of Choshu, which had fired upon American boats going through the straits of Shimonoseki. The Japanese government later paid the four powers $3,000,000 indemnity for damages to merchant vessels and for the expense of the expedition. In 1883, the United States returned to Japan its share in this indemnity.

In the Peking Congress, held after the Boxer Rebellion[w] of 1900, the United States played a leading role in frustrating attempts to dismember China by assessing an indemnity greater than the Manchu Empire might bear. The United States insisted that the indemnity should not be punitive but should be limited to actual losses and military expenses. Of the $24,440,000 received by the United States, about one half was used to indemnify American citizens for losses of life and property during the rebellion and for the cost of American participation in the military expedition. In 1908 the United States returned $10,000,000, the remainder of the indemnity, to China, which amount China devoted to the education of Chinese students in the United States.

In the Fourteen Points[w] announced by President Wilson in 1918 as the fundamentals of a peace with Germany, he called for "no punitive damages." Inasmuch as the Fourteen Points were accepted by the Allies and Germany as the basis of her surrender, the United States at the Paris Peace Conference made efforts to keep reparations strictly down to damages for violations of the laws of war. These efforts were unsuccessful and the Treaty of Versailles[w] assessed what was considered as punitive damages against Germany.

On various occasions the United States has paid indemnities for losses or injuries for which this Government has assumed responsibility. In 1887 Congress appropriated $147,748 to be paid to the Chinese government for Chinese subjects killed and injured by mob violence at Rock Springs in Wyoming. In 1892 Congress authorized the payment of 125,000 francs to the Italian government as indemnity for the lynching of eleven Italian subjects in New Orleans (see Mafia Incident; also *I'm Alone* Case).

[J. B. Moore, *Digest of International Law;* P. J. Treat,

Diplomatic Relations between the United States and Japan; W. W. Willoughby, *Foreign Interests and Rights in China;* R. S. Baker, *Woodrow Wilson and World Settlement.*]

KENNETH COLEGROVE

Indentured Servants were usually adult white persons who were bound to labor for a period of years. There were three well-known classes: the free willers or redemptioners[qv]; those who were kidnapped or forced to leave their home country, because of poverty, political or religious reasons; and convicts. The first class represented those who chose to bind themselves to labor for a definite time, usually three or five years, to secure passage to America. The best known of these were the Germans, but a great many English and Scotch came in the same way. The scarcity of labor in the colonies led to various forms of "spiriting individuals away" to the ships bound for America. This varied all the way from enticing to open kidnapping. On arrival in America their services were sold to plantation owners or farmers for what they would bring and the victims indented for a period of years. The convicts and paupers were sentenced to deportation and on arrival in America were indented unless they had personal funds to maintain themselves. Seven years was a common term of such service. The West Indies and Maryland appear to have received the largest numbers of this third class.

Most of the colonies regulated the treatment of indentured servants. A common provision was that they must be provided with clothing, a gun and a small tract of land upon which to establish themselves after their term of service. These provisions applied especially to those who were unwilling servants. There was no permanent stigma attached to indentured service and the families of such persons merged readily with the total population. Children born to persons while serving their indenture were free. This class of labor outnumbered the slaves in the Southern colonies during the 17th century and always far outnumbered the slaves in the other colonies. In the 18th century they were most numerous in the Middle colonies. Terms of an indenture were enforceable in the courts, and runaway servants could be compelled to return to their master and serve out their terms with additional periods added for the time they had been absent.

The treatment of indentured servants varied. Some were mistreated, others lived as members of the family. The presence of so many redemptioners in the later years of the colonial period would indicate that the hardships were not considered excessive.

[Edward Channing, *A History of the United States,* Vol. II.]

O. M. DICKERSON

Independence, Mo. In the 1820's when overland freighting from Missouri to upper Mexico began, the goods were shipped from St. Louis, Mo., to the town farthest west on the Missouri River. To meet the demand for a more western depot near the bend of the river, Independence was founded in 1827. For over twenty years this sprawling settlement, located ten miles from the Kansas border, served as a focal point for most of the Indian and Mexican trade and for many of the emigrants en route to the Far West. At the head of the famous Santa Fé and Oregon-California trails[qv] Independence became known as the "jumping-off place of the American frontier, the rendezvous of traders and trappers as well as of all the veriest rogues and scoundrels in America."

It is only natural that the first emigrants to the Pacific turned to this town as a point of departure. Local merchants and blacksmiths, who had sold supplies to bull-whackers[qv] as well as having done a good "truck and dicker" trade with the Indians, well served the emigrants who after 1841 annually coursed through en route west. At no time, however, did Independence outfit the whole emigration, that patronage being shared with St. Joseph[qv], Mo., and the trading posts in eastern Nebraska and western Iowa known for years as Council Bluffs[qv].

Because of its reputation, the support given by such papers as the New York *Tribune,* and advertising through handbills, Independence supplied between six and eight thousand emigrants in 1849. This town, however, which claimed 1600 inhabitants, thirty stores, two "large and fine Hotels," numerous boarding houses, and twenty wagon and blacksmith shops was doomed by the geographic fact that it did not long remain the farthest west point on the Missouri from which emigrants and freighters could depart for the West. Towns more favorably located, a number of which rose after the Kansas-Nebraska Act[qv] of 1854, outfitted the emigration and served as headquarters for the freighters in the 1850's and 1860's.

[The Missouri River Towns in the Westward Movment, a doctoral dissertation deposited in the Library of the State University of Iowa.]

WALKER D. WYMAN

Independence Hall, where the Declaration of Independence, Articles of Confederation and United States Constitution were signed, is a two-story, hip-roofed brick building, 100 feet long by 44 feet deep, on Chestnut Street, between Fifth and Sixth streets, in Philadelphia. It was erected, 1732–41, after plans drawn by Gov. Andrew

Hamilton. The white clock-steeple was added in 1781 to replace a wooden bell-tower.

Originally designed for provincial officers, it was used by the Second Continental Congress[*] and later by the legislature and the state supreme court. Independence Hall contains a museum of furniture, uniforms, documents and relics of the Revolutionary period, together with an almost complete set of portraits, chiefly by Charles Willson Peale, of the Signers. In the central rotunda stands the Liberty Bell[*].

[D. W. Belisle, *History of Independence Hall;* Wilfred Jordan and Carl Kneass, *Catalogue of Portraits and Other Works of Art in Independence Hall.*]

                                    HARRY EMERSON WILDES

Independence Rock, Wyoming. Its naming shrouded in legend, this granite boulder on the north bank of Sweetwater River is a famous Oregon Trail landmark. Pioneers to the Pacific stopped there for fresh water and trail information. The rock is approximately two fifths of the way from the beginning of the trail in Independence, Kans., to its terminus at Fort Vancouver, Wash.

[R. S. Ellison, Independence Rock and the Oregon Trail, in *The Midwest Review*, February, 1927.]

                                    ROBERT S. THOMAS

Independents. *See* Separatists.

Indian, Education of the. For a long period of time the only efforts made by the whites to educate the Indians were by missionaries and missionary organizations. The first schools were the Spanish missions established in the Southwest. French Jesuits[*] from Canada also founded schools for Indians early in the 17th century, and Protestant missionaries in the English colonies sought almost equally early to make some provision for Indian education. After the formation of the Government of the United States, the number of mission schools greatly increased. In 1819 Congress made its first appropriation for Indian education. This was $10,000, which was apportioned among various missionary organizations to administer, since the Government lacked any machinery for that purpose. Appropriations were continued and these, supplemented by funds made available for education by treaties, were administered by various missionary groups.

It was not until 1873 that the first United States Government schools were established. These were day schools, but boarding schools soon followed. In 1879 Capt. R. H. Pratt founded the Indian school at Carlisle[*], Pa., which became to a certain extent a model for boarding schools established later. The Five Civilized Tribes[*] in Indian Territory had their own system of education, which included rural day schools, as well as academies, or seminaries for more advanced students. They also subsidized certain mission schools from their tribal funds.

The number of government schools rapidly increased until by 1932 they numbered 71 boarding and 124 days schools. Many Indian children are also enrolled in the white public schools. For these the Government has usually paid tuition. It also subsidizes certain mission or state educational institutions by paying a fixed sum for each Indian student enrolled. These are known as "contract schools." In 1932 the local public schools enrolled 48,834 Indian children, while government schools had 27,006, and mission schools 7570. This indicates that eventually most Indians will be educated in the public schools.

[L. F. Schmeckebier, *The Office of Indian Affairs, Its History, Activities and Organization;* Lewis Meriam and others, *The Problem of Indian Administration.*]

                                    EDWARD EVERETT DALE

Indian, The. The aboriginal inhabitants of the United States were of one general anatomical type, regarded as Mongolian in origin. As to antiquity, there is now good evidence that the ancestors of the Indian of 1492 were in America before the mammoth, the wild horse and the ground sloth became extinct, perhaps ten to twenty thousand years ago. The Indian population of 1492 was not evenly distributed over the country, but was dense on the margins, as in the Atlantic Coastal Plain, the Gulf states and finally the Pacific Coast Belt. The sparse population areas were the Great Basin and the dry Plains. The total population in the United States at the time of white contact is variously estimated as from 800,000 to 1,000,000; in 1937 the official estimate of Indians in the United States, including mixed-bloods, was 337,336. For several years the Indians have been increasing at a faster rate than other biological classes in the national population.

The political and social order of Indian life was tribal; each tribe was independent and a self-contained social unit (*see* Indian Village; Sachem; Indian Council) . The number of such tribes is variously estimated at from 1000 to 2000. There were some confederacies of the tribes of which the most formally organized seems to have been the Iroquois League[*]. There were several other less formal groups, as the Abnaki Confederacy in New England, the Creeks in the south, the Pawnee Republics in Nebraska and the Dakota tribes along the Missouri River. Even under the Iroquois League each separate tribe reserved the right of independent action at any time. Friction with European settlers formed a few temporary group alliances but with little solidarity. For the most part the tribes were hostile to each other and more or less engaged in predatory warfare, especially in scalp and head hunting. This condition made conquest easy for the white settlers, who, when sufficiently irritated, hired other Indians to assist in the extermination of the offending tribe.

The language status of the Indian was truly primitive, for, as might be anticipated, each independent tribe had language peculiarities. The classification of Indian languages is a credit to American scholarship. The task was first sponsored by a committee of the American Philosophical Society*, appointed in 1816. The first linguistic tables and distribution map were compiled by Albert Gallatin about 1836; the final standard classification was made by Powell, about 1885. At that time fifty-one independent families of Indian languages were listed as spoken within the borders of the United States. Many of these families embraced a large number of mutually unintelligible languages, the total for the United States being in excess of 300. All the surviving Indians still speak their native tribal tongues, though more and more of them are learning English and thus becoming bilingual.

The geographical distribution of Indian languages is peculiar; of the fifty-one families, thirty are found west of the Cascade ranges, or on the Pacific coast; fifteen between these mountains and the Mississippi River and six east of the Mississippi; however, there is some overlapping. While some allowance must be made for the effect of population density upon language diversity, it nevertheless remains that most of the families are in the extreme West. The significance of this may be that the Pacific coast was the first area to be settled by Indian peoples, thus allowing a sufficient time for more languages to develop in the West. Yet this cannot be proved. The families occupying the largest territories are Algonkin, dominating in northeastern United States and eastern Canada; Siouan in the upper Mississippi and the Missouri country; the Uto-Aztecan in the western dry Plains and the Great Basin.

The economic types of Indian life were regional. Possibly excepting the village tribes of New Mexico and Arizona, the Indians of the United States were primarily hunters and gatherers of wild foods. Throughout the entire country east of longitude 100°, the secondary means of support was agriculture, with maize* the chief crop. The only other area in which agriculture was practised intensively was in parts of New Mexico and Arizona, but even here hunting was of the first importance. Beans, squashes and sun-flowers were the food plants of less economic importance. Tobacco was grown but for ceremonial uses and so a luxury. Cotton was grown in Arizona and New Mexico and the turkey was domesticated. Along the Great Lakes and the St. Lawrence, wild rice* took the place of maize, in California the acorn was dominant and in the Great Basin area certain wild seeds were gathered.

Deer was the chief food animal except in the plains and prairies where the bison was the main staple (*see* Buffalo). Fish and sea food became a staple only along the seashores and inland along streams in which the salmon and sturgeon "ran."

Skin dressing was an important craft everywhere as might be expected but most highly developed in the northern half of the United States. At the time of discovery the textile arts east of the Mississippi were primitive, but the Indians were skilled in the use of bark fibers from basswood, Indian hemp, nettle and milkweed, of which they made good cordage and some good cloth. The tribes on the lower Mississippi, when first observed, were said to weave fine cloth from vegetable fiber but trade soon destroyed this craft. Cotton was woven in Arizona and New Mexico. Along the Mississippi some coarse cloth was made from buffalo hair, and in the Columbia River country the hair of the mountain goat and the hair from a certain breed of dog were spun and woven. But in general the textile development among Indians in the United States was weak; they were predominantly a skin-and-fur-wearing people.

It is customary to divide the Indians of the United States geographically into culture areas, the tribes in each area having more or less similar modes of life. The areas are (1) the Northeastern Woodlands, all the country north of Mason-and-Dixon's Line and east of the Mississippi; (2) the Southeastern area, all the country south of said line and east of the Mississippi; (3) the Great Plains, the area between the Mississippi and the Rocky Mountains; (4) the Southwest, chiefly New Mexico and Arizona; (5) the California area, chiefly Nevada and California; (6) the Pacific area, the western parts of Oregon and Washington; (7) the Plateau area, Idaho and parts of Oregon, Washington and Montana. Among the more important tribes in history are—Area 1: Chippewa or Ojibway; Delaware; Iroquois; Miami; Pequot; Sac and Fox; Shawnee. Area 2: Cherokee; Creek; Seminole. Area 3: Blackfoot; Cheyenne; Comanche; Crow; Dakota Sioux; Pawnee. Area 4: Apache; Hopi; Zuni. Area 5: Modoc; Paiute. Area 6: Chinook. Area 7: Nez Percé.

In the colonization of the United States the Indian was, first of all, an important economic factor. He offered a market for manufactured objects in exchange for which he was prepared to give furs, hides and food. He contributed maize, tobacco, maple sugar, beans, squashes and the knowledge of how to grow them. He instructed the colonist in woodcraft, the use of the birch canoe, snowshoes and the toboggan. He contributed many medicinal plants and superstitions to the folklore of the frontier. In all these respects he was an asset; but he was a hard fighter, resisted extermination and assimilation, thus becoming a liability. His conquest was expensive in blood and property, some 200 major battles were fought, and, when subdued, he was confined to reservations where he is still dependent upon government support.

[Clark Wissler, *The American Indian.*]

CLARK WISSLER

Indian, The, as Slaveholder. The best evidence indicates that few Indian tribes within the area of the United States made slaves of people of their own race. A mild form of slavery apparently existed among several tribes in the Pacific Northwest. Elsewhere it was the general practice to adopt prisoners of war into membership in the tribe.

Negro slavery, however, existed among some of the southern Indians, notably the Five Civilized Tribes^{qv}. Individuals among these Indians early came into possession of runaway Negroes, and took slaves with them when they were removed to the region of the present state of Oklahoma between 1825 and 1840 (*see* Indian Removal). During the Civil War large portions of these tribes allied themselves with the Southern Confederacy, partly because of the sympathies of the slaveholding Indians. After the war this slavery was abolished, not only by the Thirteenth Amendment^{qv}, but by specific clauses in treaties made in 1866 with the Five Tribes.

[F. W. Hodge, *Handbook of American Indians;* Annie Heloise Abel, *The American Indian as Slaveholder and Secessionist.*]

DAN E. CLARK

Indian, The, in the Revolution. In March, 1775, the Massachusetts Provincial Congress accepted the offer of the Stockbridge Indians to serve the Patriots as minute men^{qv}. This was followed by overtures to the Iroquois^{qv}, Penobscot and St. Francis Indians seeking to attach them to the American cause. In turn, Lord Dartmouth, British Secretary of State for the colonies, instructed Sir Guy Johnson, British Superintendent of Indian Affairs in the North, to induce the Indians to take up the hatchet for England. The success of Sir Guy's plans, culminating in a council at Oswego in July, 1775, was prevented by the American invasion of Canada^{qv}, which cut off supplies. This made possible a treaty of neutrality between Continental Commissioners and some of the Iroquois at Albany in September, and another at Fort Pitt in October, securing the neutrality of the Ohio and Lake tribes (*see* Pittsburgh, Indian Treaty at).

War first broke out on the Virginia-North Carolina frontier when the Cherokee^{qv}, counting on English help in removing the white intruders from the Indian hunting grounds in the Watauga and Nollichucky valleys, plunged the frontier into a racial conflict that purged it of all Tories and resulted in an overwhelming defeat of the Indians, and the cession of the lands in question in the Treaty of Long Island^{qv} on July 2, 1777.

In the North the failure of the Canadian invasion reopened the St. Lawrence and started the conversion of the northern tribes to the British. This process was stimulated by the financial inability of the Continental Congress^{qv} to support the subsidy policy of Indian Agent George Morgan at Pittsburgh, as well as the inevitable border incidents accompanying frontier expansion. Supplied by the British, the tribes gradually went over to them, believing that British victory would save them their hunting ground and restore a satisfactory fur trade. First the Mingo^{qv}, in 1776, sought to nip the Kentucky settlement in the bud. In 1777 the Mohawk, Brant, led the Iroquois (excepting the Oneidas and Tuscaroras) in co-operating in the Burgoyne-St. Leger campaign, and terrorized the frontier, after its failure, in such massacres as took place at Wyoming and Cherry Valley, until they were silenced by the Clinton-Sullivan-Brodhead campaign in 1779^{qqv}. In 1777 the Shawnee went over to the British after the murder, by Virginia militia, of Chief Cornstalk^{qv}. In 1778 British supplies brought over the Wyandot, Ottawa, Miami^{qqv} and other Lake tribes who hesitated only momentarily in their British allegiance in 1779 until George Rogers Clark's campaign^{qv} was shown not to be in the interest of the tribes. The Delawares^{qv} went over in 1781 after years of vain waiting for the American reoccupation of Fort Laurens and a campaign against Detroit. The war ended in the Old Northwest^{qv} with the Indians confident that they had successfully defended their hunting grounds as the result, in 1782, of the victory of Blue Licks and the defeat of the expedition of Col. William Crawford, and his torture in expiation for the Moravian Massacre^{qqv}.

In the South, with the revival of British fortunes, the Cherokee had resumed the hatchet in the fall of 1780 only to be crushed again by the Virginia and Carolina militia in the battle of Boyd's Creek with the inevitable result of the forced cession of more land. The Creek Indians[qv] in general refrained from warfare until 1781 when Gen. Anthony Wayne was completing the restoration of American control in Georgia. Then a band of Creeks, under Emistesigo, made a heroic but futile attempt to relieve the British forces besieged at Savannah[qv].

[Walter H. Mohr, *Federal Indian Relations, 1774-1788.*]

RANDOLPH C. DOWNES

Indian, The Praying. *See* Praying Indians.

Indian, Treaties with the. During the colonial period the Indian tribes were regarded practically as independent nations with the right of occupancy of the lands on which they lived. The relations of the mother country and of the colonies with the tribes were regulated by means of treaties, involving extinguishment of title to Indian lands and a variety of other matters, negotiated by colonial officials or direct representatives of the crown, and signed by both parties. This same policy was adopted by the United States, which made its first Indian treaty with the Delawares[qv] in 1778. For nearly a century this practice was continued. During this period about 370 treaties, clothed in the same stately phraseology as characterized the most important international covenants, were negotiated by agents of the executive branch of the Federal Government and submitted to the Senate for ratification. Treaty-making with the Indians was abandoned in accordance with an act of Congress dated March 3, 1871. Thereafter the term "agreement" was substituted for treaty. As a matter of fact, the principal difference made by this change of policy lay in the fact that these agreements required the approval of both houses of Congress, instead of that of the Senate merely.

Many of these treaties came at the close of Indian wars. Illustrations are the Treaty of Fort Greenville in 1795 at the conclusion of Anthony Wayne's campaign in the Old Northwest; the Treaty of Fort Jackson in 1814 following Andrew Jackson's military activities in the Old Southwest; the Black Hawk Purchase Treaty of 1832[qv]; and the numerous treaties concluding the Indian wars on the Plains after the Civil War (*see* Indian Commissions). A large number of other treaties were negotiated because of the pressure of the westward movement[qv], or because the Government had plans which it wished to carry out.

Examples in this group are the Treaty of Fort Wayne made in 1809 by William Henry Harrison; the scores of treaties with both eastern tribes and the Indians of the Plains when the Indian removal policy was being carried into effect; the treaties which marked the abandonment of this policy in the early 1850's; and the treaties of Fort Laramie and Fort Atkinson in 1851 and 1853[qv], respectively, in which various plains tribes agreed to permit roads and military posts within their territories.

The pretense of regarding the Indian tribes as independent nations in any important sense had worn very thin before treaty-making was abandoned. The policy was unsatisfactory at best. The Indian chiefs met government commissioners in solemn councils where long speeches were made, and at the end the names or marks of the negotiators on both sides were affixed to the resulting document. But the Indians were slow to understand the meaning of the relinquishment of title to land (*see* Land, Indian Conception of Ownership of) ; the members of a tribe were not bound by the promises made by their leaders; and the young and ambitious warriors were difficult to control. On the other side, the westward-moving settlers, avid for land, were supremely indifferent to the sanctity of agreements with the redskins. Altogether, the story of our treaties with the Indians is not a pleasant one.

[Charles Kappler, *Indian Affairs: Laws and Treaties;* Frederick W. Hodge, *Handbook of American Indians.*]

DAN E. CLARK

Indian Affairs, Office of. Congress entrusted the management of Indian affairs to the War Department between 1789 and 1849, but not until 1832 did it create the position of Commissioner of Indian Affairs within that department. Thereafter the Indian office was variously known as the Indian Department, Indian Service, Bureau of Indian Affairs and Office of Indian Affairs. Beginning with 1849 the Commissioners' annual reports use the term Office of Indian Affairs but Congress continued to employ all four titles indiscriminately and in an act of 1916 the last three titles appear in the same paragraph.

The Secretary of War and the Commissioner of Indian Affairs had jurisdiction over trade and commerce with the Indians, their removal to the West, and later their concentration on reservations, the payment to them of annuities, their education, their punishment for such depredations as they might commit against other Indians or whites, and their protection from exploitation by white men. Dissatisfaction early developed in the West over the control of Indian Affairs by the War Department which, it was felt, was unresponsive to Western interests. Complaints were made that Indian removal[w] was not pressed aggressively, that lucrative contracts for Indian goods were given to Easterners, and that too many appointments were filled with non-Westerners. At the same time, the West demanded that the General Land Office, then a bureau of the Treasury Department, should be established in a new department where it would be disassociated from the revenue collecting agency, and would be more responsive to Western demands for quick and easy land disposal. In 1849 the Western viewpoint triumphed and the two bureaus were transferred to the newly organized Department of the Interior.

The new department was no more successful than its predecessor in preventing Indian wars, nor in eliminating the corrupt influence of the "Indian Ring," and frequent demands were made for the return of the Office to the War Department, but without effect. So shameful, however, was the record of Indian exploitation and corruption that the Board of Indian Commissioners was created in 1869 to exercise joint control with the Department of the Interior over the disbursement of appropriations.

The Office of Indian Affairs developed into a land administering agency controlling the ceded Indian trust lands, which did not become a part of the public domain[w]. It also had jurisdiction over the allotment of lands to individual Indians, a process which was speeded up after the adoption of the Dawes and Burke acts[qw] of 1887 and 1906. The Wheeler-Howard Act of 1934 reversed Indian policy and placed added responsibilities upon the Office, one of which is the repurchase for the Indians of part of their land, long since sold to white men. Today, the Office is bringing more Indians into its staff, its resident agents are largely Indians, and its principal aims are to make its wards self-governing and self-supporting.

[L. F. Schmeckebier, *The Office of Indian Affairs, Its History, Activities, and Organization;* J. P. Kinney, *A Continent Lost—A Civilization Won, Indian Land Tenure in America.*]

PAUL WALLACE GATES

Indian Agencies, more recently known as Superintendencies, are administrative centers from which are directed the affairs of one or more reservations or tribes. The system apparently originated with the British crown, which, soon after the close of the French and Indian War in 1763, appointed Sir William Johnson as crown agent to have supervision of the Iroquois In-

dians in the North and Sir John Stuart as agent for the Indians in the South (*see* Indian Policy, Colonial) . In 1786 the Congress of the United States, in imitation of the British system, established two Indian districts, one north and the other south of the Ohio River, with a superintendent and two deputies over each. In 1793, after the adoption of the Constitution, Congress authorized the President to appoint temporary agents among the Indian tribes. Under authority of this and subsequent acts, agencies were established until 1834 when the Indian Intercourse Act[w] set up a definite agency system which is still in force. This act provided for twelve agents, the President being given authority to transfer any agency to another place or tribe. The head of an agency is the agent, or superintendent, appointed under civil service regulations. Subordinates under his direction consist of clerks, teachers, physicians, matrons, farmers, shop superintendents and other employees. The physical plant usually includes a building housing the administrative offices, while about it are various others often including a school, hospital, commissary, shops, barns and employees' quarters. The number of Indian agencies varies since the recent tendency is toward consolidation, but is not far from 100 in the United States exclusive of Alaska, including large sub-agencies and independent schools. (*See also* Indian Agent.)

[Laurence F. Schmeckebier, *The Office of Indian Affairs;* Lewis Meriam and others, *The Problem of Indian Administration.*]

EDWARD EVERETT DALE

Indian Agent, The. As a civil official on the extreme frontier, it was the duty of the Indian agent to enforce the laws and regulations upon whites and Indians prescribed by a government remote from the frontier, to serve as observer and mouthpiece among the savages for Washington, by sheer personality to sway the Indians in accordance with official policies, to act as instructor in the ways of white civilization, and finally in later years to function as business guardian for the red men.

During the early colonial period individual colonies such as Massachusetts had dealt directly with Indian problems by statute (act of 1633), but the struggle between France and England for North America, with the fur trade and Indian military aid as major stakes, brought Indian affairs under British imperial control (*see* Indian Policy, Colonial) .

The general idea of a closed Indian country with admission to the area upon license issued by a superintendent of Indian affairs, as established by the Proclamation of 1763[w], was adopted after the American Revolution by the Ordinance of Aug. 7, 1786ᵠ. Under the Constitution, the act of March 30, 1802, provided for Indian agents who were to reside in the Indian country to handle licenses for fur trading, control the Indians and teach the ways of civilization.

Customarily, governors of Western territories, like William H. Harrison, William Clark and Lewis Cass, became *ex-officio* superintendents of Indian affairs, with agents under them at strategic points. Close association with the military was essential, for troops when necessary enforced the orders of the civilian Indian agents. Clark, Cass and other superintendents conducted treaty negotiations with the Indian tribes for peace and land cessions. They supervised the allotment of funds and supplies for their agencies and served as intermediaries between Washington and the Indian agents.

The average Indian agent like Maj. Lawrence Taliaferro at Fort Snellingᵠ, Minn., from 1820 to 1840 (title by courtesy only), with a salary of from $1200 to $1500, had a staff of one or two subagents, an interpreter, blacksmith, farmer and a laborer or two to control several thousand wild Indians ranging over hundreds of square miles. He issued trading licenses on proper bond, inspected cargoes for contraband liquor, held constant advisory councils with his Indians, distributed presents and annuities and promoted Indian agricultural progress, on the many reservations.

The "spoils system"ᵠ after about 1840 brought constant changes in agents, introduced the grafter to choice jobs, largely destroyed Indian confidence in their officials, and, coupled with constant removals to reserved lands (*see* Indian Removal), produced the chaos in Indian affairs of the late 19th century.

[Alban W. Hoopes, *Indian Affairs and Their Administration with Special Reference to the Far West, 1849-1860;* J. P. Kinney, *A Continent Lost—A Civilization Won;* Walter H. Mohr, *Federal Indian Relations, 1774-1788;* Arthur Pound, *Johnson of the Mohawks;* Albert T. Volwiler, *George Croghan and the Westward Movement, 1741-1782.*]

WILLOUGHBY M. BABCOCK

Indian and Liquor. There are few evidences that liquor played a role in trading between Indians and the French and English during the first decades of the 17th century. Before the middle of the century, however, its significance becomes quite apparent, and as French missions spread to the outlets of Lake Superior and Lake Michigan and to the head of Green Bay, traders and their brandy accompanied the missionaries.

In 1670 the Hudson's Bay Companyᵠ entered the field, and the competition between French and English brought so ample a flow of rum and brandy that the Indian became quite saturated. The French missionaries beseeched the governor of Canada to prohibit the trade in liquor, and official orders were issued, but the effect was not notably successful.

The trading Ottawas led other tribes to Montreal: the Hurons, Algonquins, Chippewas, Beaver, Sioux, Kishkakon, Saulteurs, Missisaugus and Crees. The French spread to the upper reaches of the Ohio and Mississippi, opened the Mississippi Valley and established claims to all of the interior. By 1713 the Mississippi was an important highway of the trader, and the Indian's demand for liquor and European goods was insatiable.

Rivalry between the French and English for the fur tradeᵠ, accompanied by lavish use of alcohol, continued in the 18th century through a long series of wars until New France passed into British hands. The monopoly of the British might be expected to bring a diminished use of liquor, but in 1783 the North West Companyᵠ of Montreal began a violent competition with the Hudson's Bay Company, and in 1801 the X Y Company opened a two-year battle that knew no bounds. Twenty-one thousand, two hundred ninety-nine gallons of liquor are recorded to have been taken into the Indian country by the X Y and North West companies in one year. When it was proposed to exclude liquor from the Indian trade, the North West Company convinced Parliament that, if it were done, three fourths of the trade would go to Americans.

The amalgamation of the X Y and North West companies in 1805 brought liquor shipments down to 9000 gallons per year; the union of the North West and Hudson's Bay Company in 1821 caused further diminution; but 200 years of liquor traffic had left an indelible mark on the native American.

As American traders offered competition in the Great Lakes region, the Mississippi and the upper Missouri country, the Hudson's Bay Company again increased the liquor supply. In 1831 the company forbade the sale of rum to Indians, and on July 9, 1832, an act of Congress brought prohibition to the American trade, yet such regulations were evaded and liquor continued to be used excessively. The United States Government steadfastly maintained on its statute books a regulation designed to protect the Indian from the ill effects of alcoholism, but it was never able to make the law effective. A reason for this appears in a list of the desirable things of this world, presented by the Arapahoes in an interview with

Col. Dodge in 1835: first, whiskey; second, tobacco; third, horses; fourth, guns; fifth, women.

[Clarence A. Vandiveer, *The Fur-Trade and Early Western Explorations;* Robert E. Pinkerton, *Hudson's Bay Company;* Harold A. Innis, *The Fur Trade in Canada;* Wm. S. Lewis and Paul C. Phillips (editors), *The Journal of John Work;* W. A. Ferris, *Life in the Rocky Mountains, 1830-1835;* Hiram Martin Chittenden, *The American Fur Trade of the Far West.*]   CARL P. RUSSELL

Indian and the Gun. The primitive weapons of the Indians were bows and arrows and clubs, with which they inflicted considerable damage both upon their enemies and the wild animals. Their first encounter with the white man's weapons or firearms always raised great amazement. Champlain was asked to fire off his musket as a "token of friendship and joy." When Nicolet landed on the shore of Green Bay^{qv} in 1634, he fired a pistol from each hand. The wondering savages thought he was a "manitou"^{qv} bringing thunder and lightning from the heavens.

The Indians from wonder and amazement turned to coveting the white man's weapons. At first they wished their new-found friends to accompany them on their war expeditions and defeat their enemies with these superior weapons. Champlain in 1609 went with a war party against the Iroquois, and as the enemy approached one shot from his arquebus felled two chiefs, even though they were clothed in Indian armor (*see* Champlain Fires a Shot).

The French governor who followed Champlain forbade his traders to sell firearms to the savages. Surrounded by so numerous a people if they acquired weapons of the white man, the colony would be endangered. The French traders, therefore, who visited the Iroquois had no guns to sell, and these tribesmen turned to the Dutch who had settled on Hudson River (*see* New Netherland). Their traders had no scruples in selling guns to the Indians. Their settlements were remote from the Iroquois cantons and their traders made excellent bargains with these tribes for their furs. The Mohawk were the farthest east of the Iroquois tribes, and were thus the first to be adequately armed with guns. They then traded with the other tribes to the west, so that by 1646 it was reported at Quebec that the Iroquois were fully armed. Then they entered upon the career of conquest that destroyed many of the other Indian nations, and made the Iroquois^{qv} the scourge of the colony of New France.

The Huron Indians^{qv}, allied in race but long at enmity with the Iroquois, were among the first to fall. In 1648 began the series of raids that by 1650 had destroyed the Huron missions and set-tlements. The nations to the west in lower Michigan next fled around Lake Michigan into Wisconsin. The Iroquois turned next upon the Susquehanna, the Neutrals and the Erie. The warriors were killed, the women and children incorporated into the Iroquois tribes. They infested the waterways of Canada and held up the fur trade flotillas. Eventually they raided as far west as the Illinois^{qv}, whom they drove in flight in 1680.

Twice French armies invaded their country. It was not until 1701, when the French allies had been armed with guns and the colonial army increased, that the Iroquois with their guns made peace with the French and their allied Indians similarly armed.

One interesting token of the change: when Champlain invaded Iroquois land their villages were protected by palisades. After acquiring guns the Iroquois dispensed with fortifications, feeling their weapons were sufficient protection.

LOUISE PHELPS KELLOGG

Indian and the Horse. The wild horse roamed over North America in late Pleistocene times, some palæontologists suspecting that it became extinct less than 10,000 years ago. That it was associated with the ancestors of the Indians has been demonstrated in cave deposits in southern Chile; but none of the historic Indians living in the New World have traditions of such an animal. The Spanish expeditions and settlements brought horses into the country during the 16th century (*see* Horse, The Spanish). In the following century the Atlantic colonists in North America were well provided with them. The Indians of the forests soon learned to use them sparingly, but the natives of Mexico and southwestern United States took to them readily, especially the Apache, Navaho^{qv} and other southwest nomads. From here horses spread rapidly northward by trade and theft, most of the Plains Indians possessing them when first noted in historical records. Lewis and Clark^{qv} found Indians using them in Washington and parts of Oregon. They were not adopted by the Indians of California, nor the tribes of Nevada, but along the main range of the Rocky Mountains and eastward to the Mississippi all of the tribes soon became horse Indians, turning more nomadic, increasing in numbers and raising their standard of living. Large camps of 100 to 200 tents were maintained, with horses enough to mount the whole population. The Kiowa^{qv}, for example, ranged more than 1000 miles in a summer. Some eastern forest tribes, formerly partially agricultural, moved out into the grassland, acquired horses and lived as hunting nomads, adopting the culture of the horse Indians. The horse-using tribes were usually at war with each other, raided white settlements to steal more horses, and in consequence, military operations against these Indians were by mounted troops.

[Clark Wissler, *Man and Culture.*]

CLARK WISSLER

Indian Art, within the United States, was limited to painting, modeling, drawing and carving. There were no large stone sculptures. The chief mediums were pottery^{qv}, textiles, wood, bone and shell. Painting and drawing were weakly developed, except for conventional designs upon skins, rarely rising above the level of picture writing^{qv}. On the other hand conventional geometric decorative art was highly developed in the 19th century, especially in bead and quill work among the Plains Indians, pottery and textiles in Arizona and New Mexico and basketry in California. In pre-Columbian times there was a high development in pottery along the Mississippi, especially between Cairo and Baton Rouge. It is agreed that the peak of pottery in New Mexico and Arizona was reached around 1100 A.D. (tree-ring dating^{qv}). There were similar art peaks in Middle-America and in Peru. Mound Builder^{qv} art, expressed in carved-stone pipes and sheet-copper cutouts, reached its climax in pre-Columbian time also. It is believed that the art cultures of all Indian peoples were on the decline in 1492. Among the Plains Indians, the tribes of California, and the Totem Pole^{qv} makers of Alaska, art reached a peak in the 19th century or in post-Columbian time. Eventually archeology may reveal the meaning of these changes.

Pottery, basketry and much painting on skins was the work of women. Totem poles were carved by men and so were the wooden "false faces" of the Iroquois. Pictographic drawing and painting was the work of men (*see* Alton Petroglyphs). The usual generalization is that Indian women specialized in geometric art, Indian men in realistic or pictographic art. In quality the art of the women is superior, possibly because beauty was the main objective, whereas the work of the men was crude, the objective being to convey information and to symbolize the mythical.

Since 1890 white people have shown an increasing appreciation for bead work, basketry, pottery and certain textiles, thus creating a market for the best Indian artists. Among the famous potters are Nampeo in the Hopi Pueblo of Hano, Arizona, and Maria Martinas in Pueblo San Ildefonso, New Mexico. Each of these women devised new techniques and achieved high levels of ex-

cellence. A number of Indian women are following the leadership of these two geniuses. Further, since 1900 an original, unique school in water colors has been developed by two Indian men, Creccencio and Awa Tsira, both in Pueblo San Ildefonso. There are now a number of Indian men proficient in this realistic art. In all this there is promise of a widespread revival of Indian art.

[Edgar L. Hewett, *Ancient Life in the American Southwest;* Clark Wissler, *The American Indian.*]

CLARK WISSLER

Indian Barrier State (Proposed). The idea of a neutral barrier state into which white settlements should not penetrate, but which should be left free for Indian trade to either of the two nations on each side of the boundary, was persistent in diplomacy concerning the Mississippi Valley. It was first proposed on a large scale in the negotiations of 1755 designed to settle the claims of France and Britain to the Ohio Valley; it was again put forward in the treaty plans of 1761–62, whereby Canada was to be ceded to Britain (*see* Paris, The Treaty of, 1763). The question was complicated by the indefinite boundary line between Canada and Louisiana. England finally obtaining the cession of Louisiana east of the Mississippi, the proposal was not needed and was dropped.

France having ceded Louisiana west of the Mississippi to Spain, the prospective approach of the British settlements toward the West alarmed the Spanish authorities, and after the revolt of the colonies the proposal for a barrier state became acute at the settlement between Great Britain on the one hand, and the United States, France and Spain on the other. France supported, in 1782, the Spanish demand for an Indian barrier state south of the Ohio, between the Mississippi and the mountains. The American commissioners held out for the colonial claims west to the Mississippi, and by a separate treaty with the British eliminated the Spanish demand for the Indian sphere of influence (*see* Definitive Treaty of Peace, 1783).

Britain, after the treaty of 1783, by which the Mississippi and the Great Lakes became the boundaries of the new nation, was very loath to lose the profitable fur trade of the Northwest, and under one pretext or another declined to surrender to the United States the Northwest military posts (*see* Border Forts, Evacuation of). The Indians of this region, who had become attached to their British traders, were actively hostile to the Big Knives (as they called the Americans) and formed a formidable conspiracy against the United States. President Washington sent an army into the Northwest, under Gen. Arthur St. Clair^{qv}, which sustained a serious defeat in November, 1791. The British attempted to mediate between the United States and the embattled Indians. Hammond, the newly appointed minister from Great Britain, proposed to Washington's administration that a barrier region be erected around the Great Lakes, in which both nations should have freedom of trade but no right of settlement. He stated that if this offer was accepted, Great Britain would surrender the Northwest posts, not to the United States but to the Indians. The latter were greatly encouraged by the British support and sympathy, and the Indians of the Confederacy strongly hoped to make the Ohio the boundary between the United States and themselves.

The American Secretary of State declined to consider the British offer, but pressed for a surrender of the posts and a fulfillment of the treaty obligations. Washington thereupon sent John Jay^{qv} to England, who negotiated in 1794 a treaty by which England surrendered the posts. Meanwhile Gen. Anthony Wayne^{qv} organized an expedition which defeated the Indian confederacy, the United States asserted its authority over the Northwest, and the idea of an Indian barrier state was dropped.

Again after the War of 1812, at the Treaty of Ghent^{qv}, the British ministry insisted as a *sine qua non* a change of boundary and the erection of an Indian neutral state west of the Great Lakes. The Indians of Canada and the West, as well as the fur trade magnates, hoped for such an arrangement. The American commissioners, however, declined, and would have broken off negotiations rather than yield. The British wanted peace, and the former boundaries were reaffirmed and the idea of an Indian barrier state was permanently laid aside.

[T. C. Pease, Anglo-French Boundary Disputes in the West, 1749-1763, in *Illinois Historical Collection*, XXVII; S. F. Bemis, *Diplomacy of the American Revolution*, and *Jay's Treaty;* L. P. Kellogg, *British Régime in Wisconsin and the Northwest;* Orpha E. Leavitt, British Policy on Canadian Frontier: Mediation and Indian Barrier State, in Wisconsin Historical Society *Proceedings*, 1915.]　　　　　　LOUISE PHELPS KELLOGG

"Indian Bible," Eliot's, was the translation into Algonkian by the Rev. John Eliot (1604–90), minister at Roxbury. Composed between 1650 and 1658, it was printed by Marmaduke Johnson on the hand press in the Harvard Yard. The 1200 pages were completed in 1663. Eliot had not only to learn the language but to invent an orthography. His version was used

among the converted Indians on Martha's Vineyard for over a century.

[Cotton Mather, *Magnalia;* Samuel Eliot Morison, *Builders of the Bay Colony*.]　　PERRY MILLER

Indian Brigade, THE, consisting of three Federal regiments composed largely of Cherokees, Creeks and Seminoles^{qv}, was formed in 1862. Two regiments were enlisted in Kansas from Indians loyal to the North who had fled to that state for safety. These, together with some white troops, invaded the Indian Territory^{qv} in the summer of 1862. Here they were joined by a sufficient number of Indians formerly allied with the South to make up a third regiment. The brigade fought many minor engagements in northeastern Indian Territory.

[Wiley Britton, *The Union Indian Brigade in the Civil War;* Annie Heloise Abel, *The American Indian as Participant in the Civil War*.]　　EDWARD EVERETT DALE

Indian Burial. In no respect does the religious nature of the American Indian so display itself as in the burial of the dead. A belief in the hereafter is shown in gifts and articles left with the dead in many burials.

Common methods of burial were: interment in graves, stone cists, mounds, or caves; embalmment and mummification; sepulture in the limbs of trees or on scaffolds; cremation; surface burial under heaps of rocks.

The huge mounds of the Mound Builder Indians^{qv} were often tombs. In Alaska, the American Southwest and elsewhere, embalmment was understood and many mummies still exist. Pacific Indians sometimes buried the dead in a canoe on high posts, while the Plains Indians habitually wrapped corpses and left them lashed in the branches of trees or on scaffolding erected where trees of proper size were not available.

Death always was an occasion of extreme manifestations of grief, particularly by women relatives of the deceased. Hair was cut off, and fingers also in frequent cases. Bodies and arms were scarified, ornaments discarded and faces painted black. Burial ceremonies sometimes were long and impressive, while it was common to destroy by fire a dwelling in which a death had occurred. Today much of the best archæological knowledge of prehistoric tribes comes from the exhumation of burial sites.

[H. H. Bancroft, *Native Races of the Pacific States;* H. C. Yarrow, *Introduction to Mortuary Customs of the North American Indians;* Bureau of American Ethnology, 1st Report.]　　PAUL I. WELLMAN

Indian Captivities. White captives taken by Indians in our early wars were variously treated.

The men, especially if they had been fighters, were sometimes, though not always, tortured to death. Women, children and adolescent males might be adopted into the tribe. Some children thus grew to maturity, regarding themselves as Indians. Some women became slaves, some were forcibly married to their captors, some sold to British or French allies. Many persons captured in Kentucky or the Northwest Territory in the latter 18th century were sold to the British in Canada, who often showed great humanity— though sometimes making a profit, too—in restoring them to their homes. At the sack of Deerfield[w], Mass., in 1704, 100 persons were carried away, most of them to Canada; some were returned in 1706, some never came back. In the seaboard colonies, the thrilling narratives of Indian captivities became a favorite form of literature, and scores of such pamphlets were published. One of the earliest (published 1682) was the story of Mrs. Mary Rowlandson, who was made prisoner at Lancaster, Mass., in 1675 and ransomed by her husband for £20 after eleven weeks. Her story has had more than thirty reprintings, appearing in a magazine as late as 1937. Increase and Cotton Mather were particularly active in collecting and publishing such narratives. John Gyles (narrative published in 1736), a garrison commander in Maine, was six years a servant to the Indians and three years to a French trader before being liberated. Mrs. Elizabeth Hanson of Dover Township, N. H., her four children and a maidservant were seized in 1724, taken to Canada, and after five months, she, two children and the servant were sold to the French, the Indians retaining two daughters. Her husband ransomed the group from the French after a year's captivity, and later with difficulty obtained another daughter. In 1727 he died while on another journey to Canada in behalf of the eldest daughter; but she was persuaded to marry a Frenchman, and never returned home. In 1780 appeared Mrs. Hanson's narrative, "the substance of which was taken from her own mouth and now published for general service." The story of Robert Eastburn, captured at Williams Fort, Pa., in 1756 and a prisoner for two years and eight months, was in 1758 "Published at the earnest request of many persons, for the benefit of the Public"—but they sold well, too.

[Samuel G. Drake, *Indian Captivities; or Life in the Wigwam.*]   ALVIN F. HARLOW

Indian Citizenship. An act of Congress approved on June 2, 1924, states that "all non-citizen Indians born within the limits of the United States be, and they are hereby declared to be, citizens of the United States." Previous to the passage of this law the legal and political status of the American Indians was anomalous. The Supreme Court in 1831 defined their status as that of "domestic dependent nations," and other decisions contained similar statements. They were not citizens and they were not aliens in the full sense of the term. Even the Fourteenth Amendment[w] did not confer citizenship on the Indians.

Prior to 1924, however, many Indians were given the rights of citizenship by treaties and by acts of Congress. Several Indian treaties, beginning as early as 1817, contained such provisions. Similarly, Congress has passed a number of acts granting citizenship to Indians under certain conditions. The most notable were the Dawes Act of 1887, the Burke Act of 1906[qw], an act of 1919 extending citizenship to honorably discharged Indian soldiers and sailors of the World War, and the act of 1924 already mentioned. Citizenship, with some exceptions, gave the Indians the right of suffrage[w] under the same conditions as those laid down for other citizens by the various states.

[Frederick Van Dyne, *Citizenship of the United States;* W. W. Willoughby, *The Constitutional Law of the United States.*]   DAN E. CLARK

Indian Commissions, THE (1865–68). The Chivington massacre[w] set the frontier ablaze. Indians attacked road stations, stagecoaches and emigrant trains, murdered settlers and their families and burned property wherever found. Sully in the Dakotas and Conner in the Powder River region[qw] punished the Indians, but did not win peace. The Government appeared to have no policy. Friends of the Indians demanded "more treaties, more kindness, more gifts." To meet this agitation and make the frontier safe, President Johnson appointed a commission of seven members, including Gen. J. B. Sanborn, Gen. W. S. Harney and Kit Carson, to make treaties with the southwestern Indians. The commission met on the upper Arkansas River in October, 1865, and signed treaties with the Cheyennes and Arapahoes[qw]. Another commission proceeded to the upper Missouri to negotiate treaties with the Sioux[w], but the aggressive element among the Indians refused to recognize it. Red Cloud[w] led the hostile Indians in a merciless war on the encroaching whites (*see* Bozeman Trail) and for over a year there was constant fighting along the frontier. Sherman, commanding the Department of the Mississippi, was subjected to bitter criticism. Another commission was appointed, but could only distribute presents and rations and abandon territory. The people in the East favored treaties to control the Indians; Congress appointed another commission (July, 1867) and appropriated large sums for its use. But still the Indians burned and murdered, and stole or destroyed property and livestock. Black Kettle's band was attacked on the Washita River and destroyed; a detachment from Fort Wallace was ambushed on Arickaree Creek and nearly annihilated^{qw}. Sentimental Easterners criticized the army for its apparently merciless methods. In spite of Indian depredations and frontier skepticism, the commission traveled along the frontier negotiating "shot gun" treaties, culminating in the treaties of Fort Laramie^{w}, April and May, 1868. Peace had been negotiated but there was no peace. The Office of Indian Affairs^{w} and its policy were in constant conflict with the Army on the Frontier^{w} and the only result of treaty-making was prompt violation, either by settlers or Indians or both. Indian depredations and punitive expeditions followed each other with monotonous regularity as the frontier moved westward.

[E. P. Oberholtzer, *History of the United States since the Civil War*.]   THOMAS ROBSON HAY

Indian Council, THE, was, technically, a gathering of all the males of mature age, roughly over thirty years, belonging to a village or community. All matters of importance were passed upon by this body. The chief had no special authority, except as delegated by the council, or such as would be spontaneously accorded because of his forceful personality.

When there was some kind of confederation, as when a number of villages or camps were considered to form a tribe, each village council would send representatives to sit in a tribal council. The numbers were rarely fixed, it being understood that the few leading, or head men, in each village would attend. The active participants usually sat around a fire, hence the designation "council fire." For example, the Dakota^{w} recognized seven autonomous tribes, so spoke of themselves as the "seven council fires." The Six Nations^{w} used the symbol of Six Fires, referring to the council fires in the respective tribes.

The Council of the Delaware Indians^{w} as described by Zeisberger (1781) proceeded as follows: When the Chief had knowledge of matters to be referred to the council, a messenger was sent to notify the council members of the time for the meeting. When they were assembled, the Chief, or usually some one designated by him, presented in detail and with clarity the question at issue. All speakers stood, spoke forcefully and

smoothly. No one interrupted a speaker, nor did they applaud, absolute silence being the rule. When all had spoken, one of the councillors summed up the discussion, formulating the prevailing opinion. This task was undertaken only by those who had special competence and experience. The discussions might be completed at one sitting, but often continued for a week or more. It was the duty of the women to bring in food at appropriate times. Each member brought his pipe, tobacco and pouch, for there was a great deal of smoking and pipe passing. These meetings were rarely secret, any one could listen, but there must be no noise. Women were rarely members or permitted to speak.

A house somewhat larger than a dwelling was used, frequently the residence of the Chief. In fine weather, the meeting might be around an outdoor fire.

Indian oratory^{w} was developed in the council, that being the only place where it functioned. The great Indian orators recorded in history, King Philip, Logan, Red Jacket, Keokuk, etc., came to notice in peace conferences with white government officials, but these conferences were not normal Indian councils.

[David Zeisberger, *History of the Northern American Indians*, ed. by A. B. Hulbert and W. N. Schwarze; Lewis H. Morgan, *The League of the Iroquois*.]
                    CLARK WISSLER

Indian Country. The term "Indian Country" was used in a general way throughout our history to designate territory to which the Indian title had not been extinguished (*see* Indian Land Cessions) . More specifically, however, it applies to the area set aside for the Indians in pursuance of the Indian removal^{w} policy formulated by Calhoun and Monroe and recommended to Congress in 1825. By 1840 a definite "Indian Country" had been created, extending from Texas to Canada. The eastern boundary, in general terms, ran west from Green Bay^{w} to the Mississippi, down that river to northeastern Iowa, southwestwardly a short distance into Iowa, south to the Missouri line, west on that line to the Missouri River, and down that river to the western boundary of Missouri, thence along that boundary and the western boundary of Arkansas to the Texas line. The western limits were the western boundary of the United States as defined by the Adams-Onís Treaty^{w} (1819) with Spain, and the eastern line of the old Oregon country^{w}. This large area, then, was for a short time called the permanent Indian country.

Within a few years, however, the pressure of settlers led to treaties with various tribes by which the boundary of the Indian country was pushed almost entirely beyond the limits of Wisconsin and Iowa. At the same time, the travel to Santa Fé and the emigration to Oregon^{qv} were dispelling the myth of an American desert, and giving rise to problems which made the existence of an inviolable Indian country increasingly embarrassing. Then the acquisition of the Oregon country in 1846 and the territorial expansion resulting from the Mexican War^{qv} foreshadowed the early abandonment of the Indian policy so confidently established by Calhoun, Monroe and Jackson.

In 1851 the eastern Sioux Indians^{qv} agreed to give up practically all claim to lands in Iowa and Minnesota; and the western Sioux, the Cheyennes and the Arapahoes^{qv} conceded the right of the Federal Government to build roads and establish military posts in their country along the Oregon-California trail^{qv}. Two years later similar concessions were made by the Comanche, Kiowa and Apache^{qv} tribes farther south. Then in 1854 the tribes which had been located along the eastern border of the Indian country were induced to make treaties ceding lands and agreeing to move. After the passage of the Kansas-Nebraska Act^{qv} in 1854, the Indian country was reduced to the region lying west of Arkansas and between Kansas and Texas, which came to be known as the Indian Territory^{qv}. When Oklahoma^{qv} was admitted in 1907 the last remnant of the old Indian country disappeared.

[Charles Kappler, *Indian Affairs: Laws and Treaties;* Annie H. Abel, *Indian Consolidation West of the Mississippi;* Frederic L. Paxson, *History of the American Frontier, 1763-1893.*]

                        DAN E. CLARK

Indian Dances. The usage now is to speak of any Indian ceremony as a dance, but in colonial literature, such terms as festival, pow-wow^{qv}, sing, busk, etc., were common. The fact that some dancing characterizes all Indian ceremonies justifies the name.

The best-known aboriginal dances, or ceremonies, are the Calumet Dance, War Dance, Scalp Dance, Green Corn Dance^{qv}, Ghost Dance, Sun Dance and Snake Dance^{qv}. All save the last-named were widely diffused among Indians, though varying in details from tribe to tribe.

The War Dance was a ceremony to arouse the community and enthuse the warriors. Among the eastern Indians the warriors danced around a post, which in a way symbolized the enemy. The Scalp Dance was a victory dance and usually danced by the women.

[James Mooney, The Ghost-Dance Religion and the Sioux Outbreak of 1890, *14th Ann. Report, Bureau of American Ethnology, Part I, 1898.*]   CLARK WISSLER

Indian Factory of Virginia, THE TRUSTEES OF THE (1757-60; 1765-67), were set up, during the French and Indian War^{qv}, to facilitate trade with and the recruitment of warriors from the Cherokee^{qv} country. The sum of £5000 was appropriated; factors were to be bonded not to engage in private transactions; goods were to be sold at cost. Supplies were ordered from England; pending their arrival, the Trustees requested patience of the Cherokee. The anti-English sentiment of the natives, quickened by a variety of reasons, was in no wise diminished by the delay in receiving promised goods. When, in 1759, the first cargo was actually approaching the Indian country, it had to be recalled, owing to the outbreak of hostilities which enlarged into the Cherokee war. The Trustees were instructed to sell their stocks and to balance accounts with the provincial Treasurer.

With the coming of peace in 1761 a number of private traders visited the mountain Indians. Temporarily, the peltry business boomed; then a slump ensued. The Assembly recreated the Trustees, appropriated £2500, and decreed trade without profit. Factor David Ross journeyed to the Cherokee and discussed with them problems of trade. He proposed the construction of a factory on the Long Island of Holston River (now Kingsport, Tenn.), but the red chieftains vigorously opposed placing the post nearer their towns than Col. John Chiswell's^{qv} lead mines (near present Wytheville, Va.).

Upon the factor's return, he reported to the Trustees that a traffic such as that projected would be attended by "Inconveniences." The Trustees dropped the scheme and made preparations to dispose of their goods, seemingly before a single cargo had been sent out. The Privy Council^{qv} in England, meanwhile, had nullified the act re-establishing the Trustees. Thereafter the Old Dominion was content to let the peltry traffic remain in private hands. (*See also* Factory System, The Indian.)

[W. N. Franklin, Virginia and the Cherokee Indian Trade, in *East Tenn. Hist. Soc. Pubs.,* V.]

                W. NEIL FRANKLIN

Indian Factory System. *See* Factory System, The Indian.

Indian Hunting Grounds. *See* Hunting Grounds.

Indian in the Civil War, THE, was conditioned by his location on the frontier—immediately west of Missouri and of Arkansas. Indian Territory^{qv} lay between Arkansas and Texas, and there, under authority of the Removal Act of 1830, lived the great tribes of the South (*see* Five Civilized Tribes) . The more influential of these Indians, half-breeds mostly, were slaveholders. The five tribes, however, distrusting both the Federal Government and the individual Southern states, would have preferred remaining neutral, but events prevented. United States troops were early withdrawn from the frontier posts and the Indians, deprived of protection, were exposed to Southern influence, without hindrance.

In May, 1861, Confederate agents appeared to negotiate treaties of amity and alliance. They began with the Cherokees, but the chief, John Ross, held out for neutrality until August. The other tribes yielded more readily; but groups, both large and small (usually full-bloods) , despite intimidation, persisted in adherence to the Union. Creek loyalists were among the most stubborn. They prepared to withstand coercion by resort to arms but soon fled northward to Kansas.

Meanwhile, "Pike's Indians," had joined Van Dorn's Confederate army in Missouri, and had participated in the Battle of Elkhorn^q. Henceforth, Pike labored to have the Indian regiments restricted to the home-guard duty for which they were originally intended. In this he only partially succeeded. Their retention in Arkansas occasioned friction, which eventually caused Pike's own displacement.

Repeated Confederate defeats in Missouri and Arkansas had a calamitous effect upon the Indian alliance, and, gradually, disgruntled elements broke away, particularly after Lincoln's Emancipation Proclamation; and still more after his Amnesty Proclamation^{qw}. Circumstances, at first, had forced the Southern Indians to cling to the Confederacy. In 1863 the Cherokees, through their National Council, nullified the Southern alliance; other tribes later doing likewise. Before long organized Indian participation had ceased altogether.

[Annie Heloise Abel, *The American Indian as Slaveholder and Secessionist*, and The Indians in the Civil War, *The American Historical Review*, Vol. XV.]

A. H. ABEL-HENDERSON

Indian Intercourse Act, THE. Before 1834 the policy of the Federal Government in removing Indians from the areas in which frontiersmen were settling was not supplemented by any guarantees that their new homes would be reserved to them against future inroads by whites. Many Indian groups hesitated to remove to new areas without such a promise and others, angered by the constant penetrations of whites into their new territories, retaliated by ravaging white settlements (*see* Indian Removal) . Congress, in

1834, adopted what many thought was a permanent solution of the Indian problem, the Indian Intercourse Act. This act and subsequent treaties with various tribes set aside a permanent Indian Country^q. White settlers were rigidly excluded from this territory, trading was only permitted under Federal license and other safeguards were authorized to protect the Indians from white men's exploitation or interference.

The guarantees remained in effect only so long as whites were not interested in the territory; but when settlers, bottled up east of the Missouri, began to look enviously upon the fertile plains of Kansas the policy was doomed. Little by little the large Indian Country of 1834 was whittled away until with the admission of Oklahoma^q as a state, in 1907, it disappeared.

[F. L. Paxson, *History of the American Frontier;* Roy Gittinger, *The Formation of the State of Oklahoma.*]

PAUL WALLACE GATES

Indian Key Massacre (Aug. 7, 1840) was an attempt, during the Seminole War^q, to destroy a settlement, consisting principally of "wreckers," on Indian Key, half-way between the present cities of Miami and Key West. The Indians were discovered before they attacked and all but six whites escaped in the darkness. Among the victims was Dr. Henry Perrine, who had brought to Florida for introduction, on a land grant from Congress, a large collection of tropical economic plants and seeds.

[Henry E. Perrine, *The True Story of Some Eventful Years in Grandpa's Life.*]

A. J. HANNA

Indian Land Cessions. The policies and procedures involved in the extinguishment of the Indians' rights to lands constitute an important chapter in the history of the United States, and present interesting comparisons with the practices of other nations in dealing with native peoples inhabiting countries over which these nations have claimed and maintained jurisdiction. At the outset it should be stated that, with a few possible exceptions, the Indians themselves had little or no conception of either individual or tribal ownership of land. To them land was like air or water—something that was necessary to life, but not capable of being bought or sold. Thus it was difficult for them to understand the full meaning of treaties in which they relinquished their rights (*see* Land, Indian Conception of Ownership of) . Furthermore, in some instances it was held by the Indians that no single tribe had the power to alienate land unless all the tribes living in a given territory were in agreement.

The English, like the other European nations

colonizing North America, based their territorial claims upon discovery, exploration or settlement. Fundamentally, therefore, they ignored the rights of the Indians. That the newly discovered lands were inhabited by native peoples was no barrier to the making of grants to individuals and companies or the planting of colonies. In fact, it was not until near the close of the colonial period that the English home government formulated any definite policy in regard to the possessory rights of the Indians (*see* Indian Policy, Colonial). The proprietors and other colonial authorities were left to deal with the Indians largely in their own way.

Policies and practices naturally differed among the various colonies. In general, it may be said that almost from the beginning it was conceded that the Indians possessed rights of occupancy of their lands which must be extinguished by purchase or treaty before such lands could be actually occupied by white men. While in many instances individuals purchased land directly from the Indians on their own responsibility, it early became the practice to prohibit such dealings without the permission of the colonial authorities. Indeed it soon became customary to require that treaties of any kind with the Indians be negotiated only by agents of the colonial government.

It would be difficult, if not impossible, to determine the date or terms of the first Indian land cession within the present boundaries of the United States. Furthermore, it would be an almost hopeless task to attempt to unravel the tangled and ambiguous accounts of Indian land cessions during the early colonial period. Boundaries were often exceedingly vague and indefinite. For instance, there were numerous "walking treaties" in which land areas were described in terms of distances which a man could walk in a day or a given number of days; and similarly, there were "riding treaties" in which the distances which a man could cover on horseback in given periods of time were used as measurements. Other treaties were even less specific in the matter of boundaries. There was also much overlapping, even in the land cessions of a single tribe to a single colony, to say nothing of the cessions by different tribes.

A few illustrations will serve to indicate something of the character of the Indian land cessions made during the colonial period. William Penn was notably successful in his dealings with the Indians, and one of his early acts was the holding of a council at Shackamaxon^{qv} (1682) at which the Indians deeded to him a vaguely defined area in return for a considerable amount

of merchandise which was itemized in the treaty. In the succeeding years several other treaties were made with the Indians of Pennsylvania, including the "Walking Treaty" of 1686^{qv}. In 1744 representatives of Pennsylvania, Virginia and Maryland concluded a treaty with the Six Nations or Iroquois at Lancaster^{qv}, Pa., in which these important tribes ceded their rights to land between the frontier of Virginia and the Ohio River. After the close of the French and Indian War^{qv} a so-called "Indian Boundary Line" was established in a series of treaties, among which three are outstanding. First was the Treaty of Fort Stanwix^{qv} in 1768 with the Iroquois in which they agreed to relinquish their claims to lands east and south of a line which ran roughly from the vicinity of Fort Stanwix in New York southward to the Delaware, then southwestwardly to the Allegheny, and down that river and the Ohio to the mouth of the Tennessee. By the Treaty of Hard Labor the same year and by the Treaty of Lochaber^{qqv} in 1770 the Cherokee Indians ceded their claims to lands in the present State of West Virginia. Finally, mention should be made of the remarkable but illegal privately negotiated Treaty of Sycamore Shoals^{qv} in 1775, between the Transylvania Company and the Cherokee Indians, who ceded to the company approximately 20,000,000 acres of land lying between the Cumberland and Kentucky rivers.

When the United States came into existence the Government from the beginning followed the policy adopted during the colonial period with respect to the rights of the Indians to their land. It has been held that the ultimate title to the soil resided in the Federal Government, but that the Indians had the right to the use and occupancy of the lands which they claimed, and that this right could be extinguished only by their consent. Negotiations for Indian land cessions could be conducted only by agents of the Federal Government except in certain cases in which the original states were permitted to act. Article IX of the Articles of Confederation^{qv} gave Congress the power to regulate the trade and manage all affairs with the Indians. A proclamation of Sept. 22, 1783, prohibited any person from "purchasing or receiving any gift or cession of such lands or claim without the express authority and direction of the United States in Congress assembled." The Constitution made no specific reference to dealings with the natives except to give Congress power to regulate commerce with them. In practice, therefore, negotiations with the Indians were based upon the treaty-making power (*see* Indian Policy, National).

As a consequence, for nearly a century Indian land cessions were accomplished by means of treaties couched in all the formal verbiage of an international covenant. These treaties were negotiated with Indian chieftains and leaders by appointees of the executive branch of the Federal Government, signed by both parties, and ratified by the United States Senate. In 1871 the fiction of regarding the Indian tribes as independent nations was abandoned; and thereafter simple "agreements" were made with them. This change of practice seems to have been dictated mainly by the determination of the lower house of Congress to have a voice in the making of commitments entailing appropriations of money, for the "agreements" required the approval of both houses of Congress.

While the United States made a treaty with the Delaware Indians in 1778, the first Indian land cession to the new nation was that made by the Six Nations or Iroquois by the Treaty of Fort Stanwix[qv] in 1784, ceding land in northwestern Pennsylvania and in the extreme western part of New York. The following are brief summaries of selections from the long list of Indian land cessions made between 1784 and 1871. They furnish some indication of the rapidity with which the Indian title was extinguished as the tide of American settlers swept westward.

Treaty of Hopewell[qv], 1785, with the Cherokee Indians, ceding land in North Carolina west of the Blue Ridge and in Tennessee and Kentucky south of the Cumberland River.

Treaty of New York City, 1790, with the Creek Indians, ceding a large tract of land in eastern Georgia (see McGillivray Incident).

Treaty of the Holston River[qv], 1791, with the Cherokee Indians, ceding land in western North Carolina and northeastern Tennessee.

Treaty of Greenville[qv], 1795, with the Wyandot, Delaware, Shawnee, Ottawa, Chippewa, Potawatomie, Miami, Eel River, Wea, Kickapoo, Piankashaw and Kaskaskia Indians, ceding large areas in southern and eastern Ohio comprising nearly two thirds of the present state, some land in southeastern Indiana, and small tracts around Michilimackinac in Michigan.

Treaty of Tellico, 1798, with the Cherokee Indians, ceding three tracts of land mostly in eastern Tennessee.

Treaty of Buffalo Creek, 1802, with the Seneca Indians, ceding lands in western New York involved in the purchase of the Holland Land Company[qv]. This was an unusual treaty in that the land was ceded directly to the company.

Treaty of Vincennes[qv], 1803, with the Kaskaskia Indians, ceding a large area in central and southeastern Illinois comprising about one half of the present state. Other tribes ceded their claims to this area in the Treaties of Edwardsville, 1818 and 1819.

Treaty of Fort Clark, 1808, with the Osage Indians[qv], ceding land between the Arkansas and Missouri rivers, comprising nearly half of Arkansas and two thirds of Missouri.

Treaty of Fort Jackson, 1814, with the Creek Indians[qv], ceding large areas of land in southern Georgia and in central and southern Alabama.

Treaty of St. Louis, 1816, with the Ottawa, Chippewa and Potawatomie Indians, ceding land between the Illinois and Mississippi rivers in Illinois, as well as some land in southwestern Wisconsin.

Treaty of Old Town, 1818, with the Chickasaw Indians, ceding land between the Tennessee and Mississippi rivers in Tennessee and Kentucky.

Treaty of Saginaw[qv], 1819, with the Chippewa Indians, ceding a large area surrounding Saginaw Bay and numerous other scattered tracts in the present State of Michigan.

Treaty of Doak's Stand[qv], 1820, with the Choctaw Indians, ceding land in west-central Mississippi.

Treaty of Chicago[qv], 1821, with the Ottawa, Chippewa and Potawatomie Indians, ceding land in southern Michigan and northern Indiana.

Treaties of St. Louis, 1823, with the Osage and Kansas Indians, ceding very extensive areas of land in the present states of Missouri, Kansas and Oklahoma.

Treaty of Prairie du Chien, 1830, with the Sac and Fox, Sioux and other tribes, ceding land in western Iowa, southwestern Minnesota and northwestern Missouri.

Treaty of Fort Armstrong, 1832, with the Sac and Fox Indians, ceding a fifty-mile strip of land along the west bank of the Mississippi in Iowa. This was the Black Hawk Purchase[qv].

Treaty of Sac and Fox Agency, 1842, with the Sac and Fox Indians, ceding all of south-central Iowa.

Treaty of Traverse des Sioux[qv], 1851, with the Sisseton and Wahpeton bands of Sioux Indians, ceding claims to lands in southern Minnesota, comprising more than one third of the present state, and in northern Iowa.

Treaty of Fort Laramie[qv], 1851, with the Sioux, Cheyenne, Arapaho and other tribes of Indians, ceding land in North Dakota, Montana and Wyoming. The provisions of this treaty were altered by the Senate and were never ratified by the Indians.

Treaty of Table Rock, 1853, with the Rogue

River Indians, ceding land in southern Oregon.

The treaties above listed have been selected to illustrate the rapidity with which the Indian tribes ceded their lands to the United States Government in the three quarters of a century following national independence. In 1854, in order to make way for the organization of Kansas and Nebraska territories, there were signed a number of treaties in which land was ceded by Indian tribes most of whom had been located along the eastern border of the so-called Indian Country[w] in accordance with the Indian removal[w] policy. The center of interest now shifted to the Far West, and especially to the region of the Great Plains, where the powerful tribes were becoming increasingly restless. In 1861, for instance, the Arapaho and Cheyenne Indians[qqw] ceded their claims to enormous tracts of land in the present states of Nebraska, Kansas, Colorado and Wyoming. Before the end of this decade the old Indian Country on the Great Plains was reduced to the area long known as the Indian Territory[w], which later became the State of Oklahoma. During the same period the extinguishment of Indian titles was proceeding rapidly from the Rocky Mountain region to the Pacific coast.

In fact, by 1871, when the making of formal treaties with the Indians was abandoned, there was comparatively little left to be done. By 1890 the process was practically complete, except for the Indian reservations on which the tribesmen resided either in accordance with treaty provisions or under authority conferred upon them by the Federal Government. Since that time many of these reservations have been abandoned, consolidated or reduced in area.

A total of 720 Indian land cessions is indicated by Charles C. Royce on the maps accompanying his digest of *Indian Land Cessions in the United States,* which covers the period from 1784 to 1894. It must be remembered, however, that it often required treaties or agreements with several tribes to clear the Indian title of a given area of land. Many treaties also dealt with the ceding of relatively small reservations set aside previously when a much larger area was relinquished.

Compensation to the Indians for the land ceded by them consisted of livestock, various kinds of merchandise (often including guns and ammunition) and annuities, or annual payments of money for a specified number of years. A government report (Donaldson's *Public Domain,* 1883) indicates that up to 1880 the Federal Government had expended more than $187,000,000 for the extinguishment of Indian land titles. How much of this sum actually reached the In-dians, either in goods or in money, would be impossible to determine. In numerous instances traders gobbled up the annuities as fast as they were paid on the ground that the Indians were indebted to them. If these figures are accepted at their face value, however, it might be contended that the United States has dealt quite liberally with the native inhabitants, since the total sum paid to Spain, Mexico and Texas for the territory acquired from them was less than $75,000,-000.

It has sometimes been asserted that the United States has never dispossessed the Indians of their right in the land without their consent. Literally speaking, with a few exceptions, this statement is true. If, however, the term "willing consent" were substituted, the case would be quite different. A survey of the history of Indian land cessions reveals the fact that they fall into three large general groups when considered in the light of the conditions or causes which produced them. In the first place, many of the cessions were made at the close of wars. In this group are the cessions made at the Treaty of Greenville, following Anthony Wayne's campaign[w]; the Treaty of Fort Jackson, following Andrew Jackson's campaign in the South; and the Black Hawk Purchase of 1832. To be sure, the Indians signed these treaties, but scarcely voluntarily.

In the second place, there are the land cessions made after the Government had exercised pressure in order to accomplish purposes which it had in mind. Illustrations of this group will be found in the treaties with both eastern and western tribes when the Indian removal policy was being put into effect from 1830 to 1840, and the treaties insisted upon when the policy of an Indian Country was being abandoned after 1853. Finally, numerous treaties ceding land were clearly brought about by the demand for more land for settlement; as, for instance, the treaties negotiated by William Henry Harrison opening up land in Indiana. It would be difficult, indeed, to find a land cession made by the Indians entirely of their own volition.

[Charles C. Royce, *Indian Land Cessions in the United States,* Eighteenth Annual Report of the Bureau of American Ethnology, Pt. II; Charles J. Kappler, *Indian Affairs: Laws and Treaties,* Vol. II; Dan E. Clark, *The West in American History.*]   DAN E. CLARK

Indian Legends. The term legend is often used to cover all fixed narratives heard among Indians. These include humorous tales, historical and migration narratives, and, finally, those accounting for the supernatural origins of life. The Indians usually distinguished between anecdotes of contemporary life and those legends assumed to have originated in the remote past, when animals could talk and perform miracles, as did the gods and supermen. While there were several hundred separate Indian tribes, each claiming a series of legends and tales as peculiarly its own, these tribal mythologies are found to have many tales in common, or at least with common plots. Fairly complete collections of tribal legends have been made for each of the more important tribes throughout the United States, the comparative study of which has produced a sizable body of literature. The American Folk Lore Society, organized in 1888, has been one of the chief agencies promoting the serious study of this subject.

Since none of the Indian tribes in the United States possessed systems of writing, these legends and myths constituted their literature. The æsthetic and literary qualities of Indian narratives seem about equal to those in the mythologies of the Old World. Some of the tales considered "classics" are "The Woman Who Married a Star," "The Twin Brothers," "The Lost Children," "Turtle's War Party," "The Bungling Host" and "Origin of the Pleiades." These are hero tales, versions of which are found in the collections from many different tribes.

One outstanding characteristic of Indian mythology is the belief in a culture-hero, a supernatural being who establishes the present order of the world by changing or transforming the then existing order. The philosophy of the Indians is to assume that the original world always existed, that there was no creator but a transformer who worked with the forms and materials at hand.

A puzzling characteristic of these transformers is that many obscene and immoral tales are associated with them. The favorite role is that of a rude, vulgar trickster, sometimes appearing to possess superhuman smartness, at other times the stupid dupe of ordinary mortals. However, when playing the hero in these antisocial antics, these transformers are masked as animals, such as rabbits, coyotes, etc. All such hero tales probably reflect the ideals, aspirations and emotions of the tribe concerned and, since human nature has much in common everywhere, Indian mythology has been enjoyed and appreciated by Americans generally.

Schoolcraft (1793–1864) was the first writer to make Indian mythology popular in the modern sense, though Longfellow's *Hiawatha*[qv] is the classic adaptation of such tales to modern literature, but good literal renderings of tribal collections are now available for the Iroquois, Ojibway, Sauk and Fox, Dakota, Blackfoot, Crow, Pawnee, Micmac, Apache, Hopi and Zuni.

Historians are interested in the class called migration legends. The best-known example is the Delaware or Lenape, *Walam Olum,* first published in 1836 by Rafinesque, and in revised form by Brinton in 1885. Though many tribes had such migration legends, few have been recorded fully by students of folklore, because they were regarded as sacred and in large part secret. For example the pueblo village tribes of New Mexico and Arizona are known to possess elaborate legends of this kind but none have been fully recorded. Judging from the known fragments, these migration narratives are in the form of a genesis, dwelling upon the miraculous but usually tracing the assumed migrations of the tribe from an unidentifiable country to the known historic habitat. A comparative study shows that these legends contain borrowed elements, thus, the same routes and events are claimed as peculiar to several tribes in turn. Since other evidence for a common history is lacking, the historical value of such Indian legends is highly questionable.

[Stith Thompson, *Tales of the North American Indians;* A. Keiser, *The Indian in American Literature.*]

CLARK WISSLER

Indian Massacres marked the course of relations between white men and red in the United States from the first settlement until the final placing of the Indians on reservations in the early 1880's. They were most common in the colonial period when Indian relations were ill regulated by the individual colonies, and the Indians themselves were used as pawns in the wars among French, Spanish and English. In this period an Indian uprising was generally initiated by a massacre of some frontier community and was almost invariably provoked by white encroachment on Indian land or by fraud and mistreatment perpetrated by the fur traders. Of such a character were the Virginia massacres of 1622 (*see* Great Massacre) and 1624, and those ushering in the Pequot, King Philip's, the Yamassee and the Tuscarora wars[qv]. The notorious Indian massacres during the intercolonial wars, such as Deerfield and Schenectady[qv], were largely due to French inspiration; Indian massacre of prisoners, as at William Henry and Fort Loudon[qv], was almost invariably due to the younger warriors defying the authority of the chiefs.

The occupation of Kentucky and Tennessee was almost unattended by Indian massacres because the early settlers were continually on guard and the frontier communities protected themselves by forts which were impregnable to Indian attack. Indian massacres were rare in the settlement of the Southwest and Northwest because by this time the United States had taken over the management of Indian affairs and the network of Indian officials made surprise impossible. In the trans-Mississippi, Indian massacres were almost unknown until the Civil War era, when land-office frauds and military mistreatment drove the Sioux[w] to desperation.

In all probability the Indians suffered as many massacres as they inflicted. No Indian massacre ever exceeded in brutality the Black Hawk massacre of 1832 or the Chivington massacre[qw] in Colorado in 1864.

R. S. COTTERILL

Indian Missions. During the colonial period efforts to Christianize the Indians were made by the Spanish Franciscans[w] in Florida and Upper California; French Jesuits[w] in the South and New York; Spanish missionaries in New Mexico, Arizona and Texas; Roger Williams, John Eliot and David Brainerd in New England and the middle Atlantic region; and the Moravians[w] among various tribes. Definite missionary work was begun by boards and societies as follows: in 1787 the Society for Propagating the Gospel among the Indian and Others in North America; in 1796 the New York Missionary Society; in 1797 the Northern Missionary Society; in 1802 the Western Missionary Society (the three latter organizations forming in 1817 the United Foreign Missionary Society, which later was absorbed by the American Board of Commissioners for Foreign Missions[w], supported by the Congregational, Dutch Reformed and Presbyterian churches); in 1803 the General Assembly of the Presbyterian Church; in 1817 the General Missionary Convention of the Baptist denomination; in 1821 the Methodist Episcopal Church; in 1842 the American Indian Mission Association; and in 1845 boards of the newly formed Southern Baptist Convention and the Methodist Episcopal Church, South. Work by the leading denominations has been carried on, until most of the tribes have come under the influence of Christianity. The missionary program has included translation, teaching, preaching, printing, farming, medical treatment and training in the crafts and domestic arts, with an attempt recently to develop native leadership. (*See also* Praying Indians.)

[G. W. Hinman, *The American Indian and Christian Missions.*]

JAMES W. MOFFITT

Indian Oil Lands are of three types. One is oil-producing land held by an individual Indian under a trust patent which grants to the holder all mineral rights. Another is land the surface of which has been allotted to individuals who hold it under either trust or fee patents, while the mineral, or subsurface, rights, are retained by the tribe as a whole. The third type is oil-bearing lands of a closed reservation where both surface and subsurface rights are held by the tribe as common property. The lands of the Five Civilized Tribes[w] in Oklahoma belong to the first class. As a result, a few of these Indians have become wealthy while many members of the same tribe are wretchedly poor. The lands of the Osage[w] Indians in Oklahoma are in the second-named class. The surface is held individually, but all money derived from leases or royalties is paid to the United States Agent for these Indians to be equally divided among the original allottees or their heirs. This has made the Osage one of the wealthiest peoples in the world. On a few Western reservations held tribally oil has been discovered and any income derived from it becomes the property of the tribe as a whole.

[Laurence F. Schmeckebier, *The Office of Indian Affairs;* Lewis Meriam and others, *The Problem of Indian Administration.*]

EDWARD EVERETT DALE

Indian Oratory. Among most tribes oratory was cultivated as a high accomplishment, and skillful speakers exerted great influence. Most Indian dialects adapted themselves well to rhetorical uses, to which the native poetical and symbolical habit of mind also lent itself.

The first white explorers remarked the eloquence of Indians, and history has preserved many Indian addresses rich in imagery, such as those of Cornplanter, Red Jacket, Big Elk, Logan and others of the East, as well as notable Western Indians, such as Chief Joseph, Sitting Bull and Satanta. Red Cloud's address at the Cooper Institute, New York City, June 16, 1870, made a deep impression on the audience although it was filtered through an interpreter.

Most native orators were men of impressive appearance with voices well calculated to stir their listeners. They had opportunity to display their art at a variety of state, religious and social occasions. Certain tribes had official orators for state events, but in most cases the practice of the art of speaking was open to all who could display ability.

[Articles by James Mooney in 14th and 17th annual reports, *Bureau of American Ethnology.*]

PAUL I. WELLMAN

Indian Paths. Without doubt some of the principal paths or trails of the American Indians were made by the mound builders[w] in traveling considerable distances between their towns. During the pre-Columbian period, as well as afterward, the buffalo[w] was chief trail-maker. By instinct he was a civil engineer; he chose the line of least resistance through mountain gaps, across valleys and along watercourses. The Indians adopted his trails as their paths, and the hunters, traders and pioneers made the paths their trails, and, later, their roads. Today many of the main highways and railroads run, broadly speaking, where the buffalo had made location and broken the way. The forests, except where fires had produced "barrens," were unbroken; the trees grew thick and tall and beneath them was a mass of matted undergrowth and vines. On the mountain heights and sides, in certain latitudes, grew thick and tangled masses of laurel and rhododendron. Through such a terrain the buffalo, by reason of his form and thick skin, was best fitted to penetrate; his hoofs and compact weight beat out a trace^w where human beings must have measurably failed. When the pioneer came to use these forest highways he found them sunken one or two feet below the surrounding surface. This wearing was due to the hoof of the buffalo rather than to the soft moccasin of the red man. The paths were not wide, only two to four feet. At portages^w they were wider. The buffaloes and bears marched in single file, as did also the Indians when traveling beyond the domain of their nation. Many of the traces of the buffalo were intercolonial in extent; his lures were vast meadows of grass and cane and the far-separated salt licks^w.

The Indian, hunter, trader or home-seeker would sometimes blaze trees along a trail so that seasonal changes might not confuse him should he see fit to make a return journey and to guide others outbound.

The paths or trails of the American Indian were used for war and trade, and were usually along relatively high ground or ridges where the soil dried quickly after rains and where the fewest streams were to be crossed; stony ground was to be avoided where practicable, because of the soft footgear. In trade the paths were followed by Indian "burdeners" loaded with peltry; later, goods of traders were taken into the Indian country by pack horses, and peltry carried back to the seacoast or a trading point in the interior. The principal paths through the territory of one tribe connected with those which ran through the country of another; and there was an interlacing of minor with major trails. Long distances were traveled in the conduct of intertribal barter or in visits on occasions of ceremony.

Among the great trails of the Amerinds were: the Iroquois trail from Albany up the Mohawk River, through the site of Rochester on to the site of Buffalo on Lake Erie; the Occaneechi trail

from the site of Petersburg, Va., southwest into the Carolinas; the Great Warrior Path leading from the mouth of the Scioto to Cumberland Gap^w into the Tennessee Country where at Long Island of Holston it joined the Great Trading Path^w which led to the Cherokee towns on the Little Tennessee, and ran on into regions of Georgia and Alabama. Over the trail through Cumberland Gap flowed early migrations into Kentucky and Middle Tennessee. It became known as Boone's Trail or the Wilderness Road^w. The Chickasaw-Choctaw Trail became the noted Natchez Trace^w between Nashville and Natchez.

[S. C. Williams, *Dawn of Tennessee Valley and Tennessee History.*]   SAMUEL C. WILLIAMS

Indian Pipes. *See* Pipe, Indian.

Indian Policy, Colonial. From the earliest colonial times the Indian title to the soil was recognized to be one of occupancy with the ultimate fee in the British crown and colony. The crown recognized the right of the Indians to occupy their lands until they had been surrendered by treaty or by conquest.

Indian affairs, prior to 1755, had been largely controlled by the individual colonies. Policies were initiated by the colonial governors; the assemblies appropriated the money to pay the expenses involved, passed laws to regulate Indian trade^w and to compel traders to secure licenses. Colonial control resulted in the natives being robbed of their lands and cheated in trade. Many tribes, therefore, allied themselves with the French during the French and Indian War^w, 1754–63. To win Indian support the British inaugurated a system of imperial management in 1755 and 1756 by creating two separate Indian departments and appointing a superintendent for each. Sir William Johnson was appointed, April 15, 1755, superintendent of Indian affairs for the northern department. He continued to serve in this capacity until his death in 1774, when his nephew, Sir Guy Johnson, succeeded him. Edmund Atkin was appointed superintendent of the southern department and held this office until 1762, when he was succeeded by John Stuart, who continued to serve until his death in 1779.

By 1761 the right to buy Indian lands was denied the American colonies, and directed by the home government. The Proclamation of 1763^w guaranteed to the Indians "for the present" the lands between the Appalachian Mountains and the Mississippi River. No colonial official could make land grants until the king's further pleasure was known within this territory, and no settlements therein were allowed. No trader was permitted within the reservation without a license obtained from the colony in which he resided.

This administrative system subordinated the Indian superintendents to the military authorities. In 1764 the superintendents, therefore, presented a plan designed to give them more independence. The proposal provided that they be permitted to regulate Indian affairs such as treaties, trade, land purchases and matters pertaining to peace or war without political or military interference; all Indian traders were to be placed under the control of the superintendent; civil cases were to be tried by the Indian agents but appeals might be taken to the superintendent; finally, all provincial laws relating to Indian affairs were to be repealed. Although Parliament never sanctioned the plan, the superintendents proceeded to administer Indian affairs according to the proposal.

In 1767 Lord Shelburne recommended the abolition of home control of Indian affairs and reversion to the earlier practice of colonial regulation. However, his proposal to abolish the Indian departments was rejected because it was felt that such matters as land purchases, treaties, boundaries and conferences should be in the hands of British officials. It was agreed, nevertheless, that the regulation of Indian trade be transferred to the colonies and a definite Indian boundary surveyed. If ever permitted, western colonization would be under imperial control. Thus the compromise between imperial and colonial control was effected. Boundary agreements were accordingly negotiated and the surveys made.

The real problem now was to prevent encroachments upon the frontier lands. The desired prevention was most difficult because the powers of the superintendents had been weakened. Despite the efforts of Stuart and Johnson to prevent Indian land cessions[w] to individuals and to companies these continued until the Revolution. The British, nevertheless, succeeded in retaining the friendship of the major tribes throughout the Revolutionary War.

The Indians were paid very little for land cessions, and permanent annuities were never granted during the colonial period. The Revolution doubtless prevented the formulation of a permanent Indian policy. Nevertheless, the Indian policy of the United States was largely inherited from the British government and the policies pursued by the colonies.

[C. W. Alvord, *The Mississippi Valley in British Politics*; W. H. Mohr, *Federal Indian Relations, 1774-1788*; Helen L. Shaw, *British Administration of the Southern Indians, 1756-1783; The Papers of Sir William Johnson.*]

GEORGE D. HARMON

Indian Policy, National. The general control which the United States Government has always exercised over Indian affairs had its origin in the course adopted by Great Britain at the time of the French and Indian War[w]. The Articles of Confederation[w] conferred the authority in express terms, saving the legislative rights of the individual states. The Federal Constitution[w] gave to Congress only the power of regulating Indian trade; but, under the doctrine of implied powers[w], the Federal Government has managed to give the grant the widest possible interpretation and to arrogate to itself the exclusive management of all Indian relations. This course was initiated in 1793, when an amendment to an Indian trade act required that all land purchased from Indians be by treaty.

In its fundamental features, also, the national Indian policy follows that of colonial times (*see* Indian Policy, Colonial). To avoid controversy private purchases were pretty generally forbidden and the theory of Indian occupancy tenure conceded. This recognition of title differentiates English and American procedure from that of most other colonizing peoples. Treaty-making was one of its attributes. President Washington's policy was shaped along these lines. It was a policy of conciliation. Washington suggested that Indian treaties should receive formal ratification and that an agency system should be devised. He also advocated a trading arrangement "to protect [the Indians] from imposition and extortion." From this recommendation there resulted the Indian Factory System[w]. At the outset, the administration of Indian affairs was entrusted to the War Department and so remained until the organization of the Interior Department[w] in 1849. Knowing well that encroachment upon Indian lands led inevitably to hostilities, President Washington urged adequate provision "for giving energy" to frontier laws; but popular pressure for cessions continued unabated and far in advance of need (*see* Indian Land Cessions). Indian wars came, and treaty after treaty was negotiated, the most obnoxious to the Indians being that of Greenville[w], which, by greatly decreasing the tribal holdings, contributed more than anything else to Indian disaffection before and during the War of 1812[w].

With the Louisiana Purchase[w] in prospect, removal and segregation suggested themselves to President Jefferson as a solution of the Indian problem for the time being; but no such plan was then worked out. Under President Monroe powerful influences, the Georgia Compact of 1802[w] predominating, were brought to bear upon the Government to revive and develop Jefferson's idea of removal. In 1824 a bureau in the War Department took exclusive charge of Indian matters. President Jackson carried on the removal[w] policy with vigor. During Jackson's administration, Congress created (1832) the post of Commissioner of Indian Affairs[w]. An Indian Intercourse Law (1834) undertook to define the Indian Country[qw]. The territorial organization of Kansas and Nebraska necessitated the breaking up of Indian areas along the Missouri, and a series of treaties ushered in a reservation[w] policy. A similar plan was initiated in the Pacific Northwest, while in California, where Spanish-derived Mexican law had not acknowledged Indian land claims, a colonization policy, resembling in some respects the Mission System, was inaugurated. The drift of the colonization scheme was toward the preservation of community life, whereas the reservation presupposed ultimate tribal dissolution, allotment in severalty and citizenship. In the ante-bellum period, innumerable treaties were negotiated, many of which were never ratified. Of those ratified, two, that of Fort Laramie (1851) and that of Fort Atkinson (1853) [qw], were significant in that they were designed to secure to the whites immunity from Indian attack and a right of way across the continent, north and south, respectively.

The Civil War had a far-reaching effect upon Indian policy, especially in relation to the Five Civilized Tribes[w]. Following its close, these tribes, who, under circumstances over which they had little or no control, had joined forces with the Confederacy (see Indian in the Civil War), were compelled to consent to reconstruction treaties greatly curtailing their rights and privileges. In 1871, by means of a simple rider to an Indian appropriation bill, came the greatest change of all; the end of Indian treaty-making and the abandonment of the conception of the Indians as domestic nations, to which several famous decisions of the Supreme Court had given force (see Cherokee Nation v. Georgia).

The post-Civil War years witnessed other important changes in policy. The Indian Commission[w] report so impressed Congress that a Board of Indian Commissioners was set up, which, until abolished by Executive Order in 1933, served effectively in an advisory capacity. Gradually the Indian Office took over the supervision of Indian education, which had formerly been almost entirely in the hands of missionaries (see Indian, Education of the). Practical farming became part of the curriculum. The institution of Indian

police was encouraged and strengthened, and reforms were made in the judicial system.

In 1887 came the Dawes, or General Allotment, Act[w], under which individual ownership, at first with a restricted title, was arranged for. The administration of the law, however, was vitiated by unnumbered frauds perpetrated upon the Government and the red men alike. The Dawes Commission[w] to the Five Civilized Tribes undertook the details of tribal dissolution, a process protracted because of the presence of free Negroes and adopted whites. It became a foregone conclusion that the extinction of tribal autonomy would eventually extend to all. With the admission of Oklahoma (1907) disappeared forever the prospect of an Indian state in the Union.

In 1934, a decade after the passage of the Snyder Act, which clothed Indians not already citizens with United States citizenship, the policy of allotments and self-government was completely reversed by the Wheeler-Howard Indian Reorganization Act[w], which was based on the belief that the course of events had too greatly hurried the process of Indian absorption into the body politic.

[A. H. Abel, *The History of Events Resulting in Indian Consolidation West of the Mississippi;* Grant Foreman, *Indian Removal;* Alban W. Hoopes, *Indian Affairs and Their Administration, 1849-1860.*]

A. H. ABEL-HENDERSON

Indian Queen, THE, on the east side of Fourth Street above Chestnut, was one of the noted hostelries of 18th-century Philadelphia. This tavern, famous for its luxurious apartments and good food, served as headquarters for many congressmen when Philadelphia was the capital of the United States. It was destroyed in 1851.

[E. P. Oberholtzer, *Philadelphia: A History of the City and Its People.*]   JULIAN P. BOYD

Indian Removal. This term is generally used to designate the removal by the Federal Government of Indian tribes from east of the Mississippi to the country west of that river, in pursuance of a national policy which received definite authorization by Congress in 1830 and was vigorously put into effect during the succeeding years. This policy was adopted in the hope and expectation that it would be a solution of the problems of conflict arising wherever whites and Indians came into contact during the rapid progress of the westward movement[w].

The idea of Indian removal seems to have originated with Thomas Jefferson at the time when he was troubled in his own mind regarding the constitutionality of the Louisiana Purchase[w]. He drafted a constitutional amendment authorizing

Congress to exchange lands west of the river for lands possessed by Indians east of the Mississippi. By this device apparently he sought to satisfy his own scruples concerning the great purchase, and at the same time to solve the Indian problems in Georgia and along the frontiers of settlement. This amendment was never submitted to Congress. The idea of Indian removal was not abandoned, however, for the act of 1804, establishing the Territory of Louisiana, contained a clause which authorized the President "to stipulate with any Indian tribes owning land on the east side of the Mississippi, and residing thereon, for an exchange of lands, the property of the United States, on the west side of the Mississippi, in case the said tribes shall remove and settle thereon."

Although the Indian removal policy received considerable support, especially in the South, for various reasons not much was achieved during the ensuing two decades. Certain tribes, such as the Delawares, the Kickapoos and a small portion of the Cherokee nation, were encouraged to migrate west of the Mississippi and there shift for themselves. Otherwise, during this period, there was a continuance of the old practice of extinguishing Indian titles by treaties which made no provision for new locations for the displaced Indians (*see* Indian Land Cessions).

The year 1825, however, witnessed a definite revival of the idea of Indian removal. By that time it was evident that the entire region east of the Mississippi would soon be included within state boundaries, and that there would then be no further place to which Indians could move on that side of the river. But beyond the Mississippi lay the Great Plains*ᵂ*, an area thought to be unsuited to white habitation (*see* Desert, Great American), but abounding in wild game and therefore adapted to the use of the Indians. Few people at that time foresaw the day when white settlers would covet this region. John C. Calhoun, Secretary of War, was therefore doubtless quite sincere when in 1825 he recommended to President Monroe that he acquire a sufficient amount of land west of Missouri and Arkansas to provide a permanent home to which the Eastern Indians could be moved. The proposal received Monroe's indorsement as one of his last official acts. During the administration of his successor treaty-making was in progress, both among the Western Indians to make room for the migrating tribes and among the Eastern Indians to induce them to move.

The Indian removal policy was pursued with real vigor and relentlessness after Andrew Jackson's accession to the Presidency. In 1830 Congress definitely authorized the President to exchange land beyond the Mississippi for lands held by tribes within the states or territories. Within a few years there was created an Indian Country*ᵂ*, to which the word "permanent" was confidently applied—a region inhabited by indigenous Western tribes and by Eastern Indians who had been moved to lands allotted to them. The Indian Intercourse Act*ᵂ* of 1834 provided for agencies, schools and farmers and prohibited the intrusion of unauthorized white men. By about 1840 the Indian removals were nearly completed and the eastern boundary of the Indian Country extended along the western boundaries of Arkansas and Missouri, along the northern line of Missouri, through eastern Iowa, northward along the Mississippi and across northern Wisconsin.

The removal of the Northern Indians was accomplished with comparatively little difficulty. There were numerous tribes, most of which were small in numbers and weakened in strength by long years of conflict. Some of these tribes had been pushed about so frequently in preceding years that they cannot be said to have become deeply attached to a given area. Among the Northern tribes moved to new homes west of the Mississippi were the Chippewas who were pushed into northern Wisconsin and Minnesota; the Sauk and Foxes, Winnebagoes and Potawatomies who were located in what is now Iowa; and the Iowas, Kickapoos, Delawares, Shawnees, Ottawas, Kaskaskias, Peorias, Miamis, and the Iroquois and other New York Indians, all of whom were assigned tracts of land in the Indian Country along the western border of Missouri.

It was in the South that the Indian removal policy encountered the most stubborn resistance and led to the most tragic results. Here lived the Cherokees, Creeks, Chickasaws, Choctaws and Seminoles, known collectively as the Five Civilized Tribes*ᵂ* because of the relative advancement of most of these tribes toward some of the features of civilization. Not only were these tribes large and powerful, but the Cherokees and the Creeks, especially, had permanent homes and farms on which they maintained herds and raised varied crops, built grist mills, carried on trade, sent their children to missionary schools and had representative government. They loved their home lands, and they put up every resistance in their power to the arguments, threats, bribes and persuasions of the agents and commissioners sent to induce them to sign and obey treaties agreeing to remove to a new and more barren country. The Seminoles*ᵂ*, particularly, were convinced of the inevitable only after a series of military campaigns. By 1840, however, all these tribes, numbering altogether about 60,000, were moved to the region immediately west of Arkansas.

The Government doubtless did not realize the difficulties and problems involved in removing large numbers of people such long distances. The officers and men of the Regular Army units detailed to escort the migrating tribes usually performed their unpleasant duties efficiently and sympathetically. Locally recruited volunteers and civilian employees, however, were generally not much concerned for the welfare of the unhappy Indians, and contractors were not over-scrupulous about the quality of the supplies furnished. As the result of all these factors the story of the removal of the Southern Indians, especially, is one of pathos and tragedy. Whether they traveled by steamboat or flatboat, in wagons or on foot, the migration of the Indians was characterized by suffering from hunger, exposure and disease and an abnormal number of deaths.

The later experiences of these Indians on the border of the Great Plains, and their conflicts with the native Western tribes, have no place in this account. It needs only to be added that the "permanent Indian Country" began to disintegrate almost before it had been completed. The Western tribes, such as the Sioux, Cheyennes, Arapahoes, Comanches, Apaches[qv] and many others were placed on scattered reservations. Beginning early in the 1850's the Eastern Indians affected by the Indian removal policy were required to move again. Ultimately they were crowded into the area long known as Indian Territory[qv]. In 1907 with the admission of Oklahoma into the Union even this last remnant of the old Indian Country disappeared. (*See also* Indian Policy, National.)

[Annie Heloise Abel, *The History of Events Resulting in Indian Consolidation West of the Mississippi;* Grant Foreman, *Indian Removal: The Emigration of the Five Civilized Tribes of Indians;* Frederic L. Paxson, *History of the American Frontier.*]

DAN E. CLARK

Indian Reservations are lands set aside for the occupancy and use of Indian tribes. The policy was inaugurated by the United States in 1786. Reservations have been set aside by treaty, by act of Congress, by executive order and by agreement. None has been made by treaty since the act of March 3, 1871. Since so often reservations have been enlarged, reduced or entirely abolished by allotting the lands in severalty, figures as to the number or total area of Indian reservations would be incorrect except for the specific date given. In 1908 the number in the United States, including the nineteen Spanish grants to the Pueblo Indians[qv], was 161 with a total area

of 52,013,010 acres. In addition there are some small state reservations in Maine, New York, Virginia and South Carolina. Indian reservations are classified as "closed reservations" where all lands are held in common, partially allotted, and wholly allotted. The term is sometimes loosely applied to an area in which most of the land is held by Indians though some may be owned by whites. In the case of the Osage tribe in Oklahoma, the subsurface is held tribally while the surface has been allotted to individual Indians and much of it sold to white farmers (*see* Indian Oil Lands).

[F. W. Hodge, *Handbook of American Indians.*]
EDWARD EVERETT DALE

Indian Slavery among Whites. Inaugurated by early Spanish expeditions to the New World, Europeans made a practice of selling into slavery captive American Indians. Carolina was early made a hunting ground by the Spaniards for Indian slaves who were sent to Cuba. The English settlers of South Carolina during the Indian wars before and after 1675 practised on a large scale the enslavement of Indians for whom they found a steady and profitable market in the West Indies. In New England during the Pequot War of 1637 and King Philip's War of 1676[qv], captive Indians were sold into slavery, the males shipped to the West Indies and the females scattered among the white settlers. The French destroyed the Natchez[qv] villages in 1730 and sold 450 captive Indians into slavery in Santo Domingo. The last-known survival of the custom was in Alabama during the enforced Indian removals[qv] of 1836 when a number of Creeks[qv] were held in servitude by white men.

[F. W. Hodge, *Handbook of American Indians;* S. G. Drake, *Indians of North America;* Grant Foreman, *Indian Removal.*]

GRANT FOREMAN

Indian Springs (Ga.), Treaties of (1821, 1825), were made between the Creek Indians[qv] of Georgia and the United States. The treaty of 1821 ceded a large tract of land east of the Flint and Chattahoochee rivers, in exchange for $200,000 and the assumption of $250,000 worth of claims. In the treaty of 1825, the Creeks agreed to migrate west of the Mississippi (*see* Indian Removal), and ceded all their lands in Georgia, together with a large tract lying west of that state. They were to receive an equal number of acres west of the Mississippi and the sum of $400,000. This second treaty caused such widespread disagreement among the Creeks that the United States rendered it null and void in the Treaty of Washington, 1826, in which the Creeks ceded all their land east of the Chattahoochee and a considerable area west of that river. Provision was made, moreover, to move a part of the nation west of the Mississippi within two years.

[Commissioner of Indian Affairs, compiler, *Treaties between the United States . . . and . . . Indian Tribes*, pp. 293-295, 323-326, 391-395.]   RICHARD E. YATES

Indian Stream Republic. Since the international boundary around the sources of the Connecticut River, in the extreme northerly part of New Hampshire, was uncertain, the remote and somewhat lawless settlers based their land titles on an Indian purchase of 1796, and drew up their own government, admitting little control by New Hampshire. The denial by that state in 1824 of the validity of the Indian deed, and the attempted exertion of Canadian rule after 1827, increased a local desire to be free of both till the line was settled. An elaborate written constitution was adopted in 1832, and legislatures met in 1833, 1834 and 1835. The claim of independence, or, failing that, of belonging to the United States, but not to New Hampshire, was rejected by both state and Federal governments. This caused many to wish to join Canada; bad feeling and violence resulted, with both Canada and New Hampshire trying to enforce their laws. Finally, in November, 1835, New Hampshire sent up militia. In April, 1836, the people voted to join New Hampshire and were incorporated as the town of Pittsburg in 1840. The Webster-Ashburton Treaty[w] of 1842 settled the boundary.

[G. Showerman, The Indian Stream Republic, *Collections of the New Hampshire Historical Society*, Vol. XI.]
HERBERT W. HILL

Indian Territory, so-called, originally included all of the present State of Oklahoma except the Panhandle. It was never an organized territory but was set aside as a home for the Five Civilized Tribes[w], who were removed to it in the period 1820–45. In 1866 they ceded the western half of this region to the United States as a home for other tribes. A part of this ceded area was opened to white settlement in 1899 and the following year was formed into the Territory of Oklahoma, which eventually came to include all the lands ceded in 1866. The reduced lands of the Five Civilized Tribes, then called Indian Territory, had an area about equal to that of Indiana and were occupied by more than 75,000 Indians. Lands were held in common and each tribe had its own government. In 1907 the two territories were again united and admitted to the Union as the State of Oklahoma.

[Roy Gittinger, *The Formation of the State of Oklahoma;* Thomas Donaldson, *The Public Domain.*]

EDWARD EVERETT DALE

Indian Trade and Traders. The expansion of Europe into the outside world was one of the most significant developments of the modern era, and as the movement proceeded Europeans invariably entered into trade relations with the native races. The Indian trade of North America, therefore, represents but one aspect of a larger world phenomenon. When explorers and settlers arrived in America they found vast potential wealth in furs and skins awaiting exploitation. The character and quality of the peltry available varied with topography and climate. The beaver was the most important fur-bearing animal and often the "beaver trade"[w] was referred to as synonymous with the "Indian trade" in general. There were other important varieties, however, including otter, muskrat, raccoon, mink, sable, fox, etc. In southern latitudes there were few fine furs and the trade was mainly in coarser skins and hides, as those of the deer, bear and buffalo[w].

The goods offered in exchange for peltry were of almost infinite variety. There is often an impression that they consisted only of valueless trinkets, but they were, for the most part, articles of real utility to the Indians. Hardware was an important item of trade, including axes, knives, traps, kettles, awls, needles, etc. Then there were woolen blankets, including the "strouds" of English manufacture. A well-assorted lot would contain small ornaments and trinkets in the nature of luxuries. Firearms and ammunition needed by the Indians for the hunt came to form a large part of almost every cargo. Lastly, there was usually liquor—English rum or French brandy (*see* Indian and Liquor). The North American tribes thus became a valuable market for European, and, later, American manufactures.

As the Indian was drawn into the orbit of European commerce, his domestic economy underwent a profound change and he rapidly made a transition from the stone to the iron age. His manner of living and hunting was altered and he became increasingly dependent upon the white man's goods, to so great a degree in fact that an interruption of trade might threaten want or actual starvation. Whatever may have been the relations between settlers and natives, contacts between the traders and Indians were normally friendly, as each group depended upon the other. The liquor traffic, however, constituted one great obstacle to the maintenance of peace and order. It is also true that certain venal and irresponsible traders did, upon occasion, cheat and otherwise impose upon the Indians, thereby arousing their hostility. Various government agencies were tireless in their efforts to win and preserve the friendship of the various tribes, and it was generally the custom to give them periodical presents. Since these presents usually consisted of goods similar to those used in the trade, the merchants were constantly on the alert to see that they were not bartered for furs by Indian agents of doubtful probity.

The Indian trade, like other forms of business enterprise, became more complex and highly organized as it expanded. The average person is prone to think of the "Indian trader" as a wilderness hunter or trapper, wearing buckskin shirt and raccoon cap, but actually there arose a vast commercial hierarchy whose interests were tied up with the traffic in furs. The trade was at first carried on by settlers or small merchants, but conditions soon demanded new methods and forms of organization. Trade was based largely upon the credit system, which required a considerable capital outlay. In the case of the British trade, for example, two or three years might elapse between the time when goods were shipped from London and the sale of the furs received in exchange for them, the merchants in the meanwhile having large sums invested. Complex problems of marketing and transportation called for more efficient business methods, while the evils of unrestrained competition furnished an incentive to large-scale organization based upon the principle of monopoly. Small firms and partnerships were formed at important trade centers which often gave way to large companies with monopoly characteristics. Commission houses were established at such centers as Montreal, New York, Philadelphia, Charleston and St. Louis, which supplied goods to traders and attended to the marketing of furs for their correspondents. Sometimes, as has been suggested, these commission merchants established companies which directly managed the business in all its stages, from the wilderness hut to the European market. Among the better known of the larger concerns were the North West Company with headquarters at Montreal; Baynton, Wharton and Morgan of Philadelphia; Astor's American Fur Company and the Missouri and Pacific Fur companies^{qw}. While the fur trade might be very profitable in some instances, its difficulties and hazards should not be minimized. A study of the correspondence reveals that all was not plain sailing by any means and one is impressed by the large number of business failures which occurred in almost every period.

Owing to the peculiar conditions under which it was carried on, the fur trade developed highly specialized methods. Transportation was a difficult and costly aspect of the business. Nat-

urally traders followed the waterways wherever possible, tracing out a far-flung network of communication, utilizing rivers, lakes and portages^{w}. The most important single highway to the interior was the St. Lawrence-Great Lakes system. The traders made use of canoes, bateaux and even sailing vessels, and the northern trade employed large numbers of French-Canadian *voyageurs^{qw}* or *engagés,* who performed the hard manual labor and added a colorful, romantic touch to the industry. Many of the *voyageurs* mingled their blood with that of the Indians, giving rise to a numerous half-breed population whose descendants are to be found scattered throughout the Northwest to this day. Where convenient waterways were not available, recourse was had to the more cumbersome and expensive method of transport by pack train. The life of the wilderness trader, who came into direct contact with the Indians, extending credit and watching over their annual hunts, was not without its picturesque side. The journals and diaries left by many of these persons afford a most interesting and valuable picture of a phase of frontier development. Here are to be found accounts of the long and lonely winters and of the thousand-and-one details which required the trader's attention. The appearance and habits of the Indians are described and there are vivid tales of the drunken "frolics" which almost invariably occurred when they visited the trader at his post.

As the Indian trade became more valuable, it frequently became involved in politics. Merchants and traders were decidedly conscious of their interests and often exerted an influence in local or international politics analogous to that of modern "pressure groups." British merchants, for example, protested vigorously against the boundary line which was agreed upon by the Definitive Treaty of Peace, 1783, and sought to delay the surrender of the posts upon the Great Lakes as long as possible (*see* Border Forts, Evacuation of). Again at the time of the War of 1812 they in vain sought the erection of an Indian barrier state^{w} between Canada and the United States. Commercial spheres of influence frequently became a basis for subsequent territorial claims.

A complete roster of the fur trade would include hundreds of persons, most of them obscure, but others well known to history. A few names, selected more or less at random, can do little more than suggest the great variety of types and the vast range of their operations. In the Great Lakes region we find Radisson^{w} and Groseilliers during the French period, and later, Alexander

Henry, John Long, Peter Pond, Robert Dickson, John Askin, John Jacob Astor and Ramsay Crooks. The "merchants of Montreal" included such personages as Isaac Todd, James McGill, Simon McTavish and Benjamin and Joseph Frobisher. George Croghan[w] and William Trent operated in the Ohio Valley, while the names of Pierre and Auguste Chouteau[w] are associated with the trade based upon St. Louis. A great many of them attained prominence in fields other than the fur trade. A complete and connected story of the activities of these and hundreds of others remains to be written.

[H. M. Chittenden, *The American Fur Trade of the Far West;* C. M. Gates, *Five Fur Traders of the Northwest;* H. A. Innis, *The Fur Trade in Canada;* Grace L. Nute, *The Voyageur;* W. E. Stevens, *The North-West Fur Trade, 1763-1800;* A. T. Volwiler, *George Croghan and the Westward Movement, 1741-1782.*]   WAYNE E. STEVENS

Indian Tribal Courts, THE, sometimes known as "courts of Indian offenses" are courts, consisting usually of one, two or three Indian judges, organized upon various reservations to try minor cases in which the parties are Indians. Such courts were created in the closing years of the 19th century by an order of the Office of Indian Affairs[w] to deal with civil disputes, domestic relations and minor criminal offenses that do not come under the jurisdiction of the United States courts. Authority for them, therefore, does not rest upon legislation but upon an administrative order; though Congress, by making appropriations for their support, may be said to have given them the sanction of law. Judges are appointed by the superintendent of the reservation and are usually older Indians with a reputation for honesty, fairness and wisdom. With the assistance of the superintendent they make their own rules as to procedure and evidence. Decisions must be approved by the superintendent before going into effect and are therefore subject to administrative rather than judicial review. In most cases these courts have proved to be an excellent influence upon the Indians of a reservation.

[Lewis Meriam and others, *The Problem of Indian Administration; Annual Reports of the Commissioner of Indian Affairs,* 1898-1904.]   EDWARD EVERETT DALE

Indian Village. In the period of exploration and colonization the term Indian village was used to designate a cluster of relatively permanent habitations in contrast to a temporary camp. Most Indians east of the Great Plains were hunters primarily, and agriculturists secondarily. Nevertheless, the latter practice required permanent residence near the cultivated plots for part of the season, at least, but permitted the use of temporary and movable shelters when engaged in hunting. The term village in historical writing of the 17th and 18th centuries, refers to the permanent places of habitation. A map of Connecticut, compiled from early historical records by Mathias Speiss, shows 106 Indian villages under seventeen sachemships, the number of villages under a sachem ranging from one to fifteen. This is typical of eastern United States. Regional variations in North American Indian house types were striking, as the Algonkins[w] north of Virginia and Kentucky usually used dome-shaped houses covered with bark or mats; the Iroquois-speaking tribes, long, rectangular, one-story bark-covered, multifamily houses, known as "long houses"; in the South among the Muskogee-speaking tribes the houses were circular, with vertical walls and conical roofs.

In eastern United States many villages north and south were fortified by palisades and often by moats, and were occasionally called "forts" in colonial literature. The village ground plans varied greatly, but in general the houses clustered irregularly around a kind of plaza, in which the council fire was kindled, and around which the inhabitants gathered for business and pleasure.

The Indians of the Great Plains were mobile bison hunters, using dogs as pack animals, until the European horse was introduced. Their habitations were usually spoken of as camps, sometimes composed of 200 tents, or tipis, with an average of ten persons to a tent. Such a camp was always on a war footing, well organized and disciplined. In New Mexico and Arizona, the Indian villages go under the Spanish name, pueblo[w], the most characteristic being the terraced apartment houses. In many cases the entire pueblo was housed in a single building of three to four stories with 200 to 500 rooms.

The size of villages varied greatly but in eastern United States the lower limit approximated fifty persons, the upper limit was around 500. The increased efficiency of iron tools and firearms, secured in trade, made possible larger villages than before. Each village was a separate community and though there was a chief, or head sachem, for several such villages, each was usually autonomous, jealous of its independence and freedom of action. This was true of all United States Indians from the Atlantic to the Pacific. Even the so-called Iroquois Confederacy[w] permitted a great deal of village autonomy.

[David I. Bushnell, Jr., *Native Villages and Village Sites East of the Mississippi,* Bulletin 69, Bureau of American Ethnology.]   CLARK WISSLER

Indiana. Until 1763, what is now Indiana

formed a part of the vast colonial empire of France in North America. Certain of the scattered French communities were within the limits of the present state, the most important being Vincennes^w. Few changes occurred within the British period, which nominally ended in 1783. In 1778 George Rogers Clark^w took possession of Vincennes, which was retaken by the British late in the same year, and again captured by Clark in 1779. When the Definitive Treaty of Peace in 1783^w made the Mississippi River the western boundary of the United States, the Old Northwest came under the jurisdiction of the Congress of the Confederation. In 1787, the Northwest Territory^w was organized. The famous Ordinance of 1787^w was a constitution for the government of colonies, unique in history. It contained provisions hostile to slavery, favorable to popular education and establishing religious freedom. There was also a clause providing for the equal division of intestate estates. The all-important clauses were, however, those that outlined the stages of government and guaranteed to the colonists settling in the district a large degree of self-government with statehood to be conferred within a reasonable time on a basis of equality with the states already in the Union (see State-Making Process).

In 1800 the original Northwest Territory was divided into the Northwest Territory and Indiana Territory (see Division Act of 1800). A Virginian, William Henry Harrison, was appointed to the governorship of the newly formed territory, which included about what is now Indiana, plus much of Michigan, all of Wisconsin and Illinois and part of Minnesota. Settlers came slowly, and, for some years, most of the problems related to the restless Indians of the Northwest. The American claim to the region was partly established by the exploits of Clark and greatly strengthened by Anthony Wayne's^w victories of 1794 and his Treaty of Greenville^w in 1795. In spite of the Louisiana Purchase^w and the earlier accomplishments of Clark and Wayne, the final showdown came during the War of 1812^w, after which, for the first time, the United States was in real possession of the valley of the Mississippi. (See also Tippecanoe, Battle of.) The organization of Michigan Territory in 1805 and of Illinois^qw Territory in 1809 left Indiana Territory with practically the limits of the present state, though the exact boundaries were not fixed until statehood was conferred.

Colonization began in earnest after 1813. A territorial census of 1815 showed a population of something over 60,000. Indiana, having passed through the stages of government provided in the Ordinance of 1787, was admitted to the Union in 1816. Though no longer a colony politically after Dec. 11 of that year, Indiana long remained a colony in regard to economic and social conditions. When the state government was set up under the constitution of 1816, and the one representative and two senators took their seats in Congress, the people of the new state lived along its southern edge within thirty-five miles of the Ohio, along the line of the State of Ohio, and along the Wabash as far north as Terre Haute. The task of colonizing the greater part of Indiana was yet to take place.

Between 1816 and 1850 the state made rapid progress. Lands were reduced to private ownership, farms were created, towns and trade appeared, counties were marked off from year to year, missionaries and itinerant schoolmasters came from the East, lawyers and preachers rode the circuits^w—in short the new state grew in population and wealth while the institutions of a civilized people were established. The population, by the census of 1820, was 147,178; by that of 1850, it was 988,416. The latter census, the first to include nativity figures, reveals that Indiana was colonized mainly by people from Virginia, North Carolina, Kentucky, Pennsylvania and Ohio. Other states and foreign countries contributed settlers, but in far smaller numbers. The total number of persons born in the three slaveholding states mentioned, who lived in Indiana in 1850, was 146,645. Those from Pennsylvania and Ohio totaled 164,438 men, women and children. All the other persons born outside of Indiana, including foreign-born who were living in the state in 1850, numbered 139,254.

In the reapportionment of representatives by Congress, following the census of 1850, Indiana was given eleven members of the lower House, the same number as Massachusetts and more than Kentucky or Tennessee. Only New York, Pennsylvania, Virginia and Ohio stood higher than Indiana in the number of representatives in the national House, or in the number of electoral votes. A second state constitution was made and ratified in 1850-51.

Between 1850 and 1860 Indiana rose from third to first place, among the states of the nation, in the production of hogs, and from sixth to second place in the production of wheat. From the War of 1812 to about 1850, pork products were the mainstay of Indiana prosperity, and furnished the economic base on which to build a civilization. Wheat became really important after the Lakes-canal line (see Indiana State Canals) and railroads connected the Northwest with the East. Since hog production tied

Indiana to the South by the river trade, and wheat caused a connection with the East, the rise of a kingdom of wheat in the Old Northwest had much to do with the parts played by Indiana and other states of this new area in the Civil War.

Because of the slow growth of industrialism in Indiana, the state has not been able to hold the high rank in population and political power to which it rose before the Civil War. Much of the time since 1865, it has, however, been a doubtful state, which has added greatly to its political importance in close presidential contests. Without the aggravated problems of a highly industrial state and yet not an agrarian commonwealth, Indiana has moved quite contentedly along a medial line. The general mellow quality of the Hoosier[w] social atmosphere has undoubtedly led to the rather large output of literature by Indiana authors and determined its character to a great extent.

[Logan Esarey, *A History of Indiana;* Charles Roll, *Indiana: One Hundered Fifty Years of American Development.*]
WILLIAM O. LYNCH

Indiana Company, THE, had its origin in a group of Indian traders and their merchant backers who lost goods at the hands of the Indians on the outbreak of Pontiac's War[w] in 1763. As compensation for these losses, the chiefs of the Six Nations, at the Treaty of Fort Stanwix[w] in 1768, presented the traders with a tract of land between the southern boundary of Pennsylvania and the Little Kanawha River. The "Indiana" proprietors sent Samuel Wharton and William Trent to England to get a royal confirmation of their title, but their claim was swallowed up in the project for the Grand Ohio Company[w]. On the outbreak of the Revolution, in 1776, the Indiana Company was reorganized, and proceeded to sell land; but its operations were blocked by Virginia, which claimed that this land lay within Virginia. The Virginia state constitution included a provision requiring legislative approval of purchases from the Indians, and on appeal by the company, the legislature refused to approve of the Indiana grant. The Indiana Company appealed to the Continental Congress[w], where the Committee on Western Lands approved the Indiana claim. But Virginia denied the jurisdiction of the Congress over Western lands, and when Congress accepted a compromise Virginia cession in 1784, Indiana was not included. New Jersey took up the claim and appealed to Congress under Article IX of the Articles of Confederation[w], but to no avail. After the Constitution became effective in 1789 the

Indiana Company brought suit against Virginia in the United States Supreme Court (Grayson v. Virginia), but the case was delayed pending the adoption of the Eleventh Amendment[w] to the Constitution, after which it was dismissed on the ground that the Court had no jurisdiction.

[Max Savelle, *George Morgan, Colony Builder;* T. P. Abernethy, *Western Lands and the American Revolution.*]
MAX SAVELLE

Indiana Plan, THE, provides a considerable measure of state control over local records, taxation and debts. In 1909 the Indiana legislature authorized uniform accounting practices and records for public offices and provided for state inspection. As a result more than six million dollars has been (1939) directly recovered. In 1919 the legislature made a beginning in extending state control to local tax levies, but it was not until 1921 that it enacted the basic law which permits any ten taxpayers affected by a proposed local tax or debt to petition the state board of tax commissioners for final review. Under this law the state tax board has rejected one third of the bond issues appealed—a saving of $35,742,985 to 1938. Annual tax cuts approximating one and one half million dollars were effected until 1932. Modifications in 1932 and 1937 established maximum local tax rates of $1.25 in rural districts and $2 in cities, exclusive of debt and welfare charges, and provided compulsory review by county boards of tax adjustment. Excess rates go automatically from county boards to the state board of tax commissioners which may increase to original levels as set by appropriating authorities, decrease, or approve. Since 1932 there has been an average annual cut exceeding half a million dollars. Despite some criticism other states have exhibited interest in the plan.

[*Yearbooks* of the State of Indiana; *Reports* of the Indiana Taxpayers Association.]
HAROLD ZINK

Indiana State Canals, THE, were one of the results of the mania for state-promoted internal improvements[w] which swept the Middle West in the first third of the 19th century. The Wabash and Erie Canal[w], to connect Lake Erie and the Ohio River through Indiana, was that state's first project, begun in 1832. In 1836 a great internal improvement bill was made law, carrying total appropriations of $13,000,000—one sixth of the state's wealth at that time. It provided for the building of a canal along the Whitewater River northward from the Ohio, another, the Central Canal, from the Wabash west of Fort Wayne via Indianapolis and White River to

Evansville; a railroad from Madison through Indianapolis to Lafayette; and some turnpikes. The Panic of 1837^{qv} greatly disturbed the plans; also there were gross incompetence, mismanagement and fraud in the state commission's operations. By 1840 the state was well-nigh bankrupt. The short completed portions of the Central Canal were sold to private interests for $2425. Before the Wabash and Erie reached the Ohio River in 1853, railroads^{qv} were destroying its reason for being. The Whitewater Canal, taken over by a private corporation in 1846, was dead before 1870. Financial failures though they were, the canals played a large part in the development of Indiana and the Middle West.

[Logan Esarey, *Internal Improvements in Early Indiana.*]

ALVIN F. HARLOW

Indies, Company of the. *See* "Mississippi Bubble."

Indigo Culture was introduced into South Carolina at the inception of that colony, but it was not until 1744 that Eliza Lucas, a youthful planter of St. Andrews Parish, demonstrated that its production was practical with slave labor. Neighboring planters promptly adopted her idea as a supplement to the cultivation of rice^{qv}. Stability was given to the industry by the granting, in 1748, by the British government of a bounty of sixpence a pound on indigo shipped to England, and by the coming to South Carolina in 1756 of Moses Lindo, an experienced indigo-sorter. For some thirty years indigo, after rice, was the colony's most important crop; on the eve of the American Revolution more than a million pounds were exported annually. But in the closing decades of the 18th century the production declined rapidly. The causes were the withdrawal of the bounty; the tedium and unhealthfulness of indigo-curing; and the development of cotton^{qv}. The dyestuff, however, continued to be cultivated in South Carolina, mostly in Orangeburg District, for local consumption until the end of the Civil War.

[D. D. Wallace, *The History of South Carolina.*]

FRANCIS B. SIMKINS

Industrial Brotherhood, THE, organized in 1868, was at first a purely fraternal order. At the 1874 convention of the Industrial Congress called by the trade unions, the Brotherhood agreed to fuse its organization with the Congress and contribute its name and ritual. Other organizations at the convention were the Patrons of Husbandry and Sovereigns of Industry^{qqv}. The Brotherhood wrote the preamble to the platform, stating fully the demands of labor which were later modified

by the Knights of Labor^{qv} in 1878. An attempt was made to organize the Brotherhood by states, but the depression of the 1870's caused loss of strength and eventual absorption in other labor organizations.

[J. R. Commons and others, *History of Labor in the United States.*]

CARL L. CANNON

Industrial Education may be defined as training toward skills and particular operations of industry, as distinguished from engineering education, which relates to the professional preparation for design and management.

In the handicraft stage of industry, all training was by means of the apprentice^{qv} system, which persisted to a degree through the 19th century, undergoing modifications to suit mechanical advances and gradually fading as a system. The introduction of mechanized industry early in the 20th century, with specialized jobs which can be learned in a few minutes or hours, leading to mass production^{qv}, gave the finishing blow to apprenticeships as industrial training.

That the apprenticeship system should be supplemented by schools became apparent early in the 19th century. The Gardiner, Maine, Lyceum (1822) was established with a two-year course for farmers and mechanics (survived ten years), followed by Rensselaer School (1824) and the Franklin Institute for the Promotion of Mechanic Arts (1824). In New York a school for the children of mechanics was established (1820) by the General Society of Mechanics and Tradesmen, and in Boston a Mechanics Institute was founded (1827) and a similar one in Baltimore (1825). These were modeled after the Mechanics Institution of Glasgow, founded a few years earlier. Some of the institutes which were originally of secondary or post-secondary grade have later advanced to collegiate level wholly or in part. Among these may be mentioned Polytechnic Institute of Brooklyn (1855), Cooper Union (1859), Worcester Polytechnic (1868) and Drexel Institute (1891). The Ohio Mechanics Institute of Cincinnati and the Rochester Athenæum and Mechanics Institute have held steadfast to their original purpose. Numerous schools in special industries such as textile, mining, electrical appliances, telegraphy, radio and auto-mechanics have been conducted as proprietary enterprises to meet special needs. The Y. M. C. A. in larger cities for the quarter century preceding the World War conducted evening schools in technological subjects. In addition, correspondence schools, which prepared textbooks designed for self study, contributed considerably to industrial education in this same period. The chief of these were the International at Scranton and the American at Chicago. Many of the state colleges with well-developed standards have continued also a program of industrial education by extension and short courses. Some of the state colleges of mechanic arts have retained the subcollegiate objectives of industrial training as their program.

With the advent of mechanized industry and mass production in the first decades of the 20th century, many of the old-line trades became obsolete and the function of specialized training was assumed largely by the separate industries, with the result that most independent industrial schools shifted character, either to assume secondary-school, quasi-college or full-college status.

Some of the larger industries have set up within their own works industrial schools suited to their needs, as, for example, the Westinghouse Evening School, New Bedford Textile School, General Motors Institute and American Institute of Laundering.

Labor organizations have attempted to establish certain "labor colleges," notably at Katonah, N. Y., and Mena, Ark., to give attention to the factor of organized labor in industry. They have not succeeded owing apparently to a lack of resources and the absence of curricular material separable from general education and suitable for their restricted purposes.

The graduates of technical institutes have generally been prepared to enter into the routine duties connected with production, their advance depending upon their abilities and training. Their early experience has been in competition with workers who lacked special education. At the same time, graduates from recognized engineering schools have frequently begun their industrial experience at this same level. The result is that sharp lines of demarcation frequently do not exist between the beginning work of graduates of technical institutes and those from standard colleges of engineering. The field of industrial education is at present a fertile area for future developments. In general, manufacturing industries require engineering[q] personnel to the extent of 2% to 3% of the forces, and operational supervision of an intermediate grade equal to 6% to 8% of the total. Engineering schools provide the former and instruction on the job provides most of the training of workmen in mechanized industries. Agencies for industrial education as herein defined for the intermediate grade are inadequately developed at the present (1939) time.

[*A Study of Technical Institutes*, by The Society for the Promotion of Engineering Education, 1931.]

CLEMENT C. WILLIAMS

Industrial Farms. Twentieth-century penology has made an increasing use of industrial or correctional farms. Antecedents of this system appeared nearly a century ago when several juvenile reform schools[q] moved onto spacious farms and developed the cottage system. Most of the adult reformatories were located on farm sites but soon faced the necessity of erecting large cell blocks and surrounding them with high walls. In the lower South several states followed the lead of Texas in 1888 and acquired large penal plantations, but they continued to rely on dogs and armed guards for the restraint of their prisoners. The Massachusetts State Farm, opened at Bridgewater in 1893, was a more direct antecedent, as were the farm annexes acquired by several of the overcrowded prisons[q] of the North after the turn of the century. When, after 1910, several city penitentiaries moved onto outlying farms, characteristic industrial farms were developed.

With the modern discovery that most criminals do not require maximum-security treatment, several states have developed minimum-security industrial farms, such as Leesburg, established by New Jersey in 1914. The Federal Government has developed several of these institutions within the last decade to care for its less vicious offenders.

[B. F. McKelvey, *American Prisons.*]

BLAKE McKELVEY

Industrial Management, the art and science of getting work done in industry, has been known as industrial engineering, scientific management and modern factory management.

Frederick W. Taylor (1856–1915), who has been called the "father of industrial management," began his experimentation at the Midvale Steel Company in Philadelphia. He explained his principles and methods in 1903 in a paper presented to the American Society of Mechanical Engineers. This was followed by other papers, articles and addresses, forming a body of literature now regarded as classic in its field. Taylor condensed his teachings into four principles, or items, in a program of industrial operation: (1) the development of a true science; (2) scientific selection of workmen; (3) scientific education and development of workmen; (4) intimate, friendly co-operation between management and men.

Henry L. Gantt (1861–1919), who had been associated with Taylor, founded a consulting practice in industrial management in 1901. His greatest contribution to the science is the humanizing influence. His "task and bonus" plan of paying wages is widely used, and his "Gantt Chart" is the best known of all management devices. During the World War Gantt's principles were applied to the production of munitions, and the building and operation of ships. Another pioneer in the field, Frank B. Gilbreth (1868–1924), developed a technique for studying motions in doing work.

There has been a steady growth of the methods and practice of industrial management with a corresponding growth of the literature of the movement, and an increase in the productivity of the American industrial worker. Together with the growing mechanization of industry, it has brought to America an unsurpassed volume of goods and services produced at an unequaled low cost in terms of human effort.

[F. W. Taylor, *Shop Management;* F. B. Copley, *Frederick W. Taylor;* L. P. Alford, *Henry Lawrence Gantt.*]

L. P. ALFORD

Industrial Relations, as the term is commonly understood in the United States, is concerned primarily with the position of the worker in relation to his employer and includes whatever is involved in the employee's selection for and relation to his job.

The beginnings of distinctive industrial relations work are found in the "welfare" activities undertaken by many employers in New England textile industries early in the 19th century. Work of this nature in behalf of employees grew in popularity for about 100 years, reached its peak approximately at the period of the World War and thereafter declined except as to those features which have survived as an essential part of good management.

The term industrial relations, as distinguished from welfare work, has grown to include all contacts between labor and all grades of management, connected with or growing out of employment. Specifically it covers items usually classified as personnel work, such as recruiting, hiring, placement, transfer, training, discipline, promotion, layoff and termination of employees, together with proper service records; also all of the financial relationships such as wages and salaries, overtime rates, bonuses and profit sharing, savings and thrift and stock plans; also education, health, safety and sanitation, recreation, housing and employees' service activities; hours of labor and other working conditions, including days of rest and vacations; reasonable provision to help meet the common economic hazards involved in temporary or total unemployment, sickness, accident, old age, disability and death; also methods used to adjust differences and to promote co-

operation between employees and management.

Most of the features in this program have been initiated by employers. Many of them, however—notably hours, wages and determining conditions under which the employee works—have been developed or influenced by collective bargaining between the employer and a labor union or other representatives of the employees.

Many of these items have been gradually covered by state and Federal legislation, starting with sanitation, accident compensation and safety measures, later dealing with child labor, hours and minimum wages especially for women and minors and more recently extended to include Federal legislation on hours and wages.

American industry, with some outstanding exceptions, has been distinctive in that it has assumed and emphasized unity of interest on the part of stockholders, management and employees, with the result that class conflict has been minimized and many broad programs of industrial relations voluntarily established. An outstanding benefit has been that, on the whole, workers—both skilled and unskilled—have not only worked under favorable conditions but shared in periods of prosperity and thus attained a higher standard of living than has been reached by similar groups in any other country.

Personnel work, which was at first a mere incident in the day's work of the foreman or superintendent, has gradually been broadened into an industrial relations program with increasing emphasis on standardization. The responsibility for developing a uniform company policy and practice as to all industrial relations activities in the individual company is increasingly being placed in the hands of an industrial relations executive, responsible to some high official of the company and having a staff relation to those directly responsible for both employee relations and production.

[E. S. Cowdrick, *Manpower in Industry;* Tead and Metcalf, *Personnel Administration;* Pamphlets of American Management Association: (a) Thomas Spates, (b) W. A. Lange.]

CLARENCE J. HICKS

Industrial Research embraces the scientific discovery and development of new materials and processes, and of new uses of products, for the improvement of manufactures. It also promotes the betterment of production and merchandising practices. Its highest purpose is the creation of new industries. Its procedures are chiefly based on chemistry, physics, biology and economics.

In the early colonial period, Emanuel Downing and his nephew, John Winthrop, Jr., conducted experiments in the preparation of indigo[w]. Later, in 1662, Winthrop read a paper on making tar before the Royal Society of London. Subsequently came efforts to encourage scientific investigations on behalf of needed American industries, by the American Philosophical Society[w] (1789), by President Washington (1790), by the Chemical Society of Philadelphia (1792–1801) and by the American Mineralogical Society (1799). Since then American scientists have in greater or less degree engaged in investigations of problems of manufacturing.

It was not until the 1920's, however, that industrial research attained a high position. Previously industrialists had sought for improvement principally through practical experience, but they are now tending more and more toward scientific aid. Our natural resources have required increased scientific attention for their efficient utilization, and the alluring but exacting markets afforded by our large population have called for scientific care in both manufacturing and merchandising. Our scientists were first stirred to apply research methods to industrial purposes by observing the progress of industrial research abroad, chiefly in Germany. A further impetus was given, about 1910, when Robert Kennedy Duncan started his industrial fellowship system, which soon led to productive effort at Mellon Institute of Industrial Research in Pittsburgh (founded 1913). Later the chemical, physical and engineering societies, and the National Research Council[w] fostered research. The necessity for cheap and quick manufacture of new products during the World War brought home to industrialists the necessity of scientific methods, and in consequence industrial research was given an opportunity that led to successful work and established many scientists in posts of importance.

At least 2000 American manufacturing companies now realize that scientific research is essential for their welfare. Particularly active in this respect are the automotive, ceramic, fine chemical, dye, electrical equipment, food, fuel, metallurgical, paint, paper, petroleum, plastic, rubber, soap and textile industries. A number of trade associations conduct co-operative research. Many educational institutions, various government laboratories and numerous consulting laboratories constantly carry on researches of industrial interest. In 1938 about $180,000,000 was spent by American concerns in sustaining industrial research in their own and other laboratories.

[Edward R. Weidlein and William A. Hamor, *Science in Action*, and *Glances at Industrial Research*.]

WILLIAM A. HAMOR

Industrial Revolution, The, in the United States had many points in common with the similar movement in England but was colored in important respects by conditions which were peculiar to this country. For one thing our abundant and varied resources directed attention both to types of invention and to routes of industrial development which were not possible across the water. Then again, since the progress of the revolution was contemporary with the opening of the greater part of this country America was spared many of the hardships which attended the shift from the old order to the new in England.

In some respects our revolution was only a counterpart of what was going on abroad. In many cases inventors worked along similar lines; ideas which were generated in one country were developed in the other; and all in all there was much unconscious exchange of ideas among discoverers and business men in England and the United States. Thus, in the standard industries such as textiles, iron and steel, and transportation[qw], the revolution developed much the same direction in both countries.

James Watt is credited with laying the foundation for the industrial revolution with the invention of a satisfactory steam engine. But, as a matter of fact, Watt was only one expression of the spirit of mechanical discovery which had its origin at least a century before, and which may have dated back to Leonardo da Vinci (1452–1519) and to the discoverers who followed in his train. Leonardo is said to have been the founder of modern mechanical engineering. He was the embodiment of the modern scientific spirit. Nevertheless, Watt's steam engine was the key invention which made possible the commercialization of all the other discoveries which followed. The significant feature was that it was a new source of power.

The so-called industrial revolution was in fact a series of revolutions each with a phase peculiar to itself, each in turn unsettling established industrial and social relations, and each making necessary industrial readjustments of great magnitude. First came the introduction of steam power which manifolded many times the work which could be done by human muscles. An experimental steam engine was set up by Christopher Colles in Philadelphia in 1773. Within twenty-five years this power was in general use in the plants along the Atlantic seaboard. In 1794 a steam engine was in use at Pittsburgh, and its employment spread rapidly not only in the factories of the interior, but in the milling of grain and in the manufacture of lumber.

Meanwhile, the textiles received their share

of inventions. Beginning shortly after the close of the War of 1812 a craze for internal improvements*w* spread over the country, including demand for canals, turnpikes and railroads*qw*. The first steamboat*w* was introduced on the Hudson in 1807, on the Ohio-Mississippi system in 1811–12 and on the Great Lakes in 1819. The Erie Canal*w* was completed in 1825, opening for development one of the greatest present commercial areas. Railroad building started in 1828 with the Baltimore and Ohio*w*, and proceeded rapidly. By 1860 the operated mileage was 30,600; it was 254,800 in 1937. With respect to ocean navigation, the construction of the *Great Western* in 1837, built expressly for regular voyages between Europe and the United States, marked a new era in ocean transportation (*see* Shipbuilding). These developments were keys which unlocked the latent possibilities of growth in industrial revolution. They widened markets, made possible mass production*w*, enhanced the opportunities for large-scale manufacture and sale, with all the economies which flow from such an industrial organization.

American farming was also a beneficiary of many improvements, with plows, harrows, reapers and threshers. At the Paris Exposition of 1855 Pitt's American thresher outdistanced all others by threshing in an hour 740 liters of wheat as compared with thirty-six liters by six men with a flail. Shortly before 1860 steam power was employed to drive the thresher*w* with the attendant increase in productivity. These inventions were of great importance in the United States with its vast potential grain area.

In America a new and greater revolution set in about the time of the Civil War, characterized by the introduction of many new inventions and by the exploitation of hitherto unused resources. Among others were the development of petroleum, aluminum, steel (Bessemer and open-hearth), the introduction of the automobile and of hoisting machinery—which revolutionized city construction and paved the way for great urban concentration of population. The great line of electrical inventions belongs to this period. Every decade from 1860 to 1900 witnessed some important new use of electricity—telegraph, telephone, electric trolley and generating plants. These created enormous demands for copper, lead and zinc, all of which entered a new phase of development.

Meanwhile, portentous changes occurred both in the external and internal forms of American business organization. Trustification went on at a rapid pace; the size of American business expanded greatly; markets became national; banking developed in various specialized fields—notably in the commercial and investment aspects. The expansion of population from about 31,000,000 in 1860 to more than 122,000,000 in 1930 supplied both new labor force and new markets to consume goods. New social problems came to the fore—a condition which affected to a marked extent the course of legislative development and the direction of Federal, state and local spending. An epitome of these developments is shown in the fortyfold expansion of capital invested in manufactures in the years from 1859 to 1919 and in the thirty-fivefold expansion in the value of manufactures from 1859 to 1929, being about $70,000,000,000 at the latter date.

A new phase of industrial revolution began about 1900. The year 1898 is said to mark the beginning of "American invasion" of foreign markets. In prior periods raw materials and partly fabricated stuffs had been our leading exports. In this new era manufactured goods forged ahead, with many kinds of machinery and a wide line of "American specialties" entering all the markets of the world. The chemical and metallurgical industries advanced to the center of the stage. Industrial research*w* became the watchword of the day, with statistics and accounting as ancillary aids in directing the course of business. Rarer base metals which had little or no industrial use twenty years before became of great importance in many manufactures—tungsten, molybdenum, vanadium and nickel being the ranking alloy metals. Among the rare gases neon and helium entered industrial uses. And the rare metals of the platinum group found increasing employment. Plastics, tank agriculture, television, mechanical cotton pickers excited popular curiosity, as was the case with moving pictures, radio and airplanes not much more than two decades ago. The present acceleration of the advance promises to carry us forward with such speed that some persons propose to plan the introduction of new industries in order to prevent what they claim will be disaster if new developments are permitted to take their course undirected.

[Isaac Lippincott, *The Economic Development of the United States.*]
ISAAC LIPPINCOTT

Industrial Workers of the World is a revolutionary industrial union organized in 1905 as a protest against craft unionism and the conservative policies of the American Federation of Labor*w*. The organization split in 1908 on the issue of political action. There emerged the Chicago I. W. W., the anarcho-syndicalist wing, which sponsored industrial unionism and opposed political activity; and the Detroit I. W. W., the socialist wing, which advocated political action in the class struggle[w]. The latter group in 1915 became the Workers International Industrial Union, which was dissolved in 1925.

The I. W. W. appeals to all workers, identifies immediate industrial strife with the ultimate revolutionary destruction of capitalism, spurns collective bargaining, and favors direct action in the form of strikes and sabotage[qw]. The militant nature of its program has resulted in considerable prosecution and severe repression under the antisyndicalist laws[w] of several states. Leaders and the rank and file have been sentenced to long terms of imprisonment.

Even at its peak in 1912, the organization did not have more than 100,000 members, and today probably has less than 10,000. Prosecution by public authorities, internal dissension, difficulties in unionizing the unskilled, lack of financial strength and loss of membership to the Committee on Industrial Organization and the Communist party[qw] have been the principal factors in its decline. (*See also* Western Federation of Miners.)

[P. F. Brissenden, *History of the I. W. W.: A Study of American Syndicalism;* J. G. Brooks, *American Syndicalism: The I. W. W.;* J. S. Gambs, *Decline of the I. W. W.*]
GORDON S. WATKINS

Industries, Colonial. During the colonial period most people engaged in agriculture, which was greatly diversified in the North, while tobacco[w] was of extreme importance in the South. However, from the earliest days of settlement many other industries developed. It was natural that the vast virgin forests should be exploited. Naval stores[w], including tar, pitch, rosin and turpentine, the products of pine forests, as well as masts and spars were exported to the mother country from all sections of the seaboard, especially from the Southern colonies. In addition to naval stores, quantities of planks, boards, shingles, barrel staves, and even house frames were produced at sawmills, and much exported to the West Indies and elsewhere. Among forest industries, the production of potash and pearl ash must be included. Mainly incidental to the clearing of land, being made from wood ashes, these two products were in demand, especially in England, for bleaching and soap making.

Shipbuilding[w] was an industry of primary importance. Wooden vessels varying from a few tons to several hundred tons were built for the fisheries, the coasting trade, the West Indies[qw], Great Britain and foreign countries. Boston, Salem, New Haven, Portsmouth and Philadelphia became shipbuilding centers. Shipbuilding created or stimulated many other industries. Among these were the making of sails, rope, nails, spikes, anchors and chain-plates, as well as calking and painting.

The coastal fisheries were carried on in all colonies, but in New England fishing for cod, mackerel[qw], bass, herring, halibut, hake, sturgeon and other deep-sea fish at the "banks" developed into a leading industry. Allied to the fishing industry and often considered a part of it was whaling[w]. By the close of the 17th century, Plymouth, Salem, Nantucket and villages on the eastern end of Long Island were doing a profitable business in supplying the demand for spermaceti, sperm oil, whalebone and ambergris. After the opening of the 18th century, whaling expanded to a remarkable extent, whalers often pursuing their prey to Arctic waters. Before the colonial period ended, several hundred vessels were engaged in this perilous industry.

The fur trade[w] was also important from the beginning of settlement. The abundance of fur-bearing animals provided opportunities for engaging in trapping, frequently as a supplemental occupation to farming. The trade in furs, large quantities of which were secured from the Indians, provided a valuable source of income. Significant in its industrial and commercial aspects, the fur trade was also of much importance in pointing the way to the West as trapper and trader pressed after the retreating fur-bearing animals. Like the fisheries, the fur trade was an important factor in colonial rivalries, especially between England and France, and was partly responsible for many of the intercolonial struggles.

The production of textiles[w] was largely a household industry. Imported textiles were expensive and therefore almost every home had its spinning wheel and hand loom to produce rough serges and linsey-woolseys[w]. Textiles were made chiefly from wool and flax, cotton being used to a much lesser extent. Before the Revolution a few shops were established in New England and in other places where several looms were brought together under one roof, thus faintly envisioning the coming factory system. Among the long list of home manufactures in addition to textiles were furniture, tools, implements, wagons, harnesses and nails. Meal, hominy, maple sugar, dried fruits, candles, lye and soap were also produced on the farms.

Ironmaking[w] was an industry which reached relatively large proportions. The basic mining and smelting processes were generally conducted on plantations or large estates where fuel for the ironworks and food for the workers could be obtained. From the bar iron produced, blacksmiths and other artisans, scattered in villages, towns and cities, fashioned tools, implements and other forms of ironmongery. Among other industrial enterprises—all conducted of course on a small scale—were tanneries and leatherworking establishments, fulling mills, grist mills, powder mills, salt works, paper mills, printing shops, glass works, brick kilns, firearms shops, copper shops, breweries and distilleries. In connection with the last-mentioned industry, the distillation of rum[w] in New England was important and lucrative.

[V. S. Clark, *History of Manufactures in the United States, 1607-1860;* R. M. Tryon, *Household Manufactures in the United States, 1640-1860.*]   ARTHUR C. BINING

Industry. *See* Manufacturing.

Industry, Fort, at the mouth of the Maumee River (now Toledo), was the scene of an important Indian treaty (July 4, 1805) whereby the leading tribes of the Ohio-Indiana-Michigan area ceded to the United States 2,726,812 acres, comprising that part of the Western Reserve[w] lying west of the Cuyahoga River and a section immediately south of this extending to the Greenville Treaty[w] line.

[C. E. Sherman, Original Ohio Land Subdivisions, *Ohio Co-operative Topographic Survey,* Vol. III.]
EUGENE H. ROSEBOOM

Inequality, The Philosophy of, has always been as deeply ingrained in Americans as that of equality. Both were embraced in the system of Jeffersonian Democracy[w]. Americans have believed in equality before the law, and, as far as possible, of opportunity, but almost more deeply in the inborn right to inequality of rewards due to individual effort and ability. In America, the French "liberty, fraternity and equality" has become "liberty, fraternity and the devil catch the hindmost." Life for Americans has always been a race against time and fortune, and they would not easily comprehend or accept a system in which they would all go at the same pace and reach the same goal at the same moment. This fundamental American philosophy is utterly opposed to the 'isms which preach the same level for all. The urge to make the most of ourselves and to get awards varying with our success has motivated practically all Americans, native and immigrant. It is the authentic American philosophy of our whole past. It has, in fact, been perhaps more influential than the doctrine of equality[w].

JAMES TRUSLOW ADAMS

Inflation. There is no generally accepted definition of inflation, but, from the standpoint of the public, inflation means rapidly rising prices of commodities and services. Such a price rise is caused by an increase in the quantity of money which is not paralleled by a corresponding increase in the quantity of goods and services coming on the market. The increased money demand for goods, without a corresponding increase in the amount of goods offered for sale, causes prices to rise and constitutes inflation.

The evils of inflation arise from the fact that prices of goods rise more rapidly than the great majority of incomes. Bondholders and other recipients of fixed money incomes suffer most since the amount of money received remains stable while the prices of various commodities are rising rapidly. Salaries and professional fees increase but slowly, and recipients of such incomes also suffer severely. Wages rise more rapidly than salaries in a period of inflation, but still do not keep pace with the rise in commodity prices[w], so that the real income of laborers is reduced, although not to the same extent as that of salaried workers or fixed-income recipients.

Debtors tend to profit from inflation since they can repay their debts in a fixed number of dollars although the dollars are worth less and less in terms of goods as the inflation progresses. However, experience shows that debtors tend to contract new debts as the inflation proceeds and, when the deflation comes, are usually in a precarious position.

Prior to the Revolution, inflation occurred in many of the colonies where bills were issued by the government and made legal tender (*see* Bills of Credit). The issue of such bills was prohibited by Parliament by acts passed in 1751 and 1764.

With the outbreak of the Revolutionary War, emission of bills of credit on a large scale by both the states and the Continental Congress[w] occurred. From 1775 to 1779 inclusive, the latter body authorized the issuance of $241,552,780 in such bills, and the various states issued an additional $209,524,776 of bills during the same period. As there was no corresponding increase in goods and services, the purchasing power of these bills decreased rapidly. By January, 1781, this currency was valued at 100 to 1 in relation to specie and by May had lost its value almost completely (*see* Currency, Continental). The Continental Congress and the various states attempted to fix prices by law, but without success.

Following the collapse of the Continental currency and the establishment of the Union, prices remained moderate until the War of 1812 when another inflation occurred. This inflation, however, was the result of the overissuance of bank notes instead of the issuance of bills by the Government. The peak of prices was reached in 1814–15 and thereafter the price level receded sharply until 1821, after which a fairly long period of relatively stable prices ensued.

The next major inflation in the United States occurred at the time of the Civl War. In order to help finance the war (*see* Civil War, Financing Problems of the, Federal), Congress authorized three issues of greenbacks*ᵂ* of $150,000,000 each. The currency was thus inflated and prices rose rapidly, reaching a peak in 1864–65 (*see* Money, Purchasing Power of). At the same time, an even more intense inflation was occurring in the Confederacy (*see* Inflation in the Confederacy). The price level dropped rapidly after 1865 until 1880.

Following the resumption of specie payments by the Government on Jan. 1, 1879, no major inflation occurred in the United States until the outbreak of the World War in 1914. Prices shortly began to rise rapidly and continued to mount after the United States entered the War in 1917. The peak was not reached until the spring of 1920 when the wholesale price index stood at 244% of the prewar level. People with fixed incomes and those receiving salaries and fees more or less fixed by custom suffered severely from the great increase in the cost of living.

The inflation during and following the World War differed from that of the Civil War period in that it was caused by an overexpansion of check currency and bank notes*ᵠᵂ* rather than by the issuance of fiat money by the Government. The Government sold bonds to the people (*see* Liberty Loans), the people borrowed at the banks in order to buy the bonds and the banks created check currency in granting such loans. Thus monetary purchasing power was expanded much more rapidly than production and prices rose accordingly.

The period from 1922 to 1929 was one of comparatively stable prices. It appeared to many economists, however, that prices should have fallen because of the vast increase in the production of goods, and that some inflation therefore existed. In any event, there was no doubt that a severe inflation of stock prices occurred between 1924 and 1929 (*see* Panic of 1929).

From the autumn of 1929 to the spring of 1933 a severe deflation occurred and the F. D. Roosevelt administration shortly decided on what was popularly termed a policy of reflation; *i.e.*, the raising of prices of commodities to the predepression level. Actually, through the sale of government obligations to the banks, a large expansion of the check currency took place. Business, however, did not respond to the increase in monetary purchasing power for a number of reasons and, at the present time (autumn of 1939), the commodity price level remains below that of the predepression period.

Nevertheless, the huge amount of monetary purchasing power thus created plus excessive bank reserves constitutes a dangerous situation which will eventually, in all probability, lead to another inflation of no mean proportions in this country.

Of the periods of inflation in the United States only those of the Continental and Confederate currencies were comparable to the extreme inflations which took place in a number of European countries following the World War, while our own postwar inflation, although severe, was less than in any of the other belligerent countries.

[D. R. Dewey, *Financial History of the United States;* G. F. Warren and F. A. Pearson, *Gold and Prices;* H. White, *Money and Banking.*]

FREDERICK A. BRADFORD

Inflation in the Confederacy began with an issue of $20,000,000 of non-interest-bearing Treasury notes, authorized on May 16, 1861, by the Confederate Congress*ᵂ*. The issuance of Treasury notes was increased throughout the remainder of the year, there being $105,000,000 of such notes outstanding at the end of 1861.

Taxation was not resorted to on any great scale and, much of the time, Confederate bonds found but a meager market. Consequently, government expenses were met in large measure by the issuance of ever-increasing amounts of Treasury notes. By the end of 1862, Treasury notes outstanding plus issues by the various Southern states totaled $500,000,000 and were worth only one third that amount in gold. A year later this amount had increased to more than $700,000,000 and gold was quoted in paper notes at 20 for 1. By the end of 1864 the amount of currency had risen to $1,000,000,000 and the gold quotation was 40 for 1 before that year-end.

The Confederacy tried various plans of compulsory refunding of Treasury notes, issuing new notes to supplant old ones, and such devices, but without success. The currency was in great confusion and the situation was complicated by state and city, as well as private, issues of notes. Large quantities of notes were also issued by the banks who had been freed from the compulsion to redeem notes in specie early in the war.

Under such circumstances, the currency was bound to collapse sooner or later. As a matter of fact, the collapse came with the loss of the war, but it would have occurred shortly in any event. The inflation in the Confederacy was thus much more severe than in the North, ending as it did in a complete loss of value of Confederate issues.

[H. White, *Money and Banking*.]

FREDERICK A. BRADFORD

Influenza. The colonists had not long been settled in the New World before they were confronted by the familiar diseases of the Old World. The first catarrh in American annals was the influenza which descended upon New England (1647). Indians, English, French and Dutch were attacked. John Winthrop, governor of the colony, described the epidemic in his *Journal,* and mourned his wife as one of its victims. In less than a decade, influenza again swept through Massachusetts and Connecticut. Since that time, America has harbored influenza in its endemic, epidemic and pandemic aspects. After the Revolution, an outbreak of influenza (1789–91) was vividly described by both Benjamin Rush and John Warren. "Buying and selling," wrote Rush, "were rendered tedious by the coughing of the farmer and the citizen who met in market places. It even rendered divine service scarcely intelligible in the churches."

All previous visitations of influenza were dwarfed by the world pandemic (1918) which in less than four months destroyed more human lives than had been lost in the four years of the World War. Repeating history, this pandemic entered America through the port of Boston. Although the world was a vast influenza clinic and morgue, little therapeutic information was gained. Subsequently, English and American investigators, exchanging views and viruses, cast doubt on both the etiology and entity of influenza. Whether influenza is an entity or a series, it remains a major infection about which our present knowledge is wholly inadequate for prevention or treatment.

[Benjamin Rush, *An Account of the Influenza, 1789-91.*]

VICTOR ROBINSON

Inherent Powers. The National Government of the United States is one of enumerated powers. As a general rule, only those powers which are expressly conferred upon national agencies by the Constitution, or which may be reasonably implied therefrom can be exercised. However, the Supreme Court has on a number of occasions asserted that the National Government has other powers which arise out of its character as a sovereign state. These powers it has called inherent. Specific examples include: the power of the President to prohibit the sale of munitions to certain warring nations (U. S. v. Curtiss-Wright Export Corporation, 299 U. S. 304); the power to acquire territory by discovery and occupation

(Jones v. U. S., 137 U. S. 202); the power to expel undesirable aliens (Fong Yue Ting v. U. S., 149 U. S. 698); the power to make such international agreements as do not constitute treaties in the constitutional sense (Altman & Co. v. U. S., 224 U. S. 583). In other cases members of the Court have referred to the power to declare paper money legal tender^w (Knox v. Lee, 12 Wall. 457) and the power of eminent domain^w as inherent in the National Government (Kohl v. U. S., 91 U. S. 367). The term "inherent power" is not used in speaking of the states since they possess residual power under the Constitution. In Kansas v. Colorado^w, 206 U. S. 46, the Court denied that the National Government possessed inherent power as to the internal affairs of the nation even though the subjects might be of national importance. Such authority is reserved by the Tenth Amendment to the states or to the people.

[W. W. Willoughby, *The Constitutional Law of the United States.*]

HARVEY WALKER

Inheritance Tax Laws. Death duties are of two types, the inheritance tax of the states based upon the shares accruing to the individual heirs, and the estate tax of the Federal Government based upon the entire net estate before distribution. Both, however, are popularly called inheritance taxes. Theoretically the laws base the tax upon the transfer of property rather than upon the property itself. The rates are ordinarily progressive both with respect to amount of the estate or distributive share and with respect to the degree of relationship of decedent to beneficiary, the state laws generally recognizing three classes of heirs: direct, collateral and strangers.

Prior to the adoption of the Federal estate tax of 1916, the Government upon three other occasions—1798 to 1802, 1862 to 1870 and 1898 to 1902—resorted to death duties. Each represented an emergency revenue use of the tax, as did also the 1916 levy with subsequent amendments. An interesting feature of the estate tax law is the credit or offset provision under which the Federal Government allows, as a credit against its tax, state inheritance taxes in an amount equal to 80% of the Federal levy that would be payable under the 1926 legislation. State legislation has been built around this credit provision in the Federal law. The estate tax, combined with a gift tax at rates three-fourths those of the former and which rise with the cumulated amount of gifts made through the years by any one donor, now yields about 7% of total Federal revenues.

There were several state inheritance taxes of a kind prior to 1885. New York in that year really began the era of state inheritance taxation with an effectively administered levy upon collateral heirs which was later extended to direct heirs. Thereafter new state laws were rapidly enacted, twenty being added to the statute books between 1885 and 1900. Today (1939) forty-seven states, Nevada being the only exception, have inheritance or estate taxes or both. The coercion of the Federal credit provision has been among the factors in this development. Most of the states tax gifts made in contemplation of death. State inheritance taxes provide about 10% of total state revenues.

Many problems have arisen under our inheritance tax laws, such as those of making property valuations, preventing evasion and avoiding multiple taxation. The last problem has been dealt with through reciprocal agreements among the states to restrict double taxation of personal property of nonresident decedents and through Supreme Court decisions which have determined taxable situs. Under these decisions real and tangible personal property can be taxed only by the state in which the property is located, and intangible property ordinarily only by the state of the decedent's domicile.

[A. G. Buehler, *Public Finance;* H. L. Lutz, *Public Finance;* Tax Research Foundation, *Tax Systems of the World,* an annual series, Commerce Clearing House, Inc.]   MARVEL STOCKWELL

Initiative. The process by which the people may propose legislation is known as the initiative. It may be either indirect or direct. The indirect type calls for the submission of the initiated law to a representative legislative body for enactment. If the body fails or refuses to act or makes changes in the proposal, the sponsors may secure its submission to a vote of the people. The direct type omits the consideration by the legislative body and proceeds at once to the popular vote. The initiative is one of two democratic devices for direct legislation, the other is known as the referendum^{qv}.

An initiative measure is drafted by its sponsors. It is then placed on a petition and signatures of a specified number of qualified voters must be secured. The petitions are filed with a public official, usually the secretary of state in a state and the city clerk in a city. They are checked for adequacy and legality. If found valid, the measure specified in the petitions is placed before the legislative body or submitted to popular vote. In the indirect type of initiative a supplementary petition is often required in order to secure the submission of a measure to poular vote after its rejection or amendment by the legislature or city council.

The initiative is used by several states and cities, but is not available in the National Government in the United States. It is used in the states not only for the proposal of laws, but also for the submission of constitutional amendments. In cities it is often available not only for the submission of proposed ordinances but also for the proposal of amendments to a city charter^{qv}. Constitutional and charter amendments are often required to be supported by petitions bearing a larger number of signatures than is required for the initiation of laws or ordinances.

The employment of the initiative in the United States dates from an early period. Georgia, in 1777, conferred upon the people the sole right to propose changes in the state constitution. Today (1939) thirteen states—California, Michigan, Ohio, Nevada, Arizona, Oklahoma, Nebraska, North Dakota, Arkansas, Massachusetts, Colorado, Missouri and Oregon—expressly authorize the proposal of constitutional amendments by popular petition. But the use of the initiative in the proposal of ordinary laws is a recent innovation. South Dakota in 1898 was the first to inaugurate the change. Utah followed in 1900 and Oregon in 1902. Since that time seventeen additional states have made similar constitutional changes. The use of the initiative in cities began to gain popularity with the advent of the commission plan^{qv} of government. The so-called Des Moines Plan was given wide publicity and a wave of adoption of direct legislative devices in cities followed in the years after 1907, reaching its peak in the decade 1910–20.

[Harvey Walker, *Law Making in the United States.*]
HARVEY WALKER

Injunctions, which are restraining court orders, play a large role in American labor history. In part, the issue developed from the conservatism and dominance of the courts, and in part from the absence of statutory regulation of strikes, picketing^{qv}, etc. The use of the injunction began in the 1880's, but became prominent for the first time with the issuance of the injunction against Eugene Debs' American Railway Union in the Pullman Strike^{qv} of 1894. A large number of labor injunctions issued after 1890, with the period from 1920 to 1930 showing the greater number. Subsequent anti-injunction legislation caused a marked decline.

Based upon the common law doctrines of conspiracy and restraint of trade^{qv} and coupled with a broad view by the courts of the "property" concept as applied to the employer's right to do business, the injunction embittered labor. The demand for remedying the alleged abuses of the labor injunction led to a long-sustained effort, particularly by the American Federation of Labor[w], to obtain statutory limitation of the courts' authority in labor injunction cases. As the injunction doctrines had largely been developed by Federal courts, efforts were concentrated primarily upon congressional enactment. Abuses of the injunction which were alleged included the lack of jury trial in contempt cases, the issuance of injunctions upon insufficient grounds, the blanket character of many injunctions, and the wide definition of "property" by the courts. Such decisions as the Buck Stove and Range Case[w] (1911) aroused dire consternation among labor leaders.

The Clayton Act[w] of 1914 was hailed by organized labor as a marked alleviation of the injunctive menace; it was believed that the act largely exempted unions from the antitrust laws, and that injunction procedure had been favorably modified. But labor was bitterly disappointed; later cases such as the Duplex Printing (1921), American Steel Founders (1921) and the Bedford Cut Stone (1927) indicated that the injunction remained a rigorous antiunion weapon. Renewed legislative activity resulted in the Norris-LaGuardia Act[w] of 1932 which imposed a number of restrictions upon the issuance of injunctions by Federal courts, specified actions by unions which might not be enjoined, and limited the doctrine of restraint of trade as applied to labor disputes. A number of states have subsequently enacted similar legislation regulating the issuance of injunctions by state courts.

[Frankfurter and Greene, *The Labor Injunction;* C. R. Daugherty, *Labor Problems in American Industry.*]

HERBERT MAYNARD DIAMOND

Inland Lock Navigation. In 1792 the New York legislature granted charters to the Western Inland Lock Navigation, to open water communication along the Mohawk River between the Hudson and Lakes Ontario and Seneca, and the Northern Inland Lock Navigation, to connect the Hudson with Lakes George and Champlain—which for lack of money the latter never quite succeeded in accomplishing. The Western company, by locks and short canals, opened a crude navigation between the Hudson and the lakes, but it never earned a profit, and was eliminated by the building of the Erie Canal[w].

[Alvin F. Harlow, *Old Towpaths.*]

ALVIN F. HARLOW

Inland Waterways Commission, THE, was appointed by President Theodore Roosevelt in 1907 to prepare "a comprehensive plan for the improvement and control" of our river systems. In 1908 it submitted a bulky *Preliminary Report* on rivers, lakes, canals and railroad competition, urging that future plans for improvement of navigation should take account of water purification, power development, flood control and land reclamation. In 1909 the National Waterways Commission[w] was created to carry on its work.

[W. S. Holt, *The Office of the Chief of Engineers of the Army,* pp. 33-34; *Preliminary Report of the Inland Waterways Commission,* Senate Document No. 325, 60th Congress, 1st Session.]

WILLIAM J. PETERSEN

Inns. *See* Taverns.

Inquiry, THE, was an organization set up by the Government shortly after the United States entered the World War in 1917, to conduct studies of the problems of peace-making which would claim attention at the close of the war. Col. Edward M. House was requested by President Wilson to assume responsibility for the general guidance of the studies, and Sidney E. Mezes became the first director. Reorganization was effected during the summer of 1918 by Isaiah Bowman, who then became executive officer. When the American delegation sailed for France in December, 1918, an organized library of books, maps, memoranda, bibliographies, and statistical material accompanied it. A series of base maps of problem areas—unique in peace conference history—permitted daily preparation of maps in duplicate for all allied commissions that required them. All delegations at Paris also made wide use of the so-called Black Book and the Red Book of the American delegation, prepared by former members of the Inquiry. These "books," documented by earlier studies, were assemblies of proposed solutions of conference problems, the Black Book of European problems mainly, the Red Book of colonial problems. Their authors served on various commissions—territorial, economic, military and labor—set up to frame specific recommendations for the consideration of the Council of heads of states.

[The archives of the Inquiry are now in the Department of State at Washington. The American Geographical Society of New York retains a partial set of duplicates and has a virtually complete book of maps prepared at Paris from pre-conference base maps.]

ISAIAH BOWMAN

Inquisition, The Spanish, or Holy Office, after a period of informal, sporadic activity in the New World beginning as early as 1524, was permanently established in Mexico City, Nov. 2,

1571, its jurisdiction extending eventually from the Isthmus of Panama to the Spanish borderlands now in United States territory. It was suppressed by decree of the Spanish Cortes in 1813, restored for a while, and definitely abolished in 1820. The tribunal took cognizance not only of heresy, but also of such offenses as blasphemy, perjury, forgery, bigamy and piracy; moreover, it exercised an elaborate censorship of books. Non-Catholics, as also the Indians, were exempt from its authority. The penalties usually imposed included fines, flogging, confiscation, imprisonment. The death-sentence was rare. Records covering 279 years, 1524–1803, show fifty-one executions in all.

The Inquisition was only slightly active in upper California, and can scarcely be traced at all in Florida, which, territorially, was within the jurisdiction of the *inquisitorial* court sitting at Cartagena. In New Mexico, where Franciscans*ᵠ* were officers of the Inquisition, differences of policy in the treatment of the Indians often set the friars at odds with alcaldes and governors, some of whom were charged with grave offenses and put on trial before the Holy Office in Mexico City. The Inquisition was never introduced into Spanish Louisiana (1762–1800). The traveler, Paul Alliot, who was in New Orleans on the eve of the Louisiana Purchase*ᵠ*, wrote: "No Inquisition exists there other than that which is exercised by men of influence."

[H. I. Priestly, *The Coming of the White Man.*]
GILBERT J. GARRAGHAN

Insane, Treatment of. In early colonial days patients with mental disorders were cared for in workhouses, the first of several being erected in the province of New York in 1736. Both Connecticut and Rhode Island passed laws for similar institutions about the same time. Later in the century mental patients were shifted from the workhouses to almshouses. Benjamin Franklin presented a petition to the Pennsylvania Assembly in 1751 pointing out the need for a hospital for mental cases. An act was passed the same year and a private home set up as a temporary hospital in 1752 which was later combined with the Pennsylvania Hospital (1756). Subsequently mental patients began to be exhibited to onlookers for an admission fee.

The first state hospital, exclusively for mental patients, was opened at Williamsburg, Va., in 1773. Massachusetts had established the first almshouse in 1662 at Boston and eventually the mental cases began to drift into this establishment. Benjamin Rush, the father of American psychiatry, started work at the Pennsylvania

Hospital in 1783 and soon initiated health reforms in psychiatric treatment and general administrative methods. In 1796 a new wing at the Pennsylvania Hospital was erected exclusively for mental patients; warm and cold baths were installed (1798); the beginnings of occupational therapy came into being (1798); "well qualified persons" who could give "kind treatment" were insisted upon (1803). In 1810 Rush advocated separate buildings for mental patients, separation of the sexes, use of occupational activities, the selection of intelligent attendants and the barring of all visitors.

The second institution exclusively for mental patients was the Friends Asylum of the Philadelphia Quakers, opened at Frankfort, Pa., in 1817. The next separate hospital was the Bloomingdale Asylum, opened in New York in 1821. An "insane" department of the Massachusetts General Hospital had previously been opened in Charlestown, Mass., in 1818 but, strictly speaking, was not a separate hospital. Kentucky opened the second state hospital in 1824 and South Carolina the third in 1828. Ohio established the "Lunatic Asylum of the Commercial Hospital" in 1827. Connecticut had opened the semiprivate Hartford Retreat in 1824. Massachusetts built the next state hospital at Worcester in 1833. New York followed at Utica in 1843. Both Tennessee and Maine opened state hospitals in 1840. Ohio erected the Ohio Lunatic Asylum at Columbus in 1838. Georgia and New Hampshire opened hospitals in 1842.

About 1840 there burst upon the field a raging fury in the form of one Dorothy A. Dix, who brought into light all of the various abuses of the insane. Starting in Massachusetts, where she attained several victories in her cry "Massachusetts must build more State Hospitals," she traveled throughout the country. Through her efforts twenty states added to their provisions for mental patients.

From these foundations the modern care of the mentally ill has sprung. Now (1939) private, state and Federal hospitals are caring for approximately 500,000 patients each year throughout the country. The patient now enters a modern hospital where he receives intense medical as well as psychiatric treatment. Adequate laboratories, X-Ray equipment, equipment for the various medical specialties, complete hydrotherapy and physiotherapy departments, trained psychologists, and psychotherapists are available for the care of the mental patient. Following discharge, adequate social service coverage for both community placement and family care of the patient is available. Out-patient services are available and help is waiting for the patient any time he may need or desire it.

[A. Deutsch, *The Mentally Ill in America.*]

NEIL A. DAYTON

Inscription Rock (El Morro), a varicolored sandstone rising 200 feet out of a lava-strewn valley in Valencia County, west-central New Mexico, derives its names from a fancied resemblance to a castle and from inscriptions carved on its sides by early Spanish and subsequent explorers. That of Don Juan de Oñate, April 16, 1606 (an error for 1605), is the earliest. Lt. J. H. Simpson and R. H. Kern, an artist, visited it, September, 1849, and were the first to record the inscriptions and bring them to the attention of the public. It was created a National Monument June 8, 1906.

[J. H. Simpson, *Report of an Expedition into the Navajo Country;* C. F. Lummis, *Some Strange Corners of Our Country.*]

F. H. H. ROBERTS, JR.

Insignia of Rank in the United States Army. Washington's orders, July 14, 1775, prescribed: commander in chief, a light blue ribbon across the heart; other generals, pink ribbon; field officers, red or pink cockades in hats; captains, yellow or buff; subalterns, green. The two stars of a major general and one star of a brigadier general were ordered for epaulets, June 18, 1780; three stars for a lieutenant general, 1798; eagle for colonel, 1832. Shoulder-straps, adopted in 1836, provided: for lieutenant colonel, a leaf of the same metal as that of the border; for major, a leaf of the opposite metal; for captain, two bars; for first lieutenant, one bar. As general, Grant (1866) wore four stars; when Sherman succeeded, a coat of arms between two stars was substituted; Pershing resumed four stars, 1917. The gold leaf for major became unique in 1872; by analogy a gold bar became the insignia for second lieutenant, Dec. 29, 1917. Sergeant's and corporal's chevrons date from 1847; worn point downward until 1861.

[H. A. Ogden and Henry Loomis Nelson, *The Army of the United States;* Robert E. Wyllie, *Orders, Decorations and Insignia, Military and Civil.*]

DON RUSSELL

Inspection, Committees of (Revolutionary). The Townshend Acts[qv] of 1767 awakened a storm of protest. To force the repeal of the objectionable duties the Non-Importation Agreement[qv] was revived. The merchants of New York City acted promptly, and on March 13, 1768, a special committee was named to "inspect all European importations." The life of this committee was short, but similar committees in the

other colonies continued to function, inspecting the correspondence and accounts of merchants, often in a high-handed and arbitrary manner (*see* Revolutionary Committees).

[C. H. Van Tyne, *War of Independence.*]

A. C. FLICK

Inspection Laws in the United States are of many varieties. While originated during the colonial period they have become increasingly numerous as the Federal, state and local governments have reached out to regulate or control economic and social activities. Often the provision for inspection is incidental to the provisions for such regulation. Federal inspection has, since the inauguration of the Government under the Constitution, been carried on in relation to imports, immigration, the postal system and navigation. The Steamboat Inspection Service and the inspectors of the Interstate Commerce Commission[qv] seek to insure the safety of transportation equipment. No more far-reaching inspection laws have been enacted by Congress than the Meat Inspection Act of 1906 and the Pure Food and Drugs Acts of 1906 and 1938[qqv]. Numerous other examples of Federal inspection might be cited.

Notable among the state inspection acts are those which, under the pretense of exercising legitimate police power, have created border "ports of entry" thus definitely setting up interstate barriers[qv] to free trade. A multitude of other state and local laws have been enacted in recent years, providing for inspection of almost every activity from conducting a restaurant to installing plumbing in a residence.

[E. Freund, *Administrative Powers over Persons and Property;* Charles A. Beard and William Beard, *The American Leviathan.*]

ERIK McKINLEY ERIKSSON

Installment Buying, Selling and Financing. Installment buying and selling, which is simply the exchanging of values by means of credit on terms which provide for liquidation by a series of predetermined partial payments, is a practice which antedates recorded history. Our Federal Government sold great portions of the public domain[qv] on installments. Early installment dealings were not confined to realty; the House of Cowperthwait and Sons, New York, applied it to furniture in 1807; the Singer Sewing Machine Company sold on installments during the middle of the 19th century; McCormick is said to have sold his reapers[qv] on installments; the piano business used it during the latter quarter of the 19th century; and in the last years of the 18th century books were thus sold.

Credit, especially installment credit, began to be commonly used in the purchase of automobiles[qv] about 1910 or 1912 and became general following the World War. From 50% to 70% of new car sales are still made on the installment basis. It was also used to sell other durable consumers' goods, durable producers' goods, store and office equipment. In the consumer goods market the general practice prior to 1930 was to confine sales on these terms to durable or semidurable goods, and to retain a lien upon the goods. Following 1930 there was further increase in the practice of selling nondurable goods on installments without lien, and many mail order houses and department stores now permit purchase on the budget plan of any merchandise carried, a single agreement covering purchases of many small items. The Bureau of the Census estimated that the total dollar volume of retail installment sales was: 1929—6.5 billions; 1935—3.6 billions; 1936—4.5 billions, which were 13%, 11% and 12% of sales, and 8%, 6.5% and 7% of national income.

In the earlier phases of the system financing of sales was done by the seller who carried the credit as he did any other credit transaction. In the period following 1913 the purchase of notes and contracts by specialized financing institutions started and developed rapidly following 1919. In 1915 the Willys-Overland Company formed the Guaranty Securities Company which in 1916 became the Guaranty Securities Corporation and handled all makes of cars. The General Motors Acceptance Corporation, a factory subsidiary, was organized in 1919. Many early financing companies were organizations which had been active in other types of credit business before entering the automobile finance business, for example, the Commercial Credit Company, Commercial Investment Trust and National Bond and Investment Company. There was a rapid increase in the number of finance companies from 1920 to 1924 and many small local companies were organized. In 1924 the National Association of Finance Companies, later named the National Association of Sales Finance Companies, the first trade association in the business, was organized. In 1934 another association, the American Finance Conference, was organized. It was estimated there were 900 finance companies in 1925; liquidations, withdrawals and consolidations reduced them until in 1938 there were about 500. This reduction was, however, accompanied by remarkably few failures.

The method developed for handling the business was to have the buyer sign an installment payment note or series of notes and a lien instrument running to the dealer. This "paper" the dealer discounted with the finance company under either recourse, nonrecourse, or repurchase agreement; which method is still used for all secured sales.

[E. R. A. Seligman, *The Economics of Installment Selling;* Evans Clark, *Financing the Consumer.*]

HARVEY W. HUEGY

Insular Cases, THE, were a succession of cases (1901–22) in which the Supreme Court determined the status of the outlying possessions and dependencies of the United States. The Court has held that such territories and possessions are of two kinds, incorporated and unincorporated; and that Congress, in legislating for incorporated territories, is bound by all provisions of the Constitution, but in legislation for unincorporated territories is bound only by certain "fundamental" provisions of the same (*see* Downes v. Bidwell).

It becomes important, therefore, to know, first, which of the territories and possessions are incorporated, and second, which provisions of the Constitution are "fundamental" and which, in the language of the Court, are merely "formal." These questions the Supreme Court has in part answered. That Hawaii and Alaska[qv] are incorporated territories was determined by the Court in the cases, respectively, of Hawaii v. Mankichi (1903) and Rasmussen v. U. S. (1905). That Puerto Rico[qv] was not incorporated, even by the Organic Act of 1917, which made its people citizens of the United States, was held in Porto Rico v. Tapia (1918) and again, with a full statement of the reasoning involved, in Balzac v. People of Porto Rico (1922). The Philippine Islands[qv] were held to be unincorporated in Dorr v. U. S. (1904).

As to what are and what are not "fundamental" provisions of the Constitution, the Court has held expressly that the provisions insuring jury trial and uniformity of tariff duties are not fundamental (Downes v. Bidwell, Hawaii v. Mankichi, etc.), but that the guarantee against deprivation of life, liberty and property without due process[qv] of law is fundamental and hence applicable in all the possessions of the United States (Balzac v. People of Porto Rico).

[F. R. Coudert, The Evolution of the Doctrine of Territorial Incorporation, *American Law Review,* Vol. LX.]

JULIUS W. PRATT

Insular Possessions of the United States include Hawaii, Guam and American Samoa in the Pacific; Puerto Rico and the Virgin Islands[qv] of the United States in the Caribbean; and a number of smaller islands of importance only as stopping places on the transpacific air routes or as sites for lighthouses or for cable and radio stations. The Philippines[v], formerly the most important of the insular possessions, have been an autonomous commonwealth since 1934 in preparation for eventual independence.

Most of these extra-continental territories were acquired at about the same time, though by various means. Hawaii was annexed by agreement with its formerly independent government in 1898, and Puerto Rico and Guam, like the Philippines, were acquired in the same year as a result of the war with Spain. American Samoa was acquired under a treaty with Great Britain and Germany in 1899. The Virgin Islands, on the other hand, were purchased from Denmark in 1917. They are administered under various forms of government. Hawaii is a territory, an integral part of the United States, with a governor appointed by the President of the United States and a locally elected legislature. Puerto Rico, without territorial status, also has an elected legislature; but the attorney general, the commissioner of education, and the auditor are appointed by the President of the United States and are not subject like other department heads to confirmation by the insular senate. In the Virgin Islands the councils of the two municipalities exercise more limited legislative functions. Formerly Puerto Rico was administered by the War Department and the Virgin Islands by the Navy Department, but both have now been placed under the Division of Territories and Island Possessions of the Department of the Interior. Guam and Samoa, on the other hand, are governed by the Navy Department.

In general, under laws passed at various dates, natives of Hawaii, Puerto Rico and the Virgin Islands enjoy American citizenship, while those of Guam and American Samoa do not. The Supreme Court has held that certain fundamental rights guaranteed by the United States Constitution apply in all territory held by the United States, but that many other provisions of the Constitution do not apply to possessions which have not been definitely incorporated as an integral part of the United States (see Insular Cases).

The insular possessions were originally acquired partly for strategic reasons, and partly, in the case of the Pacific Islands, in the hope that they might serve as bases for the development of a great American commerce with the Far East. Such importance as they have today from the standpoint of the United States, aside from the value of the Pacific Islands to the transpacific air service, arises chiefly from their rela-tionship to the problem of national defense. There are naval bases at Hawaii and Samoa, and Puerto Rico and the Virgin Islands command approaches to the Panama Canal. Hawaii and Puerto Rico are also important from a commercial standpoint.

DANA G. MUNRO

Insurance. The practice of insurance began in the colonies by means of individual underwriting, whereby individuals "wrote their names under" the agreement and stipulated the sums which they promised to pay in case of loss. This was confined to marine risks and to life policies of short duration. Distribution of risk was sought by securing many underwriters, each liable for a small sum, on each insuring contract. These contracts were usually effected at a coffee house where merchants, traders and underwriters were accustomed to gather. Thus John Copson opened a Public Insurance Office at his house in Philadelphia (May, 1721) which, however, met with little success. The first of such "offices" for underwriting marine policies in Boston was opened in 1724.

The first appeal to government regarding insurance appears to have been made in 1725 by Francis Rawle of Philadelphia, who proposed insurance facilities in a semigovernmental institution managed and financed to afford real protection. The inference from the sources is that insurance in other offices, most of which had been "dropt and prov'd abortive," involved much uncertainty as to whether claims would really be paid. Government ignored Rawle's appeal, however, and marine and life policies of short duration continued to be underwritten by individuals throughout the colonial period and for twenty years thereafter.

Fire risks during this period were underwritten by mutual insurance societies, seldom by individuals. In early days, when a building was destroyed neighbors assisted in alleviating distress, and in reconstruction. From this it was a short step to an association which bound members to make contributions in case one of them suffered loss. This step was taken in 1735 when the Friendly Society for the Mutual Insuring of Houses against Fire was organized under a royal charter in Charleston, S. C. The Philadelphia Contributionship for the Insurance of Houses from Loss by Fire, formed in 1752, still transacts business.

Individual underwriting is impracticable for long-term risks because some of the underwriters may die, others may fail financially. Realizing this, and also realizing the need for funds to support the widows and destitute families of deceased ministers, the Presbyterian Synod of Philadelphia, apparently in conjunction with the Synod of New York, under the guidance of the Rev. Dr. Francis Alison, Vice-Provost of the University of Pennsylvania, formed our first life-insurance corporation in 1759. The corporation, though changed, continues today as the Presbyterian Ministers' Fund. Alison also assisted the Rev. Dr. William Smith, Provost of the University of Pennsylvania, in founding the Episcopal Corporation in 1769. The charter of the latter provided that the accounts of the corporation be submitted to the archbishops of Canterbury and York and the Bishop of London, or their representatives in America, for examination as often as might be demanded. This foreshadowed our present system of requiring reports to the state insurance departments.

The individual underwriters charged the traditional English premium rate of 5% of the amount insured for contracts of six to twelve months' duration. The Philadelphia Contributionship required a deposit of a percentage of the face of the policy. The religious corporations promised an annuity to widows and children equal to five times the annual contribution of the minister while living, with certain limitations. These rates also were based on English experience.

Very little progress was made regarding mortality statistics. In 1761 President Stiles of Yale called attention to the high birth rate in the colonies and estimated that the population in the back settlements doubled about every fifteen years. England's Dr. Richard Price quoted statistics of births and deaths in Boston from 1731 to 1752. In 1782 Prof. Wigglesworth of Harvard determined the mortality rate in several Massachusetts towns and in 1789 he presented the first American mortality table ever compiled.

With the adoption of the Constitution and the establishment of a relatively sound financial system conditions for corporate enterprise improved. Then the outbreak of the French Revolution and the subsequent entrance of the maritime powers of Europe into war greatly enhanced the importance of our commercial and business interests. Our neutral flag secured a large share of the world's carrying trade, and the business of insurance developed along with other business. Thus from 1787 to 1799 inclusive no fewer than twenty-four charters were granted to insurance companies, and thirty-one were operating under American charters as the century came to a close. Five of these were authorized to write life as well as fire and marine policies. A few alien companies were also doing business here.

During the last decade of the 18th century, important principles of contract law were worked out or derived from English jurisprudence, in the legal and judicial interpretation of marine contracts. As the century ended a definite basis for deciding insurance cases was being evolved.

Marine insurance continued in great demand in the early 19th century, when American commerce was subjected to losses due to the Napoleonic wars, the embargo and non-intercourse acts, and the War of 1812^{qv}. Insurance companies were subjected to heavy losses also, due to the capture and detention of ships, and were therefore obliged to increase their premium rates. Attempts were made to recover damages from foreign governments for illegal captures, and some of such claims were settled. Other claims were presented to the United States Government, with no tangible results. For the most part the companies had to bear the losses themselves.

With the coming of peace, the companies began to compete for business by reducing rates. The period of general business prosperity which began about 1820 resulted in the formation of several new companies by 1825. There was a setback following 1825, partly caused by fraudulent claims due to intentional wrecking of vessels after cargoes had been surreptitiously disposed of. Revived business accompanied the period of speculation after 1832, but the panic of 1837^{qv} again caused a decline until recovery began in the early years of the next decade. Through such experiences some companies somehow managed to struggle.

By 1840 such fire-insurance companies as the Insurance Company of North America, the Hartford, the Ætna and others were firmly established. Fire insurance had experienced a much more steady growth than had marine, and the stocks of fire companies were regarded as very conservative investments. In 1835, however, an event occurred that profoundly affected the history of American fire insurance, and influenced the development of life insurance as well. On the night of Dec. 16 practically the entire business center of New York was destroyed by fire, and as a result all of the fire-insurance companies of the city except three were bankrupt. This was the first great catastrophe to be faced by our fire-insurance companies, and to this day, despite efforts by companies to limit the amount of insurance at risk in a single city, block, building or line, a portion of the fire-insurance premiums paid by property owners is assigned to "catastrophe," the nightmare of the fire underwriter. As business began to recover and New York to rebuild, capital avoided fire-insurance companies, hence the businessmen did the only thing possible under the circumstances and organized mutual companies. The mutual idea was carried over into life insurance where it has been pre-eminently successful.

During this period our first commercial life-insurance companies were formed. The early companies were organized on the stock, nonparticipating plan, with large-guarantee capital and high premium rates for safety in view of lack of experience and of adequate mortality data. One company was formed, in 1836, on the so-called mixed plan. By 1840 life insurance was on a sound financial basis, marine insurance was rich in experience but weak financially, and fire insurance was in a very humble state.

After 1840 many mutual fire-insurance companies were formed on an unsound basis, and such companies were largely discredited by the large number of failures among them. The stock fire-insurance companies which survived the conflagration of 1835, and the few new ones started thereafter, began to prosper with the business revival of the 1840's. They pushed westward into the newly formed states and organized the American agency system on a comprehensive scale. Between 1840 and the Civil War, our clipper ships^w and other vessels carried a substantial proportion of the world's ocean commerce, and were insured with their cargoes in American marine insurance companies. This business has seen no more prosperous decades in our history. Life insurance also prospered, many of the present-day mutual companies being formed during these years. Nearly all of them were formed on the participating plan in which premiums adequate to meet the requirements, with a liberal allowance for errors, were collected, any excess being returned to policyholders as experience warranted. The life-insurance companies adopted the agency system and carried the business to all parts of the country. A number of unsound companies were started, and there were failures, especially in the South and the new West; but the companies that survived the Panic of 1857^w established in the public mind the idea, still prevalent, that life insurance is our only "depression proof" financial institution.

During these decades there were refinements in premium calculations and in reserve computations. Net premium valuation, practised today, superseded gross valuation. Co-operation between companies was inaugurated on a comprehensive basis by the formation of the American Life Convention in 1859. About sixty life-insurance cases came before the courts during this period involving such matters as suicide, assignment, the married women's act, insurable interest, authority of agents, waiver, proof of death, etc., so that by 1860 the general attitude of the courts on many matters was evident. In brief, insurable interest was required, the courts were inclined to deal leniently with insured persons and to give them the benefit of any doubt as to the meaning of contracts, but to hold that persons seeking insurance should reveal material facts concerning the risk.

Until the mid-19th century each insurance company was chartered by a special act of the legislature. In 1849 an act was passed in New York to facilitate the formation of companies. To curb the formation of unsound companies another law was passed in 1851, requiring all life companies to deposit $50,000 in approved securities with the comptroller. This New York Deposit Law, mistakenly viewed by other states as an attempt to drive their companies from New York, provoked retaliatory legislation which has remained to this day an obstacle to the progress of the business. Massachusetts established the first state insurance department in 1855, and New York followed in 1859.

The Civil War, with its interruption of our commerce and its losses for our marine insurance companies, together with the development of coal-burning iron vessels by England, while we were busy with internal problems, brought our ocean marine insurance to a very low estate. Conditions in fire insurance were unsatisfactory until after the Civil War. In 1866 the National Board of Fire Underwriters was organized. The practice of allowing the agent to issue policies that could later be withdrawn if the company were not satisfied, originated shortly after the war. It forms the basis of the modern agency system which, in turn, has made it possible to spread a large company's risks over a wide range of territory. Within recent years, coverage has been extended to include hazards formerly unknown. Thus a typical state permits fire and marine insurance companies to be incorporated for making insurances on all kinds of property against loss or damage including loss of use or occupancy, by fire, smoke, smudge; by action of the elements, water damage, mine cave-ins; by aircraft, motor vehicles, inland navigation and transportation, riot, war, bombardments, collision, and by other causes, and to effect reinsurances.

Life insurance prospered greatly during the decade from 1860 to 1870, suffered reverses during and following the Panic of 1873^w, advanced steadily until the turn of the century, made tremendous strides during the first decade following the close of the World War, and has more than held its own since 1929. Industrial, or weekly premium, insurance also developed in this period. Life-insurance companies have sound assets, well diversified territorially and otherwise, amounting to about three quarters of the total United States Government gross debt.

Until the past ten years, the record of the business was characterized by increasing liberality of policies, by expanding disability and group coverages, by declining costs necessary to keep policies in force, by almost no losses on the part of policyholders due to the failure of companies. During the past ten years new policies and disability benefits have been somewhat more restricted than they were during the latter part of the previous decade, costs to policyholders have been slightly increased, and trifling losses due to failures have been suffered by those insured in companies operating only in states where supervision was inadequate. Group coverage has continued to expand, assets have steadily increased, facilities for protecting against dependent old age have been increasingly used by the public. According to the record thus far, life-insurance companies are our strongest financial institutions, and they have gained the unquestioned confidence of the public. About one half of our people are insured in them.

Accident insurance in this country began in 1864 when the president of the Travelers Insurance Company orally insured one James Bolter for $5000 against accidental death while the latter walked home from the Hartford post office, the premium being two one-cent pieces. Live-stock insurance began in the 1870's, liability insurance in the 1880's and health insurance in the 1890's. During the present century, casualty insurance has been extended to cover hundreds of hazards. Fidelity, surety, glass breakage, vehicular, automobile public liability and property damage, burglary, theft, credit, land title guarantee, workmen's compensation, employers' and public liability, steam boiler, elevator, flywheel and other types of insurance have become commonplace.

The powers of government have been freely used in regulating insurance. In 1861 the Massachusetts nonforfeiture law was passed, providing that a fair portion of the net value of a lapsed policy should be used to purchase extended-term insurance. Competition soon brought about cash-surrender values as an optional settlement. This led to the use of life insurance as a so-called "investment," which accounts for the unparalleled growth of life insurance in this country. Laws and regulations have been directed toward keeping rates high enough to maintain solvency, yet low enough to be reasonable. Also powers of government have been invoked to maintain adequate reserve and other funds necessary to solvency, to regulate investments, to supervise agents, to protect policyholders, and to retain the advantages of competition and the stimulus of private initiative within the law.

[Penn and Logan Correspondence, Vol. I, p. 353; F. Rawle, *Ways and Means for the Inhabitants of Delaware to Become Rich*, pp. 62-63; C. K. Knight, *History of Life Insurance*.]   C. K. KNIGHT

Insurance, Unemployment, was in effect in European countries, notably England, before it received any serious consideration in the United States. The outbreak of the "great depression" in 1929, with its resultant widespread unemployment, caused increasing interest in the matter. In 1930 the American Association for Labor Legislation drew up a plan for unemployment insurance. A bill for unemployment insurance was introduced in the Ohio legislature in 1931, chiefly through the efforts of the Cleveland Consumers League.

Franklin D. Roosevelt, while governor of New York, was the first prominent politician to advocate such insurance. He presented the matter to the conference of governors in 1930 and, again, in January, 1931, to a conference of seven Eastern governors.

Wisconsin was the first state to enact legislation providing for unemployment insurance. This law was adopted early in 1932, but the collection of "premiums" did not begin until July, 1934.

Meanwhile prominent leaders in the movement for old-age insurance, notably Abraham Epstein and I. M. Rubinow, became active advocates of unemployment insurance also. Early in the New Deal, Sen. Robert F. Wagner of New York, Representative David J. Lewis of Maryland and Secretary of Labor Frances Perkins joined in the movement. In February, 1934, the so-called Wagner-Lewis bill was introduced in Congress but it failed to pass. In 1935, however, the Federal Social Security Act[*q*] was passed. Included in it were provisions designed to aid the states in setting up "unemployment compensation laws." In 1938, payments amounting to over $396,000,000 were made to unemployed persons in thirty states.

On June 25, 1938, a separate Federal plan of unemployment insurance for railroad employees was adopted. It provides daily benefits of $1.75 to $3.00 for such employees who become unemployed. This act became effective on July 1, 1939.

[Paul H. Douglas, *Social Security in the United States*; 52 *Statutes at Large.*]   ERIK McKINLEY ERIKSSON

Insurance, War Risk. In this country, war risk insurance has been applied to property at sea, to property on land, to lives in the military and naval service and in the merchant marine. When not too great, these risks have been underwritten by insurance companies. To the extent that such risks have become or have threatened to become catastrophic in the past, necessarily they have been shunned by insurance companies, and in some instances have been assumed by government.

Thus on Sept. 2, 1914, provision was made for insurance by the United States Government on vessels, freight, passage moneys and cargoes against loss by war hazards. On June 12, 1917, government insurance against injury, capture or death was provided for masters, officers and crews of American merchant vessels plying between American ports and the war zone, and such insurance was made compulsory in the amount of twelve times monthly wages plus all bonuses with minimum and maximum limits of $1500 and $5000, respectively.

On Oct. 6, 1917, United States Government insurance against death or total permanent disability was afforded officers, soldiers, sailors and nurses in the service to a maximum of $10,000. Such insurance was voluntary, though great pressure was exerted by officers in effecting it. Premiums were paid by those insured at net yearly renewable term rates, American Experience, $3\frac{1}{2}\%$, averaging about $7.75 per $1000 of insurance per year. Within a period after the war, the insurance had to be converted to a level premium plan. Administrative expenses and extra war mortality costs were and are borne by the Government. After the war, much of this government insurance lapsed.

[U. S. Bureau of War Risk Insurance; U. S. Veterans' Bureau.]   C. K. KNIGHT

Insurance Investigation. Aroused by the scandals disclosed in a bitter internal struggle for control of the Equitable Life Insurance Company, Gov. Frank W. Higgins of New York convened a special legislative session in July, 1905, for the purpose of investigating the insurance business. A joint committee with William W. Armstrong as chairman and Charles Evans Hughes as counsel was created. In a brilliant and courageously conducted investigation lasting many weeks, Hughes exposed a condition in which the companies were not only making questionable investments, but also were using their funds to pay excessive salaries, commissions and gratuities; to influence political campaigns; and to further the speculative enterprises of directors. As a result of the investigation the New York insurance laws were radically amended in April, 1906.

[William W. Armstrong, *Report of Joint Committee on the Investigation of Life Insurance.*]   L. J. MEYER

Insurrections, Domestic, connote an uprising against a duly constituted or sovereign authority within a given state or political entity for the purpose of accomplishing some political end or procuring some particular advantage that may be desired by many individuals. The term insurrection implies that a number of petitioners (*see* Petition, Right of) sufficient to question the sovereign authority for a prolonged duration of time emphasize their petitions through forceful resistance to the laws or the Government. The degree of vigor in resistance may extend from concerted bloodless demonstrations to an actual civil war of extended and extensive proportions.

The immediate purposes of such uprisings usually exist in the desire of a considerable number of people to procure some practical advantage. The rebellion led by Daniel Shays[w] in Massachusetts in 1786–87 was for the purpose of preventing the creditor class, then in control of the state government, from seizing the property of the debtors through regular legal channels. The Whisky Insurrection[w] in western Pennsylvania in 1794 was a protest against the excise on spirituous liquor which the agrarian distillers believed unjust. Thomas Dorr[w] and his followers in their insurrection of 1842 in Rhode Island sought the abrogation of property qualifications for the franchise[w]. While specific local ends motivated these uprisings, an eventual overthrowing of the Government was probably contemplated. In the so-called American Civil War, eleven Southern states did seek an entirely new government for themselves (*see* Secession of Southern States) because of their desire to perpetuate their particular form of agrarian society and economy.

The sanctions and justifications for insurrections seem to be found in the philosophy that has evolved concerning the rights of man and the nature of government. Man has developed the theory that because he is a human being, because of "the nature of the universe" man has certain inalienable rights. Political philosophers have, from time to time, formulated and reiterated those rights and have asserted that life, liberty, the pursuit of happiness, property, the "unimpairment of limbs and members" and a comfortable living belong in that list of rights. Furthermore, political theorists have asserted that the chief purpose of government is to protect and nurture the rights and interests of the members of the body politic. In the United States, at least, there has been a common acceptance of the right of individuals to petition peaceably their government for redress against wrongs or relief from distress. Insurrectionists, then, justify their uprisings or their resort to petition by violence on the ground that the exercise of one or more of their so-called fundamental rights has been denied and that the sovereign authority has failed to guarantee or protect that right. To procure the exercise of that denied right, an appeal, accomplished only through domestic insurrection, is taken to a higher law, a power superior to their sovereign authority.

[Charles E. Merriam, *History of American Political Theories.*]
R. J. FERGUSON

Intelligence Tests, Army. When the United States entered the World War, the American Psychological Association offered its services to cooperate with the Government in examining recruits. No standards existed for such psychological testing and the initial stages of the work were designed primarily to develop procedure. In July, 1917, examining groups were established in camps at Indianapolis, Nashville, Syracuse and Brooklyn. By November, 1917, results of work in these four groups had crystallized the aims of army psychological examining thus: (a) to aid in segregating and eliminating the mentally incompetent, (b) to classify men according to their mental capacity, and (c) to assist in selecting competent men for responsible positions.

Under Maj. Yerkes in the Section of Psychology, Surgeon General's Office, and in co-operation with the Army's Personnel Classification Committee, mental examining units were eventually operated in thirty-five training camps. These units, from April 28, 1918, to Jan. 31, 1919, examined 1,726,966 enlisted men and officers; of this total, 221,749 were Negroes.

A recapitulation of some of the results follows: Men found with mental age below seven years, 4780; below eight, 7875; below nine, 14,814; below ten, 18,878. Recommended for discharge because of mental inferiority, 5/10% of all examined; for assignment to labor battalions because of low-grade intelligence, 6/10%; for assignment to development battalions to determine their further value to the army, 6/10%. Of all examined, 25.3% were found unable to read and understand newspapers and to write letters home.

[Psychological Examining in the United States Army, in Vol. XV, *Memoirs—National Academy of Sciences.*]
ROBERT S. THOMAS

Interchangeable Parts manufacture grew out of Eli Whitney's plan for making muskets in 1798. Thomas Jefferson reports an earlier experiment with this method in France, but most authorities give Whitney credit for the first successful operation of the system. In the artisan era, gunsmiths made muskets by hand and eye, making one part at a time and fitting it to the next part until the musket was complete. Whitney's plan was to produce each part in quantity by machine and, when the full supply had been turned out, to assemble the required number of muskets, picking the parts at random. This could only be done if all of each kind of part were identical.

Identical parts were obtained by means of the jig—a device for guiding a tool. A simple form of jig is a metal plate, in which are several holes. When it is desired to repeat the pattern of these holes, the plate is placed over the material to be drilled and the drill guided through the holes. Each piece so drilled will have the holes at the precise distances apart, and in the same relationship to one another as in the jig. The jig was Whitney's independent invention, though forms of it existed before him in watchmaking.

Whitney's scheme for the production of firearms, by jig-guided, power-operated machine tools, was perfected by his own descendants, by Simeon North, by Samuel Colt and others. English attention was drawn to it in 1851. From that time on, it became known throughout the world as the "American system." Meanwhile, it had been widely adopted in the United States in sewing-machine and farm-machinery^{qq} manufacture.

It was the basis for all mass production^{q} of machines. Its effect on industry was revolutionary. It brought the artisan era to a close. A primary reason for its development in America was undoubtedly labor shortage.

[W. F. Durfee, History of Interchangeable Construction, in *Transactions, Am. Soc. Mech. Engineers,* XIV; Joseph Wickham Roe, *English and American Tool Builders;* Thomas Jefferson, Letter to John Jay, May 30, 1785; S. N. D. and R. H. North, *Simeon North;* W. P. Blake, *History of Hamden, Conn.;* Jack Rohan, *Yankee Arms Maker;* R. Burlingame, *March of the Iron Men.*]

ROGER BURLINGAME

Interest Laws in the United States may be divided into two classes—laws affecting the rate of interest charged or paid by banks, and usury laws governing the maximum rate of interest which may be charged by any creditor entering into an interest-bearing contract.

With regard to banking laws concerning interest, the charters of the First and Second Banks of the United States^{q} prohibited these institutions from charging more than 6% per annum on loans and discounts. In respect to state banks there was no uniformity of practice, the charters of some limiting interest charges, of others, not. It was generally recognized, however, that bank interest charges must stay within the limit fixed by the usury laws of the states wherein they were located.

The National Bank Act, 1864 (*see* Banks, National), limited charges of national banks to the rate fixed by the usury laws of the states in which said banks were located under penalty of forfeiture of all interest on the loan. The Banking Act of 1933[*qv*] amplified this limitation by providing that a national bank might charge at the rate allowed by the state law or 1% in excess of the Federal Reserve Bank rate on 90-day commercial paper, whichever was higher. Where no state law prevailed, the limit was fixed at 7% or 1% above the Reserve Bank rate.

Until recently banks have not been limited as to the interest which they might pay to depositors. The Banking Acts of 1933 and 1935, however, forbade member banks to pay interest on demand deposits, and required the Board of Governors of the Federal Reserve System and the management of the Federal Deposit Insurance Corporation[*qqv*] to fix the rate of interest to be paid on time and savings deposits of member and nonmember insured banks respectively.

Usury laws in this country date back to colonial days. From 1661 (first Massachusetts statute) to 1791 (in New Hampshire) all the colonies enacted usury laws, the initial limitation varying from 6% in Connecticut, Delaware, Maryland, New Hampshire, New York, North Carolina, Rhode Island and Virginia to 10% in South Carolina. The penalties for infringement of these laws varied somewhat, being the voidance or forfeiture of the contract (or a multiple of that amount) in the majority of instances.

Since the establishment of the National Government most of the states have passed usury laws fixing the maximum rate of interest, and these laws have been amended from time to time as occasion dictated. In 1931 forty-three states had usury laws with rates varying from 6% to 12%. Since 1909 numbers of states have passed laws referring to special types of loans. Thus, in 1931, twenty-five states had a uniform small-loan law, thirty-two a credit union law, twenty-three an industrial banking law and thirty-eight a pawnbroking law.

The recent development of special laws fixing the rate of interest which may be charged on various types of small loans has come about through a realization of the inadequacy of usury laws in connection with loans to the consumer where a much higher rate must be charged by the lender in order to enable him to do business.

[F. W. Ryan, *Usury and Usury Laws;* E. Clark, *Financing the Consumer;* National Bank Act, and amendments.]

FREDERICK A. BRADFORD

"Interests, The" or "the vested interests" was an expression popularly used about the opening of the 20th century to designate the gigantic business corporations which then dominated the American scene. Among these "interests" were the so-called "money trust," the "sugar trust,"[*qv*] the "tobacco trust," the "oil trust," the "beef trust"[*qv*] and the "steel trust," all of which became subjects for strong attacks by "muckraking"[*qv*] reformers, especially during the Presidency of Theodore Roosevelt. These attacks, in books, magazines and newspapers and from the political platform, inaugurated an era of reform, local, state and national, which lasted until the United States entered the World War.

[A. M. Schlesinger, *Political and Social Growth of the United States, 1852-1933.*]   ERIK McKINLEY ERIKSSON

Interior, Department of the, was established in 1849 as the sixth department of Cabinet rank, upon the recommendation of Robert J. Walker, Secretary of the Treasury. At the time certain government bureaus had no departmental affiliation and others were overburdening departments in which, functionally, they did not fit. Walker's recommendation that these various bureaus, including the General Land Office, then in the Treasury Department, the Indian Office in the War Department, the Pensions Office scattered in both the War and Navy Departments, the Census Bureau and other minor supervisory agencies, be united in one department produced a new sectional controversy. Western interests had long complained that the General Land Office was too strongly influenced in its administration of the public domain[*qv*] by eastern control, and they now supported the measure to set up a new department which, they hoped, would be more friendly to the West. Conservatives from the East and South, however, opposed Walker's recommendation, fearing that it meant further bureaucratic growth and possibly a more liberal land policy. Another criticism that might have been directed at Walker's recommendation was that it would bring together bureaus with no functional unity, that it would set up a "catchall" department with no common objectives. Despite opposition the act to establish the "Home Department," as it was first called, was approved on March 3, 1849.

Throughout its history the Department of the

Interior has been one of the most politically minded of all government agencies and, consequently, has frequently been subject to attack by special groups, or by other departments seeking to wrest from it some of its bureaus. The War Department, smarting under the loss of the Office of Indian Affairs, made serious efforts to recover its lost child. During and after the Civil War, when the whole West was aflame with Indian troubles and the army was barely able to suppress the warlike tribes, the officials of the War Department argued that the troubles were caused by the bungling and corrupt administration of the Indian Office and that both war- and peacetime jurisdiction over the Indians should be restored to the War Department.

The Interior officials held their own in this controversy and gained a new but modest recruit in the Office of Education which was set up in 1867 as a research and tabulation agency. Then followed the creation of the Geological Survey in 1879 as a combination of surveying, geological investigations and mapping work formerly conducted by a number of government agencies. In 1902 the Reclamation Service was organized to administer the reclamation and irrigation activity being undertaken by the Government. The Bureau of Mines was established in 1910 to conduct investigations into all phases of mining and to promote the health and safety of the workers. In 1916 Congress established the National Park Service to provide administrative control for the widely scattered parks and monuments of the Federal Government. Finally, in 1934 the Division of Grazing was created to administer the 142,000,000 acres of range lands withdrawn from homestead entry and placed under organized management.

The department has thus grown by the assignment of new functions and duties but, until 1933, it had been narrowing its scope and bringing about more unity by dropping some of its ill-fitting bureaus. In 1903 the Census Bureau was transferred to the newly created Department of Commerce and Labor (later Commerce); the Patent Office was similarly transferred in 1925; and in 1930 the Pensions Office was made a part of the Veterans Administration[qv]. The Bureau of Mines was also lost temporarily to the rapidly growing Department of Commerce under its aggressive secretary, Herbert Hoover, but it later was returned to Interior.

The New Deal[qv] placed additional burdens upon the Secretary of the Interior and made his department even more of a "catch-all" than when it was first started. Either under his supervision or as bureaus in his department have been estab-lished the Public Works Administration[qv] with its vast program of public construction, the Subsistence Homestead[qv] Division, subsequently transferred to the Resettlement Administration[qv], the Soil Erosion Service, now a part of Agriculture, the Oil Administration, the National Bituminous Coal Commission[qv], the United States Housing Authority, the Administrator of the Bonneville[qv] Project and the Division of Territories and Island Possessions. No department today has a wider variety of responsibilities assigned to it, and but five have a larger personnel.

[Milton Conover, *The General Land Office;* Investigation of Executive Agencies of the Government, *Preliminary Report of the Select Committee to Investigate the Executive Agencies of the Government,* 1937, Senate Report No. 1275, 75th Congress, 1st Session.]   PAUL WALLACE GATES

Interlocking Directorates. The Clayton Act[qv] of Oct. 15, 1914, imposed certain rather complicated restrictions on interlocking directorates of industrial combinations and banks. As regards industrial combinations, the act prohibits a person from being a director in two or more corporations if one has a capital of $1,000,000 or more, when such corporations are engaged in business of such a sort that agreement between them to eliminate competition would violate the antitrust laws[qv].

With respect to banks, the act, as amended, prohibits any "private banker or director, officer or employee of any member bank of the Federal Reserve System or branch thereof," from being a director, officer or employee of any other bank or trust company or any branch thereof, "except that the Board of Governors of the Federal Reserve System[qv] may . . . permit such service" in not more than one other bank or branch. There are, however, seven exceptions to this restriction, including banks owned directly or indirectly by the United States, banks in receivership or in the hands of a conservator, banks engaged principally in foreign banking, and mutual savings banks without capital stock.

[H. R. Seager and C. A. Gulick, Jr., *Trust and Corporation Problems.*]   FREDERICK A. BRADFORD

Intermarried Citizens were persons who through marriage to an Indian became a citizen of the tribe. The term was most commonly applied to a white person who married a member of one of the Five Civilized Tribes[qv] of Indian Territory. Intermarried citizens shared equally with citizens by blood in lands and other tribal property. Cherokee[qv] laws provided that to receive a license to marry a woman of that tribe, a white man must secure a certificate of good moral character signed by ten Cherokee citizens. Laws of the other tribes were quite similar.

[J. B. Thoburn and Muriel H. Wright, *Oklahoma: A History of the State and Its People.*]

EDWARD EVERETT DALE

Intermediate Credit Banks, twelve in number, located in the Federal Land Bank cities, were created by the Agricultural Credits Act of 1923 for the purpose of advancing credit to farmers for periods of from six months to three years, that is, for periods longer than loans commonly made by commercial banks and for shorter terms than the ordinary farm mortgage. These banks are empowered to advance funds to farmers indirectly in two ways: first, by the discount or purchase from banks, agricultural credit associations, livestock companies, or co-operative marketing associations, notes or bills of exchange, the proceeds of which had been used for agricultural purposes; second, by making direct loans to co-operative associations engaged in producing and marketing staple agricultural products or livestock.

The twelve banks have an aggregate paid-in capital surplus of approximately $100,000,000 and in addition to this amount funds for their lending operations are obtained primarily through sales to the investing public of short-term consolidated collateral trust debentures secured by cash, government bonds, Federal Farm Mortgage Corporation bonds, and notes or other obligations representing their loans and discounts.

[Baird and Benner, *Ten Years of Federal Intermediate Credits.*]

FRANK PARKER

Internal Improvements. Early settlers in the American colonies were not seriously handicapped by the lack of roads because they had little surplus goods for exchange. Furthermore, water transportation was generally available to them because of their proximity to the coast and to navigable rivers. But as population pressed farther into the interior, the rivers were less accessible and frequently unsuited even to light rafts. Overland routes became necessary and the buffalo and Indian trails were commonly used. They could not stand heavy traffic, however, and when the commercial production of tobacco, salt, iron and lumber developed in interior communities, roads had to be constructed. Then was voiced the demand for internal improvements which, together with the demand for land and tariff reform, ranked as the three most vital issues of the day.

Many economic interests stood to benefit from internal improvements. Cotton and tobacco planters in the southern piedmont, the wheat producers of Maryland, Pennsylvania and New York, the grain and stock farmers of New England, the owners of western lands seeking settlers, western settlers who were beginning to produce surplus goods, iron and coal producers, traders, merchants, importers, even the artisans in eastern cities would profit from reduced transportation rates. These groups, though not always aroused to united action, provided the great bulk of sentiment for state and Federal aid to internal improvements.

The first internal improvements, such as turnpikes*w* and some short canals around falls, were begun by private groups. Even the Middlesex Canal*w* to connect Boston with the Merrimac River, the first important canal to be built, was completed without public aid in 1803. Though itself not financially successful, it brought the trade of an important industrial area to Boston and showed the commercial advantages of canal construction, something which the Erie Canal*w* was soon to demonstrate on a larger scale. But few large improvements could be financed solely with private funds. State and local governments were first importuned for aid and they responded by adopting many enterprises, some of which were quite fantastic.

The proposal to connect the Hudson River with Lake Erie by a canal was suggested in the late 18th century and efforts were made to build small parts of the project but it was not until 1817 that New York State was induced to undertake it. By that time the merchants and commercial interests of New York City were competing with the merchants of Philadelphia, Baltimore and other eastern cities for the rich trade of the trans-Allegheny country and they threw their support behind the measure. The main canal was to connect the Hudson at Troy with Lake Erie at Buffalo by way of the Mohawk River and branch canals were to lead to Lake Champlain, Lake Ontario and the Finger Lakes. The Erie Canal was completed in 1825 and its success in rapidly developing upstate New York amazed the country. Towns sprang up along its route, the counties tributary to it were soon settled and the two termini, New York and Buffalo, enjoyed unprecedented growth. But more important, cheaper transportation was provided and an admirable route into the interior now made easier the great trek of settlers into the states of Old Northwest*w*.

Other states, not to be outdone by New York and determined to prevent her from monopolizing the trade of the interior, attempted to duplicate her feat by building their own canals, but unfortunately they had to go through or across the Alleghenies and New York's canal did not. Pennsylvania spent millions of dollars in canalizing the Susquehanna, Juniata and Conemaugh, and Allegheny rivers, Virginia subsidized the James River and Kanawha Canal and Maryland the Chesapeake and Ohio Canal^{qv}, all of which were influential in developing the sections they were built through but none of which were financially sound. Most of the states which undertook canal construction severely strained their credit, some even defaulted on their obligations. Poorly developed frontier states naturally were not able to finance costly canal and road construction and they looked to the National Government for assistance.

The first national enterprise was the Cumberland Road^{qv} to connect Cumberland, Md., at the head of navigation on the Potomac River, with Wheeling, on the Ohio River. The congressional act authorizing the road involved no constitutional hair-splitting because a portion of the receipts from public land^{qv} sales was available for such purposes, and, furthermore, there could be no doubt that the road was interstate in character. Although the measure was adopted in 1806 the road did not reach the Ohio River, 130 miles distant from Cumberland, until 1818. Subsequently, it was extended through Ohio and Indiana and into Illinois but it never reached its objective, Jefferson, Mo. The road made possible overland transportation of heavy goods, and the flow of commerce over it was so heavy that parts were worn out before it was completed. The Cumberland, or National Road^{qv} as it was later called, was the first great man-made thoroughfare into the interior of America and, like the Erie Canal, was important in opening up new areas to settlement and commercial farming.

Meantime, the insistent demand of other areas for aid to canal and road construction induced Albert Gallatin, Secretary of the Treasury, to prepare a report in 1808 on internal improvements in which he outlined a comprehensive system of canals and roads for Federal construction. No action was then taken but the agitation continued and came to a head in 1816 when Calhoun and others drove through Congress the Bonus Bill^{qv} which provided that the $1,500,000 bonus to be paid by the Second United States Bank^{qv} to the Government for banking privileges and also the Government's share of the interest on the bank's stock should be used for internal improvements. Calhoun argued that the post roads and general welfare clauses of the Constitution justified such an act. But President Madison, who was more familiar with the intentions of the Constitution's framers, was not convinced by Calhoun's

eloquence and vetoed the measure. Madison and Monroe, his successor, insisted that there was nothing in the Constitution to authorize Congress to use public funds for internal improvements and urged that recourse must be had to an amendment to the Constitution. Madison was looking backward to a simpler age when the settled area was narrowly circumscribed, while Calhoun, then a farseeing nationalist, looked to the future and was keenly aware of the need for better transportation facilities throughout the country. Calhoun and his section were subsequently to revert to Madison's narrow constitutional views while the West as it grew in political power voiced an irresistible demand for Federal aid to internal improvements and found its champion in Henry Clay.

From his first appearance in the halls of Congress, Clay favored Federal aid to roads and canals. His so-called American System^{qv} included protective tariffs to encourage the development of industries, and internal improvements to make possible the easy flow of domestic commerce. He championed the Cumberland Road, the Chesapeake and Ohio Canal and numerous other projects. Clay's brilliant manœuvring and the popularity of Federal aids put the opponents of internal improvements to rout and forced President Monroe to sign measures providing for a subsidy to the Chesapeake and Delaware Canal^{qv}, a $150,000 appropriation for the extension of the Cumberland Road to Zanesville, Ohio, and smaller amounts for surveys and roads elsewhere.

Clay's views on internal improvements had the sympathetic support of John Quincy Adams during whose administration financial subsidies were granted to the Louisville and Portland Canal, the Dismal Swamp Canal and the Chesapeake and Ohio Canal, and large land donations were made to aid the Miami, the Wabash and Lake Erie and the Illinois and Michigan canals to connect Lakes Erie and Michigan with the Ohio and Mississippi rivers^{qqv}. At the same time the rivers and harbors appropriations, the "pork barrel" legislation of a later day, began to appear with ominous regularity. Few of these enterprises were of lasting significance, and most of them were scarcely completed before the railroads^{qv} began to put them out of business. But they had their part in the settlement of the territories they served and in making possible the beginnings of commercial farming therein.

Andrew Jackson, though an ardent nationalist, like most of the early national leaders allowed his political and personal prejudices to affect his constitutional views and, finding that his chief enemy, Clay, supported internal improvements, he turned against them. He endeavored to stand on the same ground that Jefferson, Madison and Monroe had taken in their opposition to grants-in-aid, and in his ringing veto of Clay's Maysville[*] Turnpike bill he rehashed all the old arguments and denounced the project as being of a local character. But Jackson could no more stay the tide of sentiment favorable to Federal aid than Monroe, and during his eight years as President annual expenditures for canals, roads, and rivers and harbors were at the same rate as they had been during the Adams administration. True, more liberal land donations were made under Adams but when Jackson retired from the White House he could well boast that, despite his veto of the Maysville Turnpike bill, Federal aids had been lavishly distributed for transportation improvements.

In the middle 1830's the craze for internal improvements seemed to seize most of the country to a degree hitherto unsurpassed. Schemes were adopted without consideration of their feasibility and ultimate cost, states piled up debts to fantastic heights to finance their elaborate programs, absurd prices were paid for necessary lands, and other costs, even wages, were driven to high levels as a result of the competition of contractors for employees. Pennsylvania with its far-flung canal system, Ohio with its three north-south canals and other feeders, Indiana with its Wabash Canal, Illinois with its Illinois and Michigan Canal[qv] and an intricate network of railroads, Michigan with its three cross-state railroads, and other states with equally extensive programs all vied with one another in their efforts to extend their transportation facilities. The Panic of 1837[*] wrought havoc with these grand programs; many of the states were forced to suspend work, dismiss employees and subsequently default on their obligations (see Repudiation of State Debts). There was a revulsion against state ownership and construction and when business conditions revived in the late 1840's private capital generally was forced to take the initiative with little state assistance. Many of the state projects were sold to private groups, notably the Michigan Southern and Michigan Central railroads[qv]. Control over others, including the Wabash and the Illinois and Michigan canals, temporarily passed out of the hands of the states.

It was the misfortune of the canal promoters that so many of their projects were approaching completion about the same time that the railroads were being built to rival them. The Chesapeake and Ohio Canal suffered from the competition of the Baltimore and Ohio Railroad[*] which was, in fact, begun in the same year, 1828.

The Rock Island Railroad paralleled the entire line of the Illinois and Michigan Canal in less than a decade after the completion of the canal in 1848, and other canals enjoyed but a short period of predominance, except for such great thoroughfares as the Erie Canal and the local canals connecting the eastern hard coal section of Pennsylvania with the rivers.

In the eastern states the early railroads were generally built to connect important cities such as Boston and Lowell, Worcester and Springfield, Syracuse and Rochester. The process of consolidation was slow, and frequent changes were necessary between such cities as Albany and Buffalo, New York and Boston, and Washington and New York. Nevertheless, by 1850, the railroad net was beginning to reveal its modern outline. Although constructed by private groups, many of the eastern railroads received aid from state and local governments. Massachusetts assisted the Great Western Railroad which connected Boston with Troy, South Carolina contributed to the Charleston and Hamburg[*], and Baltimore aided the Baltimore and Ohio. Eastern states and cities, despite their financial reverses in the 1830's, recovered quickly and were easily able to help finance railroads but the relatively undeveloped West was not as fortunate. Consequently, in that area the cry went up for Federal grants of land to aid railroads. Again the bogey of unconstitutionality was raised by that section which felt that it would profit the least from Federal aid to railroads, the states of the Old South, but it had lost its effectiveness.

In 1850 a new era in Federal aid to internal improvements began when Congress granted 3,750,000 acres of land to aid in constructing a line of railroad from Galena and Chicago in Illinois to the Gulf of Mexico at Mobile. In the next twenty-one years more than 131,000,000 acres of land were given as subsidies[*] to railroads, and large loans were made to the Union and Central Pacific railroads[qv]. Even during such a southern controlled administration as that of Franklin Pierce southern opposition failed to prevent liberal land grants (see Land Grants to Railways). The generous land grants and the financial assistance rendered by the counties and cities, which subscribed liberally to the stock and bonds of those railroads which would build through or into them, were largely responsible for the great expansion of the railroad net in the middle and far west during the years 1850 to 1890. By the latter date all parts of the country were knit together by bands of steel, and it was thought the railroads would never be replaced by more modern transportation facilities.

The 20th century has witnessed even more rapid social and economic changes than did the 19th century. The perfection of the modern high speed automobile[w] led to the "good roads movement" and as a result the Federal and state governments have in recent years been engaged in programs of road[w] construction which call for the expenditure of more money in a year than was expended by the states and Federal Government in the entire pre-Civil War period on internal improvements. Furthermore, waterways[w], once thought quite outmoded, have been revived, widened and deepened and are again competing with other forms of transportation.

Federal and state aid to internal improvements was not always a blessing. Government liberality sometimes led to extravagance, corruption, overconstruction and early bankruptcy. Little return was ever made by the canals and railroads for this liberality and the public was all too frequently charged extortionate rates. But rapid construction in advance of population made possible quick settlement of the West, and a country which its early leaders thought possessed land enough to absorb Europe's surplus population for centuries to come was, by the end of the 19th century, beginning to think of immigration restrictions[w]. To DeWitt Clinton, Henry Clay, Daniel Webster, Asa Whitney, Stephen A. Douglas and others belongs the credit for securing Federal and state aids, and to the intrepid promoters and contractors that for carrying the great projects to completion.

[C. E. McGill, *History of Transportation in the United States before 1860;* A. B. Hulbert, *Historic Highways of America;* R. E. Riegel, *Story of the Western Railroads.*]

PAUL WALLACE GATES

Internal Revenue. The revenue of the Federal Government comes from customs[w] duties and internal revenues, the administration of which is in separate bureaus. The sources of internal revenue have gradually expanded until they now include excise taxes, personal and corporate income taxes[w], estate and gift taxes, railroad employment compensation taxes, social security taxes[w] and unjust enrichment taxes.

When the early customs duties failed to produce sufficient revenue, at the advice of Secretary Hamilton taxes were levied upon a few specified articles. That these were not popular is evidenced by the Whisky Rebellion[w] and, upon the advent of the new political regime early in the 19th century, steps were immediately taken to abolish them. The contentions were advanced that they increased the number of officers, that they were obnoxious, vexatious and hostile to the genius of a free people and expensive to collect. In spite of all objections the excises were abolished as well as the machinery for their collection. The complete failure of customs duties during the War of 1812 made the return to excises imperative and a large number of articles were made subject to tax. Agitation for their discontinuance began immediately after the war and in 1817 they were again abolished, not again to be re-enacted until the advent of the Civil War.

Secretary Chase did not indicate the need of excises at the beginning of the Civil War, but upon evidence of failure of his fiscal policy and the necessity for increased revenue, Congress enacted an extensive system of excises and provided machinery for their collection. The extent of the country placed a burden upon the new and inefficient machinery which left much to be desired in the administration of the tax. After the war the machinery was strengthened, the levy reduced to apply to a few commodities, especially liquors and tobacco products, and excises occupied a place of importance equal to that of customs and finally became of much greater importance. During the World War the list of taxable commodities was greatly extended but curtailment followed the close of the war. At present (1939) a large number of articles are included in the taxable list, those which are most productive of revenue being tobacco, liquors, gasoline, automobiles and automobile parts, electrical energy, telephone and telegraph messages and sugar.

At present the most important feature in the internal revenue is the receipts from the personal and corporation income tax. This developed rapidly after the adoption of the Sixteenth Amendment[w] in 1913 and has been used as an elastic feature of the system. Rates have been increased and exemptions lowered in times of need and, as the emergency passed, modifications have been made in the opposite direction. Income taxes will doubtless continue to be the most important feature of the internal revenue system.

In most of the wars in which the Federal Government has engaged, resort for revenue has been made to a levy upon the transfer of property at death in the form of an inheritance tax[w] or an estate tax. The general practice has been to abolish the tax after the war, but this was not followed after the World War and such a tax is still in use. The primary motive, however, has not been to secure revenue but to force some semblance of uniformity in the taxation of inheritances by the states and, in recent years especially, to break up large fortunes. The uniformity in state rates is accomplished through a credit provision. The Federal Government gives a state credit for the taxes which it may levy up to 80%

of the levy made by the Federal Government. That is, if the Federal tax were $100,000 it would collect only $20,000 if the state in which the estate were taxable levied a tax of $80,000 or more. Obviously the states have increased their rates to equal 80% of those levied by the Federal Government. With the very high rates which apply to estates, to attempt to evade through the grant of gifts before death was to be expected. In an effort to stop this practice a tax is levied upon gifts at the same rate as those which apply to transfers after death.

The provision, in recent years, for social security and for old age[qw] assistance necessitated a great increase in revenue and one which would increase in amount as the demands upon the Treasury became more marked. The attempt to meet this need is found in different types of taxes upon payrolls.

To administer all the taxes which produce internal revenue necessitates an extensive machinery. This is encompassed in the Bureau of Internal Revenue, one of the divisions of the Treasury Department, under the direction of the Commissioner of Internal Revenue. The Bureau is composed of a number of divisions, each of which is in charge of a deputy commissioner. The actual collection of revenues is handled by district internal revenue officers in the sixty-four collection districts into which the country is divided.

[D. R. Dewey, *Financial History of the United States;* A. G. Buehler, *Public Finance.*]   MERLIN H. HUNTER

International Boundary Disputes. *See* Alaska Boundary Question; Mexican Boundary; Northeast Boundary; Northwest Boundary Controversy.

International Harvester Company. As a solution to the bitter competitive warfare among manufacturers of farm machinery[qw] a consolidation of the leading companies in this industry was effected in 1902 at the instigation of Cyrus Hall McCormick, son of the inventor of the reaper[qw]. It included the McCormick Harvesting Machine Company, Deering Harvester Company, Plano Manufacturing Company, the Warder, Bushnell and Glessner Company and the Milwaukee Harvester Company. It acquired other concerns as its lines diversified. The original capital stock was $120,000,000. Action was brought against the company in 1914 by the Government and the Court held that under the Sherman Antitrust Law[qw] the company was an illegal combination in undue restraint of trade and ordered that the property of the company be divided among distinct independent corporations.

[C. H. McCormick, *The Century of the Reaper;* U. S. v. International Harvester Co., 214 U. S. 987, 1914.]
ROGER BURLINGAME

International Joint Commission. Created by the Treaty of 1909, it consists of three American and three Canadian members, and has jurisdiction over cases involving the use of boundary waters or of rivers crossing the boundary. It also investigates matters referred to it by the United States or Canadian governments; and may finally settle any problem of any nature that the two governments agree to refer to it. Since its organization in 1912, the Commission has disposed of a number of important questions, and has reached in nearly every case a unanimous decision.

[*Papers relating to the work of the International Joint Commission;* C. J. Chacko, *The International Joint Commission.*]
LAWRENCE J. BURPEE

International Labor Organization, THE, was planned at the Paris Conference of 1919 by a commission of which Samuel Gompers was president. The first conference of the I.L.O. was held in Washington. The United States remained outside the Organization until 1934 because of isolationist sentiment toward the League of Nations[qw], opposition from sections of labor which feared a lowering of legislative standards, and suspicion of Socialist influence in the Organization. Individual Americans, however, accepted appointments on its commissions. In fact, American standards were in many instances lower than those of the I.L.O. conventions. This and a second consideration—that American industry with higher standards would be served by their general acceptance in competitor countries—together with the favorable attitude of President F. D. Roosevelt, prompted a joint congressional resolution in June, 1934, authorizing membership.

[James T. Shotwell, *The Origins of the International Labor Organization.*]
HAROLD S. QUIGLEY

International Law may be defined as the body of general principles and concrete rules which states, as members of the community of nations, accept as binding upon themselves in their relations with one another. Its legal character lies in the fact that through succeeding centuries the nations have on the whole been faithful to its obligations, due partly to the recognition of the necessity of such rules of conduct as a condition of peaceful intercourse and partly to respect for the sanction of public opinion. But while respected within its limited sphere, international law has never succeeded in extending its authority over a number of the most vital relations of states, which they have preferred to mark off as "matters of policy" outside and above the law.

In respect to these matters each nation tends to develop a foreign policy^{w} of its own, representing its individual attitude toward particular questions as dictated by its national interests.

On the eve of the American Revolution international law was confined to the circle of European powers among whom its principles and rules had originated some two hundred years earlier. With the Definitive Treaty of Peace of 1783^{w} the United States was the first state of the Western Hemisphere to enter the community or "family of nations." The new republic literally fought its way into the group of older states and obtained recognition^{w} of its right of membership not by reason of any principle of self-determination, such as the Declaration of Independence set forth, but solely by the fact of its independent existence as confirmed by Great Britain in the treaty. The admission of the United States into the community of nations carried with it an acknowledgment on its part that henceforth it would be bound by the rules of conduct which constituted the legal code of the community.

As early as 1793 the United States had occasion to contribute to the development of new rules of international law. At that time there was no clear principle regulating the recognition of a government coming into power by the forcible overthrow of an earlier *de jure* government. Jefferson, confronted with the *de facto* existence of the new Republic of France, declared himself ready to "acknowledge any government to be rightful which is formed by the will of the nation, substantially declared." Again, in 1794, the United States by its first Neutrality Act contributed in a constructive way to the development of more specific obligations on the part of neutral states toward belligerents (*see* Neutrality, Proclamation of). At the same time the United States came to champion more liberal rules of trade between neutrals and belligerents, and the succeeding decade was marked by the constant effort to resist what were believed to be unlawful extensions of the rules of contraband and blockade^{qw} both by Great Britain and by France. Controversies arising over these rules finally reached their climax in the declaration of war against Great Britain in 1812.

In the year 1822 new problems of international law arose in respect to the conditions under which the United States might recognize the independence of a number of Latin-American states which had thrown off the yoke of their mother country. President Monroe now applied to new states the principle of recognition based upon *de facto* control which Jefferson had applied to new governments in 1793 (*see* Latin-American Republics,

Recognition of the). The following year the President issued a warning to the powers of the Holy Alliance that an attempt on their part to extend their system to this hemisphere would be considered by us as dangerous to our peace and safety. The Monroe Doctrine^{w} thus declared against the intervention of the Quadruple Alliance in the struggle of the Latin-American states for their independence; and while the principle that it lays down has never been formally adopted as a rule of international law it has been time and again impliedly accepted as a regional rule applicable to the Western Hemisphere.

The middle of the 19th century found the United States asserting new principles with respect to the nationality of persons acquiring citizenship of the United States by naturalization^{w}. The doctrine of indelible allegiance might perhaps be said to have been the rule of international law at that time; at any rate it was the rule enforced as such by the courts of the United States. But the Executive Department found it expedient to assert the new rule that naturalization effects a change of nationality even in respect to the country of origin of the naturalized alien. This new rule was recognized in the conclusion of the Bancroft treaties of 1868, but it has not yet been completely accepted by all countries.

With the outbreak of the Civil War in 1861 the United States, reversing its position of 1793–1812, found itself in the position of a belligerent^{w} seeking to restrict the rights of neutral trade with the Confederate States. New rules of "continuous voyage"^{qw} and "continuous transports" were asserted in order to make more effective the traditional law of contraband and blockade. Moreover, the depredations of the *Alabama*^{w} led to insistence by the United States upon stricter duties of neutrality^{w}, with the result that the "three rules" of the Treaty of Washington^{w} set up a new standard in respect to the use of neutral ports for the fitting out of belligerent vessels.

The opening of the 20th century was marked by the recognition of new obligations, bilateral and multilateral, in respect to the pacific settlement of international disputes. At the second Hague Peace Conference of 1907 the United States delegation sought to create, side by side with the Hague Permanent Court of Arbitration^{qw}, a new Judicial Arbitration Court of a more permanent character, which might give continuity to international jurisprudence and develop international law by a series of precedents. In addition to methods of peaceful procedure the Conference elaborated new rules of warfare which were to find application, or rather were to be proven inadequate, when the World War broke out in 1914. Controversies over neutral rights[w] took place with the belligerents on both sides, with the result that the United States finally declared war against Germany.

The close of the war found President Wilson occupying a leading role in an effort to extend the scope of international law by the creation of a system of collective security to protect states against future acts of aggression (*see* Fourteen Points) . The failure of the United States to ratify the Treaty of Versailles[w], of which the Covenant of the League of Nations[w] constituted the first twenty-six articles, created a number of embarrassing situations due on the one hand to the uncertainty as to the position that the United States would take in the event of action by the League under Article 16 of the Covenant and on the other hand to the relations of the United States to the various international unions which had been incorporated into the League. An anomalous situation was also created by the refusal of the United States Senate to approve the ratification of the protocol containing the Statute of the Permanent Court of International Justice, which had been elaborated under the leadership of former Secretary of State Elihu Root, and which, but for the minor connection between the Court and the League of Nations, was directly in line with the policy of the United States twenty years earlier.

In the meantime the United States had taken the lead in calling the Washington Naval Conference of 1921–22[w], at which agreements were reached upon the limitation of armaments in respect to dreadnaughts and large cruisers, as well as an agreement, in the form of the Nine-Power Treaty[w], with respect to the territorial and administrative integrity of China and the principle of the "open door"[w]. This constructive action was followed in 1928 by the world-wide adoption, upon the initiative of the United States, of the Treaty for the Renunciation of War (*see* Briand-Kellogg Pact) , which extended the limitations upon resort to war first set down in the Covenant of the League of Nations, while still leaving open the loophole of wars of self-defense.

The invasion of Manchuria by Japan in 1931 proved to be the occasion for the assertion by Secretary Stimson, on Jan. 7, 1932, of the policy of nonrecognition[w] of territory acquired by means contrary to the obligations of the Kellogg Pact. This unilateral action of the United States was supported by the Assembly of the League of Nations on March 11, 1932, and in consequence the policy may be said to have become a rule of international law.

In addition to these and other contributions to general international law the United States has of recent years taken the lead in seeking to develop a regional international law for the American Republics. At the Montevideo, Buenos Aires and Lima Conferences of 1933, 1936 and 1938 (*see* Pan-American Conferences) , new rules of substantive law were adopted and new methods of peaceful procedure defined. The Declaration of Lima is a multilateral reaffirmation of the principle underlying the Monroe Doctrine, and while not drawn up in treaty form it is nevertheless to be regarded as a new development of the regional law of this hemisphere.

[C. G. Fenwick, *International Law,* 2nd ed.; C. C. Hyde, *International Law Chiefly as Interpreted and Applied by the United States;* J. B. Moore, *International Law Digest;* G. G. Wilson, *International Law,* 9th ed.]

C. G. FENWICK

International Peace Garden, THE, is located on the United States-Canadian boundary line between North Dakota and Manitoba. It comprises a total continuous area of 888 acres in the United States and 1312 acres in Canada. It originated as a monument to the friendship of nations. The suggestion to build such a garden was first made by Henry J. Moore of Islington, Ontario, Canada, in 1929. It is under the control of a New York corporation known as the International Peace Garden, Inc., with seventy-one voting members, a board of directors and other officers. Locally, the portion on the American side is being developed by the National Park Service and the State Historical Society of North Dakota, and the funds for the improvement of the grounds are provided jointly by North Dakota and the Federal Government. On the Canadian side the construction funds are provided by the Dominion Government, and the work is under the supervision of the Department of Public Works of Manitoba. National and international organizations, school children and adults also provide funds for construction.

The formal dedication ceremony took place July 14, 1932. On the boundary line between the two countries stands a rock cairn bearing this inscription: "To God in His Glory we two nations dedicate this garden and pledge ourselves that as long as men shall live we will not take up arms against one another."

The Garden is designed to serve as an international area for the use of visitors and tourists. The site, in the Turtle Mountains, was selected because of its central location on the North American Continent and because of the scenic beauty of the region.

O. G. LIBBY

Interstate Barriers originated prior to 1775, when some of the colonies raised trade barriers against their neighbors. For example, Maryland in 1704 prohibited certain importations from Pennsylvania. During the Confederation period[w] more interstate barriers were raised. In 1787 New York imposed tariff duties on products brought in from New Jersey and Connecticut. Virginia and Maryland hindered each other's trade on Chesapeake Bay and the Potomac River.

To minimize such interference with domestic free trade, the framers of the Constitution of the United States wrote into Article I, Section 10, the following provision, "No State shall, without the Consent of the Congress, lay any Imposts or Duties on Imports or Exports, except what may be absolutely necessary for executing its inspection Laws. . . ." This provision long operated to maintain substantially free intercourse between the states. In recent years, especially since the beginning of the great depression in 1929, many states, seeking more revenues, have, under the subterfuge of legitimate inspection or taxation, erected barriers which have become a distinct menace to interstate trade. By 1939 approximately a thousand restrictive laws existed. Various states had, for example, established "ports of entry" where out-of-state trucks were inspected and charged fees. Kansas led with sixty-six such "ports," closely followed by Oklahoma with fifty-eight. Twenty-four states taxed oleomargarine. New York had attempted to keep out milk from other states. Numerous states had imposed preferential taxes on liquors as in Michigan, where domestic wine was taxed four cents a gallon while wine imported from outside the state was taxed fifty cents a gallon. These, and the many other interstate barriers which had been erected, appeared in 1939 to be threatening the "Balkanization" of the United States. To deal with the problem a national Conference on Interstate Barriers was held at Chicago in April, 1939.

[De-Balkanizing, *Time*, Vol. XXXIII, No. 16; E. M. Eriksson and D. N. Rowe, *American Constitutional History*.]   ERIK McKINLEY ERIKSSON

Interstate Commerce. *See* Trade, Domestic.

Interstate Commerce Commission, THE, was set up by the Interstate Commerce Act of 1887, on the authority of the provision of the Constitution granting Congress power to regulate commerce among the states. The members of the Commission, originally five, later seven, and now eleven in number, are appointed by the President with the advice and consent of the Senate, for terms of seven years. Not more than six members

may be of the same political faith. The original act, though it gave the Commission certain regulatory powers over railroads, did not give it the degree of control necessary to develop an adequate transportation system. As a result of incessant demand for increasing the power of the Commission, the Elkins Act of 1903, Hepburn Act of 1906, Mann-Elkins Act of 1910, Valuation Act of 1913, Transportation Act of 1920 and Motor Carrier Act of 1935[qw] were passed. This legislation granted to the Commission sweeping inquisitorial and regulatory powers over rates, the character and conditions of service of railroad, motor carrier, sleeping car, express and pipe line companies engaged in interstate commerce; as well as authority to inquire into their accounts, records, financial structures and management, and power to impose penalties for refusal to comply with the Commission's orders. Authority over telegraph, telephone and cable service, granted in 1888, was transferred to the Federal Communications Commission[w] in 1934.

The staff of the Commission in 1937 consisted of about 2200 persons, and its expenditures amounted to nearly $8,000,000 annually. To expedite administration, it has subdivided its membership, each subdivision having power to act for the Commission. Most of the original hearings are conducted by attorney examiners, but may be reviewed by the entire Commission, or one of its divisions. The Commission is required to publish its findings and decisions, and to make annual reports to Congress.

[I. L. Sharfman, *The Interstate Commerce Commission;* B. C. Gavit, *The Commerce Clause of the United States Constitution.*]   GEORGE W. GOBLE

Interstate Commerce Laws. Two restrictions limit the power of Congress over commerce. The Constitution limits this power to commerce that is interstate in character, while judicial interpretations tend to confine it to matters relating to transportation and communication. Neither of these distinctions is particularly definite or clear cut. The adoption of the Interstate Commerce Act marked a change from the century-old policy of *laissez-faire*, and the beginning of a policy of regulation and control of business, increasingly extensive in its application. While innumerable laws and amendments to laws have been passed, there have been certain mileposts in the chronological development, around which this brief discussion may be centered:

(1). The Interstate Commerce Act (1887) represented the answer of Congress to the rapidly mounting public indignation at abuses in the railway business, brought into the open by the report of the famous Cullom Committee[T]. Among these were rate discriminations between shippers and between districts, the rebate[T] evil, discriminations against independent shippers in matters of car supply, use of terminal facilities, demurrage charges, and in the use of private cars and car lines. This was the first regulatory commission, and the model for many that were to follow.

(2). The Sherman Antitrust Act[T] (1890) represented the attempt of Congress to satisfy an insistent public demand for a curb on monopolies[T]. The act, which forbade "all combinations in restraint of trade,"[T] provided four methods of enforcement, with severe penalties, none of which were really effective. Extensive litigation has failed to clarify, even to this day, its meaning.

(3). The Publicity Acts (1903 and 1909) were the forerunners of the Securities and Exchange Commission Act of 1934[qT]. Commonly known as blue-sky laws[T], these measures sought to curb the sale of fraudulent securities.

(4). The Federal Trade Commission and the Clayton acts (1914)[qT] represented the adoption of a new principle in trade regulation. Whereas the Sherman Act sought to punish those who violated the law, the Federal Trade Commission Act sought to prevent the use of "unfair methods of competition in restraint of trade." Where the first was slow, expensive and ineffective, the latter was quick, cheap and effective. The Clayton Act, passed at the insistence of the American Federation of Labor[T], sought to strengthen the position of organized labor, and to exempt it from the provisions of the Sherman Act.

(5). The Shipping Acts (1916 and 1920) and the Esch-Cummins Railway Act (1920)[qT] sought respectively to encourage the American merchant marine, and the building up of the badly run-down railroads. The Shipping Act of 1916 set up the Shipping Board to govern rates and service, as a war-time agency; the Act of 1920 established it permanently on a peacetime basis. The Railway Act in effect guaranteed "a fair return upon a fair valuation," and reversed earlier legislative provisions by authorizing consolidations, with the consent of the Interstate Commerce Commission[T].

(6). Under the New Deal program of 1933 ff. there were the National Industrial Recovery Act and the Agricultural Adjustment Act (both found unconstitutional by the Supreme Court); also the Public Works Administration[qT]. Additional phases of the program included provision for the Federal Co-ordinator of Transportation, legislation affecting credit, banking, bankruptcy, labor, housing, etc.

Other important measures include the Federal regulation of radio, first by the Federal Radio Commission (1927), and later by the Federal Communications Commission (1934); of public utilities by the Federal Power Commission (1920) and the more extensive program represented by the Tennessee Valley Authority[qT] (1933).

[Thomas C. Blaisdell, Jr., *The Federal Trade Commission;* J. M. Clark, *The Social Control of Business;* J. W. Clark, *The Federal Trust Policy;* Earl W. Crecraft, *Government and Business;* Frank H. Dixon, *Railroads and Government;* Gerald C. Henderson, *The Federal Trade Commission;* Jeremiah W. Jenks and W. E. Clark, *Social Control of Business;* D. Philip Locklin, *Railway Regulation since 1920;* C. C. Rohlfing, E. W. Carter, B. W. West and J. G. Hervey, *Business and Government;* Henry R. Seager and C. A. Gulick, Jr., *Trust and Corporation Problems;* I. L. Sharfman, *The Interstate Commerce Commission;* W. W. Willoughby, *Constitutional Law of the United States;* James T. Young, *The New American Government and Its Work.*]

W. BROOKE GRAVES

Interstate Compacts. The states are forbidden by the Constitution to make treaties with one another, but they may, with the consent of Congress, enter into agreements or compacts. There is no constitutional limitation as to the subject matter of such interstate agreements, nor any regulation of the procedure, hence agreements may be made by any two or more states on any matter desired by the states concerned and agreed to by Congress.

Approximately one hundred compacts were entered into during the first century and a half of our history (1789–1939), dealing with such subjects as state boundaries, control and improvement of navigation, crime control and criminal jurisdiction, conservation of forests and other natural resources, distribution of water rights and power, flood control, control of crop production, sanitation, labor questions and a number of miscellaneous matters. Among the more notable of these compacts are the compact of 1919 between New York and New Jersey, providing for the construction of the Hudson tunnels; the compacts of 1921 and 1922 between the same states establishing the Port of New York Authority; the Colorado River or Boulder Dam[T] Compact of 1922 among seven states of the West and Southwest; and the New England Minimum Wage Compact of 1935 among Massachusetts, Rhode Island and New Hampshire.

The compact has been used much more frequently during recent years, as interstate and regional problems have become more numerous. Congress has recognized the need of expediting interstate agreements on particular problems, and has passed statutes giving blanket consent to the states to enter into compacts with respect to such matters as forest fire prevention (1911), crime control (1934), tobacco production control (1936), flood control (1936) and parks and recreational areas (1936). In several states permanent commissions have been established to formulate recommendations and to negotiate compacts as these interstate problems arise. Although the compact is a slow, cumbersome and by no means adequate means of dealing with problems of this character, it nevertheless provides a useful opportunity for overcoming some of the disadvantages of the Federal system, and for regulating matters that lie essentially within the jurisdiction of the states but that actually concern more than one state.

[Charles Warren, *The Supreme Court and the Sovereign States;* Felix Frankfurter and James M. Landis, The Compact Clause of the Constitution—A Study in Interstate Adjustments, *Yale Law Journal,* Vol. XXXIV; Jane Perry Clark, Interstate Compacts and Social Legislation, *Political Science Quarterly,* Vols. L and LI; Table of Interstate Compacts, 1789-1936, in *State Government,* Vol. IX.]   CLARENCE A. BERDAHL

Interurban Electric Lines. The first interurban electric railway was built, and so named, by Charles L. Henry in 1897. It traversed eleven miles between Anderson and Alexandria, Ind. There was rapid but steady expansion to 1917, especially in the east north-central states where 40% of the trackage was built. Historically, the interurban first provided a connecting link between city and country for both business and pleasure. After 1917 the automobile𝒯 began better to serve this purpose. The period 1917–27 was one of arrested development and retrenchment; 1927–38, abandonment, except where areas of heavy automobile traffic gave rejuvenated interurban lines an advantage. The track mileage increased from 6885 in 1902 to 18,097 in 1917. In 1932 it had decreased to 11,039; in 1937, to 7131, of which some was not in operation.

[U. S. Bureau of Census Reports, *Electric Railways,* 1902, 1907, 1912, 1917, 1922, 1927, 1932, 1937; *Electric Railway Journal,* Oct. 2, 1909; *ÆRA,* Vol. X, p. 697.]   HARVEY L. CARTER

Intervention, American Policy of. Intervention, or forcible interference in the affairs of another state with or without its consent, has been common in international practice. A chronological list of occasions on which force has been used for the protection of American interests, prepared some years ago by an official of the Department of State, cites forty-six cases before 1912, and there have been many others since that year.

Though both motives are often present, there is an important difference between intervention primarily for political purposes and intervention having as its object the protection of American lives and property. Examples of the former category are the military operations in Florida between 1812 and 1818 (*see* East Florida, Attempted Seizure of; Arbuthnot and Ambrister, Case of), the maintenance of order on the Isthmus of Panama under the Treaty of 1846 (*see* Bidlack-Mallarino Treaty) with New Granada, and more especially many of the actions of the United States in the Caribbean region between 1904 and 1933. (*See also* Caribbean Policy; Cuba; Dominican Republic; Haiti, Intervention in; Nicaragua, Relations with; Panama.) At present it is the policy of the United States to refrain from intervention of this sort, and the Convention on Rights and Duties of States, signed at the Pan-American Conference𝒯 at Montevideo in 1933, provides that "No state has the right to intervene in the internal or external affairs of another." The United States ratified this convention, and its delegation signed the additional Protocol Relative to Non-Intervention adopted by the Buenos Aires Conference of 1936 (*see* Peace Conference at Buenos Aires), which contains a still more explicit provision.

Intervention for the sole purpose of protecting foreign life and property rests on a different basis. Writers on international law𝒯 have generally upheld the right of a state to protect its citizens abroad, where the local sovereign was unable or unwilling to do so. The United States has repeatedly sent warships to foreign ports or landed armed forces where American citizens were in danger, and the continued presence of American forces in China indicates that it has not abandoned the practice.

Until within the last half-century, the chief problem was the protection of American shipping or of American merchants living in places not under the jurisdiction of any European power. On several occasions, for example, natives of islands in the Pacific or local rulers in Africa or the Near East were chastised by the United States Navy for offenses against American vessels or their crews. Operations of this sort became generally unnecessary with the expansion of European political control in these regions, but in the meantime the growth of American investments abroad and the fact that many United States citizens were going to live in countries where political disturbances were common created new demands for protection elsewhere.

The United States has intervened more frequently in China than in any other country. The Reed Treaty of 1858𝒯 authorized the stationing of American naval vessels in Chinese waters and the capture of pirates by them; and the protocol of 1901, signed after the United States and other powers had sent an expeditionary force to relieve the besieged foreign legations at Peking (*see* Boxer Rebellion), authorized the maintenance of a legation guard at that city and the occupation of several points between there and the sea. Besides the troops kept in the country under the 1901 protocol, other forces have repeatedly been landed at places where danger existed. Extremely disturbed conditions prevailed in 1911–12 and for a long period in the 1920's, and there were more than forty occasions between 1911 and 1929 where military action was taken in China for the protection of American citizens. The most sensational of these was the "Nanking incident" of March 23–24, 1927, when a British and an American warship laid down a barrage to break up an attack on the house of the manager of the Standard Oil Company, where the American consular staff and other British and American residents, with a small force of American bluejackets, had taken refuge.

Intervention of this type, solely or primarily for the purpose of protecting American citizens, has also taken place on several occasions in the Caribbean. There have been very numerous occasions when small detachments have been landed simply to maintain order temporarily in a given locality where Americans were in danger, as in Cuba in 1912 and 1917, in Honduras in 1919 and 1924, and in Nicaragua in 1912 and 1926–27. A large number of warships were sent to Cuban ports because of disturbed conditions in the latter part of 1933. Action of this sort has often served to protect other foreigners as well as Americans. The United States has not questioned the right of other powers to extend protection to their own nationals in the Caribbean region, and European naval forces have in fact frequently been landed temporarily to maintain order at Caribbean ports; but the American Government has shown a tendency to discourage such action, and to assume the responsibility for protecting all foreign interests, because of its unwillingness to permit other powers to exercise any political influence in the countries involved.

The tendency of American policy has been more and more to restrict the practice of intervention in cases where the protection of citizens and their interests is involved. Contrary to the practice of several European governments, the United States has rarely if ever used force to collect claims arising from loans or concessions[w]. At the Hague Conference[w] of 1907 it obtained the approval of an agreement by which most of the great creditor powers pledged themselves not to

have recourse to armed force for the recovery of contract debts except in cases where the debtor state refused arbitration or failed to comply with an arbitral award. In the 1920's it usually confined its intervention to cases where American lives were clearly and immediately in danger, though President Coolidge stated during the Nicaraguan troubles of 1926–27 that property as well as lives was being protected. In more recent years, the usual practice has been to insist that American citizens withdraw from disturbed areas, rather than to attempt to protect them at their homes and places of business.

[T. S. Offutt, *Protection of Citizens Abroad;* Department of State, *Right to Protect Citizens in Foreign Countries by Landing Forces;* J. B. Moore, *Digest of International Law.*]

DANA G. MUNRO

Intestate Estates. In colonial America the South, New York and Rhode Island followed the English rule of descent, under which the lands of a person dying without making a will descended to his eldest son, while chattels were distributed to the children equally. New England and Pennsylvania, influenced in part by the English local custom of gavelkind and in part by Biblical precedent, assimilated real and personal property, and provided for an equitable division to the children with a double portion for the eldest son. The New England rule was challenged in Winthrop v. Lechmere, where the Privy Council[w] denied its validity as being contrary to the common-law rule of primogeniture, but in a later decision, Philips v. Savage, the same body was induced to support these intestacy laws. Even in 18th-century New England, however, land in fee tail was generally held to descend to the eldest son.

The Revolutionary era ushered in a legislative offensive in the Middle and Southern states, as well as Rhode Island, against primogeniture[w]. Under the influence of the back-country party, partible succession was substituted for primogeniture, and the New England group, including Pennsylvania, abolished the extra dispensation for the eldest son, providing equal division among the children. While prior to the Civil War the philosophers of the Cotton Kingdom[w] advocated the reintroduction of primogeniture, for over a century the rule has obtained in the United States that, on the death of an intestate seized of real property in fee simple, such property descends to his or her children equally, subject to the varying rights of the surviving husband or wife.

[R. B. Morris, *Studies in the History of American Law;* C. M. Andrews, The Influence of Colonial Conditions as Illustrated in the Connecticut Intestacy Law, *Select Essays in Anglo-American Law*, Vol. I.]

RICHARD B. MORRIS

Intolerable Acts, THE, in part also known as the Coercion Acts[qv], were five acts of Parliament: the Boston Port Act (March, 1774); the Massachusetts Government Act; the Act for the Impartial Administration of Justice (May, 1774); the Quartering Act; and the Quebec Act (June, 1774) [qqv]. The first four acts were designed to punish Boston[qv] for the Tea Party and to reinforce royal authority at the expense of popular liberty by alterations in the Massachusetts charter; the Quebec Act, although lumped by Americans with the Coercion Acts, was not a punitive measure, but in the hands of colonial propagandists it was made to appear a menace to the religious as well as the civil liberties of the colonists. To Lord North's consternation, these acts, intended to restore peace and order in America and to isolate Massachusetts, threw the colonies into ferment and became the justification for calling the first Continental Congress[qv].

[J. T. Adams, *Revolutionary New England.*]

JOHN C. MILLER

Intolerance was a general characteristic of society in the 17th century. Anglicans, Catholics and Puritans[qqv], alike, held that views contrary to their professions were errors not to be tolerated within jurisdictions which they controlled. Although there were notable exceptions to this viewpoint in the English colonies, the degree of tolerance existing in most of them in the 17th century was an outcome of expediency rather than principle. Even in the comparatively easygoing Dutch province of New Netherland, Peter Stuyvesant persecuted those who differed from the Reformed Church.

Intolerance was an outstanding characteristic of the religious and political institutions of the first New England settlements. The ideal of self-contained communities, inherent in the theocratic[qv] system, could be reconciled neither with the immigration of settlers who were not of the "visible saints" nor with the removal from the colony of those who were steadfast in the faith. The persecution of the Quakers[qv] after 1657 was merely a continuance of the policy which had resulted in the banishment of Roger Williams and Anne Hutchinson (*see* Antinomian Controversy). Rival faiths could not be tolerated and the introduction of episcopacy into Massachusetts was "a thing more dreaded than the Indian War." But the whole course of the theocrats must be regarded as a struggle to preserve the integrity of their churches. "You know right well," a clergyman wrote after the Plymouth settlement, "that the Churches of Christ have not thrived under the tolerating government of Holland, from whence the Lord hath translated one Church already . . .; and further it is well known loose liberty cannot endure to look majesticall authority in the face." Intolerance the Puritans cultivated for their own security.

Intolerance assumed other forms in the 19th century. The Anti-Masonic party[qv] in 1831 became in many states a protest against the holding of public office by members of the order of Freemasons. This was followed a decade later by the more significant Native American or "Know-Nothing" party[qv], which sought the restriction of immigration, and the exclusion of all except native-born Americans from officeholding (*see* Nativism). It was aimed at the Catholics and especially at aliens of that faith. The justification for its platform was supplied by the riotous and corrupt behavior of the Irish in the large cities along the Atlantic seaboard.

Since the Civil War intolerance has not been the fundamental principle of any significant political party but has been the justification for many organized groups which have sought to influence public opinion. The Ku Klux Klan[qv] in the South after 1870 sought by terror to subdue the Negroes and to mitigate the evils of the "carpetbag"[qv] regimes in state capitals. A more recent revival of the Ku Klux Klan, which was extended beyond the South, has been anti-Negro, anti-Jewish and anti-Catholic in its activities. This organized group displayed its greatest power in the presidential campaign of 1928[qv]. The prohibition movement[qv] has also given rise to a great deal of intolerance. The Anti-Saloon League[qv], founded in 1893, joined with other temperance groups to attack the liquor traffic and to secure the adoption of the Eighteenth Amendment[qv].

Except in the early colonial days, intolerance has not been characteristic of the American people. On the contrary, individual liberty has prevailed. But from time to time in periods of crisis or where supposed evils have arisen, an ardent patriotism has appeared in which intolerance manifests itself through organized groups. Except in time of war, the Government has seldom embarked upon measures which could be condemned as intolerant.

[W. S. Carpenter, *Development of American Political Thought.*]

WILLIAM S. CARPENTER

Intrepid, THE, formerly the Tripolitan ketch *Mastico,* was captured by Stephen Decatur and used by him on Feb. 16, 1804, in burning the

Philadelphia[w]. On the night of Sept. 4, 1804, the vessel, carrying 15,000 pounds of powder and 150 large shells, solid shot, and combustibles, was sailed into the harbor of Tripoli by Lt. Richard Somers accompanied by two other officers and ten men, where it exploded before getting sufficiently near the enemy gunboats to destroy them. The thirteen unlucky Americans were all killed.

[Gardner W. Allen, *Our Navy and the Barbary Corsairs;* Charles Lee Lewis, *The Romantic Decatur.*]

CHARLES LEE LEWIS

Inventions, Great. The history of invention in the United States may be divided, roughly, into two phases. The Civil War marks the division. The inventions of the first phase worked, in the beginning, to bring about separation and expansion, but at the end of the period they worked toward union. The inventions of the second phase have tended to consolidate this union.

The great needs of the first phase were presented by agriculture, distance and labor shortage. The flour mill of Oliver Evans (1780) which so combined machinery that the product passed from grain sack to flour barrel without human intervention responded to two of these needs. So did the cotton gin[w] of Eli Whitney (1793). This device, however, designed as a labor saver, had the effect of multiplying slavery by increasing the planting of cotton. Thus it became a remote cause of the Civil War.

Far more important, technically, than the gin was Whitney's second labor-saving invention. In 1798 he designed for the manufacture of muskets what later became known throughout the world as the "American system." Working with jigs or patterns in automatic machines he produced identical, interchangeable parts[w] in unlimited quantity. This was revolutionary in the period. It is, perhaps, the greatest invention in American history and forms the basis of all machine mass production[w].

Western emigration which made labor-shortage acute in the East also revealed the problems of distance and soon made demands of its own. The steamboat[w], invented by John Fitch (1787) and made useful by John Stevens, Nicholas Roosevelt, Robert Livingston, Robert Fulton and others, overcame the difficulty of upstream river transport. Stevens, then, inspired the Americanization of the steam railroad. The peculiar American need of economy, because of the extent of track, was met by Stevens' son Robert with the T-rail (1830).

When agriculture increased in the fertile West the reaper of Cyrus H. McCormick[w] (1831–34) turned subsistence-farming into mass production. This, with new methods of transport, began the centralization of food supply, making other parts of the country dependent on the West and thus establishing the necessity of union. The greatest psychological stimulus to unity came, however, with the electro-magnetic telegraph[w] invented by Joseph Henry (1831) and brought into use by Alfred Vail and Samuel Morse (1844). Aided by the rotary presses (*see* Printing in America) of Richard Hoe (1847) and the resultant cheap newspapers[w], it unified public opinion and completed the process of democracy in the nation.

Industry, as well as agriculture, had now become centralized. Beginning with the reproduction of English machinery by Samuel Slater (1790), the textile[w] industry had grown enormously in New England. The boot and shoe[w] industry kept pace. Great impetus was given to both by the labor-saving sewing machines[w] of Elias Howe (1844), Isaac Singer (1851), Benjamin Wilson (1850) and James Gibbs (1850–58). These machines created the ready-made garment industry.

It is commonly supposed that the later period of American invention was the greatest. In the second phase, however, comparatively little invention was basic. Most of it was improvement in the interests of unification, consolidation, speed and the cultural impulse.

The typewriter[w], probably invented by William Burt in 1829, played no part in business until the 1870's. Meanwhile, out of the efforts by Sholes, Glidden, Clephane and many others to perfect it, came one of the greatest inventions of the century, Ottmar Mergenthaler's linotype[w] (1884). This revolutionized the one remaining slow process in printing and made modern American journalism possible.

The telephone[w] (1876), of which Alexander Graham Bell is the accepted inventor, seems from the social point of view merely a new variety of rapid communication. Psychologically, however, its effect was far more unifying than that of the telegraph because of the illusion it gave of personal contact.

The phonograph[w], a great basic invention by Thomas A. Edison (1877), belongs to the cultural phase, along with inventions in photography[w], processes for the printing of pictures, and radio[w] broadcasting. In this phase also the sound-record principle has combined with many inventions in celluloid film photography and projection to produce the modern motion picture[w] whose social effect is highly unifying and standardizing. Bearing upon this and of immense effect also in the scientific world is the invention of the incandescent lamp[w] usually attributed to Edison (1879). The improvements in dynamos and motors during the second phase are efforts at consolidation of power. Few of them are technically basic inventions. We must look to the future for the decentralizing effect of electrical energy generated by water power and transmitted by new methods.

The basic heavier-than-air flying machine by Orville and Wilbur Wright (1903–1908) has depended for its present usefulness on the collateral science of metallurgy and the technology of the internal combustion engine (*see* Aviation). Its social effect, apart from war, is still negligible. The cheap automobile*ᵂ*, an American development of the speed phase, has resulted from improved industrial machinery and processes. It has tended to standardize, democratize and consolidate national unity though it is leading, today, toward urban decentralization.

Apart from social aspects, invention itself has become collective in the second phase. The old-time individualist inventor has largely disappeared. Technology has become so complex and so dependent on the advance of all the sciences that inventions are made today by groups of anonymous technicians in laboratories often under industrial ægis.

[Roger Burlingame, *March of the Iron Men* and *Engines of Democracy*; National Resources Committee, *Technological Trends and National Policy*; Victor S. Clark, *History of Manufactures in the U. S.*; Waldemar Kaempffert, *Popular History of American Invention*; Seymour Dunbar, *History of Travel in America*; A. D. Turnbull, *John Stevens*; Stuart Chase, *Men and Machines*; J. N. Leonard, *Tools of Tomorrow*.]   ROGER BURLINGAME

Investigating Committees have frequently been used throughout our history to obtain evidence on which Congress, state legislatures and city councils have acted. Whether joint, standing or special committees, they must be expressly authorized to subpœna witnesses and papers on a specific subject. The colonial assemblies*ᵂ*, following English precedents, frequently authorized investigations of elections, finances, etc. Some state constitutions (e.g., Maryland, 1776) expressly authorized such committees, but for Congress and most legislatures it is an implied power*ᵂ*.

Congressional investigations of elections and qualifications of members have occurred at almost every session (*see* Vare Case). A bribery investigation in 1857 resulted in the expulsion of four representatives, and an act making refusal to testify before congressional committees a misdemeanor. Later instances were the Crédit Mobilier scandal*ᵂ*, the Silver Pool investigation (1891), sugar tariff bribery charges (1894), post office graft (1884 and 1903) (*see* Star Route

Frauds) and the ship subsidy lobby (1910).

The President and members of the Cabinet have been investigated at least twenty-three times, beginning with Alexander Hamilton (1793). Practically every administrative agency has been scrutinized, the War Department and the Indian Office*ᵠᵂ* perhaps most often. Nearly every war, including Indian wars, has been followed by one or more investigations. St. Clair's defeat*ᵂ* caused the first (1792). The first senatorial investigation was of Jackson's Florida campaign*ᵂ*. In 1861 was established the first joint investigating committee, on the Conduct of the War*ᵂ*. Partizanship has often caused inquiry into alleged administrative abuses, as that into the Treasury Department (1793) in connection with the Funding of Revolutionary Debt*ᵂ*, and those into the Jackson administration (1833, 1836, etc.) in connection with the Removal of Deposits, the Spoils System*ᵠᵂ*, etc. Investigations of the political activities of officials frequently furnished campaign material for the opposition party. The height of inquisitorial activity was during the Grant administration, when thirty-five investigations occurred. Investigating committees have often exposed serious abuses.

Investigations for legislative purposes have ranged widely in spite of the narrow interpretation of the investigatory power given by the Supreme Court (*see* Kilbourn v. Thompson). If the resolution authorizing the committee states that the ultimate purpose is legislation, the courts can rarely interfere with its activities, as evidenced by the Townsend case (1938). Important legislation resulted from investigations of Southern Reconstruction (1866–67), Ku Klux Klan (1871), Nicaraguan Canal Project (1899), Philippine Islands (1901), money trust (1911–13) and many others. Lately, mere "fishing expeditions" have, in general, been replaced by preliminary expert investigations, as in the senatorial inquiries into banking (1933–34), stock exchanges (1934), munitions trade (1934–35), labor conditions (1936–38), holding companies (1936) and railways (1937).

A Senate rule adopted in 1928 allows the appointment of special commissions to take testimony in any part of the country. This and other Senate rules have made senatorial investigations overshadow in number and importance those of the House. Although temporary or permanent commissions have taken over some of this work, there remains a broad field for congressional investigations.

[M. E. Dimock, *Congressional Investigating Committees*.]
    W. C. MALLALIEU

Investment Banking. Most of the early issues of securities in this country were sold through brokers directly to a few wealthy domestic investors or were distributed in foreign countries through foreign investment banking houses. These early issues consisted almost entirely of public securities, there being few stocks of private enterprises until after the War of 1812. Nevertheless, the first stock exchange was organized in Philadelphia in 1800. The New York Stock Exchange was not established formally until 1817.

In the period prior to the Civil War the United States obtained a large amount of capital from abroad. Foreign investors preferred public issues and railroad bonds, however, so that control of American industry remained at home. New stock and bond issues were offered directly to the public through brokerage houses, although large amounts of common stock were retained by promoters and later sold on the stock exchanges.

With the Civil War, Jay Cooke℗ developed the institution of the bond house, which, with its underwriting and distribution of securities, has played a prominent part in investment banking since that time. Following the Civil War powerful investment banking houses, doing an international business, handled large issues first of railroad and, later, industrial and public utility securities. Following the World War came the development in this country of the investment trust℗ and the investment affiliate, the latter institution being abolished by the Banking Act of 1933℗.

With the advent of the F. D. Roosevelt administration in 1933, the business of investment bankers and the security exchanges was subjected to regulation designed to protect investors against fraudulent or undesirable practices (*see* Securities and Exchange Commission).

[H. P. Willis and J. I. Bogen, *Investment Banking.*]

FREDERICK A. BRADFORD

Investment Trusts are financial organizations which, through the sale of their own securities, accumulate the savings of numerous investors and invest these funds in the securities of other companies in accordance with some predetermined policy. This arrangement permits individual investors to gain diversity in the security underlying their investments and expert management of their funds. Originating in Europe during the 19th century, investment trusts were brought to the United States following the World War, partly through the influence of pro-visions in the Edge Act℗ of 1919. Of rapid growth during the 1920's, American investment trusts have developed great variety in their forms of organization and investment policies, and in the aggregate have become an important force in the capital markets.

[L. R. Robinson, *Investment Trust Organization and Management*; T. J. Grayson, *Investment Trusts.*]

CHARLES C. ABBOTT

Investments Abroad. The United States entered the international investment market in a substantial way in the decade 1890–1900. The gradual accumulation of surplus capital in the United States made foreign investment opportunities appear inviting, while the increased foreign demand for goods exported from the United States augmented the funds available for investment abroad. From 1900–15 a growing number of United States manufacturers established their own sales organizations abroad. The Federal Reserve Act℗ and subsequent banking legislation provided for the establishment of foreign branches by national and state banks, and thus facilitated the expansion of United States investments in foreign countries. In the interim between the World War and the worldwide depression beginning in 1929, there was a steady and rapid increase in United States investments abroad.

United States capital has been placed abroad in two ways: First, through direct investments in American-controlled commercial and industrial enterprises located abroad; and second, through the purchase of securities of foreign governments and foreign-controlled corporations, commonly called portfolio investments. The tables opposite and continued on page 152 show the distribution of United States direct and portfolio investments, arranged according to types of investment and by geographic areas.

Investments in United States controlled enterprises doing business in foreign nations generally have yielded substantial gains to the investor. Contrariwise, the private investments in foreign dollar loans have yielded somewhat less than the return paid on United States government bonds. Investments of United States capital funds in foreign currency issues have resulted in losses of the greater part of the principal.

[Cleona Lewis, *America's Stake in International Investments.*]

FRANK PARKER

NOTE. The tables opposite and continued on page 152 illustrate the statements made in the above article on "Investments Abroad."

AMERICA'S FOREIGN INVESTMENTS, 1897-1935*
(In millions of dollars)
I. DIRECT AND PORTFOLIO, BY CLASSES OF INVESTMENTS

CLASSES	1897	1908	1914	1919	1924	1929	1935
Direct investments:							
Sales organizations	56.5	83.5	169.5	243.0	301.0	362.0	325.0
Purchasing................	5.0	5.0	9.0	11.5	12.5	16.1	20.0
Banking	10.0	20.0	30.0	125.0	125.0	125.0	125.0
Oil distribution	75.0	148.0	200.0	275.0	395.0	487.0	509.0
Oil production	10.5	75.5	143.0	328.5	572.0	854.0	872.5
Mining:							
Precious metals..........	88.0	193.6	232.7	219.0	232.5	262.3	259.3
Industrial metals	46.0	251.0	487.0	657.3	734.0	964.5	958.8
Agricultural enterprises	76.5	186.5	355.8	587.0	918.0	985.8	586.6
Manufacturing............	93.5	296.0	478.0	795.0	1,252.0	1,821.0	1,870.0
Railways	143.4	161.4	255.1	297.3	347.0	308.7	260.5
Public utilities	22.1	85.0	133.2	137.9	223.7	1,025.2	1,088.0
Miscellaneous	8.0	133.0	159.0	203.0	276.0	341.7	344.5
Total direct............	634.5	1,638.5	2,652.3	3,879.5	5,388.7	7,553.3	7,219.2
Portfolio:							
Pre-war privately taken† ..	50.0	85.0	100.0	——	——	——	——
Dollar loans	——	429.9	417.8	2,324.1	4,354.4	7,339.8	6,337.9
Foreign currency loans‡....	——	442.8	399.0	391.6	319.6	358.2	242.3
Foreign shares‡...........	——	111.6	127.7	147.4	194.9	445.3	445.3
Total.................	50.0	1,069.3	1,044.5	2,863.1	4,868.9	8,143.3	7,025.5
Less repatriations and repudiations§	——	183.0	183.0	287.0	304.0	304.0	1,404.0
Net portfolio	50.0	886.3	861.5	2,576.1	4,564.9	7,839.3	5,621.5
Short-term credits	——	——	——	500.0	800.0	1,617.0	853.0
All foreign investments	684.5	2,524.8	3,513.8	6,955.6	10,753.6	17,009.6	13,693.7

* Cleona Lewis, *America's Stake in International Investments.*

† Including market purchases abroad. Figures published by the Department of Commerce indicate that by 1924 post-war market purchases amounted to $155,000,000, but they do not show residual value, with allowance made for currency depreciation. *Trade Information Bulletin* No. 767, p. 5, published by U. S. Dept. of Commerce.

‡ Including foreign currency securities publicly offered in the United States in large blocks after the war—with outstanding amounts at the close of each period calculated at average rates of exchange for the year.

§ Loans repudiated by Russia after the 1917 revolution amounted to $104,000,000. By 1929, according to *Trade Information Bulletin* No. 767, p. 5, post-war repatriations through market transactions amounted to a net total of $184,000,000—including repatriations of foreign currency issues. Repatriated dollar loans in 1935 are entered at $1,100,000,000—as estimated by the Department of Commerce.

II. DIRECT INVESTMENTS, BY GEOGRAPHIC AREAS

AREAS	1897	1908	1914	1919	1924	1929	1935
Europe	131.0	369.3	573.3	693.5	921.3	1,340.3	1,369.6
Canada and Newfoundland ..	159.7	405.4	618.4	814.3	1,080.5	1,657.4	1,692.4
Cuba and other West Indies..	49.0	195.5	281.3	567.3	993.2	1,025.5	731.3
Mexico	200.2	416.4	587.1	643.6	735.4	709.2	651.7
Central America	21.2	37.9	89.6	112.5	143.5	250.9	160.0
South America	37.9	104.3	323.1	664.6	947.1	1,719.7	1,718.2
Africa....................	1.0	5.0	13.0	31.0	58.5	117.0	123.6
Asia.....................	23.0	74.7	119.5	174.7	267.2	446.5	487.6
Oceania	1.5	10.0	17.0	53.0	117.0	161.8	159.8
Banking	10.0	20.0	30.0	125.0	125.0	125.0	125.0
Total direct	634.5	1,638.5	2,652.3	3,879.5	5,388.7	7,553.3	7,219.2

III. Direct and Portfolio, by Geographic Areas*

AREAS	1897	1908	1914	1919	1924	1929	1935
Europe..................	151.0	489.2	691.8	1,986.8	2,652.8	4,600.5	3,026.0
Canada and Newfoundland ..	189.7	697.2	867.2	1,542.8	2,631.7	3,660.2	3,657.6
Cuba and other West Indies..	49.0	225.5	336.3	606.2	1,101.3	1,153.9	871.7
Mexico	200.2	672.0	853.5	908.9	1,005.1	975.2	912.9
Central America...........	21.2	41.0	93.2	114.8	155.3	286.3	192.0
South America............	37.9	129.7	365.7	776.2	1,411.2	3,013.8	2,574.4
Africa...................	1.0	5.0	13.2	31.2	58.7	119.2	125.8
Asia....................	23.0	235.2	245.9	309.5	671.8	1,040.4	915.3
Oceania	1.5	10.0	17.0	54.2	140.7	403.0	413.1
International, including banking.................	10.0	20.0	30.0	125.0	125.0	140.1	151.9
Total, long-term	684.5	2,524.8	3,513.8	6,455.6	9,953.6	15,392.6	12,840.7
Short-term credits	—	—	—	500.0	800.0	1,617.0	853.0
All foreign investments	684.5	2,524.8	3,513.8	6,955.6	10,753.6	17,009.6	13,693.7

* Figures for the portfolio investments take into consideration deductions made for repatriations and repudiations. They do not include debts payable to the United States Government.

Iowa. The recorded history of Iowa begins on June 17, 1673, with the advent of Jolliet and Marquette[qv]. The first explorers encountered such tribes as the Mascoutens, the Peoria and the Miami. Iowa belonged to France from 1673 to 1762, when Louisiana west of the Mississippi was ceded to Spain. The Spanish made three private land grants—to Dubuque in 1796, to Tesson in 1799, and to Giard in 1800. At Napoleon's command Spain reluctantly retroceded Louisiana in 1800 (see San Ildefonso, The Treaty of), only to see the United States acquire it three years later (see Louisiana Purchase).

Thereafter territorial jurisdiction over Iowa land was kaleidoscopic. Included in the District of Louisiana until 1805, in the Territory of Louisiana until 1812, in the Territory of Missouri until 1821, it was unorganized territory for thirteen years until attached to Michigan Territory in 1834. In 1836 Iowa formed a part of Wisconsin Territory.

Meanwhile Lewis and Clark[qv] ascended the Missouri in 1804, and Pike[qv] started up the Mississippi in 1805. These trail-blazers were followed by such men as Long, Schoolcraft, Kearny, Lisa, Beltrami, Atwater, Catlin, Nicollet, DeSmet and Marryat. Fort Madison[qv], the first American fort in Iowa, was erected in 1808, but evacuated and burned in 1813.

The Sauk, Fox and Potawatomi, the Iowa, Winnebago and Sioux[qqv] have been closely associated with the region. The only pitched battle between the Indian and the white man on Iowa soil occurred at present-day Des Moines in 1735. The Black Hawk War[qv] (1832), fought in Illinois and Wisconsin, resulted in the first Indian cession of Iowa land. Between 1832 and 1851

the United States quieted the Indian title to the land of Iowa for less than ten cents an acre. After 1851 only two significant Indian episodes occurred: the return of the Fox Indians in 1856 to purchase and establish the Tama Reservation, and the Spirit Lake Massacre[qv] in 1857.

The *Western Engineer* made the first steamboat voyage up the Missouri to present-day Council Bluffs in 1819, while the *Virginia* ascended the Mississippi to Fort Snelling[qqv] in 1823. Ten years later, on June 1, 1833, permanent settlement began. Between 1833 and 1838 churches were founded, schools, academies and seminaries established, lyceums and temperance societies organized, newspapers published and a bank opened. The first public surveys were begun in 1837 and two land offices established the following year. After stubborn Southern opposition the Territory of Iowa, including the present state of Iowa, the present state of Minnesota and that part of the present states of North Dakota and South Dakota east of the Missouri River, was created on July 4, 1838. It was named by Albert M. Lea in 1836 from the Iowa River which derived its title from the Iowa Indians. From his capital at Burlington, Robert Lucas governed the 23,242 inhabitants west of the Mississippi in 1838.

A clamor for statehood culminated in the constitution of 1844 featuring low salaries, limited debt and restrictions on banks and corporations. After a disagreement with Congress over boundaries, Iowa was admitted Dec. 28, 1846, with the present area (56,147 square miles), under a second constitution. The Democrats dominated state politics, electing Ansel Briggs as governor and Augustus C. Dodge and George W.

Jones as senators. Northern immigrants poured in and in 1854 James W. Grimes waged a successful campaign for governor on the slavery issue. Subsequently Dodge and Jones were defeated, the constitution of 1857 adopted and the capital moved from Iowa City to Des Moines. Ralph P. Lowe became first Republican governor in 1858. Only one Democrat, Horace Boies (1889–93), was elected governor between 1854 and 1932, when the New Deal[w] swept the Republicans out of office. Only one Democratic senator held office during this same period.

Iowa is an agricultural state. Farmers drew up the constitution of 1846, formed the first agricultural societies[w] in 1852, held the first state fair[w] in 1854, founded an agricultural college in 1858 and established the state dairy association in 1877. In an era of Republican domination, farmers supported third-party movements[w]. James B. Weaver was twice nominated for the Presidency (see Populist Party, The). Four Iowans have served as Secretary of Agriculture, one, "Tama Jim" Wilson, for sixteen years. The value of Iowa crops, livestock and livestock products, exceeds that of any other state. Although industry is almost as important, manufactured farm products account for one half the industrial output. The telegraph reached Iowa in 1848, the railroad in 1854. Two years later the first bridge was erected across the Mississippi at Davenport. When the Missouri was spanned at Council Bluffs in 1873 four Iowa railroads, all aided by generous land grants[w], linked the Atlantic with the Pacific. Today no point in Iowa is more than twelve miles from a railroad.

Denominational schools, supported by churchgoing citizens who have often expressed their faith in the temperance[w] movements and moral crusades, attest Iowa's claim to the title of Corn and Bible Commonwealth.

The population in 1930 was 2,470,939, of which nine tenths was native-born. Germans represent about 40% of the foreign population, with the Scandinavians, Dutch and British ranking next in importance. Although 60% of the total population is rural, one fourth of the people live in sixteen cities with over 15,000 inhabitants.

[I. B. Richman, *Ioway to Iowa;* C. Cole, *A History of the People of Iowa;* B. F. Shambaugh, *History of the Constitutions.*]

WILLIAM J. PETERSEN

Iowa Band, THE, was a group of eleven young ministers from Andover Theological Seminary who came to Iowa in 1843 as missionaries of the American Home Missionary Society, supported largely by the Congregational and New School Presbyterian churches. Their hope was that each one should found a church and that together they might found a college. In this they succeeded. Each man founded one or more Congregational churches and the group was instrumental in founding Iowa College, which opened its doors at Davenport in November, 1848. In 1859 it was moved to Grinnell. Best known of the Iowa Band was William Salter, who preached at Burlington from 1846 until his death in 1910.

[Ruth A. Gallaher, The Iowa Band, in *The Palimpsest,* August, 1930; Ephraim Adams, *The Iowa Band.*]

RUTH A. GALLAHER

Iowa Corn Song, THE, originated at the time of the Shriners' national conclave at Los Angeles, Calif., in 1912. At that time George E. Hamilton of Des Moines wrote a stanza or two and a chorus for the Iowa Shriners to sing, using the tune of "Travelling," an earlier popular song. The song, especially the rollicking chorus, caught the popular fancy and it has since appeared in various forms. The version most widely distributed was copyrighted in 1921 by Ray W. Lockard, who wrote two stanzas which Edward Riley set to music. The name of George E. Hamilton is associated with Lockard's as author of the lyrics, since the original idea was his. The music of "Travelling" was retained for the chorus, which was slightly changed but ended, as in the Shriner song of 1912, with the words, "We're from I-o-way, I-o-way. That's where the tall corn grows."

[Ruth A. Gallaher, Songs of Iowa, in *The Palimpsest,* October, 1924.]

RUTH A. GALLAHER

Ipswich Protest. Acting legally, Gov. Edmund Andros in March, 1687, ordered certain New England tax levies. Led by their pastor, John Wise, the men of Ipswich, Mass., refused payment; their formal remonstrance was the so-called "Ipswich Protest." Arrest and punishment followed; but the incident indicates the nascent colonial antagonism toward any taxation program not self-devised.

[J. T. Adams, *The Founding of New England.*]

JAMES DUANE SQUIRES

Irish Immigration. In a treatment of this subject, one is treading amid pitfalls: the impossibility of separating the Irish and Scotch-Irish[w] save on the basis of religious profession, which is not considered in statistical information, the lack of statistics prior to 1820, the unreliability of figures thereafter, the number of Irish people sailing from Scottish and English ports or migrating from British lands in America, and the emotional character of the published materials. In the 17th century there was a small number of arrivals as servants or as migrants from the West Indies. In the 18th century there may have been 50,000 Irish Catholics among the half-million Presbyterians from Ulster. In 1790, of the estimated Catholic adherents of 35,000, not over half were Irish, but on the basis of a recent name survey of the Census of 1790, 3.7% of the national population was said to be of Celtic Irish stock.

Immigrants from 1783 to 1820 are conventionally put at 250,000, of whom it is doubtful if more than a fifth were Irish Catholics. As late as 1820 there were less than 4000 Irish arrivals, and not for fifteen years was the United States more popular than British America with its official encouragement and cheaper fares, at least as a temporary resting place; nor did the Celtic surpass in numbers the Scotch-Irish division of the race. The movement, however, was under way.

In the decade preceding 1830, 54,338 Irishmen officially arrived; in the following decade, 207,-381. The industrial slack in England and Scotland, from whence unemployed Irishmen, some of long residence, were being deported back to Ireland, and the slow development of Canada popularized the western republic for emigrants, with its wages of two dollars per day for artisans and a dollar for laborers in the busy season, its demand for labor with the growth of factories and the coastal migration to the frontier, and its growing political and religious freedom. In general these immigrants came as individuals and sent for their families and friends; they were of the artisan, small-farmer class, of sturdy physique and in the prime years of life; many were the victims of land clearances and consolidations; they settled largely in coastal cities or in growing towns along the road, canal and railroad construction projects on which they worked; they account for the rapid growth of cities and provided the cheap labor necessary for the incipient industries.

In the two decades, 1841–60, official figures account for 780,719 and 914,119, with no record of those via Newfoundland and Canada or of returning immigrants, and no consideration of the numbers from the large Irish colonies in London or in the industrialized sections of north England and Scotland. Ireland's population of 8,000,-000; continuing economic difficulties in Great Britain; a wretched agrarian system; political and labor rather than religious discontent; a potato famine in the late 1840's; consolidations of small farms in the interest of landlords' economy; a shifting from tillage to grazing due in part to the competition of American agriculture; and the reduction of the cost of improved steer-

age passage from four to two pounds (as low as thirty shillings to Quebec) due to shipping competition and the rivalry between sailing and steam vessels, explain the pressure upon peasants and laborers to emigrate. The magnetism of America was in her free institutions despite some misgivings aroused by organized nativism*; in her demand for labor in the boom years between the two panics; the inducements of western states and labor agents to stimulate emigration; the relative success of their countrymen who were sending known remittances as high as £2,000,000 in later years; and the growth of the Catholic Church* in the United States which silenced Irish episcopal opposition to emigration. Despite the Civil War, during which Northern agents in Ireland sought labor, and, no doubt, potential volunteers, there was a fairly heavy emigration, so that the decade (1861–70) saw 435,778 Irishmen step from ships to American docks. In the thirty years from 1840 to 1870 the bulk of Irish immigrants were of the so-called Celtic element, and in some years as high as 80% —this separateness being emphasized by the O'Connell agitation.

Immigration in the period from 1871 to 1910, with estimates by decades of 436,871, 655,482, 388,416 and 339,065, was steady with an annual fall or rise according to economic conditions in America or depressions and troubles in the British Isles. This decline was due to the Irish competition in America with continental immigrants; improved conditions in Ireland as a result of land legislation and rising wages; an Irish population dwindling from eight to four millions; and an increased Irish movement to Australasia.

These conditions, as well as the World War and the rise of a new nationalism in Ireland, brought the number of immigrants down to 146,-181 for the decade ending in 1920. In the years 1908–23, for which figures are available, the Irish returning home numbered 46,000 or about 11% of the immigration. Under the Act of 1921, Ireland, joined with Great Britain, had a quota of 77,000; the Free State quota under the Immigration Act of 1924* was established at 28,567 as compared to 34,000 for the rest of the British Isles. The decade ending in 1930 saw 220,591 arrivals from Ireland of whom 10,567 were from the northern counties during 1925–30. From 1931–38 inclusive, 9123 are listed from the Free State (Eire) and 2016 from the six separated counties of Ulster. This decline may be assigned to American restrictive legislation and current depression as well as to relatively good economic conditions in Ireland. It is certain that far more than the official number of 4,585,080 Irishmen settled in the United States between 1820 and 1938.

[G. Shaughnessy, *Has the Immigrant Kept the Faith*; H. I. Cowan, *British Immigration to British North America*; W. F. Adams, *Ireland and Irish Emigration to the New World: 1815 to the Famine.*]

RICHARD J. PURCELL.

Irish Tract, THE. This name was applied in early colonial days to that portion of the Valley of Virginia and the bordering region on the northwest that was settled by the Scotch-Irish*ᵂ*. It may now be identified as the counties of Augusta, Rockbridge and Bath, together with the southwest fourth of Rockingham and portions of Highland, Alleghany, Botetourt, Roanoke, Craig and Montgomery. Among the prominent families of the Irish Tract were the Alexanders, Andersons, Grattans, Houstons, Lewises, McCormicks, McCues, McDowells, Pattons, Stuarts and Waddells.

[J. A. Waddell, *Virginia Magazine of History and Biography*, October, 1904, pp. 202-3.]

JOHN W. WAYLAND

Iron Act of 1750, THE, was passed by Parliament because of commercial difficulties with Sweden where England obtained most of the bar iron for her manufactures, and in the hope that the colonies would supply such iron instead. It provided that colonial pig iron could enter Great Britain free of duties, and that colonial bar iron could be imported into London duty free (extended in 1757 to include all English ports). Through the influence of English manufacturers, restrictive clauses were placed in the law. Slitting mills, steel furnaces and plating mills could not be erected in the colonies, although those already in operation could continue. The law was not very successful. Increasing amounts of colonial iron were sent to England, but not in such quantities as was expected. The restrictive aspects of the law were not observed and many forbidden ironworks were erected in the colonies.

[Arthur C. Bining, *British Regulation of the Colonial Iron Industry.*]

ARTHUR C. BINING

Iron and Steel Industry. The foundations of the American iron and steel industry were laid during the colonial period when blast furnaces and forges*ᵠᵂ* were established in the colonies. The early iron industry*ᵂ* was quite scattered. By 1800 ironworks had been built at the western boundaries of many of the older states, and a few established in eastern Ohio, Tennessee and Kentucky. Most of the iron produced served local needs. The industry was favored by the great resources of the country and by a continually growing domestic market.

From about 1800 to the Civil War, Northern river valleys, from the Hudson-Champlain region southward, became the important areas of iron production. The coastal iron industry of New England and the bog ore*ᵂ* industry of southern New Jersey gradually disappeared as anthracite*ᵂ* fuel was substituted for charcoal about 1850. The valleys of the Lehigh, Delaware, Schuylkill and Susquehanna became the chief centers of iron production. West of the mountains the industry developed rapidly in western Pennsylvania and eastern Ohio. Also, along the Cumberland River, in western Kentucky and Tennessee, much iron was produced.

The processes of early ironmaking*ᵂ* did not change until after the opening of the 19th century. The first important change was the adaptation of the puddling furnace and rolling mill, the English invention of Henry Cort. In 1817 the first mill of this type was put into operation at the Plumsock ironworks in western Pennsylvania. Others followed in the Pittsburgh district and elsewhere. Most of the iron used in early railroad development was secured from England, but by 1860 one half the rails, axles and other forms of railroad iron were rolled in this country.

Significant changes were also made in blast-furnace production. In 1840, after a few years of experimentation, it was demonstrated that anthracite could be profitably used in smelting iron. By 1855 its use had surpassed that of charcoal in the country's output of pig iron. Attempts were also made to use raw bituminous*ᵂ* coal as well as coke in blast furnaces. In 1850 several furnaces in western Pennsylvania and eastern Ohio used bituminous coal. For a few years there was an increase in the number of furnaces using this fuel; then came a decline and, like anthracite, it was displaced by coke. Although coke was used successfully in blast furnaces in the United States as early as 1837, it did not surpass coal as furnace fuel until many years after the Civil War. The substitution of steam for water power in producing the blast and the utilization of the gases which escaped from the furnace for heating the blast were important blast-furnace improvements of this period.

From 1800 to 1860 many changes also took place in the production of secondary iron manufactures. An impetus was given to the metal industries through the contemporary revolutions in agriculture and manufactures. The increased use of machinery created unprecedented demands on the iron industry. Castings, especially, were required for steam engines, machinery, stoves and for other purposes. In 1860 almost every state produced machinery; Pennsylvania, New York, Massachusetts, Ohio and New Jersey, led the others.

After the Civil War the age of iron gradually gave way to the age of steel. Until this time, relatively small amounts of blister and crucible steel were used, chiefly in making cutlery and the finer grades of tools. The Bessemer and open-hearth processes revolutionized the industry. The Bessemer method was invented in England in 1856 by Henry Bessemer, who in 1865 received a patent in the United States. Many years earlier, William Kelly of Kentucky had experimented independently and had discovered the principle of decarbonizing molten metal by forcing a stream of air through it—the essential principle of the Bessemer process. The priority of Kelly's invention was recognized by the United States Patent Office in 1857 when a patent was granted to him. It was not until 1864 that a company in Wyandotte, Mich., operating under Kelly's patent, made steel by the new method. The next year, a company at Troy, N. Y., began operating under Bessemer's patent. In 1866 the Bessemer and Kelly interests compromised their conflicting claims and thus the way was clear for the production of steel in large quantities at comparatively low cost. The Thomas-Gilchrist invention, which substituted a basic limestone lining for the acid lining of the converter, made possible the application of the Bessemer process to iron containing a high degree of phosphorus.

The open-hearth process, often called the Siemens-Martin method after its European inventors, was first used in this country in 1868. The advantage of this process, although slower than the Bessemer, lies in the fact that it can be watched and regulated in the relatively shallow bowl of the large furnace. Both the basic and acid open-hearth processes came into use.

While the total output of steel in the United States in 1875 was about 380,000 tons, production in 1900 was more than 10,000,000 tons. By 1929 a new high record of more than 56,000,000 tons was reached, mainly Bessemer and open-hearth steel. Crucible steel has been almost entirely replaced by steel made in electric furnaces.

The period since the Civil War has been marked by consolidation in the organization of the industry. Under the leadership of men like Andrew Carnegie, large combinations—such as the Carnegie Steel Company—were formed. In 1901 the crowning achievement of consolidation —in the form of a merger of combinations—was the organization of the United States Steel Corporation[q].

Integration has been a characteristic of the in-dustry during recent years. The various processes in many cases are brought together under one control from mining the ore to producing the finished materials. The modern steel works include blast furnaces, Bessemer converters, open-hearth furnaces, rolling mills, coke ovens with by-product plants, as well as foundries and machine shops.

While much of the iron and steel produced in the country today is made in the Pittsburgh-Youngstown area and eastward to the seaboard, many important plants are located in other places. The Chicago district has become highly industrialized. The great Gary, Ind., plant of the United States Steel Corporation is in this region. In its westward migrations the industry has reached the Pacific coast. In the South, Birmingham, Ala., has become the chief iron and steel center through a remarkable development during the last four decades.

[H. V. Casson, *The Romance of Steel;* V. S. Clark, *History of Manufactures in the United States, 1607-1928;* H. B. Vanderblue and W. L. Crum, *The Iron Industry in Prosperity and Depression.*]

ARTHUR C. BINING

Iron Industries, Early (Furnaces and Forges). The first attempt to build blast furnaces in the American colonies was made in Virginia while that colony was under the jurisdiction of the London Company. Before production was under way the works were demolished and the iron-workers slain during the Indian massacre of 1622 (*see* Great Massacre). It was almost a hundred years later that Gov. Spotswood[q] established his furnaces in Virginia. The first furnaces and forges to operate successfully were built by the Puritans under the leadership of John Winthrop, Jr., in 1644 at Lynn, and soon after at Braintree, Mass. While other ironworks followed in New England, especially at Concord, New Haven and Pawtucket, as well as at Shrewsbury, N. J., the American iron industry did not make much progress during the 17th century.

From the second decade of the 18th century, the development of the colonial iron industry was remarkably rapid. Before the Revolution, blast furnaces and forges had been built in every colony except Georgia. In 1775 there were more blast furnaces and forges[qq] in the American colonies than in England and Wales combined and the production of pig iron and bar iron was greater in the colonies than in the mother country. In 1700, the seaboard colonies produced about one seventieth of the world's supply of iron, while in 1775 they were producing almost one seventh. Although the industry was quite scattered, spreading from New Hampshire to South Carolina and westward to the frontier, there were forces that tended to concentrate it in certain regions. The most highly industrialized region was southeastern Pennsylvania.

The ironworks were usually organized on plantations or estates where large quantities of wood could be obtained for the charcoal fuel and where food for the workers could be raised. The ironmaster's mansion, the homes of the workers, the store, the woodlands, the farmlands, the mines, the ironworks, the gristmill, the sawmill and the blacksmith shop made up a largely self-sufficing community. This form of organization—a combination of agriculture and industry—continued until well into the 19th century.

[Arthur C. Bining, *British Regulation of the Colonial Iron Industry*.]   ARTHUR C. BINING

Iron Mining. The early ironworks of America utilized iron ores outcropping on the surface of the earth, in veins, beds, irregular deposits and also taken from bogs and ponds. Especially in New England and southern New Jersey were bog ores[w] important. All types of ores—magnetite, red hematite, brown hematite or limonite, and carbonate—were used during the colonial period. Since the ores were on the surface or just below, little or no technical knowledge of mining was necessary. The chief tools required were bars and pickaxes, for there was little boring, blasting or firing. Prior to 1800 few shaft mines existed, most mines being open trenches from which the ores were dug. In the 19th century, as the iron industry grew, the number of shaft mines increased, although old methods continued in many places.

A new era in mining began with the development of the ore deposits of the Lake Superior regions. While there were rumors of mineral wealth in this section as early as the 18th century, Michigan at the time of her admission as a state in 1836 bitterly opposed receiving the northern peninsula in lieu of a disputed strip in northern Ohio (*see* Ohio-Michigan Boundary Dispute). Even after the discovery of iron ore deposits in 1844 by United States Government surveyors, near what is now Marquette, few realized the importance of the mineral wealth of this region. In 1852 a small amount of ore was shipped to New Castle, Pa., the first shipment of Lake Superior iron ore to the East. It was not until 1856 that the Marquette range[w] began to ship ore regularly. These shipments, which marked the beginning of the development of this great ore region, were made possible by the construction of the canal around the rapids at Sault Sainte Marie

in 1855 (*see* St. Marys Falls Ship Canal). In the decades that followed many other ranges were opened up in Michigan and Minnesota, including the Menominee[w], Gogebic, Vermilion, Mesabi[w] and Cuyuna. The Gogebic range straddles the Wisconsin-Michigan line.

The iron deposits of the Lake Superior region show great variations as to the character of the ores and also as to their accessibility. In some sections the ores are very soft; in other places they are hard and difficult to mine. While the ores are found in many places close to the surface and are mined by surface methods, in other locations they occur at great depths and are secured by underground methods. Thus, while much mining is done by means of steam shovels which scoop up the soft ores in great pits, particularly in the Mesabi region, there are also many shaft mines.

Lake Superior ores are taken chiefly to Duluth, Minn., and Superior, Wis., and there loaded on large steel barges. Ingenious loading devices move the ores. The barges transport them to South Chicago, Ill., to Gary, Ind., and to Conneaut and Ashtabula, Ohio. At South Chicago and Gary are great iron and steel plants, but a part of the ores received at these two cities is transported by rail to Joliet, Ill., Milwaukee, Wis., and elsewhere. From the Lake Erie ports, the ores are shipped largely by rail to the furnaces of the great Pittsburgh district.

The ores of the Appalachian region, roughly from northeastern Pennsylvania to Alabama, are also utilized to some extent. The greatest mining development in this region is in the Chattanooga-Birmingham district. These ores had been used to a small extent before the Civil War, but during the last two decades of the 19th century their development really began. The Cornwall mines of Pennsylvania have operated for more than 200 years. Before the Lake Superior ores were utilized, and even down to more recent times the Cornwall mines produced more iron ore than any other single mining property in the country. Other ores used in the United States are obtained from scattered mines in New Mexico, Colorado, California and a few other states.

[Paul de Kruif, *Seven Iron Men;* H. R. Mussey, *Combination in the Mining Industry: A Study of Concentration in Lake Superior Iron Ore Production;* C. S. Osborn, *The Iron Hunter.*]

ARTHUR C. BINING

Iron Ship, THE, was launched at Erie in 1844 and named the *Michigan*. The first iron ship in the United States Navy, and for two generations the only naval vessel on the Upper Lakes, she was commonly called the Iron Ship. Condemned in recent years, she was given to the city of Erie, in whose harbor she is preserved as an historical memorial.

[M. M. Quaife, The Iron Ship, in *Burton Historical Collection Leaflet*, VII.]
                                                    M. M. QUAIFE

Ironclad Oath, THE, was an oath prescribed by act of Congress, July 2, 1862, by which every person elected or appointed to any Federal office of honor or profit, civil or military, had not only to swear allegiance to the Constitution but also to declare that he had never voluntarily borne arms against the United States or aided, recognized or supported jurisdiction hostile to the Constitution. This oath was the key to the disqualifications which the Radical Republicans imposed during Reconstruction[qv].

[William MacDonald, *Select Statutes and Other Documents . . ., 1861-1898.*]
                                                    ARTHUR C. COLE

Ironclad Warship, THE. Thickening ship's sides against penetration by shot was common practice in the sailing-ship era. The early American frigates afford examples. The Crimean War demonstrated the great advantage of metal armor especially against shell-fire. The advent of rifled cannon hastened the development and nearly one hundred armored warships were built or building in Europe by 1861. The first ironclad undertaken in the United States was the *Stevens Battery,* of 4683 tons and 6¾-inch side armor, begun in 1842 but never completed. In the Civil War inadequate shipbuilding facilities forced the Confederates to fit armor on existing hulls; the former steam frigate *Merrimack*[qv] (renamed *Virginia*) being the first so converted, with a waterline belt and an armored central casemate having inclined sides. Similar conversions were made by both sides on the Mississippi River (*see* Eads Gunboats) , but the Federals generally relied upon newly constructed iron or wooden vessels designed to carry metal armor. The *Monitor*[qv] was the first completed and her success against the *Virginia* (*Merrimack*) on March 9, 1862, led to the construction of many others of the same type—characterized by a very low freeboard, vertically armored sides and armored revolving gun-turrets. Vessels of other types, designed for and fitted with armor, were also built simultaneously; the large, unturreted and very seaworthy *New Ironsides*[qv] being most successful. The demonstrated worth of armor in this war led to its universal adoption for large warships. Metallurgical developments have constantly enhanced the value of armor protection.

[J. P. Baxter, *The Introduction of the Ironclad Warship.*]
                                                    DUDLEY W. KNOX

Ironclads, Confederate, on Inland Waters. The use of ironclads above tidewater was principally confined to the Mississippi River and affluents. At the Head of the Passes, on Oct. 12, 1861, the Confederate privateer ram *Manassas* became the world's first ironclad steamer in action. Though the Confederates continued to achieve individual successes, such as the *Arkansas*' single-handed passage of Farragut's and Davis' combined fleets above Vicksburg[qv], July 15, 1862, the United States, through the combined efforts of its War and Navy Departments, quickly gained ironclad superiority, which contributed largely to the splitting of the Confederacy in 1863. The ironclad war on inland waters was brought to an end with the surrender of the C. S. S. *Missouri* in the Red River, June 3, 1865. (*See also Monitor* and *Merrimack,* Battle of the; Mobile Bay, Battle of; Monitors; Mississippi Squadron.)

[A. T. Mahan, *The Gulf and Inland Waters;* J. T. Scharf, *History of the Confederate States Navy.*]
                                                    WILLIAM M. ROBINSON, JR.

Ironmaking, Early. The processes of ironmaking in the colonies were patterned after those of England. The blast furnace[qv] was built into the side of a small hill in order that the ore, limestone flux and charcoal could be put into it from the top. In front was the casting house where the molten metal was run into molds. Pig iron was usually the chief product, but pots, pans, kettles, stove plates and fire-backs were also cast. The blast was produced by huge bellows driven by a large water wheel although, before the end of the 18th century, blowing cylinders were introduced at many furnaces.

At the refinery forge[qv], pig iron was heated to a semimolten mass. Impurities were then hammered out under a large water-driven hammer. After reheating and rehammering, a bar was drawn to the required length, width and thickness. The finished bars were distributed to blacksmiths and others, who made tools, implements, locks and other forms of iron commodities. At the bloomery (bloomery forge) bars of crude wrought iron were obtained by the primitive process of heating and reheating iron ores in a hearth, and then hammering and rehammering them under a ponderous water-driven hammer.

The rolling and slitting mill provided slit iron for making nails. Bars from the forge were heated, rolled in narrow rolls, reheated and slit at the slitting rolls. Sheet iron was produced at the plating mill. Here, iron bars were hammered into thin sheets under water-driven hammers. The scant amount of steel made at small steel furnaces was blister or cemented steel. Iron bars and alternate layers of crushed charcoal were placed in two long cementation boxes or pots, which were within a furnace. After being sealed, they were kept at a certain heat for several days. The bars were transformed into steel through the absorption of carbon from the crushed charcoal. All these processes of ironmaking remained without change into the early 19th century.

[Arthur C. Bining, *Pennsylvania Iron Manufacture in the Eighteenth Century*.]   ARTHUR C. BINING

Iroquois Beaver Land Deed (1701). At a council called by Lt. Gov. Nanfan at Albany (July 10), the Iroquois deeded in trust to England their conquested Huron lands in Canada and a portion of their own ancient holdings, in all a tract 800 miles long and 400 miles broad, north and northwest of Lakes Erie and Ontario, and the southern shores. This action was designed to prevent French claims, to put the Iroquois under the protection of the British, and to secure to the English colonies the rich fur trade of the region; but neither this deed nor a more definitive one given later to lands south of the lakes was intended by the Indians to transfer title to the land itself.

[William M. Beauchamp, *History of the Iroquois*.]   ARTHUR C. PARKER

Iroquois League, THE, consisted of a confederated group of five related tribes of the Huron-Iroquois linguistic stock, these being the Mohawk, Oneida, Onondaga, Cayuga and Seneca[qv]. Their territory in 1609 extended from a line near Schenectady to the Genesee River in New York.

Each group had a distinctive dialect but could understand each other. Archæology traces the Iroquois from a point west and southwest of New York and also indicates that there were two divisions of these people, the Mohawk-Oneida-Onondaga division coming into New York from the northern bank of the St. Lawrence, and the Seneca-Cayuga by way of the hill country south of Lake Erie. Early in their history they seem to have been parts of a general group which included the Eries, Attawendaronks, Andastes and, remotely, the Tuscarora and Cherokee[qv]. Their traditions state that their league was organized sometime in the 16th century through the efforts of Hiawatha[qv], Dekanawida, Totadaho and Jikonsasa, the five tribes agreeing to unite and the others rejecting the union. Calling their government "the great peace" they established a council of forty-nine sachemships, divided unequally among the tribes, but council action was by the unanimous voice of each tribe, the Onon-

dagas, who acted as moderators, having the casting ballot in case of tie. The league had no authority to promote war, but two war captains were elected to resist invasion. Iroquois incursions and wars, in general, were the private affairs of war chiefs elected or recognized by the fighting men. A civil chief was compelled to abdicate his high position if he became a warrior. The league had no president, though the Totadaho of the Onondagas was nominally recognized as such. In practice a new chairman was chosen for each day's session of the council when convened.

Each tribe was divided into clans, the totem being hereditary through the mother. Certain hoyaneh (noble) families had the right to groom their sons for the office of civil chief, the nomination, in case of vacancy, being made by the women's council. The clans of the five tribes had three common totems, the bear, wolf and turtle, but such tribes as the Seneca had in addition the snipe, heron, hawk, beaver and deer, probably gens of the original stock.

The Iroquois were an agricultural, village-dwelling people living in stockaded towns of bark long houses[qv]. The dress of the people was as distinctive of the forest region as was their mythology. They called themselves Ongwehoweh, or the True People. Their metaphorical name was People of the Long House, because they lived in mutual peace in their chosen territory, as one family.

The cohesiveness of the league was never great but in general it stood united against invasion. Its war captains carried on a relentless war against the Erie, the Neutrals, the Hurons, the Andastes and other tribes, most of which were either exterminated or absorbed by 1675. The alliance of the French with the Hurons[qv] led the Iroquois to unite with the English during the mid-17th century in a war to destroy the power of New France[qv]. Before the American Revolution the Iroquois were generally friendly with the British colonial authorities under Sir William Johnson. This resulted in making the strongest tribes British allies in the American Revolution, though the Oneidas and the Tuscaroras (admitted as the sixth "nation" in 1722), fought for the colonists. After the Revolution the league was split, a portion going to the Grand River Valley in Canada. Those who remained accepted reservations in New York where 5000 still dwell on six reservations. Most of the Oneidas later emigrated to Wisconsin. The present status of these Indians is that of semi-dependent people, being both wards under a treaty of 1794 and citizens under an act of 1924. They have produced a number of notable professional men, but those who remain on reservations are farmers and mechanics.

[Lewis H. Morgan, *League of the Iroquois*.]

ARTHUR C. PARKER

Iroquois Theater Fire (1903). This greatest of all American theater disasters occurred on the afternoon of Dec. 30, 1903, in the "loop" district of Chicago, and resulted in burning or smothering 571 persons, mostly women and small children. Advertised to be the "finest and safest in America," the new Iroquois theater proved, upon investigation, to be a firetrap, built of the cheapest materials, much of it highly inflammable, and lacking adequate exits. As a result of the ghastly tragedy, a wave of safety legislation swept the country with effective provisions for enforcement. The custom of selling "standing room" tickets, which had aggravated the Iroquois situation, was abolished; open exits, plainly marked and swinging outward, became standardized, and special stage-door arrangements were devised to prevent such drafts as would spread flames into the audience. Schools, particularly, were compelled to adopt a widespread fire-prevention program, including "fire-drills," as well as extensive fireproof equipment.

[J. Seymour Currey, *Chicago: Its History and Its Builders*, III.]

HARVEY WISH

Iroquois Treaty (July–August, 1684). At Albany[w] on July 13, Gov. Thomas Dongan of New York; Lord Howard of Effingham, governor of Virginia; with delegates from both colonies; and Col. Stephen Cortland, one of the Council of New York, representing Massachusetts Bay[w], met in council with seventeen sachems of the Mohawk, Onondaga, Oneida and Cayuga Nations[qw]. Gov. Howard rebuked the Indians for breaking treaties and allowing their warriors to attack the settlers and Indians of Virginia. He impressed upon them that he had prevented retribution by the governor of Maryland, whom he represented, for the outrages perpetrated in his colony.

On the following day, the Mohawks denied that they had broken faith and rebuked the Cayugas, Oneidas and Onondagas, demanding that they keep the peace. They thanked Howard for having interceded with the governor of Maryland, advocated peace for all nations, and asked that the Duke of York's arms be placed upon their castles. The other nations, with ceremony, buried the hatchets[w] and agreed to live at peace with the English. On the second of August, the Onondagas and Cayugas declared themselves and their lands under the sovereignty of the Duke of York. On the fifth, the Senecas[w] arrived and confirmed the action of the other nations.

[Cadwallader Colden, *The History of the Five Nations of Canada*.]

ROBERT W. BINGHAM

"Irrepressible Conflict" was a term originating with William H. Seward in his Rochester speech on Oct. 25, 1858, in which he offered a forecast that the socio-economic institutions of the North and those of the South were headed for a collision the outcome of which would be the domination of the country at large by either a system of free labor, on the one hand, or, on the other, a system of slave labor. The same idea had been formulated by Lincoln in his famous "House Divided" speech of June 16, 1858. It had taken form even earlier, however, among both the defenders and the opponents of slavery[w]. It did not necessarily imply a program to secure one or the other objective. The use of this phrase did not include the assumption that the "irrepressible conflict" would necessarily find expression in violence or armed conflict.

[A. C. Cole, *Lincoln's "House Divided" Speech*.]

ARTHUR C. COLE

Irrigation began in the arid area of the North American continent during the Spanish regime. By the time the United States came into possession of the Mexican cession[w], irrigation institutions seem to have been rather firmly established. Irrigation by Americans began with the activities of the Mormons[w] in Utah. They established numerous farm villages of five or six thousand acres each and from this co-operative method grew the plan of reclaiming by the irrigation district. By 1860 the improved farm land of the Mormons was valued at more than one and a third million dollars.

After the gold rush, irrigation developed rapidly in California. By 1866 there were 617 ditches irrigating 37,813 acres and by 1879 there were 890 ditches irrigating 255,646 acres. In California litigation over water rights led to the establishment of what became known as the "California Doctrine" which recognized the common law of riparian rights on private land and the doctrine of prior appropriation on public lands.

During the decade of the 1860's irrigation developed along the trails to the Far West and in Colorado. Under the impetus of the *New York Tribune* several colonies were established, and from these colonies developed what became known as the "Colorado Doctrine" which held that an appropriator received his water right from the state and that the doctrine of prior appropriation should be recognized on both private and public lands.

In the following decade the people of the arid West began to urge that the Federal Government should amend the land laws to aid the development of irrigation. This movement resulted in the passage of the Desert Land Act[W] on March 3, 1877, which provided that the Government would sell up to 640 acres, at $1.25 per acre on terms, to any one who would reclaim the land within a period of three years. In spite of this encouragement, irrigation did not develop rapidly until after the break in the cattle industry in the middle of the 1880's. Land and irrigation companies then began to be formed and irrigation entered a boom period resulting in overexpansion and disillusionment in the 1890's. The census of 1890 reported 3,631,381 acres being irrigated by 54,136 irrigators.

The recession in the development of irrigation was attributed to the fact that under the Desert Land Act the land could not be made a security for the cost of reclamation since the Government did not give title until after the land was reclaimed. The West again urged a change in the land laws, and Congress, on Aug. 18, 1894, passed the Carey Act[W] which provided for the transfer of land up to a million acres to each state that would provide for the reclamation of the land. Under this act the states contracted with construction companies which reimbursed themselves by the sale of "water rights" and there followed, in the first decade of the new century, another boom. However, by 1910 it was apparent that the irrigation industry was due for another collapse, and the Carey Act bubble burst. In 1913 the general land office[W] reported that although more than seven million acres had been applied for under the Carey Act, less than a half million acres of public land had been reclaimed. Sixty-two per cent of this was in Idaho and 22% in Wyoming.

The failure of private enterprise to enter the irrigation field in the 1890's led to a movement for the construction of irrigation projects by the National Government. On June 17, 1902, the Newlands Reclamation Act was passed which provided for government construction of irrigation works from the proceeds of the sale of public lands[W]. Repayment of the cost of construction was to be by the users of water over a period of ten years, without interest on the deferred payments. Between 1902 and 1907 twenty-five projects were started. By 1910 395,646 acres had been brought under irrigation with 786,190 acres capable of being irrigated under the government system. But like private projects and the projects of irrigation districts, the projects of the Government were, in the main, financial failures. Congress was besieged to make advances to the reclamation fund and to extend the term of payment to the settlers, and, by an act of Aug. 13, 1914, the settlers were permitted to repay over a period of twenty years.

The World War was a boon to irrigation, but the close of the war, with the resulting changes in agriculture, spelled doom to success in the financing of irrigation, either private or government. Private irrigation projects were reorganized into irrigation districts and irrigation districts in a number of states had their bonds backed by the state governments. By 1930 better than 50% of the irrigation districts had failed and the states began to rescind the legislation guaranteeing the bonds. The Federal projects fared little better. A "fact-finders" committee reported in April, 1924, that the Government should write off as loss more than $27,500,000, which did not include the subsidy given to the projects by the no-interest provision.

Hectic as had been the history of irrigation, by 1930 nearly twenty million acres had been brought under cultivation; about 70% had been through the activities of private individuals or small groups, about 10% through corporate action and the remainder by the Government.

[Elwood Mead, *Irrigation Institutions*; W. E. Smythe, *The Conquest of Arid America*; F. H. Newell, *Irrigation in the United States*; R. P. Teele, *Economics of Land Reclamation in the United States*.]

JOHN T. GANOE

Island Number Ten, Operations at (1862). From March 15 to April 7, six ironclads[W] and ten mortar boats commanded by Flag-Officer Andrew H. Foote (U.) co-operated with Maj. Gen. John Pope's 25,000 men in capturing this island. Located in the upper part of a triple bend of the Mississippi, fifty-five miles below Cairo, it was protected by forty-nine guns on the island and the opposite Tennessee shore, a floating battery of nine guns and 12,000 men. The decisive factor was the running of the batteries at night by the *Carondelet*[W] and *Pittsburg*. This enabled Pope's forces to cross the river south of the island and capture about half the Confederate defenders. It was the first achievement in a campaign to divide the Confederacy by gaining control of the Mississippi.

[*Battles and Leaders of the Civil War*, Vol. I; J. M. Hoppin, *Life of Andrew Hull Foote*.]

CHARLES LEE LEWIS

Isle of Orleans is a tract of some 2800 square miles, bounded by the Iberville River[W], Lakes Maurepas and Pontchartrain[W], the Gulf of Mexico and the Mississippi. It was exempted by

France when all else east of the Mississippi was ceded to England by the Treaty of Paris, 1763^{qv}, and later, in the hands of Spain (*see* Fontainebleau, Treaty of) became a barrier to American navigation of the Mississippi (*see* Deposit, Right of). It was sought by the United States from Spain at the time of the Nootka Sound affair^{qv} (1790), and again in 1799 and 1801 was a matter of diplomatic negotiations with France which culminated in the Louisiana Purchase^{qv}.

[S. F. Bemis, *A Diplomatic History of the United States*; Edward Channing, *History of the United States*.]

JAMES E. WINSTON

Isle of Pines. Historically always Cuban, this island was specially excepted from Cuban territory by the Platt Amendment^{qv} in 1903 for its strategic value as a potential naval base guarding the Yucatan entrance to the Gulf of Mexico. By 1904, however, the United States was more interested in European routes to Panama and, having secured Guantanamo^{qv}, drafted a treaty relinquishing claim to the Isle of Pines. Under aims at Caribbean hegemony, this treaty languished unratified until, in spite of resistance by local American landowners, the Senate on March 13, 1925, ratified it in accordance with the Coolidge-Hughes policy of Latin-American friendship.

[E. Colby, The Isle of Pines Controversy, in *Bulletin of Pan American Union*, October, 1924.]

ELBRIDGE COLBY

Isleños, THE, an industrious group of Canary Islanders, came to Spanish Louisiana in 1779, settling at Terre aux Bœufs near Lake Borgne, at Galveztown near the junction of the Iberville (Bayou Manchac) and Amite rivers, and at Valenzuela on Bayou Lafourche. They long retained their peculiar old-world manners and customs.

[Charles Gayarré, *History of Louisiana*, Vol. III; V. M. Scramuzza, Galveztown, in *Louisiana Historical Quarterly*, Vol. XIII.]

WALTER PRICHARD

Isles of Shoals, ten miles off Portsmouth, N. H., consist of seven small islands of which Duck, Appledore, Cedar and Smuttynose belong to Maine, and White, Lunging and Star to New Hampshire. Visited by fishermen from the 16th century on, mentioned by Champlain in 1605, described by Capt. John Smith after his voyage of 1614, they were given to the Laconia Company in 1631, and divided between Mason and Gorges^{qv} in 1635. Long used for catching and drying fish, especially the valuable dun cod, permanent settlements were established in the 1630's and for a time the islands were the home of much

fishing and commerce, with a population of over 600, but the inhabitants had nearly all gone by the start of the 19th century, as trees and soil disappeared and a living became too hard to win.

[J. S. Jenness, *The Isles of Shoals*.]

HERBERT W. HILL

Isolation has various connotations in American usage: 1, the continental insularity of the United States (geographical isolation) ; 2, a possible policy of autarchy (economic isolation) ; and 3, the traditional American policy of "no entangling alliances" (political isolation).

Political isolation as an ideal is as old as the republic. It was evident in the hesitation of the Continental Congress^{qv} (1775–76) to enter into an alliance with France. It was revealed in the founding fathers' distrust of their wartime French allies, and in their post-Revolutionary discussions of foreign policy. Political isolation as a national policy dates from the 1790's when American statesmen declined to intervene either for or against the French Revolution, declared neutrality as to the ensuing European war (*see* Neutrality, Proclamation of, 1793), renounced the alliance of 1778 with France and formally announced their intention to enter into no commitments incompatible with neutrality and non-intervention.

This national policy was based upon several considerations. It was felt that the security, prosperity and possibly even the existence of the young republic depended upon having a period of uninterrupted peace. Alliances with European powers, it was feared, would periodically involve the United States in European wars which would not otherwise concern us. The United States, it was believed, had everything to lose and nothing to gain from close political association with Europe.

This isolation grew in vogue during the 19th century. The decline of Spanish power in this hemisphere, Great Britain's commercial and political interest in a free America, the European balance of power, the rapid growth of the United States, the New World's geographical remoteness from the Old, all these and other factors fostered the policy and tradition of political isolation.

Development of American interests abroad, especially the enlarged participation of the United States in the Far Eastern struggle (*see* Open Door Policy) and the annexation of islands in the western Pacific following the Spanish-American War (1898) ^{qv}, undermined the foundation of American isolationism without perceptibly weakening its popularity. The United States could not defend these remote dependencies single-handed, without a larger army and navy than Congress and public opinion would then support. Secretary of State John Hay (1898–1905), President Theodore Roosevelt (1901–9) and others attempted to redefine American policy in accord with these larger interests. But the United States reservations to the Hague Conventions (1899, 1907) and to the Algeciras Convention^{qw} (1906), as well as press opinion and other indicia of public sentiment, showed that the isolationist tradition still dominated American thought in the early years of this century.

The World War's impact on the national economy of the United States, the breakdown of American neutrality (1917), and especially President Wilson's crusade for the League of Nations^{w} (1918–19), threatened momentarily to destroy American isolationism root and branch. But a combination of forces, not the least of which was the resurgent strength of that ancient tradition, produced a wave of reaction which defeated the League Covenant (1919–20) and restored the isolationist pattern of policy. Among other manifestations of this trend were the attitudes of the Harding and Coolidge administrations toward the League, the Senate's votes on the World Court^{w} protocols (1926, 1935), the Senate's interpretation of the Pact of Paris^{w} (1928), the arms embargo and neutrality debates (1928–37), and the neutrality legislation (1935–37)^{w}. From about 1931 the executive branch of the Government gravitated toward a moderate internationalism. But American statesmen still felt the restraining influence of mass opinion which sanctioned little ad hoc co-operation and no commitments pledging the United States to use force in concert with other powers in some future contingency. In short, the policy and tradition of isolation are still (1939) a dominant force in American politics.

[J. F. Rippy and A. Debo, *The Historical Background of the American Policy of Isolation;* Harold H. and Margaret T. Sprout, *American Foreign Policies.*]

                    HAROLD H. SPROUT

Isthmian Canal. *See* Panama Canal.

Italian Immigration. Emigration from Italy is quite distinctly a phenomenon of the 20th century, although over one million Italians came to the United States before 1900, of whom 959,000 arrived in the last two decades. Before 1860, at the time when emigration from northern and western Europe was getting under way in earnest, only about fourteen thousand Italians, mainly from the northern provinces, migrated to the United States—"fantastic vanguard of the brawny army to follow." Among these early arrivals there were a few political refugees, of whom Garibaldi was the most famous, and a few gold-seekers who founded the Italian colony in California. From the ranks of the California Italians a number have risen to political and cultural leadership, notably Anthony Caminetti, commissioner general of immigration during Wilson's administration. In fact, until the huge wave of Italian immigration washed up on American shores after 1900, there were more Italians on the Pacific coast than there were in New England. Since 1890 more than one half of the Italian population has resided in the Middle Atlantic states, about 15% in New England, and slightly less than that percentage in the East North Central states.

Coming from a country with a rapidly increasing population, extensive tracts of unproductive soil, obsolete methods of agriculture, meager natural resources such as coal and iron, excessive subdivision of land, poor means of communication, heavy taxes, and in the south especially a high percentage of illiteracy, the Italian immigrants found inviting opportunities for employment on railroad construction gangs, on streets, in mines, in the clothing industry, as fruit venders, shoemakers, stone-cutters, barbers, bootblacks and truck farmers. The unprecedented industrial expansion of the United States in the first decade of the 20th century brought 2,104,309 Italians, the great majority of whom were single men who toiled long hours at hard work, lived frugally—even miserly—before returning to their native country in the expectation of living comfortably on their savings. Some of these immigrants were victims of the vicious padrone system.

Unlike most countries of Europe, the Italian government early embarked on a policy of protecting and encouraging emigration, instead of invoking restrictive measures. Knowing that large numbers of emigrants were "birds of passage" who would return after a few months or years, legislation was designed to protect them from exploitation en route and to furnish information about opportunities abroad. Drastic restrictive legislation inaugurated by the United States after the World War greatly reduced the volume of Italian immigration.

[R. F. Foerster, *The Italian Emigration of Our Times;* A. Stella, *Some Aspects of Italian Immigration to the United States;* F. E. Clark, *Our Italian Fellow Citizens in Their Old Homes and Their New.*]

                    G. M. STEPHENSON

***Itata* Incident,** THE (1891), was the result of an attempt on the part of the Chilean Congressional party to secure in the United States the arms needed by them in the prosecution of their struggle with President Balmaceda. They sent the *Itata* to San Diego, Calif., to take on a cargo of rifles and other military supplies. Running afoul of United States neutrality laws, it was detained on suspicion. Although it escaped and reached Chile with its cargo, the revolutionary authorities yielded to *yanqui* demands and returned the ship to San Diego. Its final release came too late to appease the Congressionalists' wrath and the incident was a prime cause of the *Baltimore* Affair[qv].

[Osgood Hardy, The *Itata* Incident, *Hispanic American Historical Review*, Vol. V.]

OSGOOD HARDY

Item Veto. As a check upon legislative extravagance, the constitutions of all but nine states permit the governor to veto separate items in appropriation bills. In Pennsylvania and a few other states, this has been construed to permit the governor not only to strike out separate items but to reduce the amount of any item. Similarly, in a number of cities, the mayor has the right to veto items in an appropriation ordinance. Down to the present (1939) the President has been without the item veto and must approve or veto a bill in its entirety. Conferring the item veto upon the President, as a check upon congressional extravagance, has been strongly urged, and was recommended by Presidents Grant (1873) and Franklin D. Roosevelt (1938).

[F. A. Ogg and P. O. Ray, *Introduction to American Government*; J. A. Fairlie, The Veto Power of the State Governor, *American Political Science Review*, Vol. XI; V. L. W., The Item Veto in the American Constitutional System, *Georgetown Law Journal*, Vol. XXV.]

P. ORMAN RAY

Iuka, Battle of (Sept. 19, 1862). To deter Rosecrans (U.) from joining Buell in opposing Bragg's (C.) advance toward Louisville, Price (C.), with 14,000 men, moved from Baldwyn to Iuka, Miss. Grant (U.) at Memphis ordered Rosecrans, with 9000 troops, to attack Price from the south while Ord (U.), 8000 strong, struck him from the northwest.

Discovering Rosecrans' approach, Price assailed his column in dense woods with Little's division, 3200 men. Little was killed but Hamilton's (U.) division was driven back. Darkness halted the operations and Ord, failing to hear the battle, did not attack. That night Price retired from a dangerous salient to Baldwyn.

[*Battles and Leaders of the Civil War*, Vol. II.]

JOSEPH MILLS HANSON

Jackson, Fort, Treaty of. *See* Creek Indians, The; Creek War, The.

Jackson, Miss., Battle of (May 13, 1863). After the Battle of Raymond[qv], Grant (U.) hurried his troops eastward to Jackson to seize that place and protect his rear when he turned westward to drive Pemberton (C.) into Vicksburg[qv]. The small force at Jackson, commanded by Gen. J. E. Johnston (C.), was no match for Grant's army. After brief resistance the Confederates withdrew. Grant marched into the city and then departed westward, leaving Sherman's division to destroy important railroad and manufacturing facilities.

[*Battles and Leaders of the Civil War*, Vol. III.]

THOMAS ROBSON HAY

Jackson and St. Philip, Forts. *See* Mississippi, Opening of the.

Jackson Hole, a valley in western Wyoming, east of the Teton Range and south of Yellowstone Park[qv], was for several years one of the best-known trappers' rendezvous[qv]. While no doubt seen earlier by trappers, it was apparently named for David E. Jackson who spent the winter of 1829 there.

[Hiram M. Chittenden, *The American Fur Trade of the Far West.*]

DAN E. CLARK

Jacksonian Democracy. Andrew Jackson was not a political philosopher as was Jefferson. Nevertheless, as President of the United States, he played a part in making democracy a success for a period at least. In every modern country where a considerable degree of self-government has appeared, a party system has speedily followed. To the present time, democracy has prevailed only where a party system has been evolved through which the people may carry on. Self-government and party government[qv] have so far proved to be inseparable—the disappearance of the one has been accompanied by the passing of the other, as the coming of the one has seen the quick advent of the other.

Gen. Jackson, the most aggressive leader to fill the presidential office before the Civil War, boldly used his party as a governing instrument. His success taught the lesson that a militant President with a loyal, organized party behind him can carry through a program even against powerful opposing forces. Jackson did not take up the Presidency with any avowed or defined purpose to promote popular rule by the party system. In this, he was not essentially different from Hamilton or Jefferson. Neither of these earlier leaders consciously planned a party system. In fact, each one merely hoped to rally behind his policies and theories of government an overwhelming support in the nation. The two-party system[qv] was evolved partly as a result of their efforts, but it was not planned by them. As political organizations to carry out the will of the voters and leaders included in their ranks, the Federalist and Republican parties lacked many features that became common to the parties of Jackson's time and since.

After the division of the Jeffersonian Republican party^{qv}, which followed the House election of 1825 (see Campaign of 1824), not only the party in power but the opposition party became more coherent and efficient. Federalists^{qv}, losing control of the government in 1801 (see Campaign of 1800), were unable to function as a party out of power, but, since the conflicts between the parties of Jackson and Clay in the 1830's, parties out of power have struggled to keep alive and perform the functions of an opposition. The American party system, sometimes weaker and sometimes stronger, has come down to the present from the days of Jackson as the chief, though imperfect, instrument of self-government in the United States.

Much of the character of Jacksonian Democracy was due to the economic changes that were taking place in his time. The westward movement^{qv} and the rapid rise of new states in the West, the conflict between foreign commerce and domestic manufacture for dominance in the East, the great expansion of the banking^{qv} system, the rise of a new sectionalism^{qv} between North and South as the latter expanded its agriculture and repudiated the protective tariff^{qv}—these were forces that arrayed party leaders and their followers in opposing groups. As a political leader in Tennessee, Jackson had not aligned himself with the more democratic elements, but, as President, he became the enemy of the Bank of the United States, and the foe of nullification^{qv}. The controversies arising in connection with these and related questions stirred men deeply, and made necessary more effective party organization and more determined leadership. Developments can come and come faster under such conditions, and, further, the results of victories are apt to be more marked and permanent.

President Jackson, in July, 1832, vetoed the Bank Bill, which was championed not only by Henry Clay, Daniel Webster and the National Republicans, but by many in his own party. In the warfare that ensued, he was able to draw the common people so largely to his side that he proved too powerful for the great bank and the allied business interests that fought under its banner. This first President from the West, who broke many precedents, also struck hard against nullification regardless of the effects on his party.

The passage of the Force Act^{qv}, at his insistence, alienated thousands of Southerners who were not nullifiers, and made possible the formation of the Whig party^{qv}, which was to fight the Jacksonian Democrats on even terms in both the North and the South for a number of years.

Jacksonian Democracy was a crude system under which a majority of the people, with vigorous leadership, were able to rule through the instrument of a political party. Popular control was enabled to survive against interests that were growing too powerful for national and state governments. Democracy was in the making, but it was not permanently established, because popular government, by its nature, must keep up an eternal fight for existence.

[Marquis James, *Andrew Jackson;* W. O. Lynch, *Fifty Years of Party Warfare.*]   WILLIAM O. LYNCH

Jackson's Valley Campaign (1862). In the early part of 1862, when McClellan (U.) removed his army to the Virginia Peninsula (see Peninsular Campaign) for a march on Richmond^{qv}, all available Confederate troops were sent to that place except a small force left in the Shenandoah Valley^{qv} under "Stonewall" Jackson. President Lincoln had directed that a large Union force under McDowell be detained at Fredericksburg and vicinity to be ready to protect Washington from attack and to watch Jackson. At the proper time it was planned to send McDowell to McClellan.

It became Jackson's mission to harass the Union troops in the valley, thus directing Lincoln's attention from Richmond to the defense of Washington. It was hoped to keep McDowell from joining McClellan. If his operations were successful, Jackson would join Lee. McClellan, as he advanced, constantly shifted his right to join with McDowell when he arrived.

In a masterly campaign of deception and unexpected maneuver, Jackson more than fulfilled his mission. Though greatly outnumbered, he usually managed to have a superior force at the point of contact. He struck first at Kernstown on March 23, 1862. Though repulsed, he created much alarm. Six weeks later, as McClellan approached Richmond, Jackson defeated Milroy (U.) at McDowell^{qv} and drove him down the valley. Two weeks later, at Front Royal^{qv} and at Strasburg, Jackson struck again. Lincoln cancelled McDowell's orders to join McClellan. Sharp fights at Cross Keys and at Port Republic^{qv} followed. The Union forces were scattered; the Washington authorities were distracted. Jackson now controlled the situation in the valley. His objective had been acomplished. In thirty-five days he had marched 250 miles, fought four battles and won them all. On June 21 he began to transfer his command to Lee's army at Richmond (*see* Seven Days Battles).

[G. F. R. Henderson, *Stonewall Jackson and the American Civil War.*]

THOMAS ROBSON HAY

Jacobin Clubs (Democratic Societies) were organized first in Philadelphia and later in other cities, after the arrival of Genêt *q.v.* in Philadelphia in 1793. Modeled after the Jacobin Clubs in Paris they sought to propagate democratic views on American politics and to arouse support for the principles of the French Revolution and for the French government in its struggle against the European powers allied against it. They opposed most of the measures of Washington's administration and bitterly assailed Washington himself.

[J. B. McMaster, *A History of the People of the United States*, Vol. II.]

ASA E. MARTIN

Jacquard Loom. This combination of French inventions, weaving patterns automatically by means of perforated cardboards controlling the warp movement, was introduced in America in 1825 by Horstman and Sons, Philadelphia ribbon manufacturers. Jacquards are used on fancy fabrics, especially silks and rayons.

[Leander Bishop, *History of American Manufactures.*]

VICTOR S. CLARK

James, Army of the (April to December, 1864), consisted of the 10th and 18th corps commanded by Gen. B. F. Butler (U.). It constituted the left wing of Grant's army (*see* Wilderness, Battles of the). Butler was instructed to occupy City Point, threaten Richmond and await Grant's arrival. He was checked at Drewry's Bluff *q.v.* and "bottled up" at Bermuda Hundred. Most of his command was later transferred to the Army of the Potomac and served, usually under Gen. E. O. C. Ord, until the surrender at Appomattox *q.q.v.*.

[*Battles and Leaders of the Civil War*, Vol. IV.]

THOMAS ROBSON HAY

James Expedition, THE, was attached to that of Maj. Stephen H. Long *q.v.* which explored the trans-Missouri country in 1820. Dr. Edwin James was a botanist and geologist. With two others he climbed Pikes Peak in July, and these three are credited with being the first white men to reach the summit. The report of the expedition was compiled by Dr. James who agreed with Pike that the plains *q.v.* were unfit for white habitation.

[W. J. Ghent, *Early Far West.*]

CARL L. CANNON

James River and Kanawha Canal, THE, began in 1785 as the James River Company *q.v.*. In 1832 the river improvement scheme was broadened to include a canal to connect Richmond with the Ohio by way of the James, Greenbrier, New and Kanawha rivers. Virginia, Richmond and Lynchburg subscribed most of the funds, and the canal was finished to Buchanan in 1851, where construction was abandoned owing to growing financial difficulties. The canal contributed materially to the development of the James River Valley and to the growth of Richmond. After the Civil War it failed to regain its prosperity, due to railroad competition, and in 1880 was sold to the Chesapeake and Ohio Railroad which abandoned the canal and used its towpath for a railroad.

[W. F. Dunaway, *History of the James River and Kanawha Company.*]

R. S. COTTERILL

James River Company. This corporation, fathered by George Washington and chartered by Virginia in 1785, proposed to improve the navigation of the James River. It was planned to construct canals and locks around the rapids and falls at Richmond and through the Blue Ridge, and thus provide a system of water transportation from the Atlantic to western Virginia. It succeeded in opening navigation about 220 miles inland to the Shenandoah Valley and became one of the most successful corporations of the day. In 1832, however, it was superseded by the more ambitious project of the James River and Kanawha Company *q.v.*.

George Washington was given 100 shares in the original company, but declined to be let in on the ground floor and gave his interest, worth $50,000, to Washington Academy, now Washington and Lee University *q.v.*. These funds are still part of its endowment.

[L. C. Helderman, *George Washington—Patron of Learning.*]

L. C. HELDERMAN

Jamestown. The Virginia Company of London *q.v.*, or London Company, sent out three ships late in 1606 to found a colony in Virginia. They were the *Sarah Constant* *q.v.*, 100 tons, Capt. Christopher Newport, Admiral; *Goodspeed*, 40 tons, Capt. Bartholomew Gosnold, Vice-Admiral and promoter of the Virginia enterprise; and *Discovery*, 20 tons, Capt. John Ratcliffe. They first sighted land at Cape Henry, April 26, 1607. The Company's sealed box of instructions was then opened, and Gosnold, Newport, Ratcliffe, Capt. John Smith, Edward Maria Wingfield, a London merchant, John Martin and George Kendall were found named as composing the governing council of the new colony. They paused at and christened Point Comfort, April 30, and on May 13 cast anchor at a marshy island thirty-two miles from the mouth of the James, one of the worst possible places to found a colony, but quite near the spot where Ayllon's colony*^w* of 1526 had its brief existence. Wingfield was elected president of the Council, and the colonists were disembarked on the 14th. On an enclosure of slightly more than an acre, rude huts covered with sedge and earth were erected. A few even made dugouts in the ground. A small fort was built and on some higher ground farther back from the river wheat was sown. An Indian attack occurred almost immediately, but was beaten off with a loss of one killed and eleven wounded. Dissension and distrust appeared among the settlers at the very beginning. Newport departed for England with small cargoes on the *Sarah Constant* and *Goodspeed,* on June 22, leaving 104 to 108 persons in the settlement. An Indian siege followed, and the inhabitants were reduced almost to starvation. They had only the brackish river water to drink, for a well was not dug until the following year. Disease next appeared, probably for the most part malaria and dysentery, and more than sixty persons died, among them Gosnold on Sept. 1. Kendall, accused of treachery, was shot, and Wingfield was deposed as president of the Council. Wingfield had made charges against Smith and John Robinson, which brought about the first jury trial in Anglo-Saxon America, Sept. 17, 1607, Smith being awarded £200 damages for slander, and Robinson £100.

By September the Indians were friendly and were sending supplies of corn and wild meat. In December Smith went on an exploring trip up the Chickahominy, but was captured by Indians, who killed his two companions, though he—saved by Pocahontas, according to tradition—was spared and returned to Jamestown. On the same day Newport returned, finding only thirty-eight or forty colonists still surviving, but bringing 120 more. Five days after Newport's return, fire destroyed the village, even the palisades. Some persons died from exposure, and the buildings were only partially replaced during the winter. Newport departed again in April, 1608, and on the 20th another ship arrived with forty additional settlers. This vessel returned in June with a cargo of cedar timber. In October, seventy more recruits came, including two women, the first to arrive. In the winter of 1609–10 famine almost depopulated the colony, and the remnant, disheartened, were starting for England in June when they met Lord Delawarr, the new governor, at the mouth of the James with provision ships, and all turned back. The cultivation of tobacco*^w*,

begun by John Rolfe in 1612, gave the colony new economic life, but in 1616 there were (according to Rolfe) only 351 inhabitants in Jamestown and thereabouts, and many were despondent. Thereafter growth was more rapid, however. In 1619 the first legislative assembly in America was held at Jamestown, and slavery*^w* was introduced when a few Negroes were brought from Africa. The fortified village was a place of refuge for those outside during the Great Massacre of 1622*^w*. In 1640 the first brick house on the continent was erected. In 1676 the town was burned during Bacon's Rebellion*^w* against Gov. Berkeley, so that it might no longer "harbor the rogues." It was during the rebuilding, between 1676 and 1684, that the brick church, whose ruined tower survives in the 20th century, was erected. But Jamestown was now doomed—in fact, it had been doomed from the very outset. Its population was dwindling, and for years there was talk of moving the capital elsewhere. When in October, 1698, another fire swept it and destroyed the little state house and the homes of the three or four families still remaining, it was decided to move the seat of government to the Middle Plantation (Williamsburg*^w*), which was accomplished in 1699. That was the end. Probably no other pioneer town had ever suffered such vicissitudes. Even the site of the place would have disappeared long ago from the river's erosion had not a sea wall been built through the efforts of the Society for the Preservation of Virginia Antiquities.

[John Fiske, *Old Virginia and Her Neighbours;* Matthew Page Andrews, *Virginia, the Old Dominion.*]

ALVIN F. HARLOW

Jamestown Exposition, THE, planned to celebrate the tercentenary anniversary of the establishment of the first permanent English settlement in America, was held at Norfolk, Va., from April 26 to Dec. 1, 1907. A popular subscription of $1,000,000 was supplemented by $1,200,000 from the Federal Government which held an international naval demonstration at Hampton Roads. The 340 acres of the Exposition itself were located across the water from Old Point Comfort*^w*. Many nations participated in the ceremonies, but the exhibits were chiefly by the State of Virginia and the Federal Government. Admissions totaled 2,850,735 during 219 days. The Exposition resulted in numerous permanent improvements.

FRANK MONAGHAN

Japanese-American Agreement (Nov. 2, 1917). See Lansing-Ishii Agreement, The.

Japanese Cherry Trees, in Potomac Park, Washington, which attract thousands of visitors each blossomtime (April), were presented by the city of Tokio as a token of good will from the people of Japan to the people of the United States. The first shipment in 1909 had to be destroyed because of insect pests. Tokio then, in a special nursery, grafted flowering cherry trees on wild cherry stock which reached Washington in perfect condition. The first two of these were planted by Mrs. Willam Howard Taft, wife of the President, and Viscountess Chinda, wife of the Japanese Ambassador, March 27, 1912.

[National Park Service, *History of the Japanese Cherry Trees.*]
FRED A. EMERY

Japanese Exclusion Acts. As early as 1890 citizens of western states began to petition Congress for laws to exclude Japanese immigration. Competition of Japanese agriculturists who maintained a lower standard of living than the average American, as well as fear of the Yellow Peril*qv*, increased friction in California and other states. In 1907, by means of the so-called "gentleman's agreement," President Theodore Roosevelt headed off the passage of legislation in Congress which would have applied to the Japanese the same exclusion applied to the Chinese in 1882 (*see* Chinese Exclusion Acts). Accordingly, the Immigration Act of 1907 contained a clause authorizing the President to enter into "such international agreements as may be proper to prevent the immigration of aliens who, under the laws of the United States, are or may be excluded from entering the United States," which supported the President in his solution of this perplexing question. The text of the "gentleman's agreement" has never been published but it is understood to be that in consideration for our refraining from the actual passage of an exclusion law the Japanese government would not issue passports to Japanese laborers who intended to migrate to the United States.

Partly with an eye to immigration difficulties as well as to sensitiveness over racial disabilities, the Japanese delegation at the Paris Peace Conference in 1919 demanded that the covenant of the League of Nations contain a clause requiring the abolishment of all distinctions in law or fact on account of race or nationality. President Wilson sympathized with these aspirations, but the Conference rejected the proposal. In an effort to reduce the tide of immigration to the United States from all parts of the world, Congress passed the Immigration Act of 1924*qv*, applying a quota limitation to the immigration from each country, save China, Japan and other Asiatic nations.

While amendments to the bill which would have exempted Japan were pending, a note from the Japanese ambassador containing a threat of "grave consequences" aroused a patriotic burst in Congress which brushed aside all efforts at conciliation. The specific exclusion of Japanese immigration under the Act of 1924 aroused bitter reproaches in Japan and has continued to be a hindrance to the good relations of the two countries.

[*Annual Reports* of the Secretary of Labor; Yamato Ichihashi, *Japanese in the United States;* Eleanor Tupper and G. E. McReynolds, *Japan in American Public Opinion.*]
KENNETH COLEGROVE

Jay-Gardoqui Negotiations. The beginning of Spanish-American diplomatic relations in 1783 found serious issues existing between the two nations: the question of the navigation of the Mississippi*qv*, which Spain claimed exclusively where it ran between Spanish banks; the southern boundary of the United States—Spain did not accept that established by the Definitive Treaty of Peace*qv*; sovereignty over the Indians within the disputed territory; and lack of any treaty of commerce. Diego de Gardoqui came to the United States in 1784 and endeavored to make a treaty with John Jay, Secretary of Foreign Affairs for the Continental Congress*qv*, to settle all these issues. The two diplomatists agreed on the main terms of a treaty (never signed, however) in 1786 by which the United States would have "forborne" to exercise the navigation of the Mississippi for thirty years in return for favorable commercial privileges in Spanish European ports, and the boundary presumably would have been settled by a compromise that would give the United States nearly all it claimed. Opposition of the Southern states, with their western (Mississippi) appanages, blocked any chance of ratification; indeed this opposition was one of the principal reasons which caused the inclusion in the national Constitution of 1787 of a provision requiring a two-thirds majority of senators present for the ratification of any treaty.

[Samuel Flagg Bemis, *Pinckney's Treaty;* Arthur Preston Whitaker, *The Spanish-American Frontier, 1783-1795.*]
SAMUEL FLAGG BEMIS

Jayhawkers, THE. A name applied to the Free State bands in the Kansas-Missouri border war (1857-59), particularly the band captained by Dr. (later Colonel) Charles R. Jennison, and to the unionist guerrilla bands during the Civil War. It was applied also to the Seventh Kansas Cavalry, commanded by Col. Jennison. Because of real and alleged depredations committed by the Jayhawkers, the term became one of opprobrium. The origin of the word is uncertain, but it appears to have been coined by a party of gold seekers from Galesburg, Ill., in 1849, and to have been used in early California. The traditional stories of its origin in Kansas are obviously apocryphal. Since the Civil War, Jayhawker has become the popular nickname for a Kansan.

[F. W. Blackmar, *Kansas: A Cyclopedia of State History*.]

SAMUEL A. JOHNSON

Jay's Treaty, signed Nov. 19, 1794, adjusted a group of serious Anglo-American diplomatic issues arising out of the Definitive Treaty of Peace of 1783^q, subsequent commercial difficulties, and distressing issues over neutral rights.

The principal issues arising out of the treaty of peace were: Great Britain's deliberate refusal to evacuate six controlling frontier forts in American territory along the northern river-and-lake boundary established by the treaty (*see* Border Forts, Evacuation of) ; obstacles of state courts to the collection of prewar debts by British creditors, despite the guarantees of the treaty of peace (*see* British Debts) ; alleged confiscation by states of property of returning Loyalists^q in violation of treaty protection against any such acts after the peace; and unsettled boundary gaps. To these grievances were added: the refusal of Great Britain to admit American ships into the ports of her remaining colonies in North America and the West Indies; to make a treaty of commerce, or even to exchange diplomatic representatives, during the period of the Confederation, 1783–89; and her active intrigue with the western Indian tribes, allies of Great Britain during the Revolution, now left within the boundaries of the United States. It was the hope of the British government to establish north of the Ohio River a "neutral Indian barrier state"^{qv} as the price of any settlement with the United States, or even to put off any settlement at all in expectation of the ultimate breakup of the feeble American Confederation.

The new Constitution of the United States of 1787, and the National Government of President George Washington established in 1789 checked these expectations. New national navigation laws, championed by James Madison in Congress, and supported by Secretary of State Thomas Jefferson, leader of the crystallizing Republican party (Jeffersonian) ^{q}, revealed the possibility of serious discrimination against British trade by its best foreign customer and induced Pitt's (the younger) government to send a minister, George Hammond, to the United States in 1791, em-

powered to "discuss" issues. These discussions had produced nothing by the time war broke out between France and Great Britain on Feb. 1, 1793, largely because Alexander Hamilton, Secretary of the Treasury, assured Hammond that he would try to block any commercial discrimination against Great Britain. Hamilton had just restored American credit by a fiscal system that depended for its revenues on import duties, and nine tenths of that revenue came from taxes on imports from Great Britain. A commercial war might thus mean the collapse of American credit and with it of the newly established American nationality.

Arbitrary British naval orders in 1793 and consequent capture of hundreds of American neutral ships, combined with a bellicose speech of Lord Dorchester, Governor General of Canada, to the western Indians, precipitated the "war crisis" of 1794. Hamilton and the Federalist leaders pressed Washington to stop short of commercial reprisals (Congress did vote an embargo for two months) while Chief Justice John Jay was sent to London as Minister Plenipotentiary and Envoy Extraordinary on a special peace mission. In the negotiations with Lord Grenville, British Secretary for Foreign Affairs, Jay could have made more of the American cause. On Hamilton's secret advice (Jefferson had now been succeeded by Edmund Randolph as Secretary of State), Jay acquiesced in British maritime measures for the duration of the war, in return for the creation of a mixed commission to adjudicate American spoliation claims ($10,345,200 ultimately paid by 1802) for damages made "under color" of British Orders in Council (not in themselves repudiated) ; Great Britain agreed to evacuate the frontier posts by June 1, 1796 (executed on time) ; the United States guaranteed the payment of British private prewar debts, the total amount to be worked out by another mixed commission (£600,000 *en bloc* settlement made in 1802) ; and two mixed boundary commissions were set up to establish correctly the line in the northwest (this one never met) and in the northeast (agreed on identity of the St. Croix).

Washington got the treaty through the Senate and the House (where the Republicans tried to block the necessary appropriations) only with great difficulty. The temporary acquiescence in British maritime measures was the price which the Federalists paid for: (1) redemption of American territorial integrity in the Northwest, (2) peace with Great Britain when peace was necessary for the perpetuation of American nationality. On her part Great Britain was anxious for a treaty: (1) to keep her best foreign customer,

(2) to keep the United States as a neutral during the European war then raging.

[Samuel Flagg Bemis, *Jay's Treaty, A Study in Commerce and Diplomacy.*]   SAMUEL FLAGG BEMIS

Jazz Age, THE, named from the syncopated dance music called jazz, is a disparaging phrase for the decade 1919–29, when the undisciplined instincts released by the World War affected civilian life. Defiance of authority and convention, a desire for speed and excitement, the worship of youth, self-expression, sexual freedom, and speculation marked the period, though tendencies in these directions were discernible before the war.

[Mark Sullivan, *Our Times.*]
STANLEY R. PILLSBURY

Jefferson, Fort, was begun during the spring of 1780, on the east bank of the Mississippi, twelve miles below the mouth of the Ohio, by George Rogers Clark to aid in his control over the Illinois country^{qv} and protect communication with New Orleans. The garrison survived an attack by Chickasaw and Choctaw^{qqv} warriors, but, owing to desertions by soldiers and settlers, the fort was evacuated in June, 1781.

[James A. James, *Oliver Pollock.*]
JAMES A. JAMES

Jefferson, Fort (Ohio), was built by Gen. Arthur St. Clair^{qv}, six miles south of the present Greenville^{qv}, Ohio, during his campaign against the Indians (1791). Chiefly a depot for supplies, it was a link in the chain of posts between Fort Washington^{qv} (Cincinnati) and the rapids of the Maumee.

[A. A. Graham, The Military Posts . . . within the State of Ohio, in *Ohio Archæological and Historical Society Publications*, III.]   FRANCIS PHELPS WEISENBURGER

Jefferson Barracks, Mo., established by the War Department in 1826, was named in honor of Thomas Jefferson, and is located ten miles south of St. Louis on the Mississippi River. Many expeditions for distant military and exploratory service started from this post. It was an important military post until the outbreak of the Civil War, when it was transformed into a general military hospital. After the close of the war and until 1867, it was used as a garrison for troops. Then it became an engineers' and ordnance depot, a cavalry post, recruiting depot, and is now (1939) a regular army station with about 1300 troops.

[Harry E. Mitchell, *History of Jefferson Barracks.*]
STELLA M. DRUMM

Jefferson-Burr Election Dispute. Jefferson and Burr were the Republican (Jeffersonian) ^{qv} candidates for the Presidency and Vice-Presidency, respectively, in the acrimonious campaign of 1800^{qv}. Due to the growing effectiveness of the Two-Party system^{qv}, the Republican candidates each received 73 votes in the Electoral College^{qv}, with the Federalist^{qv} vote split 65 for John Adams, 64 for C. C. Pinckney and 1 for John Jay. Thus, the election went to the Republicans. But as the vote for Jefferson and Burr was exactly equal, the opportunity for a quibble was presented. According to the Constitution as it then stood, "The person having the greatest number of votes shall be the president, if such number be a majority of the whole number of electors appointed; and if there be more than one who have such majority, and have an equal number of votes, then the house of representatives shall immediately chuse by ballot one of them for president." Accordingly, the election was thrown into the House. But, again by the wording of the Constitution, "in chusing the president, the votes shall be taken by states, the representation from each state having one vote; a quorum for this purpose shall consist of a member or members from two-thirds of the states, and a majority of all the states shall be necessary to a choice." The Federalists, still in control from the elections of 1798 and despite the opposition of Hamilton and other reputable leaders, and in cynical disregard of popular interest, schemed to put Burr into the highest office of the land. Jefferson received the vote of eight states; Burr of six; while Maryland and Vermont were equally divided. Thus, there was no majority as among the sixteen states then belonging to the Union. For weeks a sordid intrigue went on amid rumors of forcible resistance should the scheme succeed. On Feb. 17, on the thirty-sixth ballot, the Federalist members of Maryland and Vermont declined to vote. Jefferson now had the votes of ten states and was declared elected. The Twelfth Amendment^{qv}, correcting the procedure of the Electoral College, became effective before the next election, but the "lame duck"^{qv} Congress, an important factor in this sinister episode, remained unreformed until 1933.

[E. Stanwood, *A History of the Presidency;* A. J. Beveridge, *John Marshall.*]   W. A. ROBINSON

Jefferson Territory was a spontaneous provisional government which had a precarious existence in Colorado from 1859 to 1861. Legally, the new settlements which grew up south of the 40th parallel in the Pikes Peak country, following the discovery of gold near the site of Denver in 1858, were within the jurisdiction of Kansas; actually, they were so far from the seat of government that it appeared unlikely that the authority of that territory could be made effective. The first step toward the organization of a new government was taken in November, 1858, when the inhabitants of Denver elected a delegate to Congress and asked that a new territory be created. Torn with dissension over slavery, Congress did not act until January, 1861. Meanwhile, through several successive conventions and elections the Territory of Jefferson was formed without authorization from Congress, a constitution was adopted, and officials were chosen. The boundaries claimed were from the 102nd to the 110th meridians, and from the 37th to the 43rd parallels. Two sessions of the territorial legislature were held, laws regarding personal and civil rights were passed, counties and courts were created, but the attempt to collect taxes generally failed. This provisional government had two rivals: some settlers gave allegiance to Arapahoe County, Kans., while in the majority of mining camps the local miners' courts were the chief means of maintaining law and order. Jefferson Territory, which came to an end after Congress created the Territory of Colorado^{qv} in 1861, is significant as an illustration of that capacity for self-government in emergencies which American pioneers had already shown on earlier frontiers, as at Watauga and in the State of Franklin^{qqv}.

[J. C. Smiley, *Semi-Centennial History of the State of Colorado*; F. L. Paxson, The Territory of Colorado, in *American Historical Review*, October, 1906.]

COLIN B. GOODYKOONTZ

Jeffersonian Architecture is a term applied to a type of buildings, both domestic and public, which were planned or suggested by Thomas Jefferson, under the influence of Palladio, 16th-century Italian classicist. The buildings are a direct adaptation of classic models to present and local needs, and their proportions are calculated mathematically. Residences such as Jefferson's two homes, Monticello^{qv} and Poplar Forest, and those planned for his friends, such as Bremo and Barboursville, are marked by three distinctive features: concealed stairways in lateral corridors, semicircular terraces low in front which fall away into one-story service houses in the rear, and a central porticoed building one story higher in the rear than in front.

The public buildings were planned as a revolt against English Georgian architecture, and came directly from classical models, generally Roman. The Capitol at Richmond, reproducing with necessary modifications the Maison Carrée, beautiful Roman temple at Nîmes, marked an epoch in architecture, being the first reproduc-

tion of a classic temple for modern political use. Jefferson's architecture is seen at its best in the University of Virginia, dominated by the Rotunda, which houses the library and is adapted from the Pantheon. Carrying out the plan of "an academic village" are the East and West Lawns, with five pavilions on each side, each of a different Roman order and connected by a colonnade which is distinctly Jeffersonian in its spirit.

[Fiske Kimball, *Thomas Jefferson, Architect.*]

JAMES ELLIOTT WALMSLEY

Jeffersonian Democracy. In trying to understand Jeffersonian Democracy we have to consider Jefferson's generalizations, his more specific attitude toward democracy and his theory of the functions of government.

The most resounding and influential of the first are to be found in the Declaration of Independence^{qv} where he states that "all men are created equal" and endowed with certain inalienable rights. The interest and faith of Jefferson in the common man run through all his writings and his whole life. It is this strain which gives the peculiar flavor to Jeffersonian, as contrasted with Hamiltonian, political philosophy, and has made him one of the revered leaders of world democracy.

But it is easy to misunderstand him unless we consider carefully his more specific attitude. The America of his day was 90% agricultural, and the Virginia county, Albemarle, in which he was brought up, was a sample of frontier life at its very best. The common man, as Jefferson envisaged him in his democratic ideology, was essentially an independent farmer. Although in later years Jefferson had to alter somewhat his views as to manufactures, he always feared the influence of them and of cities. He wrote that he believed Americans would remain virtuous, politically, as long as there was free land^{qv} to be taken up but "when they get piled upon one another in large cities, as in Europe, they will become corrupt as in Europe." He believed that, with limited immigration, the country would not be filled for 1000 years. He did not foresee the industrial revolution and the age of steam and electricity^{qqv}.

An extremely able political organizer, he was the first to combine the common men of his day, the farmers and the city workers, but it must be recalled that the American cities of the period were scarce more than towns, with no such proletariat as London or Paris had to show. Even so, he feared such a development, and all the measures he advocated sprang from an unusually co-

herent and close-knit philosophy, that of a democracy which could be based safely only on agriculture, as carried on by a citizenry of small,
educated, independent freeholders[w].

Thus his fight against both primogeniture
and entail[qw] was due to his fear that the
small freeholder, even in ample America, might
be squeezed out if families could keep large landholdings permanently in their own hands. Although a firm believer in the right of private
property, he did not believe in its mal-distribu-
tion or tying it up permanently by either of
the above methods, but in its wide distribution
among the capable, energetic and saving.

His theory of state education is particularly
illuminating for his doctrine of democracy. He
considered an educated citizenry essential, and
that society would benefit by utilizing all the
talent available by paying to educate those who
could not afford it, up to the limit of their ability
to benefit, but not beyond. In his plan—the foundation for the modern French but not American
system—all children were to receive an education
in the lower grades, above which a steady sifting
process was to go on, leading certain selected
students through higher grades and college. Thus
taxes for education would pay social dividends
but not be squandered. His carefully worked out
system for state education is a most important
gloss on his generalization that all men are created equal.

To his essentials for democracy, the independence of free ownership of land and an education,
he added freedom of religion, speech, and the
press. In spite of the fact that few Presidents
have been more bitterly assailed, he never gave
up his belief in, and defense of, these last three.
Without them he believed democracy impossible.
He most certainly did not believe it possible
everywhere and under all circumstances, or in
the Europe of his time. All his writings and acts
indicate fear of democracy except in a nation of
small country freeholders and not city wage
earners.

His theory of government is succinctly and best
expressed in his first inaugural address. He believed in limiting governmental functions to the
least minimum; in a strict construction[w] of the
Constitution and retaining to the states as much
power as possible; in majority rule as a working
compromise but that such rule could not be
rightful unless it recognized the equal rights of
minorities[w]; in "the honest payment of our
debts and sacred preservation of the public
faith"[w]; in economy on the part of government
so that "labor may be lightly burthened"; in
freedom of trade[w]; and in as small a debt as pos-

sible. He was bitter against inflation[w], from
which he had deeply suffered.

Essentially an aristocrat in taste, character and
private life, he was the greatest exponent of the
democratic doctrine, and of interest in the common man (as he saw the possible common man
of his day) whom America has known. America
has changed incredibly since he lived and served
her. It is impossible to know what views he might
hold as to contemporary conditions and policies.
It may be suggested, however, that many today
(1939) who claim to be Jeffersonian Democrats
are as far as the poles from his specific doctrines.
The appeal which is made by the invocation of
his name is chiefly the appeal for interest in the
common man. Our "common man" of today is
different from any which Jefferson knew. He is
not the small freeholder in whom Jefferson solely
believed nor is he the peasant or the city prole-
tarian whom Jefferson knew in France. But it
is difficult for any party at present to call itself
Jeffersonian, if we consider either his theory as
to government functions, or his specific form of
democracy, though the generalizations remain,
often without the limitations which Jefferson
himself in writings and acts laid upon them.

[G. Chinard, *Thomas Jefferson*; W. A. Robinson,
Jeffersonian Democracy in New England; J. T. Adams, *The
Living Jefferson*, and *Jeffersonian Principles*.]

JAMES TRUSLOW ADAMS

Jeffersonian Republican Party. *See* Republican Party (Jeffersonian) .

Jefferson's Library. *See* Library of Congress.

Jefferson's Proposed States. Virginia ceded
her western land claims to the United States,
March 1, 1784. The same day Thomas Jefferson
as chairman submitted to Congress a committee
report, drafted by himself, for the future disposition of the western lands[w]. The report, variously
amended, was enacted April 23, and is known as
the Ordinance of 1784 (*see* Ordinances of 1784,
1785 and 1787) .

Although the ordinance never became operative, being superseded by the Ordinance of 1787,
some of its provisions, as reported by Jefferson,
contributed notably to the development of our
nascent constitutional system. It provided for
the division of the western country into convenient units, whose citizens might set up temporary governments, which on attaining 20,000
free inhabitants should be replaced by permanent state governments, republican in form and
duly subordinate to the United States. Slavery
(after 1800), nullification and secession were to
be forever prohibited[qw].

The solid merits of the document are sufficient to command for it the permanent interest of Americans. Unfortunately, however, the popular attention has too often been diverted from their appreciation by the impractical scheme of state boundaries and nomenclature which Jefferson embodied in the report. The area embraced by it was the entire West, from Florida northward to Canada and from Pennsylvania westward to the Mississippi. This was to be subdivided by parallels of latitude two degrees apart, beginning at the thirty-first, and by meridians of longitude running through the Falls of the Ohio and the mouth of the Great Kanawha, thereby making provision for sixteen future states. Since the states south of Virginia had not yet ceded their western claims, the report identified and named only the ten states included within the Virginia cession. Apart from that of Washington, which occupied the eastern part of modern Ohio, these states comprised two tiers, running from north to south. Beginning at the north, those comprising the eastern tier were named Cherronesus, Metropotamia, Saratoga and Pelisipia; the states of the western tier were named Sylvania, Michigania, Assenisipia, Illinoia and Polypotamia. Although Jefferson was a man of brilliant intellect, his theories frequently ignored the practical facts of life. Apart from the absurd nomenclature, the proposals for subdividing the western country into many small states, bounded by meridians and parallels, ignored the plainest facts of geography, with their consequent implications upon the economic and political interests of the people inhabiting the region. Thus the Lower Peninsula of Michigan, which constitutes a homogeneous geographical and political unit, would have been split between the four states of Cherronesus, Metropotamia, Michigania and Assenisipia; while, except for the State of Washington, the Ohio River, as a natural boundary, was completely ignored.

[Galliard Hunt, ed., *Journals of the Continental Congress*; A. C. McLaughlin, *The Confederation and the Constitution;* H. S. Randall, *Life of Thomas Jefferson.*]

M. M. QUAIFE

Jemez Indians, THE, in the 16th century occupied some twenty pueblos, northwest of modern Albuquerque, N. Mex. Decimated by intertribal fighting and by the turmoil of the Pueblo Rebellion*ᵂ*, the survivors were finally (1706) reduced to the present single pueblo, in which also were incorporated (1838) the few survivors of their linguistic cousins, the Pecos Indians.

[L. B. Bloom and L. B. Mitchell, The Chapter Elections in 1672, in *New Mexico Historical Review*, January, 1938.]

LANSING B. BLOOM

Jenkins' Ear, War of (1739–43), was a four-year struggle between England and Spain, preliminary to and merging into the War of the Austrian Succession (King George's War*ᵂ*), and ridiculously named for Robert Jenkins, a British smuggler who lost an ear in a brush with the Spaniards off the coast of Florida. Commercial rivalry on the seas and disputes over the ownership of Georgia were responsible for the conflict. War was declared in June, 1739, and was fought on land and water, with the Caribbean the center of naval operations and the Georgia-Florida borderlands the scene of military warfare.

Admiral Vernon captured Puerto Bello on the Isthmus of Panama in 1739, but the following year met with disastrous failure before Cartagena*ᵂ*. James Edward Oglethorpe, after having clinched friendship with the Creeks*ᵂ* at a great meeting on the Chattahoochee, invaded Florida in early 1740 and seized two forts on the St. Johns River. In the following summer he attacked St. Augustine*ᵂ*, but failed to take it. In 1742 the Spaniards with a force of 5000 men sought to end the Georgia colony, but were turned back at the battle of Bloody Marsh*ᵂ*, on St. Simon Island. The next year Oglethorpe again invaded Florida without success.

[H. E. Bolton and Mary Ross, *The Debatable Land, A Sketch of the Anglo-Spanish Contest for the Georgia Country;* E. M. Coulter, *Short History of Georgia;* J. T. Lanning, *The Diplomatic History of Georgia, A Study of the Epoch of Jenkins' Ear.*]

E. MERTON COULTER

Jenkins Ferry, Ark., Battle at (April 30, 1864). A campaign was planned wherein columns under Banks (U.), from Louisiana, and Steele (U.), from Arkansas, would advance and converge toward Shreveport, La. (*see* Red River Campaign). While so engaged Steele learned that Banks had withdrawn after the battle of Pleasant Hill*ᵂ*, and that Price (C.) had received reinforcements. Steele immediately withdrew toward Little Rock, harassed by Kirby Smith and Price. At Jenkins Ferry on the Saline River, Steele, delayed by the swollen stream, sustained and repulsed a severe Confederate attack.

[*Battles and Leaders of the Civil War*, Vol. IV.]

ROBERT S. THOMAS

Jenny Spinning began in America during the Revolution. The jenny, recently invented in England, contained from twenty-four to fifty-six spindles and was operated by hand. It was intermediate between the spinning wheel, the spinning jack and the mule. Such machines were installed at Philadelphia, Beverly, Worcester, New

York City and probably in South Carolina. A few may have been operated by water or horse-power. They disappeared after Samuel Slater successfully introduced more efficient Arkwright[w] machinery in Rhode Island.

[Victor S. Clark, *History of Manufactures in the United States.*]
                                        VICTOR S. CLARK

Jersey Prison-Ship, THE, was a dismantled sixty-four-gun British man-of-war, moored in Wallabout Bay, the present site of the Brooklyn Navy Yard[w], and used for the confinement of American naval prisoners during the Revolution. Though she was only one of several prison-ships moored in New York harbor, she became notorious for ill-usage of the prisoners. Rations were inadequate, often damaged and poorly cooked. Though as many as 1200 were confined aboard her at one time, all prisoners, able-bodied, sick and dying, were sent below at night, where the heat, vermin and stench were intolerable. Dysentery, smallpox and yellow fever were prevalent, and the death rate appalling.

[Thomas Dring, *Recollections of the Jersey Prison-ship;* G. W. Allen, *A Naval History of the American Revolution.*]
                                        LOUIS H. BOLANDER

Jessie Scouts, THE, were bands of Union soldiers or guerrillas[w], usually disguised as Confederates, who operated during the later years of the Civil War in northern Virginia and the adjacent sections of West Virginia. Col. Harry Gilmor states that they were organized by Gen. John C. Frémont, which may account for the name "Jessies"—for Frémont's wife, Jessie Benton. The "Jessies" were dreaded and hated by the Confederates.

[Harry Gilmor, *Four Years in the Saddle;* Charles T. O'Ferrall, *Forty Years of Active Service.*]
                                        JOHN W. WAYLAND

Jesuit Missions. The first Jesuits[w] to labor in the territory which is now the United States were a Spanish group who conducted an abortive mission during the period 1566–71 in the vast region then known as Florida. In 1566 Father Pedro Martínez, founder of the mission, was slain by Indians and in 1571 Father John Baptist Segura and seven companions met the same fate, somewhere, it would appear, in the region of the Rappahannock. In the following century French Jesuits organized the Mission of Canada or New France[w], the initial post being set up in 1611 in Acadia[w], under Fathers Pierre Biard and Ennemond Massé.

In 1625 the Jesuits were at Quebec, which they made the headquarters of their missionary operations in New France. The first of their number to reach mid-America were Fathers Isaac Jogues,

now a canonized saint, and Charles Raymbaut, who in 1641 journeyed west to attend an Indian powwow[w] at the waters connecting Lakes Superior and Huron, the rapids of which were subsequently known as Sault Ste. Marie[w]. They were followed in 1660 by Father René Ménard, Wisconsin's proto-missionary, who, until his death the following year, ministered to Indian groups of the Lake Superior region. He was in search of some scattered Hurons[w] when he perished on the way, having been, in the course of this last journey, the first member of his order to penetrate the Mississippi Valley. Next to appear on the western missionary scene was Father Claude Allouez, who in 1665 founded at Chequamegon Bay[w] near the western extremity of Lake Superior the Ottawa-Huron Mission of La Pointe du Saint Esprit. Other posts were established by him, among them, St. Francis Xavier's at Green Bay[w] and St. Mark's among the Fox Indians[w]. His career of twenty-four years, 1665–89, throbbed with activity, the range and success of his missionary labors earning for him the sobriquet of "the apostle of the West."

In 1668 Father Jacques Marquette began at Sault Ste. Marie an Algonkin[w] mission, around which grew up the earliest white settlement in the State of Michigan. Two years later, in the winter of 1670–71, was established the Mission of St. Ignace[w] on behalf of the Huron and other tribes driven from La Pointe by the Sioux[w]. Located first on Mackinac Island[w], it was later moved across the straits to the northern mainland. From St. Ignace, where he was resident missionary, Marquette set out with his fellow explorer Jolliet[w] on their famous Mississippi expedition of 1673. In 1675 the same Jesuit inaugurated among the Kaskaskia, an Illinois tribe[w], the Mission of the Immaculate Conception. This historic center of evangelical enterprise, the first in the Mississippi Valley, was moved in 1691 from its first location near Starved Rock[w] on the Illinois River to Lake Peoria, thence, 1700, to the site of the future St. Louis and, finally, 1703, to the Kaskaskia River, where it was maintained until 1763.

Other centers of Jesuit missionary activity among the western tribes were the Sioux Mission of St. Michael the Archangel, 1727, on the west bank of Lake Pepin at the present Frontenac, Minn.; the station opened, *ca.* 1739, among the Wyandot Hurons settled at Sandusky Bay in Ohio; and the Huron Mission of the Assumption, located *ca.* 1742, on Bois Blanc Island in the Detroit River and later moved to the site of Sandwich, Ontario. Nor were the aborigines in other sections of the future United States left unattended. There were Jesuit missions among the Iroquois[w] of the Mohawk Valley, the Abenaki[w] of the Kennebec, Penobscot and St. John rivers, and among the Yazoo, Alibamons, Choctaw[w] and Arkansas[w] of the South. In the Southwest the missionary career of Father Eusebio Francisco Kino, marked by the founding, 1700, of the famous Mission of San Xavier del Bac, near the site of Tucson, Ariz., was noteworthy. The California missions[w] associated with the labors of the Jesuits Salvatierra and Kino were in Lower or Mexican California.

Owing to Indian wars, lack of personnel and other circumstances, the Jesuit missions of colonial America were gradually suspended. About the last to survive were those of the Illinois country and these were swept away by the expulsion of the missionaries from that region by the Louisiana authorities in 1763. The story of the missions has been put on record in the *Jesuit Relations*[w], a rich mine of religious, geographical and ethnological data indispensable to the historian of colonial America. Yet success in converting and civilizing the Indians was not on the whole conspicuous. Typical causes of the failure of the missionaries to achieve more substantial results are detailed by one of their number, Father François Philibert Watrin, in an informing memoir in the *Relations* (Thwaites, ed.), LXX, 211 ff.

Nineteenth-century Jesuit work among the American Indians is especially identified with the career of Father Peter J. DeSmet, 1801-73, founder of the Catholic Rocky Mountain Missions, the more notable of which were those for the Flatheads, Cœur d'Alènes and Kalispel (*see* Owen, Fort). The Potawatomi and Osage[qqw] of Kansas were also successfully evangelized by Jesuits from St. Louis. Indian missions conducted at present (1939) in the United States by the Society of Jesus number sixteen, thirteen of them among the tribal groups in Montana and the Pacific Northwest, two among the Sioux of South Dakota and one among the Arapaho[w] of Wyoming.

[R. G. Thwaites, ed., *The Jesuit Relations and Allied Documents;* E. Kenton, ed., *The Jesuit Relations;* M. Kenny, *The Romance of the Floridas;* C. de Rochemonteix, *Les Jésuites et la Nouvelle France au XVIIᵉ Siècle d'après beaucoup de documents inédits;* J. Delanglez, *The French Jesuits in Lower Louisiana, 1700-63;* M. B. Palm, *The Jesuit Missions of the Illinois Country, 1673-1763;* H. M. Chittenden and A. T. Richardson, *Life, Letters and Travels of Father Pierre-Jean DeSmet, 1801-1873;* L. Palladino, *Indian and White in the Northwest;* H. E. Bolton, *The Rim of Christendom: a Biography of Eusebio Francisco Kino, Pacific Coast Pioneer;* G. J. Garraghan, *The Jesuits of the Middle United States.*]

GILBERT J. GARRAGHAN

Jesuit Relations. Each Jesuit missionary (*see* Jesuit Missions) was required to report every year to his superior the events of his mission, the prospects for exploration and all he had learned of the regions in which he dwelt. These reports were then made up into a yearly *Relation* and forwarded to the chief of the order in France or Rome. These *Relations* were published beginning with 1632 in order to stimulate the zeal and interest of the people at home. The Jesuit missionaries being educated men and careful observers wrote reports of the regions of Canada, the Great Lakes and the Mississippi Valley that could not be surpassed. They were published in annual volumes, which were known as the "Relation of 1632" or the corresponding year, sometimes including the name of the editor, as the "Relation of 1673 by Claude Dablon." In the latter year the publication was suspended; the missionaries, however, continued to send in reports, which remained in manuscript for almost two centuries.

There were in all forty-one separate *Relations* published, and it has been the aim of collectors of Americana to complete their list of *Jesuit Relations.* Several American libraries have full sets of the original *Relations.* In 1896 an edition was begun which included not only the published *Relations,* but other documents secured from many sources in America and Europe. This edition, edited by Reuben G. Thwaites, was known as the *Jesuit Relations and Allied Documents,* and extended in time from 1610 to 1791. It was published in seventy-three volumes, with the original French or Latin on the left-hand page, the translation into English opposite. It forms a source of unusual quality for the primitive conditions of the North American continent, the accounts of the fauna and flora, descriptions of the lakes, rivers and country, mention of indications of minerals and other resources. Especially is it valuable for the customs, habits, habitat and migrations of the tribesmen of this great continent, and of the impact of civilization on uncivilized barbarians. But for the *Jesuit Relations,* knowledge of the discoveries, explorations and conditions in North America in the 17th and early 18th century would be meager.

[R. G. Thwaites, ed., *Jesuit Relations and Allied Documents, 1610-1791;* James C. McCoy, *Jesuit Relations of Canada, 1632-1673: a Bibliography.*]

LOUISE PHELPS KELLOGG

Jesuits, THE, conventional designation for members of the Society of Jesus, a religious order of men founded by St. Ignatius Loyola (1491–1556) and formally approved by the Holy See Sept. 27, 1540. The Jesuits were an influence in the development of colonial America, particularly through their explorations and missions[w]. They were associated with the Calverts in the founding of Maryland[w], 1634; they inaugurated the Catholic ministry in the Middle Atlantic states, the upper Great Lakes region and the Mississippi Valley, making at the same time contributions of interest to the economic and cultural beginnings of the territory in which they worked.

Jesuit activities in post-colonial America date from the organization of the Maryland Mission of the order in 1805. From Maryland the order spread to the Middle West, opening in 1823 at Florissant, in Missouri, what proved to be a starting point of subsequent far-flung expansion. In 1841 it became established in the Pacific Northwest and in 1849 in California. Meantime, Jesuit houses had been opened in Kentucky, 1832, Louisiana, 1837 and New York, 1846. The activities of the Society of Jesus have been and continue to be highly diversified. They range from Indian Missions and the parochial ministry to the preaching of popular missions, attendance in hospitals and prisons, and other sorts of ministerial or social service. But the major interest is education. The first American Jesuit college, Georgetown, dates from 1789. St. Louis University, oldest school of university grade west of the Mississippi, has been conducted by the Jesuits since 1829. Educational institutions under their management in the United States, parochial schools apart, are fifty-seven, of which twenty-four are universities or colleges and thirty-three high schools. The American Jesuits, organized at present (1939) into seven provinces or administrative units, number 5229, the total membership of the order being 25,460.

[G. Bernoville, *The Jesuits*; G. J. Garraghan, *The Jesuits of the Middle United States*; W. J. McGucken, *The Jesuits and Education*.]

GILBERT J. GARRAGHAN

Jesup, Fort, was a United States military post on the watershed between the Red and Sabine rivers, about twenty-five miles west of Natchitoches, La., established in 1822 and abandoned after the annexation of Texas in 1845 and the Mexican War of 1846–48[w] rendered it no longer important in frontier defense.

[Alcée Fortier, ed., *Louisiana*, Cyclopedic, I.]

WALTER PRICHARD

Jews, in small numbers, were among the very early settlers of the colonies. One of the earliest of record was Elias Legardo who came to Virginia in 1621. After 1639 Jews are found in Maryland. Jacob Barsimon, from Holland, was the first Jew seen in New Amsterdam[w], this in 1654. A week

later came twenty-three more, former citizens of Holland, though of Spanish and Portuguese ancestry, who had fled from Brazil when the Portuguese took that country from the Dutch. A Jew is found on record as a witness in court at Boston in 1648; and in 1658 a group of them settled in Newport, R. I., which became a noted Jewish center. Not until 1762 was a Jew naturalized in Massachusetts, the first being Aaron Lopez, a prosperous merchant and former resident of Newport. Jews first appear in South Carolina records in 1695. Judah Monis, engaged in 1722, was the first instructor in Hebrew at Harvard University. In the 17th and 18th centuries the majority of the Jewish immigrants were of Spanish and Portuguese origin, though many came from Holland and a few from other countries. Many of the earliest were artisans, but most of them went into business and finance in America, and some soon became wealthy. The Gratz brothers, Barnard and Michael, who came from Germany in the middle 18th century and settled in Philadelphia, were within two decades among the greatest of American merchants, with agents in several foreign countries. Along with the pioneers they pushed their operations beyond the Alleghenies, and became great private landowners in the new territory, as well as members of the large land-promotion companies. Mordecai M. Noah, of South Carolina Jewish parentage, was one of New York's most famous editors and publishers in the first half of the 19th century.

In the second phase of Jewish immigration, between 1820 and 1890, the newcomers were nearly all of German birth. These scattered widely over the land, the majority of them becoming merchants. Many went into the manufacture of clothing. Others entered finance and attained high position, as the names of Schiff, Kuhn, Loeb, Speyer, Straus, Kahn, Warburg and others testify. At the close of the Civil War, 1865, there were only 200,000 Jews in the United States. But their immigration increased rapidly thereafter, and in the latter 19th century, enormous numbers of them came, fleeing from oppression in eastern Europe. Between 1880 and 1920, 2,000,000 entered our gates, of whom 70% came from Russia and 25% from Austria-Hungary and Rumania. There were 4,200,000 Jews in this country in 1930, of whom 3,500,000 were of eastern European and only 500,000 of German descent; 1,765,000 of them lived in New York City. In addition to the occupations already mentioned, some of the race, such as the Frohmans and Shuberts, had become leaders in the theatrical business, and later, yet others dominated the motion-picture industry. Before 1900 many were entering the professions and scientific research, where, in the following decades, not a few have won eminence.

[Anita Libman Lebeson, *Jewish Pioneers in America, 1492-1848*; Lee J. Levinger, *History of the Jews in the United States.*]
                                    ALVIN F. HARLOW

"Jim Crow" Laws, originally applied to acts of Southern legislatures requiring the separation of races in conveyances, now mean all aspects of the Southern color line which the dominant white caste has, since Reconstruction[w], enacted into state law. The invariable purpose of these laws is to prohibit as far as practicable all contacts between the races implying social equality. They are justified by the belief that the Negro race is both actually and inherently inferior to the white race. They define "a person of color" as one possessing a small fraction (usually one eighth) of Negro blood. Marriage between such persons and whites is universally prohibited (*see* Miscegenation). Other laws require the separation of races in schools, penal and charitable institutions, factories, restaurants, theaters, hotels and most other public places except the streets and stores. Beginning in Tennessee in 1881 all Southern states by 1907 separated the races in railroads and other public conveyances. The passage of these laws was facilitated by the Supreme Court's decision of 1883 declaring the Federal Civil Rights Act[w] of 1875 unconstitutional. But the extension of this principle to additional aspects of race relations was seemingly checked in 1917 when the Supreme Court declared unconstitutional the ordinances of various cities requiring residential segregation on racial lines. This decision, however, has not prevented the continuation and even extension, through legal subterfuge and social pressure, of the long-established custom of residential segregation. For it should be emphasized that unwritten custom, in many instances so firmly established as not to need the sanction of formal statute, keeps the Southern Negro socially subordinate.

[G. T. Stephenson, *Race Distinction in American Law.*]
                                    FRANCIS B. SIMKINS

Jingoism, in American usage, is a label for the blatant demand for an aggressive foreign policy. The word is probably derived from the "by jingo" of a music-hall song popularized by Gilbert Hastings Macdermott in England during a crisis with Russia in 1877–78:

We don't want to fight, but, by jingo, if we do,
   We've got the ships, we've got the men and
      got the money too.

By March, 1878, a "jingo" was a term of political reproach. In the United States those who have advocated the annexation of Canada, the seizure of Mexico, expansion in the Caribbean or Pacific or a bellicose interpretation of the Monroe Doctrine[w] have been charged with jingoism.
                                    STANLEY R. PILLSBURY

Jitney, THE. *See* Motor Bus, The.

Jockey Hollow, an area used by horse traders for herding their animals, was the site of the encampment of the Continental Army under Gen. Washington during the winter of 1779–80. Located about four miles southwest of the General's headquarters at Morristown, N. J., ten brigades of some 12,000 men were hutted here. Shortage of food and clothing, and cold, caused acute suffering. Here, early in 1781, occurred the mutiny of the Pennsylvania troops[w], which threatened for a time the independence movement.

[A. M. Sherman, *Historic Morristown, New Jersey.*]
                                    C. A. TITUS

"Joe Bowers" was the folk hero of the Forty-niners[w]. The song about him, dated around 1850, is a document straight from American soil.

My name it is Joe Bowers,
   And I've got a brother Ike;
I come from old Missouri—
   Yes, all the way from Pike.

To the words and haunting tune of this homely ballad[w] oxen pulled a nation westward. Nobody knows absolutely who Joe Bowers was or who immortalized him. Specifically, he was a "Piker" who had left home and "Sally" to make a stake in "Califony"; in a larger way, he expressed the bosom's core of every emigrant.

[W. E. Connelley, *Doniphan's Expedition.*]
                                    J. FRANK DOBIE

John, Fort (Colo.), named for John B. Sarpy, was built before 1839 when Wislizenus described it as a rectangle, 80 by 100 feet, protected by cottonwood pickets 15 feet high; and with towers on three sides. The name Laramie[w] later became popular and supplanted the old name which was, however, retained for the business transactions of the American Fur Company[w].

[H. M. Chittenden, *History of American Fur Trade of Far West.*]
                                    CARL L. CANNON

Johnson and Graham's Lessee v. McIntosh (1823). The decision in this case established the constitutional principle that grants of land made to private individuals by Indian tribes are invalid. The issue arose when successors to the grantees of a large tract of land in Illinois and Indiana, made by certain chiefs of the Illinois and Piankashaw[qw] tribes in 1773 and 1775, challenged the ownership of a portion of the tract by William McIntosh, whose title derived from the United States Government in 1818. The opinion of the Court presents an exhaustive survey of the attitude of civilized governments respecting the Indian tribal ownership and disposition of the soil.

[U. S. Reports, 8 Wheaton, 544-605.]

M. M. QUAIFE

Johnson Bill. *See* Immigration Act of 1924.

Johnson-Clarendon Convention, THE (Jan. 14, 1869) , covered British-American claims since 1853, without precise allusion to damages from the *Alabama[w]* and other commerce raiders. The British concessions, in the existing state of mind, were so slight that the Convention was rejected in the Senate, April 13, 1869, by a vote of fifty-four to one. Liquidation of Civil War diplomacy was thereby postponed till the Treaty of Washington, 1871[w], and the Geneva Award.

[Louis Martin Sears, *A History of American Foreign Relations.*]
                                        LOUIS MARTIN SEARS

Johnson County War, THE. *See* Rustler War.

Johnson Debt Default Act, THE (April 13, 1934) , was passed because of the failure of European governments to meet their war-debt[w] payments to the United States. It provides that the securities, issued after the passage of the act, of governments in default in the payment of debts to the American Government shall not be purchased or sold within the United States, and that private loans to such governments are prohibited. An exception is made in the case of the renewal or adjustment of existing indebtedness. The penalty for violation of the act is a fine of not more than $10,000, or imprisonment for not more than five years, or both.

[*U. S. Statutes at Large*, Vol. XLVIII, p. 574; *Opinions of Attorneys General*, Vol. XXXVII, p. 505.]
                                        BENJAMIN H. WILLIAMS

Johnson Hall, built in 1761–62, the last home of Sir William Johnson, colonial superintendent of the northern Indians, was a magnificent building for its day, sixty feet wide, forty feet deep, two stories high, and with wide clapboards cut to resemble blocks of stone. Situated half a mile from Johnstown, N. Y., and flanked on either side by stone blockhouses, the Hall was the scene of many important Indian conferences and the mecca for all travelers of note in the Mohawk Valley. Restored to almost its original appearance by the State of New York, it today is the museum of the Johnstown Historical Society.

[Arthur Pound, *Johnson of the Mohawks.*]
                                        EDWARD P. ALEXANDER

Johnson's Island, in Sandusky Bay, Lake Erie, was used as a prison for captured Confederate officers from 1862 to the end of the war. The numbers of prisoners confined there fluctuated greatly in 1862 and 1863 because of exchanges, but increased in the closing months of the war until more than 3000 were on the island. Its proximity to Canada, where Confederate agents were stationed, invited plots and attempts to escape, in which members of Northern anti-war secret societies (*see* Canada, Confederate Activities in) were also involved. The most amazing rescue attempt came in September, 1864, when Confederate agents planned to seize the lake gunboat *Michigan,* release 2600 prisoners on the island, capture Sandusky, go by train to Columbus and release the prisoners at Camp Chase[w]. This mad plot was foiled by the arrest of Capt. Charles H. Cole, as he was about to seize the gunboat. An accomplice, John Yates Beall, seized a passenger steamer but had to flee with it to Canada.

[Whitelaw Reid, *Ohio in the War*, Vol. II.]
                                        EUGENE H. ROSEBOOM

Johnstown Flood, THE, occurred simultaneously with lesser floods in twenty Pennsylvania counties and resulted from the collapse of the Conemaugh Reservoir during a period of exceptionally heavy rainfall. The dam, constructed in 1852 as part of the old Pennsylvania canal system[w], had been rebuilt during 1879–81 to a height of eighty feet by Pittsburgh sportsmen to quadruple the original size of Conemaugh Lake, situated 275 feet above the Johnstown low flats.

On Friday morning, May 31, 1889, startled engineers observed the rapid sinking of the lake as its waters poured into the reservoir. Emphatic warnings were disregarded by many inhabitants of Conemaugh Valley as exaggerated. At 3:30 P.M. the earthen walls of the dam yielded, quickly inundating the entire valley in a powerful downward thrust. Halted by the Pennsylvania railway viaduct, just above Johnstown proper, the flood receded, causing destructive vortices, inducing a huge conflagration in the

Cambria Iron Works, and annihilating most of Johnstown and its suburbs. At least 2142 persons perished; careful estimates claimed fully 5000. Property losses totaled over $10,000,000. Generous assistance came immediately from almost every civilized country, furnishing $3,742,818.

Recriminations were severe. The London *Chronicle* declared that the disaster revealed the shoddiness of American engineering. In New York City a newspaper controversy raged over the construction of the Quaker Bridge dam. To these attacks American engineers replied that the Conemaugh Reservoir did not even represent the best professional practices of an earlier generation, being the only dam in the United States over fifty feet in height without a central wall of masonry or puddle. Despite popular demands for an official investigation, none was held, but the Pennsylvania legislature permitted the legal consolidation of the Johnstown area for more effective civic co-operation.

[W. F. Johnson, *History of the Johnstown Flood.*]

HARVEY WISH

Joint Commissions. The arbitration of international disputes by joint commissions is usually distinguished from the negotiation of formal treaties by more than one diplomatic agent—such as the Definitive Treaty of Peace of 1783; the termination of Franco-American hostilities, by the Convention of 1800; the Louisiana Purchase; the Treaty of Ghent; the Webster-Ashburton Treaty; or the Peace of Paris, 1898*qqv*. Most arbitrations are, indeed, the work of joint commissions, as indicated in the monumental six-volume work on international arbitration by John Bassett Moore. Since its publication in 1898, further cases have arisen for settlement, notably the Alaskan Boundary dispute*qv* of 1903.

Among these numerous arbitrations by joint commissions, selection is capricious. But commissions were set up under the Jay Treaty*qv*; for the French Spoliation Claims*qv* in 1803, 1831, 1880; for determining various articles under the Treaty of Ghent; for claims of American citizens against Mexico, in 1839, 1849 and 1868; for claims against Colombia, in 1861; against Peru, in 1863; the Spanish Claims settlement of 1871; and the British Guiana Boundary dispute with Venezuela*qv*, 1897–99. Most significant of all was the Alabama Claims*qv* dispute, leading to the Geneva Award of 1872. To these may be added fact-finding commissions as an indispensable adjunct of modern diplomacy.

[John Bassett Moore, *History and Digest of the International Arbitrations to Which the United States Has Been a Party.*]

LOUIS MARTIN SEARS

Joint Committee on Reconstruction. Dec. 4, 1865, in the 39th Congress, Thaddeus Stevens of Pennsylvania moved the appointment of a joint committee from House and Senate to report conditions on which the late "so-called Confederate states" might be received back into the Union. Stevens and the Radical Republicans*qv*, displeased with President Johnson's plan of reconstruction, expected to take the matter from his hands, and to formulate a plan of their own.

The committee was appointed Dec. 13, 1865, consisting of: from the Senate, Messrs. Fessenden (Chairman), Grimes, Harris, Howard, Johnson and Williams; from the House, Messrs. Stevens, Washburne, Morrill, Conkling, Boutwell, Blow, Bingham, Grider and Rogers. The chief work of the committee was the formulation of the Fourteenth Amendment and of the Reconstruction Act of March 2, 1867*qqv*. In modified form the Congress adopted these measures as reported; and they became the basis of Southern Reconstruction*qv*. The committee expired with the end of the 39th Congress, March 2, 1867.

[Benjamin B. Kendrick, *The Journal of the Joint Committee of Fifteen on Reconstruction.*]

HAYWOOD J. PEARCE, JR.

"Joint Occupation." By a treaty signed Oct. 20, 1818 (*see* Convention of 1818), Great Britain and the United States determined the northern boundary of the Louisiana purchase*qv* as far west as the Rocky Mountains, but were unable to determine the boundary west of the mountains because of rival claims to the Oregon country*qv*. By this treaty it was agreed that the nationals of either nation could trade and settle in the region for a period of ten years. Aug. 6, 1827, the agreement was renewed, to continue until one party gave a year's notice of termination. Following the popular excitement characterized by the "54° 40′ or fight"*qv* campaign in April, 1846, Congress instructed President Polk to serve notice upon Great Britain that the agreement was to end. The settlement of the boundary question by treaty, June 15, 1846, ended the joint occupation of Oregon (*see* Oregon Treaty of 1846).

[Charles H. Carey, *A General History of Oregon, Prior to 1861.*]

ROBERT MOULTON GATKE

Joint Resolutions. *See* Resolutions, Legislative.

Joint-Stock Land Banks were chartered under the authority of the Federal Farm Loan Act, approved July 17, 1916. These banks were financed with private capital and were permitted to make loans in the state in which they were chartered and one contiguous state. About eighty-seven charters were granted, but not all of the banks opened for business. The joint-stock banks had their largest growth both in number and volume of business in the better agricultural areas, Iowa, Illinois, Minnesota, Missouri, Texas and California. At first the law did not limit the size of loans. The act was amended in 1923 limiting the size of loans to one borrower to $50,000. All loans were stated to be made for agricultural purposes. The land was appraised by the Federal Government appraisers. The amount of a loan was limited to a percentage of the value of the appraised land and buildings. They were permitted to issue tax-exempt bonds up to twenty times their capital. These banks did a thriving business during the World War land booms, but declined rapidly with the less profitable conditions of agriculture in the late 1920's. Many of the banks failed. Accusations of mismanagement sprang up and many of the banks reorganized or liquidated. The Emergency Farm Mortgage Act of 1933 ordered the Joint-Stock Land Banks liquidated. To aid in carrying out the liquidation of these banks the Emergency Farm Credits Act of 1933 provided the Land Bank Commission with $100,000,000 for two years and this was renewed for two more years in 1935. (*See also* Farm Credit Agencies, Federal.)

[Ivan Wright, *Farm Mortgage Financing; Annual Reports* of the Federal Farm Loan Board, 1916-1933, and Farm Credit Administration since 1933.]

IVAN WRIGHT

Jolliet and Marquette Discovery (1673). Louis Jolliet was a native of New France*q* who, after being educated at the Jesuit schools of Quebec, embarked on a career of exploration in the then far western country. On one of his voyages to Lake Superior in 1669 he met the Jesuit missionary, Jacques Marquette, then at the mission of Sault Ste. Marie*q*. Three years later the authorities of New France commissioned Jolliet to undertake the discovery of the great central river of the continent, which the Indians had described and spoken of as the Mississippi*q*. Jolliet requested that Marquette be appointed chaplain of the expedition, and late in the autumn of 1672 set out for the Northwest to prepare for the voyage. Jolliet found Marquette at the mission of St. Ignace*q* on the north shore of Mackinac Strait. Together they prepared maps and planned for the discovery during the ensuing winter; the map Marquette then drew still exists; later he traced the route of his discovery thereupon.

May 17, 1673, the two explorers left St. Ignace

in two canoes with five *voyageurs,* "fully resolved to do and to suffer everything for so glorious an undertaking." They went by way of Lake Michigan, Green Bay and Fox River (*see* Fox-Wisconsin Waterway). As far as the upper villages on Fox River the way was well known; at the Mascouten*q* village guides were obtained to lead them to the portage. Friendly Indians tried to dissuade the explorers, enlarging on the difficulties of the voyage; but the travelers pressed on, and a month from the time of departure their canoes shot out from the Wisconsin into a great river, which they instantly recognized as the stream they sought. Marquette wished to name the river the Conception for the immaculate conception of the Virgin Mary; Jolliet called it first the Buade, the family name of the Count de Frontenac, governor of New France. Ultimately he christened it the Colbert for the prime minister of France; but the Indian name has persisted.

The two explorers in their canoes drifted down the river as far as the Arkansas; they met few Indians and these for the most part friendly. They saw no monsters except painted ones on the cliffs high above the stream (*see* Alton Petroglyphs). They encountered no falls or whirlpools, and the voyage, while memorable, was not dangerous. From the Arkansas they turned back upstream, fearing to encounter Spaniards on the lower river. Acting on Indian advice they did not return to the Wisconsin-Fox waterway, but ascended the Illinois and the Des Plaines, portaging at Chicago to Lake Michigan (*see* Chicago Portage). They were thus the first white men to stand on the site of that great city.

Returning by Lake Michigan and Green Bay to the mission at DePere, Marquette remained there to recruit his health. Jolliet, after a winter of exploring around the lake, went in 1674 to Canada to report his discovery. Just before reaching Montreal his canoe overturned in the rapids, and he lost all his journals, notes and maps, his own life being saved with difficulty. Thus Marquette's journal has become the official account of the voyage, and Jolliet's share has been somewhat minimized. Jolliet was an expert map maker, later the official hydrographer of New France; his maps of the expedition, however, were drawn from memory, and the Jesuit maps superseded his. The discovery was widely heralded in France, and formed the basis for the exploration and exploitation of the Mississippi Valley by LaSalle*q* and other French voyagers in the late 17th century.

[Louise Phelps Kellogg, *French Régime in Wisconsin and the Northwest.*]   LOUISE PHELPS KELLOGG

Jonathan, or Brother Jonathan, nicknames of the American people. The story, unknown until 1846, attributing them to Washington's affection for Jonathan Trumbull (1710–85) is without foundation. In 1643 an English satirist, alluding to the "monuments" to Queen Elizabeth then common in London churches, declared that "her *Epitaph* was one of my Brother *Jonathan's* best *Poems,* before he abjured the *University,* or had a thought of *New-England.*" In a London satirical print entitled *The Yankie Doodles Intrenchments near Boston 1776,* a besieger says, "I Swear its plaguy Cold Jonathan." On vacating Bunker Hill, the British left images of hay labelled "Welcome, Brother Jonathan." Throughout the Revolution the terms were employed by loyalists and British soldiers in mild derision of patriots, but were avoided by the patriots themselves. After 1783 the terms were often applied by New Englanders to country bumpkins, and by 1812 had become established as national sobriquets. The first stage Yankees appeared as "Jonathen" in 1786, and as "Jonathan" in 1787.

[Publications of the Colonial Society of Massachusetts, VII, 94-123; XXXII, 374-86.]

ALBERT MATTHEWS

Jones Act, The, passed by Congress on Aug. 29, 1916, provided for the government of the Philippines[w], and committed the United States to the future independence of the archipelago. All inhabitants who were Spanish subjects on April 11, 1899, and their descendants were designated as citizens. The right to vote was given to all male citizens over twenty-one years of age, who could read and write. The two houses of the Philippine Congress were made wholly elective; and the President of the United States was to appoint, subject to confirmation by the Senate, justices of the Philippine Supreme Court. (*See also* Philippine Independence.)

[W. Cameron Forbes, *The Philippine Islands;* Dean C. Worcester, *The Philippines, Past and Present.*]

JOHN COLBERT COCHRANE

Jones County, Secession of, from the State of Mississippi during the Civil War, was first related by G. N. Galloway, historian of the Sixth Army Corps, in the *Magazine of American History* (1886), and assumed importance when accepted by Albert Bushnell Hart (*New England Magazine,* December, 1891). No evidence in documents or the memory of inhabitants supports the story. It apparently derives from the known anti-secession sentiment of the county, a pineywoods[w] area where there were no plantations, few Negroes and a small population, and from

the formation there (1862) of a company of 125 raiders who co-operated with the Federal Army.

[Alexander L. Bondurant, Did Jones County Secede?, *Publications of the Mississippi Historical Society,* Vol. I; Goode Montgomery, Alleged Secession of Jones County, *Ibid.,* Vol. VIII.]

MACK SWEARINGEN

Jones v. Van Zandt (5 How. 215, 1846) followed Prigg v. Pennsylvania[w] in sustaining the Federal Fugitive Slave Law[w] of 1793, despite arguments of Chase and Seward based upon the Ordinance of 1787[w] and the "inexpedience and invalidity of all laws recognizing slavery." The Court unanimously declared that the Constitution in one of its "sacred compromises" not only made slavery a political question to be settled by each state for itself, but also required each to allow the restoration of the slave property of others.

[J. W. Schuckers, *Life of Chase;* Charles Warren, *Supreme Court in United States History.*]

LAWRENCE A. HARPER

Joplin Lead Mining District. The Tri-State lead and zinc area lies in three adjoining counties of Missouri, Kansas and Oklahoma. The earliest records of lead mining in the vicinity of Joplin describe the finding of ore and the erection of a small furnace by David Campbell and William Tingle in 1849. During the same year mining began at Oronogo. The lead was freighted in four-horse wagons to Boonville on the Missouri River. The value of zinc blend was not suspected by these early miners; hence over half of the wealth of the mines was thrown out on the dump piles. In 1872 after a visit by the Missouri state geologist to Joplin the producers of the region began regular shipments of zinc.

The mining area of Galena, Kans., is continuous with the Joplin district. West of Baxter Springs are mines which form a part of the Miami-Picher area of Oklahoma. The major developments in the Oklahoma mines have occurred since 1904, although a small amount of lead was taken out at Peoria as early as 1891. In 1930 the Miami-Picher mines produced almost two thirds of the output of the Joplin district. The total value of the lead and zinc in the Tri-State area since David Campbell's discovery in 1849 has been $901,457,987.

[Joel T. Livingston, *A History of Jasper County, Mo.;* Samuel Weidman, *Miami-Picher Zinc-Lead District; Metals Industry Journal,* March, 1938.]

EDWIN McREYNOLDS

Jornada del Muerto, signifying in English the "journey of death," was a ninety-mile strip of desert extending from Valverde, N. Mex., to El Paso del Norte, later shortened to El Paso, Tex. The road follows a dry plain where soap weed grows high and the grass is dry from lack of moisture. Many tragedies occurred on the *jornada* in the old Spanish days due to the absence of life-giving water.

[J. S. Robinson, *Journal of a Santa Fe Expedition*, ed. by C. L. Cannon.]   CARL L. CANNON

Jouett's Ride. Capt. John Jouett, Jr., was spending the night of June 3, 1781, at Cuckoo Tavern, Louisa, Va., when he saw Tarleton with a detachment of British troops go by in the direction of Charlottesville, where the Virginia legislature was in session after having fled from Richmond on the approach of Cornwallis. Jouett, who knew the countryside, rode by hidden paths the forty-five miles before dawn to warn the legislature, thus saving four signers of the Declaration of Independence: Jefferson, Nelson, R. H. Lee and Harrison, in addition to Patrick Henry and Edmund Randolph.

[Mrs. Mary (Mallet) Elliott, *Colonial Days in Virginia*.]
                        JAMES ELLIOTT WALMSLEY

Journal of Congress is the official record of the proceedings of the legislative branch of the United States Government. The Continental Congress[qv] in 1774 appointed Charles Thomson, as secretary, who kept a manuscript journal recording its resolves and other decisions, and also the attendance of the members. This Journal was published contemporaneously in thirteen volumes. Thomson also kept a Secret Journal which was not published until 1821. These journals, together with information from auxiliary records and papers, were used in the Library of Congress edition of the *Journals of the Continental Congress* (Washington, 1904–37, 34 vols.) to reconstruct the fuller story of the activities of the Congress from 1774–89. The Constitution provides that "each House shall keep a Journal of its Proceedings." In the earliest Congresses the Journals were printed in parts and distributed during the session. At the end of each session since 1789 they have been published verbatim with indexes, one or more volumes for each house. Due to the burning of the Capitol in 1814 when all printed copies belonging to both houses were destroyed, the Journals of the first thirteen Congresses were reprinted (1820–26). Down to 1861 the Journals were printed by contract and thereafter by the Government Printing Office under the authority of each house. They are also substantially incorporated in the *Annals of Congress* (covering 1789–1824), in the *Register of Debates* (1824–37), in the *Congressional Globe* (1833–73), and in the *Congressional Record*[qv] since 1873. The Senate also keeps an executive journal which has been published from time to time in thirty-four volumes covering the first fifty-eight Congresses.

[L. F. Schmeckebier, *Government Publications and Their Use*.]
                        ROSCOE R. HILL

Journalism. *See* Newspapers.

Juchereau's Tannery (1702–04) was established by Charles Juchereau de St. Denys on or near the site of the present city of Cairo, Ill., in 1702. At its height, the establishment included a missionary priest, more than a hundred tradesmen, and many Mascouten hunters. Decline commenced in the summer and fall of 1703, when an epidemic caused the death of Juchereau and many of his men. Lambert Mandeville, Juchereau's second in command, attempted to carry on the enterprise, but in 1704 it was abandoned.

[C. W. Alvord, *The Illinois Country, 1673-1818*.]
                        PAUL M. ANGLE

Judicial Review. The power of courts in the United States to determine the invalidity of legislative acts deemed to conflict with constitutions had at least a preparatory background in conditions prevailing in the colonial period. Acts of colonial assemblies[qv] were subject to veto by royal governors, to disallowance (*see* Royal Disallowance) by the crown after they had gone into effect, and to disallowance in later judicial proceedings (*see* Appeals from Colonial Courts). In early state constitutions some recognition of the desirability of having a reviewing authority over the legislature was revealed in provisions for councils of revision and councils of censors[qqv]. Judges under these constitutions were selected by the legislatures, without expectation that they would serve as reviewing officers. Prior to 1787, however, the conduct of certain state courts showed bare beginnings of reviewing activities, and the belief that a part of the judicial function was the limitation of law enforcement to laws not in conflict with the state constitution.

The constitutional Convention of 1787[qv] was faced with the problem of keeping state legislatures from encroaching on the powers of the new Federal Government, as well as with the question of what, if anything, should be done to keep congressional legislation within the limits of the Constitution. These two aspects of judicial review run parallel down through the subsequent years of American history. The Constitution as adopted contained no specific grant of power to the Federal courts to prescribe the line of constitutionality with respect to either state or Federal laws, but the "supreme law of the land" provision made clear the superiority of the Federal Constitution*, laws and treaties over state enactments. The Judiciary Act of 1789 authorized the Supreme Court*q* to review cases under certain circumstances involving conflicts in this field. Alexander Hamilton, writing in the *Federalist**, supported the cause of judicial review, but in the light of the importance which it later attained the subject seems to have attracted little attention at the time.

After the adoption of the Constitution the state courts further developed the practice of declaring state laws invalid, and Federal courts began the review of state laws. The Federal courts, furthermore, while for some time arriving at no decision holding acts of Congress unconstitutional, began to examine the validity of acts of Congress and to assert the right of review. The first case in which the Supreme Court of the United States held an act of Congress unconstitutional was that of Marbury v. Madison*q* (1 Cranch 137), in 1803. The legislative act involved was a section of the Judiciary Act of 1789 which authorized the Supreme Court to issue writs of mandamus in the exercise of its original jurisdiction. The case arose out of an action for a mandamus to compel James Madison, Secretary of State under Thomas Jefferson, to deliver to William Marbury a commission as justice of the peace in the District of Columbia, which had been made out and signed under the preceding administration but had not been delivered (*see* Midnight Judges). In an opinion of the Court filled with contemporary political implications Chief Justice Marshall took the position that Marbury was entitled to the commission, and that the writ of mandamus was the proper remedy. He concluded further, however, that Congress could not enlarge the original jurisdiction of the Supreme Court by authorizing it to issue writs of mandamus, and that the act purporting to confer this power was therefore unconstitutional.

The decision and the mode of reasoning used in support of it were criticized at the time and for years to come, but no attack on the constitutional power of the Federal courts to review acts of Congress ever approached success. During subsequent years while Marshall was Chief Justice no Federal law was held invalid. Some disturbance was created by the review of cases brought up from the highest courts in the states, because of the alleged encroachment on state sovereignty (*see* Fletcher v. Peck), but the exercise of the power continued without abatement. State courts continued to measure state laws against both state and Federal constitutions, and the Supreme Court, within limits prescribed by Congress, exercised the right of additional review with respect to the Federal Constitution.

With the end of the regime of Chief Justice Marshall, and the beginning of that of Chief Justice Taney, Mr. Justice Story predicted mournfully in 1837 that never again in his day would a state or Federal legislative act be declared unconstitutional. The prediction was erroneous with respect to action on state laws, but was more than fulfilled as to acts of Congress. From Marbury v. Madison in 1803 to the Dred Scott case*q* in 1857 no Federal act was stricken down. A few acts were appraised by the Supreme Court in terms of their constitutionality, however, and the Court remained conscious of its power in this field. The explanation of the fact that no acts were held unconstitutional lies in part in the fact that during that period the scope of Federal legislation was extremely narrow.

The Supreme Court reasserted its power to declare acts of Congress unconstitutional in Dred Scott v. Sandford (19 Howard 393), in 1857, by holding unconstitutional a measure enacted in 1820 known as the Missouri Compromise*q*, by which slavery had been excluded from certain territories of the United States. The decision caused a storm of protest and indignation throughout the country, but the criticism was motivated by the nature of the decision and not by the exercise of the power of judicial review. The severity of the criticism was due in part, however, to the fact that the case could have been decided without raising the constitutional question.

The unpopularity of the Dred Scott decision placed no effective check on the development of judicial review. Ten decisions held acts of Congress unconstitutional during the regime of Chief Justice Chase from 1865 to 1873. An extensive use of the power continued down through the years thereafter. The number of state laws held unconstitutional after the Civil War likewise vastly increased, with the newly adopted Fourteenth Amendment*q* playing a prominent part in checking such legislation. An important reason for the expansion of judicial activity in both state and Federal fields was the expansion of the scope of legislation. With the growth of industrial enterprise the states enacted increased numbers of regulatory laws. As the need for effective regulation increased beyond the scope of state power as interpreted by the courts, Federal legislation expanded into the regulatory field, on the basis of powers implied from the commerce, taxation and other clauses of the Constitution (*see* Implied Powers) . The area of judicial review was correspondingly enlarged, with the Supreme Court standing as the final arbiter of the extent to which the implied and resultant powers of the Constitution should be allowed to develop. The same period saw the development of a number of complicated administrative agencies[*w*] and devices for law enforcement, and the expansion of rules and regulations in the executive and administrative field. The measurement of activities in this field against the requirements of the Constitution has become a significant sector of the area of judicial review.

The Supreme Court was sharply criticized at various times down through the years for its interference with the will of Congress and the desires of the people. (*See* the Dred Scott case, the Legal Tender cases, the Income Tax cases and others.) Various proposals were suggested from time to time for curbing its power, such as requiring more than a bare majority of the Court to hold legislation invalid, and allowing Congress to re-establish stricken legislation by a two-thirds vote. The apparent hostility of the Court to New Deal legislation in decisions rendered in 1935 and 1936, in cases involving the National Industrial Recovery Act, the Agricultural Adjustment Act[*qw*] and other statutes, led in 1937 to a concerted attempt to add new members to the Court to bring about a change in the trend of decisions (*see* Supreme Court Packing Bills) . The administration submitted to Congress a bill to authorize the appointment to the Supreme Court of a new judge for each judge sitting who had been a member of the Court for ten years and who did not retire within six months after becoming seventy years of age. The total membership of the Court was not to be increased to more than fifteen. An apparent change in the attitude of the Court toward social legislation, in cases involving the National Labor Relations Act and the Social Security Act[*qw*], revealed itself while the bill was pending, and doubtless aided in bringing about its defeat. Discussion of the bill showed in some groups a profound impatience with the use of judicial review to substitute the will of the Court for that of Congress in the making of policy. It showed in others a continuing confidence in the Court as an institution, and in the device of judicial review. After the bill was defeated normal changes in court personnel brought about much of the change in attitude which the administration had sought to achieve.

[Charles A. Beard, *The Supreme Court and the Constitu-*

tion; Charles G. Haines, *The American Doctrine of Judicial Supremacy.*]

CARL BRENT SWISHER

Judiciary, THE, of the United States, has its historical background in the legal and political institutions of England. The tribunals set up in the colonies were similar to those of the mother country, and acts of Parliament and the principles of the common law[*w*] and equity were enforced in the new country as in the old, with the added responsibility on colonial courts of enforcing the enactments of colonial assemblies[*w*]. The judiciary in the colonies (*see* Colonial Judiciary) was rudimentary in some respects. For example, among the complaints made against the king in the Declaration of Independence[*w*] were the charges that he had obstructed the administration of justice by refusing assent to laws for establishing judiciary powers; he had made judges dependent on his will alone for salaries and tenure; and he had transported people beyond the seas to be tried for pretended offenses. The office of justice of the peace[*w*], for dealing with minor civil matters and minor offenses, was well established. Above this office was the court usually known as the county court, having original jurisdiction in more important matters. A right of appeal to the colonial assembly existed in some colonies, analogous to appeal to the House of Lords in England. There was in some cases a right of appeal from colonial courts to the judicial committee of the Privy Council[*w*] in England.

After the colonies became independent states the courts remained fundamentally the same, except for the development of courts of appeals with full-time professional judges. Constitutions prescribed the governments of the states, pursuant to which state laws were made and enforced. The application of common law and equity principles was continued. After the adoption of the Federal Constitution[*w*] state judiciaries were subject to its control in that the Constitution and Federal laws and treaties were made the supreme law of the land, and binding upon all courts, notwithstanding the constitutions and laws of the states. The judiciaries in most states were largely subordinate to the legislatures in many respects, but varying degrees of separation of powers[*w*] were worked out with subsequent changes. The development of the practice of judicial review[*w*] emphasized the growing prestige and authority of the judiciary as an independent department of government.

No provision for an adequate Federal judiciary was included in the Articles of Confederation[*w*]. Congress had power to set up commissions to settle disputes among the states. Under the

Articles it set up a court of appeals to decide cases appealed from state courts involving prizes of war and piracies and felonies on the high seas. The lack of an adequate judiciary was regarded as one of the major defects of the Confederation. All the proposed plans of government submitted to the constitutional Convention of 1787^w provided for a national judiciary distinct from the judicial systems of the states.

The first three articles of the Constitution, which were drafted to provide for a high degree of separation of powers, provided respectively for the establishment of the legislative, executive and judicial branches of the Government. The judiciary article provided that the judicial power of the United States should be vested in a Supreme Court^w and in such inferior courts as Congress might ordain and establish. All Federal judges were to hold office during good behavior, and their salaries were not to be diminished during their continuance in office. By Article II, dealing with the executive, the President was authorized to nominate, and, by and with the advice and consent of the Senate, to appoint Supreme Court judges and certain other specified officers, and all other officers of the United States whose appointment was not otherwise provided for in the Constitution. Congress was authorized, however, to vest the appointment of inferior officers in the President alone, in the courts of law, or in the heads of departments (*see* Appointments and the Appointing Power). It is possible that the judges of inferior Federal courts might be included in the category of inferior officers.

The second section of the judiciary article prescribed the content of Federal judicial power. Within the limits of that power the jurisdiction of particular Federal courts was left to congressional determination, except for the original jurisdiction of the Supreme Court which was defined in the Constitution. Criminal trials, except in cases of impeachment^w, were to be by jury, in the states in which the crimes had been committed. The sixth article established a basis for review by the Federal judiciary of state court decisions involving the Federal Constitution, laws or treaties by providing that state judges should be bound by them notwithstanding any contrary provisions in the constitutions and laws of the states. Six articles in the *Federalist*^{w}, all written by Alexander Hamilton, analyzed and defended the judiciary provisions in the proposed Federal Constitution. The proposed Constitution was adopted; but the first ten amendments (*see* Bill of Rights), added in 1791 to meet criticisms voiced in the ratifying conven-

tions, included additional prescriptions with respect to the courts. Among them, suits at common law involving more than twenty dollars were to be tried by jury; criminal trials, with certain exceptions, were to be preceded by indictment by grand jury; and the resort to excessive bail, excessive fines, and cruel and unusual punishments was prohibited.

The judiciary provisions of the Constitution were given effect in the Judiciary Act of 1789^w, enacted after eleven states had ratified the Constitution. The judicial system was headed by a Supreme Court consisting of a Chief Justice and five associate justices. Below the Supreme Court were three circuit courts, which had no judges of their own but were conducted by two Supreme Court judges and a district judge. Below the circuit courts were thirteen district courts, for each of which a district judge was to be appointed by the President in the same manner as Supreme Court judges, no advantage being taken of the possibility of classifying district judges as inferior officers for whose appointment a different procedure might be prescribed. The districts established were coterminous with state lines except that two states were each divided into two districts.

The district courts were given original jurisdiction in minor offenses against Federal laws, and in a wide range of admiralty^w cases, the latter making up the burden of their work in early years. In some cases a right of appeal lay to the circuit courts. The circuit courts had original jurisdiction in cases involving larger amounts and more serious offenses. The major portion of their work in the early years was with cases involving state laws, in which Federal jurisdiction depended on the fact that the parties were citizens of different states. The Supreme Court was given the jurisdiction allotted to it by the Constitution, and appellate jurisdiction in certain cases from decisions of the circuit courts and the highest state courts.

The history of the Federal judiciary has been the history of the steady expansion of business and the consequences of this expansion. The expansion has been one of territory, an increase in the settled area requiring judicial service. It has been one of population, in that the growth of population within given areas has added to the work of the courts. It has been one of legislation, in that the bulk of Federal legislation to be applied by the courts has grown with the growth of the country and the increasing complexity of the conditions of living. The district courts in territorial United States are now (1939) more than six times as numerous as in 1789, and there are more than twelve times as many district judges.

Although the district courts survived and increased in number, they underwent drastic jurisdictional changes by which they were crowded into the field originally occupied by the circuit courts. The circuit courts had a more difficult task of survival. The circuit court system was modified early in 1801 by an act of Congress creating a number of circuit judgeships and abolishing the requirement that Supreme Court judges ride circuit (*see* Judiciary Act of 1801). Soon afterward, however, the new judgeships were abolished and the old system was largely restored. Each Supreme Court judge was assigned permanently to one circuit. The need for creating additional circuit courts to handle the increase of business resulted in pressure for the enlargement of the membership of the Supreme Court. The number reached nine in 1837 and the all-time high of ten in 1863. In 1869 Congress provided for the appointment of nine circuit judges for the circuits, which had likewise been reduced to nine in number, thereby relieving the judges of the Supreme Court of part of their circuit responsibilities. The increase in the appellate work of the Supreme Court led to demand for further relief. Congress responded with a new measure in 1891. This measure added a new circuit judge to each circuit, withdrew all appellate jurisdiction from the circuit courts, and by implication relieved Supreme Court judges of the obligation to ride circuit. The same act provided for the creation of a circuit court of appeals in each circuit. Upon these courts was conferred the appellate jurisdiction hitherto exercised by the circuit courts, and a portion of the appellate jurisdiction hitherto exercised by the Supreme Court. The result was a temporary reduction of the burden of work borne by the Supreme Court. To enable the Court to keep up with the growing stream of important cases it has been necessary to make further curtailments from time to time, particularly by limiting the classes of cases which might be taken to the Supreme Court as a matter of right, in contrast with those which might be accepted or rejected by the Court after a preliminary scrutiny to determine their public importance.

Supreme Court judges continued to be assigned to the several circuits. They were empowered to sit on the circuit courts of appeals, but they have not seen fit to exercise the privilege. The circuit courts continued to operate in each circuit until 1911, when they were abolished because of the extent to which their work overlapped with that of the district courts. The Federal judicial system proper therefore now consists of the district courts, the circuit courts of appeals, and the Supreme Court. Provisions with respect to appellate jurisdiction are exceedingly complex. For example, some cases are taken directly from the district courts to the Supreme Court. Some go from the district courts to the circuit courts of appeals, and thence to the Supreme Court. Some cannot go beyond the circuit courts of appeals. Some go directly to the Supreme Court from special courts of three judges which are made up for the trial of the particular cases. Some cases from territorial courts go to circuit courts of appeals. Orders of independent regulatory commissions, such as the Interstate Commerce Commission, the Federal Trade Commission and the National Labor Relations Board[qqv], are reviewed by circuit courts of appeals. Cases involving Federal questions go to the Supreme Court from the highest state courts having jurisdiction over them. The purpose of Congress in prescribing the appellate jurisdiction of the several courts is to provide for the expeditious appeal to the highest court of cases of greatest public importance, while moving those of a lesser importance at a slower pace, or limiting the right of appeal with respect to them, or cutting it off altogether.

The Federal judiciary, in a narrow sense, consists only of these several courts which are created pursuant to the provisions of the third article of the Constitution. In the exercise of other powers conferred upon it, however, such as the powers to govern territories, to grant patents, and to appropriate money to pay claims against the United States, Congress may create other tribunals to exercise judicial functions. These are known as legislative courts, in contrast with the so-called constitutional courts organized under Article III. Among them are the courts established in the territories of the United States, the Court of Claims, and the Court of Customs and Patent Appeals. The courts of the District of Columbia were once regarded as legislative but are now held to be constitutional courts. In providing for legislative courts Congress is not bound by the provisions of Article III with respect to salaries and tenure of judges. Bearing some resemblance to legislative courts are independent agencies such as the Interstate Commerce Commission, the Federal Trade Commission, the National Labor Relations Board and other agencies within some of the departments of the Government, which exercise functions seemingly judicial in character and commonly called quasi-judicial[qv], but which are not usually classified as judicial tribunals at all.

The appointment of Federal judges by the President and the Senate has been criticized from time to time, but there has been no serious movement for popular elections such as that which took place in connection with state judges. The provision for tenure during good behavior, on the other hand, has been regarded by many as a serious defect in the judicial system. Many judges have proved unwilling to resign from the bench even after reaching the stage of senility. In 1869 Congress authorized the continuance of full pay for Federal judges who resigned after reaching seventy years of age and after having served ten years on the bench. This promise of continued compensation proved inadequate to bring about resignations in some cases in which it was thought to be desirable. In 1919 Congress authorized the retirement of judges other than those of the Supreme Court, after the same age and service period had been attained, without the necessity of resigning. Such judges remained technically in office, and were subject to recall to the bench for such duties as they were able and willing to undertake. Their continued compensation depended, therefore, not on the promise of Congress but on the guarantee of the Constitution. This measure, likewise, failed to bring about as many early retirements as some critics of the judiciary have thought desirable.

The same act authorized the President to appoint an additional judge for each judge eligible for retirement who did not resign or retire, but who had suffered permanent mental or physical disability for the performance of his duties. The proposal to make such appointments automatic rather than dependent on findings of disability, and to include the Supreme Court along with other Federal courts, was much debated in connection with a bill submitted to Congress by the President in 1937 (*see* Supreme Court Packing Bills). The proposal failed of enactment, but during the period of debate a measure was enacted providing for the retirement of Supreme Court judges according to the procedure already prescribed for the judges of the lower courts. A constitutional amendment authorizing compulsory retirement of judges at a fixed age has been much discussed, but has attracted no widespread support. One reason lies in the fact that some judges well above the contemplated age of retirement have performed distinguished service in the courts, and there is reluctance to deprive the country of such service.

A barrier to efficiency in the Federal courts has been the technicality and diversity in rules of practice. In 1792 Congress empowered the Supreme Court to adopt uniform rules of practice for the Federal courts in equity and admiralty cases, and in 1898 the same power was given with respect to bankruptcy cases. The rules were drafted and put in operation. Concerning actions at law, however, it was provided in the Conformity Act of 1872 that the Federal courts should conform "as near as may be" to the practice currently in effect in the courts of the states. State practice varied widely. Federal practice therefore varied from state to state, and was often archaic and cumbersome. After many years of agitation, Congress in 1934 authorized the Supreme Court to adopt and promulgate uniform rules in this field for the Federal courts. The rules became effective in 1938, marking an outstanding achievement in judicial reform.

The expansion of the work of the Federal courts and the increase in the number of courts and judges created a need for central co-ordination of the judiciary. An act of Congress in 1922 provided for a Judicial Conference of the senior circuit judges, to be presided over by the Chief Justice of the United States. Pursuant to the act the Conference meets annually. It provides a forum for the discussion of ideas with reference to the business of the courts. It works out means of promoting efficiency, and makes recommendations to Congress and achieves publicity for needed reforms.

The state judicial systems differ greatly among themselves and from the Federal system in matters of appointment, tenure, jurisdiction, procedure and organization. In the early years the selection of judges was made largely by the legislature or indirectly under its control. The Jackson period saw a movement toward popular election, particularly in the newer states. In about one fourth of the states, including a number of the original thirteen and other older states, judges of appellate courts and courts of general jurisdiction are selected by legislatures or governors or by co-operation between governors and legislatures or senates. The other states resort to election by the people. The latter method is generally regarded as defective in that it involves the judiciary in politics and fails oftentimes to result in the selection of the best personnel. Tenure varies greatly from state to state and from court to court, though in only three are the judges of even the highest courts appointed for the term of their good behavior, as in the Federal system. The term is usually shortest in the lower courts, and longest in those of the highest rank. Removal of a judge before the expiration of his term is difficult. The machinery of impeachment is available but is cumbersome and hard to use. A few states authorize removal by the governor on address of both houses of the legislature without resorting to impeachment procedure. A few state constitutions provide for the recall^{qv} of judges, but little use has been made of the device. A few states provide maximum age limits beyond which judges of highest state courts, and occasionally of other courts, may not serve.

The highest appellate courts of the states have only a limited original jurisdiction or none at all. They consist of from three to nine judges. Some of them carry on their work in sections, but most of them sit as a body, as does the Supreme Court of the United States. In order to relieve the highest courts of excessive burdens of work a number of states have created intermediate appellate courts between them and the courts of original and general jurisdiction. The latter courts handle in the first instance common law civil cases, equity suits, criminal prosecutions and probate matters. All may be handled in the same court, or special courts may deal with particular subjects. The tendency has been to do away with separately organized equity courts, which were formerly provided in England and in many of the states. Juvenile courts, courts of domestic relations^{qv}, traffic courts and small claims courts illustrate the specialized tribunals which operate in some states. Municipal courts, providing oftentimes for the co-ordination of the courts of a municipality, reach down into the area formerly occupied by the justice of the peace, replacing that lay official with one professionally trained. The office of justice of the peace still survives, with perhaps a minimum of dissatisfaction in rural areas, but in more populous areas its ultimate survival is in doubt.

Complexities of procedure have embarrassed the states as well as the Federal Government. In the middle of the 19th century a movement was started for the codification of procedure with the elimination of unnecessary technicalities. It was carried forward under the leadership of David Dudley Field, of New York, and spread to many other states. A similar movement was started for the codification of substantive law. Codes were adopted in a number of states, and have been satisfactory in part, but they have never entirely fulfilled their intended purpose. An attempt at broad simplification has been made in recent years by the American Law Institute in its restatement of law in the several fields.

The expansion of court work and the increase in the number of tribunals created a need for centralized control of the judiciaries of many states. Within cities the establishment of municipal courts was a step in the direction of eliminating inefficiency arising from lack of co-ordination. A number of states, some in advance of the Federal Government and some later, organized judicial councils to aid in bringing order from chaos. The device of a supreme court of judicature has been suggested for co-ordination of all the courts of a state, but it has not as yet gone beyond the stage of piecemeal adoption in any state.

Although there is no complete separation of powers^{qv} in any state or in the Federal Government, the several judiciaries have maintained well their strength against legislative and executive departments. There has been little interference with the personnel of the bench, once the personnel has been chosen. There has been little interference with the work of the courts through the alteration of their jurisdiction. On the other hand the courts have strengthened their position down through the years by resort to judicial review, making themselves final authorities as to the meanings of state and Federal constitutions. By keeping their interpretations in harmony with powerful conservative sentiments of the times they have maintained a prestige which has given added authority to their interpretations. There have been popular outbursts against particular courts at particular times, but seldom against the courts as institutions. Outraged sentiment of many people because of constitutional interpretations defeating liberal measures of the Federal Government gave support to the concerted attempt in 1937 to liberalize the Federal courts through the addition of new blood. Opposing sentiment, based in part on opposition to the measures and in part on opposition to any attack on the courts, particularly the Supreme Court, was sufficient to prevent the success of the plan. The continuing prestige and power of the courts seem assured as long as they maintain their integrity, keep up with their business and keep their interpretations in harmony with the dominant sentiments of the times.

[William Anderson, *American Government;* Clarence C. Callender, *American Courts;* Felix Frankfurter and James M. Landis, *The Business of the Supreme Court;* Andrew C. McLaughlin, *A Constitutional History of the United States;* Carl Brent Swisher, ed., *Selected Papers of Homer Cummings;* Charles Warren, *The Supreme Court in United States History.*]   CARL BRENT SWISHER

Judiciary Act of 1789, THE, implementing the judiciary clause of the Constitution^{qv}, first organized the Federal judiciary. It provided for a Supreme Court^{qv} of six members, three intermediate Circuit Courts comprising two Supreme Court justices and a District judge, and thirteen District Courts, corresponding roughly to state boundaries, with a judge for each.

Probably most important was section 25 granting the Court, through writs of error, the right to hear and decide appeals from state courts in three categories of cases: (1) Where the validity of a Federal law, treaty or authority, under the Federal Constitution, was questioned and the state court decided against its validity; (2) where the validity of a state law or authority was similarly questioned and the state court upheld state against Federal authority; (3) where a litigant set up rights, privileges, or exemptions under Federal Constitution, treaty, or statute, and had such contention denied by the state courts.

Herein is established the doctrine of judicial review[qv] of state legislation first exercised in the case of Fletcher v. Peck[qv]. The section, through its assignment of jurisdiction to the Supreme Court on writs of error in cases of conflict between state and Federal authority, also became one of the strongest bulwarks of Federal power against the attacks of the States' Rights[qv] school. Asserted by the Court in the famous cases of Martin v. Hunter's Lessee and Cohens v. Virginia[qv], the right to hear appeals under the section was firmly established, to the chagrin of immediate advocates of States' Rights and to the permanent enhancement of the Court's prestige and of Federal authority; later decisions reviewing state legislation, such as the Dartmouth College Case, McCulloch v. Maryland and Gibbons v. Ogden[qv], exerted powerful influence upon American social and economic development.

[Charles Warren, *The Supreme Court in United States History.*]

L. ETHAN ELLIS

Judiciary Act of 1801, THE, has erroneously been viewed principally in the light of the election of 1800, leading to the frequent assertion that the outgoing Federalists[qv] erected new posts to provide offices for Federalists and perpetuate Nationalism through the judiciary. Actually, judicial reform was needed, had for some time been considered, was recommended by John Adams in 1799 and was carefully prepared in the act, which (1) reduced the membership of the Supreme Court[qv] to five and relieved its Justices of the onerous Circuit Court duty; (2) set up six Circuits, five presided over by three Circuit Judges each and the sixth by a Circuit and a District Judge; (3) established five new judicial Districts. Incoming Republicans (Jeffersonian) derided the incumbents as "Midnight Judges,"[qv] asserted that the judiciary had become a hospital for decayed politicians, and proceeded in 1802 to repeal the act. This action, at least as partisan as that of 1801, restored the Judiciary Act of 1789[qv] to full

force. The repeal debate thoroughly canvassed the issue of judicial review[qv], set forth the Jeffersonian theory of legislative supremacy and furnished the political setting for Marbury v. Madison[qv].

[Max Farrand, The Judiciary Act of 1801, *American Historical Review*, Vol. V; A. J. Beveridge, *The Life of John Marshall.*]

L. ETHAN ELLIS

Juilliard v. Greenman, 1884 (110 U. S. 421), upheld the implied power[qv] of Congress to make the United States' own notes legal tender[qv] (and therefore money) in peace time as well as in war time. In the case of Hepburn v. Griswold, the Supreme Court first held the legal-tender acts unconstitutional. Immediately thereafter in the legal-tender cases[qv] the Supreme Court (it is claimed after it had been packed by President Grant) reversed this decision and upheld the legal-tender acts as a war measure. Juilliard v. Greenman upheld them without reference to the war power, and in this decision all the members concurred except Justice Field. In this case the Supreme Court implied the power from the express power to borrow money, and the implied power to issue bills of credit.

[H. E. Willis, *Constitutional Law.*]

HUGH E. WILLIS

"Jukes, The." In 1874 Richard L. Dugdale, who was investigating county jails for the Prison Association of New York, found in a jail in a certain hilly county six persons, blood relations, who were guilty of theft, burglary, rape and murderous assault. He further learned that of twenty-nine males, immediate kin of these six, seventeen were criminals while fifteen had been convicted of some sort of offense and had received seventy-one years of sentences. Of the women, 52% were harlots in some degree. This led him to a remarkable study in heredity, a two centuries' record of a degenerate family which he called the Jukes, to protect its more worthy members. He traced it back to a man who settled in that area between 1720 and 1740. Intermarriage or cohabitation amongst themselves and with immediate neighbors of poor blood strains had brought about an appalling record of crime, licentiousness, imbecility and public dependency. Dugdale's report was published in 1884. In 1915 a continuation of it to that date by Arthur H. Eastabrook was published by the Carnegie Institution. Eastabrook studied 2820 persons, including about 1200 considered by Dugdale, and, despite an improvement in conditions, found 366 paupers, 171 criminals, 282 intemperate and 277 harlots. Their total expense to the state in prison, institutional and relief costs was estimated at $2,093,685.

[Richard L. Dugdale, *The Jukes;* Arthur H. Easta-brook, *The Jukes in 1915.*]   ALVIN F. HARLOW

"Jumping-off Places" was a term used to de-scribe the towns along the border of the settle-ments where emigrants completed their outfit-ting for the journey across the plains during the 1840's and 1850's. Independence^{qv}, Mo., was the best known of these places. Among the others were Council Bluffs, Iowa; St. Joseph, Mo.; and Fort Smith, Ark.   DAN E. CLARK

Junior College Movement. Junior colleges may be classified as preparatory or terminal. The preparatory type undertakes to co-ordinate the last two years of preparatory school with the first two years of college, so that the student may re-main in his home community and then enter the junior year of a standard college. This type is devoted to general rather than vocational sub-jects. Junior colleges of the terminal classifica-tion offer vocational and semivocational courses, including accounting, secretarial work, salesman-ship, management of individual enterprises, do-mestic economy and agriculture. There is in addition, particularly in the East, a type of junior college for women, which extends for two years the courses of private finishing and preparatory schools.

In 1892 President Harper of the University of Chicago advised the organization of junior col-leges to replace inadequately endowed four-year colleges. As a result, the Baptist denomination in Texas in 1898 reopened an institution which had failed as a four-year college. Known as Decatur Baptist College, it is the oldest existing junior college in the United States.

The University of Missouri, to obtain relief from the constantly increasing numbers in the two lower classes, early took the lead in encourag-ing junior colleges. The State of California worked out one of the best systems of public-supported junior colleges in the United States. The University of Texas gave encouragement to the organization of municipal junior colleges, to a statute for providing district junior col-leges and through liberal affiliations gave every possible encouragement to privately supported and denominational junior colleges.

In 1936 there were 535 junior colleges in the United States, with 75,000 students, 4000 instruc-tors and property valued at $250,000,000. More than half the students enrolled would not be able to attend college if there were not a junior college in their home community. A second fac-tor in their growth is the desire of many parents to keep their children at home after high school graduation. Moreover, the instruction is often more personal and intimate than in larger in-stitutions.

Some junior colleges are supported through re-ligious denominations and other private sources; others by taxpayers; others through the co-opera-tion of taxpayers and patrons where a part of the tuition is advanced by the student and the remainder is supplied by the municipality or the state.

[Walter C. Eels, *The Junior College;* Junior Colleges, *Bulletin No. 3*, U. S. Department of the Interior, 1936.]
WALTER M. W. SPLAWN

Junius, Letters of, were published in the Lon-don *Public Advertiser* (Jan. 21, 1769 to Jan. 21, 1772) signed "Junius," pseudonym of an un-identified writer, possibly Sir Philip Francis. A well-informed Whig, "Junius" poured brilliantly slanderous invective upon Tory-minded English ministers, especially the Duke of Grafton, for a "series of inconsistent measures" which allegedly ruined England and drove the colonies "into excesses little short of rebellion." Vehement, lucid, frequently reprinted in English and colo-nial newspapers, the letters were polemic master-pieces with such extraordinary knowledge and appreciation of contemporary colonial opinion that they lent moral support to the early revolu-tionary cause. "Junius" opposed the Tea Duty, but upheld the legality of the Stamp Act^{qv}, and prophesied (Dec. 19, 1769) that the colonies aimed at independence.

[*Cambridge History of English Literature*, Vol. X.]
RAYMOND P. STEARNS

Jürgen Lorentzen Prize Case. In 1861 the United States warship *Morning Light* (Capt. H. T. Moore) captured the Danish bark, *Jürgen Lorentzen,* sailing from Rio de Janeiro to Ha-vana, Cuba (*see* Confederate States, Blockade of). The papers of the bark stated that further orders might be received at Havana. Capt. Moore, suspecting the bark was bound for a Confederate port, took it to New York. The Danes complained of ill treatment. An investi-gation turned out favorably for the *Jürgen Lo-rentzen*. A joint Danish-American commission was established to ascertain the damages. Con-gress made provision for the settlement.

[S. P. Fogdall, *Danish-American Diplomacy.*]
S. P. FOGDALL

Jury Trial is the characteristic mode of deter-mining issues of fact at common law^{qv}. It developed by a process of evolution which dates far back into the Middle Ages. It came to be so highly regarded as a procedure devised for the protection of the rights and liberties of the people that Blackstone characterized it "the glory of the English law." It was transplanted from the mother country to the American colonies and became an integral part of their legal system in both civil and criminal common law cases, with the exception that a more summary procedure was allowed in petty cases. The Constitution of the United States as proposed in 1787 contained, in the second section of Article III, the provision that "the trial of all crimes, except in cases of impeachment, shall be by jury." No mention was made of jury trial in civil cases. The omission was much criticized, and it was argued by some that the failure to include the requirement of jury trial in civil cases was in effect to abolish it. In No. 83 of *The Federalist* Hamilton refuted this argument, and attempted to show that the subject was one much better left to legislation than to constitutional statement. The Constitution was adopted without any provision for jury trial in civil cases, but in the articles of amendment adopted soon afterward to quell the fears of those concerned about the omission of a bill of rights a provision was included to the effect that in common law suits involving more than twenty dollars the right of trial by jury should be preserved. The Sixth Amendment elaborated on the subject of jury trial in criminal cases by providing that "the accused shall enjoy the right to a speedy and public trial, by an impartial jury of the State and district wherein the crime shall have been committed. . . ."

In the several states the procedure of jury trial has continued to evolve since the date of the establishment of the Federal Government. Some states, for instance, have not adhered rigidly to the old common-law requirement that the jury be composed of not more nor less than twelve persons, and the requirement that the verdict be unanimous. In the Federal Government, on the other hand, these changes are held to be forbidden by the Constitution. The courts have held that the constitutional phrases mean now what they meant when they were adopted, to the extent that juries must be of twelve persons and verdicts must be unanimous.

Jury trial has not been required in cases of petty offenses, however, and in all cases, including cases of serious crimes, the right of trial by jury may be waived with the consent of the parties. The constitutional requirement does not extend to equity cases or to civil cases aris-

ing out of statutes. The jury system has undergone serious criticism in recent years, due in part to the clogging of the courts and the inadequacy of juries in dealing with complex questions beyond the limits of their experience. There has therefore been some tendency to avoid jury procedure wherever possible. On the other hand, as recently as 1914 a provision was included in the Clayton Act requiring jury trial in contempt cases where the act complained of was such as to constitute also a violation of any state or Federal law.

[John M. Mathews, *The American Constitutional System;* William Anderson, *American Government.*]

CARL BRENT SWISHER

Justice, The Department of, had its official beginning July 1, 1870. The office of Attorney General, however, which became the nucleus of the Department, had been established in 1789, along with the departments first created. Until 1870 the principal duties of the Attorney General were the argument of government cases in the Supreme Court of the United States, and the giving of legal advice to the President and the heads of the departments in connection with official business. He had no control over United States attorneys and marshals until 1861, and he was given nominally full control only after he had been designated the head of the new department.

The duties of the Attorney General for many years after the adoption of the Constitution were very light, and he devoted much of his time to private practice. Official responsibilities expanded gradually, and by the 1850's they took most or all of his time. The multiplicity of California land cases arising just before and during the Civil War added burdensome duties for the Attorney General, and made it necessary to provide assistance. Problems arising from the war, and the necessity of co-ordinating legal advice and litigation, lent weight to arguments made intermittently for a number of years for the creation of a law department of the Federal Government. The organic act was passed June 22, 1870.

The growth of litigation and of advisory legal responsibilities, and the bringing together of a variety of functions in the Department of Justice, required the Attorney General to give much of his time to problems of administration. The Solicitor General, whose office was created when the Department was organized, assumed principal responsibility for the argument of cases in the Supreme Court. That work came to be handled by or under the direction of the

Solicitor General and the Assistant Attorneys General who head the five functional divisions of the Department. Likewise, official opinions, while appearing in the name of the Attorney General, have long been prepared by subordinates, and are now the responsibility of the Assistant Solicitor General.

The work of the Department, and the establishment and expansion of divisions and bureaus for handling it have grown with the growth of the country and the extension of Federal control over varied public and private activities. The Antitrust Division, for instance, which had its formal beginning in 1903, was the product of need for organization to enforce antitrust legislation. The enactment of other laws based on the commerce clause of the Constitution has brought to the same Division work rivaling antitrust enforcement in importance. The growth of Federal criminal legislation has greatly expanded the work of the Criminal Division, and has also stimulated the growth of the Federal Bureau of Investigation[qv], with its varied G-Men activities. The growth of a Federal prison system has been responsible for the development of the Bureau of Prisons. Other agencies, such as those having to do with claims against the United States, tax problems and the acquisition of title to land, have expanded in similar fashion.

[Homer Cummings and Carl McFarland, *Federal Justice;* Albert Langeluttig, *The Department of Justice of the United States.*]

CARL BRENT SWISHER

Justice of the Peace was originally a mediæval English official authorized to keep the peace and try felonies and trespasses at the king's suit, and in more recent times to deal with numerous other affairs of local government. The office flourished in the colonies from the beginning. The justice exercised both a criminal and a civil jurisdiction, the former through the courts of Quarter or General Sessions, the latter by statutory authority, such as acts of South Carolina and Massachusetts of 1683 and 1692 respectively which authorized the justices to try all manner of debts, trespasses and other matters involving not more than forty shillings, or, in Virginia, "one hogshead of tobacco not exceeding 350 pounds." In Maryland the justices of the peace of the county comprised the county court, and later, some of their number, known as "Justices of the Quorum," were designated for court service by the governor. In New York the justices gradually supplanted the old Dutch commissaries. In North Carolina they were given exclusive jurisdiction over the crimes of slaves.

In most of the colonies the justices in court sessions exercised sweeping local executive and administrative powers, drew up the levy, collected the tax, appointed road commissioners and supervised highways, made disbursements, granted licenses to keep taverns and retail liquors, and appointed and controlled administrators, executors, and guardians. They generally took acknowledgments of deeds and depositions, and performed marriage ceremonies, but they seldom exercised the sweeping authority of the English justices of levying wage assessments of laborers.

While the institution still exists in most states, the justice's criminal jurisdiction has been curtailed, and he is in the main a committing magistrate. His civil jurisdiction is usually limited to from $100 to $300. While he was an appointive officer in colonial times, he is now generally elected, with compensation from fees paid by parties losing in the litigation. As in colonial days he is usually a layman. In urban centers there is a trend toward the abolition of this office.

[H. L. Osgood, *American Colonies in the 17th Century,* Vol. II; C. H. Smith, The Justice of the Peace System in the U. S., *California Law Review,* Vol. XV.]

RICHARD B. MORRIS

Juvenile Courts. Although the juvenile court is a comparatively new addition to the judicial system of the country, the forces which gave rise to it are not of recent origin. From a comparatively early date Anglo-Saxon jurisprudence has recognized the necessity for a special position for the child. With the development of the humanitarian[qv] spirit in the 19th and 20th centuries the welfare of the child became a matter of increasing solicitude. A great mass of protective legislation resulted, including a number of measures providing for the special handling of juveniles in criminal cases. In Massachusetts, for example, a sequence of protective statutes were passed, terminating in the act of 1877, which not only authorized separate trial of children's cases, but also used the term "session for juvenile offenders" of which session a separate docket and record was kept. New York passed a somewhat similar law the same year, and a number of other states quickly followed. It was not until 1899, however, that a juvenile court as we now know it was set up. In that year statutes were enacted in Illinois and Colorado providing for juvenile courts. In July, 1899, under the authority of the Illinois law, the Chicago Juvenile Court was established. While the Illinois law was chiefly a codification of the existing law of the state plus some additional provisions from the laws of other states, it introduced one idea of outstanding importance. The gist of this idea, which is said to have introduced a new legal concept in American Jurisprudence, was that the child who broke the law was not to be regarded as a criminal, but as a ward of the state, subject to the care, guardianship and control of the juvenile courts. The Illinois law was quickly adopted in other states. In 1901 the juvenile court of Denver, Colo., was established. This court under the administration of Judge Ben Lindsay attracted country-wide attention. In 1903 the Colorado legislature passed a special juvenile court law. In 1906 Congress established a juvenile court for the District of Columbia. The rapid spread of the movement since then has constituted one of the most remarkable developments of the American judicial system. Juvenile courts have now been established in most states, although not always as independent bodies. As a matter of fact, no uniformity exists in the provisions made for juvenile courts in the several states, or in the same state, for that matter. Generally speaking, certain features are considered essential for the organization of a juvenile court, however. These features might be outlined as follows: (1) separate hearings for children's cases; (2) informal or chancery procedure, including the use of petition or summons; (3) regular probation service, both for supervisory care and investigation; (4) detention separate from adults; (5) special courts and probation records, both legal and social; (6) provision for mental and physical examination. A significant feature of an enlightened juvenile court procedure is the tendency to supplement the orthodox criminal law and procedure with help from scientific sources, particularly from medical sciences, and those sources which deal with human behavior, such as biology, sociology and psychology. Consequently much of the evidence used in the court is taken from outside the court by court officials, and is based in great part on these sciences of human behavior plus the observations of a trained worker. Under all circumstances, the case in the juvenile court is handled with a view to the welfare of the child rather than his punishment and with an emphasis upon wide discretion and liberal procedure. In granting these special treatments to the child a decisive departure is made from the traditional point of view toward criminal justice, in which the crime was classified but the criminal was not.

[H. H. Lou, *Juvenile Courts in the United States;* William Healey, The Practical Value of Scientific Study of Juvenile Delinquents, *U. S. Children's Bureau Publication,* No. 96; The Child, the Family and the Court, *U. S. Children's Bureau Publication,* No. 193; Katherine F. Lenroot, The Evolution of the Juvenile Court, *Annals of the American Academy of Political and Social Science,* pp. 213-23, 1923; W. F. Willoughby, *Principles of Judicial Administration;* F. R. Aumann, The Juvenile Court Movement in Ohio, *Journal of Criminal Law and Criminology,* Vol. XXII, No. 4.]

FRANCIS R. AUMANN

Kaapa (Cahawba) was an Indian village, on the river of the same name, in central Alabama, probably in Perry County, from which the English in the 1730's conducted negotiations to establish trade relations with the Choctaws[w], to the vast annoyance of the French, who were then allied with the Choctaws.

[Dunbar Rowland and A. G. Sanders, *Mississippi Provincial Archives, French Dominion,* Vols. I and III.]

MACK SWEARINGEN

Kadiak Island (often spelled Kodiak) is located south of the base of Alaska Peninsula. Here, in 1784, fifteen years before the founding of Sitka on the mainland, Grigor Shelikof established the first Russian settlement in North America (*see* Russian Claims) .

[Hector Chevigny, *Lost Empire;* Joseph Schafer, *A History of the Pacific Northwest.*]   OSGOOD HARDY

Kakiate Patent, THE, located in what is now Rockland County, N. Y., was purchased from the Indians June 25, 1696, by Daniel Honan and Michael Hawdon. Known as the Hackyackawck or Kakiate patent, it was confirmed by Gov. Fletcher. Quarrels over the northern boundary with the owners of the Chesecocks patent delayed partition and settlement.

[David Cole, *History of Rockland County.*]

A. C. FLICK

Kalamazoo Case, THE, was decided by the Michigan Supreme Court in 1874. Charles E. Stuart and others, citizens of the village of Kalamazoo, sought to restrain the school authorities from collecting taxes for the support of a public high school and a non-teaching superintendent. The opinion of the court, written by Chief Justice Thomas M. Cooley, held that the levying of taxes for these purposes was consistent with the educational policy of Michigan since 1817 and was legal under the provisions of the constitution of 1850. Education beyond the rudiments, it was affirmed, had never been regarded by the state as having a merely cultural value, but rather as being "an important practical advantage" to be supplied to rich and poor alike at the option of the school district. The decision confirmed the right of the state to establish, at public expense, a complete system of education from the elementary school through the university, and, as such, constituted an important precedent in many other states.

[Charles E. Stuart et al. v. School District No. 1 of the Village of Kalamazoo, 30 *Michigan*, 69.]

WILLIS DUNBAR

Kanawha, Battle of the. *See* Point Pleasant, The Battle of.

Kanawha Salt Works, THE. Animals first, later the Indians, then white people in 1755, learned of the presence of salt along the Kanawha River, near the present city of Charleston, W. Va. The land on which these springs were located was bought by Joseph Ruffner, 1794, and leased by him to Elisha Brooks who built a furnace there, 1797, beginning the first salt[qv] industry west of the Allegheny Mountains. Later the Ruffner brothers took over the salt-making, improving the methods and drilling the first deep well, 1808. By 1817 there were twenty brine wells and thirty furnaces producing six to seven hundred thousand bushels of salt per year. Bitter competition caused the organization of a "Salt Trust," 1817, in an attempt to control production and to regulate prices. Impetus was given the business by the use of coal under the furnaces, 1817, and the introduction of a patent steam furnace, 1835. Salt-making was the dominant industry here for more than fifty years. Its decline is attributed to the discovery of stronger brine more accessible to western markets and the attraction of capitalists to more lucrative industries. Only one of these early companies continues to operate, but, today (1939) in the Kanawha Valley, the brine industry has grown from the Indian salt kettle to one of the largest chemical manufacturing centers in the world.

[*W. Va. Geological Survey*, Vol. VIII: Salt Brines of W. Va.; John P. Hale, *History of the Great Kanawha Valley.*]

INNIS C. DAVIS

Kansas was admitted into the Union Jan. 29, 1861. It occupies the geographic center of the United States. Dominated by political considerations, the boundaries were drawn without reference to geographical unities. The northern part lies in the Smoky-Kansas River watershed, the southwestern part in the Arkansas River basin, and the southeastern part is drained by large tributaries of the Missouri and Arkansas.

Early European contacts were quite casual and some of the generally accepted accounts are subject to controversy, notably of the Coronado expedition[qv]. The earliest economic penetration of the area was in exploitation of furs under the French regime, otherwise no important natural resources were subject to development until the

period of Anglo-American settlement after 1854: agricultural, coal, oil, gas, salt, gypsum, lead and zinc. After 1830, in view of apparent barrenness, the southwestern trans-Missouri River region of the United States was designated as permanent Indian country[qv], and in the portion which became Kansas, tribes from northeastern United States were relocated (*see* Indian Removal) . For frontier defense[qv] three early forts were established: Leavenworth in 1827, Scott in 1842 and Riley in 1853[qv], and later others farther westward.

Much of the region fell within the so-called Great American Desert[qv] and as such constituted a barrier to be crossed in pursuit of trade, lands, or gold beyond, by the Santa Fé Trail to the Spanish Southwest, by the Oregon Trail to the Pacific Northwest, and later to the gold region of California[qv]. When Kansas was organized as a territory in 1854 (*see* Kansas-Nebraska Act) , the primary incentive was not settlement and development for its own sake; but partly, rivalry between the North and the South over a railroad to the Pacific (*see* Union Pacific Railroad) , partly, rivalry between North and South over the issue of slavery[qv] extension which became involved with the first. To a great extent throughout its history, and partly in explanation of its unique character among the states, Kansas has stood at the crossroads of the nation, subject to the conflicts resulting from the cross flow of population, and of economic, social and cultural forces from all directions.

The first period of Kansas history after 1854 was one of trouble (*see* Kansas Struggle) . Politically Kansas was ruled for the most part, from 1854 to the late 1870's, by carpet-baggers[qv] and professional politicians, often the agents of or allied with Eastern interests. A tangible evidence of the change to home rule came in the constitutional amendments adopted in 1875 changing the organization of the state government from an annual to a biennial basis. This result had been heralded by the suicide of Jim Lane in 1866 to escape exposure for gross corruption; the bribery exposures of 1873 which drove Senators Pomeroy and Caldwell from public life in Kansas; and the departure of other politicians of lesser ill repute to newer fields of activities or to their homes in the East.

The second period of Kansas history, overlapping somewhat with the first, extends from the late 1860's to the World War, that of settlement and development, the primary theme being agricultural adaptation of Anglo-American people to a subhumid environment (*see* Agricultural Adaptation to the Plains) . Politically during this period Kansas was a nursery for various forms of radicalism, primarily agrarian in their significance; Grangerism in the 1870's, Farmers' Alliance in the 1880's, Populism in the 1890's and Progressivism in the early 20th century^{qw}. The grievances were monotonously similar for all decades of revolt; money and credit, railroads, monopolies—all characteristic of a region occupying a debtor position resulting from too heavy borrowing of outside capital to finance rapid development of resources which were slow in returning earnings on investment. A customary phenomenon in the westward movement^w, it was aggravated in the Plains states because of the new factor introduced by the difficulties of adaptation to an environment new to the American people. A second and relatively new complication was the rural-urban conflict, which was intensified by the rapid rise of the new industrialism. Kansas was a leader in several types of reform legislation growing out of this situation; in 1880 the prohibition of the manufacture and sale of intoxicating liquor, the first state to do so by constitutional amendment (see Kansas, Prohibition in); in 1889 the first state antitrust law; and in 1913 a "blue sky"^{w} law to protect investors in securities was copied by other states.

The third period overlapped somewhat with the second, but dates primarily from the World War era, and throughout the country generally was characterized by rapid urbanization and industrialization. Still essentially agricultural, Kansas found itself in a conservative position with relation to the new type of industrial radicalism of propertyless laboring classes. This conservative reaction, stemming from the exaggerated nationalism, the so-called "red" scare, and the bitterly fought coal strike of 1919, led Kansas to enact the Industrial Court Act of 1920 to protect public interest against the effects of the warfare of capital and labor (see Arbitration, Industrial). Whatever of agrarian radicalism of the 19th-century type that might remain, it was largely subordinated to the new alignment of the new conservatism against the new radicalism.

Even before the World War some steps were taken to adjust the traditional type of state government, originating in a rural age, to meet the requirements of the more complicated urban society. Centralization of control over state educational institutions began in 1913. This theme of centralization of functions continued slowly through the postwar period, as in the administration of highways, schools, taxation and social welfare, the chief driving force in most cases being compliance with conditions set by national legislation. Gov. G. H. Hodges (1913–15) pro-posed a plan of modernization of state government, but the original constitution of 1859, with minor amendments, still stands (1939). Probably the most significant change recently made was the creation of a legislative council in 1933 to conduct investigations, recommend policies and prepare legislation for consideration by the state legislature.

[No satisfactory histories of Kansas exist and such as there are deal only with the early period. Of these the better are L. W. Spring, *Kansas* (1885) and Andreas, *History of Kansas* (1883). For documents and special topics see the *Collections* of the Kansas State Historical Society and the *Kansas Historical Quarterly;* H. G. Larimer, compiler, *Proceedings of the Constitutional Convention of 1859*, with supplementary materials.]

JAMES C. MALIN

Kansas, Prohibition in. Kansas was opened for settlement just eight years after the enactment in 1846 of the first Maine Prohibitory Law^w, and the prohibition idea was brought to Kansas by New Englanders. As early as 1856 Representative John Brown, Jr., son of the antislavery crusader, presented to the free-state legislature a memorial from Topeka women petitioning for passage of a "Maine Law." While no action was taken, sentiment grew until 1880, when the people adopted a prohibition amendment to the constitution by a vote of 92,302 to 84,304.

For twenty-six years enforcement was resisted in certain localities where saloons were operated under a system of city fines, collected in lieu of licenses. Carry A. Nation advertised this flagrant violation by leading a band of women zealots in saloon-smashing raids, commencing at Kiowa in 1899 (see Hatchet, Carry Nation's). Enforcement became more effective in 1906 when Gov. Edward W. Hoch and Attorney General Fred S. Jackson hit on the plan of ousting local authorities who failed to keep their oath to support the constitution. They replaced such officers with vigilant state attorney generals, who invoked the padlock law of 1901. This provided for the closing of buildings used for liquor sales and threw the burden of enforcement on property owners, who had to keep liquor from their premises or face loss of rent.

Success of enforcement stimulated neighboring states to adopt the Kansas plan. But when the National Government adopted prohibition^w a reaction set in. Resentment in large Eastern population centers against the national amendment spread to Kansas. Following national repeal, Kansas juries, in many instances, failed to convict liquor dealers. The prohibition situation gained new strength in 1934 when a state repeal amendment was defeated by 436,678 votes to

347,644. Beer was legalized in 1937 when the legislature declared by statute that any beverage containing not more than 3.2% alcohol is nonintoxicating.

[*Kansas Historical Collections,* XV, 192-231; T. E. Stephens, *Prohibition in Kansas;* Carry A. Nation, *The Use and Need of the Life of Carry A. Nation;* Bliss Isely and W. M. Richards, *Four Centuries in Kansas.*]

BLISS ISELY

Kansas City, Mo., an outgrowth of two frontier settlements, Westport and the Town of Kansas, is named from its location at the confluence of the Kansas (Kaw) and Missouri rivers.

About 1800 Louis Bartholet (or Bertholett) established a trading camp there, but the first permanent settlement was a trading post at Randolph Bluffs, built by François Chouteau in 1821. Floods submerged this post in 1826, causing its removal two miles upstream to a point near the mouth of the Kansas. The place became important because, at the apex of the big bend of the Missouri, it was the nearest water approach to the Santa Fé and California trails[qv].

On the Santa Fé Trail, a few miles west of Independence[qv], its terminus, John McCoy laid out Westport in 1833. It was four miles south of the Kaw's mouth. A company headed by William Sublette, noted fur trader, platted the Town of Kansas on the river above Chouteau's warehouse in 1838, but a clouded title prevented its development until 1846, and it was called derisively "Westport Landing." Bent and St. Vrain, the Indian traders, hauled merchandise direct from the Town of Kansas to Fort Bent[qv] in 1845 and by the next year the settlement was competing for its share of the Santa Fé trade[qv] with Independence, Westport and Leavenworth[qv], its strategic location being a deciding factor.

In 1853 the name was changed to the City of Kansas and in 1889 to Kansas City. During the border difficulties preceding the admission of Kansas to statehood, it was a focus of proslavery activity, and near Westport[qv] the Civil War battle of that name was fought, Oct. 23, 1864. Kansas City became a railroad and packing center after the Civil War and absorbed Westport. Kansas City, Kans., a separate municipality, lies west of the Kaw's mouth.

[Roy Ellis, *A Civic History of Kansas City.*]

PAUL I. WELLMAN

Kansas-Colorado Water Rights Litigation, THE, which concerns the Arkansas River, began in 1901, when Kansas filed suit against Colorado contending, on the basis of the common-law principle of riparian ownership, that the state and its citizens had suffered material damage because of illegal diversion and use of the water of the stream by Colorado and its citizens, and asking for an injunction to prevent further diversion. Colorado in a demurrer denied the jurisdiction of the Supreme Court and asserted, on the basis of the principle of prior appropriation and public control of water, that she was well within her legal rights. The decision rendered in 1902 by Chief Justice Fuller rejected the demurrer, but gave Colorado leave to answer. Following the filing of an amended bill by Kansas in 1903, the intervening of the United States in 1904, on the grounds that approval of the contention of either party would endanger the Federal reclamation[qv] program, and the filing of answers by Colorado, the case was argued and a decision rendered by Justice Brewer in 1907. The plea of the United States was rejected as was the request of Kansas for an injunction, but the latter was given leave to file a new suit whenever it could show that the division of the water was inequitable. Such a suit was pending before the Supreme Court in 1940.

[206 *United States,* 46-118.]

GEORGE L. ANDERSON

Kansas Committee, The National (1856–57). After the sack of Lawrence[qv], emigrant aid societies and Kansas relief committees sprang up throughout the free states. July 9, 1856, representatives of these groups and of older organizations like the New England Emigrant Aid Company[qv] and the New York State Kansas Committee, met at Buffalo and formed a National Kansas Committee with headquarters in Chicago. It raised and spent some $200,000, sending arms, supplies and recruits to the Free-State Party[qv] in Kansas.

[W. E. Connelley, *A Standard History of Kansas and Kansans.*]

SAMUEL A. JOHNSON

Kansas Free-State Party, THE, originated at the Big Springs Convention, Sept. 5, 1855. Opponents of slavery[qv] in the territory, defeated in previous elections, saw the necessity of consolidating all shades of antislavery opinion. A platform, largely the work of James H. Lane, ridiculed the charge of abolitionism and urged Whigs and Democrats to unite in a party devoted to the exclusion of slavery and of the free Negro. Other resolutions, prepared by former Gov. Andrew Reeder, repudiated the "spurious" proslavery legislature. A subsequent convention, meeting at Topeka, Sept. 19, called an election of delegates to a constitutional convention and provided for the appointment of an executive committee which, with Lane as chairman, exercised the power of a provisional government and directed the party's quest for statehood. Factionalism appeared at Big Springs and became even more pronounced in the convention that framed the constitution. In the formative period of the party, Lane headed the conservative group and strongly hinted that his course was approved by the Pierce administration. Charles Robinson, Kansas agent of the New England Emigrant Aid Society[q], led the radical wing. The chief tests of strength came over the endorsement of popular sovereignty[q], which was defeated; and over the exclusion of free Negroes[q], which was referred to the voters and approved along with the Topeka Constitution[q]. The Wakarusa War[q] in December hastened Lane's transition to radicalism and gave him undisputed leadership of the western element in the territory. The Free-State party failed in its major purpose of obtaining immediate statehood. Ignoring the Lecompton movement[q], it captured control of the territorial legislature in 1857. Although the party endorsed Republican doctrine in 1856, it was not supplanted by a Republican organization until Horace Greeley visited the territory in 1859.

[W. H. Stephenson, *The Political Career of General James H. Lane.*]   WENDELL H. STEPHENSON

Kansas-Nebraska Act, THE (1854), which repealed the Missouri Compromise[q] and led to a general realignment in American politics, was initiated to aid midwestern efforts to build a transcontinental railroad line. For a decade, the South and Central West sought to best one another in this race for the Pacific. A chief southern advantage was that the whole region through which its road would pass was already organized (*see* Southern Railroad Route), while the region immediately west of Missouri and Iowa was in the hands of Indian tribes and had no political organization (*see* Union Pacific Railroad). From 1850 on, midwestern senators and representatives introduced bill after bill to organize a Territory of Nebraska. Stephen A. Douglas, Chairman of the Senate's Committee on Territories, was particularly active for such legislation. These efforts were thwarted by stubborn southern opposition, arising from the fact that the new territory, being north of the Missouri Compromise line, would therefore be free rather than slave territory. In December, 1853, a new Nebraska bill, introduced by Sen. Augustus C. Dodge, Iowa, caused Douglas to renew his quest of a formula by which it could be passed. There is some ground for believing that he thought the Missouri Compromise unconstitutional, and that climate and natural resources in the Nebraska area would ban slavery there in fact, whatever its

status in law. On Jan. 4, 1854, he reported a Nebraska bill based on the principles of Popular Sovereignty[q], as employed in the Compromise of 1850[q].

But leading Southern Ultras termed the bill "delusive" and insisted on the Missouri Compromise's explicit repeal. Douglas soon found this was the only way a territorial bill could be passed. Jefferson Davis and others secured President Pierce's active support, and the whole administration force was put behind explicit repeal of the Missouri Compromise, so that the citizens of the new area would themselves determine whether it would be free or slave territory. Likewise, because of differences in political and railroad interests between Missouri and Iowa, the Nebraska area was cut into two new territories, one west of Missouri, to be known as Kansas, the other, west of Iowa, retaining the name Nebraska.

Even before the new bill was reported to the Senate, such congressional abolitionists and antislavery leaders as Sen. Salmon P. Chase, of Ohio; Charles Sumner, of Massachusetts; and William H. Seward, of New York, saw the chance to raise a storm of passion against Douglas and the administration. Late in January they issued the "Appeal of the Independent Democrats,"[q] denouncing Douglas' original bill "as a gross violation of a sacred pledge; as a criminal betrayal of precious rights," a "monstrous" plot, a sacrifice of the people's dearest interest to "the mere hazards of a presidential game." Their appeal flamed through the antislavery states, Douglas was burnt in effigy from Iowa to Maine, and the abolitionist storm became a hurricane.

All through February Douglas defended himself stoutly in the Senate, showing by detailed historical recital that the very men who now assailed him for seeking to repeal the Missouri Compromise had, until 1848, opposed it might and main; likewise that acts of Congress had never really excluded slavery from an inch of United States soil—that free states had actually become such by self-determination rather than because of Federal law.

Closing the Senate debate, March 3, Douglas extracted Seward's admission that his chief attack on the bill had been based on a "misapprehension." Chase offered a personal apology; Sumner's egotism was pierced and he sat speechless in his seat. A few hours later the Senate passed the Kansas-Nebraska Bill, 37 to 14.

Douglas then took charge of the effort for it in the House, where the abolitionist crusade had had chief effect. Partisans went wild, fighting talk was heard, weapons were drawn. But through

March and April the administration applied pressure; the wavering were made firm, many backsliders were brought in line. Finally, May 22, 1854, the bill passed, 113 to 100. President Pierce signed it, and it became the law of the land.

[J. W. Burgess, *The Middle Period, 1817-1858;* F. H. Hodder, Genesis of the Kansas-Nebraska Act, in *State Hist. Soc. of Wis., Proceedings,* 1912; G. F. Milton, *The Eve of Conflict;* P. O. Ray, *Repeal of the Missouri Compromise,* and Genesis of the Kansas-Nebraska Act, in *Amer. Hist. Assn., Annual Report,* 1914.]

GEORGE FORT MILTON

Kansas or Kaw Indians, who gave their name to the state of Kansas and to the Kansas River, are otherwise of little historical importance. They surrendered tribal lands by treaty in 1846, relocated on a small reservation in Morris County, and removed in 1873 to the Indian Territory*ᵂ*, near the Osages. Of Siouan stock, they were closely related to the Osage Indians*ᵂ*, and intermarriage produced much confusion in the making of tribal rolls.

[F. W. Hodge, *Handbook of American Indians;* C. C. Royce, *Indian Land Cessions.*]   JAMES C. MALIN

Kansas Pacific Railroad, THE. A railroad system extending from Kansas City to Cheyenne, Wyo. Originally chartered by the Kansas Territorial Legislature in 1855 under the name of the Leavenworth, Pawnee and Western Railroad, it was included in the Pacific Railway Act of 1862 and given the right to connect with the Union Pacific*ᵂ* at the 100th meridian. The route was changed in 1864. In 1863 Gen. J. C. Frémont and Samuel Hallett secured control of the road and changed its name to Union Pacific Railway Company, Eastern Division. After many factional difficulties the road passed into the control of a group of men headed by John D. Perry who built to Denver and connected it with the Union Pacific at Cheyenne by the use of a subsidiary road, The Denver Pacific. Although operated under financial difficulties throughout the period of its history as an independent system, it served as an outlet for the Texas cattle trade and brought many immigrants to Kansas, thus aiding greatly in the rapid settlement of that state. In 1880, largely through the efforts of Jay Gould, it was consolidated with the Union Pacific to form the Union Pacific Railway Company.

[Henry Kirke White, *History of the Union Pacific Railway;* Nelson Trottman, *History of the Union Pacific.*]

WALDO CRIPPEN

Kansas Struggle, THE, began in May, 1854, with the passage of the Kansas-Nebraska bill*ᵂ*, which repealed the slavery-extension restriction of the Missouri Compromise*ᵂ* and applied the doctrine of popular sovereignty*ᵂ* to the two territories. Competition for the rich lands of Kansas began immediately. Emigrant aid societies*ᵂ* were formed in the East to promote settlement, but the lure of opportunity, a more potent factor than promotion, brought settlers from every section, especially from Missouri and the Old Northwest*ᵂ*. Important proslavery settlements were made along the Missouri River; Free-State migrants sought homes in the Kansas Valley. In elections for a delegate to Congress in November, 1854, and for a territorial legislature in March, 1855, there was illegal voting on both sides, but the proximity of Missouri gave the proslavery party an advantage and it won both contests. A slave code was enacted, friction developed between the legislature and Gov. Andrew Reeder, and he was replaced by Wilson Shannon.

Antislavery men, now a majority of the population, assembled at Big Springs in September to form a Free-State party*ᵂ*, and a few weeks later inaugurated the "Topeka Movement"*ᵂ* for statehood, with James H. Lane chairman of an executive committee. A *de facto* government, set up early in 1856 with Charles Robinson as "governor," unsuccessfully sought recognition from Congress. At Washington acrimonious debates over Douglas' proposal to authorize a constitutional convention culminated in Sumner's "Crime against Kansas" speech, May 19–20, and in Brooks' assault*ᵂ* upon the Massachusetts senator. Open warfare in the territory had been narrowly averted the previous December by Shannon's intervention to prevent "border ruffians"*ᵂ* from attacking Lawrence. As Sumner was making his speech, proslavery men again appeared at Lawrence*ᵂ* and destroyed considerable property. This act was avenged by John Brown, who, with sons and neighbors, murdered five proslavery advocates. Such proceedings greatly aroused public sentiment North and South and led to renewed activity of aid companies and committees. Sporadic outbreaks continued and "Bleeding Kansas" caused Shannon's removal in favor of John W. Geary, who established peace and thereby contributed to Buchanan's election.

Robert J. Walker, appointed governor in March, 1857, realized that slavery was doomed and labored to save Kansas for the Democratic party. Free-State men declined to participate in the framing and ratification of the Lecompton Constitution*ᵂ* which guaranteed protection of slave property already in Kansas regardless of the decision on the slavery clause, the only one submitted to the voters. Walker's rejection of fraudulent votes in the October election gave the Free-State party control of the legislature but cost the governor his position. A special session early in 1858 provided a referendum on the whole Lecompton Constitution. As proslavery men declined to vote, it was rejected almost unanimously. Despite the hostility of the great majority of actual settlers, Buchanan recommended that Kansas be admitted under it. The Senate approved notwithstanding Douglas' opposition; however, his following in the House helped to defeat it there. Congress then passed the compromise English bill[w] offering Kansas a gift of land upon becoming a state, but the bribe was rejected. The state was finally admitted in March, 1861.

[L. W. Spring, *Kansas, The Prelude to the War for the Union;* W. H. Stephenson, *The Political Career of General James H. Lane.*]

WENDELL H. STEPHENSON

Kansas Wheat Pool, THE (1920's), was a farmers' co-operative sales association calculated to eliminate the grain trade's profits, the ultimate goal being a world-wide pool, which could withhold wheat from the market until prices were "fair." At most the Kansas pool controlled 6% of the crop of its own state. Steps in development were: Kansas Wheat Growers Association, organized 1921; merged with Farmers Union pool in Kansas Co-operative Wheat Marketing Association, 1924; joined Oklahoma, Colorado and Nebraska in Southwest pool, 1926; joined pool of federally aided Farmers National Grain Corporation, 1932; Kansas Co-operative Wheat Marketing Association in receivership, 1933.

[Joseph G. Knapp, *The Hard Winter Wheat Pools.*]

BLISS ISELY

Kaposia (Pine Coulie), Battle of. Late in June, 1842, about a hundred Chippewa[w] of various bands, coming overland from Lake St. Croix, established an ambush on the east bank of the Mississippi opposite Little Crow's Sioux village of Kaposia on the site of South St. Paul, Minn. Premature firing which killed two Sioux women, wives of half-breeds, gave the alarm. In a running fight lasting several hours the Chippewa were repulsed after heavy cost in casualties to the Sioux[w].

[W. W. Folwell, *A History of Minnesota.*]

WILLOUGHBY M. BABCOCK

Kaskaskia (1703–*ca.* 1910), metropolis of the Illinois Country in the 18th century, was founded in April, 1703, when the Jesuit Gabriel Marest removed the Mission of the Immaculate Conception from the site of the present city of St. Louis[w] to the right bank of the Kaskaskia River seven miles above its then junction with the Mississippi. With him went the Kaskaskia tribe of the Illinois Indians, former inhabitants of the Great Village of the Illinois[w].

For fifteen years Kaskaskia was primarily an Indian village in which a few French lived permanently, while more drifted in and out. Growth commenced in 1717, when it became a part of the district of Louisiana[w]. In 1723 its white inhabitants numbered 196; in 1752, 350 whites and 246 Negroes were enumerated. By 1770, after the high point of its 18th century growth had been passed, it was said to contain 500 whites and nearly that many Negroes.

Meanwhile, the French and Indian villages had been separated (by Boisbriant in 1719). The population of the latter fluctuated greatly, but the trend was steadily downward. By the end of the century only a handful of indolent, degenerate Indians remained.

Under Boisbriant, commandant from 1718 to 1724, the characteristic land system of the French village was established—large commons, and common fields in narrow strips. Throughout the French period agriculture flourished, and grain was shipped as far as Detroit and New Orleans. Especially notable was the plantation of the Jesuits, which had become an "extensive estate" by 1763, when the order was dissolved.

During the last third of the 18th century many changes took place in Kaskaskia. In 1765, after the cession of the Illinois Country to Great Britain, a British garrison was established there, and traders and their employees replaced in part the former inhabitants, who moved across the Mississippi. On July 4, 1778, British rule ended with George Rogers Clark's[w] capture of the town. For a decade after the Revolution, American rule was ineffective, and Kaskaskia was sunk in anarchy. During these years its population declined to such an extent that only 349 white inhabitants were counted in a census taken in 1787.

By 1800 Kaskaskia had recovered somewhat, and had become perhaps half American. The creation of Illinois Territory in 1809, and its designation as the territorial capital, resulted in further revival. In the following decade growth continued, and by 1818, when it became the first state capital, Kaskaskia had regained its former position as the metropolis of Illinois. But its primacy was short-lived. When the state offices were removed to Vandalia in 1820 rapid decline set in, and the town soon sank into somnolence. A disastrous flood in 1844 almost destroyed it, and led to the removal of the county seat three years later. In 1881 the Mississippi broke through the tongue of land on which Kaskaskia stood and began to flow through the channel of the Kaskaskia River. Gradually it encroached upon the town site. By 1910 it had obliterated the ancient settlement.

[Mary Borgias Palm, *The Jesuit Missions of the Illinois Country, 1673-1763;* C. W. Alvord, *The Illinois Country, 1763-1818;* S. J. Buck, *Illinois in 1818;* J. R. Williams, History of Randolph County, Illinois, in *An Illustrated Historical Atlas Map of Randolph County, Ills.;* J. H. Burnham, Destruction of Kaskaskia by the Mississippi River, in *Transactions of the Illinois State Historical Society,* 1914.]

PAUL M. ANGLE

Kasson Treaties, THE, named after John Adams Kasson, charged with their negotiation, were treaties of reciprocity^{qv} authorized under the Dingley Act^{qv} of 1897. They provided for reciprocal tariff concessions with other nations. Treaties were negotiated with Denmark, the Dominican Republic, Nicaragua, Ecuador, the Argentine, France and Great Britain for certain of her smaller colonies on this side of the Atlantic. None were ratified by the Senate of the United States.

[United States Tariff Commission, *Summary of the Report on Reciprocity and Commercial Treaties.*]

DEXTER PERKINS

Kaw Indians. *See* Kansas or Kaw Indians.

Kayoderosseras Patent. Through sixty years colonial New York's relations with the Mohawks^{qv} were affected adversely by the Kayoderosseras or Queensborough patent. This huge tract of about 300,000 acres formed a rough parallelogram stretching twenty-five miles along the north shore of the lower Mohawk, with a depth northward of twenty-two miles and touching the Hudson at the Third Falls. Applied for in 1703, and granted later to thirteen persons, ownership became highly involved and title was disputed by tribal leaders alleging fraud. In 1768 joint efforts of Gov. Sir Harry Moore and Indian Superintendent Johnson effected a settlement, under which the patentees released part of the land and the Mohawks received $5000 in compensation for the balance.

[*Documents Relating to Colonial History, State of New York,* Vols. VI, VII, VIII.]   ARTHUR POUND

Kearneyites were followers of Denis Kearney, a California labor agitator, who, in 1877, organized the Workingmen's party of California as a protest against widespread unemployment, dishonest banking, inequitable taxation, land monopoly, railroad domination, Chinese coolie labor competition and other economic and political evils of the day. Fifty-one Kearneyites were

elected delegates to the California constitutional convention of 1879, but they appear to have had little direct influence in the convention. The new constitution, however, in certain respects, seemed to meet, partially at least, the demands of the Kearneyites; and Kearney himself advocated its ratification. By the presidential campaign of 1880, Kearney's party had practically disappeared.

[H. George, The Kearney Agitation in California, *Popular Science Monthly,* XVII; James Bryce, *The American Commonwealth;* article on Denis Kearney, in *Dict. Amer. Biog.,* Vol. X.]

P. ORMAN RAY

Kearny, Fort. It was with a view to protecting the frontier that Congress passed a law on July 2, 1836, providing for the opening of a military road from some point on the Mississippi near its junction with the Des Moines River, to the Red River. In accordance with this act, in the spring of 1838, Col. Stephen W. Kearny and Nathan Boone selected a site (present Nebraska City) for a fort on the Missouri River. A military post named Fort Kearny was established there in the spring of 1846, but was abandoned two years later in favor of one on the Platte. From this time on little is heard about the old fort. Lt. W. P. Woodbury was the founder of Fort Kearny on the Platte. This location on the Oregon Trail^{qv}, near Grand Island, was selected to furnish protection for emigrants who might be en route and to hold the Indians at peace. In 1851 the War Department, because of lack of appropriations, seriously considered abandoning this post. However, the Indian troubles which followed made the idea impracticable, and the fort remained in use until 1871, by which time travel on the Oregon Trail had ceased and the Indian fighting frontier had been pushed farther west. For several years, the Fort Kearny reservation remained under the control of the United States Government. Finally, by act of Congress, July 21, 1876, the land was surveyed and offered for sale to "actual settlers at a minimum price in accordance with the provisions of the homestead laws."

[Lillian M. Willman, The History of Fort Kearny, *Publications, Nebraska State Historical Society,* Vol. XXI.]

LILLIAN M. WILLMAN

Kearny, Fort Phil, principal military post on the Bozeman Trail^{qv}, was built by Col. H. B. Carrington in the Bighorn foothills on Piney Fork, in northern Wyoming. Construction, starting in July, 1866, was opposed by the Sioux^{qv}, whose warriors harassed it constantly. In the first six months of its existence, Indians made fifty-one hostile demonstrations before the fort, killed

154 persons, and drove off 700 head of stock (*see* Red Cloud War).

The Fetterman disaster[qv], Dec. 21, reduced the garrison to perilous weakness, but Portugee Phillips, a frontiersman, rode 236 miles to Fort Laramie[qv] and secured help. The Wagon Box Fight[qv], Aug. 2, 1867, was a sharp defeat for the Sioux, but at no time were there enough troops at Fort Phil Kearny for anything but defense. The fort was burned by Indians after its abandonment under the terms of the Treaty of Fort Laramie, 1868[qv].

[Frances Courtney Carrington, *My Army Life;* J. P. Dunn, *Massacres of the Mountains.*]

PAUL I. WELLMAN

Kearny-Frémont Quarrel. The quarrel between Gen. Kearny and Col. Frémont in 1847 was over the governorship of California. It had its inception in the Stockton-Kearny controversy[qv], but the open break did not occur until Commodore Shubrick succeeded Commodore Stockton as commander of the American fleet (*see* California, The Conquest of). Stockton had supported Frémont. Shubrick supported Kearny. The crisp military dispatches which Kearny began sending Frémont on March 1, 1847, indicated the change of positions. Frémont's behavior following receipt of these orders led to his arrest and to his subsequent trial by court-martial. The charges brought against him by Kearny were mutiny from Jan. 17 to May 9, 1847; disobedience to orders; and conduct prejudicing good order and military discipline. The trial began in Washington Nov. 2, and continued until the following Jan. 31, 1848. The verdict was guilty with a recommendation for clemency. President Polk pardoned Frémont and restored him to his position in the army, but he refused to accept either the verdict or the restoration, and resigned.

[Cardinal Goodwin, *John Charles Frémont, an Explanation of His Career;* Allan Nevins, *Frémont, the Pathmarker.*]

CARDINAL GOODWIN

Kearny's March to California. Gen. Stephen Watts Kearny left Santa Fé, Sept. 25, 1846, and marched to conquer and possess California. He took with him 300 dragoons, baggage, wagons and provisions enough for sixty-five days, but left all the horses, which he substituted with mules. The column marched down the valley of the Rio del Norte, and coming near to Socorro, N. Mex., on Oct. 6, met the famous scout, Kit Carson, on the way to Washington with dispatches. These messages, from Stockton and Frémont, announced the conquest of California[qv], and Kearny decided to reduce his force, depending upon the addition of the troops routed by sea for future campaigns. He sent 200 of his force back, ordered Carson to accompany him as a guide, and sent the dispatches forward by Thomas Fitzpatrick. The party soon found itself beset with hardships unexpected and almost beyond endurance. They were faced with the lack of provisions and water, and had to abandon the wagons. Near the Gila River they found evidence of many horses and the remains of a large camp. Reconnaissance revealed only a small party of Mexicans traveling to Sonora, but from them they learned that the Mexicans in California had succeeded in expelling the Americans from Santa Barbara, Los Angeles and other places. On Dec. 6 Gen. Kearny attacked a large force of the enemy at San Pasqual[qv]. Capt. Moore with about forty dragoons, together with Gen. Kearny and his staff, led the pursuit and became separated from the others, who were mounted on broken-down mules. Discovering their dilemma, more than 150 Mexicans turned upon them and did terrible execution with their lances. In fifteen minutes of hand-to-hand fighting, the Americans drove them off. With his 100 dragoons Kearny, twice wounded, fought his way through some 900 miles of grueling campaign, to reach San Diego, Calif., Dec. 12, 1846, with a loss of thirty-three men killed and wounded.

[U. S. Engineer Dept. . . . *Notes of a Military Reconnoissance from Ft. Leavenworth to San Diego, Cal.;* John T. Hughes, . . . *Doniphan Expedition and Conquest of New Mexico and California,* W. E. Connelley, ed.]

STELLA M. DRUMM

Kearny's Mission to China (1842). Despatched to the Far East to protect American trading interests in China, Commodore Lawrence Kearny arrived in Canton at the close of the Anglo-Chinese War, generally known as the Opium War. After issuing through the American consul a statement that the United States would not under any circumstances sanction trade in opium, he sent a note to the Chinese High Commissioner, on Oct. 8, 1842, expressing the hope that in any new arrangements governing foreign trade which might be made as a result of the war, the trade and citizens of the United States would be "placed upon the same footing as the merchants of the nation most favored." The reply of the Chinese High Commissioner gave assurances that this would be done. By establishing the most-favored nation doctrine[qv] as the standard for American trade relations with China, subsequently incorporated in our first treaty (Cushing's[qv]) with China, this exchange of notes constituted the genesis of the Open Door doctrine[qv] proclaimed by Secretary Hay some fifty-seven years later.

[Tyler Dennett, *Americans in Eastern Asia.*]
FOSTER RHEA DULLES

Kearsarge and Alabama (June 19, 1864). The C. S. S. *Alabama*[qv], 1050 tons, 8 guns, 149 men, Capt. Raphael Semmes, arrived at Cherbourg, France, on June 11, for repairs and to land prisoners of war. Three days later while the Confederates were awaiting Napoleon III's permission to use the imperial drydock, the U. S. S. *Kearsarge,* 1031 tons, 8 guns, 162 men, Capt. John A. Winslow, entered port for the purpose of securing the released captives. Winslow's intention being denied by the French authorities, he withdrew beyond the neutrality limits. Meanwhile, Semmes sent him word that he intended to come out and offer combat as soon as he could take on coal.

The engagement, fought five days later, on Sunday morning, within sight of crowds gathered on the Norman cliffs, was one of the most deliberately staged naval conflicts in world history. The opening gun was fired by the *Alabama* at 10:57 A.M., and the battle ended at 12:24 noon with the *Alabama* plunging stern first into the sea. Semmes sought to lie alongside his adversary to allow his well-disciplined crew to fight it out with pistol and cutlass; but the battle was decided by superior speed and ammunition. The *Kearsarge,* fresh from overhauling in a Dutch dockyard, enjoyed every advantage of condition over the *Alabama,* whose bottom was foul and powder dull from twenty-two months continuously at sea.

The *Kearsarge's* loss was one killed and two wounded; the *Alabama's,* nine killed, twenty-one wounded, and ten drowned. Little effort was made by Winslow to rescue the Confederates, most of whom were taken from the water by the boats of French and British spectators.

[W. M. Robinson, Jr., *The Alabama-Kearsarge Battle.*]
WILLIAM M. ROBINSON, JR.

Keelboats. A type of craft that was used on American rivers, chiefly in the West. The first keelboats seem to have been skiffs with a plank nailed the length of the bottom to make the boat easier to steer, but by about 1790 it had become a long narrow craft built on a keel and ribs and with a long cargo box amidships. It was steered by a special oar and propelled by oars or poles, pulled by a cordelle, or occasionally fitted with sails. Keelboats were forty to eighty feet long, seven to ten feet in beam, two feet or more in draught, and with sharp ends. A cleated footway

on each side was used by the pole men. The success of Shreve's shallow draft steamboats drove the keelboats from the main rivers by about 1820, except in low water, but they were used quite generally on the tributaries until after the Civil War. The chief utility of the keelboat was for upstream transportation and for swift downstream travel. It was used extensively for passenger travel.

[L. D. Baldwin, *Keelboat Age on Western Waters.*]
LELAND D. BALDWIN

Kegs, Battle of the, is the derisive name given to indiscriminate British firing, at Philadelphia, Jan. 7, 1778, upon David Bushnell's crudely built mines, designed to float down the Delaware River to explode upon contact with the British warships. No ships were harmed, but one gunpowder-filled keg exploded, killing four British sailors. The alarmed British garrison fired furiously upon every floating object. The panic did not subside until nightfall.

[Francis Hopkinson's poem, *The Battle of the Kegs;* John F. Watson, *Annals of Philadelphia,* Vol. II; Charles Griswold, *American Journal of Science,* April, 1820.]
HARRY EMERSON WILDES

Keith Controversy, THE (1691–95), religious in origin, had political repercussions which added to contemporary unrest in Pennsylvania. The quarrel began when George Keith, a Quaker[qv] leader formerly prominent in England, violently criticized the Pennsylvania Friends' Meetings on doctrinal grounds and for their failure to observe strictly the established Discipline. Thomas Lloyd, a Quaker minister and Penn's deputy governor, led the opposition to Keith. In 1692 Keith and his followers formed a separatist Meeting, calling themselves "Christian Quakers." Keith was forbidden to preach by the regular Meeting and also ran afoul of civil authority because of writing a seditious pamphlet attacking a Quaker magistrate. Keith went to England in 1693 to plead the orthodoxy of his group. The London Yearly Meeting, however, disowned him in 1695. As separatists, the Keithians in Pennsylvania formed a faction antagonistic to the proprietary government, but their influence faded out as the century closed.

[Charles P. Keith, *Chronicles of Pennsylvania,* Vol. I; Rufus M. Jones, *The Quakers in the American Colonies.*]
RUTH E. STILSON

Kellogg Pact. *See* Briand-Kellogg Pact.

Kelly's Ford. On Nov. 7, 1863, the Federal Army under Meade, moving forward in the early stage of the Mine Run Campaign[qv], attacked the Confederate works on the Rappahannock River

occurred the siege of Boonesborough and the battle of the Blue Licks[w].

By 1780 the Kentucky population had increased, and in that year Kentucky County was divided into three parts, which became Fayette, Jefferson and Lincoln counties. Ten conventions were held between 1784 and 1792—preparatory to the creation of the independent state of Kentucky—and on June 1, 1792, Kentucky became a member of the Union.

The new state soon became disgruntled at the national system of taxation, and between 1792 and 1794 it was deeply involved in the Spanish conspiracy[w]. Local political matters, also, kept it in turmoil, and in 1798–99 strife over the framing of a new constitution, and the Virginia and Kentucky Resolutions[w], caused a near civil war. When Thomas Jefferson became President of the United States, and the Louisiana Purchase[w] was made, Kentuckians became happier in the Union. By 1810 they were extremely patriotic, and between 1812 and 1815 they gave voice to expansionist sentiments (see War Hawks). In the War of 1812 Kentuckians did a large portion of the fighting both in the Great Lakes region and at New Orleans. Following the war, manufacturers and farmers expanded their production of goods to a high level, and in 1818 the general assembly increased the number of banks to supply currency to trade. In 1819 these banks began to fail (see Panic of 1819), and by 1820 the legislature passed laws permitting a stay of execution against debtors. Kentucky's political and economic system suffered a serious shock until the fight for "relief" was ended in 1827 (see Old Court–New Court Struggle). Between 1830 and 1860 the state enjoyed economic prosperity. It had for sale manufactured goods, distilled spirits, agricultural products, livestock and slaves. Only one major political upheaval marred the history of this period and that was the fierce struggle between proslavery and antislavery partisans over the selection of delegates to the constitutional convention in 1849. The proslavery forces won, and they controlled state politics until 1863.

When the Civil War began in 1861, Kentucky was carrying on a prosperous trade between both the North and the South. Because of its geographical location the state was a keystone between the two sections, but in reality belonged to neither (see Border States). Many families were divided in sentiment and brothers went off to fight in opposing armies. Despite its neutrality, the war was brought to Kentucky when the Confederates invaded the state on Sept. 3, 1861 (see Kentucky's Neutrality Doctrine). There was only one im-

portant engagement in Kentucky after 1861, the battle of Perryville[w], Oct. 8, 1862 (see Kentucky, Invasion of). John Hunt Morgan[w] conducted numerous raids through the state, but they were nothing more than crossroads skirmishes. Kentucky did not secede, and its slaves were not freed until 1865. Since the latter date the development of Kentucky, with the exception of the Goebel affair[w], has followed closely the lines of national development.

[T. D. Clark, *A History of Kentucky;* Mann Butler, *History of Kentucky;* W. E. Connelley and E. M. Coulter, *History of Kentucky.*]

T. D. CLARK

Kentucky, Invasion of (1862). In July, 1862, following the lull after the battle of Shiloh[w], Gen. Braxton Bragg (C.) moved his army from northern Mississippi to the vicinity of Chattanooga, preparatory to beginning a movement through middle Tennessee into Kentucky. Much of both states was strongly pro-Southern. A successful movement to the Ohio River, it was hoped, would bring many recruits into the Confederate ranks, open rich resources to the Southern cause and relieve the pressure on Lee (C.) in Virginia. Interior lines would give a controlled, well-led army an opportunity to reach the Ohio in advance of any large Union force.

Bragg's army left Chattanooga late in August and marched rapidly northward, arriving at Bowling Green, Ky., in mid-September. Buell, commanding the Union defense, hastily gathered troops to oppose Bragg. On Sept. 14, the Confederate leader, unnecessarily, digressed to attack Munfordville[w]. He wasted five valuable days of which Buell made good use.

When Bragg finally resumed his march, instead of hurrying to Louisville, his proper objective which was only weakly garrisoned, he went to Bardstown. Buell rapidly concentrated his forces at Louisville. The first phase of the campaign was over. Up to this point the advantage had been with Bragg. While Buell prepared to march southward, Bragg waited for an independent army under Kirby Smith (C.) coming from eastern Kentucky, in the meantime himself going to Frankfort to help inaugurate a secession governor of Kentucky. This ceremony completed, Bragg returned to his army.

Confused by Buell's energy, Bragg was uncertain what to do. Finally, he decided to move eastward toward Kirby Smith. Buell had gained the initiative. On Oct. 8, 1862, Bragg gathering his now scattered troops unexpectedly encountered Buell's army near Perryville[w]. A bloody battle followed, considering the numbers involved. Only portions of the two armies were engaged.

Bragg achieved a tactical success, but after dark withdrew to join Kirby Smith. Two days later it was decided to withdraw from Kentucky rather than chance defeat in enemy territory.

Divided command, unnecessary diversions and Buell's aggressive leadership all contributed to failure. Nothing of importance had been accomplished. Buell's army had not been defeated nor had the Kentuckians been persuaded to rise in revolt.

[*Battles and Leaders of the Civil War*, Vol. III.]
THOMAS ROBSON HAY

Kentucky and Virginia Resolutions. *See* Virginia and Kentucky Resolutions.

Kentucky Conventions for Separation from Virginia (1784–90). In 1784 the Kentucky frontier was subjected to frequent Indian attacks. In that year a convention of representative delegates was called to meet in Danville to petition Virginia for assistance. Between 1784 and 1790, nine conventions were held (all in Danville). A tenth convention met in April, 1792, to frame the constitution.

The first nine conventions, however, were not held in vain, for specific gains were made in the broadening of Virginia's laws for frontier defense, and in the passage of four enabling acts[qv]. These latter acts gave the Kentuckians three privileges: first, they provided specific rules for registry of land; second, they established definite terms of separation; and, third, they secured Kentucky representation in the Congress of the Confederation[qv]. In the numerous debates, pioneer statesmen were able to clarify many issues which faced the western people. Navigation and trade rights down the Mississippi River[qv] were partially guaranteed, the Spanish conspiracy[qv] was defeated and a fairly democratic constitution was drafted. Perhaps the most important accomplishment of all was the excellent political training which early Kentucky leaders secured as delegates to the Danville meetings.

[W. E. Connelley and E. M. Coulter, *History of Kentucky*.]
T. D. CLARK

Kentucky County, created by the Virginia assembly (Dec. 31, 1776) on petition of the Harrodsburg[qv] settlers, presented by George Rogers Clark and John Gabriel Jones, included all of Fincastle County[qv] south of the Ohio and west of the Big Sandy River and Cumberland Mountains. It was divided into three counties in 1780.

[Temple Bodley, *History of Kentucky*.]
W. C. MALLALIEU

Kentucky v. Dennison (24 Howard 66, 1861). The State of Kentucky petitioned for mandamus in the United States Supreme Court to compel the governor of Ohio to "honor a requisition of the Governor of Kentucky for the surrender of a violator of a state law relative to slaves." The Court, in early 1861, held the duty of the Ohio governor mandatory but also denied the Federal Government power to coerce him to perform the act. Otherwise the Federal Government could destroy the states.

[Charles Warren, *The Supreme Court in United States History;* Carl B. Swisher, *Roger B. Taney.*]
PHILIP G. AUCHAMPAUGH

Kentucky's Neutrality Doctrine. When the secession[qv] of the Southern states began in 1860, neutrality was considered by Kentucky, Tennessee and Maryland; but Kentucky was the only state to attempt to apply the doctrine. On May 16, 1861, the House resolved that the state would "take no part in the civil war now being waged, except as mediators and friends to the belligerent parties; and that Kentucky should, during the contest, occupy the position of strict neutrality. . . ." Four days later Gov. Beriah Magoffin issued a strict neutrality proclamation, warning all armed forces from entering Kentucky. The pronouncement was made complete on May 20, when the Kentucky Senate ratified neutrality.

Kentucky based her position on a long period of training and experience. Occupying a frontier between North and South, she had never been completely a part of either. Largely Southern in tradition, kindred and sentiment, she was bound to the North by economic ties and national aspirations. For years she had been fed on Clay's doctrine of compromises, to be followed by the similar teachings of John J. Crittenden. In 1861, feeling that the cotton South had precipitated the crisis without consulting the Border States[qv], and believing that by remaining neutral she could stay the forces of war, Kentucky attempted to apply her system until early September, when warring forces swamped her from all sides.

[E. M. Coulter, *The Civil War and Readjustment in Kentucky;* E. C. Smith, *The Borderland in the Civil War.*]
E. MERTON COULTER

Kermis, or *Kermess,* was an annual fair brought by the Dutch settlers to New Netherland[qv] in the 17th century. The first regular *kermis* in New Amsterdam began in October, 1659, and lasted six weeks. As in the low countries, stalls were built for the exchange of goods, a "court of pypowder" was held and dancing, processions, lovemaking and drinking made it a time of hilarious merrymaking which sometimes offended the more puritanical and led to restrictive legislation.

[M. W. Goodwin, *Dutch and English on the Hudson;* H. I. Priestley, *Coming of the White Man;* G. A. Wumkes, *Kermissen.*]

HAROLD E. DAVIS

Kernstown, Battle at (March 23, 1862). Obeying instructions to detain Union forces in the Shenandoah Valley to prevent their moving to re-enforce McClellan, Gen. Jackson (C.) engaged Shields' division at Kernstown, Va., four miles south of Winchester. Gen. Nathan Kimball (U.), commanding on the field after Shields was wounded, repulsed Jackson, who retreated up the valley toward Swift Run Gap.

[*Battles and Leaders of the Civil War,* Vol. II.]

ROBERT S. THOMAS

Kerosene Oil. Americans knew something of petroleum^w deposits as early as 1700, when the Earl of Bellomont, governor of New York, ordered samples brought from an oil spring "eight miles beyond the Senek's furthest castle." Sir William Johnson in 1767 saw the "curious oyl" from Cuba, N. Y., and Pennsylvania settlers knew that Indians sunk pits along branches of the Allegheny to procure petroleum for medicine. Soon after the Revolution men digging salt wells along the Allegheny, Kanawha and other streams found oil, then regarded as a nuisance. But in 1833 Dr. Benjamin Silliman, Sr., describing the oil springs near Cuba, N. Y., stated that the product was used as a liniment for bruises, rheumatism and sores, and that much larger quantities of medicinal "Seneca Oil" were being distributed from Venango County, Pa. In 1849 Samuel M. Kier of Pittsburgh opened an establishment at 363 Liberty Street, Pittsburgh, and began selling "Kier's Petroleum or Rock Oil, Celebrated for its Wonderful Curative Powers," in bottles on a large scale. Meanwhile other men were taking steps destined to reveal the true value of the oil. James Young of Glasgow in 1847 learned of a petroleum spring in Derbyshire and distilled from it both lubricating and illuminating oils. When it gave out he turned to the distillation of oil from coal. In Prince Edward Island as early as August, 1846, Dr. Abram Gessner distilled kerosene (which he so named from the Greek *keros,* wax, and *elaion,* oil) from local coal. He shortly brought his process to the United States and took out patents which he sold to the North American Kerosene Gas Light Company of New York, which began commercial manufacture in March, 1854. Joshua Merrill began manufacturing kerosene from coal in Boston in 1852, and in 1856 was employed by Samuel Downer as chem-

ist for the Downer Works in South Boston, where he experimented with bitumens and Cuban *chapapote.* Kerosene works were erected that same year at Cloverport, Ky., using cannel coal from the vicinity, while another establishment was opened in Perry County, Ohio. By 1859 the country had between fifty and sixty manufactories of kerosene from coal, shale and other carbons. The business was growing rapidly, and was crowding such older illuminants as whale-oil and camphene, a rectified oil of turpentine, out of the markets. It was a short step to turn from coal to petroleum.

Although Kier had begun distilling kerosene or "carbon oil" from petroleum in 1850, he made little headway and the effective pioneer was Col. A. C. Ferris of New York. Ferris in Pittsburgh during 1857 saw a tin lamp burning kerosene, and realized its possibilities. Obtaining most of the output of the Tarentum, Pa., wells, he began shipping it in quantity to New York, where various manufacturers distilled it. In 1858 the crude-petroleum business of the United States amounted to 1183 barrels, Ferris handling most of it. Then in 1859 E. L. Drake^w made his momentous oil strike in western Pennsylvania, and the supply of crude rapidly grew enormous. Works for making kerosene from coal died or were converted into oil refineries. By 1860 more than 200 patents had been granted on kerosene lamps. Within a few years kerosene became the world's principal illuminant, penetrating even China. About 1880 a safe kerosene stove was perfected by the Standard Oil Company^w, and furnished an important new use for the product. Meanwhile by-products of kerosene manufacture, such as paraffin, vaseline and lubricating oils, had taken an important place in American life.

[B. R. F. Bacon and W. A. Hamor, *The American Petroleum Industry;* Sir Boverton Redwood, *Petroleum;* James D. Henry, *History and Romance of the Petroleum Industry;* M. L. Eakin, *Technology in the Early Development of the Petroleum Industry in Western Pennsylvania.*]

ALLAN NEVINS

Ketch, a small yawllike vessel with two masts, main and mizzen, used originally as a yacht but in navies as a bomb vessel because of the clear space forward of the mainmast. The *Intrepid*^w, a captured Tripolitan ketch, is the chief one in American naval annals.

[G. W. Allen, *Our War with the Barbary Corsairs.*]

WALTER B. NORRIS

Kettle Creek, Battle of (Feb. 14, 1779). After Savannah^w had fallen to the British at the close of 1778, their troops quickly overran Georgia until rebuffed on Kettle Creek in the up-country county of Wilkes. Patriots under John Twiggs, John Dooly, Elijah Clarke and Andrew Pickens surprised and scattered about 700 loyalists[w] led by Col. Boyd. Nine Americans and seventy British, including Boyd, were killed. The British retired from Augusta, and loyalism in Georgia and South Carolina was severely checked.

[C. C. Jones, Jr., *The History of Georgia*.]

H. B. FANT

Keweenaw Waterway, THE, about twenty-five miles long, bisects the Keweenaw Peninsula which projects northward some sixty miles into Lake Superior from near the mid-point of its south shore. Begun as a private enterprise by the adjacent mining concerns of the Copper Country shortly after the completion of the St. Marys Falls Ship Canal[w], in 1855, it was taken over by the United States Government in 1891, and is now in charge of the United States Corps of Engineers[w]. It provides not only shipping facilities for the Copper Country but a harbor of refuge and safe passage for through traffic on Lake Superior. In 1936, 515,000 tons of shipping, valued at $17,620,000, passed through it. Most of the 9,000,000,000 tons of Michigan copper have been shipped by this waterway.

[Michigan Supreme Court *Reports*, Vol. X, p. 233; *Reports*, Chief of Engineers, U. S. Army.]

L. A. CHASE

Key West, Fla., southernmost city of the United States, is said to be so named from a corruption of the Spanish *cayo hueso,* or bone key, on account of heaps of human bones found there by 18th-century visitors. Grant of the island was made to Juan Pablo Salas, Aug. 26, 1815, by Don Juan de Estrada, Spanish governor of Florida. Salas sold his grant to John W. Simonton of Mobile, Ala., Jan. 19, 1822, and the latter soon disposed of three fourths of his rights to four other persons. First settlers, who were chiefly from South Carolina and St. Augustine, came in 1822.

[Jefferson B. Browne, *Key West, the Old and the New*.]

W. T. CASH

Kick Back. This expression was much used in the depression after 1929 to describe the practice by contractors or racketeers of forcing a worker to give back part of his pay as a condition of holding his job. The evil was particularly prevalent in the building trades. When it applies to public office holders the payment is usually made to the political boss. New York passed a law against it in 1935.

JAMES D. MAGEE

Kickapoo Indians, an Algonquin tribe formerly living in Wisconsin. They later removed to Illinois and Indiana where they fought in the wars of Tecumseh[w]. They then removed to Missouri and thence to northeastern Kansas where about 300 still live. In 1852 a large band migrated to Mexico. These so annoyed border settlers that in 1873 most of them were returned to the United States and settled on a reservation in what is now Oklahoma. Here they still live on individual allotments, their surplus lands having been opened to white settlement in 1895. They number a little over 200. A small band still resides in Mexico.

[F. W. Hodge, *Handbook of American Indians*.]

EDWARD EVERETT DALE

Kidder Massacre. On June 29, 1867, Lt. L. S. Kidder, 2nd Cavalry, with eleven men, left Fort Sedgwick[w], Colo., with dispatches for Gen. Custer, supposedly camped at the forks of the Republican River. Custer had moved, and in following his trail Kidder, in July, encountered 500 Cheyennes[w] under Roman Nose. Surrounded in a gully on Beaver Creek, Kidder and all his men were killed.

[Mrs. George A. Custer, *Boots and Saddles*.]

JOSEPH MILLS HANSON

Kidnapping. The first kidnapping for ransom of record in America was that of four-year-old Charley Ross in Germantown, Pa., July 1, 1874. The kidnappers demanded (by mail) $20,000 ransom, but were so fearful of detection that all attempts to make contact with them failed. On Dec. 14 two men named Mosher and Douglas were killed while attempting a burglary in Brooklyn. Douglas, dying, confessed that they were the kidnappers, but said that only Mosher, already dead, knew where the boy was. Charley was never found. The next abduction was that of the young son of E. A. Cudahy, meat packer of Omaha, in 1900 by Pat Crowe, professional criminal, who returned the boy upon payment of $25,000, but who, by a grave miscarriage of justice, was acquitted, though admitting the crime. There were other cases in 1909 and 1920. Thereafter, the evil increased enormously, and by 1930 had become a national disgrace. In 1932 the Chicago police estimated that there had been 200 kidnappings in the country in two years, with ransoms paid amounting to $2,000,000. Other agencies placed the figures much higher. The Lindbergh kidnapping[w] precipitated Federal laws in 1932 and 1934, prescribing severe penalties for interstate abduction, with the death sentence for cases in which the victim had been harmed or not returned before sentence was passed. Nevertheless, 1933's record was one of the worst of all. Among noted cases in 1933–34–

35, with the ransoms paid, were those of Charles F. Urschel, Oklahoma oil capitalist, $200,000; W. Hamm, Jr., Minneapolis, $100,000; John Factor, Chicago, $70,000; Margaret McMath, aged ten, Massachusetts, $60,000; George Weyerhaeuser, aged nine, Tacoma, Wash., $200,000—all these returned alive. But the tendency to slay the victim, thus eliminating a witness, and attempt to collect the money, anyhow, seemed to have been accelerated by the drastic law. Effective work by the Federal Bureau of Investigation[w] in wiping out criminal gangs and capturing the miscreants probably did more than the "Lindbergh Law" in slowing up the evil, though it continued in lessened degree as the years went on.

[Edward Dean Sullivan, *The Snatch Racket.*]
ALVIN F. HARLOW

Kidnapping of Free Negroes. The kidnapping of northern free Negroes and carrying them south to be sold into slavery was a common and, in some instances, organized business notwithstanding laws to the contrary in Southern states. Kidnappers were not easily punished on account of the disqualification of Negroes as witnesses. Whole families were kidnapped, but children most frequently. One enterprising Philadelphian gained a livelihood courting and marrying mulatto women and then selling them as slaves.

In 1793 and 1850 Congress passed fugitive slave laws[w] which empowered Federal officers to seize runaway slaves in free-soil states and return them to their masters. The summary character of these laws, and the lust of Federal magistrates for fees, made it easy for unscrupulous persons to seize free Negroes and hasten them into slavery, under pretext of law. Free-soil states passed statutes which afforded some protection to free Negroes. These laws usually went so far as to nullify the Constitution.

[W. H. Collins, *The Domestic Slave Trade of the Southern States.*]
LLOYD C. M. HARE

Kilbourn v. Thompson (103 U. S. 168, 1881), declared that Congress had no "general power of making inquiry into the private affairs of the citizens," and that since the inquiry being conducted was judicial rather than legislative, the House could not hold Kilbourn in contempt for refusing to answer questions. He could sue the sergeant-at-arms arresting him, but not Representatives advocating his arrest. Subsequent cases, however, have held that in legislative matters Congress has "the power of inquiry—with the power to enforce it."

[McGrain v. Daugherty, 273 U. S. 135, 1927; W. W. Willoughby, *Constitutional Law.*] LAWRENCE A. HARPER

Killdeer Mountain, Battle of (July 28, 1864). July 23, 1864, information reached Gen. Alfred Sully's Northwestern Indian Expedition[w] on the upper Heart River (N. Dak.), of a heavy concentration of Indians on Knife River. Coralling his heavy wagons and accompanying emigrant train, with 2200 mounted men and light wagons carrying provisions and supplies, Sully marched northward, and on July 28 found the united Sioux[w] forces, estimated at some 5000, strongly posted on Tahkahokuty or Killdeer Mountain (N. Dak.), in rugged, timbered country.

With dismounted men as skirmishers, supported by light artillery, flanking cavalry and reserves, Sully pushed forward, while the rear guard protected the wagons. Through skillful use of cavalry charges, while artillery shelled the ravines, the mountain was reached and fully occupied by dark, together with the abandoned Indian camp. Vast quantities of Indian provisions and equipment were destroyed. Sully's casualties were fifteen killed and wounded, while the Indian losses were estimated at upwards of one hundred.

[Official Correspondence Pertaining to the War of the Outbreak, 1862-1865, in *South Dakota Historical Collections*, Vol. VIII.] WILLOUGHBY M. BABCOCK

"King Cotton" was an expression much used by Southern authors and orators before the Civil War. The idea appeared first as the title of a book by David Christy, *Cotton Is King,* in 1855. In a speech in the United States Senate, March 4, 1858, James H. Hammond declared, "You dare not make war upon cotton! No power on earth dares make war upon it. Cotton is king." The phrase expressed the Southern belief that cotton was so essential that those who controlled it might dictate the economic and political policies of the United States and of the world.

[F. L. Owsley, *King Cotton Diplomacy;* J. A. B. Scherer, *Cotton as a World Power.*] HALLIE FARMER

King George, Fort, a cypress plank blockhouse built on the lower Altamaha, 1721, by Col. John Barnwell of South Carolina, initiated a system of American defenses endorsed by the English Board of Trade to offset French expansion. Until burned, 1725, it challenged Spanish claim to a region that Oglethorpe later dominated from Frederica[w].

[J. T. Lanning, *The Diplomatic History of Georgia.*]
H. B. FANT

King George's War (1744-48). Nominally at peace from 1713 to 1744, France and England developed irreconcilable colonial conflicts over boundaries of Acadia[w] and northern New England and possession of the Ohio Valley. When England's commercial war with Spain (1739) merged into the continental War of Austrian Succession (1740–48), England and France, first fighting as "auxiliaries" on opposite sides, threw off the mask and declared war (March 15, 1744). The Louisburg French first learned of the war (May 5, 1744), surprised and captured Canso (May 13) but failed to take Annapolis (Port Royal)[w]. In retaliation New Englanders captured Louisburg[w] (June 15, 1745), the most daring and decisive victory in the colonial war, and planned, with English aid, simultaneously to attack Quebec and Montreal. Seven colonies co-operated to raise forces, ready in 1746, but promised English help did not arrive and the colonials finally disbanded (1747). Meanwhile, France sent a great fleet under Duc D'Anville[w] (June, 1746) to recapture Louisburg and devastate English colonial seaports, but storms, disease, death of D'Anville and suicide of his vice-admiral frustrated the attempt. A second fleet sent (May, 1747) was defeated on the open sea by combined British squadrons. Gruesome raids along the New England-New York borders by both conflicting parties and their Indian allies characterized the remainder of the war, with no result except temporary check upon frontier settlement. Weary of futile, costly conflict, the warring parties signed the Peace of Aix-la-Chapelle[w] (October, 1748), granting mutual restoration of conquests (Louisburg for Madras), but leaving colonial questions unsolved.

[Francis Parkman, *A Half-Century of Conflict;* H. L. Osgood, *The American Colonies in the Eighteenth Century.*]

RAYMOND P. STEARNS

King Philip's War (1675–76). No longer of value to New Englanders, who, by 1660, produced their own food and valued fishing and commerce above fur trade[w], Indians played little part in New England economy. Their lands were coveted, their presence denounced, as New Englanders pushed forward the frontier. Conversely, Indians suspected English motives, chafed under English laws, resented missionary efforts. When Massasoit died (1662), new Indian leaders rejected friendship with the English, ignored the Pequots'[w] fate, and were suspected of conspiring against New Englanders.

Chief conspirator was Massasoit's second son, Metacom, or Philip, sachem of the Wampanoags after his elder brother died (1662). Philip renewed the peace covenant with Plymouth Colony[w], but repeated reports of plots with Narragansetts[w], the French, and others led Plymouth (1671) to demand an account. Philip haughtily protested peaceful intentions, and agreed to surrender firearms. Sullen peace followed, but the Wampanoags surrendered suspiciously few arms and when three Wampanoags were executed for the murder of John Sassamon, a Christian Indian informer, the warriors got out of hand, plundering and firing farms. Philip's alliances were not concluded, but the English were unprepared, widely scattered, tempting. On June 18, 1675, Wampanoag marauders provoked Swansea settlers to begin hostilities. Swift, devastating raids upon Swansea and neighboring towns threw the colonists into panic, intensified when the militia found no Indians to fight—for the Indians were will-o'-the-wisps and never made a stand. The war was a series of Indian raids with retaliatory expeditions by the English.

The English counter-attack was ill-planned, indecisive and antagonized other tribes. Jealous colonial commanders and troops co-operated badly, the soldiers were poorly equipped and ignorant of Indian warfare, the troops lacked scouts to track the enemy and, at first, refused to employ friendly Indians. When (June 30) combined Plymouth and Massachusetts forces drove Philip from Mount Hope into Pocasset swamps, he easily slipped into central Massachusetts. Then, suspicious of the Narragansetts, colonial forces raided their country, compelled a few lingerers to sign a treaty of neutrality (July 15), but the warriors, led by Canonchet, had joined in Philip's War. English sale of captives into West Indian slavery and slaughter of innocent Christian Indians drove Nipmucks, Abnaki and even some converted Indians into opposition—though they never united under one leader.

Before the end of 1675, disaster overtook New England on all sides. Middelboro, Brookfield, Deerfield, Northfield and other towns were devastated, abandoned, or both; two colonial forces (Beer's and Lathrop's) were ambushed and destroyed (Sawmill Brook, Sept. 3; Muddy Brook, Sept. 18). Similar raids devastated New Hampshire and Maine settlements. The English in turn destroyed the Narragansetts in the Great Swamp Fight[w]. As winter came on, the Indians encamped at Quabaug and Wachusett. Philip and a small band wintered at Scaticook, near Albany, in hopes of gaining aid from Mohawks[w] and the French.

In 1676 the war began adversely for the English. Planning to attack the eastern settlements in order to concentrate English forces there while they planted crops in the Connecticut Valley, the Indians (Feb. 9) fell upon Lancaster—where the famous Mrs. Rowlandson was captured—and threatened Plymouth, Providence and towns near Boston. Meanwhile, the colonies re-organized their forces, destroyed Narragansett food supplies (December–January, 1675–76), and, though they temporarily fell into the Indian stra-tegical trap, Maj. Palmes (April 3) captured and executed Canonchet; the Mohawks threatened to attack the valley Indians from the west, there-by helping the English; and (May 18–19) Capt. Turner with 180 men surprised and massacred the Indians at Deerfield and broke their resist-ance in the valley. By the end of May the tide had turned in the west. Capt. Benjamin Church, assisted by able scouts, harried Philip and his fol-lowers in swamps near Taunton and Bridgewa-ter, captured his wife and son (Aug. 1), sur-rounded his camp, and shot Philip as he tried to escape (Aug. 11).

Philip's death marked the end of the war, though hostilities continued in New Hampshire and Maine, where the Abnakis and others, sup-plied with French arms and encouragement, wreaked havoc upon settlement after settlement. Finally, April 12, 1678, Articles of Peace were signed at Casco[w], with mutual restoration of cap-tives and property. Since June, 1675, sixteen towns in Massachusetts and four in Rhode Island had been destroyed, no English colonist was left in Kennebec County (Maine), all along New England frontiers expansion was retarded. But the Indian problem in southern New England was solved; thereafter it was confined to the northeast and northwest where it merged with the struggle with France for control of the con-tinent.

[George W. Ellis and John E. Morris, *King Philip's War*; James Truslow Adams, *The Founding of New Eng-land.*]

RAYMOND P. STEARNS

King Philip's War, Indian Refugees from, in the West. After the Great Swamp Fight[w] (Dec. 19, 1675), the Narragansetts were dispersed and, as the war went against Philip in 1676, scattered bands of Indian refugees, harassed by the Eng-lish and their Indian allies, fled, some westward to the Mahicans and others northeastward to the Abnaki. Some Nipmucks and Narragansetts joined the Abnaki, later fled to Canada; others, with Pocumtucks, Wampanoags, Mohegans and some Pennacooks and Abnaki, fled to Scaticook on the east bank of the Hudson, where, subse-quently, they were adopted by Mohawks. In the 18th century, decimated by disease and the Iro-quois, they were induced to join French Indians at St. Francis, Quebec, or driven westward to the Illinois Country[w].

[F. W. Hodge, *Handbook of American Indians.*]

RAYMOND P. STEARNS

King William's War (1689–97). This first of the French and Indian wars was already smoul-dering on the New England frontier at the time of the English declaration of war with France in May, 1689. Angry at the plundering of St. Cas-tine's Trading House, the French had incited the Abnaki tribes of Maine to destroy the rival Eng-lish post of Pemaquid[qw], and to attack the fron-tier settlements. The Revolution in England, which forced James II from his throne, was fol-lowed by revolt against his representatives in the northern English colonies. The Dominion of New England[w] split into ten or a dozen inde-pendent parts, each jealous of its own frontiers. In New York, the civil and miltary officers of Albany, the key point for Indian relations, were at odds with Jacob Leisler[w], who had usurped control of the southern part of the province.

In Canada conditions were little better. When Count Frontenac arrived in 1689 to begin his sec-ond term as governor, he found the colony ter-ror-stricken by Iroquoian raids. To revive the courage of the French and to regain the alle-giance of his Indian allies, he sent out during the winter of 1690 three war parties, of which the first destroyed Schenectady, the second attacked and burned the little settlement of Salmon Falls on the New Hampshire border and the third forced the surrender of Fort Loyal[qw], an outpost at the site of the present city of Portland.

Terror spread throughout the English colo-nies, and Massachusetts raised a fleet of seven ships, under the command of Sir William Phips, who captured and plundered Port Royal[w]. In May, 1690, at the invitation of Leisler, represen-tatives of Massachusetts, Plymouth, Connecticut and New York met in New York City. A united attack by land on Montreal was planned with the promised co-operation of the Iroquois; Massachu-setts and the other New England colonies under-took to attack Quebec[w] at the same time by sea. Both expeditions were failures. Although a small number of New York and Connecticut troops under the command of Fitz-John Winthrop set out from Albany[w], they were unable to advance farther than the foot of Lake Champlain. Sir William Phips, who commanded the New Eng-land fleet, fared no better. Realizing that neither their financial resources nor their military or-ganization were equal to the task, the leaders of the northern English colonies made repeated ap-peals to the English government for help. In re-sponse, in 1693, a fleet was despatched under the command of Sir Francis Wheeler. This fleet, af-ter operating in the West Indies, reached Boston with fever-stricken crews, and as no preparations had been made to co-operate with it, nothing was accomplished. Frontenac, also, made urgent appeals for help, with no better luck, for the French squadron sent to capture Boston, was delayed by head winds, ran short of provisions and could do nothing.

With both the French and English colonies thus thrown back on their own resources, the results were altogether favorable to the French. Their numerous Indian allies were always available for raids on the English frontier. Pemaquid, which had been rebuilt, was again captured by the French, and the New England frontier suffered cruelly. New York suffered less, but the Iroquois, frightened by French attacks, were with difficulty held to their alliance. The peace of Ryswick^{w} (1697) ended the fighting, but did little to settle the questions under dispute.

[Herbert L. Osgood, *American Colonies in the 18th Century.*]   A. C. FLICK

King's College. *See* Columbia College.

King's Ferry, THE, was an ancient ferryboat service crossing the Hudson River from the southwest side of Verplanck's Point in Westchester County to Stony Point^{w} in Rockland County. During the Revolutionary War this territory was much disputed on both sides of the river. On Sept. 22, 1780, Maj. John Andre^{w}, attempting to regain the British lines after his conference with Benedict Arnold, crossed from Stony Point to Verplanck's Point on the King's Ferry.

[Robert Bolton, Jr., *History of Westchester County.*]   A. C. FLICK

King's Messenger was a royal official during colonial times for the arresting of prisoners of state. When the Regicides^{w}, Whalley, Goffe and Dixwell, fled to New England on the accession of Charles II, two King's Messengers were sent to arrest them.

[Thomas Hutchinson, *History of Massachusetts; New Haven Colonial Records.*]   R. W. G. VAIL

King's Mountain, Battle of. In the autumn of 1780 Maj. Patrick Ferguson, in command of a detachment of about 1000 soldiers from the army of Lord Cornwallis, made a foray into the western part of North Carolina. The "mountain men," as the dwellers in the back country were called, had been stirred up by the ill conduct of the British troops in the South; and from the western Carolinas and Virginia, as well as from the present states of Kentucky and Tennessee, there gathered about 2000 American frontiersmen under the leadership of Col. Isaac Shelby, Col. William Campbell, Col. John Sevier, Maj.

Joseph MacDowell and Maj. Joseph Winston. Hearing of this possible resistance, Ferguson beat a hasty retreat, but the American forces caught up to him at an eminence called King's Mountain, which is in what is now York County, South Carolina, about a mile and a half south of the North Carolina boundary. Here Ferguson took his position atop the mountain on Oct. 6. The next day he was entirely surrounded by the Americans. On the afternoon of the 7th the Americans attacked up the mountain from all sides. The part of the ridge which the British occupied was extremely narrow. The Americans, equipped with long rifles, but without bayonets, assaulted the hill, and the British tactics consisted of charging down the side of the hill with bayonets. However, the cover of trees and shrubs was such that the Americans were able to retreat only a little way and conceal themselves while the British had to retreat to the summit and charge down the other side of the mountain. As Light Horse Harry Lee pointed out, the hill was "more assailable by the rifle than defensible by the bayonet," and the British lost heavily from rifle fire as they tried successively to regain the height. After about an hour's fighting, Maj. Ferguson was struck by several bullets, one of which killed him. Capt. Abraham DePeyster succeeded to the command, and observing that he was being overwhelmed, raised the white flag. The British force was composed principally, not of regulars, but of Loyalists^{w}, and the bitterness felt by the mountain men against their erstwhile Tory neighbors was exceedingly deep. There were charges of atrocities on both sides, possibly with some justification. Practically all the British were either killed, wounded or captured, and they lost over a thousand stand of arms to the Americans. The significance of the battle was best pointed out by Sir Henry Clinton, the British commander in chief, who wrote that this battle "proved the first Link of a Chain of Evils that followed each other in regular Succession until they at last ended in the total Loss of America."

[L. C. Draper, *King's Mountain and Its Heroes.*]   RANDOLPH G. ADAMS

King's Province was that portion of the mainland of Rhode Island between the Pawcatuck River and Narragansett Bay, known as the Narragansett Country, claimed by Rhode Island, Connecticut and Massachusetts. In an attempt to settle the controversy, a royal commission, in 1665, erected this territory into the King's Province and placed it under Rhode Island jurisdiction; but Connecticut still claimed authority over it until the matter was settled when Sir Edmund

Andros[v] took possession of both colonies. In 1729 this territory became Kings County, Rhode Island, the name being changed in 1781 to Washington County.

[Edward Channing, *History of the United States;* S. G. Arnold, *History of Rhode Island;* C. W. Bowen, *Boundary Disputes of Connecticut.*]

R. W. G. VAIL

King's Woods. In parts of colonial New England surveyors of the King's Woods marked with a broad arrow all pine trees two feet or more in diameter suitable for use as masts in the Royal navy. Even after the land had passed into private hands, trees previously so marked were reserved to the crown, thus taking from the colonists much of their best timber. Tactless enforcement of the law by the surveyors, especially in Maine and New Hampshire where pines were more plentiful, caused friction which contributed to the growth of sentiment for independence. Various specific stands of timber were set aside for this purpose, including the township of Kingswood, N. H., chartered by the royal governor in 1737 for the "Encouragement of Setling a new Plantation for the Encrease of Naval Stores," including the production of hemp, pitch, tar and turpentine, the crown reserving "all Mast Trees growing on said Tract of land." (*See also* Naval Stores.)

[A. B. Hart, *Commonwealth History of Massachusetts;* Nathaniel Bouton, *Documents and Records Relating to Towns in New Hampshire,* Vol. IX.]

R. W. G. VAIL

Kingston, N. Y. (Esopus) , was settled in 1652 by Thomas Chambers, who was followed by Dutch settlers. Soon afterwards it became the scene of the Esopus War[v], and was later a center for trade and the third largest town in the colony. During the Revolution, when the British took New York City, the Provincial convention moved to Kingston, February, 1777, and adopted and proclaimed the first New York constitution, April, 1777. Gov. George Clinton took office in July, the legislature met in August, the courts opened in September. The British approached in October and burned the town. The government left and never returned. The Senate House (built 1676) still stands.

[M. Schoonmaker, *The History of Kingston.*]

AUGUSTUS H. SHEARER

Kinkaiders. Before 1904 homesteaders generally avoided the western third of Nebraska because of its aridity and poor soil. Some Nebraskans thought that if the homestead unit were enlarged settlers might be attracted to that part of their state, and in 1904 they persuaded Congress to adopt the Kinkaid Act which increased the size of the homestead unit in the western part of Nebraska to 640 acres. There followed a great rush of settlers, called Kinkaiders, into the region, who, however, met disappointment from the outset. Unproductive soil, drought, dust storms, warfare with cattlemen and sheepmen, and insufficient capital defeated the settlers. Within a few years there was an exodus of small farmers from the section.

[Marie Sandoz, *Old Jules.*]

PAUL WALLACE GATES

Kiowa, Fort, was built on orders of the American Fur Company[v] about 1822. It was near Fort Lookout, on the right bank of the Missouri River about ten miles above the present site of Chamberlain, S. Dak. It consisted of a range of log buildings of four rooms, storehouse, blockhouse and wooden tower. It was abandoned after the decline of the fur trade[v].

[H. M. Chittenden, *History of American Fur Trade of Far West.*]

CARL L. CANNON

Kiowa, THE. A small but extremely warlike plains Indian tribe, formerly residing in Montana but driven south by the Sioux and Cheyennes, until they crossed the Arkansas River and confederated with the Comanches[qv]. With these allies they raided the frontier from northern Kansas to Durango, Mexico, during the 1860's and 1870's. They were finally subjugated after the outbreak of 1874-75 (*see* Red River Indian War) and now live near Fort Sill, Okla.

[James Mooney, *Calendar History of the Kiowa;* F. W. Hodge, *Handbook of American Indians.*]

PAUL I. WELLMAN

"Kitchen Cabinet," THE, was a title derisively applied by President Jackson's political enemies to an informal group of advisers who were credited with exercising more influence on the President than his regular Cabinet. From 1829 until 1831 when the Cabinet was reorganized, the "kitchen cabinet" or "lower cabinet," as it was often called, was especially influential. Thereafter, President Jackson relied less on his informal advisers and more on regular members of the Cabinet. The most important members of the "kitchen cabinet" were Amos Kendall, Francis Preston Blair, Sr., William B. Lewis, A. J. Donelson, Martin Van Buren and John H. Eaton.

[John Spencer Bassett, *The Life of Andrew Jackson.*]

ERIK McKINLEY ERIKSSON

Kittanning Campaign (August, September, 1756) . During the French and Indian War[qv] the Delaware village of Kittanning, on the Allegheny

River at the site of the present town so named, was a base for Indian raids on the Pennsylvania frontier. In retaliation, Col. John Armstrong led some 300 men from Fort Shirley at Aughwick against the Indians there. In a surprise attack, the militia and volunteers burned the thirty log houses of the town, destroyed ammunition and supplies, released eleven white prisoners and killed thirty or forty Indians. Though Armstrong's losses almost equaled those of the enemy, the victory heartened the settlers and prevented further raids from Kittanning.

[C. H. Sipe, *Indian Wars of Pennsylvania.*]

SOLON J. BUCK

Kitty Hawk Airplane, THE, was the first heavier-than-air craft making a sustained and free flight under its own power and carrying a man. Constructed by the brothers Wilbur and Orville Wright, this plane was launched on Dec. 17, 1903, from a monorail track of iron-shod wood, sixty feet long, on a slope of Killdevil Hill near the small fishing village of Kitty Hawk, N. C., which location had been selected on advice of the United States Weather Bureau. It afforded constant winds of sixteen to twenty-five miles per hour as well as sand dunes for take-offs and soft ground for landing. By 1902, the brothers had succeeded in building a biplane glider with a rudder capable of sustained flight against winds of a velocity of twenty-five miles per hour. In 1903 they had constructed a four-cylinder gasoline engine weighing 750 pounds and developing twelve horsepower. The first attempt with the new combination, piloted by Orville Wright, resulted in a flight of twelve seconds covering 100 feet at a height of ten feet. The fourth attempt with Wilbur Wright at the controls produced a flight of fifty-nine seconds covering a distance of 852 feet at a speed of thirty miles per hour. This feat, witnessed by five natives, is almost universally accepted as the first flight in history. The event occurred nine days after the failure of Dr. Samuel P. Langley's experiment with a tandem monoplane on the Potomac River. The Kitty Hawk plane is now in the Science Museum at South Kensington, London.

[John R. McMahon, *The Wright Brothers; Aircraft Year Book, 1919.*]

KENNETH COLEGROVE

Klondike Rush, THE. On Aug. 16, 1896, gold was discovered on Bonanza Creek of Klondike (Ton-Dac) River, a tributary of the Yukon River in the Canadian Northwest Territory, by George Carmack and his two Indian brothers-in-law, allegedly on a tip from Robert Henderson. Carmack made known his discovery at the town of Forty Mile, and the miners from that place and other settlements came up and staked claims. At the confluence of the two streams Joseph Ladue laid out Dawson City.

News of the discovery reached the United States in January, 1897, and in the spring of that year a number of persons made preparations to depart by boat via St. Michael up the Yukon or up the Inside Passage to Lynn Canal and over the Chilcoot and White passes and thence down the upper tributaries of the Yukon. On July 14, 1897, the steamer *Excelsior* arrived at San Francisco with $750,000 in gold; on July 17, the *Portland* arrived at Seattle with $800,000. As no compelling news event was before the country when the ships arrived, the press played up the strike. Thousands of inquiries were received by chambers of commerce, railroads, steamship lines and outfitting houses, and these agencies, seeing the commercial possibilities, commenced a highly financed propaganda which precipitated the rush.

The peak of the rush occurred during 1897–99, when some 100,000 persons departed for Alaska. The passage to the Klondike was facilitated by the progressive construction of the White Pass and Yukon Railroad from Skagway to White Horse. The miners worked their claims for the coarse gold and then sold them—principally to the Guggenheim Exploration Company, which sent up dredges and introduced scientific methods of gold recovery.

The Klondike Rush had far-reaching economic results, particularly for Alaska. Those who were unable to secure claims on the Klondike spread over Alaska, finding gold at Nome, Fairbanks and at numerous lesser places. Many turned to other pursuits. Taken together, the participants in the rush were the principal factor in the diffuse settlement of Alaska and the economic development of the territory.

[Tappan Adney, *Klondike Stampede;* Jeannette P. Nichols, Advertising the Klondike, in *Washington Historical Quarterly,* January, 1922; Clarence L. Andrews, *The Story of Alaska;* A. W. Greely, *Handbook of Alaska.*]

V. J. FARRAR

Knights of Columbus, a religious fraternal order, with insurance features, for Roman Catholic men in the United States and Canada, was founded in New Haven (1882) by a half dozen men associated with Father Michael McGivney. It grew gradually as it obtained episcopal sanction until, at its height in postwar years, it approximated 1,000,000 members with a marked decline in subsequent years.

[M. F. Egan and J. B. Kennedy, *The Knights of Columbus in Peace and War.*]

RICHARD J. PURCELL

Knights of Labor, The, was founded by Uriah Stevens and other garment workers in Philadelphia in 1869. For a time the order grew slowly, but during the early 1880's its membership increased in spectacular fashion and in 1886 it included between 600,000 and 700,000 persons. Organized into mixed local and district assemblies, the whole labor movement was to be welded into a single disciplined army. All gainfully employed persons except lawyers, bankers, professional gamblers or stockbrokers, saloon keepers and (prior to 1881) physicians were eligible.

The natural consequence of this all-inclusive membership and of the structural arrangements of the order was a bent in the direction of political action and broad social reform. The underlying premise was that of an abundance of opportunity to be shared among all workers of hand and brain, and the mission of the producing classes was conceived to be to regain for themselves and to protect this opportunity.

Several factors contributed to the rapid decline after 1886. Of immediate and circumstantial character were the unsuccessful outcome of the strike policy, internal friction, and depletion of union finances consequent upon failure of the producers' co-operatives⁞ which were supported. Of more basic importance were the structural characteristics of the order and the fallacies in assumption. The centralized control and the mixed character of local and district assemblies inevitably invited difficulties with the "job-conscious" trade unions which, affiliated in the Federation of Organized Trades and Labor Unions, called American Federation of Labor⁞ after 1886, had evolved a program of worker control of jobs that attracted and held the mass of skilled craftsmen; and by 1890 their federated organization overshadowed the Knights of Labor.

[Commons and associates, *History of Labor in the United States,* Vol. II; Norman Ware, *The Labor Movement, 1868-1890;* Terence Powderly, *Thirty Years of Labor;* Samuel Gompers, *My Seventy Years of Life and Labor;* Lewis Lorwin, *The American Federation of Labor.*]

ROYAL E. MONTGOMERY

Knights of the Golden Circle, a secret order first recruited in the South, was formed about 1855 by a Cincinnati physician to support proslavery policies and promote conquest of Mexico. During the Civil War the organization was introduced into Indiana as an order of Peace Democrats or Copperheads⁞ to oppose Lincoln's war policy. Connected with many acts of minor violence, under this name the order did not promote any serious plots against the Federal Government. It was reorganized in 1863 as the Order of American Knights and in 1864 as the Sons of Liberty, the last being involved in the Northwest Conspiracy⁽ᵛ.

[Mayo Fesler, Secret Political Societies in the North during the Civil War, *Indiana Magazine of History,* Vol. XIV.]

CHARLES H. COLEMAN

Knights of the Golden Horseshoe. Gov. Alexander Spotswood is one of the most picturesque figures in the annals of Virginia history, and the western journey that he undertook in the summer of 1716 is one of the romantic episodes connected with the exploration of the western wilderness. It was on Aug. 20 that he departed from Williamsburg⁞ upon his adventurous journey. Leisurely the governor and his associates wended their way in a westerly direction up the valley of the Rappahannock River. It was a picturesque cavalcade made up of gentlemen, rangers, pioneers and Indians, followed by the pack horses and servants. At night they bivouacked "under the canopy." The forests provided an abundance of fresh meat, and a marvelous assortment of liquors had been brought along. At the end of some two weeks the party gained the summit of the Blue Ridge. Here they gazed upon the beauty of the panorama which spread itself before their eyes. Here one toast after another was offered and drunk. Two peaks were named "Mt. George" and "Mt. Alexander." The Indian name of the Shenandoah River was changed to the Euphrates. Upon its banks was buried a bottle containing a document to the effect that the region was taken possession of in the name of the king. Upon his return Spotswood had some miniature gold horseshoes made; one of these was presented to each of the gentlemen who accompanied him. Hence the participants in the enterprise were designated Knights of the Golden Horseshoe.

[Philip A. Bruce, *The Virginia Plutarch,* Vol. I.]

JAMES E. WINSTON

Knights of the White Camelia arose in New Orleans in 1867 and spread rapidly over the South as an organization to maintain the supremacy of the white race, which was threatened by Radical Reconstruction⁞. Secret, it was organized similarly to the Ku-Klux Klan⁞ in councils along state, county and community lines.

[Walter Lynwood Fleming, *The Sequel of Appomattox;* William Archibald Dunning, *Reconstruction, Political and Economic.*]

HAYWOOD J. PEARCE, JR.

Know-Nothing Party. *See* American (or Know-Nothing) Party.

"Know Ye" Party. Because of Revolutionary War debts and a depreciated paper currency worth only sixteen cents on the dollar (1785–86), Rhode Island passed a forcing act compelling creditors to accept payment in paper money at face value. If they refused payment, the money could be deposited with the court, which then issued a certificate discharging the debt. These certificates were published in the newspapers and began with the words "Know Ye," which circumstance gave the name to the Paper Money or "Know Ye" party. The forcing act made business conditions so bad that the state was sometimes referred to as Rogue's Island but the act was finally declared unconstitutional as a result of the famous case of Trevett v. Weeden.^{qv}.

[John Fiske, *Critical Period of American History.*]

R. W. G. VAIL

Knox, Fort. From 1763 to 1777, Vincennes^{qv}, though under British sovereignty, had no civil government. In May, 1777, the town was officially occupied and a small stockaded Fort Sackville was built, but not permanently garrisoned. It was occupied for George Rogers Clark in 1778, but abandoned in December on the approach of a British force. It was captured by Clark, Feb. 23, 1779 (*see* Clark's Northwest Campaign) and named Fort Patrick Henry. A small garrison remained for a few years. In 1788, when the Northwest Territory^{qv} was organized, Maj. J. F. Hamtranck built a new fort and changed the name to Fort Knox, in compliment to the Secretary of War. The post was again abandoned after Wayne's victory at Fallen Timbers.^{qv}

[L. P. Powell, *Historic Towns of the Western States.*]

THOMAS ROBSON HAY

Knox v. Lee. *See* Legal Tender Cases.

Knoxville, Siege of (November, 1863). After the battle of Chickamauga Bragg's Army of Tennessee (C.) laid siege to the defeated Army of the Cumberland (U.) in Chattanooga^{qv}. Early in November Longstreet's (C.) command was detached toward Knoxville to capture Burnside (U.) and occupy Knoxville. Longstreet was delayed and Burnside retired into Knoxville without mishap. Longstreet arrived Nov. 17 and laid siege to the town. On Nov. 29 he unsuccessfully assaulted Fort Sanders. Hearing of Bragg's defeat at Chattanooga, Longstreet withdrew into winter quarters in southwest Virginia. In the spring he rejoined Lee's army (*see* Wilderness, Battles of the). Longstreet's detachment was unnecessary. Nothing had been accomplished beyond depriving Bragg, at a critical period, of needed men and a skillful leader.

[*Battles and Leaders of the Civil War*, Vol. III.]

THOMAS ROBSON HAY

Korea, War with. Undeclared hostilities in Korea in 1871 resulted from the murder of Americans, who had illegally entered closed ports, and from the subsequent refusal of Korean isolationists to open the Hermit Kingdom to foreign trade.

By ancient custom, violation of Korean seclusion was a capital offense. In August, 1866, W. B. Preston, an American merchant of Chefoo, despatched the armed schooner *General Sherman* to Ping-yang (now Heijo) in the extreme northwest of Korea to open trade. The schooner grounded on a sandbar in the Ping-yang River. The Koreans, acting by royal command, burned the ship and murdered the entire crew.

The U.S.S. *Shenandoah,* despatched from Chefoo to investigate, was denied all communication with the capital on the ground that it had not come "in obedience to direct instructions from the sovereign of the United States." On the advice of George F. Seward, Consul General at Shanghai, a punitive expedition was authorized. Rear Admiral John Rodgers was instructed to convey Frederick F. Low, American minister to China, to the Korean capital to demand an audience with the king and to secure satisfaction for the *General Sherman* affair. The *Monocacy, Palos* and four steam launches arrived at the mouth of the Han River (then called Salée, or Seoul, River) on May 26, 1871. Local officials were advised that the squadron was friendly and sought merely to survey the coast and to confer with the king. When no favorable reply was received, the ships started up river. On June 1, masked batteries situated on either side of the stream suddenly opened fire. Two Americans were wounded. The Americans returned the fire, silenced the batteries, and shelled the ravines in which the Koreans sought cover. The Korean loss is unknown. The *Monocacy* then struck a rock and was compelled to withdraw.

Guardian-General Li, of Fu-ping prefecture, formally complained of the American penetration of Korean waters, but declared himself too humble a person to dare communicate the American message to his king. The Americans answered by sending a second expedition, June 10, to reduce the Korean forts. Five batteries were taken and burned. In the battles, which occurred June 11, 250 enemy dead were left on the field. The American loss was three killed and nine wounded. But no satisfactory reply was given the American requests for an audience, and on July 2 Edward B. Drew, acting secretary of legation at Peking, announced that the squadron would withdraw to consult with Washington concerning further steps. No treaty was secured until 1882.

[*Diplomatic Correspondence of the United States,* 1867, Part I, pp. 426-428; *Foreign Relations of the United States,* 1871, pp. 327-373; Homer B. Hulbert, *The Passing of Korea.*]

HARRY EMERSON WILDES

Kossuth's Visit. Louis Kossuth, Hungarian patriot, landed in New York in December, 1851. His visit to the United States was in response to an invitation extended by a joint congressional resolution, signed by President Fillmore. Everywhere he went, from New York and Washington to St. Louis and New Orleans, he received great ovations, reminiscent of Lafayette's visit[*w*] a quarter of a century earlier. Although the American Government did not render official aid, Kossuth aroused a nationwide support in the revolutionary causes for which he was fighting.

[John W. Oliver, *Louis Kossuth's Visit to Western Pennsylvania;* also files of New York, Washington, Pittsburgh, and St. Louis newspapers for 1852.]

JOHN W. OLIVER

Koszta Case. Martin Koszta, following the Hungarian Revolution of 1848, fled first to Turkey, and then to the United States (*see* New Buda). After taking out first citizenship papers, he returned to Smyrna in Asiatic Turkey, where he was kidnapped by the Austrians. An American warship intervened, but his captors surrendered him to the French consul general. Upon strong representations by Secretary of State Marcy, Koszta was released.

[J. F. Rhodes, *History of the United States.*]

LOUIS MARTIN SEARS

Ku-Klux Act, one of the Force Acts[*w*], was passed April 20, 1871, as the result of Republican efforts, to give the President extraordinary powers to maintain the Republican governments in Southern states (*see* Ku-Klux Klan.) The President used his power to suspend the writ of habeas corpus[*w*] only once, Oct. 17, 1871, in nine South Carolina counties. Federal troops were to be used in destroying the "conspiracy," and cases were to be tried in Federal courts. The act was declared unconstitutional, 1882 (*see* U. S. v. Harris).

[Walter Lynwood Fleming, *Documentary History of Reconstruction,* Vol. II.]

HAYWOOD J. PEARCE, JR.

Ku-Klux Klan. As a movement, the Ku-Klux Klan was relied upon by Southern whites to recoup their prestige destroyed by Radical Reconstruction[*w*]. Spontaneously organized, May, 1866, in Pulaski, Tenn., by a group of young veterans to provide activity for their unoccupied energies, its potentiality as an agency for disciplining for-

ward freedmen[*w*] was soon discovered. Its quick flowering over the South was encouraged by unprecedented economic, political and social conditions.

At least one design of Radical Reconstruction was to abolish the once dominant political power of the agrarian South by attaching the recently enfranchised freedmen to the Republican party. With leading southern whites disfranchised and with elections conducted by Federal troops, state and local governments were soon in the inexperienced and unscrupulous hands of ex-slaves, carpetbaggers and scalawags[*qw*]. As a group, the Negroes had power far in excess of their ability and fell into wanton indiscretions. Long used to sharp social distinctions and to a semblance of honest government, southern whites turned to secret means to rectify this enormity which was protected by Federal bayonets.

At Nashville, in 1867, the Ku-Klux Klan was organized into the "Invisible Empire of the South" ruled by a "Grand Wizard"; the "Realms" (states), were ruled by "Grand Dragons"; the "Provinces" (counties) were headed by "Grand Titans"; the individual "Dens" were under the authority of a "Grand Cyclops." The "Dens" had couriers known as "Night Hawks." Secret, the organization's objectives were to protect the white people from humiliation by Negroes and to open the way for the reassertion of the supremacy of the whites politically and socially.

Most of the Klan's work was directed against obstreperous blacks. To intimidate the superstitious Negroes and to escape being identified by Federal troops, the Klansmen covered their bodies in white robes, masked their faces, wore high, cardboard hats, and rode robed horses with muffled feet. One of their favorite practices was to ride out of woods, surprising Negroes walking home in the darkness from meetings of the Union League[*w*], an organization which sought to direct the Negroes' votes into the proper Republican channels. The Klan invariably rode at night.

The Klan also intimidated carpetbaggers and scalawags and played unseen influential roles in many trials in the South. It was responsible for floggings and lynchings in extreme circumstances. The trying times led it into inexcusable acts on occasions. The Klan was formally disbanded in the spring of 1869, but it did not die.

The Klan was misunderstood in the North. It brought forth presidential reference in March, 1871. In April, 1871, a "joint Select Committee" of seven senators and fourteen representatives was selected "to inquire into the Conditions of Affairs in the late Insurrectionary States. . . ." In 1871 the Ku-Klux Act[*w*] was passed, empowering the President to use Federal troops and to suspend the writ of habeas corpus in an effort to abolish the "conspiracy" against the Federal Government in the South. The gradual reassumption of political power by the whites saw the activities of the Klan gradually decline.

[William G. Brown, *The Lower South in American History;* James M. Beard, *K. K. K. Sketches.*]

HAYWOOD J. PEARCE, JR.

Ku Klux Klan (20th century), THE, traced its inspiration to the intolerance of Know-Nothingism[w] rather than to the Ku-Klux Klan of the Reconstruction era. It was founded in Georgia in 1915 by Col. William J. Simmons but remained small and local until 1920 when two professional publicity agents, Edward Y. Clarke and Mrs. Elizabeth Tyler, began a nationwide membership campaign. Their slogan of "native, white, Protestant" supremacy found favor in the nationalistic, red-baiting, alien-hating United States of the 1920's, and by 1925 between four and five million Americans had enrolled. Fiery crosses, the symbol of the new order, were burned in every part of the country, and the hooded members denounced Negroes, bootleggers, Jews, pacifists, Bolshevists, internationalists, Catholics and evolutionists with equal impartiality. This rapid growth led eventually to the Klan's downfall, for popular interest precipitated a congressional investigation and newspaper exposures of its terroristic methods and of the floggings and killings for which it was responsible. Its decline was inadvertently hastened by politicians who used the Klan's ready-made political machine to elevate themselves to positions of power in Texas, Louisiana, Oklahoma, Maine, Kansas, Indiana and other states. Their corrupt administrations, particularly in Indiana, did much to discredit the order. By 1928, when the Klan abandoned its secrecy, most of its strength was gone.

[J. M. Mecklin, *The Ku Klux Klan: a Study of the American Mind.*]   RAY ALLEN BILLINGTON

Labadists, THE, followers of Jean de Labadie (1610–74), belonged theologically to the Calvinist school. A colony settled in Bohemia Manor, Md., in 1683 under the leadership of Augustine Herrmann, and another was established in New York.

[Bartlett B. James, *The Labadist Colony in Maryland.*]

JULIAN P. BOYD

LaBalme's Expedition (1780). Col. Mottin de la Balme appeared in the West in the summer of 1780. What credentials he carried is not known. He proposed a raid against the British at Detroit[w], and, enrolling in Illinois a body of the

French inhabitants, crossed to the Wabash where a party from Vincennes[w] joined him. They advanced in October to the Miami village, where Fort Wayne[w] now stands. This village and the traders' stores were pillaged; then, not feeling strong enough to attack Detroit, LaBalme began a hasty retreat. The Miami Indians under Little Turtle pursued and gave battle. Col. de la Balme was killed and his men dispersed. This defeat long rankled in the breasts of the French and aided in destroying French prestige in the western country.

[L. P. Kellogg, *British Régime in Wisconsin* and the *Northwest;* C. W. Alvord, ed., *Kaskaskia Records, Illinois Historical Collections,* V, *passim.*]

LOUISE PHELPS KELLOGG

LaBaye. *See* Green Bay.

LaBelle Famille, Battle of (July 24, 1759). Twelve hundred French and a large force of Indians under Captains Aubry and DeLignery marching down the portage road to relieve Fort Niagara[w] were intercepted at LaBelle Famille (Youngstown, N. Y.) by the British and Indians under Lt. Col. Massey and utterly routed, only 200 of the French escaping capture or death.

[Frank H. Severance, *An Old Frontier of France.*]

ROBERT W. BINGHAM

Labor movements, attitudes and legislation have been moulded by characteristic native influences. Skilled labor was long at advantage; an open frontier contributed to the fixation of individualistic self-reliance in our mores; unparalleled alien influx created division among wage earners (*see* Immigration) ; slavery[w] indelibly marked industrial relations in a rich region; the long agricultural predominance (*see* Agriculture) delayed urban industrialization (*see* Industrial Revolution) ; internal migrations of population and industry were ceaseless; division of state and Federal authority together with the conservatism of the courts conditioned labor legislation[w]. The failure of class conflict doctrines to take substantial root, the historic weakness of organized labor (*see* Labor Unions) and the tardy development of protective labor legislation are explicable in this background.

Over this century and a half labor's gains in productivity and living standards have been incalculable; work periods were sharply reduced and working conditions immeasurably improved (*see* Wages and Hours of Labor) . Today, protective legislation touches most phases of employment, but the greater part of this development is recent. Recurrent economic difficulties have engendered frequent wage loss and unemployment (*see* Business Cycles). Accelerated industrialization has accentuated problems of security, health and safety. Labor organization has proceeded fitfully; its beneficiaries, thus far, have been a minority, chiefly among the skilled.

Subsequent to the Revolution, colonial conditions persisted for many years. Maritime occupations remained important; the indenture*ᵂ* practice continued. Skilled artisans, strategically placed, organized sporadically to press their claims. The growing dominance of the merchant-capitalist provoked defensive tactics. Vexed by conspiracy charges, as illustrated in the Cordwainer cases, 1806–9 (*see* Philadelphia Cordwainers' Case), unions were not legalized until the 1840's. Expanding textile*ᵂ* interests sought, from the beginning of the republic, the labor of women and children. The necessity for the temporary employment of young females resulted in the peculiarly protected employment known as the Waltham system. However, as early as the 1830's the child and woman labor issues were agitated, sweatshop conditions were protested, and legislation was attempted in the 1840's (*see* Child Labor). A thirteen- and fourteen-hour day generally prevailed. The first appearance of a labor movement, the Workingmen's parties, late in the 1820's, sought a ten-hour day. Prior to the Civil War, the ten-hour day had not been generally achieved. Real wages as a rule increased to 1850; practices of hiring entire families, and truck systems of wage-payment were widespread. A wave of aggressive unionism appeared in the 1830's, which faded out following the Panic of 1837*ᵂ*; and during the subsequent decade futile reformist ventures attracted followings. Meanwhile unemployment and distress prevailed. In the 1840's, also, the immigrant entered the labor market in volume, providing the basis for permanent factory populations in eastern cities, a fact not overlooked at the time. A second period of unionism ended with the disturbance of 1857 (*see* Panic of 1857). Throughout these years, and later, the frontier*ᵂ* attracted the young and energetic.

The Civil War period witnessed several foreshadowing developments. During this decade, the eight-hour movement began; a short-lived contract labor*ᵂ* law called attention to the menace of induced immigration; the foundations were laid for future development of the Socialist movement; the shoemakers fought a losing battle with the machine, signalizing that loss of skills, later to harass many trades; reviving unions sought stable national organization, not achieved until three decades had passed. Massachusetts established the first state labor bureau in 1869. In the 1870's unemployment and distress provoked labor disorders; and secret labor organizations, most important among which was the Knights of Labor*ᵂ* (1869), contested with widespread blacklisting*ᵂ* of union members. In 1877 the Socialists*ᵂ* established a national party.

Between 1880 and 1900 industrialism and big business*ᵂ* became fully established. The speed, impersonality and large-scale features of modern industry became the established order. Industrial relations shifted accordingly. Problems of unregulated child and woman labor came to the fore, as did also those of safety and health in work places. Immigration mounted in volume; its new sources in the south and east of Europe created new competitive issues for labor. Labor's attitude became increasingly restrictionist. While the eight-hour day was gained by certain unions, the greater number of workers were working nine and one-half and longer periods well into the next century. State legislation, mostly subsequent to 1880, endeavored to regulate woman and child labor; state and Federal labor bureaus were organized. Wages and living conditions generally improved. The Knights of Labor, championing the cause of the unskilled, led a great labor movement in the 1880's. Controversy with the unions resulted in the formation of the American Federation of Labor*ᵂ* in 1886. Thereafter the Knights declined to extinction, and unionism thenceforth, while stable, remained confined chiefly to certain skilled trades. Unionism failed to penetrate huge ranges of industry, until the period of the 1930's.

Between 1900 and 1929 labor gained substantially in real wages. The shorter work-day movement also progressed. By 1929, many workers and industries had achieved an eight-hour day basis. However, such gains in shorter hours and living standards were not universal. Spectacular, indeed, was the phenomenal gain in labor's productivity in well nigh every industry and occupation. After 1900 achievements in labor legislation were likewise remarkable; child labor, woman's labor, minimum wage, accident compensation, safety laws*ᵠᵂ*, etc., were enacted by many states. However, difficulties with the courts and the disparities in state laws created numerous perplexities. Due largely to demands by organized labor, the Department of Labor*ᵂ* was established in 1913, its functions, as an administrative, investigatory, and mediatory agency have constantly widened. Organized labor, facing left-wing rivalries in the Industrial Workers of the World after 1905 and the Communists*ᵠᵂ* after 1920, also contended continually against antiunion employer groups, as well as many adverse court rulings, such as the Danbury Hatters[qv] (1908 and 1915), Buck Stove and Range[qv] (1911) and Bedford (1927) cases. Gains in membership during the World War were lost, when unionism perceptibly declined in the 1920's. This last decade was significantly changeful. New techniques in industrial relations[qv] appeared in employer's personnel and welfare activities, as well as in the company union. Then, too, marked shift in population and industry occurred. European immigration virtually ceased; the South industrialized rapidly; a heavy migration from rural to urban areas took place (see Urban Drift); meanwhile new products, industries and processes further altered the labor market. The automobile became popularized, and sports[qv] attained a new vogue. Child labor definitely diminished, but women crowded further into the economic activities of the nation. An unevenness in employment, wages and hours, industrial relations and legislation perturbed many thoughtful people.

With the collapse in 1929, years of crushing distress and unemployment[qv] followed. The trend toward shorter work periods continued, culminating in the Federal legislation of 1938 providing for an eventual forty-hour week. Federal participation in relief[qv] and labor legislation is the notable aspect of the 1930's. Public works, work-relief and relief programs, largely under Federal auspices, became conspicuous in the economic, political and social life of the country (see Works Progress Administration; Public Works Administration). A series of Federal statutes, on wages and hours, child labor, social security, employment offices, collective bargaining[qv] and other welfare measures became law with startling rapidity. The Supreme Court in a series of liberal rulings appeared to have altered the legal background of industrial relations (see National Labor Relations Board). State legislation, in the East and North, followed the trend. Under favoring legislation, organized labor doubled its membership, but schism within the A. F. of L. over organizational policy provoked the rise of a rival Congress of Industrial Organizations[qv].

[J. R. Commons and associates, *History of Labor in the United States;* U. S. Bureau of Labor Statistics, Bull. 604, *History of Wages in the United States: Colonial Times to 1928,* also, *Labor through the Century, 1833-1933;* Millis and Montgomery, *Economics of Labor,* Vol. I; J. R. Commons and J. B. Andrews, *Principles of Labor Legislation; Recent Social Trends,* Vol. II (article by Wolman and Peck), *Recent Economic Changes,* Vol. II (article by Leo Wolman); Lois MacDonald, *Labor and the American Scene;* N. J. Ware, *Labor in Modern Industrial Society.*]

HERBERT MAYNARD DIAMOND

Labor, Migratory. The migratory worker has long been familiar in the economic and social pattern of America. The itinerant mechanic of the colonies, the tramp printer of the 19th century and the harvest hand of the 20th, just as the removal migrant of today, have alike characterized an epoch. North America, of all areas, has exhibited this phenomenon most prominently. In recent years, the migrant has become a national concern; California feels the problem most acutely, for, like earlier migrations, the stream flows westward. An increasing family migration is replacing the male migrant of the past. Problems of living conditions, low and irregular earnings, education of children, resettlement and relief[qv] have followed upon this change.

The industrial and agricultural migrant may be distinguished. The former follows temporary and seasonal demands for labor in lumber camps, railroad and other construction projects, the oil fields, etc. How many are so engaged no one knows.

Another group, the habitual agricultural migrants, estimated at from 250,000 to 300,000, follow the crops: cotton, sugar-beet, fruit, berries, vegetables, etc. Formerly a great army followed the wheat crop, but mechanization has reduced this necessity. Regular paths of movement for such workers are discernible in nearly every region: in the Southeast, the Middle West and on the Pacific Coast.

The removal migrant, the child of depression, drought, dust, dying enterprise and technological change, became conspicuous in the 1930's. He and his family seek relocation in new surroundings. He constitutes a major contemporary problem; his numbers are considerable, but cannot be accurately measured.

[Migratory Labor: A Social Problem (containing map showing lines of movement), in *Fortune,* April, 1939; Paul S. Taylor, Migratory Farm Labor in the U. S., in *Monthly Labor Review,* March, 1937; N. A. Tolles, A Survey of Labor Migration between States, in *Monthly Labor Review,* July, 1937.]

HERBERT MAYNARD DIAMOND

Labor, The Department of, reached its present status as the tenth unified, recognized Cabinet Department on March 4, 1913. The signing of the act that created the department marked the completion of a struggle which had begun in 1865 to give labor representation in the Cabinet[qv]. Partial fulfillment of this need was effected in 1903 with the creation of the Department of Commerce and Labor, but this amalgamation was unsatisfactory to both divisions.

Following his efforts to establish the new department, William B. Wilson, a former congressman, was appointed the first Secretary of Labor by President Wilson. Mr. Wilson has been succeeded by three other secretaries during the career of the department: James Davis, incumbent under President Harding and President Coolidge; William Doak, incumbent under President Hoover; and Miss Frances Perkin, incumbent under President F. D. Roosevelt.

According to the act creating it, the duty of the Department of Labor is to "foster, promote, and develop the welfare of the wage earners of the United States; to improve their working conditions, and to advance their opportunities for profitable employment."

At the present time the Department of Labor includes eight main divisions with subordinate services under each.

(1) The Bureau of Labor Statistics, developed from the pre-1913 Bureau of Labor, collects and publishes pertinent data on wages and hours, employment, payrolls, cost of living, labor-union statistics, employer welfare work, productivity and conditions of labor, industrial accidents and hygiene and other allied subjects. This bureau is vital in giving a clear picture of labor and industrial relations and is the primary source of statistical information necessary in construction of new labor laws.

(2) The Conciliation Service, which has been continuously vigilant in efforts to promote industrial peace. Acting chiefly at the request of interested parties in disputes, its mediators, by means of neutral and unprejudiced recommendations on the issues, attempt to bring the disputants together.

(3) The Women's Bureau, created in 1920, studies and reports on the problems of women workers and attempts to improve their employment conditions.

(4) The Children's Bureau in its own field has carried on work similar to that pursued by the Women's Bureau. It is also interested in the entire field of child welfare apart from wages, hours and working conditions.

(5) The Immigration and Naturalization Services administer the laws which Congress has passed on those subjects.

(6) The Division of Labor Standards acts as a service agency to state labor departments, industrial commissions, and labor and civic groups for the improvement of working and other job conditions, and for the enactment into law of accepted standards on such matters. It also endeavors to co-ordinate safety movements and to stimulate the efforts of state labor agencies in industrial safety and industrial health programs.

(7) The Division of Public Contracts administers the Walsh-Healey Act[w], which gives the department the power to specify "prevailing" wage rates on work to be done under government contract.

(8) The Wage and Hour Division is the administrative arm of the Fair Labor Standards Act of 1938[w], and supervises the operation of the minimum wage and maximum hour provisions of the act.

[*Monthly Labor Review*, February, 1938.]

CARROLL R. DAUGHERTY

Labor Day. On May 8, 1882, Peter J. McGuire, carpenters' union founder, proposed to the New York City Central Labor Union the designation of an annual "labor day," recommending the first Monday in September as midway between July 4 and Thanksgiving Day. This resulted in a parade and festival of the New York group the following Sept. 5. Oregon (Feb. 21, 1887) declared the first holiday, thirty-one states having followed this example when Cleveland signed the national bill (June 28, 1894). As organized labor[w] became accepted, observance changed from great parades and demonstrations to relatively fewer workers' convocations which labor leaders used as public forums.

[P. J. McGuire, Labor Day—Its Origin and Significance, *American Federationist*, October, 1897; McGuire and others, The Day We Celebrate, *ibid.*, September, 1902; R. L. Guard, *ibid.*, September, 1925.]

IRVING DILLIARD

Labor in the Colonies. Slave labor, introduced in Virginia in 1619, in time became popular in the Tobacco and Rice Colonies, and, like indentured servitude and apprenticeship[qw], was found to some extent in all the colonies. Some of the involuntary servants, as convicts, declared William Eddis, "groaned beneath a worse than Egyptian bondage." Other servants, particularly in the voluntary group, were well treated. "There is no master almost," said John Hammond, "but will allow his servant a parcell of clear ground to plant some Tobacco in for himself." St. John de Crèvecœur believed that American mechanics served an apprenticeship even when there were no gilds, but Benjamin Franklin thought that apprenticeship was designed to secure a constant supply of labor.

The scarcity of labor is evident from the use of labor impressment and labor co-operation. In New England, legislation occasionally gave constables power to compel artificers and mechanics to work in the harvest fields of their neighbors in order to save crops. Under labor co-operation, the men of the neighborhood, well fed by the women, co-operated in the construction of a house, the erection of a barn, or the accomplishment of some other big task.

Hours of work were usually from daylight till dark. Remuneration was fair, due in part to the abundance of free or cheap land, but legislation at times interfered with wages. In Massachusetts a law in 1633 set a maximum wage of two shillings a day for most skilled mechanics when they boarded themselves and fourteen pence when their employers supplied board. Constables with two associates each were allowed to set wages for inferior workers in the same trades. Employers who paid more than the maximum wage, laborers who received more and workers who remained idle were subject to penalties. The penalty against the employers was soon dropped because of the scarcity of laborers, but when the penalty against the employees was removed, another law, in 1636, gave the towns jurisdiction in the determination of wages. When prices experienced a sharp decline in 1640, the legislators ordered the laborers under penalty of a fine to accept wages corresponding with reduced prices.

During most of the colonial period wages varied from twenty-five cents a day to four times that amount, the lowest wages usually including board. In 1748, according to Peter Kalm, a manservant of ability in Pennsylvania received from sixteen to twenty pounds a year in currency and a maidservant received half as much. Both received their food, but neither received clothing. Andrew Burnaby, about a decade later, likewise commented favorably on the prosperity of workers and the dearth of beggars. Crèvecœur, citing the best board at seven shillings a week, or "less than four shillings sterling," complained of the high wages demanded by laborers: "You must give them what they ask" and "Many times have I given from five to eight shillings per day to a cradler." Notwithstanding such reports, however, both beggars and workers in need of adequate wages lived in the colonies.

[J. R. Commons, *Documentary History of American Industrial Society;* U. B. Phillips, *Plantation and Frontier Documents, 1649-1863;* James Oneal, *The Workers in American History;* U. B. Phillips, *Life and Labor in the Old South;* G. S. Watkins, *Labor Problems.*]

WALTER W. JENNINGS

Labor Legislation and Administration. Colonial labor legislation took the form of occasional statutes regulating wages, punishment for refusal to work and the like, but such laws proved ineffectual. Early in the 19th century some states passed laws prohibiting labor organizations as conspiracies (*see* Philadelphia Cordwainers' Case), but these laws were soon modified and later repealed.

The earliest protective labor legislation had to do with child labor[q], Pennsylvania prohibiting in 1848 the employment of children under twelve in cotton mills. Since then other states have restricted child labor, the age limit has been raised and the list of prohibited employments extended. Today (1939) all states have some form of child-labor legislation, but their laws vary widely in effectiveness and manufacturers have been able to evade restrictions on the use of child labor by moving to states with lax laws. Efforts made by the Federal Government in 1916 and 1919 to enter this field were declared unconstitutional (*see* Child Labor Cases), and an amendment approved by Congress in 1924 has not yet been ratified. Some restrictions on the use of child labor were achieved by the National Industrial Recovery Act and by the 1938 Fair Labor Standards Act[qq].

The regulation of working conditions was undertaken in 1877 by Massachusetts and today is found in practically all states. Such laws include the requirement of protective devices, proper lighting, heating, ventilating, sanitary devices, etc. All states require seats for women workers and some provide rest periods as well.

The idea that employers should be held liable for accidents to their employees first took root in 1907 when Maryland passed an employer liability[q] act. This and subsequent acts by other states were held unconstitutional, but finally in 1917 a New York law was upheld. Today all states save Arkansas and Mississippi hold the employer liable in the event of an accident. Several states provide compensation for occupational diseases. Compulsory health insurance laws have also been suggested, but no state has yet enacted such legislation.

Until recently, legislation regulating the length of the working day was limited to women and children and to workers in industries where long hours are dangerous to the worker or to the public. Restrictions on hours of labor were characteristic of the N.R.A. codes. The present Fair Labor Standards Act limits hours to forty-four a week for all workers covered by the act, a limit that is to be gradually reduced to forty.

Massachusetts enacted the first minimum wage[q] law in 1912 and a number of other states followed suit. These laws were not questioned as applied to children, but were held unconstitutional as applied to men and women. In 1937 the Supreme Court upheld minimum wage legislation for women (*see* West Coast Hotel Company v. Parrish), and the new Fair Labor Standards Act provides minimum wages for all workers covered by the act.

The Federal Social Security Act[w] passed in 1935 and held constitutional in 1937 provides for unemployment insurance[w] in those states which agree to co-operate with the Federal Government; and old-age[w] pensions, financed by contributions from employers and employees, for all workers covered by the act. The Federal Government also contributes up to $15 per month to care for old people not covered by the act, providing the state contributes an equal amount.

Administration of state labor laws is commonly in the hands of various state boards or labor commissioners and necessitates a regular system of inspection. Enforcement has been both good and bad, depending upon the state and the particular law involved. The Federal Social Security Act is administered by the National Social Security Board and the Fair Labor Standards Act by a Federal Administrator assisted by industrial boards.

[J. R. Commons and J. B. Andrews, *Principles of Labor Legislation.*]

                                    R. E. WESTMEYER

Labor Parties. The relations of labor and politics in the United States have been conditioned largely by factors inherent in our form of government and in the social and economic conditions of the country. Working men could not make themselves effective, as a political force, until they secured the elective franchise[w] and had organized trade unions[w]. From 1827 to 1834, several workingmen's groups, having won the right to vote and to organize, achieved modest success in a few Eastern localities, but the Panic of 1837[w] caused their disappearance. In the depression periods after 1857 and 1873, "the trade unions were literally mowed down and swept out of existence." Labor parties were not possible under such adverse conditions. Workers' activity in the political field has also been restricted because of the lack of solidarity among that group, caused, in part, by the various nationalities, classes and religions found among the workers. Free land, higher wages, and, in the governmental field, various constitutional guarantees relieved the working class of economic and political discriminations found in other countries.

After the Civil War, labor became better organized. Since 1872 several independent labor parties have appeared in national politics. The National Labor and Reform party of 1872 failed utterly. In the next two decades several other abortive labor parties or groups organized; none of them lived. The Knights of Labor[w] was not an effective political organization; although devoting much effort to political issues, they neglected the economic realities of the organized labor movement. The American Federation of Labor[w] introduced a distinct "job consciousness" among craft unionists, concentrating interest and attention upon higher wages, shorter hours and collective bargaining[w]. Most labor rejected either direct political action or affiliation with the Socialist groups. Samuel Gompers fought to maintain the nonpartisan policy. Until 1906, with one exception, the Federation remained aloof from politics. In that year a new, bipartisan policy of leverage on existing parties was introduced. Organized labor has thus become a pressure group[w]. It maintains a powerful lobby and is concerned with party policies and platforms, party nominees and many phases of governmental administration. Labor endeavors, in politics, "to reward its friends and to punish its enemies"; it has secured favorable political action and has prevented unfavorable action by that policy. Labor is divided along many lines of conflict and has no separate political tradition.

Subsequent to the World War minor parties have had certain labor support. The Farmer-Labor[w] party of 1920 was composed partly of urban workers, while the candidacy of LaFollette[w] for President in 1924 received significant endorsement from organized labor. The Communist party[w] entered the national campaigns of 1928, 1932 and 1936. It has a traditional left-wing program, recently tempered by American conditions, and is supported by a few left-wing labor elements. Two contemporary third parties, the Farmer-Labor in Minnesota and the Progressive in Wisconsin, have important labor elements.

[M. R. Carroll, *Labor and Politics;* H. L. Childs, *Labor and Capital in National Politics;* S. Gompers, *Seventy Years of Life and Labor;* A. N. Holcombe, *Political Parties of Today;* S. M. Rosen, *Political Process;* S. A. Rice, *Farmers and Workers in American Politics.*]

                             THOMAS S. BARCLAY

Labor Unions. Labor organizations existed in the United States as early as the 17th century, but these were primarily societies of skilled workers who, like the guildsmen of mediæval Europe, exercised functions of laborer, master and merchant. Labor unionism, as that term is now employed, did not emerge in this country until the late years of the 18th and the early years of the 19th centuries.

The development of unionism falls roughly into several periods which have merged into one another almost imperceptibly as the unionization movement has progressed. The following classification is indicated as one surveys the growth of the American labor movement: 1792–1827, Birth of Trade Unionism; 1827–50, Prevalence of Utopianism and Political Experimentation; 1850–57, Beginning of Nationalization; 1857–66, Revival of Trade Unionism; 1866–81, Attempted Amalgamation; 1881–1935, Predominance of Craft Federationism; 1935–39, Struggle for Supremacy between Craft and Industrial Unionism.

The rapid industrial development following the Declaration of Independence in 1776 and the adoption of the Constitution in 1789 issued in economic changes full of significance for the wage-earning class. New machine processes resulted in increasingly severe competition; employers sought to lower wages and lengthen the working day. Consequently, between 1792 and 1827, numerous unions of skilled workers were organized for protection (*see* Philadelphia Cordwainers' Case). These associations were local, ephemeral and distinctly craft-conscious. Mutual and friendly benefits, such as sickness and funeral aid, were provided, and collective action in defense of standards of apprenticeship, hours and wages was adopted. This is appropriately known as the "germinal" period of the American labor movement.

Between 1827 and 1850, the labor movement was characterized by the development of trades' unions, which were intercraft associations, the establishment of communistic societies, and the growth of political activity. Beginning with the organization of the "Mechanics' Union of Trade Associations" in Philadelphia in 1827, the movement for city associations of craft unions and for national labor unions gained considerable momentum. The idea of labor solidarity was further advanced through workers' political parties formed in Philadelphia, New York, Boston and other industrial centers. Price inflation resulted in higher living costs and stimulated labor unrest. Among the reforms demanded by the labor movement were the ten-hour day, restriction of child labor^w, abolition of imprisonment for debt, direct election of public officials and abandonment of sweatshops.

The workers gradually reacted against political and social panaceas, and again emphasized immediate, practical economic and legislative changes, particularly higher wages, shorter hours, improved factory conditions and protective labor laws. Beginning with the formation of the Typographical Union^w in 1850, many groups of skilled craftsmen organized national trade unions in an effort to keep pace with the problems incident to a widening competitive market. The economic paralysis resulting from the Panic of 1857^w affected the labor movement adversely.

The nation had not recovered from the Panic of 1857 before the Civil War broke out. Increase in productive activity meant an increased demand for labor. Because of the shift of workers from peaceful pursuits to the armies of the South and the North, labor was scarce. Such circumstances were conducive to the revival of the labor movement, and numerous local unions were integrated into national organizations. The emphasis of the movement between 1857 and 1866 was upon such practical matters as wages, hours (*see* Wages and Hours of Labor), freedom of organization and recognition of collective bargaining^w. Strikes^w were numerous and the competitive struggle was greatly intensified toward the close of the period because of alien and Negro labor.

In the years 1866–81, the National Labor Union of Baltimore (1866) and the Knights of Labor^w (1869) were organized and there was considerable expansion of unionization. In 1868 the National Labor Union had approximately 640,000 members, while the Knights of Labor had, toward the close of the period, about 700,000. The latter union obtained great numbers from among the unskilled. The unity of all workers—skilled, semiskilled and unskilled—was the aim of the Knights of Labor. The economic and political program of American unionism in this period was too comprehensive for successful attainment, and this fact, combined with unwise leadership, excessive idealism and unskillful tactics, was disastrous to the movement.

Under the leadership of the American Federation of Labor^w, which was organized in 1886 out of the existing Organized Trades and Labor Unions of the United States and Canada (1881), the pendulum of labor action swung back again from political and economic idealism to practical considerations. The national trade unions, fearing domination by the Knights of Labor, assumed control of the A. F. of L. Independent trade unionism, based upon craft autonomy and immediate economic improvement as opposed to centrally controlled general labor unions cutting across craft lines and embracing political and social programs of an idealistic character, was the objective of the new federation. From 1886 to 1935 the A. F. of L. dominated the American labor movement, rising to the peak of its numerical strength during the World War.

In the postwar period the two depressions (1921–22; 1929–35) had a serious effect upon the A. F. of L. A setback to its expansion came in the period 1935–39, because of the emergence of the Congress of Industrial Organizations^w.

American unionism experienced unprecedented growth under the protection of the New Deal^w, characterized, however, by a bitter conflict between the C. I. O. and the A. F. of L. over the question of craft v. industrial unionism. The C. I. O. not only sought the unionization of workers on an industry-wide basis rather than a craft basis, but also unionized certain "white-collar" workers and the unskilled who hitherto had been neglected by the A. F. of L. In championing the cause of industrial unionism and the unskilled, the C. I. O. attained certain of the objectives embraced by the Industrial Workers of the World*qv*.

The most prominent general organizations in the contemporary American labor movement include the American Federation of Labor (1886); the Congress of Industrial Organizations (1935); the Big Four Railroad Brotherhoods (Locomotive Engineers, 1863), Railroad Conductors (1868), Locomotive Firemen and Enginemen (1873), and Brotherhood of Railway Trainmen (1883); and the Industrial Workers of the World (1905). The I. W. W. is extremely weak, numerically and financially. Independent unions of communists which once were affiliated with the Trade Union Unity League (1928–34) have practically surrendered their separate existence. The communists now constitute the militant minorities in the A. F. of L. and the C. I. O., their policy being to "bore from within" and gradually capture the labor movement and bring it under the direction of the Communist party*qv*. Revolutionary industrial unionism in the United States is championed by the I. W. W. and the communist minorities. Practical business unionism is promoted by the A. F. of L., the C. I. O. and the Big Four Brotherhoods. Revolutionary unionism seeks the destruction of the capitalist system; business unionism seeks increasing economic advantage within the framework of the existing social order. The most optimistic reports estimated the total numerical strength of American unionism in 1939 at 9,000,000 persons, but the total varies greatly with variations in industrial and business activity.

The policies and methods of labor organizations tend to differ according to their immediate and ultimate purposes. The weapons used in attaining their objectives generally include the strike, boycott, picketing*qv*, union label and political action. Except in revolutionary unions, the strike is used only as a last resort, that is, only when grievances are not adjusted peacefully through joint conference. Boycotts and picketing are used to win strikes and compel employers to enter into collective bargaining. When collective bargaining is established, the terms of employment are embodied in the trade agreement, which usually runs for a period of one or two years.

The policy of the I. W. W. is against any such agreement with an employer, the sole object of the organization being to hasten the overthrow of capitalism*qv*. Restriction of output, limitation of apprentices, prevention or control of the introduction of machinery and the closed shop*w* are among the other traditional economic practices of American unionism.

Generally speaking, the political action of the American labor movement is indirect, that is, it consists of the "election of labor's friends and the defeat of labor's enemies." Usually, attainment of this aim is sought in and through the established Republican and Democratic parties. At various times in the nation's history attempts have been made to organize local, regional and national labor parties*qv*, but with little success. The present tendency is to organize state leagues for political action in order to consolidate the labor vote and bring more effective pressure upon existing political parties.

In addition to their activities in the industrial and the political fields, American trade unions have sought to improve the status of their members through sickness, unemployment and old-age benefits, educational programs and co-operative enterprises in production, distribution and finance. These activities have never attained great success. The provision of social insurance under governmental administration will make such programs of less importance in the future. The co-operative movement has never registered significant achievements among the American wage-earning class and is not likely to do so for a long time to come.

[F. T. Carlton, *History and Problems of Organized Labor;* G. G. Groat, *Organized Labor in America;* Herbert Harris, *American Labor;* R. F. Hoxie, *Trade Unionism in the United States.*]   GORDON S. WATKINS

Labrador Fisheries, THE, off the coast of Labrador, long ago attracted the cod and whale*qqv* fishermen of New England. The Definitive Treaty of Peace, 1783*w*, granted to American fishermen liberal privileges along the Labrador coast. Soon many codfishing vessels sailed each year from New England to Labrador. Restrictions which were placed later on American use of English colonial fisheries little affected those of Labrador, but the codfishery there no longer enjoys its former prosperity. Fishermen from New England still (1939) make the trip to Labrador, but their numbers are small compared with those engaged in the industry more than one hundred years ago.

[W. T. Grenfell and others, *Labrador, the Country and the People;* Raymond McFarland, *A History of the New England Fisheries.*]   F. HARDEE ALLEN

Lachine, Iroquois Raid at, occurred Aug. 4–5, 1689, not far from the garrisoned forts of Rémy, Roland and La Présentation (*see* Ogdensburg). Though the Indians massacred the settlers, the French officer, Subercase, was prevented by Gov. Denonville from offering resistance. The Indians departed shouting, "Onontio, you deceived us and now we have deceived you."

[Winsor, *Narrative and Critical History of America.*]
ARTHUR C. PARKER

Lacolle Mill (Canada), The Battle of (March 30, 1814). On the Lacolle River, five miles north of the international boundary, was a stone mill occupied by approximately 200 British troops. Taking a force of 4000 from Plattsburg^{qv}, N. Y., Maj. Gen. James Wilkinson marched against this outpost. The defenders stoutly resisted. With slight losses they repulsed his ill-directed attack. Threatening weather and 200 casualties caused Wilkinson to retreat.

[J. R. Jacobs, *Tarnished Warrior.*]
JAMES RIPLEY JACOBS

Laconia Grant, THE (Nov. 17, 1629). As Capt. John Mason and Sir Ferdinando Gorges were dividing their Province of Maine^{qv}, Champlain reached London a prisoner. They saw a chance to secure part of the rich fur trade^{qv} formerly held by France, and obtained a new grant of land from the Council for New England^{qv}. The area, believed to contain many lakes, was named the Province of Laconia. Its rather indefinite limits ran from Lake Champlain west halfway to Lake Ontario, and north to the St. Lawrence, embracing the land west and northwest of Maine. The proprietors were authorized to cross other lands under the Council, and to take as a coastal station as much as 1000 acres of ungranted land. Mason, Gorges and six others formed the Laconia Company to develop the grant, and sent settlers to the Piscataqua. Several attempts were made to find a trade route to Laconia; none were successful, and the grant was never located. A second patent of Nov. 3, 1631, included land on both banks of the Piscataqua and the Isles of Shoals^{qv}. The company failed to pay, and in 1634 it was dissolved and its assets divided among the partners.

[C. W. Tuttle, *Captain John Mason;* W. H. Fry, *New Hampshire as a Royal Province.*] HERBERT W. HILL

Ladd's Peace Plan. In his *Essay on a Congress of Nations,* Boston, 1840, William Ladd, a New England philanthropist and reformer, proposed a periodic congress of nations for formulating international law and for promoting the general welfare of nations, and for a related but independent court for settling disputes by judicial decision or by arbitration. The plan proposed a league of nations, not a mere league of sovereigns; and it was designed to promote peace, not merely to preserve the *status quo.* Its essential features were in part realized in the Hague Conferences, the World Court and the League of Nations^{qv}.

[Ladd's essay was reprinted, with an excellent introduction by James Brown Scott, New York, 1916. See also Dr. Georg Schwarzenberger, *William Ladd;* Merle Curti, *The American Peace Crusade, 1815–1860.*]
MERLE CURTI

Ladies' Repository, The, a monthly periodical devoted to "literature and religion," was published by the Methodist Book Concern from 1841 through 1876 (36 vols.), and continued for four more years as the *National Repository.* Started at Cincinnati under the editorship of Rev. L. L. Hamline, it speedily became prosperous, at one time boasting 30,000 subscribers.

[W. H. Venable, *Beginnings of Literary Culture in the Ohio Valley.*] EUGENE H. ROSEBOOM

Lady Elgin Disaster. Early in the morning of Sept. 7, 1860, the passenger steamer *Lady Elgin,* loaded with excursionists returning from Chicago to Milwaukee, collided with the lumber schooner *Augusta* and sank. The collision occurred about ten miles off Waukegan, Ill. Of the *Lady Elgin's* 393 passengers and crew, only ninety-six were saved.

[A. T. Andreas, *History of Chicago.*]
PAUL M. ANGLE

Lady's Book, The. See Godey's Lady's Book.

LaFamine, Treaty of (Sept. 5, 1684). Gov. LaBarre of New France, in charge of an expedition against the Senecas, was met at LaFamine (mouth of Salmon River) by the Onondaga orator, Otreouati (Hateouati) and fourteen deputies from the Onondaga, Oneida and Cayuga nations^{qv}. Otreouati countered all of LaBarre's accusations, demanded the withdrawal of the army, and reserved the right to make war upon the Illinois^{qv}. Although enraged by this defiance, sickness throughout the army forced LaBarre to make peace and withdraw his army to Montreal.

[E. B. O'Callaghan, *The Documentary History of the State of New York.*] ROBERT W. BINGHAM

Lafayette, Fort (1812–68), was situated on a shoal at the Narrows entrance to New York harbor. Begun in 1812, it was adapted only for guns of small caliber. During the Civil War it was used as a prison for political offenders, several thousand of whom were confined there at one period. Impaired by fire in 1868, it was re-placed by fortifications mounting considerably larger armament.

[*Report*, Chief of Engineers, U. S. Army, 1880; *House Ex. Docs.*, 46th Congress, 3rd Session, 1880-81, Vol. III; W. B. Hesseltine, *Civil War Prisons*.]

W. B. HESSELTINE

"Lafayette, We Are Here." On July 4, 1917, Paris enthusiastically celebrated the American Independence Day. A battalion of the 16th U. S. Infantry was reviewed by President Poincaré and then marched to the Picpus Cemetery, where several speeches were made at the tomb of Lafayette, the principal one by Mr. Brand Whitlock. Gen. Pershing was present but spoke very briefly, having designated Col. Charles E. Stanton, of his staff, to speak for him. The historic words uttered on that occasion, "Lafayette, nous voilà," translated as, "Lafayette, we are here," have been popularly, but erroneously, attributed to Gen. Pershing. He himself has stated positively that they "were spoken by Col. Stanton, and to him must go the credit for coining so happy and felicitous a phrase."

[John J. Pershing, *My Experiences in the World War*.]

JOSEPH MILLS HANSON

Lafayette Escadrille, an organization of American volunteers in French Aviation Service, was formed in April, 1916, as Escadrille Americaine No. 124. On Nov. 16, 1916, at the protest of the German ambassador, the name was changed to "Volunteer Escadrille No. 124" and on Dec. 6, 1916, it became known as "Lafayette Escadrille," continuing as such until Jan. 1, 1918, when it entered our army as the 103rd Pursuit Squadron.

[Georges Thenault, *The Story of the Lafayette Escadrille*.]

ROBERT S. THOMAS

Lafayette's Visit to America. In February, 1824, President Monroe invited the Marquis de Lafayette to visit the United States. Lafayette accepted, but would not permit a government vessel to be sent for him, as Congress wished to do. He sailed, however, in an American ship, and reached New York Aug. 16, 1824. He was so reduced in fortune that he feared he could not meet the expense of a long stay, but to his surprise, he was not permitted to pay for anything while here. After a tumultuous reception in New York and a four days' stay, he toured New England, including Albany, N. Y., visited the Harvard Commencement, returned to New York twice, then moved slowly southward through Philadelphia and Baltimore, making leisurely stays everywhere. After a long stop at Washington, where all government officials

joined in doing him honor, he visited Jefferson at Monticello and went down through the Coast states, then westward to New Orleans. Coming northward into the Middle West, he suffered shipwreck when a steamboat sank with him on the Ohio below Louisville but, despite his age, he came through the disaster without severe shock. His progress everywhere was one continuous ovation; bands and military escorts went miles along the roads to meet him, banquets and fetes greeted him at every stop. He visited Braddock's Field, Lake Erie, Niagara^{qv} and other American war scenes, returned to Boston for the celebration of the fiftieth anniversary of the Battle of Bunker Hill^{qv}, visited New York for the fourth time, and finally returned to Washington, from which he sailed for home on Dec. 7, 1825, having spent nearly sixteen months in this country. A steamboat carried him from Washington to the frigate *Brandywine*, which awaited him at the mouth of the Potomac, and on that vessel he returned to France. Congress made him a gift of $200,000 in cash and a township of land.

[*Magazine of American History*, May, 1881; John Foster, *Sketch of General Lafayette on His Late Visit to the United States*.]

ALVIN F. HARLOW

LaFollette (Progressive) Party. As a part of the general progressive movement^{qv} in the United States, led by Sen. Robert M. LaFollette of Wisconsin, there was formed in 1922 the Conference for Progressive Political Action, a loose federation of various progressive groups in the country, such as the farmers' Nonpartisan League, the Farmer-Labor party, the Single Tax League^{qv} and several labor organizations, including particularly the sixteen railroad brotherhoods. The purpose at first was not to organize another political party, but to secure the election of progressives to Congress, regardless of party, and to promote the enactment of progressive legislation.

A national convention was held in Cleveland, July 4–6, 1924, at which, in view of the dissatisfaction with the presidential nominations made by both major parties, Sen. LaFollette was nominated or "endorsed" for President and Burton K. Wheeler, Democrat, of Montana, for Vice-President. The new party, officially named the Progressive party, although generally known as the LaFollette party, was also endorsed by the Socialist party and by the American Federation of Labor^{qv}. The platform was largely a reproduction of LaFollette's personal views on public questions, with particular emphasis on the needs of agriculture and labor. It polled nearly five million votes (about 17%), chiefly in the Middle and Far West, displaced the Democratic party as the second party in eleven states and carried Wisconsin. The results were, however, disappointing to LaFollette and the other leaders of the movement, plans for a permanent party organization were abandoned, and Sen. LaFollette himself died soon thereafter.

[Harold L. Varney, An American Labor Party in the Making, *Current History*, Vol. XX; John M. Nelson, The LaFollette-Wheeler Candidacy, *Yale Review*, Vol. XIV; Fred E. Haynes, The Significance of the Latest Third Party Movement, *Mississippi Valley Historical Review*, Vol. XII; Richard Boeckel, Third Party Movements, *Editorial Research Reports*, May 16, 1928.]

                                        CLARENCE A. BERDAHL

LaFollette's Seamen's Act, also known as the Furuseth Act, was approved March 4, 1915. It applied to crews of vessels registered in the United States and to those of foreign countries while in United States ports. It was designed to improve living and working conditions on board ship, to attract American citizens to the sea and to provide greater safety for all on board vessels. Among its more important provisions were those abolishing imprisonment for desertion; reducing penalties for disobedience or neglecting to join or quitting a vessel; restricting the payment of seamen's wage allotments to certain relatives; regulating hours of work at sea and in port; fixing minimum scale and quality of daily food requirements; regulating the payment of wages; requiring a certain number and type of lifeboats; increasing the number of able seamen to 65% of the total crew exclusive of officers and seamen; and requiring 75% of the members of each ship department to understand the language spoken by the officers.

[U. S. Department of Labor, Bureau of Labor Statistics, *International Seamen's Union of America, A Study of Its History and Problems*, 1923.]   HOBART S. PERRY

LaGalette, Fort. Shortly after the foundation of the Mission of La Presentation, at the mouth of the Oswegatchie, near the modern city of Ogdensburg[q], in 1749, Father Picquet, founder of the mission, persuaded the governor of Canada to build a substantial fort, as a protection for Montreal against invasion from the Oswegatchie. One of the last French strongholds in New York, it was captured by Gen. Amherst in 1760.

[Francis Parkman, *Montcalm and Wolfe*.]
                                              A. C. FLICK

Laird Rams were two double-turreted, ironclad steamers, one equipped with a ram, and each armed with four nine-inch rifled guns, which were ordered in 1862 by James D. Bulloch, Confederate naval agent, from John Laird and Sons, shipbuilders, of Birkenhead, England. They were

designed for use in breaking the Federal blockade[q]. The North, which then had no ships able to cope with them, feared that the British government would allow them to put to sea. Work was begun on them in July, 1862. John Slidell, a Confederate agent, fearing their seizure by the British, transferred them to Messrs. Bravay and Company, a French firm, but arranged for their resale to the Confederacy after they were beyond British jurisdiction. They were both launched in the summer of 1863.

On Sept. 1, 1863, Lord John Russell, British Foreign Secretary, wrote Charles Francis Adams, American minister, that his government could not interfere with the vessels but would watch them carefully. Adams replied on Sept. 5 in a letter with this historic sentence: "It would be superfluous in me to point out to your lordship that this is war." Meanwhile, on Sept. 3, Russell, suspecting that the ironclads were destined for the Confederacy, and influenced by the Northern victories of Gettysburg and Vicksburg, ordered them detained. In October, 1863, they were formally seized by the British government, which, in May, 1864, purchased them for the Royal navy. (*See also* Alabama Claims.)

[Mountague Bernard, *A Historical Account of the Neutrality of Great Britain during the American Civil War;* C. F. Adams, *Charles Francis Adams.*]

                                          LOUIS H. BOLANDER

Laissez-Faire. The term originated among the disciples of the 18th century school of economists in France known as the Physiocrats, and means "let things alone." As conceived by the Physiocrats and expanded by the English economist Adam Smith, the doctrine was a reaction against restrictions imposed upon trade by the mediæval guilds and the Mercantilism[q] of the 16th and 17th centuries. The theory rests upon the assumption that the economic well-being and progress of society are assured when individuals are free to apply their capital and their labor without hindrance by the State. In obedience to his own self-interest the individual, it is believed, always will do that which conduces to his own best advantage and the general well-being of the community. State intervention through such agencies as protective social legislation and restrictions upon freedom of trade is condemned as socially injurious. The doctrine of *laissez-faire* involves not only a negative social policy of nonintervention but also a positive philosophy which recognizes a natural order in which harmony of individual and social interests is the rule.

In the United States there has never been an undivided allegiance to this doctrine, either theoretically or practically. The tariff[q], which has been an established policy almost from the inception of American sovereignty, is a contravention of the principle of individualism expressed in the doctrine of *laissez-faire*. The same can be said concerning the antitrust legislation represented in the Sherman Act (1890) and the Clayton Act (1914)*qw*; and the numerous examples of protective labor legislation, such as minimum-wage laws, workmen's compensation statutes, hours legislation and social security laws*qw*.

[Henry C. Adams, *Relation of the State to Industrial Action;* O. F. Boucke, *Laissez-Faire and After;* John Dewey, *Individualism Old and New.*]

GORDON S. WATKINS

Lake Champlain, Early French and English Clashes on. Both the English and the French, augmented by their Indian allies, found Lake Champlain a convenient warpath for predatory expeditions into enemy territory. As early as the 1640's the French were fortifying the Richelieu River at the northern end of the lake. French expeditions swung down the lake to the west against Schenectady and to the east against Deerfield*qw* and other New England outposts. The English retaliated. As time went on the rival expeditions began to assume larger and more organized proportions. England launched three successive but ineffectual campaigns northward (1690, 1709, 1711) in which land forces under Winthrop and Nicholson were to co-operate by way of Lake Champlain with sea forces sent into the St. Lawrence. The establishment of Fort Carillon at the southern end of the lake in 1756 gave the French control of the pathway until Gen. Amherst drove out their garrisons in 1759 (*see* Ticonderoga, Operations at) .

[P. S. Palmer, *History of Lake Champlain.*]

LEON W. DEAN

Lake Champlain as an Indian Thoroughfare. An important link in the natural highway between the St. Lawrence and Hudson rivers was Lake Champlain. Archæologists find that archaic Algonkians*qw* and ancient Esquimolike people passed along the lake several thousand years ago. An old tradition has it that the Mohawks*qw* left their lands in Canada after a quarrel with the Adirondacks, who held them subject, and entered New York by this route. In 1609 Champlain*qw* found the lake a no man's land between Algonkins and Iroquois*qw*, though his Algonkin companions told him that the Iroquois occupied its eastern shore. A Dutch map of 1616 calls it the "Sea of the Iroquois." Local tradition states that Split Rock marked the dividing line between Algonkin and Iroquois.

As soon as the Indian acquired the "thunder poles" of the white man, the lake became an even bloodier warpath. The well-organized Iroquois followed it to drive their Algonkin and Huron enemies to the very gates of Quebec. During the wars between the French and British, the practice of paying the Indians for scalps did not help matters. Small parties of red men used the lake to raid the villages of the enemy, whether they lay in Canada or in New York and New England.

[W. M. Beauchamp, *A History of the New York Iroquois.*]

EDWARD P. ALEXANDER

Lake Champlain in the French and Indian War. Fort St. Frederic, built by the French in 1731 and serving as a base for French and Indian raids, had long been "a sharp Thorne" in the flesh of New England and New York. With the outbreak of hostilities between England and France in 1754, St. Frederic became one of the prime objectives of British military policy. Col. William Johnson, the New Yorker who was so popular with the Iroquois*qw*, was sent against the fort. At the southern end of Lake George*qw*, on Sept. 8, 1755, he repulsed Baron Dieskau, but failed to follow up his advantage by moving against Crown Point*qw*. The expedition has well been described as "a failure disguised under an incidental success."

In the fall of 1755 the Marquis de Lotbinière laid out a fort at Ticonderoga*qw* as an outpost for St. Frederic, but the British campaign of 1756 under Lord Loudoun and Winslow did not get beyond Fort William Henry, which was situated at the southern end of Lake George. Meanwhile, partisan warfare was at its height: not a week passed without the French sending "a band of *hairdressers*"*qw* against the New England frontier; and Maj. Robert Rogers*qw* and his Rangers were also harassing the French posts. On March 19, 1757, the French under Rigaud failed to take Fort William Henry*qw*, but, on Aug. 9, Lt. Col. Monro, after a week's siege, was forced to surrender the fort to Montcalm. The French Indians then massacred a part of the garrison.

Gen. James Abercromby's expedition against Ticonderoga met disastrous defeat on July 8, 1758, but in the next year Sir Jeffery Amherst compelled Bourlamaque to blow up the French forts at Ticonderoga and Crown Point and to retreat to Isle aux Noix at the northern end of Lake Champlain. After a long delay Amherst moved against this place, but operations had to be suspended late in October on account of inclement weather. In 1759 Rogers and his Rangers conducted their daring raid on the village of the

St. Francis[w] Indians, and in the following year there were attacks and reprisals about the French forts at Isle aux Noix, St. Johns and Chambly. Gen. Haviland, in August, 1760, finally drove Bougainville and the French from Lake Champlain, and the fall of Montreal[w], on Sept. 8, brought the fighting to an end.

[W. H. Crockett, *A History of Lake Champlain;* Francis Parkman, *Montcalm and Wolfe.*]

EDWARD P. ALEXANDER

Lake Champlain in the Revolutionary War. The Hudson-Champlain line had for more than a century been the chief strategic highway of the continent, and both Americans and British were determined to control it. The Green Mountain Boys seized Ticonderoga and Crown Point in May, 1775, but were unable to hold St. Johns[qw]. During the summer the Montgomery Expedition against Canada, using Crown Point as a base, moved on to capture St. Johns and Montreal but was repulsed at Quebec on Dec. 31 (*see* Canada, American Invasion of). In the spring of 1776 Benjamin Franklin, Samuel Chase, Charles Carroll of Carrollton and Father John Carroll passed through the Champlain Valley on their way to Montreal to seek without success to win Canada to the American cause (*see* Canada, Attempts to Win, to American Revolution). Gen. Carleton (Br.), in the following autumn, moved up the lake with a strong flotilla, but was delayed off Valcour Island[w] by the determined stand of Benedict Arnold and his seagoing farmer boys, so that cold weather set in before the British could take the forts.

In 1777 Burgoyne's well-equipped army appeared on the lake (*see* Burgoyne's Invasion), soon compelled St. Clair to evacuate Ticonderoga, beat the retreating Americans at Hubbardton[w] and captured Skenesborough. As Burgoyne marched on to eventual defeat at Saratoga[w], Col. John Brown, of Pittsfield, failed, in September, to wrest Ticonderoga from Gen. Powell and to capture the supplies guarded by Capt. Aubrey on Diamond Island in Lake George. After Saratoga the British continued to control the Champlain Valley, though they did not usually garrison the forts. Gen. Haldimand[w] was, in 1780, seeking to induce Vermont[w] to join the British. In the same year Sir John Johnson passed up the lake on his way to raid the Mohawk Valley, and during 1781 a British fleet cruised about. In 1783, while awaiting the signing of the peace treaty, Washington visited Ticonderoga and Crown Point.

[W. H. Crockett, *A History of Lake Champlain;* Hoffman Nickerson, *The Turning Point of the Revolution.*]

EDWARD P. ALEXANDER

Lake Champlain in the War of 1812. Lake Champlain was teeming with martial activity during the War of 1812 as in previous wars, with England threatening by both land and water from the north and considerable bodies of United States regulars and militia, supported by a naval force, being stationed at Burlington, Vt., Plattsburg, N. Y., and vicinity.

In command of the American fleet was Lt. Thomas Macdonough[w]. On June 3, 1813, the Americans lost two vessels to the English. The next month Col. John Murray, with over 1400 British troops and marines, destroyed several military buildings near Plattsburg. A few days later, Aug. 2, three British ships appeared off Burlington, but were driven off by Macdonough's ships and the shore battery. At about the same time the English burned the abandoned barracks and other government property at Swanton. Macdonough sought out the English fleet, but it declined battle. In a thrust by Col. Isaac Clark several of the enemy were killed and 101 taken prisoners. Gen. Hampton, with several thousand men, crossed the border and was defeated by a smaller body of English. On the morning of March 30, 1814, the American Army, 4000 strong, advanced for an unsuccessful attack upon Lacolle Mill[w].

Meanwhile Macdonough had gone into winter quarters at Vergennes in Otter Creek and was strengthening his fleet. On April 14 the British fleet attacked the battery at the mouth of the creek and was repulsed. Land skirmishes during the summer were frequent. In the fall came the general advance of the English, the decisive engagement taking place Sept. 11, 1814, when Sir George Prevost led upwards of 14,000 British troops against an American force of some 4700 regulars and militia under Gen. Macomb, who had taken up their position on the south bank of the Saranac River near Plattsburg[w]. At the same time the British fleet attacked Macdonough off near-by Cumberland Head. The American land force and naval force were both victorious, and the outcome had an important bearing on the peace which was signed at Ghent[w] on Dec. 24.

[W. H. Crockett, *A History of Lake Champlain.*]

LEON W. DEAN

Lake George, Battle of (1755). With 3500 provincials, William Johnson (then Major General of New York militia) moved north against Crown Point[w] in midsummer, 1755. At the southern end of Lake George, his encamped force was threatened by Baron Dieskau commanding 1700 French and Indians. Sept. 8, Johnson sent 1200 men south to locate the French. Division proved costly; the French drove the surprised Americans back with severe losses, killing Col. Ephraim Williams and Hendrik, Mohawk chieftain.

At the camp barricades the reunited provincials beat off repeated charges; the day ended with the French retreating. Both commanders were wounded, Dieskau captured. Provincial forces lost 260 killed, 91 wounded; the French about as many, including most of the regulars. The battle is regarded as a draw. Johnson could not proceed, and capture of their commander stopped the French offensive.

[*Papers of Sir William Johnson*, Vol. I; Pound and Day, *Johnson of the Mohawks*.]   ARTHUR POUND

Lake of the Woods Boundary Problem, THE, was projected by the Definitive Treaty of Peace, 1783[w], which provided that the northern boundary should extend westward from the "most northwestern point" of the Lake of the Woods to the Mississippi. Since such a line was geographically impossible, it was agreed in 1818 that the boundary should be drawn south from the northwest point of the lake to the 49th parallel—an arrangement that resulted in the creation of the Northwest Angle[w].

[*Final Report of the International Joint Commission on the Lake of the Woods Reference*, 1917.]   T. C. BLEGEN

Lakes, Great. *See* Great Lakes; Ontario, Lake; Erie, Lake; Huron, Lake; Michigan, Lake; Superior, Lake.

Lakes-to-Gulf Deep Waterway. The portage between Lake Michigan and the Mississippi River by way of the Des Plaines-Illinois River was known to the French fur traders of the 17th century: in 1673 Jolliet[w] and Marquette returned to Mackinac[w] by the Illinois River and Chicago portage[w]. In 1810 Peter B. Porter proposed connecting the Great Lakes with the Mississippi; in 1822 Congress passed the first canal act; construction was actually begun in 1836 and the Illinois and Michigan Canal[w] completed in 1848. In 1871 the canal was enlarged and deepened across the Summit from Chicago to Lockport, permitting withdrawal of more water through the Chicago River. This produced the first diversion of water from Lake Michigan at Chicago by gravity, and was the forerunner of the diversion through the Sanitary and Ship Canal sponsored by the Chicago Sanitary District[w] created in 1889. Although sewage disposal was probably uppermost in the minds of Chicago until the completion of the Sanitary Canal in 1900, the problem of the Lakes-to-Gulf Deep

Waterway was doubtless in the minds of the United States engineers and those Mississippi Valley ports most likely to benefit by it. In 1906 the United States Supreme Court decided that Chicago was in the Mississippi watershed.

The Lakes-to-Gulf Deep Waterway project received a tremendous impetus during the conservation movement of 1908. At that time the Illinois constitution was amended to permit the expenditure of $20,000,000 to provide an adequate waterway across the state. The failure of the Illinois-Michigan Canal to provide ocean transportation rates led many waterways enthusiasts to adopt the slogan "Twenty-Four Feet Through the Valley." It was soon discovered that such a stupendous undertaking would be prohibitive and the depth was finally shaved down to nine feet. The efforts of Illinois to achieve a nine-foot channel were aided by the Federal Government in 1930 when Congress voted to complete the nine-foot program by authorizing $7,-500,000 for constructing four dams below Lockport—at Brandon Road, Dresden Island, Marseilles and Starved Rock—a work which was completed in 1933. Subsequently locks were constructed at Peoria, La Grange and Kampsville. Although handicapped by several bad stretches of river between Grafton at the mouth of the Illinois, and Cairo at the confluence of the Ohio and the Mississippi, the Lakes-to-Gulf Deep Waterway may be said to have been inaugurated in 1933. The decrease in the diversion of water from Lake Michigan on Jan. 1, 1939, may cause alterations and further expenditures if the present nine-foot channel is to be maintained. The construction of 2000-ton steel barges and powerful tunnel-type oil-burning towboats, the erection of modern terminals with the latest in transfer equipment, and the maintenance of regular schedules, are features of the Lakes-to-Gulf Deep Waterway project as well as other inland waterways improvements.

[B. L. Ashton, *The Geonomic Aspects of the Illinois Waterway*; G. F. Barrett, *The Waterway from the Great Lakes to the Gulf of Mexico*; Deeper Rivers: The Mid-West is Getting Them, in *Fortune*, November, 1931.]

WILLIAM J. PETERSEN

"Lame-Duck" Amendment is the name applied to the Twentieth Amendment (1933) to the Constitution of the United States, abolishing the "lame-duck" session of Congress—so-called because it included numerous members who had failed of re-election (the "lame ducks") a month before the "short" session opened in December of even-numbered years. Yet the law permitted them to sit and function until their term ended on the 4th of March following, while a newly elected Congress, with a fresh popular mandate, stood by inactive and unorganized for (usually) thirteen months. In the last lame-duck session, opening in December, 1932, there were 158 defeated members sitting in the Senate and House. The Amendment, sponsored by Sen. George W. Norris of Nebraska, did away with the lame-duck session by moving back the day on which terms of senators and representatives begin from March 4 to Jan. 3, and by requiring Congress to convene each year on Jan. 3—about two months after election. The Amendment also set back the date of the President's inauguration to Jan. 20. Other provisions related to the choice of President under certain contingencies.

[*Congressional Digest*, V, 221-240; *United States Daily*, Feb. 25, 1931, p. 3935 ff., Feb. 13, 1932, p. 2817, Feb. 17, 1932, p. 2845.]

P. ORMAN RAY

L'Amistad **Slave Case.** *See Amistad* Case.

Lamp, Incandescent. As far back as 1820 scientists all over the world began to work on this device, but it remained for Thomas A. Edison at Menlo Park, N. J., on Oct. 21, 1879, to make the first successful high resistance carbon lamp, which embodied practically all the basic features of lamps commonly in use today.

The first carbon lamp was very inefficient in comparison with our present-day lamps, giving only 1.7 lumens (light units) per watt (unit of energy). The carbon lamp was gradually improved through minor changes in construction, many of which were introduced by American inventors, so that by 1906 it produced 3.4 lumens per watt. In 1905 Dr. Willis R. Whitney, head of the Research Laboratory of the General Electric Company at Schenectady, N. Y., succeeded in changing the character of the carbon filament to give it metallic characteristics and for a few years the Gem lamp was on the market. This produced light at 4¼ lumens per watt. In 1904 two Austrian chemists, Just and Hanaman, patented a tungsten filament lamp that was remarkable from an efficiency standpoint, giving 7¾ lumens per watt. Their lamp was extremely fragile and could be used only under special conditions. At that time it was believed impossible to draw tungsten wire, but in 1910 Dr. William D. Coolidge, also of the General Electric Research Laboratory, succeeded in making ductile tungsten. This was at once used in lamps and the drawn wire tungsten filament lamp shortly superseded all other forms, being both efficient and strong.

All lamps up to this time operated filaments in a vacuum. In 1913, after much experimenta-

tion and fundamental research, Dr. Irving Langmuir, one of Dr. Whitney's assistants, discovered that with the largest sizes of lamps if the filaments were coiled and the bulbs filled with inert gases, such as nitrogen or argon, the efficiency could be increased, to as high as 20 lumens per watt. As was the case with the carbon lamp, gradual, constant improvement has taken place with tungsten lamps, many American scientists contributing their bit. Gas filling and double coiling of filament have been introduced into smaller sizes. Types and sizes believed to be physically impossible a few years ago are now in common use.

The cost has constantly been reduced and the advance can best be summed up in the following comparison: In 1907 the 60-watt lamp cost $1.75, gave 8 lumens per watt, and lost 25% of this light before burning out. Today (1938) the 60-watt lamp costs 15¢, produces 13.9 lumens per watt, and emits 90% of its original light at end of its life.

[Henry Schroeder, *History of Electric Light;* Howell and Schroeder, *History of the Incandescent Lamp.*]

A. L. POWELL

Lancaster, Fort, was a trading post on South Platte River, Colo., in use during the early days of fur trapping[qv]. It was noted by Frémont in 1843 as the trading post of a Mr. Lupton, with plenty of livestock, and was in fact more nearly a ranch. It was apparently synonymous with Fort Lupton and was of adobe construction. By 1857 it was abandoned.

[F. S. Dellenbaugh, *Frémont and '49.*]

CARL L. CANNON

Lancaster (Pa.), Treaty of (June 22–July 4, 1744), settled disputes between the Six Nations[qv] and Maryland and Virginia over land claims. Commissioners from Maryland and Virginia and representatives of the Six Nations, except the Mohawks[qv], were present. Conrad Weiser acted as interpreter. For considerations of goods and money the Six Nations surrendered claims to a large region in the western parts of Maryland and Virginia. Even more important, the Six Nations were won to the support of England in the ensuing struggle with France (*see* King George's War).

[Charles P. Keith, *Chronicles of Pennsylvania; Pa. Archives*, 8th ser., Vol. IV.]

J. PAUL SELSAM

Lancaster Pike, the first turnpike[qv] built in the United States, was begun in 1791, opened to travel in 1797 and freed from tolls, by state purchase, in 1917. Need for a public highway to connect Philadelphia with Lancaster had been felt since the founding of the latter town by Scotch-Irish and German immigrants in 1728. In 1770 commissioners were appointed to lay out a sixty-foot road, but the plan failed, probably because of war conditions. William Bingham then secured a charter for the Philadelphia and Lancaster Turnpike Company, offering for public sale 1000 shares of stock, $300 par, to be one tenth paid up at once. The offering was heavily oversubscribed, and the surplus was reduced by a lottery. In 1807 the charter was made perpetual.

The Lancaster Pike opened the interior to settlement. Conestoga wagons[w] rumbled westward in great numbers. A twelve-hour night stage service connected Philadelphia with Lancaster beginning with the spring of 1798. The Pike, however, lost heavily when the main line of the Pennsylvania Railroad[w], begun in 1846, paralleled its course. Free roads built by the state close by the Lancaster Pike also cut away its trade. The perpetual charter was, accordingly, surrendered.

[Charles I. Landis, History of the Philadelphia and Lancaster Turnpike, *Pennsylvania Magazine of History and Biography*, Vol. 42; Thomas B. Searight, *The Old Pike;* Julius F. Sacse, *The Wayside Inns of Lancaster Pike;* Thomas Scharf and Thompson Westcott, *History of Philadelphia.*]   HARRY EMERSON WILDES

Land. *See* Soil.

Land, Indian Conception of Ownership of. To the Indian, land was not susceptible of individualistic sale and transfer. Tecumseh, the Shawnee, said, "Sell a country! Why not sell the air, the clouds, the great sea as well as the land?" Land was an integral, inseparable part of nature that sustained the beings that lived upon it. These beings lived by hunting and fishing in the unity of nature which must never be disturbed by vicious exploitation. An Ohio Valley Indian told the missionary, David McClure, in 1772, "When you white men buy a farm, you buy only the land. You don't buy the horses and cows & sheep. The Elks are our horses, the Buffaloes are our cows, the deer are our sheep."

The only conception that could correspond to ownership was that geographic sections of this unity of nature were capable of being used by different tribes. Friction and warfare could thus come about between groups. But as for individuals, the Indians believed, according to the 18th-century missionary, John Heckewelder, that the "Great Spirit made the earth and all that it contains for the common good of mankind. . . . Everything was given in common to the sons of men. Whatever liveth on the land,

whatsoever groweth out of the earth, and all that is in the rivers and waters . . . was given jointly to all, and every one is entitled to his share."

Under such conditions it is easy to understand the reluctance with which Indians consented to the cession of their land at treaties (*see* Indian Land Cessions).

[F. W. Hodge, *Handbook of American Indians.*]
RANDOLPH C. DOWNES

Land Act of 1796. This was the first great land act adopted by the Federal Government. It established the office of Surveyor General and reenacted the rectangular system of survey with townships[w] of six miles square and sections of 640 acres which the Confederation had embodied in the Land Ordinance of 1785[w]. One half of the townships were to be offered in 5120-acre blocks and the smallest unit which could be bought was 640 acres. The lands were to be sold at public auction to the highest bidder at or above the minimum price of $2 per acre. Full payment was required within a year after purchase and 10% reduction was offered for advance payment. Although it was the basic law of the American land system, the act of 1796 was a failure from the start because the high minimum price and the large unit of entry deterred purchasing.

[P. J. Treat, *The National Land System;* B. H. Hibbard, *History of the Public Land Policies.*]
PAUL WALLACE GATES

Land Act of 1800. *See* Harrison Land Act.

Land Act of 1820. The credit system in the disposition of the public lands, inaugurated by the Land Act of 1796 and extended by the Harrison Land Law of 1800[qw], had become an evident failure by 1820. Large numbers of settlers found it impossible to make the deferred payments on their lands. Other hard-working farmers, seeing that nothing happened to those who failed to meet their obligations, decided to let their own installments lapse. Arrearages piled up rapidly and Congress was forced to pass law after law for the relief of the settlers. After considerable agitation Congress finally enacted the law of April 24, 1820, abolishing the credit system. The minimum price at the public auctions and at private sale thereafter was reduced from $2 to $1.25 per acre, the entire amount to be paid at the time of purchase. The smallest purchasable unit of land was fixed at eighty acres.

[Benjamin H. Hibbard, *A History of the Public Land Policies.*]
DAN E. CLARK

Land Banks. *See* Farm Credit Agencies, Federal.

Land Banks in colonial times are not to be thought of as modern banks. Francis A. Walker said that such a bank was "simply a batch of paper money." The colonists needed a circulating medium. Land was the chief article of wealth, so they tried to make it the basis of currency. In September, 1681, in Massachusetts, there was started "The Fund at Boston in New England." People turned over mortgages on real estate to the trustees, for which they got credit which could be transferred. In Massachusetts in 1714, to head off a projected private bank, a public bank was created which loaned on real-estate security. Some of the loans were not repaid. In 1740 the "Land Bank or Manufactory Scheme" was established in Massachusetts. The capital was £150,000 lawful money, but promissory notes secured by land, not money, were turned in by the subscribers, who were also borrowers. They could pay interest, and for their promissory notes, by notes of the bank or by certain commodities. The bank aroused great political opposition and was finally killed by Parliament when, in March, 1741, it extended the Bubble Act of 1720 to the colonies. Much litigation followed and a number of shareholders were ruined. Pennsylvania's public loan offices, which loaned paper money on land in 1723 and 1729, were well managed.

[D. R. Dewey, *Financial History of the United States.*]
JAMES D. MAGEE

Land Bounties. Lacking well-filled treasuries but possessing abundant supplies of land, the colonies, the states and the National Government in the early days all granted land bounties instead of cash subsidies to reward military service in past wars, to encourage enlistment in pending wars and to aid various special groups. Virginia gave more generous bounties than any other colony or state and a special Virginia Military District[w] was reserved north of the Ohio to fulfil these grants. During the Revolution, Congress promised land bounties to British deserters, and to enlisted officers and men. Again, during the War of 1812 and the Mexican War[qw] land bounties were offered as inducements to enlist and as rewards for service (*see* Bounties, Military). Land bounties were also granted to Canadian refugees in the Revolution, to earthquake sufferers and Polish exiles, and to a number of other groups and individuals whose appeals to Congress received strong political support. The warrants for the many millions of acres of land thus granted were generally sold for small sums to speculators who used them to accumulate great tracts. The Military Tracts[w] of Illinois, Arkansas and Missouri, in which land bounties of the War of 1812 had to be located, were frequently spoken of as "speculators' deserts." (*See also* Land Scrip.)

[Thomas Donaldson, *The Public Domain.*]
PAUL WALLACE GATES

Land Distribution Bill, Clay's. Land policies, tariff rates and public revenue questions were inseparable during the years 1834 to 1842. The old policy of using the public lands as a major source of income for the Government remained in effect, and throughout the boom years 1834 to 1837 Federal revenues were enormously swollen by the receipts from land sales. Faced with a surplus, the politicians sought means to rid the treasury of its unwanted millions. The West wished the Federal Government to dispose of its public domain[w] either by ceding it to the states, by granting free homesteads or by selling the land at low rates; the Old South opposed liberalization of the land policy and favored a lower tariff as a means of reducing the Federal revenue; the Northeast opposed tariff reduction and a liberal land policy and favored Clay's proposal for the distribution of the net proceeds from the public land sales among the states. Clay's distribution bill, first introduced in 1832, provided that 10% of the net proceeds of the land sales be distributed to the states in which they were located and that the remaining 90% be distributed among all the states and territories in proportion to their population. To gain support for this measure the advocates of distribution made a concession to the West by adding to Clay's bill a provision for pre-emption[w]. Before the bill was adopted it was further provided that if tariff rates were raised above the 20% level which they reached in 1841, distribution would automatically be suspended. In 1842 the tariff[w] was raised and Clay's great political measure was suspended. (*See also* Surplus Revenue, Distribution of.)

[B. H. Hibbard, *History of the Public Land Policies.*]
PAUL WALLACE GATES

Land Grant Act (1862). *See* Agricultural Education; Morrill Act.

Land Grants, Colonial. Claims to land as between European governments rested upon discovery, exploration and occupation which, when completed, vested the title in the sovereign of a particular state, who alone could terminate the claims of the natives. Consequently the title to all English America was in the king and from him all later titles stemmed. Royal land grants took the form of charters and the whole Atlantic seaboard, except Florida, was, between 1606 and 1732, parceled out to the London and Plymouth Companies, the Council for New England, James, Duke of York, William Penn^{qv} and associates, Lord Baltimore (*see* Maryland), Clarendon and associates and James Oglethorpe and associates (*see* Georgia). From some of these in turn came grants to individuals and groups which were gradually incorporated into regular colonial governments with boundaries based upon the earlier charters. Many of the original grants ran westward to the sea, and became the foundation for the western claims of the original states, which were finally surrendered to the National Government between 1778 and 1781 (*see* Western Lands).

Local land titles came from the colonial government or the proprietor, depending upon who held the direct title from the king. The practice of New England was for the General Court^{qv} in each colony to grant a considerable tract, called a township, to a body of settlers who in turn issued deeds to individual settlers. This practice tended to prevent speculation in vacant lands and engrossment.

In Maryland there were some manorial grants of 1000 acres or more, although most of the grants were small and made to actual settlers. The practice in Pennsylvania was to grant land to actual settlers in small parcels, but to retain title to vast acreage in the settled areas. Thus the proprietor not only held title to the ungranted regions but was also the largest landowner in the developed eastern counties and collected rents as from any other private estate.

In Virginia there was at first a system of grants based upon head rights—fifty acres for each person arriving in Virginia—and belonging to the individual who paid the transportation. This led to abuses and gradually degenerated into a simple fee system at the land office. Any one who could pay the fees could acquire original title to as many acres as he could pay for. Under this system large plantations grew up in excess of any possible cultivation, such as those of Byrd, Fairfax, Randolph and Spotswood.

Grants were not infrequently used to promote settlements in the back country. These were usually conditioned upon the transportation and settlement of a minimum number of families within a limited time. The best known is the Ohio Company^{qv} grant of 500,000 acres near the forks of the Ohio in 1749. The practice was common on a smaller scale in all of the colonies south of Maryland.

In New York and South Carolina there were vast individual grants and extensive engrossment. In New York the practice had begun under the Dutch by the creation of the patroon^{qv} estates which were recognized as valid by the English. Cornbury and other royal governors issued enormous grants to their favorites. In this way the Van Rensselaer, Philipse, Van Cortlandt and Livingston estates were built up and perpetuated, paving the way for the serious antirent^{qv} difficulties in New York, 1840–45.

A grant to be valid had to come from the colonial government in which the land was situated. Undefined boundaries led to conflicts over titles, such as the troubles in Vermont where settlers claimed land under grants from both New York and New Hampshire^{qv}, and the bitter dispute in the Wyoming Valley where settlers from Connecticut were expelled as trespassers by those with titles from Pennsylvania (*see* Yankee-Pennamite Wars).

Land grants as bounties for military service became especially important after 1750. The Virginia grants were made in what is now West Virginia. Individual soldiers or officers could either use their warrants or sell them, the purchaser in turn could use them singly or in groups. Thus George Washington came into possession of his vast western properties by purchasing Virginia military warrants (*see* Washington's Western Lands). The British government made extensive military grants in the Floridas after their acquisition from Spain.

Indian titles were presumed to be extinguished by the local colonial government as the representative of the king before land was granted to individual settlers. This was not always done and after 1750 there was a growing custom of frontiersmen purchasing lands directly from the Indians and securing confirmation later. In other cases, settlers secured grants before the Indian titles were extinguished; this was one of the causes of Pontiac's Conspiracy^{qv}. The Proclamation of 1763^{qv} was issued to stop encroachments of this kind. On the other hand, the expansion into Kentucky and Tennessee by Boone, Henderson, Robertson and their followers was based upon the assumption that Indian titles alone were valid.

The vast interior of the continent tempted Americans and Englishmen to seek grants to the rich lands west of the mountains. On the eve of the Revolution patents were pending in England for proprietary grants to form four new colonies in the region west of the Alleghenies and south and east of the Ohio-Mississippi rivers. These were called Vandalia, Transylvania, Georgiani and Mississippi^{qv}. Large additional purchases from the Indians north of the Ohio River also awaited confirmation.

Colonial land grants were not limited to the eastern part of the United States. Spain and France made grants similar to those made by England. When new areas came under the control of England or later the United States, the earlier foreign colonial land grants were accepted as valid. As many of these had very obscure descriptions, the boundaries became elastic and were used as the foundation for claims to large tracts of government lands. One of the most famous of these is the Maxwell land grant[w] in Colorado and New Mexico which involved litigation as late as 1887. Many of the large landed estates of the southwestern part of the United States go back to old Spanish colonial land grants confirmed after annexation to the United States (see Land Grants, Spanish and Mexican).

[Evarts B. Greene, *The Foundations of American Nationality;* C. W. Alvord, *Mississippi Valley in British Politics.*]

O. M. DICKERSON

Land Grants, Spanish and Mexican. By treaty at the close of the War with Mexico[w], the United States agreed to recognize all the land grants made by Spain and Mexico in the ceded territory. Besides the usual purposes of granting large estates for agricultural and pastoral pursuits, after the revolt of Texas a definite effort was made to colonize the frontier with Mexicans, and protect the Santa Fé trade[w] from the Indians and, especially, the aggressive *Americanos* (e.g., the Tierra Amarilla, the Maxwell, the St. Vrain, the Mora and the Las Animas grants). When these lands were ceded to the United States, many Americans rushed in and squatted on the new public lands. Innumerable conflicts arose. Three steps in the settlement of these claims followed. (1) March 3, 1851, Congress established a commission of three which confirmed 538 claims involving over 8,000,000 acres of land in California. (2) July 22, 1854, Congress provided a surveyor-general for New Mexico to investigate thoroughly all private land claims. Upon his reports, Congress confirmed seventy-one additional grants. (3) In a final effort to quiet title on these grants, Congress established "A Court of Private Land Claims" of five judges from different states. From 1891–1904, this court heard all remaining claims (301 in all) and confirmed eighty-seven grants for 3,000,000 acres.

[R. A. Twitchell, *The Leading Facts of New Mexican History,* Vol. II.]

PERCY S. FRITZ

Land Grants for Education. The practice of making land grants to aid in supporting schools was generally followed by the American colonies. The Confederation, borrowing from the New England land system, provided in the Land Ordinance of 1785[w] that the sixteenth section of each township, or one thirty-sixth of the acreage in the public-land states[w], should be granted to the states for the benefit of common schools. New states after 1848 were granted two sections in each township and Utah, Arizona, New Mexico and Oklahoma (in part) were given four sections in each township when they entered the Union. Each public-land state on entering the Union was also given a minimum of two townships of 46,080 acres to aid in founding "seminaries of learning," or state universities[w]. Such great institutions as the Universities of Michigan, Wisconsin and Indiana benefited from these grants.

The next important step in Federal aid to education came in 1862 as a result of an energetic campaign undertaken by Jonathan Baldwin Turner of Illinois, the farm and labor journals, and Horace Greeley and the New York *Tribune*. This was the Agricultural College Land Grant Act which was fathered in the Senate by Justin S. Morrill of Vermont and is generally called the Morrill Act[w]. This measure gave to the states 30,-000 acres of public lands for each Representative and Senator they had in Congress to aid in establishing Agricultural and Mechanical Arts Colleges. States which contained no public lands received scrip which could be located elsewhere on public land "subject to entry." As a result of this act agricultural colleges have been established in every state in the Union. Special land grants have, in addition, been given by the Federal Government to endow normal schools, schools of mines, military institutes, reform schools, a girls' college and a colored university.

These numerous grants reflect the ever growing interest of the United States in free public education. They encouraged the states early to create liberal educational systems and aided in financing them at a time when local resources were unequal to the task. ¶The total acreage granted by the Federal Government for educational purposes is 118,000,000, or an area practically four times the size of the State of New York. Some of the states recklessly disposed of their lands for small sums; others, like Minnesota, have received large amounts from the sale of their land grants.

[G. W. Knight, History and Management of Land Grants for Education in the Northwest Territory, *Papers of the American Historical Association,* Vol. I, No. 3.]

PAUL WALLACE GATES

Land Grants to Railways. The liberality with which Congress subsidized canal[w] construction by land grants naturally suggested to early railroad promoters that they might likewise obtain land grants to aid their enterprises. Most persistent were the advocates of a central railroad in Illinois to connect the extreme northwestern and southern parts of the state. When, in 1850, the proposed railroad was made intersectional by an extension to the Gulf of Mexico Congress adopted the measure which gave to Illinois, Mississippi and Alabama a right-of-way through the public lands[w] and the alternate sections for a distance of six miles on both sides of the road or, in other words, 3840 acres for each mile of railroad. The Government-reserved sections were priced at double the ordinary minimum of $1.25 per acre to enable strict constructionists[w] to maintain that the Government lost nothing by its liberality. Furthermore, the Government was to enjoy free transportation for troops and supplies and rate concessions on the transportation of mails.

The grant to Illinois and the rapid completion of the Illinois Central Railroad[w] aided in opening to settlement areas hitherto inaccessible and gave a great impetus to immigration and land speculation[w]. Such success produced a scramble for land grants by railroad groups and numerous donations were made from 1850 to 1871. Most important and grandest in their conception were the transcontinentals, to which were conveyed extensive grants amounting in the case of the Northern Pacific[w] to 39,000,000 acres. Altogether 131,000,000 acres were given by Congress to aid in railroad construction. (*See also* Union Pacific Railroad.)

The land-grant railroads undertook extensive advertising campaigns at home and abroad to attract immigrants to their lands, which were sold on long-term credits at prevailing prices. Unfortunately, the difficulty of making payments sometimes led to friction between the railroads and the purchasers and furthered the growing antirailroad sentiment in the West during the post-Civil War years (*see* Granger Movement). Land reformers condemned land grants as inconsistent with the free homestead idea and in 1871 they succeeded in ending the policy. The damage had been done, however, for the richest and most valuable part of our national heritage had by then passed into private hands, much into railroad ownership, and future generations were not only to regret the donations but to attempt to enforce their confiscation, with little success.

[L. H. Haney, *Congressional History of Railways in the United States;* J. B. Sanborn, *Congressional Grants of Land in Aid of Railways.*]
                                                    PAUL WALLACE GATES

Land Office, U. S. General, is a bureau of the Federal Government, established in 1812, which has as its chief functions the survey, management and disposition of the public lands[w], and the maintenance of records thereon. The Ordinance of 1785[w], the cornerstone of Federal land policy, provided for a Geographer to direct surveys of the public lands. In 1796 the Geographer was succeeded by a Surveyor General who, with his deputies, continued to survey and map the public domain[w] until 1836, independently of any other official or agency. Land sales, according to the Ordinance of 1785, were to be managed by a board of treasury consisting of three commissioners. Under the Federal Constitution this function was inherited by the Secretary of the Treasury.

The first district land offices were set up in 1800 at Chillicothe, Cincinnati, Marietta and Steubenville, all in Ohio. By act of Congress, approved April 25, 1812, the General Land Office was established as a bureau in the Treasury Department, with a Commissioner as its chief officer. Friction between the Commissioner and the Surveyor General resulted in the latter officer being placed under the Commissioner in 1836. For the next five years the Commissioner was made responsible to the President direct, but in 1841 the Secretary of the Treasury was given the power to hear and decide appeal cases. However, the Commissioner continued to enjoy considerable independence and influence for some years after the transfer of the Office in 1849 to the newly organized Department of the Interior[w], where it has since remained.

Up to 1910 surveying was done in large part by a system of contracts with private surveyors; it has since been executed by a force employed directly by the Land Office. There has been an increasing amount of resurvey work in recent years, some of it necessitated by reason of fraudulent original surveys when the work was handled through contracts. Map compiling and drafting have always been an important part of the work of the General Land Office, including the preparation of original plat maps, state maps, a biennial edition of the large United States map and many special maps. Through the years the Land Office has administered the long series of acts providing for the disposal of the public domain, including the pre-emption and homestead laws[qw]. When the acreage of public land in any district is reduced to less than 100,000 acres, the Secretary of the Interior is required by law to close the district office and transfer its business to a neighboring district office. As late as 1921 there were ninety-four district offices still in existence, but in 1938 there were only twenty-five. The records of the General Land Office in Washington, which are complete from the beginning, are the basis for all land titles in the twenty-nine public-land states[qv].

[Milton Conover, *The General Land Office;* B. H. Hibbard, *A History of the Public Land Policies.*]

OLIVER W. HOLMES

Land Ordinance. *See* Ordinances of 1784, 1785 and 1787.

Land Policy. United States land policies, so far as we have had any, have pertained largely to the disposition of the public domain[qv]. We had a vast public domain, well over a billion acres, to be disposed of. The first plan was to use this land as a source of income. Coupled with the revenue idea, however, was an equally important program of getting the land into the hands of cultivators. As matters turned out the revenue plan was a near failure. The plan to put land into the hands of actual farmers succeeded. In general terms the land policy turned out to be, primarily, a *laissez-faire*[qv] policy, based upon a minimum charge, $1.25 an acre, for the bulk of land sold direct from Government to purchaser. Eventually (1862) we offered free land to the settler, under the Homestead Act[qv] of 1862. This was, in a very real sense, the culmination of all preceding land policies, and was the result of a determined, prolonged campaign on the part of the pioneer farmers of the West.

Thus it may be said that getting the land into the hands of settlers without much regard to price was the major land policy of the Government for at least a century following the Revolutionary War. However, other policy features developed. The leading uses of land other than for direct settlement were two: first, to promote education, second, to promote internal improvements. The use of land as a basis of income for schools began during the colonial period. As soon as the nation was well started the public domain was used freely to promote and support common schools and universities. The agricultural and mechanic arts grant was made in 1862. For common schools, much the biggest item, about 76,-000,000 acres were granted—the equivalent of Michigan and Wisconsin. Much other land was added to the school grants. All school grants, i.e. for common schools, universities and colleges, reached more than 100,000,000 acres (*see* Land Grants for Education).

The largest quantity of land disposed of for any one purpose, other than grants and sales to individuals designed to promote settlement, was the donations to the railroads, aggregating at least 129,000,000 acres, or nearly one eighth of all the original public domain (*see* Land Grants to Railways).

In recent years there has been a movement toward reconstituting a public domain. This is the result of zoning, a means of planning, and limiting, the uses to which land may be put. Also the addition, inadvertently, of much tax-delinquent land to the public possessions. An item of no small importance in this connection is the expansion in size and number of national forests and parks[qv].

[R. T. Ely and George S. Wehrwein, *Land Economics;* B. H. Hibbard, *A History of the Public Land Policies.*]

BENJAMIN HORACE HIBBARD

Land Scrip was first used in the United States in 1814 when the Government issued "Mississippi Stock" to the extent of $5,000,000 in compensation for those persons claiming land under the Georgia Yazoo[qv] grants. This stock did not bear interest and was payable from the receipts of the sales of public land[qv] in Mississippi Territory. It was also receivable for public lands in the proportion of $95 scrip and $5 cash.

It was not, however, until 1830 that the United States issued land scrip under that name. The Land Scrip Act of May 30, 1830, was designed primarily to benefit the Virginia veterans of the Revolutionary War. Virginia had promised bounty lands to these soldiers and had reserved for their warrants two military reservations, one in Kentucky west of the Green River and the other in the territory northwest of the River Ohio (*see* Virginia Military Reserve in Ohio). The first was surrendered to Kentucky in 1797. According to the act of 1830, Virginia Revolutionary veterans, both of the state and continental line, might exchange their Virginia warrants for United States scrip which would be receivable for land at any land office in Ohio, Indiana or Illinois. Three years later these restrictions as to location were removed and the land scrip made receivable at any land office in the United States where public land was offered for private sale. Virginia continued to issue bounty warrants till 1852 and the United States by repeated acts authorized the issuing of scrip to be exchanged for them. In 1852 the United States authorized scrip to be issued for all the Virginia warrants and Virginia then ceded to the United States her unlocated land in the Virginia Military Reserve. The act of 1830 made the land scrip available not only to Virginia veterans but to all Revolutionary soldiers who had been given bounty warrants by the United States. Scrip was subsequently issued for the veterans of the War of 1812 and of the War with Mexico. The last resort to scrip was under the Morrill Act[w] of 1862 which provided that states having within their borders an insufficient quantity of land to satisfy their allotment might receive scrip which could be exchanged for land elsewhere. Under this provision twenty-six states received scrip representing more than 7,000,000 acres of land. Except for the Morrill Act scrip none was issued by the United States other than for exchange for military bounty warrants, of which there were by 1860 some 600,000, representing 68,000,000 acres of land (*see* Land Bounties).

The original purpose of the United States in issuing scrip was to make it possible for veterans to profit from their bounty lands even though they were unable to locate the lands themselves. The policy achieved its object apparently for it has been estimated that only one in five hundred receiving scrip used it for land purchases. The scrip was practically all bought from the original holders by speculators, and the huge land speculations[w] that were such a feature of United States history before 1860 were made possible by the land scrip. Until 1852 the speculation was chiefly in scrip, as the military warrants were not made assignable until that year. The greatest era of speculation was in the decade following the war with Mexico, when for many years bounty and scrip locations exceeded the private sales. Scrip was quoted on the market and stock manipulators dealt in it as in other commodities.

R. S. COTTERILL

Land Speculation. The favorite object of speculation in America before the era of "big business" was the public lands[w]. They could be bought cheaply in large quantities and withheld from market, if one had sufficient capital to carry them, until rising prices brought profits to the investors. Memories of high land values in the old world and of the social prestige which the possessor of broad acres enjoyed, combined with the natural land hunger of all races, produced in the American people an insatiable lust for land.

Land speculation began with the first settlements in America. The proprietors of Virginia, disappointed at the meager returns from their investment, granted to themselves great tracts of land from which they hoped to draw substantial incomes. Similarly, the Penns and Calverts in Pennsylvania and Maryland and the early proprietors of New York, New Jersey and the Carolinas speculated in an imperial way in lands. Later in the colonial period a new crop of land companies composed of English and colonial speculators sought both title to and political control over great tracts in the Mississippi Valley.

The Vandalia, the Mississippi, the Georgiana, the Wabash, the Indiana, the Loyal and the Ohio land companies[qw] attracted some of the ablest colonial leaders into their ranks, among them being George Washington, Richard Henry Lee, Benjamin Franklin, the Whartons and George Croghan. The struggles of these rival companies for charters and grants played an important role in British colonial policy[w] during the pre-Revolutionary years. Company rivalries were matched by the rival land claims of the colonies, one of the most notable being the conflict between Connecticut and Pennsylvania for the Wyoming Valley which the former had granted to the Susquehanna Land Company[w]. In western Virginia, Richard Henderson and his Transylvania Company[w], which claimed title to a great tract received from the Indians, came into conflict with Virginia and was successful in having only a small part of the area confirmed to him.

Most influential colonials tried their luck at speculating, either through the land companies or by operating on their own account. George Washington was a large land owner in Virginia, Pennsylvania and the Ohio country; Robert and Gouverneur Morris, William Duer, Phelps and Gorham and William Johnson acquired princely domains in Pennsylvania, New York and Maine. The Morrises negotiated a number of large purchases and resold tracts to others, perhaps the largest of which went to the Holland Land Company[w]. This company was composed of Dutch capitalists who bought the Holland Reserve in western New York and who were busily engaged in settling it during the first third of the 19th century. Meantime, most of upstate New York was parcelled out among speculators, some of the most prominent of whom were the Wadsworths of the Genesee country, John Jacob Astor and Peter Smith, father of Gerrit Smith. These men, unlike Robert Morris, were able to retain their lands long enough either to resell at high prices or to settle tenants upon them.

The largest purchase and the most stupendous fraud was the sale in 1795 of 30,000,000 acres of western lands by the legislature of Georgia to four Yazoo companies for one and a half cents an acre. The next legislature cancelled the sale, but the purchasers, frequently innocent third parties, waged a long fight to secure justice, claiming that the obligation of the contract clause[w] in the Federal Constitution prevented the Georgia legislature from reversing the original sale (*see* Fletcher v. Peck). The Yazoo frauds[w] became a *cause célèbre* in which John Randolph, Thomas Jefferson, John Marshall and other notables took prominent parts.

When the public domain[w] of the United States was created by the donations of the states with western land claims, speculative interest converged upon Congress with requests to purchase tracts of land north of the Ohio. In fact, the craze for land speculation was partly responsible for the adoption of the Ordinance of 1787[w] which provided for the government of the ceded territory north of the Ohio. A group of New England capitalists known as the Ohio Company of Associates[w] wished to buy a tract of land in southeastern Ohio for a New England settlement. To get the measure through Congress it seemed necessary to enlarge the original project and to create a second organization, the Scioto Company[w], which was composed of members of Congress and other influential people who planned to buy same 5,000,000 acres of land. The formation of the Scioto Company made possible the enactment of the Northwest Ordinance, but the company itself was a failure because it could not fulfil its contract with the Government. The Ohio Company of Associates did, however, succeed in planting a little New England outpost at Marietta[w]. John Cleves Symmes[w] of New Jersey likewise bought a large tract from the Congress in 1788. These purchases virtually defeated the purpose of the Land Ordinance of 1785 and the Land Act of 1796[w] because the speculators whom Congress had allowed to acquire large tracts of land at lower prices than were offered to individual settlers were thus enabled to undersell the Government.

There were three great periods of land speculation after the creation of the public domain, 1816–19, 1835–37 and 1854–57. Outstanding easterners like Daniel Webster, Caleb Cushing, Edward Everett, Amos Lawrence, Moses and John Carter Brown and James S. Wadsworth, and southerners like John C. Breckinridge, John Slidell, Eli Shorter and William S. Grayson bought western lands in large quantities. Land companies again were organized and they entered great tracts embracing entire townships. The New York and Boston Illinois Land Company acquired 900,000 acres in the Military Tract of Illinois, the American Land Company had great estates in Indiana, Illinois, Michigan, Wisconsin, Mississippi and Arkansas and the Boston and Western Land Company owned 60,000 acres in Illinois and Wisconsin.

The adoption of the Homestead Law in 1862 did not end land speculation and some of the largest purchases were made thereafter. William S. Chapman alone bought over 1,000,000 acres of land in California and Nevada, Henry W. Sage, John McGraw and Jeremiah Dwight, benefactors of Cornell University, entered 352,000 acres of timberland in the Northwest and the South and Francis Palms and Frederick E. Driggs bought 486,000 acres of timberland in Wisconsin and Michigan. Not until 1889 were effective steps taken to end large speculative purchases and by that date the Government had parted with its best lands.

Meantime, the canal and railroad land grants and the lands given to the states for drainage and educational purposes[qw] were also attracting speculative purchasing.

The accumulation of vast quantities of land in advance of settlement created many problems for the West, some of which have never been satisfactorily settled. The Indians were pushed back more rapidly than the actual needs of the population dictated and the frequent clashes between settlers and Indians might have been avoided had there been more social control of westward expansion[w] and land purchases. In some places "speculator's deserts" were created where large amounts of land were owned by absentee proprietors who withheld them from development while waiting for higher prices. Settlers were widely dispersed because they could not find land at reasonable prices close to existing settlements. The problem of providing transportation facilities was consequently aggravated and as a result of the importunities of settlers, thousands of miles of railroads were built through sparsely settled country which could provide but little traffic for the roads. Nevertheless, the speculators and land companies were an important factor in the development of the West. Their efforts to attract settlers to their lands through the distribution of pamphlets and other advertising literature which described the western country lured thousands from their homes in the eastern states and countries of northern Europe to the newly developing sections of the West. They also aided in building improvements such as roads, canals and railroads to make easier the life of the immigrant.

[T. P. Abernethy, *Western Lands and the American Revolution;* A. M. Sakolski, *The Great American Land Bubble;* P. W. Gates, The Homestead Law in an Incongruous Land System, *American Historical Review,* July, 1936; S. Livermore, *Early American Land Companies: Their Influence upon Corporate Development.*]

PAUL WALLACE GATES

Land Surveying. *See* Public Lands, Survey of.

Land System, National. Our land system was, almost as a matter of course, an adaptation of European land systems brought over by the colonists, or in some instances imposed by England, or Holland, on their respective colonies. The land in the English colonies, according to English law, in the first instance, belonged strictly to the crown.

Land was granted liberally to single individuals, groups of individuals, or joint-stock companies, proprietors who undertook settlements. These proprietors in turn granted land to settlers, generally pretty freely, but often under the stipulation that rents should be paid. Down through these patentees, sometimes three or four in succession, title to the land passed into the hands of occupier and tiller. The latter usually paid little if anything for it, in the way of a purchase price. He was in many colonies granted a fee simple title. Such was the case in the New England colonies. In most of the others there was an attempt to collect "quit rents"^{qv} in the form of very small payments, such as a halfpenny per acre, or a shilling per hundred acres. Money being scarce, provision was made for payment in kind, usually in wheat or tobacco.

There was much difficulty attendant upon the collection of the rental payments, and eventually it gradually fell into disuse, although under its provisions title to much land was lost. This was no great calamity, since land was so plentiful, and the colonies so anxious to have it settled that almost any one who wanted land could get it. Land, thus, came to be widely distributed in ownership, held in fee simple, and serving at once as a "homestead" and a farm.

Two general land systems, so far as the character of the holding was concerned, prevailed. In New England the holding was patterned after the farms of England and consisted of several separate pieces of land, altogether making a small unit. There was the "home lot," usually in a village; a modest sized tract of arable land; a smaller piece of meadow, in typical localities where such were available; a wood lot; and last, but not least, a share in a commons. This latter right might also include woods in lieu of a separate wood lot. The commons was used largely for pasturage, available for feeding all kinds of farm animals. These farm lands were parcelled out under direction, located within a prescribed "town." The surveying was done in advance of distribution of the parcels, and the distribution carried out by lot. Thus the whole procedure was democratic in the extreme.

In the South the farm was essentially different in character. To begin with it was large. The grants of land were generally, to a family, a matter of a few hundred acres, and not infrequently, to the influential, a few thousand acres, some reaching the equivalent of a modern township.

These tracts were surveyed privately, and the sites chosen by the grantee virtually at will. Through these liberal grants, coupled with the adaptation of the country to large field undertakings in the growing of staple products, the foundation was laid for the plantation system^{qv} which long characterized the South.

The system of the North was found suitable for the settlers as they moved farther west. The complications characterizing the New England farm were broken down, even before the Green Mountains were reached. Farms came to be of one piece. The village idea was abandoned as fear of the Indians disappeared. For a long time the farms of the North were small, due to the fact that each family did most of its own work, and, until about the middle of the 19th century, with comparatively little machinery.

All told the land system as found in the United States is adapted to a regime of extreme, individualistic, private ownership (see Land Titles), modified mainly by the power of taxation. More recently a system of zoning^{qv} has been applied; first to city property; now to much land adapted to agriculture, forestry and recreation. The proportion of public land to private is still, however, small. Zoning implies, and embodies, the right of the public to decide, in general terms, the use to which land shall be put: whether or not, for example, a given tract, large or small, shall be provided with schools or roads, or shall be designated as forest, or recreational land.

The general plan respecting land, for a century and a half, has been to put the public domain^{qv} into the hands of the user as fast as possible. Recent movements have been in a contrary direction.

[Payson J. Treat, *The National Land System, 1785-1820;* B. H. Hibbard, *A History of the Public Land Policies.*]

. BENJAMIN HORACE HIBBARD

Land Tenure, as here considered, applies to farm land and the status of the farmer who holds it either temporarily or permanently. The two classes of people from the tenure standpoint are the owner or landlord, on the one hand, and the tenant, or lessee, on the other. In England the tenant is ordinarily called the farmer. While early America was the land of farm ownership outstandingly, there were, even so, a considerable number of tenants during colonial times. It is, however, only since the Civil War that tenancy has been a matter of public concern. The first census of farm ownership was taken in 1880. At that time just over a quarter of the farmers of the country were tenants, 25.6%. These were by no means evenly distributed.

Tenancy then, as now, was highest in the

South, and lowest in the Mountain states, then quite new. In the South it was, when this census was taken, but fifteen years after the close of the Civil War. The major part of the work in the cotton and tobacco fields was done by the Negroes. After the war it was found impossible to hire the Negroes and keep them on the job from the time the crop was planted until it was harvested. The device hit upon was that of renting small pieces of land to tenants, both whites and Negroes. Thus the plantations were broken up, and a system of tenancy started which has grown in proportion to ownership with hardly an interruption until it has come to occupy the major part of the cotton belt, and much of the other farm land of the whole South. In 1880 the census showed 36% of the Southern farms to be worked by tenants. This had grown to 54% in 1935.

In the North tenancy was comparatively low, 19%, in 1880. In 1935 it was 32%. In contrast with the South where tenancy is high in all states, there is a wide difference from state to state, and section to section in the North. In New England, the tenancy percentage, always low, was still lower in 1935 than it was fifty years before, having fallen during that time from 8.5% to 6%. This is not tenancy enough to attract attention. The highest tenancy section in the North is found in the West North Central states where in 1935 it averaged 43%. Even within this group of seven states there was considerable range, Minnesota showing 34%; Iowa, 50%.

Until within recent years tenancy, outside the Southern states, where different conditions prevailed, was a rung on the agricultural ladder, leading very certainly to ownership. At the present time tenancy is still a step toward ownership, but does not result in ownership so early in life, or so certainly for all farmers. For example, in 1910 nearly a quarter, 23.3%, of the farmers under 25 years of age were owners; in 1930 this had fallen to 12.7%. But the great majority of those who stayed in the business until the age of 65 were owners in each period: 84.5% in 1910; 83.2% in 1930. Correspondingly, most of the young farmers are tenants, while only about a sixth of the farmers 65 years old are still in that class. Were the analysis carried out in greater detail it would be seen that most of the older tenants, which means a class, or at least a group, of farmers remaining tenants substantially all their lives are to be found in our Southern states. It appears that quite beyond half of the Negroes remain tenants for life. While farmers are, or have been until very recently, achieving ownership of farms, it has been at a constantly later time in life. This in itself would account for an

increase in tenancy, but so long as ownership was reasonably certain the postponement of the time of its accomplishment was not extremely serious.

Certain types of farming lend themselves to tenancy operation while others do not. For example, very few crops or products, the production of which extends over a period of years, are likely to be found in quantity on tenant farms. On the contrary, annual crops, and especially those which can be produced with comparatively little outlay of cash and equipment per acre, are grown in quantity by tenants. The two outstanding major crops produced by tenants are cotton and corn. These are both strictly annuals; are both salable as soon as harvested; and can easily be divided into shares for the two parties. The outlay on the part of the tenant in growing cotton is traditionally small, a very few hundred dollars covering the outlay in acceptable shape, while a corn tenant may get along moderately well on a thousand or two thousand dollars of capital. In both instances the tenant may come onto the farm anew in the early spring, and move to another farm a year later with little loss. This is the extreme of its kind. Wheat and tobacco also are crops which are much grown by tenants.

In contrast with the simple operations in growing corn or cotton are, at the other extreme, the complex, prolonged, scientific operations involved in a high grade fruit farm. On an orange ranch the main investment is in the trees rather than the land. Such trees must be cared for constantly and intelligently. Almost no owner would, or does, trust them to a tenant.

Livestock lies between the extremes as a tenant product. In general, ownership is more prevalent than tenancy in animal husbandry. However, a somewhat different type of tenancy, approaching the partnership status, with a landlord who usually lives near by, and who takes a direct and constant interest in the affairs of the farm, overcomes the objection to such tenancy. As a result, a quarter of our distinctive dairy farms are in the hands of tenants.

In considering tenancy in this country, the question of family relationship between tenant and owner should not be overlooked. This kind of tenancy amounts to about one fifth of the total, but reaches 30% for the East North Central states. It is highest in Wisconsin, 39%, followed by Utah with 35%, Nebraska 34.8% and Iowa 32%. Related tenancy is lowest in the Southern states.

Until within a few years it was taken for granted that farmers desired, and hoped, to own farms. They worked through the preliminary stages with this goal in mind. Now, although no doubt the majority still prefer to own the farms they operate, there is a growing number who are not so anxious for ownership. This is the result of the relatively high price of land since the World War, which has meant a big mortgage for all recent buyers, involving a heavy interest payment. To this is to be added a tax bill which, after very material reductions, is still more than 50% higher than twenty years ago. Still more significant is the price situation, which has been against the farmer from 1920 to the present (1939). This fact is of profound importance with respect to farm tenure. Obviously a constant disparity between the prices received by farmers in relation to prices paid means constant difficulty in meeting bills. If, for example, it requires 15% to 50% more produce in recent years to meet certain fixed charges, such as taxes and interest, and about the same added proportion to pay for building material, skilled labor and machinery, a tenant is likely to revise his views regarding the desirability of becoming a "mortgaged owner." Faced with expenses which have not come down in proportion to the level of farm produce prices, many tenants are glad to have a landlord to furnish a farm, keep buildings in repair, assume responsibility for a considerable part of current cash expenses, and who must be the most lenient of creditors with respect to collections of the rent whenever the tenant finds it hard to meet the obligation.

[U. S. Census Reports; Agricultural Yearbooks, especially for 1923; L. C. Gray, *The History of Agriculture in Southern United States to 1860*; P. W. Bidwell and J. I. Falconer, *History of Agriculture in the Northern United States, 1620-1680*; T. N. Carver, *Readings in Agricultural Economics*.]

BENJAMIN HORACE HIBBARD

Land Titles. In the United States land titles are called, in the terminology of English law, allodial, or fee simple, which terms, with us, have come to be synonymous. Allodial means free of rent or services demanded by some lord, or other claimant, leaving the exclusive right to land, or real estate, in the hands of an owner, subject only to the demands of the state, or to the demands of some third party to which the right of eminent domain[qv] has been granted. Fee simple means, in contrast to fee tail, or any condition or limitation imposed respecting the exclusive right to real property, exclusive ownership limited only as noted in the definition of allodial.

Titles as recognized in the English-speaking world are required to go back to grants made by the state, and, to be perfect, must show that at no time, no matter how remote, has any claim been left unsatisfied, or unacknowledged. Names must be meticulously correct and all formally attested by notaries.

The title must normally start with a grant, or, in case of direct conveyance of title to an individual, with a patent, A patent is in every respect a deed, giving the recipient full fee-simple ownership. Where a grant, usually of a larger tract, is made to a company, such as a colonizing company or a railroad, the company comes into possession of the land in fee simple and can therefore sell, passing all rights possessed on to the buyer.

This type of title is found in all parts of the country which at any time belonged to the Federal Government as a part of the public domain, and amounts to about half of the whole area of the country. In the thirteen original states the land systems varied. In many colonies the old English tradition prevailed under which it was assumed that all land titles were vested in the crown. Thus the kings of the 17th century granted land to colonies, to colonizing companies and to individuals. In general, the colonial authorities were given the right to grant land to individuals. Hence the title came from the king to the colony, and from the colony to a town, or land company, and from town or company to the individual. In several colonies the right of primogeniture[qv] prevailed, as it had in other European countries, but it hardly survived the Revolutionary War, and disappeared almost entirely before 1800.

In the case of settlement on land before it became United States territory, as in the Florida and Louisiana purchases, and the Mexican cession[qv], an agreement was made to the effect that bona fide settlers should be respected in their titles. Especially in the Spanish territory of the Southwest the Spanish grants to their own citizens had been lavish and vague. The titles to these lands are now on a par with other titles of the country, but they became such through court action, involving, in many cases, much litigation and expense (*see* Land Grants, Spanish and Mexican). Some such titles have been settled within the present century.

The most unfortunate feature of our land titles is the insistence, supported by the legal profession and court decisions, of the requirement of a complete schedule of all transfers, called an abstract of title, showing all transfers from the beginning to date. The result has been in numerous cases that certain small tracts of land, usually pieces split off from larger tracts, are not worth the cost of the abstracts. A way out of this difficulty is provided in the "Torrens system."[qv] This is a system of registering titles and involves a state guarantee of their validity. The system is undoubtedly excellent where started in a new country, as was this system in Australia in 1858. It is used in several of our states on a voluntary basis, and has not, as a matter of fact, made great progress. It has come into use to a considerable extent in England and other parts of Europe. In our country the Government grants the title in the first place, keeps records of transfers, but leaves it to the individuals to keep such titles valid and correct.

[L. C. Gray, *History of Agriculture in Southern United States to 1860;* Jacques Dumas, *Registering Titles to Land;* Edward L. McKenna, *State Insurance of Land Titles in the United States.*]

BENJAMIN HORACE HIBBARD

Landgrave was the title proposed for the second order of provincial nobility provided for in the Fundamental Constitutions of Carolina[w] by the Lords Proprietors. Their inability to enforce the Constitutions made the title of little meaning save as an occasion for gifts of land to favorites, and as a title for the governors.

[E. McCrady, *South Carolina under the Proprietary Government.*]

R. L. MERIWETHER

Lands, Public. *See* Public Domain, The.

Landslides (Political). This is a term used to denote an overwhelming defeat, particularly of the party in power, due to a revulsion of public opinion against it shown either at a presidential or a mid-term congressional election. Until recently "landslides" have been relatively rare. The election of McKinley in 1896 was hailed as a "landslide" because of the one-sidedness of the electoral vote, though only 51% of the popular vote was cast for him as against 47% for his opponent, Bryan, and 2% for third parties. There was more justification for the expression in 1904, when Theodore Roosevelt received 56.4% of the vote to 37.6% for Parker. Even more striking was the rejection of Democratic control in 1920 when Harding received 60.3% of the popular ballots to Cox's 34.2%, the record "landslide" until 1936. Yet Hoover's victory (1928) approached it, being 58% to Smith's 40.7%, which appeared all the more remarkable when four years later F. D. Roosevelt received 54.7% to Hoover's 39.7%. In 1936 F. D. Roosevelt surpassed, somewhat, the Harding "landslide" and set a new all-time high of 60.7% to Landon's 36.4%.

The term "tidal wave" also is applied to one-sided congressional elections as, for example, the "tidal wave of 1874" in the midst of Grant's second term, when the Republicans, after having controlled the Presidency, Senate and House of Representatives for fourteen years, saw their majority of 115 suddenly reversed to a Democratic majority of 76. In the mid-term elections of 1890 the extremely unpopular McKinley Tariff Act[w] turned a Republican advantage of 166 to 159 Representatives into a Democratic majority of 235 to 88. Again, the mid-term elections of 1910, after fourteen years of Republican supremacy in all branches of the Government, brought a reversal of the Republican advantage of 219 to 172 in the House of Representatives to a disadvantage of 228 to 162.

[A. M. Schlesinger, *Political and Social Growth of the United States.*]

W. E. BINKLEY

Lane v. Oregon. In December, 1868, the United States Supreme Court ruled that the Legal Tender Act[w] of 1862 could not interfere with state taxation. Under the Constitution the state has its own government and controls the problems pertaining to taxation. It was a victory for states' rights and strict construction[qw].

[J. W. Ellison, The Currency Question on the Pacific Coast during the Civil War, *Mississippi Valley Historical Review,* June, 1929.]

J. W. ELLISON

Lansing-Ishii Agreement, THE, was concluded by an exchange of notes between Secretary Lansing and Viscount Ishii on Nov. 2, 1917. Its ostensible purpose was to reconcile conflicting viewpoints in American and Japanese policy in the Far East as a measure of wartime co-operation, but Japan also undertook to win from the United States recognition of what Viscount Ishii termed Japan's "paramount interest" in China. Secretary Lansing opposed this move but finally accepted a compromise whereby the two governments' reaffirmation of the Open Door policy[w] and of the territorial integrity of China was supplemented by American recognition of Japan's "special interest in China, particularly in the part to which her possessions are contiguous." Despite Secretary Lansing's disclaimers, Viscount Ishii subsequently insisted that this clause in the agreement implied definite acknowledgment of Japan's special position in Manchuria. His interpretation was generally accepted in the Far East and the agreement was widely condemned in China as a betrayal of the principles of the Open Door. Its ambiguity was recognized at the time of the Washington Conference[w] and soon thereafter, on March 30, 1923, a further exchange of notes between the American and Japanese governments declared that "in the light of the understanding arrived at by the Washington Conference," the correspondence between Secretary Lansing and Viscount Ishii

would be considered canceled and "of no further force or effect."

[Robert Lansing, *War Memoirs;* Viscount K. Ishii,
Diplomatic Commentaries.]   FOSTER RHEA DULLES

LaPointe, Treaty of (Oct. 5, 1842). The Chippewa[qv] by this treaty ceded to the United States
the western half of the Upper Peninsula of Michigan and a large tract in northern Wisconsin,
extending westward to Minnesota. The cession
opened the rich mineral deposits of the Lake
Superior region to white exploitation and the
settlement and development of the copper country was at once begun.   M. M. QUAIFE

Lapwai (Idaho) Indian Council was held in
May, 1877, in an endeavor to induce the non-
treaty part of the Nez Percé[qv] tribe to retire to
a reservation. The Federal Government had lost
patience with those who refused to abide by the
treaties previously signed with some of the Nez
Percés. Gen. O. O. Howard was sent to enforce
obedience. The arrest of Too-hul-hul-suit, the
holy man, or "tu-at," of the tribe, on the third
day of the council aroused the non-treaty Indians
to rebellion and the Nez Percé War[qv] followed.

[C. J. Brosnan, *History of the State of Idaho;* C. A. Fee,
Chief Joseph.]   CORNELIUS JAMES BROSNAN

Lapwai Mission, THE (1836–47), was established in November, 1836, by the Rev. and Mrs.
Henry Harmon Spalding, co-workers of Dr.
Marcus Whitman, at a site eleven miles above
Lewiston, Idaho, where the Lapwai Creek empties into the Clearwater River. Here Spalding
had the first white home, church, school, flour
mill, sawmill, blacksmith shop and loom in
what is now Idaho. In 1839 the mission secured
a printing press from Hawaii and sent it to
Lapwai. This was the first press in the Pacific
Northwest. The mission was closed by the Whitman massacre[qv]. In 1871 the Presbyterian Church
resumed the work, which is still being carried
on among the Nez Percés.

[C. M. Drury, *Henry Harmon Spalding;* Cornelius James
Brosnan, *History of the State of Idaho.*]
                        CORNELIUS JAMES BROSNAN

Laramie, Fort, was established in June, 1834,
by William Sublette and Robert Campbell, fur
traders from St. Louis, Mo. The first structure,
built of logs, was named Fort William for the
senior founder. Located near the junction of
the Laramie and North Platte rivers, in the land
of the Sioux and Cheyennes[qv], it became the
trade center for a large area, serving white trappers and Indians alike. The American Fur Company[qv] purchased the fort in 1836. They replaced

the log stockade with adobe walls in 1841 and
christened the structure "Fort John." But the
name did not "take"; "Fort Laramie" supplanted
it.

First missionaries to Oregon and earliest overland emigrants used this fort, on the Oregon
Trail[qv], as a supply and refitting depot. The
growing emigrant tide, greatly augmented by
the goldseekers of 1849, demanded protection
from Indians. The Government purchased the
post from the trading company on June 26, 1849,
for $4000 and converted it into a military fort.
New wooden and adobe buildings were erected.
It became the great way station on the principal
road to the Far West. The Grattan (1854) and
the Harney (1856) massacres[qv] near the fort
foreshadowed the general Indian war that followed. Fort Laramie became headquarters for
the military campaigns. When the Indians were
finally subdued and placed on reservations, need
for the fort ended. It was abandoned April 20,
1890.

[L. R. Hafen and F. M. Young, *Fort Laramie and the
Pageant of the West, 1834-1890.*]   LEROY R. HAFEN

Laramie, Fort, Treaty of (1851). Thomas
Fitzpatrick, first Indian agent to the tribes of
the upper Platte and Arkansas, asked, in 1849,
authorization and funds for a general treaty
with his wards. In February, 1851, Congress responded with a $100,000 appropriation. Couriers
were sent to the Indians appointing a council
for Sept. 1 at Fort Laramie[qv]. Sioux, Cheyennes,
Arapahoes[qv] and Shoshones were the principal
tribes that gathered, forming perhaps the largest
and most colorful Indian council ever assembled
in the West. For twenty days negotiations continued, being prolonged to await arrival of the
wagon train of presents. Indian feasts and demonstrations occurred daily. Companies of soldiers
placed between tribes hereditarily hostile avoided conflict. The treaty as signed provided peace,
territorial boundaries for individual tribes, a
$50,000 annuity to the Indians and permitted
establishment of forts and roads in the Indian
country[qv].

[L. R. Hafen and W. J. Ghent, *Broken Hand, the Life
of Thomas Fitzpatrick.*]   LEROY R. HAFEN

Laramie, Fort, Treaty of (1868). In 1866 the
Sioux had agreed to permit the opening of the
Bozeman Trail[qv] to Montana. Before negotiations were completed, Col. Carrington arrived
with troops and began erection of forts on the
new road. The Indians objected, attacks began
and war ensued (*see* Red Cloud War). Peace
advocates in the East now won ascendency with

the slogan "cheaper to feed than to fight the Indians." The Government changed policy and in 1867 sent Peace Commissioners (*see* Indian Commissions), but the hostiles refused to negotiate while the new forts remained. The Commissioners came again in April, 1868, acceded to Indian demands and drafted a treaty. They agreed to withdraw the Bozeman Trail forts and to recognize the country north of the North Platte and east of the Big Horn Mountains as unceded Indian territory. No whites might settle in this region. All that part of present South Dakota, west of the Missouri River, was formed into a Sioux Reservation. To induce Indians to settle upon it the Government agreed to construct agency building, a schoolhouse, sawmill, gristmill, etc., on the Missouri River and to furnish food supplies for four years and clothing for thirty years. The Indians promised to refrain from capturing and killing whites, attacking coaches and wagon trains, and to withdraw all opposition to the construction of railroads being built across the plains. Some of the Indians signed the treaty in April, but Red Cloud and the distrusting bands refused to sign until November, after the hated forts in the Powder River country had actually been abandoned. With these concessions made and with annuities provided, generally peaceful relations were to prevail until gold discoveries in the Black Hills[w] brought a new white tide into Dakota and precipitated the wars of the middle-1870's.

[George E. Hyde, *Red Cloud's Folk;* L. R. Hafen and F. M. Young, *Fort Laramie and the Pageant of the West, 1834-1890.*]   LEROY R. HAFEN

Larned, Fort, named for Col. B. F. Larned, then Paymaster-general of the United States Army, was established on the Pawnee fork of the Arkansas River, Oct. 22, 1859. Built first of adobe[w], it was later reconstructed of stone. Gen. Winfield Scott Hancock used it as a base for his expedition against the Cheyennes[w] in 1867, and troops operated from it in the Dull Knife campaign[w] of 1878. The post was abandoned in the latter year.

[Rolland R. Jacquart, article in *Kansas City Star*, April 11, 1926.]   PAUL I. WELLMAN

LaSalle, Explorations of. Until New France[w] became a royal colony in 1663, its development was painfully slow. Following this change, a period of marked progress set in. The Iroquois[w] were subdued, industry and commerce were fostered and geographical expansion was vigorously prosecuted.

Foremost in promoting this renaissance of

New France were Intendant Jean Talon and Gov. Frontenac. Among the galaxy of explorers whose names adorn the period, the most notable was René Robert Cavelier, Sieur de LaSalle (1643–87), who came to Canada in early manhood in 1667 and began near Montreal the development of a seigniory. Soon, however, his active mind became absorbed in the possibilities inherent in the Indian trade, and the coming of Count Frontenac as Governor in 1672 offered him an opportunity to exploit them.

Frontenac was an imperialist and the fur trade[w] offered the prospect of recouping his ruined fortune. In 1673 he founded Fort Frontenac[w] (modern Kingston) in the Iroquois country, and next year sent LaSalle to France to enlighten the king concerning his expansionist designs. The royal approval was obtained, and LaSalle returned with a patent of nobility for himself and the grant of Fort Frontenac as a seigniory.

In 1677 LaSalle again went to France to seek royal approval of a far greater design. He now desired to establish a colony in the country south of the Great Lakes, and to this end desired a trade monopoly of the region to be developed, and authority to build forts and govern it. The king was willing to approve all but the idea of colonizing, and in 1678 LaSalle was back in New France making preparations for the actual invasion of the West, to be launched the following season. A small vessel, the *Griffon*[w], was built above Niagara and in August, 1679, LaSalle set sail for Green Bay[w]. Here the *Griffon* was sent back to Niagara, laden with furs, while LaSalle himself journeyed southward by canoe around Lake Michigan to the mouth of the St. Joseph.

Here he tarried until December, building Fort Miami[w] and awaiting the return of the *Griffon*, which had vanished forever on its maiden voyage. At length he ascended the St. Joseph to South Bend, where he crossed to the Kankakee and descended that stream and the Illinois to Lake Peoria where he built Fort Crèvecœur[w] and a vessel in which to descend the Mississippi. He also dispatched Father Hennepin[w] and two companions to explore the Upper Mississippi, while he himself set out in midwinter for distant Fort Frontenac to procure badly needed supplies.

Iroquois raids and other obstacles were now encountered, but LaSalle doggedly fought on and the close of 1681 found him again at Fort Miami, ready to renew his push for the sea. Descending the Illinois, he reached the Mississippi on Feb. 2, 1682, and on April 9 was at the Gulf of Mexico, where with fitting ceremony he formally claimed the entire Mississippi Valley for his king and named it Louisiana^qv.

The way to Mexico was open, and the realization of his plans seemed assured, when Count Frontenac was replaced by a new Governor who proved a bitter enemy of LaSalle. Facing utter ruin, he again went to France to appeal to his monarch in person. His requests were approved, and in 1684 he sailed for the Gulf of Mexico, equipped with men and means to establish a post on the Lower Mississippi to serve as the southern outlet of his colony. Unable to find the river-mouth, however, the colonists were landed on the coast of Texas, where most of them eventually perished (*see* St. Louis of Texas; LaSalle, Spanish Searches for). LaSalle himself was murdered in 1687 while still seeking to find the Mississippi and establish contact with his post in Illinois. Although his life closed in seeming failure, his dream survived and in the following century Louisiana became the fairest portion of New France. In the eyes of history, LaSalle will forever be deemed its father.

[Francis Parkman, *LaSalle and the Discovery of the Great West;* Pierre Margry, *Découvertes et Établissements des Français dans l'ouest et dans le sud de l'Amérique Septentrionale.*]
                                        M. M. QUAIFE

LaSalle, Spanish Searches for (1685–89). The alarm felt by the Spaniards over LaSalle's intrusion in the Gulf of Mexico was revealed by the intensity of their search for his colony. Between 1685 and 1688 five maritime expeditions combed the Gulf coast, but failed to find the French settlement on the Garcitas. By land, one expedition searched westward from Florida, four expeditions, led by Alonso DeLeon, went northeastward from Mexico, and a number of minor searches were instituted by provincial officials. On his fourth expedition (1689) DeLeon found the remains of LaSalle's colony, three months after it had been destroyed by Indians.

[Carlos E. Castañeda, *The Finding of Texas;* William E. Dunn, *Spanish and French Rivalry in the Gulf Region of the United States, 1678-1702.*]
                                        C. T. NEU

Las Animas Land Grant. On Dec. 9, 1843, the Mexican Government granted to Cornelio Vigil and Ceran St. Vrain a tract of 4,000,000 acres lying southwesterly from the Arkansas River to the Sangre de Cristo Mountains with the valleys of the Huerfano and the Purgatory (Animas) rivers as side lines. It was one of the many large grants made by Mexico to settle and protect the border. June 21, 1860, Congress confirmed only 97,651 acres of this grant on the

grounds that more than eleven square leagues to one individual was illegal under Mexican law. Dissatisfied claimants appealed unsuccessfully to a special Court of Private Land Claims (1891–1904) and finally to the United States Supreme Court.

[L. R. Hafen, Mexican Land Grants in Colorado, *Colorado Magazine*, May, 1927; *U. S. House Reports*, 36th Cong., 1st Sess., No. 321; 179 *U. S. Reports* 201-06.]
                                        PERCY S. FRITZ

Lassen's Trading Post and Ranch, near the mouth of Deer Creek in northeastern California, stood at the head of Sacramento Valley and was an important center both in early exploration and in the gold rush. It was named after Peter Lassen, an early pioneer. Frémont was using the ranch as his headquarters when war was declared against Mexico in April, 1846.

[F. S. Dellenbaugh, *Frémont and '49;* Rensch and Hoover, *Historic Spots of California.*]
                                        CARL L. CANNON

Last Chance Gulch. *See* Helena Mining Camp.

Last Island Catastrophe. Last Island, in the Gulf of Mexico opposite the mouth of Bayou Lafourche, which had become a favorite summer resort for Louisiana families who wished to escape the intense heat of the interior, was devastated by a tropical hurricane on Sunday, Aug. 10, 1856, in which more than 100 persons perished.

[Walter Prichard, ed., The Last Island Disaster of August 10, 1856, in *Louisiana Historical Quarterly*, XX.]
                                        WALTER PRICHARD

Latin America, United States Investments in, including direct and portfolio, represented about 33.2% of the total foreign holdings of the United States in 1935. Direct investment, beginning early in the 19th century in small trading ventures, expanded to its present proportions principally during the 20th century. American funds have been widely placed in railways, mining (gold, silver, copper, nitrates), agriculture (tropical fruits, sugar, cotton), petroleum, industry and public utilities. The total of American capital placed in Latin America in 1935 was estimated at $3,300,000,000. Complaints of exploitation have been frequent, and, on the other hand, investors have often appealed to the United States Government for protection of their interests. Since the World War, the Latin-American countries have tended to place increasing restrictions on the employment of foreign capital, and American investors have suffered from the exchange control measures which recently have been put in force.

Portfolio investments, consisting of loans to

governments and sub-divisions thereof, began about 1900. To 1914, the total loans to Latin America amounted to $236,000,000, with over half being to Mexico and Central America. Post-war issues increased this amount to $1,800,000,-000 ($1,500,000,000 outstanding) in 1935, representing about 23% of the foreign lending. At that time due to changing economic conditions and the depression, over 75% of these bonds were in default. The losses suffered have made these investments unsatisfactory, and the effect upon the debtor governments has not been the best. Some countries are burdened with obligations which will never be paid. Investments in the Latin-American republics have been one of the factors of the relations of the United States with those countries. Many steps have been taken by the Department of State to protect American interests, and this activity is often termed "dollar diplomacy"[q].

[Cleona Lewis, *America's Stake in International Investments.*]

ROSCOE R. HILL

Latin-American Relations with the United States have been varied and complex. Though as early as 1823, Colombia passed a law to encourage emigrants by grants of lands, yet with the exception of Brazil, at the end of the Civil War, and Mexico under Díaz, there have been no marked currents of emigration from the United States to Latin-American countries. From 1880 to 1915 only some 6000 Americans migrated to Argentina, an element that constituted only one tenth of one per cent of the total immigration into that country during the given period. Most American citizens residing in Latin America are engaged in commercial or industrial enterprises. Leading Latin Americans have, from time to time, sojourned in the United States and have been influenced by her civilization. Many teachers from the United States have been employed in schools in Latin-American countries.

Ministers of various Protestant sects in English America have served as teachers in schools and academies established in those countries in connection with missions and churches. In 1836 Methodist missionaries were sent from the United States to Buenos Aires and Rio de Janeiro. Prominent among institutions of higher learning founded by Protestant sects in Latin America are the Evangelical Seminary in Mexico City, Mackenzie College at São Paulo, the American Institute at La Paz, Santiago College and the English Institute at Santiago de Chile. By 1916 forty-seven religious societies in the United States had become interested in missionary work in Latin-American countries. It has been esti-

mated that, at that time, there were over 1000 Protestant missionaries from the United States in towns and cities of Cuba, Mexico, Central and South America. These missionaries had direction of 1051 churches and 1876 missionary stations, with 82,000 communicants. Not only did this activity promote primary and higher education in Latin-American countries but it also had at times a liberal influence upon the attitude of governments in western South America toward civil and religious liberty.

The custom observed by the élite of Latin America of sending their sons abroad to complete their education has not been without influence. During the struggle for independence from Spain, the practice began of sending young men to the United States to study. The Liberator Simón Bolívar sent his nephew there to be educated. Latin-American governments soon adopted the custom of sending students on stipends to the United States to prosecute their education. From Argentina they have been sent to study agriculture, mechanic arts and electricity. From Peru they have been sent to study medicine and the military art. In general, the studies pursued by Latin-American youth in the United States have been of a practical sort—engineering, medicine, commerce and agriculture. It was estimated that in 1918 there were 2000 students from Latin-American countries in the United States.

Latin America has furnished an attractive field of study, especially for scholars interested in geography and allied sciences. At one time or another, the Smithsonian Institution, the National Geographic Society and the American Museum of Natural History have promoted investigations into the archæology, ethnology and culture of Latin America. Among others, Yale University, the University of Pennsylvania and Tulane University have subsidized research expeditions to Latin-American countries. In 1865 the distinguished scientist Louis Agassiz made a trip up the Amazon River during which he not only investigated the geology of Brazil but also studied the distribution of fish. In 1912 an expedition to Peru, under the auspices of Yale University and the National Geographic Society, and led by Hiram Bingham, explored the forgotten refuge of the Incas in an Andean fastness at Machu Picchu. In 1914, by the aid of the Brazilian Col. Rondon, Theodore Roosevelt's expedition, which was organized under the auspices of the American Museum of Natural History, explored the Rio da Duvida and collected many specimens of birds and mammals. Notable work in medical science has been advanced by the Rockefeller Foundation in prosecuting research concerning yellow fever^{qv}.

Commercial relations between the United States and Latin America hark back to colonial days. After the government at Washington acknowledged the independence of Latin-American countries, it proceeded to negotiate commercial treaties with them. A treaty with Colombia, Oct. 3, 1824, incorporated the most-favored-nation doctrine^{qv}, and defined contraband of war^{qv} in a narrow sense. These provisions and that declaring against paper blockades were later included in other treaties between the United States and her southern neighbors. During the years from 1850 to 1875, the United States promoted the adoption by Latin-American nations of the principle that when rivers flowed through more than one country they should be open to navigation by the vessels of all countries. In 1868 sales to the countries lying south of the Rio Grande were but 20% of the total exports of the United States; in 1878, a little less than 10%; in 1888, a fraction over 10%; and in 1898, only 7% of the total exports. The chief imports of Latin-American countries from the United States were manufactured articles, while their exports were largely raw materials. Reciprocity^{qv} in trade relations of the United States was not applied to Latin America until Blaine launched his Pan-American policy. The reciprocity provisions of the McKinley Tariff Act^{qv}, however, were abruptly ended in 1894. In 1903 a reciprocity treaty was negotiated between Cuba and the United States which much stimulated commercial intercourse between those countries. From 1900 to 1914 there was a great increase in the trade between the United States and Latin America. During the World War that trade increased prodigiously. By the midsummer of 1917, the import and export trade of the United States with Latin-American countries was over five times as large as in 1900. With the revival of keen European competition upon the close of the World War, however, this trade relatively decreased. With regard to certain countries, the decline was intensified by the nationalistic tariff policy of the United States. The Fordney-McCumber Tariff Act^{qv} laid import duties on wheat and meat. And when the United States proceeded to enforce rigorously certain sanitary regulations so as to shut meat from the pampas out of her markets, the Argentinians became resentful. Not until President F. D. Roosevelt inaugurated his "good neighbor policy"^{qv} was an attempt made to appease this discontent by the negotiation of reciprocity treaties with Latin-American countries.

During recent decades commercial relations with Latin-American countries have improved partly because of the important industrial enterprises of Americans there. Among other interests may be mentioned mines in Mexico, Peru and Chile, railroads in Mexico, Ecuador and Peru, and branches of the National City Bank in South American capitals. In 1930 it was estimated that between five and six billion dollars of American capital were invested in Latin-American countries—an amount presumably only exceeded by that invested by the English. This enormous outlay has not infrequently provoked questions concerning the right and duty of the United States to protect her citizens' investments under foreign skies.

With respect to influence upon the political ideals and institutions of Latin America, the United States has not gained much ground recently. During the protracted struggle for independence and for some years afterwards, leaders in divers sections of Middle and South America viewed the Republic of the North as a great exemplar. Translations of the Declaration of Independence, the Constitution of the United States and the constitutions of various states were circulated among the patriots. Some of the early constitutions in Mexico, Central America, Chile and Argentina were patterned after the Constitution of the United States. Though the national constitutions of Argentina, Brazil, Venezuela and Mexico still show many traces of their grand model, and though here and there the transformation of local administrative areas into states has been advanced, yet during recent decades there has been in certain quarters a great tendency toward centralization.

Commercial and political relations have often been related to diplomatic intercourse. The Monroe Doctrine^{qv} with its varying interpretations has often furnished issues for discussion. Upon occasion Latin-American publicists have praised that doctrine when it has been applied to protect their countries against foreign aggression. On the other hand, they have denounced it when used to sanction interference with a nation's sovereign rights, as in Haiti and the Dominican Republic. In particular, the "Roosevelt Corollary of the Monroe Doctrine"^{qv} caused bitter criticism of the United States which was only brought to an end by the disavowal of that corollary by President F. D. Roosevelt. The role of the United States in the New World was also placed at stake by her refusal to accede to the Covenant of the League of Nations^{qv}, while almost all of the Latin-American states joined that society. Many important problems involved in inter-American relations have been considered by international conferences of the American states. Historical and scientific congresses have discussed various phases of intellectual and cultural relationships, while Pan-American conferences[TW] have framed protocols concerning inter-American commercial and political intercourse.

[W. S. Robertson, *Hispanic-American Relations with the United States;* C. H. Haring, *South America Looks at the United States;* J. H. Latané, *The United States and Latin America.*]

WILLIAM SPENCE ROBERTSON

Latin-American Republics, Recognition of the. Both the Government and public opinion in the United States were openly sympathetic to the cause of Latin-American independence from the beginning of the revolution against Spain. In 1810 Joel Poinsett was sent to Buenos Aires and Chile to promote commercial relations with the revolted colonies and to express the friendly feeling of the United States. Other agents and consuls were sent in the following years. Officially the United States was neutral in the war, but private citizens engaged in filibustering[TW] and many Latin-American privateers were fitted out in American ports despite official opposition.

The uncertain character of the struggle postponed for some years any serious consideration of diplomatic recognition. In 1817, however, three commissioners were sent to Buenos Aires to investigate the propriety of entering into relations with the government there. They returned with conflicting reports and no action was taken. Later in the same year Henry Clay began ardently to advocate recognition in a series of speeches in Congress, chiefly perhaps with the idea of causing embarrassment to the Monroe administration. In 1821 he procured the passage of a resolution in the House of Representatives expressing sympathy with Latin America and a readiness to support the President when he felt that the time for recognition had come.

Meanwhile Monroe and Adams, his Secretary of State, had proceeded cautiously in the matter, though the President's message to Congress in 1819 had spoken sympathetically of the Latin-American cause. The treaty with Spain for the purchase of Florida, signed Feb. 22, 1819 (*see* Adams-Onís Treaty) , was still pending, and the administration did not wish to offend Spain until this matter was finally disposed of by the exchange of ratifications on Feb. 22, 1821. By this time the patriots in South America had won a series of important victories, and later in the same year Mexico proclaimed its independence. Strong Spanish forces still held the greater part of Peru, but the revolution in Spain had made their situation difficult.

On March 8, 1822, President Monroe recommended in a message to Congress that the Latin-American republics be recognized. A bill authorizing diplomatic missions to them was signed by the President on May 4, and on June 19 Manuel Torres was formally received by the President as *chargé d'affaires* from Colombia. In the following months the United States also entered into diplomatic relations with Argentina, Chile, Mexico, Brazil and Central America.

[F. L. Paxson, *The Independence of the South American Republics;* W. R. Manning, *Diplomatic Correspondence of the United States Concerning the Independence of the Latin-American Nations.*]

DANA G. MUNRO

Latin Schools. These, the earliest type of educational institutions set up in the American colonies, grew out of the influence of the Renaissance and were patterned on the Latin schools of England. These schools appeared in all the colonies except Georgia, but reached their greatest growth in New England. An attempt to establish a Latin school in Virginia was made as early as 1621 but the Great Massacre[TW] of the following year and the failure of the Virginia Company[TW] ended the project. The first successful attempt to establish a Latin school was made in Boston in 1635; it was the principal school in that city for nearly a half century. The purpose of these schools was to prepare boys for college. The Massachusetts law of 1647, requiring a grammar school in every town having 100 families, stimulated these schools, which also quickly appeared in neighboring colonies. Latin schools were planned, supported and managed by the well-to-do. Tuition fees were generally charged and the curriculum, which was confined almost entirely to a study of Latin and Greek, was intended to teach boys to read and write Latin and possibly to speak it. Some of these schools had distinguished teachers. The Latin schools began to decline in importance by the middle of the 18th century when they began to give way to the academies[TW].

[E. P. Cubberley, *Public Education in the United States;* Edgar W. Knight, *Education in the United States.*]

EDGAR W. KNIGHT

Latitudinarians is the name applied to a school of thought in the Church of England in the 18th century which emphasized the fundamental principles of the Christian religion rather than any specific doctrinal position. In America the name has been given to such religious leaders as have not been primarily concerned about the interpretation of a creed, but have been liberal and

propriation of public funds by lawless political groups like the Tweed Ring[q] in New York and the more "honest" graft of special favors to real-estate or public-service interests, went hand in hand with widespread crime and lax law enforcement as pictured in Brand Whitlock's *On the Enforcement of Law in Cities* (1913).

Lawlessness appeared in national life in the Crédit Mobilier and reached the President's official family in the Whiskey Ring[qq] and the scandals of Indian trade of Grant's administration (*see* Belknap Scandal). Business and industry began systematically to evade state taxation and regulation by incorporation in states with more lenient laws. Employers resorted to maintaining private armed forces, like the Pinkerton detectives who fought with the strikers in the Homestead Strike (1892), while labor unions openly defied court injunctions in the Pullman Strike (1894) [q]. The Molly Maguires[q] in Pennsylvania mining towns in the 1870's show the lawlessness which grew out of post-Civil War industrial unrest, while private interests exploiting the land, mineral and timber resources of the West flirted with actual law violation in a mad race for wealth.

Organized lawlessness reached a high stage of development in American cities after the World War. Gangs like that of Al Capone, organized to exploit bootlegging[q] of liquor in violation of the Eighteenth Amendment[q], developed into a widely ramified system of "rackets" and "racketeers"[q] exploiting gambling, organized vice, narcotics, gun-running, abortions and lawless labor activities. A general conviction that organized lawlessness had become stronger than the forces of law brought the investigation of the Wickersham Commission on Law Enforcement[q] (1931) and of a Senate Committee (1934) and resulted in increased Federal activity, especially through the Federal Bureau of Investigation[q], for the efficient co-operation of all law-enforcing agencies.

[R. M. Coates, *The Outlaw Years;* H. H. Bancroft, *Popular Tribunals;* A. B. Hart, *American Ideals Historically Traced;* M. Mooney, *Crime Incorporated.*]

HAROLD E. DAVIS

Lawrence, THE, a twenty-gun brig built by O. H. Perry at Erie, in 1813, and his flagship at the battle of Lake Erie[q]. In July, 1815, it was sunk as useless, but was raised in 1875 and exhibited at the Centennial Exhibition[q] until accidentally destroyed by fire.

[W. W. Dobbins, *History of the Battle of Lake Erie.*]

WALTER B. NORRIS

Lawrence, The Sack of (May 21, 1856), was the beginning of actual civil war in the Kansas conflict (*see* Border War). A proslavery grand jury had indicted several of the Free-State[q] leaders for treason, and had "presented" the Emigrant Aid Company's[q] Free-State Hotel, believed to have been built as a fort, and the newspapers, the *Herald of Freedom* and the *Free State,* as nuisances. A United States marshal appeared before the village with a posse of seven or eight hundred men to serve the warrants. Having made his arrests unopposed, he relinquished his posse to the proslavery sheriff S. J. Jones who, since the Wakarusa War[q], had sought the destruction of this "hotbed of abolitionism." Led by Jones, ex-Senator Atchison of Missouri, Maj. Buford of Alabama and others, the mob entered the town and, making a pretext of the grand jury "presentment," burned the hotel and wrecked the newspaper offices. Accounts disagree as to how much more property was destroyed or stolen. A few days later John Brown retaliated in the Pottawatomie Massacre[q], while, at the request of Gov. Shannon, troops were sent to Topeka to effect the dispersal of a Free-State legislature. News of the sack aroused the entire North, led to the formation of the National Kansas Committee and provided the Republican party with the issue of "Bleeding Kansas."

[Richard Cordley, *A History of Lawrence, Kansas;* L. W. Spring, *Kansas, the Prelude to the War for the Union.*]

SAMUEL A. JOHNSON

Lawrence Raid, THE (1863). *See* Quantrill's Raid.

Lawrence Strike, THE, of textile workers in Lawrence, Mass., against a wage cut which employers alleged was necessitated by legislation curtailing working hours, lasted from Jan. 11 to March 14, 1912. Perhaps its most sensational feature was the success of the Industrial Workers of the World[q] in organizing the polyglot mass of low-paid mill workers into a militant co-operative body. The I. W. W. had hitherto been a minor factor in eastern labor disputes and its appearance in New England created widespread perturbation. The strike involved most of the lawless practices common in American industrial warfare but resulted in important successes for the strikers. Increased wage scales were granted, resulting in improved standards in other New England textile centers.

[P. F. Brissenden, *The I. W. W., A Study of American Syndicalism;* Report on Strike of Textile Workers in Lawrence, Mass., 62nd Congress, 2 Sess., *Senate Document No. 870.*]

W. A. ROBINSON

"Laws, Concessions and Agreements," THE, were provisions for the colonization and government of West Jersey[w]. The work of William Penn, they were approved and signed before leaving England by 151 emigrants (March 3, 1676/77), and became operative four months later. To encourage orderly and speedy settlement the land acquired was divided into ten equal parts, each part subdivided into tenths or proprieties (units of representation) and generous grants made to settlers subject only to the annual quitrent[w]. Government rested upon a bill of rights including absolute religious freedom, public trial by jury, right of petition, freedom from arbitrary arrest or imprisonment for debt, and equal taxation by representatives. A general assembly, annually elected by secret ballot by all resident proprietors, freeholders[w] and inhabitants, exercised supreme governing authority. The assembly (first meeting Nov. 21, 1681) was charged with lawmaking, choosing chief executives, constituting courts, punishing murder and treason and, above all, with maintaining the supremacy of the fundamental law. The province was governed by the "Concessions" until 1702.

[Leaming and Spicer, *Grants, Concessions and Original Constitutions of the Province of New Jersey;* C. M. Andrews, *The Colonial Period of American History,* Vol. III.]
C. A. TITUS

Lead Mining. Lead ore was worked in Dutchess County, N. Y., by 1740, and at Southampton, Mass., in 1754. Col. Chiswell[w] opened lead mines in Virginia about 1750, but they ceased production before 1776. During the Revolution lead production was stimulated by bounties, but there was no large production east of the Mississippi prior to 1800.

The deposits of the Mississippi Valley were discovered as early as the middle of the 17th century and began to be worked by Perrot about 1690. Renault made a more ambitious attempt in 1720 and by the time the region came into United States possession, in 1803, a considerable amount had been produced. By 1855 the production of the Galena[w] district had reached 55,000,000 pounds.

Gold and silver were the principal objects of search in the development of the Far West after 1850, and lead smelting was one of the most feasible methods for treating ores rich in silver. Before railroad transportation became available the silver was recovered from the lead and the latter not shipped, but as transcontinental railroads were built Montana and Nevada began shipping lead. In 1876 rich silver-lead ores were discovered at Leadville[w], Colo., and for a time Colorado was the largest lead-producing region

of the world. Lead production in Idaho steadily increased in importance after the discovery of the Bunker Hill & Sullivan in 1885. There are many lead-producing districts in Utah which have from time to time shifted in relative importance. Since 1900 the Mississippi Valley, Idaho and Utah have been the most important lead-mining regions, Colorado's output having severely declined. (*See also* Ste. Genevieve Lead Mining District; Joplin Lead Mining District.)

[H. B. Pulsifer, *Notes for a History of Lead;* T. A. Rickard, *A History of American Mining.*]
T. T. READ

Lead Plates. *See* Céloron's Lead Plates; Verendrye Plate.

Leadville Mining District, THE, named for a lead carbonate ore which abounded in the region and contained large amounts of silver, is located near the headwaters of the Arkansas River. The first settlement resulted from the discovery in 1860 of rich placer[w] deposits in California Gulch, which yielded over $3,000,000 in gold before they were exhausted in 1867. For nearly ten years sporadic prospecting was carried on, which finally culminated, in 1875, in the discovery of the true nature of the carbonate ore by W. H. Stevens and A. B. Wood. Then occurred a mining rush on a grand scale. The Little Pittsburg, Matchless, Robert E. Lee and other famous mines were developed. On Jan. 26, 1878, the city of Leadville was organized with H. A. W. Tabor, who was to become the district's best-known Bonanza King[w], as the first mayor. During the period 1858–1925 the district produced nearly $200,000,000 of silver and over $50,000,000 of gold.

[G. F. Willison, *Here They Dug the Gold.*]
GEORGE L. ANDERSON

League of Armed Neutrality, THE. *See* Armed Neutrality.

League of Nations, THE, in the words of President Wilson, "is a great idea which has been growing in the minds of all generous men for several generations . . ., the dream of the friends of humanity through all the ages." The "great idea" was embodied in such works as Pierre Dubois' *Recovery of the Holy Land* (1305), Henry of Navarre's (probably Sully's) *Great Design,* published in 1662, and the Abbé de St. Pierre's *Plan for a Perpetual Peace* (1712) . William Penn's *Essay Toward the Present and Future Peace of Europe* (1693) and William Ladd's *Essay on a Congress of Nations* (1840) were notable American contributions to this remarkable literature on world organization. On the practical side, the framers of the Covenant relied upon the experience of the numerous public administrative unions—such as the Universal Postal Union—the Permanent Court of Arbitration and the international conferences like those of 1899 and 1907 at The Hague^{w} of which the purpose and result were the provision of principles and rules of international law^{w}. In all of these steps toward an integrated international system the United States had participated, American official and private effort having been particularly directed toward the establishment of international judicial machinery.

During the World War^{w} various societies were formed in the United States, as in European countries, to consider and plan for an international political structure that would, *inter alia,* provide legal methods of settling controversies and thus reduce the likelihood of war. The most effective of these societies was the League to Enforce Peace, organized at Philadelphia in June, 1915. William Howard Taft was its president, and its twenty-two vice-presidents were highly distinguished leaders in public life, business and the professions. Political party lines were disregarded in its membership. Henry Cabot Lodge and A. Lawrence Lowell as well as Mr. Taft were ardent advocates of its four-point program: (1) a world court, (2) a council of inquiry and recommendation to deal with political issues, (3) economic and military sanctions and (4) periodical law-codification conferences. Ninety-six per cent of American Chambers of Commerce voted "that this country take the lead in forming a league of nations," 77% for economic sanctions and 64% for military sanctions.

President Wilson made the conception of a league the fourteenth point of his peace program laid before Congress on Jan. 8, 1918: "A general association of nations must be formed under specific covenants for the purpose of affording mutual guarantees of political independence and territorial integrity to great and small states alike." He received in March the report of a British committee, headed by Sir Walter Phillimore, which had been working on a plan for a league of nations. Col. House did not use this report in preparing a draft plan which Wilson revised and took to Paris. There he further revised the document. The plan submitted to the commission appointed by the Versailles Conference to "work out the details of the constitution and functions of the League" was a combination of British and American ideas prepared by Sir Cecil Hurst and David Hunter Miller from the drafts above mentioned.

President Wilson insisted that the Covenant should be part of the Treaty of Versailles^{w}. He was chairman of the Peace Conference commission to draft the Covenant, of which Col. House also was a member. Wilson's emphasis upon Article X^{w}, which he regarded as a universalizing of the Monroe Doctrine^{w}, is well-known, but Article XI was his favorite. Suggestions from American senators and congressmen were incorporated in the text during the drafting process. Besides Articles X and XI, the American contribution to Articles IV, VIII, XII, XV, XVI, XVIII, XIX, XXI, XXII and XXIII was especially noteworthy.

The Treaty of Versailles was submitted to the Senate on July 10, 1919. Sen. Lodge, who had previously withdrawn from his advocacy of a league, was, as chairman of the Foreign Relations Committee, the principal opponent of the Covenant. Outside the Senate, Mr. George Harvey, editor of *Harvey's Weekly* and the *North American Review,* was vigorously antagonistic. Because of the strong popular feeling favoring entrance into the League, the senatorial opposition feared a direct vote and resorted to reservations and delay. This opposition was motivated by party politics, by traditional repugnance to "entanglement" in foreign affairs and by resentment against certain sections of the treaty. On the final vote upon the treaty with fifteen reservations, taken on March 19, 1920, the ayes mustered but thirty-five, the noes forty-nine votes; twenty supporters voted against the treaty at Wilson's request rather than have it passed in emasculated form. Although by that date public sentiment had cooled, it was still so favorable to League membership that Warren G. Harding, the Republican candidate in the 1920 election, felt obliged to propose an "association of nations," thereby confusing the electorate as to his real attitude.

For six months after President Harding took office the Department of State ignored all communications from the agencies of the League. Undoubtedly Secretary Hughes was controlled in this procedure by the feeling among the "irreconcilable" Republican senators. However, American interest in many of the subjects of League conferences soon forced a co-operative attitude. At first "unofficial observers" were sent to such meetings, but as these men and women were usually experts and sincerely concerned, their participation was of great value to the League's activities. Beginning in 1924 the American Government has been officially represented in various League conferences, among them the Second Opium Conference of 1924–25 and the Opium Conference^{w} of 1931, the Conference on the Traffic in Arms of 1925, the Conference for the Limitation and Reduction of Armaments, 1932–34, and the Economic Conferences of 1927 and subsequent years. It has also appointed official representatives to such League committees and commissions as the Preparatory Commission for a Disarmament Conference, the Economic Committee and the Opium Advisory Committee. In 1931 an official of the American Government represented the United States as a full voting member of the Council Committee on assistance to Liberia[w]. A number of American citizens have accepted appointment by the Council or Secretariat on other agencies, notably on the Health Committee and the Committee of Intellectual Co-operation. A few are members of the Secretariat. In 1934 the United States agreed to register all treaties and other international agreements with the Secretariat. A special group of Foreign Service Officers is maintained at Geneva to observe and have contact with the work of the League.

Co-operation in political questions began with the Sino-Japanese controversy in Manchuria, 1931–33 (see Lansing-Ishii Agreement). Secretary Stimson not only sent notes of protest paralleling those of the Council but appointed a representative to sit with the Council for consultation upon the applicability of the Pact of Paris and approved the acceptance by Maj. Gen. McCoy of membership in the Lytton Commission of Inquiry. Approval of the League's nonrecognition[w] resolutions, which were similar to the statement of Secretary Stimson on Jan. 7, 1931, and of the Assembly resolution of Oct. 6, 1937, in which Japanese action in China was declared to be contrary to Japan's treaty obligations, was expressed by the incumbent secretaries of state. However, the American Government gave no direct intimation of readiness to co-operate with the League in economic or military sanctions.

A Commission of Neutrals, on which the United States was represented, attempted unsuccessfully to collaborate with the League toward assisting in a settlement of the Gran Chaco boundary dispute between Bolivia and Paraguay, 1932–33. Subsequently the United States accepted membership on certain League commissions seeking to settle the dispute. Similarly cordial co-operative measures were taken in connection with the League's handling of the Peruvian-Columbian dispute over Leticia, 1932–35. The relation of this country to the Italo-Ethiopian case was indirect, but the application of the Neutrality Act of 1935[w], like the public endorsement by President F. D. Roosevelt and Secretary Hull of League measures in the premises, was assurance to the League that the United States at least

would not support Italy morally or by the sale of arms and munitions of war.

[Benjamin H. Williams, *American Diplomacy, Policies and Practice.*]   HAROLD S. QUIGLEY

League of United Southerners, THE (1858), was an organization of Southern leaders created by Edmund Ruffin and William L. Yancey to promote Southern political unity and to spread propaganda for secession[w]. It met with such indifference that the founders, in 1859, abandoned it. Nevertheless, some of the local clubs remained to campaign effectively for secession in 1860–61.

[Avery Craven, *Edmund Ruffin, Southerner.*]
HENRY T. SHANKS

League of Women Voters, National, founded in 1920 to help the newly enfranchised women make intelligent use of voting privileges, has become an outstanding agency for nonpartisan political education and a sponsor for legislation and policies it believes desirable for public welfare.

[*Publications* of the National League of Women Voters.]
LOUISE B. DUNBAR

***Leander* Incident, THE** (April, 1806), was an acute manifestation of impressment[w]. A British man-of-war, on patrol duty off the three-mile limit at New York, fired across the bow of an American merchantman, killing John Pierce, the captain's brother. American indignation mounted high, in part foreshadowing the War of 1812[w].

[Samuel Flagg Bemis, ed., *The American Secretaries of State and Their Diplomacy*, III.]   LOUIS MARTIN SEARS

Learned Societies. The types and aims of learned societies in the United States have in general reflected the social and intellectual characteristics of the period of foundation. Thus, the earliest societies, founded in the 18th century, are of the so-called European or Academy type, with restricted membership and generalized interests, embracing at least in theory the entire field of intellectual endeavor. Representative are the American Philosophical Society[w], arising from a club founded by Benjamin Franklin in Philadelphia in 1727 (and hence the oldest learned society in the country), and the American Academy of Arts and Sciences, founded in Boston in 1780.

But with the growth of democratic ideas in the early years of the 19th century the organization of learned societies tended to assume a form which has been regarded as typically American, namely that of a society of unrestricted membership comprising both professional scholars and less active but interested laymen. Further, societies tended to limit themselves to a single discipline or field of knowledge, in keeping with the general intellectual trend, which throughout the 19th century was steadily toward greater specialization of interest, as a means of promoting most effectively the scientific approach. This tendency toward specialization became more and more marked following the Civil War, as the industrialization of the country proceeded and the influence of contemporary European and particularly German methods of scholarship became widely operative. It is possible to mention here only a few of the scores of important societies founded within this general period and embodying the characteristics just described. Representative societies are the American Oriental Society (1842), the American Association for the Advancement of Science (1848), the American Philological Association (1869), the American Chemical Society (1876), the Modern Language Association of America (1883), the American Historical Association*[gv]* (1884), the American Economic Association (1885), the Geological Society of America (1888), the American Psychological Association (1892), the American Philosophical Association (1900) and the American Anthropological Association (1902).

Paralleling the development of national societies, there was, beginning in the latter part of the 18th century and carrying through the 19th into the 20th, a steady growth in the number of regional societies. At the present time, most of the states, as well as various lesser geographical areas, have their own historical societies, medical societies, academies of arts and sciences, etc. In some cases, these regional societies have been given a national focus through some type of Federal organization; examples of such organization are the American Medical Association (1847) and the Conference of Historical Societies (1904).

The general social and intellectual changes intensified and in part occasioned by the World War are clearly reflected in the development of learned societies during the post-war period. There has been first of all an increasing self-consciousness and social consciousness, a recognition of the responsibility of scholarship in educational and social terms. This consciousness, manifested first in societies directly concerned with the social sciences, has in the last decade or so spread widely to other societies, as the realization has grown of the essential community of interests shared by all branches of learning and of the necessity of pooling all possible intellectual resources in the attempt to solve pressing social and cultural problems.

Accompanying this new awareness of responsibility has been a growing recognition of the drawbacks inherent in specialization. While in general there has been since 1915 a marked slackening in the rate of founding new societies, certain of the societies which have been founded illustrate very clearly a conscious attempt to transcend specialization while preserving such of its features as are indispensable to any true scholarship. An example of such a society is the Mediæval Academy of America (1925), a society designed to cut across and at the same time co-ordinate the various scholarly disciplines in the study of an extensive historical period.

Specific effects of the World War may be noted in the impetus given to research of all kinds and to the tendency toward organization in the interests of co-operative effort. Various activities arising out of war needs later assumed a more permanent form, as the needs of a changing society seemed to make their continuance desirable.

All these trends in society development which have been mentioned as characteristic of the post-war period would seem to make inevitable some sort of official co-ordination, and it is in fact the establishment of the three national councils of learned societies which is the most salient feature of the period. These bodies, the National Research Council (1916—natural sciences), the American Council of Learned Societies (1919—humanities) and the Social Science Research Council (1923—social sciences), represent most of the important societies in their respective fields, and have proved themselves the means of putting into effect, more efficiently than could be done by societies working alone, many of the new objectives in society activity which have come into existence as a result of general social change.

G. W. COTTRELL, JR.

Leasehold was a system of land tenure characteristic of the southeastern portion of the colony and State of New York, whereby the tenant was bound to a perpetual payment of rent in money, produce or labor, or all three. In the central part of the state and on the land included in the Holland Purchase*[gv]* in the six western counties, the system of long-term sales, whereby the title of the land did not pass until the final payment, was also upon occasion spoken of as "leasehold." This leasehold system was abolished by the middle of the 19th century by the constitution of 1846 and the decisions of the courts (see Antirent Agitation).

[A. C. Flick, ed., *History of the State of New York*, Vol. VI.]

A. C. FLICK

Leatherwood God, The. The Leatherwood Valley in Guernsey County, Ohio, was the scene of a camp meeting[w] in 1828. During the meeting a mysterious stranger appeared, who later gave his name as Joseph C. Dylks. With a tremendous voice he would shout "Salvation!" and then make a strange sound like the snort of a frightened horse. He claimed to be a celestial being. Men and women began to believe in him, and he made bolder claims that he could perform miracles and that he was the true Messiah. He disappeared from the community as mysteriously as he had appeared.

[R. H. Tanneyhill, *The Leatherwood God.*]

HARLOW LINDLEY

Leave to Print is a parliamentary device used in the House of Representatives as a substitute for the unlimited debate which exists in the Senate. Under the five-minute rule the member usually succeeds only in getting started; he then asks unanimous consent to extend his remarks in the *Congressional Record*[w]. This leave to print is rarely denied, for each member expects that he will desire a like privilege at some future time.

[Robert Luce, *Legislative Procedure.*]

W. BROOKE GRAVES

Leavenworth, Fort. In 1824 some citizens of Missouri, at the suggestion of Sen. Benton, petitioned Congress for a military post at the Arkansas Crossing of the Santa Fé Trail[w] to protect traders journeying to New Mexico. Although no action was then taken, the Secretary of War in 1827 decided to erect a fort near the western boundary of Missouri, which would, at least in part, meet the wishes of the petitioners. On March 7 the adjutant-general ordered Col. Henry Leavenworth to select a site for the cantonment, an assignment which he completed on May 8. It was named Cantonment Leavenworth. Due to an epidemic of malaria between 1827 and 1829, it was practically evacuated in May, 1829; but late that summer it was reoccupied. During 1832 it was renamed Fort Leavenworth.

The post became important as a starting point for a number of military expeditions to the Far West, as a meeting place for Indian councils and as a supply depot for forts and camps on the frontier. Before 1846 its garrison usually included portions of the Sixth Infantry or First Dragoons. It rose to national prominence during the Mexican War, when the Army of the West was organized there and began a long march to occupy the Far Southwest (*see* Kearny's March to California). Throughout the 1850's it continued to be a point of departure for many military expeditions. Occupying a strategic position in the West during the Civil War, it was at various times headquarters of the Department of the West, the Department of Kansas and the Department of Missouri. Although the Fort Leavenworth military reservation was for a time the seat of an arsenal (1859–74) and of the United States Disciplinary Barracks (1874–95, 1906–29), today it includes, in addition to a military post, the United States Penitentiary (since 1895) and the Command and General Staff School (since 1881), the latter an important training school for officers.

[E. Hunt and W. E. Lorence, *History of Fort Leavenworth, 1827-1937;* E. Bandel, *Frontier Life in the Army, 1854-1861.*]

RALPH P. BIEBER

Leavenworth, Kans., located near Fort Leavenworth on Delaware Indian lands, was settled in June, 1854, by squatters[w] from Weston, Mo., who soon formed a town association. It was incorporated in 1855 and received title to its site in November, 1856. Accessible by the Missouri River and overland trails, it became the headquarters of the freighting firm of Russell, Majors and Waddell[w], and the terminus of a number of overland mails. The Kansas border troubles[w] brought a reign of terror to the town. It prospered during the Civil War. With the advent of railroads during the 1860's, it became an important commercial center in eastern Kansas.

[H. M. Moore, *Early History of Leavenworth.*]

RALPH P. BIEBER

Leavenworth and Pikes Peak Express, The, was launched by W. H. Russell and J. S. Jones to serve the newly revealed gold region of Colorado (*see* Pikes Peak Gold Rush). The meager first discoveries hardly warranted establishment of an expensive express, but the first coach reaching Denver, May 7, 1859, received news of important finds that saved the stage-line venture. The first route, a new one along the Republican River, was changed to the Platte River trail[w] in June, 1859. The express ran weekly. Fare to Denver was $100, board included; letters twenty-five cents, newspapers ten cents. The Central Overland California and Pikes Peaks Express[w] absorbed the L. & P. P. Ex. in 1860.

[L. R. Hafen, *The Overland Mail, 1849-1869.*]

LEROY R. HAFEN

Leavenworth Expedition (1823). At the Arikaree villages on the upper Missouri a party of the Rocky Mountain Fur Company[w] under Gen. Ashley, en route to the Yellowstone, was attacked on June 2 and twenty-six men killed or wounded.

Informed of this outrage, Gen. Henry Leavenworth promptly started up the Missouri from Fort Atkinson[qv], at Council Bluffs, Nebr., with six companies of the 6th Infantry and some artillery. Joined on the way by Joshua Pilcher's party of the Missouri Fur Company[qv], by Ashley's survivors and 750 Sioux Indians[qv], Leavenworth reached Grand River, Aug. 9. Next day he attacked the Arikarees' fortified, dirt-lodge villages, forcing their submission.

[*South Dakota Historical Collections*, Vol. I; Doane Robinson, *Encyclopedia of South Dakota*.]

JOSEPH MILLS HANSON

LeBœuf, Fort, Washington's Mission to. In 1753 the French erected forts at Presque Isle[qv] and at LeBœuf (Waterford, Pa.) and, seizing an English trader's house at Venango[qv], converted it into a French fort. Gov. Dinwiddie of Virginia selected the youthful George Washington to deliver a letter to the French demanding their withdrawal. With Christopher Gist and five others, Washington traveled from Wills Creek over the trail later known as Braddock's Road to the forks of the Ohio and thence to Logstown[qv]. Guided by friendly Indians, the party then proceeded to Venango and LeBœuf. St. Pierre, the commandant at LeBœuf, received Dinwiddie's letter and answered that he would forward it to Duquesne. At LeBœuf Washington and his companions noted the strength of fort and garrison and the large number of canoes there, indicating a contemplated expedition down the Ohio.

After two narrow escapes from death on the return journey, Washington arrived at Williamsburg Jan. 16, 1754, and delivered to Dinwiddie his journal and St. Pierre's letter. The journal, published and widely reprinted in the colonies and in England, not only helped arouse the English against the French advance, but also brought Washington for the first time to the attention of the world.

[C. H. Ambler, *Washington and the West;* Francis Parkman, *Montcalm and Wolfe*.]   SOLON J. BUCK

Lecompton Constitution, THE, was framed by a convention of proslavery Kansans[qv], Sept. 7–Nov. 7, 1857, Free State men having abstained from voting at an election of delegates on the preceding June 15. The convention adjourned on Sept. 11 to await the outcome of the territorial legislative election; a Free State victory discouraged moderates and the convention, which reassembled on Oct. 19, could not obtain a quorum until the 22nd. A constitution was framed which provided the usual forms and functions of a state government. A clause in the bill of rights excluded free Negroes. The slavery article declared slave property inviolable, denied the power of the legislature to prohibit immigrants from bringing in slaves or to emancipate them without compensation and the owners' consent, and empowered that body to protect slaves against inhuman treatment. The schedule provided a referendum on the alternatives, the "Constitution with Slavery" and the "Constitution with no Slavery." If the latter prevailed, the slavery article should be deleted, but there should be no interference with slave property already in Kansas. Other provisions prevented amendment before 1865 and placed responsibility for canvassing returns upon the presiding officer.

On Dec. 21 the slavery clause was approved, 6226 to 569, Free State men declining to vote. The legislature called an election for Jan. 4, 1858, at which the whole constitution was submitted. Proslavery men did not participate and the document was rejected, 10,226 to 162. Against the advice of some of his friends, Buchanan recommended on Feb. 2 that Kansas be admitted under it. The constitution was approved by the Senate, but Republicans, Douglas Democrats and other opponents in the House united to defeat it. Congress then passed the English bill[qv] which provided a referendum on the whole constitution and promised the future state over 5,000,000 acres of land if the instrument were ratified. An election on Aug. 2 rejected it, 11,300 to 1788.

[W. E. Connelley, *A Standard History of Kansas and Kansans;* D. W. Wilder, *Annals of Kansas*.]

WENDELL H. STEPHENSON

Lecture Days were midweek gatherings in the New England churches for sermons on doctrinal points. In 1633 the General Court[qv] ordered the lectures confined to afternoons so that the people would not lose a full working day, and in 1639 attempted to reduce the number; when the clergy protested, it rescinded the order, but shortly thereafter lectures were generally abandoned. The Boston lecture continued to be given at the First Church by ministers of the city in rotation until 1845, when the church resumed control in order to exclude Theodore Parker, whereupon the institution died of inanition.

PERRY MILLER

Lecturing. Public lectures have been semireligious and semieducational, but oftentimes chiefly entertainment for middle-class people opposed to "frivolous amusements." Now that movies and radio have attracted the amusement seekers, the semieducational aspect again predominates. Popular interest in science has been evident for over 200 years. Among early science lecturers were Isaac Greenwood (1734), Ebenezer Kinnersley (1751–52), Benjamin Silliman (*ca.* 1839–50) and L. J. R. Agassiz (*ca.* 1846–56). The Lyceum movement[*qv*] developed interest in lectures on literature, biography, history and philosophy. Emerson, most of whose writings were revised lectures, lectured throughout the nation for over twenty years (1849–72). Other popular literary lecturers were James Ogilvie, George Lippard, John Lord and John Fiske. Early reformers, lecturing on woman's rights, diet, public schools, peace and especially abolition, included Frances Wright, Sylvester Graham, Josiah Holbrook, Henry Barnard, Elihu Burritt, Wendell Phillips, Henry W. Beecher, etc.

After 1865 lecturing grew in popularity, partly because of the promotional activities of the lyceum bureaus. Woman's suffrage and prohibition replaced abolition as the chief reform topic. J. B. Pond's "lecture kings" were John B. Gough (most popular), Wendell Phillips (most polished), Henry W. Beecher (most elevating) and Mary A. Livermore (outstanding woman lecturer). Other reform lecturers were Julia Ward Howe, Susan B. Anthony, Frederick Douglass, T. D. Talmage, W. J. Bryan and Anna Howard Shaw. Lesser speakers, especially in the traveling chautauquas[*qv*], dealt with "mother-home-heaven" and personal advancement (e.g., R. H. Conwell's "Acres of Diamonds," given over 6000 times). Other important topics were evolution and religion, with Robert G. Ingersoll and Andrew D. White attacking religion and John Fiske, F. J. Cooke and M. J. Savage attempting to reconcile it with Darwinism. Later E. E. Slosson popularized modern science. The travel lecture, first popularized by Bayard Taylor, had wider appeal through John L. Stoddard's use of the stereopticon and E. M. Newman's "Traveltalks." Humorous lectures, begun by Artemus Ward and Josh Billings, reached their zenith with Mark Twain and were continued by Bill Nye, Petroleum V. Nasby, Will Rogers, etc.

[J. S. Noffsinger, *Correspondence Schools, Lyceums, Chautauquas*; J. B. Pond, *Eccentricities of Genius.*]

W. C. MALLALIEU

Lederer's Exploring Expeditions. John Lederer, a German traveler, in 1670–72 made tours of western exploration for Sir Wm. Berkeley, governor of Virginia and one of the proprietors of Carolina. Lederer, starting from the site of Richmond, claimed to have reached the summit of the Appalachian Mountains, but in fact he only reached the eastern foothills of the Blue Ridge. In a town of the Occaneechi Indians he met "stranger Indians" who lived two months'

distance to the westward and who well described their country as marked by waves (mountain ranges). From this Lederer drew the wild conjecture that "the Indian Ocean does stretch an arm or bay from California into the continent as far as the Apalataean Mountains." The explorer did reach as far south as upper South Carolina, visiting as he went a number of Indian tribes, some of whose customs he recorded in a book published by Sir Wm. Talbot in London, 1672.

[John Lederer, *The Discoveries of John Lederer, in Three Several Marches*; James Mooney, *The Siouan Tribes of the East.*]

SAMUEL C. WILLIAMS

Lee, Fort (N. J.), originally called Fort Constitution, was built by Washington's orders on the summit of the palisades, opposite Fort Washington[*qv*], during the summer of 1776. The two forts, with obstructions placed in the river between them, were intended to prevent the passage of enemy vessels, but failed in this purpose. After the fall of Fort Washington, Fort Lee, with large stores, was abandoned when Lord Cornwallis crossed the Hudson.

[George Bancroft, *History of the United States of America*, Vol. V.]

C. A. TITUS

Leech Lake, Indian Council at. On Feb. 16, 1806, Maj. Zebulon M. Pike[*qv*], who had been sent by Gen. James Wilkinson to reconnoiter to the source of the Mississippi, held a council with local Chippewa[*qv*] bands at the North West Company's[*qv*] trading post on Leech Lake. The Indians agreed to make peace with the Sioux[*qv*], to yield up their British flags and medals and to send two warriors to St. Louis with Pike.

[Elliott Coues, ed., *The Expeditions of Zebulon Montgomery Pike.*]

GRACE LEE NUTE

Leech Lake Uprising (1898). The previously friendly Pillager band of Chippewas[*qv*] in northern Minnesota had, by 1898, been irritated beyond primitive patience. Neglect of natives, haled long distances to court as liquor witnesses and then abandoned, caused Pillagers to resist apprehension as material witnesses. United States sheriffs called in troops to help make arrests. Seventy-seven regular soldiers from Fort Snelling[*qv*] crossed Leech Lake to corral the fugitives. A gun accidentally discharged by a raw recruit upset a tense situation. General shooting followed. Soldiers, pinned to the ground in a clearing, and under hostile fire from noon to dark on Oct. 5, suffered several casualties before being rescued two days later. Re-enforcement rushed up; Indians disappeared; agents induced many red men to surrender; troops were withdrawn; executive clemency reduced prison sentences; but the principal Indian protester never surrendered and was never captured.

[E. Colby, Our Last Indian War, in *Infantry Journal*, March, 1936.]   ELBRIDGE COLBY

Legal Tender is anything which, by law, a debtor may require his creditor to receive in payment of a debt, in the absence of any agreement for payment in some other manner, appearing in the contract itself. The tender is an admission of the debt and in some jurisdictions, if refused, discharges the debt.

There were two periods of American history when the question of legal tender was an important political issue. The first was in the period between 1776 and 1789; the second was in the years just after the Civil War. In the first case the question was whether the states should be permitted to print currency and require its acceptance by creditors regardless of its severe depreciation in value. In the second case it was whether Congress had power, under the Constitution, to cause the issuance of paper money (greenbacks[*w*]) which would be legal tender in payment of private debts.

The amount of circulating medium in the newborn states was insufficient to finance a costly war. Nearly every state early had recourse to the printing presses in order to meet its own expenses and the quota levies made by the Continental Congress[*w*]. At first, these issues were small and notes passed at their face value. Soon, however, they began to depreciate and the state legislatures resorted to laws requiring the acceptance of state bank notes at par. In Connecticut, in 1776 for example, the legislature made both Continental and state notes legal tender and ordered that any one who tried to depreciate them should forfeit not only the full value of the money he received but also the property which he offered for sale. Attempts were also made at price regulation. The South particularly went to excess in the abuse of public credit. Virginia, for example, practically repudiated her paper issues at the close of the Revolution.

The leaders in business and finance in the states were not slow to see the undesirability of a repetition of this financial orgy. So when the Constitutional Convention[*w*] met in 1787 there was general agreement upon the desirability of providing for a single national system of currency[*w*] and of prohibiting note issues by the states. Accordingly Article 1, Section 10 of the Constitution contains the following prohibitions upon the states, "No state shall . . . coin money; emit

bills of credit; make anything but gold and silver coin a tender in payment of debts; pass any . . . *ex post facto* law or law impairing the obligation of contracts."

The question raised after the Civil War related to the constitutionality of the Legal Tender Act[*w*] passed by Congress in 1862. It was alleged that Congress, in requiring the acceptance of greenbacks at face value was violating the Fifth Amendment, which forbade the deprivation of property without due process[*w*] of law (*see* Legal Tender Cases). It is now a clearly recognized power of Congress to make paper money legal tender. The Constitution itself clearly denies such powers to the states.

[Allan Nevins, *The American States during and after the Revolution;* Charles Warren, *The Supreme Court in United States History.*]   HARVEY WALKER

Legal Tender Act (1862). To provide funds to carry on the Civil War, Congress issued fiat money[*w*]. By the act of Feb. 25, 1862, and by successive acts, the Government put into circulation about $450,000,000 of paper money dubbed "greenbacks."[*w*] No specific gold reserve was set aside nor any date announced for their redemption. To insure their negotiability, Congress declared these notes legal tender[*w*] in "payment of all taxes, internal duties, excises, debts and demands of every kind due to the United States, except duties on imports, and of all claims and demands against the United States . . . and shall also be lawful money and legal tender in payment of all debts, public and private, within the United States." Wall Street[*w*] and the metropolitan press opposed this measure. On the Pacific coast the law was frequently evaded through the passage of a "specific Contract Act." In 1870 the Supreme Court declared the Legal Tender Act unconstitutional and void in respect to debts contracted prior to its passage. Upon filling two vacancies, however, the Court reversed its decision (*see* Legal Tender Cases) .

[W. C. Mitchell, *A History of the Greenbacks with Special Reference to the Consequences of Their Issue, 1862-1865;* Joseph Ellison, The Currency Question on the Pacific Coast during the Civil War, in *Mississippi Valley Historical Review,* June, 1929; D. R. Dewey, *A Financial History of the United States.*]   J. W. ELLISON

Legal Tender Cases, THE, involved the question of the constitutionality of the measures enacted during the Civil War for the issue of treasury notes to circulate as money without provision for redemption. The constitutional question hinged not on the power of the Government to issue the notes, but on its power to make them legal tender[*w*] for the payment of debts, particularly those contracted before the legislation was enacted. The Supreme Court of the United States decided the question on Feb. 7, 1870, in the case of Hepburn v. Griswold (8 Wallace 603). The majority of the Court held that Congress had no power to enact the legal-tender provisions. The vote of the Court members, when taken in conference, had been five to three, with the obvious senility of Mr. Justice Grier, one of the majority, casting doubt on the weight of his opinion. He retired before the decision was announced, leaving the alignment at that time four to three. The opinion against the constitutionality of the legislation was written by Chief Justice Salmon P. Chase, who as the Secretary of the Treasury had shared responsibility for the original enactments.

Nominations of two new members of the Supreme Court were sent to the Senate on the day on which the decision was announced. At the ensuing term, over the protest of the four members who had hitherto constituted the majority, the Court heard the reargument of the constitutional question in another case. On May 1, 1871, the Court reversed the Hepburn decision in Knox v. Lee and Parker v. Davis (12 Wallace 457), which are listed in the United States Reports under the title of The Legal Tender Cases. The question as to whether President Grant deliberately packed the Court to bring about a reversal of the original decision is still a matter of debate. Some of the notes issued were withdrawn by the Treasury but some were reissued under a later statute enacted without reference to war-time conditions. This statute was upheld on March 3, 1884, in Juilliard v. Greenman[w].

[Charles Warren, *The Supreme Court in United States History;* Carl B. Swisher, *Stephen J. Field: Craftsman of the Law;* Sidney Ratner, Was the Supreme Court Packed by President Grant? *Political Science Quarterly,* Vol. L.]

CARL BRENT SWISHER

Legislation, Quantity of, Federal and State. Much critical comment has been written on the quantity of legislation in the United States. In presenting the findings of such tabulations as have been made on the subject, it is suggested that too much importance should not be attached to mere numbers of bills or laws. Many of the measures that are adopted do not actually add to the total volume of legislation in force. Many are appropriation measures, whose life extends only to the end of the fiscal period for which they are adopted. Many more amend and some repeal existing laws. Others are supplements, restatements, validations, codifications, corrections or revisions, or temporary laws. While the resulting volume of session laws may look imposing, there may be no appreciable growth in the amount of substantive law.

It is reported that for the twenty-seven years from 1906 to 1933, inclusive, Congress and the legislatures of the states produced 1,259,253 bills, of which 301,578 were enacted. The following table, based on each fifth Congress, indicates the quantity, character and fate of Federal legislation.

Congress	Bills Introduced	Resolutions Introduced	Total	Bills Passed	Resolutions Passed	Total
1st (1789-91)	144	——	144	102	16	118
5th (1797-99)	234	——	234	153	2	155
10th (1807-09)	266	——	266	104	1	105
15th (1817-19)	507	——	507	237	20	257
20th (1827-29)	612	20	632	226	9	235
25th (1837-39)	1,566	65	1,631	514	18	532
30th (1847-49)	1,305	128	1,433	396	50	446
35th (1857-59)	1,544	142	1,686	274	38	312
40th (1867-69)	3,003	720	3,723	531	180	711
45th (1877-79)	8,413	322	8,735	685	61	746
50th (1887-89)	16,664	414	17,078	1,754	70	1,824
55th (1897-99)	17,817	646	18,463	1,329	108	1,437
60th (1907-09)	37,981	407	38,388	584	62	646
65th (1917-19)	21,919	675	22,594	397	56	453
70th (1927-29)	23,238	659	23,897	1,605	117	1,722
Total 1-74 Congresses	689,433	22,339	711,772	54,408	3,975	58,383

These figures indicate clearly the growth in the volume of legislative business, due partly to the increase in the number of members, and partly to the growing number and complexity of governmental problems. From 1908 to 1921 the percentage of the bills passed varied between 1% and 3%; from 1922 through 1925 it was very much higher. Since the latter date it has ranged between 6% and 8%, although this is considerably lower than the percentage in the lowest state, as will be seen below.

The beginning of careful tabulations of the quantity of legislation in the states seems to coincide with the development of the legislative reference idea in the early 20th century. Since then, figures extending back over a number of years are obtainable in most states. In North Carolina, for instance, the total number of bills and resolutions introduced in regular sessions, 1907–35, has averaged around 2000, of which about 1100 or 1200 have been enacted. About one third originated in the upper house, two thirds in the lower. The sifting process is much more effective in eliminating proposed measures in some states than in others. Thus in Pennsylvania for the same period, the average number of bills introduced runs well over 2000, while the average number passed runs well under 1000. A study made in 1934 by the Duke University Law School, for the regular sessions of 1933 and 1934 in all states, showed that, of the total number of bills introduced, New York stood first with 4427 and Wyoming last with 338. On the total number of bills passed, Florida stood first with 1914, and Utah last with 98. On the percentage of bills passed, Florida was highest with 74.65, and Kentucky lowest with 11.54. On average cost per bill introduced, Ohio stood first at $1694.74, and Tennessee last, at $34.40, due to the low compensation of members and the failure to print bills. These figures reflect the diversity among the states, both in the effectiveness of their lawmaking machinery and in the number and importance of their legislative problems. Another study made by the Wisconsin Legislative Reference Bureau in 1934 covers the total number of bills introduced and laws enacted by twelve representative states from 1911 through 1933. These states produced an average of 21,357 bills per regular session, or of 1779 per state per session; an average of 5801 laws, or of 484 per state per session. The average percentage of bills passed for the twelve states was 27.43.

[Chester J. Best, *Volume of Proposed and Enacted Legislation in Congress and the Several States*, Wisconsin Legislative Reference Library, 1934; Duke University Law School, *The Cost of Legislation*; W. Brooke Graves, *American State Government*; William E. Hannan, *Legislation in the United States, 1906 to 1933, inclusive*, New York State Library, 1933; Joint Legislative Committee on Finances, *Survey of the Government of Pennsylvania*; Thomas I. Parkinson, *Legislative Contribution to Progress*.]

W. BROOKE GRAVES

Legislature, THE, in the United States is one of the three major organs of National and state governments, the others being the executive and the judiciary. Its function is to enact law—to declare the public will in objective form.

Colonial legislatures usually consisted of an assembly, elected by vote of the freemen[qv] of the colony, and a council, appointed by the crown or proprietor. There were no councils in Georgia or Pennsylvania, resulting in legislatures of but one house. The first state legislatures followed colonial models, except that senates were substituted for councils as the upper house. Suffrage was restricted by property or taxpaying qualifications, often larger for the upper than for the lower house. The legislature appointed the governor and judges. Its powers were not subject to check by gubernatorial veto or judicial review. This was the period of legislative supremacy.

The first half of the 19th century witnessed the rise of gubernatorial and judicial power in the states and the corresponding decline of legislative authority. The state legislature has never regained its early position of supremacy over the other two branches of state government. In addition state constitutions have become longer and contain more and more limitations upon the power of the legislature. Initiative and referendum[qv] have increased popular control over legislative questions. The impossibility of dealing with administrative details in a general law has led to the delegation of rule-making power (*see* Delegation of Power) to administrative officers, boards and commissions further restricting the sphere of legislative action (*see* Quasi-Judicial Agencies).

The form of the legislatures in the states has generally followed the national model. Georgia and Pennsylvania entered the Union with single houses but abandoned them in 1789 and 1790 respectively. Vermont used but one house from 1777 to 1836. In 1934 Nebraska amended its constitution to substitute one house for two. Unicameralism[qv] is a live issue in most of the states. One important reason lies in the fact that rural areas retain representation in one of the houses out of all proportion to their population. A single house consisting of members chosen on the basis of population is widely advocated as a remedy.

[R. Luce, *Legislative Assemblies*; H. Walker, *Law Making in the United States*.]   HARVEY WALKER

Leisler Rebellion (1689). The revolution in England, which forced James II to abdicate, was followed by revolution in America. May 31, 1689, Fort James on Manhattan Island was "seized by the Rable" and shortly afterward Capt. Jacob Leisler usurped complete control of southern New York. The following spring at his suggestion representatives of Massachusetts, Plymouth, Connecticut and New York met in New York City to concert measures for a united offensive against Canada. Leisler assumed energetic charge of operations, but lack of co-operation from the other colonies, and his own tactlessness, spoiled his efforts. In March, 1691, Col. Henry Sloughter was commissioned governor of New York by William and Mary. Leisler was tried for treason and executed, but the flame which he had kindled burned long and the agitation caused a further examination of the case in England, resulting in a reversal of the attainder and restoration of his estates.

[A. C. Flick, ed., *History of the State of New York*, Vol. II.]   A. C. FLICK

Leisure, loosely defined, may be considered as time free from attention to the important matter of securing the necessary means of existence according to one's accustomed standard of living. In America the attainment of leisure for the general public has been a very gradual evolution. In colonial times and throughout frontier days there was little leisure for the average person. On the one hand there was little pauperism; on the other there was little accumulated wealth. Merit was attributed to work, while leisure was viewed with condescension or scorn. Colonial Americans were little worried about the uses and abuses of leisure.

For two centuries after 1607 American life remained predominantly agricultural. Never has leisure been conspicuous in agricultural life. Time taken from farm duties was usually employed in productive social activities. Leisure was, as a rule, used rather than abused. Only on the largest plantations was leisure attained for a few by assigning responsibility to others.

With the rise of the factory system of industry, a profound economic change took place with important later results in the matter of leisure. But for fifty years life in factory towns provided very little leisure for any one. Before 1825 hours of labor[w] for men, women and children in factories averaged twelve or more a day. And even the fortunate few who possessed leisure time generally made productive use of it in busy work of some kind.

But the growth of labor unionism[w] produced a shortening of hours of labor in industry and business. In 1835 the ten-hour day was adopted in Philadelphia and Baltimore. In 1840 the Federal Government adopted the ten-hour day for its employees. Slowly shorter hours became almost universal. Leisure thus came to a larger number of people. The use made of this leisure is an important aspect of social history.

At first, Americans, unaccustomed to leisure, hardly knew what to do with it. Sheer relaxation was foreign to tradition and mores. Many turned ardently to fraternal orders[w], which enjoyed a mushroom growth. Some frequented the theater[w], which thereby enjoyed its greatest period of prosperity. Others devoted leisure hours to games and sports[w]. Only the agricultural class continued largely the earlier life of incessant attention to the necessities of living.

Unfortunately intensive urbanization[w] followed industrialization and commercialization and the increased leisure was spent, not in repose and relaxation, but in search of excitement and entertainment. The result was the rapid commercialization of many forms of entertainment and amusement[w], a commercialization which reached its climax with the coming of motion pictures[w], daily attended by many millions of people.

The role of automobiles[w] in leisure has been significant. Leisure hours are often spent in motoring around the country. But automobiles are also used to go long distances to commercialized amusements. Individuals, however, have used them to facilitate access to music, art and personal activity in games.

People in large numbers waste leisure hours in ways individually and socially injurious. Leaders of American thought are aware of the problem of the use or abuse of leisure. Education for leisure must be a feature of the future.

[George B. Cutten, *The Threat of Leisure*.]
                                        ALFRED P. JAMES

Leisy v. Hardin. *See* Original Package.

Leprosy. The introduction of leprosy into continental United States probably occurred through the Spanish conquests, slave trade and immigration, which latter has perpetuated it subsequently within other than a few Southern states in which it has spread indigenously. Its incidence has never been comprehensively recorded; however, forty cases were admitted to the first hospital established in 1785 in New Orleans, and the national official survey conducted by mail during 1902 reported 278 cases. The National Leprosarium at Carville, La., contained 172 patients shortly after it was provided in 1921, and 441 in 1936. It has been estimated recently that there are 1200 cases in the country.

[O. E. Denny, *Public Health Reports*, XLI, 20; H. E. Hasseltine, *Hospital News*, III, 16, issued by U. S. Public Health Service.]   N. E. WAYSON

"Let Us Have Peace." Gen. Grant in his letter of May 29, 1868, accepting the Republican nomination for President endeavored to speak a word to calm feelings excited by civil war, reconstruction and impeachment[qw]. His phrase "Let us have peace" became the keynote of his successful campaign (*see* Campaign of 1868).

[J. F. Rhodes, *History of the United States since the Compromise of 1850*.]   THEODORE M. WHITFIELD

Lethal Gas, a deadly fume used by Arizona, California, Colorado, Nevada, North Carolina and Wyoming, to carry out the death penalty (*see* Capital Punishment). Nevada, the first state to adopt this method, in 1924, uses hydrocyanic, HNC, pellets, about the size of a hen's egg. When dropped into an earthen jar filled with sulphuric acid the gas is produced. Ten seconds after the condemned person, strapped in a chair in a steel, airtight chamber, breathes the wild-peach-smelling vapor, he is senseless; ten to fifteen minutes later his heart stops beating.   EFFIE MONA MACK

Letters from a Pennsylvania Farmer. See Farmer's Letters, Dickinson's.

Levee System. The outstanding example of a levee system in the United States is that of the lower reaches of the Mississippi River. Unlike the river Nile, where the yearly overflows bring down from Upper Egypt a wealth of sediment that enriches the soil and creates the fertile Nile Valley, the floods from the Mississippi River devastated the plantations of the early settlers, and as early as 1717 local levee systems had been started by large landowners along the lower river near New Orleans. Grants of land from the king of France obliged the owner to build his share of the levee by his own labor and resources, and by 1812, when Louisiana*ᵂ* became a state after the purchase of the Louisiana Territory from France, the levees extended approximately 170 miles on each bank. These levees were extended in later years by local and state aid until the 1850's, but much of the system was damaged by the devastating floods of 1858–59 and during the Civil War.

As the economic condition of the South improved after Reconstruction days, agitation for strengthening of the levee system was resumed, resulting in the organization of the Mississippi River Commission in 1879 and the initial participation of the Federal Government in levee construction. From that time on the levees were built higher and stronger after each break revealed the fact that they were inadequate, until in 1927 a flood of unprecedented proportions resulted in congressional action to adopt a plan for supposedly complete protection. As a result, the levee system was completed on both sides of the river from Cairo to the Gulf, comprising a total length of 2000 miles of levees, the longest and most expensive levee system in existence. This plan was proved inadequate by the floods of 1936 and 1937, and it is still inadequate to take care of the largest floods to be anticipated. Consequently, plans are now (1939) under way to reduce the flood flows by means of tributary storage reservoirs and diversion channels (*see* Flood Control).

[Andrew A. Humphreys and Henry L. Abbott, *Report on the Physics and Hydraulics of the Mississippi River*, War Dept., 1861; Arthur DeWitt Frank, *Development of the Federal Program of Flood Control on the Mississippi River*.]   ARTHUR E. MORGAN

Lever Act, THE (Aug. 10, 1917), sponsored by Representative A. F. Lever to mobilize food and fuel resources for the World War, authorized price fixing of commodities and licensing of producers and distributers, and prohibited "unfair" trade practices. Subsequently the Price-Fixing Committee, the Food and Fuel Administrations*ᑫᵛ* and the Grain Corporation were created by executive orders to administer the law.

[Reports of the United States Food and Fuel Administrations, 1917, *House Doc. no. 837,* 65 Cong., 2 sess.; F. M. Surface, *The Grain Trade during the World War.*]   MARTIN P. CLAUSSEN

Levy, THE (1803–5), was an English project to recruit recent British arrivals in the United States and Canada for an enterprise against Napoleon's French possessions in the West Indies. Charles Williamson, formerly agent of the Pulteney Associates*ᵂ*, was delegated to organize the Levy. He proposed to co-operate with Miranda*ᵂ* in an attack against Spanish possessions in Florida, Mexico and South America. The Levy may have been offered to Burr (*see* Burr Conspiracy). No organization was ever effected. Miranda and Burr both failed; Williamson returned to England.

[T. R. Hay, Charles Williamson and the Burr Conspiracy, *The Journal of Southern History*, May, 1936.]   THOMAS ROBSON HAY

Lewes, Bombardment of, was a British attempt to stop shipping in the Delaware River and Bay during the War of 1812. On March 14, 1813, a squadron of ten British vessels anchored off Lewes, ravaged shipping, demanded provisions and threatened to destroy the town if the provisions were not received. By delaying their reply the Americans gained time to march militia to complete the construction of batteries. Finally, on April 6, the British squadron began firing at the town and continued until ten o'clock at night. Firing began again at daybreak and continued until five or six o'clock in the afternoon. The British shots passed high over the town with the result that after twenty-two hours of bombarding, during which time nearly 900 shots and bombs were fired, no one at Lewes was killed or wounded and only a few houses damaged. Shortly afterward the British vessels withdrew.

[J. Thomas Scharf, *History of Delaware.*]   LEON DEVALINGER, JR.

Lewis and Clark Expedition (1804–6). The problem which Lewis and Clark undertook to solve originated with the dawn of American history. Columbus was intent upon finding a new way to the Orient, and the accidental discovery of America was for him a great tragedy. As soon as contemporaries perceived that America barred the way to the Indies, they took up the task of finding a way around or through the troublesome continent, and for centuries this goal afforded one of the chief incitements to further American exploration. President Jefferson was deeply interested in scientific discoveries, and the acquisition of Louisiana*ᵂ* in 1803 afforded him a pretext for sending an expedition to explore the western country.

Meriwether Lewis, Jefferson's private secretary, was appointed to command the expedition, and he associated his friend, William Clark, younger brother of Gen. George Rogers Clark, in the leadership. The party was assembled near St. Louis*ᵂ* late in 1803 in readiness to start up the Missouri the following spring. This season it ascended the river by flatboat and keelboat to the group of Mandan and Arikara towns in west central North Dakota.

Here the winter was passed, and from here on April 7, 1805, while the flatboat returned to St. Louis, the explorers, in six canoes and two keelboats, set their faces toward the unknown West. Besides the two leaders, the party included twenty-six soldiers, George Drouillard and Toussaint Charbonneau, interpreters, Clark's Negro servant, York, and last but not least, Charbonneau's squaw-wife, Sacajawea (the Bird Woman), and her infant son.

On Nov. 7, 1805, the explorers gazed upon the Pacific Ocean. They had ascended the Missouri and its Jefferson fork to the mountains, which by a rare combination of skill, perseverance and luck they had crossed to the Snake; thence down the Snake and the Columbia to the sea. The winter was passed in a shelter (named Fort Clatsop) near present-day Astoria, and in March, 1806, the return journey was begun. After crossing the Rockies the explorers separated into three groups to make a more extensive examination of the country than a single party could accomplish. Thus both the Missouri and the Yellowstone were descended, near whose junction the groups reunited. From here the party passed rapidly down river to St. Louis on Sept. 23, 1806, where the expedition ended.

A great epic in human achievement had been written. Thousands of miles of wilderness inhabited by savage beasts and savage men had been traversed; an important impulse to the fur-ther extension of American trade and settlement had been supplied; important additions to the existing body of geographical and scientific knowledge had been made; in the person of humble, patient, loyal Sacajawea a precious addition to the world's roster of heroines had been disclosed.

[Reuben G. Thwaites, ed., *Original Journals of the Lewis and Clark Expedition, 1804-1806;* M. M. Quaife, ed., *The Journals of Captain Meriwether Lewis and Sergeant John Ordway;* Paul Allen, *History of the Expedition under the Command of Captains Lewis and Clark to the Sources of the Missouri.*]

M. M. QUAIFE

Lewis and Clark Exposition, THE, held at Portland, Oregon, from June 1 to Oct. 15, 1905, commemorated the historic expedition of Lewis and Clark*ᵂ* in opening up the Oregon country to settlement. It occupied 402 acres on the site of Willamette Heights. The Federal Government and nineteen states participated. Some statuary and exhibits were sent from the Louisiana Purchase Exposition*ᵂ*. Twice the estimated number of visitors attended and made it a conspicuous financial success.

FRANK MONAGHAN

Lexington, Mo., Siege of (Sept. 12–20, 1861). After the battle of Wilson's Creek*ᵂ*, Gen. Sterling Price of the Missouri State Guard moved his army of 1500 men northward toward Lexington, the most important town on the Missouri River between St. Louis and St. Joseph, and in the midst of the counties having a large slave population. Lexington was defended by 2640 men under Col. J. A. Mulligan (U.), who entrenched on a hill around the Masonic College. Price surrounded him and, cutting him off from the town, the river and his water supply, constructed a breastwork of hemp bales which enabled him to move within close range of the defenders in comparative safety. On Sept. 20 Col. Mulligan surrendered after hopes of reinforcement were gone and his men were suffering from thirst. Price captured commissary stores valued at $100,000 and considerable war materials, but he abandoned Lexington in the face of superior Federal forces. Losses on each side were comparatively light.

[*Battles and Leaders of the Civil War,* Vol. I.]

W. FRANCIS ENGLISH

Lexington, THE. (1) Continental brig which, under John Barry, captured the British sloop *Edward,* April 7, 1776, off the Chesapeake. In 1777 it cruised about Ireland under Henry Johnson, but was captured on Sept. 19. (2) Store ship which, in 1848 under Theodorus Bailey, captured San Blas, Mexico, in final naval operation of

Mexican War. (3) Union sidewheeler, later armored, which fought at Belmont, Fort Henry and on the Red River[qw] in 1861–63. At Shiloh[w] it saved Grant's army from being driven back in utter defeat the first day.

[G. W. Allen, *The Naval History of the American Revolution; Battles and Leaders of the Civil War*, Vol. I.]

WALTER B. NORRIS

Lexington and Concord. On the evening of the 18th of April, 1775, the British military governor of Massachusetts sent out from Boston a detachment of about 700 regular troops, to destroy military stores collected by the provincials at Concord. Detecting the plan, the Whigs in Boston sent out Paul Revere[w] and William Dawes with warnings. The detachment consequently found at Lexington, at sunrise on the 19th, a part of the minute-man[w] company already assembled on the green. While it was unwillingly breaking ranks at the command of the British Maj. Pitcairn, the regulars fired and cleared the ground. Eight of the Americans were killed, ten wounded. The regulars marched for Concord after but a short delay.

Here the provincials, outnumbered, retired over the North Bridge and waited reinforcements. The British occupied the town, held the North Bridge with about a hundred regulars, and searched for stores. Of these they found few; but the smoke of those which they burned in the town alarmed the watching provincials who (reinforced to the number of about 450) marched down to the bridge, led by Maj. John Buttrick. The regulars, seeing them, hastily formed on the farther side to receive them, and began to take up the planks of the bridge. Buttrick shouted to them to desist. The front ranks of the regulars fired, killing two provincials and wounding more. Buttrick gave the famous order, "Fire, fellow soldiers, for God's sake, fire!" The response of his men, and their continued advance, were too much for the British, who (with two killed and several wounded) broke and fled. The Americans did not follow up their success, and after a dangerous delay the British marched for Boston about noon.

At Meriam's Corner their rear guard was fired upon by the men of Reading, and from there to Lexington a skirmish fire was poured upon the British from all available cover. By the time they reached that town the regulars were almost out of ammunition and completely demoralized, and were saved from slaughter or surrender only by the arrival of a column from Boston, under Lord Percy, with two fieldpieces which overawed the militia and gave the troops time to rest. When they marched on again, however, the militia

closed in once more and dogged the regulars all the way to Charlestown, where before sundown the troops reached safety under the guns of the fleet.

The casualties of the day bear no relation to its importance. Forty-nine Americans were killed, seventy-three British, with a total of the killed and wounded of both sides of 366. But the fighting proved to the Americans that by their own methods they could defeat the British. In that belief they stopped, before night, the land approaches to Boston, thus beginning the siege of Boston[w].

[Peter Force, *American Archives*, Series 4, Vol. 2; Justin Winsor, *Narrative and Critical History of America;* Harold Murdock, *The Nineteenth of April, 1775;* Allen French, *The Day of Concord and Lexington*, and *General Gage's Informers.*]

ALLEN FRENCH

Lexington and Ohio Railroad, THE, was chartered Jan. 27, 1830, to be built from Lexington to some point on the Ohio River. Louisville was selected as the western terminus, and in 1831 the first rail was laid. In 1835 the road was completed to Frankfort. In 1842 the company failed financially. The state of Kentucky leased the line and equipment to a private company, and in 1852 the road was completed between Lexington and Louisville.

[T. D. Clark, The Lexington and Ohio Railroad—A Pioneer Venture, *Kentucky State Historical Register*, January, 1933.]

T. D. CLARK

Lexow Committee, THE, appointed by the New York Senate (Jan. 30, 1894) to investigate the New York City Police Department, revealed a corrupt machine, called "the system." It represented a half-century's growth. While it was above party, "the system" became reckless during the Tammany[w] leadership of Richard Croker, and its opponents "were abused, clubbed and imprisoned, and even convicted of crime on false testimony by policemen and their accomplices." Legitimate business, from pushcart peddlers to steamship companies, was forced to pay graft. But the underworld was the chief source of revenue, estimated at $7,000,000 annually. Crooked patrolmen and detectives fattened on street walkers, thieves and the like. Dishonest officials grew rich on brothel keepers, gamblers and liquor dealers. The monthly levies were: saloons, $2 to $20; poolrooms, $200; $20 on each of the 1000 policy shops; bawdy houses, a minimum of $5 per inmate; each new brothel paid an average of $500 to open. The bawdy-gambling-liquor graft was thus divided: 20% to the patrolman-collector; 35% to 50% to the precinct commander; the rest to the inspector. It was also testified that it cost $300 to become a patrolman; $300 to be promoted to roundsman; $1600 to be made a sergeant; and as high as $15,000 for a captaincy. The comparative success of the committee, of which Sen. Clarence Lexow, Republican, was chairman, was due chiefly to its fearless counsel, John W. Goff, Democrat. In the ninth month of the committee's labors, the Republicans, after being out of office for several years, swept the city and state. One of the new police commissioners was Theodore Roosevelt. But "the system," somewhat camouflaged, went marching on.

[*Report and Proceedings of the Senate Committee Appointed to Investigate the City of New York*, Transmitted to the Legislature Jan. 18, 1895.]   DENIS TILDEN LYNCH

Libby Prison was, after Andersonville[w], the most notorious of Confederate prisons. When the captives from the battle of First Bull Run[w] arrived in Richmond, Gen. John H. Winder, provost marshal of the city, commandeered a number of vacant tobacco warehouses, among them one belonging to the firm of Libby and Son. Commissioned officers were confined here until after the fall of Richmond. The prison contained eight rooms, 103 by 42 feet, each equipped with a stove upon which the prisoners cooked their rations. After the failure of the cartel for the exchange of prisoners[w], Libby became crowded and a shortage of food supplies during December, 1863, and January, 1864, caused extensive suffering among the inmates. In February, 1864, 109 officers escaped through a tunnel, and 61 made their way to the Union lines. Feb. 28 and March 4, 1864, saw two Federal cavalry raids on Richmond for the purpose of releasing the prisoners (*see* Dahlgren's Raid). As a result of these events, the Confederates established a new officers' prison at Macon, Ga., in May, 1864. Thereafter Libby Prison was used only as a temporary station for captives en route to Macon.

[W. B. Hesseltine, *Civil War Prisons*.]
    W. B. HESSELTINE

Libel in Anglo-American law comprises defamatory matter in some such permanent form as writing, printing or painting, the less permanent or oral form being designated as slander. In Tudor and Stuart England published libels attacking public officers were rigorously dealt with, and as a result a distinction developed between civil suits for libel and criminal prosecutions. In the latter, truth did not constitute a defense. To a lesser extent the English political libel suits could be paralleled in colonial America. The most celebrated prosecution was that of John Peter Zenger[w], New York printer, in 1735.

In this case the prosecution contended that only the fact of publication could be determined by the jury, while the court was to determine whether the publication were libelous. Andrew Hamilton, counsel for the prisoner, persuaded the jury, however, to judge both law and fact, and secured Zenger's acquittal. This trial has generally been regarded as the first great victory for the freedom of the press[w] in America. Reports of the trial were widely circulated in Great Britain and her colonies, but in neither English nor colonial law was the Zenger trial considered a precedent.

The Sedition Act[w] of 1798 allowed the defense to give evidence of the truth of the matter contained in the publication charged as a libel, the jury having the right to determine the law and the fact. Although the law expired in 1801, the whole question was brought to a head by the famous trial in New York of Croswell[w] for a libel on President Jefferson. As a result of Alexander Hamilton's arguments, the same ruling as in the Zenger case prevailed, and a precedent was set for the American common law. In 1805 a statute was enacted embodying the result of this decision, permitting the defendant to give truth in justification provided it was published "with good motives and for justifiable ends."

While technically at common law[w] oral defamation was a tort rather than a crime, in the colonial courts a flood of criminal prosecutions, as well as civil suits, for defamatory utterance gave unusual color and vitality to the court minutes of that period. In modern times criminal slander is not recognized in law, and civil suits for oral defamation have greatly declined in number and frequency.

[W. S. Holdsworth, *History of English Law*, III, V, VIII; V. V. Veeder, The History and Theory of the Law of Defamation, in *Select Essays in Anglo-American Law*, Vol. III; M. W. Hamilton, *Country Printer*.]
    RICHARD B. MORRIS

Liberal Construction. The principle of liberal construction of the Constitution had its origin in 1791 in connection with the argument over the power of Congress to set up the first United States Bank[w]. President Washington asked his Cabinet for opinions concerning its constitutionality. Arguing for a strict interpretation of the powers delegated to the Federal Government by the Constitution, Jefferson held that the establishment of a bank would be an unwarranted extension of such power.

On the other hand, Hamilton argued for a liberal interpretation of the Constitution. He found ample authority for the bank in the "necessary and proper" clause. He declared, "The powers contained in a constitution of government . . . ought to be construed liberally in advancement of the public good. . . . If the end be clearly comprehended within any of the specified powers, and if the measure have an obvious relation to that end, and is not forbidden by any particular provision of the Constitution, it may safely be deemed to come within the compass of the national authority."

Washington accepted Hamilton's views and the principle of liberal construction was definitely established. Even Jefferson as President followed it, his purchase of Louisiana^{qv} and his methods in defense of neutral rights being wide extensions of the Constitution.

John Marshall, in an opinion upholding the bank in McCulloch v. Maryland^{qv}, in 1819, stated the doctrine of liberal construction in classic language, "Let the end be legitimate, let it be within the scope of the constitution, and all means which are appropriate, which are plainly adapted to that end, which are not prohibited, but consist with the letter and spirit of the constitution, are constitutional." Jackson probably came the nearest to being a strict constructionist President. In general the party in power has adhered to liberal construction and the minority party to assertions of strict construction. The doctrine has been of distinct historical significance, giving flexibility to a rigid constitution, making it adaptable to changing conditions.

[A. C. McLaughlin, *A Constitutional History of the United States.*]   GLENN H. BENTON

Liberal Republican Party, THE, represented a revolt of the reform element in the Republican party^{qv} during Grant's first administration. They advocated a conciliatory Southern policy (*see* Reconstruction) and civil service^{qv} reform, and condemned political corruption. Some favored tariff^{qv} revision. The movement was led by B. Gratz Brown, Carl Schurz, Charles Sumner, Charles Francis Adams, Horace Greeley and others. Greeley was named for President and Brown for Vice-President in 1872 (*see* Campaign of 1872). Both candidates were later endorsed by the Democrats. In the ensuing campaign Greeley was overwhelmingly defeated by Grant.

[Edward Stanwood, *A History of the Presidency from 1788 to 1897.*]   GLENN H. BENTON

Liberals. In the United States we have never had a political party which has designated itself officially as Liberal. For what corresponds roughly to the Liberal party in England we have preferred such terms as Democratic, Progressive, and so on. Liberal has been, with us, a term applied to individuals and to general attitudes. In the absence of a party and a definite program, the definition becomes subjective rather than objective, and the word is variously applied.

Although liberalism is often considered a halfway house between conservatism and radicalism, its real nature removes it from such a graduated scale. Both conservatives and radicals tend to intolerance of the opinions of others, whereas we may consider one of the special attributes of the liberal to be tolerance. In this respect either a radical or conservative may be "liberal." We also attribute to the liberal a willingness to try new ways, a dislike of the fetters of the past, an insistence upon freedom of speech and religion and a strong sympathy with others of any class or creed.

Although the term came into use rather late in our religion, politics, and social life, the whole tendency toward freedom in America, engendered by the frontier and other conditions, has built up a tradition of what we would now designate as liberalism, that is, a lack of confining restrictions in life and thought. The movement started early, and we may perhaps cite Roger Williams as our first great liberal. The founders of Massachusetts, though they had come to America to seek religious freedom for themselves, would not allow it to others who differed with them, whereas Williams, escaping from Massachusetts as the Puritans^{qv} had from England, allowed freedom of opinion, although not license of crime, in his new colony.

Probably the American who has been of most influence on liberal thought among us was Thomas Jefferson, who remained a liberal after such radicals as Patrick Henry and Samuel Adams had turned reactionaries. In these two instances, Williams and Jefferson, we glimpse the difference between genuine liberalism and the seeking of mere personal freedom or the intolerance of mere radicalism. We can delimit the meaning of the term, again, if we compare Jefferson and Lincoln with Andrew Jackson. All were great democrats in the broad sense, but we would hardly consider Jackson as a liberal; and the same may be said of some later leaders and Presidents who have been considered as "progressive" but who proved themselves intolerant and even vindictive.

At present (1939) the term has fallen into some disrepute, partly because men not genuinely liberal have assumed it, and partly because liberalism, being an attitude toward programs rather than a program itself, tends to be crushed between parties fighting for immediate and definite objectives, as the Liberal party in England has been crushed between the Conservatives and the Laborites. It is often claimed that the liberal has nothing definite to offer, and that therefore liberalism is bankrupt. If, however, we consider liberalism somewhat in the terms suggested above, and as a mental attitude toward problems, which might well be shared by both conservatives and radicals as well as those more specifically designated as liberals, it would seem that liberalism has a role to play at present more essential than ever.

[L. T. Hobhouse, *Liberalism;* W. L. Blease, *Short History of English Liberalism.*]   JAMES TRUSLOW ADAMS

Liberator, THE, was a weekly antislavery newspaper edited by William Lloyd Garrison*ᵂ* and published in Boston, Jan. 1, 1831, to Dec. 29, 1865. Its circulation never exceeded 3000. The subscription price was $2. Though never a success financially, this paper was largely influential in changing the antislavery movement*ᵂ* from the advocacy of gradual emancipation to a demand for immediate, uncompensated emancipation. It greatly aided Garrison's work in organizing the New England Anti-Slavery Society*ᵂ* in 1832 and the American Anti-Slavery Society*ᵂ* in 1833. In its first issue he sounded its keynote in these words: "I am in earnest—I will not equivocate—I will not excuse—I will not retreat a single inch—AND I WILL BE HEARD."

[Edward Channing, *A History of the United States.*]
ASA E. MARTIN

Liberia is a Negro republic on the west coast of Africa between Great Britain's Sierra Leone and France's Ivory Coast. The area is approximately 40,000 square miles; and the population is slightly less than 2,000,000, of whom about 20,000 are descendants of American Negroes.

The early history of Liberia is associated with "The American Society for the Colonization of the Free People of Color of the United States" (*see* American Colonization Society) organized in 1816. Partly as a result of the influence of this society, Congress in 1819 authorized the President to send an agent to locate a site for a colony in Africa on which Negroes taken from slave-smuggling ships together with the free Negroes*ᵂ* assembled for colonization by the Society might be settled. After purchasing from the natives a strip of country at Cape Mesurado, agents of the Society and of the United States Government settled a shipload of free Negroes on the site in 1822, after an abortive attempt at colonization two years previously. Though the Society founded a number of settlements along the coast during the next decade and expended approximately $100,000 in the undertaking, its

work was hampered by lack of funds, the hostility of the natives and the unwillingness of the free Negroes to offer themselves for transportation. Finally, in 1847, at the request of the Society, an independent republic of Liberia was established with a Negro president. In 1848 and 1849 the new government was recognized by most of the great powers, but not until 1862 by the United States. Because of internal strife, boundary controversies and trouble with the natives, the United States, in 1912, co-operating with Great Britain, France and Germany, arranged for a loan of £340,000 to the republic. Liberia in return pledged the customs duties and certain taxes as security for the loan and accepted an American receiver-general as financial advisor to the government. The frontier police, also, were placed under the direction of officers of the United States Army.

[H. F. Reeve, *The Black Republic;* R. C. F. Maughan, *The Republic of Liberia;* J. B. McMaster, *History of the People of the United States.*]   ASA E. MARTIN

Liberty is a word which has been used in America ever since the first English colonization. In verse and song, as well as in formal declarations, America, since attaining independence, has been extolled as a "sweet land of liberty."

During the national prohibition*ᵂ* era from 1920 to 1933, many persons insisted on their "personal liberty" to secure and consume alcoholic liquors. An examination of history will reveal, however, that "liberty" has never been considered in America to mean freedom to do as one pleases. Gov. John Winthrop of Massachusetts Bay made this clear as early as 1645 when he wrote in his *Journal* that there were two kinds of liberty, "natural" and "civil." The first, common to man and beasts, meant doing as one wished; it was "a liberty to evil as well as to good," which was "incompatible and inconsistent with authority." On the other hand, "civil" liberty was limited by authority; it was "a liberty to that which is good, just, and honest." Gov. Winthrop and his fellow Puritans, it should be observed, did not hesitate to prescribe the limits of liberty within the bounds of their "Bible Commonwealth."*ᵩᵂ*

Obviously, the Winthrop concept of liberty has generally prevailed in America. Liberty is, and has been, "liberty within the law." As society has become increasingly complex, governments have tended to place more restrictions on the individual's freedom of action. In the exercise of police power*ᵂ*, the Federal, state and local governments have placed thousands of laws and ordinances on the statute books to limit liberty.

Regulative agencies and police officers by the scores of thousands have been set up to apply the limitations. Only the written guarantees of civil liberties in the Federal and state constitutions stand as bulwarks against the complete curtailment of liberty by statutes, ordinances and police actions.

[Everett Dean Martin, *Liberty;* Harry T. Warfel, et al., eds., *The American Mind.*]

ERIK McKINLEY ERIKSSON

Liberty, The Song of, was written in 1768 by John Dickinson to unite Americans against British oppression by expressing in popular verse his convictions of the necessity of colonial union. The song enjoyed immense popularity among the Sons of Liberty[qv] and played an important part in creating that unanimity of thought and action which Dickinson believed essential to the preservation of American liberty.

[M. C. Tyler, *The Literary History of the American Revolution.*]

JOHN C. MILLER

"Liberty and Union Now and Forever, One and Inseparable." *See* Webster-Hayne Debate.

Liberty Bell first proclaimed American independence from the State House, Philadelphia, following the reading there on July 8, 1776, of the Declaration of Independence[qv]. Originally ordered by the Provincial Council in 1751 for the Golden Jubilee of Penn's 1701 Charter of Privileges[qv], it was cracked in testing upon arrival and recast by Pass and Stow, Philadelphia. During the Revolution it was hidden in Allentown (1777–78). Rung frequently for celebrations, it was first strained tolling the obsequies of Chief Justice Marshall (1835), but was fatally cracked and silenced on Washington's birthday, 1846. The antislavery movement in 1839 first called it Liberty Bell. It weighs over 2080 pounds, cost £60, and is inscribed: "Proclaim Liberty throughout all the land unto all the inhabitants thereof."

[J. B. Stoudt, *The Liberty Bells of Pennsylvania.*]

JULIAN P. BOYD

Liberty Boys, THE. *See* Sons of Liberty (Revolutionary).

Liberty Cap, THE, with a sharp-pointed apex tilted forward, was much used in the late 18th century. Probably Asiatic (Phrygian) in origin, and seemingly used in Rome as a token of manumission, this form of cap was used by revolutionists in France after 1789. The red cap or *bonnet rouge* of the extremists became notorious (*see* Jacobin Clubs). With the extension of French revolutionary sentiment in America in the next decade, radical Jeffersonian Republicans[qv] sometimes donned liberty caps.

ALFRED P. JAMES

Liberty-Cap Cent. A United States cent, somewhat smaller than a modern half dollar, struck by the mint at Philadelphia, 1793–96. On the obverse is a bust of Liberty with a pole over the left shoulder surmounted by a liberty cap[qv].

[Government Document, *Catalogue of Coins of the United States Mint.*]

THOMAS L. HARRIS

Liberty Loans. Upon the entry of the United States into the World War in April, 1917, it at once became apparent that large sums in excess of tax receipts would be needed both to provide funds for our European allies and to conduct the war activities of this country. To obtain the necessary funds, the Treasury resorted to borrowing through a series of bond issues. The first four issues were known as "Liberty Loans," while the fifth and last was called the "Victory Loan."

These issues were brought out between May 14, 1917, and April 21, 1919, in the total amount of $21,478,356,250. The separate issues were as follows: 1st Liberty Loan, $2,000,000,000; 2nd Liberty Loan, $3,808,766,150; 3rd Liberty Loan, $4,176,516,850; 4th Liberty Loan, $6,993,073,250; and Victory Loan, $4,500,000,000. The Liberty Loans were long-term bonds bearing from $3\frac{1}{2}\%$ to $4\frac{1}{4}\%$ interest, while the Victory Loan consisted of two series of 3–4 year notes bearing interest at $3\frac{3}{4}\%$ and $4\frac{3}{4}\%$. The issues were all oversubscribed.

The disposal of this vast amount of obligations was accomplished by direct sales to the people on an unprecedented scale. Liberty Loan Committees were organized in all sections of the country and practically the entire population was canvassed. Four-minute speakers gave high-powered sales talks in theaters, moving-picture houses, hotels and restaurants. The ministers of the country made pleas for the purchase of bonds from their pulpits. Mass meetings were held upon occasion and the banks assisted by lending money, at a rate no higher than the interest on the bonds, to those who could not afford to purchase the bonds outright. In this way it was possible to secure the funds wanted and to obtain oversubscriptions on each issue.

Some issues of Liberty Bonds have matured and have been paid or refunded. The remaining issues have been refunded at a considerable saving of interest and now bear the name of Treasury bonds.

[D. R. Dewey, *Financial History of the United States;* A. D. Noyes, *The War Period of American Finance.*]

FREDERICK A. BRADFORD

Liberty Party, THE (1839–48), the first anti-slavery political party, was formed by anti-Garrison abolitionists and cast 7059 votes in the campaign of 1840^w. James G. Birney was its candidate in that year and again in 1844, when a total of 62,300 was attained, drawing enough from Clay to give New York and the election to Polk. In 1848 it nominated John P. Hale who withdrew and the party merged in the Free Soil^w organization. Its leaders included Salmon P. Chase, Gerrit Smith, Myron Holley and Charles Torrey.

[T. C. Smith, *History of the Liberty and Free Soil Parties in the Northwest.*]   THEODORE W. COUSENS

Liberty Poles, or Liberty Trees, were symbols before which Sons of Liberty^w assembled and "pledged their fortunes and their sacred honors in the cause of liberty." Numerology played a part in the erection of poles, particularly the numbers *Ninety-two* and *Forty-five*. *Forty-five* symbolized the issue of John Wilkes' newspaper which had criticized the king. *Ninety-two* typified the votes in the Massachusetts legislature against rescission of the Circular Letter. Ninety-two Sons of Liberty raised a Liberty Pole forty-five feet high, or dedicated a tree with ninety-two branches after seventeen had been lopped off in detestation of the seventeen Tories^w who had voted to rescind the Circular Letter.

The best-known Liberty Pole was erected in New York City (1766), with approval of the royal governor, in celebration of repeal of the Stamp Act^w. Raised in harmony, it soon became the focus of brawls between British soldiers and Liberty Boys, attended by lively street fights and bloodshed.

The original Liberty Tree was an elm at the intersection of Washington and Essex streets, Boston; a rallying place for Sons of Liberty who met under its boughs, denounced British oppression, drank toasts, sang songs and hanged unpopular officials in effigy. It was cut down by British soldiers in 1775, and converted into fourteen cords of firewood.

[W. C. Abbott, *New York in the American Revolution;* Justin Winsor, *Memorial History of Boston.*]
                                        LLOYD C. M. HARE

Libraries. The origin of the public-library movement in the United States is easily traced to the establishment of the Harvard College Library under the terms of the will of the Rev. John Harvard, whose collection of 300 volumes formed its nucleus. Thus in 1636 the first library of anything like a public nature was formed in this country. Sixty years later the Rev. Thomas Bray (1656–1730) developed his idea of parochial libraries, and by 1699 he had established twenty such libraries in the colonies (sixteen of them in Maryland). Although these were intended for the use of ministers only, they did service as public libraries and led to the enactment of the first American library law in 1700, when the General Assembly of South Carolina passed an act regulating the use of another of them to which it referred as the "Provincial Library." A new stage in the development occurred when Benjamin Franklin's prolific mind conceived the subscription or shareholding library, and in 1732 the Library Company of Philadelphia was formed as an outgrowth of the literary society, the "Junto," which was to become the American Philosophical Society^w. Another subscription library, Redwood Library, was established in Newport, R. I., in 1747. To it belongs the honor of erecting, in 1752, the first building to be used solely for library purposes (still used by the Library). Other such associations were formed, and from them developed the mercantile, mechanics' and apprentices' libraries in which the membership fees were lower and within the means of the classes of people indicated by their titles (Boston, 1820; New York, 1820; Philadelphia, 1821, etc.). It was not until well into the 19th century that free public libraries, supported from public funds, came into being. The oldest library of this type in continuous use is that at Peterborough, N. H., established through the efforts of the Rev. Abiel Abbot in 1833. Fifteen years later the Massachusetts legislature passed an act enabling Boston to establish a tax-supported library (a law, which was amended in 1851 to permit any community in the state to do the same). Thus the great Boston Public Library came into being. It still ranks as the second largest public library, and was not overshadowed until 1895, when the New York Public Library was formed by merging the foundations established by James Lenox, Samuel J. Tilden and John Jacob Astor.

Meanwhile, in 1853, Charles C. Jewett, then librarian of the Smithsonian Institution^w, was instrumental in calling together a conference of librarians, which was attended by such men as Edward Everett Hale, Henry Barnard and others interested in public education. This conference was the forerunner of another in 1876 which resulted in the formation of the American Library Association by Justin Winsor, William F. Poole, Charles Ammi Cutter, Melvil Dewey and others, and in the publication of *The Library Journal.* In that same year the United States Bureau of Education published a lengthy survey called *Public Libraries in the United States of America:*

Their History, Condition, and Management.
Thus the free public library idea became an accepted fact and free library service was nationally recognized as a proper corollary of the free public school. The movement was accelerated by the generosity of Andrew Carnegie who began his benefactions to libraries in 1881 and during the remainder of his life gave over $60,000,000 to establish and aid them (his work being continued after his death by the Carnegie Foundation*ⁱᵛ*).
In the 1890's state library extension agencies came into being and through them library service was extended to those living in rural districts and communities without local library facilities. Today many of the states have officially recognized the library as an educational agency and require by law the establishment of libraries in public schools, especially secondary schools. In a few states, notably New York, librarians serving tax-supported libraries must hold certificates similar to those held by teachers.

Private libraries, too, have their place in American life, for in the United States as in no other country these have tended to become public property through gift or bequest. Most private libraries have always been rather miscellaneous collections of books accumulated in the course of a lifetime of reading and study and hardly deserve the name library. But many have deliberately formed around some central idea, such as that gathered by the Rev. Thomas Prince (1687–1758) to display the intellectual and social history of New England (this collection is now incorporated in the Boston Public Library). Many other private libraries of note have been formed and some of them have become part of public institutions. For example, Thomas Jefferson's library became the nucleus of the Library of Congress*ⁱᵛ*, the national reference library in Washington. James Lenox gave his great collection of Americana to New York City, and his rival collector, John Carter Brown, of Providence, R. I., established his in the John Carter Brown Library at Brown University. Henry E. Huntington's great private library, with its hundreds of unique items, and a heavy endowment, went to the State of California. J. Pierpont Morgan's great collection and the building housing it were given to New York City. Edward E. Ayer's collection of material pertaining to the American Indian was bequeathed to the Newberry Library, a privately endowed public library in Chicago, established by another public-spirited man, Walter Loomis Newberry. William L. Clements' fine collection of books and manuscripts pertaining to colonial America, and a building to house it, was donated to the University of Michigan. Henry Clay Folger directed that his collection of 50,000 books pertaining to Shakespeare and the Elizabethan dramatists be housed in a special building in Washington, adjacent to the Library of Congress, and given to the nation. These are but a few of the outstanding private collections which have come to public institutions, partly, to be sure, through a desire to perpetuate a name, but largely through the recognition of the public library as a vital factor in the education of the citizens of the United States.

[B. C. Steiner, *Rev. Thomas Bray and His American Libraries*, in *The American Historical Review*, October, 1896; C. C. Jewett, *Notices of Public Libraries in the U. S.*, 1851; H. B. Adams, *Public Libraries and Popular Education*, 1900; American Library Association, *Survey of Libraries in the U. S.*, 4 vols., 1926-27; A. E. Bostwick, *The American Public Library*, 4th ed., 1929; G. B. Utley, *Fifty Years of the American Library Association*, 1926.]

GILBERT H. DOANE

Libraries, Traveling. These libraries, consisting of small collections of selected books, general or special, are an effort to reach the population beyond the radius of public libraries. Generally a state authority, as the state library commission or state library, sends the libraries. These go to organized groups, as study clubs, high-school debaters, Americanization classes, granges, churches; also to rural schools, and small public libraries. Books for adult foreigners are sent to different agencies. Individuals can get books under special circumstances. City libraries reach people by deposit stations, or traveling libraries to school classrooms (Buffalo plan), to fire-houses, hospitals, prisons, settlements. In rural districts, the book-wagon was first used in 1905 (Miss Mary L. Titcomb, Hagerstown, Md.). The use spread, and became a feature of the county library in its effort to reach people beyond library limits.

These traveling libraries, although tried in Wales, Scotland and Germany in the 18th century, and in America during the lyceum and early Chautauqua*ᵠᵛ* periods, were really started as a public institution in New York State under Melvil Dewey, 1893. Other states immediately followed.

AUGUSTUS H. SHEARER

Library of Congress, THE, was established by act of Congress, April 24, 1800, and was located in the Capitol until 1897. The library of Thomas Jefferson, numbering 6457 volumes, purchased from him in 1815, formed the nucleus of the present collections.

The period 1815 to 1897 was one of gradual growth. Events of this period which left an impress upon the scope or service of the collections were the purchase in 1829 of the manuscripts from the estate of Thomas Jefferson; the purchase for the Government of the Washington, Madison and Hamilton papers; the deposit of the Library of the Smithsonian Institution in 1866; the purchase of the Peter Force collection of Americana (60,000 volumes) ; and the establishment of the Library as the office of copyright registry and deposit in 1870. By 1881 the position and function of the Library were becoming clearer, and the need for a separate building to house its collections and activities became apparent. In 1897 this building was ready—the largest ever constructed for library purposes.

The period 1899–1938 was marked by rapid increase and diversification of the collections by purchase, gift and transfer from about 1,000,000 volumes in 1897 to 5,591,710 in 1938. This period was also marked by organization of a definitive bibliographical apparatus; by the formation of an effective personnel; by ampler provision for necessary purchase; by a scheme of classification, systematic and elastic, with an appropriate nomenclature; by adoption of processes of cataloging, now standardized for American libraries; by actual application of the classification and cataloging to a substantial portion of the collection of printed books; and by many new activities of a cultural sort, aided in part by private subvention.

The collections comprised on June 30, 1938: books, 5,591,710; manuscripts not numerable; maps, 1,402,658; music, 1,194,697 volumes and pieces; prints, 542,074; and, also, about 2,500,000 folios of reproduction of American historic material in foreign archives. Annual accessions of printed books are about 196,600. Special divisions administer the collections of periodicals, documents, law, science, aeronautics, manuscripts, maps, music, Hispanica, Semitica, Slavica, Orientalia and Rare Books. Service divisions include those of Legislative Reference Service, Bibliography, Reading Rooms, etc.

Its collections are pre-eminent in American history and politics, bibliography and library science, publications of learned societies, public documents (state, Federal and foreign) , files of American and foreign newspapers (including 95,000 volumes in bound form) , maps and atlases; eminent in law, economics, political science, religion, technology, aeronautics and the sciences. It contains a comprehensive collection of musical scores and literature; the largest collection of Chinese books outside of China and Japan, and of Russian books outside of Russia; a considerable collection of Semitica; and, with-

in the Fine Arts, over 500,000 prints. The manuscripts include papers of nearly all the Presidents and of many other Americans distinguished in public life. The Rare Book collection has about 70,000 volumes of first editions, rare bindings, etc., upwards of 1600 volumes of American 18th-century newspapers and nearly 5000 incunabula.

The results of its cataloging processes are cheaply available through the purchase of printed cards now subscribed to by upwards of 6500 libraries and other learned institutions. Its Union Catalog (developed by a Rockefeller grant) is a finding list of 10,000,000 entries for books in 700 American libraries. The official printed publications include basic texts (e.g., Journals of Continental Congress, Records of Virginia Company, etc.) , manuals, bibliographies, lists of atlases, calendars of manuscripts, etc.

Endowments provide "chairs" for special collections, e.g., aeronautics, history, fine arts, music and cartography, to administer, develop and interpret the collections. Other grants provide "consultants" in other fields to develop and interpret the collections. Individual benefactions have provided (1) the Elizabeth Sprague Coolidge Foundation for certain activities in the production and performance of music, including a chamber-music auditorium; (2) the Gertrude Clarke Whittall Foundation, established for the active use of the quintet of Stradivarius stringed instruments presented by her.

Special services to investigators include study tables, study rooms, access to bookshelves, interlibrary loan and photoduplication (photostat and film) service.

The present building and Annex together contain 1,563,189 square feet of floor space (35.88 acres); 414 miles of steel shelving; eight reading rooms; a practically unlimited number of study tables and 226 study rooms for those pursuing advanced research. The cost of the Main Building and Annex has been, to date, $18,747,000. The capacity of the Annex will be about 9,000,000 volumes.

Annual appropriations ($2,773,224 in 1938) are offset in part by moneys turned over to the United States Treasury from copyright fees, sales of card indexes and sales of photoduplications ($584,925.02 in 1938) . The Library of Congress Trust Fund Board administers endowments, the income from which is available for specified objects. From 1925 to 1938 these amounted to $1,338,804.77. Other endowments amounted to $650,000 and gifts for direct application by the Library were $1,632,018.65.

By the act of April 24, 1800, the primary service of the Library was to Congress. By extension, its range of service came to include all the governmental establishments. Now, retaining all its original functions, it has come to be the National Library of the United States, serving Congress, the governmental establishments and the public at large.

MARTIN A. ROBERTS

License Cases, THE (1847), involved state laws fixing conditions of, and requiring licenses for, the sale of certain goods imported from other states. In upholding the laws the Supreme Court of the United States weakened the doctrine of exclusive Federal control of interstate commerce as laid down in Gibbons v. Ogden[q]. The doctrine was reasserted, however, with modifications, when, in Cooley v. Port Wardens[q] (1851), the Court held that with reference to subjects not demanding uniformity states might impose regulations on interstate commerce until Congress exercised its right to establish uniform regulations.

[W. W. Willoughby, *The Constitutional Law of the United States.*]

J. HARLEY NICHOLS

Licenses to Trade. During the 19th century licenses to trade were used chiefly by state and municipal governments, with varying plans of operation. Usually the primary object was regulation of activities that might otherwise be inimical to public health and welfare. The list of licensed activities ranged from the strictly professional services of physicians to the strictly trade operations of shops selling intoxicating liquors.

During the 20th century the trend has been toward a more extensive use of licenses by municipalities. In cities having a population over 30,000, fees for licenses increased from about $40,000,000 in 1903 to more than double this amount in 1933. The increase was due partly to desire for additional revenue; partly to the recognition of new professions and services, such as accountancy and insurance brokerage; and partly to increasing control of stores selling food products.

Largely because of the fear of political manipulation, Federal licensing has not been favorably considered until recently. As a war measure for controlling foreign trade and conserving shipping space, Federal licenses were required for exports and imports in 1917–18, and have since been required for the export of munitions. The Agricultural Adjustment Act of 1933[q] provided for licensing distributors of various farm products. In 1938 a strong campaign was begun for the passage of an act requiring Federal licenses for all corporations engaged in foreign or interstate trade.

G. B. HOTCHKISS

Licks were saline springs or oozes to which herbivorous animals resorted for the quota of salt needed in their diet, which they obtained by licking the mud banks or rocks near the water. In some cases the lick was not near a flowing spring, but was a spot, usually muddy and, in at least one case, nearly an acre in extent, where the earth was so impregnated with salt that the animals licked it until they excavated considerable depressions. Important deposits of salt were frequently found thus. That prehistoric animals used the licks is indicated by the mastodon fossils found near Big Bone Lick[q] in Kentucky. Well-beaten trails made by the animals led to the licks, which therefore became favorite places for the stalking of deer and buffalo, both Indian and white hunters constructing blinds near by for the purpose. Licks were numerous in New York, Pennsylvania, the Middle States, Louisiana, Texas, etc. Their frequency in Kentucky accounted for the swarms of game found there when the white men came, and there they left behind them more place-names, such as Bank Lick, Berry's Lick, Paint Lick, Lick Creek—not to mention the Licking River—than in any other state. It has been said that it was the discovery of the licks and saline springs along the Holston, the Kanawha and Kentucky rivers which enabled colonization to cross the mountains. Daniel Boone located his first settlement, Boonesborough[q], at a salt lick on the Kentucky River. It was while making salt at the Blue Licks[q] some thirty miles distant, that he and several other colonists were captured by Indians in 1778. The Blue Licks later became a fashionable health resort. When Boone in after years moved to Missouri, he settled near another lick, which thereafter bore his name.

[Jeremiah Van Rensselaer, *An Essay on Salt;* Lewis and Richard H. Collins, *History of Kentucky.*]

ALVIN F. HARLOW

Lifeguard, Washington's, was a corps of infantry and cavalry attached to the person of George Washington, and to insure the safety of baggage and papers. Organized 1776, it was augmented at Valley Forge[q] by the addition of 120 picked men as a model corps to be trained by Baron von Steuben. The membership was selected of men "with uniforms and arms," of soldierly bearing, "neat and spruce." Its official title was the Commander in Chief's Guard.

[G. W. P. Custis, *Recollections of Washington.*]

LLOYD C. M. HARE

Lifesaving Service. In 1789 the Massachusetts Humane Society began erecting huts on dangerous and lonely portions of that state's coast for the shelter of persons escaped from shipwrecks. In 1807 the Society established at Cohasset the first lifesaving station in America, and soon afterward another at Lovell's Island. It continued to be the only organized agency in the nation for saving life and property from the sea until 1837, when Congress authorized the President to employ ships to cruise along the shores and render aid to distressed navigators. William A. Newell, afterward governor of New Jersey, saw a wreck off Barnegat from which many bodies were washed ashore, and, entering Congress in 1848, at once introduced a bill for aiding shipwrecked persons. An appropriation of $10,000 was made, and eight lifesaving stations set up between Sandy Hook and Little Egg Harbor, N. J. The crews were all volunteers—fishermen, etc., from the neighborhood—and were under the direction of officers appointed by the Revenue Marine Service and the Life Saving Benevolent Society of New York, organized in 1849. This society awarded medals for bravery and otherwise aided the work. Another appropriation that year financed the establishment of four more stations on the New Jersey and Long Island coasts, all with volunteer crews. Sumner I. Kimball, chief of the Revenue Cutter Service, induced Congress in 1870–71 to appropriate $200,000 and authorize the organization of a Government Lifesaving Service, under control of the Treasury Department. On Jan. 28, 1915, this service lost its identity, it being merged with the Revenue Cutter Service to form the Coast Guard[w]. It then had 203 stations on the coasts of the Atlantic and Gulf of Mexico, 62 on the Great Lakes, 19 on the Pacific Coast and one at the falls of the Ohio River at Louisville.

[T. B. M. Mason, The Preservation of Life at Sea, *Journal of the American Geographical Society*, 1879, No. 2.]
                                         ALVIN F. HARLOW

Lighthouse Service. The first lighthouse in America was completed at the entrance to Boston Harbor in 1716, and used candles for illumination. While British troops held Boston in 1775, parties of Americans twice seized the tower, took the lamps and burned the wooden parts. The British restored the light, but when they left the city in 1776, they blew up the structure. A new one was built in 1783, which, with some alteration, still stands. Under British rule, all lighthouses were built by the colonies. In 1789 there were ten such, of which seven were on the New England coast. Among them, those at Sandy Hook, built 1764, and at Cape Henlopen, at the entrance of Delaware Bay (1765), were still in use in the 20th century. Some 18th century lighthouses were of wood, and three such on Nan-

tucket Island were destroyed by fire. Most of the lights used candles at the beginning, but by 1789 all were using oil lamps. The existing lighthouses were ceded to the new government in 1789 and the service placed under the Secretary of the Treasury, who proceeded as rapidly as feasible to light the whole Atlantic coast—though even as late as 1796 North Carolina built a lighthouse of her own at the mouth of the Cape Fear River. Emerson found opposition to lights on Cape Cod, "because it injured the wrecking business." Between 1832 and 1841 there were forty wrecks on the reefs off Cohasset, Mass. An iron lighthouse was set up on one of the submerged reefs, Minot's Ledge, in 1849, but fell during a storm two years later. A stone tower was then essayed, and proved to be one of the most difficult construction jobs in history. Beginning in 1855, two years were required to obtain a foundation and three years more to build the tower. Lighthouses were under the Treasury Department until 1852, when a Lighthouse Board was set up. This was transferred to the Department of Commerce in 1903 and reorganized as the Bureau of Lighthouses, Jan. 1, 1910. In 1920 there were 14,550 warning lights and signals on the American coast. The first lightship was stationed in Chesapeake Bay near Norfolk in 1821; the first in the open sea, near Sandy Hook in 1823.

[George R. Putnam, *Lighthouses and Lightships of the United States.*]
                                         ALVIN F. HARLOW

Lighting. The first American settlers employed candlewood or pine knots, which were dipped in pitch and burned with a bright but smoky flame. When they could afford it they used candles[w], which were generally manufactured at home, but the mass of the people used grease lamps with wicks of reed or twisted rag. The so-called Betty lamps, small oval or triangular basins of metal with a short spout and a handle and chain for carrying or hanging, were popular. In the more elaborate colonial homes candle fixtures of crystal and brass imported from France and England were installed.

At the beginning of the 18th century whale oil (*see* Spermaceti Trust), abundant and cheap, was used extensively, although tallow candles were much preferred. Wealthy colonists used astral oil burned in glass shades to protect the flame from drafts. With the discovery of oil[w] in Pennsylvania about 1860 kerosene was the accepted illuminant and is still in common use in communities with no electric or gas service.

Illuminating gas produced by distilling coal was a real advance in artificial lighting. Tried experimentally in England in 1798 it did not reach America until 1816. By 1875 it was the accepted method of lighting in all the cities. The "fish tail" burner was used exclusively until Welsbach's invention of the mantle, which gave a whiter and more brilliant light than any previous source. Gas lighting was widely used until about thirty years ago for stores, factories, theaters, churches and the better-class homes within reach of the mains.

The electric arc lamp was a practical thing before the incandescent lamp[w] and in the late 1870's began to be introduced for street lighting using the series system. Electric lighting indoors, however, had to await the development of Edison's multiple system, the incandescent lamp and the establishment of central stations to supply current. The first permanent central station in the world was that of the Edison Electric Illuminating Company in Pearl Street, New York City, which started operation on Sept. 4, 1882, with fifty-nine customers who had a total of 1284 sockets.

For nearly thirty years all that was available for electric lighting were high-powered arc lamps and rather weak (2, 4, 8, 16 and 32 candlepower) carbon lamps. General illumination in stores, theaters and other public buildings was accomplished by arc lamps or clusters of incandescent lamps in a single reflector. In most offices and factories lighting was provided by individual lamps in tin or glass shades, known as drop lights. There was little general illumination and extreme contrasts between the brightly lighted work area and the rest of the room. In the homes most of the fixtures were converted gas chandeliers and table lamps.

With the introduction of the efficient and more powerful tungsten filament lamps, general lighting for all types of interiors became common. Soon such a range of sizes was available that any illumination problem could be solved effectively. Today (1939) for regular lighting circuits, lamps are available from 3 watts (3 candlepower) to 50,000 watts (150,000 candlepower).

With the introduction of the modern movement in architecture, lighting equipment became a component part of the structure rather than something which was supplied after the building was finished, and the more progressive architects are installing modern lighting in all new structures.

Since present-day light sources are far more brilliant than the inefficient lamps of the past, they cannot be used exposed without creating severe glare and eyestrain. Proper lighting today conceals all lamps save those which are of low wattage and used only as decorative points. Indirect illumination, where the ceiling and side walls are used as secondary light sources, is a very important factor. Inbuilt and cove lighting are essentially modern.

[*Transactions* Illuminating Engineering Society, 1906 to 1938.]   A. L. POWELL

Ligonier, Fort, at the site of the Pennsylvania town so named, was built by Col. Bouquet in 1758, as the Forbes expedition[w] made its way slowly westward toward Fort Duquesne[w]. After the battle of Grant's Hill[w], French and Indians attacked Bouquet at Ligonier but were repulsed (*see* Loyalhanna, Battle of the). Thereafter the fort was an important link in the chain of communications between eastern Pennsylvania and Fort Pitt[w]. During Pontiac's War[w] Ligonier was the only small fort west of the mountains in Pennsylvania that did not fall in the early attacks; its retention made possible the relief of Fort Pitt by Bouquet's forced march in 1763.

[C. H. Sipe, *Fort Ligonier and Its Times;* S. J. and E. H. Buck, *The Planting of Civilization in Western Pennsylvania.*]   SOLON J. BUCK

Lily-White Movement, THE. This term has been used for half a century in the politics of the South. It signifies opposition to the participation of the Negro[w] in the political life of the Southern states. A lily-white Republican advocates the elimination in Republican politics of Negroes, including voters, committeemen, convention delegates and all forms of party activity. Those white Republicans favoring the idea contend that, until the party is purged of Negroes, it will not attract white persons of normal Republican proclivities. The origins of the movement are found in the local, factional differences in the Republican organizations in certain Southern states. Republicans representing this point of view have been spasmodically active in all states of the Solid South[w]. The struggle for control between the regular or "black-and-tan" Republican faction and the lily-white faction assumed significance in national politics periodically from 1908 to 1928. In 1901 Theodore Roosevelt had criticized the Republican control in the South, with its interest in Federal patronage and its alleged venality. In 1928 it was apparent that the lily-white movement could benefit greatly by the factors of Southern industrialism, opposition to a one-party area, the character of the regular Southern Republican organizations, and discontent with the candidacy of Alfred E. Smith. Subsequently, President Hoover supported the lily-white group and by depriving the regulars, especially certain Negroes, of their patronage and position, instituted attempted reforms in the ten states of the Solid South. Other Northern Republican leaders, however, did not endorse the reforms; either they condoned the use of the older practices or they feared the effects on the Northern Negro Republican vote of a lily-white Southern policy. No permanent results were obtained by Hoover's efforts.

[*New York Times*, March (various days), 1929; Paul Lewinson, *Race, Class, and Party*.]

THOMAS S. BARCLAY

Lima Conference, THE (1938), was the eighth International Conference of American States, held at Lima, Peru, Dec. 9–27. All of the twenty-one American republics were represented. The United States, apprehensive of the efforts of Nazi Germany to extend its economic and political influence in certain states of Latin America, sought approval of an inter-American consultation committee, to meet periodically to discuss common measures of defense. Argentina firmly opposed this proposal and was supported by Uruguay, Paraguay, Bolivia, Chile and Brazil. After vigorous debate the Declaration of Lima, alternatively entitled the Declaration of the Solidarity of America, was passed. It omitted reference to particular states, merely affirming the "determination [of the signatories] to make effective their solidarity," in case of any threat, by means of the procedure of consultation; the states, however, "will act independently in their individual capacity." The Conference also passed a resolution on reduction of trade barriers and a declaration of American principles. Secretary of State Cordell Hull headed the American delegation, which included ex-Gov. Alfred M. Landon of Kansas.

[*Department of State, Press Releases*, Dec. 10, 24, 31, 1938; Jan. 14, 1939.]   HAROLD S. QUIGLEY

Limitations, Statutes of. All of the American states have statutes limiting the time within which a person having a cause for court action is permitted to bring suit for the recovery of his rights. As time passes, witnesses die, papers are destroyed and the conditions of transactions are forgotten. By such laws stale claims are prevented from being enforced which might earlier have been successfully defended. Thus legal titles and the possession of property are made more secure, and much malicious or frivolous litigation is prevented.

[Bouvier's *Law Dictionary*.]

EARL E. WARNER

Limping Standard. The laws of 1878, 1890 and 1934 provided for the coinage of a limited number of silver dollars[v] and gave these dollars, actually "token coins," a fictitious status as standard money. Historically this type of money system has been known as the "limping" standard, in America as well as in France.

NEIL CAROTHERS

Lincoln County War, THE, was a struggle between two rival groups of ranchers and businessmen in southeastern New Mexico. One faction was headed by Maj. L. G. Murphy and the other by John Chisum and Alexander A. McSween. Murders and depredations extending over a long period culminated in July, 1878, in a three days' battle at the town of Lincoln, in which McSween and several others were killed. William H. Bonney, better known as Billy the Kid, was a prominent figure in this struggle.

[Walter Noble Burns, *Saga of Billy the Kid.*]

EDWARD EVERETT DALE

Lincoln-Douglas Debates, THE, most noted events in Abraham Lincoln's senatorial campaign in Illinois against Stephen A. Douglas, took place at Ottawa, Freeport, Jonesboro, Charleston, Galesburg, Quincy and Alton, Aug. 21–Oct. 15, 1858. The Little Giant's[v] opening speeches in his re-election drive, with their effective frontal attack on Lincoln's "House Divided"[v] doctrine, alarmed Lincoln's managers and led him to challenge Douglas, "for you and myself to divide time and address the same audiences the present canvass." Douglas' speaking dates were already set through October, but he agreed to one debate in each of the above seven congressional districts.

About 12,000 gathered at Ottawa, Aug. 21, for the first debate, which was preceded and followed by parades, and punctuated by shouts and cheers. Douglas was well-dressed, with a ruffled shirt, a dark blue coat with shiny buttons and a wide-brimmed soft hat. Lincoln wore a rusty, high-topped hat, an ill-fitting coat with sleeves too short and baggy trousers so short as to show his rusty boots. Their speaking manners likewise contrasted. Douglas talked fast and steadily, in a heavy voice. He would shake his long, black hair and walk back and forth across the platform with great effectiveness. Lincoln's voice was light, almost nasal, and at the start had an unpleasant timbre, but carried well. Both gave a sense of profound earnestness.

Douglas' theme at Ottawa was the sectional bias, the strife-fomenting nature, of Republican doctrine. He read a series of resolutions he mistakenly believed had been adopted when the party was formed in Illinois in 1854, and pressed

Lincoln to deny his own indorsement of them. Douglas likewise assailed the "House Divided" doctrine. Lincoln seemed troubled by the questions.

He went to Freeport determined to impale Douglas on the horns of a dilemma. There he asked the famous Freeport questions, as to the Dred Scott decision[qq]. Either Douglas must accept the Supreme Court's decision, which would mean that slavery could go anywhere; or he must cease urging the sanctity of Supreme Court decisions.

It was not a new question for Douglas, who was more realist than dialectician. "Slavery cannot exist a day," he answered, "or an hour, anywhere, unless it is supported by local police regulations." This was an effective counter in debate, and would seem one in fact. Without the support of local laws and administration, no national law can be effectively enforced, as was shown in the national prohibition[q] experiment.

The other debates were hard fought and colorful, but Ottawa and Freeport had set the main tone for the rest of them. The third took place Sept. 15 at Jonesboro, a little town deep in "Egypt"[q] where Lincoln had few friends— and Douglas had few, for it was "Danite"[q] territory. At Charleston, three days later, the crowd was fairly evenly divided. Lincoln, smarting under Douglas' Negro equality charges, toned down his earlier statements. Thereupon Douglas said his opponent's views were "jet black" in the North, "a decent mulatto" in the center and "almost white" in Egypt.

Three weeks later the fifth debate occurred at Galesburg, an Abolition stronghold. On Oct. 13 the two men grappled at Quincy, and the last debate was two days later at Alton. Here the two men epitomized again their points of view. Lincoln repeated the charge that the trouble with Douglas was "that he looks to no end of the institution of slavery." But Douglas said: "I care more for the great principle of self-government, the right of the people to rule, than I do for all the Negroes in Christendom. I would not endanger the perpetuity of this Union."

The Lincoln of the debates was a strong antagonist at grips with one quite as strong. At times both men seemed political wrestlers crafty in verbal clutches, who spent much time in fumbling about for or escaping from effective holds. Judged as debates, they do not measure up to their reputation. On neither side did the dialectic compare with that in the debates between Webster, Hayne and Calhoun.

[George Fort Milton, *The Eve of Conflict.*]

GEORGE FORT MILTON

Lincoln Highway. The idea of a coast-to-coast highway originated with Carl G. Fisher of Indianapolis in 1912, when the automobile was in comparative infancy and when there was no system of good roads covering even one state. In September, 1912, Fisher laid the proposition before the leaders of the automobile industry, and, giving $1000 himself, obtained pledges of more than $4,000,000 for the building. To add a patriotic touch, he gave the name "Lincoln" to the road in 1913, and the Lincoln Highway Association was formed to further the project. States and individuals the country over made contributions, cement manufacturers donated material for "demonstration miles." By an act of 1921 the United States increased its aid to states in road building, which greatly helped this project. From Jersey City the route chosen passed through Philadelphia, Gettysburg, Pittsburgh, Fort Wayne, near Chicago, through Omaha, Cheyenne, Salt Lake and Sacramento to San Francisco. The original course was 3389 miles, later cut by more than fifty miles. Work began in October, 1914, but proceeded slowly. When the Association closed its offices on Dec. 31, 1927, and $90,000,000 had been spent, the road was usable throughout its length, though there were still sections of gravel, some even of dirt road, which were slowly improved thereafter. In 1925 the road became U. S. Highway No. 30.

[Lincoln Highway Association, *The Lincoln Highway.*]

ALVIN F. HARLOW

Lincoln's Assassination. On April 14, 1865, at 10:15 P.M., while attending a performance of "Our American Cousin" at Ford's Theatre, Abraham Lincoln was shot in the back of the head by John Wilkes Booth. As soon as the fatal nature of the wound was apparent, Lincoln was carried to a lodging house opposite the theater. There, without regaining consciousness, he died at 7:22 on the following morning.

In spite of the fact that Booth broke his leg in jumping from the presidential box to the stage, he made his way from the theater, and, with David E. Herold, escaped from Washington in the direction of Virginia before midnight. All the forces of the Government were directed toward his capture, but hysteria, greed for the reward and incompetence hindered the pursuit to such an extent that it was not until April 26 that Booth and Herold were surrounded in a tobacco shed on the Garrett farm near Port Royal, Va. There Herold surrendered, but Booth defied his captors and was shot—possibly by Boston Corbett, possibly by his own hand.

Before the death of Booth, the Government

had implicated nine persons in the assassination —George A. Atzerodt, Lewis Payne, David E. Herold, Mary E. Surratt and her son John H. Surratt, Edward Spangler, Samuel Arnold and Michael O'Laughlin. All except John H. Surratt were tried before a military commission, May 9–June 30, 1865. All were found guilty, although the verdict in the case of Mrs. Surratt was certainly a miscarriage of justice. Atzerodt, Payne, Herold and Mrs. Surratt were hanged on July 7; the others were imprisoned in Fort Jefferson, Dry Tortugas. John H. Surratt was brought to trial in 1867, but the jury failed to agree, and his case was later dismissed.

The assassination of Lincoln was a national tragedy in the broadest sense. It removed a President who was averse to vindictive measures, and by transforming widespread Northern inclination to leniency into a passion for retribution, gave Reconstruction[q] its popular sanction.

[Otto Eisenschiml, *Why Was Lincoln Murdered*; D. M. DeWitt, *The Assassination of Abraham Lincoln and Its Expiation*; Lloyd Lewis, *Myths after Lincoln*.]

PAUL M. ANGLE

Lind, Jenny, Tours America. Opening at Castle Garden, New York City, Sept. 11, 1850, Jenny Lind toured the eastern United States under the astute management of P. T. Barnum, giving ninety-five concerts, the last one on June 9, 1851. Tickets were auctioned before the concerts and often sold at fantastic prices (one at $650!). Miss Lind received $176,675 for her services and Barnum cleared over $500,000. Thereafter the singer gave a number of concerts under her own management before returning to Europe in 1852.

[P. T. Barnum, *Struggles and Triumphs*.]

ALVIN F. HARLOW

Lindbergh Flies across the Atlantic. The first nonstop flight between New York and Paris, and the first one-man crossing of the Atlantic by air, was made by Charles A. Lindbergh on May 20–21, 1927. Previously, several attempts had been made to win the Orteig prize of $25,000, offered in 1919, for the first continuous flight between New York and Paris over the Atlantic. In 1926 Fonck had crashed when taking off from Roosevelt Field, two American naval officers had been killed on a trial flight and the French aviators, Nungesser and Coli, had been lost over the Atlantic while attempting the difficult east-to-west crossing.

Backed by a group of St. Louis businessmen, Lindbergh supervised the construction of a Ryan monoplane, christened the "Spirit of St. Louis." It had a wing spread of forty-six feet and a chord of seven feet, weighed 5135 pounds, and was propelled by a 225-horsepower Wright Whirlwind motor. On the morning of May 20, 1927, taking advantage of an area of high pressure reported over the Atlantic, Lindbergh took off from Curtiss Field on Long Island with a load of 425 gallons of gasoline. Encountering fog and sleet, the aviator was compelled to fly blind part of the way at an altitude of 1500 feet. Later he dropped closer to the water, flying at times ten feet above the waves. Sighting the coast of Ireland he turned his course toward France. Flying over England, he crossed the Channel and at ten o'clock in the evening saw the lights of Paris. After circling the Eiffel Tower he made for the field Le Bourget where he landed after having flown 3605 miles in thirty-three hours and thirty-nine minutes.

The reception of the young aviator in the capital of France was cordial and demonstrative. Under the guidance of Myron T. Herrick, the American ambassador at Paris, Lindbergh made a most favorable impression on the French public. A round of fêtes in his honor failed to mar his attractive modesty, and he became a symbol of daring, courage and international fraternity. In Brussels, Berlin and London he was received with equal enthusiasm. He returned to America from Cherbourg on the U.S.S. *Memphis* sent by command of President Coolidge.

[Charles A. Lindbergh, *We*; *Aircraft Year Book*, *1928*.]

KENNETH COLEGROVE

Lindbergh Kidnapping Case. On the night of March 1, 1932, the eighteen-months-old son of Col. Charles A. Lindbergh was abducted from his parents' country home near Hopewell, N. J. The kidnapper climbed to the window of the second-story nursery by a ladder brought with him. He left a note demanding $50,000 ransom. After some futile attempts at closer contact with him, Dr. John F. Condon, a retired New York teacher, acting as intermediary, succeeded in having two night interviews with the man in a cemetery. On the second occasion, April 8, the money was paid to the latter upon his promise to deliver the child—a false promise, as it had been slain immediately after the abduction. Its body was found on May 12 near its home. The serial number of every note of the ransom money was made public. On Sept. 15, 1934, a carpenter named Bruno Hauptmann passed one of the bills at a New York filling station and was arrested. More than $14,000 of the ransom money was found concealed about his home. At his trial at Flemington, N. J., in January-February, 1935, the ladder was identified as having been made with plank taken from his attic. He was convicted, and executed on April 3, 1936.

[P. J. O'Brien, *The Lindberghs;* Sidney B. Whipple, *The Lindbergh Crime.*]   ALVIN F. HARLOW

Lind's Mission to Mexico (August, 1913–April, 1914). After the overthrow of President Madero in February, 1913, the Government of the United States refused to recognize the government set up by Victoriano Huerta; and John Lind of Minnesota was commissioned by President Wilson as his personal representative and adviser to the American embassy in Mexico City to use his influence to set up a constitutional government worthy of recognition. Lind's efforts failed, in spite of seven months of "watchful waiting"^{qv} at Vera Cruz.

[G. M. Stephenson, *John Lind of Minnesota.*]
                              G. M. STEPHENSON

Linen Industry. Flax was the principal textile fabric in colonial America where it was raised and made into linen on the farm. Some colonies subsidized its manufacture into sail cloth. For two centuries dressed flax and yarn were common articles of barter, homespun was familiar merchandise in country trade, and linsey-woolsey^{qv}, made of flax and wool, was a common clothing fabric.

With the coming of the gin and Arkwright machinery^{qqv} cotton displaced flax. Small linen mills were established subsequently but few were permanent and none grew into sizable enterprises. The most successful manufactured thread and canvas. The Civil War cotton shortage stimulated efforts to revive the industry but the high cost of dressing domestic flax and duties on imported fiber prevented its extension. Some linen goods, mostly thread and towels, are still manufactured in America, but the industry is a minor one and nearly all its raw materials are imported.

[Victor S. Clark, *History of Manufactures in the United States;* U. S. Census of Manufactures, 1935.]
                              VICTOR S. CLARK

Linotype, THE (1886), most important printing invention since movable type, transformed typesetting into a mechanical process. Many had sought faster composition when J. O. Clephane, Washington stenographer, promoted an experiment in multiplying typewriting in 1876. This failed but it inspired Ottmar Mergenthaler, Baltimore machinist, who for a decade worked on a series of machines, each nearer the goal. Finally, Mergenthaler devised a machine for casting molten metal in lines, automatically spaced, from individual matrices, assembled by keyboard

and returned to a magazine after use. The first patent was issued in 1884. On July 3, 1886, a "Linotype" was successfully operated by the New York *Tribune*. Within eighteen months there were sixty machines in newspaper composing rooms; by 1895 more than 3100 were in use. An immediate effect was impetus to afternoon newspapers through faster news presentation. The tramp printer^{qv} was dispossessed, but the way opened for undreamed-of publishing expansion. Thus, the Linotype is a striking example of the machine which, although producing technological unemployment, develops demand and increases opportunities for work.

[Thomas Dreier, *The Power of Print—and Men;* Waldemar Kaempffert, *A Popular History of American Invention;* A. M. Lee, *The Daily Newspaper in America;* G. E. Barnett, The Introduction of the Linotype, *Yale Review*, Vol. XIII.]   IRVING DILLIARD

Linsey-Woolsey was a stout homespun cloth having a wool weft and commonly a flax warp, though hemp or cotton was sometimes used, extensively manufactured in the American colonies and on the frontier. Its name, which is of British origin, first appears in colonial records soon after settlement. It was a homely fabric suitable for backwoods use, conveniently made in country households from materials raised on the farm. Not only was it widely used for men's and women's garments by servants, laborers and rural workers and therefore consumed for the most part in the households where it was made, but it also appeared in local store accounts and was occasionally receivable for taxes. No trustworthy statistics of the quantity produced in America exist but linsey-woolsey probably formed a substantial fraction of the eighteen or twenty million yards of mixed fabrics reported by the census of 1810.

[William B. Weeden, *Economic and Social History of New England;* Rolla M. Tryon, *Household Manufactures in the United States.*]   VICTOR S. CLARK

Liquor. *See* Rum Trade; Whiskey.

Liquor, Use of, in the Fur Trade. No sooner had the Indian tasted the white man's liquor, whether brandy, rum or whiskey, early in the 17th century, than its importance in the fur trade^{qv} became evident. By 1625 Thomas Morton was reaping a harvest of beaver skins at Merry Mount^{qv}, the present Quincy (Mass.), through the sale of liquor and firearms to Indians, and Massachusetts by 1641 had a special trader liquor licensing system. Other colonies likewise vainly attempted to legislate against whiskey sales to Indians. Under the French regime in the Great Lakes region Champlain in 1633 prohibited the sale of liquor except under strict regulation, and Bishop Laval in 1660 threatened excommunication against offenders. A decree of Louis XIV in 1679 provided fines and corporal punishment for sales to Indians, but liquor was thereupon given to the savages. Commandants like Cadillac, and soldiers as well, engaged in the contraband trade.

The ever-increasing bitterness of competition for furs, first between the French and English during the early 18th century, and, late in that century among rival English companies and traders, naturally emphasized the importance of the liquor trade. In 1769 two traders secured licenses at Michilimackinac[w] for canoes carrying 512 gallons of liquor, and by 1777 four traders for Grand Portage[w] (Minn.) alone took in 3956 gallons. It became difficult to purchase provisions for northern posts without liquor. Under the North West Company[w] and its rivals, liquor consumption ranged from 9600 gallons to 19,400 gallons between 1793 and 1804. Not all this liquor went to Indians, for the *voyageur*[w] ration was computed at one gill per day per man. The traders, according to a report in 1790, claimed to furnish liquor to the Indians in moderation, as gifts at feasts and talks, and progressive dilution of the high wines and alcohol with water, as intoxication developed, was customary.

American control, while attempted, was equally ineffective. Under the act of March 30, 1802, regulating intercourse with the Indian tribes, reinforced by subsequent legislation and executive orders, sale or distribution of spirituous liquors to Indians was prohibited, yet the fur trader and even the government official virtually required whiskey for use as a business "lubricant." Indian agents customarily examined cargoes on traders' boats for contraband rum, but seizures were difficult to substantiate in the courts. By various ruses liquors were smuggled past the inspecting officers.

On the Great Lakes, by permission of Superintendent Lewis Cass at Detroit, the American Fur Company[w] in the 1820's shipped to the northern Minnesota boundary posts substantial quantities of whiskey "for the purchase of provisions," in competition with the Hudson's Bay Company[w], and large consignments went into the Indian country through Prairie du Chien[w] (Wis.), a white community adjoining the closed area. The Fur Company further secured permits for liquor at the rate of one gill per *voyageur* per day, under bond, and in 1830–31 over 3000 gallons thus went into the Missouri country. In 1833 Kenneth McKenzie at Fort Union (N. Dak.)[w] even established a distillery, but governmental

disapproval closed it in 1834. To the **fur trader** it was liquor or ruin

[Harold A. Innis, *The Fur Trade in Canada;* Frederick J. Turner, The Character and Influence of the Indian Trade in Wisconsin, in *Johns Hopkins Studies in Historical and Political Science,* 9; Francis X. Moloney, *The Fur Trade in New England, 1620-1676;* Ida M. Johnson, The Michigan Fur Trade, in *Michigan Historical Publications, University Series,* 5; H. M. Chittenden, *The American Fur Trade of the Far West;* Wayne E. Stevens, *The Northwest Fur Trade;* Elliott Coues, ed., *Forty Years a Fur Trader on the Upper Missouri.*]

WILLOUGHBY M. BABCOCK

Liquor Laws. Drinking proved a problem very early in American history. In 1619 the colony of Virginia enacted a law against gaming, drunkenness and other excesses. A little later, among other liquor acts, it legislated against drunkenness among the clergy, and in 1676 penalized judges who got drunk on court days. Massachusetts passed laws against drunkenness in 1633, 1635, 1637, 1638, 1639, etc. In fact, at intervals of from one to three years throughout that century, Massachusetts is found imposing penalties or tightening restrictions on the liquor trade. It imposed the first real revenue taxes in the colonies in 1644. New York began restricting the business in 1638, and the other colonies followed closely behind it. Beginning with Connecticut in 1645, one colony after another forbade the selling of liquor to Indians. Likewise, one after another, they took up the imposition of excise taxes on liquor and derived a considerable income thereby. In 1658 Plymouth disfranchised drunkards; then Maryland disfranchised them for three years and Virginia deprived them of the right to testify or hold office. Maryland and Virginia defined a drunkard as one who had been intoxicated three times. New Hampshire prohibited the sale of liquor to such persons in 1719. Liquor legislation was less frequently heard of in the 18th century, but by 1800 drunkenness was again becoming a matter of great concern; the temperance movement[w] arose, and states again began making laws. Mississippi in 1839 forbade the purchase of less than one gallon of liquor at a time, hoping thus to curb tavern drinking. Massachusetts the year before had even enacted a fifteen-gallon law, but soon repealed it. An era of Local Option[w] began about 1830. By 1845 the country was becoming ripe for prohibition[w], but at that time no one thought of national legislation on the subject; it was regarded as a state problem. Beginning with Maine[w] in 1846, several states "went dry," though most of the state-wide laws were repealed within a few years. Another movement developed west of the Mississippi between 1880 and 1900, resulting in state-wide prohibition in Kansas[qv], Iowa and the Dakotas. Congress attempted to protect the dry states from liquor shipments by the Wilson Act in 1890 and the more effective Webb-Kenyon Act[qv] in 1913; but from 1907 on, states, especially in the South, were rapidly passing their own state-wide prohibitory laws, building up a sentiment which finally resulted in the creation of the Eighteenth Amendment[qv] in 1918 and its quick ratification.

[Ernest H. Cherrington, *The Evolution of Prohibition in the United States of America;* D. Leigh Colvin, *Prohibition in the United States.*]   ALVIN F. HARLOW

Lisa, Fort, near the present site of Omaha, Nebr., was established by Manuel Lisa probably in the spring of 1813, when he was forced to abandon Fort Manuel[qv]. The most important post on the Missouri River from 1813 to 1822, it controlled the trade of the Omaha, Pawnee, Otoe and neighboring Indians. (*See also* St. Louis Missouri Fur Company.)

[Hiram Chittenden, *American Fur Trade of the Far West;* John C. Luttig, *Journal of a Fur Trading Expedition, 1812-1813.*]   STELLA M. DRUMM

Lisa (Manuel) & Co. consisted of Manuel Lisa, Gregoire Sarpy, François M. Benoist and Charles Sanguinet. After Auguste and Pierre Chouteau[qv] failed in their endeavor to renew their monopoly, and moved their activities to the Arkansas River, Manuel Lisa & Co., in the year 1802, sought and obtained the exclusive trade with the Osage Indians[qv] on the waters of the Missouri and Osage rivers. The territory involved was about 120 miles from the mouth of the Missouri. This monopoly ended with the transfer of Upper Louisiana to the United States in 1804. In 1807 another firm called Manuel Lisa and Company was organized by Lisa, William Morrison and Pierre Menard, with a capital of $16,000. An expedition consisting of about twenty-five men left St. Louis for the Upper Missouri River country on April 19, 1807. The party reached their wintering ground Nov. 21, 1807, and immediately built a trading house. In the following spring Fort Raymond was built on the Yellowstone at the mouth of the Big Horn River. (*See also* St. Louis Missouri Fur Company.)

[Walter B. Douglas, Manuel Lisa, in *Missouri Historical Society Collections,* Vol. IV.]   STELLA M. DRUMM

Litchfield Law School, THE, was established by Tapping Reeve in about 1784. In 1798 he was succeeded by James Gould, who developed an institution which in the early years of the 19th century gave legal training to hundreds of young men from almost every state in the Union and numbered among its graduates some of the most prominent men in the public life of the next generation. Before it closed its doors in 1833, the Litchfield school had sent out over a thousand graduates.

[A. A. Reed, *Training for the Public Profession of the Law;* W. D. Lewis, ed., *Great American Lawyers.*]
                              FRANCIS R. AUMANN

Literacy Test. The literacy test has been used to determine qualifications for voting and the eligibility of aliens to enter the country. In the first connection, it has often been accompanied in the southern states with the requirement that the applicant for registration shall be able to interpret the portion of the state constitution indicated. In practice, this has enabled the registration officer to discriminate against Negro voters. Of the northern states, New York was first to adopt a literacy test act in 1923.

A Federal literacy test act was passed, applicable to immigrants, in 1913, and vetoed by President Taft. In 1915 Congress passed another act, which was vetoed by President Wilson. Finally, in 1917, it was passed over his veto. The issue aroused much controversy. It was argued for the bill that it would exclude only persons we did not want anyway; against it, that it placed further barriers in the way of those who had been denied the opportunity for education, and who might be coming here as adults eager to secure it for themselves or their children. The tests imposed have been very reasonable, and no question has arisen regarding them, since the policy became established.

[Finla G. Crawford, The New York State Literacy Test, in *American Political Science Review,* May, 1923; *ibid.,* November, 1925.]   W. BROOKE GRAVES

Literary, THE, sometimes called the literary society, was an institution common in rural districts throughout the West during the last quarter of the 19th century. Its origin is uncertain but was probably much earlier. In some remote communities, it was common well into the 20th century. Its purpose was both educational and social since it sought to create or stimulate interest in "things literary" and at the same time provide entertainment and an opportunity for closer social contacts. Possibly it represented an unconscious revolt against both the narrow, puritanical group, which seemed to find its chief pleasure in long sermons, prayer meetings and hymn singing, and the wild, boisterous element found in virtually every frontier or backwoods community. If so, it succeeded admirably. The most ardent churchgoers could find in it little to condemn while even the rowdiest of the rougher spirits gladly attended its meetings, because of the fun and good fellowship they afforded.

Meetings were generally held once or twice a month, usually at the schoolhouse, and the local schoolteacher often took a prominent part. Officers commonly consisted of a president, secretary and program committee. This might be a standing committee, or in some cases a new one was appointed for each meeting. There was seldom a formal membership list, but, instead, all interested persons were invited to attend and urged to take part in the programs. These consisted of readings, short plays, commonly called "dialogues," and sometimes a vocal solo, duet or quartet. A debate on some such subject as: "Resolved that fire is more destructive than water," or "There is more pleasure in pursuit than possession," sometimes formed a part of the evening's entertainment. Often a "newspaper" was prepared and read aloud to the audience. This gave some bits of news, but was more often given over to clever gibes directed at various local leaders. Readings were humorous, dramatic or pathetic, and new ones as well as new dialogues were eagerly sought in various books produced by publishers seeking to exploit this market. Such favorites as *Curfew Must Not Ring To-night, The Face on the Barroom Floor,* and *The Lips That Touch Liquor Can Never Touch Mine* were widely read. A clever program committee sought to provide a well-balanced entertainment with enough comedy, pathos, drama and ethical or religious teaching to cause every one to be pleased with at least some part of the program.

[W. L. Wilkerson and B. A. Botkin, The Oklahoma Literary Society, in *Folk-Say, A Regional Miscellany,* Vol. II.]   EDWARD EVERETT DALE

Little Big Horn Battle (June 25, 1876). The Indians in Dakota territory bitterly resented the opening of the Black Hills[w] to settlers in violation of an earlier treaty. Owing also to official graft and negligence they were facing actual starvation for the coming winter. In the fall of 1875, therefore, they began to leave their reservations contrary to orders, to engage in their annual buffalo hunt. Here they were joined by lawless tribesmen from other reservations until the movement took on the proportions of a serious revolt. The situation was one that called for the utmost tact and discretion, for the Indians were ably led and the treatment they had received had stirred the bitterest resentment among them.

Unfortunately, by some inexplicable blunder, an order, originating with the Indian Bureau, was sent to all reservation officials early in December, directing them to notify the Indians to return by Jan. 31, under penalty of being attacked by the United States Army. This belated order could not be carried out in the dead of winter even if the Indians had been inclined to obey it.

Early in 1876 Gen. Sheridan, from his headquarters at Chicago, ordered a concentration of troops on the upper Yellowstone River, to capture or disperse the numerous bands of Dakotas who were hunting there. In June Gen. Terry, department commander, and Lt. Col. George A. Custer with his regiment from Fort Abraham Lincoln[w], marched overland to the Yellowstone, where they were met by the steamboat *Far West*[w] with ammunition and supplies. At the mouth of Rosebud Creek (a tributary of the Yellowstone) Custer received his final orders from Terry: to locate and disperse the Indians. According to official records there is now no longer any doubt that Gen. Terry gave Custer absolutely free hand in dealing with the situation, relying upon his well-known experience in this kind of warfare.

With twelve companies of the 7th Cavalry, Custer set out on his march and soon discovered the Indians camped on the south bank of the Little Big Horn River. He sent Maj. Reno with three companies of cavalry and all the Arikara scouts across the upper ford of this river to attack the southern end of the Indian camp. Capt. Benteen, with three companies, was sent to the left of Reno's line of march. Custer, himself, led five companies of the 7th Cavalry down the river to the lower ford for an attack on the upper part of the camp. One company was detailed to bring up the pack train.

This plan of battle, thoroughly typical of Custer, was in the beginning completely successful. Suddenly faced by a vigorous double offensive, the Indians at first thought only of retreat. At this critical juncture, Reno became utterly confused and ordered his men to fall back across the river. Thereupon the whole force of the Indian attack was concentrated upon Custer's command, compelling him to retreat back from the river to a position where his force was later annihilated. The soldiers under Reno rallied at the top of a high hill overlooking the river and here they were joined by Benteen's troops and two hours later by the company guarding the pack train.

An official inquiry into Reno's conduct in the battle was made in 1879 and he was cleared of all responsibility for the disaster. Since that time, however, the sober judgment of military experts has tended to reverse this conclusion and to hold both Reno and Benteen gravely at fault.

In Gen. Philip H. Sheridan's *Memoirs* it is stated: "Reno's head failed him utterly at the critical moment." He abandoned in a panic the perfectly defensible and highly important position on the Little Big Horn River.

As to Benteen, at the military inquiry he admitted he had been twice ordered by Custer to break out the ammunition and come on with his men. Later, at 2:30 P.M., when he had joined Reno, there was no attacking force of Indians in the vicinity and he had at his disposal two thirds of Custer's entire regiment as well as the easily accessible reserve ammunition. Gen. Nelson A. Miles in his *Personal Recollections* can find no reason for Benteen's failure to go to Custer's relief. He says, after an examination of the battlefield, that a gallop of fifteen minutes would have brought reinforcements to Custer. This expert opinion makes it hard to understand why, for more than an hour, while Custer's command was being overwhelmed, Reno and Benteen remained inactive.

[Chas. F. Bates, *Custer's Indian Battles;* Nelson A. Miles, *Personal Recollections;* Philip H. Sheridan, *Personal Memoirs;* The Arikara Narrative in *Collections of the State Historical Society of North Dakota*, Vol. VI.]

O. G. LIBBY

"Little Church Around the Corner." In 1870 the rector of a New York church refused a burial service to George Holland because he had been an actor, but remarked, "I believe there is a little church around the corner where they do such things." He referred to the Church of the Transfiguration on 29th Street, built 1849–50, which thereupon became a favorite sanctuary for actors, and still retains its whimsical nickname.

[George MacAdam, *The Little Church Around the Corner.*]

ALVIN F. HARLOW

"Little Giant," THE, was the title given Stephen Arnold Douglas at a political rally in Jacksonville, Ill., 1834. So well did the youthful lawyer-politician uphold President Jackson and denounce "Emperor" Biddle and his panic (*see* Panic of 1837) that the crowd hailed the diminutive Democrat by the soubriquet by which he was thereafter known.

[George Fort Milton, *The Eve of Conflict.*]

GEORGE FORT MILTON

"Little Group of Willful Men." By a five-day filibuster ending Sunday, March 4, 1917, Senators LaFollette, Norris, Cummins, Gronna, Clapp, Works (Republican) , and Stone, O'Gorman, Kirby, Lane, Vardaman (Democrat) , pre-

vented the passage of a bill to arm merchant ships against German submarines, which had passed the House of Representatives, 403–13. President Wilson in a public statement stigmatized them as "a little group of willful men, representing no opinion but their own [who] have rendered the great Government of the United States helpless and contemptible."

[F. L. Paxson, *Democracy and the World War: Pre-War Years, 1913-1917;* Mark Sullivan, *Our Times*, Vol. V.]

HARVEY L. CARTER

Little Niagara, Fort. *See* Niagara, Carrying Place of.

Little Nine Partners' Patent, THE, granted April 10, 1706, to Samuel Broughton and seven associates, was in the northeastern part of Dutchess County, N. Y., and included the present towns of Milan and Pine Plains, the north half of North East and small portions of Clinton and Stanford. The colonial assembly authorized its partition in 1734.

[Frank Hasbrouck, *History of Dutchess County.*]

A. C. FLICK

Little Red Schoolhouse. The old-time country school became a symbol of American democracy and civilization founded upon the "three R's." The small, one-room school building, located usually on a small piece of waste land which the farmers could readily spare, was painted, if at all, with red or yellow ochre, the cheapest possible paint, hence the "red" in the title. Such schoolhouses were found, from the 18th century on, along country roads throughout New England and states farther west, ministering to several farm families in a central place. Pictures of the building became a sort of patriotic fetish with the American Protective Association, successor of the Know-Nothing[qv], anti-Roman-Catholic movement, at the close of the 19th century, as a seal of unadulterated Americanism.

[Clifton Johnson, *Old-Time Schools and School-Books.*]

ROBERT P. TRISTRAM COFFIN

Little Sarah, THE, was an English ship captured by French privateers[qv] in 1793 and interned at Philadelphia. The French minister, Genêt[qv], by equipping the vessel and permitting its departure under the name *Little Democrat,* in defiance of Jefferson's protest of July 12, forfeited the confidence of Washington and even of Jefferson, whose pro-French sympathies were outraged. Demand for Genêt's recall became insistent. The *Little Sarah* thereby imposed a strain upon Franco-American relations.

[J. B. McMaster, *History of the People of the United States.*]

LOUIS MARTIN SEARS

"Little Steel" was a name given a group of steel companies whose aggregate output was exceeded (1939) only by the United States Steel Corporation[w]. Bethlehem, Republic, Inland, and Youngstown Steel & Tube constitute the group.

THOMAS ROBSON HAY

"Little Theater" Movement, an effort of small groups to produce art for art's sake rather than great profit, often experimentally in small theaters with repertory companies (and in the smaller towns, with amateur actors), arose in 1911–12. In the first season three little theaters appeared—that of Maurice Brown in Chicago, Mrs. Lyman's Toy Theater in Boston and Winthrop Ames' in New York—though the last-named was not strictly true to type, being rather a commercial venture. The growth of the idea was rapid, and within five years fifty theaters had been opened. Storerooms, dwellings, remodeled barns were turned into theaters, while in other cases, lodge halls, chapels and museum auditoriums were utilized. Some universities set up experimental or laboratory theaters in connection with their dramatic courses, that of Prof. George Pierce Baker of Harvard being especially famous. That at the University of North Carolina also ranked high and produced at least one noted playwright, Paul Green. A remarkable little theater was established by Alfred Arnold in an unused chapel at the North Dakota Agricultural College at Fargo, with students for actors. In New York the pioneer Washington Square Players were succeeded by the Provincetown Players, launched in 1916 in an old wharf building at Provincetown, Mass., and giving first presentations of some of the earlier, yet now famous, plays of Eugene O'Neill. The Hedgerow Theater, founded in 1924 by Jasper Deeter in an old mill, with 168 seats, at Moylan, near Swarthmore, Pa., remains the only self-sustaining, continuous repertory theater in existence. The summer theater—this, too, often in remodeled barns or mills—which grew enormously in popularity after 1925, especially in the resort regions of New England and other Eastern states—stock companies giving weekly bills, with one or more guest stars—is another phase of the movement.

[Constance D'Arcy Mackay, *The Little Theater in the United States.*]

ALVIN F. HARLOW

Livestock Industry, THE, epitomizes the economic transformation of the nation from diffused primitive self-sufficiency to concentrated specialized commercialism. All classes of farm animals of Europe were brought to the colonies as a basic element of formative equipment and in general, with considerable variations and certain necessitated acclimatizations, proved remarkably adaptable to the new environments. Livestock in the different groups of colonies was fitted into the various colonial economies: the common field system of New England necessitating group action in regulation and efforts at breed improvement; the more diversified husbandry of the Hudson Valley and southern Pennsylvania; and the open ranging in the southern Piedmont. Export and regional markets early developed. Cured and pickled meats from the Connecticut Valley, New York and Philadelphia found increasing demand in the West Indian trade[w]. Locally organized market centers developed with selling and slaughtering regulation.

With the trans-Allegheny expansion following the Revolution, livestock production entered upon its large-scale phases. Localizing influences of availability to market, natural pasturage and breeder initiative centered production in the Old Southwest[w] before the Civil War, but from the 1830's extension to the Northwest was increasingly marked. The river trade at best provided a limited outlet and the main market centers were reached by the overland drovers. The Erie Canal[w] inaugurated a direct western competition with eastern production and with the trunk line railroad of the 1850's the invasion was overwhelming. Cincinnati[w] was the great packing center before the Civil War though western cities in Missouri and Illinois were profiting from availability of supplies.

In the two decades following the Civil War the forces that were to produce the modern industry came into full operation. The open range[w], involving the finishing of the southern-bred cattle on the northern plains and the shipment from convenient points on the new railroads to the primary markets, provided the cattle for a major industry, and with the closing of the "long drive"[w] by the middle 1880's production was more stabilized on the ranch. The best combination of localizing influences was making Chicago, by the time of the establishment of the Union Stock Yards in 1865, the permanent center of the industry. Promotive genius of the "big four" packers[w] and others laid the basis of the processing and shipping business. Specialized refrigeration[w] from the middle 1870's extended the fresh meat market to the East and to Europe. Raising, processing and marketing on such a vast scale have occasioned problems of vital social concern involving major applications of governmental control. The problem of the adjustment of output that has arisen since the World War has tried the efforts of both Government and the interests directly involved.

[R. A. Clemen, *The American Livestock and Meat Industry;* L. B. Schmidt and E. D. Ross, *Readings in the Economic History of American Agriculture.*]   EARLE D. ROSS

Llano Estacado. *See* Staked Plains.

Loan Offices, Colonial New York, were established in 1737 to remedy "a great want of Medium" and "to Revive the Commerce Trade and Navigation" of the colony. Paper bills of credit^{qv} were lent out by loan commissioners in each county on the security of real-estate mortgages. Thus did the province provide a land-bank organization. The State of New York continued the system as a device for investing its funds long after the function of note issue had disappeared.

[*Colonial Laws of New York*, II-V.]

EDWARD P. ALEXANDER

Lobbies consist of one or more persons who seek to influence legislators either to support or to oppose a proposed measure. Entreaties, promises, threats and, perhaps, even bribery are used to secure the results desired by a particular lobby. Since the 1880's lobbies have been especially active whenever tariff changes have been considered by Congress. The influence of the protective tariff lobby first attracted wide public notice in 1883 when it was able to block any effective tariff reform. There is hardly a subject of legislation that is not the concern of some lobby. So powerful have lobbies become, especially in the post-World War period, that they have been referred to by alarmed critics as a "government outside of government."

Maintained at Washington are scores of lobbies of various types. Lobbies are maintained by industrial groups, such as the National Association of Manufacturers; by farmers' groups, such as the American Farm Bureau Federation; by labor organizations, such as the American Federation of Labor; by professional groups, such as the American Bankers Association; by reform groups, such as the Anti-Saloon League; by patriotic associations, such as the American Legion; by peace organizations, such as the American Peace Society; by religious groups, such as the Federal Council of the Churches of Christ in America; and by women's groups, such as the League of Women Voters^{qqv}.

After the beginning of the New Deal^{qv}, the country witnessed the phenomenon of administrative agents lobbying even to the extent of participating in the closed sessions of congressional committees. Another new type of lobbying became observable by 1939 in the activity of the Workers' Alliance, composed of persons on relief^{qv}. A feature of lobbying which also became apparent in the 1930's was the attempt by pressure groups^{qv} to persuade people in all parts of the country to send letters and telegrams to members of Congress opposing or favoring certain proposals. For example, a Senate committee revealed that this was done in 1935 by public utilities in an attempt to defeat a bill designed to curb utility holding companies.

Since, in the final analysis, lobbying is a form of petition^{qv}, it probably cannot constitutionally be stamped out, but it can be regulated. This has been demonstrated by legislation in Wisconsin and a few other states. Wisconsin legislation, enacted chiefly in 1899 and 1905, required lobbyists as well as their employers to register. No effective action has been taken by Congress. In 1928 the Senate passed a bill to require lobbyists to register but nothing resulted. During the period of the F. D. Roosevelt administration, a special Senate committee was active in exposing the activities of lobbies, especially those opposed to the New Deal, but little if anything of practical value resulted. Lobbies were just as active as ever in 1939.

[Frederic A. Ogg and P. Orman Ray, *Introduction to American Government;* Rodney L. Mott, *Materials Illustrative of American Government.*]

ERIK McKINLEY ERIKSSON

Local Government. The number of units of local government in the United States is so great that no one knows exactly how many there are. The two most reliable tabulations are given in the following table:

Unit	Bureau of the Census[1]	Professor Wm. Anderson[2]
States (incl. D. C.)	49	49
Counties	3,062	3,053
Incorporated Places[3]	16,442	16,365
Townships	19,978	20,262
Other civil divisions[4]	14,572	8,580
School Districts	128,548	127,108
	182,651	175,417

[1] C. E. Rightor, Chief Statistician, Statistics of States and Cities, Bureau of the Census.
[2] William Anderson, *The Units of Government in the United States,* Public Administration Service, Chicago, 1934.
[3] Cities, Towns, Villages and Boroughs.
[4] Including drainage, road, park, sanitary, irrigation, reclamation, fire, lighting, cemetery, navigation, port, waterworks, etc.

The town and the county were the two original forms of local government. The climatic and physiographic conditions in New England, together with the dangers from the Indians and from wild animals, were all such as to encourage the establishment of small, compact settlements. The presence of water power, and the eventual development of industrial communities tended to preserve the established governmental traditions. In similar manner, the climatic and physiographic conditions in the South, and the virtual absence of danger from the Indians, made possible the more extended settlements out of which developed the Southern counties. The soil was fertile, and the types of crops for which it was adapted encouraged the maintenance of the plantation system^w, as did the absence of water power and other influences toward industrialization. Thus the town form was indigenous to New England, the county to the South, the strength of each form varying directly in proportion to the distance from the locale of its origin.[5]

In the Middle Atlantic States, where the two types come in contact with each other, hybrid forms developed. The North Central type, characterized by New York, had both the town and the county, with the town stronger and more important. The South Central type, characterized by Pennsylvania, had both the township and the county, with the county the stronger and the more important. As the settlers moved west, they took with them the forms of local government to which they had become accustomed in the East, making only such changes in these forms as were required to adapt them to the conditions of the frontier.[6]

Regardless of the form of local government established, there were certain important functions which it was expected to perform; among these were the maintenance of peace and order, the administration of justice, the settlement of estates, the conduct of poor relief, the maintenance of the schools, the protection of the public health, the construction and maintenance of roads, the administration of elections and the recording of land titles. The local units also served as units for military purposes. Vitally important to all of these was the assessment and collection of taxes.

The Town. The New England town was an excellent illustration of the functioning of pure democracy, perhaps the best available. The freemen^w of the community came together in the town meeting to select the town officers and to determine questions of public policy. As the settlements spread out and increased in size, as the

danger from the Indians and wild animals decreased, it became necessary to develop the representative principle, in partial substitution for that of pure democracy. The character of the General Court^w was changed by the dispersion of the towns, a portion of the membership consisting of deputies of those who, on account of numbers and dispersion, could not themselves attend the court. In time, the district system developed, with small districts and a consequently large total membership. The tradition of local self-government, however, was firmly established; included in the setup were such institutions of English origin as jury trial, the grand jury, the justice of the peace, etc. The town form of organization, characteristic of New England, appeared also in New York, became the township in Pennsylvania, and ceased to exist in Maryland and other states to the south.

The County. The county seat constituted the political and economic center of a number of adjacent plantations. Its location and the size of the county itself were determined by the distance that a man could travel between morning and nightfall, allowing some time at the county seat in which to transact his business. The prevailing form of organization called for a board of county commissioners, consisting usually of three members, who had the power to levy taxes and to provide for the usual governmental functions. There was no executive officer, but the county court was a very important institution. This form appeared in Pennsylvania, but in New York the board of commissioners became a board of supervisors, in which each town or city was represented by at least one member, often resulting in a body of considerable size. While counties were laid out in New England, they had no important functions of government to perform; in Rhode Island, for instance, they served only to establish the limits of the judicial districts.

The other county officers included that group of elected officers often referred to as the row offices: the sheriff; the prosecuting attorney, district attorney or state's attorney; the coroner; the county clerk; the court clerks; the treasurer, auditor or comptroller; the register of wills; the register of probate, the probate judge or the surrogate; the recorder of deeds; and such others as the jury commissioners, jail commissioners, prison wardens, prison inspectors, mercantile appraisers, election boards, superintendent of schools; director, overseer or superintendent of the poor; superintendent of the workhouse; surveyor or engineer; road or highway commissioner; board of assessors, and board of review. The more important of these offices were closely

[5] The states in the South and Far West, which followed the lead of the South in this matter, are: Alabama, Arizona, *California*, Colorado, Delaware, Florida, Georgia, Idaho, Kentucky, Louisiana, Maryland, Mississippi, *Montana, Nevada,* New Mexico, *North Carolina*, Oregon, *South Carolina*, Tennessee, Texas, Utah, Virginia, Washington, West Virginia and Wyoming. Townships exist in those states whose names appear in italics, but they are merely justice of the peace districts and do not possess the charactertistic township organization.

[6] The North Central group includes Illinois, Michigan, Nebraska, New Jersey, New York and Wisconsin, while the South Central group includes Arkansas, Indiana, Iowa, Kansas, Minnesota, Missouri, North Dakota, Ohio, Oklahoma, Pennsylvania and South Dakota.

patterned after the English models, particularly the sheriff and the coroner.

City Government. City government in the United States has passed through four different forms or stages—the weak mayor and council plan, the strong mayor and council plan, the commission type and the manager type. The first of these, once universally used, was a reproduction in miniature of the machinery of the Federal Government. There was a mayor, who had little real power. The council consisted of two chambers, a large common council and a smaller select council. While the judges in the courts were selected locally, the courts themselves were a part of the state judicial system. The Federal form of governmental organization is best adapted to meeting the needs of a large number of people in a broad expanse of territory; the effort to adapt it to the need of even a fairly large number of people in a small and compact area was a dismal failure. It was of cities so governed that Bryce was able to say, in all truthfulness, that municipal government was the one conspicuous failure in American politics. It was in cities so governed that the Tweed Ring$^{q\!v}$ developed in New York, the Gas Ring$^{q\!v}$ in Philadelphia and similar rings of one sort or another in cities throughout the land.

Out of these experiences grew a general dissatisfaction with the existing situation. This first found expression in the strong mayor and council plan, in which the powers of the mayor were considerably increased, he being authorized to appoint the heads of the various administrative departments in the city government. These department heads formed an advisory body frequently called the cabinet, the members of which were directly responsible to the mayor. It thus became possible for the mayor to be in fact as well as in theory the head of the administration. The old, cumbersome, bicameral council was abolished and a small, compact, unicameral council substituted for it. The judicial branch of the government was not affected by this reorganization. Where the mayor and council form of municipal organization is still in use it is of this type, since the old weak mayor and council form has practically passed out of existence.

While some cities were trying to remodel and improve the existing machinery for municipal government, others were experimenting with new devices. First of these was the commission form, which owed its origin to the occurrence of a great natural catastrophe—the tidal wave which swept over and largely destroyed the city of Galveston$^{q\!v}$, Tex., in the year 1900. As soon as the extent of the damage could be estimated,

the survivors determined to rebuild their city. For this purpose they selected a commission of five outstanding citizens, who performed their duties with such honesty and efficiency that there was no hint of fraud or graft or corruption; the people were so impressed by what had been accomplished that they decided to retain the commission to govern the new city, instead of returning to graft-ridden conditions that had existed in the city prior to the flood. The city of Des Moines copied the plan in a new city charter; from here, it spread rapidly to 200 or 300 communities in various parts of the country. The commission plan$^{q\!v}$ represented some measure of improvement over the old mayor and council form, but it developed certain conspicuous weaknesses of its own, which prevented its acquiring any permanent standing as a form of municipal organization.

Next to develop was the city manager$^{q\!v}$ form. More or less by accident, in 1908 the city of Staunton, Va., evolved the precedents upon which the city manager form is based. A railroad maintenance engineer was employed by the city to make some repairs in the water supply system, at a considerable saving to the city as compared with contractor's estimates. The idea was extended to other similar operations, with the result that the engineer, Charles E. Ashburner, was retained by the city as a sort of business manager. After a rather unhappy two years, this creator of a new profession resigned in disgust, and vowed never again to undertake such an assignment. He showed up again, however, as manager of the city of Norfolk, and in the meantime, the city of Dayton, Ohio, adopted the plan, attracting nation-wide attention to it. It has been adopted in cities and towns in all sections of the country, until today it is functioning in about 500 communities.

Home Rule. The question of home rule has long been a troublesome one in the field of local government. All of the units—counties, cities, boroughs, towns, townships, villages and special districts—were created by, and the nature and extent of their powers were defined by, the legislature. The legislature can today abolish most of the units, and modify or withdraw their powers as it sees fit, except in so far as the units themselves are protected by the provisions of home rule amendments, such as exist in about one third of the states. For many years, nearly every small detail in the government of any city had to be submitted to its state legislature; this was bad for the cities and bad for the legislature, until the powers of the latter to adopt special legislation were restricted by constitutional prohibitions, or by provision for the classification of cities according to population. The home rule idea was first applied in the case of municipalities, leaving them free to select their own form of governmental organization and either draft their own charter or select one to their liking, under an optional charter plan; its application is now being extended to the counties, in similar ways. The home rule idea always presents the conflict between the right of local self-government, on the one hand, and the right of the state to exercise reasonable regulatory and supervisory powers, on the other.

Metropolitan Areas. The metropolitan area*ᵟᵛ* constitutes the most recent and one of the most difficult problems in the field of local government, due to the interstate aspects of the problem, and to the large number of overlapping units and the duplication of responsibility.

[Patrick Abercrombie, *Town and County Planning;* Thomas Adams, *Outline of Town and City Planning;* William Anderson, *The Units of Local Government in the United States;* Roger J. Bounds, *A Bibliography of the Reorganization and Consolidation of Local Government;* W. Brooke Graves, *American State Government;* Herman G. James, *Local Government in the United States;* Lane W. Lancaster, *Government in Rural America;* K. H. Porter, *County and Township Government in the United States;* Murray Seasongood, *Local Government in the United States: a Challenge and an Opportunity;* Bruce Smith, *Rural Crime Control;* Raymond C. Atkinson, *Principles of a Model County Government;* Arthur W. Bromage, *American County Government;* John A. Fairlie and Charles M. Kneier, *County Government and Administration;* Henry S. Gilbertson, *The County, the Dark Continent of American Politics;* Frank W. Hoffer, *Counties in Transition;* Howard P. Jones, *Constitutional Barriers to Improvement in County Government;* Wylie Kilpatrick, *Problems in Contemporary County Government;* Theodore B. Manny, *Rural Municipalities, a Sociological Study of Local Government in the United States;* Chester C. Maxey, *County Administration;* Edward B. Schmidt, *County Consolidation.*

Municipal Government and Administration: William Anderson, *American City Government;* Tso-Shuen Chang, *History and Analysis of the Commission and City Manager Plans of Municipal Government;* Morris L. Cooke, *Our Cities Awake;* Ernest S. Griffith, *The Modern Development of City Government in the United Kingdom and the United States,* 2 vols.; Charles M. Kneier, *City Government in the United States;* Howard L. McBain, *Law and Practice of Municipal Home Rule;* Joseph D. McGoldrick, *Law and Practice of Municipal Home Rule, 1916-1930;* Chester C. Maxey, *Readings in Municipal Government,* and *Urban Democracy;* William B. Munro, *Municipal Government and Administration, The Government of American Cities,* and *Municipal Administration;* Thomas H. Reed, *Municipal Government in the United States;* Clarence E. Ridley, *The City Manager Profession;* Paul Studensky, *The Government of Metropolitan Areas;* Lent D. Upson, *Practice of Municipal Administration;* Schuyler C. Wallace, *State Administrative Supervision over Cities in the United States;* Leonard D. White, *The City Manager.*]

W. BROOKE GRAVES

Local Option, a development of the late 19th century, gave to the people the right to decide by petition or direct popular vote whether or not the liquor traffic should be licensed within their locality. First recognized by Massachusetts and incorporated in her state laws in the early 1880's, many communities throughout the country became dry through popular elections.

The formation of the Anti-Saloon League*ᵟᵛ* in 1893 gave a strong impetus to the movement. The League inaugurated a nation-wide campaign, molding public opinion, to abolish the liquor traffic through local option (*see* Temperance Movement). The cause rapidly gained momentum during the first decade of the 20th century, many states passing local option laws. A growing public conviction regarding the direct relation of liquor to health and corrupt politics, the demand of business for sobriety in the interest of efficiency and safety, the Church, and the Women's Christian Temperance Union*ᵟᵛ* supplemented the Anti-Saloon League and added strength to the movement.

At first the principle of local option was applied in rural and village communities; later it was used in the larger centers of population. The results of a local option election generally obtained from one to four years, at the end of which period another election might be held. The units in local option elections were counties, townships, municipalities, wards and precincts.

During the early years of the 20th century local option greatly increased the dry territory in the rural sections of the Middle West and the South. Moreover, several of the states adopted state-wide prohibition*ᵟᵛ*. By 1917-18 the number of such states had mounted to thirty-two. Much of the remaining territory, mostly rural, in wet states where state-wide prohibition was impossible, had been won to the dry cause through local option. By 1918, 90% of the land area of the United States was dry and two thirds of the people were living in dry territory.

[Ernest H. Cherrington, *The Evolution of Prohibition in the United States of America.*]

GLENN H. BENTON

Lochaber, Treaty of (Oct. 18, 1770), with the Cherokees*ᵟᵛ*, was negotiated by Col. John Donelson for Virginia. Its purpose was to exclude from the Indian lands many whites who had settled west of the line fixed by the Treaty of Hard Labor*ᵟᵛ*. The treaty effected these changes: the dividing line was moved westwardly to begin six miles east of Long Island of the Holston, running thence to the mouth of the Kanawha River. However, in the running of Donelson Line*ᵟᵛ* a wide departure from the treaty was made in fixing the northern terminus.

[S. C. Williams, *Dawn of Tennessee Valley and Tennessee History.*]   SAMUEL C. WILLIAMS

Lochner v. New York (198 U. S. 45, 1905). At about the same time that Utah attempted to regulate hours of labor for men in dangerous industries, New York sought to extend this type of regulation to workers in baking and confectionery establishments. While the Supreme Court upheld the Utah statute in Holden v. Hardy (169 U. S. 366, 1898), it declared the New York statute invalid seven years later. The law provided for a maximum sixty-hour week, with an average ten-hour day. Lochner, proprietor of a Utica bakery, was arrested, tried and convicted for violation of the law. On appeal to the Supreme Court, attorneys for the defendant argued that while such protections might be justified in dangerous industries, they were quite unnecessary in industries which, by their very nature, required extreme care in matters of cleanliness and sanitation. The Court accepted this reasoning, holding the act void as a violation of freedom of contract. It held that this right is a part of the liberty of the individual, protected by the Fourteenth Amendment^{qv}, along with the right to purchase or sell labor. The statute did not come under the legitimate police power^{qv} of the state as a proper regulation of the health, safety or morals of the people.

[C. K. Burdick, *The Law of the American Constitution;* J. R. Commons and J. B. Andrews, *Principles of Labor Legislation;* W. Brooke Graves, *American State Administration.*]   W. BROOKE GRAVES

Lochry's Defeat. When George Rogers Clark's proposed expedition of 1781 against Fort Detroit^{qv} mobilized at Wheeling^{qv}, Col. Archibald Lochry and some hundred Pennsylvania volunteers had not arrived. On Aug. 8 Clark started down the Ohio with his Virginia and regular troops, leaving word for Lochry to follow. Separated thus from Clark, Lochry and his men were attacked on Aug. 24 about twenty miles below the site of Cincinnati^{qv} by a band of Indians under Joseph Brant and Alexander McKee. A third of Lochry's men were killed, the rest captured; and of the captives several, including Lochry, were later killed. This defeat contributed to Clark's abandonment of his projected expedition.

[J. A. James, *Life of George Rogers Clark;* C. H. Sipe, *Indian Wars of Pennsylvania.*]   SOLON J. BUCK

Locke's Influence on American Political Thought. John Locke (1632–1704) was one of the leading English philosophers of the 17th century who carried political theory to an advanced state of democratic development. His most characteristic contribution was in his doctrine of natural rights^{qv}. He maintained that life, liberty and property were the inalienable rights of every individual. He believed that the happiness and security of the individual were the ends for which government came into existence.

Locke believed in the social contract not only as a means of securing the grant of political authority but also as a means of securing political and social liberty. The contract not only originates and delegates the powers which a government is to possess but also it indicates the extent of liberty which the individual should retain. Locke justified the right of revolution not upon the ground of hostile acts of the people but upon usurpations of authority upon the part of those to whom such authority has been delegated. In other words, the possession of authority by governmental officials was strictly upon a fiduciary basis. However, the popular right of revolution should not be exercised for trivial reasons but only with the consent of the majority of the people. A controlling public opinion has the right to pass upon the acts of government.

At the time of the American Revolution John Locke was perhaps the most influential political authority and his theories were regarded with the greatest respect by the leaders in the American cause. "Almost every writer seems to have been influenced by him, many quoted his words, and the argument of others shows the unmistakable imprint of his philosophy . . . no better epitome of the Revolutionary theory could be found than in John Locke on civil government" (C. E. Merriam). Locke's influence still remains supreme today in the political thought of large numbers of the American people.

[W. S. Carpenter, *The Development of American Political Thought;* C. E. Merriam, *American Political Theories;* W. A. Dunning, *Political Theories from Luther to Montesquieu.*]   WILLIAM STARR MYERS

Lockout, THE, is a temporary withholding of work by an employer or group of employers in order to effect acceptance by employees of certain terms of employment. While government data indicate lockouts to be much more frequent than strikes, the distinction between the two is often without substantive meaning except as an indication of which party initiated a stoppage of work. At common law in the United States the right of employers to lock out their employees has been almost unrestricted, and has stood in sharp contradistinction to the right of workers to strike^{qv}. The effect of the National Labor Relations Act[w] of 1935 and similar legislation in a number of the states has, however, been to prevent lockouts when their intent was avoidance of the requirements of this legislation.

[U. S. Bureau of Labor Statistics, Bulletin No. 651, *Strikes in the United States, 1880-1936;* J. R. Commons and J. B. Andrews, *Principles of Labor Legislation;* C. E. Bonnett, *Employers' Associations in the United States;* R. F. Hoxie, *Trade Unionism in the United States.*]

ROYAL E. MONTGOMERY

Locks and Waterways. In the latter 18th century, dams and locks began to be employed to make rough rivers, such as the Mohawk, navigable for arks and flatboats[qw]. Usually short canals with locks in them were built around falls or rapids; as for example, one around the rapids of the James at Richmond, built 1785-89, five along the Potomac, built 1785-1808, several on the Connecticut and Merrimac rivers in New England and one at the Conewago Falls in the Susquehanna, all constructed between 1790 and 1800. The height of locks was then very modest. The Bellows Falls Canal on the Connecticut required nine locks in less than a mile to overcome a fall of fifty feet—or less than six feet of lift to each lock. The Blackstone Canal, built 1824-28, had forty-eight locks of cut granite in its 45-mile length. The Chemung Canal, completed in 1833, connecting Seneca Lake with the headwaters of the Susquehanna River, though only twenty-three miles long had forty-nine locks!

For the sake of cheapness, the lock walls of some early canals, such as the Chemung and Chenango in New York and the Middlesex[w] between Boston and Lowell (built 1794-1803), were of wood, and in some cases began to bulge and warp almost as soon as completed. Until cement[w] rock was discovered in central New York in 1818, most stone lock walls had to be built with ordinary lime mortar, as cement imported from Europe was too costly. With the aid of cement, locks became higher, and in 1830 one with a lift of seventeen feet was built on the Delaware Division of the Pennsylvania Canal system[w].

Larger rivers were "canalized"—i.e., improved with dams and locks—early in the 19th century. When the canal fervor swept Pennsylvania (1826 and after), not only was the Monongahela thus improved for a hundred miles, but even small streams, such as Bald Eagle Creek and Conestoga Creek from Lancaster to the Susquehanna. In Ohio nearly a hundred miles of the Muskingum was canalized (1836-40) and here for the first time in America the locks—36 feet wide and 180 feet long—were made large enough for steamboats. Before the end of the 19th century, navigation dams and locks were placed upon the upper Ohio, and later, upon the Mississippi. With the development of steamboat traffic, and the declaring of small rivers and small creeks to be navigable streams, their improvement by locks became a favorite congressional method of distributing "pork."

[Alvin F. Harlow, *Old Towpaths.*]

ALVIN F. HARLOW

Loco Foco Party, a radical faction of the Democratic party in New York allied with Jacksonian Democracy[w]. At a meeting in Tammany Hall[w], Oct. 29, 1835, it wrested control of the city caucus from the conservatives by producing candles, lighting them with loco foco matches and continuing the meeting, when their opponents turned off the gas. Newspapers derisively called this faction the "Loco Foco Party." Its program embraced suppression of paper money, curtailment of banking privileges and protection of labor unions[w]. From 1837 to 1860, the term was applied to the National Democratic party by its opponents.

[William Trimble, Diverging Tendencies in New York Democracy in the Period of the Locofocos, in *American Historical Review,* Vol. XXIV.]

W. B. HATCHER

Locomotives. In 1825, Col. John Stevens of Hoboken, N. J., constructed an experimental locomotive, operating it on a circular track. The "Tom Thumb," built in 1829 by Peter Cooper, made its first run, Aug. 25, 1830, on the Baltimore and Ohio Railroad[w] between Baltimore and Ellicott's Mills, Md. "The Best Friend of Charleston," the first locomotive built in the United States for actual service on a railroad, was constructed in 1830 for the South Carolina Canal and Railroad Company, at the West Point Foundry in New York City, which also built the "De Witt Clinton" for the Mohawk and Hudson (1831).

Matthias Baldwin's "Old Ironsides," the beginning of construction by the Baldwin Locomotive Works, went into service in 1832. The American Steam Carriage Company of Philadelphia announced in 1833 its readiness to build locomotive engines and tenders. In 1838 a report on "Steam Engines" submitted by Secretary of the Treasury Levi Woodbury contained the names of twenty-seven American builders of locomotives. In following years, other locomotive works were organized and some of the railroads began construction, the Altoona Works of the Pennsylvania Railroad[w] building its first locomotive for passenger service in 1866. With its tender, this locomotive weighed 137,700 pounds—about equal to the weight of two pairs of drive wheels of today's standard passenger locomotives. How far the making of locomotives in America has extended may be judged by a comparison of the engines of the early period with the steam, electric and Diesel locomotives of the present day.

[*Proceedings of American Railway Master Mechanics Association*, 8th Annual Meeting, May, 1876, pp. 84-91; S. C. Derrick, *Centennial History of S. C. Railroad Company*; W. H. Brown, *History of the First Locomotives in America*; *American Railroad Journal*, Dec. 14, 1833, p. 800, Dec. 17, 1836, p. 785, Dec. 24, 1835, p. 801; Railway and Locomotive Historical Society, *Bulletin*, No. 6, pp. 22-31; H. W. Schotter, *The Growth and Development of the Pennsylvania Railroad.*]   JULIUS H. PARMELEE

Lode Mining. Gold, silver and other metals are generally found in narrow streaks from a few inches to many feet in width and frequently traceable for a mile or more in length. This is a lode or vein or ledge. A lode has been legally defined as mineral-bearing rock in place. Extracting this mineral-bearing rock from the earth is lode mining. It is hard rock mining and almost entirely underground, as distinguished from placer mining in which the metals are found in alluvial deposits near the surface. The ore is mined either by shafts sunk vertically downward or by tunnels driven horizontally into the mountainside.

The discoverer of a new lode, according to the laws of the early mining districts, could stake out two claims, but no more, along the lode. Others could stake one claim. Local laws and regulations determined the size of the claim—usually 100 or 200 feet—which was recognized by the first United States mineral patent law^{qv} (1866). May 10, 1872, Congress fixed the size of lode claims at 600 feet wide and 1500 feet along the lode. Consequently, there can be many rich mines on the same lode. Famous lodes are the Mother Lode in California and the Comstock Lode^{qv} in Nevada.

[W. R. Crane, *Ore Mining Methods*; R. S. Morrison, *Mining Rights.*]   PERCY S. FRITZ

Lodge Reservations, THE. In the duel between Woodrow Wilson and his opponents over incorporation of the League of Nations Covenant within the Treaty of Versailles^{qv}, the Lodge Reservations played an important part. Designed to safeguard national sovereignty, they were unacceptable to Wilson. Nevertheless, had Lodge secured his Reservations, Wilson might have had his League.

Including the preamble, there were fifteen resolutions, notably the following: (2) In the event of her withdrawal from the League, the United States must be sole judge of whether its obligations had been met; (3) No obligation existed to uphold the celebrated Article X^{qv}, insuring permanence to existing territorial boundaries; (5) The United States reserved the sole determination of what questions fell within domestic jurisdiction; (6) The Monroe Doctrine^{qv} was specifically exempted from foreign interference; (7) Full liberty of action was reserved concerning certain contingencies that might arise between China and Japan; (8) No American might represent his country in organizations created by the League, save in accordance with an Act of Congress; (10) All contributions toward League expenditures must first be authorized by Congress; (11) Any agreements covering a limitation of armaments must be subject to reversal by the United States if "threatened with invasion or engaged in war"; (12) Nationals of a Covenant-breaking nation residing in the United States might continue their usual relations with our citizens; (14) The United States must assume no responsibility toward "the government or disposition of the overseas possessions of Germany." Finally (15) The United States must be the exclusive judge of what questions affected "its honor or its vital interests."

These Reservations, first ordered printed on Nov. 6, 1919, were modified somewhat as the controversy gained momentum. In the calm of retrospection they seem mild enough and probably quite unavoidable. To Wilson at the time they seemed a base betrayal of idealism. He fought them to his own paralysis and death. The Reservations ultimately gave way to entire negation of the League and to a policy of isolation.

[*Proposed Reservations to the Treaty of Peace with Germany*, 66th Congress, 1st Session, *Senate Document* No. 150; *Reservations to the Treaty of Peace with Germany, Statements made to the Press regarding the Bipartisan Conference on Reservations to the Treaty of Peace with Germany*, by Sen. Henry Cabot Lodge and Sen. Gilbert M. Hitchcock, presented by Mr. Lodge, Jan. 31, 1920, 66th Congress, 2nd Session, *Senate Document* No. 193.]   LOUIS MARTIN SEARS

Loewe v. Lawlor (1908). In this case, commonly known as the Danbury Hatters' Case, the Sherman Antitrust Act^{qv} was held to have been violated by a combination of members of a labor organization in the nature of a boycott to prevent the manufacture and sale of hats intended for interstate commerce. The Court emphasized that where the general purpose and effect of the organization was to restrain trade the separate acts, though in themselves acts within a state, were illegal as tested by Federal law.

[W. W. Willoughby, *The Constitutional Law of the United States.*]   J. HARLEY NICHOLS

Loftus Heights, the high eastern bank of the Mississippi, first called *Roche à Davion* for a French missionary (1699), is just north of the 31st parallel. It took its present name from an incident of the expedition led by the British Maj. Arthur Loftus in 1764 from Mobile to take possession of the Illinois country in accordance with the Treaty of Paris of 1763*ᵂ*. At *Roche à Davion* the Loftus party, consisting of 300 men, was fired upon by Tunica Indians. Several men were killed and Loftus retreated precipitately down the Mississippi. Dominating the Spanish-American boundary on the Mississippi (*see* Southern Boundary, Survey of the) it became the site of Fort Adams*ᵂ*, 1798–99.

[J. F. H. Claiborne, *Mississippi;* Charles Gayarré, *History of Louisiana;* Justin Winsor, *The Mississippi Basin.*]

MACK SWEARINGEN

Log Cabin, THE. Log buildings were in use in northern Europe before the discovery of America. It has been asserted that log construction was introduced by the Swedes who settled on the lower Delaware in 1638; but a log blockhouse, the "McIntyre Garrison" at York, Maine, far distant from the Delaware, built about 1640–45, is cited by others as evidence that the New England colonists, somewhere between 1620 and 1640, had learned log construction for themselves—though some one among them might have seen one of the Norse or German log buildings in Europe. Anyhow, such construction increased rapidly in the 17th century, and the one- or two-room log cabin became the typical American pioneer home, being also supplemented by log outbuildings. For the dwelling the sides of the logs facing each other were adzed flat, and the chinks between were luted with flat stones or chips of wood embedded in clay. In stables the crevices were usually left unfilled. Furthermore, as the frontier was pushed westward across the continent, small log buildings became the first churches and schools, the first mills, stores and hotels, the first seats of town and county government and of the courts. In the South, tall tobacco barns were built of long logs with wide, unfilled chinks between, so that the wind might blow through and dry the leaf tobacco racked inside. Many a solitary pioneer had to build his little log hut singlehanded or with the aid of his wife and family; but where there was a settlement, a house-raising became a pioneer social function, the neighbors gathering and practically completing the cabin in one day. More prosperous farmers or villagers might erect two-story log houses of several rooms, which in New England would be shingled on the outside or, farther west, per-

haps weatherboarded, though in Pennsylvania they were occasionally stuccoed.

[Henry C. Mercer, Origin of Log Houses in the United States, *Bucks County Historical Society Papers,* Vol. V; William J. Petersen, The Pioneer Cabin, *Iowa Journal of History and Politics,* October, 1938.]

ALVIN F. HARLOW

"Log Cabin and Hard Cider Campaign." *See* Campaign of 1840, The.

Log College, THE (1726–42), at Neshaminy, Pa., was a log schoolhouse, about twenty feet square, erected and conducted by William Tennent, an Irish Presbyterian minister. It served to emphasize the need for an institution for the instruction of Presbyterian ministerial candidates. The Presbyterian Synod recognized this need and in 1746 the charter for the organization of Princeton University was issued.

[James Mulhern, *A History of Secondary Education in Pennsylvania.*]

H. H. SHENK

Logan's Fort (St. Asaph) was located near Stanford, Ky. Its founder was Benjamin Logan who arrived in Kentucky in 1775. On May 20, 1777, the fort was assaulted by Indians. Logan spurred his companions in the defense, and by sheer courage and surprising athletic prowess, became the mainstay in his fort's defense. Stories of these exploits have given this station an important place in Kentucky's history.

[Richard Collins, *History of Kentucky.*]

T. D. CLARK

Logan's Speech, popularly regarded as the most famous example of Indian oratory, was made by the Mingo*ᵂ* warrior, Capt. James Logan, sometimes called John Logan (Indian "Tahgahjute"), to John Gibson who had been sent from Camp Charlotte*ᵂ* (in present Pickaway County, Ohio) by Gov. Dunmore of Virginia to persuade Logan, then at his cabin a few miles distant, to attend the peace negotiations at the close of Dunmore's War*ᵂ* (1774). The Indian refused to come and recited his grievances in a speech so strangely moving that Gibson translated and recorded it from memory after returning to Dunmore's camp. Thomas Jefferson later inserted it in his *Notes on The State of Virginia,* but the family and friends of Capt. Michael Cresap, whom Logan mistakenly charged with the murder of his relatives, took offense at the speech and denied its authenticity. A long controversy ensued. Most historians since have reached the cautious conclusion that Gibson probably caught at least the spirit of Logan's impassioned remarks, if not the exact words.

[E. O. Randall amd D. J. Ryan, *History of Ohio;* Theodore Roosevelt, *The Winning of the West.*]

EUGENE H. ROSEBOOM

Logrolling is a practice among members of Congress of trading votes for each other's pet bills. The term is derived from pioneer days when the frontiersmen were accustomed to help one another in cutting down trees and rolling up the logs for building or burning. Usually one logrolls with his friends. They work together to secure appropriations, each seeking to benefit his own district. The pressure of local interests for these Federal appropriations convinces the congressman of the necessity of seeking favors for his constituency in an effort to insure his reelection. While the practice normally obtains with reference to legislation applicable to local interests, it may be applied in national affairs when parties trade votes on certain bills on purely party grounds.

The practice of logrolling often results in wastefulness and ill-advised legislation. Many such laws would not pass on their own merits. Logrolling has obtained since the early days of the Republic. To secure the passage of his bill for the assumption of state debts[qv], Hamilton in 1790 logrolled with Jefferson, pledging northern votes to locate the National Capital[qv] on the Potomac in return for southern votes to carry assumption.

[Charles A. Beard and Mary R. Beard, *The Rise of American Civilization.*]

GLENN H. BENTON

Logstown, an Indian village eighteen miles below the forks of the Ohio[qv] near the present Ambridge, Pa., was probably established by Shawnee some time after 1728, but it later became a mixed village of Shawnee, Delaware and Iroquois[qqv]. In the critical period from 1747 to 1753 it was the most important Indian village on the upper Ohio, the center of trade and the scene of Indian councils. It was visited by Conrad Weiser in 1748; by Céloron's expedition[qv] in 1749; by Christopher Gist[qv] in 1750; by Washington on his journey to Fort LeBœuf[qv] in 1753; and by Christian F. Post in 1758. When the French and Indian War[qv] began, most of the Logstown Indians removed to Aughwick[qv], and parties of them fought for the English in the battle of Fort Necessity[qv] and joined Braddock's expedition[qv].

[J. H. Bausman, *History of Beaver County, Pa.;* S. J. and E. H. Buck, *The Planting of Civilization in Western Pennsylvania.*]

SOLON J. BUCK

Logstown, Treaty of (June 13, 1752), opening to settlement lands west of the Allegheny Mountains, was negotiated with Iroquois, Delaware, Shawnee, Wyandot and Miami Indians[qqv] resident in what are now western Pennsylvania, Ohio and Indiana. In 1751 negotiations with the same Indians had been conducted at Logstown[qv] by George Croghan of Pennsylvania and presents had been distributed, but the Pennsylvania Assembly had refused funds for erecting forts to hold the region against the French. In 1752 commissioners from Virginia distributed a royal present to the Indians and, with the help of Croghan and of Christopher Gist representing the Ohio Company[qv], secured permission for the Virginians to make settlements south of the Ohio and to build two fortified trading houses on the river. One of these was erected on the Monongahela at Redstone Old Fort[qv], and the other, in process of erection at the site of Pittsburgh, was surrendered to the French at the outbreak of hostilities in 1753 (*see* Duquesne, Fort).

[S. J. and E. H. Buck, *The Planting of Civilization in Western Pennsylvania.*]

SOLON J. BUCK

Logwood Trade. Logwood, alias "blockwood," sometimes known as Campeachy-wood or improperly as Brasiletto or Jamaica-wood, comes from the leguminous tree, *Hæmatoxylen campecheanum,* found in Central America and the West Indies, and derives its name from the dark brownish red blocks in which shipped. Its chief use (prohibited in England from 1581 to 1662) was in dyeing blacks and blues.

English activity in the trade, commenced by the buccaneers and soon supplemented by colonial traders, centered in Spanish territory, first at Cape Catoche, then at Campeachy Bay and finally around Belize (now British Honduras) and along the Mosquito Coast. Spain made protests, occasional raids and frequent seizures, but in 1763 conceded limited wood-cutting rights to the British. Before 1670 England received practically all her logwood from Spain, and one ninth in 1698; but in 1773 she obtained 862 tons direct from Spanish America, 771 tons from Jamaica, 548 tons from her other colonies and only 16 tons from Spain—less than she exported there.

Most of the colonists' logwood came from Yucatan and Honduras but some came from surprisingly varied sources—to New York, for example, from Curaçao, Martinique, the Virgin Islands[qv], Hispaniola, Havana, Vera Cruz, St. Augustine and eight British colonies. Logwood grown in an English colony was regulated by the Navigation Acts[qv], but foreign logwood could be exported freely, and approximately one fifth of the 3480 tons exported in 1770 from the continental colonies went directly to Europe, which also was the ultimate destination of most of England's imports.

[G. L. Beer, *Old Colonial System;* M. Postlethwayt, *Dictionary.*]   LAWRENCE A. HARPER

London, Declaration of (Feb. 26, 1909), was a code of laws relating to maritime warfare drafted by the London Naval Conference. Ten naval powers, representing different viewpoints, thereby achieved a compromise agreement in the hope of enabling the international prize court, proposed at the Second Hague Conference*qv*, to function.

Conspicuous in the Declaration was the treatment of contraband and continuous voyage, questions entailing peculiar difficulties between belligerents and neutrals*qv*. Agreement was reached on definite lists of absolute and conditional contraband, and on a third classification of goods which could not be declared contraband. Barring this third classification, a belligerent might add to the absolute and conditional lists. Noteworthy in the free list were raw cotton and metallic ores. Continuous voyage was restricted in application to absolute contraband, thus voiding in large part the precedents of the American Civil War. To illustrate: arms (absolute contraband) were seizable anywhere on the high seas, if destined for the enemy; foodstuffs (conditional contraband), cotton and copper (on the free list) only for violation of blockade*qv*. Since a blockading force could not bar access to a neutral port, neutral commerce would be free from interruption except in cases of absolute contraband.

The Declaration illustrates the strength and weakness of international legislation. It went unratified, but the United States, with the experience of the Napoleonic wars in mind, tried to make it an important instrument of policy. To persuade Britain to follow the Declaration during the World War, Secretary of State Lansing secretly promoted a scheme to extend continuous voyage to conditional contraband. Britain might, by proclamation, attaint the ports of neutral countries adjoining Germany with enemy character with respect to trade in contraband. This would permit her to seize foodstuffs and supplies en route to Germany, but would free American cotton, copper, etc., from molestation. Britain rejected the plan, and the United States fell back on the traditional principles of international law*qv*.

[Carlton Savage, *Policy of the United States toward Maritime Commerce in War;* R. W. Van Alstyne, The Declaration of London Policy of the United States at the Outbreak of the Great War, *Journal of Modern History,* VII.]   RICHARD W. VAN ALSTYNE

London, Treaty of (Aug. 18/28, 1604), brought to an end the formal warfare which had been waged since 1585 between England and Spain, endangering all English colonizing projects in the New World. The treaty temporarily eradicated this danger and, among other things, reopened "free Commerce" between the two kingdoms "where commerce existed before the war." Spain intended this clause to exclude English merchants from her colonies overseas, but the English gave it the opposite interpretation, causing continued warfare "beyond the Line" (*see* "No Peace Beyond the Line") and the rise of the buccaneers.

[Frances G. Davenport, *European Treaties Bearing on the History of the United States and Its Dependencies to 1648; The Cambridge History of the British Empire,* I.]   RAYMOND P. STEARNS

London Company, THE. *See* Virginia Company of London.

London Naval Treaty of 1930, THE. Through the efforts of Ramsay MacDonald, British prime minister, a naval conference met at London in 1930 attended by representatives of the United States, Great Britain, Japan, France and Italy. The object was an agreement to limit the size and number of warships left unlimited by the Washington Treaty of 1922*qv*. The clash between the United States and Great Britain over parity and large cruisers which had disrupted the Geneva Conference was settled by a compromise arranged by Premier MacDonald with President Hoover prior to the conference. The success of the conference was endangered, however, by the French demand for a tonnage beyond Italian needs and for a security pact with Great Britain, and by the Japanese claim for a 10:10:7 ratio in place of the 5:5:3 ratio of the Washington Conference. The British were unwilling to give a guarantee to the French without American support, and the United States utterly rejected the idea. The final treaty thus was confined to a three-power pact with provisions to include France and Italy if agreeable in the future. The 5:5:3 ratio was applied to large cruisers, but Japan won a 10:10:7 ratio in small cruisers and destroyers, and equality in submarines, each nation being permitted to maintain a tonnage of 52,700 in the latter category. Not including capital ships and aircraft carriers the total tonnage limitation under the treaty was 541,700 tons for Great Britain, 526,200 tons for the United

States and 367,050 for Japan. In order to meet the situation caused by the fact that neither France nor Italy signed the treaty, the so-called "escalator clause" provided that if the national security of any signatory power was endangered by the new construction of ships by a non-signatory power, the signatory power might increase its tonnage. Ratification of the treaty in Japan was obtained only after a struggle with the militarists. In 1931, after the invasion of Manchuria, the Japanese government took an expanded view of the naval requirements of Nippon. Japanese demands for parity were rejected by the United States and Great Britain in parleys in London in 1934. Accordingly, under the provisions of the treaty, on Dec. 29, 1934, the Japanese government gave notice of its denunciation of the Washington Naval Treaty of 1922, to take effect on Dec. 31, 1936.

[*Proceedings of the London Naval Conference of 1930, Department of State: Press Releases.*]

KENNETH COLEGROVE

London Naval Treaty of 1936. The Japanese government having, on Dec. 29, 1934, denounced the Washington Naval Treaty of 1922[w], a conference of the principal naval powers was held in London from Dec. 9, 1935, to March 25, 1936. Great Britain and the United States refused to recognize the Japanese claim to parity or to accept a "common upper limit" for naval construction. Japan thereupon withdrew from the conference. By the treaty of March 25, 1936, Great Britain, France and the United States agreed to maximum limits of the various types of warships which they would not exceed (35,000 tons and 14-inch guns for battleships) and to exchange information concerning their building programs. But it was provided that the limits agreed upon might be set aside in the event of war or if these limits were exceeded by a power not a party to the treaty. Italy, indignant at the application of sanctions in the Ethiopian war, refused to sign the treaty, which was, however, left open for her adherence and that of Japan. The treaty, unlike those of 1922 and 1930 (*see* Naval Limitation Conferences), contained no provisions for quantitative limitation. In 1938 the contracting parties, unable to obtain information from the Japanese government about its building program, agreed to set aside the limit of 35,000 tons for capital ships.

[*Survey of International Affairs*, 1936.]

BERNADOTTE E. SCHMITT

Lone Jack, Action at (Aug. 16, 1862), was fought in southeastern Jackson County, Mo., between a body of Union state militia under Maj.

Emory S. Foster and a Confederate force under Gen. Upton Hays, Col. John F. Coffee and Col. Vard Cockrell. The Confederates attacked early in the morning and a six-hour fight ensued. The Union artillery was captured, recaptured and finally captured and held by the Confederates. About 800 men were in each force, and each side sustained losses of 125 killed and wounded. The intense feeling between the two sides in this part of Missouri accounts for the vindictive nature of the struggle.

[*Encyclopedia of the History of Missouri; The Missouri Historical Review*, Vol. XXII, No. 3.]

W. FRANCIS ENGLISH

Loneliness, of various types, has been an important factor in molding American character and social and political institutions. On the frontier "the stores of pent-up loneliness" found vent, on the rare occasions when people met together, in emotional outbursts. The wild frenzy of religious camp meetings[w], lasting sometimes a week or so, can be traced to the effect of the lonely weeks or months intervening between them. House-raisings and all social occasions were boisterous, and political meetings became festivities at which the style of oratory had to fit the need of emotional outlet (*see* Frontier Oratory). The "goings-on" at a national political convention today, forming perhaps the worst possible background for sober thought and choice, stem straight from the loneliness of earlier America.

The characteristic trait of joining innumerable organizations is probably also a reaction from the earlier solitude. Various traits, such as self-confidence and versatility, may be traced in part to the same cause. The desire that loneliness should be relieved by the clearing growing into a community is also one of the elements making for the American concept of "bigger and better" which originally had a real basis, long lost. We can also trace to the time when every stranger was a godsend in lonely lives, that trait of hospitality for which Americans are famous, as well as talkativeness. The ready talk with strangers in the Pullman "Smoker" is a reaction from the lonely log cabin.

Another effect, now happily passing with the radio, telephone, automobile and other means of keeping in touch with others, was for long the appallingly high rate of insanity of farmers' wives, whether on the frontier or on isolated farms in older sections.

Among our best traits, which have had deep effect on our life and institutions, are generosity and mutual helpfulness, which spring largely from the isolation of early times and later frontiers, and perhaps also from the recollections on the part of millions of another form of loneliness, that of the immigrant arriving alone in a strange land without friends or often even knowledge of the language.

Particularly in the past century there was a loneliness of yet another sort, that of the artist who in the roaring world of business and development found himself without congenial or understanding society. It was this in large part which sent the stream of expatriates[w] to Europe —Story, Abbey, Whistler, Sargent and a host of lesser men.

[There is no study of the topic. F. L. Paxson, *History of the American Frontier*, has a suggestive paragraph on it, p. 115.]

            JAMES TRUSLOW ADAMS

Long Drive, THE (1866–90) . At the close of the Civil War cattle were plentiful and cheap in Texas. High prices in the North led cattlemen to seek a market. The building of the Pacific railroads opened the way. Beginning in 1866 cowboys drove herds of cattle, numbering on an average 2500 head, overland to rail points on the Northern Plains. Gradually homestead settlement pushed the trails westward, extinguishing them at the base of the Rocky Mountains about 1890. The average time consumed in driving a herd these hundreds of miles was from six weeks to two months (*see* Cattle Drives) .

[Edward E. Dale, *The Range Cattle Industry.*]

            EVERETT DICK

Long Expedition, THE, was a movement of protest against the Adams-Onís Treaty[w] with Spain in 1819 by which the United States relinquished claims to Texas. A meeting of the citizens of Natchez[w], Miss., was held that year and the expedition planned. Gen. Adair of Kentucky was proffered the leadership but declined it. Dr. James Long of Virginia, a favorite of Andrew Jackson, was then chosen as leader.

He left Natchez for Texas in June, 1819, with about seventy-five men; the number had increased to more than 300 soon after his arrival at Nacogdoches[w]. At this place he promptly declared Texas free and independent and set up a provisional government, a republic. Long was elected president of it. He made immediate military arrangements for conquering and holding the entire province. However, failing to receive expected aid from the pirate, Jean Lafitte, and facing an overwhelming Spanish force, his entire scheme speedily collapsed.

In 1821 he returned to Texas from New Orleans with reinforcements and captured La Bahia, south of San Antonio. After holding this place for a few days he learned of Mexican independ-

ence from Spain and accepted an invitation from the new government to visit Mexico City, where he was killed, either by accident or design, in 1822.

[H. S. Foote, *Texas and Texans;* H. H. Bancroft, *History of North Mexican States and Texas.*]

            J. G. SMITH

Long Houses of the Iroquois were structures of heavy poles covered with large sheets of bark, and varied from 50 to 160 feet or more in length. The roof was either angular or arched but usually the latter. Long houses sheltered several families and had individual compartments for each.

[Lewis H. Morgan, *Houses and House Life of the American Aborigines.*]

            ARTHUR C. PARKER

Long Hunters (1760–70) was the term applied to residents of settled communities who in groups spent months, sometimes eighteen, in hunting game in the western wilds. Daniel Boone was one of the earliest and the most noted. Another and more typical was Elisha Walling or Walden. Customarily each hunter took along two horses (one a pack horse) , a trap and a large supply of powder and lead, and each group carried a hand vise, bellows, files and screw-plates to repair rifles. Long hunting required courage, initiative and endurance, but the returns yielded a handsome profit, and enabled those engaged to select choice lands later on; most of the hunters later settled in the West. Successive parties went farther and farther into the West; and their reports to their neighbors gave a decided impetus to migration to the countries described by the explorers. The Kentucky and Cumberland river valleys were favored hunting grounds. Comparatively few of the hunter-explorers lost their lives.

[S. C. Williams, *Dawn of Tennessee Valley and Tennessee History.*]

            SAMUEL C. WILLIAMS

Long Island, a part of New York State, 118 miles long, and 1682 square miles in area, lies parallel to the southern shore of Connecticut. As early as 1620 it was included in the grant given by James I to the Virginia Company of Plymouth. In 1635 the territory held by the Plymouth Company's successor, the Council for New England[w], was divided into eight parts, and Long Island was assigned to William Alexander, Earl of Stirling.

In 1636, when Wouter Van Twiller was director general of New Netherland[w], Jacobus Van Curler (or Corlaer) was given the first Dutch patent for land on Long Island. During the Dutch period farms spread along the Long Island shore opposite Manhattan, and several settlements, both Dutch and English, sprang up in the interior, Hempstead, Flushing, Gravesend, Newtown and Jamaica being English; and Breuckelen (Brooklyn), Midwout (Flatbush), Amersfoort (Flatlands), New Utrecht and Boswyck (Bushwick) being Dutch.

While the western end of the island was thus being settled as a part of New Netherland, Puritan towns which reproduced the characteristic features and religious polity of New England were planted along the northern and southern shores of its eastern end. In 1640 English settlers from New Haven^w laid out Southold, and others from Lynn in Massachusetts Bay settled Southampton. Similar New England communities were established elsewhere, such as that at Oyster Bay in 1653 and those at Huntington and Setauket in 1660. An attempt was made to settle conflicting Dutch and English claims by means of a treaty signed at Hartford in 1650^w, which fixed a boundary by drawing a line southward across the island from the point where Oyster Bay was afterward located. The eastern towns in time fell under Connecticut jurisdiction, and thus eastern Long Island was politically a part of New England when the English conquered New Netherland (1664). Charles II at that time granted all of Long Island to his brother, James, Duke of York^w, who cleared his title by promises of payments to Stirling and to Lord Berkeley who had bought a half interest. Reconquest brought the Dutch back to the western district in 1673, but the Treaty of Westminster^w (1674) finally established Long Island's status as part of the English colony of New York^w.

Long Island has become one of the most prosperous and populous areas of its size in the United States. Its primary industries were agriculture, fishing and shipbuilding, but during the past century there has been a varied and constantly increasing industrial development. Its two western counties comprise two of the five boroughs of the city of New York, the boroughs of Brooklyn and Queens.

[Benjamin F. Thompson, *A History of Long Island;* Ralph Henry Gabriel, *The Evolution of Long Island;* Charles M. Andrews, *Colonial Period of American History,* Vol. III, p. 58 n.; Jacqueline Overton, *Long Island's Story.*]
        RALPH FOSTER WELD

Long Island, Battle of (Aug. 27, 1776). Howe brought all but one of his brigades across from Staten Island, landing them on Gravesend Bay beach. Washington's outpost line was along Brooklyn Heights, a series of low hills crossed by four roads, through Jamaica, Bedford and Flatbush passes, and along the shore from the Narrows. He strengthened his force by placing nearly a third of the entire American army on Long Island—under command of Putnam.

The night of Aug. 26–27, Howe attacked, captured Miles' rifle regiment and most of Stirling's command. Following this victorious outpost action, the British struck Washington's main position. Had this attack been pushed, all American forces on Long Island could have been captured. Instead, Howe switched to siege tactics. Realizing his danger, Washington determined to withdraw his forces to Manhattan, while giving the impression he was reinforcing. Withdrawal, begun the night of Aug. 29–30, was successfully completed, without interference from the British, by 7:00 A.M., on the 30th.

[Oliver L. Spaulding, *The United States Army in War and Peace;* Francis V. Greene, *The Revolutionary War and the Military Policy of the United States;* John W. Wright, Notes on the Continental Army, in the *William and Mary Quarterly,* 1931, 1932, 1933.]   ROBERT S. THOMAS

Long Island Flats, Battle of. In June, 1776, the Overhill Cherokees^w, under British incitement, determined to make war on the whites settled in what is now upper east Tennessee and southwest Virginia. The invading force consisted of about 700 warriors, divided into three parties, the right wing, under Chief Old Abraham, to strike Fort Caswell on the Watauga^w, the center, under Chief Dragging Canoe, to attack Eaton's Fort near Long Island of Holston^w, while a smaller detachment was to strike settlers in Carter's Valley^w. Near Long Island and Eaton's Fort were level lands called "the flats," where, on July 20, 1776, a sharp battle was fought. After a severe conflict, the Indians were routed, with a loss of more than forty killed in addition to the wounded. The loss of the defending pioneers was five wounded and not a man killed.

[J. M. G. Ramsey, *Annals of Tennessee.*]
        SAMUEL C. WILLIAMS

Long Island of Holston, Treaty of. The militia of southwest Virginia and North Carolina under Col. William Christian and Col. Joseph Williams made a successful punitive expedition in the fall of 1776 against the Cherokees^w, following the Indians' raid and the battle of Long Island Flats^w. A pledge was extorted from the Cherokees that they would come into a treaty the following year. In June and July, 1777, the Indians met and negotiated with commissioners of the two states at Long Island, and ceded lands. North Carolina received a cession, the south line of which ran from Chimney Top Mountain past the mouth of McNamee's Creek of the Nolachucky to the Allegheny range.

[John Haywood, *History of Tennessee.*]
        SAMUEL C. WILLIAMS

Long Knives. *See* Big Knives.

Longhorns, Texas. Although predominantly of the blood that Spaniards began bringing to Mexico in 1521, the longhorn achieved character and fame (roughly 1845–95) as a Texas product. A strain out of cattle imported from southern states and the climate and ranges of Texas combined to develop an animal heavier and more "rangy" than straight Mexican cattle but at the same time severely differentiated from the "American" cattle of Colorado, Kansas and elsewhere. In color the breed was earthlike, brindles, duns, smokies, blues, browns, dull reds, blacks, paints of many variations, all mingling. Long of legs, body and tail, a "Texas steer" carried a pair of horns that spread from three to five feet from tip to tip, occasionally over eight feet.

The longhorn could, if necessary, go without water for days; many animals of this hardy breed are known to have thriven for months at a time while deriving all liquid nourishment from prickly pear and yucca stalks. Fortified by range grasses and browse, they could withstand the worst blizzards[w] of the Northwest. The masses survived stampedes[w] and milling roundups that would have killed other breeds. A longhorn cow was prepared to fight the fiercest panther or a pack of lobos off her calf; the bulls at times challenged grizzly bears. Hide and hoofs were tough against dagger thorns and the stones in trails over the Rocky Mountains. For driving thousands of miles and for stocking vast ranges vacated by buffaloes and Indians, the breed was ideal (*see* Cattle Drives).

For the same reason that razorbacks[w] have been supplanted by meatier hogs, the longhorn has been supplanted by bovine breeds that will better convert forage into beef—rather than into horns and bones. Only an occasional remnant can now be found along the lower Rio Grande, the animal being far nearer extinction than the buffalo[w] ever was. Nevertheless, the longhorn made more history than any other "cow brute" the civilized world has known. As a picturesque character, and as the maker of the American cowboy[w], the longhorn is not likely to be forgotten.

[Andy Adams, The Poker Steer, in *Cattle Brands;* E. E. Dale, *The Range Cattle Industry;* J. Frank Dobie, *On the Open Range;* J. Evetts Haley, *Charles Goodnight, Cowman and Plainsman.*]

J. FRANK DOBIE

Long's Explorations (1819–20, 1823). In the summer of 1819, Maj. Stephen H. Long, in the steamboat *Western Engineer*[w], left St. Louis in command of the scientific part of the Yellowstone Expedition[w]. Because of the delay and expense of the latter expedition, Congress refused further funds. As a compromise Long was authorized to make a scientific exploration to the Rocky Mountains.

On June 6, 1820, Long and twenty men set out to explore the Platte, the Arkansas and the Red[qw]. Marching up the Platte to the mountains, he discovered Long's Peak. Dr. Edwin James of his staff climbed Pikes Peak[w]. Capt. J. R. Bell marched down the Arkansas with part of the force; but Long, misled by Spanish information, explored the Canadian River and found it was not the Red when he came to its confluence with the Arkansas. The expedition added little to the world's knowledge of geography; but the four scientists of the party, including Dr. Thomas Say, added much to knowledge of the botany, zoology, geology and Indian lore of the Plains.

On April 20, 1823, Long set out on another exploration, from Fort Snelling[w] and thence up the St. Peter's (Minnesota) River. His mission was to explore the country, locate the 49th degree of latitude and take possession of all the territory below this newly authorized boundary line (*see* Convention of 1818 with England). Lord Selkirk's Colony at Pembina and North West Company[qw] posts in the Red River country were visited. The return trip was begun in August, the party going down Red River to Lake Winnipeg and thence eastward to Lake Superior, through the Great Lakes to Niagara Falls, and on southward to Philadelphia where they arrived Oct. 26, 1823.

[Cardinal Goodwin, ·*The Trans-Mississippi West.*]

BLISS ISELY

Lookout Mountain, Battle on (Nov. 24, 1863), was an action in which Hooker (U.), commanding the right wing of Grant's army of about 56,000 men, cleared Lookout Mountain of the enfeebled and disheartened Confederate troops who had held it since the battle of Chickamauga[w]. This initial stroke in Grant's effort to raise the siege of Chattanooga[w] was dramatic, even if easily accomplished. It is popularly known in history as the "battle of the clouds" owing to the fact that low-hanging clouds hid the contending forces from observers below in the valley of the Tennessee. The withdrawal of Longstreet's (C.) corps from Lookout Mountain had left the Confederate left wing dangerously weak. Hooker's troops scrambling up the mountain drove off the remaining Confederates, swept on across Chattanooga Creek and the next day participated in the fighting on Missionary Ridge[w], lying farther to the east. The battle, though not a hard fight, marked the beginning of final Union triumph in the Chattanooga campaign.

[*Battles and Leaders of the Civil War*, Vol. III.]

ALFRED P. JAMES

Loom, THE. Primitive English looms, brought to America by the first settlers, were soon displaced by improved Dutch looms to which the fly shuttle, which speeded their operation, was added before 1800. Power looms were invented in England, but original American types were perfected by the Boston Manufacturing Company^{qv}, and adapted from the Scotch loom. Between 1825 and 1850 Samuel Bachelor, William Mason and William Crompton of Massachusetts improved these looms to weave wool as well as cotton and to make pattern as well as plain fabrics, and Erastus Bigelow of the same state invented machinery to weave ingrain and eventually Brussels and Wilton carpets. Another era of rapid improvement occurred after the Civil War when James Northrop and George Draper perfected improvements which automatically changed shuttles and stopped a loom when a single warp thread broke. Early in the present century further refinements were embodied in the Crompton^{qv} and Knolls looms and their successors.

[Leander Bishop, *History of American Manufactures;* Victor S. Clark, *History of Manufactures in the United States.*]

VICTOR S. CLARK

Loomis Gang, THE, consisting chiefly of the six Loomis brothers, terrorized Madison County, N. Y., during the 1850's and 1860's. Burglary, horse stealing and even murder finally aroused the community. Vigilantes killed the oldest brother, burned the Loomis farmhouse and frightened the remainder of the gang into quiescence.

[Carl Carmer, *Listen for a Lonesome Drum.*]

EDWARD P. ALEXANDER

Loose Construction is a term applied in interpreting powers supposedly warranted by the Federal Constitution. Alexander Hamilton, original advocate of the liberal ("loose") construction theory, and founder of the Federalist^{qv} party, contended that Congress could exercise not only powers specifically "expressed," but such "implied" powers^{qv}—when not forbidden—as might be deemed "necessary and proper" for the attainment of the purposes contemplated in Article I, Section 8 of the Constitution^{qv}. Opposing Hamilton was Jefferson, leader of the Anti-Federalists^{qv}, who advocated a strict ("narrow"), literal interpretation. (*See also* Strict Construction.)

[J. T. Young, *The New American Government and Its Work;* N. W. Stephenson, *History of the American People,*

Vol. I; F. A. Ogg and P. O. Ray, *Introduction to American Government.*]

JOHN B. CLARK

Lopez Filibustering Expeditions (April, 1850 and August, 1851) were armed attempts by Cuban revolutionists, led by Narciso Lopez, and American annexationists, chiefly Southerners, to free Cuba from Spain. Both expeditions were recruited and at least partly financed in the United States, and both set out from New Orleans. The first, consisting of 750 men, reached Cuba but dispersed, and the second, 450 men, was captured and its members either executed or imprisoned (*see* Atares Massacre). So extensive was popular approval of filibustering that the American Government was powerless to enforce its own laws. This included inability to prevent the escape of the filibusters in the first instance, and inability to effect conviction of an illegal act upon their return.

Lopez wanted independence for Cuba, but his American supporters desired annexation (*see* Ostend Manifesto). So grave a peril to the balance of power in the Caribbean did these expeditions appear to England and France that they threatened to intervene, and they further urged a tripartite self-denying convention (1852) upon the United States.

[Samuel Flagg Bemis, *A Diplomatic History of the United States.*]

RICHARD W. VAN ALSTYNE

Loramie's Store, a trading post on the Miami-Maumee portage in present Shelby County, Ohio, was founded by Pierre Louis Lorimier (Anglicized into "Peter Loramie") about 1769. It remained an important center of British influence among the Ohio Indians until destroyed by George Rogers Clark in 1782, because of Lorimier's participation in Indian raids during the Revolution. Gen. Anthony Wayne later (1794) erected a fort on the site. "Loramie's" was used as a significant point of identification for the Indian boundary in the Treaty of Greenville^{qv}.

[Henry Howe, *Historical Collections of Ohio*, Vol. II; W. R. McFarland, Forts Loramie and Pickawillany, *Ohio Archæological and Historical Society Publications*, VIII.]

EUGENE H. ROSEBOOM

"Lords and Gentlemen" was a designation applied by the Massachusetts people to Lord Saye and Sele, Lord Brooke and others who, under the Old Patent of Connecticut^{qv}, designed a settlement at Saybrook^{qv} in 1635.

[C. M. Andrews, *The Colonial Period of American History*, Vol. I.]

R. V. COLEMAN

Lords of Trade and Plantation. Constitutional practice provided that English provinces outside the realm were charges of the Privy Council[qv]. Beginning in 1624, British colonial administration was directed by special committees advising the Privy Council. As these committees were short-lived and often unskilled, confusion and inefficiency in imperial control resulted. To create an informed personnel with vigor and continuity in colonial policy, Charles II organized, by Order in Council (March 12, 1675), the Lords of Trade and Plantation of twenty-one Privy Councillors, nine of whom held "the immediate Care and Intendency" of colonies, any five constituting a quorum. Though the Lords represented nothing new in method and held powers only advisory to the Privy Council, because they were men of informed ability and great administrative capacity and had continuous existence for twenty years with relatively few changes in personnel, they achieved more systematic administration than any previous agencies for colonial affairs, serving as a transition to and a model for the Board of Trade and Plantations[qv] which succeeded them (May 15, 1696). Holding 857 meetings (1675–96) and maintaining permanent offices in Scotland Yard, they established a permanent, salaried secretary (Sir Robert Southwell), assistant secretary (William Blathwayt) and clerical staff to handle colonial correspondence; became a bureau of colonial information by sending inquiries to colonial governors, and agents (notably Edward Randolph) to colonies; recommended appointees as royal governors to crown colonies and prepared their commissions and instructions; developed the technique of judicial review of colonial cases appealed to the Privy Council; assaulted, in the interests of unity and efficiency, the charters of colonies—forcing surrender of two and instituting *quo warranto* proceedings against five others by 1686—and instituted the policy of consolidating colonies (the Dominion of New England[qv]). Though vigorous in its early years, the Popish Plot (1678) lessened activity, and as death took older members and political disorders (1685–89) interfered, the Lords of Trade became weak and ineffective. Their last meeting was on April 18, 1696, a month before the Board of Trade superseded them.

[Ralph Paul Bieber, *The Lords of Trade and Plantations, 1675-1696.*]   RAYMOND P. STEARNS

Lords Proprietors, THE. *See* Proprietary Provinces.

L'Orient, an important French port and naval base from which, early in 1777, the ship *Amphitrite* cleared with a cargo of cannon, ammuni-

tion, tents, etc., for the American army and succeeded in landing it safely at Portsmouth, N. H. In November, 1777, two American frigates brought prizes into L'Orient and sold them. This port was thereafter a place of departure for American munitions and of entry for American products sold to the French during our Revolutionary War[qv].

[*Papers in the Case of Silas Deane.*]   ALVIN F. HARLOW

Lorimer Case, THE. On May 26, 1909, the Illinois legislature, after a deadlock of nearly five months, elected William Lorimer, a Republican, as United States senator. About a year later sensational charges of bribery and corruption were made in connection with this election. After an investigation the Senate by a close vote (March 1, 1911) declined to unseat him. A committee of the Illinois senate having produced new evidence of corruption, the United States Senate ordered a second investigation, and on July 13, 1912, ousted him from his seat.

[*Compilation of Senate Election Cases from 1789 to 1913,* Senate Document No. 1036, 62nd Congress, 3rd Session, pp. 1002-1113.]   CLARENCE A. BERDAHL

Los Adaes was a Spanish garrison established east of the Sabine River about 1718 to prevent French encroachment from Natchitoches[qv], twenty miles eastward on Red River. It remained a Spanish military and trading post on the route between Natchitoches and San Antonio[qv] until surrendered to the United States in the Louisiana-Texas boundary settlement of 1821 (*see* Adams-Onís Treaty).

[Isaac J. Cox, The Louisiana-Texas Frontier, in *Quarterly of the Texas State Historical Association* (continued as *Southwestern Historical Quarterly*), X, 1906, 1-75, *passim;* XVII, 1913, 1-42, 140-187, *passim.*]   WALTER PRICHARD

"Lost Battalion" (Oct. 2–8, 1918) is a misnomer applied to part of the American 77th Division which, during the Meuse-Argonne offensive[qv], was surrounded in Charlevaux Ravine by German troops. The force was composed of Companies A-B-C-E-G and H, 308th Infantry; Company K, 307th Infantry; and two platoons from Companies C and D, 306th Machine Gun Battalion, all under command of Maj. Charles W. Whittlesey. Adjoining French and American attacks launched Oct. 2 failed, whereas Whittlesey penetrated to his objective where he was promptly encircled. For five days (morning of Oct. 3–evening Oct. 7) he maintained a heroic defense against great odds until American relief troops broke through. Strictly speaking,

Whittlesey's force was not a battalion nor was it at any time lost.

[The Epic of the Lost Battalion, *New York Times Magazine*, Sept. 30, 1928; Thomas M. Johnson, *The Lost Battalion.*]

ROBERT S. THOMAS

"Lost Cause," THE, a symbolic term descriptive of the ideals, aspirations and memories of the Southern Confederacy. It was probably first used by E. A. Pollard, a Richmond newspaper man, in a book *The Lost Cause*, published in 1866.

THOMAS ROBSON HAY

"Lost Colony," THE. *See* Raleigh's Colony.

Lost Order, Lee's (September, 1862). As the Confederate Army advanced into Maryland[w], Lee planned to capture Harpers Ferry and concentrate his army for an advance into Pennsylvania. Accordingly, on Sept. 9, 1862, he issued Special Order No. 191, outlining routes and objectives. Copies were sent to division commanders concerned. D. H. Hill's division, heretofore under Jackson's orders, had been transferred. Jackson, receiving the order before learning of Hill's transfer, sent him a copy in his own hand. Hill preserved this copy. Another copy from Lee's headquarters, also sent Hill, in some manner was lost and later found by a Federal soldier. It was sent to McClellan (U.) who was thus informed of Lee's plans. It is not certain that Lee knew until several days later that McClellan was informed as to his plans. The loss nearly brought about Lee's complete defeat and created one of the most unusual situations in American military history.

[D. S. Freeman, *R. E. Lee*, Vol. II.]

THOMAS ROBSON HAY

Lotteries, until a comparatively recent time, were considered in this country a legitimate method of raising money for a wide variety of purposes. Their history dates from 1612, when James I authorized the Virginia Company[w] to make "a good supply to ye colonie" by this means. Although this venture was apparently restricted to England, the idea was speedily transmitted across the Atlantic, and by 1699 lotteries were sufficiently numerous here for a New England ecclesiastical assembly to denounce them as "a cheat" and their agents as "pillagers of the people." Nevertheless, the earliest printed reference to a lottery occurs in Bradford's *American Weekly Mercury*, for Feb. 23, 1720. Thereafter, throughout the remainder of that century, lotteries were increasingly employed on behalf of schools, roads, bridges, canals, etc. In 1748

part of Philadelphia's fortifications were built with funds thus obtained. Lotteries for churches were especially popular. Franklin's *Pennsylvania Gazette*[w] announced one in 1759 "Solely for the promotion of honor and religion . . . in imitation of . . . neighbors in this and adjacent provinces." The idea of lotteries for private gain was largely a growth of later days.

The fact that the early lotteries were generally projected for public causes long blinded to their evils many who would otherwise probably have opposed them. Franklin, Washington, Jefferson and other distinguished citizens favored them. As late as 1826 a lottery was considered a dignified method of relieving Jefferson's financial embarrassments.

Philadelphia was the principal center of lottery activities in this country in the 18th and early 19th centuries. There were, however, lotteries in many other places, some sporadic, some permanent. Boston, for instance, built the existing Faneuil Hall[w] with the proceeds of a lottery in 1761. Harvard, Dartmouth, Yale, Williams and other colleges replenished their building funds by the same device. In 1793 the District of Columbia commissioners paid for improvements in Washington through a lottery. In New York City, in 1790–91, lotteries were numerous and permanent enough for the lists of drawings to fill half a column in a local newspaper.

Between 1820 and 1833 the traffic in lottery tickets rose to extraordinary proportions. Philadelphia's lottery offices, of which there were three in 1809, increased by 1833 to more than 200. In 1830 New York had fifty-two drawings, involving prizes aggregating $9,270,000. It is estimated that 420 lotteries were then functioning in the country, offering annual prizes of about $53,000,000. Most were indigenous enterprises, but many were foreign-owned.

The earliest legislation restricting lotteries was enacted by Pennsylvania in 1729, but affected only those not operating under special legislative grants. No consistent attempt was made to suppress lotteries, as such, until about 1831. Pennsylvania and Massachusetts passed laws to that purpose in 1833; New York followed in 1834. The earliest antilottery society appeared in Philadelphia in 1833. Its educational work did much to direct attention to the essential immorality of lotteries. During the ensuing two decades one state after another took steps to end them. Louisiana, after chartering in 1868 the greatest lottery in American history (*see* Louisiana Lottery), abolished it in 1892. In 1890 Congress made illegal the distribution of lottery tickets or advertising through the mails. In 1895 they were excluded from interstate commerce (*see* Lottery Case). These acts proved a deathblow to the business.

[A. R. Spofford, Lotteries in American History, in *American Historical Association Annual Reports*, 1892.]

JOHN S. KENDALL

Lottery Case. The issue was whether the Lottery Act of Congress, passed in 1895, prohibiting the sending of lottery[tw] tickets through interstate commerce, was a valid exercise of power under the commerce clause[tw]. In 1903 the Supreme Court held, in Champion v. Ames, that Congress could do so, in order to guard the people of the United States from the "pestilence of lotteries." This has given rise to what some authorities term a "Federal police power" and in line with this principle Congress has passed and the Supreme Court has upheld laws excluding from interstate commerce such articles as obscene literature, impure food, prize-fight films and other articles deemed injurious to the health, welfare or morals of the people.

[A. C. McLaughlin, *A Constitutional History of the United States*; R. E. Cushman, *Leading Constitutional Decisions.*]

LEONARD C. HELDERMAN

Loudon, Fort (southeast of the present Loudon, Pa.), was built by Col. John Armstrong of the Pennsylvania militia in 1756 as a protection against Indian forays into the Conococheague Valley. During the Forbes expedition[tw] it was used as a military storehouse and convalescents' camp. Lt. Charles Grant with a detachment of Highlanders occupied the post when, in November, 1765, the "Black Boys"[tw] demanded the return of several guns which Grant had impounded following an assault upon a pack train of trading goods. Refused, they fired upon the fort, forcing its surrender and evacuation.

[G. O. Seilhamer, Old Fort Loudon and Its Associations, *Kittochtinny Historical Society Publications*, Vol. VI.]

E. DOUGLAS BRANCH

Loudoun, Fort. In 1756, to meet the French menace in the Old Southwest[tw], two forts were erected on Little Tennessee River west of the Alleghenies, one by Virginia and the other by South Carolina. The latter, named in honor of the Earl of Loudoun, commander of the British forces in America, was garrisoned by troops from South Carolina, and stood until 1760, when, under French incitement, it was besieged by the Cherokees[tw], and surrendered on Aug. 7. The troops marched out only to be attacked by the Indians early in the morning of the 10th, when four officers, twenty-three privates and some

women and children were massacred. The fort was burned.

[S. C. Williams, *Dawn of Tennessee Valley and Tennessee History.*]

SAMUEL C. WILLIAMS

Louisburg Expedition, THE (1745). After the loss of Acadia[tw] (1713), France settled Louisburg (Cape Breton Island), constructing a mighty fortress and naval station to dominate the North Atlantic. A seat of Popery, privateers and pirates, Louisburg threatened Nova Scotia and preyed upon New England commerce, fishing and peace of mind, though after long peace (1713–44) France neglected it. When King George's War[tw] began (1744), New Englanders, led by Gov. William Shirley of Massachusetts, determined to attack Louisburg. Well advised about French conditions, Shirley prevailed upon the General Court (Jan. 25, 1745) to raise 3000 men and necessary supplies, and enlisted support from neighboring colonies. Without assurance of English assistance, Shirley hoped to capture Louisburg before the French spring fleet arrived. On March 24 about 4300 men, commanded by William Pepperell, sailed from Boston. Landing at Canso, they were cheered by the arrival (April 23) of Commodore Peter Warren with three English warships (eight others arrived later). On April 30, while Warren blockaded Louisburg harbor, Pepperell landed his men at Gabarus Bay and laid siege to the town. Fortunate in capturing (May 3) the French Royal Battery of thirty heavy cannon, which they turned upon the town, the colonials forced Louisburg to capitulate (June 15), and captured the vessels of the French fleet as they arrived. Primarily achieved by colonial troops, this first important English victory in America was the result of careful planning, reckless fortitude and good luck. The colonists held Louisburg despite ill-fated attempts at recapture, and were embittered when, in the Treaty of Aix-la-Chapelle[tw] (1748), England sacrificed Louisburg for Madras, though England's reimbursements to the colonies for their expenses in the capture rescued Massachusetts, at least, from financial doldrums.

[C. H. Lincoln, ed., *The Correspondence of William Shirley*; Francis Parkman, *A Half-Century of Conflict*; H. L. Osgood, *The American Colonies in the Eighteenth Century.*]

RAYMOND P. STEARNS

Louisiana, as a French and Spanish Colony. Spanish explorers touched the Louisiana coast before 1520, and DeSoto[tw] died in the interior in 1542 while searching vainly for mines of precious metals. Spain then abandoned the region, which remained a sort of "no man's land" for nearly a century and a half, until LaSalle[tw], coming from Canada, followed the Mississippi[w] to its mouth in 1682 and claimed the entire valley for Louis XIV of France, in whose honor it was named "Louisiana." LaSalle's expedition to plant a colony at the mouth of the Mississippi in 1684 missed its intended destination and landed on the Texan coast, and in 1687 he was assassinated while trying to make his way back to Canada by land. The War of the English Succession (*see* King William's War) delayed the completion of LaSalle's project, but when peace returned Iberville and Bienville planted the first permanent French colony on the Gulf coast in 1699 (*see* Biloxi). The War of the Spanish Succession (*see* Queen Anne's War) forced France to neglect the colony. In 1712 Louis XIV, still anxious to develop Louisiana but with an empty treasury, granted to Antoine Crozat[w] the exclusive privilege of exploiting Louisiana. Crozat exhausted his resources in futile searches for sources of quick wealth, and in 1717 surrendered his charter without having effected much development in the colony.

John Law, a Scotchman recognized in France as a successful banker and financier, organized the Western Company, which assumed control of Louisiana on Jan. 1, 1718. The scope of the company's operations was soon enlarged and its name changed to the "Company of the Indies." The anticipated immense and immediate profits were not realized, and in 1720 the company failed, the "bubble" burst and Law passed off the scene (*see* Mississippi Bubble). However, the company retained control of Louisiana until a series of bad harvests and the disastrous war with the Natchez Indians[w] caused the surrender of the charter in 1731. Profiting by Crozat's mistakes, the company brought some substantial development to the colony, but failed to make it a financial success.

Louisiana then passed under French royal control, thus to remain for three decades. The colony developed slowly, handicapped by strife between France and England. France undertook to unite Louisiana with Canada by erecting fortified posts to exclude the English from the Mississippi Valley. The British quickly accepted the challenge, and the ensuing War of the Austrian Succession (*see* King George's War) and the Seven Years' War (*see* French and Indian War), culminating in the expulsion of the French from the mainland of North America, seriously retarded the progress of Louisiana. In 1762 Louisiana west of the Mississippi and the Isle of Orleans[w] were ceded to Spain, and the remainder of Louisiana was surrendered to England in 1763 (*see* Fontainebleau, Treaty of; Paris, Treaty of, 1763).

Resentment of the French inhabitants at the transfer, Spain's tardiness in taking possession of the colony, general economic distress and the unpopular measures of Antonio de Ulloa, the first Spanish governor, led to his expulsion in the so-called Revolution of 1768. But Alexandro O'Reilly crushed the "Revolution" and firmly established Spanish authority in 1769. Louisiana experienced a steady development under Spanish rule, in spite of many difficulties. The international confusion accompanying the American and French revolutions kept alive the hope of the Louisianians for eventual reunion with France. Spanish Louisiana played an important part in the American Revolution. Needed supplies were forwarded from New Orleans to the patriot forces in the West (*see* Pollock's Aid to the American Revolution), and when Spain entered the war as an ally of France in 1779, Bernardo Galvez, operating from Louisiana, captured the British posts in West Florida. Spanish discontent with the Definitive Treaty of Peace, 1783[w], led to intrigues with the Indians and with some of the western leaders for protecting Louisiana by holding back the influx of American settlers, or detaching the trans-Allegheny region from the United States (*see* Western Separatism). The Nootka Sound controversy between England and Spain in 1790 and the Genêt episode[qw] of 1793, involving threats of western attack upon Louisiana, alarmed the Spanish authorities. Disputes between the United States and Spain over navigation of the Mississippi and the northern boundary of West Florida were adjusted by the Pinckney Treaty[w] of 1795, but Spain still feared the outcome of American expansion in the southwest.

When Napoleon became head of the French government in 1799, he planned a new colonial empire, and by the Treaty of San Ildefonso[w] (Oct. 1, 1800) Spain retroceded Louisiana to France. But Napoleon's inability to subjugate the blacks in Haiti, threat of renewal of the European war, discontent of the United States over commercial restrictions at New Orleans (*see* Deposit, Right of), and his pressing need for money induced him to sell Louisiana to the United States by the Louisiana Purchase Treaty[w] of April 30, 1803, before he had taken possession of the colony. In spite of Spanish resentment and threats, Louisiana was formally transferred by Spain to France on Nov. 30, 1803, and by France to the United States on Dec. 20, 1803.

[Charles Gayarré, *History of Louisiana;* Alcée Fortier, *History of Louisiana;* François Xavier Martin, *History of Louisiana;* Albert Phelps, *Louisiana, A Record of Expansion;* Henry E. Chambers, *History of Louisiana.*]

WALTER PRICHARD

Louisiana, State of, the first carved from the Louisiana Purchase^ᵂ, was admitted to the Union in 1812. The War of 1812^ᵂ threatened Louisiana near its close, but Andrew Jackson repulsed the British invasion on Jan. 8, 1815 (*see* New Orleans, Battle of). Aligned at first with Jeffersonian Republican national politics, Louisiana's interests later coincided with the principles of the Adams-Clay "American system" and with those of the Whigs, until the sectional controversy made her definitely Democratic after 1850^{qᵂ}. The American^ᵂ (Know-Nothing) movement, being anti-Catholic, never gained much strength in Louisiana. New constitutions were adopted in 1845 and 1852, each more democratic than its predecessor.

Louisiana developed like all new states of the West and South. Agriculture and commerce expanded rapidly. Sugar^ᵂ culture, stimulated by tariff and the introduction of hardier varieties of cane and improved processes of manufacture, became the favorite crop in lower Louisiana, extending to Red River by 1845. Cotton^ᵂ culture expanded greatly, particularly after the settlement of the region north of Red River about 1840. The steamboat^ᵂ made New Orleans the commercial emporium of the entire Mississippi Valley. Agricultural and commercial expansion necessitated better transportation and banking facilities, and the state adopted the unsound policy of combining internal improvements with banking, chartering several "improvement banks" backed by state credit, which brought financial distress in the Panic of 1837^ᵂ. This disaster produced good results. A sound state banking system was developed (*see* Louisiana, Specie Reserve, Banking System) and internal improvements put on a saner basis. Agriculture and commerce soon revived, followed by a new era of railroad and levee construction^{qᵂ} in the 1850's.

Ante-bellum Louisiana experienced important cultural development. The public school system, revised from time to time, was fairly adequate by 1850, though private and parochial schools still flourished. An important literary development, in both French and English, was manifest. The Louisiana press was outstanding in the decade preceding the Civil War. Catholicism ceased to be the sole religion in the state. Enlightened principles were introduced in the care of unfortunates and criminals.

The sectional crisis of 1860 found Louisiana definitely aligned with her sister slave states. The sixth state to secede, she early suffered from Federal military and naval superiority, New Orleans being captured on May 1, 1862 (*see* New Orleans, Capture of), and vital sections of the state

remaining in Federal hands throughout the war. Reconstruction^ᵂ began earlier and lasted longer in Louisiana than in any other Confederate state, and during the war Lincoln used this state as an experimental laboratory for testing his reconstruction theories. The war left Louisiana with capital exhausted and the labor system demoralized, and the radical reconstruction regime retarded economic revival.

After the return of home rule^ᵂ in 1877 Louisiana soon recovered much of her ante-bellum prosperity. Agriculture regained its prewar level in the 1880's, and southwest Louisiana was transformed from a grazing region into an important rice-growing^ᵂ section. A new era of railroad and levee construction followed, and the timber resources were exploited. Economic revival was accompanied by rehabilitation of the state's educational, charitable and penal institutions. The horrors of reconstruction aligned Louisiana politically with the "Solid South"^ᵂ, and the Negro problem prevented the Granger, Populist and "Lily White"^{qᵂ} Republican movements from endangering Democratic supremacy. The constitution of 1879, designed to establish white supremacy, but later condemned as undemocratic, was replaced in 1898 by a more liberal one, with special provisions for excluding the Negro from politics (*see* Grandfather Clause). Other constitutions were adopted in 1913 and 1921.

Louisiana's great industrial development began about 1900, with the exploitation of her petroleum and natural gas^{qᵂ} resources, as well as salt, sulphur and timber, which had previously become important. Social progress followed economic prosperity. The public educational system was revised and extended, yellow fever^ᵂ was eliminated and malaria brought under control, better levees were constructed, a more equitable system of taxation was introduced and other evidences of progress appeared prior to the World War.

A mild spirit of progressivism entered Louisiana politics about 1920, and became militant with the advent of Huey P. Long as governor in 1928. Though bitterly assailed by the opposition, Long carried through in record time an elaborate program of public improvement and social amelioration. Paved roads and free bridges replaced gravel roads and toll ferries on main highways, a magnificent new state capitol was erected, more adequate financial support was accorded to all state educational, charitable and correctional institutions, free textbooks were supplied to all children and the burden of taxation was more equitably distributed. Long's policies are still in effect. The program of public improvement continues (1939), and an elaborate system of social security is being developed.

[Charles Gayarré, *History of Louisiana;* Alcée Fortier, *History of Louisiana;* François Xavier Martin, *History of Louisiana;* Henry E. Chambers, *History of Louisiana;* Albert Phelps, *Louisiana, A Record of Expansion;* William O. Scroggs, *The Story of Louisiana;* Harriet Magruder, *History of Louisiana;* John R. Ficklen, *Reconstruction in Louisiana through 1868;* Ella Lonn, *Reconstruction in Louisiana after 1868; Publications of the Louisiana Historical Society; The Louisiana Historical Quarterly.*]

WALTER PRICHARD

Louisiana, Upper, was the Spanish designation for that part of Louisiana stretching from Hope Encampment (nearly opposite Chickasaw Bluffs^{qv}) northward to Canada and westward to the Rocky Mountains. Beginning with 1770 St. Louis^{qv} was the seat of government, presided over by a lieutenant governor, subordinate only to the governor of Louisiana at New Orleans. The first lieutenant governor was Pedro Piernas and the last Carlos Dehault Delassus. The United States called Upper Louisiana the District of Louisiana, distinguishing Lower Louisiana with the name of Territory of Orleans^{qv}. Upper Louisiana was further divided by the United States after the purchase into five districts denominated respectively: St. Louis, St. Charles, Ste. Genevieve, Cape Girardeau and New Madrid.

[Amos Stoddard, *Sketches, Historical and Descriptive, of Louisiana;* Louis Houck, *History of Missouri.*]

STELLA M. DRUMM

Louisiana (Specie Reserve) Banking System (1842–62). The Panic of 1837^{qv} destroyed the loose banking system of Louisiana. As a result of the distress there was a banking reform movement which culminated in the act of 1842 setting up a board of currency with large powers of supervision over all banks. The banks were required to separate their loans into two types: those made from capital and those made from deposits. Capital loans could be made on long-term paper, but those from deposits were limited to ninety-day paper, nonrenewable. In addition to this deposit protection was a requirement for a one-third specie reserve. Banks were prohibited from dealing in speculative ventures and daily exchanges of notes and weekly specie settlements were required.

The strength of the Louisiana system was demonstrated during the Panic of 1857^{qv}, which had less effect in New Orleans than in any commercial city of the nation. This drew the attention of financiers and explains why the Louisiana system exerted such a marked influence on the National Banking System^{qv}. Its influence was second only to that of the New York act of 1838.

[Leonard C. Helderman, *National and State Banks — A Study of Their Origins.*]   LEONARD C. HELDERMAN

Louisiana Lottery, THE, was chartered by the Louisiana legislature August, 1868, for a period of twenty-five years. The capital stock was fixed at $1,000,000, but operations were to begin when $100,000 was paid in. In return for its monopoly of the lottery business in Louisiana, the company paid $40,000 annually to the state, but was exempt from other taxation. The business soon became immensely profitable. In March, 1879, the legislature repealed the charter, but the United States District Court for Louisiana held that this was a violation of contract. In 1890, when the charter was about to expire, the company, through John A. Morris, one of its founders, offered the state $500,000 annually for an extension of twenty-five years. This offer was subsequently raised to $1,000,000 and then to $1,250,000. Opposition immediately developed. Gov. Nicholls sent to the legislature a message denouncing the proposal. Nevertheless, an act calling for a constitutional amendment embodying the lottery company's franchise was passed. This was vetoed by Nicholls. The House passed the bill over his veto, but the Senate failed to do so. The latter body, however, approved a resolution denying the governor's right to veto a bill proposing a constitutional amendment, whereupon the House sent the bill to the Secretary of State to be promulgated. This the official refused to do. Morris took the matter into the courts, which decided against the Secretary of State. On Sept. 19, 1890, the United States Post Office Department denied the lottery company the use of the mails (*see* Lotteries). Morris thereupon withdrew his proposition. In the meantime a political organization unfavorable to the lottery had been formed, and held a convention in Baton Rouge, Aug. 7, 1890. The agitation thus initiated resulted in the election of Murphy J. Foster to the governorship. After his election, Foster approved acts (June 28 and July 12, 1892) making the sale of lottery tickets unlawful in Louisiana. The lottery company continued in business in New Orleans till 1895 (*see* Lottery Case), when it transferred its domicile to Honduras. Thence it continued to sell tickets in the United States till April, 1906, when the United States Department of Justice^{qv} succeeded in breaking up the business.

[Alcée Fortier, *Louisiana;* Thomas C. Johnson, *Life and Letters of Benjamin M. Palmer.*]

JOHN S. KENDALL

Louisiana Purchase. The province of Louisiana embraced the Isle of Orleans^{qv} on the east bank of the Mississippi and the vast area between that river, the Rockies and the Spanish possessions in the Southwest (*see* Louisiana Purchase, Boundaries of). The purchase of the colony from Napoleon by the United States in 1803 ended forever France's dream of controlling the Mississippi Valley, and began a program of expansion destined to carry the American flag to the Pacific.

For a generation Louisiana had been a pawn in European diplomacy. France ceded it to Spain in 1762 (*see* Fontainebleau, Treaty of). Genêt[w] planned to attack it from the United States in 1793, but France turned to diplomacy as a means of recovering it between 1795 and 1799. By the Treaty of San Ildefonso[w], Oct. 1, 1800, and the Convention of Aranjuez, March 21, 1801, Napoleon acquired Louisiana in return for placing the Prince of Parma, son-in-law of the Spanish king, on the newly erected throne of Etruria.

The acquisition of Louisiana was part of an ambitious plan by which Napoleon and Talleyrand hoped to build a colonial empire in the West Indies and the heart of North America. The mainland colony would be a source of supplies for the sugar islands, a market for France and a vast territory for settlement. Two million francs were spent upon an expedition for Louisiana assembled in Holland, at Helvoët Sluys, in the winter of 1802–3. Fortunately for the United States the ships were icebound in February, just as they were ready to sail.

By the Treaty of San Lorenzo[w], Spain, in 1795, had granted American citizens the privilege of depositing their goods at New Orleans for reshipment on ocean-going vessels. The United States was deeply aroused when Juan Ventura Morales, the acting intendant of Louisiana, revoked this right of deposit[w] on Oct. 16, 1802, and failed to provide another site, as the treaty required. It was assumed at the time that France was responsible for the revocation but all available documentary evidence indicates that the action was taken by Spain alone, and for commercial reasons.

President Jefferson handled the crisis in masterly fashion by appointing James Monroe as a special envoy to assist Robert R. Livingston, the minister at Paris, in securing American rights. Monroe's instructions authorized an offer of $10,-000,000 for the Isle of Orleans, on which New Orleans stood, and the Floridas[w], erroneously thought to be French. If France refused this proposition the ministers were to seek a commercial site on the Mississippi, or at least permanent establishment of the right of deposit at New Orleans.

In the meantime, Livingston had pursued his country's interests with a zeal deserving better results. He proposed the cession of New Orleans and the Floridas, belittled the economic value of

Louisiana for France and, after the closing of New Orleans, urged the cession to the United States of the Isle of Orleans and all the trans-Mississippi country above the Arkansas River. This was the first hint by any one that France surrender any part of the right bank of the Mississippi.

By the spring of 1803, Napoleon's plans for his American empire had all gone astray. Spain refused to round out his possessions by ceding the Floridas. Negro resistance and yellow fever thwarted the attempt to subjugate Santo Domingo. War with Great Britain was imminent. In the United States there was growing hostility to France and talk of an Anglo-American alliance. Particularly disturbed at such a prospect, Napoleon decided to reap a nice profit and placate the Americans by selling them all of Louisiana.

When Monroe arrived in Paris on April 12, the first consul had already appointed François Barbé-Marbois, Minister of the Public Treasury, to conduct the negotiations. On April 11 Talleyrand had amazed Livingston by asking what the United States would give for the entire colony. Barbé-Marbois conferred with Livingston on the evening of April 13, thereby initiating the negotiations before the formal presentation of Monroe. Some jealousy arose between the American ministers but it did not handicap their work. Monroe was at first less inclined than Livingston to exceed their instructions and purchase all of Louisiana. By a treaty and two conventions, all dated April 30, the United States paid $11,-250,000 for Louisiana, set aside $3,750,000 to pay the claims of its own citizens against France and placed France and Spain on an equal commercial basis with the United States in the colony for a period of twelve years.

Serious barriers to American ownership of Louisiana yet remained. Napoleon's action required the confirmation of the French legislature, and the sale was a violation of his solemn pledge to Spain never to alienate the colony to a third power. There was also grave doubt regarding the constitutionality of such a purchase by the United States. None of these dangers materialized. Napoleon ignored the legislature, Spain did nothing more than protest and Jefferson put his constitutional scruples conveniently aside. On Nov. 30, 1803, Spain formally delivered the colony to Pierre-Clément Laussat, the French colonial prefect, who on Dec. 20 transferred the territory to William C. C. Claiborne and Gen. James Wilkinson, the American commissioners. The Anglo-Saxon had vanquished the Latin in the long struggle for the Mississippi Valley.

[François Barbé-Marbois, *Histoire de la Louisiane;*

Henry Adams, *History of the United States;* F. P. Renaut, *La question de la Louisiane, 1796-1806;* E. Wilson Lyon, *Louisiana in French Diplomacy, 1759-1804;* Arthur P. Whitaker, *The Mississippi Question;* Samuel Flagg Bemis, *A Diplomatic History of the United States.*]

E. WILSON LYON

Louisiana Purchase, Boundaries of the. The United States purchased Louisiana "with the same extent that it now has in the hands of Spain, and that it had when France possessed it; and Such as it Should be after the Treaties subsequently entered into between Spain and other States." The treaty of cession, incorporating these words, quoted verbatim from the treaty by which Spain retroceded Louisiana to France in 1800. When the United States commissioners requested a definition Napoleon is reported to have said that "if an obscurity did not already exist, it would perhaps be good policy to put one there." The resultant series of diplomatic and territorial controversies is still not settled.

France, original settler of Louisiana, had not reoccupied it at the time of our purchase, but the extent of the region as then "in the hands of Spain" was ill defined. Before 1763 France claimed the entire Mississippi watershed eastward to the Alleghenies and westward to undetermined limits, as well as the Gulf Coast eastward to the Perdido River[qv]. French explorers had traversed Texas, and French traders controlled the Texas Indian trade, but the Arroyo Hondo, between Nacogdoches[qv] (Tex.) and Natchitoches[qv] (La.), was tacitly accepted as the frontier in the 18th century. Between French Louisiana and French Canada no clear line had been drawn.

France ceded western Louisiana to Spain in 1762 (*see* Fontainebleau, Treaty of), but there is no evidence that they made a boundary delineation. Great Britain, by the Treaty of Paris[qv], in 1763 completed her possession of all North America east of the Mississippi except New Orleans, making that river the eastern boundary of Louisiana. The province of West Florida[qv] was joined with the province of Louisiana, in administration only, from 1783, when Spain recovered both Floridas (*see* Definitive Treaty of Peace, 1783), until 1803 when Louisiana was surrendered to France and in turn to the United States (*see* Louisiana Purchase). But Spain governed West Florida separately after 1803 and asserted its independence of Louisiana. The United States claimed it and took over part of it in 1810 (*see* West Florida, Annexation of), further complicating the West Florida controversy.

Meanwhile Spain's acquisition of Louisiana in 1762 had postponed the need for a Texas-Louisiana delineation. Frontier disturbances began after 1803, and in 1806 rival commanders effected the "Neutral Ground Agreement"[qv], mutually limiting their activities by a strip between the Arroyo Hondo and the Sabine River. The United States took French colonial exploration and the instructions to the intended French captain general of Louisiana in 1802 as bases for its claim that the purchase extended to the Río Grande.

The State of Louisiana as admitted in 1812 included part of West Florida and employed the Sabine River as its western limit, though without treaty sanction. In the Adams-Onís Treaty of 1819[qv] Spain relinquished West Florida, though the negotiators consciously avoided saying whether or not it belonged to Louisiana before 1819, and in exchange for other concessions the United States yielded Texas beyond the Sabine.

The natural limit between New Mexico and Louisiana was at the headwaters of the Río Grande and the Arkansas River. But to keep the line far from Santa Fé, the Adams-Onís delineation left the Red River at 100° W. Long., and proceeded west along the Arkansas to its source. Since colonial occupation gave no ground for boundary claims farther north, it was logical to assume that the purchase included the natural watershed of the Mississippi. Jefferson's claim that Oregon was included had no foundation and no international recognition. The drawing of the line to the Pacific on the 42nd parallel, N. Lat., in the Adams-Onís Treaty was the result of bargaining on a larger scale.

An assertion that the northern boundary was defined in the Treaty of Utrecht of 1713[qv] was ignored. In the Convention of 1818[qv] a practical agreement between this country and England placed the boundary at 49° N. Lat., from the Lake of the Woods to the Rocky Mountains. The United States had thus effected its ownership of practically the whole western Mississippi watershed through rights acquired in the Louisiana Purchase.

[Henry Adams, *History of the United States;* Samuel F. Bemis, *Diplomatic History of the United States;* Thomas M. Marshall, *History of the Western Boundary of the Louisiana Purchase.*]   PHILIP COOLIDGE BROOKS

Louisiana Purchase Exposition, THE, was held in St. Louis, Mo., from April 30 to Dec. 1, 1904. Its 1240 acres made it the largest of international expositions; its cost was over $31,586,000 and its attendance 19,694,855. The total deficit was considerable. Six years of preparation went to the celebration of the centennial of the purchase of the Louisiana territory. The technical marvel popularized by the exposition was the automobile, of which more than 100 were placed on display, including one that had made the trip all the way from New York "under its own power." There were great chemical exhibits from Germany, thousands of articles from Japan, and an immense Philippine Reservation to show Americans the extent of the empire they had so recently acquired from Spain. Architecturally the Fair followed the grandiloquent French style and the ensemble formed an astonishing pattern of elaborate and universal chaos. The foreign governments contributed to this by building, for the most part, replicas of great European buildings and palaces—thus enhancing the architectural confusion.

FRANK MONAGHAN

Louisiana Revolution of 1768. The French inhabitants of Louisiana keenly resented being transferred to Spain by the Treaty of Fontainebleau[w] of Nov. 3, 1762, and Spain's tardiness in taking possession of the colony induced the inhabitants to hope that the actual transfer would never take place. Economic distress, loyalty to France and the unpopularity of Antonio de Ulloa, the first Spanish governor of Louisiana, culminated in Ulloa's expulsion from the colony in the so-called "Revolution" of October, 1768.

[Charles Gayarré, *History of Louisiana*.]

WALTER PRICHARD

Louisville and Nashville Railroad, THE, was constructed because of Louisville's need of dependable transportation, sufficient to compete with the projected railroads of other cities. Through the Lexington Railroad, completed in 1851, Louisville expected to retain commercial dominance in the Kentucky Bluegrass region. Its supremacy was threatened when Nashville, planning connection with Charleston via Chattanooga, planned also a rail invasion of western Kentucky. To meet this challenge, a Louisville mass meeting favored a municipal subscription of $1,000,000 for a project to connect Louisville and Nashville by rail. Charters were secured (1850), and by 1853 cities, counties and individuals had subscribed $4,085,000. However, most of the funds for the early construction were borrowed in Europe (1853–54). The line was completed to Nashville in 1859, at a total cost of $7,221,204.91.

[T. D. Clark, *The Beginning of the L. and N.*]

W. C. MALLALIEU

Louisville and Portland Canal, around the Falls of the Ohio[w], was constructed by a Kentucky corporation chartered in 1825. The original construction (1826–31) cost $742,869.94. The

Federal Government, which had already subscribed heavily to the project, acquired complete possession of the canal in 1872, reducing the tolls to a nominal sum, and none after 1880. The canal was twice enlarged (1861–66 and 1870–82).

[*History of the Ohio Falls Cities and Their Counties*.]

W. C. MALLALIEU

Lovejoy Riots. The Rev. Elijah P. Lovejoy established a weekly newspaper, *The Observer*, at St. Louis (1833). Threatened with violence by proslavery men for editorials against slavery (1834), he made a point of his rights to free speech and free press. Moving his press to free soil (Alton, Ill.) in 1836, it was smashed on the Alton dock by local citizens. Sympathizers helped to purchase a new press, but when Lovejoy came out for immediate abolition and a state antislavery society (July, 1837), a mob destroyed the press (August), smashed a third (Sept. 21) and, in an effort to destroy the fourth (Nov. 7), shot its defenders and killed Lovejoy who immediately became a martyr to the cause of Abolition[w].

[Joseph C. and Owen Lovejoy, *Memoir of the Reverend Elijah P. Lovejoy;* Edward Beecher, *Narrative of Riots at Alton.*]

RAYMOND P. STEARNS

Lovely's Purchase. W. L. Lovely, Cherokee Indian agent in Arkansas, in informal peace conference between Osage and Cherokee at the mouth of the Verdigris River, on July 9, 1816, obtained consent of the Osage[w] to cede a large tract of land lying east of that stream if the Government would pay claims for depredations held against them by white people. At St. Louis, Sept. 25, 1818, representative members of the Osage tribe ratified this cession in consideration of payment by Government of claims amounting to $4000.

[Grant Foreman, *Indians and Pioneers.*]

GRANT FOREMAN

Lovewell's Fight occurred at Pigwacket (Fryeburg), Maine, Sunday, May 9 (o.s.), 1725. Capt. John Lovewell, with thirty-three volunteers, was out for scalp bounty[w], and Chaplain Frye had just scalped an Indian, when the troop was ambushed by about eighty Indians. Twelve white men, including Lovewell, fell at the onset; one deserted under fire; twenty-one were left. Ensign Seth Wyman, the only officer, placed his men for a finish fight, a pond at their backs and two large, fallen pines for breastworks. Toward nightfall, seeing the Indians powwowing for a fresh attack, Wyman still-hunted and shot the medicine man at his incantations. This ended the fight. Eighteen of the men eventually reached home. Rev. Thomas Symmes in his account changed the date from May 9 to May 8, supposedly to divert from Chaplain Frye, who died, the odium of scalp hunting on Sunday.

[Rev. Thomas Symmes, *Historical Preface, or Memoirs of the Battle at Piggwacket;* Frederic Kidder, Expeditions of Captain John Lovewell, in *Magazine of History,* Extra Number—No. 5; F. H. Eckstorm, Pigwacket and Parson Symmes, in *New England Quarterly,* Vol. IX.]
                                    FANNIE HARDY ECKSTORM

Lower (Baja) California, discovered in 1534–35 by Fortún Jiménez, a navigator in the service of Hernán Cortés, was separated from Spanish Upper (Alta) ^{qv} California in 1772. The cession of the peninsula by Mexico was vainly sought by Nicholas P. Trist in making the peace treaty of Guadalupe Hidalgo ^{qv} in 1848. It was also the objective of William Walker's futile filibustering expedition of 1853–54, and James Gadsden failed to obtain it as part of the Gadsden Purchase ^{qv} completed in 1854. A number of efforts to purchase it for the United States in 1857, 1859 and later years have been equally fruitless. The United States Navy for several years made use of Magdalena Bay on the west coast of the peninsula as a maneuvers base, by courtesy of the Mexican government; and an alleged Japanese effort to lease the bay in 1910–11 was the occasion leading to the Lodge Resolution of 1912, with its notable elaboration of the Monroe Doctrine ^{qv}, concerning the use by non-American governments of New World harbors and strategic points.

[H. H. Bancroft, *The North Mexican States and Texas;* J. M. Callahan, *American Foreign Policy in Mexican Relations.*]
                                    RUFUS KAY WYLLYS

Lower Counties-on-Delaware, The, which comprised the counties of New Castle, Kent and Sussex, or the present state of Delaware ^{qv}, evolved from the earlier Swedish and Dutch settlements. They were conveyed by the Duke of York (*see* York's, Duke of, Proprietary) in 1682 to William Penn, and shortly afterward annexed to the Province of Pennsylvania by the Act of Union. Because of disagreement in the Provincial Assembly the Lower Counties, in 1704, seceded from that body and formed, at New Castle, their own assembly, by which, and the provincial governor of Pennsylvania, they continued to be governed until the adoption of the constitution of the State of Delaware in 1776.

[J. Thomas Scharf, *History of Delaware;* Henry C. Conrad, *History of the State of Delaware.*]
                                    LEON DeVALINGER, JR.

Lower Lakes. *See* Upper, and Lower, Lakes.

Lower South is that part of the South lying wholly within the cotton belt ^{qv}, including South Carolina, Georgia and the Gulf states of Florida, Alabama, Mississippi, Louisiana and Texas. In the later ante-bellum period these states (Florida excepted) secured political leadership in the South, based upon large scale, slave-labor cotton culture and its concomitants.

[William G. Brown, *The Lower South in American History.*]
                                    HAYWOOD J. PEARCE, JR.

Loyal, Fort, Capture of (May 20, 1690). Two of Count Frontenac's lieutenants, Hertel and Portneuf, commanding a mixed force of French and Indians, besieged this Casco Bay fort and compelled its commander, Capt. Sylvanus Davis, to surrender. The pledge of kind treatment and quarter to the vanquished was grossly violated and many of them were tortured and murdered.

[William D. Williamson, *The History of the State of Maine;* Francis Parkman, *Count Frontenac and New France.*]
                                    ROBERT S. THOMAS

Loyal Land Company (1748). The spirit of speculation in western lands was rife in Virginia in the later years of the first half of the 1700's. The first grant to a company organized to deal in such lands was to the Loyal Land Company. A grant of 800,000 acres was made to it by the Council of State of Virginia, on July 12, 1748, John Lewis, founder of Staunton, Va., being the leading spirit for four years. In launching the company's activities Dr. Thomas Walker was chosen on Dec. 12, 1749, as field agent, and soon became the directive force of the enterprise. In 1750 he led a group on a tour of exploration into the Tennessee and Kentucky country in the interest of the company and kept a journal which is one of the most valuable sources on the early history of that region. On that tour Walker named the Cumberland Mountains, Gap and River in honor of the Duke of Cumberland.

However, the lands actually taken up by the company were located east of the Cumberland Mountains. By the autumn of 1754 lands were sold to about 200 settlers. The French and Indian War ^{qv} brought a cessation of activities for some years; and the Proclamation of 1763 ^{qv} gave Walker and his associates concern and trouble. In order to render lands west of the proclamation line available, Walker took an active part in removing the claims of the Indian tribes to the region. He participated in negotiating the treaties of Fort Stanwix and Lochaber ^{qqv}. Until his death in 1794, Walker was persistent in salvaging all he could for the company. Southwest Virginia owes much to his enterprise and assiduity in bringing in settlers.

[Archibald Henderson, Dr. Thomas Walker and the

Loyal Land Company, in *Proceedings, American Antiquarian Society,* 1931.]
SAMUEL C. WILLIAMS

Loyal Leagues, known generically as the Union League, were formed to restore Northern morale which was shaken by military and political reverses in 1862. The movement had its origin at Pekin, Ill., where the "Union League of America" was formed on June 25, 1862. Eventually leagues were set up in every Northern state and clubs were organized in many cities and towns. A convention which assembled at Cleveland, May 20–21, 1863, created a national Grand Council with headquarters at Washington. Public meetings were sponsored and broadsides, pamphlets and posters were circulated by the millions. Union Leagues insisted upon unconditional loyalty, promoted the formation of the Union party, contributed to the renomination and election of Lincoln, and aided in state and local contests. In the Reconstruction period pamphlets on Southern "outrages" and the Negro problem were issued, but many leagues continued mainly as local social clubs. Agents sent South were welcomed by upland loyalists who joined the Union League to wrest political control from the lowland aristocracy. Most native whites deserted upon the admission of Negroes who were organized into local lodges by secret and mysterious ritualistic ceremonies. As a political machine designed to inculcate the tenets of Radical Republicanism, the League was partly responsible for the Klan movement[qqv]. By 1870 the League ceased to exert influence in the South.

[H. W. Bellows, *Historical Sketch of the Union League Club of New York;* G. P. Lathrop, *History of the Union League of Philadelphia;* W. L. Fleming, *The Sequel of Appomattox.*]
WENDELL H. STEPHENSON]

Loyal Legion, Military Order of the, a society resembling that of the Cincinnati[v], was organized at Philadelphia in 1865 by a group of officers in the Federal Army who had served in the Civil War. Membership was limited to such officers and their eldest male descendants, according to the laws of primogeniture.

[Henry S. Burrage, *Historical Address at Fiftieth Anniversary of the Maine Commandery, Loyal Legion,* Dec. 7, *1916.*]
ALVIN F. HARLOW

Loyal Publication Societies were formed during the Civil War to distribute "journals and documents of unquestionable loyalty." Strongly opposing Copperheads and Democrats[qqv], they were active in state politics and the national campaign of 1864[v]. Under the leadership of Francis Lieber, the New York society from 1862

to 1865 raised $30,000 with which they published 900,000 copies of ninety pamphlets. The New England Loyal Publication Society, at Boston, spent $4000 to print more than 200 broadsides. The two organizations co-operated with each other. In addition to their own publications, they distributed newspapers, pamphlets and broadsides favorable to the Union cause.

[E. E. Ware, *Political Opinion in Massachusetts during the Civil War and Reconstruction;* Loyal Publication Society of New York, *Annual Reports.*]
FRANK FREIDEL

Loyalhanna, Battle of the (Oct. 12, 1758), at Ligonier, Pa., was an unsuccessful attack of about 600 French and Indians under M. Aubry, upon 1500 men, in an entrenched encampment, commanded by Col. James Burd. Its purpose was to delay the Forbes Expedition[v] by destroying horses and cattle and, if possible, capture the post. Baffled by artillery behind fortifications, M. Aubry, after four hours conflict and slight losses, retired. Burd's losses were considerable.

[Alfred P. James, *Fort Ligonier,* 1758-1765, in *West Pennsylvania Historical Review,* XVII, 1934.]
ALFRED P. JAMES

Loyalists, or Tories, those who were loyal to Great Britain during the Revolution, comprised about one third of the population of the thirteen revolting colonies. In Georgia and South Carolina they were a majority; in New England and Virginia a minority; elsewhere they were more or less evenly matched by the patriots. Included in their ranks were all classes: great landowners such as the DeLanceys, Jessups and Philipses of New York; rich merchants like the Whartons and Pembertons of Philadelphia, and the Higgins and Chandlers of Boston; large numbers of professional men—lawyers, physicians and teachers; prosperous farmers; crown officials and Anglican clergy and laity; and dependents of loyalist merchants and landlords. While a few of the more conservative stood for the rigid execution of imperial law, the majority opposed the objectionable acts of the British Parliament, served on the early extralegal committees and were not hostile to the calling of the first Continental Congress[v] in 1774, in fact working hard to elect delegates of their own convictions to it. Although anxious to maintain their rights by means of petition and legal protest, and in some cases not even averse to a show of force, they were strongly opposed to separation from the British Empire. The Declaration of Independence[v] gave finality to their position.

Before April, 1775, few efforts were made to arrest or suppress the loyalists, but after the battle of Lexington[v] the war fervor rapidly grew more intense. Great numbers of loyalists flocked to the royal colors or, in a few instances, organized militia companies of their own under commissions from the crown. Although they probably contributed 60,000 soldiers, yet much to the disappointment of the British authorities their military service was not commensurate with their numerical strength, their only outstanding exploits being an expedition against the coast towns of Connecticut; frontier raids in conjunction with the Indians; and a savage guerrilla warfare between patriot and loyalist in the South.

As the struggle progressed the patriots resorted to more and more drastic measures against the loyalists. All who refused to take an oath of allegiance to the new governments were denied the rights of citizenship, and could not vote, hold office or enjoy court protection. In many cases they were forbidden to pursue professions, or to acquire or dispose of property. Free speech was denied them, and they were not allowed to communicate with the British. When these laws failed to accomplish their purpose, the more ardent loyalists were jailed, put on parole, sent to detention camps, and tarred and feathered[*]. Nearly all of the new state governments eventually enacted legislation banishing those who refused to swear allegiance. Before the war was over probably 200,000 loyalists died, were exiled, or became voluntary refugees to other parts of the Empire—a large number of citizens for struggling frontier communities to lose.

To banishment was added confiscation of property. In the early days of the Revolution Thomas Paine advised confiscation of loyalist property to defray the expenses of the war, and several states followed this suggestion. The definition of treason by Congress on June 24, 1770, supplied a legal basis for action. Late in 1777 Congress advised the states to confiscate and sell the real and personal property of those who had forfeited "the right of protection" and to invest the proceeds in Continental certificates. Although some of the more conservative patriots protested that confiscation was "contrary to the principles of civil liberty," statutes of condemnation and forfeiture were enacted in all the states before the end of the war.

Many persons were inevitably the victims of private grudges and persecution. Evidence abounds that the execution of the sequestration laws was frequently attended with scandal and corruption. The amount of property seized is uncertain. Claims totaling £10,000,000, however, were filed with the commission established by the British Parliament, and less than £1,000,000 were disallowed (*see* British Debts).

On the whole, throughout the conflict the loyalists lacked organization and good leadership. They were conservatives who were suspicious of the innovations demanded by a crisis. The triumph of the patriots accentuated their hesitancy. They had placed implicit trust in the invincibility of the British army, and the unexpected development of the conflict dazed them.

All things taken into consideration, the treatment of the loyalists was moderate and fair. The period was one in which the most bitter and most harsh human emotions were aroused—a civil war within a state. Although the laws of banishment and sequestration were severe, there was no such slaughter and terrorism as prevailed in the French Revolution, and surprising care was taken to make sure that punishment of loyalists was carried out only in accord with law.

[C. H. Van Tyne, *The Loyalists in the American Revolution;* A. C. Flick, *History of the State of New York*, Vol. III.]

                                        A. C. FLICK

Ludlow Resolution. This proposed constitutional amendment was a by-product of the Senate Munitions Investigation (1934) and the keep-America-out-of-war movement which culminated in the Neutrality Acts[*] of 1935–37. Proceeding on the theory that the people who have to do the fighting should make the decision, this proposal limited the power of Congress by requiring a popular referendum to ratify a declaration of war except in case of actual attack on the United States or its outlying territories. First introduced in 1935 by Representative Louis Ludlow, Democrat, of Indiana, it grew steadily in popularity, and only strenuous efforts by the F. D. Roosevelt administration prevented its coming to a final vote in the House in January, 1938.

[Stephen and Joan Raushenbush, *The Final Choice, America between Europe and Asia;* and *New York Times,* Jan. 11, 1938, p. 1:1.]   HAROLD H. SPROUT

Ludlow's Code (1650). A common complaint of the early colonists was that, in the absence of an established body of laws, the decisions of the magistrates tended to be capricious. To meet this situation the General Court[*] of Connecticut in 1646 requested Roger Ludlow, a member of the court and trained in the English law, to compile a body of laws for the Commonwealth. The result was Ludlow's Code of 1650 which, under seventy-eight headings, established the law of the colony—prefaced by the assurance that no man's life, reputation or goods should be endangered "unless it be by the virtue or equity of some express law of the country warranting the same, established by a General Court, and sufficiently published. . . ." Though many times revised, this code remains as the foundation of the laws of the State of Connecticut.

[*Colonial Records of Connecticut*, 1636-1665, pp. 509-563.]

R. V. COLEMAN

Lumber Industry, THE. Making lumber began with the first colonists, and one of the earliest commercial sawmills was operated by water of the Salmon Falls River in South Berwick Township, Maine, in 1631. But the industry remained a purely local business until shortly after 1800, when, because of its natural advantages, Bangor, Maine, became the first of the great "lumber cities." By 1840 Bangor was making boards and timbers for the world.

The first quest was for white pine only, and when this species became scarce in New England the lumberjacks moved westward, pausing briefly in New York and Pennsylvania before attacking the vast stands in Michigan. From 1869 to 1885 Michigan dominated the industry. Wisconsin came next, and when its pine was gone (about 1904), the lumberjacks migrated to two regions— the South and the Pacific Northwest. Since about 1920 lumber production has centered in the latter region.

Aggregate production, 1801–1935, of six leading states is estimated by the United States Forest Service in millions of feet as follows: Washington, 187,500; Michigan, 182,800; Wisconsin, 134,700; Pennsylvania, 126,100; Louisiana, 117,700; Oregon, 102,500.

Technically, the industry was backward. Oxen and horses, augmented by rivers for "driving" logs, were the chief motive power for logging until 1890, when steam donkey engines were introduced; and logging railroads took the place of rivers. Today, the steam engine and the locomotive are being replaced by the caterpillar tractor and the gasoline-driven truck.

Sawmills adopted steam power long before it was used in the logging woods. By 1836 there were thirty-six steam-powered sawmills in Maine. Invention of the circular saw brought greatly increased mill capacity. Other improvements quickly followed. Modern sawmills are comparatively automatic, requiring few men to operate, and there are many large plants which can cut 1,000,-000 board feet of lumber in eight hours.

Waste marked the lumber industry until well into the 20th century. Timber was cheap, in fact, a nuisance to those who wanted farms. The Federal and state governments sold it cheaply, gave it to homesteaders, and granted it to road, canal and railway companies[qw]. Homesteaders[w] were urged to cut and pile their trees and to burn them. Many lumber concerns were involved

in timber "scandals." This condition obtained until after 1900, when the Government started acquiring lands for its National Forests and Parks[qw].

The loss of markets, due to the inroads of other building materials, has brought about a "conservation" that is no less real because it was enforced. Peak of lumber production was in 1906 and totaled 45,000,000,000 feet. In 1935 it was 18,000,000,000 feet. During the same period per capita lumber consumption dropped from 523 feet to 135 feet.

Since 1920 actual conservation of timber has made great strides. States have followed the Government in acquiring forests. Many large private concerns have adopted a policy of "sustained yield" and maintain tree nurseries from which stock is taken for planting on ground not suitable to natural reforestation[w]. All agencies are active in fire prevention and suppression.

[Ovid Butler, ed., *American Conservation;* Stewart H. Holbrook, *Holy Old Mackinaw, A Natural History of the American Lumberjack.*]

STEWART H. HOLBROOK

Lumber Rafts. Both logs and lumber have been moved by means of rafts. Lumber was rafted from Penobscot River sawmills to tidewater at Bangor in the late 18th century; and later, on many streams as far west as the Mississippi. The great period of lumber rafting was during the latter part of the 19th century when many billions of feet were moved down the Mississippi to St. Louis from the mills in Wisconsin and Minnesota. The trip from LaCrosse, Wis., to St. Louis averaged sixteen days.

The earliest attempt to build an ocean-going raft was made in 1791 at Bath, Maine, when Dr. James Tupper sought to take squared timbers to England by that method. It was not successful, nor were later attempts to bring log rafts from Halifax to Boston. The sea pounded them to pieces. In 1906, however, Simon Benson and his crew of Portland, Ore., devised a cigar-shaped raft of logs that made the 1200-mile voyage from the Columbia River to San Diego, Calif., without trouble. Since then more than 100 similar but much larger rafts have been moved. They average 835 feet in length, draw 28 feet of water and are bound with 175 tons of chain. Each contains enough material "to build an entire village."

[Stewart H. Holbrook, *Holy Old Mackinaw, A Natural History of the American Lumberjack.*]

STEWART H. HOLBROOK

"Lunatic Fringe" was a phrase used by Theodore Roosevelt in his *Autobiography* to characterize the "foolish fanatics," such as extreme pacifists, "who form the lunatic fringe in all re-form movements." The term has since been used by journalists to describe "crack-pots" and "rab-ble-rousers" who proclaim impractical schemes.

STANLEY R. PILLSBURY

Lundy's Lane, Battle at (July 25, 1814). Three weeks after his victory at Chippewa*, Maj. Gen. Jacob Brown's invading army encountered the British under Riall at Lundy's Lane, in Canada near Bridgewater and Niagara Falls. Winfield Scott's First Brigade failed to carry the position in a frontal attack and was reinforced by Ripley's and Porter's brigades. Jesup, with the 25th Infantry, executed a turning movement, driving in the British left and capturing Riall himself. Lt. Gen. Drummond, arriving with reinforce-ments, took command. Protracted and savage fighting ensued. Miller's 21st United States Infantry stormed the hill and took the British artillery, the Americans repulsing determined counterattacks until midnight. Brown and Scott, both severely wounded, withdrew. Ripley, left in command, brought off the army when ammu-nition failed, but lacking horses, abandoned the captured cannon. Both sides claimed victory, but Drummond remained in possession of the field. Losses were heavy, the British 30%, American slightly less.

[B. J. Lossing, *Pictorial Field-Book of the War of 1812;* E. A. Cruikshank, *The Battle of Lundy's Lane.*]

CHARLES WINSLOW ELLIOTT

Lusitania, **Sinking of the.** The Cunard liner *Lusitania* was sunk without warning by the German submarine U-20 off Old Head of Kinsale, Ireland, on May 7, 1915. Of the 1959 passengers and crew, 1198 perished, including 128 (out of 197) Americans. Since on May 1, the day of sail-ing, the German embassy in Washington had published an advertisement in American papers warning Atlantic travelers that they sailed in British or Allied ships at their own risk, it was widely believed that the sinking was premedi-tated. The log of the U-20, published years later (*Journal of Modern History,* VIII), shows, how-ever, that the submarine had sunk other ships, met the *Lusitania* by chance, and sank her from fear of being rammed. The ship carried 4200 cases of small-arms ammunition and 1250 shrap-nel cases, this being allowed by American law; this cargo, stored well forward, about 150 feet from the spot where the torpedo struck, may have exploded and contributed to the rapid (eighteen minutes) sinking of the ship. A thor-ough examination prior to sailing revealed no evidence that the liner was armed. Why the captain of the ship had reduced speed, failed to follow a zig-zag course and kept close to shore, in violation of orders from the British admiralty, was not satisfactorily explained.

The catastrophe created intense indignation in the United States. On Feb. 10, 1915, the Amer-ican Government had denied the legality of sub-marine warfare (as practised by Germany) and had warned that it would hold the German gov-ernment to "a strict accountability" for the ob-servance of American rights on the high seas. In May, President Wilson resisted considerable pop-ular clamor for war (chiefly in the East), and in three successive notes (May 13, June 9, July 21, 1915) demanded that Germany make repara-tion for and disavow the sinking; the last note concluded with the statement that a repetition of the act "must be regarded by the Government of the United States, when they affect American citizens, as deliberately unfriendly." Secretary of State Bryan thought the American demands too severe and likely to lead to war, and resigned on June 8. The German government agreed to make reparation and eventually gave a promise (after the sinking of the *Arabic*) that liners would not be sunk without warning and without safety for the lives of noncombatants; but it steadfastly refused to disavow the sinking of the *Lusitania.* No settlement of this question was reached be-fore the United States entered the World War*.

[*Papers Relating to the Foreign Relations of the United States,* 1915, supplement, *The World War;* Charles Sey-mour, *American Diplomacy and the World War;* T. A. Bailey, The Sinking of the Lusitania, *American Historical Review,* Vol. XLI.]

BERNADOTTE E. SCHMITT

Lusk Committee, THE, was authorized in 1919 by the New York legislature and headed by state senator Clayton R. Lusk. It published a monu-mental report of 4450 pages on radical and sedi-tious activities.

[*Revolutionary Radicalism,* Report of the Joint Legisla-tive Committee of the State of New York Investigat-ing Seditious Activities.]

W. BROOKE GRAVES

Luther v. Borden (7 How. 1, 1848) was an at-tempt to make the Supreme Court decide be-tween the old government and the "convention" government in Rhode Island (*see* Dorr's Rebel-lion). Chief Justice Taney's opinion evaded that issue, recognized state law and state courts as completely competent, and declared existing state authority legally empowered to use martial methods to maintain itself against violence. (*See also* Martial Law.)

[Charles Warren, *Supreme Court in United States His-tory.*]

ELBRIDGE COLBY

Lutherans, THE, one of the largest denominational families in the United States, contained in 1937 thirteen separate bodies with a membership of 4,454,373. The Dutch in New York and the Swedes on the Delaware formed the first Lutheran congregations in America. Of much greater importance, however, was the large 18th-century German immigration. Congregations began to be formed among these German settlers as early as 1703, Daniel Falckner being one of the first Lutheran ministers among them. Salzburg*qv* Lutherans settled in Georgia in 1734. The outstanding personality among colonial Lutherans was Henry Melchior Mühlenberg who came to America in 1742. Through his influence the first Lutheran Synod, the Ministerium of Pennsylvania, was formed in 1748.

The first national Lutheran organization, the General Synod, dates from 1820, the earlier synods being state organizations. The Civil War caused the formation of the United Synod of the South, and in 1867 the more conservative element withdrew to form the General Council. In 1918 these divisions were healed when the United Lutheran Church was organized.

The large influx of Germans after 1830 and the great immigration from Scandinavian countries after 1860 resulted in the formation of numerous independent Lutheran bodies, their maintenance as separate bodies being largely due to language differences. The principal German bodies are the Missouri Synod, the Wisconsin Synod, and the American Lutheran Church formed in 1930 through the merger of three independent synods. The largest Scandinavian churches are the Norwegian Synod, the Augustana (Swedish) Synod and the United Danish Synod.

All the Lutheran bodies maintain colleges and theological seminaries and several of the more conservative synods have important parochial school systems. Altogether, American Lutherans support more than 100 periodicals and maintain numerous boards of missions, education and other charities.

[A. R. Wentz, *The Lutheran Church in American History;* G. M. Stephenson, *The Religious Aspects of Swedish Immigration;* H. E. Jacobs, *A History of the Evangelical Lutheran Church in the United States.*]   WILLIAM W. SWEET

Lyceum Movement, THE, was an important phase of the early adult education and public school*qv* movements. It was begun by an article in the *American Journal of Education* (October, 1826) by Josiah Holbrook, containing a plan of a "Society for Mutual Education." The first society was organized by Holbrook in November, 1826, at Millbury, Mass. Within a year more than

a dozen lyceums had sprung up in Worcester County, Mass., and in Windham County, Conn. The movement was endorsed by a meeting of eminent Bostonians, presided over by Daniel Webster (1828). By 1831 lyceums existed in all the New England states and in northern New York. State lyceums were organized in 1831 in Massachusetts, Maine and New York. The same year, the New York State Lyceum called a meeting in New York City to organize a national lyceum. Holbrook journeyed as far west as Missouri, and found active interest in the Western states, including Kentucky and Tennessee. National lyceums were held each year until 1839, although often poorly attended. The town lyceums, estimated by Holbrook at 3000 in 1835, were the heart of the movement. Their number probably increased greatly thereafter. After 1840 the main emphasis was upon self-improvement by means of lectures, readings and discussions on science, literature, morality, etc. Politics and religion were generally avoided because of their controversial nature, but the lyceums often developed interest in topics which later became political issues, such as slavery and prohibition. (*See also* Lecturing.)

The lyceums continued to grow until the early 20th century. In 1915 their number was estimated at 12,000. In 1924–25, it was found that they existed mostly in small towns and gave mostly semipopular music and "sanitated vaudeville." Besides improving the public schools and giving a supplementary education to those unable to attend high school or college, the early lyceums led to certain permanent institutions, such as Lowell Institute and Brooklyn Institute. A Lyceum Village was founded at Berea, Ohio (*ca.* 1837–42). Holbrook conducted a Central Lyceum Bureau (1842–49). In 1867–68 a number of commercial lecture bureaus were founded, among them the Boston Lyceum and Musical Bureau of J. C. Redpath, whose successor, J. B. Pond, was a successful lecture promoter. Some lyceums developed into historical or literary societies, public libraries, or museums. Later the same idea was developed by the chautauqua movement and women's clubs*qv*.

[C. B. Hayes, *The American Lyceum.*]
W. C. MALLALIEU

Lygonia was a grant, commonly called the Plough Patent, made by the Council for New England*qv*, June 26, 1630, of an area forty miles square, west of the Kennebec River. Settlement by the original grantees having failed, the grant was purchased, April 7, 1643, by Sir Alexander Rigby, an influential member of Parliament, whose interest had been aroused by George Cleeve, whom he appointed deputy president of the province. Cleeve was involved in a bitter quarrel, over land, with John Winter, agent of the Trelawney plantation[w], and the revival of the dormant Lygonia patent gave him not only a legal basis for his own defense but actually placed the Trelawney grant within his jurisdiction. The Rigby title was confirmed March 27, 1647, by the Warwick Commission[w]. Thus Sir Ferdinando Gorges[w] was deprived of over half of his Province of Maine, including Saco, Black Point, Spurwink, Richmond's Island and Casco. Litigation between Gorges' deputy governor and Cleeve was a chief cause of the difficulties of Gorges' government in its formative years, while Cleeve's constant appeals to Massachusetts Bay[w] for aid paved the way for that colony's expansion northward to include jurisdiction over Lygonia in 1658 (see Maine under Massachusetts). The records of the province have disappeared and only a few official documents dealing with its brief history have survived. The king's commissioners of 1664 did not recognize the legality of the Rigby claim, and, in 1686, Edward Rigby, Alexander's grandson and heir, filed a claim with Massachusetts which was not accepted. In 1691 the new Massachusetts charter put an end to the Province of Lygonia.

[James Phinney Baxter, *George Cleeve of Casco Bay.*]
ROBERT E. MOODY

Lyman's Colony. *See* Georgiana.

Lynching, or the extralegal execution of an offender by a mob, has long been practised in the United States. The word is thought to have been derived from a Virginian named Lynch, who in Revolutionary times led a small organization which meted out punishment to desperadoes and Tories. Under frontier conditions, when regular law enforcement agencies were weak or lacking, lynching served as a substitute method of social control. In the South, however, lynching has crystallized into a traditional method of summary execution, particularly of Negro offenders against white people.

Fairly reliable statistical data on lynching have been available only since 1882. A compilation made at Tuskegee Institute and published in *The Negro Year Book* shows that from 1882 to 1936 there were 4672 persons lynched in the United States, of whom 3383 were Negroes and 1289 were whites. All states except the six New England states had one or more lynchings during this period and all except eleven lynched one or more Negroes. Although the annual number of lynchings fluctuates considerably, the trend has been consistently downward for the past forty years. The annual average number of lynchings was 154 for the decade 1890–99; 31 for the decade 1920–29; and 15 for the period 1930–37. Lynching tends more and more to be confined to the South and to Negro victims. Whereas from 1890 to 1899, 13% of the lynchings were outside the South, since 1930 fewer than 5% have been outside. In the decade of 1890–99, 72% of mob victims were Negroes but in the period 1930–37, 91% were Negroes.

In the list of offenses resulting in lynching from 1882 to 1937 homicide led, accounting for 41% of the cases; rape and attempted rape accounted for about 25%; and relatively trivial offenses figured in over 10% of the lynchings.

[J. E. Cutler, *Lynch-Law*; W. F. White, *Rope and Faggot*; M. N. Work, *The Negro Year Book.*]
GUY B. JOHNSON

Lynching Legislation. Generally speaking, the states have relied on ordinary homicide laws for the prosecution of members of lynch mobs. The record indicates, however, that neither these laws nor special state laws have had any substantial effect. In over 99% of the lynching cases there have been no arrests, indictments or convictions. Since almost three fourths of all lynched persons have been Negroes, the National Association for the Advancement of Colored People[w] has persistently demanded national legislation to deal with the matter. The Dyer antilynching bill passed the House in 1922, but failed in the Senate. The campaign was carried on, reaching a climax in 1937 when no less than fifty-nine antilynching bills were introduced in Congress. One of these, the Gavagan bill, passed the House. In 1938 what was known as the Wagner-Van Nuys bill failed in the Senate because of a filibuster conducted by senators from Southern states, who argued that states' rights[w] would be violated by its enactment. The proposed bills provided for Federal prosecution of offenders; fine or imprisonment, or both, for negligent local officers; and indemnity to be paid by the county to the family of a lynched person, if official negligence were proved.

[James Harmon Chadbourn, *Lynching and the Law*; Black's White, *Time*, Vol. XXXI, No. 4.]
ERIK McKINLEY ERIKSSON

Lyon, Fort (Colo.), was built near Bent's[w] new fort on the Arkansas River, thirty-eight miles below Bent's old fort, destroyed in 1852. It was named successively Fort Fauntleroy, Fort Wise and Fort Lyon, the last after the hero of Wilson's Creek[w]. In 1866 the river cut the banks so that Fort Lyon was moved twenty miles upstream to its present site, two miles below the mouth of the Purgatoire.

[George Bird Grinnell, Bent's Old Fort and Its Builders, *Kansas State Historical Society Collections*, Vol. XV.]

PAUL I. WELLMAN

Macadam Roads. *See* Hard Roads.

Macdonough's Fleet on Lake Champlain. When Lt. Thomas Macdonough took command of the American naval force on Lake Champlain, Sept. 12, 1812, it consisted of two gunboats. By acquisition and construction he gradually built it up to approximately a dozen active vessels, two or three of which compared favorably with some of the famous seagoing war craft of the period. After a few minor brushes with the enemy, in which no serious damage was done to either side, Macdonough went into winter quarters at Vergennes on Otter Creek to prepare for the 1814 campaign. A heavy English attack by land and water from Canada was pending. Ships were built and stores accumulated to meet it. To maintain control of the lake was imperative. On April 14 the British fleet appeared off the mouth of Otter Creek, but was driven away by a land battery. The British advance came in September. Macdonough met the English fleet, Sept. 11, 1814, off Cumberland Head, near Plattsburg[qv], where between 15,000 and 20,000 British and American troops had joined battle. The American fleet consisted of fourteen battle craft, mounting eighty-six guns and carrying 882 men. The English had sixteen fighting vessels, ninety-two guns and approximately 937 men. The fight, one of the most bitter naval engagements of the war, was won by Macdonough through superior seamanship and strategy.

[Theodore Roosevelt, *Naval War of 1812*.]

LEON W. DEAN

Macedonian. In 1821 Chilean forces in southern Peru under Lord Cochrane seized $70,400 in silver from the captain of the American merchant ship *Macedonian,* asserting that it was Spanish property. Twenty years later the United States submitted a claim for repayment. After a long diplomatic controversy, the matter was arbitrated by the King of Belgium, who, on May 15, 1863, awarded the American owners three fifths of the amount claimed.

[J. B. Moore, *International Arbitrations*, Vol. II.]

DANA G. MUNRO

Machault, Fort, was built on the site of Franklin, Pa. (*see* Venango, Pa.), in 1754, by the French under Chabert Joncaire, as a link in their chain of communications from Lake Erie to the Ohio. With other small posts in western Pennsylvania it was abandoned when the loss of Fort Niagara[qv], 1759, cut off communications with Canada.

[F. H. Severance, *An Old Frontier of France.*]

SOLON J. BUCK

Machine, Party, is the term employed in American politics to convey an unfavorable impression regarding a given party organization. It was claimed that certain of the delegates to the Republican National Convention which nominated Grant in 1872 became conscious of the fact that the management of the party had passed into the hands of the officeholders and that a party machine was being formed to exclude party members from the control of the party. The New York *Nation* made use of this term during the 1870's.

Writing in the 1880's, Theodore Roosevelt indicated that outsiders nicknamed the party organizations "machines" because of the "clockwork regularity and efficiency with which they played their parts, alike for good and for evil." He pointed out that the term was one of reproach because the party organizations were run by the leaders very largely as business concerns to benefit themselves and their followers, with little regard to the community at large. In the same decade, Bryce described American party machines at great length, stressing as an outstanding characteristic the perversion by rings and bosses[qv] of the nominating machinery of primaries and of conventions by fraud and trickery.

In more recent times the term has been employed as a general label of opprobrium. In New York the Republicans and the reform groups refer to the Tammany Hall[qv] machine; in Philadelphia the Democrats and independents refer to the Republican machine, and in or near Wisconsin the conservative newspapers refer to the LaFollette machine. Any political faction which maintains rigid discipline and holds power for a considerable length of time is likely to be called a machine by the opposing groups.

The most common use of the term is to describe city, county or state party oligarchies led by ruthless political bosses who collaborate with officeholders, gangsters, election crooks, unscrupulous lawyers and businessmen to manipulate the confused and apathetic voters by special favors, fraud and force.

The type of political organization that is now called a machine emerged at the beginning of American national history. Orth points out that Aaron Burr was organizing Tammany Hall into a party machine at the time that Thomas Jefferson was making his bid for political power. The Clintons constructed the first state machine in

New York during the same era. Following in their footsteps. Martin Van Buren established an efficient party organization which won the title "Albany Regency."[qv]

The territorial expansion of the United States westward, the broadening of the franchise, the death of the caucus[qv] and the rise of the convention system[qv] for making nominations, the adoption of a four-year term for appointive offices and the growing specialization in business and politics were among the influences which brought about the widespread use of the machine methods in our national affairs. Beginning with the "Kitchen Cabinet"[qv] of Jackson, the devices of political manipulation have been employed more or less in national politics ever since.

However, it is not in national politics that the party machine has reached its fullest development. As the industrial revolution progressed, urban communities began to multiply and expand at a rapid rate. The development of new municipal services, the growth of municipal public utilities[qv] and the need for their regulation, the rise of a new urban plutocracy based upon the exploitation of rising land values and urban improvements, the flooding of the cities by peasant immigrants from abroad, and waning interest of the older families in political affairs afforded the machine politicians unequalled opportunities. In New York City from the days of Wood and Tweed[qv] there has been a continuous line of political bosses and party machines. The longest reign was that of Boss Murphy, who controlled the political destinies of the metropolis for twenty years. In many other cities the experience of New York was duplicated on a smaller scale. Philadelphia had its Vare machine[qv], Cincinnati its Cox, Pittsburgh its Magee, Chicago its Nash, New Orleans its Behrman, Boston its Lomasney and Kansas City its Pendergast.

Certain conditions in America have aided the establishment and perpetuation of party machines by professional politicians. The huge size of the electorate, the long ballot, the technical character of the voting arrangements, the multiplicity of elections, the small size of the election districts, the single member district system with its accompanying abuses of gerrymandering[qv] and rotten boroughs, the lack of adequate safeguards against fraud, the disparity between economic and political power and the widespread use of direct and indirect bribery as a technique for gaining power, the spoils[qv] tradition, the theory of rotation in office[qv], the presence of poorly assimilated minority groups, and the lack of civic pride are all factors which have played into the hands of the political bosses.

In any democratic country there must be a well-trained body of party workers who are willing to perform the routine tasks of the electoral process such as canvassing, circulating petitions, holding neighborhood meetings, addressing envelopes, distributing literature, looking after the technical details of the election process and getting out the vote. In the United States those who do this work expect some kind of concrete reward in the form of money, jobs or favors. Campaign funds (see Campaign Resources and Uses) are raised by levying upon officeholders and candidates, businessmen who are in a vulnerable position, underworld leaders who wish to be protected against police interference, labor union officials who wish to gain special privileges and others who might respond to appeals or pressure. Party funds and political jobs are distributed by those party leaders who have been successful in nominating their candidates at primary elections or in the party conventions. These bosses and their adherents have shrewdly observed that if they divide the spoils into small enough parts, a great many individual citizens may be put under personal obligations to them. As a result of the many favors which the machine can perform, its agents are able to get a hearing when they come to ask for votes.

[S. P. Orth, *The Boss and the Machine;* J. Bryce, *The American Commonwealth;* L. Steffens, *Autobiography.*]

HAROLD F. GOSNELL

Machine Guns. The inventions and most of the improvements of machine guns have been made by Americans—Gatling[qv], Hotchkiss, Gardner, Maxim[qv], Benet, Lewis, Browning and Thompson.

A few Gatlings were used in the Civil War, four were employed effectively at Santiago (*see* Spanish-American War). For several years prior to 1917 each regiment of infantry and cavalry had a platoon of two machine guns—Maxims, Benet-Mercie or Lewis.

During the World War each infantry regiment had a company of twelve guns and each division two animal-drawn battalions of four companies each and one motorized battalion of two companies—total of 168 guns per division. The machine guns became the backbone of the defense and important auxiliaries in the attack. In 1938 a division had 211 machine guns and 780 automatic rifles, all Brownings. The "streamlined" division, adopted 1939, contains 108 light (cal. .30), 150 heavy (cal. .30) and 18 caliber .50 Brownings; also 111 Browning automatic rifles. The machine gun now is a major weapon in war.

WALTER C. SHORT

Machines. It will be convenient here to consider the machine as a power-operated device as distinguished from the prime mover which translates energy into power. Thus examples of the machine will be the loom, the gin, the typesetter rather than the steam engine, the electric motor, etc.

The development of the machine in the United States was retarded by the dominance of agriculture and the consequent delay in the industrial revolution[w]. Other factors in this delay were transportation needs, England's colonial policy projected in her attitude toward the new nation and the slow exploitation of native iron.

In the earliest phase, however, appear the beginnings of the prevailing American trend toward machines for mass production[w]. In the last quarter of the 18th century came nail-making machines, Oliver Evans' epoch-making machine for the manufacture of wool cards which combined three operations, Evans' flour mill which has been described as possibly "the first instance of an uninterrupted process of mechanical manufacture, from raw material to finished product, in the history of industry." (Clark, I, 179.) At the end of the century, Eli Whitney designed the interchangeable parts[w] system which laid the basis for mass production of machines. At about the same time, the textile industry[w] became successful as a result of two events: the reproduction (from 1790) in Rhode Island of the Arkwright[w] spinning machinery by the English immigrant, Samuel Slater, and the invention of the cotton gin[w] by Eli Whitney (1792–93). This success greatly stimulated the invention of labor-saving machines.

In the next phase, the stimulus to American industry given by the Napoleonic wars when importation ceased was nullified by the flood of imported manufactures after 1815, and the resulting financial depression (see Panic of 1819). During this period, however, notable achievements were made in transportation machinery (from 1830) and farm machinery[w] beginning with the McCormick reaper[w] (1831). Other inventions, such as the profile lathe (1818), the power loom for wire weaving (1826), the power knitting machine (1832), the shoe-pegging machine (1833), pin and match-making machinery (1842) and the turret lathe (from 1845), laid the foundations for the great industrial recovery of the 1850's. In this decade, the sewing machine[w] (from 1846) established the garment and shoe industries on a large scale.

With the Civil War over, large transportation systems established and the steel industry in operation, mechanization advanced rapidly. In the later period, concentration was on increased automaticity, efficiency, adaptation and arrangement rather than on basic invention. While there were brilliant exceptions in such machines as the typewriter[w] (1868), typesetters and casters (from 1884) and web presses (from 1865) as well as certain domestic labor savers, most mechanization developed through the adaptation of older or foreign inventions to cheap mass production. It was this genius for improvement and adaptation which brought the United States into world leadership in industry. A striking illustration is in automobile[w] manufacture. Here an assembly of foreign inventions, the motor vehicle, is manufactured by machine tools largely invented abroad, adapted to the American interchangeable parts system and co-ordinated by the American assembly line. The result is that more than 75% of the world's automotive vehicles are produced in the United States. Similar situations have developed in the production of locomotives, electric motors and equipment, internal combustion engines and plumbing devices, all basic European inventions.

Important factors in American mechanical advance have been rigid standardization and extreme simplification. The co-operation of industries, aided by government regulation, has resulted in a set of rules and standards for the manufacture of machine parts. The application of the "Taylor System" (see Industrial Management) brought about simplification not only in machine design, but especially in arrangement and co-ordination of machinery, industrial organization and manufacturing method.

What has been called the "second industrial revolution" began with electrification (see Electricity, Utilization of). With the use of a separate motor for each machine unit, old belts, shafts and gearing incident to steam power disappeared, resulting in increased cleanliness, safety, ease of control, economy of space and power. As machines became more compact, the science of metallurgy provided the new steel and aluminum alloys, new case hardening methods and other matters to decrease weight and increase durability. Another phase of this revolution is the use of water-power generators and the long-distance transmission of current.

With the new so-called revolution have come certain opposing economic and social factors. One is the rapid obsolescence of machines under revolutionary changes. The extent of this may be estimated from a survey made in 1935 showing that, due to changes in machine design, metalworking machinery becomes obsolete within ten years. No adequate solution has yet been found,

Another factor is unemployment[w] caused by increased automaticity. Specific examples of this are the bottle-making machine (1903) and the cotton picker (1936).

Several philosophies have grown up about this latter problem. One, technocracy[w], has proposed readjustment of working hours. Another school teaches that, as in the past, the slack will always be taken up by increased production. A group which might be designated as the "Frankenstein school" believes that mechanization has brought us to a destructive materialism, while an opposing philosophy contends that the machine has elevated mankind by lessening the burden of manual labor.

[R. Burlingame, *March of the Iron Men;* National Resources Committee, *Technological Trends and National Policy;* V. S. Clark, *History of Manufactures in the United States;* J. W. Roe, *English and American Tool Builders;* A. P. Usher, *A History of Mechanical Inventions;* G. and D. Bathe, *Oliver Evans;* J. N. Leonard, *Tools of Tomorrow;* W. Bowden, *Industrial History of the United States.*]

ROGER BURLINGAME

Mackenzie's Treaty (1831). Kenneth Mackenzie, director of the Upper Missouri Outfit of Astor's American Fur Company[w], anxious to keep the rich domain under his governorship open to his traders, arranged a peace between warring Indian tribes. This treaty between Blackfeet and Assiniboins[qw] was signed at Fort Union[w] in 1831. It pledged the two tribes and certain related groups to perpetual peace, thus opening a large section of the Upper Missouri Country to exploitation by the American Fur Company.

[H. M. Chittenden, *History of the Fur Trade in the Far West.*]

THEODORE G. GRONERT

Mackerel Fisheries, The, occupy a place in the development of New England of only less prominence than that of the cod fisheries[w]. The first public free school, opened in 1671, received aid directly from the profits of the mackerel fishery of Cape Cod. Mackerel supported the codfish in supplying a profitable trade with the West Indies[w] that became very important during the 18th century. However, the taking of the mackerel lagged far behind the cod until after the conclusion of the Convention of 1818[w] with England. The failure of this instrument to provide facilities for the mackerel fisheries became an important factor in the fisheries question when Americans began sending large mackerel fleets to the Gulf of St. Lawrence. In 1840 Gloucester passed Boston as the leading mackerel port. To Gloucester went the credit for the introduction of such improvements as the clipper fishing schooner. The adoption about the middle of the century of the purse-seine enabled the mackerel vessels to fish profitably off the New England coast. Fishing vessels also went as far south as Cape Hatteras to take mackerel. The fisheries reached their height in the decade from 1880 to 1890, after which they suffered an abrupt decline. The varying abundance of the fish from time to time has often determined the extent of the industry.

[G. B. Goode and others, *Materials for a History of the Mackerel Fishery;* Raymond McFarland, *A History of the New England Fisheries.*]

F. HARDEE ALLEN

Mackinac. *See* Michilimackinac.

Mackinaw Boat, a light, strongly built, flat-bottomed boat, pointed at both ends, utilized for travel, more especially for transportation of goods, on the rivers of the interior of the continent. Mackinaw boats varied greatly in size; they were commonly propelled by oars, and when conditions permitted, by a sail. Apparently the Mackinaw boat was adapted from the Indian Northwest canoe, long the favorite vehicle of the fur trader and explorer.

[Henry R. Schoolcraft, *Narrative Journal of Travels through the Northwestern Regions of the United States . . . in 1820;* Charles Larpenteur, *Forty Years a Fur Trader on the Upper Missouri;* Mrs. Juliette Kinzie, *Wau Bun: the "Early Day" in the Northwest.*]

M. M. QUAIFE

Macomb Purchase, The. In accordance with an act of the legislature for the sale and disposition of lands of the State of New York, Alexander Macomb contracted with the commissioners in 1791, for the purchase of 3,635,200 acres of land in the present counties of St. Lawrence, Franklin, Jefferson, Lewis and Oswego at eight pence per acre. The application was accepted and a patent issued to Macomb who, soon becoming financially embarrassed, deeded the tract to William Constable and others.

[E. B. O'Callaghan, *Documentary History of New York,* Vol. III.]

ROBERT W. BINGHAM

Macon, Fort (N. C.), Capture of (April 26, 1862). In April, 1861, North Carolina state troops seized this fort. A year later, besieged by Burnside's (U.) combined land and sea force from March 23 to April 26, the Confederates surrendered.

[*Battles and Leaders of the Civil War,* Vol. I.]

ROBERT S. THOMAS

Macon, The. *See* Dirigibles.

Macon's Bill No. 2 was enacted May 1, 1810, for the purpose of compelling Great Britain and

France, the major belligerents, to desist from their illegal seizures of American commercial vessels. Designed as a substitute for the unsuccessful Nonintercourse Act[qv], it forbade British and French armed vessels to use American waters, unless forced in by distress, except for the carrying of dispatches. The measure opened American trade to the entire world. If France removed its restrictions on neutral commerce by March 3, 1811, and Great Britain failed to do likewise within three months, the President should continue to trade with the former and prohibit it with the latter and vice versa.

[*American State Papers, Foreign Relations*, III; *Annals of Congress*, 11th Congress, part 2; *Public Statutes at Large of the United States*, II.]

GEORGE D. HARMON

Madison, Fort, sometimes called Fort Bellevue, was built during the winter and spring of 1808–9, on the west side of the Mississippi River where the city of Fort Madison, Iowa, now stands. Housing a garrison for protection of a government post for Indian trade (*see* Factory System, The Indian) , Fort Madison from its occupation had a precarious existence among tribes which were under the influence of English traders, and suffered repeated attacks both before and during the War of 1812. On Sept. 3, 1813, its garrison, out of firewood, food and ammunition, and closely besieged by hostile Indians, set fire to the buildings and escaped through a trench to boats in the Mississippi.

[Jacob Van der Zee, *Iowa and War*, Old Fort Madison, 7th in series, State Historical Society of Iowa, 1918; Fort Madison, *Annals of Iowa*, Vol. III.]

KATE L. GREGG

Madison County Antislavery War, The. The existing controversy over slavery in Madison County, Ky., became more serious in 1853 and 1855 when Cassius M. Clay, a well-known native Emancipationist, caused Rev. John G. Fee to establish a union church and a school in opposition to slavery at a place later called Berea in the southern part of the county. Naturally this movement was opposed by the slaveowners of the community, and disorder arose. Even Clay disapproved the "higher-law"[qv] teachings of the Bereans and gave them little support after 1856. In 1859 mass meetings were held in Richmond, the county seat, and ten families of Berea were warned to leave the state. Gov. McGoffin refused to protect them and they promptly went to Cincinnati. One of the fugitives returned to the county early in 1860, "and for a time a warfare similar to that previously in Kansas seemed imminent." The work at Berea, however, was resumed in 1865.

[John G. Fee, *Autobiography of John G. Fee;* John A. R. Rogers, *The Birth of Berea;* Cassius M. Clay, *The Life, Memoirs, Writings, and Speeches of Cassius M. Clay;* Jonathan T. Dorris, *Old Cane Springs*.]

JONATHAN T. DORRIS

Madison Square Garden. Gilmore's Concert Garden in New York was remodeled and given this name in 1879. P. T. Barnum bought it in 1880. The old buildings were torn down and a vast new structure erected (1890–91) designed by McKim, Mead & White and topped by St. Gaudens' famous statue of Diana. Great athletic contests, horse shows and balls were held there. This building was demolished in 1925 and the name given to a new one far uptown from Madison Square.

[I. N. Phelps Stokes, *The Iconography of Manhattan Island*.]

ALVIN F. HARLOW

Madison's Island. The name given by Capt. David Porter, U. S. N., to the island of Nukahiva in the Marquesas group. Porter, commanding the U. S. frigate *Essex,* spent several weeks at Nukahiva in 1813, erected a fort and on Nov. 19 formally proclaimed United States sovereignty. The United States never ratified Porter's act of annexation, and the Marquesas Islands became a French colony in 1842.

[David Porter, *Journal of a Cruise Made to the Pacific Ocean by Captain David Porter in the U. S. Frigate Essex, in the Years 1812, 1813, and 1814.*]

JULIUS W. PRATT

Madrid, The Treaty of (1670) , between Spain and Great Britain, provided for peace between the colonial possessions of the respective powers, excluding the subjects of each party from trade and navigation to the other's colonies; thus by implication Spain for the first time recognized the legal existence of British colonies in the New World over which she had hitherto (with Portugal, now annexed to Spain, 1581–1640) asserted a monopoly of sovereignty based on the papal decrees of 1493 and afterward, and the Treaty of Tordesillas[qv] of 1494.

[Francis Gardiner Davenport, *European Treaties Bearing on the History of the United States and Its Dependencies,* Vol. II.]

SAMUEL FLAGG BEMIS

Madrid Conference, The (1880) , was the first international conference arising from imperialistic rivalry in Morocco, an antecedent of the Algeciras Conference[qv]. Great Britain and Spain tried to strengthen the Sultan's government and to limit extraterritorial[qv] rights, especially that of protection to natives in foreign employ. France, backed by Germany, insisted on earlier treaty rights. The conference accomplished little beyond a convention defining current practices. The United States, not closely involved, participated for the first time in a European political conference, partly because of humanitarian interest in the welfare of Moroccan Jews. Secretary Evarts' instructions show a firm but moderate assertion of extraterritorial rights important to the United States in the Far East.

[J. B. Moore, *A Digest of International Law;* S. F. Bemis, *A Diplomatic History of the United States.*]

CHARLES C. GRIFFIN

Mafia Incident, THE (March 14, 1891), caused an interruption of diplomatic relations between the United States and Italy (1891–92). David C. Hennessey, chief of police, was assassinated at the gate of his home in New Orleans (Oct. 15, 1890) by a lurking group of men with sawed-off shotguns. Hennessey had been relentless and courageous in efforts to curb local groups which, using the name made infamous by a Sicilian secret society, Mafia, had a record of a dozen murders. His murder was certainly the work of such a group. Nineteen Italians were indicted, and nine of these were the first put on trial. The case made by the state was overwhelming. Yet the jury brought in a verdict of acquittal for four; there was a mistrial for three; two were cleared by direction of the judge, and by public feeling. There was strong conviction that improper influences had defeated elementary justice. A mass meeting of the most prominent citizens the next morning (Saturday, March 14) denounced this, and marched from Canal and St. Charles streets to the old Parish Prison, on what was then Congo (now Beauregard) Square. Eleven accused Italians were put to death by the leaders of this committee, most of them being shot; the two known to be innocent were not harmed; there was no rioting. President Harrison and Secretary Blaine expressed regrets to Italy, and paid a small indemnity.

[New Orleans *Times-Democrat,* and *Picayune,* of period; John S. Kendall, *History of New Orleans.*]

PIERCE BUTLER

Magazin Royal (1720). *See* Niagara, Carrying Place of.

Magazine Publishing in America began with the almost simultaneous appearance in January, 1741, of Andrew Bradford's *American Magazine, or Monthly View* and Benjamin Franklin's *General Magazine, and Historical Chronicle.* Franklin indignantly alleged that Bradford had stolen his idea. It did not matter very much, since neither lasted out the year, and thereafter American magazine publishing remained a perilous undertaking. Noah Webster observed in 1788 that "the expectation of failure" was "connected with the very name of a Magazine." In spite of this doleful and only too accurate view of the matter, short-lived magazines, largely reprinting British material, continued to increase in number. But it was not until the 19th century that magazine publishing, though always perilous, began to be genuinely profitable in some instances.

The change came as printing processes improved; as education increased both the reading public and the number of authors; and as improved postal organization, with special privileges for periodicals, made it possible to reach readers more easily. Advertising[w] was in the beginning a relatively negligible source of revenue, and as late as 1864 *Harper's* carried none except notices of Harper books. The publishers were greatly insulted when offered $18,000 worth of sewing machine advertising.

Among the early successes were *Godey's Lady's Book[w],* Robert Bonner's *New York Ledger* and magazines of the "quality" type like *Atlantic* and *Harper's,* which began in the 1850's. They were followed by *Century, Scribner's* and *Forum.* In more recent years, as the reading public has become larger and less educated, they have yielded ground to cheaper and more popular magazines, which were given great impetus by the success of S. S. McClure. Selling for much less than their production cost, most modern magazines now depend almost entirely upon their advertising revenue. Modern methods of printing and engraving have greatly increased illustration, and have helped the development of a host of special journals, catering to special interests in news, fashions, pictures, various industries and pure sensation.

[John Bakeless, *Magazine Making;* Frank Luther Mott, *History of American Magazines, 1741-1885;* Lyon N. Richardson, *History of Early American Magazines.*]

JOHN BAKELESS

Magdalena Bay Resolution, THE, has been designated the Lodge Corollary of the Monroe Doctrine[w]. In 1912 American statesmen became suspicious that a Japanese syndicate was aiming to secure control of land on Magdalena Bay in Lower California. A committee of the Senate advised that body to express its views "regarding this and similar cases." Sen. Lodge, accordingly, introduced "a statement of policy, allied to the Monroe Doctrine," which was adopted by that body on Aug. 2, 1912, by a vote of 51 to 4. This resolution declared that when "any harbor or other place in the American continents" is so located that its occupation "for naval or military purposes might threaten the communications or the safety of the United States," she could not without grave concern see that land pass into the possession of any corporation or association which would ensure its control by a non-American power. This was the first time the Monroe Doctrine was applied to an Asiatic power.

[F. A. Ogg, *National Progress, 1907-1917.*]

WILLIAM SPENCE ROBERTSON

Magee-Gutiérrez Expedition. *See* Gutiérrez-Magee Expedition.

Magee-Kearny Expedition (July, 1820). War Department plans for the simultaneous movement of troops up the Missouri toward the Yellowstone, and up the Mississippi to the mouth of the St. Peters or Minnesota River in 1819, contemplated contacts and close co-operation between the two forces in case of Indian hostilities (*see* Yellowstone River Expeditions). Col. Henry Atkinson's force, wintering at old Council Bluffs[w], Nebr., on April 10, 1820, received orders to open roads from this camp to Chariton and to Col. Leavenworth's post on the St. Peters.

July 2, 1820, Capt. M. J. Magee of the Rifles, commanding a detachment comprising a lieutenant, an engineer officer and fifteen soldiers, and accompanied by Lt. Col. Willoughby Morgan and Capt. S. W. Kearny, left Council Bluffs to lay out the road to St. Peters. After traveling twenty-three days through unsettled, sparsely timbered country, the party reached St. Peters and reported this route impracticable. The force returned to St. Louis by boat (*see* Long's Explorations).

[Edgar B. Wesley, *Guarding the Frontier;* Valentine M. Porter, ed., Journal of Stephen Watts Kearny, in *Missouri Historical Collections*, Vol. III.]

WILLOUGHBY M. BABCOCK

Magna Carta. By the early spring of 1215 England was in the throes of a civil war. King John's blundering foreign policy had disrupted the Angevin Empire and had alienated a goodly number of his former followers. His clash with Rome over the vacant See of Canterbury had outraged the nation's religious sentiments. More significant were his repeated violations of feudal and common law. The accumulative effect of these factors, plus unrivaled despotism, led to armed revolt by most of John's barons. Military success crowned the efforts of the latter and John capitulated at Runnymede, June 15, 1215. Here he gave his consent to Magna Carta.

No document in all English history equals Magna Carta, though none has been more misunderstood or misinterpreted. Stripped of its wording, the Great Charter was a treaty won by a victorious barony from a defeated king. In its essence, the Charter simply meant that John, like all other Englishmen, was to be subject to the spirit and letter of law. His past conduct was condemned; in the future he was to rule in accordance with law and custom. The Charter, however, was not a document of human liberties. It contained no reference to habeas corpus, jury trial in criminal cases, or Parliament's control over taxation. Several centuries were to pass before these basic rights became an integral part of England's organic law. One does not hear during the period between the 13th and 17th centuries of Magna Carta having been drafted in the interests of the masses. Indeed, though it was frequently reissued during these years, it was gradually shoved into the background and ultimately forgotten. The civil conflicts attending the War of the Roses and the strong arm of the Tudors blotted out the memory of Magna Carta. Contemporary literature of the Tudor period (1485-1603) is strangely silent about the Charter, and Shakespeare in *King John* has no reference to what probably was the most important event in the life of that monarch. Had the great dramatist known of the Charter, he would hardly have passed over so significant an episode.

It remained for the Puritans[w] of the 17th century, in their contest with the Stuarts, to resurrect Magna Carta and interpret it as an impregnable bulwark of democracy. Although they were wrong in their conclusions and laid the foundation of the "Myth of Magna Carta," they fashioned it into an obstacle to arbitrary government and paved the way for the present constitutional monarchy. Many of these Puritans migrated to the New World and imbedded their ideas in American political philosophy. And when these United States came into being, Magna Carta was viewed as a priceless heritage, never to be lost sight of, and bravely to be defended. Historical research has removed the myth and fancy which have surrounded the Charter, but its essential truths have become more significant than when John reigned. Human rights, individually or collectively, are not to be destroyed by arbitrary and despotic government. The law of the land is supreme and inviolable; it must be respected. No individual or government may transcend law. This is what the barons declared at Runnymede, and this is the present meaning of Magna Carta.

[W. S. McKechnie, *Magna Carta.*]

W. F. GALPIN

Maguaga, Battle at (Aug. 9, 1812). Commanding a force consisting of Michigan and Ohio volunteers and the 4th Regular Infantry, Col. James Miller defeated a British and Indian force at Maguaga, Mich. The enemy was commanded by Maj. Muir and the Indian, Tecumseh, the latter being commissioned brigadier general in the British army for his part in this fight.

[Benson J. Lossing, *Pictorial Field Book of the War of 1812.*]   ROBERT S. THOMAS

Mahican Indians, an Algonkian group of five divisions, occupied both banks of the upper Hudson River northward almost to Lake Champlain (*ca.* 1650). The Dutch called them the River Indians while the French classed them with the Munsees and Delawares under the name Loups. The Mahicans, who had about forty villages, joined the Wappingers on the south near the present Poughkeepsie and extended east into Massachusetts, holding the upper Housatonic Valley. Their capital was at Schodac Island near Albany. In 1730 they had lost most of their territory and had removed to Wyoming, Pa. A few survivors joined the Stockbridges and later the Oneidas[qv].

[F. W. Hodge, *Handbook of American Indians;* E. N. Ruttenber, *History of the Hudson River Indians.*]
ARTHUR C. PARKER

Maiden's Rock, in Pepin County, Wis., is a picturesque rocky bluff overhanging the eastern shore of beautiful Lake Pepin. It was from this rock, according to an Indian legend long believed and possibly true according to old pioneers, that Winona (Wee-no-nah), the comely Dakota maiden, hurled herself to death rather than be espoused to an Indian brave of another tribe, probably a Winnebago, of parental selection.

[*Narrative of Major Stephen H. Long's Expedition;* F. Curtiss-Wedge, *Wabasha County, Minnesota.*]
RICHARD J. PURCELL

Mail-Order Houses. Business has long been done by mail and private messenger. Mail-order houses, receiving all or most of their business by mail, developed in the 1870's and 1880's when the railroads began to give quick, safe and cheap transportation. They were helped greatly by the rural free delivery[qv] service started in 1896 and the parcel post service[qv] established in 1913. They obtained most of their business in rural areas and small towns. People bought by mail because they could secure goods not obtainable in the local stores or because of lower prices. The low prices of the mail-order houses aroused the hatred of the rural merchants. By the middle of the 1920's the automobile was in general use and the rural population could visit towns where the stores carried larger assortments of goods. It appeared that the mail-order business had reached its peak, so the larger mail-order houses opened chains of retail stores.

Mail-order houses operate under a distinct handicap as the buyers cannot examine the goods before purchasing, there is delay in delivery and there is no personal salesmanship. For these reasons they have never obtained a large proportion of the business and in 1929, according to census figures, they did only 1% of the total retail business.

A. Montgomery Ward is usually credited with starting the first mail-order house. He with his partner, George R. Thorne, started business in Chicago in 1872 in a room 12x14 feet. Their first catalog was a single sheet 8x12 inches. They were for a time the official supply house of the Grange[qv]. Sales grew to more than $150,000,000 before they opened a chain of stores. John D. Larkin entered the soap business in Buffalo in 1875 and soon adopted the club plan of selling by mail. Butler Brothers started a wholesale notion business in Boston in 1877 and soon adopted the mail-order method, which was used exclusively for many years. The company, now (1939) located in Chicago and other cities, is one of our largest wholesalers, although it no longer sells exclusively by mail. Richard W. Sears started selling watches by mail while a railroad agent at Redwood Falls, Minn., in 1886, at first writing his advertisements by longhand. At the end of the year he quit the railroad and moved his business to Minneapolis and then to Chicago, where he operated the R. W. Sears Watch Company. He advertised for a watch repairman and hired A. C. Roebuck. Sears sold his business in 1889 and returned to Minneapolis where he started a mail-order watch and jewelry business under the name of A. C. Roebuck & Co., later changed to Sears, Roebuck & Co. In 1894 the business was moved to Chicago and a line of general merchandise added. Julius Rosenwald joined the company in 1895. Growth was rapid and sales grew to $250,000,000 before opening its chain of stores. The National Cloak and Suit Company started selling women's clothing by mail in New York in 1888. The Chicago Mail Order House was started in the early 1890's. There have been many others but the houses mentioned were among the leading pioneers.   P. D. CONVERSE

Maine, a part of Massachusetts until its separation in 1820, has had a long and involved history. Situated in the extreme northeastern part of the United States, covering approximately 31,500 square miles, the state is strategically located with reference to the Atlantic seaboard and the St. Lawrence River. Historians differ as to possible visits by Europeans before the 17th century, but that Gosnold (1602), Pring (1603), Champlain (1604), Weymouth (1605), Popham [w] (1607) and Capt. John Smith (1614) visited Maine before the first permanent settlement in New England in 1620, there can be no doubt.

First falling within the colonial schemes of France, Maine was included in the patent obtained by Sieur de Monts from the king of France, November, 1603, and was subsequently explored by Champlain in 1604–5. However, Maine also fell within the limits of the grant made to the Plymouth Company by the king of England in 1606, confirmed in 1620 by the king in his grant to the Council for New England [w], and included in the charter given to Capt. John Mason and Sir Ferdinando Gorges in 1622. By this latter grant the proprietors had possession of all the lands between the Merrimac and Kennebec [w] rivers, reaching sixty miles inland, with all the islands within five leagues of the shore. The name "Maine" was first used in this charter, and therefore antedates the names of all other states with the exception of Virginia and Massachusetts. In 1629 Mason and Gorges divided their claim, Sir Ferdinando taking for his share the land between the Piscataqua and Kennebec rivers. Ten years later, 1639, Gorges' charter was renewed by Charles I, and in it was inserted a clause to the effect that the land "shall forever, hereafter be called and named the Province or County of Maine & not by any other name or names whatsoever."

With colonizing impulse proceeding directly from England in this early period, settlements for the most part were confined to the southern limits of the state in the region of the Piscataqua. By 1630 there were eighty-four families in Pemaquid [w] and trading posts in Monhegan [w], Richmond's Island, Kittery, Saco Bay and Damariscove. In England Gorges worked tirelessly for the success of this colonial venture. A representative of the lesser feudal class of landed proprietors in England, he failed completely to visualize the needs of the settlers in a colony he had never visited, and when he died in 1647 he left as a legacy an ill-governed community made up largely of adventurers whose background was at variance with that of the settlers to the south in Massachusetts Bay (see Gorges and His Province of Maine). In the meantime civil wars in England had their repercussions in New England. Puritan Massachusetts began her encroachments on Anglican Maine in 1651 and a year later Maine was annexed to Massachusetts, a relationship that underwent various changes until 1692, when the Province of Maine became officially a part of the royal colony of Massachusetts by charter of William and Mary (see Maine under Massachusetts).

Governmental changes and conflicting grants made to landed proprietors in Maine were but a small part of its involved colonial history. The contest between France and England for the land north of the Kennebec, begun in 1613 when Capt. Samuel Argall sacked LaSaussaye's French colony on Mount Desert [w], continued for 150 years, during which time parts of Maine were surrendered to France by the Treaty of St. Germain-en-Laye (1632), returned to England by the Treaty of Westminster (1655), ceded to France by the Treaty of Breda (1667), captured by Sir William Phips (1690), annexed to Massachusetts (1691), returned to France by the Treaty of Ryswick (1697) and surrendered by her to England in the Treaty of Utrecht (1713), although France did not relinquish absolute claim until the Treaty of Paris in 1763 [qw]. During this period tribes of Algonquin [w] Indians were incited by French allies to attack the English colonists, and few settlements in Maine escaped their depredations.

From the close of the Revolution to 1820, when Maine was admitted to the Union, such differences in political ideology developed as to make separation from Massachusetts desirable. Commercial in a capitalistic sense, Massachusetts had little in common with the frontiersmen to the north who wanted cheap money, low tariffs, and who, with rivers and harbors, felt little need for internal improvements. Ill feeling was further engendered by Boston capitalists who speculated in Maine lands, thereby creating an artificial scarcity which increased the price of land at a time when the Napoleonic wars raised the market price of agricultural products.

State history, less eventful, has had several significant developments. The rise and decline of the shipping and lumbering industries, the Northeastern boundary dispute, the Aroostook war and Maine's identification with certain reform movements, notably the Prohibition movement, have been peculiar to her history [qw]. Politically the state has been something of an enigma. With a preponderance of its administrations in Democratic control up to 1856, and with a basic frontier philosophy democratic in the extreme, Maine was, nevertheless, one of the first states in the Union to elect a Republican governor (Hannibal Hamlin in 1856) and has been predominantly Republican ever since.

[W. D. Williamson, *The History of Maine;* L. C. Hatch, *Maine.*]

ELIZABETH RING

Maine, **Destruction of the** (Feb. 15, 1898). In January, 1898, the second-class battleship *Maine,* Capt. Charles D. Sigsbee, was ordered from Key West to Havana on a friendly visit but before the objections of the Spanish authorities were ascertained. For three weeks the ship lay moored to a buoy 500 yards off the arsenal. There was considerable ill feeling against the United States among the Spaniards, but no untoward incident took place until 9:40 P.M., Feb. 15, when two explosions threw parts of the *Maine* 200 feet in the air and illuminated the whole harbor. A first dull explosion had been followed by one much more powerful, probably that of the forward magazines. The forward half of the ship was reduced to a mass of twisted steel; the after part slowly sank. Two officers and 258 of the crew were killed or died soon afterward. Most of these were buried in Colon Cemetery, Havana.

Investigations were soon made by the American and Spanish authorities separately. Their decisions differed: the Spaniards reported that an internal explosion, perhaps spontaneous combustion in the coal bunkers, had been the cause; the Americans that the original cause had been an external explosion which in turn had set off the forward magazines.

News of the disaster produced great excitement in the United States, and accusations against the Spaniards were freely expressed by certain newspapers. Without doubt the catastrophe stirred up national feeling over the difficulties in Cuba, crystallized in the slogan "Remember the *Maine.*" The wreck remained in Havana harbor until 1911, when United States Army engineers built a coffer dam about the wreck, sealed the after hull of the ship, the only part still intact, and floated it out to sea. There, on March 16, 1912, appropriate minute guns boomed as it sank with its flag flying. The remains of sixty-six of the crew which were found during the raising were buried in the National Cemetery, Arlington.

During the removal of the wreck a board of officers of the navy made a further investigation. Their report, published in 1912, stated that a low form of explosive exterior to the ship caused the first explosion. "This resulted in igniting and exploding the contents of the 6-inch reserve magazine, A–14–M, said contents including a large quantity of black powder. The more or less complete explosion of the contents of the remaining forward magazine followed." The chief evidence for this was that the bottom of the ship had been bent upward and folded over toward the stern. European experts, perhaps influenced by several internal explosions in warships in the intervening years, still, however, maintained the theory of an internal explosion. No further evidence has ever been found to solve the mystery.

[Charles D. Sigsbee, *The Maine;* F. E. Chadwick, *The Relations of the United States and Spain, Diplomacy; Report of Vreeland Board on Destruction of the Maine; Final Report on Removing Wreck of Battleship Maine.*]
                              WALTER B. NORRIS

Maine, Prohibition in, was the result of a vigorous crusade against intemperance by the people of a frontier state who early recognized the abuses of too much drinking (*see* Temperance Movement). In 1821 the Maine legislature passed a license law and in 1846 a prohibitory law was enacted, based largely upon the report of Gen. James Appleton, a member of the legislature. While prohibitory legislation was not at first the goal of the reformers, under the leadership of Neal Dow it became injected into the movement, and resulted in the enactment of the "Maine Law," May 26, 1851, which prohibited the manufacture and sale of intoxicating liquors. This law was repealed in 1858, but was subsequently re-enacted and put beyond legislative reach in 1885 when it became a part of the state constitution. Enforcement, always a problem, was never achieved, and the amendment was repealed in September, 1934, following repeal of the Eighteenth Amendment*q* to the Federal Constitution.

[*The Reminiscences of Neal Dow: an Autobiography;* L. C. Hatch, *Maine.*]   ELIZABETH RING

Maine Boundary Dispute. *See* Northeast Boundary; Aroostook War; Webster-Ashburton Treaty.

Maine under Massachusetts (1652–1820). During the 17th century scattered settlements on the Maine coast from the Piscataqua to the St. Croix River, loosely organized in separate political divisions, were united under Massachusetts Bay*q* as the Province of Maine. Massachusetts extended her charter rights over the patents of Gorges*q* in 1652, and Rigby (*see* Lygonia) in 1658, and combined them into the county of Yorkshire with orderly local government and representation in the General Court. These rights were denied by the king in 1664, reclaimed by Massachusetts in 1668, challenged by the heirs in 1677 and finally established through the purchase, in 1678, of Gorges' Patent for £1250 sterling. The territory was again organized in 1680, with a provincial president and an assembly of two houses, but in 1686 this government was destroyed by the establishment of the Dominion of New England*q*. By the victorious arms of William Phips in 1690, the Charter of William and Mary in 1691 and the Treaty of Utrecht[w] in 1713, the St. Croix River became the eastern boundary of "The Province of Massachusetts Bay." Large numbers of farmers, fishermen, foresters and fur traders[w] who settled here continued this union for more than a century, but geographical, political and economic differences made separation inevitable. This was advocated in 1785, and consummated March 15, 1820, when Maine became a state (see Maine).

[W. D. Williamson, *The History of the State of Maine from Its First Discovery A.D. 1602, to the Separation, A.D. 1820, Inclusive.*]   THOMAS MORGAN GRIFFITHS

Maize, or Indian Corn, was extensively cultivated in aboriginal America. It was the chief cereal for the civilizations in Mexico, Central America and the highlands of South America. Archæology has demonstrated that the earliest agriculture in prehistoric United States was based upon such native plants as the sunflower and the giant ragweed. Later maize and beans were introduced from Mexico. Tree-ring dating[w] for Arizona and New Mexico suggests that maize appeared there about the fifth century B.C. and beans about 200 A.D.

Presumably these plants reached the mound builders[w] a few centuries later and were handed on to the proto-historic Indians east of the Mississippi. The only Indians depending primarily upon maize and beans were the pueblo dwellers[w] of Arizona and New Mexico. Hunting was with them secondary. In addition, maize was grown by most of the tribes east of the 100th meridian and south of 48° N. Lat. The modern cultivation of maize is limited to the same areas.

The colonists planted maize in the Indian way, in hills, tended it with hoes and used fish for fertilizer. In the making of meal, corn bread and hominy, the Indian methods were followed. The Indians planted beans and squashes among the maize, which is still the white custom. Both popcorn and sweet corn were developed by Indians. Throughout the Mississippi Valley and eastward, the historic Indians were primarily hunters, using maize as a reserve food. Traders encouraged the forest Indians to abandon agriculture and to become more nomadic in order that all their time be given to hunting and fur production. (See also Corn.)

[S. F. Will and S. E. Hyde, *Corn among the Indians of the Upper Missouri.*]   CLARK WISSLER

Majority Rule. A fundamental American concept, evolved from the principle of the sovereignty of the people, is that, when two candidates are running for an office, the one who receives more than half of the total votes cast shall be elected and his policies shall be entitled to a fair trial. If three or more candidates are seeking the same office, the concept holds that an absolute majority is not required but that the one who receives a mere plurality, or more votes than any other candidate, shall be elected.

The operation of majority rule was well illustrated when the election of Thomas Jefferson (see Campaign of 1800) to the Presidency was accepted as sufficient warrant for refusing to approve Federalist changes in the judiciary (see Judiciary Act of 1801) . President Jackson interpreted his re-election in 1832 as approval of his hostility to the Second Bank of the United States[w]. During the Reconstruction[w] period, the Radical Republicans[w] believed their 1866 election victories justified them in imposing a harsh program of military reconstruction on the South. In 1933 President Franklin D. Roosevelt and people generally interpreted his overwhelming victory at the polls as authority for inaugurating his far-reaching New Deal[w].

Majority rule, it should be noted, is limited somewhat by the Constitution. Civil liberties[w] are specifically protected by the fundamental law and cannot be suppressed by a temporary majority. The Constitution itself cannot be amended without the consent of three fourths of the states. Because of constitutional guarantees of freedom of speech and of the press[qw], and other liberties, minority groups in the United States are able to oppose the majority. Minority criticism and the ever-present possibility that the minority will become the majority have operated to make majority rule work well.

[James Bryce, *The American Commonwealth*, Vol. II; Alexis DeTocqueville, *Democracy in America.*]
                    ERIK McKINLEY ERIKSSON

Malaria, the ancient disease responsible, in part, for the degeneracy of Greece and the downfall of Rome, appears to have been brought to America by slaves from Africa—invisible cargo which the *Anopheles* sucked from their blood and transmitted to their masters. Under a variety of names, malarial fevers occupy much space in early American medical literature—thousands of pages of professional ignorance. The parasitic origin of malaria, as advocated by the Virginian, John Kearsley Mitchell (*On the Cryptogamous Origin of Malarious and Epidemic Fevers,* 1849), could find no support from contemporaries, who declared the carbonic-acid origin violated no cardinal principle of philosophy. A leading student of malariology, Col. Charles Smart, of the United States Army, reviewed (1887) without condemnation the theory that malaria is caused by phases of the moon, high and low tide, electricity and exhalation of flowerpots, reserving his ridicule for the conception of the proboscis of the mosquito as nature's inoculating needle ("Perhaps the most amusing, as well as the most puerile, of the theories offered as a substitute for the marsh miasma is that which refers malarial diseases to mosquito-bites").

Thomas Stewardson's demonstration of the bronzed liver of malaria (1841), George Troup Maxwell's first description of blackwater fever, or malarial hematuria, in this country (1860), George Dock's differentiation of the varieties of the malarial parasite in the United States (1890–92), William George MacCallum's discovery of the method of sexual fertilization of the malarial plasmodium (1897), Charles Cassedy Bass' first successful cultivation of the malarial parasites in test tubes (1911), are striking American contributions. A French army surgeon in Algiers found the plasmodium of malaria, an English army surgeon in India discovered the mosquito transmission of malaria, and it was reserved for an American Army surgeon (W. C. Gorgas) in Panama to become the most effective of mosquito hunters in his practical elimination of yellow fever[w] and malaria.

[Daniel Drake, *Principal Diseases of the Interior Valley of North America*, Vol. II.]   VICTOR ROBINSON

Malefactors of Great Wealth. Aug. 20, 1907, President Theodore Roosevelt defended his antitrust policy in an address at Provincetown, Mass., blaming the depression of that year (*see* Panic of 1907) partly on "certain malefactors of great wealth" who he believed had brought about some of the financial stress in order to force the Government to relax its control over corporations.

[Mark Sullivan, *Our Times*, Vol. III.]
STANLEY R. PILLSBURY

Mallet Brothers Explorations (1739–42). The first known Santa Fé[w] traders to cross the plains from the Missouri were eight Canadians led by Pierre and Paul Mallet, who, in 1739, driving pack horses, explored a route from the Platte River's mouth to Santa Fé. Returning, they explored the Arkansas from the Rockies to the Mississippi in 1740. They guided Fabry de Bruyere on a second Santa Fé expedition from New Orleans by boat up the Mississippi, Arkansas and Canadian rivers to the present central Oklahoma. Inability to float boats in the shallow Canadian, and Fabry's reluctance to use Indian horses, caused abandonment of the expedition in 1742.

[Pierre Margry, *Découvertes et Établissements des Français dans l'Amérique*, Vol. VI.]   BLISS ISELY

Malvern Hill, Battle of (July 1, 1862), last of the Seven Days[w] battles, ended Gen. McClellan's (U.) Peninsular Campaign[w]. After the battle of Frayser's Farm[w], McClellan fell back to a prepared position on Malvern Hill, a plateau protected by streams on its flanks, with an open field of fire at the immediate front. When Gen. Lee's (C.) artillery attack failed, through poor organization and staff inefficiency, several divisional attacks were launched against Malvern Hill. These assaults were not successful in driving the Union Army from its position that day, but on July 2 McClellan felt forced to withdraw to his base at Harrison's Landing.

[Matthew Forney Steele, *American Campaigns*.]
GEORGE FREDERICK ASHWORTH

Mammoth Cave, Edmonson County, Ky., is mentioned in county records as early as 1797. Evidences of Indian occupation were found for miles inside its entrance by early explorers. Saltpeter was taken from it to make gunpowder during the War of 1812. Within a quarter century afterward it began to be a tourists' objective. The first official guide, Stephen Bishop, a Negro, did much of the dangerous work of exploring the cave as it is known today. A large area surrounding it became a national park in 1936.

[Helen F. Randolph, *Mammoth Cave and the Cave Region of Kentucky*.]   ALVIN F. HARLOW

Managed Currency. Although plans for stabilizing the purchasing power of the money unit through management of the currency date back more than 100 years, active suggestions for such management in the United States date back only to 1879, when an article on the standard of value by the late Simon Newcomb appeared in the *North American Review* for September. Years later, in 1911, Prof. Irving Fisher outlined a plan for stabilizing the dollar in his *Purchasing Power of Money*. But little attention was paid to these or other suggestions, however, until after the World War.

In his *Stabilizing the Dollar*, in 1920, Prof. Fisher elaborated his earlier proposal and presented the text of a suggested law, worked out in detail. In 1925 an organization known as the Stable Money Association was formed and carried on an extensive campaign for a stabilized price level for a number of years. Various books and numerous articles dealing with the subject were also published.

Although Prof. Fisher's proposed bill (which involved altering the weight of gold in the dollar from time to time to offset changes in the price level) never received detailed consideration from Congress, several bills requiring the Federal Reserve Board[qv] to operate to stabilize the commodity price[qv] level have been the subjects of extended hearings in the House Committee on Banking and Currency and one actually passed the House. These were the Strong bill in 1927, a second Strong bill in 1929, the Goldsborough bill in 1932, the amended Goldsborough bill which was passed by the House on May 2, 1932, and the Patman bill in 1937, modified in 1938. The Goldsborough and Patman bills required the price level to be first raised and then stabilized.

In the matter of practice, President F. D. Roosevelt, on two occasions in 1933, announced the intent of the administration to raise and then stabilize commodity prices. On the latter occasion, in his Oct. 22 address, the President actually stated, "We are thus continuing to move toward a managed currency." The gold purchase plan[qv], inaugurated Oct. 25, 1933, was the attempt at managed currency referred to. It was dropped with the actual devaluation[qv] of the dollar on Jan. 31, 1934. Since the latter date, the Federal Reserve Board has attempted to raise commodity prices to the pre-depression level and then stabilize them, but with no marked success.

[I. Fisher, *Stabilizing the Dollar;* A. D. Gayer, *Monetary Policy and Economic Stabilization;* J. Donaldson, *The Dollar.*]

FREDERICK A. BRADFORD

Manassas. *See* Bull Run.

Manchac was a British trading post established shortly after 1763 at the junction of Bayou Manchac (Iberville River[qv]) with the Mississippi, from which an extensive trade was conducted with French planters along the Mississippi as far down as New Orleans, until Manchac was captured by Spanish forces under Galvez in September, 1779.

[Charles Gayarré, *History of Louisiana;* Alcée Fortier, *History of Louisiana.*]

WALTER PRICHARD

Manchuria and Manchoukuo, American Policy toward. A specific policy was first defined by John Hay in his so-called open door[qv] notes to the major powers having interests in China (Sept. 6–Nov. 21, 1899) . In main the American Government was interested in guarantees that the principle of equal commercial opportunity should be maintained in Manchuria. This policy was expanded during the Boxer Uprising[qv] by the Hay circular notes (July 3, 1900) affirming American support of the principle of "Chinese territorial and administrative entity." While not recognizing officially the existence of "spheres of influence" in China, the United States aided in

negotiation of the Treaty of Portsmouth[qv] (Sept. 5, 1905) by which Japan acquired the former Russian "sphere" in South Manchuria. Dollar Diplomacy[qv], which received little encouragement from Theodore Roosevelt or Root (*see* Root-Takahira Agreement) was actively supported in the Taft-Knox railroad neutralization proposal (1909–10). Secretary of State Bryan (March 13, 1915) admitted that Japan had "special relations" with Manchuria—a statement reaffirmed as "special interests" in the Lansing-Ishii notes[qv] (Nov. 2, 1917), later abrogated (April 14, 1923) . The Nine-Power (open door) Treaty[qv] (Feb. 6, 1922) pledged the United States, among other signatories, to respect "the sovereignty, the independence, and the territorial and administrative integrity of China," which was regarded as including Manchuria.

Following the so-called Manchurian Incident (Sept. 18, 1931), the United States, both by independent action and by partial co-operation with the League of Nations[qv], sought to exert pressure on Japan. The doctrine of nonrecognition[qv] of the *de facto* situation created by Japan in Manchuria was proclaimed by Secretary of State Stimson (Jan. 7, 1932) . In a word, the United States would not recognize any situation or any treaties brought about by means which it interpreted as in violation of the Nine-Power Treaty, or the Pact of Paris. When the new state of Manchoukuo was formed (March, 1932) its appeal for recognition was ignored by all powers save Japan. As late as the spring of 1939 the United States had not abandoned its policy of nonrecognition toward Manchoukuo.

[Eleanor Tupper and G. E. McReynolds, *Japan in American Public Opinion;* F. R. Dulles, *Forty Years of American-Japanese Relations;* P. H. Clyde, *A History of the Modern and Contemporary Far East.*]

PAUL H. CLYDE

Mandan, Fort, was built by the Lewis and Clark expedition at Five Villages[qqv], now Stanton, N. Dak. The party remained there from Oct. 26, 1804, to April 7, 1805. This was an advantageous wintering place because of neighboring Mandan and Hidatsa villages.

[*Original Journals of the Lewis and Clark Expedition, 1804-6.*]

O. G. LIBBY

Mandans, THE, belong to the Siouan family. Some evidence of their origin may be found in their most sacred relics, four huge turtle shells, claimed to have come from the Atlantic Ocean. They were sedentary in habit and lived in earth lodges of a fixed type in villages along the Missouri River from the Grand River, S. Dak., to Fort Berthold, N. Dak. They have been associated with the Hidatsa, also of Siouan stock, from about 1790, and were found by Lewis and Clark[qv], 1804, at the Five Villages[qv]. After being almost entirely destroyed in 1837 by smallpox, they moved northward and were joined by the Arikara[qv] at Fort Berthold in 1861. A few survivors are located on separate holdings in the vicinity of Elbowoods.

[Matthews, *Ethnography and Philology of the Hidatsa Indians.*]   O. G. LIBBY

Mandates, United States and. Under the treaties of Versailles and Lausanne, and the Covenant of the League of Nations[qv], conquered German and Turkish colonies were assigned for administration to individual powers, subject to general supervision by the League. The United States, although not a party to the treaties nor a member of the League, has taken a keen interest in these mandates and insisted on equal rights with the other powers in them. Its claims were based on the provision in the Treaty of Versailles turning the German colonies over to the principal allied and associated powers, of which the United States was one even though it did not ratify the treaty, and on the ingenious argument that although the United States was not at war with Turkey, it had by its participation in the war with Germany helped win the war with Turkey and was entitled to share in the results.

Both claims were finally granted by the other powers, and the United States thereupon insisted on being consulted concerning the terms of the individual agreements. Again it won its point. Treaties were negotiated incorporating the text of the mandate agreements entered into between the mandatory power and the League council and making its terms applicable to the United States. Ten such treaties, securing for the United States all the rights it would have had automatically had it joined the League of Nations, have been ratified by the Senate. They include: treaties with Japan respecting the mandate over Yap[qv] and other Pacific islands (Feb. 11, 1922); with France respecting the French Cameroons and French Togoland (Feb. 13, 1923); with Belgium respecting Ruandi-Urundi (April 18, 1923, and Jan. 21, 1924); and with Great Britain respecting Palestine (Dec. 3, 1924), British Cameroons, British Togoland and Tanganyika (all Feb. 10, 1925), and Iraq (Jan. 9, 1930).

[Quincy Wright, *Mandates under the League of Nations; Mandate for Palestine,* State Department Publication, 1927.]   CLARENCE A. BERDAHL

Mangas Coloradas Wars (1835–63) were a series of Apache[qv] hostilities led by the celebrated chief Mangas Coloradas, who took command of the Mimbres Apaches after his predecessor Juan José was killed in a massacre engineered by American trappers under James Johnson, for the purpose of collecting bounties offered in Mexico for scalps.

Mangas Coloradas and his warriors made a large part of the Southwest untenable for settlers, and in the early years of the Civil War virtually devastated Arizona, New Mexico and western Texas. Troops under Gen. James H. Carleton eventually inflicted severe reverses on the Apaches, and Mangas Coloradas surrendered. He was killed Jan. 19, 1863, by his guards, on the pretext that he was attempting to escape.

[J. P. Dunn, *Massacres of the Mountains;* John C. Cremony, *Life among the Apaches.*]

PAUL I. WELLMAN

Mangeurs de lard was a term applied to the new crop of recruits for the fur trade[qv] imported annually and bound for a period of five years' service. While en route from Canada they were fed on pea soup, bread and pork, but chiefly on the latter, whence the term of pork eaters. They were scorned by the aristocracy of the trapping fraternity, assigned only the most menial tasks and their wages were so low that they customarily ended the five years' apprenticeship in debt to the company, and were forced to remain as employees. The term was frequently applied to any newcomer in the sense of greenhorn or tenderfoot.

[H. M. Chittenden, *History of American Fur Trade in Far West.*]   CARL L. CANNON

Manhattan Island was discovered by Verazzano in 1524 and visited by Hudson in 1609. Its insularity and name are first shown on a printed map (Dutch) of 1617. The name is derived from that of a small tribe of Indians—variously called Manahata, Manhatoes, etc.—then living on the island. There were white settlers on it in 1613–14. In 1626 Peter Minuit, an agent of the Dutch West India Company[qv], bought the beautiful island, then covered with forest and abounding in game and wild fruits, from the Canarsie Indians, who had no claim to it, for, it is said, about $24 worth of trinkets. Later, other payments had to be made to the Manhatoes, the true claimants. New York City spread rapidly over it in the 19th century, and by 1860 streets were being planned to the northernmost tip of Manhattan. The city was confined to this island alone until Greater New York was created in 1898.

[I. N. Phelps Stokes, *The Iconography of Manhattan Island.*]   ALVIN F. HARLOW

"Manifest Destiny" was a phrase in common use in the 1840's and 1850's, suggesting the supposed inevitability of the continued territorial expansion of the United States (*see* Westward Movement). The phrase first appeared in the *Democratic Review* for July-August, 1845, in an article in which the editor, John L. O'Sullivan, spoke of "our manifest destiny to overspread the continent allotted by Providence for the free development of our yearly multiplying millions." While this article referred specifically to the annexation of Texas[w], the phrase was quickly caught up by the expansionists of the period and utilized in the controversy with Great Britain over Oregon[w] and in the demand for annexations of territory as a result of the war with Mexico[w] in 1846–48. It was also used, in the next decade, in connection with the desire to annex Cuba[w].

Believers in "manifest destiny" derived their faith in part from the phenomenal rate of population growth in the United States, in part from a conviction of the superiority of American talents and American political institutions over those of neighboring countries. Though at first a tenet chiefly of the Democratic party, "manifest destiny" also had its devotees among Whigs or Republicans—notably William H. Seward, who as Secretary of State purchased Alaska[w] and sought vainly to annex sundry Caribbean and Pacific islands. "Manifest destiny" was revived as a Republican doctrine in the 1890's and was in evidence in connection with the annexation of Hawaii[w] and the islands taken from Spain in 1898 (*see* Spanish-American War).

[Julius W. Pratt, The Origin of "Manifest Destiny," *American Historical Review*, Vol. XXXII; A. K. Weinberg, *Manifest Destiny*.]   JULIUS W. PRATT

Manila Bay, Battle of (May 1, 1898). Selected for the Asiatic command through the influence of Assistant Secretary of the Navy Theodore Roosevelt, Commodore George Dewey thoroughly fitted out at Hong Kong his four cruisers, *Olympia* (flagship), *Baltimore, Boston* and *Raleigh* (6000–3000 tons), and the gunboats *Concord* and *Petrel*. Upon the declaration of war with Spain (*see* Spanish-American War) he received orders to attack Admiral Montojo's fleet at Manila—"You must capture vessels or destroy." On April 30 Dewey was outside Manila Bay and entered safely at midnight, disregarding serious risks from shore batteries and mines. Off Manila at dawn, he sighted Montojo's force ten miles westward under the guns of Cavite dockyard. It consisted of some ten small, wretchedly equipped cruisers and gunboats, mounting not one-third

the American broadside. At 5:41 A.M. Dewey opened fire, swinging his column in long ovals past the enemy ships at 5000–2000 yards' range. On a mistaken report of ammunition shortage he withdrew at 7:35, but renewed action at 11:16 and ended it an hour later, when the shore batteries were silenced and every Spanish ship, to quote Dewey's report, "was sunk, burned, or deserted." The Spanish suffered 381 casualties, the Americans but nine slightly wounded. Manila was blockaded, and surrendered Aug. 13 after merely formal bombardment. For his easily won victory Dewey's promotion to full admiral (1899) was high reward, yet justified by his prompt, resolute movements, and correct discounting of the dangers in entering enemy waters defended by mines and heavy guns on shore.

[H. W. Wilson, *The Downfall of Spain*.]
      ALLAN WESTCOTT

Manila Galleon, THE, was the instrument by which Spain kept a contact via Mexico with the Philippine Islands[w]. The first trading voyage went from Acapulco, Mexico, to Cebú, Philippine Islands, in 1566. In 1571 Manila became the oriental terminus, and annual sailings of the galleon were maintained until 1815. Prior to 1769, except for a few outstanding voyages, only the galleons visited Alta California[w]. Apparently they never entered San Francisco Bay, and on their eastern voyage first saw land near Monterey. The desire to establish a way station here was a prime cause for Spanish expansion to Alta California.

[C. E. Chapman, *History of California: The Spanish Period*.]   OSGOOD HARDY

Manitou is an Algonkin Indian[w] word of uncertain meaning, but used with reference to supernatural beings or gods, or to a quality or power of an animistic kind which may reside within any specified object, temporarily or permanently. Manabus, Nanabozho, etc., is a supernatural hero in Algonkin mythology, or the chief manitou. The term Kitchi Manito is often used for Great Spirit[w].

[W. T. Thomas, ed., *Source Book for Social Origins*.]
      CLARK WISSLER

Manitoulin Islands, THE, stretch across northern Lake Huron from east to west, and include Drummond, Great Manitoulin and Little Manitoulin islands. They became known to the Jesuit missionaries of Huronia about 1640, and were subsequently seen, or skirted, by most voyagers between Lower Canada and the Upper Lakes. St. Lusson wintered on or near Great Manitoulin in 1670–71, when the island teemed with big game. Following the War of 1812[w] the Joint International Boundary Survey Commission[w] awarded Drummond Island to the United States and the remainder of the group to Canada.

M. M. QUAIFE

Mann, Fort (Kans.), is supposed to have been built about 1845, as part of Gilpin's battalion was quartered there in 1847–48 (*see* Doniphan's Expedition). The exact location is in doubt. Marcy in his *Prairie Traveler,* 1859, located Fort Mann near the Arkansas River on the route from Fort Leavenworth to Santa Fé, about 359 miles from Fort Leavenworth and 423 miles from Santa Fé. A later writer, R. M. Wright, says: "At this side of Point of Rocks, 8 miles west of Dodge City, used to be the remains of an old adobe fort. Some called it Ft. Mann; others, Ft. Atkinson."

[F. W. Blackmar, Kansas.]
CARL L. CANNON

Mann Act. In 1910 Congress enacted the so-called Mann Act, the title of which was: "An Act Further to Regulate Interstate and Foreign Commerce by Prohibiting the Transportation therein for Immoral Purposes of Women and Girls, and for Other Purposes." The object of the legislation was the suppression of the white-slave traffic[w]. The law is an example of Federal police legislation for the protection of public morals, based constitutionally upon the commerce power[w]. Although attacked as denying to American citizens the privilege of free access in interstate commerce, as invading the legislative domain of the states, and as exceeding the proper scope of the commerce power, the law was declared constitutional. The Court held that no person has any constitutional right to use the channels of interstate commerce to promote objectionable or immoral transactions, that the act is a proper exercise of the power to regulate commerce, and, as such, its effect on the normal scope of state police power is irrelevant. The act was further upheld where there was involved the interstate transportation of women for immoral purposes without any pecuniary element; "the mere fact of transportation" was sufficient. The act is significant in the extension of congressional control over a social and economic problem for the general welfare of the country.

[36 Stat. 825, c. 395; Hoke v. United States, 1912, 227 U. S. 308; Caminetti v. United States, 1916, 242 U. S. 470; R. E. Cushman, National Police Power, 3 *Minnesota Law Review,* 1918-19.]

THOMAS S. BARCLAY

Manners. The development of manners in the United States from the first settlement up to the present (1939) must be interpreted in the general framework of Western culture, but as taking its distinctive expression as a result of the characteristics of the immigrants who came to this country, the peculiar environmental conditions and changes, the ways in which social control has shaped itself as a special part of the native cultural situation, and the influence of inventions[w] as they have changed the habits of life of the people.

From the beginning, the chief motive of those entering the country has been the expectation of lifting their standard of living. In spite of this the colonial settlements represented different classes, leading to an aristocracy that leaned more or less toward a reflection of European, especially English, manners and a democracy militant in its stress of the self-made man. With the expansion of the United States, the first took deepest root in the South (*see* Plantation System of the South) and the second, in the Western expansion over the Appalachian Mountains. The Western proverb that "the rifle and axe make all men equally tall" expressed the sentiment behind native manners, so expressive of pride of independence as to suggest a fundamental inferiority feeling.

Slavery[w], as it developed, anchored more firmly the dominant aristocratic code in the South. Elsewhere the dictum of "shirt-sleeves to shirt-sleeves in three generations" revealed the popular clinging to the doctrine of social equality and an open pathway to self-advancement.

Manners, as they developed in the United States, registered not only sectional and class differences, the influence of the frontier, rural and city conditions, but also the influence of separate groups, especially those built upon religious foundations. The Quakers[w] were among the first of these peoples who kept to themselves and maintained a distinct system of manners. The Oneida Community[w] was one of the most spectacular of such groupings, and the peculiar dress of the women that resulted from the effort to have garments adapted to their working conditions attracted more popular attention than did their marriage scheme.

American manners were indicted by European travelers, particularly during the period 1825 to 1845, for their coarseness. Much of this criticism was justified. The widespread habit of chewing tobacco, the prevailing carelessness of dress, intemperance, and crudity of conversation were in part a product of the rough life characteristic of frontier conditions. Apart from this defect of the culture that fashioned itself in the total situation of the American people, the lack of sympathy with democratic aspirations on the part of European critics, including Harriet Martineau, Charles Dickens and Capt. Marryat, led them to a selection and emphasis that distorted the picture of American manners as a whole, even though they reported with accuracy what they saw. At a later time Anthony Trollope and James Bryce were more discriminating in their statements regarding American characteristics (*see* British Travelers in the United States, Early).

In spite of a prevalent coarseness, a taboo against any open recognition of anything suggestive of sex was maintained by a prudery so extreme that Power's nude statue of "The Greek Slave," modeled in 1843, both thrilled and shocked people as it was exhibited in various parts of the country. At Cincinnati, before it was shown to the public, it was partially clothed by a group of prominent women in the city. Corsets displayed in the window of A. T. Stewart in New York brought him a flood of protest against his immorality. The practices, especially, of men who maintained the double standard were by no means consistent with this stress of delicacy which led to such an astonishing convention as the description in Lady Gough's *Etiquette* of the perfect hostess:

> "The perfect hostess will see to it that the works of male and female authors be properly separated on her bookshelves. Their proximity unless they happen to be married should not be tolerated."

Chaperonage was insisted upon from about 1850 onward, even into the 20th century in the polite society of Eastern cities and especially in the South. The rest of the country generally resisted this imitating of European customs "except among those belonging to the most fashionable social groups in the larger cities." Although after the Civil War women greatly extended their social influence, there was less advancement in manners than advocates of the rights of women[qw] had assumed would happen. Indeed, feminine patronage of art has been charged with being the cause of our "anemic, uncreative cultural atmosphere."

The growth of popular education, although it has increased the power of the masses, has not as yet elevated American manners as its promoters prophesied it would. The greatest influence on manners at the present time, unquestionably, is the motion picture[qw]. Its chief effect has been a widespread sophistication based upon sentimental and false standards. It has, however, lessened some of the crudities of American manners and, with commercial advertising, has tended to make men more careful of their dress and has led

women away from the overdressing for which they had so long been indicted by European critics. On the whole, American manners have improved.

[Allan Nevins, *American Social History as Recorded by English Travellers;* Dixon Wecter, *The Saga of American Society: A Record of Social Aspiration, 1607-1937.*]

ERNEST R. GROVES

Manors were self-sufficient agricultural communities, embracing one or more villages or towns over which seignorial rights and privileges generally obtained and within which both independent farmers and servile tenants lived. At the time of colonial settlement the manor was the prevailing mode of agricultural life in the mother country, but the manorial lord was becoming more and more a country proprietor and less and less an administrative figure. It was owing to the desire of the country gentlemen to secure landholdings in the New World that the manorial system was established in the proprietary colonies[qw], principally in New York, Maryland and South Carolina.

Under the Dutch regime in New Netherland numerous patroonships[qw], virtually manors, were authorized, but only one, that of Rensselaerswyck, was successfully established. The early English governors of New York created numerous manors in Westchester, on Long Island and elsewhere, whose legal and political characteristics were feudal, and confirmed the manorial jurisdiction of Rensselaerswyck. The manorial jurisdiction, however, could not withstand the encroachments of town and county authority, although the manorial landlords, through their control of the sheriffs and the manorial or local courts, and through their influence in the provincial legislature, dominated for long the local government of the province. From the point of view of the tenants the chief grievances in the manor system were insecurity of tenure and perpetual rents. The tenants on the Van Rensselaerswyck manor agitated against their leasehold estates and perpetual rents, and the controversy was a burning one down into the 19th century.

In Maryland the proprietors set up the manorial system extensively, erecting some sixty manors in the 17th century, not including those which the proprietary and his relations laid out in 6000-acre tracts, each for his own use. The manors were divided more or less unevenly into demesne land reserved for the lord and freehold lands, both called plantations, where tobacco was cultivated.

Under the Fundamental Constitutions of Carolina[qw] of 1669 an aristocratic system of landholding was set up, two fifths of the land being granted to the hereditary nobility and three fifths to the manorial lords and the common freeholders. Seignories, baronies and manors were provided for, although no seignory or barony ever contained more than 12,000 acres, and there is no evidence available of any manor in the strict sense actually having been set up. In these large estates manorial jurisdiction such as found in Maryland and New York in the 17th century (*see* Court Leet) does not appear to have existed. Over a hundred proprietary manors were set up by Penn for his colony, but in no case does it appear that manorial jurisdiction was ever exercised.

[The Order of Colonial Lords of Manors in America, *Publications*, Nos. 1-25; C. M. Andrews, *Colonial Period of American History;* Nissenson, *Patroon's Domain;* Johnson, *Old Maryland Manors;* Kilty, *Land-holder's Assistant;* Spencer, *Land System in Colonial New York.*]

RICHARD B. MORRIS

Mansfield, Battle of. *See* Sabine Cross-Roads, Battle at.

Manuel's Fort (1807-11), first American outpost in the present Montana, was built by Manuel Lisa, St. Louis fur trader, at the junction of the Yellowstone and Big Horn rivers in 1807, to serve as a trading post for Crow Indians[qv] and as headquarters of trapping brigades. Various trapping expeditions started from this post and explored the region. Most noted were two ventures of John Colter, who, traveling alone, explored what is now Yellowstone Park and first reported the geysers. He later explored a route to the three forks of the Missouri, where he narrowly escaped the Blackfeet Indians[qv].

Hostility of the Blackfeet caused the abandonment of the fort, first in 1810, and finally in 1811. Trappers returning to the site after the War of 1812 found no remains of the fort. Later trading posts built at this location were headquarters for trappers who explored most of the present Wyoming. (*See also* St. Louis Missouri Fur Company.)

[Hiram Martin Chittenden, *The American Fur Trade*, pp. 119, 126-7, 138-44, 704-15.]   BLISS ISELY

Manufactures, Colonial. *See* Industries, Colonial.

Manufactures, Restriction of, in Colonies. During the 17th century the colonies were regarded by Englishmen as sources of supplies, chiefly raw materials, which England did not produce herself. By the 18th century the plantations came to be prized as markets for English manufactured goods in addition to being reservoirs of raw materials. English manufacturers now felt that it was imperative to keep the colonies from manufacturing goods which they themselves could produce. For this reason, attempts were made in various ways to restrict the development of colonial manufactures. It was partly for this reason, also, as well as to free Great Britain from dependence on Baltic countries for naval stores[qv] and other supplies that a policy of granting bounties[qv] on such commodities was inaugurated in 1705.

Restrictions of colonial manufactures were attempted not only through the passage of laws, but also by administrative action. For instance, the Board of Trade[qv] in its inquiries and reports was constantly concerned with the problem. In its instructions to royal governors the Board frequently emphasized that the restriction of colonial manufacturing was one of the duties of governors, but in few cases were such instructions taken seriously. Another example can be seen in the action of the Privy Council[qv], when in 1724 it ordered the colonists to refrain from imposing tariffs on English goods, thus discouraging colonial legislation which favored manufacturing.

The first important step in the direction of Parliamentary restriction of colonial manufactures was made in connection with the production of woolens. In 1699, at the demand of English woolen manufacturers, a law was passed which forbade the export of wool, raw or manufactured, from one colony to another "or to any other place whatsoever." The law was not prohibitory, for any colony could still manufacture woolen goods for consumption within its own borders.

Another colonial enterprise which became the subject of restrictive legislation was the beaver hat industry[qv]. An inquiry in 1731 disclosed that thousands of hats were being manufactured annually in the colonies, especially in New England and New York. The Hat Act of 1732 provided that no American-made hats could be exported from any colony, that no one could engage in hat making who had not served an apprenticeship of seven years, that no hat maker could have more than two apprentices, and that no Negroes should be employed in the industry. The Iron Act of 1750[qv] prohibited in the colonies the further erection of slitting mills, steel furnaces and plating mills. However, it also encouraged the production of colonial pig iron and bar iron by relaxing the duties when imported into England.

The colonists, whenever they wished, disregarded all administrative measures and laws which restricted manufactures. The reason why manufacturing did not develop more rapidly in the colonies was due to other causes, such as the difficulty of securing skilled labor, poor transportation, the lack of capital, and competition from agriculture.

[G. L. Beer, *British Colonial Policy, 1754-1763*; Arthur C. Bining, *British Regulation of the Colonial Iron Industry;* Eleanor Lord, *Industrial Experiments in the British Colonies of North America;* Curtis Nettels, The Menace of Colonial Manufacturing, *New England Quarterly*, Vol. IV.]

ARTHUR C. BINING

Manufacturing. Most manufacturing in the United States was still in the handicraft stage when Washington became President. The only power-using plants were mills for making flour, lumber, paper and gunpowder and for grinding plaster. Establishments in the fuel-using industries were limited to charcoal furnaces and forges for working iron, kilns for making lime, tar and potash, distilleries, brickyards, and a few small glass works and potteries.

During the next quarter of a century, ending with the War of 1812, such enterprises increased in size and number. More significant, however, was the introduction of Arkwright[qv] spinning, the erection of nearly 200 cotton mills in New England and the Atlantic states and the use of steam to move machinery. Meanwhile a manufacturing interest, which had been vocal in a small way when the first Federal revenue laws were drafted in 1789, had acquired sufficient influence by 1816 to give a protectionist[qv] color to subsequent customs legislation.

Between the War of 1812 and the Civil War American manufacturing acquired its characteristic pattern. Faced by a scarcity of accumulated funds and entrepreneurial experience, its leaders adopted corporate organization as a device for assembling capital and economizing management. This was particularly true in New England. Funds came at first from the accumulations of merchants engaged in the European and East Indian trade. Later the investment reserves of insurance companies and other financial institutions were a source of capital. The mercantile origin of many factories accounted for the early appearance of the agency or factor system and through it of larger corporation groups.

During this period the growth of manufacturing was encouraged by a rapidly expanding market protected to some degree by tariffs[qv] but even more by proximity to newly settled territories and by the adaptation of American products to pioneer requirements. Industry progressed under a frontier economy. Factories specialized in the quantity production of standardized goods to supply the multiplying demands of middle-class consumers. Native ingenuity and scarcity of labor stimulated the use of power devices. Yankee inventors designed textile[qv] machinery that enabled relatively inexperienced operatives to make cheaply and efficiently plain fabrics for common use. Americans developed interchangeable[qv] mechanism and its correlative, automatic machinery, for working wood and metals, in order to produce on a large scale and at low cost the tools, agricultural implements, household utensils, firearms, shelf clocks and vehicles demanded in ever larger quantities by the expanding population of the older settlements and the rapidly growing West. Simultaneously imperative traffic demands called into being shops and foundries to build steamboat machinery and locomotives, and improved transportation hastened the urbanization of industry.

During these fifty years the advent of factory goods in place of household and homespun manufactures revolutionized consumption. Although in 1860 plain fabrics, hats, footwear, axes and nails, plowshares and hoes still dominated manufacturing output, refinements and modifications of these staples as well as new inventions and novelties already held a conspicuous position in the market. The production of machine-knit goods, collars and cuffs, garment accessories and silks had become important industries. Manufactures of rubber were familiar. Pressed glass and porcelain, plated metal wares, lamps and numerous minor conveniences turned out in quantities by machinery had ceased to be luxuries. Changing fashions increasingly determined consumer demand and the industries that served it.

Quantitative evidence of progress was even more imposing. Between 1810 and 1860, or within the memory of people still alive at the latter date, the number of factory cotton spindles in the country increased from a few hundred thousand to over 5,000,000, each doing far more work than its predecessors. Output of pig iron rose from less than 60,000 tons to nearly 1,000,000 tons. The factory system extended from textiles to the production of clocks and watches, firearms, sewing machines and other metal manufactures. In 1853 American methods of making interchangeable mechanism with automatic machinery had aroused European attention and were studied by special commissioners from Great Britain.

Meanwhile a division of labor developed along sectional lines so that by 1860 the northeastern states were engaged chiefly in mechanical production, the South in growing staple crops like cotton*, and the West in producing and processing other raw materials and provisions.

American manufacturing was influenced profoundly by the Civil War. Military requirements advanced the art of working large masses of metal to exact dimensions as well as methods of treating metals to secure special qualities anticipatory to the coming age of alloys. Exigencies of the blockade of Southern ports stimulated improvements in steam engineering. Army demands caused a shortage of civilian man power that accelerated the development of the harvester and other farm machinery*. The war's outcome gave the industrial states control over Federal policies and inaugurated a period of high protection during which new branches of manufacture were brought to America from Europe. An era of expansion followed the restoration of the Union which revolutionized the national economy. The discovery of petroleum, the introduction of Bessemer steel, the opening of new mines on Lake Superior and in the South, the growth of inland cities, a great influx of immigrants from Europe, the approaching exhaustion of public lands and the disappearance of the frontier*** combined to turn the nation's energy increasingly toward manufacturing and to move industries from older sites to centers near new sources of raw material and recently created markets. This phase of American manufacturing development was passing at the close of the century and terminated with the World War.

Inventions* and scientific discoveries multiplied at an accelerated rate as the industrial organism grew more complex. Some of these, suggested at first by an immediate need, later created new industries. In the 1840's, ten years after the advent of railways, the electric telegraph*** arrived to facilitate their operation. But a major electrical industry did not arise until forty years afterwards, when the growth of cities called for better illumination and power distribution, and enlarged manufacturing plants outgrew shaft and belt transmission (*see* Electricity, Utilization of). In 1851 William Kelly, a Kentucky ironmaster, invented a rudimentary Bessemer process which enabled him to make better boiler plates for steamboats*. The perfected process came to America, however, nearly twenty years later, after heavier traffic made steel rails and bridges* a necessity. Petroleum appeared at the opportune moment to provide lubricants for millions of machine-age bearings and subsequently suggested the development of internal combustion engines which made it an indispensable source of power (*see* Oil Industry).

During this second half century also the nation became manufacturing-minded. Ancient rural prejudice against factories and factory life, which had moved New England mill owners to provide model boardinghouses for their employees and which was especially strong in the slaveholding South, made way for general recognition of the benefits of production by power machinery. Two years after the Crystal Palace Exhibition at London in 1851, where American manufacturers first exhibited their skill to Europe, a similar though smaller exhibition in New York testified to a national awakening on the subject (*see* Exhibition of the Industry of All Nations). America was officially represented at the Paris Exposition of 1867 and subsequent international fairs in Europe and learned much from this participation. At home the Centennial Exhibition* at Philadelphia in 1876 for the first time enabled the public to compare in a systematic way foreign and domestic manufacturing attainments. This exposition* movement, which has not ceased today, reached a climax at the World's Columbian Exposition* of 1893, with so impressive a record of America's industrial advance as to make the nation fully aware of its manufacturing destiny.

Quantity expansion was as characteristic of this period as of its predecessor (*see* Mass Production). Between 1869 and 1914 the number of wage earners engaged in manufacturing more than trebled. Meanwhile, however, the horsepower employed in factories increased nearly tenfold and the gross value of manufactured products rose from $3,400,000,000 to $24,200,000,000.

Before the turn of the century important manufacturing enterprises had begun to assemble under unified control all operations from extracting raw materials to marketing finished products. Along with this vertical integration occurred a horizontal grouping of plants engaged in similar processes of production but situated in different parts of the country under the ownership and direction of giant companies such as the United States Steel Corporation* formed in 1901. This movement necessitated large-scale financing from a capital focus like New York City and caused control over industrial policies to pass from operating proprietors to bankers (*see* Trusts). Simultaneously plant management was entrusted increasingly to salaried administrative technicians rather than to owners. Although proprietary establishments and moderate size corporations continued, numerous big companies thereafter dominated big industry and gave a characteristic pattern to American manufacturing.

During the 19th century most manufacturing

consisted of processing or shaping materials with hand tools or power machinery. The development of new substances was a relatively minor part of industrial activity. The factory overshadowed the laboratory. It is only during the most recent stage of economic history that organized research, made possible in part by the concentration of industrial capital in great corporations, has been directed consciously and continuously to the discovery of processes and products hitherto unknown and has made it the task of large-scale manufacturing to deal with molecules and atoms as well as masses (*see* Industrial Research). As early as the Civil War, to be sure, when Abram Hewitt watched his furnace assays and introduced gun metal from Great Britain, research into the structure and qualities of metals and alloys began slowly to emancipate American metallurgy from rule of thumb limitations. A line of advance indicated by the requirements of the Bessemer process in the 1870's and of high test armor ⌐late in the 1880's, and the development of electrolytic processes and the commercial production of aluminum in the same decade eventually gave industry the metals that make airplanes and automobiles*qv* possible. By the time of the World War chemistry was contributing much more than before to the country's industrial progress. By-product coke ovens, an established dye manufacture, and the production of rayons and plastics followed in quick succession. The latter opened the way for radios and moving pictures*qv* and added a major branch to textile manufacturing.

Industry's trend toward larger plants, scientific organization and financier control has placed price and wage fixing in fewer hands than formerly and provoked protest from workers and consumers. As a result government regulation*qv* has now become an important influence affecting manufacturing history. Industrialization has continued to extend from its early centers in the Northeastern states to those of the West and South, occasionally by the transfer of old works and factories to new locations, but in the main by the growth of manufacturing regions near more recently developed sources of raw materials*qv* and markets.

Early cultural manufactures in America were mostly limited to a few musical instruments and the products of the press. Today the publishing business is one of the largest in the country, mechanical art reproductions have multiplied enormously, and artistic design is almost as important as price and durability in creating market appeal for manufactured articles. In this field also the demands of the masses have been a first consideration as exemplified by the quantity production of cabinet organs and pianos in the last century and by the popularization of the camera (*see* Photography).

This is still the age of steel, however, and the furnace capacity of the country has expanded over 1000% in half a century (*see* Iron and Steel Industry). Between 1914 and 1935 the gross value of manufactured products and the power used in factories about doubled but the number of establishments declined and the wage earners they employed increased less than 10%. Meanwhile, however, the proportion of all manufacturing enterprises reporting an annual product valued at $1,000,000 or more rose from 49% to 69%. Classed according to value added by manufacture to raw materials, in 1935 industries with an output valued at more than a billion dollars annually ranked in the following order: food products, textiles, machinery, iron and steel, printing and publishing, chemical industries and transportation equipment—including automobiles and airplanes.

[Victor S. Clark, *History of Manufactures in the United States, 1893-1938;* J. L. Bishop, *A History of American Manufactures from 1608 to 1860;* Caroline F. Ware, *Industrial Revolution in the New England Cotton Industry, 1790-1846;* James F. Swank, *History of the Manufacture of Iron in All Ages;* Williams Haynes, *Men, Money, and Molecules;* Roger Burlingame, *March of the Iron Men.*]

VICTOR S. CLARK

Manufacturing, Household, employed a substantial part of the annual working time of American colonists and settlers for 200 years and continued in rural and frontier communities until after the Civil War. During much of this period, clothing, household goods, tools, implements and other articles of home consumption were made largely by members of the family. Wool cards, flax hatchels, spinning wheels, hand looms and dye tubs were even more universal than the sewing machine is today.

Throughout their history the American colonies experienced cycles of prosperity and depression comparable for their day with those under the republic. In hard times household manufactures expanded. In good times, when the people had money to pay for imported goods, they declined. Since periods of distress and their accompanying indebtedness to British merchants were commonly ascribed to the colonists' buying too many imported goods, public and private agencies exerted themselves at such times to encourage household manufacturing by establishing spinning schools, levying taxes payable in homespun yarn, and similar measures.

No comprehensive statistics exist concerning these manufactures. Contemporary observers before the Revolution testified to their prevalence except in towns and on plantations producing export crops. British colonial governors described them in reports to their London superiors, for they curtailed the market for British goods. Alexander Hamilton's[w] report on manufactures in 1791 was the first systematic attempt to gather information about them. A more ambitious effort was made to enumerate them in the census of 1810 but its figures are fragmentary. Thereafter factory goods rapidly replaced the products of family industry, though values of household manufactures were reported by the census until 1860 (see Manufacturing).

The most important of these were textiles and garments. According to the incomplete returns of 1810 over 72,000,000 yards of cotton, flax, woolen and mixed fabrics valued at nearly $38,000,000 were made in households. Maple sugar, cheese, cider, soap, candles, shoes, harness, furniture, woodenware, plows, harrows, tools, nails and other unrecorded or imperfectly recorded articles of household production probably added several million dollars to this total. Already, however, the output of local factories and workshops was displacing household products. According to later censuses the total value of family-made goods produced in the United States declined from $29,000,000 in 1840 to less than $25,000,000 in 1860, and by the latter date their per capita value, which had exceeded $5 in 1810, had fallen to less than $1.

[Rolla Milton Tryon, *Household Manufactures in the United States, 1640-1860.*]   VICTOR S. CLARK

Manumission (1790–1860) was the formal liberation of a slave by means of an instrument of writing, such as a will or a deed of manumission, as prescribed by state law. Often the slaves purchased their freedom, especially in the border states, over a period of years. Personal considerations, religion, the doctrine of natural right and the schemes for African colonization (see Liberia; American Colonization Society) influenced the slaveowners to free their Negroes. Changes in the attitude toward slavery within each state were reflected in the changing laws on manumission. Manumission was advocated by the moderate antislavery groups in opposition to the extreme abolitionist program for immediate, unconditional emancipation. By 1831 the Northern states had adopted measures for the gradual emancipation of their Negro population, but fear for the loss of white supremacy and increasing sectional strife caused the Southern and border states to restrict or prohibit manumissions. In 1860 Maryland had the largest number

of free Negroes, 49% of its black population, with Virginia holding second place. In the United States slaves increased from 697,897 to 3,950,531 between 1790 and 1860. During the same period free Negroes increased from 59,527 to 488,070, due largely to manumissions and the natural growth of population.

[A. D. Adams, *The Neglected Period of Antislavery in America;* James Wright, *The Free Negro in Maryland.*]
ELIZABETH W. MEADE

Maple Sugar. The Indians were familiar with maple sap, either drinking it fresh or boiling it down to syrup and sugar, usually in bark troughs into which hot stones were dropped. The French in Canada soon learned of its merits, but not until the late 17th century do we find the English settlers taking it up. Then the sugar rapidly became an article of food and commerce, especially in the Northern states, with Vermont leading all the rest. It was said in 1809 that probably two thirds of Vermont's population worked in spring at making sugar and syrup. In one town alone in 1794, eighty-three families produced 14,080 pounds of sugar; whence the state's total output was guessed at 1000 tons. The sap was first boiled in iron kettles; the introduction of shallow pans in the middle 19th century was revolutionary. On the frontier, where cane sugar and molasses were scarce or unprocurable, the maple tree sweetened the pioneer's food and drink, its sugar was his confection. Small quantities of maple sugar were made even in the Gulf states in early days, but this soon ceased. The use of the sugar declined in the 19th century, but the syrup gained in popularity. By 1900 Ohio was competing sharply with Vermont in its production.

[W. F. Fox and W. F. Hubbard, *The Maple Sugar Industry;* H. A. and Sybil C. Schuette, Maple Sugar: A Bibliography of Early Records, *Wisconsin Academy of Science, Arts and Letters Publications*, Vol. XXIX.]
ALVIN F. HARLOW

Maps, Coastal (1492–1900). Every phase of exploration and discovery in America is represented by one or more contemporary maps. Columbus plotted his course to the westward in 1492 either from Toscanelli's world map (1474) or from Martin Behaim's globe (1492). On his return to Spain with news of islands in the "Great Western Sea" between Europe and the Orient, Columbus drew a map of his discoveries. Only a copy, after the original, survives in the "Admiral's Map" (*ca.* 1507), first published in the 1513 edition of Ptolemy's *Geographia*. By the end of the 15th century several voyages had been completed, a series of explorations which probed the coastlines of both North and South America in an attempt to find a passage through the land barrier to the Orient. The mapping of America was a slow process, made slower by the unwillingness of navigators to exchange information and maps. In 1500 Juan de la Cosa, experienced navigator and pilot, compiled a large map of the world based on his own voyages across the Atlantic with Columbus and also Ojeda. On it he incorporated all he knew of the Spanish, Portuguese and English discoveries in America, including those of Vespucius and the Cabots. Two years later (1502), the discoveries of Corte-Real were outlined on a map drawn by Alberto Cantino. But only four maps are known which were actually printed between 1492 and 1510, so closely were new discoveries guarded in Spain and Portugal. And those four were printed in other countries. The earliest, by Giovanni Contarini (1506), was closely followed in 1507 by a globe and large wall map by Martin Waldseemüller. The globe gores of Waldseemüller were published with a text (*Cosmographiæ Introductio*) which suggested for the first time that the New World be called America. The fourth printed map, by Johann Ruysch, appeared in 1508.

Two general theories became current regarding the size and shape of America. The first, propagated in a series of maps by Oronce Finé, whose heart-shaped world was published in 1531, assumed that America was joined to Asia, that by sailing far enough north or south along the Atlantic coast a passage would be discovered which would lead to Asia, lying not far beyond. Others believed that America was a continent beyond which, at some distance, lay the Orient. But just how far beyond, nobody knew. This second theory was championed by Waldseemüller, whose ideas were developed and extended in a long series of maps by Johannes de Stobnicza. After Magellan had circumnavigated South America in 1520, and Cortés had launched several expeditions in the Pacific Ocean, the western coast of America began to take shape. It was first drawn on a map in 1529, but there was no other good map of the coast until 1544, when one attributed to Sebastian Cabot was published, probably based on the *Padron Real* in Seville. This master chart, maintained under the supervision of the Casa de Contraction, was supposed to have added to it all new discoveries, as soon as they were made. Many inaccuracies crept into this chart, and many discoverers failed to report their findings. The first authentic map of the coast of California, undated, but based on the discoveries of Cortés in 1535, was followed by a map of the same region by Alonso de Santa Cruz (1542–45).

The latter half of the 16th century saw many map-publishing firms spring up in Europe. From them issued hundreds of maps of America and parts thereof, strange combinations of factual and legendary information. Two cartographic productions by Gerard Mercator (Krëmer) led to a revolution in the mapping of America. On his world map of 1538 and his globe of 1541, Mercator, though unfamiliar with the discoveries of Cortés, separated America from Asia and rejected the Asiatic names commonly found in the heart of the New World. Meanwhile, three manuscript maps were produced in the Dieppe school of cartography (1541–53), to which we owe our cartographic knowledge of the three voyages of Jacques Cartier along the northeast coast. These maps incorporated much that was new, including the discoveries of Giovanni Verrazano (1524–28). With the publication of Gerard Mercator's large-scale chart of the world (1569), revised and improved by Edward Wright in 1655, the science of cartography came into its own, and mariners were able to navigate with a degree of certainty. Mercator's projection, in a modified form, is still in use today.

In the 17th century, three maps made by Capt. John Smith added to the knowledge of the Atlantic coast; these were a map of Virginia, 1608, a map of New England, 1614, and a general map of the Atlantic coast, 1624. Samuel Champlain's map of the northeast coast, published in his *Voyages*, 1613, represents the first attempt to lay down the latitudes and longitudes of the region, at the same time adding a great deal of information on the interior of the country. (For maps of the interior of the United States *see* Topographic Mapping.) On the west coast, beginning with a map in the 1622 edition of Herrera, and later on the Briggs map of 1625, California was shown as an island. This erroneous idea persisted for many years, although not all cartographers subscribed to it. Chief among the notable maps of the west coast printed in the 17th century were those of Robert Dudley, an expatriated Englishman who explored the entire west coast. His large-scale map of the region was included in his atlas, the *Arcano Del Mare*, Florence, 1646–47. On this map he supplied the world with a precise and elaborate nomenclature for the west coast.

In the 18th century an elaborate survey of the Atlantic coast was projected by the British government. The work was begun in 1765 under the direction of Capt. Samuel Holland, who worked with a detail of men until 1772. At that time it was estimated that it would take five more years to complete the job. In 1774 Capt. J. F. W. Des Barres replaced Capt. Holland, and from that date until 1781 his charts were printed and published as they were completed. Later they were bound in various atlas formats and issued under the title *The Atlantic Neptune* (1774–81). On the west coast Capt. George Vancouver[w] completed two years of surveying in 1792 and published his findings in three volumes (1798) including a valuable atlas, giving the world the first accurate maps of the region. Surveys of the Pacific coast were climaxed by Alexander von Humboldt and Aimé Bonpland, whose monumental works including many maps, published over a period of nearly fifty years, added greatly to our knowledge of the Northwest. The mapping of the United States by the Coast Survey, a branch of the Federal Government, began in 1807; the field work of this agency has been practically uninterrupted since its inception. After the Civil War geodetic operations were added to the function of the Coast Survey, and in 1878 the name of the agency was changed to Coast and Geodetic Survey[w].

[H. Harrisse, *The Discovery of North America*; J. G. Kohl, *Substance of a Lecture . . . on a Collection of Charts and Maps of America*; Walter Thiele, *Official Map Publications*; H. R. Wagner, *The Cartography of the Northwest Coast of America to the Year 1800*; Justin Winsor, *Narrative and Critical History of America*.]

LLOYD A. BROWN

Maps, Interior. *See* Topographic Mapping of the United States.

Marais des Cygnes Massacre, THE (May 19, 1858), was an incident of the Kansas Border War[w]. Charles A. Hamilton, a proslavery settler from Georgia, with a party of about thirty men, arrested a number of Free State men, eleven of whom were taken to a ravine near the Marais des Cygnes River and shot. All were left for dead, though five were only wounded, and one, falling with the rest, escaped unhurt. The shooting, without political significance, was probably an act of revenge. Whittier commemorated the event with a poem.

[L. W. Spring, *Kansas, The Prelude to the War for the Union.*]

SAMUEL A. JOHNSON

Marbury v. Madison (1 Cranch 137) was decided by the Supreme Court of the United States on Feb. 24, 1803. The importance of the decision in American constitutional history lies chiefly in the position taken that the Court would declare unconstitutional and void acts of Congress in conflict with the Constitution[w]. By this decision the doctrine of judicial review[w] was firmly entrenched in the governmental system, and the position of the judiciary was strengthened in the balance of powers among the legislative, executive and judicial branches of the Government.

The case grew out of the attempt of William Marbury to compel James Madison, Secretary of State, to turn over to Marbury a commission as justice of the peace which had been made out to Marbury by Madison's predecessor in office. The Supreme Court had to decide whether it could and should issue a mandamus to compel the Secretary of State to act. Intimately involved were issues of contemporary politics. The appointments of Marbury and other Federalists to newly created offices had been made as the Federalist[w] administration under John Adams retired to be succeeded by Republicans under the leadership of Thomas Jefferson (*see* Midnight Judges). At the head of the Supreme Court was Chief Justice John Marshall, a staunch Federalist. Granting the writ of mandamus would therefore be regarded not merely as an exertion of judicial power upon the Executive, but of Federalist power upon Republican (Jeffersonian)[w] party leadership as well. The customs of the Constitution were not yet well established, and it was not known whether the writ would be obeyed even if issued.

The opinion of the Supreme Court, written by the Chief Justice, began not with the constitutional question, the existence of which was not generally recognized, but with the question as to Marbury's right to the commission. He found that Marbury had such a right. Reasoning from accepted principles of government he concluded that the laws of the country must provide a remedy for the violation of a vested legal right, and that the writ of mandamus was the proper form of remedy. The remaining question was whether the Supreme Court could issue the writ. The power was not included among the grants of original jurisdiction made to the Supreme Court in the Constitution, but it was given by a section in the Judiciary Act of 1789[w], which had the effect of expanding the original jurisdiction of the Court beyond the group of powers enumerated in the Constitution. The Chief Justice argued that Congress could not expand the original jurisdiction of the Court. The act was therefore in conflict with the Constitution, and it became necessary to decide whether an act repugnant to the Constitution could become the law of the land. The Court answered in the negative. It held the statutory provision unconstitutional, and decided that the writ of mandamus could not issue from the Supreme Court.

Contemporary interest lay less in the doctrine of judicial review than in the political aspects of the case. The Chief Justice succeeded in condemning the acts of the Jefferson administration, and then, by a step which appeared superficially an act of judicial self-restraint, avoided a resulting decision which might have terminated in mutiny when it came to enforcement. It was only gradually that emphasis in appraisal of the case shifted to the topic of the power of the courts to invalidate Federal legislation deemed by them to be in conflict with the Constitution.

[A. J. Beveridge, *The Life of John Marshall;* Charles Warren, *The Supreme Court in United States History.*]
CARL BRENT SWISHER

March to the Sea, Sherman's. *See* Sherman's March to the Sea.

Marcy-Elgin Treaty. *See* Elgin-Marcy Treaty.

Marcy's Exploring Expedition of 1852 was ordered by the War Department for the purpose of exploring the Red River to its source. Capt. R. B. Marcy by reason of his previous exploration of the territory between Fort Smith (Ark.) and Santa Fé to determine the best route to California from the Mississippi, and his experience in exploring the Canadian and locating sites for forts in that region, was selected to command the expedition. His report, printed by Congress in 1853, disclosed that there were two main branches of Red River, whereas earlier treaties, including the one between Mexico and Texas, admitted but one. Between the two stretched valuable lands which were made the object of litigation between the United States and Texas in 1896 (*see* Greer County Dispute). No survey of the Red to its source had been made before Marcy's expedition. In addition to mapping the country, Marcy brought back much valuable scientific information and wrote one of the most interesting reports of the Southwest which we possess.

[G. Foreman, ed., *Adventure on Red River.*]
CARL L. CANNON

Marcy's March (1857). Because of menacing conditions in the Mormon country a military department was constituted in Utah. In the summer of 1857 troops commanded by Col. A. S. Johnston were sent there (*see* Mormon Expedition). The command wintered at Fort Bridger[w]. A detachment, under Capt. R. B. Marcy, was sent to New Mexico for supplies. It marched, Nov. 24, 1857, into a mountainous wilderness, without pathway or habitation, through deep snow and in bitter cold, to Fort Massachusetts, N. Mex. Preparing to return, Marcy was instructed to delay for re-enforcements, because of information that hostile Mormons planned to intercept him and destroy the supplies. On June 9, 1858, Marcy reached Fort Bridger.

[O. L. Spaulding, *The United States Army in Peace and War.*]
THOMAS ROBSON HAY

Mardi Gras is the name applied to the elaborate series of outdoor pageants and indoor balls held annually during the winter social season in New Orleans, and culminating on Shrove Tuesday, the day next preceding the beginning of Lent. Introduced on a small scale from Paris in 1827, this interesting spectacle still survives, in a greatly enlarged and refined form, after many lapses and revivals. The unique and colorful pageants, each sponsored by one of the numerous carnival organizations, are based upon themes drawn from history, fiction or mythology; and the balls given by the several groups are elaborate and exclusive.

[John S. Kendall, *History of New Orleans;* Lyle Saxon, *Fabulous New Orleans.*]
WALTER PRICHARD

Mare Clausum is a term in international law[w] indicating the principle of the "closed sea" as against *Mare Liberum,* or a "free sea." America's record has been in favor of the free sea (*see* Freedom of the Seas) , though she asserted the principle of *Mare Clausum* when she sought to break up pelagic sealing in Alaskan waters. She seized, summer of 1886, three English sealers operating well upon the high seas. America contended that with Alaska[w] she had acquired the privilege of closing the sea. A Russian ukase of 1821 was cited. In arbitration, America had to surrender the principle. Too often had she invoked the principle of *Mare Liberum,* including a protest against the ukase in question, which had resulted in Russian treaties with United States (1824) , and Britain (1825) , keeping the Bering Sea open.

[John Bassett Moore, *International Arbitrations.*]
JIM DAN HILL

Maria Monk Controversy, THE, originated in 1836 with the publication of the *Awful Disclosures of the Hotel Dieu Nunnery of Montreal,* which, although purporting to be Maria Monk's autobiography, was actually written by a group of New York clergymen. Its stress on priestly immorality aroused a storm of controversy which persisted even after several committees had investigated the Hotel Dieu Convent and pronounced Maria Monk a fraud. She retained some prestige until after her death in 1849 in a Five Points house of ill-fame, and her *Awful Disclosures,* an immediate best seller, inspired dozens of other revelations from fence-climbing nuns and has itself remained as the most influential single piece of nativistic[w] propaganda ever printed in the United States.

[R. A. Billington, Maria Monk and Her Influence, *Catholic Historical Review,* XXII; R. A. Billington, *The Protestant Crusade.*]
RAY ALLEN BILLINGTON

Mariana, the territory between the "Naumkeck" River (Salem) and the Merrimac from the sea to their heads and including Cape Ann, was granted to Capt. John Mason[qv] by the New England Council[qv] March 9, 1621/2. The evidence of Mason's actual occupation is slight. In 1679 his heirs claimed that his agent, Ambrose Gibbons, took possession in 1622 or 1623 and that he was ousted in 1630 by the Massachusetts Bay Company[qv]. Neither Mason nor his heirs were ever able to make good their title to the territory, which by the charter of 1629 was incorporated in that of the Massachusetts Bay Colony.

[J. W. Dean, ed., *Captain John Mason*.]
ROBERT E. MOODY

Marietta, the first settlement made under the provisions of the Ordinance of 1787[qv], was settled on April 7, 1788, when forty-eight men under the leadership of Gen. Rufus Putnam of the Ohio Company of Associates[qv] concluded their journey from Massachusetts to the mouth of the Muskingum River in the present State of Ohio. It was at first named Adelphia, but on July 2, 1788, in honor of Queen Marie Antoinette of France, the name was changed to Marietta. The machinery of government in the Northwest Territory[qv] first functioned here, on the arrival of Gen. Arthur St. Clair, governor of the Territory, July 9, 1788.

[*Ohio Archæological and Historical Society, Publications*, II.]
T. N. HOOVER

Marin, Expedition of (1753), planned by Duquesne and executed by Marin, established French authority in western Pennsylvania. Routes and sites were reconnoitered in 1752. Moving by water from Montreal in 1753, Marin occupied Presqu'île[qv]. Later LeBœuf and Venango[qv] were garrisoned. The expedition alarmed the Indians and precipitated British-American resistance.

[William Kingsford, *The History of Canada*, III; Frank Hayward Severance, *An Old Frontier of France*.]
ALFRED P. JAMES

Marine Corps, United States. An organization of marines, as a regular branch of our country's service, first came into existence by an act of the Continental Congress[qv] passed Nov. 10, 1775. During the Revolutionary War the marines saw service with the Continental navy, with the navies of several states and with Washington's army. After that war they suffered the same fate as the navy and went out of existence. The Marine Corps, as it exists today, was formed by the act of July 11, 1798, to help meet a national emergency—the Naval War with France[qv]. During that war and the Barbary War, as well as the War of 1812[qv], the marines took part in many naval battles. They played an heroic part in the ill-fated defense of Washington in August, 1814, and were with Jackson at New Orleans[qv]. During the succeeding three decades they helped the army fight the Indians and served with the navy throughout the world.

It was during the Mexican War, however, that the marines first won their spurs. They took part in the numerous naval operations along both coasts of Mexico, fought with Scott around Mexico City and played a conspicuous part in the conquest of California[qv]. In the Civil War their services were almost entirely on board vessels of the navy. They were almost lost sight of during the Gilded Age[qv] but with the coming of the Spanish-American War[qv] they again won fame by being the first to land in Cuba, and taking part in the two great naval victories. Several battalions of marines helped suppress the Philippine Insurrection[qv] and played a conspicuous part in the relief expedition to China in 1900 (*see* Boxer Rebellion).

The marines are best known today for the many interventions they have recently made in the countries of the Caribbean area. From the turn of the century until 1934 they were continually engaged in one or more efforts to restore peace in that troubled area—always acting as the strong arm for the nation's foreign policy. In three Caribbean countries they carried out extensive campaigns against disorderly elements and in each country trained a native force to keep order after they withdrew. In Haiti they fought two wars with *Cacos;* in the Dominican Republic it took them six years to suppress banditry; in Nicaragua they fought the bandit elements for an equal period but were recalled as the result of modified foreign policy before completing the job.

In the World War the marines did the hardest fighting in their history. A brigade served as one of the infantry brigades of the Second American Division and not only fought the desperate battle of Belleau Wood[qv] but was in the drive at Soissons, in the reduction of the St. Mihiel[qv] salient, in the attack on Blanc Mont, in the last great battle—the Argonne—and in many other far-flung operations. The primary role of the corps is to provide an auxiliary force for the United States Fleet[qv], called the Fleet Marine Force, to support the fleet in landing operations, and to defend temporary fleet bases. In addition it has for a number of years maintained a force in China.

[C. H. Metcalf, *A History of the United States Marine Corps; Annual Reports* of the Secretary of the Navy.]
C. H. METCALF

Marion, Battle at (Dec. 18, 1864). Gen. George Stoneman (U.), raiding southwestern Virginia from eastern Tennessee, struck the Confederates under Breckinridge at Marion, Va. During the battle Stoneman detached a force which moved back to Saltville and destroyed the salt works there. This was his original purpose, even though he could gain no decision against Breckinridge.

[*Battles and Leaders of the Civil War*, Vol. IV.]
ROBERT S. THOMAS

Marion, Fort, at St. Augustine, Fla.,[w] called by the Spaniards (at various times) San Juan de Pinos, San Augustine and San Marco, and by the British (1763–83) St. Marks, was finally brought to completion, at enormous cost, in 1756. In the meantime it had withstood Gov. Moore's attack in 1702 and James Oglethorpe's siege in 1740. The fort is a regular, coquina (shell-stone) structure of four equal, huge outer walls and four equal *bastiones,* each with a tower. It has about thirty rooms (one was the chapel), which inclose an open court 103 by 109 feet. A moat, drawbridge and portcullis suggest a mediæval castle. When the United States acquired Florida in 1819 the place was renamed for Gen. Francis Marion. The fort and the great coquina pillars of the ancient gate to St. Augustine stand today as monuments of the Spanish regime in America.

[J. T. Connor, The Nine Wooden Forts at St. Augustine, *Florida Historical Quarterly*, Vol. IV; Charles B. Reynolds, *Old Saint Augustine;* Herbert E. Bolton and Mary Ross, *The Debatable Land;* Amos A. Ettinger, *James Edward Oglethorpe, Imperial Idealist.*]
JONATHAN T. DORRIS

Maritime Commission, an independent Federal maritime regulatory agency created June 29, 1936, replaced the Shipping Board Bureau and was vested with all its duties, functions and powers as well as those of its predecessor, the Shipping Board[w]. The commission is directed by Congress to make such studies as are necessary to develop a merchant fleet that will serve as an effective naval and military auxiliary, provide a satisfactory service on all essential trade routes and transport a substantial portion of the United States water-borne international commerce. It is required to devise ways and means of inducing American exporters and importers to give preference to vessels of American registry; collaborate with vessel owners and shipbuilders in developing modern, efficient and economical vessels and power plants; remove, under its regulatory powers, all discriminatory rates, charges, classifications and practices; prescribe maximum or minimum rates in domestic interstate commerce, excepting that conducted on the Great Lakes; ascertain foreign and American ship-

building and operating costs; and grant subsidies which will equalize adverse capital and operating differentials and those created by foreign government subsidy programs.

It is required also to develop an efficient ship-operating personnel; encourage collective bargaining[w]; investigate employment and wage conditions in ocean-going shipping, in order to determine minimum manning scales and minimum working conditions for all officers and crews employed on vessels which have been awarded an operating differential subsidy or are operating a chartered government vessel. Should it not be able to negotiate agreements with private American ship operators to purchase new vessels in accordance with its long-term construction program, it is directed to build, recondition or remodel vessels for its own account and to charter them to private operators on a bare-boat basis. These vessels, however, must be sold to American shipowners whenever possible upon conditions specified in the act.

[United States Maritime Commission, *Annual Report to Congress*, 1937 and 1938.]
HOBART S. PERRY

"Mark Twain." On the old Mississippi River steamboats[w], the leadmen created a series of characteristic terms for the various markings on the leadline which were chanted as they called the soundings, thus: "quarter twain" indicating two and one-quarter fathoms; "mark twain," two fathoms or twelve feet. "Mark Twain" was first used as a *nom de plume* for newspaper articles by the old Mississippi River pilot, Isaiah Sellers. It was later adopted and made famous by Samuel L. Clemens.

[Mark Twain, *Life on the Mississippi.*]
ROBERT W. BINGHAM

Marketing. *See* Distribution of Merchandise.

Marketing Research, authoritatively defined as "the study of all problems relating to the transfer and sale of goods and services from producer to consumer" was developed between 1911 and 1926, and in the latter year received official recognition as a definite field of scientific activity through the publication of *Market Research Agencies* by the United States Department of Commerce. This guide to the organizations and publications of the field has since been revised periodically and issued under the title *Market Research Sources.* The 1938 edition listed 1040 sources, of which 219 were provided by Federal and state governments.

Prior to 1911 the chief examples of systematic fact-finding for marketing purposes were in the form of market news and statistics of demand for staple raw materials. Some isolated studies had been made of advertising media and methods. In 1911 the Commercial Research Department of the Curtis Publishing Company was established, and began a series of market analyses for important groups of manufactured goods. Similar departments were soon established by other publishers, by large advertising agencies, by universities, by trade associations and others. The problems investigated covered a wide range, including such physical factors as trade areas, channels of distribution and costs; also mental factors, such as advertising and sales appeals. The movement was stimulated by progress in product research and scientific factory management, and after 1920 by the necessity of developing peace-time markets to absorb the enlarged plant capacity of American industries. Largely through the efforts of the National Association of Marketing Teachers and the American Marketing Society (merged Jan. 1, 1937, into the American Marketing Association) the technique of marketing research was developed to a high degree of scientific accuracy.

[Lyndon O. Brown, *Market Research and Analysis*.]

G. B. HOTCHKISS

Markets, Public. When America was settled every European town of any importance had its public market and so in laying out their towns it was not unusual that the early settlers provided for them. There was a market place in Jamestown[w] as early as 1617 and one in New Amsterdam[w] as early as 1647. As in Europe, forestalling, regrating and engrossing were generally prohibited. The sale of meats and vegetables was permitted only in the public market. A sale of these articles at any other place was an illegal sale. The system was quite general in America in the colonial and early national periods. By the time of the Civil War, however, the public market system was well on its way to disintegration. It was inconvenient for the city householder to travel some distance to make daily purchases. As a result meat shops, although at first illegal, were established outside the public market but near the householder. The public market buildings were then abandoned, or in some instances were converted into wholesale private markets.

[Thomas F. DeVoe, *The Market Book*.]

FRED M. JONES

Marque and Reprisal, Letters of, are papers from a belligerent government authorizing privately owned vessels, commonly known as privateers, to engage in warfare against enemy commerce. The Constitution gives Congress power to "grant letters of marque and reprisal, and make rules concerning captures on land and water." According to former practice, the legality of captures was decided in prize courts[w], and the profits went chiefly to the privateer owners, officers and crews. During our earlier wars, privateering was widely practised and highly profitable. In the Revolution, letters of marque were issued by both Congress and state governments to 1150 vessels, and in the War of 1812 privateers numbering 515 captured about 1450 prizes. Among European nations privateering was abolished by the Declaration of Paris[w] (1856). It was practised only briefly by the South in the Civil War, and in subsequent wars commerce destroying has been limited to government-owned vessels.

[E. S. Maclay, *History of American Privateers*.]

ALLAN WESTCOTT

Marquette Iron Range, THE, is in upper Michigan near the midpoint on the south shore of Lake Superior. The oldest and largest mines are at Negaunee and Ishpeming, where iron was first discovered in the Lake Superior district, September, 1844, by United States land surveyors. The Jackson Mining Company was incorporated in 1848, and others were soon established. There was in the district abundant wood for charcoal to weld the iron into blooms and smelt it in blast furnaces, and Lake Superior charcoal iron became a standard product in the American market until superseded by coke furnace iron produced in the lower lake region. In order to connect the ore with the Great Lakes transportation routes it was necessary to build first a road and then a railroad from mines to ports. The "Iron Mountain" railroad, built in 1857 to serve this range, was the first railroad in the Upper Peninsula. The known ore resources will last for many years. The aggregate output of ore since inception to 1938 has been 181,000,000 tons.

[Rickard, *A History of American Mining*.]

L. A. CHASE

Marriage. Economic opportunity, the prevalence of domestic production, social and religious attitudes up to the 20th century generally encouraged marriage among the American people. The most distinct feature of the American marriage system during the colonial period was the break in New England with English tradition and the establishment of marriage as a civil contract. This anticipated by more than 200 years changes in the law and sentiment of the motherland. These early colonial laws generally required that marriages should be celebrated before justices of the peace[w] and in some cases nullity was the penalty for failure to comply. In the middle states choice was, as a rule, permitted between civil and ecclesiastical marriage. This was true at first in Maryland, but later the law required that a marriage be solemnized by a clergyman. In the Southern states the sacramental idea of marriage, brought from England, prevailed, and at first only members of the established Church of England[w] could perform the ceremony. During the first half of the 18th century there was a gradual trend toward the more tolerant policy of the middle states.

Throughout the colonies there was general disapproval of adults remaining unmarried, especially if they violated the custom of being connected with some family and maintained an independent life. Laws were frequently passed taxing bachelors[w]. It was customary for fathers to attempt to control the courtship of both sons and daughters, and laws were sometimes passed to enforce this power of the parent. In New England the custom of formal public betrothal led to a rigorous code in problems of sexual misconduct. Throughout the colonies the following provisions were generally enforced: The giving of notice of marriage; the presenting of evidence of the parents' consent; the celebrating of marriage before authorized persons, although common law marriage was sometimes also recognized; and the registering of the marriage in some form of public records. Frontier conditions, during the development of the West, continued the colonial trend toward early marriage, placed a premium on marriage on account of its economic advantages and stimulated the influences that were lifting woman's status.

The chief departures from orthodox marriage were the polygynous system of the Mormons[w] and the group marriage scheme of the Oneida Community[w]. The first was so administered by the Church as to emphasize eugenics. Although the idea of plural marriages was held as a Church doctrine, based upon Old Testament teachings, the proportion of such marriages never exceeded 4%. The Oneida experiment came to an end because of internal dissension and outside hostility. The Shaker[w] communities were founded on a religious basis of chastity and, therefore, gradually dwindled.

In spite of the industrial and social changes associated with modern culture, proneness to marry remains an American trait. Each ten-year period from 1890 to 1930 has seen an increase in the percentage of the married among the population, which is only in part due to the larger proportion of persons who fall within the mid-dle-age period. This increase in the percentage of married people was found especially among those from fifteen to nineteen years of age, but obstacles to such early marriage have become greater in recent years. During 1920 to 1930 there was evidence of a lessening trend of marriage in this age group. The history of the laws of domestic relations in the United States reflects an increasing recognition of the rights of women[w] and the emergence of the individuality of the wife.

[Willystine Goodsell, *A History of Marriage and the Family;* Ernest R. Groves, *The American Family;* Ernest R. Groves and William F. Ogburn, *American Marriage and Family Relationships,* Part II.]

ERNEST R. GROVES

Married Women's Property Rights. According to English common law, husband and wife were one, and that one was the husband. Hence, a married woman's property and earnings were at the complete disposal of her husband. In the colonies, however, by prenuptial agreements wives at times kept control of their property. The first legal concession to married women appears to have been made in 1809, when Connecticut gave them the right to make wills. Around the middle of the 19th century several states recognized the right of married women to their property or earnings, or both. By the beginning of the 20th century in every state married women could will away their property; in about three fourths of the states they had the right to administer and dispose of their property; and in about two thirds, they were permitted full control of their earnings. After the Nineteenth Amendment[w] was passed in 1920 discriminations were removed more rapidly; but in 1938 there were still a few states which, as regards married women's property rights, held to the old English common law.

[R. B. Morris, *Studies in the History of American Law;* Willystine Goodsell, *A History of the Family as a Social and Educational Institution;* A. W. Calhoun, *A Social History of the American Family from Colonial Times to the Present.*]

MARY WILHELMINE WILLIAMS

Marshall Convention, THE, was a gathering of the governors of Texas, Louisiana, Mississippi and Arkansas at Marshall, Tex., in May, 1865. It was called by Gen. Kirby Smith (C.) for the purpose of obtaining more favorable terms of surrender than had been granted by Grant and Sherman. The Confederate Army in the Southwest was rapidly disintegrating after the news of Lee's surrender and a strong effort was made to check this and try for time and better terms. The convention drew up terms and attempted to present them directly to Washington, but failed.

[C. W. Ramsdell, *Reconstruction in Texas.*]

J. G. SMITH

Martha's Vineyard, an island off the coast of Cape Cod, Mass., was granted by derivation from the crown of England to Thomas Mayhew, an English merchant, and his son as a proprietary with rights of government. The first settlement was made at Edgartown, 1642. The community was an outpost of feudalism in a new world of democratic tendencies. The Mayhew family held manors and offices for life until the Revolution put an end to hereditary pretensions.

[L. C. M. Hare, *Thomas Mayhew, Patriarch to the Indians.*]

LLOYD C. M. HARE

Martial Law, in American procedure, is the exercise of control by a state or by the National Government over the civil population, through its military forces, after civil authority has shown itself ineffective in meeting the emergency. The term does not apply, though often employed, to the exercise of authority by a belligerent in enemy territory under the laws of war^{qv}, as in Puerto Rico following American occupation of the island in 1898. A more common error in terminology appears in the frequent confusion of "military aid to the civil power"^{qv} with martial law. The President may legally furnish aid, short of a declaration of martial law, to a state government whose authority has been impaired by domestic disturbances, and may move separately to protect United States property, with or without the consent of the states in which such property may be located. Correspondingly, the state executive may act on his own initiative in parallel situations.

An historical summary of the instances of actual martial law in the United States may be divided into three classes: first, where the President of the United States promulgated the declaration *eo nomine;* second, where such proclamations issued from state executives; lastly, where military commanders on their own initiative invoked the law of necessity during an emergency, either in peace or war. There are but two instances of the first type: the presidential proclamations of Sept. 24, 1862, and July 5, 1864. The authority invoked under the latter led to the decision by the United States Supreme Court in the case of *Ex Parte* Milligan^{qv} (1866). The Court was unanimous in holding that the President and his military subordinates had violated the constitutional rights of the defendant, a citizen of Indiana, in denying trial by jury. The results of

the case were summarized later by Charles Evans Hughes: "Outside the actual theater of war, and if, in a true sense, the administration of justice remains unobstructed, the right of the citizen to normal judicial procedure is secure." The Whisky Insurrection^{qv}, in 1794, and President Cleveland's use of regular army troops in Chicago to prevent interference with the mails (*see* Pullman Strike) were not instances of actual martial law.

More frequent have been the declarations of martial law by state executives. Among the more notable instances was the Dorr Rebellion^{qv}, which occurred in Rhode Island in 1842. It gave rise to a declaration of martial law by the state legislature, probably the one instance in our history of such an occurrence. In 1877 widespread strikes in fourteen states, from New York to Texas, caused conditions which state executives attempted to meet by the use of state military forces. Where such forces were inadequate, President Hayes dispatched Federal troops; but in all instances where it did not appear that state authorities had used all means at their disposal for the restoration of order, Federal troops were under orders only to protect United States property (*see* Railroad Strike of 1877). Idaho in 1892 and again in 1899 was the scene of martial rule, declared by the governor (*see* Cœur d'Alene Riots). Federal troops were used in each instance to support the civil authorities. Colorado went through three serious periods of domestic disturbance: 1903–4, 1913–15, 1927–28, and in each instance martial rule was established in the disaffected areas (*see* Colorado Coal Strikes). In West Virginia, 1912–13, Gov. Glasscock declared the existence of a "state of war," and exercised war powers through military commissions and the state militia. Demobilization^{qv} after the World War virtually stripped several states of armed forces, and in consequence regular army units were used to restore order in Gary, Ind. (1919), and in the West Virginia coal fields (1920–21).

An instance of the third class of martial law—when a military commander acts on his own initiative—occurred in December, 1814, when Andrew Jackson, facing the threat of a British attack against New Orleans^{qv}, established martial law in that city and its vicinity. There were many cases of martial law in the zone of operations during the Civil War. A notable peace-time instance occurred when Gen. Funston, immediately following the San Francisco earthquake^{qv} of April, 1906, declared himself martial-law ruler of the stricken community. Floods and other disasters have similarly impelled the nearest military commander to assume full control.

[C. M. Dowell, *Military Aid to the Civil Power;* Charles

Fairman, *The Law of Martial Rule;* C. E. Hughes, *War Powers under the Constitution; Federal Aid in Domestic Disturbances, 1903-1922,* Senate Documents, Vol. XIX; *Report on Colorado Strike Investigation,* House Document No. 1630, 63rd Congress; *Cœur d'Alene Mining Troubles,* Senate Document No. 142, 56th Congress; *Report on Labor Disturbances in the State of Colorado from 1880-1904,* Senate Document No. 122, 58th Congress; Opinion of Justice Oliver Wendell Holmes in the case of Moyer v. Peabody, 212 U. S. 78; Opinion of Chief Justice Hughes in the case of Sterling v. Constantin, 287 U. S. 378.]

HERMAN BEUKEMA

Martin-Tolliver Feud, THE. In an election brawl in Morehead, the county seat of Rowan County, Ky., in 1884, John Martin was wounded by Floyd Tolliver. Later, Martin killed Tolliver and while he was under arrest for the shooting, he in turn was slain by Tolliver kinsmen. A vendetta ensued, lasting three years, causing such a state of anarchy that many peaceable citizens left the county and the population of Morehead shrank from 700 to 300. The Logan family was drawn in on the Martin side, and after twenty-three men had been killed in the war, Daniel Boone Logan armed a large force, closed in on Morehead, June 22, 1887, and in a pitched battle killed the Tolliver leaders, ending the feud.

[Charles G. Mutzenberg, *Kentucky's Famous Feuds and Tragedies.*]

ALVIN F. HARLOW

Martin v. Hunter's Lessee (1 Wheaton 304, 1816) upheld the right of the United States Supreme Court to review the decisions of state courts, which right had been challenged by the Virginia court of appeals. The opinion of Justice Story (Chief Justice Marshall not participating because of personal connection with the litigation) held that the Supreme Court's jurisdiction depended upon the nature of the case rather than upon the court from which it was appealed, and that Congress could confer appellate jurisdiction upon the Supreme Court in all cases involving the laws, treaties and Constitution of the United States.

[A. J. Beveridge, *Life of John Marshall;* Charles Warren, *Supreme Court in United States History.*]

LAWRENCE A. HARPER

Martin v. Mott (12 Wheaton 19, 1827). Considering an incident of the War of 1812, the Supreme Court decided that, when under the Constitution Congress authorizes the President to call militia[qv] against actual or imminent invasion, his decision "whether the exigency has arisen" is "conclusive upon all persons." Prompt obedience, said Justice Story, obviates maintaining huge standing forces.

[J. Story, *On the Constitution.*]

ELBRIDGE COLBY

Martling Men, THE, were a faction of the Jeffersonian Republican[qv] party of New York City, composed of followers of Burr and Lewis, who opposed DeWitt Clinton. They received their name from the fact that they met in the Long Room of Martling's Tavern, at the southeast corner of Nassau and Spruce streets, which was also the first "wigwam" of the Tammany[qv] Society, to which most of the Martling Men belonged.

[D. R. Fox, *The Decline of Aristocracy in the Politics of New York.*]

STANLEY R. PILLSBURY

Mary and John, THE, was the ship which, sailing from Plymouth on March 20, 1630, landed the pioneers of the Great Migration[qv], on May 30, at Massachusetts Bay where they founded a town to which they gave the reminiscent name of Dorchester[qv].

[*Memoirs of Roger Clap.*]

R. V. COLEMAN

Maryland. The Province or Palatinate of Maryland was carved out of Virginia by virtue of the patent granted in 1632 by Charles I to George Calvert, Lord Baltimore. George died before the patent had passed the royal seal, so that the province was colonized under the direction of his eldest son, Cecil. On Nov. 22, 1633, the *Ark*[qv] and the *Dove* sailed from Cowes via the West Indies, the settlers landing on Maryland soil early in March, 1634. On March 25, a cross was erected at St. Clement's Island in the Potomac; and, two days later, permanent settlement was begun some twenty-odd miles down the river. Here the provincial government was proclaimed, an event of peculiar interest in that it marked the separation of church and state, whereby religious freedom was first established on the American continent. The first capital was named St. Mary's City. The province was granted by an Anglican monarch to a Roman Catholic subject; and while Lord Baltimore provided a refuge for coreligionists, he welcomed without distinction all who cared to unite in the enterprise.

From 1634 to 1649 governmental attention to religious differences was confined to penalties imposed upon those who sought to interfere with the practice of "security of conscience." In 1649, after the advent of a number of Virginia-exiled Puritans, the General Assembly passed an Act Concerning Religion. The first part of this act affirmed the principles of toleration previously practised but imposed penalties upon non-Trinitarians. This restriction was invoked in the trial of Jacob Lumbrozo, a Jew. Prosecution, however, was delayed and finally abandoned on the restoration of the Calvert regime subsequently to the Cromwell interregnum. The Act Concerning Religion has been described as the "Toleration Act," whereas it delimited the practice of religious freedom that had preceded its enactment.

Following his brother's instructions, Gov. Leonard Calvert was careful to initiate and maintain friendly relations with the near-by natives. Although Sir John Harvey paid Calvert a friendly visit in the first conference of American colonial governors, the people of Virginia resented the intrusion of a separate colony under Roman Catholic leaders, whom they associated with the church and government of Spain. Furthermore, William Claiborne[q], secretary of state for Virginia, had established a settlement at Kent Island. This planting, Claiborne declared, invalidated Calvert's charter covering land "hitherto uncultivated." Lord Baltimore had, however, the ear of the king, and Claiborne was dispossessed in 1638. In all controversies affecting the principles underlying the management of his province, Cecil Calvert showed a high degree of courage. In 1666–67 he defied the will of the autocratic Sir William Berkeley, governor of Virginia, who attempted to force Maryland into an agreement to limit tobacco production and fix prices. Again, in the matter of acquiring and holding land within the bounds of his grant, he long contended with members of the Society of Jesus until his position was vindicated by the General of the Order and at the Vatican.

Cecil Calvert died in 1675, so that he did not live to see the encroachments upon his domain by William Penn, whose claims for a proprietary province below the 40th parallel were unsuccessfully disputed by Charles Calvert (see Pennsylvania). Following the accession of William and Mary, Calvert was deprived of his political prerogatives. In 1694 the seat of government was removed from St. Mary's to Anne Arundel Towne (Annapolis), where King Williams School, now St. Johns College, was founded in 1701. Albeit William III had issued instructions "to permit freedom of conscience to all," the Anglican Church[q] was established. Benedict Calvert renounced the Roman Catholic faith, and proprietary rights were restored to his son Charles in 1715.

During the period of controversy prior to the outbreak of the Revolution, the people of Maryland were active in opposition to the Stamp Act and to the principle of imposts exemplified in the duty on tea[qq]. The magistrates of Frederick County repudiated the Stamp Act; and, at Annapolis, the owner was compelled to burn a ship that had included in its cargo some of the for-

bidden leaf. The Maryland Convention summed up the reasons for resistance to Parliament as follows: "To continue to the legislatures of these colonies the sole and exclusive right of regulating their internal polity."

While Maryland declared her independence and formulated a constitution in 1776, she did not become a member of the Confederation until 1781, when Virginia yielded her claims to the Northwest (see Western Lands). This unique attitude in no way hampered her services in the common cause, the courage and discipline of the Maryland Line earning for the former province the title of the Old Line State. As a result of the successful defense of Baltimore in 1814, Francis Scott Key gave the nation the "Star-Spangled Banner"[q].

In 1860–61 Maryland was opposed to secession[q] and worked for reconciliation between the sections. When, however, coercion of the seceded states came up, the majority of the people in the East opposed a war of invasion, and thousands of volunteers crossed the Potomac to join the Southern Confederacy, a movement immortalized in Randall's "Maryland! My Maryland!"[q] Plans for secession had been blocked by the action of the Federal Government in causing the arrest of political and civic leaders. By the middle of May, Federal troops were in complete command of Baltimore and Annapolis. The Emancipation Proclamation[q] specifically excepted the slaves in regions under Federal control, and, in 1864, the General Assembly anticipated the Thirteenth Amendment[q] by abolishing slavery within the state.

[J. T. Scharf, *History of Maryland;* Matthew Page Andrews, *History of Maryland: Province and State.*]

MATTHEW PAGE ANDREWS

Maryland, Invasion of (September, 1862). The defeat of Pope (U.) in the Second Battle of Bull Run[q], and his retreat to the Washington lines, imposed upon Lee (C.) the necessity of adopting a new plan of operations. He wrote President Davis (C.), "The present seems to be the most propitious time . . . to enter Maryland." Regardless of objections, Lee added, "We cannot afford to be idle." Aggressive movements, he thought, would insure the safety of Richmond.

On Sept. 2, 1862, marching orders were issued. Within a week troops were concentrating at Frederick[q]. McClellan (U.), who had been restored to command, began organizing a force to defend Maryland. The "uncertainty" as to Lee's intentions was dispelled by the finding of the "Lost Order"[q]. McClellan accelerated his movements.

Meantime, Lee detached Jackson to capture

Harpers Ferry[w] while he led his army westward to an expected junction with Jackson in the vicinity of Hagerstown. Once across South Mountain[w] Lee's line of supply would be through the Shenandoah Valley[w].

On Sept. 13, McClellan reached Frederick. He hurried troops after Lee. Sharp fights took place at gaps in South Mountain; Lee sent re-enforcements, but by nightfall, finding the positions no longer tenable, he directed a retirement toward Sharpsburg. McClellan advanced slowly, diverted by Jackson's movement against Harpers Ferry. As soon as that place surrendered, Jackson hurried to Sharpsburg, leaving A. P. Hill to dispose of captured property and prisoners and then follow promptly.

McClellan reached Sharpsburg Sept. 16 and spent the day testing Lee's line. His attacks the following day brought on the battle of Antietam[w], characterized by more hard fighting than any other battle of the war. Lee, outnumbered, remained in possession of the field, but severe losses and heavy odds made it inadvisable to stay. McClellan did not again attack. On the night of Sept. 18, Lee recrossed the Potomac "without loss or molestation." The campaign was over.

[*Battles and Leaders of the Civil War*, Vol. II.]
THOMAS ROBSON HAY

"Maryland! My Maryland!" was written by James Ryder Randall in April, 1861. Randall, a college professor in Louisiana but a native of Maryland and a strong Southern adherent, was inspired to write this famous poem when he heard that Massachusetts troops had been attacked as they passed through Baltimore (*see* Baltimore Riot). In the hope that this episode would swing Maryland to the Southern cause, Randall made his appeal to the people of his state in verses that, set to the music of the old German song, "O Tannenbaum," soon became one of the marching songs of the Confederate Army.

[M. P. Andrews, *The Poems of James Ryder Randall.*]
E. H. O'NEILL

Mascouten, THE. Their name meant prairie people, but often they were spoken of as "people of the fire." Their earliest habitat was in lower Michigan whence with kindred Algonquian[w] tribes they took refuge in Wisconsin, building, about 1667, a village with the Kickapoo[w] on the upper Fox. There they were visited by Allouez, Perrot and other missionaries and traders. La Salle[w] enticed them, about 1682, to the neighborhood of his fort on Illinois River. In 1698 a band was on the Milwaukee River, whence

Juchereau[w] in 1702 engaged them as hunters for his enterprise on the Ohio River. Then they united with the Kickapoo and lived on Rock River. The latest mention was in the late 18th century.

[F. W. Hodge, *Handbook of American Indians.*]
LOUISE PHELPS KELLOGG

Mason, Fort, was established by the Federal Government in Mason County, Texas, in 1851, as frontier protection against the Comanche and Kiowa Indians[qw]. It was situated on the divide between the Llano and San Saba rivers. When Texas seceded in 1861, it was abandoned. There was also a fort of that name in Missouri, and one called Mason's Fort in Pennsylvania.

[F. W. Johnson and E. C. Barker, *History of Texas.*]
CARL L. CANNON

Mason and Dixon Line (1763–69) is the southern boundary line of Pennsylvania, and thereby the northern boundary line of Delaware, Maryland and a part of Virginia which is now West Virginia. It is best known historically as the dividing line between slavery and free soil in the period of history before the Civil War, but to some extent has remained the symbolic border line between North and South, both politically and socially.

The present Mason and Dixon Line was the final result of several highly involved colonial and state boundary disputes, at the bottom of which was the Maryland Charter of 1632, granting to the Calverts lands lying "under the fortieth degree of Northerly Latitude." Acute trouble arose with the grant and charter to William Penn in 1681, containing indefinite and even impossible clauses in regard to boundaries. The terms of the two charters were inconsistent and contradictory. A full century of dispute in regard to the southern boundary of Pennsylvania was the result. At first the trouble was between Pennsylvania and Maryland. Had all Pennsylvania claims been substantiated, Baltimore would have been included in Pennsylvania, and Maryland reduced to a narrow strip. Had all Maryland claims been established Philadelphia would have been within Maryland. There were conferences, appeals to the Privy Council[qw], much correspondence, attempted occupation, temporary agreements, all without permanent solution. The Maryland and Pennsylvania proprietors continued the quarrel until 1760, when an agreement was finally made, and under its terms, in 1763, two English surveyors, Charles Mason and Jeremiah Dixon, began the survey of the boundary line. Completed after four years' work, it was ratified by the crown in 1769. In the meantime, Virginia contested the boundary west of Maryland in a dispute which lasted for many years and ended finally with the extension of the Mason and Dixon Line westward, a settlement not completed until 1784. Historically the line embodies a Pennsylvania boundary triumph. (*See also* Pennsylvania-Maryland Boundary Dispute; Pennsylvania-Virginia Boundary Dispute.)

[James Veech, *Mason and Dixon's Line: A History;* John E. Potter, Pennsylvania and Virginia Boundary Controversy, *Pennsylvania Magazine of History and Biography,* XXXVIII; *Report on the Re-Survey of the Maryland-Pennsylvania Boundary, Part of the Mason and Dixon Line,* Harrisburg, 1909.]   ALFRED P. JAMES

Mason and Slidell Incident. *See* Trent Affair.

Mason Band, THE, of which Samuel Mason was a leader, consisted of highwaymen and river pirates who operated in pioneer days at Cave-in-Rock[qv], and upon the Ohio and Mississippi rivers and over the Natchez Trace[qv]. Mason was killed by two of his men in 1804.

[Otto A. Rothert, *The Outlaws of Cave-in-Rock.*]
OTTO A. ROTHERT

Mason Title, THE. Capt. John Mason commanded an expedition against the Hebrides in 1610 for which he advanced money never recovered. This debt was indirectly repaid by land grants later. From 1615 to 1621 he was governor of Newfoundland, and while there explored New England's coast. On returning to England he became associated with Sir Ferdinando Gorges[qv] and others on the Council for New England[qv], and received from it on March 9, 1622, the grant of Mariana[qv] in Massachusetts, and on Aug. 10, jointly with Gorges, the Province of Maine[qv] between the Merrimac and Kennebec rivers. European wars hindered settlement. With peace, the proprietors divided their land, the Council on Nov. 7, 1629, granting to Mason the Province of New Hampshire[qv], extending from the Merrimac to the Piscataqua and running inland sixty miles up each river. On Nov. 17 he and Gorges were granted Laconia[qv]. Mason sent over settlers to the Piscataqua and spent about £22,000, with no return. In 1635 the Council, breaking up, confirmed Mason, by then its vice-president, in his title to Mariana, New Hampshire, Masonia on the Kennebec, and the south half of the Isles of Shoals[qv]. He died soon after and his widow allowed the colony to shift for itself.

In 1675 his heirs recovered title, but collected little money from the settlers. Samuel Allen bought the title in 1691 for £2750, and likewise profited nothing. The sale was voided by the Privy Council[qv] in 1739 and in 1746 John Tufton Mason, the heir, sold his lands in New Hampshire to a group of twelve leading citizens, called the Masonian Proprietors. Their offer to sell to the Province of New Hampshire was not met, and they granted out about two million acres. The last meeting of the Proprietors was in 1846; their records have been printed by the state. The long quarrels between the people and government of New Hampshire, the heirs of Mason, and those of Allen were very important in determining the political and economic history of the state, its settlement, its boundaries and indeed its separate existence.

[C. W. Tuttle, *Captain John Mason;* W. H. Fry, *New Hampshire as a Royal Province;* Otis G. Hammond, The Mason Title and Its Relation to New Hampshire and Massachusetts, in *Proc. American Antiquarian Society,* 1916; J. T. Adams, *The Founding of New England;* C. M. Andrews, *The Colonial Period of American History.*]
HERBERT W. HILL

Masonry. Jonathan Belcher, governor of Massachusetts 1730–41, became a Freemason when in England in 1704, and on his return to Boston, was said to have been the only member of the order in the city. A lodge of Masons, supposed to have been British soldiers, met for a time in King's Chapel, Boston, in 1720. A Masonic lodge is believed to have assembled in Philadelphia as early as 1730. Benjamin Franklin, in his weekly newspaper published there, printed an alleged exposure of Masonry, written in England; but a year later he was initiated into a Masonic lodge. A Philadelphia member installed a lodge in Boston in 1733. Masonry died out in Philadelphia in 1738, but was revived by Franklin in 1749. Lodges appeared in other cities. George Washington was initiated at Fredericksburg, Va., in 1752; he took the oath of office as President upon his Masonic Bible, and in laying the cornerstone of the Capitol at Washington, he used a Masonic trowel. The participation thereafter of Masons in cornerstone layings was often strongly opposed by Anti-Masonic factions. The first Scottish Rite lodge in America was installed at Albany in 1768. The first Grand Encampment of the Knights Templar of which there is record was in South Carolina in 1780. The first shaft on the site of the present Bunker Hill Monument was a memorial to Dr. Joseph Warren, a Grand Master of the order, who was killed in the Battle of Bunker Hill[qv]. The Masons donated this with its plot of ground to the Bunker Hill Monument Association, on condition that a model of the original structure be kept in the base of the newer one. Lafayette, a French Mason, laid the cornerstone of the great monument in 1824. At its dedication in 1842, Daniel Webster, the chief orator, made no reference to Masonry, to the indignation of members of the order. Anti-Masonic feeling was at its height then. John Quincy Adams was a bitter opponent. Henry Clay had joined the order in youth, but in later life practically disowned it. Strong feeling had been aroused in 1826 by the kidnapping and alleged slaying of one William Morgan of Batavia, N. Y., who had revealed Masonic secrets, and an Anti-Masonic political party[qv] existed for some years thereafter. The feeling against secret orders died away in the latter 19th century. In 1775 a British army lodge in Boston initiated Prince Hall and fourteen other Negroes as a new lodge; and Negro Masonry has ever since that time pursued an existence separate from that of the whites.

[Robert F. Gould, *A History of Freemasonry;* J. E. Craig, *A History of Freemasonry.*]

ALVIN F. HARLOW

Mass Impression, Agencies of, include newspapers and widely circulated periodicals, radio broadcasting stations and motion pictures[qqv]. The average daily circulation (1939) of English language daily and Sunday newspapers in the United States is approximately 41,300,000; radio broadcasting stations have a potential listening audience of 50,000,000; and the weekly attendance at motion pictures is estimated to be about 85,000,000.

Technical improvements in the process of gathering news, manufacturing and distributing newspapers; spread of literacy and educational facilities; growth of population; large-scale production accompanied by lower unit costs and reduced rates; growth in advertising revenues, as well as improvements in transportation, have contributed to the rise of newspapers with large circulations. Although newspaper circulation has increased since 1900, the number of independently owned papers has decreased due to the economies of large-scale operation, the growth of newspaper chains, voluntary consolidations and forced liquidations. By 1930 over 900 cities were served by only one paper each. An increasing number of papers have a national circulation. The rise of newspapers with mass circulations has been accompanied by significant changes in content: improvement in news reporting, standardization, extensive use of syndicated features, widespread use of pictorial methods of presentation, declining importance of the editorial, and the increasing importance of the political essayist and feature writer. A few periodicals such as *Collier's, The Saturday Evening Post, Life,* etc., may properly be called agencies of mass impression because of the size of their circulations.

Of considerable significance is the increasing number of news and pictorial magazines.

Radio attained its majority as an agency of mass impression after the World War. There are about 27,000,000 families owning radio receiving sets in the United States, served by nearly 700 domestic broadcasting stations. The program content of radio broadcasts has been greatly influenced by the mass audiences served. Great emphasis has been placed upon programs appealing to all classes at the same time; there is less opportunity for differentiation; a pronounced tendency toward standardization. Music and entertainment are the principal features. The effect of specific broadcasts is quicker and more widespread than in the case of newspaper items.

Radio broadcasting was first used politically in the presidential campaign of 1924 and has been used extensively since then by political parties and governmental agencies. Although privately owned and operated, it is subject to government regulation and the supervision of a Federal Communications Commission[qv] established in 1934. Its increasing use as an advertising medium, as a source of entertainment, as a news agency, and as an instrument of party warfare and political comment, has had a profound although indeterminate effect upon social, political and economic history. Television[qv] promises to be another instrument of mass impression of unprecedented importance. It has passed through the experimental stage and is now functioning in the large population centers of the United States.

The significance of the motion picture as an agency of mass impression is due in part to its general appeal to persons of all ages and classes, of both sexes; to the controlled surroundings and receptive character of the audience; to the attention time at the disposal of the exhibitor; and to the unrivalled opportunity available for using visual as well as auditory stimuli. The motion picture business is privately owned and operated, is subject to some regulation by the states but none by the Federal Government.

Agencies of mass impression tend to produce a more closely knit and unified culture; increase the influence of groups and individuals able to use them effectively; accelerate the process of social change by producing widespread changes in public attitudes simultaneously; emphasize the need for social control, and lessen the relative influence of the home, the church and the school in the formation of public attitudes. (*See also* Public Opinion; Propaganda.)

[Broadcasting and the Public—A Case Study in Social Ethics, *Department of Research and Education of the*

Federal Council of the Churches of Christ in America; A. M. Lee, *The Daily Newspaper in America;* Howard T. Lewis, *The Motion Picture Industry;* O. W. Riegel, *Mobilizing for Chaos: The Story of the New Propaganda;* Malcolm M. Willey and S. A. Rice, *Communication Agencies and Social Life.*]   HARWOOD L. CHILDS

Mass Production, in general practice, may be described as the application of machinery in simultaneous or successive operations to the manufacture of identical articles. Standardization of process and continuity of operation are two essentials and the corollaries are large, continuous and standardized markets. In this sense it is probably American in origin though its background is large-scale production (from which economists differentiate it sharply) which began in the English industrial revolution. As attention came to be concentrated on operation rather than organization—on efficient mechanization and close co-ordination of all contributory processes rather than mere departmentalism, specialization and division of labor—the influences are primarily American.

For the origin of the pattern of all mass production of machines, we must go far back to Eli Whitney who, in 1798, with jigs and machine processes of his own invention, introduced the interchangeable parts[qv] system in the manufacture of firearms. In mass production of goods other than machines, a great pioneer was Oliver Evans in the same period; his contribution was the combination of several different operations in the same machine and in the co-ordination of different machines in a continuous process.

Following Whitney's pattern, manufacture moved toward mass production through other firearms, notably the Colt revolver, through the sewing machine and farm machinery to the automobile[qqv] in which true mass production may be seen at its highest degree of perfection. From Evans' card-making machine and flour mill, we may trace the steps toward mass production of hardware, shoes, ready-made clothing, food products and many other manufactures. In the late 19th century, new methods introduced by William Richard Jones in the steel industry and by the first efficiency engineer, Frederick Winslow Taylor, were further American steps (*see* Industrial Management), though mass production did not reach anything approaching its present stage of efficiency until the 20th century.

Probably Henry Ford has contributed most to true mass production. In his design of multiple assembly lines leading into a final assembly line and in the co-ordination of men and machines, the simplification of processes and the reduction of work to a point where each man or machine unit in a long series performs a single specialized operation, he has evolved what seems to the observer a miracle of timing and continuity. His cardinal principles are that the work must be brought to the man (in practice by conveyor belts) ; that no portion of the entire process must at any time be idle; and that all material shall be in constant transit. This last principle is carried to the point where there are no warehouses or static inventories in a Ford plant.

Ford methods have been adopted by other manufacturers of motor vehicles and, in general, by makers of such machines as small electric motors and every variety of domestic machinery for which there is a large, continuous market and a fairly standardized demand, with the result that more of such articles are available in America to every level of society than in any other country.

But we must examine the social factors in this development. The original patterns such as those laid down by Whitney, Evans, Slater, Howe, Lowell, McCormick and many others (*see* Inventions, Great; Machines) were undoubtedly designed under duress of labor shortage so characteristic of our earlier agricultural and industrial society. Later, however, there arrived another factor which may be called the democratic spirit. It is notable that many of our so-called necessities such as automobiles, domestic machines, plumbing, are regarded as luxuries in other countries and restricted to certain classes. Some of these, like the motor vehicle, are artificially restricted in Europe by taxes reflecting government attitude toward class tradition, and mass production of such commodities has therefore been inhibited.

With the breakdown of a class hierarchy in America another attitude evolved. This was greatly stimulated by the cheap press (from 1833) under the influence of such men as Benjamin Day and James Gordon Bennett. The penny newspaper[qv] was something closely approximating a mass-produced commodity; it not only proved that, by such efficient method, daily news and comment (formerly something of a luxury) could be made available to every one, but the newspaper itself became a vehicle for the spread of the democratic spirit. Further, as it carried advertising, there arrived the implication that whoever could read could buy. Thus was crystallized in the social consciousness the equality articulated in the Declaration of Independence, and politically adapted in the Constitution. With the growing, popular American conviction that each citizen was "as good as the next man"—a conviction fostered by pioneer equalities of hardship and opportunity—a kind of socialization of goods came into the pattern and manufacturers saw, in the absence of any psychological class inhibition, an endless demand providing commodities could be made cheap enough.

Through the late 19th century we see an incessant effort in this direction. Rigid standardization became necessary in every industry engaged in large-scale production. Prices, in consequence, fell to a point where such luxuries as the sewing machine and the bicycle became virtual necessities in almost the lowest income brackets. With the new mechanization, scientific methods and the collaboration of such sciences as chemistry and metallurgy, any reduction in quality due to large-scale production was overcome and mass production extended the "necessity" range to motor cars, plumbing facilities, radio receiving sets, mechanical refrigerators, washing machines, building materials, electric razors and so on.

The interplay of the democratic and mass-production impulses is undoubtedly responsible for America's leadership in industry—a single statistical demonstration of this being that more than 75% of the world's motor vehicle production is in the United States.

[R. Burlingame, *March of the Iron Men*, and *Engines of Democracy;* H. E. Stearns, ed., *America Now*, chapters on Industry, Invention, Science; H. Ford and S. Crowther, *My Life and Work*, and *Today and Tomorrow;* E. H. Schell, The Future of Production, in *Annals*, *American Academy of Political and Social Science*, CXLIX, Part I, May, 1930; G. and D. Bathe, *Oliver Evans;* J. W. Roe, *English and American Tool Builders;* S. Chase, *Men and Machines;* Lewis Mumford, *Technics and Civilization;* F. B. Copley, *Frederick W. Taylor, Father of Scientific Management.*]   ROGER BURLINGAME

Massac, Fort (1757–64; 1794–1814), was erected in 1757 by Charles Philippe Aubry by order of the commandant of the Illinois. Originally named Fort Ascension, it was renamed Fort Massiac in 1758 in honor of the Marquis de Massiac, French minister of marine. In 1763 Aubry described it as "a Picqueted Fort with four Bastions and eight pieces of Cannon" garrisoned by 100 men, but in the following year it was abandoned and soon afterward destroyed by the Indians.

The site remained unfortified until 1794, when Maj. Thomas Doyle, under orders from Gen. Anthony Wayne, erected a new fort. Mistakenly attributing the former name to a legendary massacre, the post was called Fort Massac. The fort was built of pickets with a small bastion at each angle. Its garrison, which was maintained until 1814, varied from a handful to nearly 100 men.

Fort Massac was of minor military significance, and is known today principally because George

Rogers Clark[qv] landed on its site at the outset of his Illinois campaign.

[C. W. Alvord and C. E. Carter, *The Critical Period*, *1763-1765;* C. W. Alvord, *The Illinois Country, 1673-1818;* Mrs. M. T. Scott, Old Fort Massac, in *Transactions of Illinois State Historical Society*, 1903.]

PAUL M. ANGLE

Massachusetts, Fort, at Williamstown, Mass., was one of the three "Province Forts" erected for the protection of the Deerfield Valley. It was built in 1744 by order of the Massachusetts Court. In August, 1746, it was attacked by a party of French and Indians, led by de Vaudreuil, and its garrison, which had been depleted to render assistance in the war to the eastward, destroyed. It was rebuilt in 1747, put in command of Capt. Ephraim Williams, and came to serve as headquarters for the surrounding forts and blockhouses. On Aug. 2, 1748, it was again subjected to attack.

[Justin Winsor, *Narrative and Critical History of America*, Vol. V.]   LEON W. DEAN

Massachusetts, Fort, was established in 1852, at the foot of Blanca Peak on Ute Creek in the San Luis Valley, Colo., by Maj. George A. H. Blake, of the U. S. Army, in order to protect the settlers on the upper Rio Grande against the Ute Indians[qv]. The buildings and stockade of pine logs accommodated 150 men, infantry and cavalry. In 1858 the post was moved six miles south and the name changed to Fort Garland.

[M. L. Crimmins, Fort Massachusetts, in *Colorado Magazine*, July, 1937.]   COLIN B. GOODYKOONTZ

Massachusetts, State of. The events which marked the end of Massachusetts as a royal colony[qv] presaged war, and in April, 1775, an effort of Gen. Gage to secure military stores of the colonists brought on the first battles at Lexington and Concord[qv]. On June 17 occurred that of Bunker Hill[qv] and the following month Washington arrived to take charge of the colonial forces with the resultant evacuation of Boston[qv] by the British and large numbers of Loyalist Bostonians. During the remainder of the war the tide of military operations flowed to other colonies though Massachusetts contributed liberally in men and money.

The state had adopted a constitution in 1780, but as a result of economic distress in 1786 there was a serious rebellion, led by Daniel Shays[qv], which was of national importance in that it helped to stir conservatives everywhere to form the Federal Constitution of 1787. Massachusetts became strongly Federalist in politics and, as one of the leading maritime states, was bitterly opposed to Jefferson and his Embargo policy, as it was to the War of 1812[qw]; and in 1814, in the Hartford Convention[w], the question of secession was broached. Sharing the separatism of New England[w] as a section, the state was also opposed to westward expansion, notably in the Louisiana Purchase and the Mexican War[qw].

The completion of the Erie Canal[w], favoring New York and opening the rich farm lands of that state, hurt Massachusetts' agriculture, and turned her attention still more to fisheries[w], manufacturing and overseas trade, especially that with China[w]. The era of the famous clipper ships[w] extended from about 1843 to the opening of the Suez Canal, 1869, and was a glorious chapter in the history of the state.

In this same period, Boston became the publishing and literary center of the country, the group of writers there and in Concord including such names as Parkman, Lowell, Longfellow, Whittier, Emerson, Hawthorne, Thoreau and others. It was a time of intellectual and social ferment in which the state took a leading part resulting in such movements as Brook Farm, Abolitionism under the lead of William Lloyd Garrison, and the formation of the Free Soil Party[qw]. In education, also, although educational facilities in the earlier periods have been much overestimated, the state was of wide influence, particularly as exemplified in the labors of Horace Mann (1796–1859), and the later development of Harvard[w] and the establishment of colleges for women, such as Smith, Wellesley, Radcliffe and others.

When the Civil War came, unlike that of 1812, the state was wholeheartedly on the side of the Union. From that time also it has been strongly Republican and, on account of its manufactures, devoted to a high tariff, though in the past few decades there has been disturbing transfer of much of its textile industry to the South, which has raised serious problems. In the later 19th century there was likewise a great change in population due to foreign immigration, especially Irish but followed by French Canadians, Poles and others. Westward emigration also drained off much of the old stock. If, with our present vast population and territory, no one state can again occupy the dominant position of Massachusetts in the past, there is no other which has in so many different ways so deeply influenced our history and thought.

[J. T. Adams, *New England in the Republic, 1776-1850*; A. H. Clark, *The Clipper Ship Era; New England's Prospect 1933*, Am. Geog. Soc.]

JAMES TRUSLOW ADAMS

Massachusetts as a Royal Colony. This new phase in the history of the colony may be considered as lasting from the annulment of its charter in 1684 (*see* Massachusetts Bay Company) to the revolutionary establishing of the Massachusetts Provincial Congress[w] to administer government in 1774. The insistence of the Massachusetts leaders on a larger measure of independence than could be allowed at the time by the British authorities if they were to exert any imperial control had, in 1684, laid the colony prostrate. It now had no charter, and in 1686 a royal government was inaugurated provisionally with a native son, Joseph Dudley, as "president." He was soon replaced by Sir Edmund Andros who as royal governor of the Dominion of New England[w] (including New York) greatly irritated the colonists by lack of tact and unwise laws, though not essentially tyrannical. When word came of the overthrow of the Stuarts in Britain Andros was imprisoned, and in 1691 the colony received a new charter, adding Maine and Plymouth[qw] to the former Massachusetts. Although it much diminished the power of the old theocratic[w] party it was a reasonable instrument, and the colony was not harshly treated, though henceforth it would have a royal governor. The first under the new charter was Sir William Phips, a New England man who had unsuccessfully attacked Quebec[w] in 1690, almost bankrupting the colony by a debt of £200,000.

It was the lowest period in the colony's history and the most sterile intellectually. In 1691–92 came the witchcraft[w] delusion, but after the turn of the century Massachusetts began to take a larger share in the life of empire, and her troops played honorable parts in imperial expeditions against Jamaica, 1702, Canada, 1709–11, and Cartagena[w], 1740. The colony was also chiefly responsible for the capture of Louisburg[w] in 1745, and the loss of the old charter was proving a benefit rather than a detriment to its life. It had got into serious financial difficulties with overissues of paper money[w] but the payment to it of £183,000, sterling, by England for its services in the Louisburg expedition enabled it to redeem about £2,000,000 of its depreciated currency, which greatly assisted its now rapid economic development. Thought had also become much more liberalized, including Harvard[w].

Commerce had expanded and during the French and Indian War[w] there had been much smuggling and trading with the enemy. In 1756 England introduced a system of general search warrants (already authorized locally by the Massachusetts courts), against which James Otis made his famous speech opposing Writs of Assistance[w] in 1761. The colonists were conscious of their growing wealth and power, and protested vigorously against the measures passed by Parliament after the peace of 1763, notably the Stamp Act[w]. In especial, Samuel Adams, an extremely able agitator, organized resistance and manipulated public opinion. Building up his system of Committees of Correspondence[w] he probably did more than any other man in America to prevent any settlement with the mother country.

In 1768 British troops were stationed in Boston and on March 5, 1770, a clash occurred between them and citizens, of which latter five were killed. The mob, led by a halfbreed Negro, had been the aggressor, but the affair was skilfully employed to stir public emotion and was dubbed the "Boston Massacre"[w]. New laws as to trade had led to acts of violence and in 1773 the famous "Boston Tea Party"[w] was staged. A band of Bostonians, slightly disguised as Indians, boarded a British ship and threw overboard the cargo of tea, estimated to be worth £15,000. The repercussion of anger in England was immediate and Parliament closed the port of Boston to all trade. This Boston Port Bill[w] went into effect June 1, 1774, and on that day the royal governor, Hutchinson, sailed for England, turning over the administration of the colony to the British commander in chief in America, Gen. Gage.

Meanwhile, there was mob violence in many parts of Massachusetts and government was rapidly breaking down. Members of the colonial council who lived in the country were hunted from their homes and forced to resign or take refuge with Gage in Boston. Gage canceled the writs for the autumn elections to the General Court[w], and the towns, claiming this to be illegal, elected representatives to a "Provincial Congress," which became the revolutionary government of the colony. The royal government had ended, and this may be taken as the close of the period, though Gage was still in Boston with his troops. Meanwhile, in wealth, population and influence, Massachusetts and Virginia had become the most important colonies in America, and were to take the lead in the struggle now to follow.

[J. T. Adams, *Revolutionary New England, 1691-1776.*]
JAMES TRUSLOW ADAMS

Massachusetts Ballot. Previous to July 20, 1629, all voting in New England was by acclamation or by the uplifted hand, but on that date the Salem church used the ballot[w] in choosing a pastor. By 1634 the ballot was used in electing the governor of Massachusetts. In 1645 Dorchester ordered that all "elections be by papers," that is, by ballots. Paper being scarce, kernels of wheat and Indian corn were sometimes used, the wheat for the affirmative and the corn for the negative; in Dedham, in 1643, Assistants[w] were chosen by the use of Indian beans, white for the affirmative and black for the negative, hence the term "black ball" to signify a negative vote. The Australian, or secret, ballot was introduced into the United States by Massachusetts in 1878.

[A. B. Hart, *Commonwealth History of Massachusetts;* J. F. Sly, *Town Government in Massachusetts.*]
R. W. G. VAIL

Massachusetts Bay, Franchise in, was limited to church membership under the first charter and to property holders under the second. The charter of 1629 contained no such specific provisions, but because it gave to stockholders, or freemen[w], the right to vote in the trading company's General Court[w], and to the General Court the authority to admit new freemen, the Puritan leaders, after the Great Migration[w], were able to limit suffrage to those in sympathy with their religious beliefs. Only about one fifth of the adult males had any share in the colony government. Charles II's protest against the suffrage limitations brought occasional gestures of compliance, but the Massachusetts leaders could not submit to such demands without endangering the theocracy[w] itself. This close union of church and state was broken by the annulling of the charter in 1684. Under the Dominion of New England[w], 1686–89, there was, in the absence of a representative assembly, no colony franchise, but when the leaders of revolution in 1689, without authority from England, re-established the old charter government, they made a wide extension of suffrage in order to win support to the movement for restoring the charter. To their disappointment, the new charter of 1691 did not confirm the old freemanship, but gave the suffrage to forty-shilling freeholders[w] and to others who had property of the value of forty pounds sterling. The state constitution of 1780 contained a similar property qualification, but when a general national movement for a freer suffrage set in, Massachusetts fell into line, abandoning the property qualification first in favor of a small taxpaying restriction and later adopting the generally accepted white manhood suffrage (*see* Franchise) .

[F. N. Thorpe, *The Federal and State Constitutions.*]
VIOLA F. BARNES

Massachusetts Bay Company (1629–84). Its history is in reality not the history of a trading company, but of a theocracy, one of the most interesting of the early American experiments in utopias. The royal charter of 1629 confirmed to a group of merchants and others land already granted to them, presumably, by the Council for New England^w in 1628, with power to trade and colonize in New England between the Merrimac and the Charles rivers. Under the Council's patent the Massachusetts group had local powers of self-government, subject to the general government to be established by the Council over all New England. The royal charter removed Massachusetts from its position of dependence on the Council's general government and allowed the company to establish whatever government it chose for its colony, subject to no superior authority except that of the king. The company in its beginnings closely resembled other trading companies operating in the New World, but almost immediately after receiving its charter, it changed the emphasis of its interest from trade to religion. Puritan stockholders who considered prospects for religious and political reforms in England increasingly hopeless under Charles I, decided to migrate to New England with their families, possessions and the company charter (*see* Cambridge Agreement). Some compromises concerning the business administration were made with the merchants remaining behind, but control of the enterprise for the future lay with those who left England in the Great Migration^w of 1630, and the government designed for the trading company in England became that of the colony of New England.

The charter of 1629 provided for the usual organs of government; governor, assistants, and General Court^w of the stockholders, but omitted the clause requiring the company to hold its business sessions in England. This omission made it possible for Puritan leaders among the stockholders to transfer the company with its charter to the colony in New England and to superimpose upon the colony the government designed for the company. By so doing they could use the power of the General Court to admit new members as a means of limiting the suffrage (*see* Massachusetts Bay, Franchise in) in the colony to those of their own religious faith and in a few years to transform the enterprise from a trading company existing for profit into a theocracy^w practically free from outside control. As a further safeguard, the assistants tried to govern the colony without the share of the General Court except in annual elections, but when this breach of charter terms was objected to, the General Court received back its legitimate authority. With the expansion of settlement, representative government evolved and the General Court came to be comprised of deputies from the towns, who sat with the governor and assistants until a bi-

cameral court was established in 1644. Dissent within the theocracy resulted in the voluntary exile of the group which founded Connecticut^w, and the forced exile of Roger Williams and Anne Hutchinson, founders of Rhode Island^w towns.

The Council for New England under the leadership of its president, Sir Ferdinando Gorges^w, almost immediately charged that the charter had been surreptitiously obtained, and, aided by leading officials of government, including Archbishop Laud, began a campaign to have it annulled. In 1635 the Council surrendered its own charter and asked the king to regrant the land in eight charters to eight members of the Council, a process which would give to the new patentees an opportunity to inspect all previous grants for purposes of confirmation. It was expected that the Massachusetts charter would be caught in this net. The plan failed of its purpose because only one of the eight patents, that for Maine, passed the seals before the outbreak of the Puritan Revolution.

Massachusetts Bay Company remained neutral during the Puritan Revolution in England, but joined with Plymouth, Connecticut and New Haven in a defensive confederation in 1643, perhaps partly as a protection against being drawn into the struggle (*see* United Colonies of New England). Although the Massachusetts government considered itself an independent commonwealth after 1649, nevertheless when the monarchy was restored in 1660 the company recognized the relationship to the mother country which the charter defined. After the passing of the Navigation Acts^w, however, the leaders in the theocracy found it extremely difficult to be reconciled to the dependent position of the colony. Because they refused to accept many features of England's new colonial policy^w, they gradually incurred the displeasure of the crown. The commission sent over in 1664 to conquer New Netherland was instructed also to visit the New England colonies and investigate conditions. The commission and others reported Massachusetts at error in many respects: coining money without authority, extending government over the region of Maine and New Hampshire at the north, restricting the suffrage to church members, denying freedom of worship to dissenters, and, most important of all, refusing to obey the Navigation Acts or to recognize Parliament's authority over them (*see* Nicholl's Commission). The company avoided trouble for a while by a policy of procrastination and evasion, but in 1676 Edward Randolph^w was dispatched on another mission of investigation. His report was even more damning than that of the 1664 commission. At the king's demand the company sent over agents to negotiate some sort of compromise, but thereafter failed to fulfill the promises made by the agents. The Lords of Trade[w], exasperated by the long delays and the failure to accomplish results, finally recommended annulling the charter on the ground that the company had not lived up to its terms. Formal charges were made against the company and the charter withdrawn by *scire facias* proceedings in 1684, after which the company as a corporation ceased to exist. Its government, however, continued to function without legal status until the establishment of the Dominion of New England[w] in 1686.

Although the company very early lost its character as a trading company, and became a theocracy, the charter itself was necessary to the maintenance of that theocracy because of the almost complete governmental control it gave to the company's General Court. Under that outer shell the colony developed a very close union of church and state, a theocracy more or less on the Calvin pattern. To maintain the purity of the religious ideals of the leaders, the very limited suffrage was necessary, as was the weeding out of dissenters, the control of the school system and the refusal to recognize the power of Parliament over them. Yet the colony was too weak to resist the authority of the mother country by force and therefore had to resort to strategy. The faith of the leaders in God's protection of them led them to believe that in a crisis He would come to their aid. It was this faith which made them dare to procrastinate and at times even to defy the mother country. If they had been more conciliatory they might have preserved the charter. As it was, their actions and attitude made England believe that no policy of colonial administration could ever be successful as long as the Massachusetts Bay theocracy existed. The only way to destroy it was to destroy the company through its charter.

[H. L. Osgood, *The American Colonies in the Seventeenth Century*, Vol. I; C. M. Andrews, *The Colonial Period in American History*, Vol. I.]

VIOLA F. BARNES

Massachusetts Body of Liberties (1641). To curb the power of the magistrates, deputies in the Massachusetts General Court[w] agitated for a code of laws (1635). Committees appointed (May 6, 1635; May 25, 1636; and March 12, 1638) accomplished little, though a member of one, John Cotton, presented (October, 1636) a code not accepted. Finally (June, 1639), the court referred the task to Cotton and Nathaniel Ward, formerly an English lawyer, each to frame a model. Both models were referred to a com-

mittee (November, 1639) which adopted Ward's code. Sent to the towns for suggestions and reduced to 100 items by the court, the code was adopted as law (Dec. 10, 1641). This Body of Liberties was to be in force for three years and, if found satisfactory, made perpetual. Similar to Bills of Rights and based largely upon English common law, the code left too much authority to magistrates; deputies, at the end of the probation period, renewed the agitation and, after a long survey, replaced the Body of Liberties with *The Book of the General Lawes and Libertyes* . . . (1648).

[Charles M. Andrews, *The Colonial Period of American History*, I; J. W. Dean, *A Memoir of the Reverend Nathaniel Ward*. . . .]

RAYMOND P. STEARNS

Massachusetts "Circular Letter" (Feb. 11, 1768). The Massachusetts House of Representatives, fearing the commercial, political and constitutional effects of the Townshend Acts[w] (1767), petitioned George III and his ministers, and drafted a letter to all colonial legislatures "to inform them of the measures this House has taken" with regard to the acts, a step toward colonial unity punished by dissolution (July 1, 1768) of the General Court[w].

[Edward Channing, *A History of the United States*, III; John C. Miller, *Sam Adams: Pioneer in Propaganda*.]

RAYMOND P. STEARNS

Massachusetts Government Act, or Regulating Act, second in order of the Coercion Acts[w], was passed by the English Parliament in May, 1774, with the intention of quelling the recent disturbances created by New England merchants and radicals protesting against the tea tax. Its purpose, Lord North announced, was "to take the executive power from the hands of the democratic part of the government." To this end, the act provided that the charter of Massachusetts be abrogated; that members of the council be appointed by the governor instead of by a convention of the preceding council and assembly, as formerly; that salaries of councillors be paid by the crown rather than by appropriation of the assembly, and that all councillors be subject to dismissal at the king's pleasure. The judges were also to be chosen by the governor and receive their stipend from the crown. Sheriffs were to be appointed in like manner, and they alone had the right of selecting juries. Last and most drastic, the town meeting[w] was abolished, except for the function of electing municipal officers. The immediate reaction to the act was one of intense indignation throughout English North America, and in Massachusetts it crystallized public opinion in favor of an armed revolt, if need be, to safeguard the liberties of the colony.

[John Fiske, *The American Revolution*; C. H. Van Tyne, *The Causes of the War of Independence*.]

FRANK J. KLINGBERG

Massachusetts Provincial Congress (Oct. 7, 1774–July 19, 1775) was the real, though illegal, government from the breakdown of royal government to the "resumption" of the "Old Charter" (July 19, 1775). When Gen. Gage (Sept. 28) withdrew writs issued (Sept. 7) for a new General Court*ᵂ*, representatives of ninety towns ignored their withdrawal and met at Salem (Oct. 5). When the governor failed to appear, the delegates, following instructions, organized themselves into a provincial congress*ᵂ* (Oct. 7) which assumed legislative and executive powers. Consisting of three consecutive bodies representing about 200 towns, meeting in different places (Salem, Concord, Cambridge, Watertown), the Congress severed administrative, judicial and commercial connections with England, and undertook, with great popular support, the control of provincial affairs. In co-operation with the Continental Congress*ᵂ*, the Congress, through committees, managed public finance, enforced British boycott, regulated industry and trade in the interests of provincial self-sufficiency, enlisted support of other colonies and superintended the enormous detail of recruiting, organizing and equipping the provincial army. Orderly and responsible, the Congress served as an admirable transition from colonial to commonwealth government.

[Harry A. Cushing, *History of the Transition from Provincial to Commonwealth Government in Massachusetts*; Allan Nevins, *The American States during and after the Revolution*.]

RAYMOND P. STEARNS

Matamoras Expedition, THE, was an incident in the Texas Revolution*ᵂ*. After the capture of San Antonio*ᵂ* in December, 1835, many Texans wished to carry the war to Mexico by launching an expedition to seize Matamoras. The provisional government of Texas was divided over the plan; a violent quarrel between Gov. Smith and the council disorganized the military forces of Texas and wrecked the proposed expedition. Meanwhile, the rival commanders, Fannin and Johnson, who had been commissioned by the council to lead it, were left on the frontier where their forces were annihilated by the Mexicans early in 1836 (*see* Goliad, Massacre at).

[George P. Garrison, *Texas: A Contest of Civilizations*; H. H. Bancroft, *History of the North Mexican States and Texas*.]

C. T. NEU

Matanzas, Fort, was constructed by the Spaniards in 1743 on an islet at the south entrance to the Matanzas River as a part of the defenses of St. Augustine*ᵂ*, Fla. The immediate occasion for the fortification was fear of the British after Oglethorpe's victory on St. Simon's Island in 1742 and his second attack on St. Augustine in March, 1743. This coquina (shell-stone) structure is now kept in condition by the Federal Government.

[Herbert E. Bolton and Mary Ross, *The Debatable Land*; Amos A. Ettinger, *James Edward Oglethorpe, Imperial Idealist*.]

JONATHAN T. DORRIS

Matches. The friction match is not an American invention. A match which could be lighted by striking on any surface (an outgrowth of the chlorate of potassium and sulphide of antimony "lucifer") arrived in New England in the early 1830's. The first American patent was issued to Alonzo D. Phillips of Springfield, Mass., in 1836. On this patent Ezekiel Byam, also of Massachusetts, manufactured the "loco foco"*ᵂ* celebrated in the presidential campaign of 1840.*ᵂ*

America's great contribution was in matchmaking machinery. This was developed by Jonathan Morgan (1839), Thaddeus Hyatt (1840), Hervey Law (1844) and finally by William Gates, Jr., and H. J. Harwood, who, in 1854, patented the first continuous match machine in the world. This was improved in detail until it became the standard machine.

So much industrial disease developed from the use of phosphorus in American match factories that President Taft in 1911 urged preventive legislation. The Diamond Match Company*ᵂ* met this objection by the purchase of a foreign process using sesqui-sulphide of phosphorus instead of white phosphorus.

[Herbert Manchester, *The Diamond Match Company*; R. Burlingame, *March of the Iron Men*.]

ROGER BURLINGAME

Matilda Lawrence Case (1837). A slave, Matilda Lawrence, left a steamboat at Cincinnati, and later, through her attorney, Salmon P. Chase, claimed her freedom on the ground that she had been brought by her master to free soil. The local court remanded her to slavery, but a conviction of James G. Birney for harboring her was reversed by the Ohio Supreme Court as a result of Chase's defense.

[J. W. Schuckers, *Life and Public Services of Salmon Portland Chase*; A. B. Hart, *Salmon P. Chase*.]

EUGENE H. ROSEBOOM

Maumee Indian Convention (August, 1793). At this fateful conference the confederated Indian tribes of the Northwest Territory[w], encouraged by the British through their agent, Alexander McKee, and puffed up by two recent defeats of the American army (see Harmar's Expedition; St. Clair's Defeat), decided to insist that the United States give up to the Indians all the lands of the Northwest Territory. As a result, United States Commissioners, who were on their way to Sandusky with compromise proposals concerning the Indian-American boundary, declined to meet with the tribes, and the American army under Gen. Anthony Wayne[w] proceeded to carry out its final campaign against the Indians.

[R. C. Downes, *Frontier Ohio, 1788-1803.*]
RANDOLPH C. DOWNES

Maurepas, Fort, was erected by Iberville in 1699 on the Bay of Biloxi, near the present town of Ocean Springs, Miss., as the seat of the first French colony in Louisiana, after he had explored the lower reaches of the Mississippi River without finding a suitable site for a colony on its banks. The seat of colonial government was removed from Fort Maurepas (Biloxi) to Dauphine Island[w], near Mobile, in 1702, but the fort appears to have been occupied continuously until destroyed by fire in 1719. When Louisiana was divided into districts for local administration, Biloxi[w] became the chief post in the new district of that name.

[Alcée Fortier, ed., *Louisiana,* Cyclopedic; Dunbar Rowland, *History of Mississippi, the Heart of the South;* J. F. H. Claiborne, *Mississippi, as a Province, Territory and State;* Robert Lowry and William H. McCardle, *A History of Mississippi.*]
WALTER PRICHARD

Maury's Charts (1840's). In the autumn of 1847 Matthew Fontaine Maury, then in charge of the Depot of Charts and Instruments of the Navy Department, published his first *Wind and Current Chart of the North Atlantic,* founded on information collected from old discarded naval log books. Through the co-operation of navigators all over the world, Maury secured data which enabled him not only to revise this chart but also to prepare similar charts for the South Atlantic, North Pacific, South Pacific and Indian Ocean. To explain and illustrate these charts he issued first a pamphlet of ten pages, which grew to 1257 pages in two quarto volumes, called *Sailing Directions.* By demonstrating to navigators how to take advantage of winds and currents and thus shorten the time of their voyages, Maury saved enormous sums to shipowners. It has been estimated that the annual saving to British commerce alone in the Indian Ocean, thus effected, amounted to at least $1,000,000;

while the United States saved annually in the outward voyage alone from Atlantic and California ports to South America, Australia and the Far East at least $2,250,000. For this achievement Maury has been called the "Pathfinder of the Seas."

[Charles Lee Lewis, *Matthew Fontaine Maury: Pathfinder of the Seas.*]
CHARLES LEE LEWIS

Mauvilla, Battle of (October, 1540). The only surviving sources, the partly historical, partly romantic Portuguese accounts, record the southwesterly march of DeSoto[w] to meet the cacique, Tuscaluza, near the present site of Montgomery, Ala. DeSoto, contemptuous of the Indians' kindness, held Tuscaluza practically a prisoner, forcing him finally to lead the way to Mauvilla, a populous and splendidly fortified town. Tuscaluza, outwardly friendly but inwardly resentful, forwarded a secret message, warning of the Spaniards' vicious characteristics. Unsuspecting, De Soto entered Mauvilla. A few hours later a Spaniard killed an Indian in a street brawl. In the ensuing fight, Mauvilla was burned, hundreds of its citizens perishing; Tuscaluza committed suicide; DeSoto was seriously wounded; while the Spaniards suffered eighty casualties, lost many horses and practically all baggage.

[Lambert A. Wilmer, *The Life, Travels and Adventures of Ferdinand de Soto;* Theodore Irving, *The Conquest of Florida;* Narratives of the Career of Hernando de Soto, translated by Buckingham Smith.]
ROBERT S. THOMAS

Maverick. In 1845 Samuel A. Maverick, lawyer in San Antonio, Tex., reluctantly took over 400 head of stock cattle on a $1200 debt. He kept them for eleven years under charge of a thriftless Negro and had fewer cattle than he started with. Neighbors had done most of the branding of the increase. They came to refer to any unbranded animal too old to suck and running at large as "one of Maverick's." The usage spread, the noun becoming common. After the Civil War there were hundreds of thousands of maverick cattle in Texas. Mavericking became an occupation that sometimes bordered on and often led to thieving, though any range man had—and yet has—a right to brand any maverick found on his range.

[J. Frank Dobie, *A Vaquero of the Brush Country;* Mary A. Maverick, *Memoirs.*]
J. FRANK DOBIE

Maxent, Laclede and Company was a firm established some time in 1762 by Pierre Laclede Ligueste, Antoine Maxent and others for stimulating and maintaining a large-scale commerce with Indians. An exclusive license to carry on this trade with the Indians of the Missouri and all nations residing west of the Mississippi was granted to them, and confirmed in 1763 by M. D'Abbadie, Director General of Louisiana. They imported from Europe large supplies of goods for the purpose. Laclede, a man of great experience, skill and prudence, was placed in charge of a considerable armament which left New Orleans, Aug. 3, 1763. Proceeding into the Illinois country he stored his goods at Fort Chartres[w]. Locating the present site of St. Louis[w] for his post, from which to control the territory included in the grant, he ordered his lieutenant to clear the spot and form a settlement; meanwhile he traded with various tribes of Indians. In May, 1769, Laclede bought the three-fourths interest of Maxent for 80,000 livres in silver, and the partnership was dissolved. The trade established by Laclede extended as far north as St. Peter's River and came in competition with the British traders. Laclede carried on the trade until his death in 1778.

[John Francis McDermott, The Exclusive Trade Privilege of Maxent, Laclede and Company, in *Missouri Historical Review*, Vol. XXIX.]

STELLA M. DRUMM

Maxim Gun. Hiram S. Maxim (1840–1916), a native of Maine, invented the first automatic, quick-firing gun. He conceived the idea and made the first drawings while on a visit to Paris, and going thence to London, perfected the gun in 1884. It used a belt of cartridges, the first model firing more than ten times per second. Maxim manufactured automatic guns of various calibers (up to 12-pounders) for many governments, modifying them to suit the ideas of each. His guns' aid to Great Britain in winning the Egyptian campaigns of 1897–99 brought about his knighting in 1901. He had become a British subject several years before.

[Sir Hiram S. Maxim, *My Life*.]

ALVIN F. HARLOW

Maxwell Land Grant, THE, was made by the Mexican government, Jan. 11, 1841, to Guadalupe Miranda and Carlos Beaubien. It included roughly a rectangle of land whose eastern boundary was the line connecting Trinidad, Colo., and Springer, N. Mex., and reaching west to the Sangre de Cristo[w] Range. Congress confirmed the title June 21, 1860, and Beaubien's son-in-law, Lucien Maxwell, eventually acquired 1,714,-765 acres by inheritance and purchase. His successor, the Maxwell Land Grant Company, successfully maintained its title to this vast estate in four suits before the Supreme Court and against armed resistance of the settlers.

[J. Henderson, et al., *Colorado: Short Studies of Its*

Past and Present; R. E. Twitchell, *Leading Facts of New Mexican History.*]

PERCY S. FRITZ

May Day. The festivity at Merry Mount[w] in 1627 seems to have marked the introduction of the Maypole to America. Naturally, such frivolity could not continue in Puritan Massachusetts; nor was the mediæval May Day much celebrated anywhere else in early America. During the 19th century it became in cities the traditional family moving day. In 1889 an International Socialist Congress selected it as a world labor holiday; and on May Day, 1890, for the first time, there were demonstrations in Europe and America in favor of the eight-hour working day. Thus began a radical practice which became fixed in the calendar.

[Mary Caroline Crawford, *In the Days of the Pilgrim Fathers*.]

ALVIN F. HARLOW

Mayflower, THE, a three-masted, double-decked, bark-rigged merchant ship of 180 tons, with a normal speed of 2½ miles per hour, Christopher Jones her master since 1608 and in 1620 quarter owner, was chartered in London to take the Pilgrims[w] to America. They left Leyden, Holland, on July 31, 1620 (all dates are New Style[w]), for Delfthaven, from where, the next day, they sailed for Southampton, England, aboard the *Speedwell,* a smaller but older craft which they had outfitted for the voyage to America. There they met the *Mayflower,* took on supplies for the voyage and the two ships sailed on Aug. 15, but put back into Dartmouth harbor about Aug. 23 because of the leaky condition of the *Speedwell*. They sailed again about Sept. 2, but the *Speedwell* continued unseaworthy and they were again forced to return, this time to Plymouth harbor, where the smaller ship was abandoned, some of the passengers returned to shore and 102 passengers and crew finally sailed on the *Mayflower* on Sept. 16, sighted Cape Cod on Nov. 19 and arrived in what is now the harbor of Provincetown, Cape Cod, on Nov. 21. Some time was spent in taking on wood and water, in mending their shallop and in exploring the bay and land, so that they did not reach the site of Plymouth until Dec. 21, 1620. The *Mayflower* followed the land-exploring party and sailed into Plymouth harbor on Dec. 26, where she remained until houses could be built for the new settlement. She finally sailed for England on April 5, 1621, reaching London safely. She was in the port of London again in 1624, after which her history is uncertain because of confusion with several other contemporary ships of the same name.

[G. Mourt (George Morton), *Relation*, 1622, 1865

ed.; William Bradford, *History of the Plymouth Planta-tion;* W. S. Nickerson, *Land ho!—1620.*]

R. W. G. VAIL

"Mayflower Compact," THE, was the agree-ment signed on Nov. 11, 1620, by the male pas-sengers on the *Mayflower*[w], before coming ashore, that they would form a body politic and submit to the will of the majority in whatever regula-tions of government were agreed upon. Its pur-pose, according to Bradford, was to hold in check the restless spirits on board who had threatened to strike out for themselves when the Pilgrim[w] leaders decided to land in New England instead of Virginia. The Pilgrims held a patent from the Virginia Company[w] granting rights to the soil and to local self-government, but this pat-ent was of no use after they began settlement in New England. The compact appears therefore to have been a voluntary agreement to establish a local government which, though having no legal status until a patent could be obtained from the Council for New England[w], would at least have the strength of common consent. Its significance lies rather in its similarity to later ideas of demo-cratic government than in any new philosophy of popular government in the minds of its au-thors. Plymouth[w] Colony, though never so com-pletely theocratic[w] as Massachusetts, neverthe-less leaned more toward theocracy than toward democracy.

[H. L. Osgood, *The American Colonies in the Seven-teenth Century.*]

VIOLA F. BARNES

Maynard Tape Primer consisted of a water-proofed paper roll of fifty fulminate caps and a mechanism to operate it, designed to speed oper-ation of the percussion lock rifle. Offered to an ordnance board Jan. 29, 1845, by Edward May-nard (1813–91), it was used, with some improve-ments, on many Civil War firearms, notably the rifle and rifle-musket, models of 1855.

[E. A. Allin, *Rules for the Management and Cleaning of the Rifle-Musket,* Model 1855; Claude Fuller, *United States Shoulder Arms, 1795-1865.*]

DON RUSSELL

Mayo Foundation, THE, for Medical Education and Research, which has been an integral part of the Graduate School of the University of Min-nesota since 1915, was the first, and is the largest, graduate department to offer training in the clini-cal branches of medicine. Its offerings are not restricted, however, to clinical fields, and a con-siderable percentage of its fellowship holders are awarded degrees by the University in one of the laboratory sciences related to medicine.

Between 275 and 300 fellows are usually in service, most of them at Rochester, Minn., site of the Mayo Clinic. The average period of a fellow-ship covers between three and four years, which time the graduate student spends partly in diag-nosis, partly as clinical assistant to a physician or surgeon, and partly in laboratory research. Their studies are carried on under a faculty composed in part of selected members of the Mayo Clinic staff, who are members of the graduate faculty of the University of Minnesota, and partly of similarly selected members of the faculty of the University of Minnesota Medical School. Gov-erning the activities of the Mayo Foundation is a joint committee from the faculties at Minne-apolis and Rochester, over which the dean of the Graduate School presides. The Foundation was created by gifts of Drs. William James and Charles Horace Mayo, and their associates, total-ling more than $2,600,000.

[G. S. Ford, *On and Off the Campus.*]

GUY STANTON FORD

Maysville Veto, THE, is important in Ameri-can history as an episode in the long struggle over internal improvements[w]. In 1830 Congress passed "A Bill Authorizing a subscription of stock in the Maysville, Washington, Paris and Lexington, Turnpike Road Company." In veto-ing the bill President Jackson pointed out that the project lay entirely within one state, that it had no connection with any established system of improvement, and therefore violated the prin-ciple that such works, to receive Federal aid, should be national and not local in character. The attitude of Jackson was in accord with pre-vailing Democratic principles but he was perhaps not unmindful of its political effect. "The veto," wrote Van Buren, "was the wedge which split the party of internal improvements, a party which was wielded by a triumvirate of active and able young statesmen as a means through which to achieve for themselves the glittering prize of the Presidency."

[Archer Butler Hulbert, *Historic Highways of America.*]

J. HARLEY NICHOLS

Mazzei Letter, THE. A letter by Thomas Jef-ferson to Philip Mazzei, April 24, 1796, was pub-lished in translation at Florence, Jan. 1, 1797. Retranslated for the French *Moniteur,* it was republished in English for the *Minerva,* May 14, 1797. An attack upon Washington and the Fed-eralists[w], it precipitated a permanent rupture be-tween Washington and Jefferson.

[*The Works of Thomas Jefferson,* Ford Edition, Vol. VIII.]

LOUIS MARTIN SEARS

McAllister, Fort, Capture of (Dec. 13, 1864). This fort, six miles from Ossabaw Sound and eighteen miles southwest of Savannah, Ga., commanded the mouth of the Ogeechee River and held up Sherman's "March to the Sea"^{qv} for several days. At 5:00 P.M. on Dec. 13 Gen. W. B. Hazen (U.) effected its capture. This made possible Sherman's junction with the gunboat fleet, and opened the gates to Savannah^{qv}.

[*Battles and Leaders of the Civil War*, Vol. IV.]

ROBERT S. THOMAS

McCardle, ex parte (7 Wall. 506, 1869), marked the summit of Radical Republican^{qv} power (*see* Reconstruction) by confirming the supremacy of a legislative majority over the executive and judicial branches of the Government. President Johnson's impeachment^{qv} trial was under way and the Fourteenth Amendment^{qv} was about to become effective. The boot of the military was on the neck of the prostrate South; the Negro, the carpetbagger and the scalawag^{qqv} reveled in extravagance while wielding new-found power.

In two cases—Mississippi v. Johnson and Georgia v. Stanton^{qqv}—an effort had been made to restrain Congress from effecting military reconstruction in the South, but in each case the Supreme Court had refused jurisdiction. Another case soon reached the Court. McCardle, a Mississippi editor, had criticized Gen. E. O. C. Ord, the military commander in the "conquered province" of Mississippi. Worse, he had criticized the policy of Congress. He was promptly arrested and jailed and denied the benefit of habeas corpus^{qv}. (*See also* Freedom of the Press.) To secure freedom, McCardle endeavored to take advantage of a Radical law providing for an appeal to the Supreme Court of "all cases where any person may be restrained of his or her liberty in violation of the Constitution or of any treaty or law of the United States," a statute passed to protect Federal officials and other "loyal persons" against the state courts of the South.

As a decision in the McCardle case was imminent, the alarmed Radicals hastened to restrain the Supreme Court from fear that the precedent of *ex parte* Milligan^{qv} might be used to declare the Reconstruction acts^{qv} unconstitutional. After failure of a proposal to require a two-thirds vote of the Court to invalidate a law, the Court was stripped of its power of judicial review^{qv} so far as it concerned the Reconstruction acts. President Johnson vetoed the act, but the Radicals promptly repassed it. The Supreme Court, unanimously decided it had no jurisdiction, because of the new restriction, and dismissed the case.

[W. A. Dunning, *Reconstruction, Political and Economic;*

W. L. Fleming, *The Sequel to Appomattox;* G. F. Milton, *The Age of Hate: Andrew Johnson and the Radicals.*]

THOMAS ROBSON HAY

McConnelsville Ordinance, THE. Citizens of McConnelsville, Ohio, passed an ordinance in April, 1869, for the purpose of restraining the liquor traffic. This first ordinance proved unsatisfactory and a new one was unanimously adopted in September, 1869. This was repealed in 1871 but was re-enacted March 14, 1874. This ordinance, which was taken to the Supreme Court and declared constitutional, was adopted in many cities and villages.

[Charles Robertson, *History of Morgan County, Ohio;* T. W. Lewis, *History of Southeastern Ohio and the Muskingum Valley.*]

HARLOW LINDLEY

McCormick Reaper, THE. The machine with which the name of Cyrus Hall McCormick will be forever associated had many inventors, notably Obed Hussey, who patented his machine in 1833, a year before the first McCormick patent and whose machine was the only practicable one on the market before 1840. It was the McCormick reaper, however, that invaded the Middle West, where the prairie farmer was ready for an efficient harvester which would make extensive wheat growing possible. In 1847 McCormick moved from the Shenandoah Valley in Virginia, where the first machine was built, to Chicago.

Perhaps, as his biographer contends, McCormick, or his father, Robert McCormick, did most effectively combine the parts essential to a mechanical grain cutter. Other improvements came in the 1850's and 1860's, the self raker, which dispensed with the job of raking the cut grain off the platform, and then the binder, first using wire to bind the sheaves and later twine. In this development McCormick was by no means the first. The first self raker was sold in 1854, seven years before McCormick produced such a machine. The first wire binder was put on the market in 1873, two years before the McCormick binder. Through effective organization the McCormick reaper came to dominate the field.

[H. N. Casson, *The Romance of the Reaper;* Victor S. Clark, *History of Manufactures in the United States;* W. T. Hutchinson, *Cyrus Hall McCormick.*]

ERNEST S. OSGOOD

McCray v. U. S. (1904). An act of Congress imposing a prohibitory tax of ten cents per pound upon artificially colored oleomargarine was upheld by the Supreme Court as a valid exercise of the constitutional power to lay taxes.

[Charles K. Burdick, *The Law of the American Constitution.*]

EARL E. WARNER

McCrea, Jane, Murder of (1777). Jane McCrea of Fort Edward[w] was seized by some Indians and accidentally shot when her captors were pursued by the colonials. She was scalped by an Indian in revenge for losing the reward given for white prisoners. This act contributed to Burgoyne's[w] defeat, for the frontiersmen were greatly aroused and rallied to Gates' support. Many Indians deserted Burgoyne, angered by his orders to end murder and pillage, leaving the English without sufficient scouts or guides.

[W. L. Stone, *The Campaign of Lt. Gen. John Burgoyne*.]   NELSON VANCE RUSSELL

McCulloch v. Maryland (4 Wheaton 316) was decided by the Supreme Court of the United States on March 6, 1819. The immediate question involved was whether the State of Maryland could tax notes issued by the Baltimore branch of the Second Bank of the United States[w], which had been created pursuant to an act of Congress of April 10, 1816. The present-day importance of the case lies in Chief Justice Marshall's discussion and broad interpretation of the implied powers[w] of Congress, and in the denial of the power of a state to tax an instrumentality of the Federal Government. The Bank of the United States was created as the successor to an institution of the same name which had gone out of existence in 1811. It was intended to aid in restoring stability to currency and credit after the chaos created by the War of 1812. The power which it exerted over state banks[w] and a measure of looseness in its own operations resulted in jealousy and distrust which expressed themselves in hostile legislation in a number of states. The Maryland tax measure was one such piece of legislation. Similar measures were enacted in other states. The case was undoubtedly argued and decided with the situation as a whole in mind. William Pinkney, Daniel Webster and William Wirt argued for the bank, and Luther Martin, Joseph Hopkinson and Walter Jones for Maryland.

Chief Justice Marshall wrote the opinion for a unanimous court upholding the power of Congress to charter a bank as a government agency, and denying the power of a state to interfere with the agency by taxation. The establishment of a bank or the creation of a corporation was not listed in the Constitution as among the powers granted, but such an instrumentality might facilitate the exercise of powers which were specifically granted. The Chief Justice measured the discretion of Congress in such matters as follows: "Let the end be legitimate, let it be within the scope of the constitution, and all means which are appropriate, which are plainly adapted to that end, which are not prohibited, but consist with the letter and spirit of the constitution, are constitutional."

The denial of state power to tax the notes of the bank was based on the argument that "the power to tax involves the power to destroy." This part of the decision became the parent of a long line of subsequent decisions dealing with the power of state and Federal governments to tax the instrumentalities of each other. Important issues remain unsettled, however, and still provide grounds for serious controversy (*see* Taxation, Reciprocal Immunity from) .

[A. J. Beveridge, *The Life of John Marshall;* Charles Warren, *The Supreme Court in United States History*.]

CARL BRENT SWISHER

McDonald's Expedition (1774). Angus McDonald, a Scotchman, living at Winchester, Va., responded to Dunmore's[w] call for an expedition against the hostile Indians. Enrolling 400 militia, he left Wheeling July 26 and marched ninety miles across country to the Shawnee[w] villages on the Muskingum River, known as the Wapatomica. The Indians had previously deserted these villages, but had returned and were in ambush. After a skirmish they retreated; the whites then cut up the standing corn and retired. The expedition only led to fresh hostilities by the Shawnee.

[R. G. Thwaites and L. P. Kellogg, *Dunmore's War*.]   LOUISE PHELPS KELLOGG

McDowell, Va., Battle at (May 8, 1862). The combined Confederate forces of Generals Jackson and Edward Johnson gained a decisive victory in this engagement. Union forces were compelled to retreat toward Franklin, suffering the loss of great quantities of stores and ammunition (*see* Jackson's Valley Campaign) .

[*Battles and Leaders of the Civil War*, Vol. II.]   ROBERT S. THOMAS

McFadden Banking Act, THE, of Feb. 25, 1927, permitted national banks to operate home-city branch offices in cities where the state banks were allowed similar privileges. It also tended to delimit the growth of out-of-town branches by providing that no state bank which was a member of the Federal Reserve System[w] might establish such a branch after date of passage of the act, and that no nonmember bank might join the Federal Reserve System, after the same date, without relinquishing any out-of-town branches established after that date. The act also changed the restrictions on real-estate loans of national banks and provided indeterminate charters for national and Federal Reserve banks.

[F. A. Bradford, *Money and Banking.*]

FREDERICK A. BRADFORD

McGillivray Incident, THE (also known as the Treaty of New York). On Aug. 7, 1790, Alexander McGillivray and other Creek chiefs signed, in New York, with Henry Knox, sole American commissioner, two treaties, one public and one secret, having to do with peace, boundary and trade, and abrogating in effect the Creek-Spanish Treaty of Pensacola*ᵠᵛ* (June, 1784). McGillivray was commissioned an American brigadier general, with a salary of $1200 a year, twice his Spanish salary as Indian *comisario*.

Creek and Spanish opposition prevented ratification of these treaties. Spanish intrigues, including gradually raising his *comisario* salary almost sixfold, finally induced McGillivray to sign a convention with Carondelet (July 6, 1792) abrogating the New York treaties. McGillivray's death (Feb. 17, 1793) left both Spanish and American treaties unratified.

[J. W. Caughey, *McGillivray of the Creeks;* American State Papers, *Indian Affairs,* Vol. I; A. P. Whitaker, Alexander McGillivray, in *North Carolina Historical Review,* Vol. 5.]

ELIZABETH HOWARD WEST

McGuffey's Readers formed a series of textbooks which moulded American literary taste and morality, particularly in the Middle West, during the sixty years preceding 1900. The total sales reached 120,000,000 copies. Only the Bible and *Webster's Spelling Book*ᵠᵛ have enjoyed equal acceptance in the United States. William Holmes McGuffey undertook the preparation of the Eclectic Series of school readers at the request of Winthrop B. Smith, a Cincinnati publisher interested in books adapted to the Western schools. The *First Reader* (1836) followed the conventional pattern of readers, as indeed did its successors. Its fifty-five lessons with accompanying pictures taught principles of religion, morality and patriotism. The *Second Reader* (1836) contained eighty-five lessons and sixteen pictures. It included considerable lore about nature, games and sports, manners, and attitudes toward God, relatives, teachers, companions, unfortunates and animals. Here the pioneer youth found a code of social behavior to carry him safely through any experience. This book plagiarized *Worcester's Readers;* in 1838 damages were paid and the offending pages changed. In 1837 the *Third Reader* and *Fourth Reader,* for older pupils, completed the series. The *Third,* with only three pictures, contained many rules for oral reading. The *Fourth,* an introduction to standard British and American literature, elaborated the objectives of the whole series, the ability to read aloud with sense, clearness and appreciation. Several revisions were made: in 1844 a *Fifth Reader* was added; in 1857 the material was regraded and a *Sixth Reader* (by Alexander H. McGuffey, a brother) and a *High School Reader* were added; in 1879 the books were completely remade; in 1901 and 1920 the series was recopyrighted with slight changes.

The popularity of the McGuffey Readers arose partly from the happy adaptation of the substance to frontier interests. The lessons enforced proverbial wisdom, advising accuracy, honesty, truthfulness, obedience, kindness, industry, thrift, freedom and patriotism. The problems of the world were simplified, so that in the end right always conquered and sin or wrong was always punished. In defense of the many religious selections McGuffey wrote: "In a Christian country that man is to be pitied who at this day can honestly object to imbuing the minds of youth with the language and spirit of the word of God."

[H. C. Minnich, *William Holmes McGuffey and His Readers.*]

HARRY R. WARFEL

McHenry, Fort, built in 1799 on a small island in Baltimore harbor at the time of Franco-American difficulties*ᵠᵛ*, was named for James McHenry. After the burning of Washington*ᵠᵛ* a British fleet in Chesapeake Bay bombarded the fort (Sept. 13, 1814). A spectator, Francis Scott Key, who watched through the night, was moved to write a poem, "The Star-Spangled Banner"*ᵠᵛ*. Subsequently the fort was used as a storage depot and an army headquarters post.

[B. C. Steiner, *The Life and Correspondence of James McHenry.*]

THOMAS ROBSON HAY

McIntosh, Fort, on the north bank of the Ohio River within the limits of the present Beaver, Pa., was built in 1778 by Gen. Lachlan McIntosh as a base for a projected expedition against Detroit*ᵠᵛ*. From October of that year to the following spring it was the headquarters of the Western Department of the Revolutionary Army. In 1783 the fort was transferred by the War Department to the State of Pennsylvania, and in 1788 it was demolished.

[J. H. Bausman, *History of Beaver County, Pa.*]

SOLON J. BUCK

McIntosh, Fort, Treaties of (January, 1785). After the second treaty of Fort Stanwix*ᵠᵛ* in 1784 it was thought desirable to extinguish the claims of western Indian tribes to some of the lands covered by the Iroquois cession. United States and Pennsylvania commissioners therefore met at Fort McIntosh with representatives of the Wyandot, Delaware, Chippewa and Ottawa Indians[qw]. By the treaty, signed Jan. 21, these tribes ceded much of what is now the State of Ohio and agreed to give hostages for the return of prisoners taken during the Revolution. By the Pennsylvania treaty, signed Jan. 25, the Wyandot and Delaware, for a consideration of goods worth $2000, deeded to Pennsylvania the lands previously claimed by them within the limits of that state. Many of the western Indians later repudiated these treaties, and stable peace in the region involved was not secured until the Treaty of Greenville[w].

[J. H. Bausman, *History of Beaver County, Pa.*]
SOLON J. BUCK

McKinley Tariff, THE (1890–94), named after the chairman of the Ways and Means Committee, embodied the protectionist[w] view that the high duties of the Civil War and thereafter were not temporary expedients for revenue purposes, but were proper methods of fostering industry .To reduce the accumulating surplus in the Treasury it enlarged the free list from 33.4% to 52.4% of the imports, the most important addition being sugar, but the rates on dutiable imports were increased, attaining an average of 48.4%, exceeded only under the Hawley-Smoot Tariff[w] of 1930. Duties were levied on tin plate, not to protect but to create an industry, with a proviso for their abandonment unless successful within six years; and an effort was made to bring the farmers within the protectionist fold by providing many new duties for agricultural products. Innovations included a bounty of two cents per pound offered sugar growers, and a reciprocity[w] bargaining clause authorizing the President to suspend the free entry of sugar, molasses, tea, coffee and hides if he considered that the duties imposed on American produce by the country exporting the goods were reciprocally unjust. The tariff proved unpopular, however, and its Republican proponents met an overwhelming defeat immediately following its enactment (*see* Campaign of 1892).

[E. Stanwood, *American Tariff Controversies;* F. W. Taussig, *The Tariff History of the United States.*]
LAWRENCE A. HARPER

McKinney, Fort (Wyo.), was established in 1877 on the north bank of Clear Creek, a short distance west of the present town of Buffalo, Wyo. Its establishment was recommended by Gen. George Crook, then engaged in a campaign against the Sioux and Cheyenne[qw]. The fort was improved on Gen. Sheridan's orders in 1882, but

abandoned in 1895 and the grounds donated to the State of Wyoming.

[F. B. Beard, *Wyoming.*]
CARL L. CANNON

McLane-Ocampo Treaty, THE, between the United States and Mexico, was signed Dec. 14, 1859. Its terms granted the United States right of way over the Isthmus of Tehuantepec, including the right to transport troops across the Isthmus and other parts of Mexico. It also provided for reciprocal trade relations, and for a loan of $4,000,000 by the United States to Mexico. The treaty was ratified by Mexico, but not by United States.

[William R. Manning, *Diplomatic Correspondence of the United States, Inter-American Affairs, 1831-1860,* IX.]
N. ANDREW N. CLEVEN

McLeod Case, THE, arose out of the arrest at Lockport, N. Y., of Alexander McLeod, deputy sheriff of Niagara, Upper Canada, on Nov. 12, 1840, on charges of arson and of murdering Amos Durfee when the *Caroline*[w] was destroyed on Dec. 29, 1837. Despite British demands for McLeod's release on the ground that the destruction of the *Caroline* was a public act, the New York Supreme Court held that he had been rightfully indicted for murder and remanded him for trial in a lower court, where he was acquitted on Oct. 12, 1841, by proving an alibi.

Meanwhile much excitement was generated in England over a bellicose report on foreign affairs in Congress, and the New York court's decision. Minor naval preparations for war were undertaken in case of McLeod's execution. Both Federal and New York state governments took every precaution to safeguard McLeod's person. In both the United States and Canada additional appropriations were made to strengthen border defenses. To prevent jurisdictional conflicts in similar cases in the future, a congressional act of 1842 provided for the removal of an accused alien from a state court to a United States court on a writ of habeas corpus[w].

[J. M. Callahan, *American Foreign Policy in Canadian Relations.*]
ALBERT B. COREY

McLoughlin Land Claim (1829–62). Dr. John McLoughlin, a chief factor of the Hudson's Bay Company[w], laid claim in 1829 to the land at the falls of the Willamette River where he later platted Oregon City. Because of disputed national possession until 1846 (*see* Oregon Question) all land claims rested upon squatters' rights. As a nonresident, Dr. McLoughlin found his claim contested by a group of early settlers, which contest was settled by a compromise. Even after becoming a resident at Oregon City in 1846 his claim was disputed, and by the terms of the Federal law known as the Donation Land Law^{w} of 1850 a portion of McLoughlin's claim was given to a rival claimant, and the remainder, with its valuable water power rights, was given to the territory of Oregon for the benefit of a university. While this injustice was not corrected within McLoughlin's lifetime, the land claim was restored to his heirs by act of the state legislature in 1862.

[Charles H. Carey, *A General History of Oregon.*]
ROBERT MOULTON GATKE

McNamara Case. Efforts of union labor to organize Los Angeles, culminated Oct. 1, 1910, in the bombing of the plant of the *Times,* which had campaigned for an open shop. Twenty persons were killed, and the building demolished. Labor leaders claimed the explosion was due to escaping gas, but James B. McNamara, his brother, John J. McNamara, and Ortie McManigal, an accomplice, were arrested and charged with the crime. McManigal confessed, but the brothers pleaded "not guilty."

Following their arrest, the prisoners became symbols of labor's struggle against capital, and their trial a national issue. Employers' organizations supported the prosecution, while the American Federation of Labor^{w} issued an official appeal to the working class to stand by the McNamaras. Samuel Gompers visited the brothers and declared the trial a "frame-up." McNamara Defense Leagues raised a large fund, with which Clarence Darrow was hired as defense attorney.

The trial began on Oct. 11, 1911, coinciding with a heated political campaign in Los Angeles. It proceeded slowly, and was marked by the arrest of two of Darrow's agents on charges of jury-bribing. After asserted negotiations with the prosecution, the defense on Dec. 1 withdrew its pleas of "not guilty." James B. McNamara pleaded guilty to bombing the *Times,* and John J. McNamara to bombing the Llewellyn Iron Works, a Los Angeles concern. They were sentenced to life imprisonment and fifteen years respectively. Their confessions were a decided blow to the organized labor movement throughout the country.

[Louis Adamic, *Dynamite, The Story of Class Violence in America.*] FRANK FREIDEL

McNary-Haugen Bill, THE, had for its purpose the rehabilitation of American agriculture by raising the domestic prices of farm products. At the end of 1920, overexpansion of agricultural lands, the decline of foreign markets, the effects

of the protective tariff^{w}, the burdens of debt and of taxation had created a serious agricultural depression. It grew steadily worse in the middle 1920's. The basic idea of the McNary-Haugen, or equalization-fee, plan was to segregate the amounts required for domestic consumption from the exportable surplus. The former were to be sold at the higher domestic price (world price plus the tariff), using the full advantage of the tariff rates on exportable farm products, and the latter at the world price. The difference between the higher domestic price and the world price, received for the surplus, was met by the farmers of each commodity, in the form of a tax or equalization fee. The legislation was before Congress from 1924 to 1928. It received powerful and united support from the agricultural interests in 1927 and in 1928, respectively, when it passed both houses, only to meet two vigorous vetoes by President Coolidge. (*See also* Export Debenture, Farm.)

[J. D. Black, *Agricultural Reform in the United States;* George M. Peek, in *Current History,* November, 1928.]
THOMAS S. BARCLAY

Meat Industry. See Packing, Meat.

Meat Inspection Laws in the United States originated with the campaign for pure food^{w} legislation. After 1887 the publications of the Department of Agriculture, under the supervision of H. W. Wiley, did much to stimulate national and state interest. Spurred to action by the "embalmed beef"^{w} scandal at the time of the Spanish-American War, Congress passed in 1906 a comprehensive meat inspection statute. This act gave the Secretary of Agriculture, under the interstate commerce clause, power to inspect all meat and condemn such products as are "unsound, unhealthful, unwholesome, or otherwise unfit for human food." Although modified and amended, this enactment has remained the basis of activity by the Federal Government.

[C. W. Dunn, ed., *Food and Drug Laws, Federal and State;* Gustavus Weber, *The Food, Drug and Insecticide Administration.*]
BENJAMIN F. SHAMBAUGH

Mechanicsville, Battle of, sometimes called Beaver Dam Creek (June 26, 1862). Aware that McClellan (U.), endeavoring to contact McDowell's (U.) advance from Fredericksburg (*see* Jackson's Valley Campaign), had dangerously extended his right, consisting of Porter's 5th Corps, north of the Chickahominy, Lee (C.) determined to crush the exposed wing. Leaving 21,000 troops east of Richmond to contain the 75,000 of McClellan's center and left, he threw 36,000 across the Chickahominy toward Porter's front, east of Mechanicsville. Jackson (C.), marching from the Shenandoah Valley via Ashland with 18,500 troops, was to envelop the Federal flank. Five brigades of A. P. Hill's and Longstreet's divisions of Lee's army assaulted McCall's (U.) division, entrenched behind Beaver Dam Creek, and were severely repulsed. Jackson arrived too late to participate. During the night McCall withdrew and Porter concentrated behind Boatswain's Creek. (*See also* Peninsular Campaign.)

[*Battles and Leaders of the Civil War*, Vol. II; Douglas S. Freeman, *R. E. Lee*, Vol. II.]

JOSEPH MILLS HANSON

Mecklenburg Declaration of Independence (May 20, 1775). On April 30, 1819, the *Raleigh Register* printed what was purported to have been a document adopted by the citizens of Mecklenburg County, meeting at Charlotte, N. C., May 20, 1775, in which they declared themselves "a free and independent people, are and of right ought to be a sovereign and self-governing association under the control of no other power than that of our God and the General Government of Congress." This account was based on the recollections of old men, who insisted that there had been such a meeting and that the original records had been destroyed by fire in 1800. Jefferson denounced the document as "spurious," but its authenticity was not seriously questioned until 1847, when a copy of a Charleston newspaper of June 16, 1775, was found containing a full set of the Resolves[?] adopted at Charlotte, May 31, 1775. The available evidence leads one to believe that there was only one meeting. Confusion as to dates probably arose because of the old style and new style calendars. The Resolves of May 31 did not declare independence and they were drafted by the same men who claimed the authorship of the May 20 document, and who, after 1819, insisted that there was one meeting and one set of resolutions. Although the date May 20, 1775, is on the state seal and the state flag, most historians agree that the Mecklenburg Declaration of Independence is a "spurious document."

[William Henry Hoyt, *The Mecklenburg Declaration of Independence*.]

HUGH T. LEFLER

Mecklenburg Resolves. On May 31, 1775, a committee of Mecklenburg County (North Carolina) citizens, meeting at Charlotte, drew up a set of twenty resolves, declaring "that all laws and commissions confirmed or derived from the authority of the King and Parliament are annulled and vacated and the former civil constitution of these colonies for the present wholly

suspended." One resolve stated that the Provincial Congress of each colony under the direction of the Continental Congress[?] was "invested with all legislative and executive powers within their respective Provinces and that no other legislative or executive power does or can exist at this time in any of these colonies." The committee proceeded to reorganize local government, elected county officials, provided for nine militia companies, and ordered these companies to provide themselves with proper arms and hold themselves in readiness to execute the commands of the Provincial Congress. Any person refusing to obey the Resolves was to be deemed "an enemy to his country." The Resolves were to be "in full force and virtue until instructions from the Provincial Congress shall provide otherwise or the legislative body of Great Britain resign its unjust and arbitrary pretensions with respect to America." This revolutionary document must not be confused with the so-called Mecklenburg Declaration of Independence[?] of May 20, 1775, the authenticity of which has never been established.

[Hugh T. Lefler, *North Carolina History Told by Contemporaries*.]

HUGH T. LEFLER

Medal of Honor, THE, is the primary military and naval valor recognition, authorized for navy enlisted men, 1861; extended in 1862 to enlisted men of the army; extended in 1863 to include officers of the army, and in 1915 to officers of the navy and marine corps. Army and navy have different decorations, authorized by different acts of Congress, though conditions of award are identical. Officers or enlisted men to win the medal must have performed an act of heroism under fire, conspicuous bravery all above and beyond the call of ordinary duty, and at risk of life. Originally worn on breast; now worn at neck as position of highest honor.

[Robert E. Wyllie, *Orders, Decorations, Insignia, Military and Civil; Decorations, United States Army,* Government Printing Office; *Decorations, Medals, and Badges of the United States Navy,* Government Printing Office.]

LELAND P. LOVETTE

Mediation. *See* Arbitration, International; Arbitration, Industrial.

Medical Schools. Before 1800 most medical students were apprenticed to physicians for six years. Of about 3500 physicians in 1775, less than 400, largely in the Southern and Middle Colonies, were M.D.'s, most of these having studied in London, Edinburgh, etc. Medical schools developed from lecture courses, and originally supplemented apprenticeship. Philadelphia College (merged with the University of Pennsylvania, 1792) elected John Morgan and William Shippen medical professors in 1765. King's College medical department (1768) was suspended in 1775 and merged with Columbia College (1792–1813). Columbia University medical school (1891) was originally New York College of Physicians and Surgeons (1807). New England medical education began at Harvard (1783), and was promoted by Nathan Smith, who helped found medical schools at Dartmouth (1797), Yale (1810), Bowdoin (1820) and Vermont (1822). The first southern medical school was at the University of Maryland (1807). The first western school was Transylvania University (1817–59), where B. W. Dudley was the outstanding teacher. Daniel Drake left Transylvania to found the Medical College of Ohio (1819), now in the University of Cincinnati. Charles S. Caldwell led Transylvania seceders who founded the Louisville Medical Institute (1837). Other early schools were South Carolina (1824), Jefferson (1826), Georgia (1830), Louisiana-Tulane (1835). About 400 schools were founded up to 1900, but many were short-lived or only on paper. The highest number at one time was 162 (1906). The incentive was the profit resulting from the simple equipment required and the large numbers of students (28,142 in 1904). City hospitals provided material for dissection and clinics, causing the abandonment or removal of the small-town schools.

The American Medical Association (founded 1846–47) unsuccessfully advocated higher standards. In 1871 Harvard adopted a three-year graded course (four years in 1892) and was widely imitated. In 1891 the Association of American Medical Colleges specified certain high-school subjects as admission requirements. Johns Hopkins (1893) admitted only college graduates, and its great teachers (Osler, Welch, Thayer, Kelly, etc.) emphasized the scientific attitude. Full-time professorships began at Hopkins and were stipulated in certain subjects by the General Education Board and the Carnegie Foundation[qqv].

The Council on Medical Education (1904) established minimum standards in 1914, raised in 1932. This and the survey made by Abraham Flexner for the Carnegie Foundation (1908–10) caused many schools to combine or dissolve, so that by 1932 only seventy-six were extant. One year's internship is now almost universal. Institutions for training specialists have increased, supervised by such organizations as the American College of Surgeons.

[H. E. Sigerest, *American Medicine.*]

W. C. MALLALIEU

Medicine and Surgery. Colonial America studied its medical alphabet in British books. Thomas Thacher, Boston preacher and physician, issued in 1677/8 a broadside which he called "A Brief Rule to guide the Common People of New-England how to order themselves and theirs in the Small Pocks, or Measles." It is apparent from the title that "the well wisher to the sick," as Thacher styled himself, did not make a differential diagnosis between the two diseases. This single sheet—a double-columned poster, printed on one side of the paper, 15½ inches long and 10 inches across—was the first and only medical publication in the colonies during the 17th century. In the 18th century, Benjamin Franklin gave a decided impetus to early American medicine, and demonstrated in his own person that science had found an accomplished votary in the New World. Thomas Cadwalader's account and autopsy (1742) of a case of osteomalacia, or softening of the bones (printed and sold by Benjamin Franklin, 1745), is the first description of this disease on record. John Morgan, in the year that he established America's first medical school (1765), delivered the address, "A Discourse upon the Institution of Medical Schools in America," remarkable for its forecast of modern methods.

American achievements in the 19th century include: John Conrad Otto's original description of hemophilia, or bleeder's disease (1803); Ephraim McDowell's first ovariotomy (1809, reported 1817); William Beaumont's pioneer study of the stomach (*see* St. Martin's Stomach) in life (1825); William Wood Gerhard's differentiation of typhoid fever and typhus fever (1837); Oliver Wendell Holmes' recognition of the cause of childbed fever (1843); John Collins Warren's major operation under ether anæsthesia[qv], the first in the world (1846); James Marion Sims' conquest of vesico-vaginal fistula (1852); Austin Flint's description of the mitral murmurs (Flint's murmur, 1862); John Shaw Billings' *Index Medicus* (1879) and *Index Catalogue of the Surgeon-General's Office* (1880), herculean labors in bibliography which amazed the medical scholars of Europe; Reginald Heber Fitz's baptism and localization of appendicitis (1886) and clarification of pancreatitis (Fitz's syndrome, 1889); William Stewart Halsted's injection of cocaine into nerves (1885) and introduction of the rubber glove into surgery (1890).

Walter Reed's incrimination of the yellow fever mosquito in Cuba (1900), followed by William Crawford Gorgas' eradication of yellow fever[qv] in Havana and Panama, set the pace for sanitary efficiency (*see* Health, Public). Outstanding achievements of the 20th century are:

Charles Wardell Stiles' finding of a new species of hookworm[qv] (*Uncinaria americana,* 1902); Charles Franklin Craig's description of a new intestinal parasite of man (*Paramœba hominis,* 1906); Theobald Smith's classic on Texas cattle fever and his discovery of serum susceptibility (Theobald Smith phenomenon, 1906); Leo Buerger's delineation of thrombo-angiitis obliterans, or presenile spontaneous gangrene (Buerger's disease, 1908); Howard Taylor Ricketts' investigation of tabardillo (1910); Hideyo Noguchi's demonstration of the parasite of syphilis in the brain of paretics and in the spinal cord of tabetics ("I am the first to cultivate the spirochete of syphilis," 1910); Joseph Goldberger's conquest of pellagra (1914); Edward Francis' study of the new American disease, tularemia (Francis' disease, 1921). The work of Nicholas Senn in bone surgery, of John Benjamin Murphy in abdominal surgery, of George Crile in surgical shock, of Harvey Cushing in cerebral surgery, the scalpel of the brothers Mayo, and the bronchoscope of Chevalier Jackson, have raised American surgery to first rank.

The Nobel prize in medicine was awarded to the following American workers: Alexis Carrel (vascular ligature and grafting of blood vessels and organs, 1912); Karl Landsteiner (discovery of the human blood groups, 1930); Thomas Hunt Morgan (discoveries relating to the hereditary function of the chromosomes, 1933); George Hoyt Whipple, William Parry Murphy, George Richards Minot (liver therapy against anemias, 1934).

[Medicine in America, in Victor Robinson's *The Story of Medicine.*]
                                    VICTOR ROBINSON

Medicine Creek Council, THE (October, 1867), was conducted by the Commissioner of Indian Affairs of the Department of the Interior with the Kiowa, Comanche and Apache tribes and some parts of the Arapahoe and Cheyenne tribes[qv], on Medicine Creek, eight miles south of the Arkansas River. The Comanche and Kiowa tribes agreed to relinquish their claims to the lands embraced in the Texas Panhandle, while they and all the other Indians participating accepted removal to new reservations set aside for them. Though the negotiations did not bring final peace on the southwestern frontier, they went far toward doing so, and after 1875 Indian disturbances there practically ceased.

[Annual Report of the Secretary of War, 1867.]
                                    JOSEPH MILLS HANSON

Medicine Man is a white man's name for any Indian who practises magic, conjuring, or heal-ing in all forms. The term shaman is often used as a synonym. Really, the term medicine man signifies a profession or a function in Indian society, and when any one exercises that function he is, for the moment, a medicine man. How the white man came to apply the name medicine to Indian magic is not known, but we assume that the most obvious function of magical power was to cure the sick.

The medicine man was an influential person, for aside from being intelligent and well-informed, he was feared because he could bring evil as well as good. If game was wanting, he was called upon to "make medicine" and restore it; if enemies threatened he was to cause them to turn back; if any one was ill he was called in. The One-eyed-prophet, half brother of Tecumseh and a famous medicine man, sat on a rock, at a safe distance, "making medicine" while the Battle of Tippecanoe[qv] was fought in Indiana, Nov. 7, 1811. In this instance he failed.

Sleight of hand was often resorted to, to increase the prestige of the medicine man, as, among the Mandan and Pawnee, making a corn stalk appear to grow up quickly. The most famous tricks were those of the juggler, or Jésako, of the Ojibwa and neighboring tribes. A small tent or booth was set up, the medicine man entered, presently he was heard convening with the spirits, from whom he learned the cause of his patient's illness or answers to any other questions propounded to him. Some jugglers allowed themselves to be tied with cords, but when inside threw objects out the top of the lodge, as modern mediums sometimes do.

[B. Drake, *Life of Tecumseh and of His Brother, the Prophet.*]
                                    CLARK WISSLER

Medicine Show. About 1830 Gideon Lincecum, a practising physician and Indian trader of Mississippi who was later to earn a name as botanist and entomologist, went to live alone in the wilderness with a Choctaw medicine man[qv] in order to absorb his herbal knowledge—some of it secret. Lincecum represented a public that believed in some herbs as strongly as a preceding age had believed in the fabled Fountain of Youth. If the American Indians could not show the gold of Cíbola and the Gran Quivira[qv] to the Spaniards, they had more precious valuables in the form of a new pharmacopœia. The widespread dissemination of patent medicines[qv] was at hand. The stage was prepared for the medicine show, though it existed in the 18th century.

The showman understood all that Barnum expressed about the public. He had a cure-all medicine to sell. In order to sell this bottled magic, he gave his show free, on town squares, on street corners, wherever he could find a drawing place for crowds. Often he claimed to be Indian or part Indian, or he might be accompanied by a human being of complexion and garb professedly Indian. He employed blackface comedians. Songs and repartee jokes were his stock in trade. He was an artist at "kidding" the crowd while he mixed in praise of the supernal drug. The medicine show is not altogether obsolete yet, but other forms of quackery, not so diverting, have generally supplanted the medicine.

[R. Wright, *Hawkers and Walkers in Early America*.]

J. FRANK DOBIE

Mediterranean Fund, THE, was projected in 1786 by Thomas Jefferson while minister to France. It provided for international co-operation against the Barbary Pirates. Jefferson proposed that, "As miscarriages often proceed from the want of harmony among officers of different nations the parties shall now consider & decide whether it will not be better to contribute their quotas in money to be employed in fitting out, and keeping on duty, a single fleet of the force agreed on." The project was too visionary to be realized.

[*The Works of Thomas Jefferson*, Ford Edition, Vol. I.]

LOUIS MARTIN SEARS

Meeker Massacre (1879). Because of his arbitrary ways, Agent N. S. Meeker of the Ute agency on White River, Colo., created so much ill will among the Indians that on Sept. 10, 1879, one of them assaulted him. He asked military aid and Maj. T. T. Thornburgh marched with 200 men, Sept. 24, from Fort Fred Steele, Wyo., bearing also orders to arrest Indians suspected of setting forest fires in the district. The Utes ambushed this detachment near Milk River, Sept. 29, killing Thornburgh and nine men and wounding forty-three others. The survivors were besieged six days in hastily prepared barricades. Meanwhile, on Sept. 29, other Utes attacked the agency, thirty miles south of Milk River, killing Meeker and seven employees, and carrying away three women. Gen. Wesley Merritt relieved Thornburgh's men Oct. 5, the Utes disappearing. Through efforts of Ouray, Ute chief, who was absent deer hunting during the fights, further hostilities were averted and the three captured women released.

[J. P. Dunn, *Massacres of the Mountains;* Philip H. Sheridan, *Record of Engagements with Hostile Indians*.]

PAUL I. WELLMAN

Meetinghouse, THE, became best known in connection with the New England Puritan (Congregationalist)ᵂ churches. Reserving "church" to designate a covenanted ecclesiastical society, the Puritansᵂ used "meetinghouse" for the church's assembly place, the more appropriately because the same place often served for town meetings and other public gatherings. Church membership was restricted but attendance at church services was a community requirement. Services included baptism and the Lord's Supper, lengthy sermons, prayers and psalm singing, but marriages and funerals were excluded from the meetinghouse although commemorative "funeral sermons" were preached there for notable persons. Early square meetinghouses, with central towers, gave way to an oblong style with end tower topped by a spire, most typically a white frame structure. The pulpit dominated the simple but dignified interior. In much of New England taxes as well as offerings and pew receipts long were available to support the meetinghouses' religious activities. Population expansion necessitated new meetinghouses for new churches, closely related to the increase of new townships. In late colonial times the meetinghouse became a center of revolutionary activities. Always it fostered local responsibility and community spirit.

[W. Walker, *A History of the Congregational Churches in the United States;* N. Porter, The New England Meeting House, Connecticut Tercentenary Historical Publications Committee, *Tercentenary Pamphlet Series*, No. 18; *The Pageant of America*, Vol. XIII.]

LOUISE B. DUNBAR

Meigs, Fort, was built in 1813, on order of Gen. William Henry Harrison, on the south bank of the Maumee River opposite the present town of Maumee, Ohio, primarily as a general depot for supplies and a base of operations against Detroit and Canada. It was in the form of an irregular ellipse, with blockhouses equipped with cannon. April 28 to May 9, 1813, it was besieged, unsuccessfully, by Gen. Proctor with a force of British, Canadians and Indians, aided by Tecumseh. During this siege Col. Dudley exceeded orders given him by Harrison, and, as a result, he and his men were ambushed and killed by the Indians.

[Randall and Ryan, *History of Ohio*, Vol. III; *Ohio Archæological and Historical Publications*, Vol. X.]

HARLOW LINDLEY

Melungeons, THE (or malungeons, from French *mélange*) , are a people of mixed blood who have long lived in a remote mountain section of Hancock County, Tenn. The Bureau of American Ethnology classed them as an offshoot of the Croatan Indians but Dromgoole said that the original stock was Cherokee Indianᵂ which had settled on Newman's Ridge in 1797 and intermarried with the English and the Portuguese traders and settlers. There have been many disputes over alleged Negro blood; most of the families alleged to have such blood have lived separately. Intermarriage with neighboring people and emigration are causing the melungeons to lose their identity.

[Will Allen Dromgoole, The Malungeon Tree and Its Four Branches, *Arena*, May, 1891; Paul D. Converse, The Melungeons, *Southern Collegian*, December, 1912.]

P. D. CONVERSE

Memorial Day. *See* Decoration Day.

Memorial of the Planters and Merchants of Louisiana (1768). Immediately after the Louisiana Revolution of 1768*w*, in which the Spanish governor, Ulloa, was expelled from the colony, the leading citizens of Louisiana drew up and sent to Louis XV of France a lengthy Memorial, in which they sought to justify the recent revolutionary proceedings against Spanish authority. The Memorial set forth a sort of "bill of indictment" against Ulloa, whom they charged with having ruined the colony by oppressive restrictions on commerce, navigation and industry, prohibition of importation of slaves, and the granting of monopolies to favorites. They also complained of his introduction of the Spanish legal system, and of his contempt for the ecclesiastical laws of the colony. They stressed the great value of Louisiana to France and its uselessness to Spain, professed their love for Louis XV, and begged him to take back the colony. The Memorial may be regarded as a sort of antidote or rebuttal to the reports on the Revolution which they knew Aubry, the last French commandant, and Ulloa, the expelled Spanish governor, would send to their respective governments. Their pleadings were ineffective. Louis XV refused to consider taking back the colony, and Spain sent Alexandro ("Bloody") O'Reilly who crushed the "Revolution" and firmly established Spanish authority in Louisiana in 1769.

[Alcée Fortier, *History of Louisiana;* Charles Gayarré, *History of Louisiana;* B. F. French, ed., *Historical Collections of Louisiana*, Vol. V, 218-230.]

WALTER PRICHARD

Memphis, Naval Battle before (June 6, 1862). About sunrise the Federal western flotilla, of five ironclad*w* gunboats mounting sixty-eight guns, under Flag Officer Charles H. Davis, was anchored across the Mississippi two miles above Memphis. Here it was attacked by the Confederate River Defense Fleet, of eight improvised steam rams carrying twenty-eight guns, commanded by Capt. J. E. Montgomery. Col. Charles

Ellet with three unarmed Federal rams ran down past Davis' flotilla and broke the double Confederate line. The gunboats followed, firing rapidly, and Montgomery's fleet was destroyed in an hour and ten minutes. Three Confederate vessels were sunk, four captured and one escaped. Memphis immediately surrendered to Davis. The Federals lost four men wounded, including Col. Ellet, who subsequently died. (*See* Mississippi Squadron, The.)

[*Battles and Leaders of the Civil War*, Vol. I; A. T. Mahan, *Gulf and Inland Waters.*]

JOSEPH MILLS HANSON

Memphis, Tenn. While Memphis is, comparatively speaking, a modern city, its site (the lowest Chickasaw Bluff) figured in the dawn of the history of the Mississippi Valley. The legend of the Chickasaws fixed it as the place of their crossing the Mississippi in their migration from the West. A number of historians place there the crossing of that river by DeSoto*w* in 1541. Father Marquette in 1673 stopped there on his journey down the river. Fort Assumption was built by Bienville on the Bluff in 1739 as base for his campaign against the Chickasaws*w*. In 1795 Gayoso, for the Spanish government, erected on the site Fort San Fernando, which stood until 1797, when it was dismantled (*see* Guion's Expedition). The town was laid out in 1819 and given the name of the ancient city on the Nile. It soon became the trade center for western Tennessee, northern Mississippi and eastern Arkansas.

[S. C. Williams, *Beginnings of West Tennessee.*]

SAMUEL C. WILLIAMS

Memphis and Charleston Railroad, THE. Between 1830 and 1850, by means of railroads, the principal Atlantic ports sought to break the monopoly of New Orleans on the lucrative export trade of the Mississippi Valley. Charleston, no less than New York, sought to obtain this commerce for itself by constructing an east-west railroad terminating at some point on the Mississippi. Such a rail route was begun in 1829. By 1845 the road had reached Atlanta, and in the same year Memphis*w* was selected by the Charleston promoters as the western terminus. In 1857, after twelve years of further construction, both from Atlanta westward and Memphis eastward, the Memphis and Charleston Railroad was completed.

[R. S. Cotterill, Southern Railroads and Western Trade, *Mississippi Valley Historical Review*, Vol. III.]

GERALD M. CAPERS, JR.

"Men of the Western Waters" was a term used by people living along the frontiers of the Eastern states, 1642–1785. There was no specific group of men to whom this applied, but it referred generally to persons hunting or exploring in the neighborhood of the Ohio and Mississippi rivers and their tributaries. The Long Hunters[w], Daniel Boone and, later, George Rogers Clark's men, were referred to as "Men of the Western Waters." Sometimes settlers of Kentucky were referred to as living on the Western Waters.

[C. W. Alvord and Lee Bidgood, *The First Explorations of the Trans-Allegheny Region by the Virginians;* Charles Kerr, *History of Kentucky.*]
           T. D. CLARK

Mendoza Expedition, THE (1683–84). In 1683 the Jumano Indians who lived in central Texas appealed to the governor of New Mexico for missionaries. In response to this request Juan Dominguez de Mendoza and Father Nicholás López, starting from El Paso in December, 1683, traveled to the country of the Jumanos where they hoped to meet a delegation of Tejas Indians. They established a temporary mission on the Colorado River which, on their return to El Paso in July, 1684, they recommended be made permanent. Their recommendation was not followed because the LaSalle[w] intrusion had drawn the attention of Spanish officials to eastern Texas.

[Carlos E. Castañeda, *The Winning of Texas;* Herbert E. Bolton, *Spanish Exploration in the Southwest, 1542–1706.*]
           C. T. NEU

Menéndez in Florida and Georgia. On Aug. 28, 1565, Pedro Menéndez de Avilés arrived at St. Augustine, Fla., with 2646 persons, for the purpose of colonization and driving out the French. In a short time most of the French were exterminated (*see* Florida, French in) and the first Jesuit missionaries[w] began their work in Florida. To Menéndez, Florida meant the whole of eastern North America and he intended to make it self-supporting and rich. Within two years he had established a line of posts between Tampa Bay and Santa Elena, S. C., and had made an attempt to colonize Virginia. He erected forts at Guale in northern Georgia, at Tampa and Charlotte bays on the west coast of the peninsula, and at Biscayne Bay and the St. Lucie River on the east coast. The projected settlement at Chesapeake Bay failed and the missionaries left. In 1570 more missionaries were sent to Virginia but the next year they were killed by the Indians. In 1572 Menéndez was recalled to Spain to take charge of the Invincible Armada, but he died in 1574. His work gave Spain another important colony in America, and by 1615 more than twenty missions were established in Florida, Georgia and South Carolina (*see* Florida, Spanish Catholic Missions in).

[H. E. Bolton, *Spanish Borderlands;* J. T. Lanning, *The Spanish Missions of Georgia.*]
           LILLIAN ESTELLE FISHER

Mennonites, THE, a religious body founded in 1525 in Switzerland by Conrad Grebel, and in 1533–36 in Holland by Obbe Philips and Menno Simons, orthodox in theology, but advocating separation of church and state, nonresistance and renunciation of war, and mutual aid. It spread to South Germany (1650 f.). From Switzerland and South Germany about 5000 Mennonites went to eastern Pennsylvania 1683–1756, founding settlements in Bucks, Montgomery, Chester, Berks and Lancaster counties. A second emigration from the same regions (1815–60) brought about 3000 to Ohio, Indiana, Illinois, Iowa and Ontario. Their descendants constitute today the main body of the Mennonite Church, with about 60,000 baptized members, located chiefly in compact rural settlements in eastern Pennsylvania, the Shenandoah Valley of Virginia, east central and western Ohio, northern Indiana, central Illinois, eastern Iowa, eastern Nebraska and southern Ontario. Seven schismatic bodies with a total of over 30,000 members have left the main body. The Amish Mennonites[w] are represented chiefly by the so-called "Old Order Amish" with about 10,000 baptized members. From 1873 to 1880 about 10,000 South Russian-German Mennonites settled in the prairie states and Manitoba, and in 1923–25 about 20,000 more went to western Canada. American Mennonites have created outstanding rural communities by their industry, intelligence, solidarity, piety and simple living. In recent years there has been a tendency toward assimilation in their respective communities.

[C. H. Smith, *The Mennonites, a Brief History,* and *The Mennonites of America;* J. C. Wenger, *History of the Mennonites of Franconia Conference;* E. G. Kaufman, *The Development of the Missionary and Philanthropic Interest among the Mennonites of North America;* H. S. Bender, *Two Centuries of American Mennonite Literature, A Bibliography of Mennonitica Americana, 1727–1928; The Mennonite Quarterly Review,* 1927-.]
           HAROLD S. BENDER

Menominee Iron Range, THE. About 85% of the iron produced in the United States comes from six iron ranges adjacent to Lake Superior. Three of these are in Michigan and three in Minnesota. Of these six ranges, the Menominee is the second to have been developed, the Marquette Range[w] being the oldest. The Menominee Range is situated mainly in the valley of the Menominee River which lies on the boundary between the Upper Peninsula of Michigan and northern Wisconsin. That iron was located here seems to have been known before the Civil War, but mining dates from the 1870's. The Breen Mine was opened in 1872 and other locations were made soon thereafter, but active shipments had to await the construction of a branch of the Chicago and North Western Railroad^w from Powers on the main line of the Peninsular Division, which reached the district in 1877. The best outlet for the Range was at Escanaba on Bay De Noc of Lake Michigan, to which the North Western constructed a direct line. The Chicago, Milwaukee and St. Paul Railroad^w also penetrated the region and shipped ore over the Escanaba and Lake Superior line until it reached a pooling^w agreement for shipment over the North Western. Mines were opened at Vulcan, Norway, Iron Mountain and Iron River, and at Florence, Wis., from which eventually more than 180,000,000 tons of iron were shipped to the end of 1936. The most remarkable producer was the Chapin Mine at Iron Mountain which produced nearly 26,000,000 tons of iron ore from its opening in 1879 to its closing in 1934. Most of this ore reached Lake Michigan at Escanaba where ore docks were erected, whence bulk freighters carried the ore to lower lake ports. A few well-integrated corporations operate the mines.

[*Lake Superior Mining Institute Proceedings*, 1905 and 1911; *Wisconsin Magazine of History*, Vol. VII, No. 4.]

L. A. CHASE

Mercantile Agencies grew up following the Panic of 1837^w when there was an urgent need for credit information. The first agency was started in 1841 in New York by Louis Tappan who had accumulated a great deal of credit information for the wholesale firm of A. Tappan & Co. He offered this information for sale following the failure of the Tappan company, and the demand was such that the business grew from the first. In 1859 it became R. G. Dun & Company. In 1849 the Bradstreet Company was started by John M. Bradstreet, a Cincinnati lawyer who had accumulated a great deal of credit information while settling an estate. Many other agencies were started, but these were the only two general agencies to survive and they were merged into Dun & Bradstreet, Inc. in March, 1933. There are several special agencies which cover only particular trades or limited areas. Dun & Bradstreet, Inc. supply financial and credit ratings and information on concerns in all trades in all parts of the United States and in many foreign countries.

P. D. CONVERSE

Mercantilism, as applied to the British colonies, did not follow the general theories of that doctrine very closely. It was always tempered by the fact that the colonies were self-governing subdivisions of the British Empire, inhabited by Englishmen. The mercantilist trading company^w was used to initiate the first colonies, but was soon abandoned for direct imperial control (*see* Colonial Policy, The British). This control took the form of many measures intended to regulate the trade, production and manufacture of both England and the colonies with the object of promoting the prosperity of all. These included the Navigation Acts^w by which the trade within the Empire was confined to English seamen and English ships. The word English in these and subsequent acts referred to nationality and not to residence, thus a merchant from Boston was just as English as was a resident of London.

Other phases of the Navigation Acts enumerated certain colonial products and required that they be shipped from their place of production to England, or to another British or colonial port, and not directly to a foreign country. Asiatic goods and European manufactured goods were in turn required to reach the colonies only by way of England. This program permitted the profits from colonial trade and commerce to center in England, promoted English shipping, and enabled the British government to support itself by taxing this trade as it flowed through England.

The colonies were chiefly producers of raw materials, homes for surplus British population, and markets for goods produced in the home country. Colonial manufacture^w for an export trade that competed with that of the home country was discouraged by prohibitive legislation: wool in 1699, hats in 1732, and wrought iron and steel in 1750. On the other hand, colonial production of articles needed within the Empire was encouraged. The sugar islands were given a practical monopoly of the colonial market for molasses^w (1733). Virginia and her neighbors were given a monopoly of the tobacco^w market in England by acts forbidding the growing of tobacco in England and by prohibitive tariffs on competing Spanish tobacco. Direct bounties, paid from the British treasury, were used to promote the colonial production of hemp, tar, pitch and other naval stores^w, and very large sums were paid out for this purpose between 1705 and 1774. Other colonial products that benefited from bounties were raw silk, masts, lumber and indigo^w. Payments from the British treasury on this account averaged more than £15,000 a year in the decade preceding the Revolution. Preferential tariffs gave colonial products favored treatment in the British markets. Colonial products like sugar and tobacco that were not needed for the British market were, on exportation, assisted by drawbacks of the import duties so that they reached their European markets burdened by a minimum of British taxes. Drawbacks also were used to promote American colonial use of goods from the British colonies in Asia, as tea[w] after 1767. The total export drawbacks paid out by Great Britain in an average year, as 1772, amounted to £2,214,508 in a total export trade valued at £16,159,412, nearly one third of which was exports to America. Exports from Scotland show a similar relationship. Thus colonial and foreign goods flowed through Great Britain to the colonies without too much burden.

The colonial markets were developed by favors instead of compulsion. The usual inducement was export bounties, especially in the case of British manufactures that had foreign competition. The chief articles so aided were cordage, gunpowder, linen, sail cloth, silk manufactures and refined sugar. The total payments by England alone averaged about £40,000 a year at the close of the colonial period, but amounted to more than £61,000 in 1771, according to treasury reports. In this way the British market was made attractive to colonial purchasers. Both England and the colonies profited from this 18th-century policy of enlightened mercantilism.

The opposition to mercantilism in its later stages came from free traders like Adam Smith, who admitted that the system worked, but insisted it was wrong in theory. It is difficult to find opposition to the system among Revolutionary Americans, so long as measures were purely regulatory and did not levy a tax upon the colonists. The system was specifically approved by the First Continental Congress in the Declaration of Rights[w] of Oct. 14, 1774.

[Lawrence A. Harper, *English Navigation Laws.*]
O. M. DICKERSON

Mercer, Fort, Engagements at (Oct. 22 and Nov. 20, 1777). Lord Howe despatched Count Donop with 1200 Hessian[w] troops to attack Col. Christopher Greene's force of 400 at Fort Mercer, a dirt fort, mounting but fourteen guns, located at Red Bank, N. J.

When Donop's command attacked, Greene's men raked them with grapeshot and musketry fire, forcing their retreat with heavy losses, including Donop, left mortally wounded on the battlefield. A month later (Nov. 20), Cornwallis, with greater numerical strength, compelled Greene to evacuate the fort, which was then dismantled.

[B. J. Lossing, *Pictorial Field-Book of the Revolution.*]
ROBERT S. THOMAS

Merchant Adventurers. *See* Adventurers.

Merchant Fleet Corporation, United States Shipping Board, successor to the Emergency Fleet Corporation[w], directly or through agents operated the government-owned merchant fleet from 1927 until superseded by the United States Maritime Commission[w] in 1937. During this decade the fleet, by sale to operators and wreckers, was reduced from 770 vessels of 6,000,000 dead weight tons (two-thirds idle) to 225 vessels of 1,300,000 tons (85% idle). Losses on aggregate fleet operations totaled, 1928–36, about $40,-000,000. (*See also* Merchant Marine.)

[*Annual Reports,* United States Shipping Board and Bureau, 1928-1936.]   FRANK A. SOUTHARD, JR.

Merchant Marine. During the era of the wooden, wind-propelled ship Americans possessed natural advantages in shipbuilding and ship operation which made government aid unnecessary and expanded the American merchant marine from 202,000 tons in 1789 to 5,354,000 in 1860. With the Black Ball Line[w] (1818), New York to Liverpool, the first attempt to maintain a scheduled transoceanic service, the distinction between "liner" and "tramp" emerged (*see* Packets, Sailing). In the clipper ship[w] era (1843–60) Americans gave a last boost to the sailing vessel. The first clipper was built at Baltimore in 1843, five years after the *Sirius* (British) had initiated regular transatlantic steam-navigation. Before steam power won the struggle the long, narrow clipper ships made brilliant records. The clipper *Thornton,* for example, in 1854 sailed the 3000 miles from Sandy Hook to Liverpool in thirteen days, nine hours.

But with the growing supremacy of iron and (after 1870) steel ships and steam propulsion, the United States lost shipbuilding advantage to England. Moreover, American enterprise was absorbed in westward expansion and in the development of tariff-protected manufacturing. Shipbuilding[w] and ship operation could not compete with more lucrative opportunities; 1860 proved to be a peak in the American foreign-trading fleet which was not regained until the World War. By 1910 American-flag ships engaged in foreign trade had only one third the tonnage of 1860; and whereas they carried 90% of American waterborne foreign trade in 1830 and still 66% in 1860, from 1896 to 1910 they carried only 10%. In 1817, however, the coastwise and freshwater trade of the United States had been closed to ships of foreign registry (*see* Coasting Trade; Navigation Act of 1817). This protection from the competition of foreign carriers so stimulated the growth of the domestic trade merchant marine that by 1910 it was 290% larger than in 1860. Consequently whereas 69% of the American merchant marine was engaged in foreign trade in 1810, only 10% was in 1910.

Prior to 1860 there was little occasion to extend government aid to the steadily expanding shipping industry. Only for a brief period was Congress tempted into a shipping subsidy. England in 1838 granted a mail subvention to Samuel Cunard for a North Atlantic service. In 1845 Congress responded with the first subsidy act, authorizing the Postmaster General to conclude mail contracts with the operators of ships (preferably steam) of American construction. The most important aid extended was to the temporarily successful but ill-fated Collins Line, American competitor of Cunard. Although England had increased shipping subventions in 1852, Congress discontinued payments in 1858. This first act foreshadowed the combination of aid to both shipbuilding and ship operation which is typical of much subsequent shipping legislation.

The steady decline of the foreign trade fleet after 1860 induced Congress to turn again to ocean mail payments as a means of keeping American ships in transoceanic trade. For about a decade following 1865 a Philadelphia-Rio de Janeiro line was subsidized and very liberal payments were made to the Pacific Mail Steamship Company for a service to the Orient. But exposure of corruption in Pacific Mail contracts was a factor in the discontinuance of all ocean mail contracts in 1877, although the poundage rates for mail carrying continued to be generally higher than competition would have decreed. By the act of 1891 mail contracts were resumed with operators of ships of American registry, payments varying from sixty-six cents to $4 per mile of outward voyage depending on size and speed of vessel, regardless of amount of mail carried. This system of operating subventions was continued with modifications (notably in the act of 1928) until replaced by the cost-differential principle in 1936. In 1914 the Government spent $1,200,000 on six services.

Thus, up to the World War American merchant marine policy consisted of excluding foreign ships from domestic trade and of relatively modest subventions to selected mail lines. There were no aids to tramps and no direct assistance to shipbuilders. It is therefore not surprising that the International Mercantile Marine Company (1893, 1902), greatest shipping combine under American (Morgan) leadership, registered the bulk of its tonnage under foreign flags. In

so doing it lost little in subsidies and gained in lower operating costs.

The World War was the cause of gigantic growth in the American merchant marine, as is shown in the following table:

Per cent of 1860	1910	1922
Total fleet	140	340
Domestic trade fleet	250	290
Foreign trade fleet	33	455
Per cent of world fleet. . . .	12	24
Per cent of U. S. foreign trade carried in U. S. ships	10	33
Shipbuilding in U. S. as per cent of world. . . .	(1915–20) 46 10	(1921–25) 12

Most of this expansion resulted from the government-financed program authorized by the Shipping Act of 1916[w] and the Emergency Shipping Act of 1917, and carried out by the Emergency Fleet Corporation[w] of the United States Shipping Board[w] at a cost of about $3,200,000,-000. With the completion of this greatest shipbuilding program in history the Shipping Board owned some 1700 steel vessels totaling almost 12,000,000 tons. The period 1920–36 marked the efforts of the Board and the Fleet Corporation to operate and to dispose of this fleet under the Merchant Marine Acts of 1920 and 1928[w]. Most of the time after 1922 the greater part of the vessels were idle; hundreds were sold to wreckers, many—notably passenger-cargo ships—were sold to private operators at a small fraction of their original cost per ton. These operators were then, in most cases, granted ocean mail subsidies. From 1928 to 1937 the Government spent $176,000,000 under mail contracts at the sharply higher rates of the act of 1928, plus poundage payments at about three times the foreign rate. In addition, the Government appropriated, 1923–37, $222,-000,000 to cover Shipping Board and Fleet Corporation deficits.

But by 1936 the state of the American merchant marine was not encouraging. About one tenth of the wartime fleet was still government-owned, but only some forty ships were in operation on seven services. Of the total fleet, in domestic and foreign trade, 90% was fifteen years or more old. Moreover, except for "industrial carriers," supported by strong parent companies, American ship operators as a whole were not financially able to provide replacements without further government aid. A congressional investigation in 1932 had created widespread dissatisfaction with the ocean mail contract system as a means of providing operation subsidies, and the construction loan provisions of the acts of 1920 and 1928 had not materially encouraged new building. Consequently the Merchant Marine Act of 1936[qv] declared a new policy based—according to Maritime Commission[qv] survey—on the necessity of an American-flag merchant marine for purposes of national defense[qv] and commerce, with government aid to consist primarily of payments to cover the construction and operation differentials between American and foreign merchant marine costs. Through this subsidy principle, whose application presents most of the difficulties of the cost of production tariff formula, the Commission proposed to maintain ships on twenty foreign trade routes at a Government outlay of approximately $30,000,000 per year.

[United States Maritime Commission, *Economic Survey of the American Merchant Marine*, Washington, 1937; Abraham Berglund, *Ocean Transportation*.]

FRANK A. SOUTHARD, JR.

Merchant Marine Acts (1920, 1928, 1936). The act of 1920 empowered the Shipping Board[qv] to operate and to dispose of the wartime merchant fleet (*see* Emergency Fleet Corporation), and to make loans for the construction of new vessels under such terms as the Board deemed suitable. If practicable, United States mails were to be carried on American ships at rates determined conjointly by the Postmaster General and the Board. The act of 1928 increased the size of the construction fund, specified the terms of loans, and stated the ocean mail compensation per mile for each of seven classes of vessels. The act of 1936, reasserting Congress' determination to develop a merchant marine, continued low-interest-rate construction loans, but abandoned concealed aid through ocean mail contracts in favor of outright subsidies to offset the construction and operating disadvantage suffered by the American foreign trade fleet in competition with foreign-flag ships. The act also created the Maritime Commission[qv]. (*See also* Merchant Marine.)

[*The Shipping Act of 1916 . . . and other laws relating to the United States Maritime Commission*, Washington, 1936.]

FRANK A. SOUTHARD, JR.

Merchantmen, Armed, for defense against pirates and hostile privateers[qv], have been in established use in America since colonial days. Their armament consisted generally of three- and six-pounders. On March 3, 1805, Congress provided that all armed American-owned vessels clearing American ports must post bonds, amounting to double the cost of the ship, that its guns would be used for defense only. This act soon expired and a similar law was passed April 20, 1818. The

Supreme Court upheld this law in January, 1832. In 1877 and again in 1894 the State Department ruled that merchant ships might carry arms for defense. But the world-wide suppression of piracy and the abolition of privateering rendered the practice of arming merchantmen gradually obsolete. During the World War all neutrals conceded the arming of merchantmen as justifiable, although our State Department in January, 1916, attempted unsuccessfully to prevent this practice. After German diplomatic relations were broken off the United States began arming her merchantmen for submarine[qv] defense.

[H. I. Chapelle, *History of American Sailing Ships;* U. S. State Department, *Policy of the United States toward Maritime Commerce in War.*]

LOUIS H. BOLANDER

Meridian Campaign, THE (February, 1864). In preparation for the spring campaign, Grant (U.) sent a force of 20,000 men under Sherman to Vicksburg[qv] for advance eastward to Meridian, Miss., to destroy Confederate supply depots and railroads. If advisable, Sherman was authorized to move on to Selma or southward toward Mobile. He left Vicksburg, Feb. 3, 1864, opposed only by weak Confederate forces under Polk (C.). Sherman expected co-operation from cavalry under Sooy Smith coming from Memphis. On Feb. 20 Confederate cavalry under Forrest stopped Smith's advance and at Okalona, Miss., decisively defeated him. Lacking Smith's co-operation and fearing for his communications Sherman returned to Vicksburg, having accomplished nothing of importance. Several weeks later his troops were ordered to Chattanooga[qv] to prepare for the campaign against Atlanta[qv].

[*Battles and Leaders of the Civil War.*]

THOMAS ROBSON HAY

Merit System, THE, is the method of recruiting personnel on an open, competitive basis. Though frequently so used, it is not synonymous with the term Civil Service[qv], since the latter applies to the entire civil personnel no matter how recruited. Thus the Federal Government has had a Civil Service from its origin in 1789, but did not have a merit system until 1883 when the Pendleton Act[qv] was passed. The proportion of the entire Civil Service that is selected on the merit principle varies from time to time. In 1789 the percentage was zero; in 1884 the percentage was thirteen; in 1932 it was eighty; in 1936 it had dropped to sixty per cent. Nor is the merit system exclusively confined to use in the Civil Service. It is used by the Foreign Service, by the Military Service, by the Interstate Commerce Commission, by the Social Security Board and by the Tennessee Valley Authority. Moreover, state and municipal civil services are incorporating the merit system to an increasing degree. Even private industry has seen the value of the merit system and since 1914 has adopted the idea of competitive tests for use in its own personnel recruitment.

Originally the merit system was confined to the technique of selection by competitive examination. It has now expanded from a simple system of recruitment to an elaborate system of personnel maintenance. Examinations are widely publicized in scientific journals, colleges and universities, in order to attract career men. Various types of written, performance and oral tests have been perfected. Eligible registers are created with a limited duration to keep the available reserves up to date. Appointment is generally made from one of the three highest names on the eligible list. A probationary period, carefully supervised by the personnel agency, supplements appointment. Service ratings are kept to indicate job performance. Modern transfer and promotion systems have been developed. Permanency of tenure, advancing salaries and adequate pensions have all become necessary attributes of the merit system.

[William E. Mosher and J. Donald Kingsley, *Public Personnel Administration*.]
 F R A N C E S   L.   R E I N H O L D

Merrimac, Sinking of (June 3, 1898). When Cervera's squadron was blockaded by Sampson at Santiago[q], in the Spanish-American War[q], Assistant Naval Constructor Richmond Pearson Hobson with seven men volunteered to sink the collier *Merrimac* across the narrow entrance, blocking Cervera's escape. Under heavy enemy fire the *Merrimac* was anchored in position about 2 A.M., but her steering gear was injured, only two of her sinking-charges exploded, and as finally sunk she did not lie athwart the channel or close it effectively. Surviving almost miraculously after their hazardous exploit, Hobson and his crew were taken prisoners and courteously treated till their exchange on July 7.

[R. P. Hobson, *The Sinking of the Merrimac*.]
A L L A N   W E S T C O T T

Merrimack. *See Monitor* and *Merrimack*, Battle of the.

Merrimack Destroys the *Cumberland* and *Congress* (1862). On March 8 the Confederate ironclad *Virginia* (the reconstructed steam frigate *Merrimack*), commanded by Capt. Franklin Buchanan, attacked the Union blockading ships *Congress* and *Cumberland* off Newport News.

Pouring a destructive fire into both vessels, the ironclad then drove her iron ram into the starboard side of the *Cumberland*, which quickly sank with 121 of her crew of 376. The *Congress* went aground while trying to escape and, forced to surrender by the *Virginia's* heavy broadsides, was then destroyed by hot shot and incendiary shells. She lost 136 men, killed, wounded or missing. The *Virginia* had two killed and nineteen wounded.

[Charles Lee Lewis, *Admiral Franklin Buchanan; Battles and Leaders of the Civil War*, Vol. I.]
C H A R L E S   L E E   L E W I S

Merry Mount, or Mount Wollaston, in Quincy, Mass., was the site of an early conflict between the public interest and commercial greed. About 1625 one Thomas Morton, Gent., established an Indian trading post there, and later added a Maypole, around which he and his men sported with the "lasses in beaver coats." Of the dozen settlements then scattered along the New England coast only that at Plymouth[q] would have objected to the customary May Day[q] promiscuity which Morton, according to his own story, gleefully introduced, and Plymouth was too busy trying to get out of debt; but the combination of neglected Indian husbands, liquor and gunpowder was recognized as a public menace. Every settlement from Maine to Nantasket (none of them Puritan) complained. Plymouth, being near by, was asked by the others to suppress Morton. Twice the Pilgrims protested to him that he was endangering the common safety, but each time he insisted that he would "trade peeces [guns] with the Indeans in despite of all." As a result, Miles Standish was sent in June, 1628, to arrest him in the king's name. Fortunately Morton's crew was so drunk that the only bloodshed came from one of his men who ran his nose onto a sword. Morton was sent off to England, whence he returned shortly to set up the Maypole again and resume his practices. The Massachusetts Bay Colony[q] having been founded in the interval, it was Gov. Endecott who cut down the pole this time. The Puritans offered to take Morton into the fur-trading monopoly, but he refused because its methods were less profitable than his practice of getting the Indians drunk before trading. So he was again shipped off to England, where he got revenge by writing his amusing *New English Canaan*, the first of the attacks on the New Englanders.

[S. E. Morison, *Builders of the Bay Colony*.]
C L I F F O R D   K.   S H I P T O N

Merryman Case, THE (1861), involved President Lincoln's exercise of extraordinary war powers, specifically his right to suspend habeas corpus[W]. John Merryman, a Baltimore County secessionist, was imprisoned in Fort McHenry by military order, May 25, 1861. The commanding officer refused to comply with a writ of habeas corpus issued by Chief Justice Roger B. Taney, on the grounds that he had been authorized by the President to suspend the writ. Taney wrote an opinion, widely denounced in the North, that it could be suspended constitutionally only by Congress, not by the President. Lincoln, however, did not alter his policy (*see* Milligan Case).

[C. B. Swisher, *Roger B. Taney;* Charles Warren, *The Supreme Court in United States History.*]

RANSOM E. NOBLE, JR.

Mesa Verde, Prehistoric Ruins of. In the southwest corner of Colorado stands Mesa Verde National Park, created in 1906 to preserve the ruins known as the "cliff dwellings." Not all the remains of cliff dwellings[W] are found in Colorado; many have been located in the adjacent parts of New Mexico, Arizona and Utah. But the most extensive and best preserved, particularly the communal houses, lie in the canyon walls of this sloping plateau. There are hundreds of ruins scattered through these canyons, among the most important being Spruce Tree House, Cliff Palace, Balcony House and Sun Temple. The builders were a race of Indians, supposedly the predecessors of the present Pueblos[W]. For purposes of defense, they constructed their communal houses in recesses high up on the sides of precipices, the dwellings and temples being composed of stone, clay and supporting poles. The cliff dwellers flourished in the 11th and 12th centuries, and it is supposed that they were forced to abandon the mesa canyons by a severe drought which came upon the land in the year 1276.

[U. S. Department of the Interior, *Mesa Verde National Park.*]   ROBERT PHILLIPS

Mesabi Iron Range of Minnesota became of economic importance with the discovery of workable iron ore in November, 1890, though references to the region occur as early as 1810. Over 4000 tons of ore were shipped from the district in 1892; railroads reached the deposits the following year; and ten years later the output had increased to over 13,000,000 tons annually. Steam shovels were used for mining the ore almost from the beginning, and in 1916 the output from the district was over 40,000,000 tons. The Merritt brothers, who discovered the first ore, early secured the financial participation of John D. Rockefeller in a program of opening mines and building railroads and ore docks. Following the Panic of 1893[W] the properties fell into Mr. Rocke-

feller's hands, and were later sold to Andrew Carnegie and his associates, who subsequently merged them, as the Oliver Iron Mining Co., into the United States Steel Corporation[W]. Various other mining companies are now (1939) operating in the region, which is the most important iron-ore producing district of the world. The Hull-Rust-Mahoning-Susquehanna pit is the largest surface excavation made by man.

[C. K. Leith, The Mesabi Iron-bearing District of Minnesota, *Bulletin XLIII, U. S. Geological Survey;* Paul deKruif, *Seven Iron Men.*]   T. T. READ

Mesas (Spanish for table) are flat-topped areas of land with bluffy walls, sometimes hundreds of feet high, standing above eroded terrain. A mesa may comprise an acre or a thousand acres. This geological formation is characteristic of the Southwest. Acoma[W], the "city in the sky," is a noted example.

[C. F. Lummis, *Mesa, Cañon and Pueblo.*]

J. FRANK DOBIE

Mesilla (messeéya), a village in Doña Ana County, N. Mex., was originally situated on the west side of the Rio Grande, but since 1865, due to a change in the river's channel, is on the east. It was founded after the conclusion of the Mexican War[W] by persons who wished to retain Mexican citizenship. However, a conflict over jurisdiction ensued, which threatened a renewal of hostilities, until the Gadsden Purchase[W] definitely placed the region within the United States. During the Confederate invasion of New Mexico in 1861–62, Mesilla was made the capital of a Confederate territory of Arizona. It has subsequently declined in importance, owing especially to the lack of railroad facilities.

[*New Mexico Historical Review*, Vols. V and VI.]

P. M. BALDWIN

Mesquite, THE, characterizes the Southwest. Its astounding root system enables it to withstand the severest drouths and produce beans, which horses thrive on, cattle can exist on, and of which Indians and Mexicans make brew and bread. Its leaves afford browse, its trunks fence posts, its limbs and roots aromatic fuel. The more arid the land, the slimmer are its leaves—to avoid evaporation. It is always spinous. For many a man it connotes "home on the range." (*See also* Chaparral.)

J. FRANK DOBIE

Messiah War, THE (1890–91), was an outgrowth of the Ghost Dance[W] excitement, which so affected the Sioux Indians that R. F. Royer, the agent at Pine Ridge, S. Dak., wired for troops.

On the arrival of the soldiers, Oct. 19, 1890, thousands of Indians fled to the Badlands[qv], and many settlers left their homes in fear of a major Indian war.

Gen. Nelson A. Miles, commanding the troops in the area, ordered the apprehension of the chief, Sitting Bull, then living on Grand River, but on Dec. 15 the chief was killed, together with six Indian police and eight of his own followers, while resisting arrest.

Skirmishing in the Badlands followed, but on Dec. 28 Maj. S. M. Whitside, 7th Cavalry, discovered the principal band of hostile Indians, under Big Foot, camped on Wounded Knee Creek. Big Foot surrendered but the following morning while his warriors were being disarmed by the troops, fighting broke out, and the so-called Battle of Wounded Knee[qv], really a massacre of the Indians, followed. An estimated 200 to 300 Indians were killed and 29 whites lost their lives.

This was the only important action. After a few more skirmishes, the overwhelming force under Miles overawed the Sioux and compelled their surrender at Pine Ridge Agency early in January, 1891.

[James Mooney, The Ghost Dance Religion, *14th Annual Report, Bureau of American Ethnology*; Stanley Vestal, *Sitting Bull*.]

PAUL I. WELLMAN

Meteorology. *See* Weather Bureau, The.

Metes and Bounds was the ancient system of indicating boundaries of land holdings by reference to natural objects such as trees, stones, etc., as opposed to the modern system based on astronomical lines as first exemplified in the National Survey System[qv]. The Metes and Bounds system, which prevails generally in that portion of the country settled before 1785, is productive of much uncertainty concerning legal titles and boundaries of holdings.

M. M. QUAIFE

Methodists, THE, although their origin in England dates from 1739, did not begin in any organizational sense in America until 1766. By that time two Methodist classes had been formed in the colonies, one under the leadership of Robert Strawbridge, one of Wesley's Irish preachers, on Sam's Creek in Maryland, and the other in New York by Philip Embury, also an immigrant from Ireland. News of these beginnings in America caused John Wesley to send out two missionaries in 1769. Two years later (1771) two others were sent, one of whom, Francis Asbury, was to become the principal leader of the Methodist movement until his death in 1816. Later four others came, making eight in all. Meanwhile a

native ministry was arising, largely in Maryland and Virginia, while Devereux Jarratt, an evangelical Anglican minister in Dinwiddie County, Va., gave full co-operation, administering the sacraments to the newly gathered Methodist classes wherever possible.

With the approach of the Revolution all of Wesley's missionaries, with the exception of Asbury, returned to England. Wesley's political pamphlets and his activity in support of the policies of King George III complicated the situation for the American Methodists and led to the persecution of some of the preachers in Maryland and Virginia. Once independence was won the American Methodists were not content to remain under Wesley's control, and he was wise enough to see the necessity of setting them apart as an independent body. Up to this time none of the American Methodist preachers had been ordained and the people were demanding the sacraments. Accordingly, Wesley ordained two of his English preachers and sent them to America with Dr. Thomas Coke, an Anglican clergyman, whom Wesley appointed superintendent of the American Methodists. He also appointed Asbury as joint superintendent with Coke. Asbury, unwilling to accept his appointment without the consent of the preachers, called a conference to meet at Baltimore in Christmas week, 1784. Here within eleven days the Methodist Episcopal Church was formed, preachers were ordained, and a book of discipline and a service and hymn book adopted.

The circuit[qv] system which had been brought from England by Asbury and his co-laborers proved to be ideally suited to the task of following a moving population, while the Methodist gospel of free grace and individual responsibility won a ready response on the democratic frontier. As a result Methodism grew rapidly, and by 1820 there was a Methodist membership in America of 259,890. Twenty years later (1840) it had increased to 740,000.

American Methodism has had two great controversies, each of which resulted in a serious division. The first culminated in 1830 with the formation of the Methodist Protestant Church; the second in 1845 with the organization of the Methodist Episcopal Church, South. The first was over the question of the power of the bishops; the second grew out of the slavery controversy. Three large Negro Methodist churches have also arisen.

Until 1831 the American Methodists had established no permanent colleges, but after that date a national educational policy was adopted and by 1860 thirty-four colleges had been formed. In the development of Methodism the press has had an influential place. The Methodist Book Concern was formed in 1789 and is now one of the largest publishing houses in the country, issuing a large number of official papers as well as books.

Since 1872 a movement had been under way to unite the three main Methodist bodies. After years of negotiation a plan of unification was finally worked out and in 1938 was adopted by the Methodist Episcopal Church, the Methodist Episcopal Church, South, and the Methodist Protestant Church to form a united body of nearly 8,000,000.

[W. W. Sweet, *Methodism in American History;* H. E. Luccock and Paul Hutchinson, *The Story of Methodism;* A. Stevens, *History of the Methodist Episcopal Church in the United States of America,* 3 vols.]
                                        WILLIAM W. SWEET

Metropolitan Aqueduct. *See* Colorado River Aqueduct, The.

Metropolitan Areas. In recent years, it has become customary to refer to an urban center, with the surrounding suburban area, as a metropolitan area. This realistic term is intended to include the entire territory whose social and economic interests are centered in the city in question, without regard to state lines or other political boundaries. Thus the metropolitan area of Chicago includes approximately 1500 governmental units in three states. Metropolitan New York consists not only of the five counties of the Greater City but of those on Long Island and adjacent in southeastern New York State, of a portion of southwestern Connecticut, and of northern New Jersey. Similarly, Metropolitan Philadelphia includes portions of three states— Delaware, New Jersey and Pennsylvania.

[Charles E. Merriam and Albert Lepawsky, *The Government of the Metropolitan Region of Chicago;* Paul Studenski, *The Government of Metropolitan Areas.*]
                                        W. BROOKE GRAVES

Meuse-Argonne Offensive (Sept. 26–Nov. 11, 1918). Marshal Foch entrusted to the American army the task of beginning the Allied general offensive which he designed to disrupt the German Western front. Gen. Pershing planned to attack in the sector Argonne plateau (inclusive)—Meuse River, and advance northwest on the axis Montfaucon-Romagne-Buzancy toward Sedan, thirty-five miles distant. At Sedan breaking of the enemy's main railways would compel evacuation of his four entrenched zones from that place to the English Channel.

Nine American divisions supported by 2700 guns attacked the eleven small German divisions of Gen. Gallwitz' Army Group holding the 20-mile Argonne-Meuse front. This was the pivot of the enemy's salient in France, protected by three of his entrenched zones, ten miles in total depth. Co-operating constantly with Gen. Gouraud's 4th French army, west of Argonne, the Americans captured Montfaucon, Sept. 27, and by the 29th had progressed six miles in places, piercing the second entrenched zone. Gallwitz now introduced six more divisions and progress became slower. However, on Oct. 7 and 8 attacks on the Argonne heights and those east of the Meuse deprived the Germans of formidable flanking positions and relieved the American center of artillery cross-fire.

In mid-October Gen. Liggett took the 1st American army and Gen. Bullard the new 2nd army, Gen. Pershing assuming command of the Group of American Armies. The 1st army's renewed general attack, Oct. 14, encountered bitter resistance, but Romagne was taken and the line straightened by Oct. 31 confronting the third German retirement position, held by thirty-one divisions.

Attacking Nov. 1 with seven divisions west of the Meuse and six east of it, the 1st army immediately broke the German center, advancing five and one-half miles the first day. Nov. 2 Buzancy was captured and the Gallwitz Army Group began withdrawing east of the Meuse. When hostilities ceased, Nov. 11 (*see* Armistice), the Americans had crossed in pursuit at many points and their left had reached Sedan, interdicting the German rail communications.

This was America's greatest battle. Aiding and aided by French and British advances averaging fifty miles between the Argonne and the sea, the 1st American army employed over 1,000,000 troops during seven weeks, broke the hinge of Germany's defenses, defeated forty-seven divisions, more than one fourth of her total, and captured in action 26,000 prisoners and 4000 cannon and machine guns. American losses totalled 117,000 killed and wounded.

[*Final Report of General John J. Pershing;* Frederick Palmer, *Our Greatest Battle;* J. M. Hanson, History of the American Combat Divisions, in *The Stars and Stripes.*]
                                        JOSEPH MILLS HANSON

Mexican Association, THE (1805 f.), was one of several similar organizations formed to secure liberation of Mexico from Spanish rule. It consisted of some 300 men who were interested in reviving the commerce of New Orleans, securing the spread of American ideas and the building up of a sentiment favorable to the United States. Any undertaking that gave promise of furthering these objectives was readily supported. Burr hoped to utilize the Mexican Association (*see* Burr Conspiracy). In spite of government opposition, the Association continued to function actively and was one of the backers of Mina's and of Long's filibustering expeditions[qv].

[W. F. McCaleb, *The Burr Conspiracy*.]

THOMAS ROBSON HAY

Mexican Boundary, THE. The history of the boundary between the United States and Mexico may be said to begin in 1803 with the Louisiana Purchase[qv]; thereby the frontier of the United States marched with the possessions of Spain along the western limits of the Louisiana Territory; but the western boundary of the Louisiana Territory was not, either then or thereafter, internationally or juridically delimited.

After prolonged negotiations, a conventional line was established between American and Spanish sovereignties by the Adams-Onís Treaty[qv] of Feb. 22, 1819. The boundary fixed by that treaty, with a reference to Melish's Map of 1818, began in the Gulf of Mexico at the mouth of the Sabine River, ran up that river to latitude 32°, thence north to and up the Red River to longitude 100°, and thence north to and up the Arkansas River; from the source of the Arkansas the line extended north to the 42nd parallel and followed that parallel from near longitude 109° (in Wyoming) west to the Pacific. Adams had given up the American claim to Texas[qv] and in return had acquired for the United States the Spanish rights to the Oregon country[qv], north of California, as well as a definitive cession of all Spanish territory east of the Mississippi, i.e., the Floridas[qv].

The treaty of 1819 did not go into effect until Feb. 22, 1821; in the same year came Mexican independence; so the line of the treaty of 1819 became the first boundary between the United States and Mexico. This was declared by the two countries in the treaty of Jan. 12, 1828, which did not enter into force until April 5, 1832; before survey of the line, events intervened; the independence of Texas (March 2, 1836) was recognized by the United States on March 7, 1837. Accordingly, the boundary of the treaty of 1819 was not demarcated either with Spain or with Mexico.

The boundary between the United States and Mexico during the period of Texan independence (1836–45) is not internationally definable; not only was there great divergence of view as to the western and northern limits of Texas, but the independence of Texas was at no time recognized by Mexico; and there was but a brief interval between the admission of Texas into the Union (Dec. 29, 1845) and the outbreak of the Mexican War[qv] on May 13, 1846.

The boundary of the treaty of peace, signed at Guadalupe Hidalgo[qv] on Feb. 2, 1848, ran from the Gulf of Mexico up the Rio Grande to the southern boundary of New Mexico (i.e., Nuevo-México) "which runs north of the town called Paso" (Ciudad Juarez), thence along the southern and western boundaries of New Mexico (as those boundaries were laid down in Disturnell's Map[qv] of 1847) to the intersection of the western boundary of New Mexico with the river Gila, thence down the Gila to its junction with the Colorado, and thence by a straight line to a point on the Pacific one marine league due south of the southernmost point of the Port of San Diego (as shown on a plan of that port drawn in 1782).

Owing to inaccuracies of Disturnell's Map, controversy arose during the demarcation of the boundary between the Rio Grande and the Colorado. The Mexican Boundary Commissioner proposed a line beginning on the Rio Grande at latitude 32° 22′ north (this being the latitude at the Rio Grande of the southern boundary of New Mexico according to Disturnell's Map), running thence about one degree west to the Mimbres, up that stream to its source, and therefrom by direct line to the Gila. The line agreed upon by the two Boundary Commissioners (April 24, 1851) ran from the Rio Grande at 32° 22′ three degrees west, and thence due north to the Gila; but the Surveyor of the United States, whose assent was necessary under the treaty, did not accept the line of the Commissioners, and contended (correctly) that the beginning point at the Rio Grande should be at 31° 52′ N. Lat., according to the position of the Chihuahua-New Mexico boundary on Disturnell's Map relative to the true latitude of Paso; this starting point is some thirty miles south and a few miles east of the point on the Rio Grande at latitude 32° 22′; the line of the Surveyor ran from the Rio Grande at 31° 52′ three degrees west and thence due north to the Gila. The territorial difference between the line of the Surveyor and the line of the Commissioners was about 6000 square miles. Congress approved the line of the Surveyor; the work of demarcation ceased; the boundary of the United States with Mexico between the Rio Grande and the Colorado under the Treaty of Guadalupe Hidalgo was never internationally agreed upon.

Dispute as to the boundary from the Rio Grande to the Colorado under the Treaty of Guadalupe Hidalgo was ended by the Gadsden

Purchase[w]; by the Gadsden Treaty of Dec. 30, 1853, as it went into force on June 30, 1854, after extensive Senate amendments, the line westward from the Rio Grande ran, as it does now, from 31° 47′ N. Lat. due west one hundred miles, thence south to 31° 20′ N. Lat., thence along that parallel to 111° W. Long., thence in a straight line to a point on the Colorado River twenty English miles below the junction of the Gila and Colorado, and, finally, up the middle of the Colorado some twenty miles to a point nearly seven miles to the west of the junction of the Gila and Colorado and about ten miles by water below that junction, meeting at that point the boundary from the Colorado to the Pacific. That line of the Gadsden Treaty is now the boundary with Mexico of the states of New Mexico and Arizona, and throughout its entire course from the Rio Grande to the Colorado is well to the south of any possible line under the Treaty of Guadalupe Hidalgo. No change from the treaty of 1848 was made by the Gadsden Treaty in the line from the Pacific to the Colorado River (the southern boundary of California) or in the boundary of the Rio Grande between Texas and Mexico, from 31° 47′ to the Gulf of Mexico.

The boundary resulting from the treaties of 1848 and 1853 remains the boundary between the two countries, except for the reciprocal elimination, pursuant to various agreements, of *bancos,* which have been defined as "small tracts of land in the valleys of the Rio Grande and the Colorado which are isolated by the river when it cuts through a sharp bend and forms a new channel"; and from the shifting course of the Rio Grande arose one question of the boundary which technically has not been settled; this involves the Chamizal Tract of some 630 acres in El Paso, Tex.

[C. O. Paullin, *Atlas of the Historical Geography of the United States,* with maps showing the various lines; J. F. Rippy, *The United States and Mexico;* T. M. Marshall, *History of the Western Boundary of the Louisiana Purchase;* P. C. Brooks, *Diplomacy and the Borderlands: The Adams-Onís Treaty 1819;* J. H. Smith, *The War with Mexico;* P. N. Garber, *The Gadsden Treaty;* Hunter Miller, *Treaties and Other International Acts of the United States of America; Reports of International Boundary Commission, United States and Mexico.*]   HUNTER MILLER

Mexican Cession. *See* Guadalupe Hidalgo, Treaty of.

Mexican Decree of April 6, 1830, THE, sought to save Texas for Mexico by stopping immigration from the United States and substituting for it an inflow of native Mexicans, and perhaps Europeans. Garrisons were sent to Texas to en-

force the law. This abrupt change in policy so adversely affected the Americans already in Texas that to a large extent they ignored its provisions, resorted to violence and finally seceded from Mexico by their Declaration of Independence, March 2, 1836.

[Alleine Howren, Causes and Origin of the Decree of April 6, 1830, *Southwestern Historical Quarterly,* XVI.]
                                                      JIM DAN HILL

Mexican Gulf Ports, Blockade of (1846–48). War with Mexico was declared on May 13, 1846. Not long afterward Commodore David Conner, in command of the Home Squadron, was ordered to blockade or seize the Mexican Gulf ports. The first success was the capture of Frontera at the mouth of Tabasco River, on Oct. 23, by Capt. Matthew Calbraith Perry, commanding the *Mississippi* and six gunboats. He also forced Tabasco, eighty miles up the river, to surrender on Oct. 26, but the same day returned to Frontera. On Nov. 14 Commodore Conner captured Tampico. On Dec. 8 the brig *Somers,* commanded by Lt. Raphael Semmes, while chasing a blockade runner off Vera Cruz, capsized with the loss of about forty men. Commodore Conner was replaced, on March 20 during combined naval and military operations against Vera Cruz, by a younger and more aggressive officer, Capt. M. C. Perry. Only a week later the city surrendered to Perry and Gen. Winfield Scott. Meanwhile the gunboat *Hunter* was lost in a gale on March 21, though all her crew were saved. Lt. C. G. Hunter, commanding the *Scourge,* captured Alvarado, March 30, prematurely against orders, and for this was dismissed from the service. Perry proceeded with his squadron of sixteen vessels to Tuspan. On April 18 the town, located five miles above the mouth of the Tuspan River, was captured by ships' barges towed by six small gunboats. Leaving two vessels here, Perry sailed with the rest to Frontera. Ascending the river again to Tabasco on the 15th and 16th of June, in spite of serious resistance from the fortifications he took and held the place. With all Mexican Gulf ports taken, Perry's squadrons cruised up and down the coast until the signing of the Guadalupe Hidalgo[w] Treaty on Feb. 2, 1848, the yellow fever[w] having proved a more dangerous foe than the Mexicans.

[Charles Lee Lewis, *Admiral Franklin Buchanan;* Edward M. Barrows, *The Great Commodore: Exploits of Matthew Calbraith Perry.*]
                                              CHARLES LEE LEWIS

Mexican Oil Controversy. The first successful Mexican oil well was drilled in the Ebano field in 1901 by Edward L. Doheny and associates, but the phenomenal growth of the industry began ten years later. By 1921 an annual production of 193,397,587 barrels made Mexico the second largest petroleum-producing nation. The industry was developed principally by United States and British capital, and centered in Vera Cruz and Tabasco.

The Mexican Revolution early adopted a program of nationalization of natural resources. President Carranza, recognized (1915) by the United States with the understanding that he would respect foreign property interests, tried to secure more taxes from petroleum. The Mexican constitution of 1917 (Article 27) vested in the government power to direct the use of natural resources.

Gradual application of this provision is the essence of the heated dispute which followed. Later Carranza measures were radical enough to contribute to the strong interventionist agitation in the United States, culminating in the Fall Committee hearings in 1919.

The Obregón regime, established in 1920, decreed export and production taxes considered confiscatory by the oil interests. The resulting diplomatic impasse, complicated with unsettled claims, and default on the foreign debt, prevented American recognition of Obregón until the Bucareli Conference (1923), which brought a tacit understanding that the Obregón government would not implement the constitutional provision in a manner hostile to valid titles acquired before 1917.

A new Petroleum Law (1925) required oil companies to accept fifty-year concessions on all their lands. Americans considered this law a violation of the Bucareli understanding. An extremely bitter controversy was settled only when Ambassador Dwight W. Morrow arranged a compromise granting permanent concessions for developed lands, and preferential rights for those undeveloped. The Mexican Six Year Plan (1934–40) called for more complete nationalization of the oil industry, partly because of its strategic importance in the government program to increase wages and raise the Mexican standard of living. Oil workers' demands for increased wages and better conditions brought official intervention (1937), and upon refusal of the companies to comply with an award of $7,200,000 annual wage increases, and other workers' benefits, the Mexican government expropriated (March 18, 1938) all the properties of seventeen British and American companies, variously valued from $250,000,000 to $450,000,000. A sharp protest from Great Britain caused Mexico to break off diplomatic relations, while efforts of the United States and Mexico to agree to the amount and

method of compensation proved unsuccessful to the summer of 1939.

[J. R. Clark, Jr., in *Foreign Affairs*, June, 1938; F. S. Dunn, *Diplomatic Protection of Americans in Mexico; Foreign Policy Report*, Aug. 15, 1937.]

HAROLD E. DAVIS

Mexican Relations. The relations between the United States and Mexico are based primarily upon geographical propinquity and essential raw materials. The long, almost imaginary frontier of some 1800 miles is a constant invitation to violation. Not only is Mexico a vast storehouse of precious metals, particularly silver, but it has large deposits of copper, lead, iron and tin, and its subsoil is permeated with oil.

In the period of the westward expansion^{qv} of the United States this rich, sparsely settled country contiguous to an aggressively pioneer people succumbed to the principle of manifest destiny^{qv}. The annexation of Texas in 1845, the Mexican War of the following year and the purchase at a very nominal price of New Mexico, Arizona and Upper California were the normal developments of an imperialistic age. A remarkable feature of subsequent political relations with Mexico has been the definite cessation of further territorial encroachments on the part of the United States at the expense of its weaker neighbor to the south.

Not only did the United States restrain its own territorial appetite, but it threw its influence strongly against European aggrandizement in this region. The Monroe Doctrine^{qv}, although often dormant, served as the underlying cause for the withdrawal of the French troops and the downfall of Maximilian in 1867, and, although frequently suspected, it has nevertheless remained a potent safeguard of Mexican territorial integrity.

But political independence must be based upon a firm economic foundation. Mexico possessed raw materials in abundance but needed foreign capital for their development. The long regime of Porfirio Díaz (1876–1910) gave encouragement to foreign investment and American citizens poured millions of dollars into Mexican railroads, mines and agricultural lands. The country prospered but the peon did not. Democratic principles became revolutionary watchwords and Mexico was ripe for revolution. Madero, Carranza, Obregón, Calles and Cardenas have improved the position of the Mexican worker and have slowly but effectively restricted foreign exploitation of Mexican wealth. Their revolutionary program, however, has been at the expense of legally established rights of Americans, and as a result diplomatic relations with the

United States have been strained on many occasions. In 1914 matters reached a crisis in the shelling of Vera Cruz[qv] which brought about the complete severance of diplomatic relations, while in 1916 the Villa raids[qv] resulted in the Pershing expedition into Mexico (see Mexico, Punitive Expedition into).

The United States has a certain responsibility to protect its citizens and their property abroad. The question of claims has been a prolific cause of diplomatic negotiation between the United States and Mexico, and four important arbitration commissions have been established to pass upon these controversies, those of 1839, 1849, 1868 and in 1923 (see American-Mexican Mixed Claims Commissions). The Mexican constitution of 1917 and laws enacted under it have permitted wholesale expropriation of American property in land and oil (see Mexican Oil Controversy). Fair and adequate compensation in cash is impossible, and Mexican bonds do not have a high marketable value. The United States has variously threatened, refused recognition, attempted friendly co-operation, and, as attested by the silver purchase policy (see Silver Purchase Act of 1934), even sacrificed its own financial interests in its efforts to deal fairly with Mexico.

Officially, the United States can take no cognizance of the unfortunate situation created by the disestablishment of the Church in Mexico. But on numerous occasions our ambassadors, both of the diplomatic corps and those of "good will," have been able to persuade the Mexican officials to ameliorate some of the distress inherent in the execution of the religious laws. The Coolidge administration was successful, with Dwight Morrow as ambassador, in obtaining a temporary respite from both religious and political questions, and Secretary Hull made valiant efforts to carry out a good neighbor policy[qv] in acts as well as words. Yet, whereas the religious problem is no longer acute, American property rights in Mexico are seriously jeopardized and American business enterprise is not welcome in the country south of the Rio Grande.

A new policy of Pan-American solidarity was laid down at Buenos Aires in 1936 (see Peace Conference at Buenos Aires), and Mexico subscribed to it. But Mexico's internal problems of reform and expropriation have affected her foreign policy, and in 1938 Great Britain severed diplomatic relations as a protest against the confiscatory policy of the Mexican government. The United States is in a difficult position. Manifestly, even the Monroe Doctrine does not permit flagrant violations of international right and the good neighbor policy must be reciprocal to be effective. The geographical situation compels the United States to tackle the problem.

Nor is the great investment of United States capital in Mexico our only concern in Mexican-United States comity. The volume of trade between the United States and Mexico flows in both directions and Mexico suffers proportionately even more than do we at its curtailment. But above all the relations of these two adjacent states are a most important index of effective Pan-Americanism and the keystone of the arch of the good neighbor policy.

[J. M. Callahan, *American Foreign Policy in Mexican Relations*; J. F. Rippy, *The United States and Mexico.*]

GRAHAM H. STUART

Mexican War, THE, had remote or indirect causes in the increasing distrust arising from diplomatic indiscretions, quibblings and misunderstandings of the first decade of American-Mexican diplomatic relations (see Mexican Relations). Its more immediate cause was the annexation of Texas[qv], which the Mexican government regarded as equivalent to a declaration of war and which was followed by withdrawal of the Mexican minister from Washington in March, 1845, and the severance of diplomatic relations. Another cause was the American claims against Mexico arising from injuries to and property losses of American citizens in the Mexican revolutions.

The American Government strove to preserve peace. It adopted a conciliatory policy and made the first advances toward renewal of diplomatic relations. Recognizing that the chief American foreign policy was the annexation of California, Polk planned to connect with that policy the adjustment of all difficulties with Mexico, including the dispute concerning jurisdiction in the territory between the Nueces and the Rio Grande.

In September, 1845, assured through a confidential agent that the new Mexican government of Herrera would welcome an American minister, and acting upon the suggestion of James Buchanan, Secretary of State, Polk appointed John Slidell as envoy-minister on a secret peaceful mission to secure California and New Mexico for fifteen to twenty million dollars if possible, or for forty millions if necessary—terms later changed by secret instructions to $5,000,000 for New Mexico, and $25,000,000 for California. In October, before Slidell's departure, Secretary Buchanan sent to the American consul Larkin at Monterey, in California, a confidential statement of the American "good will" policy to acquire California without war and with the spontaneous co-operation of the Californians.

However, Mexico refused to reopen diplomatic relations. In January, 1846, following the first news that the Mexican government under various pretexts had refused to receive Slidell, partly on the ground that questions of boundary and claims should be separated, Polk ordered Gen. Taylor to advance from Corpus Christi to the Rio Grande, resulting shortly in conflicts with Mexican troops (see Palo Alto, The Battle of; Resaca de la Palma, The Battle of).

On May 11, after arrival of news of the Mexican advance across the Rio Grande and the skirmish with Taylor's troops, Polk submitted to Congress a skillful war message, stating that war existed, and that it was begun by Mexico on American soil. He obtained prompt action authorizing a declaration of war, apparently on the ground that such action was justified by the delinquencies, obstinacy and hostilities of the Mexican government; and proceeded to formulate plans for military and naval operations to advance his purpose to obtain Mexican acceptance of his overtures for peace negotiations.

The military plans included an expedition under Col. Stephen W. Kearny to New Mexico and thence to California, supplemented by an expedition to Chihuahua; an advance across the Rio Grande into Mexico by troops under Gen. Taylor to occupy the neighboring provinces; and a possible later campaign of invasion of the Mexican interior from Vera Cruz.

In these plans Polk was largely influenced by assurances received in February from Col. Atocha, a friend of Santa Anna, then in exile from Mexico, to the effect that the latter, if aided in plans to return from Havana to Mexico, would recover his Mexican leadership and co-operate in a peaceful arrangement to cede Mexican territory to the United States. In June, Polk entered into negotiations with Santa Anna through a brother of Slidell, receiving verification of Atocha's assurances. Polk had already sent a confidential order to Commodore Conner who later, Aug. 16, permitted Santa Anna to pass through the coast blockade to Vera Cruz (see Mexican War, The Navy in). Having arrived in Mexico, Santa Anna promptly began his program which resulted in his own quick restoration to power, but he gave no evidences whatever of his professed pacific intentions.

On July 3, 1846, the small expedition under Col. Kearny received orders to go via the Santa Fé Trail^{qv} from Fort Leavenworth to occupy New Mexico (see Kearny's March to California; Doniphan's Expedition). It reached Santa Fé on Aug. 18, and a part of the force (300 men) led by Kearny marched to the Pacific at San Diego.

From there it arrived (Jan. 10, 1847) at Los Angeles to complete the work begun at Sonoma by insurgents under Frémont, and at Monterey and San Francisco Bay by Commodore Sloat, shortly succeeded by Stockton (see California, The Conquest of).

The expedition of Gen. Taylor into northern Mexico, which was organized to carry out the plan for an advance southward into the interior of Mexico, began to cross the Rio Grande to Matamoras on May 18, 1846, and advanced to the strongly fortified city of Monterey^{qv}, which after an attack was evacuated by Mexican forces on Sept. 28. Later, in February, 1847, at Buena Vista^{qv}, Taylor stubbornly resisted and defeated the attack of Santa Anna's Mexican relief expedition.

Soon thereafter the theater of war shifted to Vera Cruz, from which the direct route to the Mexican capital seemed to present less difficulty than the northern route. In deciding upon the campaign from Vera Cruz to Mexico City, Polk probably was influenced by the news of Sloat's occupation of California, which reached Washington on Sept. 1, 1846. In November, 1846, Polk offered the command of the Mexico City expedition to Gen. Winfield Scott, who promptly accepted. After the capture of the fortress of Vera Cruz^{qv}, March 29, 1847, Scott led the army of invasion westward via Jalapa to Pueblo, which he entered May 15, and from which he began (Aug. 7) his advance to the mountain pass of Cerro Gordo^{qv}.

Coincident with Scott's operations against Vera Cruz, Polk began new peace negotiations with Mexico through a "profoundly secret mission." On April 15 Secretary Buchanan had sent Nicholas P. Trist^{qv} as a confidential peace agent to accompany Scott's army. In August, after the battles of Contreras and Churubusco^{qqv}, Trist arranged through Scott an armistice as a preliminary step for a diplomatic conference for discussion of peace terms—a conference which began on Aug. 27 and closed on Sept. 7 by Mexican rejection of the terms offered.

Scott promptly resumed his advance. After hard fighting (Sept. 7–11) at the battles of Molino del Rey and Chapultepec, he captured the city of Mexico^{qqv}, Sept. 14, and with his staff entered the palace over which he hoisted the American flag.

Practically, the war was ended. Santa Anna, after resigning his presidential office, made an unsuccessful attempt to strike at the American garrison which Scott had left at Pueblo, but was driven off and obliged to flee from Mexico. The chief remaining American question was to find a government with sufficient power to negotiate a treaty of peace to prevent the danger of American annexation of all Mexico. Fortunately, Trist was still with the army and in close touch with the situation at the captured capital. Although recalled, he determined (Dec. 3–4) to assume the responsibility of remaining to renew efforts to conclude a treaty of peace even at the risk of disavowal by his government. After some delay, he was able to conclude with the Mexican commissioners a treaty in accord with the instructions which had been annulled by his recall. The chief negotiations were conducted at Mexico City, but the treaty was completed and signed, Feb. 2, 1848, at the neighboring town of Guadalupe Hidalgo[qv]. By its terms, which provided for cessation of hostilities, the United States agreed to pay $15,000,000 for New Mexico and California. Polk received the treaty on Feb. 19, and promptly decided to submit it to the Senate, which approved it on March 10 by a vote of thirty-eight to fourteen. Ratifications were exchanged on May 30, 1848.

Among the chief results of the war were the following: expansion of American territory; increased American interest in problems of the Caribbean and the Pacific and in the opening and control of isthmian interoceanic transit routes at Panama[qv], Nicaragua and Tehuantepec; and ebullitions of "manifest destiny" in the period of "Young America"[qv] from 1848 to 1860. In domestic affairs the result of the large acquisition of territory was reflected in political controversies relating to the slavery problem (see Wilmot Proviso; Compromise of 1850).

[Justin H. Smith, *The War with Mexico;* G. L. Rives, *The United States and Mexico;* Roswell S. Ripley, *The War with Mexico;* J. M. Callahan, *American Foreign Policy in Mexican Relations;* Jesse S. Reeves, *American Diplomacy under Tyler and Polk.*]   J. M. CALLAHAN

Mexican War, The Navy in. The dry cactus barrens of southern Texas in conjunction with wider and mountainous wastes of northern Mexico constituted a greater barrier to military invasion of Mexico from the United States than did the Mexican armies. Gen. Zachary Taylor, from his navy supported base at Brownsville, easily vanquished, or drove off, all military opposition on his front, but experienced supply troubles as soon as his lines of communication became extended. In Washington it was decided the main effort should be made from a naval supported base at Vera Cruz[qv], hundreds of miles closer to Mexico City than Brownsville.

Meanwhile the Pacific Squadron was circumventing distance and wilderness in another direction by seizing Monterey, San Diego, San Francisco and other key points on the Pacific. This guaranteed American possession of California. Thereafter the squadron not only rendered mobility, re-enforcements and indispensable aid to the military commands of Kearny and Frémont, but also blockaded, threatened and harassed the principal Mexican seaports in that ocean.

While Gen. Taylor was invading from the north, and long before Gen. Scott's Vera Cruz disembarkation, March 9, 1847, men-of-war under Commodore David Conner were engaged in blockading Tampico, Vera Cruz and lesser Gulf ports. Raids by landing parties were frequent. The most pretentious expedition was Capt. Matthew C. Perry's capture of Frontera and Tabasco. During the nineteen-day siege of Vera Cruz, the navy rendered invaluable assistance by covering landing parties, bombarding forts and providing a siege battery.

[Justin H. Smith, *The War with Mexico.*]
                                        JIM DAN HILL

Mexican War Claims were settled by a commission created under a convention of 1867 with the Mexican government. American citizens presented 1017 claims against Mexico amounting to $470,126,613, and Mexicans countered with 998 claims totaling $86,661,891.15. To the former, 186 awards, totaling $4,125,622.20, were allowed; to the latter, 167 awards amounting to $150,498.41. Claims against the United States arose largely from Indian depredations, and excesses committed by American soldiers. Those presented against Mexico were largely for the seizure and destruction of property, forced loans, illegal arrests and imprisonments, and murder. The work of the commission was not completed until November, 1876.

[J. F. Rippy, *The United States and Mexico.*]
                                        FRANK FREIDEL

Mexico, Confederate Migration to. After the Civil War many Confederate military and civil leaders sought homes in Mexico. They were despondent and dreaded Reconstruction[qv]. The exact number who went to Mexico will probably never be known, but an estimate of 2500 seems reasonable. Southerners settled in all parts of the empire—on farms, in seaport towns and in villages of the interior. Colonies were planted in the provinces of Chihuahua, San Luis Potosi, Jalisco and Sonora. The best known was the Córdova Valley Colony (see Carlotta, Confederate Colony of).

Maximilian (see Mexico, French in) encouraged migration to Mexico by offering low priced public lands, free transportation for the needy, and toleration for the Protestant churches and schools, but the movement failed because of unforeseen circumstances. There was a hostile Northern and Southern press; the United States Government opposed the movement; and the settlers had little cash. The disturbed political conditions under Maximilian's regime aided in the downfall of the project. By 1867 most of the adventurers had returned to the United States.

[George D. Harmon, Confederate Migration to Mexico, in *The Hispanic American Historical Review*, Vol. XVII.]

GEORGE D. HARMON

Mexico, French in. In October, 1861, England, France and Spain signed a treaty by which they undertook coercive action to secure reparation for their subjects and the execution of certain obligations contracted by Mexico. They agreed to refrain from intervention in Mexico's internal affairs and neither to make any territorial aggrandizements nor to influence her form of government. Armed forces of Spain promptly seized Vera Cruz. After French and English soldiers arrived on the Mexican coast, a conference of commanders of the allied forces held at Orizaba could not agree. The English and the Spaniards decided to withdraw from Mexico. The French army, which was strongly reinforced, captured the city of Mexico in June, 1862. An Assembly of Notables convoked there by the invaders, decided in favor of the establishment in Mexico of a monarchy headed by Ferdinand Maximilian, Archduke of Austria, who had been selected by Napoleon III.

Attracted by the glittering dream of a throne in a fair land over which his ancestors had ruled, Maximilian accepted the invitation. He expected that Napoleon III would support the exotic empire for a term of years. After Maximilian's arrival in Mexico, he sought to secure recognition by the United States, but that government continued to support the republican leader, President Juárez, who took refuge on the northern frontiers of his country.

The fortunes of the Empire of Maximilian largely depended upon the outcome of the Civil War. During that struggle the United States made mild protests against French intervention in Mexico, but after Lee's surrender, the French secretary of foreign affairs was informed by Secretary Seward that the "presence and operations of a French army in Mexico and the maintenance of an authority there resting upon force and not the free will of the people of Mexico is a cause of serious concern to the United States." In vain did France attempt to secure the recog-

nition of Maximilian's government by the United States or to postpone the withdrawal of her troops. Finally, in the spring of 1867, the last detachment of French soldiers left Mexican soil. The soldiers of Juárez soon captured Maximilian, who was deserted by his Mexican followers. The unfortunate prince was court-martialed, and, despite the pleas of the United States for mercy, was shot on June 19, 1867. Thus a clear violation of the Monroe Doctrine[qv] was repelled and republican government restored in Mexico.

[E. C. Corti, *Maximilian and Charlotte of Mexico;* D. Perkins, *The Monroe Doctrine, 1826-1867.*]

WILLIAM SPENCE ROBERTSON

Mexico, Punitive Expedition into (1916). As a result of Villa's[qv] attack on Columbus, N. Mex., on the night of March 8–9, 1916, Gen. John J. Pershing was directed to pursue Villa into Mexico for the purpose of capturing him and preventing any further raids by his band. On March 15 Gen. Pershing crossed the border with a force consisting of a provisional division, mostly cavalry. The advance was conducted in two columns, each column engaging in minor skirmishes with small groups of Villa's troops. Progress was exceedingly difficult, both because the Carranza government refused Pershing's troops the use of railroads and because the United States had given instructions that villages could not be occupied. The Mexican government troops were also hostile to what they considered an invasion, and on two occasions, one at Parral and one at Carrizal[qv], clashed with Pershing's forces. These clashes occurred in spite of the fact that the United States Government had agreed to withdraw its troops as soon as the Mexican government could give assurance that the border situation could be handled by the Mexicans themselves. Pershing's force advanced 400 miles into Mexico and, although it was unable to capture Villa, his followers were scattered into small, unorganized bands. On Feb. 5, 1917, Pershing's punitive force was ordered to return to the United States. In the meantime sufficient troops of the National Guard and Regular Army were stationed along the border to prevent further incidents such as occurred at Columbus.

[W. A. Ganoe, *History of United States Army;* Frank Tompkins, *Chasing Villa.*]   C. A. WILLOUGHBY

Mexico, The Gulf of, which by its form and position has had a profound influence on the climate of the southeastern part of the United States and all the eastern coast, has also had a large influence in American national history, especially on American foreign policy. Its early importance was determined by the Spanish search for a possible water passage through the continental barrier, the Spanish settlement at Havana in 1519, the expedition of Cortés into the interior from Vera Cruz, and the subsequent discovery of gold in Mexico. Later it was also influenced by several settlements along the northern coast, a Spanish permanent settlement at Pensacola in 1696 and French settlements at Mobile in 1702 and New Orleans in 1718[qqw].

Its subsequent increased importance was especially due to its relations as the receiver of the Mississippi drainage and as the natural commercial outlet of the trans-Allegheny West. Its strategic geographic importance was recognized by the British seizure of Havana in 1762, and by the British colonial opposition to the surrender of Havana in 1763, by the American hope to secure the Floridas from England in the Revolution, by Napoleon's dreams of a circum-Gulf colonial empire before 1803, by the American acquisition of Louisiana[w] by purchase in 1803 in order to secure for the increasing American trans-Allegheny settlements free access to the Gulf via the mouth of the Mississippi, and by the consequent American claim to the entire Gulf coast from the Perdido on the east to the Rio Grande on the west.

Later, in 1819, influenced in part by the British use of Spanish harbors on the Gulf in the War of 1812, the American Government obtained a cession of all the Floridas (see Adams-Onís Treaty) in order to secure the safety of a logical American abutment on the Gulf and the complete control of the American rivers which reached the Gulf through this territory, and to prevent the danger of a transfer of the strategic territory by Spain to some other European power. In the decade of 1825–35, the United States unsuccessfully negotiated to extend the Gulf frontage west of the Sabine, and in 1845 it was able to extend it to the Rio Grande by annexation of the independent state of Texas[w].

Meantime, as a result of increasing interest in the Gulf after it obtained control of the mouth of the Mississippi, the American Government naturally had a vital interest in the political condition and destiny of Cuba[w], which guarded the commercial portal water between the Gulf and the Atlantic and which was regarded as the strategic key to the Gulf, and therefore to the Mississippi.

After the Mexican War[w], and the subsequent opening of practical transit routes across Panama[w] and Central America, American interest in the Gulf was extended by the increasing use of the Yucatan Channel, the natural line of communication between the mouth of the Mississippi and the new interoceanic transits. In the decades of the 1850's prominent Southern quixotic leaders, as Toombs and Benjamin, urged the acquisition of Cuba (see Ostend Manifesto) as a means of making the Gulf a *mare clausum*, on the ground that the Gulf was the reservoir of the Mississippi and must be practically an American lake for purposes of American security.

The commercial and political interests and relations which were influenced or determined by geographic conditions of the Gulf region finally reached a logical consequence in the expulsion of Spain (in 1898) from its last foothold in the Western Hemisphere (see Spanish-American War), in the later significant advance of American influence and control and ascendency in the Caribbean and in Panama and Central America, and in the subsequent growing commercial importance of the American southern seaboard.

[Ellen C. Semple, *American History and Its Geographic Conditions;* J. M. Callahan, *Cuba and International Relations.*]
            J. M. CALLAHAN

Mexico City, Capture of (Sept. 13–14, 1847). The fall of Chapultepec[w] made possible a combined advance by Worth's and Quitman's divisions against the western gates of Mexico City. By dusk (Sept. 13) Worth, despite desperate resistance, arrived at the San Cosme gate. Quitman, on the Belén Causeway, was held up before the Citadel. During the night Santa Anna evacuated the city, the Citadel surrendering to Quitman at dawn. Marching immediately to the Plaza, Quitman raised the flag on the Palace. Worth's troops, followed by Scott himself, then entered and the General in Chief announced the capture of the capital.

[J. H. Smith, *The War with Mexico;* C. W. Elliott, *Winfield Scott.*]   CHARLES WINSLOW ELLIOTT

Miami, Fort, or Miamis, at the juncture of the St. Mary and Miami (St. Joseph) rivers, at the present site of Fort Wayne, Ind., was built by the French about 1749. It replaced an older fort of the same name. It was garrisoned by the British under Lt. Robert Butler, of Rogers' Rangers[w]. In May, 1763, the fort was evacuated, and shortly thereafter it was seized by the Indians in Pontiac's uprising[w].

[E. O. Randall and D. J. Ryan, *History of Ohio;* C. Moore, *The Northwest under Three Flags.*]
         RANDOLPH G. ADAMS

Miami, Fort, at the foot of the Maumee rapids, on the left bank of the Maumee River, in the present State of Ohio, was built by the British in April, 1794, under orders of Lt. Gov. J. G. Simcoe of Upper Canada. The command was given to Maj. William Campbell. The position of the fort, "an encroachment of nearly forty miles upon the American soil," was protested by Washington, Jefferson and Jay. On July 26, 1796, according to Article II of the Jay Treaty*, signed in 1795, the fort was yielded to the Americans. During the War of 1812 it was retaken by the British and used as Gen. Henry Proctor's headquarters.

[E. O. Randall and D. J. Ryan, *History of Ohio;* J. Winsor, *Narrative and Critical History;* B. Lossing, *The Pictorial Field-Book of the War of 1812.*]
RANDOLPH G. ADAMS

Miami, The, of the Algonquin family, often referred to as Twightwees, were originally divided into six bands, of which the Weas and Piankashaws became practically separate tribes. Pushed from the Wisconsin region by other tribes, they settled in the St. Joseph, Wabash and Maumee (Miami of the Lakes) valleys and adjacent regions, finally spreading as far south as the Miami valleys of southwestern Ohio. After 1763 they retired to Indiana. By various treaties from 1795 to 1854, they ceded their Ohio-Indiana lands and moved west of the Mississippi, except for a band remaining permanently in Wabash County (Ind.). Though few in numbers and mild in disposition, they long resisted the white advance. Little Turtle, who signed the Treaty of Greenville*, was their most famous leader.

[F. W. Hodge, *Handbook of American Indians.*]
EUGENE H. ROSEBOOM

Miami and Erie Canal. *See* Ohio State Canals.

Miami Purchase, The, the next important colonization project in the Old Northwest* after the grant to the Ohio Company of Associates*, was first settled about eight months after Marietta*. The Miami Purchase represented an important step in the American advance on the north bank of the Ohio. Extending northward from the Ohio, between the Miami and the Little Miami rivers, in addition to the increasingly important Ohio River route it commanded the Miami-Maumee roadway to Lake Erie, while southward the Licking River gave ready access to the Kentucky bluegrass* region. Benjamin Stites, an Indian trader, represented the possibilities of the Miami country to Judge John Cleves Symmes, of Morristown, N. J., an influential member of the Continental Congress. After a personal inspection Judge Symmes enlisted the support of Jonathan Dayton, Elias Boudinot and other important men, to found a colony between the two Miamis. A contract with the Treasury

Board, Oct. 15, 1788, granted Judge Symmes and his associates 1,000,000 acres, for which, under the Land Ordinance of 1785*, they agreed to pay $1 per acre, with certain deductions, in Continental certificates, and one seventh in military warrants*. As in the Ohio Company Purchase, section sixteen in each township was reserved for the support of education, and section twenty-nine for that of religion. Also, one entire township was set aside for a college. Eventually, Judge Symmes could not meet the payments in full, and in 1794 he received a patent for the Miami Purchase that covered only 311,682 acres.

Judge Symmes started for his new colony in July, 1788, and made a temporary stop at Limestone, Ky. The first permanent settlement in the Miami Purchase was made Nov. 18, 1788, by Benjamin Stites, at Columbia, at the mouth of the Little Miami. The next settlement, Dec. 28, 1788, opposite the mouth of the Licking, was led by Israel Ludlow and Robert Patterson, and was given the fanciful name, Losantiville, which Gov. St. Clair changed to Cincinnati*, in honor of the Society of the Cincinnati*. The third settlement Judge Symmes himself founded, Feb. 2, 1789, at North Bend. At first the constant danger of Indian attacks confined the settlers, the majority of whom were from New Jersey, to the vicinity of Fort Washington*, but gradually they went up the watercourses into the interior. Fort Hamilton*, founded in 1791, became the nucleus of an advanced settlement, and after the Treaty of Greenville*, population quickly spread through the Miami Purchase.

[Beverley W. Bond, Jr., ed., *The Correspondence of John Cleves Symmes;* Charles T. Greve, *Centennial History of Cincinnati,* Vol. I.]
BEVERLEY W. BOND, JR.

Miami Trail, The, an early Indian trail running from the towns of the Miami Indians* in the valleys of the two Miami rivers of southwestern Ohio to the Cherokee* country of the South. It had several branches north of the Ohio but these converged to cross that river near the mouth of the Licking River. From that point it followed the Licking and Kentucky valleys to the watershed between the Cumberland and Green rivers where it divided, one branch joining the Scioto Trail leading to Cumberland Gap*, the other passing southward into the Cherokee country of Tennessee. It was much used in Indian invasions of Kentucky.

[A. B. Hulbert, *Indian Thoroughfares.*]
EUGENE H. ROSEBOOM

Miamisburg Mound is the largest conical mound in Ohio, base about three acres and height at the apex about seventy feet, situated a few miles south of Dayton. It has not been excavated, but is assigned to the Adena Mound Culture[w], contemporary with Hopewell[w] Culture and in the middle period of prehistoric mound development (see Mounds and Mound Builders).

[H. C. Shetrone, *The Mound Builders*.]
                                        CLARK WISSLER

Michabous, God of Michilimackinac. The island of Mackinac, at the junction of Lakes Superior, Michigan and Huron, was regarded by the surrounding Indians as the home of their greatest supernatural sponsor, known as Michabous, Manabozhu, Manitou, etc. The term Michilimackinac[w], with various spellings, was originally applied to the whole region embracing the union of the lakes but eventually was restricted to Mackinac Island. Jesuit missionaries[w] first visited the region about 1641 but the name does not occur in the Jesuit Relations[w] until 1670. Forms of the term Michabous appear among all Algonkin tribes with such synonyms as Gloskap and Wisakedjak (corrupted into whiskey jack). Ethnologists prefer to speak of the basic concept implied in these terms as the Manitou[w], for although in Algonkin mythology the various names given above apply to animal as well as human gods, these are in turn but personifications of the "life force" in the world as formulated in Algonkin philosophy.

[Ellen R. Emerson, *Indian Myths or Legends;* Reuben G. Thwaites, Story of Mackinac, in *Wisconsin Historical Collections*, Vol. XIV.]
                                        CLARK WISSLER

Michigan. The story of Michigan properly begins with the founding of the Huron mission on Georgian Bay less than a dozen years after the establishment of Quebec. The murderous Iroquois[w] eventually destroyed the Huron[w] nation, and the mission was abandoned in 1650, the Fathers returning to Quebec. During their years in Huronia they naturally learned much concerning adjoining Michigan and had made a beginning of exploring it.

Activities in the Upper Country closed for a few years, but toward 1660 they were renewed and by 1670 the entire coast of the Upper Peninsula[w] had been explored. About the same time the eastern coast from Sault Ste. Marie to Lake Erie was traversed, and the following decade witnessed the exploration of the Lake Michigan coast and southwestern Michigan.

Meanwhile, at Sault Ste. Marie[w] on June 14, 1671, the entire Great Lakes area was formally annexed to France. Although the state was thus explored and its settlement was begun in the 17th century, its subsequent development was exceedingly slow. For 200 years (ca. 1634–1837) it remained a wilderness outpost successively of New France, Great Britain and the United States. To the end of the French regime Michigan was exploited as a center of Indian trade[w]. By the Proclamation of 1763[w] the British set up the entire Northwest as an Indian reserve. In 1774, after long years of hesitant muddling, they attached it to Quebec Province (see Quebec Act). The Definitive Treaty of Peace[w] (1783) divided the western country between Great Britain and the United States, the boundary running through the middle of the Great Lakes, but all Michigan remained under British rule until 1796. In 1788 it was included in the District of Hesse, with a county form of local government. In 1791 this was replaced by the province of Upper Canada, the Detroit River settlements being divided between Kent and Essex counties. Kent County extended northward and westward as far as British dominion ran, embracing uncounted hundreds of thousands of square miles.

The Northwest Territory[w], to which Michigan nominally belonged, was created by the Ordinance of 1787[w]. By the Jay Treaty[w] the British agreed to evacuate the northwestern posts, and on July 11, 1796, the American flag was raised at Detroit (see Border Forts, The Evacuation of). Shortly thereafter Wayne County, with boundaries embracing almost all of Michigan and much of Ohio, Indiana and Wisconsin, was organized, with Detroit as the county seat.

Until 1800 Michigan remained a part of the Northwest Territory. On the organization of Indiana Territory, it was divided between the two, and when Ohio became a state in 1803 all of Michigan was attached to Indiana. The resounding complaints of Michigan's residents over this status were soon heeded by Congress, which created Michigan Territory, July 1, 1805. Until 1818 the territory embraced only the southern peninsula plus the eastern end of the upper one. When Illinois was admitted in 1818 the remaining portion of the Old Northwest, north of Illinois and west of Lake Michigan, was attached to Michigan. Finally, in 1834, the boundary was extended to embrace Iowa and Minnesota and the eastern half of the Dakotas.

Michigan's territorial era was prolonged and stormy. Separated from the settled portion of the United States by a wide wilderness, there was almost no immigration, and as late as 1820 the white population was less than 9000. The extinction of the Indian title to the land, and the completion of the Erie Canal[w] in 1825 finally brought Michigan within the sweep of the westward movement[w] of American settlement. From 1830 on, the tide of immigration rose steadily higher and the territory quickly became eligible for statehood.

The story of Michigan's transition from territory to state is unique in American history. The Ordinance of 1787 provided that Congress should organize three states in the Northwest Territory, and at its discretion might create two more north of a line drawn due east and west through the southern extreme of Lake Michigan. Five states were eventually created, but the boundary provision proved a fruitful source of discord among them. Indiana in 1816 and Illinois in 1818 were admitted with material extensions northward of the Ordinance line. When Michigan applied for admission with this Ordinance line as its southern boundary, Congress, catering to Ohio's demands, required the people, as the *sine qua non* of admission, to assent to the present Ohio-Michigan boundary, which is the eastward projection of a straight line drawn northeastwardly from the southern extreme of Lake Michigan to the northeast corner of Maumee Bay. The tract in dispute was a triangular strip about 470 square miles in area and seven miles wide at its eastern end, running from Lake Erie to the western boundary of Ohio, and embracing the mouth and lower portion of Maumee River. But few issues have so united the people of Michigan as this one. Under its influence a political revolution was consummated; the territorial government was banished and a state government established, which functioned for a year and a half unrecognized by the United States (*see* Ohio-Michigan Boundary Dispute). This impasse was finally resolved by a characteristic political subterfuge, and Michigan, "compensated" for the loss of the southern boundary by the unasked donation of the Upper Peninsula, was admitted to the Union, Jan. 26, 1837 (*see* Ohio-Michigan Boundary Dispute; Toledo War).

The succeeding century of statehood has been one of marvelous change and development. Michigan was a hotbed of antislavery agitation and Jackson in 1854 became the reputed birthplace of the Republican party, which dominated the state for almost eighty years. Half a century of ceaseless and insensate slaughter sufficed to destroy the magnificent forest which originally covered most of Michigan, entailing economic and social burdens which the present and future generations must continue to bear. A century of experience has not sufficed to demonstrate the wisdom of attaching the Upper Peninsula to Michigan. The phenomenal industrial progress of southern Michigan in the 20th century has attracted a vast number of immigrants to the state, imposing on it most of the evils as well as the benefits which characteristically attend a high degree of industrial and urban development.

[No adequate single history of Michigan has yet been produced. Much material of varying value is contained in the forty volumes of the *Mich. Pioneer and Hist. Colls.* and in the *Michigan Hist. Mag.* Silas Farmer's *History of Detroit and Michigan* is encyclopædic in character. Other general works of varying content and value are: Henry M. Utley et al., *Michigan as a Province, Territory, and State;* C. M. Burton, *City of Detroit, 1701-1922;* Charles Moore, *History of Michigan;* Thos. M. Cooley, *Michigan: A History of Governments.* For the French and British periods, a wide range of publications is available; among the more important are the *Works* of Francis Parkman, the publications of the Ontario, Quebec and Dominion archives departments, and the two co-operative histories of Canada: *Canada and Its Provinces,* and *Chronicles of Canada.* A convenient guide to Canadian historical material is R. G. Trotter's *Canadian History, A Syllabus and Guide to Reading.*]   M. M. QUAIFE

Michigan, Lake, the largest lake lying wholly within the United States, extends some 335 miles from north to south. The first known European discoverer was Jean Nicolet[w] in 1634, but not until four decades later did the French (Marquette, Jolliet, LaSalle[qw]) become familiar with the lake's entire shore line. From this time forward Lake Michigan became a highway of travel to explorers, traders and others. Following 1760 the British developed a naval establishment on the Upper Lakes, and occasional voyages for commercial or military reasons were made to Lake Michigan, at whose northern outlet lay the important fur trade center of Michilimackinac[w]. The chief historical importance of Lake Michigan, however, dates from the early 19th century, when the tide of American settlement began pouring into the adjacent country and such thriving cities as Milwaukee, Kenosha, Chicago and Michigan City were founded. The vast importance of Lake Michigan as a highway of travel and commerce during the last century can only be suggested here. Because the Ordinance of 1787[w] fixed an east and west line through the southern extreme of Lake Michigan as the boundary between the three southern and the two northern states of the Old Northwest[w], and because in every instance this provision was later violated, Lake Michigan figured importantly in the determination of the boundaries of the states of Ohio, Indiana, Illinois, Michigan and Wisconsin.

[Louise P. Kellogg, *The French Régime in Wisconsin and the Northwest;* Louis C. Karpinski, *Bibliography of the Printed Maps of Michigan, 1804-1880.*]

M. M. QUAIFE

Michigan Central Railroad, THE, was projected as early as 1831 to connect Detroit with Lake Michigan. Little progress was made until 1836 when the new State of Michigan adopted the enterprise as one of three cross state railroads it undertook to build. In common with most canal and railroad schemes begun by the western states in the speculative years 1836 and 1837, the Michigan plan ended in failure and near bankruptcy for the state. The Michigan Central was sold, in 1846, to a group of eastern capitalists including George Griswold of New York and John C. Green and John Murray Forbes of Boston. These men had little experience in railroad affairs but they possessed a good deal of shrewd Yankee ability.

The new owners decided to extend their line west to Chicago and they succeeded in reaching New Buffalo on Lake Michigan in 1849 and Michigan City, Ind., by 1850. There the railroad was temporarily stalled as a result of the strenuous efforts being made by its rapidly growing rival, the Michigan Southern*w*, to prevent it from reaching Chicago. Both railroads strained every nerve to reach the Illinois line first and there bar its rival from building farther. The fight was carried into the legislative halls of Michigan, Indiana and Illinois, into the common council of Chicago, and the courts. Both projects were delayed but each, by secret agreements with other lines, secured trackage rights into Chicago and entered that city almost simultaneously, in 1852. Chicago was thus given two competing railroad connections with the East.

The Michigan Central became part of the "Joy Lines" running from Suspension Bridge, through Canada, via Detroit to Chicago and from there by the Chicago, Burlington and Quincy*w* into Missouri, Kansas, Iowa, Minnesota and states farther west. In 1878 competition with its old rival ceased when the Michigan Central passed into the control of the Vanderbilt group which made it a part of the New York Central*w* system. In 1930 it was leased for ninety-nine years to the New York Central.

[C. E. MacGill, *History of Transportation in the United States before 1860;* P. W. Gates, *The Illinois Central Railroad and Its Colonization Work.*]

PAUL WALLACE GATES

Michigan Southern Railroad, THE, was begun by the State of Michigan in 1836 to connect Lake Erie with Lake Michigan by a line of railroad through its southern tier of counties. The state built a strap line railroad from Monroe to Hillsdale where, its finances exhausted, work was suspended. The railroad was sold in 1846 to a group of eastern capitalists, chief of whom were George

Bliss of Springfield, Mass., and John B. Jervis and Edwin Litchfield of New York. As Chicago had already become the greatest port on Lake Michigan the new owners decided to build their line to that city. They deflected the road southward to the Indiana boundary, where it joined the Northern Indiana Railroad, which was under the same management. The Michigan Southern and Northern Indiana (as the road was now called) then rushed its construction as rapidly as possible in order to reach Chicago before its rival, the Michigan Central*w*. It entered the Illinois city in 1852. The Michigan Southern and Northern Indiana soon came under the control of the Lake Shore Railroad, running from Buffalo to Toledo, and in 1869 was consolidated with it to form the Lake Shore and Michigan Southern Railroad. Although it retained its corporate identity until 1914, the Michigan Southern was operated practically as a unit of the rapidly developing Vanderbilt system. In 1914 it was consolidated with the New York Central Railroad*w*.

[C. E. MacGill, *History of Transportation in the United States before 1860.*]

PAUL WALLACE GATES

Michigan Territorial Road, THE, was authorized by the territorial legislature in 1829 and laid out in 1830. It ran from Detroit to the mouth of the St. Joseph River and followed approximately the route of the present highway U. S. 12. It paralleled the national turnpike (*see* Chicago Road) from Detroit to Fort Dearborn (now highway U. S. 112) which was authorized in 1824. These two roads are sometimes called "extensions of the Erie Canal" and were the chief routes followed by immigrants who settled the southern part of the Lower Peninsula of Michigan. A stage line over the territorial road connecting at St. Joseph with steamers for Chicago was established in 1834.

[M. M. Quaife, *Chicago's Highways Old and New.*]

WILLIS DUNBAR

Michilimackinac (Mackinac) Strait and Island. The waters of Lakes Michigan and Superior unite with Lake Huron by the Strait of Michilimackinac and the St. Marys River. Lying at the crossroads of the Upper Lakes, in the middle of the Strait and within striking distance of the outlet of the St. Marys, is Michilimackinac Island, widely famed for its scenic beauty, and today a popular summer resort. In the period when waterways were the chief highways of travel it was renowned as a strategic center of military and commercial operations.

Historically considered, the name Michilimackinac applies not only to the Strait and to the adjacent mainland, but also specifically to three distinct place-sites, the Island, Point St. Ignace on the northern mainland and Mackinaw City on the southern mainland. Although today the final syllables of both Island and mainland names—*nac* and *naw*—are pronounced alike (rhyming with "paw"), originally the French pronounced *nac* as they spelled it (rhyming with "pack").

For almost a century prior to 1761 Michilimackinac was under French rule. From 1761 to 1796 (*see* Border Forts, The Evacuation of) and from 1812 to 1815 (*see* War of 1812) the rule of Britain prevailed; from 1796 to 1812 and since 1815 Michilimackinac has belonged to the United States. The advent of the railroad wrought the doom of Michilimackinac as a military and commercial center, but its scenic beauty and its rich and colorful history remain as permanent possessions. A Jesuit missionary labored for some months on the Island (1670–71); thereafter until 1706 white activity centered at St. Ignace[q]; from about 1712 to 1781 it was at Mackinaw City; for two generations following 1781 both military and commercial activities again centered on the Island; since the advent of American settlement communities have existed at all three places.

To the red man Michilimackinac was an enchanting earthly paradise. Here the whites maintained missionaries to convert, soldiers to subdue, and traders to exploit him. Here labored pious Father Marquette, the fiery imperialist Lamothe Cadillac, the renowned scientist Dr. Beaumont; here Jolliet[q] launched the successful expedition for the discovery of the Mississippi in 1673, and Robert Rogers his unsuccessful effort a century later to unlock the golden door of the Indies (*see* Northwest Passage). Near here LaSalle's *Griffon*[q] vanished in 1679, the first marine disaster on the Great Lakes, and the Mormon Kingdom of God on Earth flourished briefly in the 19th century (*see* Strangite Kingdom). Here occurred the dreadful Indian massacre of 1763 (*see* Pontiac War). Here civilization and savagery, France, England and America, contended for the spoils of Empire.

[E. O. Wood, *Historic Mackinac;* M. M. Quaife, The Romance of the Mackinac Country, in *Michigan History Magazine*, XIII.]

M. M. QUAIFE

Midcontinent Oil Region, THE, includes the oil fields between the Mississippi River and Colorado on the one hand and from a line approximately 150 miles north of the Gulf of Mexico northward to Nebraska on the other. Some geol-ogists also include southeastern New Mexico, which is structurally similar, and others include the Gulf Region of southern Texas and Louisiana for geographical convenience.

The earliest pioneers found gas and oil in this region. Gas in sufficient quantities to burn on the surface of the water was found as early as 1825 in a 400-foot water well in Natchitoches Parish, La. Travelers on the old Santa Fé Trail procured axle grease for their wagons from accumulations of oil which seeped to the surface in springs on the upper Osage and Neosho rivers in the present Kansas. Similar tar springs were similarly utilized in Missouri and Texas.

With the perfection of the process for refining coal oil, wells were sunk in the vicinity of tar springs. Near Paola, Kans., the Lykins No. 1 Well yielded a barrel of oil a day. It was struck at 275 feet in 1860. Shortly thereafter oil wells were sunk in western Missouri and in Nacogdoches County, Texas. Drillers, however, were discouraged by the small returns of the wells of the 1860's. Interest revived in the 1880's. Gas for street lighting was developed at Paola in 1886 and wells were drilled in Texas, Missouri, Kansas and Indian Territory, now Oklahoma. In 1889 the Midcontinent produced 600 barrels.

This attracted the attention of William M. Mills, who had lost everything in the Pennsylvania oil fields (*see* Oil Industry) and started anew in Kansas. He induced businessmen at Neodesha, Kans., to risk money in a well, drilled in 1893, that produced twelve barrels a day. This stimulated rapid development of fields in Kansas and across the state line in Oklahoma. Until 1905 Kansas led the Midcontinent in oil production. In that year Oklahoma gained the lead and in 1930 northern Texas became the major producer. Northern Louisiana became a commercial producer in 1907 and Arkansas in 1921.

Oil became a major industry with the perfection of motor vehicles. Oil geologists were engaged to discover new fields and deeper pools. Depth of wells varies from pools just below the surface to a well in the Binger sector, Caddo County, Okla., which produces from a depth of 9982 feet. Production of wells varies from a barrel a day to a well in the Yates pool, Pecos County, Texas, 1200 feet deep, which had an initial yield of 204,681 barrels a day. Up to 1938 the Midcontinent Region had produced more than 11,000,000,000 barrels of oil, or 58% of the entire output of the United States, besides being the nation's chief gas producer.

[Walter A. Ver Wiebe, *Oil Fields in the United States;* Ralph Arnold and William J. Kemnitzer, *Petroleum in the United States and Possessions.*]

BLISS ISELY

Middle-of-the-Road Populists, THE, objected to fusion with either of the older parties, and insisted that the proper policy was to "keep in the middle of the road." In 1896 they were unable to prevent the People's party (Populist[q]) convention from accepting Bryan as its candidate for President (see Campaign of 1896), but they forced it to nominate a Populist, Thomas E. Watson of Georgia, for Vice-President. After 1896 the Middle-of-the-Roaders formed a separate organization, which endured feebly for a dozen years.

[J. D. Hicks, *The Populist Revolt.*]
JOHN D. HICKS

Middle Passage was the term applied to the trip from Africa to America, the second leg of the triangular voyage of a slave ship. During the passage the slaves, packed in holds eighteen inches to five feet deep, and allowed above only for air, food and exercise, died in large numbers.

[U. B. Phillips, *American Negro Slavery;* J. R. Spears, *The American Slave Trade.*]   FLETCHER M. GREEN

Middlesex Canal, THE, was constructed, 1793–1803, between Boston and the Merrimac River near the site of Lowell, to bring that river's commerce to Boston without a sea voyage. It was of great economic value in developing the State of New Hampshire, but the building of railroad lines ruined it, and the last boat passed through it in 1852.

[Alvin F. Harlow, *Old Towpaths.*]
ALVIN F. HARLOW

***Mide-wiwin* or Grand Medicine Lodge, THE,** was a secret society of medicine men, widespread among the Algonquins[q], which attracted the attention of early missionaries by its use of the cross in ceremonies of initiation. The order centered around the cult of Minabozho, traditional source of men's knowledge of medicine. Candidates for membership (either men or women) served an apprenticeship with older Midé, and prepared for admission to each of the degrees of the lodge with sweat baths, fasting, ceremonial smoking and by giving gifts to the Midé. The initiation ceremonies centered around shooting the sacred *mīgis* (shell) into the body of the candidate. The Midé possessed an extensive native pharmacopœia, practised blood-letting and simple surgery, and used songs and formulæ of exorcism. The *djesakid* class interpreted dreams and foretold the future. The sorcerers were known as *wabeno*. The *Mide-wiwin* was the principal means for transmitting legends, songs and traditional religious lore preserved in pictographs on birch bark. Because the order represented a tendency to evolve into a mystic, priestly religion, and because it was so widespread, its members resisted Christianization stubbornly. Remains of the organization and its practices still exist among the Ojibwas[q].

[Frances Densmore, *Chippewa Customs;* F. W. Hodge, *Handbook of American Indians;* W. J. Hoffman, *The Mide-wiwin or Grand Medicine Society of the Ojibwa.*]
HAROLD E. DAVIS

Midnight Judges refers to the judicial appointments made by John Adams just before he was succeeded in the Presidency by Thomas Jefferson. The action of Adams was assailed as an attempt "to make permanent provision for such of the Federalists and Tories as cannot hope to continue in office under the new administration." Congress, dominated in the next session by the partisans of Jefferson, reconstructed the inferior courts and legislated out of their commissions most of the midnight judges (see Judiciary Act of 1801). In the case of a justice of the peace for the District of Columbia the delivery of his commission was refused. This led to the famous case of Marbury ·. Madison[q].

[W. S. Carpenter, *Judicial Tenure in the United States.*]
WILLIAM S. CARPENTER

Midnight Order, THE, was issued Dec. 5, 1872, by United States District Judge E. H. Durell. It cited in contempt the members of a board appointed by the governor of Louisiana, H. C. Warmoth, to canvass the returns in the gubernatorial election of that year. Durell had previously enjoined this board from functioning save under very great restrictions. It had nevertheless ignored the injunction, and declared the Democratic ticket elected. The order also directed the United States marshal to prevent the state legislature from meeting on Dec. 9, pursuant to Warmoth's call. The "midnight order" had the effect of making the Republican candidate, W. P. Kellogg, governor of Louisiana.

[Albert Phelps, *Louisiana*, 372-375.]
JOHN S. KENDALL

Midway Islands, THE, covering scarcely three square miles, belong to the Hawaiian group and lie 1400 miles northwest of Honolulu. They were formally occupied on behalf of the United States, on Aug. 28, 1867, by Capt. Williams Reynolds, of the *Lackawanna*. In 1905 the islands became the junction in the first submarine cable between San Francisco and Guam, and since then have remained a strategic point in the electrical communications of the Pacific. In 1936 they served as a station on the fortnightly transpacific flights from San Francisco to Manila, and in 1937 to Hong Kong, by the Pan-American Airways Corporation.

KENNETH COLEGROVE

Midway Plaisance (1893) was the amusement center of the World's Columbian Exposition[w]. Extending from the exposition grounds to Washington Park, it was lined with restaurants, music halls and concessions contrived by the people of all nations to draw profit from the exposition's visitors. Most memorable were a huge Ferris wheel[w] and the Streets of Cairo, featuring "Little Egypt," the hoochee-coochee dancer. The Midway has been preserved as a parkway, which is bordered by the University of Chicago, and the term is regularly used as a Chicago place name.

[*Official Guide to the World's Columbian Exposition;* Edgar Lee Masters, *The Tale of Chicago.*]

PAUL M. ANGLE

Midwinter International Exposition, THE, first international exposition held on the Pacific Coast, formally opened Jan. 27 and closed July 4, 1894. The Exposition covered 100 acres in San Francisco's Golden Gate Park and cost $1,193,-260; there were 1,315,022 paid admissions. The purpose was to "enhance the commercial and industrial interests of the Pacific Coast." It was directly inspired by the World's Columbian Exposition[w], of which it was a smaller edition in many respects. Many of the exhibits were transported directly from Chicago to San Francisco. Four American states, exclusive of California, and nine foreign nations participated officially.

FRANK MONAGHAN

Mier Expedition, THE. Mexico refused to recognize the independence of Texas[w] in 1836 and as late as 1842 made an invasion and took possession of San Antonio for a short time. A counter expedition into Mexico was ordered by President Houston. This expedition left San Antonio for the border in November, 1842, under Gen. Somervell, with 750 troops. Because of lack of enthusiasm of the leaders and dissension among the troops, only 250 crossed into Mexico and these surrendered to an overwhelming Mexican force at Mier on the lower Rio Grande. After an attempt to escape, one tenth were shot and the others marched to a prison near Mexico City. Here some died, some escaped and the others were released two years later.

[H. H. Bancroft, *History of North Mexican States and Texas;* Thos. J. Green, *Journal of the Texian Expedition against Mier.*]

J. G. SMITH

Mifflin, Fort, was originally built as Mud Fort in 1762 on Mud Island, Delaware River, below the mouth of the Schuylkill. The most important of Philadelphia's Revolutionary defenses, it was besieged by the British from Sept. 27 to Nov. 16, 1777, when, razed by gunfire, it was abandoned. After the British evacuation of Philadelphia, it was rebuilt and named for Thomas Mifflin, the then governor of Pennsylvania. It has been frequently modernized and is still in active use.

[Scharf and Wescott, *History of Philadelphia.*]

MARION V. BREWINGTON

Migration, Group. The single family was the typical unit in the westward movement[w] which resulted in the settlement of America. Nevertheless, a large number of communities in the West were settled by groups of people previously associated with each other who migrated in one body to a new home. Usually, although not always, the destination of these groups was predetermined by agents sent out in advance to select favorable locations, and often even to purchase land before the movement was undertaken.

These group migrations fall into two classes. The first class was made up of groups of people who were governed by the same motives that in general impelled settlers westward, but who decided to move and settle in a body for mutual aid and protection, or in order to make sure of having friendly neighbors in the new home, or for other reasons. The second class was composed of religious groups or experimental colonies seeking more favorable environments in which to carry out their particular purposes. In both classes were to be found not only groups migrating westward from eastern communities, but also other groups which came directly from Europe. A few illustrations will serve to indicate the nature of these two types of group migration.

From earliest colonial times the westward advance presented examples of groups of the first class moving into the interior. The first settlements in the Connecticut Valley were made by the groups that followed Roger Ludlow from the Massachusetts Bay colony (*see* River Towns of Connecticut). In fact community migration into new lands previously surveyed was quite typical of the method of early frontier expansion in the New England colonies. The original settlement of Germans and their subsequent migrations in New York were of this type, as were many of the German and Scotch-Irish[w] movements to Pennsylvania. In the early 1770's there was mention of a group of "adventurers" from Connecticut who settled on a tract of land on the Mississippi in West Florida (*see* Georgiana).

Frequent examples of the same phenomena were found throughout the years when the country west of the Alleghenies was being occupied by settlers. One authority states that Rev. Lewis Craig's congregation moved in a body from Virginia to Kentucky in 1781. In 1788 the Ohio Associates[w] from New England founded Marietta in Ohio. Two decades later *Niles' Weekly Register*[w] commented on the tendency of the people of Connecticut to move in groups, after previous investigation, to new homes in the Western Reserve[w] in northern Ohio. About the same time a New York editor described "a cavalcade of upwards of twenty waggons containing one company of 116 persons, on their way to Indiana, and all from one town in the district of Maine." In 1819 a party of 120 persons led by Captains Blackman and Allen was seen on its way to Illinois. In Michigan in 1822 there were said to be numerous individuals spying out lands for groups of settlers who were to follow. A colony of Quakers on the River Rouge was mentioned the following year.

In 1839 an Iowa editor reported that "whole neighborhoods in Illinois, Indiana and Ohio are 'organizing' for emigration." To one locality in Wisconsin a few years later came a group of more than 100 persons from Rochester, N. Y., of whom sixty-two were members of the Allen family. During the 1850's the rush to the newly opened Kansas-Nebraska country contained many groups, such as the one made up of friends and acquaintances from Outagamie County, Wis., which founded Fremont, Nebr., in 1856. Illustrations of this nature might be multiplied indefinitely to show the part played by groups in the westward movement.

Turning now to the second class of group migrations, a few illustrations may be cited among the various experimental colonies and religious groups which migrated westward. The Harmony Society[w], led by George Rapp, and made up of a sect from southern Germany, established a settlement in western Pennsylvania in 1805 and moved to Indiana ten years later. The Zoarites[w] came to Ohio in 1817 from Württemberg, Germany. In the 1830's a group of ministers in the Mohawk Valley, New York, drew up a plan for a religious and educational community in the West. An exploring committee sent out in 1835 selected land in Illinois and the result was the founding of Galesburg and Knox College. The establishment of Oberlin, Ohio, and Oberlin College were accomplished in a similar manner a few years earlier. The Mennonites[w] nearly always moved in groups, after previous investigations of localities, when they established their various communities

throughout the country, whether they came directly from Europe or moved from their earlier centers of settlement in America. Another instance of group migration may be found in the history of the Iowa community known as Amana[w] —a religious colony which until recently was communistic in organization.

The final illustration of this type of group migration may well be one that is in many respects the most notable of all. The Mormon Church[w] had its origin around 1830 in western New York. In that year a temporary domicile was selected at Kirtland, Ohio, but at the same time Independence, Mo., was chosen as a permanent location and by 1831 more than 1000 members of the sect had moved thither. Two years later the Mormons were forced to move to Far West[w], north of the Missouri River. In 1839 the hostility of the neighboring settlers caused another removal, this time to Nauvoo[w], on the eastern bank of the Mississippi River in Illinois. After seven years at Nauvoo, the leaders decided to seek an asylum in the Rocky Mountains, and the result was the historic hegira of the Mormons to Utah, which began in 1846.

[There is no general work dealing with group migrations. For illustrations see R. V. Coleman, *The Old Patent of Connecticut;* Bertha M. H. Shambaugh, *Amana: The Community of True Inspiration;* Earnest E. Calkins, *They Broke the Prairie;* and William A. Linn, *The Story of the Mormons.*]

DAN E. CLARK

Milan Decree. *See* Napoleon's Decrees.

Mileage is an allowance toward the expense of legislators in traveling to and from sessions of their respective bodies. Members of Congress receive twenty cents per mile, to be estimated by the nearest route usually traveled in going to and returning from each regular session. The allowance is sufficient to cover transportation, Pullman fares, meals and incidental expenses of a member and his family. In the case of state legislators, mileage allowances vary from three cents a mile in Ohio and five cents a mile for one round trip for regular sessions in California, to actual traveling expenses in Nebraska, five cents a mile for round trips once a week during sessions in Pennsylvania and twenty cents a mile in Arizona and Indiana. Mileage is also commonly provided by law for national and state officials who are required to travel in the performance of their duties, and for witnesses summoned to testify in state and Federal courts or before legislative committees.

[*Code of the Laws of the U. S.*, 1934; *Book of the States,* II, 249.]

P. ORMAN RAY

Military Academy, The United States, dates legally from an act of Congress signed by President Jefferson, March 16, 1802. Credit for its foundation belongs above all to George Washington, who from 1776 to the day of his last message to Congress in 1796 worked for the establishment of an institution where the officers of America's armies would receive their training and education. Maj. Gen. Henry Knox is credited with the initial proposal. Alexander Hamilton and Baron von Steuben, among others, supported him. Their efforts met with no success until 1794, when Congress established at West Point a "School for Artillerists and Engineers." The act provided for fifty-six cadetships, the cadets being attached to the troops in garrison. Their training, however, could scarcely be called an education; it was no more than a military apprenticeship.

The deficiencies in the program were corrected in part by the act of 1802. It provided for a Corps of Engineers, consisting of five officers and ten cadets. The Chief of Engineers was designated Superintendent of the Academy, Jonathan Williams being the first to hold that office. In addition, Congress provided for 176 cadetships in troops of the line, but these cadets were not eligible for admission to the Academy. West Point was to be a school of engineering, the first in the country's history. The educational weaknesses of the new program were at once apparent. It set no standard of entrance examinations, provided no curriculum or buildings, and left the cadets to shift for their own maintenance on their monthly pay of ten dollars. Worse still, the Superintendent was absent from West Point most of the time, supervising construction of harbor defenses on the seaboard.

The darkest days of this period occurred in the administration of President Madison. His Secretary of War, William Eustis, gradually dispersed the officers and cadets to various duties in the army, and failed to send to West Point some 300 candidates appointed to cadetships. When the War of 1812 opened, the Academy existed on paper only. Congress reopened the Academy the following year. By 1816, 200 cadets were enrolled.

The following year, bringing the appointment of Brevet Major Sylvanus Thayer as Superintendent, marks the true inception of the West Point system of education which remains today. His breadth of vision, human sympathy, knowledge of educational methods and purposes and enthusiasm all contributed to qualify him for the task he had set himself. He found at West Point a curriculum which included mathematics, engineering, natural philosophy, drawing and French. To these he added shortly chemistry, general history, moral philosophy, law, geography and ethics. It is not his expansion of the curriculum to which he owes chief recognition as "Father of the Military Academy," but rather to methods of instruction and discipline established. Classes were divided into sections of not more than twelve men each. Assignments to sections were based on demonstrated ability. Daily recitations, weekly reports of grades, term examinations and ruthless elimination of the unfit made for a thoroughness of performance previously lacking.

The Corps was organized into a two-company battalion, its officers and noncommissioned officers chosen from the upper classes. In all of his activities—study, recitation, drill and ceremony —the cadet lived under a rule of strict discipline. Important as were these contributions in discipline and education, they were surpassed by the establishment of a code of honor for the Corps of Cadets. Rigid to the point of tolerating no infraction however slight, its success then and always has depended on its full and frank acceptance by the Corps. The measure of its influence is evident from the fact that, from the outset to the present day, the cadets themselves have been the principal instrument of its enforcement.

Following the close of Col. Thayer's sixteen-year term as superintendent, no noteworthy change occurred for several decades. The steady increase in the number of congressmen and senators brought a corresponding increase in the size of the Corps. Keeping step with educational progress the curriculum was expanded gradually. Its basis remained in the sciences.

The War with Mexico brought to the American public the first full realization that West Point was paying dividends in terms of military efficiency. That fact was driven home more sharply by the records of its graduates in the Civil War, in both the Union and Southern forces. At its outbreak sixty-five cadets from Southern states resigned to accept commissions under the Confederacy. More than half of the 296 West Point graduates who espoused the Confederate cause became generals in the Southern armies. On the Union side nearly 300 graduates attained that rank.

That West Point was no longer a school of engineering, but was training officers for all branches of the Service was recognized by Congress in the act approved July 13, 1866. Supervision was transferred from the Corps of Engineers to the War Department. At the same time entrance requirements were stiffened materially.

Subsequent development of the educational plant and curriculum came sporadically, influenced largely by the nation's experience in war. Thus after the Spanish-American War, an extensive building program gave West Point its most distinctive architecture, the work of Cram, Goodhue and Ferguson. For a brief period the plant was adequate for its purpose. Then came the World War, and an increase of the Corps to 1334 cadets. The most recent increase, provided in the act of June 7, 1935, raised the Corps strength to 1960 cadets.

The most severe test to which the Military Academy and its traditions has been put occurred during the World War and early post-war years. The pressing need of officers for the nation's huge armies resulted in the graduation of five West Point classes between April, 1917, and Nov. 1, 1918. One class remained at West Point—with less than five months' service to its credit. The Military Academy had become a training camp. Urgent representations by Gen. Pershing and others resulted in action by Congress to restore the full four-year course, beginning with the class graduated in 1923.

The present-day cadet receives pay and allowances aggregating $1072 yearly, enough to cover the cost of his board, uniform, books and supplies, as well as the cost of his initial equipment as an officer after graduation. He pursues a four-year course aimed to give him a balanced development in three spheres: mental, physical and military. His academic year, from Sept. 1 to June 4 (with a brief holiday at Christmas), covers the following curriculum: Mathematics, English (two years), French (two years), History, Physics, Chemistry, Electrical Engineering, Mechanics, Thermodynamics, Hydraulics, Aerodynamics, Spanish, Civil and Army Engineering, Military Art and History, Ordnance and Gunnery, Automotive Engineering, Economics, Government, Law, Military Hygiene and a four-year course in the Tactics of all arms and branches of the Service. The summer months are wholly devoted to practical military training, as are also the daily afternoon hours after 3.00 P.M. in the academic year. And to ensure proper development of the cadet's physique, military training is supplemented by a program of intramural athletics which runs through the full year.

Upon graduation a cadet is granted the degree of Bachelor of Science, and may be commissioned as an officer in the Regular Army. With the exception of foreign cadets and the few Americans who resign to enter civil pursuits, all give their lives to the Service. Slightly more than 53% of the total of cadets who entered the Academy from its foundation to June, 1939, were graduated; and 6042 of these 11,790 graduates were on that date in service as officers of the Regular Army.

Keeping pace with the increase in the Corps, the West Point Military Reservation has been added to from time to time. It comprises now approximately 2500 acres in West Point proper and nearly 1300 acres more in near-by areas. The act of Congress approved March 1, 1931, looks to the early purchase of an additional nine or ten thousand acres.

[E. C. Boynton, *History of West Point; The Centennial of the U. S. Military Academy;* R. C. Richardson, *West Point;* H. J. Hancock, *Life at West Point; The United States Military Academy,* a pamphlet published by the Department of Economics, Government and History, West Point.]

HERMAN BEUKEMA

Military Aid to the Civil Power. Federal troops have been employed in more than 100 instances for the suppression of domestic disturbances. Similar actions by state authorities have been much more numerous. Usually the armed forces have given aid to civil officers temporarily obstructed in the execution of their functions. Less frequently the military commander has had to establish "martial rule" (not "martial law,"^{qv} when troops operate under the law of necessity, without statutory sanction), terminative whenever conditions permitted resumption of civil control.

The President is the sole judge of the exigency demanding the use of Federal troops. Their employment is based on Article IV, Section 4, of the Constitution^{qv} and acts of Congress which have been incorporated under the title "Insurrection" (Revised Statutes of the United States, Sections 5297–5301). These laws provide that the President may order out troops: (*a*) on the request of the legislature of a state, or of the state executive, if the legislature is not in session and cannot be convened in time; (*b*) without the request, or even against the protest of state authorities, to maintain the guarantees of the Federal Constitution; (*c*) in any case of interference with the execution of the Federal laws, the transportation of the mails, the flow of interstate commerce, or of danger to United States property.

The governors of Hawaii, Puerto Rico and the Virgin Islands have emergency powers comparable to those of the President; however, such authority ends as soon as the governor can communicate with the President and place himself under the latter's direction. The Philippine Independence Act provides for intervention by the United States for the preservation of the government of the Commonwealth, and for the maintenance of its obligations under the Philippine constitution.

The employment of National Guard[qv] units by state authorities for the suppression of domestic violence presents a confused picture; in law and practice and in judicial action there is a complete lack of uniformity of procedure. In general, there is a tendency to declare martial law when the situation requires no more than military aid to the civil power.

[C. M. Dowell, *Military Aid to the Civil Power;* Charles Fairman, *The Law of Martial Rule;* C. E. Hughes, *War Powers under the Constitution;* Federal Aid in Domestic Disturbances, 1903-22, *Senate Documents,* Vol. XIX.]

HERMAN BEUKEMA

Military Companies, Voluntary. These organizations were a feature of the social and recreational activities of the youth of the 1850's. The companies appeared in considerable numbers as a result of the interest in military affairs aroused by the Mexican War. Young men joined the companies because they combined athletic activity with social recreation. In 1856–59 every important newspaper carried records of their activities which included dress parades, competitive drills and interstate encampments. These companies sometimes received aid from the state, but generally maintained an independent existence, depending on some rich patron, and the proceeds from military balls and other entertainments for funds.

The movement developed simultaneously in every section of the country, and spread from the larger cities to the towns and villages. The Chicago Zouaves attained a national reputation for their discipline and their military proficiency. Most of the voluntary companies had disbanded before the Civil War began and did not contribute much to the officer personnel of the war.

[T. G. Gronert, The First National Pastime in the Middle West, *Indiana Magazine of History,* Vol. XXIX, No. 3.]

THEODORE G. GRONERT

Military Company of Adventurers (1773). *See* Georgiana.

Military Intelligence is information of the enemy, collected, valued and disseminated to the commanders, upon which they may base their offensive or defensive plans. Securing such information is a practice as old as war. Though techniques have changed with the passing years and the development of new military tools, the basic rules of getting and using information of the enemy's strength, situation and plans have, like the never-changing principles of war, remained the same. To secure information of the enemy

troops and country is described as positive intelligence work and to prevent the enemy from getting similar information is characterized as negative intelligence activity. Land and air reconnaissance, prisoners, maps and aerial photographs, combat, economic, political, geographic and psychological estimates of the enemy country, enemy newspapers and spies[qv], are some of the tools utilized in compiling positive military intelligence. Detection and frustration of enemy agents, and censorship[qv] of means of communication are common negative intelligence activities. Public relations is also a phase of military intelligence work.

Prior to the World War the development of the military intelligence service in the United States was slow and halting. A permanent unit was first established in the War Department during 1885 when a bureau was formed in the Adjutant General's office. The Congress appropriated money in 1889 to send army officers abroad, thereby inaugurating the present military attaché system, which is responsible for the major part of the work of gathering military information during times of peace. The Bureau developed satisfactorily and in 1903, when the General Staff[qv] was created, became the second division of that organization. Nearly a quarter of a century of steady development was interrupted in 1908, when the Military Intelligence Division was transferred in its entirety, including its personnel, records, library and maps, to the War College Building. This move was designed to facilitate the use of the Division's materials by the faculty and students of the Army War College[qv] and was not to affect its functions or organization. Shortly, however, the Division was consolidated with the War College to form a new Second Division of the General Staff and its personnel and materials were distributed throughout the War College. From 1910 until the World War, the Military Intelligence function was exercised by a committee of the War College Division of the General Staff, only two members of which were actually engaged in military intelligence work. Soon after the United States entered the World War, a Military Intelligence Section of the War College Division of the General Staff was organized, which expanded and carried on the wartime military intelligence duties. Finally, on Aug. 26, 1918, the Military Intelligence Division, G–2, of the General Staff, was established. The staff of each army unit, down to and including the battalion, now has a military intelligence section. The commissioned officer personnel of the Regular Army establishment can be augmented during time of war by the mobilization of a Military Intelligence Reserve composed of specially trained reserve officers.

[Walter C. Sweeney, *Military Intelligence, a New Weapon in War.*]   GEORGE FREDERICK ASHWORTH

Military Law, as comprehended in the United States, is the legal system adopted for the regulation of the military establishment, including naval and marine attachments and, under certain circumstances, camp retainers and followers; is both disciplinary and administrative; and is distinct from martial law*qv* and the laws of war and hostile occupation. It is a branch of municipal law and is specifically authorized in the Constitution. The Articles of War*qv*, together with other statutory enactments and such executive promulgations as the Army Regulations, general and special orders and decisions by the War Department and by commanding officers, constitute the written law. The customs of the Service form the unwritten law. The first Articles of War were enacted by the Second Continental Congress on June 30, 1775, and were predicated on the British Code of 1765 and the articles adopted by the Provincial Congress of Massachusetts Bay on April 5, 1775. They were enlarged and modified in 1776, supplemented in 1786, rewritten in 1806 to conform better to the republican form of government, amended during the War of 1812, the Seminole wars and the Civil War, restated in 1874, generally recast in 1916 and were revised in 1920. Jurisdiction for the trial of offenders against military law is exercised by general, special and summary courts-martial*qv*. The Confederate states adopted the United States Articles and regulations with few modifications, but introduced marked improvements in the scheme of courts.

[G. B. Davis, *A Treatise on the Military Law of the United States;* War Department, *A Manual for Courts-Martial, Courts of Inquiry, and of Other Procedure under Military Law.*]   WILLIAM M. ROBINSON, JR.

Military Policy of the United States. We have often found ourselves on the verge of war, entirely unprepared. This has sometimes led writers to say that we have no military policy.

There may be some truth in this criticism, if we mean merely that there has been inconsistency in the conduct of our military affairs. But a military policy, in this sense, is not an independent thing capable of study by itself. The dictum of Clausewitz holds true—that war is a continuation of state policy by other means. Thus our conduct of military affairs has been dictated by our civil situation and policy; these are continually changing, our military requirements are therefore con-

tinually changing and if we study our military legislation and administration alone there may seem to be no continuity.

But they should not be so studied. The question of the use of military force is not for the soldier, but for the statesman. The military problems of the statesman vary widely; and the statesman is engrossed with a multitude of civil problems, generally more important, or at least more urgent, in his eyes, than the military problems. The natural result is an apparent inconsistency in military policy, which is really only symptomatic of changes in the civil situation. And in the execution of changing policies, civil and military, it is not unnatural to find that the statesman gives little thought to his military machinery, with the result that emergencies find us unprepared.

If, however, we mean by military policy our customary national attitude toward military affairs, we shall find a fairly definite trend of thought.

Our military policy in that sense was inherited from England during our colonial period (*see* Army, United States) . England had two types of military organization, existing side by side. There was a militia force, maintained by the counties, and available for duty in civil disturbances within the county only. The king held command over the whole militia, and it was available, within the national boundaries, for repelling invasion.

For military service of any other kind this force was not adapted. Hence it was necessary to raise a separate force under the king's prerogative, available for duty anywhere. These troop units came to be more and more permanent and professional, and formed the basis for the present Regular Army. There was always a certain popular distrust of these king's troops, as compared with the "constitutional force," the militia, and a desire to keep them under control. In the English Bill of Rights of 1689 it was provided that "the raising or keeping a standing army within the kingdom in time of peace, unless it be with the consent of parliament, is against law."

This system was transplanted to America, as a matter of course, by the colonists. Its development in this country is traced in the article referred to above, and the discussion will not be repeated here. But a review of that development from the point of view just indicated will show that we do possess a military policy in the sense here defined, and that its evolution has been, on the whole, reasonably consistent and logical. Like so many of our national institutions, this policy is flexible enough to permit ready adaptation to changing conditions, and yet stable enough to furnish a balance wheel.

[Emory Upton, *Military Policy of the United States;* Frederic L. Huidekoper, *The Military Unpreparedness of the United States;* Oliver L. Spaulding, *The United States Army in War and Peace.*]

OLIVER L. SPAULDING

Military Roads. No highways designed primarily for military purposes have been constructed in the United States in recent years. But during the century and more of the westward movement[qv] many such roads, of a primitive sort, were built by or for troops on expeditions through the wilderness, or for communications between remote military posts and the settled frontier.

Among such routes were the Braddock Road, built in 1755 from Alexandria, Va., nearly to Fort Duquesne, on the Ohio, and George Rogers Clark's Road from Fort Massac, Ill., to Kaskaskia and Vincennes, in 1778–79[qv]. Many others later threaded the plains and mountains from the Mississippi to the Pacific during the era of the Indian wars.

The Civil War saw many military roads built, some for communication between the works of great fortified areas, such as Washington and Petersburg, Va., others for temporary needs in active campaigns. In the field, however, maintenance or improvement of existing roads was generally sufficient. This was also true in 1918 in France, where the American Expeditionary Forces[qv] learned how necessary substantial hard-surfaced roads have become for supporting the continuous motorized traffic of modern armies.

A future war within our own territories would find us dependent upon the existing public highway system. Whether this system would meet all requirements is questionable. In 1938 two bills were introduced in Congress, framed, in part, "to provide additional facilities for the national defense." The McKellar bill proposed the construction of a four-lane automobile highway between Washington and New York, with three similar highways spaced across the entire United States from east to west, and three more from north to south. The Bulkley bill provided for seven north-and-south and three east-and-west "superhighways" across the country, each at least 300 feet wide. Neither bill was acted upon. But a prudent policy of national preparedness is likely in future to require some construction of modern military roads, if only to supplement the existing highway network in certain localities.

[*The Military Engineer*, Vols. XI, XII, XVIII, XX; 75th Congress, 3rd Session, Senate bills 3211 and 3428.]

JOSEPH MILLS HANSON

Military Supplies. *See* Army Supply; Munitions, The Manufacture of.

Military Tracts. Military land bounties[qv] were offered in the early national period by the states and the Federal Government to attract people into the armies or to reward soldiers and officers for their services. In the Revolutionary War such bounties varied in size according to military rank, the upper limit being 5000 to 10,000 acres in some cases. To satisfy the warrants issued for these bounties military tracts were set aside in which the warrantee must locate his land. New York set up two such reserves, one in the Finger Lakes district and the other in the extreme northern part of the state. North Carolina created a military tract in the Cumberland basin of Tennessee, and Virginia established a similar tract in western Kentucky. When it was seen that the Kentucky tract would not satisfy outstanding warrants of Virginia a second military tract, consisting of 3,850,000 acres, was created in south central Ohio which Virginia reserved to itself from the cession it made of its western lands[qv] to the Federal Government. In this latter tract the United States had no control over the lands and it is the only part of Ohio which was not surveyed in rectangles in advance of lawful settlement (*see* Virginia Military Reserve in Ohio) .

The United States created four military tracts to satisfy its warrants given in the Revolutionary War and the War of 1812. The first of these was located in central Ohio, adjacent to the Virginia Military Tract[qv], and consisted of 2,539,000 acres. Warrantees of the Revolutionary War located their lands here. The other three tracts of 2,000,-000 acres each were originally located in Michigan, Illinois and Arkansas; but when it was reported that the Michigan tract was poorly drained and unsuited to farming, it was abandoned and the Illinois tract was increased to 3,500,000 acres and a tract of 500,000 acres was established in Missouri. In these three tracts soldiers of the War of 1812, who received 160 acres each, were required to locate their warrants by lottery.

Most of the soldiers or their heirs refused to move to these tracts to take up their claims, as the law contemplated, because they were too far distant from zones of settlement. Instead, they sold their warrants or locations to speculators for prices as low as ten cents an acre. The result was a high percentage of absentee or speculative ownership in each of the military tracts. For example, twenty-four persons, including such well-known individuals as Nathaniel Massie, Duncan McArthur and Thomas Worthington, owned

1,035,000 acres in the Virginia Military Tract of Ohio. In the Military Tract of Illinois, located in the triangle between the Illinois and Mississippi rivers, the New York and Boston Illinois Land Company acquired 900,000 acres, Romulus Riggs of Philadelphia owned 40,000 acres and other easterners had large possessions.

Such large-scale land monopolization in the military tracts aroused all the latent frontier hostility against absentee speculators. Squatters*ᵥ settled upon the absentee-owned lands, plundered them of their timber, defied ouster proceedings and flouted all efforts to make them pay rent for their use of the land. Local governments frequently levied discriminatory taxes on absentee-owned lands, raised their valuations and built public improvements in their vicinity to force higher taxes. The speculators with little capital might lose their lands at tax sales; others, better financed, sooner or later would sell or lease to tenants. Residents of the military tracts long cherished their dislike of nonresident proprietors.

[P. J. Treat, *The National Land System, 1785-1820;* B. H. Hibbard, *History of the Public Land Policies.*]
PAUL WALLACE GATES

Military Warrants. *See* Land Bounties.

Militia. Settlers brought to America with them the militia idea, that all men "joined in some measure," as Adam Smith said, "the trade of a soldier to whatever other trade or profession they happened to carry on." It was tied to traditional fears of standing armies, in ancient as in British history the tools of despotic rulers. In the Declaration of Independence*ᵥ, George III was accused of permitting standing troops to be maintained in the colonies without the consent of their legislatures. In the Constitution*ᵥ, and debates leading to its formulation and adoption, militia was considered indispensable to republicanism. Militiamen required "for the common defense" were to be requisitioned by the President only in emergencies and through the governors according to state quotas. An act of May 2, 1792 (1 Stat. 259), re-enacted Feb. 28, 1795, authorized the President to call federally "such number of the militia of the states most convenient to the scene of the action as he may judge necessary." It was thus that, for want of a standing army, troops had been raised for the disastrous Harmar (1790) and St. Clair (1791) expeditions against the Indians, and were raised for the Whiskey Rebellion (1794) *ᵠᵥ. In the last instance local disaffection kept Pennsylvania militia out of the contingent, although that called from New Jersey, Maryland and Virginia participated. Political

rather than practical considerations kept the militia of Massachusetts and Connecticut home in 1812, the governors of those states claiming priority for local control and local authority. The governor of Vermont in 1813 tried to recall his militia from campaigning in New York, but his troops flouted his orders. (Also political were the defiances of Virginia, North Carolina, Kentucky, Tennessee, Arkansas, Maryland and Delaware— "border states"—to Lincoln's militia calls after the bombardment of Fort Sumter*ᵥ in 1861.) Mutinies and refusals of troops to cross into Canada in 1812, as well as these other incidents, had been based upon an assumed constitutional right regarding state authority and merely local service. The Supreme Court in 1820 declared the Federal authority supreme. An act of May 27, 1908 (35 Stat. 400), attempted to grant the President authority to call militia for foreign service, but this was considered beyond his powers (29 Ops. Atty. Gen. 322, 1912). However, in 1917 the difficulty was avoided by basing the Selective Service Act on "war powers" to "raise armies" in general rather than on the militia principle (*see* Draft).

To secure more effective training than the one or two days a year of universal musterings first required, formation of "a select militia" was resorted to by the states. This became our "National Guard"*ᵠᵥ—volunteers for state service, officered by state appointees, practising about once a week. Called to check insurrections like the Whiskey Rebellion, the secessions of 1861*ᵠᵥ, and foreign invasions in New York, Maryland and Louisiana during the War of 1812*ᵥ, they were suddenly assembled, deliberately used—unseasoned as they were—as soon as called, and allowed to return home at the end of their specified terms, whatever the current military situation might be. The result was often disorder, disaster and waste. The Morrill Act*ᵥ of 1862 attempted to produce, through the land-grant colleges, efficient leaders for state forces. The "select militia," organized by the states as the National Guard, improved little, and even in suppressing serious local disorders was often ineffective. The Dick Act of Jan. 21, 1903, offered Federal pay for militia training, provided Regular Army inspectors and instructors, and organized, armed and equipped local units according to Federal standards. During the next decade, as a result of this legislation, this select force participated with regulars in combined maneuvers and improved immeasurably. In 1916 it formed a large part of the force protecting the Mexican border against bandit inroads, and in 1917, drafted into Federal service, comprised many of the combat divisions of the A. E. F.[w] It was integrated into the new force provided by the National Defense Acts of 1916 and 1920[w] at twice the strength of the regulars, and was purposely by Congress given preference over alternative suggestions for a new wholly Federal militia and for universal compulsory service. Always maintained, the general "militia idea" has been only partially applied, on a voluntary basis and parallel to, instead of replacing, the regular or standing army (*see* Volunteers). Militia training and organization have progressively, though slowly, improved. (*See also* Army, United States.)

[E. Upton, *Military Policy of the United States;* O. L. Spaulding, *United States Army in War and Peace;* Longstreet, *Georgia Scenes;* Abner R. Small, *The Road to Richmond;* R. H. Rogers, Military Powers, National and State, in *American Law Review,* Vol. I, pp. 321-328; Houston v. Moore, 5 Wheaton 1, 13, 1820; Arver v. United States, 245 U. S. 366, 1918; Cox v. Wood, 247 U. S. 3, 1918; George W. Wickersham, Powers of the President, in 29 Ops. Atty. Gen. 322, 1912.]

ELBRIDGE COLBY

Militia, Colonial, is a general term denoting a variety of local defense organizations from the days of Dale or Standish to the time of Gen. Washington. It includes such types of fighters as "trained bands," "embattled farmers," "prime riflemen." The generally accepted idea was that every adult male inhabitant, with special exceptions, should possess arms and participate in the defense of the commonwealth. Naturally, training was imperfect and discipline a problem.

More specifically, colonial militia consisted of units enlisted, paid, armed and sometimes uniformed by provincial governments. Such troops fought the French and the Indians and also participated in internal struggles such as Leisler's Revolt or Bacon's Rebellion[qw].

In the intercolonial wars, each province provided the troops it saw fit and chose their commanders. Misunderstandings with British officers and "regulars" were common. The militiamen occasionally gave good accounts of themselves, however, as at Louisburg in 1745 and at Lake George[qw] ten years later.

[H. L. Osgood, *The American Colonies in the Seventeenth Century,* and *The American Colonies in the Eighteenth Century.*]

DONALD R. ALTER

Mill Springs, Encounter at, took place on Jan. 19, 1862, in Pulaski County, Ky., between about 4000 Confederates led by George B. Crittenden and an equal number of Federals under George H. Thomas. Before the end of the day, with the arrival of about 8000 reinforcements, the Fed-

erals disastrously defeated the Confederates and killed Felix K. Zollicoffer, second in command. This was one of a number of disasters which overtook the Confederates and resulted in their expulsion from Kentucky.

[L. and R. H. Collins, *History of Kentucky;* E. M. Coulter, *Civil War and Readjustment in Kentucky.*]

E. MERTON COULTER

Mill Streams. That the pioneers could think of no more appropriate name than Mill Creek or Mill River for dozens of streams in the eastern United States attests the widespread use of water power[w]. There are two Mill Rivers flowing into the Connecticut in Massachusetts alone. When dams and short canals[w] with locks began to be constructed in the latter 18th and early 19th century for the improvement of navigation by arks, flatboats and rafts[qw] of such rough rivers as the Merrimac, the Connecticut, the Blackstone, the Mohawk, the Potomac, the James, the Schuylkill and others, the fall of the water at the locks was often employed to operate mills and factories. The village of Manchester, N. H., was developed into an important industrial city after 1800 through the utilized water power of the little canal around the Amoskeag Falls in the Merrimac River. Those early mills had to be actuated, of course, directly by a water wheel or turbine, and must therefore be close to the fall or rapid. So Woonsocket and Pawtucket, R. I., were built up on the Blackstone by the power from that stream and from the canal locks later (1824–28) built alongside it. Paterson, N. J., and Rochester, N. Y., became large cities because of the cataracts of the Passaic and the Genesee, around which they were built. So also did the Falls of St. Anthony in the Mississippi create Minneapolis. The name of the city of Fall River, Mass., tells its own story. Lowell on the Merrimac, Turner's Falls, Holyoke and Chicopee on the Connecticut, Richmond on the James are some other cities made large and prosperous by the adjacent water power which in their earlier history was almost their only reason for being. Even larger canals often sold water power at their locks; one frequently finds the prospectus of a new canal project estimating that the water power would operate, say, "thirty run of millstones."

ALVIN F. HARLOW

Mille Lacs, Battle of (*ca.* 1745). As part of their general tribal advance, Lake Superior Chippewa[w], equipped with firearms, surprised three Sioux[w] villages on the southwest shore of Mille Lacs Lake (Minn.). In a fierce three-day battle, the Sioux were decisively defeated and, retreating down Rum River, abandoned these villages. Sometimes called the Battle of Kathio.

[W. W. Warren, *History of the Ojibway Nation.*]
WILLOUGHBY M. BABCOCK

Millerites. *See* Adventists.

Milligan Case (1866). This decision by the Supreme Court invalidated the trial and conviction of Lambdin P. Milligan by a military commission in 1864. Milligan had been arrested at his Indiana home by order of the general in command of the military district of Indiana (*see* Martial Law) charged with conspiring against the United States, with giving aid and comfort to the enemy, and with inciting insurrection and disloyal practices (*see* Copperheads). The charges grew out of Milligan's activities as an officer of a secret order whose general purpose was to cooperate with the Confederate government. Milligan was tried before a court-martial established under the authority of the President, found guilty, and sentenced to be hanged. Before execution of sentence, proceedings were instituted in the Federal circuit court denying the legality of the military trial, and asserting that Milligan had been deprived of his constitutional right to trial by jury.

The Supreme Court held that neither the President nor Congress has the power to set up military tribunals except in the actual theater of war, where the civil courts are no longer functioning; and that elsewhere courts-martial[w] have jurisdiction over only persons in the military or naval service of the United States. Milligan was not in the military or naval service; war did not exist in Indiana; nor was the state invaded or threatened with invasion; and the civil courts were open and in the proper and unobstructed exercise of their jurisdiction. The substitution of trial before a court-martial for the regular civil procedure was therefore unwarranted, and Milligan had been deprived of his constitutional right. He was released, after having been held in confinement for eighteen months. Later, because the decision seemed to cast grave doubt upon the legality of the military government established by Congress in former rebellious states, the Court was widely denounced, especially by Radical Republicans[w].

[*Ex parte Milligan, 4 Wallace 2*; B. Pitman, *Trials for Treason at Indianapolis*; J. F. Rhodes, *History of the United States since the Compromise of 1850*; W. D. Foulke, *Life of Oliver P. Morton*; S. Klaus, ed., *The Milligan Case.*]
P. ORMAN RAY

"Millions for Defense, but not a Cent for Tribute," a toast offered by Robert Goodloe Harper, congressman from South Carolina, at the dinner given by Congress in Philadelphia on June 18, 1798, in honor of John Marshall on his return from the diplomatic mission to France, which eventuated in the XYZ Affair[w]. The naval war with France[w] followed soon afterwards. (*See also* Franco-American Misunderstanding.)

[A. J. Beveridge, *Life of John Marshall; South Carolina Historical and Genealogical Magazine*, January, 1900; E. McK. Avery, *A History of the United States.*]
CHARLES LEE LEWIS

Mims, Fort, The Massacre at, occurred Aug. 30, 1813, when the fort was attacked by a force of about 1000 Creeks[w]. The fort was a mere stockade built the preceding July around the house of Samuel Mims on the eastern bank of Lake Tensaw, near Mobile. In it the white and half-breed families of the vicinity had taken refuge, fearing a Creek uprising in revenge for the Burnt Corn[w] attack in July. At the time of the massacre there were 553 people within the fort, about 100 of whom were enlisted soldiers. Deceived as to the intentions of the Creeks and not expecting an attack, the commanding officer, Maj. Daniel Beasley, neglected to keep out patrols, to maintain a watch, or even to keep the gates closed. The Creeks surprised the fort, entered through the open east gate, and after desperate fighting burned the fort and massacred all the people except thirty-six who managed to escape. The Creeks themselves lost heavily.

[A. J. Pickett, *History of Alabama;* T. M. Owen, *History of Alabama and Dictionary of Alabama Biography.*]
R. S. COTTERILL

Mina Expedition (1816–17). Francisco Xavier Mina, a Spanish exile, came to the United States and plotted the liberation of Mexico. Going to Galveston, Texas, in November, 1816, with some 200 volunteers, he landed at Soto la Marina, Tamaulipas, the following April. Receiving additional recruits from New Orleans, he marched into the interior of Mexico. After some preliminary successes most of his followers deserted him. On Oct. 17 he was surprised and captured by a superior Spanish force, and sent to Mexico City, where he was executed on Nov. 11, 1817.

[H. I. Priestley, *The Mexican Nation;* H. H. Bancroft, *History of Mexico;* Philip Young, *History of Mexico and Her Civil Wars;* W. S. Robertson, *Rise of the Spanish-American Republics.*]
WALTER PRICHARD

Mine Run Campaign (1863). The Army of the Potomac[w] under Meade (U.) forced its way across the Rappahannock River on Nov. 7–8, 1863; then, after some delay, crossed the Rapidan unopposed on the 26th. Lee (C.) took a strong position in the forest back of a brook called

Mine Run. Here Meade, confronting him on the 29th, ordered flanking movements by Warren on the left and Sedgwick on the right. Warren's advance was detected by Lee and blocked in such force that Warren refused a major attack. Meade thereupon halted Sedgwick, and on the following day the Federal Army retired across the Rapidan.

[*Battles and Leaders of the Civil War*, Vol. IV.]

ALVIN F. HARLOW

Mine Sweeping became of great importance during the World War[w] because of constant mine laying by the principal belligerents to block hostile harbors and sea lanes. In all, nearly 250,-000 mines were laid, principally in the North Sea. German submarines laid mines off American harbors on the Atlantic coast, necessitating daily sweeping, to insure clear channels for shipping, by more than eighty mine sweepers. In addition, many large vessels used paravanes for their own protection.

Clearing the seas of mines after the war was an herculean task allocated among several navies. The American Navy cleared its own coast and in addition the 56,000 American mines constituting a barrage nearly across the North Sea (*see* Northern Mine Barrage). The latter was especially difficult and hazardous to sweep up because of climatic conditions, distance from home, and the novel type of antennae mine having a very sensitive electric firing device. A force of eighty mine sweeping vessels under Admiral Joseph Strauss finally cleared the 6000 square-mile area of scattered mine fields in September, 1919. Five vessels were seriously disabled or sunk and ten men killed in this great sweeping operation.

[Navy Department Historical Section, Publication Number 4, *The Northern Barrage: Taking up the Mines.*]

DUDLEY W. KNOX

Mineral Patent Law of the United States. When gold was discovered in California and Colorado the United States had no mining code. Mining law consisted of the rules and regulations drawn up and enforced by the miners themselves (*see* Mining Camp, Law of the). Based on these laws, Congress passed the first national mining act July 26, 1866. This law, amplified by the act of May 10, 1872, established the rules for obtaining patent to the mineral lands of the United States. The principle adopted was the sale of the lands, even those containing gold and silver mines, to the first occupant for a nominal sum. Upon discovering a mineral lode[w] any citizen could stake off a claim 1500 feet long by 600 feet wide and obtain title to it after making $500

worth of improvements and paying $5 per acre. Placer[w] claims were limited to twenty acres at a price of $2.50 per acre. No great nation has been as liberal as the United States in disposing of its mineral deposits. Special acts govern mining in the Philippines and Alaska. The mineral patent laws apply only to the public domain[w] of the United States, hence do not apply to the original thirteen states or Texas. Some lead mining states like Michigan, Wisconsin and Minnesota are governed by the agricultural land laws instead of the mineral patent law.

[G. P. Costigan, *Handbook on American Mining Law;* 14 *U. S. Statutes* 251-3; 17 *U. S. Statutes* 91-6.]

PERCY S. FRITZ

Mineral Springs, estimated at 10,000 in the United States, influenced location of settlements. Salt deposits (licks[w]) attracted deer and buffalo; abundance of game made desirable sites. With crude diet, intemperance and primitive medicine, convenient medicinal waters were a blessing. The most famous springs were Saratoga (N. Y.) and White Sulphur (W. Va.); colonists learned of both from Indians (1767 and 1778). After settlement, springs were important as resorts; visiting "spas" became fashionable. In 1809 Natchez ladies "took the waters" at near-by springs. Saratoga was nationally popular by 1820, White Sulphur by 1830. Most abundant east of the Mississippi, springs were especially important in the South. After 1870 improved transportation boomed resorts. Many were small, drawing patronage only from surrounding areas, but they were an important part of social routine until recent years. They were the scene of famous entertainments, of honeymoons, family vacations, protracted "cures," political horsetrading and semiprofessional gambling.

MACK SWEARINGEN

Mines were a source of interest to the pioneers in the colonies in North America; the early Spanish expeditions had a keen eye for gold and silver, while the French also sought them in the North. Unfortunately, they mostly eluded discovery, and the gold deposits of the southern Appalachian region were not developed until after the founding of the United States. The English colonists were more interested in useful minerals, and the story that the settlers of Jamestown[w] sent a shipload of "fool's gold" to England is untrue. They did build an iron smelter, but the colony was almost wiped out before it got started. Iron smelting began in Massachusetts in 1645, using bog ores[w], and the industry spread south and west. The early iron furnaces of Connecticut, New York, New Jersey and Pennsylvania had attained much importance before the

Revolution, and British attempts to control iron making in the colonies were an important factor in bringing it about. Charcoal was used as fuel; there was no coal mining until the middle of the 18th century, since wood fuel was abundant and coal from England could be delivered at the cities on the seacoast cheaper than it could be brought from inland.

John Winthrop's concession for metal mines in Connecticut (1651) never produced anything of importance and the copper deposit at Simsbury was the first one worked. Its short life only extended over the period 1707-45. The copper mine which Arent Schuyler discovered at Arlington, N. J., in 1714 was more lasting, and the first steam engine in America was used to operate pumps there about 1755. The first engine built in America was also constructed in its shops. This mine had closed down by the time of the Revolution, which greatly stimulated the production of iron for cannon balls and industrial uses, and of lead for bullets. The latter was derived from numerous small deposits now only of historic interest but the iron industry continued to thrive, always working westward.

The lead[w] deposits of the Mississippi were early discovered by French missionary explorers and LeSueur made an attempt to exploit them in 1699 that was a fiasco. Crozat's[w] concession in 1712 also produced nothing, and actual production began with Philippe Renault in 1721, who was disappointed to find the lead contained no silver (see "Mississippi Bubble"). There was some production both in southeast Missouri and in northwestern Illinois before the Louisiana Purchase, and vigorous American exploitation after 1810, lead mining being an important factor in the settlement of these regions. Mines on public land were leased on a royalty basis, but much confusion developed, and payments eventually ceased although production continued.

The copper[w] deposits of the Keeweenaw peninsula, though long known, were not worked until 1844, when treaty rights with the Indians were finally adjusted. The deposits were rich and about 1850 this was the most active mining region in the United States. The iron[w] deposits of the Lake Superior region, which eventually were more important, were also discovered in 1844 and a little ore began to be smelted locally and also shipped to the Pittsburgh region, but it was not until 1873 that the iron ore output reached 1,000,000 tons annually.

Meanwhile, the discovery of gold in California (see California Gold Rush) diverted public interest from the production of more useful minerals, which, however, continued, especially iron and coal mining. Anthracite[w] had begun to be shipped to Philadelphia for domestic heating and power purposes about 1800 and its production grew steadily; bituminous coal[w] had also become a commodity of importance after steam engines came into use and it was also used to produce coke for iron smelting. There was always more mineral production east of the Mississippi River than west of it, though in popular interest the West far exceeded the East.

California gold not only furnished a supply of that metal at a time when it was economically important but was also a powerful incentive for rapid settlement. The slightly later discovery of gold in Colorado had a similar effect there, and the same is true of mineral production in South Dakota, Montana, Idaho, Nevada and the southwest region. Utah, on the contrary, was settled as an agricultural region and only later became of great importance as a mineral producing region. Some districts, especially in Nevada, were short-lived while others, like the Homestake, South Dakota, have been persistent, but all facilitated the establishment of a normal society in the unsettled regions of the West. Mining on public land caused the passage of the Federal mining laws of 1866 and 1872, and the defects in this legislation created many difficulties that were interwoven in a complex way into the gradual development of a public land policy, and the final enactment of a leasing law, in 1920, under which petroleum, coal and certain other types of deposits would thereafter be leased, not sold. Though mineral production in the United States after 1900 amounted to more than in all its previous history, the mineral deposits had by that time mostly passed into private hands and, with few exceptions, mineral production from claims located on public land is now only of historic interest.

[T. A. Rickard, *A History of American Mining.*]
                                    T. T. READ

Mines, United States Bureau of, was established in the Department of the Interior[w] by act of Congress approved May 16, 1910. Presidential orders transferred the bureau to the Department of Commerce[w], July 1, 1925, and back again to the Department of the Interior, April 24, 1934. Its functions are: (1) to promote safer practices and healthier conditions in a hazardous occupation, (2) to conduct technological researches and disseminate scientific information of general benefit to the industry, and (3) to promote economic production and consumption and in other ways encourage the conservation of irreplaceable mineral resources.

[F. W. Powell, *The Bureau of Mines: Its History, Activities and Organization.*]   OLIVER W. HOLMES

Mingo Bottom (Ohio), a region about three miles south of Steubenville, so named from Mingo[qv] Indians who frequented it in the 18th century. During the Revolutionary War it became a rendezvous for white expeditions against Indians farther west. From Mingo Bottom, March 4, 1782, frontiersmen under Col. David Williamson marched to Gnadenhutten[qv] and massacred nearly 100 Christian Indians. The expedition of Col. William Crawford assembled there in May, 1782, and thither the survivors fled after a disaster made famous by the capture and burning of Crawford[qv].

[Theodore Roosevelt, *Winning of the West.*]
ALFRED P. JAMES

Mingos, or Mingoes, were Indians of the great Mengwe family, better known as the Iroquois of the Five Nations[qv], who once dominated the upper reaches of the St. Lawrence, Hudson, Susquehanna and Ohio rivers. Their main habitat was in New York, but scattered groups dwelt elsewhere, sometimes as overlords of other Indians. These outlying Mengwes, as in the Ohio Valley were, by the whites, called Mingoes. They proved a great trouble to early frontiersmen.

ALFRED P. JAMES

Miniature, THE, in America, like its European prototype, was a small portable portrait painted on ivory, generally oval, that was highly popular during the 18th and early 19th centuries. Whereas both portraits in oil and in miniature were considered primarily as family documents, the oil portrait, with its frame, served as an article of interior furnishing, while the miniature, with its gold case, was used for personal adornment as a locket or as part of a bracelet.

John Singleton Copley (1738–1815), better known as a portrait painter in oils, his half brother, Henry Pelham (1749–1806), John Ramage (*ca.* 1748–1802), James Peale (1749–1831), and Charles Willson Peale (1741–1827) were some of the prominent 18th-century miniature painters.

The most important miniature painters during the 19th century were Edward Greene Malbone (1777–1807), who worked in Boston, New York and Charleston; Charles Fraser (1782–1860), who worked in Charleston; Benjamin Trott (*ca.* 1791–1841), who worked in Philadelphia and Baltimore; and Robert Field (died 1819), an Englishman who worked in Boston, Washington and Halifax, N. S.

In spite of their artistic quality for which they are now collected, miniatures have largely an historic value as records of likenesses. There is a small but excellent collection of miniatures at the Metropolitan Museum of Art.

[A. H. Wharton, *Heirlooms in Miniatures;* T. Bolton, *Early American Portrait Painters in Miniature;* H. B. Wehle, *American Miniatures.*]
THEODORE BOLTON

Minié Ball, THE, was invented in 1849 by Capt. Minié of the French army. This bullet had a deep tapered cavity in the base with a hemispherical iron cup fitted into it. The bullet was easily fitted into a muzzle-loading rifle, and the force of the explosion expanded the base of the bullet against the rifling of the barrel with resultant greater accuracy and range. The Minié ball was used extensively in the Civil War in the Model 1842 U. S. Rifle, caliber .69. In the American service a wooden plug was substituted for Capt. Minié's iron ring; the force of the explosion driving the plug into the cavity and expanding the bullet.

[A. O. P. Nicholson, *Reports of Experiments with Small Arms for the Military Service.*]
H. A. DeWEERD

Minimum-Wage Legislation and Cases. Minimum-wage legislation has been applied chiefly to industries employing women and minors. Appearing first in New Zealand (1894) and Australia (1896), it spread eventually to Great Britain and the United States. Massachusetts, the first American state to pass such a measure, enacted a minimum-wage law in 1912. Between 1912 and 1923 fourteen other states, the District of Columbia and Puerto Rico enacted similar legislation.

Early in 1914 the constitutionality of the Oregon law was questioned in the case of Stettler v. O'Hara (243 U. S. 649, 37 Sup. Ct. 475, 1917). The statute had been upheld (1914) by the Supreme Court of Oregon as a valid exercise of the police power[qv] of the state. Appeal was made to the United States Supreme Court, which in 1917 approved the law in a four to four decision, Justice Brandeis abstaining from voting because he had previously defended the law as counsel before the Oregon Supreme Court.

In spite of this favorable decision, the movement has progressed with great difficulty. The Nebraska law was repealed in 1919, and the Texas law in 1921. Also, less favorable treatment awaited this type of legislation in the courts, for on April 9, 1923, in the Adkins v. Children's Hospital case[qv], the United States Supreme Court by a five to three decision held that the District of Columbia minimum-wage law was unconstitutional. The majority opinion declared that the statute limited women's freedom of contract as well as that of employers by setting wages without regard to the value of the workers' services, and hence was a violation of the "due process"[qv] clause in the Fifth Amendment. The Court's negative attitude was again manifested in the Arizona case (Sardell v. Murphy, 1925) and the Arkansas case (Donham v. West Nelson Manufacturing Co., 1927) in which such laws were held invalid as violations of the Fourteenth Amendment[W]. As a consequence, the courts of Kansas and Puerto Rico declared their respective statutes unconstitutional, and the attorney general of Minnesota held the law unconstitutional except for girls under eighteen years of age.

Depression conditions led to a revival of the movement in 1933. Seven states (Connecticut, Illinois, New Hampshire, New Jersey, New York, Ohio, Utah) passed minimum-wage laws. Massachusetts followed in 1934 and Rhode Island in 1936. All sought to avoid the danger of unconstitutionality. Prior to the decision in the District of Columbia case most of the laws fixed a minimum wage on the basis of the cost of living. This new type of measure did not attempt to regulate wages, but provided for investigation of any occupation in which a substantial number of women and minors were receiving less than a living wage, and then, on the basis of discovered facts, set a wage "fairly and reasonably commensurate with the value of services rendered" and sufficient to meet the minimum cost of living necessary for health and well-being.

In 1936 minimum-wage legislation was dealt another severe blow by the United States Supreme Court when, by a five to four decision, the New York law was held unconstitutional (Morehead v. Tipaldo). As in the District of Columbia case, the Court judged the statute an unreasonable interference with the freedom of employers and employees to contract in the realm of wages. The situation changed quickly, however, when in 1937 the Court upheld the validity of the minimum-wage law of the State of Washington (West Coast Hotel Co. v. Parrish[W]). In a five to four decision the Court held that such measures do not constitute an unwarranted interference with the right of freedom of contract. The decision in effect validates all minimum-wage legislation and makes it clear that it is quite within the police power of the several states to safeguard the standard of living of women and minors. By July 1, 1939, the District of Columbia, the territory of Alaska, Puerto Rico and twenty-eight states had enacted minimum-wage laws. The states included Arizona, Arkansas, California, Colorado, Connecticut, Illinois, Kansas, Kentucky, Louisiana, Maine, Massachusetts, Minnesota, Nebraska, Nevada, New Hampshire, New Jersey, New York, North Dakota, Ohio, Oklahoma, Oregon, Pennsylvania, Rhode Island,

South Dakota, Texas, Utah, Washington and Wisconsin.

One of the important developments in minimum-wage legislation in the United States was the passage of the Fair Labor Standards Act[W], signed by the President on June 25, 1938. This measure provided for the establishment of minimum-wage rates for employees engaged in industries in or affecting interstate commerce.

[Barbara N. Armstrong, *Insuring the Essentials*; J. R. Commons and J. B. Andrews, *Principles of Labor Legislation*; E. M. Burns, *Wages and the State*; U. S. Bureau of Labor Statistics, *Minimum Wage Legislation in Various Countries*, Bulletin No. 467, 1928.]

GORDON S. WATKINS

Mining. *See* Coal Mining and Organized Labor; Iron Mining; Gold Mines and Mining; Silver Prospecting and Mining; Lead Mining; Salt.

Mining Camp, The Law of the. The early mining camps of California and Colorado had a law of their own because the United States had not yet established civil government in the regions suddenly made populous by the gold seekers. When a group of miners found a promising spot they quickly formed a mining district, defined its boundaries, passed laws regulating the filing and working of claims and elected officers. A president and recorder kept track of each miner's claims. A sheriff preserved order. Disputes were settled by the miners' court, an open meeting of miners at which both sides were heard and decisions rendered by those present. To promote discovery the finder of a new vein or placer[W] could have two claims. To insure equality of opportunity others could then pre-empt one claim each on that vein. The size of claims varied in each district, but 100 feet long by 50 feet wide was most common for lode[W] claims. Claims must be recorded and must be worked a specified number of days each year. Usual punishments were hanging, shaving of head with banishment, whipping or paying fine. This born-of-necessity and extralegal law of the mining camps established titles to the mines which were recognized by the United States in its mineral patent law[W] of 1866.

[C. H. Shinn, *Mining Camps*; T. M. Marshall, *Early Records of Gilpin County, Colorado*; P. S. Fritz, *Constitutions and Laws of Early Mining Districts*.]

PERCY S. FRITZ

Mining Towns. The location of mining towns is determined by the location of the deposits, whether mineral, coal or oil. All are monuments to the drama of mining, but none more so than the mining towns born in a gold rush. The towns originate in the desire of the miners to be near their place of work. Others come flocking to serve the miners' needs.

The towns are usually boom towns. Flimsy temporary structures dominate. Because of this fact practically every mining town has been destroyed by fire. After this they are usually more substantially rebuilt. San Francisco, gateway to the California mining towns, had five fires in the million dollar class, 1849–51. The fire of May 4, 1851, almost completely destroyed the city. Denver, born in the Colorado gold rush (*see* Pikes Peak Gold Rush), was swept by fire April 19, 1863. Central City, Colo., completely destroyed by fire in 1874, was rebuilt mostly of stone. More recent mining towns have not escaped the same fate, e.g., Cripple Creek, Colo., in 1896 and Nome, Alaska, in 1934.

Another characteristic of mining towns is their rapid growth. Leadville, Colo., started in 1877, grew to a city of 10,000 inhabitants within two years. Nevada City, Calif., was another town which showed phenomenal growth in a few months. Mining towns show a much greater fluctuation in population than other towns, except seasonal resorts. Some early mining towns have already developed other dominant interests, like Oroville, Calif., with its fruit raising, or Gold Hill, Colo., which is a mountain resort. Other mining towns are today "ghost cities," their buildings still standing, but deserted. Kokomo, Colo., a ghost town, claims historic interest because it is the highest incorporated town (altitude 10,618 feet). Nevadaville, Colo., and Rhyolite, Nev., are other ghost cities. But as some die, new ones are born as, for example, Climax, Colo., the site of the greatest molybdenum mine in the world, and Uravan, Colo., whose prosperity like its name is based on the two rare metals, uranium and vanadium.

[H. H. Bancroft, *Works*, Vol. XXIII; C. H. Shinn, *Mining Camps;* G. C. Quiett, *Pay Dirt.*]

PERCY S. FRITZ

Minisink Indian Raid (1779). To divert attention from the Sullivan-Clinton expedition[w] against Iroquois strongholds, Joseph Brant and his Indians raided Minisink, N. Y., on July 20, 1779. They were pursued by 149 men under Col. Hathorne and attacked on July 22 near Lackawaxen ford. Though considerably outnumbering the combined troops of Hathorne, Tusten and Meeker, Brant won only after a hard struggle, losing many men. The principal object was not achieved; Sullivan and Clinton proceeded as planned and Brant considered the Minisink raid a disappointment.

[Howard Swiggett, *War out of Niagara;* H. E. Twichell, *History of the Minisink Country;* C. E. Stickney, *History of the Minisink Region.*]

ARTHUR POUND

Minisink Patent, THE, granted in 1704 by Lord Cornbury to Stephen DeLancey, Matthew Ling and twenty-two associates, was a vast tract, lying in the southern parts of Orange and Sullivan counties, N. Y., bounded on the south by Pennsylvania and on the north by the Hardenbergh patent.

[C. E. Stickney, *A History of the Minisink Region;* Russel Headley, *The History of Orange County.*]

A. C. FLICK

Minneapolis. *See* Twin Cities, The.

Minnesota bears a Sioux name, meaning sky-tinted or turbid water, which originally was applied to the river that joins the Mississippi near the Twin Cities[w]. Among geographic factors that have influenced the state's history are its more than ten thousand lakes and its central position. Within its borders are three river systems, the Mississippi, St. Louis and Red, flowing, respectively, southward to the gulf, eastward to the St. Lawrence and northward toward Hudson Bay.

French explorers, taking advantage of this water highway system, were early on the scene. Radisson[w] and Groseilliers, traders and adventurers, probably visited Minnesota on their "voyages" to the Northwest between 1654 and 1660, and they were followed by a long line of explorers, including DuLhut[w] from 1679 to 1689, Father Hennepin[w] in 1680, LeSueur in 1700, LaPerrière in 1727, and the Vérendryes[w] in the 1730's and 1740's. Among French outposts in the Minnesota wilderness were Forts L'Huillier, Beauharnois[w] and St. Charles[w].

Eastern Minnesota remained under French control until 1763, when it became British. Among the explorers and traders of the British period were Jonathan Carver, 1766–67; Peter Pond, 1773–75; and David Thompson, noted cartographer, 1797–98. The British developed an extensive Indian trade, with Grand Portage[w] on the north Superior shore serving as the western headquarters of the North West Company[w] until about 1803. Minnesota east of the Mississippi came under American sovereignty by the Definitive Treaty of Peace of 1783[w], and four years later it became part of the Northwest Territory. British traders continued to operate in Minnesota, however, until after the War of 1812. The American Fur Company[w] then took over the field.

White men in Minnesota came into contact with two Indian nations, the Sioux and the Chippewa[ww]. About the middle of the 18th century, the Chippewa, an Algonquian people migrating westward and armed with guns, forced the Sioux from their ancient wooded lands into the prairie country farther south and west. Conflict between these tribes continued until well after Minnesota was settled by white men. Zealous missionaries worked among both the Sioux and the Chippewa.

Minnesota west of the Mississippi was nominally part of the Spanish empire for forty-one years preceding its transfer to the United States as part of the Louisiana Purchase^{qv}. To explore the new region, conciliate the Indians and obtain fort sites, Zebulon M. Pike^{qv} was sent into the Minnesota country in 1805. At the mouth of the Minnesota River he secured from the Sioux the site of the post later known as Fort Snelling^{qv}, established in 1819.

Explorers of the Northwest henceforth made this fort the objective or point of departure for their expeditions. Among them were Lewis Cass, 1820; Giacomo C. Beltrami and Maj. Stephen H. Long^{qv}, 1823; Henry R. Schoolcraft, who discovered Lake Itasca, the source of the Mississippi, in 1832; and Joseph N. Nicollet, who mapped the Northwest in the late 1830's.

By treaties in 1837 the United States purchased from the Indians the triangle of land between the lower St. Croix and the Mississippi. Settlements, such as Stillwater, Marine and St. Paul, began to appear as lumbermen, farmers and town builders arrived. In 1849 Minnesota Territory was established, its boundaries extending northward from Iowa to the Canadian line and westward from Wisconsin to the Missouri. Alexander Ramsey of Pennsylvania was appointed its first governor.

Much of the southeastern and central part of Minnesota was opened to settlement by treaties with the Sioux in 1851 (*see* Traverse des Sioux, Treaty of); and large areas farther north were made available by Chippewa treaties in 1854 and 1855. After 1851 southeastern Minnesota was rapidly settled, large numbers of Germans, Scandinavians, Irish and English joining the native American pioneers. A great boom came on and Minnesotans, increasing from 6077 in 1850 to 157,037 in 1857, asked for statehood. The Kansas question delayed admission, but finally, on May 11, 1858, Minnesota, with its present boundaries, took its place among the states. The first state governor was the Democratic Henry H. Sibley, who had settled at Mendota as an agent of the American Fur Company in 1834. The land boom was checked by the Panic of 1857^{qv} and the young state soon faced the double ordeal of the Civil War and the Sioux Uprising^{qv}, the latter occurring in August, 1862, when the Sioux rose against the whites.

Railroad building began in 1862 with the completion of ten miles (from St. Paul, the capital, to St. Anthony, later incorporated into Minneapolis) by the St. Paul and Pacific. This road, reorganized under James J. Hill's leadership after the Panic of 1873^{qv}, eventually became the Great Northern^{qv}. The Northern Pacific^{qv}, completed in 1883, was the first railroad to connect Minnesota with the Pacific coast. In the modern development of the state, railroads have played an important role, as have lumbering, wheat raising, flour milling and dairying. The exploitation of the Vermilion, Mesabi^{qv} and Cuyuna ranges made Minnesota a national center for iron^{qv} mining. A special feature of Minnesota industry has been the growth of co-operative marketing, especially in dairying. Minnesota's population increased from 172,023 in 1860 to 2,563,953 in 1930.

Ramsey, succeeding Sibley as governor, opened a long period of Republican control, leaders including such men as John S. Pillsbury, Cushman K. Davis and Knute Nelson. Agrarian opposition, however, was voiced by third parties from Grangers to Populists^{qv}, with Ignatius Donnelly as an outstanding leader; and three Democrats, John Lind, John A. Johnson and W. S. Hammond, served as governors, respectively, from 1899 to 1901, from 1905 to 1909 and in 1915. Prominent in the more recent political history of the state were such men as Charles A. Lindbergh, Sr., Moses E. Clapp and Frank B. Kellogg. The Nonpartisan League appeared during the World War years, and the Farmer-Labor party^{qv}, organized soon thereafter, was strong enough to send two senators to Washington in 1922-23. In 1930 this party won power in state affairs with the election of Floyd B. Olson as governor, and it maintained control until 1939, when the Republicans, successful in the fall election of 1938, were returned to power.

[W. W. Folwell, *A History of Minnesota; Minnesota History: A Quarterly Magazine; Minnesota Historical Collections;* T. C. Blegen, *Building Minnesota* and *Minnesota: Its History and Its People.*]   T. C. BLEGEN

Minnesota Massacre. *See* New Ulm, Defense of.

Minnesota Moratorium Case (Home Building and Loan Association v. Blaisdell et al., 290 U. S. 398, 1934) . At the height of the depression which began in 1929, many property owners whose properties were covered by a mortgage were unable to meet the regular interest payments. Under long-established rules of law, the holders of these mortgages had a right to foreclose. Property owners importuned their legislators for relief. In 1933, in Minnesota and some other states, so-called mortgage moratorium^{qv} acts were adopted. These acts were immediately attacked on constitutional grounds. On the one hand, it was contended that they constituted a violation of the contract clause in the Federal Constitution (*see* Fletcher v. Peck), and of the due process and equal protection clauses of the Fourteenth Amendment*qv*, while on the other the existence of an emergency situation was stressed. The Minnesota act was sustained by the state supreme court, and later, on appeal, by the United States Supreme Court. While the latter contended that an emergency does not create power, it admitted that an emergency may furnish occasion for the exercise of power. The conditions upon which the period of redemption was extended did not appear to the majority of the Court to be unreasonable; furthermore, the act was definitely temporary in character, its life being limited to the exigency which called it forth.

[Robert E. Cushman, *Constitutional Law in 1933-34*, American Political Science Review, February, 1935.]
W. BROOKE GRAVES

Minor v. Happersett (21 Wallace 162, 1875). The first section of the Fourteenth Amendment*qv* provides that "no state shall make or enforce any law which shall abridge the privileges or immunities of citizens of the United States." Virginia L. Minor, a citizen of Missouri, the wife of a St. Louis lawyer, when rejected in her attempt to register in 1866 as a voter in that state, maintained that the right of suffrage was a privilege of United States citizenship. In rejecting this contention, the Supreme Court held that the right of suffrage is not coextensive with citizenship, that the Fourteenth Amendment does not add to the privileges or immunities of citizens of the United States, but merely furnishes an additional guarantee for those in existence, and that, if the purpose of the Amendment had been to make all citizens voters, it would have been unnecessary to adopt the Fifteenth Amendment*qv*. In the opinion, the Court, for the first time, also gave a definition of citizenship, declaring that a citizen is one who owes allegiance to the state of which he is a member, and to whom the state owes protection.

[K. H. Porter, *A History of Suffrage in the United States;* B. R. Trimble, *Chief Justice Waite.*]
THOMAS S. BARCLAY

Minority, Rights of the. On Feb. 8, 1788, the 51st number of the *Federalist*qv pointed out that a republic must not only be on guard against oppression by its rulers but must also protect "one part of the society against the injustice of the other part. . . . If a majority be united by a common interest, the rights of a minority will be insecure." Separation of powers*qv* and constitutional limitations would check abuses by rulers, and the diversity of "interests, parties, and sects" would render unlikely the control of the National Government by oppressive coalitions. On the other hand, the *Federalist* declared, the narrow limits of a state, if left to itself, would produce insecurity of rights against "factious majorities." The course of American history has, on the whole, verified these predictions.

The Fourteenth Amendment*qv* added a protection against arbitrary state action. While frontal attacks on minority rights were infrequent, possession of police power*qv*, control of education and the taxing power enabled the states to encroach on minority rights under the guise of general legislation. Such recent decisions of the Supreme Court as Meyer v. Nebraska, 262 U. S. 390, 1923, Near v. Minnesota*qv*, 283 U. S. 697, 1931, or Norris v. Alabama, 294 U. S. 587, 1935 (*see* Scottsboro Case), show that minority and individual rights need constant protection. With the growth of Federal regulatory power similar problems have appeared in the national field. Here the guarantees of the first ten amendments are a vital factor and here, too, as James Bryce pointed out, the Supreme Court, "the conscience of the people," performs an all-important function as "the guarantee of the minority, who, when threatened by the impatient vehemence of a majority, can appeal to this permanent law, finding the interpreter and enforcer thereof in a court set high above the assaults of faction." Constitutional guarantees are not self-executing but are most effective when formal legislation or acts of government are involved. It is well to remember that the United States has had an unenviable record of popular violence against minorities, aggravated in many cases by lack of efficient administrative machinery for keeping the peace and insuring justice.
W. A. ROBINSON

Minstrel Shows. The first appearance of a comic Negro character on the stage is said to have taken place in Boston in 1799. There were few such appearances until 1830, when Thomas D. Rice introduced his enormously popular song, "Jim Crow," in blackface makeup. The first known minstrel troupe was a quartette—including Dan Emmett, who later wrote "Dixie"*qv*—which appeared on the Bowery*qv* in 1843. Thereafter, many new troupes sprang up and grew in size. By 1857, when the famous Christy Minstrels appeared, the performance had settled into the standard pattern which endured ever afterward; a "first part," with the company seated in a semicircle, a white interlocutor and two "end men" who bandied jokes with him between vocal solos by others in the circle. Following this came the "olio," a variety entertainment, with dances, comic sketches and acrobatic turns. In the latter 19th century, when such entertainment was highly popular and there were scores of companies on the road, Haverly's was perhaps most famous, though Lew Dockstader, Primrose & West, Al G. Fields and others shared popularity with him toward the end and carried on after him. Beginning in 1853, Philadelphia had a permanent minstrel organization for three quarters of a century. Minstrelsy gradually died in the 20th century and was practically extinct by 1930, though the "first part" was heard in its original form on the radio as late as 1935.

[Edwin LeRoy Rice, *Monarchs of Minstrelsy*.]

ALVIN F. HARLOW

Mint, Federal. Robert Morris, Secretary of Finance, urged the Continental Congress*ᵠ*, in 1782, to establish a mint. In 1786 Congress ordered the Board of the Treasury to study the subject, but not until April 2, 1792, three years after the birth of the new government, was the creation of a mint authorized. It was set up in Philadelphia, then the national capital, in 1793, and remained there permanently after other government agencies had been removed to Washington. Silver coinage began in 1794 and that of gold in 1795. The staff at first consisted of eleven officers and clerks, nineteen workmen in the coining department and seven at the furnaces. The total coinage produced in 1794–95 was less than $500,000. Not until 1807 did the output exceed $1,000,000; but in 1851 nearly $63,500,000 was struck, all of it gold save about $800,000. In the earlier years the mint often lacked gold and silver with which to work. In 1820 it operated only part of the time because of this scarcity and the small demand for copper coins. In 1835 Congress established three branch mints—one at New Orleans and two in the new gold fields, at Charlotte, N. C., and Dahlonega, Ga. The one at New Orleans was taken over by the Confederates at the beginning of the Civil War and operated thus from Jan. 26 to May 31, 1861, then suspended. It did not resume work until 1879; ceased to coin in 1909 and became an assay office*ᵠ*. The mint at Dahlonega closed in 1861; that at Charlotte was used as barracks by Confederate soldiers and never operated thereafter. A branch mint was installed at San Francisco in 1854. Another was legally established at Denver in 1862, but no coins had yet been made there when in 1870 it was turned into an assay office. In 1895 it was again authorized to coin, but no money was made there until 1906. A sixth branch mint

began work at Carson City, Nev., in 1870; but its production was not great, and it closed in 1893. Another, authorized in 1864 at The Dalles, Oregon, was in process of construction in 1871 when destroyed by fire, and the project was abandoned. A mint authorized in 1902 at Manila, P. I., has had comparatively small output. By acts of 1846 and later, the various mints were made public depositories. The Bureau of the Mint was created by Congress, Feb. 12, 1873.

[Jesse P. Watson, *The Bureau of the Mint*.]

ALVIN F. HARLOW

Mints, Private, frequently appeared in new gold-producing areas, up to about 1860—first in Georgia and North Carolina, later in the West—and their coins, of original design, circulated freely. In California, in 1849–51, government money was so scarce that several private mints were set up; their coins, though not legal tender, were often accepted as such, they circulated widely and were accepted on deposit by banks. A little later, private mints functioned in Oregon, Utah and Colorado.

[John S. Dye, *Dye's Coin Encyclopedia*.]

ALVIN F. HARLOW

Minutemen. While the phrase "minute-man" goes back at least to 1756, the famous body developed under that name first appeared in the reorganization of the Massachusetts militia by the Worcester convention and the Provincial Congress*ᵠ* in 1774. To get rid of Tories*ᵠ* in the older militia, in September resignations of officers were called for in the three Worcester regiments, which were broken into seven and new officers elected. These officers were to enlist a third of the men in new regiments, which were specifically called (Sept. 21) regiments of minutemen, who were to elect their officers. The Provincial Congress, meeting in October, found the same process voluntarily going on in the militia of other counties, and directed its completion (Oct. 26). Thus a double system of regiments was established in the province, the minutemen to be ready for any emergency "at a minute's warning."

The formation of the minuteman regiments proceeded slowly. On Feb. 14, 1775, as returns which had been called for were not forthcoming, the Provincial Congress set May 10 for a complete return. None was ever made, and only scattered records show that while Marblehead organized its company on Nov. 7, 1774, Woburn, though close to Boston, did not vote to establish its minutemen until April 17, 1775, two days before the outbreak of war. No complete list of minutemen companies and regiments was possible, and only from town records, a few lists and the "Lexington alarm lists" of minutemen and militia alike can a fragmentary roster be patched together of an organization that never was finished.

On April 19 militia and minutemen turned out together to resist the British expedition to Concord. The men whom the British killed on Lexington^{qv} green were minutemen, and minutemen led the march down to Concord bridge. But militia were also in the column, and men of both kinds harried the British back to Boston. The minuteman organization was then abandoned by the Provincial Congress in organizing the Eight Months Army (*see* Washington's Eight Months Army). As this was formed, it drew men from both minutemen and militia; those who could not join went back into the militia, and the minutemen thenceforth disappeared in Massachusetts.

Other colonies organized their minutemen on the recommendation of the Continental Congress^{qv} (July 18, 1775) to enlist them for rounds of service on special brief enlistments. Maryland (August), New Hampshire (September) and Connecticut (December) are on record as accepting this plan, and Connecticut minutemen are credited with resisting Tryon's expedition against Danbury. There are statues to minutemen in Concord and Lexington, Mass., and Westport, Conn.

[Proceedings of each Provincial Congress, Massachusetts, Boston, 1838, containing also records of county conventions, 32 f., 99, 643 f.; or the same passages, for Provincial Congress only, in Force's *American Archives*, series 4, Vol. I; Lexington Alarm Lists (Applications for pay of individual companies) in *Massachusetts Archives*; Allen French, *First Year of the American Revolution*.]
                                            ALLEN FRENCH

Miramar, Convention of, was a treaty between France and Mexico infringing upon the Monroe Doctrine^{qv}. It was signed April 10, 1864, in Maximilian's Miramar castle, overlooking the Adriatic from near Trieste, immediately after his acceptance of the proffered Mexican throne (*see* Mexico, French in). The French army was to withdraw, but 25,000 Frenchmen would stay to become a part of Maximilian's Mexican army. Mexico was to pay 1000 francs a year per man, other sustaining costs extra, and an additional 270,000,000 francs for previous costs of intervention. Bonds were to be issued to liquidate claims of French citizens. Thus Maximilian, before leaving Europe, saddled his regime with commitments that might well have doomed it without the subsequent American pressure.

[Percy F. Martin, *Maximilian in Mexico*.]
                                            JIM DAN HILL

Miranda's Intrigues. Threatened with incarceration in Cuba in 1783, Francisco de Miranda, a native of Caracas, fled from the Spanish military service to the United States. During a tour of this country which ended in December, 1784, Col. Miranda made the acquaintance of Gen. Washington, Gen. Knox and Alexander Hamilton. To several Americans he disclosed in more or less detail his plan to emancipate the Spanish Indies by the aid of foreign powers. From London, on the occasion of the Nootka Sound Controversy^{qv} in 1790, Miranda attempted in vain to interest Knox and Hamilton in the separation of the Spanish colonies from the motherland. After war broke out between England and Spain in 1796, he tried to get the American Government to enter into an alliance with England and with alleged Spanish American emissaries for the revolutionizing of the Indies, but largely because of the reluctance of President Adams this scheme was frustrated. Still, he continued to correspond with parties in America. Upon landing in New York from London, in the end of 1805, Miranda renewed his acquaintance with Col. W. S. Smith, Richard Rush and Rufus King; he met Aaron Burr, Secretary Madison and President Jefferson. Ex-Senator Jonathan Dayton, Dr. Thornton of the State Department, a merchant named Samuel Ogden, and a sea captain called Commodore Lewis also became interested in Miranda's revolutionary schemes (*see* Levy, The). Largely by the aid of Smith and Ogden, the promoter of revolutions succeeded in inducing some 200 recruits to embark on an ill-fated filibustering expedition which in February, 1806, was allowed to sail from New York City for South America.

[W. S. Robertson, *The Life of Miranda*.]
                                    WILLIAM SPENCE ROBERTSON

Miro, Fort, was the Spanish post established on the Ouachita River in 1785 by Don Juan Filhiol, on the site of the modern Monroe, La. First called "Ouachita Post" and later "Fort Miro," after Estevan Miro, Spanish governor of Louisiana from 1785 to 1791, it was given the modern name of Monroe in 1819.

[J. Fair Hardin, Don Juan Filhiol and the Founding of Fort Miro, the Modern Monroe, Louisiana, in *Louisiana Historical Quarterly*, XX.]
                                            WALTER PRICHARD

Miro-McGillivray Treaty. *See* Spanish-Indian Relations.

Miscegenation. Race mixture in the United States began soon after the early colonists settled along the Atlantic seaboard. Most of the mixed marriages were between whites of low status and

Indians or Negroes. These marriages were regarded with disfavor, especially those with Negroes, and as early as 1663 were forbidden by law in Maryland. As Negro slavery increased, marriages between whites and Negroes were forbidden quite generally in the Southern states, while they were permitted in several states of the North. But even in the North such marriages have been relatively infrequent. Curiously enough, most of these have been between Negro or mulatto men and white women; rarely the reverse. Marriages between white men and Indian women were fairly common during the pioneering days in the West.

Unquestionably most of the mulatto stocks in the United States originated in illegitimate unions between whites and blacks. Under slavery and for several years after emancipation, miscegenation went on rapidly, but for the past few decades, owing in part to an increasing sentiment against it in both races, it has been growing less frequent. The proportion of mulattoes to the total Negro population increased from 11.2% in 1850 to its maximum of 20.9% in 1910, and, if the census returns can be taken at their face value, declined to 15.9% in 1920, the last date at which mulattoes were separately recorded as such in the census.

[E. B. Reuter, *Race Mixture;* S. J. Holmes, *The Negro's Struggle for Survival.*]   S. J. HOLMES

Mischianza, THE, was the most elaborate, extravagant and romantically feudal *fête champêtre* given in 18th-century America. It was held at the Wharton estate, "Walnut Grove," on May 18, 1778, in honor of Sir William Howe, then occupying Philadelphia as commander of the British forces. The directing geniuses were Maj. John André and Capt. Oliver Delancey. The entertainment lasted from four o'clock on the afternoon of May 18 until four o'clock in the morning of the following day. Seven hundred and fifty invitations were issued, 330 covers were laid. The staff officers paid 3312 guineas and a London firm sold, it is said, £12,000 worth of silks, laces and other fine materials.

[*Century Magazine,* André's Account, Vol. XLVII; *Pennsylvania Magazine of History and Biography,* Vol. LX.]   JULIAN P. BOYD

Misiones Award was the decision ending an Argentine-Brazilian dispute over part of the Misiones Territory between the Iguassú and Uruguay rivers. After direct negotiations failed, the two governments asked President Grover Cleveland to arbitrate. On Feb. 5, 1895, he rendered an award upholding Brazil's contentions.

[M. W. Williams, The Treaty of Tordesillas and the Argentine-Brazilian Boundary Settlement, *Hispanic American Historical Review,* February, 1922.]   MARY WILHELMINE WILLIAMS

Missionaries and Diplomacy. American missionaries to foreign lands have represented, inevitably, more than the Christian Gospel. They have represented the American nation, as well, whether merely through their citizenship, their "unofficial good offices" as foreign counsellors in times of political conflict, or through services rendered as formally designated consular and diplomatic representatives of the American Government. As missionaries, they have often had unusual technical knowledge of languages, usages, etc., valuable in negotiations. And they have enjoyed an unusual degree of esteem and confidence throughout the range of international intercourse. Their citizenship, however, has involved controversy, at times, when their "treaty rights" have been in question. But often they themselves have been the agents of diplomatic adjustments—at whatever risk to their standing and influence as agents of the Christian Gospel. Examples: Dr. James L. Barton counseled with the American Government in certain phases of its dealings with Turkey and the Near East; S. Wells Williams served as interpreter with the Perry expedition*ᵛ* to Japan in 1853, and in 1856 was secretary and interpreter in Peking with the American legation. He was several times *ad interim* in charge of the legation. He was responsible for the clause in the Treaty of Tientsin, 1858, guaranteeing Chinese tolerance toward Christian workers.

[S. F. Bemis, *Diplomatic History of the United States;* J. W. Foster, *American Diplomacy in the Orient;* R. E. Speer, *Christianity and the Nations.*]   JOHN CLARK ARCHER

Missionary Activity in the Pacific. American missions in the Pacific were preceded by those of the Jesuits and other Catholic orders as well as by the London Missionary Society which began its labors in the South Seas in 1797. The American missionary activity in this area had its origin with the American Board of Commissioners for Foreign Missions, founded in 1810 in Massachusetts. Interest in Hawaii*ᵛ* was stimulated by the finding of an Hawaiian boy, Obookiah (a refugee from tribal wars who had been brought to America), weeping at the door of a classroom in Yale College because of his desire for an education. In 1820 the American Board sent a party of seventeen led by Hiram Bingham and Asa Thurston to Honolulu to build churches and schools and to heal the sick. Members of the royal family of Hawaii were among the early adherents. American missions were established in

Samoa and the Micronesian Islands. Previous to 1898 American missionary effort was not directed toward the Philippine Islands. There is abundant testimony regarding the beneficent work of American missions in the South Seas. Especially in Hawaii, they gave the natives an alphabet, grammar and dictionary and preserved their language from extinction, translated the Bible and scientific books, established schools and taught the people to read and write.

[Rufus Anderson, *History of the Sandwich Islands Mission;* J. J. Jarves, *History of Hawaii;* Sheldon Dibble, *History and General Views of the Sandwich Islands.*]

KENNETH COLEGROVE

Missionary Association, The American, was formed by Congregationalists[qv] on Sept. 3, 1846, in Albany, N. Y., for the more effectual prosecution, especially of work previously undertaken by certain other Congregational societies among Negroes and Indians. It was actively opposed to Negro slavery, and as the crisis in this issue approached, it concentrated (1859 ff.) on work among Negroes. Its missionaries had been serving, also, in Africa, Egypt, Siam, Hawaii, Jamaica and Canada, as well as in the southern and western portions of the United States. Hampton Institute developed from work begun by it in 1861 among fugitive slaves on the shore of the bay into which the first American slave ship had sailed in 1619. It also founded Fisk University (independent since 1917), and many colleges (e.g., Talladega, LeMoyne, Tillotson) and schools which it still administers. In 1870 it resumed work among the Indians. In 1882 it transferred its foreign missions to another board. It entered Puerto Rico after the war with Spain, where it still shares in the work of the Evangelical Church. It operates more than 100 churches and mission stations, along with its many schools and several hospitals, as a division of the home boards of the recently united Congregational and Christian churches.

[*In America for America:* report of the Board of Home Missions of the Congregational and Christian Churches, New York, 1937.]

JOHN CLARK ARCHER

Missionary Ridge, Battle of (Nov. 25, 1863). To prevent reinforcement of Longstreet (C.), besieging Knoxville, Tenn.[qv], on Nov. 24, 1863, Grant (U.) ordered Hooker to attack Bragg's (C.) left on Lookout Mountain[qv]. The movement was successful. The next morning Thomas (U.) was directed to assault the Confederate center on Missionary Ridge; Sherman (U.) was ordered to turn Bragg's right and sever his communications southward; Hooker was to advance from Look-

out Mountain and get across Bragg's line of retreat. Sherman made repeated unsuccessful attacks against the Confederate right commanded by Hardee and Cleburne; Hooker's attack was held up. To prevent Bragg from reinforcing either wing of his army, Thomas, about noon, was ordered forward.

Bragg's defense was faulty. He had disposed one half his center at the foot of Missionary Ridge, with orders to retire and join the other half, stationed on the crest of the Ridge, if Thomas' advance should get within 200 yards. Bragg's artillery was nearly useless as it could not be sufficiently depressed to sweep the slope of the Ridge effectively. The Union troops had orders to halt at the foot of the Ridge, but as the Confederates promptly retreated, the Union soldiers took matters into their own hands. They must either go forward or retreat. Stopping only momentarily, the men rushed on, driving the disorganized Confederates from their positions on the top. Bragg's routed center and left moved eastward to the protection of Cleburne's command, which had successfully resisted Sherman. Before dark the battle was practically over. It only remained for Bragg to withdraw his defeated troops as best he could southward to Chickamauga Station and Dalton. Cleburne covered the retreat, halting Hooker's vigorous pursuit at Ringgold Gap[qv]. A week later Bragg relinquished his command of the Army of Tennessee[qv]. Hardee, temporarily in command, was soon succeeded by Gen. J. E. Johnston.

[*Battles and Leaders of the Civil War*, Vol. III.]

THOMAS ROBSON HAY

Missionary Societies, Home, are voluntary associations, usually under denominational control, for the advancement of religion in the needy parts of the United States. In the 18th century missions to the new settlements were sponsored on a small scale by such ecclesiastical units as Presbyterian synods, Baptist or Congregational associations[qv]. A revival of interest in evangelical religion, the growing spirit of humanitarianism[qv], and the realization of the vastness of the expanding frontier resulted in the establishment of many local missionary societies, especially in New England and New York, in the latter part of the 18th and early part of the 19th centuries; among these were the Missionary Society of Connecticut (1798), Massachusetts Missionary Society (1799), Maine Baptist Missionary Association (1804) and the United Domestic Missionary Society of New York (1822). Competition among the local societies led to the formation in 1826, by members of Congregational, Presbyterian, Associate Reformed and Dutch Reformed churches, of the American Home Missionary Society; it was intended to be national in scope and, within limits, interdenominational. Successive withdrawals of three of the constituent groups left this society entirely Congregational after 1861 (name changed to Congregational Home Missionary Society in 1893); the chief agency for those Presbyterians who did not co-operate with the American Home Missionary Society was the General Assembly's Board of Missions (1816). In order to advance their own interests, as well as to spread the gospel, the principal Protestant denominations have created similar organizations; examples, in addition to those mentioned above, include the Missionary and Bible Society of the Methodist Episcopal Church (1819), the Domestic and Foreign Missionary Society of the Protestant Episcopal Church (1821), the Baptist Home Mission Society (1832). The slavery controversy and church schisms on the eve of the Civil War resulted in the formation of the antislavery American Missionary Association^{q} (1846) and, on the other hand, of missionary societies affiliated with the Southern churches.

Throughout most of the 19th century the chief aim of home missionary societies was to send preachers to, and maintain churches on, the Western frontier; in recent years more attention has been paid to the foreign-born in the cities, to Negroes and to decadent rural communities in the Eastern states. The formation in the latter part of the 19th century of national denominational societies composed chiefly of women showed the influence of the feminist movement. Although concerned primarily with preaching, the home missionary movement has helped in the establishment of many colleges and academies in the West.

[*Baptist Home Missions in North America;* H. L. Burleson, *The Conquest of the Continent;* J. B. Clark, *Leavening the Nation;* H. P. Douglass, *The New Home Missions;* O. W. Elsbree, *The Rise of the Missionary Spirit in America; Historical Sketch of Board of Home Missions of the Presbyterian Church;* J. M. Reid and J. T. Gracey, *Missions and Missionary Society of the Methodist Episcopal Church;* Colin B. Goodykoontz, *Home Missions on the American Frontier.*]

COLIN B. GOODYKOONTZ

Missions. *See* California Missions; Dominicans; Franciscans; Indian Missions; Jesuit Missions.

Missions, Foreign, constitute a phase of the expansion of Christianity. More specifically, they represent a modern movement of the last two centuries, analogous to the rise in earlier times of the orders of preaching friars. Protestant missions followed, at first, Dutch, English and Dan-

ish conquests and colonization, whether in India, the East Indies or North America. The German Moravians were the first Protestants to undertake (in 1732) foreign missions apart from colonial expansion. The American movement received its initial impulse from England, where William Carey, the first great missionary herald, founded (1792) the Baptist Missionary Society, and himself undertook service in 1793 in India. In England began the formation by Protestant churches of missionary societies, which were organized for the spread of the gospel to the "uttermost parts" of the world, and for the conversion of all non-Christian peoples. There was at the time little critical reckoning with certain substantial elements in the non-Christian cultures and religions.

American participation began in 1810–11 with the organization of the American Board of Commissioners for Foreign Missions, a society which served the interests of Congregational, Presbyterian and Reformed churches. Thereafter, separate societies were formed by Baptists (1813), Methodist Episcopalians (1819), Protestant Episcopalians (1820), Presbyterians (1836–37), Lutherans (1839), and others, in turn. Bible societies, e.g., the American Bible Society^{q}, undertook the translation of Holy Scripture into the tongues of mission lands. The development of the foreign-missions enterprise was most notable between 1850 and 1930. In 1920, 236 American Protestant societies were operating through about 9000 missionaries, on an income of about $30,000,000. There has been recently considerable recession caused by reduction of income, unrest in mission lands, opposition from foreign cultures and religions and a reappraisal by the churches themselves of the gospel in relation to non-Christian faiths. There is reason to expect a continuance, however, of this essential enterprise in co-operation with universal religious factors, if not with the sole motive of conversion by a change of name.

[K. S. Latourette, *The Expansion of Christianity.* Among recent evaluations of the movement, one of the most exhaustive investigations of missions ever undertaken was the Laymen's Foreign Missions Inquiry, whose report was published in 1933.]

JOHN CLARK ARCHER

Missions, Frontier, grew out of the feeling among Christians in the older parts of the United States that it was their duty to send the gospel to the new settlements in the West. The frontier^{q} was usually regarded in the East as a region of crudeness, lawlessness and low moral standards. In religion it was thought to be characterized paradoxically both by irreligion and by excessive emotionalism (*see* Camp Meetings) ; unorthodox creeds, such as Mormonism[w], were thought to flourish there. But as the new territories increased in population and were admitted to the Union it became evident that the West would some-time hold the balance of power in the nation; hence it was imporant that "sound principles" be established in the frontier communities. An-other powerful motive was the rivalry between the various denominations to win adherents and to hold their own constituents in the new settle-ments; the spread of Roman Catholicism[w] espe-cially was an incentive for Protestant mission-ary activity. Disinterested Christian benevolence, however, is the chief explanation of home mis-sions.

Missions to the frontiers began early in the 18th century. By the opening of the 19th century the rapidly expanding field led to the organiza-tion of many local home missionary societies[w] in New England and New York. These in turn generally grew into or merged with national de-nominational societies between 1820 and 1835. Preachers and churches were the chief agencies employed, but academies and colleges were use-ful adjuncts. Among the more important Protes-tant denominations it appears that a majority of their congregations west of the Alleghenies have at some time received missionary assistance. In-dian missions, since they normally operated be-yond the frontier of settlement, were regarded as foreign missions.

[J. B. Clark, *Leavening the Nation;* O. W. Elsbree, *The Rise of the Missionary Spirit in America;* P. G. Mode, *The Frontier Spirit in American Christianity;* W. W. Sweet, *The Rise of Methodism in the West;* Colin B. Goody-koontz, *Home Missions on the American Frontier.*]

COLIN B. GOODYKOONTZ

Missions of the Southwest, THE. As a Spanish frontier institution the mission was meant to be a temporary, not a permanent device. It en-visaged the training of the aborigines for citizen-ship and economic self-dependence, a process which the first lawmakers expected would last some ten years only, after which period the mis-sion regime was to give way to civil and parochial organization. Along with the mission went the presidio or military guard. The two mutually supporting institutions formed in combination the essential spearhead of the Spanish advance into the wilderness.

In 1539 Fray Marcos de Niza made his famous journey along the road to Cíbola[w], and the year following Coronado[w] led his expedition in the same direction. With the latter were four Fran-ciscans[w], whose missionary activities in present New Mexico and beyond are the earliest record-ed for the Southwest. One of their number, Fray Juan de Padilla, settled among the Indians of Quivira, but while on his way to evangelize a tribe farther afield was slain by the natives, *ca.* 1544, being the first missionary so to die on Amer-ican soil. In the religious sphere the Southwest was pre-eminently Franciscan land, the bulk of missionary enterprise in that region being due to members of the Order of St. Francis.

Numerous missions were established within the limits of present-day New Mexico, Arizona and Texas. In New Mexico Fray Francesco de López and the lay brother Agustín Rodríguez were at work as early as 1581 among the Tigua Indians at Puaray, now Sandía, where they were mar-tyred. Mission centers multiplied with the years. In 1630 they were twenty-five in number, staffed by fifty friars and serving ninety pueblos with a Christian population of some 60,000. In 1680 the New Mexico missions, then numbering thirty-three, were destroyed in the great Pueblo revolt[w] of that year, which cost the lives of twenty-one missionaries. With the reconquest of New Mex-ico under Gov. de Vargas, in the last decade of the 17th century the missions were restored. In Arizona the three missions set up among the Hopi[w] or Moqui Indians, the first of which dated from 1628 or 1629, were swept away in the Pueblo revolt. Near the site of Tucson the Jesuit[w], Euse-bio Kino, "superb missionary, church-builder, explorer and ranchman," founded in 1700 the Mission of San Xavier del Bac. Within the two years following he founded also San Gabriel de Guevavi and San Cayetán del Tumacácori, all three missions being within the limits of Arizona. On the expulsion of the Jesuits in 1767 the three missions were taken over by the Franciscans, one of whom, Fray Francisco Garcés, labored at San Xavier del Bac with distinguished zeal. The first of the Texan missions was planted among the Jumano of La Junta near the present Presidio, 1683; the last foundation, Refugio, on Mission River, was in 1791. Outstanding among the Tex-an missionaries was the saintly Fray Antonio Margil de Jesús.

The missions of the Southwest declined during the 18th century and by the time of the Mexican War were practically nonexistent. Chief among the causes of decay was the process of seculariza-tion, which withdrew the Indians from the tute-lage of the friars and transferred administration of the mission temporalities from the latter to civil functionaries.

[J. G. Shea, *History of the Catholic Missions among the Indian Tribes of the United States;* H. E. Bolton, *The Rim of Christendom: a Biography of Eusebio Francisco Kino,* and *Spanish Explorations in the Southwest, 1542-1706;* C. E. Castañeda, *The Mission Era:* I, *The Finding of*

Texas, 1519-1693, II, *The Winning of Texas, 1693-1731*; Z. Engelhardt, *The Franciscans in Arizona.*]

GILBERT J. GARRAGHAN

Mississinewa, Battle of, was a result of an expedition led by Col. John B. Campbell against the Miami Indian villages on the Mississinewa River within the limits of the present Grant County, Ind. Nearly all the Miamis[qv] were in the service of the British. Gen. Harrison, then at Franklinton (Columbus, Ohio), decided to destroy them. Col. Campbell left Nov. 25, 1812, but was delayed at Dayton until Dec. 14. By forced marches he covered the remaining eighty miles in three days. In the early morning of Dec. 17 the troops attacked an Indian town, which was captured and burned. Following this three other villages were destroyed.

[Logan Esarey, *History of Indiana.*]

HARLOW LINDLEY

Mississippi, Army of (C.). On March 27, 1862, the Confederate troops under Gen. A. S. Johnston, known as the Army of Kentucky, retiring from Kentucky to Corinth, Miss.,[qv] were united with other troops gathered from various Southern points. The combined forces were called the Army of Mississippi. Gen. Beauregard was made second in command. At the death of Johnston at Shiloh[qv], Beauregard became commander of the army, but was soon succeeded by Gen. Braxton Bragg. In the summer of 1862, the army unsuccessfully invaded Kentucky. Following the return to Tennessee, it was reorganized, and on Nov. 20, 1862, was designated as the Army of Tennessee[qv].

[F. Phisterer, *Statistical Record.*]

THOMAS ROBSON HAY

Mississippi, Army of the (U.), was first constituted late in March, 1862, and consisted of troops, under Gen. John Pope, gathered to operate against Island No. 10[qv]. Later the army joined the forces collected by Halleck after the battle of Shiloh[qv] to besiege Corinth. When Pope was ordered to Virginia, Rosecrans assumed command. The Army of the Mississippi with that "of the Tennessee," combined under Grant, fought Confederate forces at Iuka and Corinth[qqv]. On Oct. 24, 1862, the Army of the Mississippi became the 13th Army Corps. In January, 1863, under McClernand, it enjoyed a brief existence as an independent army during the operations against Arkansas Post[qv].

[F. Phisterer, *Statistical Record.*]

THOMAS ROBSON HAY

Mississippi, Opening of the (1861–63). The strategic importance of controlling the Mississippi was recognized by both Federals and Confederates early in the Civil War. In the hands of the former it would afford an easy avenue for penetrating into enemy territory and separating the important states of Arkansas, Louisiana and Texas from the rest of the Confederacy; to the latter it served as a valuable artery for transporting troops and supplies and a connecting link between two important sections of their territory.

Thwarted in 1861 in their plan to hold the line of the Ohio River, the Confederates fortified Columbus, Ky., on the Mississippi; but the Federal capture of Forts Henry (Feb. 6, 1862) and Donelson[qqv] (Feb. 16, 1862) led to the evacuation of Columbus. Island No. 10[qv], in the Mississippi River near the Kentucky-Tennessee boundary, was then fortified by the Confederates, but Federal gunboats captured the island on April 7, 1862, leaving Fort Pillow, about midway between Island No. 10 and Memphis, as the northernmost river defense. However, Federal occupation of Corinth[qv], Miss., soon rendered Fort Pillow useless to the Confederates and it was abandoned; and on June 6, 1862, Memphis[qv] fell into Federal hands, thus opening the Mississippi as far south as Vicksburg.

Meanwhile, a Federal squadron under Farragut, operating from the Gulf of Mexico, had forced its way past the Confederate defenses at Forts Jackson and St. Philip, some sixty miles below New Orleans, and appeared before that city on April 25, 1862. New Orleans[qv] surrendered on May 1, 1862, and other river points as far up as Baton Rouge[qv] soon fell into Federal hands. The Confederates now strongly fortified the high bluffs at Port Hudson, twenty-five miles above Baton Rouge, and at Vicksburg, 200 miles to the northward, in an effort to preserve the valuable communication between the fertile Red River Valley and Confederate territory east of the Mississippi.

After several months of preliminary operations, Grant closed in on Vicksburg in the early summer of 1863, and Banks soon attacked Port Hudson[qv] from the rear, after Farragut had made an unsuccessful attempt to pass the fortifications with his gunboats on March 14, 1863, to go to the aid of Grant before Vicksburg. After a siege of nearly two months Vicksburg[qv] surrendered on July 4, 1863; and when the news reached Port Hudson that post also surrendered on July 9, 1863, being no longer of value to the Confederates. This completed the opening of the Mississippi, and Lincoln could write: "The Father of Waters again goes unvexed to the sea."

[James Ford Rhodes, *History of the Civil War, 1861-*

1865; James Kendall Hosmer, *The Appeal to Arms, 1861-1863;* Alcée Fortier, *History of Louisiana;* John S. Kendall, *History of New Orleans.*]

WALTER PRICHARD

Mississippi, Territory and State of, was first explored by DeSoto*ᵂ* who entered the present limits of the state in 1539. In 1682 LaSalle*ᵂ* descended the Mississippi River to its mouth and claimed possession of the entire basin for France, giving it the name Louisiana. Biloxi*ᵂ*, near the present town of that name, was founded by Iberville in 1699, and Natchez*ᵂ* was founded by Bienville in 1716. France ceded Louisiana to Spain in 1762 (*see* Fontainebleau, Treaty of), but Great Britain gained the portion east of the Mississippi as a result of the Treaty of Paris, 1763*ᵂ*. The lower third of the present states of Mississippi and Alabama was made part of the new British province of West Florida*ᵂ*. Spain occupied West Florida during the American Revolution, but the United States claimed that part north of the 31st parallel under the treaties with Great Britain of 1782 and 1783 (*see* Definitive Treaty of Peace, 1783) . Spain accepted this parallel as the northern boundary of West Florida in 1795 (*see* Pinckney's Treaty) .

Mississippi Territory was organized under the act approved April 7, 1798. It included the area between the 31st parallel and the parallel of the mouth of the Yazoo River, and between the Mississippi and Chattahoochee. The addition, in 1804, of the country south of Tennessee, and, in 1812, of the region between the Pearl and Perdido rivers, enlarged the Territory to what is now included in Alabama and Mississippi.

The territorial government was similar to that provided for Ohio under the Ordinance of 1787*ᵂ* except that slavery was permitted. As first constituted, the government consisted of a governor, secretary and three judges, all appointed by the President. Until provision was made for a legislature by the act approved May 10, 1800, all laws were enacted by the governor and judges, a circumstance which made the first administration, that of Winthrop Sargent, very unpopular. The territory was first administered from Natchez, and after 1801, from the near-by town of Washington.

Mississippi was admitted as a state Dec. 10, 1817, and at the same time the eastern half was organized as Alabama Territory. The opening to settlement of the Indian lands within the state in 1830 and 1832 (*see* Indian Removal) brought a rush of immigration, and the total population increased from 75,448 in 1820 to 375,651 in 1840. Jefferson College had been founded at Washington in 1803, and in 1844 the University of Mississippi was established at Oxford. Other educa-

tional facilities were provided by such private schools as Franklin Academy, established in 1821 at Columbus, and Hampstead Academy, established in 1826, now Mississippi College, at Clinton. There was virtually no public education.

Agriculture was the dominant interest of the state. However, the plantation system*ᵂ* of the western delta country supported a type of society which was quite different from that of the small upland farms in the northern part, and vastly different from that of the "Piney Woods"*ᵂ* area east of Pearl River. By 1840 these differences were discernible in the political alignments of the time, with the conservative Whig party*ᵂ* drawing its strength from the planter-dominated society of the river counties, and the Democrats*ᵂ* being supported by the less prosperous landholders of the rest of the state. This sectionalism has continued to be of fundamental importance in the history of the state. Politics in the period 1830–50 centered on the questions of banking, bond repudiation and internal impovements*ᵠᵂ*.

Majority opinion in Mississippi opposed secession when the issue was raised during the nullification*ᵂ* controversy in South Carolina in 1833, and the question remained largely academic in the years thereafter. Most of the people acquiesced in the Compromise of 1850, but the infractions of the fugitive slave law, the Kansas struggle and the rise of the Republican party, led to a militant advocacy of secession*ᵠᵂ*. Mississippi seceded Jan. 9, 1861, and one of her citizens, Jefferson Davis, was elected President of the Confederacy*ᵂ*.

The struggle for control of the Mississippi River inevitably made the state a main theater of the war. Corinth, Iuka, Holly Springs*ᵠᵂ* and Oxford were occupied in 1862. The capital, Jackson*ᵂ*, was captured in May, 1863, and the state government was moved first to Columbus, and then to Macon. The surrender of Vicksburg*ᵂ*, July 4, 1863, was followed by Sherman's march*ᵂ* from Meridian across the state in January, 1864. By the end of the war most places had at some time been occupied by Federal troops.

Mississippi declared slavery illegal and the act of secession void in a constitutional convention which met Aug. 14, 1865. The legislature, however, rejected the Thirteenth Amendment, and enacted the "Black Code"*ᵠᵂ* to control the Negroes. With the advent of congressional reconstruction*ᵂ*, the so-called "Black and Tan Convention" was elected in 1868. This convention, largely composed of Negroes, "carpetbaggers" and "scalawags,"*ᵠᵂ* formulated a second constitution which virtually restricted the suffrage to the freedmen*ᵂ* and their white cohorts. It was not accepted by the people until 1869, after its objectionable features had been removed.

Mississippi was readmitted Feb. 23, 1870, but continued under a reconstruction government until 1875. In that year a threat of armed force from the organized white citizens of the state induced Gov. Ames to dismiss his Negro militia, and a "white election" was held which swept the carpetbag government from office. Political reconstruction was completed with the adoption of the constitution of 1890. This prescribed a literacy test[w] for voters which has effectively prevented the exercise of Negro suffrage. The 1890 constitution, which succeeded those adopted in 1817, 1832 and 1869, is the present law of the state.

Economic reconstruction was retarded by the disastrous floods of 1867 and the yellow fever[w] epidemic of 1878. The share cropping[w] system, a legacy of the war, hindered advancement in agriculture. Moreover, certain depressing factors: an undiversified agriculture, an absence of manufactures and an inadequate educational system, had been present before 1861.

In 1870 the counties were compelled to provide for public education. Schools such as the Agricultural and Mechanical College, established at Starkville in 1879, and the agricultural high schools, started in 1910, improved farming methods. The construction of a market road system, the restoration of certain depleted and eroded areas and the development of the long-leaf pine industries are important recent advances, but the basic problem of land tenure has yet to be met. The need for new industries was recognized as early as 1882 by Gov. Robert Lowry, and in recent years the influx of factories into the state has assumed significant proportions.

[J. F. H. Claiborne, *Mississippi as a Province, Territory and State;* Dunbar Rowland, *History of Mississippi;* P. L. Rainwater, *Mississippi: Storm Center of Secession, 1856-1861;* J. W. Garner, *Reconstruction in Mississippi.*]

EDGAR B. NIXON

"Mississippi Bubble" is the term commonly applied to the disastrous failure of John Law's scheme for exploiting the resources of French Louisiana. After Antoine Crozat[w] surrendered his charter in 1717, John Law, a Scotchman who had previously gained an enviable reputation in France as a successful banker and financier, organized the Compagnie de l'Occident (Western Company), also known as the Mississippi Company, to assume control of Louisiana on Jan. 1, 1718. Law's reputation caused the stock to sell readily, and the organization soon enlarged the scope of its activities by absorbing several other commercial companies, its name then be-

ing changed to the "Company of the Indies." Enormous profits were anticipated from the operations of the company, and the increasing demand for its stock led to wild speculation which drove the price of shares to high figures, without any sound basis in tangible assets. Many Frenchmen invested their all in the company's stock. A few, who sold at the right moment, reaped fortunes from their speculation; but the majority held their stock in expectation of greater profits. The anticipated immense and immediate profits were not realized, and soon the scheme revealed itself as a purely speculative venture. In 1720 the company failed, the "bubble" burst, and the stockholders lost their entire investments, many being completely ruined. Law's connection with the venture ceased, but the company retained control of Louisiana until 1731.

[Charles Gayarré, *History of Louisiana;* Alcée Fortier, *History of Louisiana.*]   WALTER PRICHARD

Mississippi Company of Virginia, THE (1763), was organized by a group of men, most of whom were members of the original Ohio Company of Virginia[w], including Thomas and Arthur Lee, George Washington and others, for the purpose of procuring a huge tract of land at the junction of the Ohio and Mississippi rivers. Their hopes were soon dampened, however, by the Proclamation of 1763[w] which prohibited land grants and settlements west of the Appalachian Mountains. The company continued its existence, however, and Arthur Lee was its representative in London in 1768 when the Treaty of Fort Stanwix[w] again opened opportunities for western settlements. He pressed the claims of the Mississippi Company which was now asking for 2,500,000 acres to lie between the Alleghenies and the Ohio and the 38th and 42nd parallels. From that time to 1775 the British secretary of colonial affairs was besieged by the Ohio Company, the Indiana Company and the Vandalia Company[qw] for grants of land which overlapped the grant sought by the Mississippi Company. The approach of the American Revolution terminated the hopes of the Mississippi Company, as well as the hopes of the other companies.

[Clarence W. Alvord, *The Mississippi Valley in British Politics.*]   R. J. FERGUSON

Mississippi Deltas, The Blockade off the. Prior to the capture of New Orleans[w] the chief task of Federal naval ships in the Gulf was to blockade the mouths of the Mississippi River. Late in May, 1861, the two main ship channels, Pass à L'Outre and South West Pass, were blockaded by Commander C. H. Poor in the screw sloop *Brooklyn* and Lt. D. D. Porter in the side-wheeler *Powha-tan*. Deep draft and poor maneuverability in narrow waters prevented these vessels from entering the river in chase of suspicious craft, and unsupported by light auxiliaries they could do little to police the four secondary passes between the two main channels. When Commander Poor ill-advisedly left his station on June 30 to block a secondary pass, Commander Raphael Semmes in the Confederate raider *Sumter* made his famed escape through Pass à L'Outre. The difficulty of stopping all the mouths of the Mississippi from the outside led to an effort to establish a base within the river at Head of the Passes; but this was thwarted by the Confederate ironclad ram *Manassas*. Since New Orleans had, in addition to the Delta passes, lateral outlets via Lake Pontchartrain*ᵠ* and Barataria Bay, it proved impossible for the Federals with their shortage of ships to establish an effective blockade: a fact which materially influenced the decision to attempt the capture of New Orleans itself.

[*Official Records . . . Navies*, Ser. I, Vol. IV; R. S. West, Jr., *The Second Admiral*.]

RICHARD S. WEST, JR.

Mississippi Plan, THE (1876 f.) , was a practice occurring generally in the South in the 1870's, and even as late as the 1890's, under various names such as the Edgefield or Shotgun Policy, to discourage Negroes from voting. In contrast to the violence of the earlier Ku Klux Klan*ᵠ*, this device was a more subtle means of intimidation, and it did not become customary until Federal troops were withdrawn. Roughly, it refers to the practice by Southern whites of carrying firearms on Election Day, ostensibly for hunting, but actually as a veiled threat to the Negro. Occasionally a gun would "accidentally" go off in the direction of some Negro around the polls.

[J. G. Randall, *The Civil War and Reconstruction*.]

GERALD M. CAPERS, JR.

Mississippi Plan, THE (1890 f.) , disfranchising the Negro, adopted by the Mississippi constitutional convention of 1890, required every citizen, twenty-one to sixty, to be able to display his poll tax*ᵠ* receipt; one had to be able to read the Constitution, or understand it when read to him, or give a reasonable interpretation thereof. This permitted registration officials to discriminate between white and black illiterates. Furthermore, citizens were disfranchised for crimes Negroes were prone to commit, as theft, arson and wife beating. Six other Southern states made similar constitutional changes, 1895 to 1910. In Williams v. Mississippi*ᵠ* (1896) the Supreme Court upheld these suffrage provisions.

[Kirk Porter, *A History of Suffrage in the United States*.]

OSCAR S. DOOLEY

Mississippi River, Free Navigation of, from its headwaters to its mouth was important to inhabitants of the interior Mississippi Valley at a time when the river was their main highway of commerce and its mouth was owned by a foreign power. The establishment of the right was an important step in the world-wide liberation of commerce. It was first granted by France, which then owned Louisiana*ᵠ*, in favor of Great Britain and was a by-product of the territorial settlement at the end of the French and Indian War (*see* Paris, Treaty of, 1763). At the same time France ceded Louisiana to Spain (*see* Fontainebleau, Treaty of) . During the American Revolution both British subjects and American citizens claimed the right of free navigation and Spain permitted both of them to navigate it for a time —the British until 1779, when Spain went to war with Britain, and the Americans until 1784, when Spain closed the river to all foreigners, mainly in the hope of checking the growth of American settlements in the West. During and just after the Revolutionary War, the United States sought repeatedly, but in vain, to obtain from Spain treaty recognition of its claim, which was based upon natural law, its inheritance of the British right of 1763, and its treaty of peace with Great Britain (*see* Definitive Treaty of Peace, 1783), by which the two powers guaranteed the right to each other. Spain persisted in her refusal when the subject was discussed in the Jay-Gardoqui negotiation*ᵠ* of 1785–87. In 1786 Jay, convinced that Spain would not yield, advised Congress to agree to suspend the claim for a term of years in return for commercial privileges which would have been mainly beneficial to the Middle and Northern states. By a sectional vote Congress instructed Jay to negotiate on this basis; but its action aroused such vehement protest in the South and West that he decided not' to proceed, especially since the creation of a new Federal Government was already in prospect. The negotiation hung fire until 1795. In 1788 Spain undertook a separatist intrigue (*see* Spanish Conspiracy) with the Westerners and, in order to promote it, granted them limited privileges of navigation; but they were not satisfied, French revolutionary influence soon increased their unrest, and by 1794 their threats of violent action had become so menacing that the governments of both the United States and Spain were prodded into renewed activity. Further alarmed by the Jay Treaty*ᵠ* of 1794 (by which Britain and the United States renewed their mutual guarantee of free navigation) and by the ill success of her war with France, Spain at last yielded in the Pinckney[w]-Godoy Treaty of San Lorenzo (Oct. 27, 1795). Art. IV established the free navigation of the Mississippi by the United States, which also gained the ancillary right of deposit at New Orleans (*see* Deposit, Right of). These rights gave a great impetus to American commerce on the Mississippi, which was shared by the Eastern seaboard as well as the West, and paved the way for the Louisiana Purchase[w] of 1803. The right of free navigation, as distinguished from the right of deposit, was never thereafter disturbed and this phase of the question was ended by the Louisiana Purchase. The British right was lost by the War of 1812[w] and never recovered.

[S. F. Bemis, *Pinckney's Treaty;* E. W. Lyon, *Louisiana in French Diplomacy;* A. P. Whitaker, *The Mississippi Question.*]

A. P. WHITAKER

Mississippi River, Navigation on. The primitive craft used on the Mississippi were the bull boat[w], or coracle, made of buffalo hide stretched on a frame, and the pirogue[w], or dugout canoe. The French introduced the bateau[w], which was essentially a large flatbottomed skiff propelled by oars, and the barge, which was built with keel and ribs and propelled by sails, oars or cordelle. The Spanish maintained on the river a fleet of galleys which were probably large barges or small ships.

The Americans seem to have introduced the flatboat[w], or ark, which handled much of the downstream transportation until the Civil War. The keelboat[w] also seems to have been an American adaptation. It was a long, narrow craft built on ribs and keel and propelled by setting poles or cordelle. The barge and the keelboat were the most important upstream carriers until the period of steamboat[w] dominance began, shortly after 1820.

The first Mississippi steamboat was the *Orleans* or *New Orleans*[w], built at Pittsburgh by Nicholas Roosevelt, which entered the Natchez–New Orleans trade in 1811. The steamboat was not successful on the western rivers, however, until in 1816 Capt. Henry Shreve built the *Washington,* which carried the boilers on deck and skimmed the surface of the water instead of plowing the depths as did Fulton's steamboats. Steamboats multiplied rapidly after 1820 and this multiplication necessitated river improvements. Some dredging of sandbars was done by the Government after 1824 and Henry Shreve invented a snag-pulling apparatus with which he cleared river channels and picked apart the famous Red River raft[w].

By 1840 steamboat traffic had reached its zenith, though even then much heavy freight was brought downstream in flatboats. East-west railroads soon began sapping trade from the steamboats. The western phase of the Civil War was largely based upon the Union campaign to open the Mississippi. Fleets of armored river gunboats aided in this effort (*see* Mississippi Squadron), and other fleets of boats were essential in supplying the armies. After the war steamboat commerce revived for almost twenty years, but the railroads finally conquered. The navigation of the river is now important for the carriage of bulky freight, much of it on steel barges, and for the check it provides to railway rates.

In the early years ocean vessels came as high as New Orleans, and that city is still the most important transfer point. There has been much difficulty in keeping bars from forming in the mouth of the river and the problem still requires constant vigilance.

The modern system of improvements, since 1879 largely under the direction of army engineers, has provided vast lines of levees[w], dams, dikes, cutoffs, reservoirs, spillways and dredged channels over more than 2000 miles of river. The present low-water channel above St. Louis is six feet deep, and below St. Louis nine or more feet deep. These operations have also aided in flood control[w].

LELAND D. BALDWIN

Mississippi River, THE. Although other Spaniards had doubtless seen the mouth of this great river, its discovery is rightly accredited to Hernando DeSoto[w], who reached it near the site of Memphis, Tenn., early in May, 1541. There is no indisputable evidence that another European saw the Mississippi River until 1673, and then the new discoverers were Frenchmen. On June 17 of that year Louis Jolliet[w] and Father Jacques Marquette paddled their canoes out of the Wisconsin River into the larger stream. They proceeded down the river to a point near the mouth of the Arkansas River, where they turned back. In 1682 LaSalle[w] explored the river from the Illinois to its mouth, where on April 9 he took possession of the country for France and named it Louisiana[w].

LaSalle realized the full significance of the Mississippi River, and planned to establish a colony at its mouth. Unfortunately, when in 1684 he sailed from France to carry out the purpose, he missed the mouth of the Mississippi and landed on the coast of Texas. Three years later he was murdered by one of his followers and his plan for a French colony seemed to have perished with him.

Scarcely more than a decade elapsed, however,

before two Frenchmen, Iberville and Bienville, sailed from Brest in two vessels carrying 200 soldiers and colonists. In March, 1699, they entered the Mississippi, explored it for some distance and warned away an English vessel which had arrived on a mission similar to their own (*see* Carolana). The French established themselves first at Biloxi*ᵠ*, then on Mobile Bay, and in 1718 they founded New Orleans*ᵠ*. Thereafter for nearly a half-century the Mississippi was used and controlled by the French.

At the close of the French and Indian War*ᵠ* France lost her possessions in the New World (*see* Fontainebleau, Treaty of; Paris, Treaty of, 1763), and the Mississippi River became an international boundary. From 1763 to 1783 Spain and Great Britain confronted each other across the "Great River." During the American Revolution the river witnessed hostilities between the British and the Spanish, and was the avenue for the supplies by means of which George Rogers Clark was able to maintain his hold on the Illinois country (*see* Spanish Military Supplies from New Orleans). According to the Definitive Treaty of Peace, 1783*ᵠ*, the United States was to extend to the Mississippi between Spanish Florida*ᵠ* and the Canadian boundary, and Americans were to have the free navigation of the river (*see* Mississippi River, Free Navigation of).

The Spanish were not party to this treaty and they had their own ideas about the navigation of the Mississippi—ideas which they were able to enforce because they controlled the mouth of the river. They imposed duties which were regarded as exorbitant and prohibitive by the settlers in the Ohio Valley*ᵠ* for whom the river was the only feasible outlet to market. The West seethed with unrest, intrigues and threats of disunion (*see* Western Separatism; Spanish Conspiracy), and the "Mississippi Question" became one of the most troublesome problems facing Federal officials and diplomats. Finally, in 1795, in accordance with Pinckney's Treaty*ᵠ* with Spain the river was opened to Americans (*see* Deposit, Right of). In 1800, however, Spain ceded Louisiana back to France (*see* San Ildefonso, Treaty of). Shortly afterward the river was closed once more and again there was consternation and turmoil in the West until the Louisiana Purchase*ᵠ* settled the question and made the Mississippi an American river.

Thereafter the Mississippi River served without restriction as the great artery of trade and commerce for the whole upper valley (*see* Mississippi Valley). The first successors of the canoes or pirogues of the Indians and traders were the flatboats*ᵠᵠ* on which the farmers floated their produce to market. Then came the keelboats*ᵠ* which could be propelled upstream by prodigious effort. But river transportation received its greatest impetus in 1811 when the steamboat *New Orleans*ᵠ* made its historic trip from Pittsburgh to New Orleans. The number of steamboats*ᵠ* on the Mississippi and Ohio increased slowly at first, but by 1825 there were 125, and by 1860 more than 1000 were in service. It was not without reason, therefore, that the Southerners counted on the Mississippi to bind the Middle West to them in economic interest. That it failed to do so at the critical time was due to the counteracting influence of the railroads*ᵠ* and other factors.

During the Civil War the vital importance of the Mississippi to the Confederacy was recognized by both sides, and the struggle for its control was one of the principal aspects of the war. When, after the fall of Vicksburg, the river came into full possession of the Federal forces, the Confederacy was cut in two and seriously weakened (*see* Mississippi, Opening of the).

Since the close of the Civil War the Mississippi River has never regained its earlier significance as a highway of transportation. Steamboating revived somewhat after the war and still continues, but the railroads, with their greater speed, convenience and certainty, have largely frustrated all hope of a return of the glamorous river life about which Mark Twain wrote so vividly. Disastrous floods*ᵠ*, such as those in 1912, 1927 and 1936, have made flood control*ᵠ* one of the principal problems connected with the Mississippi in recent years.

[Julius Chambers, *The Mississippi River;* Charles H. Ambler, *A History of Transportation in the Ohio Valley;* Arthur P. Whitaker, *The Spanish-American Frontier, 1783-1795,* and *The Mississippi Question, 1795-1863;* Mark Twain, *Life on the Mississippi.*]   DAN E. CLARK

Mississippi River Bridge at New Orleans (constructed Jan. 1933–Dec. 1935) is a double-track railroad bridge with an over-all length of 4.73 miles and an 18-foot highway driveway of 1.52 miles on each side of the tracks. The main river structure is .6 miles including one span of 790 feet; from underside of bridge, height above high water, 135 feet; above low water, 155 feet. The construction cost of $13,000,000 was financed by the Louisiana Highway Commission and the New Orleans Public Belt Railroad Commission.

[Louisiana Highway Commission.]

W. B. HATCHER

Mississippi Squadron, THE. At the beginning of the Civil War the importance of controlling the great river system of the Mississippi Valley stimulated both Union and Confederate governments to construct war vessels to co-operate with their land forces. By the end of July, 1861, the Union Flotilla in the Western Waters consisted of three wooden gunboats converted from river packets by Commodore John Rodgers II under orders from the War Department. In December and January the completion of nine ironclad^{qv} vessels placed the fleet on a formidable basis.

The first major operation of the flotilla was the capture of Fort Henry^{qv} and the ascent of the Tennessee River into Alabama. The fleet also contributed to the capture of Fort Donelson^{qv} and the occupation of Nashville. The reduction of the Confederate strongholds at Columbus, Island No. 10 and Fort Pillow, and the naval victory at Memphis, June 6, 1862, opened the river to Vicksburg^{qqv}, and led to the attack on its fortifications during June and July. To guard the rivers against incursions by guerrilla bands^{qv}, large numbers of light-draught steamers were purchased, armed and kept on patrol duty. Additional ironclads and monitors were added as rapidly as they could be completed. This expansion of the fleet necessitated its transfer to the Navy Department, and on Oct. 1, 1862, it was rechristened the Mississippi Squadron.

A second unsuccessful attack on Vicksburg in December was followed by the capture of Arkansas Post^{qv}, Jan. 11, 1863. Henceforth, much of the squadron was in close co-operation with Gen. Grant in his campaign against Vicksburg^{qv}. Also, the vessels in the upper rivers were frequently called on to help defeat the plans of the Confederate cavalry raiders. After the fall of Port Hudson^{qv}, July 9, 1863, the only important variation from the monotony of patrol and convoy duty was the Red River Campaign^{qv}, April 8 to May 22, 1864, when a sudden fall in the river threatened the destruction of many of the best vessels of the squadron. During the summer of 1865 most of the squadron was taken out of commission and the vessels either returned to peace-time traffic or dismantled and sold for scrap.

[A. T. Mahan, *Gulf and Inland Waters.*]

T. R. PARKER

Mississippi v. Johnson (4 Wall 475, 1867) was a suit filed April 5, 1867, by Gov. William L. Sharkey of Mississippi, Alexander H. Garland and Robert J. Walker, asking from the Supreme Court of the United States permission to file a plea to perpetually enjoin Andrew Johnson from "executing or in any manner carrying out" the Reconstruction acts^{qv} passed a few weeks before by the Radical^{qv} Congress. Although he had vetoed them as unconstitutional, the President ordered Attorney General Stanbery to oppose the Mississippi plea before the Court. Charles O'Conor argued for the petitioners. Speaking for an unanimous Court, Chief Justice Chase denied the petition for lack of jurisdiction. The Court pointed out that no question of person or property was involved. Furthermore, "the Congress is the legislative department of the government," he said. "The President is the executive department. Neither can be restrained in its action by the judicial department." Mississippi's counsel sought desperately to introduce person or property. But after reargument, by a four-to-four vote, the plea was disallowed.

[G. F. Milton, *The Age of Hate: Andrew Johnson and the Radicals.*]

GEORGE FORT MILTON

Mississippi Valley, THE. Until it came into the possession of the United States the Mississippi Valley was the prize sought by the leading nations of Europe. Spaniards were the discoverers of the lower valley (DeSoto and Coronado^{qqv}, 1541), but Spain did not follow up the discoveries and more than two centuries elapsed before she became really interested in the region. It was far different with the French. Their explorers and *coureurs de bois* (Nicolet, 1634; Radisson and Grosseilliers, 1654–60; Jolliet and Marquette, 1673; LaSalle, 1669–84; and many others^{qqv}) penetrated far and wide into the valley. When in 1699 Iberville and Bienville established a colony near the mouth of the river (*see* Biloxi), the French were in almost undisputed control of the great valley—a control which they maintained for half a century. Although claiming the region on the basis of their sea-to-sea charters, the English colonists were slow in finding their way to the "western waters." But when English traders and land companies became actively interested in the Ohio Valley^{qv}, about the middle of the 18th century, there was precipitated the great struggle between the French and English for the Mississippi Valley, which is known as the French and Indian War^{qv}.

At the close of this war France lost her possessions in America, relinquishing her claims west of the Mississippi to Spain and the region east of that stream to the English. In the Definitive Treaty of Peace, 1783^{qv}, the new United States received jurisdiction westward to the Mississippi and north of Spanish Florida^{qv}. Twenty years later the Louisiana Purchase^{qv} gave the United States the entire valley, after Spain had ceded Louisiana back to France in 1800 (*see* San Ildefonso, Treaty of). Even before the Revolutionary War there were American settlements in

Kentucky and Tennessee[qv]. After 1783 the flood-gates were opened and Americans poured across the mountains in ever-increasing numbers to take possession of their new domain (*see* Westward Movement) .

The influences and problems arising out of the settlement of the Mississippi Valley made the United States a strong nation. In meeting the demands of the Westerners for protection against the Indians, for autonomous local governments, for roads and river improvements, for mail service and for liberal land legislation, the powers of the Federal Government were vastly extended and strengthened. It was in the Mississippi Valley that the frontier had its most characteristic influence on American life and institutions. At the same time it was in the Mississippi Valley that the sectionalism which culminated in the Civil War developed its greatest bitterness.

[James K. Hosmer, *A Short History of the Mississippi Valley;* Dan E. Clark, *The West in American History.*]
DAN E. CLARK

Mississippi Valley Historical Association, THE, was organized in Lincoln, Nebr., in 1907 by seven men, historians of the Middle West, called together by Clarence S. Paine, superintendent of the Nebraska Historical Society. The Association rapidly expanded its activities until it included in its membership students and teachers of American history from every part of the country. Ten volumes of *Proceedings* have been published. The principal organ of the Association is the quarterly *Mississippi Valley Historical Review* (since 1914) containing scholarly articles, important documents, and reviews of the latest books in the various fields of American history.
MRS. CLARENCE S. PAINE

Missouri history virtually begins in the last half of the 17th century. The French were the first real explorers, traders and white settlers, the Canadian-French being in the majority among the settlers and the Louisiana-French in the minority. Chief among the explorers between 1673–1723 were Jolliet[qv], Marquette, LaSalle[qv], LaHontan, DuTisne and Bourgmont[qv]. Others followed and a large part of Missouri was explored by 1804. Lead[qv] mines and salt springs were discovered and made productive, and profitable fur trading[qv] was established. Trade with Santa Fé[qv] and the upper Missouri was attempted, and war and peace were made with the Indians. A temporary settlement was made as early as 1700 when French Jesuits[qv] from Canada established a mission where St. Louis now stands. The first permanent settlement was Ste. Genevieve[qv], possibly about 1735. St. Louis[qv], the second permanent

settlement, was founded by Laclede in 1764. In 1762 France secretly ceded her territory west of the Mississippi to Spain (*see* Fontainebleau, Treaty of) . It was 1767, however, before the first Spanish officer came to St. Louis, and 1770 when the French lieutenant-governor in St. Louis, St. Ange de Bellerive, officially surrendered upper Louisiana[qv] to Don Pedro Piernas, Spanish lieutenant-governor and military commandant. French population increased after England won the eastern side of the Mississippi (*see* Paris, Treaty of, 1763) , and American immigration began during the Revolutionary War, increasing after 1795 because Spain encouraged American settlement. The simple Spanish government did not affect the character of the easygoing French and more energetic Americans, and French influence remained dominant in colonial Missouri.

The Louisiana Purchase[qv] was consummated by the United States in 1803 but upper Louisiana was not formally transferred to the United States until March 10, 1804, when Capt. Amos Stoddard took command in St. Louis. Following a period of military government (March 10–Oct. 1, 1804) , the area which became Missouri passed through three stages of territorial government as a part of the District of Louisiana (Oct. 1, 1804–July 4, 1805) , the Territory of Louisiana (July 4, 1805–Oct. 1, 1812) , and finally the Territory of Missouri (Oct. 1, 1812–1820) . In 1818 and 1819, when popular and legislative petitions from Missouri Territory were presented asking for statehood, Congress engaged in a bitter sectional controversy of nation-wide significance. The Missouri Compromise[qv], effected in 1820, gave Missouri the right to form a state constitution and government without restriction on slavery[qv], and also provided that slavery should not exist elsewhere in the Louisiana Purchase north of 36° 30′, N. Lat. Missouri drafted and adopted a constitution on July 19, 1820, held a state election in August, and set in operation a state government in September of that year. The constitution guaranteed the existence of slavery and forbade the immigration of free Negroes[qv] into the state. This latter provision provoked congressional conflict again, which ended in a second compromise whereby Missouri agreed never to deprive citizens of other states of their rights. Missouri was formally admitted into the Union on Aug. 10, 1821, with the boundaries which she has today, excepting the addition of the Platte Purchase[qv] area which by act of Congress was ceded to Missouri in 1837.

Certain distinctive developments have combined with diversified agriculture to foster economic stability in Missouri. The Missouri-Santa

Fé trade and the fur trade were very important in promoting prosperity between 1800 and 1860. During the first half-century of statehood, steamboating[w] on the Mississippi and Missouri rivers was also of outstanding importance. Railroad building began in the 1850's and was practically completed by the close of the century. Lead mining, in which the state still leads, became profitable as early as 1725. Lead, coal and zinc are mined extensively and other metals in smaller quantity. Stone and clay products are especially valuable. Manufacturing industries placed Missouri tenth among the states in 1933 in total number of industries established and in total value of products. Recently, remarkable development has taken place in harnessing water power, resulting in the formation of such artificial bodies of water as Lake Taneycomo and the Lake of the Ozarks. Improved highways and the Ozark resort areas of beautiful scenery and springs of unusual size and beauty have contributed much to the state's attractiveness.

The Mormon[w] troubles occupy a most tragic period in the social history of Missouri. Mormon settlers began to come from Ohio to Jackson County, Mo., in 1831. Hostility soon developed over religion, Mormon opposition to slavery, and possession of property. The Mormons fled to Clay County in 1833, and in 1836 the state legislature created Caldwell County for them. As the Mormons increased in Caldwell County, conflict developed between them and the people of adjoining counties. In 1838 the state militia was ordered to move against them, and the Mormons were expelled in 1839.

An unhappy phase of Missouri life immediately preceded the Civil War. After the passage of the Kansas-Nebraska Act[w], Missourians and Kansans became embroiled in the so-called "border wars"[w]. Missourians invaded Kansas between 1855 and 1857 to aid the establishment of proslavery government. Retaliation followed from 1857 to 1860, and the state militia was called to intervene upon several occasions.

During the Civil War Missouri's position made her a border state with a divided people subject to bitter conflicts both regular and guerrilla in nature. The pro-Southern state government was deposed and a Union provisional government held control from the spring of 1861 to the fall of 1864. Eleven per cent of the total number of the combats of the war were fought in Missouri though few were classified as first-rank battles.

With every decade, the Federal census figures have shown an increase in population over the previous census. The largest per cent of growth (236.6) occurred between 1810 and 1820, and the lowest (3.4) was recorded 100 years later between 1910 and 1920. Increase was not so rapid between 1820 and 1830 (110.9) but was accelerated between 1830 and 1840 (173.2). After 1840 the percentage of increase declined steadily until 1920 when the smallest increase occurred. A slight rise appeared by 1930 when the population was 3,629,367, an increase of 6.6%. In recent years urban and rural population have tended to balance, and, in 1930, the urban population composed 51.2% of the total.

Missouri is now a Central, representative American state, although she was originally Western because of her position, and Southern due to the early American settlers, who came chiefly from Kentucky, Virginia, North Carolina and Tennessee. Immigration followed from the Middle and Eastern states, and today near-by states in the Mississippi Valley add to the population. An influx of German immigration came between 1830 and 1860, and the Irish increased between 1850 and 1860; nevertheless, Missouri's population has been predominantly native-born. Negroes have never constituted a large portion of the population.

Politically, Missouri has been chiefly Democratic since personal politics ended in 1831, excepting provisional government and Radical Republican[w] rule from 1861 to 1870. The Republican party gained gradually after its defeat in 1870, and Missouri has been termed a doubtful state since 1904.

[Louis Houck, *A History of Missouri, from the Earliest Explorations and Settlements until the Admission of the State into the Union;* Walter B. Stevens, *Centennial History of Missouri: One Hundred Years in the Union, 1820-1921;* William F. Switzler, *Switzler's Illustrated History of Missouri, from 1541 to 1877;* Walter Williams and Floyd C. Shoemaker, *Missouri, Mother of the West.*]

FLOYD C. SHOEMAKER

Missouri, Kansas & Texas Railway. The outgrowth of several pioneer lines in four Southwestern states, with its earliest unit dating from incorporation in Kansas on Sept. 29, 1865, the "Katy" railway was instrumental in the post-Civil War development of Texas and Oklahoma. By 1870 its main line operated 140 miles southward from Junction City to a point near Parsons, Kans. After the addition of the Tebo & Neosho Company line northeastward to Moberly, Mo., and other branches giving access to St. Louis and Kansas City, construction was resumed southward across the old Indian Territory[w]. The objective was a crossing of the Red River near Preston Bend in Texas. Each advance toward the cattle country shrunk the overland trail drives[w] by the same distance. On Jan. 1, 1873, the first train of the railroad entered the new town of Denison, Texas, which had been reached one year earlier by the Houston & Texas Central Railroad. This junction afforded the first through rail connection between Texas and the remainder of the United States. During the next four decades the railroad continued construction and additions to include water terminals at Houston and Galveston, Texas, and entry into San Antonio. It was operated under lease as a part of the Missouri Pacific Railway[w] by Jay Gould from 1880 until 1888 but then regained its separate identity. Its present name of the Missouri-Kansas-Texas Lines was acquired under a subsequent reorganization. Its chief subsidiary is the Missouri-Kansas-Texas Railroad of Texas.

[*The Texas Almanac*, 1869, 1870 and 1872; corporate records of the railway company at Dallas and St. Louis.]

SAM ACHESON

Missouri, Three Forks of the, is a picturesque and strategically important spot in Montana, so named because three principal source streams of the Missouri unite there—the Jefferson, the Madison and the Gallatin. They were named by Lewis and Clark[w], who camped at the junction on their exploratory trip to the Pacific in 1805. A fort was established there by the Missouri Fur Company[w] in 1810 but persistent attacks by the Blackfeet[w] caused its abandonment in the same year.

[Q. D. Wheeler, *The Trail of Lewis and Clark*.]

CARL L. CANNON

Missouri Compromise. The Missouri Territory comprised that part of the Louisiana Purchase not organized as the State of Louisiana[qqv] in 1812. Ever since it had been a French province slavery had existed in the Territory. From 1817 to 1819 the Missouri Territorial Assembly petitioned Congress for statehood, with boundaries limited to approximately those of the present state. In 1819 there was an equal number of slave and free states. When the House of Representatives reported a bill authorizing Missouri to frame a constitution, James Tallmadge[w] of New York proposed an amendment prohibiting the further introduction of slaves into Missouri and providing that all children born of slaves should be free at the age of twenty-five. The amendment was passed, Feb. 16–17, 1819, but rejected by the Senate. Congress adjourned without further action but the South was stricken with fear.

When Congress reconvened in December, 1819, Maine had formed a constitution and was requesting admission as a free state. The House passed an act admitting Maine. The Senate joined this measure to the one admitting Missouri without mention of slavery. Sen. J. B. Thomas of Illinois offered an amendment to the Senate bill for the admission of Missouri as a slave state, but with the provision that, in the remainder of the Louisiana Purchase, slavery should be prohibited north of 36° 30′ N. Lat. A debate followed that startled the nation. It came, said Thomas Jefferson, "like a fire bell in the night." A sectional alignment threatened the Union.

The House passed a bill, March 1, 1820, admitting Missouri as a free state. The Senate took up the measure, struck out the antislavery provision, and added the Thomas amendment. A compromise was effected by admitting Maine as a free state, March 3, 1820 (effective, March 15) , and by authorizing Missouri to form a constitution, with no restriction on slavery, March 6, 1820. The region of the Louisiana Purchase north of 36° 30′, except the State of Missouri, was thus dedicated to freedom.

Missouri called a constitutional convention to meet at St. Louis, June 12, 1820. The constitution empowered the legislature to exclude free Negroes[w] and mulattoes from the state. This restriction caused another bitter debate in Congress. A second compromise was, therefore, effected, March 2, 1821. This stipulated that Missouri would not be admitted until she agreed that nothing in her constitution should be interpreted to abridge the privileges and immunities of citizens of the United States. The pledge was secured. On Aug. 10, 1821, Missouri became a state.

The Compromise was respected and regarded as almost sacred until the Mexican War, when the power of Congress to exclude slavery from the territories was again questioned (*see* Wilmot Proviso) . In 1848 Congress passed the Oregon Territory bill prohibiting slavery. President Polk signed it on the ground that the Territory was north of the Missouri Compromise line. Soon afterward proposals were made to extend the Compromise line of 1820 through the Mexican Cession[w] to the Pacific. These efforts failed to secure the extension of the 36° 30′ line across the continent. Instead, the principle of popular sovereignty prevailed in the Compromise of 1850[qqv]. The admission of California in 1850 gave the free states a majority of one. In 1854 the Missouri Compromise was repealed (*see* Missouri Compromise, Repeal of the; Kansas-Nebraska Act) .

[J. A. Woodburn, The Historical Significance of the Missouri Compromise, in American Historical Association *Reports*, 1893; F. H. Hodder, Side Lights on the Missouri Compromise, in American Historical Association *Reports*, 1909; Louis Houck, *History of*

Missouri, Vols. II and III; *Annals of Congress*, 15 Cong., 2 Sess.; *Ibid.*, 16 Cong., 1 Sess.]

GEORGE D. HARMON

Missouri Compromise, Repeal of the (1854). Without warning, the proposal to repeal the Missouri Compromise*ᵂ* appeared in Congress early in 1854—less than two years after both the Democratic and Whig*ᵠᵂ* platforms of 1852 had emphatically endorsed the Compromise of 1850*ᵂ* as a final settlement of the slavery question, and condemned in advance all attempts to renew the slavery controversy. Agitation burst forth anew, however, in January, 1854, when a bill to organize a territorial government west of Missouri and Iowa was found to contain an oddly worded section that repealed the Missouri Compromise prohibition of slavery in that region. Over this Kansas-Nebraska Bill*ᵂ*, a gigantic and picturesque parliamentary duel followed, in which Sen. Douglas of Illinois was the outstanding champion of repeal; and most historians have assumed that he was its real author. They fail to explain, however (1), why the passage of the territorial bill occurred in 1854 and not sooner or later; and (2) why the repealing provision was added, when less than a year before (March, 1853) a Nebraska bill with no repeal provision had passed the House and probably would have passed the Senate if it could have been brought to a vote.

An explanation that rests upon something more than conjecture may be found in certain western political events of 1853–54, which form a chain leading directly to the congressional action of 1854; and so far as any individual can be regarded as the originator of the repeal, both circumstantial and direct evidence points more strongly to Sen. David R. Atchison of Missouri than to Sen. Douglas. In 1853–54, the Wyandot Indians in Nebraska and the people of western Iowa and Missouri had become intensely and actively interested in the organization of Nebraska Territory, in the construction of a Pacific railroad across it and in the question of slavery therein. Of even greater importance were the dissensions that had rent the Democratic party in Missouri during the preceding decade and culminated in the bitter senatorial struggle of 1853–54. Sen. Atchison, leader of the slavery extensionists in western Missouri, was strenuously seeking re-election to the Senate. Opposing him was Thomas H. Benton, leader of the slavery restrictionists, whose strength lay mainly in the eastern part of the state. Benton was now a member of the House of Representatives, to which he had been elected in 1850 following his defeat for re-election to the Senate. Neither candidate

was leaving any stone unturned to win a majority of the Missouri legislature that was to be elected in August, 1854, and which would choose the next senator. In competing for votes, both Atchison and Benton pledged themselves in 1853 to work for the early organization of Nebraska and to promote action by Congress that would hasten construction of a Pacific railroad across this territory. But the chief issue between them was nothing less than the retention or repeal of the Missouri Compromise prohibition of slavery therein. Benton was opposed to repeal, while Atchison was heart and soul for it, since it would enable his slave-owning constituents in the western counties to move into Nebraska with their slaves. All of these matters were peculiarly within the scope of congressional authority; and so the factional contest was certain to appear in one form or another at Washington when the Thirty-third Congress convened in December, 1853. There alone could the issues of the Missouri conflict be finally determined. Apparently after some pressure, Sen. Douglas, chairman of the committee on territories, reported the Kansas-Nebraska Bill in January, 1854, and included in the measure an ingenious provision for repeal of the old prohibition by indirection. The bill declared that the idea of a geographical line had been "superseded" by the compromise measures of 1850 in favor of leaving the question of slavery to be decided by the inhabitants of the territories. This method of settling the question of slavery in the territories had long been advocated by Douglas; and its inclusion now in the territorial bill seemed well calculated to strengthen Atchison's position in the approaching Missouri election, not only because the Missouri legislature had been formally on record since 1845 in favor of this mode of settlement, but especially because the Kansas-Nebraska Bill placed Benton upon the horns of a dilemma. If he voted for the repealing measure, he would go counter to his free-soil opinions and sympathies, and lose support in eastern Missouri; if he opposed the bill, he would be violating his recent campaign pledges to work for the immediate organization of a territorial government in Nebraska, and lose a following in the western counties that he had taken great pains to attract. In the end he spoke and voted against the bill, and his vote largely explains his defeat in the ensuing August election. Later, however, Atchison himself failed to win re-election in the legislature of 1854–55, although he had been the mainspring to congressional action that had opened the Nebraska country to settlement by his slave-owning constituents.

However much historians may differ concerning the origin and authorship of the repeal of the Missouri Compromise, they are agreed that it immediately led to the formation of the Republican party[qv] and to the series of events that culminated in disruption of the Union.

[F. J. Turner, *Rise of the New West;* J. W. Burgess, *The Middle Period;* P. O. Ray, *The Repeal of the Missouri Compromise: Its Origin and Authorship;* P. O. Ray, The Genesis of the Kansas-Nebraska Act, American Historical Association *Report,* 1914, I.]

P. ORMAN RAY

Missouri Fur Company. *See* St. Louis Missouri Fur Company.

Missouri Pacific Railroad, THE, chartered March 12, 1849, by the Missouri legislature as the Pacific Railroad Company, was the first railway west of the Mississippi. Climaxing nearly twenty years of western railroad agitation, it owed much to Sen. Thomas H. Benton's enthusiastic support. Ground was broken July 4, 1851, in St. Louis, whose leading businessmen were its backers, and the first five miles were opened Dec. 9, 1852. Panics, labor strife, cholera, management troubles and bridge collapses were weathered and on Oct. 2, 1865, service was opened to Kansas City, 283 miles distant, over a route paralleling the Missouri River. Private subscriptions were generously supplemented by Federal, state and county aid, the cost of almost $14,000,000 greatly exceeding estimates. Western migration brought the line immediate prosperity and Jay Gould purchased it in 1879 as the basis for his projected transcontinental system.

[Robert E. Riegel, *The Story of the Western Railroads;* Dorothy Jennings, The Pacific Railroad Company, *Missouri Historical Society Collections,* Vol. VI.]

IRVING DILLIARD

Missouri River, THE, known to Marquette in 1673 as the Peki-tan-oui, so named on some of the early maps, and later as Oumessourit, drains a watershed of nearly 600,000 square miles. Stretching from its source northwest of the Yellowstone Park, where the Jefferson, Gallatin and Madison rivers join together in southern Montana, it winds around hills and bluffs, through the most fertile valley in the world, a distance of 2546 miles to its junction with the Mississippi. The Missouri River was first explored from its mouth to its source by Lewis and Clark[qv]. The lower part of the Missouri was known to the French trappers, traders and *voyageurs,* who ascended it as far as the Kansas River in 1705. In 1720 a Spanish caravan was sent from Santa Fé to the Missouri to drive back the French (*see*

Villasur Expedition). The early French called the river "St. Philip." They probably did not go higher than the Platte, which was considered the dividing line between the upper and lower river. In 1719 Claude Charles du Tisne and party went up the Missouri in canoes as far as the Grand River. Credited with being the first white man to visit the upper Missouri country, Sieur de la Verendrye[qv] led a party from one of the posts of the Hudson's Bay Company in 1738 to the Mandan villages. Other explorations followed, searching for the "Western Sea"[qv] by way of the Missouri River. Although it was thought for years that no keelboat[qv] could ascend the Missouri, it later became the great highway into the West. While Gregoire Sarpy is said to have first introduced the keelboat, the real father of navigation on the Missouri was Manuel Lisa[qv]. The first steamboat ever to ascend the river was the *Independence* which pushed off from St. Louis in 1819, reached Old Franklin in thirteen days and turned back at Old Chariton, in Missouri. In 1831 Pierre Chouteau[qv] succeeded in ascending the Missouri in his steamboat *Yellowstone*[qv]. As a result of steamboating[qv] many cities grew up along the edge of the river and several states built their capitals upon its bank. This river has always carried in suspension an immense amount of solid matter, mostly very fine light sand, discoloring the water, and justifying the name of "Muddy Waters." The water has always been considered exceptionally pure otherwise—a condition attributed to the peculiar sand. It is said that the yearly average of solid matter carried into the Mississippi by this river is over 500,000,-000 tons, brought along for an average distance of 500 miles. While the Missouri has a greater annual flow of water than the Mississippi above its mouth, it is subject to greater fluctuations. These have affected its navigability in certain seasons and caused the shore line to shift, farms and villages to disappear, and others to be left far back through deposits of the soil in front of them.

[J. V. Brower, *The Missouri River and Its Utmost Source.*]

STELLA M. DRUMM

Missouri River Fur Trade. This river and its tributaries constituted one of the three great systems of importance to the fur trader and trapper. The several companies engaged in the fur trade operated, generally speaking, in distinctive fields, usually identified with some one or another of the great drainage systems that mark off the natural divisions of the country. The Spanish Commercial Company, St. Louis Missouri Fur Company, and thereafter in succession the Missouri

Fur Company, the Columbia Fur Company and the American Fur Company[qw], all confined their operations to the Missouri and Mississippi watersheds. While the Rocky Mountain Fur Company[w] competed with these to some extent at the headwaters of the Missouri, its operations were largely confined to some of the tributaries and to regions farther inland. Many establishments, variously designated as forts, posts and houses, were scattered along the Missouri in the wilderness long before the tide of western immigration set in. After the Verendrye expedition[w] in 1738, whose main purpose was one of exploration, came one Menard, fourteen years earlier than Jacques D'Eglise, 1791–95, and then Jean B. Truteau of the Spanish Company. This last-named company erected, in 1794, Truteau's Post. In 1800 Regis Loisel's post, known also as Cedar Post, was established in the Sioux country, thirty-five miles below the present site of Pierre, S. Dak. The most important early post was that of the St. Louis Missouri Fur Company, known as Fort Lisa[w], and located near Council Bluffs. Outstanding forts of the American Fur Company were received from the Columbia Fur Company. The largest and most important of the American Fur Company's forts was Fort Union[w]. The Missouri River made St. Louis[w] the greatest center of the fur trade. All of the early expeditions were outfitted and started from this point. In 1843 in the country tributary to St. Louis there were 150 fur trading posts, a great majority of which lay along the Missouri River. Although the upper reaches of the Missouri were at first walled off by the British and certain Indians under their influence, these obstacles were finally overcome. The tribes giving the most trouble were the Blackfeet and Arikara[qw]. The fur trade was the principal commerce of the early days in the West and its development to the great size attained was made possible by the Missouri River. As facilities for navigation improved the fur trade increased. The pirogue, bateau[qw] and barge of the French *voyageur* gave way to the keelboat and mackinaw boat, and these in turn yielded to the steamboat[qw] in 1831. Although the Missouri River is said to be the most difficult to navigate in the world, nevertheless, it was the most dependable medium of transportation in the days of the fur trade.

[Phil E. Chappell, *A History of the Missouri River;* Hiram M. Chittenden, *The American Fur Trade of the Far West.*]

STELLA M. DRUMM

Missouri v. Holland (252 U. S. 416, 1920). The question involved was whether the treaty-making power extends the exercise of Federal power to a field not specifically delegated to the National Government. Two Federal district courts had held an earlier Migratory Birds Act, passed under the commerce power, unconstitutional. An identical statute of 1918, passed after the ratification of the Migratory Bird Treaty with Great Britain of 1916, was upheld on the grounds, first, that it contravened no express limitations of the Constitution and, second, that the treaty-making power is not limited by any "invisible radiation from the general terms of the Tenth Amendment."

PHILLIPS BRADLEY

Mitchell's Map (Feb. 13, 1755), on a scale of 1:2,000,000, was published in London under the auspices of the Board of Trade[w] by Dr. John Mitchell, a successful physician and botanist who practised medicine in Urbana, Va., between 1735 and 1746. He wrote well on many subjects, but is best remembered for his large-scale *Map of the British and French Dominions in North America with the Roads, Distances, Limits, and Extent of the Settlements.* On the fourth English edition, London, 1775, the title was changed to read *British Colonies* for *British and French Dominions.* The map, engraved on copper and printed on eight sheets, measures when joined 52¾ x 76¼ inches.

More than twenty editions were published before 1792, after which parts of the map were published with new titles by numerous authors, many times without acknowledgment to Mitchell.

Since its publication, "the most important map of America" has figured in nearly every boundary dispute involving the United States or parts thereof. On it (Paris, 1783) were laid down the first boundaries of the United States of America. (*See also* Red Line Map.)

[*Dictionary of American Biography*, Vol. XIII, pp. 50-51, sketch of life of John Mitchell.]

LLOYD A. BROWN

Mixed Commissions have been a favorite device of American diplomacy for the arbitral adjustment of controversial legal questions involving particularly damages claimed as arising out of torts and spoliations, and for the compromise or delimitation of boundaries. The diplomatic settlement of 1794 achieved by Jay's Treaty[w] with England set up four of these mixed commissions, each having representatives from both sides, and an umpire. A mixed commission was set up by Pinckney's Treaty[w] in 1795 with Spain for the settlement of maritime spoliations. Similar claims arising out of the Napoleonic wars, against France and Portugal, were settled by mixed commissions (*see* French Spoliation Claims). Many miscellaneous minor Anglo-American claims have been settled by mixed commissions, following the precedent of Jay's Treaty: for example, the slave indemnity claims of 1822, miscellaneous routine claims settled by the Claims Conventions of 1853, and the Washington Treaty of 1871^{qv}. Today there are treaties between Mexico and the United States which provide standing mixed commissions for the routine settlement of boundary disputes arising along the common frontier, with its shifting water courses. Routine claims with Mexico have been adjudicated by special claims commissions as in 1840 and 1867; but the vast category of claims submitted in 1924 to two separate claims commissions, one for the settlement of routine claims arising since 1867, and the other for the settlement of special claims arising out of the Mexican revolution, broke down in wrangles leaving the problems to be settled by diplomacy (*see* American-Mexican Mixed Claims Commissions). Mixed claims commissions are really a form of arbitration. Sometimes they have been arranged by treaties; but where the claims ran only against foreign governments, the United States has usually provided, by a mere executive agreement, for arbitral settlement through a mixed commission. The functioning of these commissions has been an undramatic but steady example of the peaceful settlement of international disputes.

[Samuel Flagg Bemis, *A Diplomatic History of the United States.*]

SAMUEL FLAGG BEMIS

DICTIONARY OF AMERICAN HISTORY